The Blackwell Encyclopedic Dictionary of Organizational Behavior

THE BLACKWELL ENCYCLOPEDIA OF MANAGEMENT

About the Editors

Cary L. Cooper is Professor of Organizational Psychology in the Manchester School of Management at the University of Manchester Institute of Science and Technology. He was the Founding President of the British Academy of Management and served as its president for four years. He is a Fellow of the British Psychological Society, a Fellow of the Royal Society of Arts and is the editor-in-chief of the international quarterly journal *The Journal of Organizational Behavior*. He is the author of numerous books and scholarly articles in the fields of organizational behavior, and has been an adviser to two UN Agencies (The World Health Organization and The International Labor Office).

Chris Argyris is the James B. Conant Professor, Graduate School of Business, Harvard University. He is the author of thirty books and research monographs as well as numerous articles. He is a consultant to many corporations, governmental organizations, and universities in the United States and Europe. Professor Argyris, who received his Ph.D. from Cornell University, is the holder of six honorary degrees.

The Blackwell Encyclopedic Dictionary of Organizational Behavior

Edited by Nigel Nicholson

Advisory Editors

Randall S. Schuler
Andrew H. Van de Ven

First published 1995

Blackwell Publishers Inc.
238 Main Street
Cambridge, Massachusetts 02142, USA

Blackwell Publishers Ltd
108 Cowley Road
Oxford OX4 1JF
UK

Library of Congress Cataloging-in-Publication Data

The Blackwell encyclopedic dictionary of organizational behavior / edited by Nigel Nicholson ; advisory editors, Randall Schuler, Andrew Van de Ven.
p. cm.
Includes bibliographical references and index.
ISBN 0-631-18781-2
1. Organizational behavior–Dictionaries. I. Nicholson, Nigel. II. Schuler, Randall S. III. Van de Ven, Andrew H. IV. Blackwell Publishers. V. Title: Encyclopedic dictionary of organizational behavior.
HD58.7.B57 1995
302.3′5′03–dc20 95-5490
CIP

British Library Cataloguing in Publication Data
CIP catalogue record for this book is available from the British Library.

ISBN 0631187812

Typeset in 9½ on 11pt Ehrhardt by Page Brothers, Norwich
Printed in Great Britain by T. J. Press (Padstow) Ltd

This book is printed on acid-free paper

—— Contents ——

—— Preface ——

Organizational Behavior – Coming Of Age

Organizational Behavior (OB) is the study of human action and experience *in* organizational contexts, and the behavior *of* organizations within their environmental contexts. The subject takes as its starting point the idea that organizations are human creations. This means that what they generate in terms of varieties of experience, social value and practical consequences are matters of choice – choice which can be informed by knowledge and ideas.

This definition implies that much of what we prize most dearly about our ways of living, and also what we most abhor, are created or conditioned by Organizational Behavior. The Great Wall of China, the Nazi holocaust, the Gobelin tapestries, the automobile, every major war, disaster relief effort, all the religions of the world, and the welfare, transportation and communication systems of society, and much more besides are the product of organization and behavior. At the level of personal experience, it is also true that many of the greatest achievements and failings of individuals can be traced to the liberating or oppressive effects of organizational structures and relationships.

This is not a new insight. From the earliest oral traditions of reflective inquiry to the modern social sciences, people have pondered upon how we should organize to live – to fulfill human potential in harmony with each other and with the living planet which sustains us. Plato, Confucius, the authors of the Talmud, the Gospels, the Bhagavad Gita and the Koran, all, in different ways, sought to answer this question by explaining and prescribing secular human relations, but within frameworks which pronounce about spirituality and the meaning of existence. For much of our history this metaphysical legacy has inhibited the search for insights about human organization through systematic methods of inquiry, in contrast to the relatively liberated growth of other bodies of knowledge, such as the natural sciences. Normative social philosophies have often discouraged and sometimes punished the separation of the empirical from the doctrinal when it came to thinking about human conduct (an effect not exclusive to self-declared religions; Marxist-Leninist orthodoxy has also exhibited this character where it has held sway).

For this reason, the applied social sciences are relatively new. It has only been in the last hundred years that they have found institutional legitimacy for their pedagogy, empirical research, dissemination and practice. Within this volume, the reader will find reference made to the historical cornerstones of OB as we find it presently constituted: writings at the turn of the century by psychologists about human capacities in work environments, by sociologists about the consequences of industrial organization, and by administrative theorists about the tasks of management. But *The Blackwell Encyclopedic Dictionary of Organizational Behavior* is not a history book. Contributors are reaching towards the future as much as reflecting on the past, and our collective aim has been to provide a contemporary atlas of the field, its key ideas, its major findings, and their implications. Over 180 worldwide experts have provided definitive statements about these developments. The maturity of the field can be seen in the confidence and authority with which they have set about their task. Demonstrably, OB come of age.

Indeed, this book would not have been possible even a few years ago, such has been the explosion in knowledge and activity within the field. The interest and enthusiasm this project has raised among all who have shared in its creation also owes to the fact that OB's interests have never been more important than at the present time. We are moving into an age of increasing uncertainty and choice about how we organize and work. These developments are extensively documented in this book. Although the nature of work and organization, as defined above, are matters of choice, those decisions have in the past often been heavily constrained by prior choices about technologies and institutional forms. This has often cast OB scholars in the role of powerless observers or critical commentators on the dysfunctions of organization, such as monotonous work, autocratic management, interpersonal and intergroup conflict and inefficient production. The disciplines of engineering and finance have tended to set the organizational agenda, with SCIENTIFIC MANAGEMENT[1] as their operational paradigm, leaving PERSONNEL MANAGEMENT to pick up the pieces, i.e. deal with the human consequences of operational imperatives.

This industrial order is being dismembered before our eyes, as a function of several developments. First, there is a vast increase in the complexity of technical and financial problems in business, and complexity means choice. Second, new business disciplines such as marketing and strategy have raised awareness of the need to satisfy multiple STAKEHOLDERS, and the inherently open-ended nature of this challenge. This implies for organizations the need to be proactive as well as responsive in their DECISION MAKING about market positioning, resourcing and external relationships. Third, competitive pressures, intercultural exchange, INFORMATION TECHNOLOGY, regulatory pressures, and demographic developments in LABOR MARKETS are having the simultaneous effect of increasing the diversity of organizational forms visible in society and making apparent the implausibility of "one best way" solutions to the problems of managing. Fourth, the human and material costs of poorly designed jobs, unskilled management practices, and ill-conceived ways of organizing and communicating, are being laid bare, not just as a result of pressures to reduce costs, but also through a growing awareness that the satisfaction of human needs and values is essential to firms' ability to rise above the mediocre in the quality of their products and services. Fifth, and finally, all of this implies change, often on a profound scale. Throughout organizations of all kinds and among people at all levels, one finds a primary and urgent desire to know how best to manage change, and to understand what factors help or hinder human adaptive processes.

As a result of these recent developments, we are now witnessing the curious irony that ideas with a long pedigree of vigorous promotion in scholarly articles but almost universal neglect in business practice, have suddenly become prime concerns to managers. COMPETITIVENESS is newly perceived as linked with long-familiar concepts such as JOB ENRICHMENT, SELF-MANAGEMENT, PARTICIPATION, LEADERSHIP STYLE, TEAMBUILDING, DECENTRALIZATION, ORGANIZATIONAL CULTURE and STRATEGIC CHOICE. OB is now in demand as never before, from individual managers struggling to make sense of their experience and take charge of their careers, to business leaders realizing that competitive success means drawing creatively upon their prime asset – human adaptability, tacit knowledge and talent.

How To Use This Book

This *Encyclopedic Dictionary* is a reference work but its entries give much more than definitions. Some 500 essays by over 180 leading authorities provide definitive statements of current knowledge and thinking about all the key concepts and ideas of OB. Entries vary in length according to the significance or specificity of a term, but most are 500–1000 words long, and follow a format which includes the following elements:

definition – state of knowledge – current significance – future trends & applications

This is designed to be especially useful to people new to the field, cutting through the jargon barrier with clear, concise and informative explanations of key concepts and issues, with an emphasis on

[1] Words set in small capital letters are entry cross-references, i.e. they are the titles or "headwords" for substantive entries to be found in this volume.

current and developing trends. These qualities are also intended to make the book a valuable resource for educators, graduate students, researchers, practising managers and any other inquiring minds.

The format of the volume means it can be used in many ways – it is an almost-infinite matrix. Because entries are substantive essays, and each contains multiple cross-references (terms set in capitals in the text, plus additional cross-references at the end of each entry), any number of entries may form a continuous and developing chain or program of reading. This makes the volume ideal for executive, short-course reading, core MBA modules, other programs, or just personal exploration of related themes.

Since each entry provides key references and further reading on topics, it can also be seen as 500 gateways into specialist areas for students and educators. The Subject Index at the end of the volume is designed to help reader searches. (Entry headwords are marked in bold).

Possibilities for usage are further extended by the wide coverage of the volume. The field as represented here is much broader than is to be found in the curriculum of a single OB course, and has been defined to embrace the broadest interests of writers on organizations. In addition to core OB issues it encompasses key topics in HUMAN RESOURCES MANAGEMENT, BUSINESS ETHICS, INTERNATIONAL MANAGEMENT, ORGANIZATION THEORY and STRATEGIC MANAGEMENT.

Since the volume is committed to reporting what is known at the leading edge of the field, we are also committed to regular future editions of *The Encyclopedic Dictionary*. Readers can help us here. We would be pleased to hear from you, what topics you would like to see included in future editions, and what trends that you detect in the field which should be represented.

The Field as Represented By The Dictionary

The reader's first impression on leafing through the contents of this volume may be the enormous breadth of the interests of OB scholars and practitioners. Even similar sounding headwords (entry titles) have widely diverging contents – see, for example, the quite different ideas described under LEARNING ORGANIZATION and ORGANIZATIONAL LEARNING. This diversity comes from four dimensions: level of analysis, domain, pedigree, and controversy.

Level of analysis (see LEVELS OF ANALYSIS) Within OB it is common for scholars to describe themselves or each other as working at a micro or macro level, though in reality this represents a continuum of interacting themes from individual experience and behavior (see INDIVIDUAL DIFFERENCES), through group and intergroup functioning (see GROUP DYNAMICS; WORK GROUPS), to the characteristics and behaviors of organizations as units of analysis (see ORGANIZATIONAL DESIGN; STRATEGIC MANAGEMENT). Many entries have an even wider focus, such as the nature of OCCUPATIONS, the POPULATION ECOLOGY of firms within sectors, and the effects of CULTURE on organizations. The chosen focus of a scholar's interest can often be traced to their academic origins – psychologists at the individual level, social psychologists at the group level, sociologists at the organizational level, and anthropologists and economists at the societal level.

Yet this academic division of labor is weakening as a result of two developments. First, as OB becomes more instituted as a defined subject area (mainly in business education) scholars have become increasingly aware of work outside their original disciplinary specialism and its relevance to their interests. Within specialist university departments, social scientists studying organizations may still call themselves I/O (Industrial/Organizational) Psychologists or Organizational Sociologists, but in interdisciplinary contexts, such as business schools, these labels become less useful as circumscribing and understanding the breadth of OB scholars' interests. Second, the problems which OB seeks to address, as presented by the business environment, do not come neatly wrapped in discipline-shaped parcels. To understand individual behavior or performance in an organization requires a developed sense of contextualism, i.e. an understanding of the nature of the "macro" forces bearing down upon the individual or the group, constraining their scope for action. Conversely, ideas about how organizations are designed or function benefits from awareness of the "micro" diversity and dynamics of INDIVIDUAL DIFFERENCES in MOTIVATION, VALUES, and PERSONALITY.

It is helpful, therefore, to draw a distinction between the nature of a field of study and a discipline. Fields are defined by the content of their topics. Disciplines are defined by how they define their approach to topics – the type of knowledge they seek, the kinds of theories they construct, and the character of the methods they use. This makes OB an interdisciplinary field of study. It is defined, as we have seen above, by a bounded range of issues and problems, and within it, different social sciences meet, often with common cause.

Domain Domain denotes four kinds of activity in which one finds scholars displaying differing balances of interest: theory building/testing, empirical investigation, methodological development/ practice, and intervention/application. However, the interdependence of these domains points to the danger of individual scholars becoming over-identified with any of them. Theorizing without data drifts into armchair dreaming. The pursuit of data without theoretical foundation becomes trivial or empty cataloging. The pursuit of methodological rigor for its own sake degenerates into technical game playing. Application without conceptual, empirical and methodological discipline become mere selling. However, readers will find entries and authors differing in the emphasis across these domains, according to the state of knowledge about a topic. For example, there are topics whose primary challenge is theoretical, such as EXCHANGE RELATIONS, areas where the descriptive accumulation of data is the main objective, such as AGE; fields in which methodological development is a priority, such as NETWORK ANALYSIS; and areas where different methods of application are compared, such as SELECTION INTERVIEWING. However, most topics (including all of the above) offer challenges in all four domains.

Pedigree Entry topics also differ in terms of their historical and cultural positioning. Some are represented here because of their importance to the past development of the field, such as MOTIVATOR/HYGIENE THEORY, whose insights have now largely been absorbed into current thinking. Others stand at the leading edge of the field and look likely to be areas of major future growth and application, such as PUNCTUATED EQUILIBRIUM and BUSINESS ETHICS, though one can never be too sure. The field of knowledge creation is a treacherous arena in which to try to second-guess the future and pick winners. This is not the same as identifying the unanswered questions, untested applications or future research needs of a topic, and in most entries authors have sought to do this.

Controversy The fourth way in which topics differ is the degree to which they are contested. Contributors were asked to provide definitive statements about their topics, but at the same time to be open about controversies or substantive debates within them. Readers should not be alarmed if what they read in one entry is qualified or challenged in another – indeed the cross-referencing is intended to help surface these debates (compare, for example, EMOTION with EMOTIONS IN ORGANIZATIONS, or CHANGE METHODS with EVALUATION RESEARCH). Some entries offer more explicit challenge to orthodoxy than others (see, for example, POSTMODERNISM or CRITICAL THEORY). Others summarize the status quo in fields where a substantial consensus has emerged (e.g. GOAL-SETTING and MINORITY GROUP INFLUENCE). These contrasts are healthy in any field of inquiry where theories compete to give more complete explanations of phenomena, where new empirical studies are continuing to accumulate evidence, and where relevance is critically tested through application and practice. In other words, if you detect apparent contradictions between entries, they represent the vitality of competition in a growing field.

The Method: How The Dictionary was Conceived and Developed

The Blackwell Encyclopedic Dictionary of Organizational Behavior is one of those projects which, when one hears of it, one's reaction is, "what a great idea – I could really use something like that." Well, that was my response on first thinking about it with the publisher, and it was a reaction pretty universally shared by contributors. Very few people approached to contribute declined the invitation. Unsolicited enthusiasm was the most common response: "this is a wonderful project – my graduate students/executive classes/researchers/and I will find this really helpful."

Clearly, to fulfil this potential required an organization and method. The key elements in the chronology of this were as follows:

A model of the field The first major editorial task (in November 1991) was to develop a model of the field in terms of broad topic areas to be covered, with sample headwords to illustrate each. Feedback from Blackwell Publishers and external referees subsequently refined the categories into the following list: 1. individual differences; 2. job and role attitudes and behaviors; 3. management and leadership; 4. groups and group processes; 5. power, politics and intergroup relations; 6. human resources management; 7. organization theory; 8. organizational strategy and effectiveness; 9. human factors and technology; 10. culture and change; 11. metatheory and method.

This formed the framework for the first draft of the headword list, and is the structure underlying the alphabetical sequence which appears in the volume.

Generating the headword list In April 1992 Advisory Editors, Professors Randall Schuler and Andrew Van de Ven, were recruited, not just to offer their specialist expert advice respectively in human resources management and organization theory, but also as scholars renowned for their breadth and mastery of the wider field. Our first collective task was to develop and refine the headword list, with the aim of achieving balance of content across domains, and a balance of specificity/detail across topics. To this end all headwords were classified, specifying target wordcount length and number of references. The length categories ranged from 50 words for a glossary entry to 4,000 for a few major feature entries. The final distribution by length was a bell-curve: the most frequent allocations were 500 and 1000 words, with fewer in the shorter and longer categories.

Identifying contributors Once the provisional headword list was complete (October 1992) the editorial team set about drawing up a contributor list. Selection and allocation was designed to achieve an international mix, but allowing for a North American preponderance, in keeping with the field's distribution of scholarship worldwide. It was also designed to draw upon a mix of established authorities and mid-career scholars and young rising stars. More senior authors were more often allocated major fields with wide boundaries and long histories, and newer scholars invited to write on specialist and emerging topics. Around April 1993, the list was complete and letters of invitation were sent out, accompanied by sample entries and guidance *Notes for Contributors*. In the months following, the contributor and headword list were extended and refined in response to contributor feedback.

The editorial process Writing a concise, informative and definitive essay within a very limited wordcount is no easy task. Most contributors did an outstanding job with their first drafts. Editorial feedback, typically, was to suggest ways of tightening text to fit within limits, queries for clarification of key points, and requests for additional material. The most common request of the latter kind was for contributors to expand on how their topic related to organizational experience, or to add comment on what future questions and developments might be foreseen for their topic. From mid-1994, with the bulk of entries now submitted, copy-editing commenced. Apart from minor adjustments to remove anomalies, overlaps and solecisms, the main task here was cross-referencing. This not only meant highlighting and adding textual headwords, but making additional suggestions at the end of entries, often to make connections which might not be obvious to readers.

Production The final stages of the project were those associated with production – final copy-editing, type-setting, proof-reading and printing.

You hold the result in your hands. Read, use, enjoy.

—— Acknowledgments ——

The name of my secretary Angie Quest easily merits top billing for help way beyond the call of duty toward the creation of this book. Angie's name is well-known to contributors, since she has had continuing dialog with them all and has been absolutely indispensable to the smooth running of this project. There were times when we were simultaneously commissioning new contributors, receiving new manuscripts, suggestions, revisions, and receiving revised or finished copy. The complexity of this task with over 180 contributors writing over 500 pieces was, frankly, mind-boggling. It didn't boggle Angie's mind, and she handled the task and the contributors superbly throughout, always cheerful, tactful, insistent when necessary and unfailingly accurate and efficient in this multi-track operation. Most heartfelt thanks, not just from me but also from anyone who profits from or enjoys this book, are owed to her. A truly brilliant job.

Randall Schuler and Andy Van de Ven also gave outstanding assistance at various stages of the project. Most of all, they gave deep and considered thought to the vital issues of content, balance and design to ensure the book represented the newest as well as the most traditional interests of OB scholars across a wide-ranging field. They also did a great job in helping suggest and commission the wonderful contributor list we assembled, also giving occasional additional advice on feedback to authors where I needed additional opinions. The fine quality of this book is a tribute to their contribution.

The staff at Blackwells have also been terrific. First thanks are due to the editorial team of Alyn Shipton, Alison Mudditt and Tim Goodfellow, whose combined commitment from Blackwell's Reference, Psychology and Business divisions helped the interdisciplinary vision of this volume to flourish, and were essential to its continuity and efficient production. Successively, Judith Harvey, Jason Pearce, Denise Rea, Sarah McNamee and other staff, provided first-class backroom support – circulating contributors, detecting problems to be solved, logging copy and providing technical advice. Thanks to you all.

I also want to thank all my professional colleagues, at London Business School and beyond for their consistent support, encouragement and advice at all points on the long journey from inception to completion. Special thanks here are due to the OB Group at London Business School, for the excellence of their contributions to the volume, for their insights and ideas about its conception, and their tolerance of my absorption with it during some very busy periods of the academic calendar. Without these supports, the book would have been a near impossible task, and much less enjoyable and meaningful as a project.

My wife and partner Mary, I thank too, for her patience at my regular distraction day and night by piles of manuscripts, and for her unflagging and generous support.

Last, but by no means least, I thank our contributors, for their outstanding work, their good-natured responsiveness to editorial suggestions and progress-chasing, and for their belief in this project. Financial rewards for short reference entries are necessarily limited, but clearly this was never the source of their high motivation to take part and produce work of the highest quality standards (see INTRINSIC/EXTRINSIC MOTIVATION!). Throughout the process, I have continued to receive numerous notes from them affirming that this was a great project and expressing thanks and encouragement to me and the team. That meant a lot. Thank you.

Nigel Nicholson

Acknowledgments

Contributors

Seymour Adler
Stevens Institute of Technology

Stuart Albert
University of Minnesota

Teresa M. Amabile
Harvard Business School

Deborah Ancona
Massachusetts Institute of Technology

Philip Anderson
Dartmouth College

Chris Argyris
Harvard University

Richard Arvey
University of Minnesota

Stephen Barley
Stanford University

William P. Barnett
Stanford University

Jay B. Braney
The Ohio State University

Bernard Bass
SUNY, Binghamton

Max Bazerman
Northwestern University

Avner Ben-Ner
University of Minnesota

Kenneth Bettenhausen
University of Colorado at Denver

John Bigelow
Boise State University

Paul Blyton
University of Wales

Jeanne Brett
Northwestern University

Philip Bromiley
University of Minnesota

William Brown
University of Cambridge

L. David Brown
Boston University

John G. Burgoyne
Lancaster University

W. Warner Burke
Teachers College, Columbia University

Richard Butler
University of Bradford

Kim Cameron
University of Michigan

Andrew Clarkson
Boston University

Chris W. Clegg
University of Sheffield

Stewart Clegg
UWS MacArthur

A. P. Cockerill
London Business School

Adrienne Colella
Rutgers University

Mary Ann Collins
Brandeis University

Thomas D. Cook
Northwestern University

Arnold C. Cooper
Purdue University

Cary L. Cooper
University of Manchester Institute of Science and Technology

John Cordery
University of Western Australia

Thomas G. Cummings
University of Southern California

Sandra Dawson
University of Cambridge

Angelo De Nisi
Rutgers University

Gerardine DeSanctis
Duke University

David L. Deephouse
Louisiana State University

Theresa Domagalski
University of South Florida

Robert Drazin
Emory University

William Dyer
Brigham Young University

P. C. Earley
University of California, Irvine

Jack E. Edwards
Defense Manpower Data Center

P. K. Edwards
University of Warwick

Miriam Erez
Technion–Israel Institute of Technology

Paul Evans
INSEAD

Daniel C. Feldman
University of South Carolina

Mark Fenton-O'Creevy
London Business School

Alan C. Filley
University of Wisconsin

Stephen Fineman
University of Bath

Clive Fletcher
Goldsmiths College, University of London

Charles Fombrun
New York University

John A. Fossum
University of Minnesota

Arthur Francis
University of Glasgow

John Freeman
University of California, Berkeley

Michael Frese
University of Giessen

David Fryer
University of Stirling

A. G. Gallagher
Queens University, Belfast

Jennifer M. George
Texas A&M University

Barry Gerhart
Cornell University

Connie Gersick
University of California, Los Angeles

Robert A. Giacalone
University of Richmond

Rob Goffee
London Business School

Irwin L. Goldstein
University of Maryland

Brian Graham-Moore
University of Texas at Austin

Lynda Gratton
London Business School

Jerald Greenberg
Ohio State University

Hal B. Gregerson
Brigham Young University

Ricky W. Griffin
Texas A&M University

David Guest
Birkbeck College, London

Barbara A. Gutek
University of Arizona

J. Richard Hackman
Harvard University

Jerald Hage
University of Maryland

Colin L. Hales
University of Surrey

Donald C. Hambrick
Columbia University

Kathy A. Hanisch
Iowa State University

Michael M. Harris
University of Missouri-St Louis

Jean Hartley
Birkbeck College, University of London

Torsten Heinbokel
University of Giessen

Peter Herriot
Sundridge Park Management Centre

Beryl Hesketh
University of New South Wales

Linda Hill
Harvard Business School

Wendy Hirsh
Institute for Employment Studies (University of Sussex)

Joyce C. Hogan
University of Tulsa

Edwin P. Hollander
Bernard M. Baruch College, CUNY

Dian Marie Hosking
Aston University

Robert House
Wharton School

Graham Hubbard
Royal Melbourne Institute of Technology

Anne Sigismund Huff
University of Colorado

John W. Hunt
London Business School

Daniel Ilgen
Michigan State University

Susan E. Jackson
New York University

Marie Jahoda
University of Sussex

Mariann Jelinek
College of William and Mary

John M. Jermier
University of South Florida

Gary Johns
Concordia University

Ruth Kanfer
University of Minnesota

Tony Keenan
Heriot-Watt University

John Kelly
London School of Economics and Political Science

Manfred Kets de Vries
INSEAD

Richard Klimoski
Ohio State University

P. L. Koopman
Free University, Amsterdam

Kenneth Koput
University of Arizona

Kathy E. Kram
Boston University

Roderick Kramer
Stanford University

Michael Lawless
University of Colorado

Barbara S. Lawrence
University of California, Los Angeles

Gerald E. Ledford, Jr
University of Southern California

Karen Legge
Lancaster University

Ariel S. Levi
Wayne State University

Alessandro Lomi
London Business School

Robert G. Lord
University of Akron

Judi Marshall
University of Bath

Joanne Martin
Stanford University

Mark J. Martinko
Florida State University

Michael Masuch
University of Amsterdam

Thomas C. Mawhinney

Nigel Meager
University of Sussex

Elizabeth O. Mellon
London Business School

Marshall W. Meyer
University of Pennsylvania

Stephen Mezias
New York University

Susan Miller
Durham University

Henry Mintzberg
McGill University and INSEAD

Lawrence B. Mohr
University of Michigan

Allan M. Mohrman Jr
University of Southern California

Tim Morris
London Business School

J. Keith Murnighan
University of British Columbia

Nigel Nicholson
London Business School

Stella M. Nkomo
University of North Carolina at Charlotte

Greg Oldham
University of Illinois

J. Douglas Orton
Hautes Études Commerciales, Paris

Richard Osborn
Wayne State University

Roy L. Payne
University of Sheffield

Maury Peiperl
London Business School

Johannes M. Pennings
University of Pennsylvania

Jeffery T. Polzer
Northwestern University

Scott Poole
University of Minnesota

Walter W. Powell
University of Arizona

Robert D. Pritchard
Texas A&M University

Derek Pugh
Open University

Elizabeth C. Ravlin
University of South Carolina

Gordon Redding
University of Hong Kong

Peter Smith Ring
Loyola Marymount University

Catherine A. Riordan
University of Missouri-Rolla

Ivan T. Robertson
University of Manchester Institute of Science and Technology

David Rogers
New York University

James E. Rosenbaum
Northwestern University

Paul Rosenfeld

Sara Rynes
University of Iowa

John Schaubroeck
University of Nebraska

Randall S. Schuler
New York University

Viv Shackleton
Aston University

Noel P. Sheey
Queen's University, Belfast

Henry P. Sims Jr
University of Maryland – College Park

John W. Slocum
Southern Methodist University

Sabine Sonnentag
University of Amsterdam

Paul Sparrow
Manchester Business School

Paul E. Spector
University of South Florida

R. B. Stammers
Aston University

Linda Stroh
Loyola University

Robert I. Sutton
Stanford University

Marie D. Thomas
California State University, San Marcos

Cheryl J. Travers
Loughborough University Business School

Linda Trevino
The Pennsylvania State University

Roger Undy
Templeton College, University of Oxford

John Van Maanen
Massachusetts Institute of Technology

Andrew Van de Ven
University of Minnesota

Marc J. Ventresca
Northwestern University

Mary Ann Von Glinow
Florida International University

Toby D. Wall
University of Sheffield

John P. Wanous
The Ohio State University

Peter Warr
University of Sheffield

Karl E. Weick
University of Michigan

David T. H. Weir
University of Bradford Management Centre

Michael A. West
University of Sheffield

Roy Westbrook
London Business School

David A. Whetten
Brigham Young University

Uco J. Wiersma
Hong Kong Baptist University

Charles R. Williams
Texas Christian University

Paul Willman
London Business School

Donna J. Wood
University of Pittsburgh

Stephen Wood
London School of Economics & Political Science

Richard W. Woodman
Texas A&M University

Stuart A. Youngblood
Texas Christian University

Edward J. Zajac
Northwestern University

Dale E. Zand
New York University

Fred Zimmerman
University of St Thomas

— A —

ability This concept denotes competence in an activity (*see* COMPETENCIES). It is the capacity to act – it is realized talent. Ability is a synonym for mental power, although there are other human abilities beyond the cognitive domain. Ability, a construct inferred from human performance, is a product of inherited genetic predispositions and acquired characteristics. Basic or general abilities are important for performance of a wide range of tasks (*see* PERFORMANCE, INDIVIDUAL).

Historically, intelligence was seen as the basic human ability, and perhaps the most classic controversy in psychology is whether intelligence is a general ability (g) or a collection of specific abilities. Spearman, at the turn of the century, studied the relations between various mental measures and concluded that intelligence (*see* INTELLIGENCE, TESTING) has one general component and several secondary components. Thorndike and Thurstone argued that there are multiple components of intelligence; the most comprehensive conceptualization of intelligence is Guilford's structure of intellect model, which proposes 120 cognitive abilities. Cattell and Horn, in a more recent interpretation, suggest two dimensions – fluid intelligence, based on the individual's biological inheritance, and crystallized intelligence, based on fluid ability combined with experience. Measures of basic intellectual abilities almost always include verbal comprehension and quantitative reasoning (*see* COGNITIVE PROCESSES). In addition to the cognitive domain, abilities underlying physical, perceptual, and psychomotor task performance have been identified (Fleishman & Quaintance, 1984).

See also **Assessment; Psychological testing; Skill**

Bibliography

Fleishman, E. A. & Quaintance, M. K. (1984). *Taxonomies of human performance*. New York: Academic Press.

JOYCE C. HOGAN

absenteeism The term can be defined as the failure to report for scheduled work. Absenteeism is distinguished from lateness or tardiness, which indicates a failure to show up for scheduled work on *time* and from TURNOVER, which indicates a permanent break in the employment relationship. Traditionally, managers have been interested in absenteeism because of its cost to organizations, while academic researchers have been interested in absenteeism on the assumption that it indicates something about employees' social or psychological attachment to the organization (*see* COMMITMENT; PSYCHOLOGICAL CONTRACT).

The Measurement of Absenteeism

Many organizations are notoriously lax when it comes to recording systematically instances of absence. When they do so, they often codify absence instances with attributions as to cause which are of suspect accuracy (*see* ATTRIBUTION). Consequently, contemporary researchers most often simply divide absenteeism into *time lost*, the number of days missed over some period, and *frequency*, the number of inceptions or spells of absence over some period irrespective of the duration of each incident. To permit comparisons of employees with a different number of scheduled days or to characterize absenteeism at the group level (*see* LEVELS OF ANALYSIS) these figures can also be expressed as rates. Following the logic that absence is missing *scheduled* work, not reporting due to jury duty, vacation, or maternity leave is not generally counted as absence.

Absence is a low base rate behavior, in that most employees exhibit relatively low absence levels while a few exhibit higher levels. Thus, a frequency distribution for absenteeism is truncated on the low end and positively skewed. Because it is a low base rate behavior, absence measures for individuals must be aggregated over a reasonably long period of time (3 to 12 months) to achieve adequate RELIABILITY of measurement. Even then, the reliability of absence measures (indexed by interperiod stability or internal consistency) is tenuous and varies across samples. Some VALIDITY evidence suggests that frequency of absence is more likely than time lost to reflect a voluntary component (Chadwick-Jones, Nicholson, & Brown, 1982; Hackett & Guion, 1985). Because of its nonnormal distribution, researchers should give serious consideration to transforming absence data or using alternative statistical procedures (e.g., tobit) in its analysis (*see* STATISTICAL METHODS). Managers should be aware that a few extreme absentees can have a disproportionate effect on means calculated from absence distributions, especially for small samples.

The Correlates and Causes of Absenteeism

A longstanding tradition concerns the correlation between demographic variables and absenteeism. This research reveals reliable associations between AGE and absence among men (younger workers exhibit more absence (Hackett, 1990)) and GENDER and absence (women are absent more than men) (*see* SEX DIFFERENCES; WOMEN AT WORK). However, little theory has emerged to explain these associations, and they tend to be confounded by differences in OCCUPATION and job STATUS.

Johns (1987) presents several "models" of absenteeism that correspond to both popular explanations and research-based explanations for absenteeism. Concerning the *medical model*, there is very little evidence regarding the association between verified illness and absence. However, self-reported health status is correlated with absence, and people tend to attribute the majority of their own absence to minor medical problems. The ultimate accuracy of such attributions is questionable, since "sickness" absence has motivational correlates, medical diagnoses often reflect prevailing community standards, and people sometimes adopt sick roles that manifest themselves in absence (*see* MENTAL HEALTH).

The *withdrawal model* suggests that absenteeism is an attempt to remove oneself temporarily from aversive working conditions (*see* WITHDRAWAL, ORGANIZATIONAL). The voluminous literature on the relationship between JOB SATISFACTION and absenteeism reveals a very modest relationship, with dissatisfaction with the work itself being the facet most associated with absenteeism (Hackett & Guion, 1985). The progression-of-withdrawal hypothesis posits a movement from temporary absence to permanent turnover. In fact, there is a positive relationship between these variables at the individual level, a condition that is necessary but not sufficient to prove such a progression.

The *deviance model* derives from the negative consequences of absence for organizations. In its more elaborate form, it suggests that absentees harbor negative dispositional traits that render them unreliable (*see* PERSONALITY). People tend to make negative attributions about the causes of others' absenteeism, and absenteeism is a frequent cause of employee/management conflict. People also have a tendency to underreport their own absenteeism and to see their own behavior as exemplary compared to that of their coworkers and occupational peers (Johns, 1994). Evidence for an actual connection between negative traits and absenteeism is sparse and indirect. A necessary condition would be cross-situational consistency in absenteeism, and there is some evidence for that. More rigorous proof would be an association between absenteeism and other negative behaviors. Bycio's (1992) review indicates that more frequent absentees tend to be poorer performers and notes that "a disposition for delinquency" is one possible explanation.

The *economic model* of absence suggests that attendance behavior is influenced by economic and quasi-economic constraints and opportunities. Those who value highly their nonwork time are more likely to be absent, and looser contractual provisions regarding attendance result in more absence (*see* NONWORK/WORK). Absence tends to increase when unemployment falls and when lucrative overtime pay is available. Some INDUSTRIAL RELATIONS scholars have argued that absence is a form of unorganized conflict that substitutes for some of the functions of COLLECTIVE ACTION.

The *cultural model* of absence begins with the observation that there is often more variance between aggregates of individuals (such as work groups, departments, organizations, occupations, industries, and nations) than within these aggregates. Mechanisms of social influence and control subsumed under the label absence CULTURE have been advanced to account in part for these differences between groups (Chadwick-Jones et al., 1982; Johns & Nicholson, 1982). Some rich case studies of absence cultures exist, and work unit absence has been shown to account for individual absence over and above individual-level predictors. What is needed currently is more rigorous evidence on the formation and content of absence cultures (*see* ORGANIZATIONAL CULTURE).

In addition to the research subsumed under the above models, other eclectic themes can be seen in contemporary research. These include investigations of mood and absence (*see* AFFECT; EMOTION), the self-regulatory and coping functions of absence (*see* SELF-REGULATION), and the prediction of absence using within-person rather than between-person models.

Managing Absenteeism

The deviance model has tended to dominate management approaches to absence. As a result, surveys show that PUNISHMENT and discipline systems are the most common methods of controlling absence. Used alone, they are not especially effective because of negative side effects and because few employees are actually punished. More effective are mixed consequence systems that punish extreme offenders but reward good attenders with money, time off, and so on (Rhodes & Steers, 1990) (*see* REWARDS). JOB ENRICHMENT and FLEXITIME have both been associated with reduced absence, as have SELF-MANAGEMENT programs that teach employees to regulate their own attendance behavior. Badly needed are theories that translate the likely causes of absenteeism into credible interventions and organizations with the foresight to experiment with these interventions. Obsession with extreme offenders has distracted managers from giving attention to the attendance behavior of *all* employees.

See also **Job characteristics; Motivation and performance; Person–job fit; Performance, individual; Stress**

Bibliography

Bycio, P. (1992). Job performance and absenteeism: A review and meta-analysis. *Human Relations*, **45**, 193–220.

Chadwick-Jones, J. K., Nicholson, N. & Brown, C. (1982). *Social psychology of absenteeism*. New York: Praeger.

Goodman, P. S. & Atkin, R. S. (Eds), (1984). *Absenteeism*. San Francisco: Jossey-Bass.

Hackett, R. D. (1990). Age, tenure, and employee absenteeism. *Human Relations*, **43**, 601–619.

Hackett, R. D. & Guion, R. M. (1985). A reevaluation of the absenteeism–job satisfaction relationship. *Organizational Behavior and Human Decision Processes*, **35**, 340–381.

Johns, G. (1987). Understanding and managing absence from work. In S. L. Dolan & R. S. Schuler (Eds), *Canadian readings in personnel and human resources management* 324–335. St. Paul, MN: West.

Johns, G. (1994). Absenteeism estimates by employees and managers: Divergent perspectives and self-serving perceptions. *Journal of Applied Psychology*, **79**, 229–239.

Johns, G. & Nicholson, N. (1982). The meanings of absence: New strategies for theory and research. *Research in Organizational Behavior*, **4**, 127–173.

Martocchio, J. J. & Harrison, D. A. (1993). To be there or not to be there? Questions, theories, and methods in absenteeism research. *Research in Personnel and Human Resources Management*, **11**, 259–329.

Rhodes, S. R. & Steers, R. M. (1990). *Managing employee absenteeism*. Reading, MA: Addison-Wesley.

GARY JOHNS

accidents "Accident" normally refers to a chance event or consequence which, being unexpected, seems to lack an obvious cause. Investigations of industrial or organizational accidents commonly attribute cause either to machine failure, environmental factors, human error, or a combination of these (*see* ERGONOMICS; ERRORS). Applied psychologists and ergonomists have traditionally seen their organizational role to include accident analysis, particularly when accidents might be due to human error (Sheehy & Chapman, 1987).

A number of methods have been devised to assist in the investigations and analysis of accidents. Task analysis permits the design of work practices according to regulated sequences of behaviors (*see* JOB ANALYSIS). This makes it possible to identify human error from a reliable and well-established reference point. However, in the modern workplace the increasing flexibility in work roles and responsibilities and the increased sophistication of industrial equipment, means that highly regularized work sequence reference points are less common. This type of analysis is probably inadequate in large-scale socio-technical systems (Rasmussen, 1990) (*see* SOCIOTECHNICAL THEORY). Another type of accident analysis involves tracing the causal path from consequences back to an identified source and to contributing factors. The advantage of this approach is that it allows the enumeration of a broad range of factors, and the identifications of inter-relationships between them, and can guide the design of countermeasures. However, it can lead to biases in the sampling and analysis of error behaviors (Brown & Groeger, 1988) (*see* BIAS). This occurs because only error behaviors resulting in a recorded accident are studied. We have no indication of the frequency of occurrence of that behavior, nor of its variability, under circumstances which do not lead to accidents. Limitations in accident analysis methods may explain why some types of accident or patterns of accident are difficult to predict or explain. For example, Guastello (1988) describes the phenomena of small groups being subject to a highly variable accident rate (even bimodal) whereas large groups often display consistent rates over time (*see* GROUP SIZE).

The study and prevention of accidents is not simply a matter of identifying abnormal events and practices. Many accidents are "normal" in the sense that they are an inevitable consequence of the design and management of certain kinds of work practice. Dwyer and Raferty (1991) have offered a sociological theory of industrial accidents using this idea. They suggest accidents are a product of three levels (not necessarily hierarchical), of social relations of work: (1) REWARDS; (2) command; and (3) organization. The reward level refers to the work that is produced through the manipulation of recompense (monetary or symbolic) in return for work effort (e.g., price-work, overtime, or BONUS PAYMENTS). The command level refers to work produced through the use of POWER, overt or covert, such as when risks at work are accepted as normal. Organizational level refers to the division of labor through task structure, the relationship between tasks and the knowledge or information that workers possess.

See also **Crises; Safety; Stress; Information processing**

Bibliography

Brown, I. D. & Groeger, J. (1988). Risk perception and decision taking during the transition between novice and experienced driver status. *Ergonomics*, **31**, 585–597.

Dwyer, T. & Raferty, A. E. (1991). Industrial accidents are produced by social relations at work: A sociological theory of industrial accidents. *Applied Ergonomics*, **22**, 167–178.

Guastello, S. J. (1988). Catastrophe modeling of the accident process: Organizational subunit size. *Psychological Bulletin*, **103**, 246–255.

Rassmussen, J. (1990). The role of error in organizing behaviour. *Ergonomics*, **33**, 185–1199.

Reason, J., Manstead, A., Stradling, S., Baxter, J. & Cambell, K. (1990). Errors and violations on the road: A real distinction? *Ergonomics*, **33**, 1315–1332.

Sheehy, N. P. & Chapman, A. J. (1987). Industrial accidents. In C. L. Cooper & I. T. Robertson (Eds), *International review of industrial and organizational psychology 1987*. Chichester, UK: Wiley.

NOEL SHEEHY and A. G. GALLAGHER

accountability The term denotes responsibility for particular activities, results, or outcomes; specification of the person(s) or group(s) who hold such responsibility in an organization; the practice of holding designated individuals responsible, in an effort to insure that tasks are accomplished on time and according to agreed-upon methods and criteria. Literally, the term implies that the responsible party will be expected to account for outcomes, positive or negative, explaining how and why they occurred.

Accountability has roots in CLASSICAL MANAGEMENT THEORY, in the DIVISION OF LABOR into parts, and in explicit job specifications. Consistent with Taylor's SCIENTIFIC MANAGEMENT, as well as with widespread norms of fairness, employees in organizations are deemed accountable for that portion of the work under their direct control; it is assumed that they can and will cause agreed-upon results for that work. Accountability thus also assumes that results can be directly linked to the actions of specific individuals or groups. More generally, accountability carries an assumption of POWER as well as responsibility to affect specified results, often including profit or loss. Accounting systems, performance ASSESSMENT systems, and organizational arrangements generally are characterized by accountability if responsibility for identified outcomes is charged to specified individuals.

See also **Job analysis; Job description; Delegation; Hierarchy; Organizational design**

Bibliography

Hoghland, J. C. & Wood, J. R. (1980). Control in organizations and the commitment of members. *Social Forces*, **59**, (1), 92–104.

MARIANN JELINEK

achievement, need for This denotes a motivational disposition toward performance improvement and achievement under challenging or competitive conditions. Need for achievement, or nAch, has since 1947 been the subject of an impressive program of research by McClelland (1985), his students and others. This research has shown that those high in nAch are distinguished by a preference toward effort-based tasks on which they have a moderate – rather than a very high or low – probability of success and that provide them with concrete performance FEEDBACK. Tasks of this sort allow those high in nAch to more accurately diagnose the degree of effort required to improve and, ultimately, to succeed. A key developmental predictor of high nAch is early independence TRAINING. McClelland has measured societal differences in nAch and demonstrated how these differences are predictive of subsequent economic development. The preferred method for measuring individual differences in nAch is through the Thematic Apperception Test (TAT) or a similar, fantasy-based measure of achievement need (*see* PERSONALITY TESTING); self-report measures of achievement motivation are only weakly correlated with fantasy-based measures of nAch and are less predictive of achievement outcomes.

See also **Personality; Motivation; Power**

Bibliography

McClelland, D. C. (1985). *Human motivation*. Glenview, IL: Scott, Foresman.

Spangler, W. D. (1992). Validity of questionnaire and TAT measures of need for achievement: Two meta-analyses. *Psychological Bulletin*, **112**, 140–154.

SEYMOUR ADLER

action research "Action research aims to contribute both to the practical concerns of people in an immediate problematic situation and to the goals of social science by joint collaboration within a mutually acceptable ethical framework" (Rapoport, 1970, p. 499).

Its origin has been traced back to Kurt Lewin's concern that THEORY should not only be used to guide practice and its evaluation but that, equally important, results of evaluation should inform theory in a cyclical process of fact-finding, action, and evaluation (Ketterer, Price, & Politser, 1980) (*see* EVALUATION RESEARCH).

Action research can be a rich source of accurate, detailed and authentic understanding of informants' assumptive worlds and contribute to both theory development and the prevention/intervention of psychological distress (*see* STRESS). Action researchers also emphasize the importance of the dissemination and use of the findings of research, ensuring that results are readily available in a comprehensible and meaningful form to the people involved.

Much research "dealing with organizations from an action–research base" (Trist, 1980, p. 148) has been carried out from a socio-technical systems theory (STST) perspective (*see* SOCIO-TECHNICAL THEORY). Classic STST action research redesigned the work of coal miners and weavers in the 1950s. More recent job redesign studies have also included action research components (Kemp, Wall, Clegg, & Cordery, 1983) (*see* ORGANIZATIONAL DEVELOPMENT).

Action research has also been carried out within a community psychology perspective. Action researchers have illuminated the social impact of new TECHNOLOGY by facilitating the development of computer applications by women, ethnic minorities, older people, the disabled, and unwaged people collectively in the community (Cassell, Fitter, Fryer, & Smith, 1988). Others have investigated the role of poverty in psychological distress through action research which simultaneously empowers informants in their dealings with state organizations by offering financial advice as part of the research process (Fryer & Fagan, 1994). Other researchers have empowered tenants' groups in lobbying state organizations for housing improvements by enabling tenants to demonstrate the physical and MENTAL HEALTH consequences of damp housing through research (Martin, Platt, & Hunt, 1987).

Action research is especially valuable when investigating difficult to access, exceedingly complex, or sensitive issues, or when working with informants who would be otherwise unlikely to become constructively involved in research. These include those who are: low in confidence; confused; apathetic; emotionally fragile; distressed; suspicious; or who have limited COMMUNICATION skills. It is interesting that Eric Trist's first published paper was based on research "methods of investigating and giving some kind of service to the community in order to gain legitimate access" (Trist, 1980, p. 146).

Jahoda's seminal study of an unemployed community is a classic example of such research. Her team distributed shoes and clothing, ran courses, provided free medical consultations and medications, and facilitated political party activity, amongst many other interventions, to build close and insight-yielding researcher/informant relationships. It was "a consistent point of policy that (none) of our researchers should be... a mere reporter or outside observer. Everyone was to fit naturally into the communal life by participating in some activity generally useful to the community" (Jahoda, Lazarsfeld, & Zeisel, 1972, p. 5). More recent Scandinavian action research in the same spirit is reported by Levi, Brenner, Hall, Hjelm, Salovaara, Arnetz, & Pettersson, (1984).

The main attraction of action research is, indeed, that it facilitates the development of ethically and ideologically more acceptable ways for persons as researchers to relate to persons as research informants, methods which do not reinforce distress or further disadvantage.

See also **Research methods; Consultancy intervention models; Empowerment**

Bibliography

Cassell, C., Fitter, M., Fryer, D. & Smith, L. (1988). The development of computer applications by non-employed people in community settings. *Journal of Occupational Psychology*, **61**, 89–102.

Fryer, D. & Fagan, R. (1994). The role of social psychological aspects of income on the mental health costs of unemployment: An action research perspective. *The Community Psychologist*, **27**, 2, 16–17.

Jahoda, M., Lazarsfeld, P. F. & Zeisel, H. (1972). *Marienthal: The sociography of an unemployed community*. London: Tavistock.

Kemp, N. J., Wall, T. D., Clegg, C. W. & Cordery, J. L. (1983). Autonomous work groups in a greenfield site: A comparative study. *Journal of Occupational Psychology*, **56**, 271–288.

Ketterer, R. F., Price, R. H. & Politser, P. E. (1980). The action research paradigm. In R. H. Price & P. E. Politser (Eds), *Evaluation and action in the social environment*. London: Academic Press.

Levi, L., Brenner, S., Hall, E. M., Hjelm, R., Salovaara, H., Arnetz, B. & Pettersson, I. (1984). The psychological, social and biochemical impacts of unemployment in Sweden. *International Journal of Mental Health*, **13**, 18–34.

Martin, C. J., Platt, C. D. & Hunt, S. M. (1987). Housing conditions and ill health. *British Medical Journal*, **294**, 1125–1127.

Rapoport, R. (1970). Three dilemmas of action research. *Human Relations*, **23**, 499–513.

Trist, E. L. (1980). Eric Trist, British Interdisciplinarian, interviewed by Marshall Sashkin. *Group and Organisation Studies*, **5**, 2, 144–166.

DAVID FRYER

action theory The theory offers an account of how human action is structured cognitively, and is of special relevance to JOB DESIGN, TRAINING, GOAL-SETTING, and other applications. It originated over 20 years ago in Germany and has been highly influential in European Industrial/Organizational Psychology since that time (Frese & Zapf, 1994; Hacker, 1985; Volpert, 1974). It is both a cognitive and a behaviorally oriented theory (*see* COGNITIVE PROCESSES). One basic assumption is that action is goal-oriented behavior. Action is described from a process-oriented and a structural viewpoint that are integrated in a hierarchical–sequential model.

From a process-oriented perspective, an action consists of developing goals, choosing between competing goals, orienting and making prognoses for future events, generating and selecting plans, executing and monitoring the plan, and processing FEEDBACK. These steps are not necessarily performed in this order, their sequence may appear rather chaotic, for example, when a goal is changed during the execution of a plan.

Regarding the structural aspects of action, actions are organized hierarchically. High level and global goals that cannot be achieved directly are divided into lower level subgoals. Generally, this means that units at lower levels are nested in units at higher levels (e.g., via TOTE units, see Miller, Galanter, & Pribram, 1960). One can distinguish four levels of action regulation along both the dimension of conscious to automatic regulation and the dimension of thoughts to muscular movements: Heuristic level, intellectual level, level of flexible action patterns, and sensorimotor level.

Operative image systems build the knowledge base of action regulation. They are internal long-term action-regulating representations and are comprised of movement-oriented, flexible actions, as well as complex schemata, strategies, metaplans, and heuristics. These image systems are task-oriented, selective, schematic, and "cost optimizing." Appropriate operative image systems are necessary for efficient action regulation.

Action Theory conceptualizes action as a mediator between the working person and the objective world of work objects such as material and outcome. Action is necessary in order to change work objects, but also the objective world has an impact on actions. Personal prerequisites influence actions, and actions have an impact on the PERSONALITY of the working person as well (*see* SOCIALIZATION).

Within this framework, Action Theory has developed applications for central phenomena in Industrial/Organizational Psychology: classifications of task characteristics (*see* JOB CHARACTERISTICS), instruments for job analysis, strategies for work design, ERRORS, the effects of competence on performance, training, and the developmental impact of work experience on personality.

One of Action Theory's most important contributions to OB is its analysis of competence for efficient actions and its methodology for enhancing competence through training. For example, effective managers demonstrate more causal thinking and better PLANNING, better diagnostic information seeking, and better synthetic thinking than do average managers (Klemp & McClelland, 1986). This is also true of blue and white collar workers.

Action Theory can well explain why goal setting methods (*see* GOAL SETTING) have been found to work so well, and why people will fall back on old routines even when new approaches are actually necessary (the principle of automatization).

See also **Cognition in organizations; Performance, individual; Human-computer interaction; Self-regulation**

Bibliography

Frese, M. & Zapf, D. (1994). Action as the core of work psychology: A German approach. In M. D. Dunnette, J. M. Hough & H. C. Triandis (Eds), *Handbook of industrial and organizational psychology* (vol. 4, 2nd edn, pp. 271–340). Palo Alto, CA: Consulting Psychologists Press.

Hacker, W. (1985). Activity: A fruitful concept in industrial psychology. In M. Frese & J. Sabini (Eds), *Goal directed behavior: The concept of action in psychology* (pp. 262–283). Hillsdale, NJ: Erlbaum.

Klemp, G. O. & McClelland, D. C. (1986). What characterizes intelligent functioning among senior managers. In R. J. Sternberg & R. K. Wagner (Eds), *Practical intelligence: Nature and origins of competence in the everyday world* pp. 51–83. Cambridge, UK: Cambridge University Press.

Miller, G. A., Galanter, E. & Pribram, K. H. (1960). *Plans and the structure of behavior*. London: Holt.

Volpert, W. (1974). *Handlungsstrukturanalyse als Beitrag zur Qualifikationsforschung*. Köln: Pahl–Rugenstein.

SABINE SONNENTAG and MICHAEL FRESE

adhocracy *see* DECISION MAKING; GARBAGE CAN; ORGANIZATIONAL DESIGN

administrative theory *see* ORGANIZATION THEORY

advanced manufacturing technology The term "advanced manufacturing technology" (AMT) describes computer-based manufacturing machinery and support systems. In other words, AMT is the manufacturing application of INFORMATION TECHNOLOGY. Closely related terms, often used as synonyms, include "new manufacturing technology," "microelectronic-based manufacturing technology," and "computer-aided manufacturing." A distinction can be made between direct and indirect applications of AMT (Sharit, Chang, & Salvendy, 1987). The former include stand-alone computer numerically controlled machine tools, assembly machines, and robotics installations. Where several such pieces of equipment are integrated under shared computer control, through various materials handling and transfer devices, they form a flexible manufacturing system (*see* FLEXIBILITY). Indirect applications include COMPUTER-AIDED DESIGN and computer-aided engineering, process planning, and production scheduling systems.

Two features of AMT make it a particularly significant development. First, because different applications are based on a common information technology there is the potential for greater functional integration through the transmission of information between direct and indirect applications (*see* INFORMATION PROCESSING). For example, information on materials use from shopfloor equipment can be downloaded to immediately update an inventory control system; data on machine utilization can be fed into production scheduling systems to optimize output; and design to production lead times can be reduced through computer-aided design functions being directly linked to part programming. This offers the prospect of full "computer integrated manufacturing," though in practice logistic and economic factors constrain the extent to which such integration is being realized. However, there is a second feature of AMT which is being more widely exploited. Computer control not only supports accurate and rapid machine operation but, because it can be programmed, also enables machinery to be used to make a wide variety of parts and to readily accommodate new ones. For the same reason, set-up and changeover times are often very short. Consequently, AMT represents a flexible and more widely applicable form of AUTOMATION which is also highly compatible with JUST-IN-TIME inventory control and TOTAL QUALITY MANAGEMENT. Indeed, because of the interdependencies among these three initiatives they have been identified as core components of a "new paradigm" of "integrated manufacturing" (Dean & Snell, 1991).

Much of the initial interest in AMT concerned its impact on JOB DESKILLING. Research has shown that while it can encourage the simplification of shopfloor work, it does not necessarily do so. The effect depends on the choices made in the associated JOB DESIGN. Correspondingly, increasing attention is being paid to the relationship of operator job design to the effective use of AMT systems, where initial findings suggest that, at least for more complex applications, an enskilling strategy is best. That in turn, from a HUMAN–COMPUTER INTERACTION standpoint, has raised the question of the appropriate allocation of function between AMT and operator, and how one can bring "human-centered" criteria into the system design process. Also of current interest are the wider implications of AMT for HUMAN RESOURCES MANAGEMENT strategies and ORGANIZATIONAL DESIGN. Research in these and other areas is in its early stages, but is gathering momentum.

See also **Productivity; Ergonomics; Business process reengineering; Operations management**

Bibliography

Dean, J. W. & Snell, S. A. (1991). Integrated manufacturing and job design: Moderating effects

of organizational inertia. *Academy of Management Journal*, **34**, 776–804.
Majchrzak, A. (1988). *The human side of factory automation*. San Francisco: Jossey–Bass.
Sharit, J., Chang, T. & Salvendy, G. (1987). Technical and human aspects of computer-aided manufacturing. In G. Salvendy (Ed.), *Handbook of human factors* pp. 1587–1616. New York: Wiley.
Wall, T. D., Clegg, C. W. & Kemp, N. J. (Eds), (1987). *The human side of advanced manufacturing technology*. Chichester, UK: Wiley.
Wall, T. D. & Davids, K. (1992). Shopfloor work organization and advanced manufacturing technology. In C. L. Cooper & I. T. Robertson (Eds), *International review of industrial and organizational psychology* (vol. 7, pp. 363–398). Chichester, UK: Wiley.

TOBY D. WALL

affect This is a generic term which refers to the wide range of feeling states that people experience. In ORGANIZATIONAL BEHAVIOR, the primary concern is with affective or feeling states that are experienced on the job. Affective states vary in intensity. Relatively strong affective states that interrupt cognitive processes and/or behavior are typically referred to as EMOTIONS. Typical day-to-day affective states that do not interrupt cognitive processes and/or behavior, but rather provide the affective context for daily experiences are often referred to as moods. While mood states do not interrupt current thought processes and activities, they have been demonstrated to have profound effects on them.

Mood at work refers to feeling states workers typically experience on the job. While there is a tendency to think of mood as varying along a single continuum from positive to negative, a substantial body of literature suggests that mood states are characterized by two predominant and independent dimensions, positive mood and negative mood. Positive moods and negative moods have different antecedents, different consequences, and have different relationships with life events.

Mood at work is determined by both PERSONALITY and situational factors. Two personality traits, positive affectivity and negative affectivity, are the key dispositional determinants of positive and negative mood states, respectively. Positive and negative moods at work are also influenced by situational factors which can be either work or nonwork related (*see* NONWORK/WORK). While situational factors may help to initiate a particular mood state, mood states are generally pervasive and not directed at any particular object or event.

Mood at work has been neglected by organizational behavior researchers, but this situation is changing and mood is currently receiving increasing attention. It is important to realize that affective states (and moods at work) are conceptually and empirically distinct from the often studied construct, JOB SATISFACTION, which connotes an attitude toward one's job rather than how one feels on the job (Clark & Isen, 1982).

Mood at work has been linked to various work-related behaviors such as ABSENTEEISM, helping behavior, and the extent to which individuals perform extra-role behaviors such as forms or organizational spontaneity (George, 1989; 1990; George & Brief, 1992). Mood states of group leaders have been shown to affect group outcomes such as group performance (*see* GROUP DYNAMICS). Additionally, it has been argued that certain processes may result in members of WORK GROUPS experiencing similar mood states on the job. When this occurs, groups are said to possess an affective tone which has been shown to be related to group outcomes such as performance (*see* CULTURE, GROUP).

See also **Attitude, theory; Performance, individual; Emotions in organizations**

Bibliography

Clark, M. S. & Isen, A. M. (1982). Toward understanding the relationship between feeling states and social behavior. In A. H. Hastorf & A. M. Isen (Eds), *Cognitive social psychology* pp. 73–108. New York: Elsevier.
George, J. M. (1989). Mood and absence. *Journal of Applied Psychology*, **74**, 317–324.
George, J. M. (1990). Personality, affect, and behavior in groups. *Journal of Applied Psychology*, **75**, 107–116.
George, J. M. & Brief, A. P. (1992). Feeling good–doing good: A conceptual analysis of the mood at work-organizational spontaneity relationship. *Psychological Bulletin*, **112**, 310–329.

JENNIFER M. GEORGE

affiliation, need for This dispositional motive reflects a concern with establishing and maintaining affectively positive relationships with other people (McClelland, 1985; 1989). In common with other dispositional motives such as the NEED FOR ACHIEVEMENT and need for power, the preferred method for measuring individual differences in need for affiliation is the Thematic Apperception Test (TAT) (*see* PERSONALITY TESTING). Those high in need for affiliation (nAff) more frequently interact with others. Friendship, rather than SKILL or expertise, more strongly governs their choice of a work partner. There is a strong element of fear of rejection in nAff; consequently, those high in nAff act to avoid CONFLICT or direct competition. They will only demonstrate higher levels of CONFORMITY if conformity is instrumental in the particular situation for achieving social acceptance or avoiding conflict or rejection. In pursuit of approval, those high in nAff will demonstrate strong task performance and in the presence of social incentives demonstrate strong achievement tendencies. High nAff is a key component of what McClelland (1989) has labeled the Relaxed Affiliative Syndrome, or Affiliative Trust, which is associated with lower rates of hypertension, lower levels of STRESS, and higher levels of immunochemicals.

See also **Type-A; Need theory; Group cohesiveness**

Bibliography

McClelland, D. C. (1985). *Human motivation*. Glenview, IL: Scott, Foresman.

McClelland, D. C. (1989). Motivational factors in health and disease. *American Psychologist*, **44**, 675–683.

SEYMOUR ADLER

age Within ORGANIZATIONAL BEHAVIOR, two questions about age are paramount. What are the effects of age on work PERFORMANCE and attitudes, and how do different conditions of work affect the pace of aging? (*see* PERFORMANCE, INDIVIDUAL).

On the first question, meta-analyses of studies published in the past four decades have shown that the average association between age and job performance is around zero; in the extensive review by McEvoy and Cascio (1989) the mean correlation was 0.06. However, there are wide variations between individual studies, with age–performance correlations ranging from -0.44 to 0.66.

In all cases we need to ask what are the underlying causal factors. *Negative* age gradients in any behavior are likely to be due to a decline in basic capacities, deriving from physiological processes which tend to deteriorate over the years, especially after the age of RETIREMENT. *Positive* associations between age and performance are likely to arise from accumulated knowledge and SKILLS over years of relevant experience.

In general, positive associations between age and job performance are likely to be found in relatively stable situations, where knowledge and skills can continue to be acquired by older workers. Models of age-related gains in cognitive performance are sometimes presented in terms of "selective optimization with compensation" (Baltes & Baltes, 1990b). As people age, they increase their effectiveness in areas of specialization. Continued interest and practice in a limited number of areas permit the growth of knowledge-based expertise; and at the same time individuals are sometimes able to learn how to compensate for limitations from deteriorating basic capacities.

In many jobs, declines in basic capacities (typically small during the years of employment) will be balanced by improvements associated with relevant experience and possible compensation for limited deficits. For example, older people's successful compensation in cognitive activities was documented in relation to transcription-typing by Salthouse (1984). Although older typists were found to respond more slowly in a choice reaction–time task, there was no age difference in actual typing speed. That was because older staff were more likely to look further ahead along the line than their younger counterparts; it was this additional preparation time which permitted them to type as rapidly as their younger colleagues, despite their slower reactions.

On the other hand, a negative relationship with age is expected in tasks where basic capacities are exceeded and experience cannot help. This is seen in continuous rapid INFORMATION-PROCESSING or in any kind of strenuous physical activity which becomes more difficult with advancing years. For example, slight negative age gradients are found in "fluid" intelligence, over the span of working life, in situations where new material (usually abstract and nonverbal) has to be processed under time pressure.

Age differences of a similar kind are found in LEARNING and memory. Older people in general do not learn as quickly and they sometimes lack confidence in training situations. Within specific jobs, older employees thus tend in general to have more difficulty where job content is changing rapidly, and where their knowledge and skills can become obsolete. However, it is clear that older as well as younger employees are able to learn complex new material, despite the operation of negative STEREOTYPING in this area (Sterns & Doverspike, 1989; Warr, 1994).

It is important to stress that many job activities are unaffected by either type of age effect. Work is in many settings routine and nonproblematic, requiring either limited skill or skill sufficiently firmly established for behavior to be fairly automatic. Age differences in task performance are not expected in the many roles where employees are not required to perform at high levels nor to respond quickly to new stimuli.

However, age DISCRIMINATION is common in the SELECTION and promotion of staff (*see* SELECTION METHODS). Research has shown that age discrimination harms an organization's effectiveness as well as being unethical. The variation in employees' performance within age-groups is typically greater than that between them.

Research has also examined job attitudes at different ages. Overall JOB SATISFACTION is typically found to be significantly higher among older workers (e.g., Doering, Rhodes, & Schuster, 1983), although the positive correlation is not high, usually falling between 0.10 and 0.20. Even after controlling for factors such as tenure, income, positive job features, or job level there still remains a positive age gradient. Part of that gradient is likely to be attributable to nonwork differences between older and younger people, associated with differences in LIFE STAGE and general MENTAL HEALTH (Warr, 1992).

The second major question about age is: How do different conditions of work affect the pace of aging? Are some environments more conducive than others to "successful aging" (Baltes & Baltes, 1990a)?

Evidence about the long-term influence of jobs on aging tends to be indirect, since any job is located in a broader socio-economic structure and it is difficult to disentangle job from nonjob factors (*see* NON-WORK/WORK). However, research has pointed to the causal importance of the "environmental complexity" provided by different jobs. Kohn and Schooler (1983) have demonstrated longitudinally that several forms of "intellectual flexibility" are enhanced by prolonged exposure to complex jobs. Avolio and Waldman (1987) have reported that age and mental performance are differently interrelated among skilled and unskilled employees. Negative correlations of reasoning ABILITY with age (holding constant level of education) were significantly greater for the unskilled group (exposed to less complex work environments) than for the skilled workers.

As part of the wider concern of organizational behavior for the impacts of different JOB CHARACTERISTICS, it is thus important to examine long-term effects across a period of years. Cognitive aging is likely to be accelerated or slowed down by the nature of a person's employment.

See also **Individual differences; Career stages; Training**

Bibliography

Avolio, B. J. & Waldman, D. A. (1987). Personnel aptitude test scores as a function of age, education, and job type. *Experimental Aging Research*, **13**, 109–113.

Baltes, P. B. & Baltes, M. M. (Eds), (1990a). *Successful aging*. Cambridge, UK: Cambridge University Press.

Baltes, P. B. & Baltes, M. M. (1990b). Psychological perspectives on successful aging: The model of selective optimization with compensation. In P. B. Baltes & M. M. Baltes (Eds), *Successful aging* (pp. 1–34). Cambridge, UK: Cambridge University Press.

Doering, M., Rhodes, S. R. & Schuster, M. (1983). *The aging worker: Research and recommendations*. Beverly Hills, CA: Sage.

Kohn, M. L. & Schooler, C. (1983). *Work and personality: An inquiry into the impact of social stratification*. Norwood, NJ: Ablex.

McEvoy, G. M. & Cascio, W. F. (1989). Cumulative evidence of the relationship between employee age and performance. *Journal of Applied Psychology*, **74**, 11–17.

Salthouse, T. A. (1984). Effects of age and skill in typing. *Journal of Experimental Psychology: General*, **113**, 345–371.

Sterns, H. L. & Doverspike, D. (1989). Aging and the training and learning process. In L. L. Goldstein (Ed.), *Training and development in organizations* (pp. 299–332). San Francisco: Jossey-Bass.

Warr, P. B. (1992). Age and occupational well-being. *Psychology and Aging*, **7**, 37–45.

Warr, P. B. (1994). Age and employment. In H. Triandis, M. Dunnette & L. Heugh (Eds), *Handbook of industrial and organizational psychology*, 485–550. Palo Alto, CA: Consulting Psychologists Press.

PETER WARR

agency restriction Agency Restriction Metatheory (ARM) is based on two hypothesis-generating assumptions. The first is that people are socially embedded agents actively striving for purposeful self-determination, attempting to make sense of, initiate, influence, and cope with events in line with personal VALUES, goals, and expectations of the future in a context of cultural norms, traditions, and past experience (*see* SELF-REGULATION).

The second assumption is that agency is frequently undermined, restricted, and frus trated by formal and informal social forces including: powerful constituting and regulating social institutions and organizations; required social relationships entailing strain-inducing obligations combined with minimal collective and individual rights; inadequate personal, family, social, community, and material resources; and powerful, socially constructed, norms, role expectations, and disentitlements.

ARM was first developed within the UNEMPLOYMENT field out of a critique of the underlying assumptions of Jahoda's MANIFEST AND LATENT FUNCTION theory in an attempt to generate alternative working hypotheses (Fryer, 1986). It was developed further to focus research on the way unemployment undermines future orientation, on the extent and nature of active coping strategies and on the FRUSTRATION of personal agency by relative poverty.

Although first applied to individuals, ARM also helps to explain the impact of unemployment and relative poverty on families and on the broader community, and the psychological costs of JOB INSECURITY, and low JOB SATISFACTION amongst young people, as well as negative labor market experience more generally.

Support for ARM comes from literature reviews, conceptual analysis, small scale qualitative research ACTION/INTERVENTION RESEARCH, and large scale, orthodox quantitative studies.

See also **Locus of control; Mental health; Stress; Quality of working life**

Bibliography

Fryer, D. (1986). Employment deprivation and personal agency during unemployment. *Social Behaviour*, **1**, (1), 3–23.

DAVID FRYER

agency theory This theory examines the problems – and partial contractual solutions (*see* CONTRACT) – that exist when a principal delegates DECISION-MAKING responsibility to an agent who is paid a fee, but whose own objectives may conflict with those of the principal. This economics-based theoretical perspective, like TRANSACTION COST THEORY, has grown enormously in scope and influence (and with some controversy) since the 1970s, and has been used in analyses of executive compensation contracts and other corporate governance issues (*see* GOVERNANCE AND OWNERSHIP). In applying or adapting agency theory to these organizational issues, it is useful, however, to distinguish between what Jensen (1983, pp. 334–335) refers to as two "almost entirely separate" agency literatures: a normative principal–agent literature emphasizing the design of compensation contracts with optimal risk-sharing properties (Levinthal, 1988), and a positive, empirically-based, agency literature focusing primarily on questions relating to the separation of corporate ownership and control, and the role of boards of directors (Jensen & Murphy, 1990).

Organizational research using agency theory has tended to draw from the positive, rather than the normative, agency literature. For example, while the positive agency literature highlights the value of placing greater amounts of managerial compensation and managerial wealth at risk by tying it closer to firm performance, the normative agency literature stresses the need to consider the potential *disadvantages* of forcing managers to bear "excessive" compensation risk (Beatty & Zajac, 1994) (*see* RISK TAKING). Organizational research, however, has generally placed greater emphasis on the importance – from an incentive and control standpoint – of imposing strong pay-for-performance linkages, rather than the possible disadvantages of imposing risk-bearing in managerial compensation contracts (*see* PERFORMANCE RELATED PAY). Interestingly, the lack of debate in the recent organizational literature on this issue is somewhat surprising, given that the organization behavior literature on compensation has historically recognized that different forms of compensation, such as pay-for-performance, vary in their attractiveness to individuals, and therefore, vary in their appropriateness as incentive–motivational tools (Zajac, 1992) (*see* PAYMENT SYSTEMS).

Agency problems typically emerge because of the two fundamental conditions that underlie principal–agent relationships: goal incongruence and information asymmetry (Zajac, 1990). Goal congruence is an assumed condition, without which the agency problem reduces to a more easily solvable contracting problem. The second dimension, information asymmetry, is a critical variable in the principal–agent relationship, and has generated a substantial body of research within the information economics literature (*see* ORGANIZATIONAL ECONOMICS). Information asymmetry refers to the fact that in the typical principal–agent relationship, the principal has less information than the agent about:

(1) the characteristics of the agent; and
(2) the decisions made and the actions taken by the agent.

These two aspects of information asymmetry have been labeled formally in the information economics literature as *adverse selection* and *moral hazard*, respectively.

The moral hazard problem is typically discussed in the positive agency literature that examines problems between owners and top managers (Fama and Jensen, 1983) or between boards and CEOs (Westphal & Zajac, forthcoming). For that literature, the issue is whether owners are able to adequately monitor and control the actions and decisions of self-interested CEOs. Interestingly, organizational research has tended to focus on the effectiveness (or ineffectiveness) of boards of directors as monitors of top management, without considering explicitly the possible cost/benefit trade-offs between the relative use of incentives versus monitoring as alternative sources of controlling managerial behavior (Zajac & Westphal, 1994). Beatty and Zajac (1994) suggest that three fundamental elements underlie agency relationships in organizations (incentives, monitoring, and risk-bearing), and that all three should be included in theoretical and empirical analyses of contractual relations. Future research that considers these three elements jointly, and explicitly considers the conflicts, trade-offs, and substitution possibilities among them, may have the greatest potential to further advance our understanding of top executive compensation, ownership, and corporate governance.

See also **Exchange relations; Governance and ownership; Strategic management**

Bibliography

Beatty, R. P. & Zajac, E. J. (1994). Top management incentives, monitoring, and risk sharing: A study of executive compensation, ownership, and board structure in initial public offerings. *Administrative Science Quarterly*, **39**, 313–336.

Fama, E. F. & Jensen, M. C. (1983). Separation of ownership and control. *Journal of Law and Economics*, **26**, 301–325.

Jensen, M. C. (1983). Organization theory and methodology. *Accounting Review*, **58**, 319–339.

Jensen, M. C. & Murphy, K. J. (1990). Performance pay and top-management incentives. *Journal of Political Economy*, **98**, 225–264.

Levinthal, D. (1988). A survey of agency models of organizations. *Journal of Economic Behavior and Organization*, **9**, 153–185.

Westphal, J. D. & E. J. Zajac (1994) Substance and symbolism in CEOs' long-term incentive plans. *Administrative Science Quarterly*, **39**, 367–390.

Zajac, E. J. (1990). CEO selection, succession, compensation and firm performance: A theoretical integration and empirical analysis. *Strategic Management Journal*, **11**, 217–230.

Zajac, E. J. (1992). Relating economic and behavioral perspectives in strategy research. In P. Shrivastava, A. Huff & J. Dutton (Eds), *Advances in strategic management* (vol. 8, pp. 69–96). Greenwich, CN: JAI Press.

Zajac E. J. & Westphal, J. D. (1994). The costs and benefits of managerial incentives and monitoring in large US corporations: When is more not better. *Strategic Management Journal*, **15**, 121–192.

EDWARD J. ZAJAC

alcohol and substance abuse Alcohol and illegal substance use is regarded as a major problem in the United States and many other countries. While precise figures are impossible to estimate, a commonly used estimate is 30 billion dollars of lost productivity due to illegal substance use and 60 billion dollars of lost PRODUCTIVITY due to alcohol abuse in the United States annually. Alcohol and illegal substance use is viewed as a workplace problem in many other countries as well. In an attempt to alleviate such losses, some have argued that companies should address the *causes* of alcohol and substance abuse. One of the most commonly mentioned causes is job conditions (e.g., STRESS). Despite the adage "my work is driving me to drink," empirical studies have found little support for a link between job conditions and alcohol and substance abuse. There is relatively stronger evidence for a relationship between workforce characteristics, such as AGE and substance abuse (i.e., younger workers are more likely to engage in substance abuse than older employees).

A great deal of attention has focused on organizations' attempts to reduce alcohol and substance abuse through testing and Employee Assistance Programs (EAPs). With regard to testing, many U.S. companies have adopted programs to screen for a variety of illegal substances (Roman, 1990). These testing programs may be performed at the pre-employment stage (*see* SELECTION METHODS), "for cause" (e.g., after an accident occurs), or on a random basis. The research on drug testing has been somewhat mixed; although some studies have found drug testing to be somewhat predictive of job outcomes (e.g., ACCIDENT rates, terminations) (*see* TURNOVER), others have challenged the cost-benefits of such testing. Drug testing has also been criticized by those who feel that it produces a high false positive (i.e., applicants or employees who may be mistakenly labeled as drug users) rate. Again, the research evidence is quite mixed as to how high the false positive rate is for various drug tests. In terms of legal status, there are numerous federal, state, local, and industry (e.g., Department of Transportation) regulations in the United States that may limit the conditions under which drug testing can be performed. In some cases, however, these regulations may mandate drug testing. Other U.S. laws potentially affect the employment rights of alcohol and substance abusers; under certain conditions, for example, an alcoholic may be protected from discrimination under the Americans with the Disabilities Act. Workplace drug testing in other countries is practically nonexistent.

Employee Assistance Programs (EAPs) are workplace-based programs designed to identify troubled employees (e.g., those who are alcohol or substance abusers), and help them obtain treatment or counseling (*see* COUNSELING IN ORGANIZATIONS). Such programs are widely available in many U.S. companies, particularly among larger companies. Similar programs are becoming much more common in other countries, such as Sweden and Germany. Despite their popularity, there has been little rigorous research regarding their effectiveness. The focus, from an organization's perspective, has been on the cost-benefits of such programs compared with other treatment sources. At least in some cases, organizations have reported that their EAP provided lower cost treatment than other health providers. One frequently reported problem that remains is the reluctance of employees to use EAPs. Despite some criticisms of EAPs, they remain prevalent in many companies.

See also **Mental health; Performance, individual; Justice, procedural; Absenteeism**

Bibliography

Harris, M. & Heft, L. (1992). Alcohol and drug use in the workplace: Issues, controversies, and directions for future research. *Journal of Management*, **18**, 239–266 [A summary of recent literature addressing drug use, drug tests, and EAPs].

Roman, P. (Ed.) (1990). *Alcohol problem intervention in the workplace*. New York: Quorum Books.

Sonnenstuhl, W. J. & Trice, H. M. (1986). *Strategies for employee assistance programs: The crucial balance*. Ithaca, NY: ILR Press.

Zwerling, C., Ryan, J. & Orav, E. J. (1992). Costs and benefits of pre-employment drug screening. *Journal of the American Medical Association*, **266**, 91–93.

MICHAEL M. HARRIS

alienation The concept of alienation originated in Marxist thought, to denote the separation of proletarian workers from the means of production and its capitalist control. Subsequent sociological writings by Durkheim, Simmel, Weber, and Merton extended its use to denote the psychological and social consequences – anonymity, inequality, fragmentation, isolation – of industrial production and DIVISION OF LABOR, especially under conditions of MASS PRODUCTION and BUREAUCRACY. Blauner introduced the concept into industrial sociology in the 1960s, and it was subsequently developed by Seeman (1972) as a six-facet construct consisting of powerlessness, meaninglessness, normlessness, social isolation, self-estrangement, and cultural estrangement. It has tended to fall out of favor as a concept in ORGANIZATIONAL BEHAVIOR, though some studies continue to use it, but with varying definitions and measures. This decline parallels the relative reduction in use of the term QUALITY OF WORKING LIFE, both of which trends might be attributed to the decline of smokestack industrial production, with which alienation has been traditionally associated. However, it may be argued that alienation remains a highly relevant experience in many OCCUPATIONS, perhaps especially among certain types of office work and casualized or part-time employment (*see* HOURS OF WORK; FLEXIBILITY). It is possible that alienation will remain an important focus of some academic attention, perhaps within the compass of the fast growing field of BUSINESS ETHICS (Kanungo, 1992).

See also **Job characteristics; Job design; Job insecurity; Job satisfaction; Power**

Bibliography

Kanungo, R. N. (1992). Alienation and empowerment: Some ethical imperatives in business. *Journal of Business Ethics*, **11**, 413–422.

Seeman, M. (1972). Alienation and knowledge-seeking: A note on alienation and action. *Social Problems*, **20**, 3–17.

NIGEL NICHOLSON

altruism This term refers to human action that is motivated by concern for the interests of others. Although neoclassical economists argue that all human behavior is driven by self-interest, research supports the existence of significant amounts of altruistic behavior, suggesting that individuals are motivated by both self-interest and moral COMMITMENTS (Etzioni, 1988). Within ORGANIZATIONAL BEHAVIOR, altruism has been studied primarily as a dimension of ORGANIZATIONAL CITIZENSHIP behavior.

See also **Business ethics; Corporate social responsibility; Values**

Bibliography

Etzioni, A. (1988). *The moral dimension*. New York: Free Press.

LINDA TREVINO

ambiguity *see* UNCERTAINTY; ROLE AMBIGUITY

analyzers *see* STRATEGIC TYPES

anticipatory socialization This process occurs prior to organizational entry, and is typically considered to be the first stage of organizational SOCIALIZATION (Feldman, 1976). The sources of such influence are virtually unlimited; including, family, peers, schools, local/regional/national culture, and the organization itself (Van Maanen, 1976, discusses these). The primary organizational influence is the RECRUITMENT/selection process, including, where they apply, REALISTIC JOB PREVIEWS. Because CAREER ENTRY precedes the JOINING-UP PROCESS, all of the formal and informal factors associated with a career choice are also relevant anticipatory socialization factors.

Anticipatory socialization influences both specific expectations about organizational life (e.g., How will my boss treat me?), basic work beliefs (e.g., accepting authority), work VALUES (e.g., hard work is good, or the "Protestant work ethic"), and an individual's valences (the desirability of various work outcomes, such as job security versus pay) (*see* VIE THEORY). The congruence of an individual's expectations with organizational realities is particularly important for newcomers (Wanous, Poland, Premack, & Davis, 1992), and is primarily influenced by the realistic job preview. The congruence of an individual's basic beliefs, work values, and valences with the reinforcement received from the organization remain important long after organizational entry, because they are major influences on JOB SATISFACTION, COMMITMENT, and TURNOVER. Organizational socialization tactics are designed to increase the congruence of beliefs, values, and valences by changing the newcomer individual.

See also **Career choice; Career transitions; Selection methods; Selection interviewing; Training**

Bibliography

Feldman, D. C. (1976). A contingency theory of socialization. *Administrative Science Quarterly*, **21**, 433–452.

Van Maanen, J. (1976). Breaking in: Socialization to work. In R. Dubin (Ed.), *Handbook of work, organization, and society* (pp. 67–130). Chicago: Rand-McNally.

Wanous, J. P., Poland, T. D., Premack, S. L. & Davis, K. S. (1992). The effects of met expectations on newcomer attitudes and behavior: A review and meta-analysis. *Journal of Applied Psychology*, **77**, 288–297.

JOHN P. WANOUS

anxiety The construct of anxiety can be viewed as a state or a trait. When viewed as a state, it refers to aroused levels of negative AFFECT or EMOTION. Anxiety as a state fluctuates over time and refers to affective experience in the short-run; such as when an employee is worried about the future and potential problems. Anxiety as a trait refers to the disposition to experience negative emotional states; relatively enduring personality characteristics making the individual more likely to experience anxiety over time and across situations (Tellegen, 1983).

In ORGANIZATIONAL BEHAVIOR, anxiety is related to the concept of job STRESS. Anxiety (as a state) may be viewed as a consequence of exposure to workplace stressors. Considering anxiety as a trait suggests that some individuals are more likely to experience distress at work over time and across situations. Self-reports of levels of distress at a single point in time are likely to contain aspects of both state and trait anxiety. Therefore, organizational researchers need to control for trait anxiety when investigating anxiety as a state.

Anxiety can interfere with thought processes, behaviors, and job performance (*see* PERFORMANCE, INDIVIDUAL). A considerable body of literature focuses on how individuals cope with stressors which has implications for the management of anxiety at work.

See also **Organizational neurosis; Personality; Emotions in organizations**

Bibliography

Burke, M. J., Brief, A. P. & George, J. M. (1993). The role of negative affectivity in understanding relationships between self-reports of stressors and strains: A comment on the applied psychology literature. *Journal of Applied Psychology*, **78**, 402–412.

Tellegen, A. (1985). Structures of mood and personality and their relevance to assessing anxiety, with an emphasis on self-report. In A. H. Tuma & J. D. Maser (Eds), *Anxiety and the anxiety disorders* (pp. 681–706). Hillsdale, NJ: Erlbaum.

JENNIFER M. GEORGE

appraisal *see* PERFORMANCE APPRAISAL

aptitude This term means readiness to learn. It is the capacity to acquire SKILL – potential for talent. Aptitudes predict subsequent performance and can be used to forecast achievement in a new situation. Traditionally, aptitudes refer to relatively homogeneous and narrowly defined segments of ability. Aptitudes reflect the cumulative experience of daily living under unknown conditions (Anastasi, 1988). Interest in measuring aptitude comes from the need to make specialized distinctions from the more general intelligence test (*see* INTELLIGENCE, TESTING). From this practical need and the availability of factor analysis and high-speed computers, distinctive aptitude measures were developed for educational advising, CAREER counseling, and occupational classification. Today, available multiple aptitude test batteries include assessments of mechanical reasoning, clerical speed and accuracy, spelling, language use, manual dexterity, and CREATIVITY; these are used widely by the armed services and civilian agencies for vocational counseling (*see* VOCATIONAL GUIDANCE). It should be noted that tests of ability, aptitude, and achievement (*see* ACHIEVEMENT, NEED FOR) – where achievement is defined as learning information under controlled conditions – correlate very highly, making statistical distinctions between these test types difficult.

See also **Psychological testing; Assessment; Ability; Individual differences**

Bibliography

Anastasi, A. (1988). *Psychological testing*. New York: Macmillan.

JOYCE C. HOGAN

Assessment This practice in the field of ORGANIZATIONAL BEHAVIOR generally involves judgments being made about someone's personal qualities. When the assessment is made against a standard or criterion (e.g., whether an employee shows sufficient competence to be promoted) the assessment is criterion-referenced. When people are compared with each other the assessment is norm-referenced. Assessment of people is conducted in organizational settings for a variety of reasons including the selection of new entrants or the appraisal of existing personnel for development and promotion/placement. Assessment is a broad topic and there is a great deal of relevant literature. At the most general level assessment practices need to be linked to the strategic goals of the organization; the literature on HUMAN RESOURCE STRATEGY and HUMAN RESOURCE MANAGEMENT contains useful guidance here. At the more specific level of individual assessment, material concerning personnel SELECTION METHODS, INDIVIDUAL DIFFERENCES, PERFORMANCE APPRAISAL, and PSYCHOLOGICAL TESTING, is of substantial importance.

Some form of assessment takes place in most organizations. It is common for supervisors or managers to be asked to assess their subordinates although other forms of assessment, such as self-assessment or upward assessment, also take place. Tact, sensitivity, and SKILL are needed when one person makes an assessment of another and assessors should always be trained. There is a lot of material to draw on for the training of assessors and the development of assessment procedures but there is no single, correct approach. The assessor TRAINING needed and the procedures to be followed vary according to the purpose of the assessment, the circumstances and the use to which the information will be put. It is always important for assessors to be taught to focus on actual events and behavior, and some understanding of the psychology of person PERCEPTION is important. Any assessment must be as reliable (i.e., free from random error) and as valid (i.e., provide relevant information) as possible (*see* RELIABILITY; VALIDITY).

Research has shown that, when making assessments, people are prone to certain kinds of error, including a tendency to attribute too much influence to personal factors, such as personality, and too little to the circumstances surrounding an individual's behavior. This tendency is so pervasive that it is known as "The FUNDAMENTAL ATTRIBUTION ERROR" (Ross, 1977) (*see* ATTRIBUTION). Other errors include being influenced by stereotypes and irrelevant personal features (e.g., RACE or GENDER) (*see* STEREOTYPES; BIAS), making norm-referenced judgments when criterion-referenced judgments are needed, giving distorted information due to rating ERRORS such as leniency or restriction of range (*see* HALO EFFECT). Most general OB or industrial/organizational psychology texts will provide an overview of these errors and advice on how to overcome them.

The FEEDBACK of information to the assessee is of crucial importance in any assessment process. It is well established that FEEDBACK can be an important ingredient in performance improvement (Algera, 1990) but only when it is accurate, interpretable, and delivered in a supportive and constructive fashion.

See also **Assessment centers; Personality testing; Competencies; Selection interviewing**

Bibliography

Algera, J. A. (1990). Feedback systems in organizations. In C. L. Cooper & I. T. Robertson (Eds), *International review of industrial and organizational psychology* (vol. 5). Chichester, UK: Wiley.

Ross, L. (1977). The intuitive psychologist and his shortcomings: Distortions in the attribution process. In L. Berkowitz (Ed.), *Advances in experimental social psychology* (vol. 10). New York: Academic Press.

IVAN ROBERTSON

Assessment centers These do not refer to physical locations but to a combination of several personnel SELECTION METHODS (e.g., PSYCHOLOGICAL TESTING, SELECTION INTERVIEWING, work sample testing). A typical assessment center will take place over a day or two, and candidates will be assigned to small groups (6–8 people) so that they can participate in the various exercises. Generally, the assessors will be senior managers from the organization who have been specially trained; it is quite common for psychologists to be involved in both the training and ASSESSMENT process. Detailed information on the research base for assessment centers and clear guidance on their development may be found in Thornton and Byham (1982) and Woodruffe (1990).

Like other selection methods assessment centers should be designed after a JOB ANALYSIS has been conducted and used to clarify the major dimensions on which candidates should be assessed. Typical dimensions used in an assessment center include planning and organizing, INTERPERSONAL SKILLS, and business acumen. Each dimension should have been derived from job analysis and needs to be defined clearly in conceptual and behavioral terms so that assessors have a clear grasp of the constructs involved. Centers vary in terms of the number of dimensions used. Some use as few as seven but others use as many as 20. Candidates are required to undertake a variety of exercises and assessors observe their behavior in these exercises and make judgments about the candidates on the various dimensions. It is common for specific exercises to be focused on specific dimensions. For example, a group discussion may provide information about interpersonal skills and judgment, an intray exercise may be designed to provide information on business acumen and problem analysis, and a presentation may provide evidence of oral COMMUNICATION skills.

Evidence on the criterion-related validity of assessment centers is good. Several large-scale validation studies have reported positive findings and a meta-analysis (Gaugler, Rosenthal, Thornton, & Bentson, 1987) of results from a large number of these studies found good criterion-related VALIDITY for assessment centers against various criteria (e.g., job performance, career advancement) (*see* VALIDITY GENERALIZATION).

Although the majority of validation studies have concentrated on assessment centers as a whole, the validity of the component parts of assessment centers has been explored. Most assessment centers incorporate several work sample exercises which have been derived from job analysis. Work sample exercises literally sample the key tasks of a job and build these into an assessment procedure. Probably the most common exercises in assessment centers are Group Discussions and In-Trays. In general, evidence on the validity of In-Trays is good and they have been shown to make a unique contribution to the prediction of managerial success (e.g., Wollowick & McNamara, 1969; Kesselman, Lopez, & Lopez, 1982). Group Discussion exercises have been less extensively studied and some investigations have found problems with their reliability. Although the exercises may be standardized for group discussions there is no established procedure for taking account of differences in group composition (*see* GROUP STRUCTURE). Gatewood, Thornton, and Hennessy (1990) found problems with the alternate form RELIABILITY of Group Discussions and suggested that measurement reliability may be influenced by differences in group membership.

Although the results from meta-analysis suggest that assessment centers have a useful role to play in personnel selection, there have been some troubling findings concerning the extent to which assessment centers provide valid measures of the underlying dimensions that they are designed to examine. In a landmark study Sackett and Dreher (1982) discovered that the correlations between assessments of candidates on the same dimension but different exercises (monotrait–heteromethod) were smaller than correlations between different dimensions on the same exercises (heterotrait–monomethod). This is exactly the opposite of what should have been the case. It seems from this research that either assessors' evaluations of candidates do not provide clear measures of the dimensions, that candidate performance on the dimensions is not consistent across exercises, or that candidate performance is exercise (rather than dimension) specific. The true picture is probably some combination of these possibilities. The original findings from Sackett and Dreher have been reproduced many times and place a large question mark over the construct validity of assessment centers. These results make it difficult to explain why assessment centers show good criterion-related validity (*see also* Klimoski & Brickner, 1987) but do not detract from their good criterion-related validity.

Assessment centers involve multiple assessors and candidates. The problems of pooling information and arriving at a clear view of each candidate have been resolved in a variety of ways and many assessment centers incorporate an assessors' meeting at which candidates are discussed. Research evidence suggests that a fairly mechanical approach to this task, in which scores are combined with minimal discussion, is likely to produce the best results.

Assessment centers are complex procedures and there is evidence to show that validity can vary from one situation to another. The meta-analysis of Gaugler et al. (1987) and other research (e.g., Schmitt, Schneider, & Cohen, 1990) revealed that the type of assessor used, number of exercises, use of peer evaluation, degree of prior contact between assessor and candidate, and other factors moderate the effectiveness of assessment centers. These results demonstrate clearly that simply using assessment center exercises does not guarantee success. Like other selection and assessment processes, assessment centers need careful design and monitoring.

As well as being used for personnel selection purposes, assessment center technology has also been adapted for use in TRAINING and MANAGEMENT DEVELOPMENT. Used in this way, development centers make use of assessment center exercises to provide an evaluation of a person's COMPETENCIES. With suitable preparation, counseling, and follow-up, the procedure can make a useful contribution to training needs diagnosis and to the preparation of a tailored development program.

See also **Human resources management; Recruitment; Management of high potential; Succession planning**

Bibliography

Gatewood, R., Thornton, G. C. & Hennessey, H. W. (1990). Reliability of exercise ratings in the leaderless group discussion. *Journal of Occupational Psychology*, **63**, 331–342.

Gaugler, B., Rosenthal, D. B., Thornton, G. C. & Bentson, C. (1987). Meta-analysis of assessment center validity. *Journal of Applied Psychology*, **72**, 493–511.

Kesselman, G., Lopez, F. M. Jr. & Lopez, F. E. (1982). The development and validation of a self-report, scored in-basket test in an assessment center setting. *Public Personnel Management*, **11**, 228.

Klimoski, R. & Brickner, M. (1987). Why do assessment centers work? The puzzle of assessment center validity. *Personnel Psychology*, **40**, 243–260.

Sackett, P. R. & Dreher, G. F. (1982). Constructs and assessment center dimensions: Some troubling empirical findings. *Journal of Applied Psychology*, **67**, 401–410.

Schmitt, N., Schneider, J. R. & Cohen, S. A. (1990). Factors affecting validity of a regionally administered assessment center. *Personnel Psychology*, **43**.

Thornton, G. C. & Byham, W. C. (1982). *Assessment centres and managerial performance*. London: Academic Press.

Wollowick, H. B. & McNamara, W. J. (1969). Relationship of the components of an assessment centre to management success. *Journal of Applied Psychology*, **53**, 348–352.

Woodruff, C. (1990). *Assessment centres*. London: IPM.

IVAN ROBERTSON

attitude measurement *see* ATTITUDE, THEORY

attitude, theory This connotes the body of extant knowledge concerned with the structure of attitudes and the determination and consequences of attitudes. Attitude theory has generally tended to focus on the components of attitudes, the formation of attitudes, and the formation of quasi-consistent construct systems comprised of different attitudes, VALUES, and beliefs.

Central to this body of knowledge is work concerned with attitudes that manifest themselves in and/or that are relevant to the workplace. An attitude is a relatively enduring feeling, belief, and behavioral tendency directed toward specific individuals, groups of individuals, ideas, philosophies, issues, or objects (*see* Ajzen & Fishbein, 1980). Thus, in an organization a person may (and likely will) have attitudes about various coworkers and colleagues, supervisors, subordinates, various organizational policies and practices, physical WORKING CONDITIONS, REWARDS and other compensation, opportunities for advancement, the organization's culture and climate, and a wide variety of other organizational characteristics.

The dominant approach to characterizing the structure of an attitude is in terms of three components. The *affective component* of an attitude is the EMOTION, feeling, or sentiment the person has toward something (*see* AFFECT). For example, the statement "I do not like that particular work group" reflects affect. The second component of an attitude, the *cognitive component*, is the actual belief or knowledge the individual presumes to have about something. The statement "The people in that work group are lazy and are too political" represents cognition (note that cognitions may or may not be accurate, or true, but are only believed to be by the individual). Finally, the *behavioral intention component* of an attitude reflects how the individual intends to behave toward something. For example, the statement "I would resist a transfer to that work group." reflects a behavioral intention. These components are not discrete phenomenon that are formed sequentially but instead interact among themselves and are manifested in a variety of forms and mechanisms.

An alternative view of attitudes that has received moderate attention is the so-called situational model of attitudes (*see* Salancik & Pfeffer, 1977). This approach suggests that attitudes represent socially constructed realities based on social information available in the workplace (*see* SOCIAL CONSTRUCTIONISM). Any given person's attitudes are seen as being a function of social cues about the object of the attitude that are provided by "significant others" in the workplace.

Attitudes are of interest in part because of their presumed connection with workplace behavior. Common sense suggests that attitudes will affect behaviors. In reality, this relationship is not straightforward. Only specific attitudes actually predict specific behaviors. For example, a strong attitude about one's pay being too low may cause that person to resign for a position with higher pay. General attitudes such as overall JOB SATISFACTION are not precise predictors of specific job behaviors. Likewise, specific attitudes such as satisfaction with one's vacation schedule are not precise predictors of overall job performance. While people develop a wide array of attitudes in the workplace, much organizational research on attitudes has tended to focus on the key attitude of job satisfaction (*see* Fisher, 1980).

See also **Individual differences; Cognitive dissonance; Attitude, measurement**

Bibliography

Ajzen, I. & Fishbein, M. (1980). *Understanding attitudes and predicting social behavior*. Englewood Cliffs, NJ: Prentice-Hall.

Fisher, C. D. (1980). On the dubious wisdom of expecting job satisfaction to correlate with performance. *Academy of Management Review*, **5**, 607–612.

Salanick, G. & Pfeffer, J. (1977). An examination of need-satisfaction models of job attitudes. *Administrative Science Quarterly*, **22**, 427–456.

RICKY W. GRIFFIN

attitudes, dispositional approaches Within the last decade, a stream of research has emerged to challenge the view that job attitudes (*see also* Attitude, measurement; Attitude, theory) can be easily modified through organizational intervention. Within this new perspective, job attitudes are seen to be a function of stable traits of the worker in addition to being a reaction to a specific situation (*see* PERSONALITY TRAITS). Perhaps the most convincing evidence for a dispositional component to job attitudes was a longitudinal study by Staw, Bell, and Clausen (1986). Affectivity measures obtained from Californian children in the classroom were significantly correlated with job attitudes measured later in life.

Laboratory studies subsequently implicated individual dispositions in JOB SATISFACTION, but it was also found that task enrichment manipulations had a stronger effect on satisfaction.

Field studies suggest that individual job attitudes have some stability over time, and experimental studies indicate that traits and mood influence task satisfaction. On the other hand, the degree of stability in attitudes is not very strong, and no study has yet shown that that stability can be attributed to traits rather than constancy in the situation. Moreover, the effects of traits do not in any way account for the satisfaction effects of task perceptions. While there may be some dispositional component to job attitudes, this would not seem to be an impediment to organizational interventions designed to improve job attitudes.

See also **Attitude theory; Personality; Affect**

Bibliography

Gutek, B. A. & Winter, S. J. (1992). Consistency of job satisfaction across situations: Fact or framing artifact? *Journal of Vocational Behavior*, **41**, 61–78.

Staw, B. M., Bell, N. E. & Clausen, J. A. (1986). The dispositional approach to job attitudes: A lifetime longitudinal test. *Administrative Science Quarterly*, 31, 56–77.

JOHN SCHAUBROECK

attribution An attribution is a causal explanation. Attribution theory is concerned with the COGNITIVE PROCESSES and consequences of the processes by which individuals explain the behavior and outcomes of others as well as their own behavior and outcomes (Martinko, 1994).

Heider (1958) is most often credited as the founder of attribution theory. His basic thesis was that people are motivated to predict and control their environments. An essential prerequisite for control is an understanding of the basic causal mechanisms operating in the environment. Thus, average people can be viewed as "naive psychologists" attempting to understand and explain cause and effect relationships so that they can attain mastery in their environments.

Although there are many variations of attribution theory, Kelley and Michela (1980) note that research on attributions has focused on two primary areas:

(1) the ACHIEVEMENT MOTIVATION model (*see* ACHIEVEMENT, NEED FOR) which emphasizes how individuals explain their own successes and failures (see the work of Weiner (1986) and his colleagues); and
(2) the process by which observers account for and explain the outcomes of others (see Kelley (1973); Green & Mitchell, 1979; Martinko & Gardner, 1987).

Attribution theories have been applied to a wide range of phenomena including STEREOTYPING, LEADERSHIP, performance evaluation processes, interpersonal CONFLICT, IMPRESSION MANAGEMENT, and accounts of organizational responsibility.

Several models of attributional processes have been developed to describe the role and function of attributions in motivating individual behavior. The achievement motivation models of Weiner (1986) and his colleagues as well as the learned helplessness models suggested by Abramson, Seligman, and Teasdale (1978) and Martinko and Gardner (1982) all show the role of attributions with regard to individual behavior. While the achievement motivation models focus on the role of attributions regarding individual success and failure, the learned helplessness models focus specifically on passive and maladaptive reactions to failure. Thus, learned helpless individuals often display passive behavior and fail to exert effort even when success may be possible because they believe that prior failures were due to stable and internal characteristics such as lack of ability (*see* LOCUS OF CONTROL). The learned helplessness models are most helpful in understanding and explaining the behavior of poor performers whereas the achievement-oriented models address the more general process of explaining and predicting reactions to success and failure.

In both the learned helplessness and achievement motivation models, individuals process information about prior outcomes to arrive at causal attributions. These attributions are believed to affect most directly subjects' expectancies, which, in turn, influence individuals' affective states (e.g., depression and ANXIETY) and affect the probabilities of target behaviors and the consequences (outcomes) generated (*see* VIE THEORY). A basic assumption of both these models is that attributions can be classified within a limited number of underlying cognitive dimensions. The models almost always include the dimensions of internal/external and stable/unstable. The internal/external dimension is concerned with whether the locus of causality is inside the person or in the environment. The stability dimension is concerned with whether or not the cause is likely to remain constant or change over time. Combining the polar opposites of these two dimensions, attributions can be classified as: stable/internal (e.g., ability); stable/external (e.g., task); unstable/internal (e.g., effort); and unstable/external (e.g., chance/luck). In addition, other dimensions such as intentionality, controllability, and globality have also been proposed (Abramson et al. 1978; Weiner, 1986) but have less research support (*see* SELF-REGULATION).

Research has generally supported attributional models of learned helplessness and achievement motivation. In particular, there appears to be reasonably clear relationships between attributions and expectations. It has also been found that certain types of attributions are related to particular affective states (*see* AFFECT). Thus, for example, attributing failure to an internal and stable characteristic such as lack of ABILITY has been associated with depression. On the other hand, the linkage between attributions and behaviors is not as clear. Attributions affect behaviors primarily through the influence that they have on expectations.

Several models have also been developed to describe how individuals make attributions for the behavior of others. The majority of these responsibility assignment models (e.g., Green & Mitchell, 1979) generally use the three factors described by Kelley's cube to explain the attribution process. Essentially, these models indicate that observers evaluate the environment and the target person to determine which of three causal factors is responsible for the outcome. The belief about causation then drives the observer's response (behavior) toward the actor. The three types of causal factors that are believed to be responsible for the outcome are: the person, the stimuli, and the specific occasion. To make a determination of the causal factor that is primarily responsible, observers are posited to evaluate the behavior of the target along the dimensions of:

(1) the distinctiveness of the response – performance on this versus other tasks;
(2) consistency – over time and occasions; and
(3) consensus – comparison to others (*see* SOCIAL COMPARISON).

The final assignment of responsibility is made according to the principle of covariation which attempts to determine whether or not changes in causes are related to different outcomes. Thus, there must be multiple observations and causes must vary for analysis to occur. As Kelley (1967) indicated: "The effect is attributed to that condition which is present when the effect is present and which is absent when the effect is absent." Thus a leader is most likely to blame a subordinate for poor performance if he observes that the subordinate typically performs poorly on other tasks, has consistently performed this task poorly on other occasions, and that everyone else performs this same task well. In general, the research has documented that information regarding the dimensions described by Kelly's cube is related to the nature and severity of leaders' reactions to poor subordinate performance.

Two issues appear to recur in the attributional literature and research regarding ORGANIZATIONAL BEHAVIOR. First is the effect of attributional processes on LEADERSHIP behavior and leader–subordinate interactions. Particular attention has been devoted to the impact of attributional biases such as the FUNDAMENTAL ATTRIBUTION ERROR on leader evaluations of employee performance. Another key issue has been the validity of descriptions of attributional processes within organizational contexts. Lord and Maher (1990) have suggested that the rational process depicted by attributional models may not always provide a realistic description of the processes by which people assign causality in specific organizational situations. Thus, for example, as a result of experience, leaders may develop cybernetic short-cuts or schemata in assigning causality regarding the outcomes associated with a particular job and set of workers, thereby bypassing the more thorough causal analyses suggested by attribution theory. In addition, some researchers have questioned whether or not other cultures have the same need for causal analysis and suggest that other dimensions or depictions of the process of responsibility assignment and achievement motivation may be appropriate for other cultures (*see* CULTURE, NATIONAL).

See also **Perception; Role; Motivation; Minority group influence**

Bibliography

Abramson, L. Y., Seligman, M. E. P. & Teasdale, J. D. (1978). Learned helplessness in humans: Critique and reformulation. *Journal of Abnormal Psychology*, **87** (1), 49–74.

Green, S. & Mitchell, T. (1979). Attributional processes of leaders in leader–member interactions. *Organizational Behavior and Human Performance*, **23**, 429–458.

Heider, F. (1958). *The psychology of interpersonal relations*. New York: Wiley.

Kelley, H. H. (1967). Attribution theory in social psychology. In D. Levine (Ed.), *Nebraska symposium on motivation, 1967*. Lincoln: University of Nebraska Press.

Kelley, H. H. (1973). The process of causal attribution. *American Psychologist*, **28**, 107–128.

Kelley, H. H. & Michela, J. L. (1980). Attribution theory and research. *Annual Review of Psychology*, **31**, 457–501.

Lord, R. G. & Maher, K. J. (1990). Alternative information processing models and their implications for theory, research, and practice. *Academy of Management Review*, **15** (1), 9–28.

Martinko, M. J. (Ed.), (1995). *Attribution theory: An organizational perspective*. Delray Beach, FL: St. Lucie Press.

Martinko, M. J. & Gardner, W. L. (1982). Learned helplessness: An alternative explanation for performance deficits. *Academy of Management Review*, **7 (2)**, 195–204.

Martinko, M. J. & Gardner, W. L. (1987). The leader member attribution process. *Academy of Management Review*, **12** (2), 235–249.

Mitchell, T. R. & Wood, R. E. (1980). Supervisor's responses to subordinate poor performance: A test of an attributional model. *Organizational Behavior and Human Performance*, **25**, 123–138.

Weiner, B. (1986). *An attribution theory of motivation and emotion*. New York: Springer-Verlag.

MARK J. MARTINKO

authoritarian personality This term denotes a personality syndrome characterized by rigidity of thinking, deep suspicion of outgroups, an aggressively domineering and harshly critical attitude toward those in a subordinate position, an excessively submissive attitude toward those in positions of authority (*see* OBEDIENCE and CONFORMITY), and a generally conservative or "old-fashioned" outlook on life (Ray, 1990). Authoritarianism was identified and studied in a remarkable program of research begun during World War II to better understand the psychological origins of PREJUDICE and totalitarianism. One of the unique characteristics of the authoritarian research program was the blend of psychoanalytically-oriented concepts (*see* PROJECTION) and methods with more traditional psychometric approaches. Authoritarianism was measured by a self-report measure, the California F-Scale (F stood for Fascism), which became one of the most widely used personality instruments (Christie, 1991). Publication of *The Authoritarian Personality* generated much criticism and debate which in turn stimulated several important contributions to the study of PERSONALITY. For one, by focusing on the disposition toward fascist beliefs the researchers had overlooked a more general rigidity and conventionality of thought that characterized authoritarians irrespective of political orientation. Rokeach developed a measure of authoritarianism that was politically neutral, labeling the construct Dogmatism, or close-mindedness (Christie, 1991). Research also revealed that scores on the F-scale were affected by an acquiescence response set, or the tendency to agree with self-report items (*see* BIAS; ERROR). In the decades since the original authoritarian research, response sets of different sorts have been identified and studied. Organizational behavior researchers have become more sensitive to the need to control these response sets in their measures.

See also **Leadership style; Managerial style; Power; Theory X and Y; Organizational neurosis**

Bibliography

Christie, R. (1991). Authoritarianism and related constructs. In J. P. Robinson P. R. Shaver & L. S. Wrightsman (Eds), *Measures of personality and social psychological attitudes*. San Diego, CA: Academic Press.

Ray, J. J. (1990). The old-fashioned personality. *Human Relations*, **43**, 997–1013.

SEYMOUR ADLER

authority This concept denotes the legitimate POWER in a social system associated with a particular person or position. Legitimate power is consented to or accepted by members of the social system (*see* LEGITIMACY). The power exercised by an authority includes not only the expectation of COMPLIANCE or OBEDIENCE with orders but also the ability to reward or punish.

Weber outlined four types of authority. Katz Kahn (1978) condensed two of them into the rational–legal type; ideally, it is rule-bound, formal, and based on positions, not personalities. Prevalent in modern organizations, rational–legal authority is manifested by HIERARCHY or BUREAUCRACY. Occasionally charismatic authority, Weber's second type, is prevalent in organizations and is derived from the visionary characteristics of a particular leader (*see* LEADERSHIP, CHARISMATIC); this authority is personal and not characterized by rules. Weber's third form of authority is traditional, based on the sanctity of customs, VALUES, and experience; interest in traditional authority in organizations is evidenced by ORGANIZATIONAL CULTURE.

See also **Classical design theory; Formal organization; Management, classical theory; Status**

Bibliography

Katz, D. & Kahn, R. L. (1978). *The social psychology of organizations* (2nd edn), New York: Wiley.

DAVID L DEEPHOUSE

automation In his seminal study of automation, Bright (1958) credits D. S. Harder, then Vice-President of Manufacturing of the Ford Motor Company, with coining the word in 1946. Initially used to describe automatic work feeding and material handling devices, the meaning of the term soon broadened to cover the more general case of the automatic control of the manufacture of a product through successive stages. Thus, as reflected in the use of the prefix "auto," which comes from the Greek word "autos" meaning "self," "automation" refers to machinery or equipment characterized by SELF-REGULATION, which operates independently of real-time human CONTROL. The term also has a relative connotation. It is used both to describe TECHNOLOGY which performs functions previously carried out manually, and to characterize technology which is more automatic than its predecessor. For these reasons, it is common to identify different levels or degrees of automation.

Manufacturing automation traditionally has been based on built-in mechanical or electro-mechanical control devices such as cams, timers, and counters. These are designed for particular requirements, which results in a technology dedicated to one or at most a few products. The initial capital outlay, and the cost of modification to meet different product requirements, effectively restricts the use of such "hard" automation to MASS PRODUCTION (Sharit, Chang, & Salvendy, 1987). The advent of numerical control and computer numerical control, however, has made it possible to develop more flexible or "soft" forms of automation (*see* ADVANCED MANUFACTURING TECHNOLOGY). A key feature of such computer-based control systems is that they can be programmed to determine the selection, sequence, and duration of different machine operations. The same technology can thus be used to make a much wider range of products and can more easily be adapted to accommodate new ones. This has extended the sphere of application of automation to BATCH-PRODUCTION, which represents the larger part of the manufacturing base in industrialized countries.

Although the term automation remains closely associated with manufacturing technology its use is no longer restricted to that domain. It is now common, for example, to refer to "office automation" to describe computer-based information input, storage, manipulation, retrieval, and COMMUNICATION systems which provide word-processing, spreadsheet, electronic filing, messaging and a wide range of other facilities (*see* INFORMATION PROCESSING). Czaja (1987) suggests that such applications do not represent automation in a strict sense, since rather than substituting for human activity they enhance or augment it. However, that is a subtle distinction which is ignored in practice.

Within the study of ORGANIZATIONAL BEHAVIOR automation bears upon several areas of inquiry. For example, from a human factors and HUMAN–COMPUTER–INTERACTION perspective, it raises the question of the appropriate allocation of function between operator and technology (*see* ERGONOMICS). There is evidence that over-automation can impede the operator's ability to respond correctly to malfunctions which threaten output or safety. Another set of issues concerns the relationship of automation with JOB DESIGN. Here there is concern about the implications of automation for JOB DESKILLING, and interest in how to design operator jobs so as to promote system efficiency and reliability. Automation is also a component of the more inclusive concept of technology, and hence central to the wider issue of the relationship of technology to ORGANIZATIONAL DESIGN.

See also **Business process reengineering; Operations management; Productivity**

Bibliography

Bright, J. R. (1958). *Automation and management*. Boston: Harvard University Press.

Czaja, S. J. (1987). Human factors in office automation. In G. Salvendy (Ed.), *Handbook of human factors* (pp. 1587–1616). New York: Wiley.

Sharit, J., Chang, T. & Salvendy, G. (1987). Technical and human aspects of computer-aided manufacturing. In G. Salvendy (Ed.), *Handbook of human factors* (pp. 1694–1723). New York: Wiley.

TOBY D. WALL

autonomous work groups These are groups of employees with overlapping skills who collectively perform a relatively whole task (e.g., manufacturing a complete product), whilst exercising a high level of discretion over the conduct of work. Sometimes called "self-regulating," "self-managing," "semiautonomous," or "internally led" work groups (*see* SELF-MANAGEMENT), they are the most common structural outcome associated with sociotechnical systems interventions (*see* SOCIOTECHNICAL THEORY; SELF-MANAGED TEAMS). According to this perspective such work designs enhance productivity by encouraging the control of key variances at source and locating intertask coordination requirements within a single work unit. They are held to be more performance effective than individual JOB DESIGNS when technically required cooperation is high and when there is a high level of uncertainty or variability associated with boundary transactions or work processes. A positive effect on employee MOTIVATION and ATTITUDES is also predicted, since such structural arrangements yield jobs which are congruent with psychologically significant human VALUES, such as the needs for variety, AUTONOMY, meaningful work, opportunities to learn, and social support (Pasmore, 1988). Autonomous work groups often feature as part of an overall HUMAN RESOURCES STRATEGY oriented toward labour flexibility and employee COMMITMENT.

In practice, the degree of autonomy exercised by these WORK GROUPS varies, but typically involves three categories of workplace DECISION MAKING (Susman, 1979). First, there are decisions associated with regulating the immediate production or work process. These concern the coordination of task performance or the allocation of resources within the group. Second, there are decisions which affect the work group's overall level of independence within the organization, such as determining the order of production. Finally, there are decisions concerning the internal governance of the group, such as the process whereby collective decisions are reached.

The capacity of an autonomous work group to operate effectively depends on the degree of:

(1) *task differentiation* – the extent to which the group's task is independent of others within the organization;
(2) *boundary control* – the degree to which employees can influence transactions with their work environment and protect work boundaries from external intrusions; and
(3) *task control* – the extent to which employees are free to regulate their own behavior to convert inputs (e.g., information, raw materials) into a completed product or service, such as by varying the pace of work (*see* SELF-REGULATION).

Therefore, autonomous work groups require first-level management practices which clearly define and protect the boundaries of the group's discretion, avoid close direct supervision, and ensure that members possess the necessary information, knowledge, and SKILL to exercise control effectively (Manz & Sims, 1987). Group-based performance FEEDBACK and REWARD systems are also common, whilst skill-based pay is often used as a means of encouraging the development of multiskilling (*see* PAYMENT SYSTEMS).

Studies confirm that appropriately designed autonomous work groups positively affect PRODUCTIVITY and some specific work attitudes (e.g., intrinsic JOB SATISFACTION). However, they have not consistently given rise to improvements in performance motivation, ABSENTEEISM, or LABOR TURNOVER (Goodman, Devadas, & Hughson, 1988), leading some researchers (e.g., Wall, Kemp, Jackson, & Clegg, 1986) to question motivational explanations of their effects.

See also **Group decision making; Organizational design; Team building**

Bibliography

Goodman, P. S., Devadas, R. & Hughson, T. G. (1988). Groups and productivity: Analyzing the effectiveness of self-managing teams. In J. P. Campbell, R. J. Campbell & Associates (Eds), *Productivity in organizations*. San Francisco: Jossey-Bass.

Manz, C. C. & Sims, H. P. (1987). Leading workers to lead themselves: The external leadership of self-managing teams. *Administrative Science Quarterly*, **32**, 106–128.

Pasmore, W. A. (1988). *Designing effective organizations: The sociotechnical systems perspective*. New York: Wiley.

Susman, G. I. (1979). *Autonomy at work: A sociotechnical analysis of participative management*. New York: Praeger.

Wall, T. D., Kemp, N. J., Jackson, P. R. & Clegg, C. W. (1986). Outcomes of autonomous work groups: A long-term field experiment. *Academy of Management Journal*, **29**, 280–304.

JOHN CORDERY

Autonomy This concept, in work settings, means the degree to which an individual is free to decide how to accomplish a task, or goals of a job. Considered a basic human need, it is also a motivational characteristic of jobs. Employees who perceive themselves as choosing to perform an activity, as opposed to being directed to do so, are intrinsically motivated and accept more personal responsibility for the consequences of their work (*see* MOTIVATION; INTRINSIC/EXTRINSIC MOTIVATION). Workers relinquished autonomy in the eighteenth century during the Industrial Revolution and the consequent DIVISION OF LABOR; but better educated workforces, technologically complex jobs, service-based economies, and international competition have spurred attempts over the past 40 years to increase autonomy. Organizations have changed the distribution of POWER through decentralization and participative decision making, (*see* PARTICIPATION; DECISION-MAKING) and have improved oversimplified work through JOB ENRICHMENT. Findings (Spector, 1986) show that high levels of perceived control are associated with high levels of JOB SATISFACTION, COMMITMENT, involvement, performance and motivation, and low levels of physical symptoms, emotional distress, role STRESS, ABSENTEEISM, and LABOR TURNOVER. However, because organizations are OPEN SYSTEMS which must adjust to their environments, they will vary in the degree to which they are able to provide autonomy (*see* MECHANISTIC/ORGANIC).

See also **Locus of control; Job design; Job characteristics; Democracy; Job deskilling; Leadership style; Delegation; Self-regulation; Employee involvement; Theory X and Y; Theory Z**

Bibliography

Spector, P. (1986). Perceived control by employees: A meta-analysis of studies concerning autonomy and participation at work. *Human Relations*, **39**, 1005–1016.

UCO J. WIERSMA

— B —

bargaining *see* COLLECTIVE BARGAINING; NEGOTIATION.

barriers to entry Economic theorists generally argue that under perfect competition a firm's profits should be equal to its cost of capital. When firms make profits above the cost of capital they are said to generate "rents."

When researchers look across industries or portions of industries' STRATEGIC GROUPS, they often find significant profitability differences unrelated to cost of capital. They argue that with a few firms in the industry, the firms can collude to raise prices and profits. This raises a serious question: If firms in this industry make unusually high profits, why don't other firms enter this industry until the industry simply makes normal profits?

Researchers have proposed that "barriers to entry" prevent other firms from entering the industry. A barrier to entry can be any of a number of things that keep other firms from entering an unusually profitable industry. Some barriers and how they might work include:

> *1. Government Action* For a variety of reasons, government actions can directly and indirectly create barriers to entry. Regulatory monopolies constitute the most direct barrier. Firms are restrained from offering services (e.g., telephone, cable television) which would compete with an existing firm. Patent and other property rights laws may also protect firms in an industry by denying potential entrants access to essential intellectual property. Environmental, labor, and other regulations may create barriers by raising the cost of entry, minimum scale for entry, and so forth.

2. Economies of Scale In some industries, both costs and competitive ability may vary such that only large producers are competitive. This might come from a need for large-scale production facilities or some economies of scale in advertising or any of a number of sources. If current producers have reached such efficient scales, then entrants unable readily to attain a similar scale will find entry difficult. This is particularly true if the demand for a product is not large relative to the efficient scale of production.

3. Limit Pricing Competitors within an industry may not price to maximize their profits, given current industry participants, but rather control price and output to deter new entrants.

4. Absolute Competitive Advantages Current competitors in an industry may have factors of production (e.g., control of ore deposits) that can be denied to any potential entrant, putting new entrants at a cost disadvantage. This is particularly true where the factors have value within current competitors but may not be readily sold or transferred (e.g., REPUTATION or know-how). Competitive advantages can also derive from control over other stages of the value chain than the one of primary interest (*see* COMPETITIVENESS). For example, control over distribution channels may deny other manufacturers the ability to market their products. Alternatively, a vertically integrated firm may deter entry into later stages in the production process because it can control earlier stages (*see* VERTICAL INTEGRATION). For example, a firm might use dominance in the mining of ore to keep other firms out of smelting and other materials processing industries.

5. Product Differentiation Long-term development of loyal or even legally or technically bound customers greatly increases the difficulty for new entrants.

A number of these barriers can also be seen as "first mover advantages," i.e., advantages that accrue to the early participants in the industry. For example, early participants are likely to be able to lock up absolute competitive advantages or attain economies in production due to learning curve effects (*see* ORGANIZATIONAL LEARNING).

See also **Strategic management; Organizational design; Organization and environment; Stakeholders**

Bibliography

Geroski, P., Gilbert, R. J. & Jacquemin, A. (1990). *Barriers to entry and strategic competition.* Chur, Switzerland: Harwood Academic.

PHILIP BROMILEY

batch production This is a method of transforming inputs into outputs in lots or groups so that any single type of product is produced only intermittently. This is generally considered the least complex PROCESS TECHNOLOGY, compared to MASS PRODUCTION and continuous production. Manufacturers employing batch processes typically produce heterogeneous items targeted to different customer groups; batch sizes are small if customers demand modest amounts of different types of goods.

Batch production is important in organizational research because many studies generally suggest that ORGANIZATIONAL DESIGN is linked to the process technology the firm employs, and that high organizational performance requires matching technology with structure (*see* CONTINGENCY THEORY). Batch production usually involves more UNCERTAINTY than mass production or continuous-flow processes. Consequently, it is usually associated with more flexible, organic organizations (*see* MECHANISTIC/ORGANIC). Woodward (1970), for instance, found that organizations employing batch processes use more ambiguous performance measures, have market-oriented as opposed to functional departments, and less carefully rationalized work patterns than did organizations using more complex forms of process technology.

Historically, batch production has been more adaptive but also more costly than mass production or continuous-flow production. However, ADVANCED MANUFACTURING TECHNOLOGY may lead to general-purpose machine tools that can process batches of one unit as cost-effectively as mass quantities of an item can be produced (Lengnick-Hall, 1986).

See also **Automation; Productivity; Technology; Organizational effectiveness**

Bibliography

Lengnick-Hall, C. A. (1986). Technology advances in batch production and improved competitive position. *Journal of Management*, **12**, 75–90.

Woodward, J. (1970). *Industrial organization: Theory and practice* (2nd edn) Oxford, UK: Oxford University Press.

PHILIP ANDERSON

Behavior modification (Kazdin, 1978) This is the systematic application of scientific principles of learning (including but not limited to those mentioned elsewhere, e.g., LEARNING INDIVIDUAL; and REINFORCEMENT) to change behavior on a person-by-person or case-by-case basis. Individuals may seek the services of a qualified behavior modifier to change behaviors they personally consider dysfunctional and beyond their own ability to control without professional assistance. Common problems addressed and solved by behavior modification specialists include elimination of phobias, body weight goal achievement (gaining or reducing), smoking cessation, and elimination of drug abuse. Supervisors are sometimes taught behavior modification methods so they can determine why one or several subordinates have learned dysfunctional behaviors on the job. The supervisors then create new environmental experiences for subordinates that increase the rate of functional behaviors or eliminate dysfunctional and replace them with functional behaviors.

See also **Conditioning; Influence; Learning, individual**

Bibliography

Kazdin, A. K. (1978). *History of behavior modification*. Baltimore, MD: University Park Press.

THOMAS C. MAWHINNEY

behavioral decision research The rational model of DECISION MAKING is based on a set of assumptions prescribing how a decision *should* be made rather than describing how a decision *is* made. In contrast, behavioral decision research focuses on the systematic inconsistencies in the decision-making process which prevent humans from making fully rational decisions (*see* RATIONALITY).

Kahneman and Tversky (1979) and Tversky and Kahneman (1974) have provided critical information about specific systematic biases that influence judgment. Their work, and work by subsequent researchers, has elucidated our modern understanding of judgment. People rely on a number of simplifying strategies, or rules of thumb, in making decisions. These simplifying strategies are called heuristics. Unfortunately, these heuristics lead to a number of biases. A number of the predominant biases described in this literature are reviewed below (this summary is based on Bazerman (1994)):

Ease of Recall. Individuals judge events which are more easily recalled from memory, based upon vividness or recency, to be more numerous than events of equal frequency whose instances are less easily recalled.

Retrievability. Individuals are biased in their assessments of the frequency of events based upon how their memory structures affect the search process.

Presumed Associations. Individuals tend to overestimate the probability of two events co-occurring based upon the number of similar associations which are easily recalled, whether from experience or social influence.

Insensitivity to Base Rates. Individuals tend to ignore base rates in assessing the likelihood of events when any other descriptive information is provided – even if the information is irrelevant.

Insensitivity to Sample Size. Individuals frequently fail to appreciate the role of sample size in assessing the RELIABILITY of sample information.

Misconceptions of Chance. Individuals expect a sequence of data generated by a random process to look "random," even when the sequence is too short for those expectations to be statistically valid.

Regression to the Mean. Individuals often ignore the fact that extreme events tend to regress to the mean on subsequent trials.

The Conjunction Fallacy. Individuals falsely judge that conjunctions, i.e., two events co-occurring, are more probable than a more global set of occurrences of which the conjunction is a subset.

Anchoring. Individuals make estimates for values based upon an initial value (derived from past events, random assignment, or whatever information is available) and typically make insufficient adjustments from that anchor when establishing a final value.

Conjunctive and Disjunctive Events Bias. Individuals exhibit a bias toward overestimating the probability of conjunctive events and underestimating the probability of disjunctive events.

Overconfidence. Individuals tend to be overconfident in the infallibility of their judgments when answering moderately to extremely difficult questions.

The Confirmation Trap. Individuals tend to seek confirmatory information for what they think is true and neglect the search for disconfirmatory evidence.

Hindsight. After finding out whether or not an event occurred, individuals tend to overestimate the degree to which they would have predicted the correct outcome.

Framing. Individuals are influenced by irrelevant information concerning how questions are framed.

During the 1980s and 1990s, these biases have had a profound influence on the field of organizational behavior. Decision making and a decision perspective to negotiation have emerged as central themes in OB research and the development of new OB courses. Our knowledge of biases has been used to help organizational members better understand their limitations, and have been extended to the organizational level of analysis to help account for the systematic errors of organizations.

See also **Attribution theory; Bounded rationality; Errors; Commitment, escalating; Negotiation; Prospect theory**

Bibliography

Bazerman, M. H. (1994). *Judgment in managerial decision making* (3rd edn). New York: Wiley.

Kahneman, D. & Tversky, A. (1979). Prospect theory: An analysis of decision under risk. *Econometrica*, **47**, 263–291.

Tversky, A. & Kahneman, D. (1974). Judgment under uncertainty: Heuristics and biases. *Science*, **185**, 1124–1131.

MAX H. BAZERMAN

behaviorism *see* LEARNING, INDIVIDUAL

benchmarking This has become a highly fashionable "buzzword" in business, especially in the areas of OPERATIONS MANAGEMENT and STRATEGIC MANAGEMENT. It denotes the identification of best practice in another organizational unit, followed by its analysis and adoption. An early example of the method being taken to an extreme was the Xerox Corporation's fightback against surgent Japanese competition in the copier market, where a wide range of business and operational processes were improved as a result of systematic benchmarking (for a case study report of the Xerox experience, *see* Jick, 1993). The car industry also contains numerous examples.

From an ORGANIZATIONAL BEHAVIOR perspective it can be seen as a substitute for INNOVATION, practiced by "Analyzer" companies (*see* STRATEGIC TYPES) who seek to minimize first mover risks whilst reaping the benefits of EXCELLENCE and COMPETITIVENESS. Companies can benchmark their own best practice as well as that of others, and increasingly do so in the "soft" areas of HUMAN RESOURCES MANAGEMENT through the use of employee attitude SURVEYS and the like.

Usually, companies benchmark the practices of their best performing competitors, though commentators have pointed out the dangers of this, since bad practice or conservatism may predominate in a sector. It is said that companies should benchmark *activities* not other companies, and may accrue the benefits of benchmarking most dramatically where the focus is on organizations quite dissimilar to themselves in type. This is more likely to lead to adoption and diffusion of new forms in a business (*see* INNOVATION ADOPTION; INNOVATION DIFFUSION), though inevitably raises issues of whether benchmarked practices are transferable and implementable. Other recommendations for effective benchmarking are that it should be creatively applied, rather than an exercise in mere imitation, and that it should be a continuous monitored activity, rather than a one-off effort at improvement (*see* CONTINUOUS IMPROVEMENT).

See also **Five forces framework; Organizational change; Organizational effectiveness; Productivity; Risk-taking**

Bibliography

Jick, T. D. (1993). *Managing change: Concepts and cases*. Homewood, IL: Irwin.

NIGEL NICHOLSON

bias Any systematic deviation of an estimate given by a STATISTICAL METHOD from the true value the estimate is meant to represent is called bias (Oakes, 1986). As such, bias is a property of a procedure for estimating a value, rather than of any particular value of an estimate obtained from such a procedure. Bias can take many forms. The most common in organizational research are sample-selection, aggregation, model-selection, and omitted-variable biases.

Sample-selection bias occurs when an investigator selects a sample for observation without proper randomization. Examples of nonrandom selection abound, as when individual units are included in the sample because they are successful on the outcome variable of interest, because they are convenient, or because they are willing. Researchers using the CASE METHOD need to guard against bias in the process of selecting evidence. Studies done via SURVEYS, on the other hand, are especially prone to concerns about a particular sample-selection problem known as response bias.

Aggregation biases can occur when observations on individual units or variables are combined. These biases are closely tied to questions concerning the choice among LEVELS OF ANALYSIS. Time-aggregation bias is a particular form that arises in POPULATION ECOLOGY or similar work where continuous durations are rounded, either solely up or down, to discrete intervals.

Model-selection bias occurs when an investigator presumes the relationship between the predictor and outcome variables follows a certain form without verifying that form for a particular set of data. Often a convention emerges to use a particular model for reasons of expediency, and it becomes taken for granted. Omitted-variable biases are extremely difficult to eliminate. These occur when an important predictor variable is unobserved, but at least partially correlated with other variables in a model.

SIMULATION is often used to demonstrate the bias of a statistical procedure or to explore ways of reducing biases in statistical methods. Other biases are of a nonstatistical nature. Foremost among these are personal biases. Personal biases can only be mitigated through careful scrutiny of an investigator's entire methodology.

See also **Errors; Reliability; Research design; Research methods; Validity**

Bibliography

Oakes, M. W. (1986). *Statistical inference: A commentary for the social and behavioral sciences*. New York: Wiley.

KENNETH W. KOPUT

big five personality model *see* PERSONALITY; PERSONALITY TESTING

biodata There are many selection situations where the ratio of candidates to posts available is so high that many have to be screened out on the basis of biographical data contained in the application form (*see* SELECTION METHODS). Not only is the process of reading large numbers of application forms very time-consuming, but also the judgments made are highly subjective and of doubtful validity. Biodata offers an alternative method of dealing with biographical data which is both economical in time and objective in terms of the method used to evaluate the information.

The procedure involves allocating scores to individual items of biographical data provided by applicants. These individual scores are then summed to obtain a total score for each individual. Only those whose total score is above a predetermined cut off point proceed to the next stage of the selection procedure. A central feature of the biodata approach is the method used to develop scoring keys for the individual items. The procedure is essentially an empirical one. It involves a development stage of identifying the extent to which each of a series of trial items is answered differently by successful versus less successful existing employees and allocating weights to these items accordingly to create scoring keys. England (1971) provides a detailed description of one of the most popular techniques for constructing biodata scores.

As with any selection device, a central issue is VALIDITY. The evidence here is generally favorable, the indications being that biodata can be one of the more valid predictors of job performance (Hunter & Hunter, 1984). Despite this evidence, there are some areas of current concern relating to the exact meaning and applicability of biodata.

First, as Mael (1991) points out, there is no clear definition as to what actually constitute biodata. On the one hand, there are "hard" biodata items consisting of essentially verifiable factual information. On the other hand, there are a wide variety of "soft" biodata items covering attitudes, opinions, reactions to hypothetical events, and the like. With this latter group in particular, it is not at all clear what the defining characteristics of a biodata item actually are. Two other issues are the possibility of faking and of unintentional DISCRIMINATION against particular social or racial groups (*see* RACE). Because "hard" biodata items can be checked, it seems plausible to assume that they will be less susceptible to faking, and indeed there is some evidence that this is the case. Nonetheless, there are real possibilities of unintentional discrimination here. Suppose, for example, individuals living in a certain location performed better, say in terms of job tenure. Weighting this item could be discriminatory should it turn out that very few members of a particular racial group happened to live in that location. The dangers of unintentional discrimination may be less for "soft" items, but, because these are not readily verifiable, they may be more susceptible to applicants' "faking good" by guessing the "correct" response. Another limitation on the use of biodata is the time-consuming nature of the procedure to develop scoring keys coupled with the widely held view that scoring keys developed in one job situation cannot be used for another. However, recent research suggests that well-developed biographical items may be more robust across job situations than was previously assumed (Rothstein, Schmidt, Erwin, Owens, & Sparks, 1990).

See also **Assessment; Recruitment**

Bibliography

England, G. W. (1971). *Development and use of weighted application blanks*. Minnesota: Minnesota Industrial Relations Center.

Hunter, J. E. & Hunter, R. F. (1984). The validity and utility of alternative predictors of job performance. *Psychological Bulletin*, **96**, 72–99.

Mael, F. E. (1991). A conceptual rationale for the domain and attributes of biodata items. *Personnel Psychology*, **44**, 763–792.

Rothstein, H. R., Schmidt, F. L., Erwin, F. W., Owens, W. A. & Sparks, C. P. (1990). Biographical data in employment selection: Can validators be generalizable? *Journal of Applied Psychology*, **75**, 175–184.

TONY KEENAN

bonus payments These are cash payments received in addition to, or in lieu of, base salary increases. Bonuses may be linked to individual performance (e.g., merit ratings), group performance (e.g., new product development), facility performance (e.g., cost savings, product quality, customer satisfaction) business unit/organization performance (e.g., profits, stock returns), or any combination thereof. From a financial point of view, bonus payments have the advantage of being paid out, in the case of profit sharing, only when the organization is profitable. In addition, it has been argued that bonuses, which must be re-earned, in contrast to base salary increases which roll into the base permanently, provide a more direct link between current performance and pay, and also control the growth of fixed labor costs. On the other hand, employees, especially those at lower levels, who have less discretionary income, may view bonuses as unnecessarily putting their income stream at risk.

Whereas bonus payments for production workers were fairly rare until recently, middle and top level managers in the United States have typically had a bonus plan as an important part of their total compensation (*see* CEOs). Among top executives, bonus payments can easily exceed base salary. Short-term (quarterly or annual) bonus pools for executives are typically tied to meeting net income or return on stockholders' equity targets (Berton, 1990) and individual performance (Gerhart & Milkovich, 1990). Long-term incentives can also be based on such objectives, although stock performance is usually the key factor in such plans.

See also **Payment systems; Performance, individual; Performance related pay; Rewards**

Bibliography

Berton, L. (1990, April 18). Calculating compensation. *Wall Street Journal*, p. R26.

Gerhart, B. & Milkovich, G. T. (1990). Organizational differences in managerial compensation and financial performance. *Academy of Management Journal*, **33**, 663–691.

BARRY GERHART

boundary spanning To understand this term, we must first understand the idea of boundary. Boundary implies limit or separateness; a boundary therefore limits or establishes something to be separate from something else. This something can be physical – e.g., a wall – psychological or sociological – e.g., one's role, title or ethnic identity – or even imaginary – e.g., "People who work in that part of the organization should be avoided." Boundary spanning then becomes any process or activity that bridges, links or perhaps even blurs the separateness of two or more boundaries (*see* ORGANIZATIONAL BOUNDARIES).

Organizationally, boundaries exist interpersonally between and among individuals, particularly in the form of roles (*see* ROLE). Job descriptions also establish boundaries. Regardless of how desirable it might be to link if not blur roles, spanning a role can create stress and conflict. Kahn, Wolfe, Quinn, Snoek, and Rosenthal (1964) defined a boundary role person as one located in two or more groups within the organization or within more than a single organization. Such a person can experience conflicting demands (*see* ROLE CONFLICT).

Organizational subsystems (*see* FORMAL ORGANIZATION; FUNCTIONAL DESIGN; ORGANIZATIONAL DESIGN) establish boundaries within the organization. Marketing is one subsystem, finance another, etc. The classic organizational studies of Burns and Stalker (1961) and Lawrence and Lorsch (1964) distinguished between dividing labor (differentiation) and coordinating work (integration) (*see* MECHANISTIC/ORGANIC). In one organization that Lawrence and Lorsch (1964) studied, product INNOVATION was desperately needed, requiring strong interdependence between research and sales groups and between research and production groups. They pointed out that management hierarchy alone could not bridge the gap across such wide differences. Consequently, Lawrence and Lorsch advocated the development of *integrating* roles and *cross-functional teams*, recommendations for spanning boundaries within the organization.

Thompson (1967) has described boundary-spanning structures, particularly between the organization and its external environment (*see* ORGANIZATION AND ENVIRONMENT). In this context, procurement is an example of an organizational function that is boundary spanning. Thompson proposed that the more the organization's environment was large, complex, and unpredictable, the more management would need to establish boundary-spanning structures to monitor – e.g., market research – and respond rapidly to the environment with decentralized, local units (*see* DECENTRALIZATION).

More recently Kanter (1989) has identified at least three examples of boundary spanning across organizations:

(1) service alliances, where a group of organizations band together to create a new organization to serve some need for all of them, e.g., an industry research consortium;
(2) opportunistic alliances, where usually two organizations seize an opportunity to gain a competitive advantage by joining forces, typically referred to as a joint business venture; and
(3) STAKEHOLDER alliances, where pre-existing interdependencies are strengthened, such as with suppliers, customers, and employees, i.e., between labor organizations and management. (*See also* Strategic alliances.)

By 1990 a new term had entered the scene – the boundaryless organization, popularized by Welch of GE and others. The point being made, albeit in an exaggerated form, is that since organizations by their very nature are often overly hierarchical, protective of domains, and unnecessarily competitive and conflictual, spanning processes and activities are required to decrease the boundaries and increase permeability.

See also **Linking pin; Division of labor; Span of control; Managerial roles; Integration**

Bibliography

Burns, T. & Stalker, G. M. (1961). *The management of innovation*. London: Tavistock.

Kahn, R. L., Wolfe, D. M., Quinn, R. P., Snoek, J. D. & Rosenthal, R. A. (1964). *Organizational stress: Studies in role conflict and ambiguity*. New York: Wiley.

Kanter, R. M. (1989). *When giants learn to dance: Mastering the challenge of strategy, management, and careers in the 1990s*. New York: Simon & Schuster.

Lawrence, R. R. & Lorsch, J. W. (1964). *Organization and environment*. Homewood, IL: Irwin.

Thompson, J. D. (1967). *Organizations in action*. New York: McGraw-Hill.

W. WARNER BURKE

bounded rationality Classical economic theories of management assume that decision makers make choices in completely rational ways, selecting the best alternative to achieve optimal outcomes. They assume a complete set of alternative solutions is readily available to the decision maker, who has full knowledge of the consequences of each. The choice is arrived at after a thorough evaluation of each alternative against explicit criteria.

These assumptions are unrealistic in many cases and, although individuals are "intendedly" rational, their RATIONALITY is bounded – constrained by the environment in which they operate and their own human limitations.

The complexity of the environment means that decision makers have to simplify to make sense of it. It also means they are faced with UNCERTAINTY. Individuals cannot absorb all the information needed to formulate a complete set of alternatives from which to choose. Information may not be available and evaluation may be subject to personal biases.

A boundedly rational process involves limiting information to what can be easily managed. Alternative solutions are evaluated sequentially, not all together; if the first is acceptable, further search ceases. Decisions are made using "rules of thumb," heuristics, and, where possible, tried and tested routines for problem solving. A suboptimal, or SATISFICING, decision is the result of this process, which is neither absolutely exhaustive nor completely rational.

See also **Decision making; Group decision making; Behavioral decision theory; Cognitive processes**

Bibliography

March, J. G. & Simon, H. A. (1958). *Organizations*. New York: Wiley. (2nd edn., 1993; Oxford: Blackwell).

SUSAN MILLER

brainstorming The brainstorming technique is an informal technique or tool for GROUP DECISION MAKING. Group participants informally generate as many ideas, regardless of their apparent practicality or even relevance, as possible, without evaluation by others. In this way, brainstorming generates a large number of alternatives to issues, problems, and concerns (Ackoff & Vergara, 1988). Using the same informal and relaxed format, the brainstorming group is then used to generate creative solutions based upon those alternatives. Again, during the process of solutions generation, evaluation is suspended until everyone has had the opportunity to contribute. By these means the brainstorming technique is regarded as a highly effective process for groups to generate, at relatively low cost and in an informal atmosphere, many potentially creative and useful alternatives and solutions.

The method is used by business and governmental organizations to help groups overcome barriers to DECISION MAKING, such as HIERARCHY which tends to suppress the contributions from lower status members. By generating contributions from all group members, the method creates member understanding and ownership of alternatives and solutions. This can then result in less resistance to solutions and greater recognition of the usefulness of change (Delbecq, Van de Ven, & Gustafson, 1977) (*see* RESISTANCE TO CHANGE).

Used in conjunction with more formal and more structured techniques of group decision making such as the nominal group technique and the Delphi technique, brainstorming offers organizations an effective means to foster and facilitate CREATIVITY in organizational and group decision making (Whiting, 1978).

See also **Nominal group technique; Delphi; Innovation**

Bibliography

Ackoff R. L. & Vergara, E. (1988). Creativity in problem solving and planning, in R. L. Kuhn (ed.), *Handbook for creative and innovative management* pp. 81–92. New York: McGraw-Hill.

Delbecq, A., Van de Ven A. & Gustafson, D. (1977). *Group techniques for program planning*. Glenview, IL: Scott, Foresman.

Whiting, C. S. (1978). Operational techniques of creative learning, in M. Richards (ed.) *Readings in management*, (5th edn) pp. 131–142. Cincinnati: South-Western.

RANDALL S. SCHULER

bureaucracy This widely used concept has a variety of meanings, some positive, some less so. The sociologist Weber (1946) thought bureaucracy synonymous with rational organization (*see* RATIONALITY): bureaucracies embodied the ideals of rational–legal Authority such that all but policy decisions are based on rules, which themselves are internally consistent and stable over time (*see* DECISION MAKING). Political scientists tend to think of bureaucracy as governance by bureaus having the following characteristics: they are large, they are staffed by full-time employees who have careers within the organization, and they rely on budget allocations rather than revenues from sales since their outputs cannot be priced in voluntary *quid pro quo* transactions in the market (Downs, 1967; Wilson, 1989). There is a third definition of bureaucracy, which is far less flattering; bureaucracy is inefficient organization, is inherently antidemocratic, cannot adapt to change, and, worse, exacerbates its own errors (Crozier, 1964). Discussion of bureaucracy tends to be ideologically tinged (*see* IDEOLOGY). The political left emphasizes the rationality and neutrality of government while downplaying the power of bureaucracy itself, while the right uses bureaucracy as an epithet or shibboleth and focuses on bureaucracy's antidemocratic tendencies and inefficiencies.

Properties of Bureaucracy

The properties of bureaucracy are best understood in comparison with other forms of organization. Weber, for example, focuses on comparisons between bureaucracy and traditional forms of administration. Compared to traditional organizations, the structure of bureaucracy exhibits much greater DIFFERENTIATION and INTEGRATION. With respect to differentiation, there is intensive DIVISION OF LABOR, a HIERARCHY of authority, and, perhaps most importantly, a clear separation of official duties from personal interests and obligations, what Weber calls separation of home from office. With respect to integration, bureaucracies have written rules and regulations, codified procedures for selection and advancement of officials, and a specialized administrative staff charged with maintaining these rules and procedures (*see* ROUTINIZATION). And compared to traditional organizations, bureaucracies constrain the conduct of officials while offering powerful incentives for compliance. The constraints lie in strict super- and subordination requiring all actions to be justified in terms of the larger purposes of the organization, the norm of impersonality that requires detachment and objectivity, and advancement contingent on both seniority and performance (*see* CONTROL). The incentives consist of the prospect of a lifetime career, salaries paid in cash rather than in kind, and (in Europe if not the United States) a modicum of social esteem attached to the status of official or *fonctionnaire*. The elements of differentiation, integration, constraints, and INCENTIVES render bureaucratic organizations both more powerful and more responsive to central authority than traditional administration. The power of bureaucracies results from their capacity for coordinated action. Their responsiveness to centralized authority arises from the dependence of individual bureaucrats on their salaries and other emoluments of office. These four elements, according to Weber, also render bureaucracy more efficient than traditional forms of organization. "Precision, speed, unambiguity, knowledge of the files, continuity, discretion, unity, strict subordination, reduction of friction and of material and personal costs – these are raised to the optimum point in the strictly bureaucratic administration . . ." (Weber, 1946, p. 214).

Compared to modern business organizations, bureaucracies have somewhat different and in some respects less attractive properties. One must ask, to begin, whether comparison of business and bureaucracy is warranted given Weber's insistence that the bureaucratic model describes both private and public administration. Public and private administration were remarkably similar at the time Weber was writing. Indeed, much of the United States public sector was modeled explicitly after the private sector at the beginning of the twentieth century. It is not accidental that the reform movement in the United States, which called for administration devoid of politics, coincided with the emergence of scientific management, which called for active management of firms. Nor is it accidental that in the 1940s the same theory of organization was believed to apply to public- and private-sector enterprises (*see* ADMINISTRATIVE THEORY and CLASSICAL DESIGN THEORY). Public and private organizations have diverged in the last 50 years, however. Divergences have occurred in several domains, most notably organizational design, accounting practices, and performance measurement. With respect to organizational design, virtually all large firms have moved from functional to divisionalized organizational structures, that is, from designs in which the principal units are responsible for different activities (such as purchasing, manufacturing, and sales) to designs in which the principal units are self-contained businesses responsible for profit as well as for other objectives (*see* DECENTRALIZATION). To be certain, patterns of divisionalization have changed over time – firms typically have fewer and somewhat larger business units as a result of several waves of DOWNSIZING – but until very recent times there have been no comparable innovations in the public sector (*see* ORGANIZATIONAL DESIGN). For the most part, public agencies have retained the same organizing principles – organization by function – they used 90 years ago. With respect to accounting, public-sector agencies have departed substantially from private-sector practices. At the beginning of this century, public entities issues consolidated financial reports and maintained capital accounts just like private businesses. Consolidated accounting gave way to much more complicated fund accounting during the 1920s, when it was believed necessary to segregate revenues and expenditures intended for different purposes into separate funds. Capital accounting has all but disappeared from the public sector, though accounting for long-term indebtedness remains out of necessity. With respect to performance measurement, the public sector lags substantially behind private businesses (*see* ORGANIZATIONAL PERFORMANCE). In business operations, not only is financial analysis necessary and universal, but firms' internal operations are often typically gauged against industry BENCHMARKS assembled by consultants and trade associations. By contrast, very little comparative performance assessment exists for government. In the United States, at least, performance comparisons across governmental units are strongly resisted. Just as at the beginning of the twentieth century, some efforts to make government more businesslike are now underway (*see* GOVERNMENT AND BUSINESS; GOVERNMENT AGENCIES). Some services have been privatized altogether. Others have been placed in public corporations, which are held responsible for breaking even if not making a profit. And some government agencies now measure customer satisfaction, just as businesses do.

Liabilities of Bureaucracy

If public-sector bureaucracies suffer in comparison with private-sector management, one must ask whether these liabilities arise from systematic causes, that is, the structure of bureaucracies themselves, or from other causes. Both sociologists and economists have argued that at least some of the liabilities of bureaucracy are systematic, although for different reasons. Sociologists have focused on bureaucratic dysfunctions of various kinds, including displacement of goals, so-called VICIOUS CYCLES in which different dysfunctions feed on one another, and spiraling bureaucratic growth. Economists, by contrast, have emphasized the efficiency disadvantages of bureaucracies compared to firms, asking whether, in general, nonmarket transactions are inefficient compared to market transactions and, specifically, the funding of bureaucracies through budgets rather than market transactions is conducive to overproduction of bureaucratic services. These potential liabilities of bureaucracy should be reviewed seriatim.

Displacement of goals. Bureaucracies are known for rigid adherence to rules and procedures, even when rules and procedures appear to impede the objectives of the organization. The notion of goal displacement provides both a description and an explanation for this seemingly nonrational conduct. Goal displacement, following Merton (1958), describes the process whereby means become ends in themselves, or "an instrumental value becomes a terminal value." The displacement of goals is especially acute in settings, such as bureaucracies, where the following conditions obtain: the technical competence of officials consists of knowledge of the rules, advancement is contingent on adherence to the rules, and peer pressure reinforces the norm of impersonality, which requires rules and procedures to be applied with equal force in all cases. What is important is goal displacement, at least as originally conceived, argues that bureaucracies are efficient in general – under conditions anticipated by their rules and procedures – but inefficient in circumstances that cannot be anticipated. The implications of goal displacement for INNOVATION and new product development have been realized only gradually: bureaucracy can be antithetical to innovation.

Vicious cycles. A more thoroughgoing critique of bureaucracy argues that dysfunctions are normal rather than exceptional and, moreover, that dysfunctions accumulate over time such that organizational stasis is the expected outcome. The elements of the vicious cycle of bureaucratic dysfunctions are impersonal rules that seek to limit the discretion of individual workers, centralization of remaining decisions, isolation of workers from their immediate supervisors as a consequence of limited DECISION-MAKING authority, and the exercise of unofficial power in arenas where uncertainty remains. Thus, as Crozier (1964) observes, maintenance people exercise undue influence in state-owned factories because their work is inherently unpredictable and cannot be governed by rules. The logic of vicious cycles, it should be pointed out, yields several consequences. To begin, new rules will arise to eliminate whatever islands of POWER remain in the organization, but these rules will trigger further centralization, isolation, and power plays as new sources of UNCERTAINTY arise. Second, to the extent that the organization is opened to uncertainties arising externally, line managers have the opportunity to reassert power that would otherwise erode through the dynamics of vicious cycles. External crisis (*see* CRISES), in other words, may be an antidote to bureaucracies' tendency toward rigidity over time.

Spiraling growth. Bureaucratic systems also tend toward growth other things being equal (Meyer, 1985). Until recently, growth of government and of administrative staff in private firms was endemic. The causes of growth lie in several factors, but chief among them are people's motives for constructing organizations in the first place. People construct formal organizations in order to rationalize or make sense of otherwise uncertain environments; organizations, in fact, succeed at making the world more sensible; as a consequence, there is continuous construction of bureaucracy and hence bureaucratic growth as people attempt to perfect their rationalization of an inherently uncertain world (*see* ORGANIZATION AND ENVIRONMENT). Two comments are in order. First, the logic of bureaucratic growth is built into administrative theory as developed by Simon (1976) and others (*see* ORGANIZATION THEORY). Irreducible uncertainty in the environment in conjunction with the belief that administrative organization can rationalize uncertainty will result in continuous growth in administration. Second, the growth imperative is so strong that deliberate campaigns to "downsize" or "restructure" organizations must be launched in order to achieve meaningful reductions in staff (*see* RESTRUCTURING). Downsizing continues to occur at record rates in United States' firms but may have reached a limit now that modest industrial expansion is underway.

Inefficiency. Economists have asked persistently without resolution whether public sector bureaucracies are inherently less efficient than private-sector enterprises. Several answers have been proffered, none fully satisfactory. From the 1940s to the present time, the Austrian school of economics, von Mises (1944) and others, have argued that any departure from market principles yields both inefficient transactions and antidemocratic tendencies. This position has proved difficult to reconcile with contemporary transaction–cost theories (*see* TRANSACTION COST THEORY), which argue that hierarchies may be more efficient than markets under some circumstances. In the 1970s, the efficiency question was cast somewhat differently: might bureaus, which depend on budgets for their sustenance, overproduce compared to firms subject to the discipline of the market (Niskanen, 1971)? Here too the answer was equivocal, as analysis showed that rent-maximizing monopolists would have similar incentives to overproduce whether they were located in public bureaucracies or private firms. Despite the absence of strong analytic underpinnings for the belief that bureaucracies are more apt to harbor inefficiencies than private-sector organizations, PRIVATIZATION of governmental functions is occurring rapidly and with positive results in many countries. It is unclear whether the liabilities of public bureaucracies are simply the liabilities of established organizations that have been shielded from extinction for too long, or whether bureaucracies suffer disadvantages in comparison with private organizations regardless of their age.

Research on Bureaucracy

Organizational research and research on bureaucracy were once synonymous or nearly so, as the bureaucratic model was believed descriptive of all organizations, for-profit and non-profit, and governmental (*see* NOT-FOR-PROFIT ORGANIZATIONS). Case studies of bureaucracy written during the 1950s and 1960s encompassed government agencies and industrial firms alike as evidenced by titles like Gouldner's (1954) *Patterns of Industrial Bureaucracy*. Early quantitative research on organizations, such as the work of the Aston group and the studies emanating from the Comparative Organization Research Program in the United States, focused mainly on relations among elements of organizational structure (size, hierarchy, administrative ratio, formalization, centralization, etc.) that flowed from the bureaucratic model implicitly if not explicitly (Blau & Scheonherr, 1971). As attention shifted to external causes of organizational outcomes, the bureaucratic model lost some of its relevance to research. Thus, for example, the key causal variable in RESOURCE DEPENDENCE models of organizations is control of strategic resources, which is more germane to businesses than to government bureaus. The key dependent variables in organizational POPULATION ECOLOGY are births and deaths of organizations, which are infrequent in the public sector. And institutional organizational theory has very much downplayed Weber's notion of bureaucracy as rational administration and has substituted for it the notion that all organizations, bureaucratic and nonbureaucratic alike but especially the former, seek social approval or legitimation rather than efficiency outcomes (*see* LEGITIMACY).

Some research on bureaucracy remains. Development economists continue to study the role of national bureaucracies in promoting or retarding economic growth. Others, again mainly economists, pursue the comparative efficiency of private- versus public-sector service deliver and possible advantages of creating competition among public agencies. And the study of public administration remains a viable although by no means a growing field. But research on bureaucracy is no longer at the core of organizational theory even though most of the public sector and much of the administrative component of the private sector continues to be organized along bureaucratic lines.

See also **competitiveness; alienation; organizational size**

Bibliography

Blau, P. M. & Schoenherr, R. (1971). *The structure of organizations*. New York: Basic Books.

Crozier, M. (1964). *The bureaucratic phenomenon*. Chicago: University of Chicago Press.

Downs, A. (1967). *Inside bureaucracy*. Boston: Little-Brown.

Gouldner, A. W. (1954). *Patterns of industrial bureaucracy*. Glencoe: Free Press.

Merton, R. K. (1958). Bureaucratic structure and personality. In *Social theory and social structure*, (2nd edn, pp. 195–206). Glencoe: Free Press.

Meyer, M. W. (1985). *Limits to bureaucratic growth*. Berlin and New York: de Gruyter.

Niskanen, W. (1971). *Bureaucracy and representative government*. Chicago: Aldine.

Simon, H. A. (1976). *Administrative behavior*, (3rd edn). New York: Free Press.

Weber, M. (1946). Bureaucracy. In H. Gerth and C. Wright Mills (Eds), *From Max Weber: Essays in sociology* (pp. 196–244). Glencoe: Free Press.

von Mises, L. (1944). *Bureaucracy*. New Haven: Yale University Press.

Wilson, J. Q. (1989). *Bureaucracy*. New York: Basic Books..

MARSHALL W. MEYER

burnout The technical use of the concept of burnout originated with Freudenberger who wrote about Staff Burnout in 1974. Its importance grew directly as a result of the development of a measure, The Maslach Burnout Inventory (Maslach & Jackson, 1981). The definition of the concept was implicit in the three factors derived from this 22-item measure: emotional exhaustion; depersonalization of feelings toward clients; and reduced personal accomplishment in helping clients.

Burnout was originally conceived to be the result of job STRESS, particularly arising from caring for other people. Questions were soon raised as to whether burnout was different from job stress. More recently, it has been asked how it differs from depression and negative affectivity, as empirical studies have shown that the emotional exhaustion scale correlates moderately strongly with these constructs (Cordes & Dougherty, 1993).

In a study of 600 nurses, Schaufeli and van Dierendonck (1993) show the concept of exhaustion is the core element in measures of burnout and recommend it is best reserved for studies of people in caring professions. It remains an interesting theoretical and empirical issue as to whether there is advantage in continued use of the burnout concept, if superior measures of psychological strain provide better scope for comparative studies across occupations.

See also **Affect; Job satisfaction; Mental health; Performance, individual; Repetitive work**

Bibliography

Cordes, C. L. & Dougherty, T. W. (1993). A review and integration of research on job burnout. *The Academy of Management Review*, **18, No. 4**, 621–656.

Maslach, C. & Jackson, S. E. (1981). The measurement of experienced burnout. *Journal of Occupational Behaviour*, **2**, 99–113.

Schaufeli, W. B., Maslach, C. & Marek, T. (Eds), (1993). *Professional burnout: Recent developments in theory and research.* New York: Hemisphere.

ROY L. PAYNE

business ethics This subject is becoming an increasingly well established and institutionalized field of management study. Institutionalization is evidenced by the existence and development of professional associations (e.g., Society for Business Ethics, Social Issues in Management Division of the Academy of Management, International Association of Business and Society, and European Business Ethics Network) and professional journals (e.g., *Business Ethics: A European Review, Journal of Business Ethics, Business Ethics Quarterly,* and *Business and Society*), and the growth of business ethics course offerings in the United States and some European business schools.

The business ethics field is comprised of two somewhat distinct subfields:

(1) normative (or prescriptive) business ethics – traditionally the province of philosophers; and
(2) descriptive (or empirical) business ethics – traditionally the province of social scientists.

The key differences between these approaches include different underlying assumptions about human agency, different research goals and questions, and different methodologies. The normative approach is openly value driven, focusing attention on questions of **what ought to be** (how the morally autonomous individual and/or business ought to behave) and on developing methods for making these normative decisions. The empirical approach assumes a degree of researcher objectivity in its attempts to answer social scientific questions about **what is** – how individuals and organizations can be expected to actually behave, given INDIVIDUAL DIFFERENCES and external influences on their behavior (Trevino & Weaver, 1994).

Despite recent calls for integration of business ethics into a single unified field (Kahn, 1990), these key differences in the two approaches make integration a difficult challenge (Weaver & Trevino, 1994). Because they remain essentially separate, and because the descriptive approach is more in line with the domain of ORGANIZATIONAL BEHAVIOR, this entry will focus on the descriptive/empirical approach.

Within the descriptive/empirical approach, the business ethics area can be further divided into micro and macro levels. The macro level concerns the organization/environment interface (e.g., corporate social responsibility, social performance, and relationships with STAKEHOLDERS). The micro level addresses individual and group ethical or unethical behavior within the business organization context. Because other entries will focus on the more macro level concerns (*see* CORPORATE SOCIAL PERFORMANCE), this entry is limited to the micro level.

As this field of inquiry grows, more attention is paid to research quality and methodology (*see* RESEARCH METHODS). Randall and Gibson (1990) critiqued the methodology of business ethics research in their review of three decades of published empirical research (94 academic journal articles) on ethical beliefs and behavior in business organizations. The large majority of these articles were published in the *Journal of Business Ethics*, but thirty-eight academic journals were represented. Atheoretical surveys of managers' beliefs and attitudes predominated. The researchers concluded that business ethics studies have been seriously lacking in theory development and rigorous research methodologies. Further, an entire issue of *Business Ethics Quarterly* (Volume 2, No. 2, 1992) was devoted to methodological issues. It included articles on the use of experimental approaches, scenarios, interviews, and specific techniques to overcome social desirability biases and to increase the cooperation of SURVEY subjects (*see* BIAS).

More recent business ethics research has focused on developing and testing models of individual ethical behavior in organizations. These models have generally proposed that some combination of individual and situational factors influence ethical behavior in organizations.

Ferrell and Gresham (1985) developed a broad framework for understanding ethical DECISION MAKING in marketing that included individual factors (knowledge, VALUES, attitudes, and intentions) and external factors (significant others and opportunity).

Trevino (1986) proposed an interactionist (*see* INTERACTIONISM) model of ethical decision making in organizations that began with the assumption that individuals think about ethical dilemmas based upon their individual stage of cognitive MORAL DEVELOPMENT. The model proposed a direct relationship between cognitive moral development and ethical behavior, and then proposed that this relationship would be moderated by other individual differences (ego strength, field dependence, and LOCUS OF CONTROL and situational influences (e.g., the organizational reward system, ORGANIZATIONAL CULTURE, and characteristics of the work) (*see* PERSONALITY; PAYMENT SYSTEMS). Trevino and Youngblood (1990) tested aspects of the model and found support for a mutual influences model of ethical decision-making behavior. The two individual differences they studied (cognitive moral development and locus of control) influenced ethical decisions directly. The reward system (vicarious reward) influenced ethical decisions indirectly through outcome expectancies (*see* VIE THEORY). No interactions were found.

Jones incorporated characteristics of the moral issue itself in his issue-contingent model of ethical decision making (Jones, 1991). Jones proposed that the intensity of the moral issue would influence an individual's likelihood of recognizing the moral issue, making a moral judgment, establishing moral intent, and engaging in moral behavior. Moral intensity is based upon five issue characteristics:

(1) magnitude of the consequences;
(2) social consensus about what is right or wrong;
(3) probability of harm;
(4) temporal immediacy of the consequences; and
(5) proximity to victims or beneficiaries of the act.

Still others have focused their research attention on particular types of ethical or unethical behavior, the emphasis of this research being on the social context of ethical decision making. For example, Grover (1992) developed and tested a model of dishonesty among professionals based upon ROLE THEORY (*see* EMPLOYEE THEFT; HONESTY TESTING). He found that dishonesty was greater in professional role conflict situations, particularly for those at lower levels of moral development. Trevino and Victor (1992) studied peer reporting of unethical behavior. They found that role responsibility and the interest of group members both influenced the inclination to report a peer's unethical behavior.

Victor and Cullen (1988) focused systematically on the social context to propose a theoretical typology of ethical work climates (*see* ORGANIZATIONAL CLIMATE). The typology was built upon three ethical criteria derived from normative ethical theory (egoism, benevolence, and deontology) and three levels of reference (individual, local, and cosmopolitan), creating nine theoretical ethical work climate types. Empirical tests of the theory supported the existence of five ethical climate types across companies, and differences within companies by position, nature and work group membership. Subsequent research has found an indirect association between ethical climate types and ethical decisions through their influence on the decision-making criteria used (Gaertner, 1991).

More work will be required to further develop theoretical models of ethical organizational behavior and to test these models in a methodologically rigorous fashion. Additional work will also be required to determine the appropriate ongoing relationship between descriptive/empirical and prescriptive/normative approaches to business ethics (Weaver & Trevino, 1994). Finally, despite the growth in business ethics courses, questions remain about whether teaching business ethics results in any real or lasting changes in students' ethical attitudes or behaviors.

See also **Codes of conduct; Dilemmas, ethical; Justice, distributive; Justice, procedural**

Bibliography

Ferrell, O. C. & Gresham, L. G. (1985). A contingency framework for understanding ethical decision making in marketing. *Journal of Marketing*, **49**, 87–96.

Gaertner, K. (1991). The effect of ethical climate on managers' decisions. In *Morality, rationality and efficiency: New perspectives on socio-economics*. Armonk, NY: Sharpe.

Jones, T. (1991). Ethical decision making by individuals in organizations: An issue-contingent model. *Academy of Management Review*, **6**, 366–395.

Kahn, W. A. (1990). Toward an agenda for business ethics research. *Academy of Management Review*, **15**, 311–328.

Randall, D. M. & Gibson, A. M. (1990). Methodology in business ethics research: A review and critical assessment. *Journal of Business Ethics*, **9**, 457–471.

Trevino, L. K. (1986). Ethical decision making in organizations: A person–situation interactionist model. *Academy of Management Review*, **11**, 601–617

Trevino, L. K. & Weaver, G. (1994). Business ETHICS/BUSINESS Ethics: One field or two?. *Business Ethics Quarterly*, **4**, 113–128.

Trevino, L. K. & Youngblood, S. A. (1990). Bad apples in bad barrels: A causal analysis of ethical decision making behavior. *Journal of Applied Psychology*, **75**, 3378–3835.

Victor, B. & Cullen, J. B. (1988). The organizational bases of ethical work climates. *Administrative Science Quarterly*, **333**, 101–125.

Weaver, G. & Trevino, L. K. (1994). Normative and empirical business ethics: Separation, marriage of convenience, or marriage of necessity. *Business Ethics Quarterly*, **4**, 129–144.

LINDA TREVINO

business process reengineering Also called "business process redesign" and "BPR." BPR is a technique for corporate transformation which came to prominence in the early 1990s. Since the term is relatively new, definitions vary, but there is some consensus on key elements. Fundamental is the prescription that companies should be organized around key business processes rather than specialist functions. Proponents of BPR maintain that a business process (such as new product development, for example) typically involves several departments or functions – to its detriment. The vertical orientation of each function breeds inefficiency and retards responsiveness. Reorganizing along business process lines claims to save time and cost, and to produce an organization better able to respond swiftly to market needs. There is thus a clear link between the currency of BPR and aspects of ORGANIZATIONAL RESTRUCTURING such as DELAYERING. Also many BPR schemes involve replacing the narrow specialist with multiskilled workers often working in SELF-MANAGED TEAMS. The presence in BPR case studies of familiar ideas such as these, and a few spectacular BPR failures have led to a negative reaction in some quarters. Opponents feel BPR offers nothing new and is little more than the next oversold trick in the consultants' repertoire. But the bringing together of all these elements into a holistic package with a radical aim is arguably the new and valuable contribution of BPR. In particular, its breakthrough orientation is often contrasted with incremental techniques such as CONTINUOUS IMPROVEMENT, which are seen as actually harmful – evolution doing just enough to stave off revolution. The role of INFORMATION TECHNOLOGY is also of importance – its role in worker empowerment (*see* EMPLOYEE INVOLVEMENT) via the swift availability of key data is just one of the ways in which information aids reengineering schemes. Even if not all companies radically re-engineer themselves in the next decade, the exhortation of BPR to see a company as a set of business processes rather than specialist functions is likely to affect both JOB DESIGN and many aspects of HUMAN RESOURCE MANAGEMENT.

See also **Organization development; Organizational change; Productivity; Technology; Sociotechnical theory**

Bibliography

Hammer, M. & Campy, J. (1993). *Reengineering the corporation: A manifesto for business revolution.* London: Brealey.

ROY WESTBROOK

C

career A career is the evolving sequence of a person's work experiences over time, usually with reference to a particular social setting and outcome.

The work experiences, social settings, and outcomes that define a career may be construed broadly or narrowly. Narrowly, an individual may hold a career within an OCCUPATION or organization. The work experiences are jobs, seen as related from an external perspective (*see* CAREER THEORY), and the outcome is being promoted. More broadly, an individual may hold a career within society, ranging across multiple occupations and organizations. The work experiences are also jobs, but they may be seen as unrelated from either an internal or external perspective. The outcome is earning a livelihood. Other examples of careers include a family career, in which the outcome is developing and maintaining ties to spouses, children, and relatives, and a volunteer career, in which the outcome is contributing to the community (*see* NONWORK/WORK).

This definition contrasts with the dictionary definition of career, in which career is "a course of continued progress (as in the life of a person or nation): a field for or pursuit of consecutive progressive achievement especially in public, professional, or business life (*Webster's Third New International Dictionary of the English Language Unabridged*, 1976)." The dictionary definition provides a narrow view of career, in which individuals work within a small set of institutions toward an outcome tightly defined by increased hierarchical STATUS and social recognition.

The etymological origins of the term career consistently denote the narrow view. However, modern careers diverge from this perspective. The rate of change and uncertainty in industrial society increasingly produce careers characterized by fragmentation, discontinuities, and diversity. As personal meanings acquired through work environments lose focus and continuity, people necessarily rely more on self-identity to define, make sense of, and evaluate their own "continued progress."

See also **Career development; Career transitions; Labor markets; Psychological contract**

Bibliography

Arthur, M. B., Hall, D. T. & Lawrence, B. S. (Eds), (1989). *Handbook of career theory*. Cambridge, UK: Cambridge University Press.

Webster's third new international dictionary of the English language unabridged (1976). U.S.: G. & C. Merriam.

BARBARA S. LAWRENCE

career anchor A career anchor is an individual's occupational self-concept, composed of his or her self-perceived talents and abilities, motives and needs, and attitudes and VALUES (*see* NEED THEORY; MOTIVATION; ATTITUDE, THEORY). Individuals discover their career anchors over time through personal work experiences in real-life settings. "By definition, there cannot be an anchor until there has been work experience, even though motives and values may already be present from earlier experiences. It is the process of integrating into the total self-concept what one sees oneself to be more or less competent at, wanting out of life, one's value systems, and the kind of person one is that begins to determine the major life and occupational choices throughout adulthood" (Schein, 1978, p. 171). Once identified, a career anchor provides a growing source of stability for individuals. Although individuals typically hold and explore many abilities and interests, when presented with occupational choices, they will make decisions congruent with the career anchor.

The career anchor concept emerged from a longitudinal panel study by Edgar H. Schein of 44 male alumni of MIT's Sloan School of Management (Schein, 1975). The panelists were interviewed in 1961 and then again in 1973. Schein identified five career anchors during this study: technical/functional competence, managerial competence, security, CREATIVITY, and AUTONOMY/independence (*see* COMPETENCIES).

Technical/Functional Competence. The occupational self-image of individuals with a technical/functional anchor is tied to their feelings of competence in the "actual technical or functional *content* of the work they are doing" (Schein, 1978, p. 129). Individuals with a technical/functional anchor see their ideal job as the top job within an organization or occupation that fits their specific functional area (*see* PROFESSIONALS IN ORGANIZATIONS).

Managerial Competence. The occupational self-image of individuals with a managerial anchor is tied to their feelings of analytical, interpersonal, and emotional competence. In contrast to individuals with a technical/functional career anchor, individuals with a managerial career anchor see technical or functional jobs as a means of getting to general management positions, rather than as an end in and of themselves.

Security. The occupational self-image of individuals with a security anchor is tied to their organizations' evaluations of them. These individuals value stability and continued job employment over job content or choice (*see* JOB INSECURITY).

CREATIVITY. The occupational self-image of individuals with a creativity anchor is tied to their need to build or produce something that is entirely their own – something that they can point to and say "I did that." These individuals have motives that overlap with those in other anchors, but the need to create something is paramount.

AUTONOMY. The occupational self-image of individuals with an autonomy anchor is tied to control over their own lives. These individuals "have found organizational life to be restrictive, irrational, and/or intrusive into their own private lives and have therefore left business or government organizations altogether . . ." (Schein, 1978, p. 156).

Research extending this concept is limited. Other anchors, such as service and variety have been hypothesized, and a Career Anchor Orientation Questionnaire is available.

See also **Career; Career theory; Career development.**

Bibliography

DeLong, T. J. (1982). The career orientation of MBA alumni: a multidimensional model. In R. Katz (Ed.), *Career issues in human resource management* (pp. 50–64). Englewood Cliffs, NJ: Prentice-Hall.

Schein, E. H. (1975). How career anchors hold executives to their career paths. *Personnel*, **52 (3)**, 11–24.

Schein, E. H. (1978). *Career dynamics: matching individual and organizational needs.* Reading, MA: Addison-Wesley.

BARBARA S. LAWRENCE

career breaks A career break scheme enables employees to leave and subsequently reenter a job following an agreed period of absence (Leighton & Syrett, 1989). Such schemes are found mainly in organizations where a high proportion of the workforce is female (*see* WOMEN AT WORK). While being consistent with EQUAL OPPORTUNITIES policies, employers may also introduce career breaks to help retain access to scarce SKILLS during periods of LABOR MARKET shortage and avoid additional RECRUITMENT and TRAINING costs. Career breaks remain rare, however, and those in existence vary considerably. Ones guaranteeing reentry at the same level are typically available to only a small proportion of high-level staff. Other schemes embody less employer COMMITMENT, for example, concerning which jobs are available to returners. The spread of career breaks is restricted by several factors. Market uncertainties mean that many employers are unwilling to commit themselves to rehiring staff several years in the future. TECHNOLOGY changes also mean that rehiring can entail substantial retraining (thus reducing the benefit of schemes in terms of training cost savings). Also, the widespread weakening of labor market pressures in recent years, coupled with the tendency for many organizations to reduce the size of their work forces, has restricted the growth of career breaks.

See also **Career transitions; Career development; Flexibility**

Bibliography

Leighton, P. & Syrett, M. (1989). *New work patterns: Putting policy into practice.* London: Pitman.

PAUL BLYTON

career choice CAREER choice is a major construct in career development (Meier, 1991). It is used to refer to a person's statement about the area of work or occupation they intend to follow as well as to the actual area of work or occupation finally entered. As such, it is one of the most frequently used outcome or dependent variables in research undertaken to test theories in the careers domain and to evaluate VOCATIONAL GUIDANCE programs. Understanding career choice is an advantage to HR professionals who have traditionally ignored the individual's perspective in selection (*see* SELECTION METHODS). Individual career choices influences who apply for jobs and whether or not an offer is accepted. Understanding career choice is also critical for HR practitioners involved in setting up career development systems within organizations.

Theories of career choice address the factors that influence work-related decisions and the processes by which individuals make career choices. Factors influencing career choice have been studied within an economic, sociological, or cultural perspective as well as a psychological perspective. The former address issues, such as the internal and external labor market, labor force trends, the availability of educational and other work opportunities, and the social background of individuals. The latter psychological approaches explain choice in terms of individual capabilities (intelligence, specific abilities, COMPETENCIES, intelligence, and work experiences), motivational orientations (needs, interests, and values) as well as the opportunity structure. Individuals are viewed as using these factors to make a choice that optimizes their "fit" with the environment (*see* PERSON-JOB FIT).

Two dominant theories within the psychological perspective are Holland's (1985) typological theory and the Minnesota Theory of WORK ADJUSTMENT. Holland's theory argues that both people and environments can be described in terms of six types: realistic, investigative, artistic, social, enterprising, and conventional. These six types are organized in a hexagon, with adjacent types being most similar. Individuals who choose occupations of the same or similar type to themselves are predicted to be more stable, satisfied and productive compared with those who choose occupations further removed from their type on the hexagon. Recently, questions have been raised about the notion of "fit" implicit in both Holland's theory and the Minnesota Theory of Work Adjustment (Hesketh, 1993). Research demonstrates a stronger direct relationship between job characteristics and satisfaction and between general cognitive ability and performance than implied by the theories.

Social learning, psychoanalytic, and developmental theories of career choice emphasize developmental influences (Brown & Brooks, 1990). Adult developmental theories usually offer loosely defined adult CAREER STAGES, while other theoretical approaches address the transition process following the implementation of choices involving change (Nicholson, 1984) (*see* CAREER TRANSITIONS). Normative decision theories of career choice draw on Subjective Expective Utility and other classical decision theory approaches. Descriptive approaches outline how individuals actually make choices, with nonoptimal strategies such as SATISFICING being common and with time pressure and decision stress reducing vigilance in processing relevant information (Brown & Brooks, 1990).

See also **Personality; Joining-up process; Realistic job previews**

Bibliography

Brown, D. & Brooks, L. (Eds), (1990). *Career choice and development* (2nd edn). San Francisco: Jossey-Bass.

Hesketh, B. (1993). Toward a better adjusted theory of work adjustment. *Journal of Vocational Behavior*, **43**, 75–83.

Holland, J. H. (1985). *Making vocational choices: A theory of vocational personalities and work environments*. Englewood Cliffs, NJ: Prentice-Hall.

Meier, S. T. (1991). Vocational Behavior, 1988–1990: Vocational choice, decision-making, career development interventions, and assessment. *Journal of Vocational Behavior*, **39**, 131–181.

Nicholson, N. (1984). A theory of work role transitions. *Administrative Science Quarterly*, **29**, 172–191.

BERYL HESKETH

career development This denotes the sequence of changes that occur throughout individuals' careers (*see* CAREER), usually with reference to either individuals' inner psychological evolution or their status within a social entity, for instance, functional area, hierarchical level, or degree of inclusion (organizational centrality). Career development represents a subset of CAREER THEORY that focuses on individuals (Arthur, Hall & Lawrence, 1989). The outcome of interest is the individual's career, and the time period involved is usually the individual's working life, although shorter segments are also studied.

The term career development generally assumes either an explanatory or prescriptive meaning. First, the term refers to theories or research that explain what happens to individuals over their careers. Thus, such work might include studies of CAREER CHOICE, CAREER STAGES, career typologies, SOCIALIZATION, or MENTORING. Second, the term refers to programs designed to facilitate individuals' career growth. These programs are usually developed by career development specialists outside organizations or by human resource managers (*see* HUMAN RESOURCE MANAGEMENT) within organizations. For example, individual counselors may provide private career counseling to individuals, and organizations may furnish special developmental career tracks to employees, such as dual-track engineering/management careers (*see* COUNSELING IN ORGANIZATIONS). The following discussion of career development focuses on the former rather than the latter meaning.

The history of career development theory begins with, and has been heavily influenced by, studies of vocational choice (Super 1953; Roe, 1956) (*see* VOCATIONAL GUIDANCE). Early versions of these theories through the 1950s assume that people select vocations during young adulthood and that, once selected, vocations generally do not change. Because later life experiences make no contribution to such initial selections, these theories did not examine adult lives. However, during the 1950s and 1960s changes in working patterns challenged this single-vocation assumption. Then, in the 1970s adult development research focused scholars on psychological change in mature men and women. As a result, scholars revisited vocational choice theories and considered career choices throughout life. Further, they developed new types of career development theory: career stage theories, which propose career-related developmental changes at given ages, situational theories, which focus on career development within social settings, and career typologies, which identify distinct career development patterns.

Vocational Choice Theories. These can be loosely categorized into trait-factor and PERSONALITY theories. Trait-factor theories assume that people's abilities and interests can be matched with available vocations, and that once matched, the match remains relatively stable for life. Widely used standardized tests, such as the Strong–Campbell Vocational Interest Inventory and the Differential Aptitude Tests (DAT), are based on trait-factor theory. Personality theories assume that people select vocations that meet their needs. Studies from this perspective examine people's needs as identified in the vocational choice process as well as personality characteristics associated with different occupations.

Career Stage Theories. These assume that career development follows human development, that career development represents an evolutionary process, and that it must be examined throughout the life course. Most career stage theories are based on developmental psychology and focus on the maturation of people's self-concepts over time. These theories divide life up into segments loosely related to LIFE STAGES and specify the developmental tasks that produce career growth within each segment.

Situational Theories. These assume that social settings influence people's career development. Situational theories primarily come from ORGANIZATIONAL BEHAVIOR and sociology. Organizational theories within this category might examine the process by which organizations socialize individuals or how identity and psychological success are related over time within organizational careers (Hall, 1990). Sociological examples in this category might include studies of the impact of socio-economic class on career choice, or the distinction between hereditary and meritocratic cultures in determining occupational entry.

Career Typologies. These assume that people's careers fall into distinct patterns. Typologies do not explain development so much as they describe different developmental forms. Psychological typologies distinguish careers using people's inner experiences of work. For example, different self-concepts may produce a CREATIVITY or security CAREER ANCHOR. Social psychological typologies distinguish careers using people's relationships with institutions. For example, "fast track" (*see* FAST TRACK DEVELOPMENT) and "slow-burn" identify different careers within an organizational or occupational context. Sociological typologies distinguish careers using institutional criteria, for example, the JOB CHARACTERISTICS that distinguish occupations such as a brick-layer or radiologist.

These four categories provide a flavor for different types of career development theory. However, many theories fall across categories. Dalton and Thompson (1986), for example, present a career stage theory that is situationally-based. They propose that PROFESSIONALS IN ORGANIZATIONS experience four career stages, segmented by changes in work-related activities, relationships, and psychological issues. In contrast to most career stage theories, people do not move inexorably through each stage. The stages fall in chronological order, but they are not age-linked. Thus, a person might get stuck in Stage II and never experience Stages III and IV. Further, and again in contrast to most career stage theories, the stages are segmented by changes in a person's work relationship with the organization rather than by changes in the person's inner psychological evolution.

As with all social science, career development theory is tied to the social and historical times in which it evolved. Much of the situational literature matured during a time when people held fairly stable relationships with their work organizations. However, the dramatic DOWNSIZING, DELAYERING, and reengineering of organizations in the 1980s and 1990s created a more tenuous relationship between employees and employers. Thus, similar to the evolution of vocational choice theories in the 1950s and 1960s, situational theories seem ripe for reconsideration and revision.

See also **Joining-up process; Career transitions; Management development**

Bibliography

Arthur, M. B., Hall, D. T. & Lawrence, B. S. (1989). *Handbook of career theory*. Cambridge, UK: Cambridge University Press.

Dalton, G. W. & Thompson, P. H. (1986). *Novations: strategies for career management*. Glenview, IL: Scott, Foresman.

Hall, D. T. (1990). Career development theory in organizations. In D. Brown, L. Brooks & Associates (Eds), *Career choice and development*, (2nd edn, pp. 422–454). San Francisco: Jossey-Bass.

Holland, J. L. (1973). *Making vocational choices: a theory of careers*. Englewood Cliffs, NJ: Prentice-Hall.

Osipow, S. H. (1985). *Theories of career development*, (3rd edn). Englewood Cliffs, NJ: Prentice-Hall.

Roe, A. (1956). *The psychology of occupations*. New York: Wiley.

Schein, E. H. (1978). *Career dynamics: matching individual and organizational needs*. Reading, MA: Addison-Wesley.

Super, D. E. (1953). A theory of vocational development. *American Psychologist*, 8, 185–190.

BARBARA S. LAWRENCE

career entry *see* CAREER CHOICE; JOINING-UP PROCESS

career mobility *see* CAREER TRANSITIONS; LABOR MARKETS

career orientation *see* CAREER; CAREER CHOICE

career plateauing The phenomenon of CAREER plateauing in organizations presents an important and perplexing challenge to HUMAN RESOURCES MANAGEMENT (HRM), and an array of conceptual and empirical problems to ORGANIZATIONAL BEHAVIOR scholars. The first problem is definitional. How do we decide when an employee is plateaued? Three types of criteria can be found in the literature. First, many researchers have adopted time in current position as a measureable and objective benchmark. Employees more than 5 years in a post would typically be counted as immobile or "plateaued" by this standard, though this or alternative cutoffs have the drawback of looking worryingly arbitrary, and, at the same time, liable to mischaracterize the experience and career positions of many groups, such as professionals (*see* PROFESSIONALS IN ORGANIZATIONS). A second alternative is to use a subjective criterion – individuals' expectations of future advancement, defining as plateaued those who expect no or minimal further STATUS increase. The problem with this approach is the questionable accuracy of people's reading of future opportunities and their own capabilities. A less common third alternative, of increasing interest, is the concept of implicit AGE-grade timetables (Lawrence, 1988). These may be assessed subjectively – whether employees believe themselves to be on-track relative to peers, or ahead/behind schedule. Individuals' positions relative to company norms may also be assessed objectively (Nicholson, 1993).

Plateauing by any of these definitions is an organizational problem to the degree that the people to whom it applies have desires or expectations which have not or are not being fulfilled. This is regarded as especially problematic for managerial ranks, whose career expectations are more deeply socialized (*see* SOCIALIZATION) and hierarchical than other workers, and whose MOTIVATION and COMMITMENT organizations are most concerned to maintain.

Research has shed light on several aspects of the phenomenon. First, career success is often foretold by rapid early upward movements in a person's history (*see* CAREER TRANSITIONS; MANAGEMENT OF HIGH POTENTIAL), and conversely, people who get off-track early typically fail to recover momentum (*see* TOURNAMENT PROMOTION). Second, it is mistaken to assume plateauing is necessarily associated with loss of motivation and effectiveness. The distinction needs to be drawn between mere immobility and frustrated feelings of being "stuck." Some people are contentedly plateaued, often called "solid citizens," as distinct from "high fliers" and "deadwood" (Veiga, 1981). Third, people's aspirations and interests change over the career cycle (*see* CAREER DEVELOPMENT; LIFE STAGES). Early career ambition may, as the person matures and the realities of limited horizons sink in, become deflected into other life spheres (*see* NON-WORK/WORK). Not all forms of this displacement need detract from the individual's organizational contribution, though in some cases "insurgent" and "alienated" orientations may develop if there is resentment and FRUSTRATION at perceived unfairness of career opportunities (*see* ALIENATION; JUSTICE, DISTRIBUTIVE).

Finally, the phenomenon of plateauing is becoming more common as organizations restructure toward "delayered" or "flattened" structures (*see* ORGANIZATIONAL RESTRUCTURING). One recent survey estimated that 25 percent of the United States workforce was plateaued. Plateauing presents a challenge to HRM to the degree that employees maintain hierarchical views of career fulfilment – the view that "up is the only way" (*see* HIERARCHY). One solution is increased lateral mobility, sabbaticals, and alternative developmental paths (*see* CAREER BREAKS). To date, organizations have been slow to seek these remedies, often more aware of the short-term costs than the long-term benefits to the ORGANIZATIONAL CULTURE.

See also **Career theory; Labor markets; Succession planning**

Bibliography

Chao, G. T. (1990). Exploration of the conceptualization and measurement of career plateau: A comparative analysis. *Journal of Management*, **16**, 181–193.

Feldman, D. C. & Weitz B. A. (1988). Career plateaus reconsidered. *Journal of Management*, **14**, 69–90.

Lawrence, B. S. (1988). New wrinkles in the theory of age: Demography, norms, and performance ratings. *Academy of Management Journal*, **31**, 309–337.

Nicholson, N. (1993). Purgatory or place of safety? The managerial career plateau and organizational agegrading. *Human Relations*, **46**, 1369–1389.

Veiga, J. F. (1981). Plateaued versus nonplateaued managers: Career patterns, attitudes, and path potential. *Academy of Management Journal*, **24**, 566–578.

NIGEL NICHOLSON

career stages The career stage concept is embedded in developmental theories of CAREER CHOICE (Swanson, 1992). From developmental psychology it takes the idea that developmental tasks are appropriate for particular stages, with successful resolution of these tasks prerequisite for moving on to the next stage (Mussen, Conger, & Kagan, 1975). Typically, career stages are defined in terms of AGE bands. Super and others suggested that career development could be divided into fantasy, exploration, establishment, maintenance, and decline stages, each with various substages and associated vocational developmental tasks. More recently in the HUMAN RESOURCES MANAGEMENT literature, the concept of adult career development stages has received considerable attention, with a focus on the career concerns that predominate at particular stages. The Adult Career Concerns Inventory (ACCI) (Super, Thompson, & Lindeman, 1984), is a measure designed to locate individuals in a particular stage according to their dominant career concern. Future work might use the concept of FUZZY SETS to assign individuals a grade of membership for each stage rather than locating them in one particular stage. Fuzzy classification could prove more accurate, since locating individuals in a particular stage is seldom an all-or-nothing affair.

Levinson's (1986) theory offers another view of career stage, with a cyclical rotation through stability and change at roughly 5-year intervals in adulthood. The theoretical, empirical, and rational bases for these precise predictions are yet to be established. Most traditional approaches to the concept of career stage have been normative, with assumptions about common patterns of career development at particular ages for most individuals. Although intuitively appealing, career stages with precisely specified age bands are difficult to justify theoretically, and there are scant empirical data to support this model (Ornstein & Isabella, 1990). Recent approaches to the concept of stage include notions of a personal career clock, which acknowledges individual variations in both the timing and sequencing of career stages. However, the departure from an age-related definition of career stage raises fundamental questions about the utility of the concept.

Future developments in the concept of career stages will need to integrate what is known about the biological aging processes, family lifecycles, society norms, and expectations for age-appropriate career-related behaviors, and the differing opportunity structure at different ages. Organizations should take account of the changing needs and values of employees at different stages of the life-span in order to retain and motivate staff (*see* CAREER PLATEAUING). In doing this it will be necessary to consider work and nonwork domains (*see* NON-WORK\WORK). Specifically, organizations should provide flexibility with respect to child care responsibilities in early career, programs for reducing the impact of plateauing in mid-career, and RETIREMENT programs to optimize the WITHDRAWAL process for both individuals and organizations.

See also **Life stages; Management development; Individual differences; Career transitions**

Bibliography

Levinson, D. J. (1986). A conception of adult development. *American Psychologist*, **41**, 3–13.

Mussen, P. H., Conger, J. J. & Kagan, J. (Eds), (1975). *Basic and contemporary issues in developmental psychology*. New York: Harper & Row.

Ornstein, S. & Isabella, L. (1990). Age versus stage models of career attitudes of women: A partial replication and extension. *Journal of Vocational Behavior*, **36**, 1–19.

Super, D. E., Thompson, A. S. & Lindeman, R. H. (1984). *The Adult Career Concerns Inventory*. Palo Alto, CA: Consulting Psychologists Press.

Swanson, J. L. (1992). Vocational Behavior, 1989–1991: Life-span career development and reciprocal interaction of work and non-work. *Journal of Vocational Behavior*, **41**, 101–161.

BERYL HESKETH

career theory Career theory is a generalizable explanation of a CAREER or career-related phenomenon. The qualifier "generalizable" is used to distinguish career theory from situation-specific career descriptions derived from personal experience or local practices (Arthur, Hall, & Lawrence, 1989). Thus, while an ethnographic career description may explain that career and prove useful in generating career theory, the description itself is not a THEORY (*see* ETHNOGRAPHY).

Career theory examines a fundamental area of management studies: the relationship between individuals, their work, and the social systems within which they work over time. Careers are a temporal product of what the individual contributes to the social system and what the social system returns to the individual (*see* PSYCHOLOGICAL CONTRACT). As a result, career theory involves a multidisciplinary perspective, including, but not limited to, contributions from psychology, sociology, economics, and anthropology. Topics covered by career theory include phenomena as diverse as self-identity, work role transitions, occupational mobility, and human capital (*see* CAREER TRANSITIONS).

Career theories are distinguished by six dimensions: work, time, level of analysis, perspective, social setting, and outcome. *Work* is any set of activities directed toward a specific goal. Thus, one could study the work of a dishwasher, an architect, a volunteer fire fighter, or a delinquent. Each constitutes a set of activities that is recognized as connected and purposeful by the individual, or by others observing the individual. *Time* is a measurable period during which actions, processes, or conditions occur. Time provides an important dimension because work represents a process: a sequence of activities begining at one time and ending at another. Work may involve a short time, such as the task of managing breaks in a blue collar job, or a long time, such as intergenerational changes in occupational STATUS (*see* OCCUPATION). Further, work may be defined by chronological time, i.e., time as measured by a clock, or sociotemporal time, i.e., time as measured by people's perceptions (Lawrence, 1984).

LEVEL OF ANALYSIS is the position on a scale of social entities, ranging from small to large, selected for research focus, where "small" might be individuals and "large" might be a society. For example, careers can be studied at the individual level by examining individuals' self-concepts within work settings, at the organizational level by examining how vacancy chains influence mobility, at the social network level by examining how social contacts lead to jobs (*see* NETWORKING; NETWORK ANALYSIS), or at the societal or national level by examining the impact of economic conditions on LABOR MARKETS (Blau & Duncan, 1967).

Independent of level of analysis is the *perspective* from which the career is studied. For instance, the career can be viewed from the individual's perspective, i.e., how the individual sees him or herself, from the organization's perspective, i.e., how organizational managers perceive, define, or evaluate the individual's career, or from a regional perspective, i.e., how the inhabitants of a specific geographic area define or evaluate the individual's career. Other terms for distinctions in perspective include internal versus external and objective versus subjective.

Social setting is the context within which careers occur. Because careers include all points where the lives of individuals touch the social order, careers do not exist without social settings. Many scholars study career-related phenomena without concurrent study of the social setting in which they occur: a typical example is studying individuals' promotions and career success without examining their organization or occupation. However, research suggests that social settings play an important role in careers.

A final dimension of career theory is *outcome*, the result or consequence of the work that individuals perform. Outcomes are specified either by the researcher, the individual, or the social setting. For an individual, the defining outcome of an organizational career might be self-perceived career success or simply making a living. For an organization, the defining outcome might be organizational performance. For a network, the defining outcome might be a typology of boundaryless careers.

The history of career theory begins in psychology and sociology. In psychology, career theories originated with studies of vocational choice in the 1940s and 1950s. The idea was understanding how individual differences and self-knowledge translated into career choices characterized by JOB SATISFACTION and MOTIVATION. Two types of theories emerged: matching theory and process theories (*see* PROCESS THEORY). Matching theories examine vocational choice as the match between the individual's traits and those of people currently in the occupation (*see* PERSON-JOB FIT; WORK ADJUSTMENT). These theories led to psychological instruments used for vocational counseling. In contrast, process theories focus on how people make vocational decisions, examining the sequence of development and motivations involved throughout the life course (*see* CAREER CHOICE; CAREER DEVELOPMENT; CAREER STAGES).

Sociologists started with a different notion of career. In the 1920s and 1930s, scholars at the University of Chicago began using life histories to study the sequence of events underlying various social problems such as delinquency. These unfolding sequences were defined as "careers," and subsequent research by Everett Hughes and his students produced the beginnings of the sociology of work and occupations (Barley, 1989). Their studies included an array of ethnographies, embracing medical careers, funeral directors, marijuana users, and "taxi dancers" (partners for hire). The focus was on connecting the individual's interpretation and experience of career with institutional definitions. Later sociologists objected to the breadth of this career vision and began narrowing their scope, concerned with providing depth about more focused topics.

In the early 1970s, a group of management professors, energized by the connections they saw between these disciplinary approaches and armed with a view of careers as a fundamental component of social systems, began broadening the theoretical and research agenda once again. The development of this agenda can be seen in a series of books about career theory and research published during the subsequent two decades. The topics this group examined included CAREER ANCHORS, scientific and engineering careers, SOCIALIZATION, sense-making; MENTORING, and career "styles," emphasized professional careers within organizations (Hall, 1976; Osipow, 1983; Schein, 1978).

This much abbreviated history presents a central dilemma of career theory. The dizzying breadth of topics and interactions encompassing career theory make it easy for big picture theories to be "a mile wide and an inch deep." As a result, interest in the topic waxes and wanes as scholars search for middle ground. Interest is highest when the concept remains broad, but narrowly defined studies produce more concrete results. However, when narrowly defined, scholars seem to retreat toward disciplinary boundaries and the concept seems to lose its broad, general appeal.

Notwithstanding this dilemma, the importance of maintaining a broad definition of career theory has never been more important than it is today. The global economy, corporate DOWNSIZING, massive shifts in job types, and technological changes have dramatically changed the nature of careers (Kanter, 1989). These systemic changes in the fabric of work challenge all career theories and provide a potent reminder of the importance of historical period and cohort effects in theory and research. Career theories that are truly generalizable will hold to the test of such change. Others may not, becoming more conditional, middle-range theories. Certainly, these striking changes in modern work life are putting career theory to the test.

See also **Career plateauing; Succession planning; Management of high potential; Motivation and performance; Nonwork/work; Tournament promotion.**

Bibliography

Arthur, M. B., Hall, D. T. & Lawrence, B. S. (Eds), (1989). *Handbook of career theory*. Cambridge, UK: Cambridge University Press.

Barley, S. R. (1989). Careers, identities, and institutions: The legacy of the Chicago school of sociology. In M. B. Arthur, D. T. Hall & B. S. Lawrence (Eds), *Handbook of career theory* (pp. 41–65). Cambridge, UK: Cambridge University Press.

Blau, P. & Duncan, O. D. (1967). *The American occupational structure*. New York: Wiley.

Hall, D. T. (1976). *Careers in organizations*. Santa Monica, CA: Goodyear.

Howard, A. & Bray, D. W. (1988). *Managerial lives in transition: Advancing age and changing times*. New York: Guilford Press.

Kanter, R. (1989). Careers and the wealth of nations: A macro-perspective on the structure and implications of career forms. In M. B. Arthur D. T. Hall & B. S. Lawrence (Eds), *Handbook of career theory* (pp. 506–521). Cambridge, UK: Cambridge University Press.

Lawrence, B.S. (1984). Historical perspective: Using the past to study the present. *Academy of Management Review*, **9**, 307–312.

Osipow, S. H. (1983). *Theories of career development* (3rd edn). Englewood Cliffs, NJ: Prentice-Hall.

Rosenbaum, J. E. (1984). *Career mobility in a corporate hierarchy*. New York: Academic Press.

Schein, E. H. (1978). *Career dynamics: Matching individual and organizational needs*. Reading, MA: Addison-Wesley.

Super, D. E. (1963). *Career development: Self-concept theory*. New York: CEEB.

BARBARA S. LAWRENCE

career transitions CAREER or work role transitions can be defined as any major change in work roles or ROLE requirements. This definition is designed to encompass not just major job switches, but also situations where the role changes radically "around" the incumbent, without their mobility to a new post, such as instances of significant job redesign (*see* JOB DESIGN) and changes of boss and coworkers.

The term career transitions is potentially misleading, if taken to connote order and logic in succession between positions, for a significant proportion of transitions are between tenuously related roles, i.e., traversing sectors and functions quite radically.

TURNOVER has been a heavily researched career transition, but usually with exclusive interest in its causes. The transitions perspective on this and other job changes has developed in recent years to turn attention toward the *consequences* of mobility, which can have great significance for individuals and organizations. These have been relatively under-researched, compared with the extensive literature on predictors of mobility. For individuals, transitions can be turning points, a significant force for identity change in the job mover (*see* MANAGEMENT DEVELOPMENT; PERSONALITY). For organizations, transitions of key personnel can be significant catalysts for change and development (*see* ORGANIZATION DEVELOPMENT), e.g., via the succession of a new CEO (*see* CEOs; SUCCESSION PLANNING).

The outcomes of adjustment to transitions include Stress and well-being, personal change, role INNOVATION (changes effected to how roles are performed), and success in job performance (*see* WORK ADJUSTMENT) (Nicholson, 1984). These outcomes are determined by the interaction of three sets of factors:

1. The Nature of the Change

The definition of transitions embraces a wide range of mobility types (Schein, 1978), including lateral (functional), inclusionary (to or from the center to the periphery of an organization), vertical (promotion/demotion), interorganizational, cross-cultural (*see* EXPATRIATES), and between states of employment (*see* UNEMPLOYMENT; REDUNDANCY). The adjustment challenge varies greatly in terms of the novelty of change, the scale of the demands, and the amount of discretion in the new role. Research suggests that radical high-discretion roles have more positive outcomes on some dimensions, such as innovation and personal change, but also entail significant risks on others, such as stress and failure. The high personal impact of expatriation, and the high rate of failure (as signified by premature return home), illustrates both of these tendencies (Black, Mendenhall, & Odou, 1991).

2. The State of the Person

INDIVIDUAL DIFFERENCES in dispositions, expectations, preparation, motives, SKILLS and related attributes affect the adjustment process in various ways, but principally in terms of the adjustment strategies individuals adopt and how they react to experiences. For example, people with high SELF-EFFICACY will be more likely to achieve successful proactive adjustment (Nicholson & West, 1988), and individuals high in HARDINESS better withstand stresses. Research indicates that preparation for change can help, but that previous experience is less important than how *successful* has been prior experience of transitions (Brett, Stroh, & Reilly, 1992).

3. The Management of the Change

The idea of a "Transition Cycle" (Nicholson, 1990) helps to point out the different strategies, supports, and resources which aid adjustment at various stages: preparation, encounter, adjustment, and stabilization. Most research has concentrated on the early phases of the cycle (*see* JOINING-UP PROCESS), and the role of management, coworkers and other agencies in easing the transition and supporting individuals' "sense-making" in their new role or setting (Louis, 1980). A number of distinctive SOCIALIZATION tactics have been identified, which have differentiated effects upon adjustment outcomes (Van Maanen & Schein, 1979).

The combined effects of these forces are little understood in the absence of definitive research untangling their complex and varied interactions. To do so is clearly of the utmost importance since transitions have the power to shape significantly the identity of individuals, and to affect significantly the effectiveness of organizations. This also implies that the strategic management of transitions – who moves, over what boundaries, and with what support – is a potentially powerful tool for ORGANIZATIONAL LEARNING, the management of ORGANIZATIONAL CULTURE, and the maximization of ORGANIZATIONAL EFFECTIVENESS. Unfortunately, most organizations' management of transitions is ad hoc rather than planful, driven by necessity rather than vision, and concerned more with causes than with outcomes. This is understandable, given the complexity of the subject, but it also represents a missed opportunity, since the information and resources needed for a strategic outcome-oriented approach to all forms of mobility already exist in most organizations (*see* HUMAN RESOURCES STRATEGY).

Future scholarly interest can be expected to focus increasingly on radical, i.e., cross-functional, interorganizational, and intercultural career transitions, which are becoming more common as a function of the accelerating globalization of business and the restructuring of organizations (*see* INTERNATIONAL MANAGEMENT; ORGANIZATIONAL RESTRUCTURING).

See also **Career choice; Career theory; International human resource management; Organizational change; Retirement; Tournament promotion**

Bibliography

Black, S. J., Mendenhall, M. & Oddou, G. (1991). Toward a comprehensive model of international adjustment: An integration of multiple theoretical perspectives. *Academy of Management Review*, **16**, 291–317.

Brett, J. M., Stroh, L. K. & Reilly, A. H. (1992). Job transfer. In C. L. Cooper & I. T. Robertson (Eds) *International Review of Industrial and Organizational Psychology, 1992*. Chichester, UK: Wiley.

Louis, M.R. (1980). Surprise and sense-making: What newcomers experience in entering unfamiliar organizational settings. *Administrative Science Quarterly*, **25**, 226–251.

Nicholson, N. (1984). A theory of work role transitions. *Administrative Science Quarterly*, **29**, 172–191.

Nicholson, N. (1990). The transition cycle: Causes, outcomes, processes and forms. In S. Fisher & C. L. Cooper (Eds) *On the move: The psychology of change and transition*. Chichester, UK: Wiley.

Nicholson, N. & West, M. W. (1988). *Managerial job change*. Cambridge, UK: Cambridge University Press.

Schein, E. H. (1978). *Career dynamics*. Reading, MA: Addison-Wesley.

Van Maanen, J. & Schein, E. H. (1979). Toward a theory of organizational socialization. In B. M. Staw (Ed.) *Research in organizational behavior* (vol. 1). Greenwich, CT: JAI Press.

NIGEL NICHOLSON

case study research It has become increasingly popular in the research of ORGANIZATIONAL BEHAVIOR to study phenomena in large numbers (*see* RESEARCH METHODS). The advantage of such a large sample size is greater reliability, but the cost can be a loss of richness, due to a certain detachment or distance from the phenomenon. For example, the work of a large number of managers can be studied by the diary method, in which they fill out forms of predetermined categories for each of their activities (e.g., Stewart, 1967) (*see* MANAGERIAL BEHAVIOR). But when the pace of their work gets hectic, or their work itself is highly nuanced, managers may have difficulty filling out such forms. The difficulties may become even more severe when a mailed questionnaire is used, which seeks to reduce all of the manager's work to some broad overall categories (*see* SURVEYS).

Case study research forfeits large sample size for greater sample depth. The researcher selects one or a few sites ("cases") and probes into each thoroughly. Data collection may be somewhat systematic – certain aspects of the phenomenon can be documented carefully, such as the contacts a manager has with his or her people – but never so structured that the researcher cannot probe aspects of the phenomenon that did not occur to him or her before the work started. In other words, case study research always maintains a certain flexibility. Another way of putting this is that the research tends to be significantly, if not primarily, inductive, developing its interpretations from its findings and, in some of the best of this work, often surprising the researcher. Often, though by no means necessarily, case study research tends to be largely qualitative as well, and focused on the processes people in organizations engage in more than the contents of their results.

The researcher may be physically present to watch behavior as it unfolds, which is known as "participant observation" (*see* RESEARCH DESIGN; ETHNOGRAPHY) of managerial work (e.g., Mintzberg, 1973, 1993). Alternatively, the researcher may study the case through documents, which is necessary when the behavior in question is either historical or simply inaccessible to an observer, such as tracking the strategies of organizations across decades (e.g., Mintzberg & McHugh, 1985). Such studies may be supported by interviews or, of course, be based on interviews in the first place.

What distinguishes case study research is the probing in depth into particular situations. Nuances can be appreciated; the experiences of the actors can be recounted, in their own terms; unanticipated lines of inquiry can be pursued; complex connections can be made; so that situations can be described holistically. But all of this works only so long as the researcher is sensitive to what he or she hears, reads, sees, or otherwise uncovers.

In effect, this is fundamentally idiosyncratic research, for better and for worse. It all depends on the personal capabilities of the researcher (as, of course, does any research, only more transparently so here, since there can be no hiding behind "sophisticated" techniques). The result, therefore, cannot be predictable – it is not as if once the data goes into the computer, it will get processed in a predetermined way.

That is why case study research tends to produce the best and worst of results. A number of our most famous studies – the classics, that truly endure – are of this form, for example, Whyte's *Street Corner Society* (1943), participant observation of a street gang during the 1930s, with some wonderful insights on LEADERSHIP, or Chandler's *Strategy and Structure* (1962), which described the evolution of the major American corporation by studying the histories of four firms in particular; and Crozier's *The Bureaucratic Phenomenon* (1964, in English), an intense probe into two agencies of the French government (*see* BUREAUCRACY). Needless to say, the failures of this method are not well known. But, tricky though it may be, this is an exciting way to do research, and arguably the source of many, if not most, of our really significant conceptual advances.

A final word is necessary on what case study research is not. If true research marries empirical data with conceptual insight, then, on one side, the so-called "case study method," in which experiences from practice are written up for the pedagogical purposes of the classroom, is not research. Data may be collected, sometimes even as much as in case study research, but there is no intent to draw the conceptual lessons of the experience. On the other side, conceptual interpretations of experience per se cannot be labeled case study research either. Such works can be greatly insightful, as in Barnard's classic *The Functions of the Executive* (1938) about his own experiences as President of the New Jersey Bell Telephone Company. But these are not usually based on probes into cases per se so much as the drawing on general experience. Of course, when the author relates the conceptual interpretation to his or her own experiences directly and somewhat systematically, then the label case study research may well apply.

But in research, the object of the exercise is understanding, not methodological elegance and so it hardly matters what the approach is called, so long as it is applied carefully and honestly, nor where the ideas come from, so long as they are insightful.

See also **Generalization; Levels of analysis; Validity**

Bibliography

Barnard, C. I. (1938). *The functions of the executive*. Cambridge, MA: Harvard University Press.

Chandler, A. D. (1962). *Strategy and structure: Chapters in the history of the industrial enterprise*. Cambridge, MA: MIT Press.

Crozier, M. (1964). *The bureaucratic phenomenon*. Chicago: University of Chicago Press.

Mintzberg, H. (1973). *The nature of managerial work*. New York: Harper & Row.

Mintzberg, H. (1993). *Rounding out the manager's job*. Working Paper #93–04–05, Montreal: McGill University.

Mintzberg, H. & McHugh, A. (1985). Strategy formation in an adhocracy. *Administrative Science Quarterly*, **30 (2)**, 160–197.

Stewart, R. (1967). *Managers and their jobs*. London: Macmillan.

Whyte, W. F. (1943). *Street corner society: The social structure of an Italian slum*. Chicago: University of Chicago Press.

HENRY MINTZBERG

centralization *see* ORGANIZATIONAL DESIGN; ORGANIZATIONAL RESTRUCTURING

CEOs The chief executive officer, or CEO, is the executive who has overall responsibility for the conduct and performance of an entire organization, not just a subunit. The CEO designation has gained widespread use since about 1970, as a result of the need to draw distinctions among various senior executive positions in today's elaborate corporate structures. For example, sometimes a chief operating officer (COO) who is responsible for internal operational affairs is among the executives who reports to a CEO, who in turn is responsible for integrating internal and external, longer-term issues such as acquisitions, government relations, and investor relations.

In publicly traded corporations, sometimes the chairman of the board of directors is also the CEO, while the president (if such a title even exists) is the COO. In other cases (particularly European companies), the chairman is not an executive officer at all, but rather is an external overseer, while the president is the senior-ranking employed manager or CEO. Other variations exist as well. Further complicating the scholar's task of identifying the CEO of a company is that the label may not be explicitly bestowed on anyone. Still, theorists and other observers of organizations are drawn to the idea that some one person has overall responsibility for the management of an enterprise and that, in turn, that person's characteristics and actions are of consequence to the organization and its STAKEHOLDERS.

The roles of a CEO are many and varied (Mintzberg, 1973; Kotter, 1982), including DECISION MAKING (on major and sometimes minor issues), monitoring and transmitting information (both inside and outside the company), and interacting with internal and external parties (many constituencies believe they warrant the CEO's personal attention). Another way to think about CEO roles is as in the domain of substance (tangible actions) and symbols (the intangible, added meaning that is attached to a senior leader's behaviors, because of the position he or she holds in the organization). Far more research has been done on CEO substantive actions than on SYMBOLISM, but recent theory and investigations have pointed to the great significance of the latter (Pfeffer, 1981).

Most writings on senior executives, and CEOs in particular, have focused on the effects these individuals have on the form and fate of their companies. Some of these works, often referred to as the "Great Man" view, attempt to describe the traits and behaviors of CEOs who have achieved remarkable successes (*see* LEADERSHIP, CHARISMATIC; TRANSACTIONAL/TRANSFORMATIONAL THEORY). These inquiries are usually qualitative and, while rich in detail, are difficult to use as a reliable basis for a generalizable theory of LEADERSHIP.

Some research has taken a more limited approach, seeking to understand the associations between certain measurable CEO characteristics and specific actions taken or subsequent organizational profiles. For example, research has documented the tendencies of new CEOs hired from outside the company to make major immediate strategy and staffing changes; for CEOs with certain types of personalities to adopt certain structural characteristics for the organization; and for CEOs who are large shareholders of the company to take larger strategic risks than CEOs who are only paid employees (*see* RISK-TAKING). In terms of quantity of significant findings, this stream of research is mounting. But as the few ilustrations here suggest, the patterns are diffuse and generally lacking a coherent theoretical framework, that is, unless the broadest possible perspective is taken, in which case it can be said that CEOs matter.

Actually, the issue of whether (or how much) CEOs matter to organizational outcomes is of long-standing debate among scholars. The earliest perspective, often called the strategic choice perspective, posits that executives engage in major adaptive decisions in the face of shifting environmental requirements and internal resources (*see* STRATEGIC MANAGEMENT). Namely, CEOs make big choices and those choices matter. A contrary perspective, gaining currency in the 1970s and early 1980s, is that organizations are so confined by external constraints, institutional pressures, and internal inertia, that CEOs are not allowed (or choose not to undertake) many major strategic actions – that managers do not matter much.

A recent theoretical bridge between these two polar perspectives is the concept of executive discretion, defined as latitude of action (Hambrick & Finkelstein, 1987). Executive discretion emanates from factors in the environment, in the organization, and within the executive him- or herself; thus, sometimes CEOs have considerable discretion, sometimes none at all, and usually somewhere in between. This concept of executive discretion is proving very important for untangling the debate about whether CEOs matter and is further shedding light on other phenomena such as executive pay levels, executive TURNOVER, and executive demographic and PERSONALITY characteristics.

The prevailing literature on CEOs has focused on the effects they have on their organizations, but a secondary and still notable stream has focused on the factors that affect CEO characteristics. Namely, why do certain people get appointed to CEO positions? When and why do they get dismissed? Theoretical perspectives for addressing these questions range widely. At the broadest level is the theory of social elites, arguing that individuals of the highest socio-economic and educational backgrounds, as well as those with the strongest connections with other elites, are chosen for CEO positions and are only reluctantly dismissed (*see* STATUS). A related theory, but narrower in its level of analysis, argues that successive CEOs are clones of each other – that there is a strong institutional tendency toward continuity of leadership profiles; moreover, CEOs who depart on good terms are allowed to INFLUENCE, if not CONTROL, the selection of their replacements, who often strikingly resemble them. Finally, RESOURCE DEPENDENCE theory argues that specific identifiable pressures from outside or from within the organization give rise to the appointment of CEOs with certain characteristics. For example, trends in an industry may favor certain perspectives among top executives; strategic plans for a company may necessitate a certain CEO profile; and so on. Unfortunately, the actual processes of CEO selection, understandably very sensitive phenomena, are not well documented or understood.

See also **Top management teams; Governance and ownership; Fast-track development; Succession planning; Managerial behavior**

Bibliography

Barnard, C. (1948). *The functions of the executive.* Cambridge, MA: Harvard University Press.

Fredrickson, J. W., Hambrick, D. C. & Baumrin, S. (1988). A model of CEO dismissal. *Academy of Management Review*, **13**, 255–270.

Hambrick, D. C. & Finkelstein, S. (1987). Managerial discretion. A bridge between polar views of organizational outcomes. In L. L. Cummings & B. M. Staw (Eds), *Research in organizational behavior* (pp. 369–406). Greenwich, CT: JAI Press.

Kotter, J. (1982). *The general managers.* New York: Free Press.

Levinson, H. & Rosenthal, S. (1984). *CEO: Corporate leadership in action.* New York: Basic Books.

Mintzberg, H. (1973). *The nature of managerial work.* New York: Harper and Row.

Pfeffer, J. (1981). Management as symbolic action: The creation and maintenance of organizational paradigms. In L. L. Cummings & B. M. Staw (Eds), *Research in organizational behavior* (pp. 1–52). Greenwich, CT: JAI Press.

Romanelli, E. & Tushman, M. L. (1988). Executive Leadership and organizational outcomes: An evolutionary perspective. In D. C. Hambrick (Ed.), *The executive effect: Concepts and methods for studying top managers* (pp. 129–140). Greenwich, CT: JAI Press.

Vancil, R. F. (1987). *Passing the baton: Managing the process of CEO succession*. Boston, MA: Harvard Business School Press.

DONALD C. HAMBRICK

chain of command *see* CLASSICAL DESIGN THEORY; MANAGEMENT, CLASSICAL THEORY

change, evaluation The field of ORGANIZATIONAL BEHAVIOR needs effective methods for assessing organizational change for two basic reasons – one related to practice and one related to theory. From a managerial perspective, there is the need to assess validly the effectiveness of ORGANIZATIONAL CHANGE programs. At the same time, understanding change phenomena and processes in complex human systems can contribute to theory development in the organizational sciences (Woodman, 1989). In OB, we have drawn heavily from the field of EVALUATION RESEARCH primarily developed by sociologists and other social scientists (e.g., Sechrest & Figueredo, 1993).

There are a variety of issues surrounding the valid evaluation of organizational change. These tend to center around: (a) what should be measured; and (b) how such assessment might proceed. These issues sound deceptively simple – however, at their heart lie philosophically complex issues concerning the nature of reality itself and how knowledge about that reality can be obtained (Legge, 1984). For example, debates over positivistic versus interpretative research PARADIGMS are frequently found in the literature on organizational change (*see* RESEARCH DESIGN). One manifestation of this debate surrounds the well-known concern with alpha (behavioral change), beta (scale recalibration), and gamma (concept redefinition) changes introduced almost 20 years ago by Golembiewski, Billingsley, and Yeager (1976).

Often, in the assessment of change programs, evaluators have relied upon participant PERCEPTIONS to evaluate organizational change. When dealing with individual cognitions and perceptions, the concern becomes separating changes in external reality from changes in perceptions of that reality. It is crucial that evaluators can distinguish among, for example.

(a) actual changes in behavior;
(b) recalibration of measurement scales; or
(c) redefinition of concepts in the minds of organizational participants.

Many would consider an effective strategy of evaluation to be one that does not rely exclusively on organizational member perceptions, but rather utilizes objective criteria (such as PRODUCTIVITY, ABSENTEEISM, and so on) to assess change effort effectiveness. Logical as this is, it is unfortunately no panacea. It is typically quite difficult in complex organizations to link outcome variables (such as productivity or performance), which by their very nature are multidetermined, to specific change methods and activities. Further, considerable disagreement exists concerning whether quantitative or qualitative assessments of organizational change make the most sense (Legge, 1984; Sechrest & Figueredo, 1993). Woodman (1989) has argued for combining the two. "Managing organizational change effectively is both an art and a science, so perhaps our evaluation paradigms need to better reflect this reality. . . . The nature of change . . . would seem to require research paradigms that, at least, attempt to match the complexity that is being investigated" (Woodman, 1989, p. 177).

Regardless of the approach taken, evaluation of organizational change is likely to be most useful, for both practice and theory, when the following criteria are met:

(1) When feasible, assessment should be based not upon ad hoc choice of outcomes and other variables to be measured, but rather upon some theoretical model of organizational behavior and change (*see* THEORY).
(2) To the extent possible, an assessment program should rest upon information obtained in a describable and replicable way.
(3) The design of the evaluation program should allow the elimination of plausible but invalid interpretations of the findings (Lawler, Nadler, & Mirvis, 1983).

See also **Organizational effectiveness; Change methods; Validity**

Bibliography

Golembiewski, R. T., Billingsley, K. & Yeager, S. (1976). Measuring change and persistence in human affairs: Types of change generated by OD designs. *Journal of Applied Behavioral Science*, **12**, 133–157.

Lawler, E. E., Nadler, D. A. & Mirvis, P. H. (1983). Organizational change and the conduct of assessment research. In S. E. Seashore, E. E. Lawler, P. H. Mirvis & C. Cammann (Eds), *Assessing organizational change: A guide to methods, measures, and practices* (pp. 19–47). New York: Wiley.

Legge, K. (1984). *Evaluating planned organizational change*. London: Academic Press.

Sechrest, L. & Figueredo, A. J. (1993). Program evaluation. *Annual Review of Psychology*, **44**, 645–674.

Woodman, R. W. (1989). Evaluation research on organizational change: Arguments for a 'combined paradigm' approach. In R. W. Woodman & W. A. Pasmore (Eds), *Research in organizational change and development*, pp. 161–180 (Vol. 3). Greenwich, CT: JAI Press.

RICHARD W. WOODMAN

change, methods Specific methods used to change organizations are often referred to as *interventions* (*see* INTERVENTION RESEARCH) Interventions are the planned change activities designed to increase an organization's effectiveness (Cummings & Worley, 1993, p. 163). In the ORGANIZATION DEVELOPMENT paradigm, effectiveness includes both PRODUCTIVITY and QUALITY OF WORK LIFE.

Antecedents and Conditions for Effective Change

Effective change depends in large measure on valid diagnosis of organizational functioning and problems (Woodman, 1990). A valid identification and exploration of what the organization does well and poorly is a natural precursor to change. Argyris (1970), for example, has argued that effective ORGANIZATIONAL CHANGE depends upon three things:

(1) valid and useful information about the organization and its problems;
(2) free and informed choice on the part of organizational members with regard to courses of action that they might take; and
(3) internal commitment by participants in the change effort to the actions chosen (*see* DOUBLE-LOOP LEARNING).

Absent these antecedents, effective change is seen as quite problematic.

In a similar vein, Cummings and Worley (1993) see effective change management as based on the following antecedents:

(1) motivating change by creating a readiness for change among employees and attempting to overcome resistance to the change (*see* RESISTANCE TO CHANGE);
(2) creating a shared vision of the desired future state of the organization; and
(3) developing political support for the needed changes.

Porras and Robertson (1992) have reviewed the literature dealing with change methodology in order to identify conditions that would seem to be related to effective interventions. In brief, these conditions include:

(1) The organization's members must be the key source of energy for the change, not some external consultant or change agent.
(2) Key members of the organization must recognize the need for change and be attracted by the potential positive outcomes from the change program.
(3) A willingness to change norms and procedures, in order to become more effective, must exist.

Key members of the organization must exhibit both attitudes and behaviors that support new norms and procedures (*see* GROUP NORMS).

Finally, recent meta-analyses (*see* VALIDITY GENERALIZATION) of systematically evaluated organizational change programs (*see* CHANGE, EVALUATION), have provided strong support for the notion that organizational change efforts are most effective when they are systemwide and "multifaceted" (Macy & Izumi, 1993; Robertson, Roberts, & Porras, 1993). Multifaceted interventions are those that take place in multiple subsystems of the organization, seek change in multiple variables of interest, and/or employ multiple change methods.

Focus of Change Efforts

Managers and change agents must have some means to link the conclusions from the diagnosis with effective action. Such attempts at identifying linkages have often taken the form of a model or typology that would categorize interventions by their focus or change targets. The "classic" forerunner of such categorization schemes is the dichotomy of human processual and technostructural interventions developed by Friedlander and Brown (1974). Human processual interventions focus on processes, such as COMMUNICATION, problem solving, and decision making, through which individuals accomplish the organization's work (*see* PROCESS CONSULTATION). Technostructural interventions are targeted on changing the organization's TECHNOLOGY (e.g., task methods and processes, work design) and structure. A more recent example of such a categorization scheme is that used by McMahan and Woodman (1992) in a survey of *Fortune* 500 industrial firms. McMahan and Woodman were able to identify the change methods used by these organizations as falling into one of the four following categories:

Human Processual. Emphasis on human relationships, TEAM BUILDING, work team interaction, process consulting, or CONFLICT RESOLUTION.

Technostructural. Emphasis on sociotechnical systems, task and technology work designs, or organization and group structure (*see* JOB DESIGN; SOCIOTECHNICAL THEORY).

Strategic Planning. Emphasis on strategic business PLANNING processes, strategic change or visioning; primarily top management involvement (*see* TOP MANAGEMENT TEAMS; MISSION STATEMENTS).

Systemwide. Emphasis on organization-wide improvement activities; LEADERSHIP, CULTURE, quality improvement, and transformation-type organizational change projects (*see* TOTAL QUALITY MANAGEMENT; TURNAROUND MANAGEMENT).

Implementation Theory

The applied theories that can serve to guide change methods are called implementation theories (Porras & Robertson, 1992). (For a discussion of the theory domains involved in organizational change, (*see* ORGANIZATION DEVELOPMENT). Implementation theories can be further broken down into three categories, each corresponding to a different level of specificity in terms of prescribing change actions. At the most general level of specification are *strategy theories*, which describe broad strategies that can be used to change human systems. *Procedure theories*, at a higher level of specificity, include descriptions of major steps to be taken in order to complete a process of change. The most specific category of implementation theories, called *technique theories*, focuses tightly on, say, a single "step" identified in a procedure theory.

Weisbord's (1988) "practice theory" of OD provides an example of an implementation theory. Weisbord proposes four guidelines for effective organizational change:

(1) assess the potential for action;
(2) get the whole system in the room;
(3) focus on the future; and
(4) structure systems tasks people can do for themselves.

The ideas and concepts in Weisbord's implementation theory are themselves theoretically grounded, being drawn from the theory and practice of Fred Emery, Kurt Lewin, Douglas McGregor, and Eric Trist, among others (*see* FORCE-FIELD ANALYSIS).

Many years ago, Kurt Lewin stated that there was nothing as practical as a good THEORY. Implementation theories provide the field with a means for identifying important antecedents and conditions necessary for effective organizational change. Further, implementation theories provide guidance that can link the problems identified during organizational diagnosis with the solutions or action steps needed to address them. In sum, implementation theory summarizes what the field knows about change methods, why they work, and how they might be successfully used.

See also **Consultancy intervention models; Organizational restructuring; Politics**

Bibliography

Argyris, C. (1970). *Intervention theory and method: A behavioral science view*. Reading, MA: Addison-Wesley.

Cummings, T. G. & Worley, C. G. (1993). *Organization development and change*, (5th edn). St. Paul, MN: West.

Friedlander, F. & Brown, L. D. (1974). Organization development. *Annual Review of Psychology*, **25**, 313–341.

Macy, B. A. & Izumi, H. (1993). Organizational change, design, and work innovation: A meta-analysis of 131 North American field studies—1961–1991. In R. W. Woodman & W. A. Pasmore (Eds), *Research in organizational change and development*, (Vol. 7, pp. 235–313). Greenwich, CT: JAI Press.

McMahan, G. C. & Woodman, R. W. (1992). The current practice of organization development within the firm. *Group & Organization Management*, **17**, 117–134.

Porras, J. I. & Robertson, P. J. (1992). Organizational development: Theory, practice, and research. In M. D. Dunnette & L. M. Hough (Eds), *Handbook of industrial and organizational psychology*, (2nd edn, vol. 3, pp. 719–822). Palo Alto, CA: Consulting Psychologists Press.

Robertson, P. J., Roberts, D. R. & Porras, J. I. (1993). An evaluation of a model of planned organizational change: Evidence from a meta-analysis. In R. W. Woodman & W. A. Pasmore (Eds), *Research in organizational change and development*, (vol. 7, pp. 1–39). Greenwich, CT: JAI Press.

Weisbord, M. R. (1988). Towards a new practice theory of OD: Notes on snapshooting and moviemaking. In W. A. Pasmore & R. W. Woodman (Eds), *Research in organizational change and development*, (vol. 2, pp. 59–96). Greenwich, CT: JAI Press.

Woodman, R. W. (1990). Issues and concerns in organizational diagnosis. In C. N. Jackson & M. R. Manning (Eds), *Organizational development annual*, Vol. 3: *Diagnosing client organizations*. Alexandria, VA: American Society for Training and Development.

RICHARD W. WOODMAN

change agents *see* CHANGE METHODS; CONSULTANCY; ORGANIZATION DEVELOPMENT

chaos theory Social entities with virtually identical initial internal states, embedded in virtually identical environments, can exhibit totally different, or chaotic, behaviors even though their behavior is governed by the exact same set of rules or "laws." In social systems, there seem to be at least two useful indicators of chaos:

(1) highly iterative recursive structures that change over time; and
(2) highly discontinuous behavior in the system.

Social systems that fit these criteria (e.g., NEGOTIATION processes, organizational decline, and CAREER TRANSITIONS) will often exhibit chaotic behavior over some part of their domain. While the study of chaos is new to social science, the examination of chaotic systems has made rapid progress in the physical sciences (Gleick, 1987). Examples of systems that seem to exhibit chaos are turbulence in fluid flows, stellar configurations, and human physiological patterns. Surprisingly, natural systems such as these are best understood and simulated, but not predicted, by using very simple nonlinear equations. Moreover, certain characteristics of chaotic systems in the physical sciences are similar to characteristics of social systems, suggesting that many social systems may also be chaotic (Gregersen & Sailer, 1993).

More importantly, knowing a social entity's state, its environment, and the "laws" which govern the transformation of the state from one time to the next are not sufficient to guarantee that the long-run behavior in some systems can be predicted. While an entity's behavior in a chaotic system can be simulated *ex post facto* to understand it better, its behavior cannot be predicted *a priori*. This inability to predict would occur even if no variables have been omitted, measurement has been perfect, and no stochastic ERROR is present. As a result, future organizational behavior research may profit by relying less on quantitative methods and more on SIMULATIONS and qualitative methods to understand chaos in social systems. In addition, collecting more data points and knowing the behavior and environment of a larger number of extremely similar entities is also insufficient to predict behavior in a chaotic domain. Unfortunately, such is the nature of chaotic systems where traditional statistical analyses (e.g., means, regressions, etc.) are useless (*see* STATISTICAL METHODS). Moreover, to understand a chaotic social system through quantitative analysis, thousands of synchronic observations would be necessary, spaced out over a long enough time period that potential divergent behavior would manifest itself. Furthermore, these data points would need to avoid potential reactivity BIAS from respondents providing information repeatedly over time.

Finally, chaotic systems can exhibit nonchaotic (i.e., predictable) behavior over much of their domain. As a result, the social scientist's question is not simply whether or not chaos exists, but the degree to which chaos occurs and the degree to which it is relevant to a particular study. At present, no systematic methodologies exist to identify chaotic domains in social arenas (*see* RESEARCH METHODS). Thus the future of chaos theory in organizational contexts would benefit from the development of diagnostic methods for identifying the existence of chaos.

Until critical methodological and statistical challenges to examining chaos are overcome, chaos theory in organizational behavior will continue to be used primarily as an explanatory, yet exploratory, metaphor to describe phenomena exhibiting potentially chaotic characteristics. For example, numerous recent books (e.g., Wheatley, 1992) have taken this metaphoric approach to explaining behavior in organizations; however, without further advances in the identification and study of chaotic behavior in organizational settings, the application of chaos theory will remain primarily at the conceptual level, mimicking prior applications of physical science theories to organizational phenomena.

See also **Systems theory; Theory; Fuzzy sets**

Bibliography

Gleick, J. (1987). *Chaos: Making a new science*. New York: Viking.

Gregersen, H. B. & Sailer, L. (1993). Chaos theory and its implications for social science research. *Human Relations*, **46** (7), 777–802.

Wheatley, M. (1992). *Leadership and the new science*. San Francisco: Group West.

HAL B. GREGERSEN

citizenship *see* ORGANIZATIONAL CITIZENSHIP

class *see* LABOR PROCESS THEORY; OCCUPATIONS; STATUS; STRATIFICATION

classical design theory Classical theory is often contrasted with CONTINGENCY THEORY, the latter attempting to specify conditions under which particular ORGANIZATIONAL DESIGNS are most appropriate.

Classical design theory refers to the application of a number of tenets of management emanating mainly from a diverse group of early twentieth century management thinkers and writers. They were usually practicing managers (Gulick, Urwick, and Brech), often engineers (F. W. Taylor and H. Fayol), usually American, but some were British and Fayol was French. Many also had a military background. These theorists were particularly concerned to lay down grand principles of organizational design.

The tenets of classical design theory are not dissimilar to the theory of BUREAUCRACY and can be summarized:

Universal management functions exist. These are to forecast, plan, organize, coordinate, command, and control (*see* PLANNING).

Unity of command. A subordinate should be accountable to one manager and there should be a clear line of authority. This is also sometimes referred to as the scalar principle.

Specialization. An individual should perform one function only.

Span of control. Should not exceed five or six.

Delegation. Duties should be delegated to as low a level in the hierarchy as possible.

The term SCIENTIFIC MANAGEMENT has been coined to describe the ideas of F. W. Taylor who set out to measure work by timing component activities for jobs as diverse as cutting metals and shoveling pig iron. It is from this work that time and motion study came to be widely used in industry. Taylor was more concerned than the other theorists with the design of work in such a way to make the most effective use of human resources. The term "Taylorism" is also used to describe Taylor's ideas of work measurement.

Classical theory also presents a view of organization that is often typified by Henry Ford's original factory which used the principles of MASS PRODUCTION and the assembly line. Hence the term "Fordism" is sometimes used to describe the design of large-scale organizations based on repetitive meaningless jobs (*see* REPETITIVE WORK; JOB DESIGN).

The principles of classical theory have been extensively criticised (e.g., by March & Simon, (*see* PUGH & HICKSON, 1989), on the basis that they are too simplistic for complex organizations, many are mutually incompatible and that to restrict a worker to one activity only makes delegation difficult (*see* ROLE). They are given as universal principles but no account is taken of the variation in situations found in practice. Such a restricted view of management cannot survive more complex situations which have arisen since these tenets were advocated. For example, the MATRIX ORGANIZATION requires reporting to two bosses, the use of TEAMBUILDING requires a more flexible DIVISION OF LABOR.

Mary Parker Follett is another classical theorist who sought general principles but her emphasis upon reciprocal coordination between people presented a more flexible approach to organization. Chester Barnard's book *The Functions of the Executive* (1938) is a landmark in a move away from over-reliance upon classical design principles. Barnard emphasized the problem of coordination under conditions of COMPLEXITY and proposed a theory of organization based upon COOPERATION, COMMUNICATION, and DECISION MAKING.

The classical theorists were writing from experience rather than from systematic scientific observation. It is doubtful whether they ever intended these principles to be used in such a rigid way as is sometimes suggested. Many also described the need for judgment in DECISION MAKING and to take into account the needs of employees.

See also **Human relations movement; Managerial behavior; Management, classical theory**

Bibliography

Pugh, D. S. & Hickson, D. J. (1989). *Writers on organizations* (4th edn). Newbury Park, CA: Sage.

RICHARD BUTLER

coalition formation This state occurs when some but not all members of a group organize themselves to push their perspective on an issue (*see* GROUP DYNAMICS; POLITICS). Thompson (1967, p. 126) wrote that "coalition behavior is undoubtedly of major importance to our understanding of complex organizations." But even though the concepts of coalitions and coalition formation have been used to describe organizations and organizational action (e.g., Cyert & March, 1963; Pfeffer & Salancik, 1978), ORGANIZATIONAL BEHAVIOR has paid little attention to the literature on coalitions in social psychology, GAME THEORY, or political science (Murnighan, 1978; 1994).

Early results found that the least endowed tended to coalesce and exclude the most endowed. These "strength is weakness" findings, which suggested the supremacy of the underdog, were soon debunked. New research showed that when POWER BASES vary, strength is weakness only when parties with different resources are effectively interchangeable. Partners with just sufficient resources to do the job appear optimal: Fewer resources may imply smaller outcome demands, and greater attractiveness. When parties are not interchangeable, however, strength is extremely valuable, and no longer the harbinger of exclusion (i.e., weakness). The political and the social psychological literature also suggest that small but sufficient coalitions are most frequent.

Founders tend to possess a diverse network of weak ties, rather than strong links to only a few others (*see* NETWORKING). Thus, a coalition's strength may rest on infrequent, nonrepetitive interaction with many others, rather than on frequent, well-established interactions with a few close contacts. Political models also suggest that coalitions form incrementally, as interconnected sets of interacting dyads. Put simply, *coalitions form one person at a time* (Murnighan & Brass, 1991). Once a coalition is successful at achieving a critical mass, continued growth becomes considerably easier.

Being surreptitious may be critical in the success of many organizational coalitions: Keeping quiet helps blunt the formation of an organized opposition, i.e., counter-coalitions, which von Neumann and Morgenstern's (1947) classic, original model assumed would be excluded parties' natural reaction to a coalition forming. Successful coalitions tend to be fluid, forming quickly, expanding and bursting at decision time, and quickly disappearing (Murnighan & Brass, 1991).

Political models suggest that founders add similar members to ensure their own centrality in the final coalition. New parties are invited to balance each other's IDEOLOGY, on either side of the founder's position. The coalition can grow until it is just large enough, keeping the range of its ideologies at a minimum and increasing the likelihood that its final policy positions will most closely resemble the founder's (*see* GROUP STRUCTURE). This kind of political strategy, which may be well understood by astute organizational tacticians, has not found its way into the organizational literature.

Within an organization, executives who are involved in many productive projects (i.e., organizational coalitions) are viewed as politically powerful (*see* POWER). A few organization members may be in several dominant coalitions: They represent Thompson's (1967) concept of *the inner circle*, a select few whose interconnectedness provides them with considerable influence. These are the people who wield considerable coalitional and political influence in organizations (*see* INFLUENCE; LEADERSHIP).

See also **Intergroup relations; Interorganizational relations; Joint ventures; Cooperation; Collaboration**

Bibliography

Cyert, R. & March, J. G. (1963). *A behavioral theory of the firm*. Englewood Cliffs, NJ: Prentice-Hall.

Murnighan, J. K. (1978). Models of coalition formation: Game theoretic, social psychological, and political perspectives. *Psychological Bulletin*, **85**, 1130–1153.

Murnighan, J. K. (1994). Game theory and organizational behavior. In B. M. Staw & L. L. Cummings (Eds), *Research in organizational behavior*. Greenwich, CT: JAI Press.

Murnighan, J. K. & Brass, D. J. (1991). Intraorganizational coalitions. In Bazerman, M. H., Lewicki, R. J. & Sheppard, B. H. (Eds), *Research on negotiation in organizations*. Greenwich, CT: JAI Press.

Pfeffer, J. & Salancik, G. (1978). *The external control of organizations*. New York: Harper & Row.

Thompson, J. D. (1967). *Organizations in action*. New York: McGraw-Hill.

von Neumann, J. & Morgenstern, O. (1947). *The theory of games and economic behavior*. Princeton, NJ: Princeton University Press.

J. KEITH MURNIGHAN

codes of conduct A code of conduct is a formal document that communicates the organizations standards of behavior (*see* COMMUNICATIONS). In response to concerns about unethical conduct, ethics code usage has grown in recent years. According to one recent survey, 83 percent of large United States corporations, 68 percent of Canadian firms, and 50 percent of European firms have codes (Berenbeim, 1992).

The most frequently stated code purpose is the encouragement of ethical conduct in the organization. To accomplish this purpose, codes take a variety of forms ranging from short statements of values (sometimes called credos) to lengthier specifications of rules and regulations in such areas as conflicts of interest and customer/supplier relations.

Other, less explicitly stated code functions have also been acknowledged (Weaver, 1993). These include attracting employees, managing a firm's public image, avoiding government regulation and legal penalties, and boosting employee morale (*see* STAKEHOLDERS).

Code effectiveness is generally discussed in relation to how well it encourages ethical conduct. Although honor codes have been found to be associated with reduced academic dishonesty in colleges and universities, the minimal research that exists provides little support for an association between codes of ethics and reduced unethical behavior in other types of organizations.

See also **Business and government; Business ethics; corporate social responsibility; Mission statements; Values**

Bibliography

Berenbeim, R. (1992). *Corporate ethics practices*. New York: The Conference Board.

Weaver, G. (1993). Corporate codes of ethics: Purpose, process, and content issues. *Business and Society*, **32**, 44–58.

LINDA TREVINO

cognition in organizations This term includes PERCEPTION, INFORMATION PROCESSING, analysis, decision, LEARNING and memory by individuals and groups, and the relationship of these COGNITIVE PROCESSES to organization activity. The basic definition of these subjects is informed by work on cognition across the social sciences, but the organizational setting requires specific theoretic and empirical attention.

The study of cognition in organizations can be divided into three streams of research. The first assumes that cognitive processes result in rational DECISION MAKING (*see* RATIONALITY), although researchers in this tradition have paid attention to the differential impact of the decision-maker's cognitive style, the effects of GROUP SIZE, GROUP STRUCTURE, and ROLES. Even intuition (Pondy, 1983) has been studied, but the basic assumption is that cognition is intentional, representational, and computational (Stubbart, 1989). The second stream of work draws on BEHAVIORAL DECISION THEORY and presumes that rationality is more difficult to achieve. Work from psychology has been used to explain systematic ERRORS in individual judgments (Duhaime & Schwenk, 1985); other research has considered the effect of social processes and POLITICS on cognition. A third stream of work argues that through ENACTMENT (Daft & Weick, 1984) individual cognition and action create the environment within which further cognition and action takes place. This perspective focuses on the interpretive content of cognitive processes and the importance of shared understanding for coordinated action (Smirchich & Stubbart, 1985).

A key distinction among these approaches has to do with the presumed impact of the organizational setting. Those adopting a rational perspective often de-emphasize the importance of the organization setting, but do recognize that coordination facilitates more, and more complex, problem solving. Those taking a behavioral approach see the organization as a more influential, multifarious setting for individual cognition; group settings and processes encourage BIAS but also provide diverse experience and opinions that can be used to reduce bias. Some who follow this general line of thought argue that the organizational setting dominates individual cognition so completely (especially through organizational routines) that concepts like organization knowledge, organization learning, and even organization mind, have meaning independent of individual cognition (*see* LEARNING ORGANIZATION). An interpretive perspective does not allow such an easy dichotomy, because this approach finds it impossible to explain either individual cognition or broader context without simultaneously considering the other.

At present, one of the most important issues for all those interested in cognition in organizations is to establish a stronger empirical link between cognition and action, paying special attention to LEVELS OF ANALYSIS. Organization researchers have long claimed that what organizational members think and believe has a profound impact on organization activities (Barnard, 1938), and interesting action research is being done which maps cognitive information from organization members for use by decision makers (e.g., Eden, 1992) (*see* ACTION/INTERVENTION RESEARCH). Nevertheless, the relationship between cognitive processes and individual behavior, as well as the link between collective cognitive processes and organization activity, have not been adequately explored empirically. A number of interesting case studies have linked interpretation to ORGANIZATIONAL CHANGE (e.g., Dutton & Dukerich, 1991; Barr, Stimpert, & Huff, 1992), but much remains to be done to establish the impact of cognition in organizations.

See also **Strategic management; Group culture; action theory**

Bibliography

Barnard, C. I. (1938). *Functions of the executive*. Cambridge, MA: Harvard University Press.

Barr, P. S., Stimpert, J. L. & Huff, A. S. (1992). Cognitive change, strategic action, and organizational renewal. *Strategic Management Journal*, **13**, 15–36.

Daft, R. & Weick, K. (1984). Toward a model of organizations as interpretation systems. *Academy of Management Review*, **9**, 284–295.

Duhaime, I. D. & Schwenk, C. (1985). Conjectures on cognitive simplification in acquisition and divestment decision-making. *Academy of Management Review*, **10**, 287–95.

Dutton J. E. & Dukerich, J. M. (1991). Keeping an eye on the mirror: Image and identity in organizational adaptation. *Academy of Management Journal*, **34**, 517–554.

Eden, C. (1992). On the nature of cognitive maps. *Journal of Management Studies*, **29**, 261–265.

Pondy, L. R. (1983). Union of rationality and intuition in management action. In Suresh Srivastava (Ed.), *The executive mind*. San Francisco: Jossey-Bass.

Smircich, L. & Stubbart, C. I. (1985). Strategic management in an enacted world. *Academy of Management Review*, **10**, 724–736.

Stubbart, C. I. (1989). Managerial cognition: A missing link in strategic management research. *Journal of Management Studies*, **26**, 4, 325–347.

A. SIGISMUND HUFF

cognitive appraisal *see* COGNITIVE PROCESSES; JOB INSECURITY

cognitive dissonance This is an element of ATTITUDE THEORY, which arises when there is an inconsistency among an individual's attitudes, behaviors, and/or VALUES (*see* Festinger, 1957). For example, an individual who strongly dislikes his or her job (i.e., who has a negative attitude toward his or her job) but who must work long hours in order to perform that job (i.e., a job-related behavior) will likely experience dissonance between intended behavior (as predicted by the negative attitude) and actual behavior (working long hours).

A person who experiences cognitive dissonance will be motivated to resolve it in some fashion. For example, the worker noted above may alter her or his attitude by focusing more on positive aspects of the work. Alternatively, the worker may alter her or his behavior by working fewer hours. Prolonged periods of dissonance tend to have dysfunctional consequences for the individual. For example, the worker is likely to experience higher levels of STRESS, FRUSTRATION, and ANXIETY. Job performance may suffer (*see* PERFORMANCE, INDIVIDUAL). Extreme dissonance may also cause the individual to withdraw from the situation by being absent more frequently or resigning altogether (*see* WITHDRAWAL).

See also **Job satisfaction; Turnover; Absenteeism; Cognitive processes.**

Bibliography

Festinger, L. (1957). *A theory of cognitive dissonance*. Palo Alto, CA: Stanford University Press.

RICKY W. GRIFFIN

cognitive processes This term refers to the internal cognitive operations involved in sensing and interpreting information, encoding and storing information, retrieving information, and transforming information into more meaningful or more useful forms. Cognitive processes are the basis by which environmental information, memories, and SKILL are translated into ORGANIZATIONAL BEHAVIOR. It is also the basis for affective responses (*see* AFFECT). Thus, understanding cognitive processing lies at the heart of understanding human behavior and emotions. Cognitive processes also provide the basis for SELF-REGULATION in a number of domains.

During the 1980s and 1990s there was a dramatic increase in the application of INFORMATION PROCESSING theories, principles, and methods (e.g., protocol analysis) to understanding organizational behavior. Individual level phenomena such as PERFORMANCE APPRAISALS (Ilgen, Barnes-Fanell, & McKellin, 1993), MOTIVATION and skill development (Kanfer & Ackerman, 1989), LEADERSHIP perceptions (Lord & Maher, 1993) and job simulations have all been explained in terms underlying cognitive processes. Organizational level researchers have also effectively used such concepts as mental models, cognitive maps, cognitive categories, and cognitive scripts to explain strategy, competitor perceptions, and DECISION MAKING.

This varied and eclectic borrowing of principles, terms, and procedures has produced a diverse range of findings and activities. Yet there are also useful integrative reviews. Lord and Maher (1989) summarize and critique much of this research in terms of content areas, and these same two authors provide a summary of developments in cognitive science (Lord & Maher, 1991). There are also excellent books by cognitive scientists that explain information processing and cognitive science in terms geared for more advanced readers (Newell, 1990; Posner, 1989).

A coherent approach to understanding cognitive processes is provided by conceptualizing information processing as occurring within a *cognitive architecture*. Cognitive architectures define:

(a) the nature and organization of memory;

(b) easily performed (primitive) cognitive operations; and
(c) a control structure that sequences information processing operations (Lord & Maher, 1991).

Currently, debate exists in cognitive science over the level at which cognitive architectures should be addressed.

The more established perspective is that architectures should be defined at a symbolic level, the level involving conscious mental operations. Symbolic architectures describe processing in terms of serial manipulations of symbols (e.g., language) as a way of solving problems or understanding environments (*see* METAPHOR; SYMBOLISM). Processing activities involve accessing symbols from memory or the external environment and manipulating symbols according to rule-based mental operations.

This approach has demonstrated a number of successes in terms of understanding problem solving (Simon, 1990) and intelligent behavior (Newell, 1990). It is consistent with the emphasis in the OB literature on mental models and conscious, deliberative information-processing activities. Symbolic architectures represent LEARNING and skill development in terms of the accumulation of domain or task specific rules. Performance results from a trade-off between accessing previous knowledge or rules and composing new rules or insights on the spot (Newell, 1990). In terms of time, symbolic level explanation is appropriate for processes taking on the order of one second or longer.

A contrasting perspective is to define cognitive architectures at a more basic, neurologically based level. *Connectionist* or parallel distributed processing architectures conceptualize processing in terms of the flow of activation and inhibition between networks of neuron-like processing units. Such processing occurs in parallel rather than serial steps. It is comparatively fast, providing a reasonable explanation for cognitive processes occurring in less than half a second. Connectionist processes are particularly useful for understanding the control of motor activities, perceptions, and the regulation of mental or motivational activities through processes such as spreading activation (priming) or spreading inhibition (negative priming) (Lord & Levy, 1994). Learning in connectionist architectures is much slower than in symbolic architectures. It involves changes in weights connecting units rather than changes in rules. Connectionist processes also seem to provide a more natural explanation of preconscious implicit processes associated with phenomena such as intuition and the more basic aspects of EMOTION. Finally, changes in older workers such as a general slowing of information processing and reduced inhibitory capacity are nicely explained in connectionist terms (*see* AGE).

Current research in cognitive science and artificial intelligence is addressing the interface between symbolic level and connectionist processes. Two fundamental areas of concern for the OB field pertain to this interface. One area addresses the nature and extent of the cognitive (attentional) resources that support symbolic level operations. The biologically based connectionist perspective implies that people have multiple cognitive resources that can be used to perform organizational tasks. This view emphasizes that evolution, not an engineer, designed the human brain, resulting in many distinct processing units and capacities. Each processing capacity had significance for survival at one point in time, but in modern man, these capacities interact in performing most tasks. The obvious implication is that work tasks may be done in many ways and that human potential can be best used by designing jobs and organizational systems that utilize these multiple human capacities.

In contrast, the symbolic perspective emphasizes the effective use of a limited attentional resource that supports symbolic operations (Kanfer & Ackerman, 1989). There may be substantial differences among individuals in the amount of attentional capacity or working memory they can use to hold or manipulate symbols, and these differences are strongly related to general intelligence (*see* INTELLIGENCE TESTING). From this perspective, increased performance largely results from greater attentional resources or from substituting learning for on-the-spot processing (Newell, 1990). Further, as Kanfer and Ackerman note, task and self-regulatory activities may compete for use of the same limited attentional resources.

A second and related concern pertains to the nature of process control in connectionist and symbolic architectures. Being concerned with sequencing of activities, process control is critical to understanding coherence in thinking and task activities. It involves the interface between selective attention and purposeful motivational activities. Symbolic level approaches to process control emphasize the use of aggregate mental structures like scripts and schema (see Lord & Maher, 1991). Connectionist approaches, on the other hand, emphasize processes like the spread of activation and inhibition from highly activated cognitive units. A critical function of process control is to protect current operating objectives from interference (Lord & Levy, 1994). Purposeful functioning and emotional regulation deteriorate if connectionist level, automatic self-regulatory capacities diminish with age, FATIGUE, or disease.

See also **Performance individual; Perception; Ability cognition in organizations**

Bibliography

Ilgen, D. R., Barnes-Farrell, J. L. & McKellin, D. B. (1993). Performance appraisal process research in the 1980s: What has it contributed to appraisals in use? *Organizational Behavior and Human Decision Processes*, **54**, 321–368.

Kanfer, R. & Ackerman, P. L. (1989). Motivation and cognitive abilities: An integrative/aptitude-treatment approach to skill acquisition. *Journal of Applied Psychology*, **74**, 657–690.

Lord, R. G. & Levy, P. E. (1994). Moving from cognition to action: A control theory perspective. *Applied Psychology: An International Review*, **43**, 335–398.

Lord, R. G. & Maher, K. M. (1989). Cognitive processes in industrial and organizational psychology. In C. Cooper & I. Robertson (Eds), *International review of industrial and organizational psychology 1989*. New York: Wiley.

Lord, R. G. & Maher, K. M. (1991). Cognitive theory in industrial/organizational psychology. In M. E. Dunnette (Ed.), *Handbook of Industrial/Organizational Psychology*, (vol. II). Palo Alto, CA: Consulting Psychologists Press.

Lord, R. G. & Maher, K. J. (1993). *Leadership and information processing: Linking perceptions and organizational performance*. Cambridge, MA: Routledge, Chapman & Hall.

Newell, A. (1990). *Unified theories of cognition*. Cambridge, MA: Harvard University Press.

Posner, M. I. (Ed.), (1989). *Foundations of cognitive science*. Cambridge, MA: MIT Press.

Simon, H. A. (1990). Invariants of human behavior. In M. Rosenzweig & L. Porter (Eds), *Annual review of psychology*, (vol. 41, pp. 1–19). Palo Alto, CA: Annual Reviews.

ROBERT G. LORD

cognitive resource theory The theory seeks to account for differences in leaders' performance in terms of their cognitive resources and situational demands. Leaders who are intelligent, as measured by intelligence tests, but less experienced, do poorly if they are stressed by conflict with their boss. Conversely, those leaders who are experienced, but less intelligent, exhibit better performance under conditions of job STRESS and CONFLICT with their boss. The reverse is also found. In the absence of job stress due to a hostile or threatening boss, intelligent leaders do better and experienced leaders do worse. The theory has been validated in field studies with army infantry leaders, fire service officers, coast guard officers, and petty officers, and in-basket experiments. The theory explains these results by assuming that stress interferes with the use of cognitive abilities on intellectual tasks. Experience provides overlearning. Experienced leaders can also rely on their intuition.

See also **Competencies; Leadership; Leadership contingencies, Cognitive processes; Intelligence testing**

Bibliography

Fiedler, F. E. & Garcia, J. E. (1987). *New approaches to effective leadership: Cognitive resources and organizational performance*. New York: Wiley.

Fiedler, F. E., Potter, E. H., III, Zais, M. M. & Knowlton, W., Jr. (1979). Organizational stress and the use and misuse of managerial intelligence and experience. *Journal of Applied Psychology*, **64**, 635–647.

BERNARD M. BASS

cognitive style *see* COGNITIVE PROCESSES; PERSONALITY

cohesiveness *see* GROUP COHESIVENESS

Collaboration The interest in the increasing array of collaborations in today's global economy is intense (Borys & Jemison, 1989). These forms have become a permanent part of the business scene. Beyond rich description, however, there is a lack of agreement on what theory provides the best basis for predicting when collaborations should occur, or what makes some collaborations more strategic than others. Three bodies of theory provide important, but limited, guidance on this issue: TRANSACTION COST THEORY, INTERORGANIZATIONAL RELATIONS (IOR), and the so-called RESOURCE BASED THEORY of the firm.

Oliver (1990) explores the question of collaboration within an IOR framework. The IOR approach, in general, however, does not provide enough guidance on where collaboration may not be likely, and the reasons why this may be so. The resource based approach (Barney, 1991), combined with a RESOURCE DEPENDENCE perspective in the interorganizational relations framework (Pfeffer & Salancik, 1978), provides a basis for predicting collaboration based on the needs to gain access to the kinds of resources that an organization may need to create a basis for sustained competitive advantage (*see* COMPETITIVENESS).

Transaction cost economists argue that when a firm needs resources it has three basic choices: it can acquire them in the market, it can make them itself, or it can transact for them through "mixed" modes (Williamson, 1991). To an extent, all three involve collaboration. In contrast to the IOR approach, institutional economists largely have ignored mixed or hybrid forms of governance (in which a collaborative effort is more likely to be found (*see* GOVERNANCE AND OWNERSHIP). This is one of its obvious shortcomings, as Williamson observes.

The results of recent research seems to indicate that strategic collaboration occurs when one or more of four elements is present. First, access to, or exchange of, **organization specific assets** (e.g., proprietary TECHNOLOGY, human resources) is required by one or both parties to achieve sustained competitive advantage. Second, country specific assets (e.g., raw materials) or the assets of a governmental agency are needed because they can provide sustained competitive advantage. Third, collaborating organizations face a common threat to their assets affecting their collective survival which cannot be efficiently countered by a single organization. Fourth, market-based contracts cannot be employed in transacting for the assets in question. In some cases, access to assets may not be available through arm's length, contract-based market transactions because of home or host country policies. In other instances, the assets simply cannot be sold; that is, they are not private property. The first three conditions imply that strategic collaboration might take place between business firms and other kinds of organizations (e.g., governmental agencies). Thus, strategic collaboration can be defined as an interorganizational relationship not governed by arm's length, contract-based market transactions to create, exchange, or protect assets essential to creating or preserving sustained competitive advantage.

Strategic collaboration will either involve organizations operating within the same resource environment or will occur between organizations operating within different resource environments (*see* ORGANIZATION AND ENVIRONMENT). Collaboration between organizations operating within the same resource environment is commensualistic, while that between organizations from different resource environments is symbiotic (Astley & Fombrun, 1983).

Commensualistic collaboration occurs when organisms place the same kinds of demands on the environment. In business, those demands are reflected in the need for assets. Within a very specific industry group we except that all firms will need the same kinds of assets in order to survive. As a general rule, we should not expect to find collaboration among firms competing for the same or very similar types of assets, because of the risk that one or more of the parties might engage in opportunistic behavior.

Where the legal, regulatory, or normative regime designed to guard against unlawful appropriation of assets is strong, however, we have conditions that favor commensualistic collaboration. First, a strong regime dampens opportunistic behavior by competitors by providing a context in which it is possible to design effective endogenous safeguards. Second, effective institutional guarantors typically are available to the parties in strong regimes. Third, industry norms may be strong enough to discourage opportunism.

Symbiotic collaboration occurs when the organizations involved make demands on their respective environments for different types of assets. A symbiotic collaboration typically will be composed of two or more firms from different industries; however, it also may be composed of firms from within the same industry, but whose primary production activities are located almost exclusively at different points on the industry's value chain. Symbiotic collaboration also may be composed of organizations from different sectors of the economy, i.e., between firms and GOVERNMENT AGENCIES (*see* GOVERNMENT AND BUSINESS).

See also **Strategic management; Strategic alliances; Strategic choice; Joint ventures**

Bibliography

Astley, W. G. & Fombrun, C. J. (1983). Collective strategy: The social ecology of organizational environment. *Academy of Management Review*, **8**, 567–587.

Barney, J. (1991). Firm resources and sustained competitive advantage. *Journal of Management*, **17**, 99–120.

Borys, B. & Jemison, D. (1989). Hybrid arrangements as strategic alliances: Theoretical issues in organizational combinations. *Academy of Management Review*, **14**, 234–249.

Oliver, C. (1990). The determinants of interorganizational relationships: Integration and future directions. *Academy of Management Review*, **16**, 241–265.

Pfeffer, J. & Salancik, G. (1978). *The external control of organizations: A resource perspective*. New York: Harper & Row.

Williamson, O. E. (1991). Comparative economic organization. *Administrative Science Quarterly*, **36**, 269–296.

PETER SMITH RING

collateral organization The first formal definition of collateral organization to appear in the organization's literature was offered by Zand (1974; 1981), who defined it as a parallel, coexisting organization used to supplement the existing formal organization. The utility of this structural adaptation was based on the notion that different types of problems require different "modes" of organization. AUTHORITY/production-centered organizations (e.g., the classic BUREAUCRACY) work best with "well-structured" problems. "Ill-structured" problems (i.e., problems in which key pieces of information are unknown or unknowable) require a more flexible "knowledge or problem-centered" organizational form. Zand argued that a collateral organization has different norms than those operating in the formal organization. For example, using the collateral structure, managers and employees can communicate freely without being restricted to the formal channels of the organizational HIERARCHY leading to a rapid and complete exchange of relevant information on problems and issues. Further, managers can approach and enlist others in the organization to help solve a problem; they are not restricted to their formal subordinates. Zand proposed the collateral organization as a form of ORGANIZATION DEVELOPMENT intervention intended to help managers create flexible, problem-solving organizations (*see* FLEXIBILITY; LEARNING ORGANIZATION).

In their operation: "Collateral organizations are intended to be responsive, flexible, and adept at solving ill-structured problems and to endow the full organization with these attributes." Collateral organizations coexist side by side with the formal organization; they are permanent – or relatively so; they are staffed by members drawn from several or all strata of the formal organization, using no new or "extra-organizational" people. The collateral organization consists of a web of fresh problem-solving linkages, mainly vertical, that slice through the formal structure" (Rubinstein & Woodman, 1984, p. 3 (*see* VERTICAL INTEGRATION)).

Most recently, the term collateral organization is perhaps being supplanted by the label of "parallel learning structures." Bushe and Shani (1991) define the parallel learning structure as a generic label to cover interventions where:

(a) a 'structure' (i.e., a specific division and coordination of labor) is created that;
(b) operates 'parallel' (i.e., in tandem or side-by-side) with the formal hierarchy and structure; and
(c) has the purpose of increasing an organization's learning (i.e., the creation and/or implementation of new thoughts and beha-

viors by employees (1991, p. 9) (*see* ORGANIZATIONAL LEARNING).

There is a genre of OD interventions which proceed by the creation of collateral or parallel organizational structures to aid in problem solving, learning, and change. Somewhat unfortunately, these supplemental structures go by a variety of names. The reader is referred to the work of Bushe and Shani (1990; 1991) for a deeper understanding of these structural interventions.

Most evaluation of the efficacy of collateral organizations has been qualitative in form. Improved PRODUCTIVITY, DECISION-MAKING quality, INNOVATION, employee satisfaction (*see* JOB SATISFACTION), and ORGANIZATIONAL EFFECTIVENESS are among the outcomes reported (e.g., Bushe & Shani, 1990; 1991). However, little systematic empirical work has been done to evaluate the effectiveness of this structural adaptation. Based upon case experience, linkage of the collateral structure with the formal organization would appear to be a key criterion for success.

See also **Organizational boundaries; Organizational design; Subunits**

Bibliography

Bushe, G. R. & Shani, A. B. (1990). Parallel learning structure interventions in bureaucratic organizations. In W. A. Pasmore & R. W. Woodman (Eds), *Research in organizational change and development*, (vol. 4, pp. 167–194). Greenwich, CT: JAI Press.

Bushe, G. R. & Shani, A. B. (1991). *Parallel learning structures: Increasing innovation in bureaucracies.* Reading, MA: Addison-Wesley.

Rubinstein, D. & Woodman, R. W. (1984). Spiderman and the Burma raiders: Collateral organization theory in action. *Journal of Applied Behavioral Science*, **20**, 1–21.

Zand, D. E. (1974). Collateral organization: A new change strategy. *Journal of Applied Behavioral Science*, **10**, 63–89.

Zand, D. E. (1981). *Information, organization, and power: Effective management in the knowledge society*. New York: McGraw-Hill.

RICHARD W. WOODMAN

collective action When there is CONFLICT between workers and managers, collective action is one means of resolving the difference. In comparison with other forms of conflict, collective action reflects more explicit demands or grievances and requires more deliberate organization (Hyman, 1989). The best-known form of such action is the strike, but there are many others including bans on overtime and "sick-ins" (coordinated ABSENTEEISM). Much research sees action as an indicator of workers' protest, but the role of the employer is equally important. In some countries, the lock-out, the employer's equivalent of the strike, is a significant tactic. More generally, employer tactics are crucial in whether a dispute reaches the stage of overt action.

Most research examines strikes, with systematic information on other action being much harder to produce. However, workplace surveys in Britain and Australia suggest that other forms are at least as common as the strike.

Research on strikes (Kaufman, 1992; Shalev, 1992) reveals dramatic differences in patterns between countries (with very long and quite large disputes in North America; large but short strikes in Italy; and very low levels of action in Austria, the Nordic countries, and Japan). This reflects the role of institutions which bring together TRADE UNIONS, employers, and the state to regulate conflict (*see* CONFLICT RESOLUTION). Where such institutions are weak, strikes remain weapons of leverage or protest; they are less necessary where means to coordinate the interests of the parties have developed.

Strikes have also occurred in waves, with peaks of activity in many countries around the First World War and during the 1960s (Edwards, 1992). Rates declined rapidly during the 1980s and 1990s in many countries, notably the United States and Britain, though they also rose in others such as Sweden. Main reasons for the decline are economic conditions (with recession tending to make collective action more difficult to sustain), the shift of employment from manufacturing, a weakening of trade unions, and new managerial initiatives to promote INDIVIDUALISM (*see* HUMAN RESOURCE MANAGEMENT).

Connections between collective action and conflict or morale have to be made with care. There are alternative means of protest such as Absenteeism and TURNOVER. In some cases one form can be substituted for another but there is no straightforward correlation. Japanese firms, for example, are low on both dimensions. Whether or not there is a correlation depends on the wider system of employment relationships.

The effects of collective action can be immediate or broader. On specific effects, the time lost in strikes is much less than that due to absence or ACCIDENTS, and there are few clear-cut effects on PRODUCTIVITY. More broadly, major waves of strikes have symbolized substantial industrial and political change, as in the United States in the 1930s or many European countries in the 1960s. At the level of the enterprise, high levels of action can reflect a "low TRUST syndrome." Concerted action is one means by which employees can use "voice" mechanisms to indicate their concern on an issue and it thus has important implications for the functioning of the enterprise.

See also **Collective bargaining; Intergroup relations; Interest groups; Interorganizational relations**

Bibliography

Edwards, P. K. (1992). Industrial conflict. *British Journal of Industrial Relations*, **30**, 361–404.

Hyman, R. (1989). *Strikes*, (4th edn). London: Fontana.

Kaufman, B. E. (1992). Research on strike models and outcomes in the 1980s. In D. Lewin, O. S. Mitchell and P. D. Sherer (Eds). *Research frontiers in industrial relations and human resources* (pp. 77–130). Madison: Industrial Relations Research Association.

Shalev, M. (1992). The resurgence of labour quiescence. In M. Regini (Ed.), *The future of labour movements* (pp. 102–132). London: Sage.

Wheeler, H. N. (1985). *Industrial conflict*. Columbia: University of South Carolina Press.

PAUL EDWARDS

collective bargaining This is the term applied to those methods of managing the employment relationship which explicitly acknowledge a role for TRADE UNIONS (Clegg, 1960; 1976). In contrast with the approach of, say, autocratic paternalism or worker COOPERATIVES, the employer who engages in collective bargaining accepts the right of independent representatives of employees, acting as a collectivity, to argue their point of view on matters that affect their interests. The most obvious outcome will be a collective agreement, which may be anything from a single, written document to an accumulation of agreed rules and common understandings of varying degrees of informality and precision. Pay, HOURS OF WORK, and WORKING CONDITIONS are the most common subjects, but collective bargaining can deal with any aspect of management (*see* PAYMENT SYSTEMS).

Webb (1897) coined the term in 1891, later contrasting it with individual bargaining, in that the employer, instead of making separate deals with individual workers, ". . . meets with a collective will and settles, in a single agreement, the principles on which, for the time being, all workmen of a particular group, or class, or grade, will be engaged." The most influential modern treatment of the subject has been that of Flanders (1975). He emphasized that collective bargaining is best seen as a political, rather than an economic process. It is joint regulation. The two sides meet in the awareness of their POWER relationship, of their ability to inflict mutual damage, in order to establish for the forseeable future the rules governing work. The collective agreement commits no-one to buy or sell any labor; it only specifies the terms on which such a transaction must be conducted.

The character of collective bargaining owes much to two essential features of the employment relationship. They are its open-endedness and its continuity. It is open-ended because the recruitment of an employee does not ensure the performance of work. The employee has to be motivated, by whatever means, to perform to the required standard. Since proximal SOCIAL COMPARISONS play an important part in the MOTIVATION and demotivation of labor, the standardization of terms of employment, which is a necessary feature of collective agreements, tends to fit well with bureaucratic personnel techniques (*see* BUREAUCRACY). The continuity of the relationship is significant because employer and employees are bound together for an indeterminate duration, with normally intermittent and incremental changes to the workforce. Of the myriad potentially contentious issues in the collective relationship, only a minority will be at issue at any moment, many affecting a minority of the workforce. Any one issue of grievance cannot be dealt with in isolation; it is no more than a single fiber in the rope of regulation maintained through collective bargaining.

The coverage of collective agreements is generally wider than is implied by the extent of trade unionism. Employers often follow the terms of collective agreements even when their workforces are not unionized. But for most industrialized Western countries, after a high tide of both coverage and unionization in the 1960s and 1970s, both have ebbed in the 1980s and 1990s. In Britain, for example, the proportion of all employees covered by collective agreements fell from around three-quarters to under a half over the course of the 1980s. Among the many causes of this worldwide decline are increased international competition, the decline of mass-employment manufacturing, shrinkage of public sector employment, a shift to more individualistic employment practices, and changes in the structure of bargaining.

The most conspicuous feature of the structure of collective bargaining is the organizational level at which the bargaining takes place. This is directly related to the unit of bargaining, that is, the group of employees covered by a particular agreement. The crucial decision that has faced employers over the years has been whether, on the one hand, to bargain with unions alone in what is now called "enterprise bargaining" or, on the other hand, to group together in an industry-wide employers' association and, by confronting labor together through a single, national, or regional industry-wide agreement, to "take wages out of competition."

The European tradition had been one of industry-wide bargaining, whereas in Japan and the United States enterprise bargaining became established earlier. Over the past 20 years establishment bargaining has gained overwhelming importance in Britain and is steadily spreading elsewhere, driven as much as anything by the internationalization of markets. Against the advantages offered by enterprise bargaining for more flexible employment practices has to be balanced the disadvantages of the loss of orderly national training arrangements and of nationwide wage restraint which are generally favored by industry-wide bargaining (*see* FLEXIBILITY). The crumbling of national employer solidarity under the impact of international competition is forcing firms to put more resources into managing their own enterprise-based bargaining.

Bargaining structure has been demonstrated by Clegg (1936) and Crouch (1993) among others to have substantial implications for a country's industrial relations experience and its economic performance (*see* COMPETITIVENESS). The reform of this structure is, however, hard to achieve. Employer strategy is of prime importance but slow to change. The legislative framework, which establishes fundamental conditions such as trade union security, the status of the employment CONTRACT, and limits on the right to strike, is also crucial (*see* COLLECTIVE ACTION). But for most countries the principal labor legislation was enacted at some historic period of crisis – war, defeat, depression, or extreme industrial unrest – and in more serene times the accretion of voluntary institutional structures makes it hard to alter these underlying legal foundations.

Viewed in this longer perspective, collective bargaining can be seen to have a deeper political significance. The victorious Allies ensured that collective bargaining would play a central part in the recovery of Japan and Germany after the Second World War because they saw it as a grass-roots democratic institution that might inhibit the return of militarism. Although it has been under challenge in Britain, the United States, and some other countries recently, there has been a deeply rooted view in most Western countries that collective bargaining offers the best means of achieving a practical form of industrial DEMOCRACY. In the central tradition of pluralism, acknowledging that there can never be identity of interest between employer and employee, collective bargaining offers an orderly means to modify employer actions in the light of employee interests, insofar as their organized power permits. Collective bargaining may never regain the significance it enjoyed in the third quarter of this century, but its roots and its rationale will ensure that its decline is not terminal.

See also **Industrial relations; Intergroup relations; Labor process theory; Negotiation; Trust**

Bibliography

Clegg, H. A. (1960). *A new approach to industrial democracy*. Oxford, UK: Blackwell.

Clegg, H. A. (1976). *Trade unionism under collective bargaining*. Oxford UK: Blackwell.

Crouch, C. (1993). *Industrial relations and European state traditions*. Oxford, UK: Clarendon.

Flanders, A. (1975). *Management and unions*. London: Faber and Faber.

Kochan, T. A. (1980). *Collective bargaining and industrial relations*. Homewood, IL: Irwin.

Webb, S. & B. (1897). *Industrial democracy*. London: Longmans Green.

WILLIAM BROWN

commensalism *see* COMMUNITY ECOLOGY

commitment This is concerned with the level of attachment and loyalty to an organization amoung its employees. Organizations increasingly compete to attract and retain the most able staff and those committed to the organization might be expected to have longer tenure. Demands to compete through high quality require a workforce willing to display the MOTIVATION, flexibility, and belief in product or service that produces high performance, and commitment should help to ensure this. Indeed, Walton (1985) has contrasted a traditional relationship between employer and employee based on control with one based on commitment, arguing that all organizations need to pursue a high commitment approach if they are to survive. This has been one of the factors behind advocacy of HUMAN RESOURCE MANAGEMENT.

Despite its intuitive appeal, commitment is a complex phenomenon. Interest has focused on four main issues. These are: the focus or target of commitment; the definition and measurement of commitment; the causes of variations in levels of commitment; and the consequences of commitment. The picture is made more complex by the presence of two rather different strands of scholarship, one concerned with commitment as an attitude, the other with commitment as behavior.

Attitudinal or Organizational Commitment

Interest in commitment as an attitude has been mainly concerned with commitment to an organization. It is equally plausible to consider commitment to a job, a work team, a profession, to one's family, or to a range of other foci. Indeed, the possibility of multiple and potentially competing commitments has led to a strand of research on dual commitment (*see* COMMITMENT, DUAL).

In their influential work on organizational commitment, Mowday, Porter, and Steers (1982) define it as "the relative strength of an individual's identification with and involvement in an organization." They elaborate this to incorporate: belief in the VALUES and goals of the organization, willingness to exert effort on behalf of the organization, and desire to be a member of the organization. They have developed a widely used scale, the Organizational Commitment Questionnaire (OCQ) to measure these elements. Both the definition and the measure have been criticized for conflating commitment with outcomes such as effort and propensity to stay.

Meyer and Allen (1991) have proposed alternative definitions and measures, distinguishing affective and continuance commitment. Affective commitment emphasizes identification with the organization and is predicted to impact on job performance. Continuance commitment borrows from the work of Becker (1960) and others who have given emphasis to the exchange component inherent in the concept of commitment. Individuals will wish to stay with an organization as long as they gain a positive exchange. This exchange may be financial but over time "side bets" such as pensions, career prospects, and friendship develop. For both financial and nonfinancial reasons, staff cannot then "afford" to leave. Continuance commitment therefore predicts tenure. There is some support for the distinction between continuance and affective commitment, and this approach holds out promise for the future.

Much research has sought to identify antecedents of organizational commitment (Mathieu & Zajac, 1990). The evidence is inconsistent but supports the importance for high commitment of providing jobs with some AUTONOMY and scope for self-expression and policies which ensure fairness of treatment and, particularly for newcomers to the organization, confirmation of expectations about working in the organization.

The general theory of organizational commitment predicts that high commitment should result in greater motivation and performance, lower ABSENTEEISM and lower labor TURNOVER. Despite the more specific predictions of Meyer and Allen and evidence from at least one study linking organizational commitment and PERFORMANCE (Meyer, Paunonen, Gellatly, Goffin, & Jackson, 1989), most research shows that organizational commitment has little impact on performance or on absenteeism but does have some ability to predict labor turnover. In general, the impact of organizational commitment on a range of outcomes has been less than theory would predict (*see* PERFORMANCE, INDIVIDUAL).

Behavioral Commitment

The second main strand of research is concerned with the process whereby individuals become bound or committed to their actions. Drawing on cognitive dissonance theory, Salancik (1977) proposed that the propensity to act will be greater when an individual volunteers to act, when the action to be taken is explicit, when it is done in the presence of other people, and when the decision is hard to revoke. This approach underpins organizations such as Weightwatchers and Alcoholics Anonymous but can equally well be applied to decisions to join an organization or to decisions taken in WORK GROUPS and committees. A commitment to act is expected to increase the probability of subsequent action and of attitudes moving in line with behavior. This approach has been successful in predicting tenure based on analysis of the circumstances surrounding the process of CAREER CHOICE (Kline & Peters, 1991). Indeed, insofar as comparisons are possible, behavioral commitment appears to have more impact on performance than organizational commitment.

After two decades of research on organizational commitment, evidence about the causes remains blurred and evidence on the effects of organizational commitment remains disappointing. One reason for the initial interest of some researchers was disillusion at the failure of JOB SATISFACTION to predict behavior. Yet in many studies where the two have been compared, commitment has fared no better than job satisfaction as a predictor of performance and tenure. It appears that the concept may need further unbundling to build on the work of Meyer and Allen in separating out the various components and to clarify the focus of commitment. More attention also needs to be paid to the dynamics of commitment and the processes through which levels of organizational commitment can be changed among long-tenure workers. Ethical questions associated with commitment should not be ignored; the "exchange" may become very one-sided and the temptation to enhance quit rates through policies to reduce commitment may appeal to some managers irrespective of its impact on worker well being. Finally, current trends in employment, including the decline in job security (*see* JOB INSECURITY) and rapid RESTRUCTURING and delayering of organizations presents a growing challenge to the viability of organizational commitment, increasing the possibility of a shift in the focus of individual commitment to their profession, their work-group, or even to themselves.

See also **Joining-up process; Psychological contract; Employee involvement; Professionals in organizations**

Bibliography

Becker, H. (1960). Notes on the concept of commitment. *American Journal of Sociology*, **66**, 32–42.

Kline, C. J. & Peters, L. H. (1991). Behavioral commitment and tenure of new employees: A replication and extension. *Academy of Management Journal*, **34**, (1), 194–204.

Mathieu, J. & Zajac, D. (1990). A review and meta-analysis of the antecedents, correlates, and consequences of organizational commitment. *Psychological Bulletin*, **108**, (2), 171–194.

Meyer, J. & Allen, N. (1991). A three-component conceptualization of organizational commitment. *Human Resource Management Review*, **1**, 61–89.

Meyer, J., Allen, N. & Gellatly, I. (1990). Affective and continuance commitment to the organization: Analysis of measures and analysis of concurrent and time-lagged relations. *Journal of Applied Psychology*, **75**, 710–720.

Meyer, J., Paunonen, S., Gellatly, I., Goffin, R. & Jackson, D. (1989). Organizational commitment and job performance: It's the nature of the commitment that counts. *Journal of Applied Psychology*, **74**, 152–156.

Mowday, R., Porter, L. & Steers, R. (1982). *Employee–organizational linkages*. New York: Academic Press.

Salancik, G. (1977). Commitment and the control of organizational behavior and belief. In B. M. Staw & G. R. Salancik (Eds), *New directions in organizational behavior*. Chicago: St Clair Press.

Walton, R. (1985). From control to commitment in the workplace. *Harvard Business Review*, 63, 76–84.

DAVID GUEST

commitment, dual Can a worker be committed to both company and trade union? A traditional INDUSTRIAL RELATIONS perspective would argue that the different interests and values of employers and workers makes dual COMMITMENT difficult. Consequently, unions have been suspicious of the rise of human resource policies (*see* HUMAN RESOURCES MANAGEMENT) designed to generate organizational commitment at a time when union membership is declining.

One of the key questions is whether the causes of union and company commitment are the same. If they are different, then it should be possible to manipulate the causal variables independently and therefore be high or low on both. If the causes are the same, but at opposite ends of a dimension such as, for example, perception of fair treatment by the company, then dual commitment is impossible. The balance of the research to date suggests that the causes are largely different and therefore dual commitment is possible. Angle and Perry (1986) have highlighted the importance for dual commitment of a positive industrial relations climate (*see* ORGANIZATIONAL CLIMATE). This is reinforced by evidence suggesting that dual commitment is higher in countries such as Germany and Sweden where institutional arrangements foster a positive industrial relations climate.

Although dual commitment has been mainly concerned with commitment to company and union, there is growing interest in the possibility of multiple and potentially competing foci of commitment both inside and outside the company, making dual or multiple commitment a challenging research and policy issue.

See also **Identification; Socialization; Trade unions**

Bibliography

Angle, H. J. & Perry, J. L. (1986). Dual commitment labor–management relationship climates. *Academy of Management Journal*, **29**, 31–50.

DAVID GUEST

commitment, escalating *Escalation* is the degree to which an individual commits to a previously selected course of action beyond a level that a rational model of DECISION MAKING would prescribe. Research suggests that decision makers committed to a particular course of action have a tendency to make subsequent decisions which continue that COMMITMENT beyond the level that RATIONALITY would suggest is reasonable. In Staw's initial (1976) study of escalation, one group of subjects (labeled the high responsibility subjects) was asked to allocate research and development funds to one of two operating divisions of an organization. The subjects were then told that after 3 years the investment had either proved successful or unsuccessful, and that they were now faced with a second allocation decision concerning the same division. A second group (labeled the low responsibility subjects) was told that another financial officer of the firm had made a decision that had been either successful or unsuccessful (both groups were provided the same information regarding success or failure) and that they were to make a second allocation of funds concerning that division. When the outcome of the previous decision was negative (an unsuccessful investment), the high responsibility subjects allocated significantly more funds to the original division in the second allocation than did the low responsibility subjects. In contrast, for successful initial decisions, the amount of money allocated in the second decision was roughly the same across subjects.

There are multiple reasons why escalation occurs (Bazerman, 1994). First, the individual's PERCEPTION may be biased by his/her previous decision (*see* BIAS). That is, the decision maker may notice information that supports his/her decision, while ignoring information that contradicts the initial decision. Second, the decision maker's biased judgments may cause him/her to perceive information in a way that justifies the existing position. Third, negotiators often make subsequent decisions which justify earlier decisions to themselves and others. Finally, competitiveness adds to the likelihood of escalation; unilaterally giving up or even reducing demands may be viewed as a defeat, while escalating commitment leaves the future uncertain.

See also **Behavioral decision research; Risk taking; Game theory; Decision making; Negotiation; Persistence**

Bibliography

Bazerman, M. H. (1994). *Judgment in managerial decision making* (3rd edn). New York: Wiley.

Staw, B. M. (1976). Knee-deep in the big muddy: A study of escalating commitment to a chosen course of action. *Organizational Behavior and Human Performance*, **16**, 27–44.

MAX H. BAZERMAN

communication Through communication, organizations and their members exchange information, form understandings, coordinate activities, exercise influence, socialize, and generate and maintain systems of beliefs, symbols, and VALUES (*see* SYMBOLISM). Communication has been called the "'nervous system' of any organized group" and the "glue" which holds organizations together.

Claude Shannon's classic mathematical theory of communication defined seven basic elements of communication (Ritchie, 1991): a *source* which encodes a *message* and *transmits* it through some *channel* to a *receiver*, which decodes the message and may give the sender some FEEDBACK. The sender and receiver may be individuals, machines, or collectives such as organizations or teams. The channel is subject to a degree of *noise* which may interfere with or distort the transmission of the message. Other distortions may come during encoding or decoding, if errors are introduced or if the source and receiver have different codes. The process of communication occurs through a series of transmissions among parties, so Shannon's single message is only the basic building block of larger interchanges among a system of two to N entities. This system may be represented as a *communication network* in which communicators are nodes and the various types of communication relationships links (*see* NETWORK ANALYSIS). Distortion may also be introduced as the message passes through multiple links, with small changes at each node. Communication is dependent on its *context*; many scholars argue that the interpretation of messages is only possible because the receiver has contextual cues to supplement message cues.

Due to the complexity of the organizational communication process and the many levels at which communication occurs, there is no generally agreed theory of organizational communication. Different positions have been advanced on several issues.

A major controversy concerns *what is communicated, i.e., the substance of communication.* One position assumes that messages transmit *information*, defined as anything which reduces the receiver's uncertainty (Ritchie, 1991). This stance, first advanced in Shannon's theory, portrays communication as something amenable to precise analysis. The amount of information in a given message can, in theory, be measured, and messages compared on metrics of uncertainty reduction. This view has been adopted metaphorically by a wide range of analysts who view organizations as INFORMATION PROCESSING systems or focus on uncertainty reduction. The information perspective has been criticized for reducing ideas, feelings, and symbols to a set of discrete bits pumped through a conduit from sender to receiver (Axley, 1984). An alternative position is that the essence of communication is *meaning*, encompassing ideas, EMOTIONS, VALUES, and SKILLS which are conveyed via symbolization and demonstration. Meaning cannot be reduced to information, because it depends on associations among symbols grounded in the surrounding CULTURE and the communicators' experience. The meaning of a message or interaction is grasped through a process of interpretation which requires communicators to read individual signs in light of the whole message and its context, but simultaneously understand the whole by what its constituent signs signify. This *hermeneutic circle* implies that meaning can never be established finally or unequivocally. Interpretation is a continuing process, always subject to revision or qualification. The information-centered and meaning-centered conceptions of communication represent two quite different approaches, the former being favored by empirical social scientists and the latter by ORGANIZATIONAL culture and critical researchers (*see* CRITICAL THEORY).

There are also at least two positions on *the role of communication in organizations*. One regards communication as a *subprocess* which plays an important role in other organizational processes. For example, communication serves as a channel for the exercise of LEADERSHIP or for the maintenance of interorganizational linkages (*see* INTERORGANIZATIONAL RELATIONS). The other position argues that communication is the process which *constitutes* the organization and its activities. Rather than being subsidiary to key phenomena such as leadership, communication is regarded as the medium through which these phenomena and, more generally, organizations are created and maintained. This viewpoint is reflected in a wide range of organizational research, including Herbert Simon's *Administrative Behavior*, analyses of leadership as a language game, and most studies of organizational culture. The two positions have quite different implications for practice. For example, in the case of leadership communication the subprocess view implies that a leader should make sure that leadership functions are conveyed effectively, while the constitutive view implies that the leader should try to use communication to create and maintain leader–follower relationships and to generate a shared vision.

Another way of describing the role of communication is to delineate the functions it plays for organizations and their members. While the list is potentially endless, at least seven critical functions can be distinguished. Communication serves a *command and CONTROL* function in that it is the medium by which directives are given, problems identified, MOTIVATION encouraged, and performance monitored (*see* UPWARD COMMUNICATION). The Weberian BUREAUCRACY emphasizes this function of communication, and the first wave of formal information systems for accounting attempted to automate it, with mixed results. The *linking* function of communication promotes a flow of information between different parts of the organization, enabling the organization to achieve a degree of coherency among disparate units and personnel (*see* BOUNDARY SPANNING). The linking function plays a key role in INNOVATION and in the diffusion of innovations within organizations (*see* INNOVATION DIFFUSION). Important to linking are upward and lateral communication flows. A third function of communication is *enculturation*, which refers to the creation and maintenance of organizational cultures and to the assimilation of members into the organization. Rituals, myths, METAPHORS, MISSION STATEMENTS, and other symbolic genres contribute to this function (*see* RITES AND RITUALS).

In addition to the three intraorganizational functions, communication also serves two additional interorganizational functions. The fourth function is *interorganizational linking*, which serves to create and maintain interorganizational fields. This linking function is accomplished via BOUNDARY SPANNING personnel and units and through shared information systems used to monitor interorganizational ventures. The fifth is *organizational presentation*, which defines the organization to key audiences, such as potential customers, other organizations, the state, and the public at large. This function contributes to the maintenance of an organization's institutional legitimacy. It is carried out through such diverse activities as public information campaigns, corporate advocacy advertisement, and maintenance of proper records and certifications.

Two functions of communication apply to both intra- and interorganizational situations. The *ideational* function of communication refers to its role in the generation and use of ideas and knowledge in the organization (*see* GATEKEEPERS; IDEOLOGY). Simon's description of decision premises and their circulation through the organization is one example of the ideational function. This function is critical to the processes of social reasoning and ORGANIZATIONAL LEARNING which contribute to ORGANIZATIONAL EFFECTIVENESS. There is also an *ideological* function of communication: it is the vehicle for the development and promulgation of ideologies, systems of thought which normalize and justify relations of POWER and CONTROL. Postmodern analysis of organizations asserts that the reigning discourse in organizations defines what is correct and incorrect and who is able to decide matters of truth and falsehood (*see* POSTMODERNISM). This arbitrary allocation of power leaves some groups with unquestioned control and omits others from consideration. Such processes are hard to uncover and change, because they occur in the course of normal, everyday communication and thus seem natural and nonproblematic.

Organizations have two distinct communication systems, formal and informal. The *formal communication system* is a part of the organizational structure and includes supervisory relationships, WORK GROUPS, permanent and ad hoc committees, and management information systems. In traditional organizations the major design concern was vertical communication, focusing on command and control; more contemporary forms such as matrix or networked organizations also focus on formal lateral communication (*see* MATRIX ORGANIZATION). Formal channels, especially vertical ones, are subject to a number of communication problems. These include unintentional distortion and omission of information as it is passed up the HIERARCHY, delays in message routing, and intentional distortions by subordinates attempting to manipulate superiors or protect themselves.

The *informal communication system* emerges from day-to-day interaction among organizational members. Ties in the informal network are based on proximity, friendship, common interests, and political benefits more than on formal job duties (*see* POLITICS). The informal system includes the "grapevine" and the "rumor mill." The informal communication network is usually more complex and less organized than the formal network. Messages pass through the informal network more rapidly, and members often regard them as more accurate and trustworthy than those from the formal system. An organization's informal communication system is important for several reasons. First, it often compensates for problems in formal communication. Members can use informal channels to respond to CRISES and exceptional cases rapidly. They can use informal contacts to make sense of uncertain, ambiguous, or threatening situations. Second, use of informal networks may improve organizational decision making, because it allows members to talk "off the record" and "think aloud," hence avoiding the negative consequences of taking a public position. This is especially valuable when problems are ill defined or solutions unclear. Third, informal networks foster innovation, because they are more open and rapid, and because they often connect people from different departments or professions.

The nature of *communication channels* exerts an important influence on its functions and effectiveness. The archetypal communication situations occur in face-to-face interactions or in public speeches to large audiences. However, communication occurs through many other MEDIA, including written formats, telephone, fax, electronic mail, teleconferencing, computer conferencing, and broadcast technologies. INFORMATION TECHNOLOGIES such as electronic mail and computer networks vastly increase the connections among members and may stimulate a greater flow of ideas and innovations and change power relations. Studies have shown that the nature of the medium used affects the communication process; for example, NEGOTIATION generally is more effective through face-to-face and (to a lesser extent) audio media than through video or written media. In order to guide communicator's media choices, researchers have attempted to rank order these media in terms of their *social presence*, the degree to which they convey a sense of direct personal contact with another, and in terms of *media richness*, the degree to which a medium allows immediate feedback, multiple channels, variety of language, and personal cues. Generally, face-to-face communication is classified as the richest and highest social presence medium, followed by meetings, videoconferencing, telephone and teleconferencing, e-mail, written memos, and, finally, numerical information. Achieving the correct match between media richness and the communication situation is an important determinant of effectiveness. Variables governing media choice include a degree of equivocality and uncertainty in the situation (the more uncertain, the richer the medium needed), sender and receiver characteristics, and organizational norms (*see* GROUP NORMS). Also important in media choice is what the medium symbolizes; a personal meeting might signal the importance the convener attaches to an issue, whereas an electronic mail message might suggest the same issue is less critical. While social presence, richness, and symbolism are important to consider, studies have shown variations in the ranking of media on these dimensions; so, media choice is also dependent on the nature of the organization.

Numerous prescriptions and recommendations have been offered to improve organizational communication. Perhaps the most common is that the organization's communication system should be as open as possible. However, more communication is not necessarily better communication. At the personal level open communication can be threatening and exhausting to those who have to deal with difficult issues and personal problems they might otherwise avoid. At the organizational level open communication can result in communication overload and in CONFLICT. Another common prescription emphasizes the importance of clarity and uncertainty reduction, but this too may be somewhat overrated. Eisenberg (1984) discusses the value of purposefully ambiguous communication. Its uses include the downplaying of differences in order to build consensus and masking negative consequences of ORGANIZATIONAL CHANGE in order to promote acceptance of innovations. A final common admonition is to promote rational argumentation and discussion. While this certainly is good currency, overemphasis can blind us to the creative potential of inconsistency and logical jumps and to the importance of the emotions (*see* CREATIVITY). Like many things that seem simple and straightforward, communication conceals considerable complexity.

See also **Communications technology; Integration**

Bibliography

Axley, S. (1984). Managerial and organizational communication in terms of the conduit metaphor. *Academy of Management Review*, **9**, 428–437.

Conrad, C. (1990). *Strategic organizational communication* (2nd edn). Fort Worth, TX: Holt, Rinehart, & Winston.

Eisenberg, E. M. (1984). Ambiguity as strategy in organizational communication. *Communication Monographs*, **51**, 227–242.

Jablin, F. M., Putnam, L. L., Roberts, K. H. & Porter, L. W. (1987). *Handbook of organizational communication*. Newbury Park, CA: Sage.

Ritchie, L. D. (1991). *Information*. Newbury Park, CA: Sage.

Sitkin, S. B., Sutcliffe, J. M. & Barrios-Choplin, J. R. (1992). A dual-capacity model of communication media choice in organizations. *Human Communication Research*, **18**, 563–598.

Weick, K. (1979). *The social psychology of organizing*. Reading, MA: Addison-Wesley.

MARSHALL SCOTT POOLE

communications technology COMMUNICATION is the glue that binds organizations. As a result, there has been great incentive to develop and apply technologies that might enhance and speed communication. Communication technology refers to the hardware, software, organizational structures, and social procedures by which individuals collect, process, and exchange information with other individuals (Rogers, 1986).

While it is natural to think of it in terms of modern electronic communication systems, communication technology has a long and complex history (Yates, 1989). The oldest communication technology, writing, fostered ancient empires and commerce. Later, the printing press laid the groundwork for literacy and education which made Weber's BUREAUCRACY possible. In the late nineteenth and early twentieth centuries, techniques for systematic storage and retrieval of documents, such as vertical filing systems, greatly enhanced the ability of businesses to marshall information, while the evolution of communication genres such as the memo and the business letter changed the way in which internal and external communication was handled.

The first electronic technologies, the telegraph and the telephone, had profound effects on organizations, allowing them to spread over much greater distances and work more rapidly. Originally intended primarily as a business tool, the telephone also transformed interpersonal communication in general, changing both work and social relationships in organizations.

Videoconferencing came next, but it remained largely unsuccessful until the late 1980s, when the technology finally matured. The most recent wave of communication technologies involve computer-supported communication (*see* INFORMATION TECHNOLOGY). The earliest entries – electronic mail and computer conferencing – have already changed the nature of organizational communication. More recent developments – WORKGROUP support, multimedia systems, virtual reality – promise even more profound changes (Grant & Wilkinson, 1993). Communication technologies are becoming so important to modern organizations that some theorists have ventured that they are the limiting factor on ORGANIZATIONAL DESIGN and growth.

This brief overview hints at the complex nature of communication technologies. Their most obvious aspect is the ever-expanding array of hardware. However, reflection indicates that the hardware operates within a broader context of social norms which define adequate communication, organizational structures which influence the application of the hardware and motivate members to use it, and the larger societal and international systems within which technologies develop and standards for their design are set. This context is as essential to the communication technology as the hardware.

Media choice theories have attempted to define dimensions that help organizational members select among the wide variety of communication modes available to them. Communication technologies can be characterized in terms of their *social presence*, the degree to which they convey a sense of direct personal contact with another, and in terms of *media richness*, the degree to which a medium allows immediate FEEDBACK, multiple channels, variety of language, and personal cues (see entry on COMMUNICATION for a more complete discussion). A related dimension is *interactivity*, which describes the degree to which a communication technology supports active PARTICIPATION in interchanges and interaction among users.

The expanding array of new communication technologies have had major impacts on organizations, and these should increase in the future. These technologies have greatly influenced organizational design. The capacity of electronic mail, teleconferencing, videoconferencing, and fax to enable coordination and collaboration at a distance permits organizations to adopt more dispersed forms. For example, Hewlett–Packard product development teams are often spread around the world at several facilities and do much of their work via electronic media. Various new organizational forms, such as the dynamic network and federated organizational structure (*see* DECENTRALIZATION), rely on new communication technologies to hold them together and to give them the ability to restructure rapidly (Sproull & Keisler, 1941). Combined with accounting and other information technologies, communication technologies greatly enhance the ability to coordinate and control a wide variety of contracting and JOINT VENTURE relationships among individual firms. This has promoted the increasing use of "modular" organizations composed of temporary aggregations of firms and contractors which pursue a limited term project. Communication and information technologies also permit telecommuting and outsourcing of work to the home, both of which promise to alter the nature of work fundamentally.

New communication technologies also affect organizational behavior. If members are permitted to use technologies such as electronic mail with few restrictions, the result is often an "opening up" of the organization. Ideas flow more freely and INNOVATION increases. Boundaries between different levels or parts of the organization become more permeable, and lower level members feel freer to engage in UPWARD COMMUNICATION. The downside of this is that those at the top of the organization are often overloaded.

Communication technologies such as group-decision support systems and computer conferencing alter DECISION-MAKING, meeting, and NEGOTIATION processes. Their effects include:

(1) the possibility of enhanced member participation in meetings;
(2) more thorough consideration of options, alternatives, and ideas;
(3) greater surfacing of differences and CONFLICT;
(4) greater difficulty in achieving CONSENSUS if the systems do not have features which support CONFLICT RESOLUTION, but greater ability to resolve conflict if the systems do have CONFLICT MANAGEMENT features; and
(5) more organized meetings and negotiation processes.

Accompanying these group level impacts are several on the individual level. Initially users tend to report lower satisfaction with these technologies than with more traditional group methods, though this difference fades with continued use. Computer-mediated communication technologies also seem to alter the individual's attentional focus, centering it more on the self and less on others. However, the widely discussed phenomenon of "flaming," the use of exteme, abusive, and negative language in computer-mediated communication, is not as widespread as was originally presumed; generally, organizations and user communities develop norms which control or prohibit it (*see* GROUP NORMS).

With the exception of the telephone, new communication technologies are not yet fully integrated into society. From the onset, unmediated, face-to-face communication has been taken as the standard which should be emulated and achieved by communication technologies. However, as was true for the telephone, over time, new norms develop and the ideal standard of effective communication changes. Novel communication technologies promise to change the nature of communication and of organizations in the coming years.

See also **Human–computer interaction; Information processing; Integration**

Bibliography

Grant, A. E. & Wilkinson, K. T. (1993). *Communication technology update: 1993–94*. Austin, TX: Technology Futures.

Rogers, E. M. (1986). *Communication technology: The new media in society*. New York: Free Press.

Sproull, L. & Keisler, S. (1991). *Connections: New ways of working in the networked organization*. Cambridge, MA: MIT Press.

Yates, J. (1989). *Control through communication: The rise of system in American management*. Baltimore, MD: Johns Hopkins University Press.

MARSHALL SCOTT POOLE

community ecology An organizational community is a collection of interacting organizational populations. The community ecology of organizations investigates the evolution of community structure in terms of patterns of community succession – the process by which new organizational forms emerge and replace old ones. Community ecology considers how interactions among organizational populations affect the likelihood of survival of the community as a whole.

In ecological theories, organizations are thought to be interdependent when they affect each other's life chances. The interdependence between and among organizational populations may be neutral (growth in one population has no effect on growth in the other), competitive (the presence of one population suppresses the other's growth), or mutualistic (growth in one population stimulates growth in the other). Interdependence among organizational populations is conceptualized in terms of niche overlap, defined as a pattern of jointly occupied positions in a resource space (*see* RESOURCE BASED THEORY).

The impact of American TRADE UNIONS on the vital dynamics of American trade associations provides an illustration of neutral interdependence between organizational populations. Aldrich, Staber, Zimmer, and Beggs (1994) show that trade unions' density had no effect on the founding and disbanding of trade associations during the twentieth century.

In their study of organizational mortality in the populations of American national craft and industrial labor unions from 1836 to 1985, Hannan and Freeman (1988) found evidence of asymmetric patterns of interpopulation competition. While density of craft unions had a significantly positive effect on the disbanding rate of industrial unions, no consistent effect of industrial union density was found on the disbanding rates of craft unions. Apparently, craft unionism suppressed industrial unionism, but the reverse was not so.

In his classic statement of the principles of human ecology, Hawley (1950) distinguished two different bases for mutualism: commensalism – or positive interdependence based on supplementary similarities – and symbiosis – or positive interdependence based on complementary differences. Commensalism and symbiosis are important ecological relations because they give unitary character to organizational communities.

In contemporary organizational ecology research, commensalism between two populations is defined as a situation where one population benefits from the presence of the other without affecting it directly (Brittain &

Wholey, 1988). Examples of commensalism are the presence of small photocopy shops in the vicinity of a college campus, and of street orchestras performing for people in line at the ticket counter of concert halls.

Symbiosis can be defined as a situation where each organizational population benefits from the presence of the other. Examples of symbiosis include institutes of management and executive development located within hotels, and liquor stores located in the proximity of unlicensed restaurants.

Mutualistic and competitive interdependence may be direct – i.e., it may occur between pairs of organizations each identifiable to the other – or diffuse – i.e., it may occur among many anonymous competitors. For example, Barnett and Carroll (1987) found evidence of diffuse competition among early telephone companies in Southeast Iowa. Barnett and Carroll also found that mutual telephone companies – companies owned by their subscribers and located in dispersed rural areas – were commensal with neighbouring companies and decreased their death rate. Evidence of symmetric symbiosis was found between mutual and commercial forms of telephone companies, with each organizational form increasing the other's probability of offering long-distance service.

See also **Population ecology; Organization theory; Strategic management; Organizational change**

Bibliography

Aldrich, H., Staber, U., Zimmer, C. & Beggs, J. (1994). Minimalism, mutualism, and maturity: The evolution of The American trade associations population in the 20th century. In J. Baum & J. Singh (Eds), *Evolutionary dynamics of organizations* (pp. 223–239). New York: Oxford University Press.

Barnett, W. & Carroll, G. (1987). Competition and mutualism among early telephone companies. *Administrative Science Quarterly*, **32**, 400–421.

Brittain, J. & Wholey, D. (1988). Competition and coexistence in organizational communities: Population dynamics in electronic components manufacturing. In G. Carroll (ed.), *Ecological models of organizations* (pp. 195–222). Cambridge, MA: Ballinger.

Hannan, M. & Freeman, J. (1988). The ecology of organizational mortality: National labor unions, 1836–1985. *American Journal of Sociology*, **94**, 25–52.

Hawley, A. (1950). *Human ecology: A theory of community structure*. New York: Ronald Press.

ALESSANDRO LOMI

compensation *see* PAYMENT SYSTEMS; REWARDS

competencies The word "competency" has been given various meanings by different researchers and practitioners. In general, it is used to denote the qualities needed by a job holder, as in Boyatzis' (1982) definition: "A job competency is an underlying characteristic of a person which results in effective and/or superior performance in a job." The different competency approaches usually begin by identifying the attributes of individuals who occupy a given type of ROLE – such as managerial or clerical jobs. Hence, jobs are classified into different types, and possibly subtypes, and the individual attributes applicable to each are then identified. For some practitioners, such as Boyatzis (1982), a wide range of attributes – including motives, traits, aptitudes, and behaviors – are identified by job competency analysis (*see* JOB ANALYSIS). For others, and this is the direction taken by the most recent research, attention is focused on the behaviors enacted by job holders. In addition, as Boyatzis' definition suggests, a very important distinction is drawn between "relevant" behavior and "performance-related" behavior. Relevant behavior is used by job holders. Performance-related behavior is both used by job holders and is associated with superior job performance. For example, in his work on the competence of managers, Boyatzis (1982) found "Concern with Close Relationships" (the behavior of spending time talking with subordinates and coworkers when there is no particular task requirement) to be behavior used by managers but not associated with superior performance. Concern with Close Relationships can be regarded, therefore, as *relevant* behavior. In contrast, Boyatzis found "Conceptualization" (the behavior of developing a concept to recognize a pattern or structure in a set of information) to be both used by managers and to be associated with superior performance. Hence, Conceptualization is performance-

Table 1 Definitions of the Eleven High Performance Managerial Competencies.

HPMC	BEHAVIORAL DEFINITION
Information search	Gathers many different kinds of information and uses a wide variety of sources to build a rich informational environment in preparation for decision making in the organization.
Concept formation	Builds frameworks or models or forms concepts, hypotheses or ideas on the basis of information; becomes aware of patterns, trends, and cause/effect relations by linking disparate information.
Conceptual flexibility	Identifies feasible alternatives or multiple options in planning and decision making; holds different options in focus simultaneously and evaluates their pros and cons.
Interpersonal search	Uses open and probing questions, summaries, paraphrasing, etc., to understand the ideas, concepts, and feelings of another; can comprehend events, issues, problems, opportunities from the viewpoint of others.
Managing intervention	Involves others and is able to build cooperative teams in which group members feel valued and empowered and have shared goals.
Developmental orientation	Creates a positive climate in which staff increase the accuracy of their awareness of their own strengths and limitations; provide coaching, training, and developmental resources to improve performance.
Impact	Uses a variety of methods (e.g., persuasive arguments, modeling behavior, inventing symbols, forming alliances, and appealing to the interest of others) to gain support for ideas and strategies and values.
Self-confidence	States own "stand" or position on issues; unhesitatingly takes decisions when required and commits self and others accordingly; expresses confidence in the future success of the actions to be taken.
Presentation	Presents ideas clearly, with ease and interest so that the other person (or audience) understands what is being communicated; uses technical, symbolic, nonverbal, and visual aids effectively.
Proactive orientation	Structures the task for the team; implements plans and ideas; takes responsibility for all aspects of the situation even beyond ordinary boundaries – and for the success and failure of the group.
Achievement orientation	Possesses high internal work standards and sets ambitious, risky, and yet attainable goals; wants to do things better, to improve, to be more effective and efficient; measures progress against targets.

related behavior. Usually, relevant behaviors are called "Threshold" or "Basic" Competencies, whilst performance-related behaviors are called "Competencies" or "High Performance Competencies".

A significant trend is for increasing attention to be given to the identification, validation (*see* VALIDITY), and development of behavioral High Performance Competencies (HPC). An example is the work of Schroder (1989) and Cockerill (1989), identifying and validating eleven High Performance Managerial Competencies or "HPMC" – see Table 1. A major reason for the interest in HPC is the contribution it can make to raising organizational performance to very high levels – a matter of increasing concern as the environment of organizations becomes increasingly dynamic, complex, and competitive on a global scale (*see* COMPETITIVENESS). These environmental conditions have led organizations to become very dissatisfied with traditional approaches to the development of people which are usually unable to demonstrate empirically their efficacy in raising organizational performance (*see* ORGANIZATIONAL EFFECTIVENESS). As McClelland (1973) has observed, the growth of the (HPC) approach in response to an increasing demand for organizational improvement has resulted in a fundamental shift in methodology. Traditionally, the first step in research is to identify and measure INDIVIDUAL DIFFERENCES. Then researchers strive to find out whether these characteristics are able to explain any variations in job performance. The results of these endeavors have been very disappointing in general, as Schmitt, Gooding, Noe, and Kirsch (1984) demonstrate. As Klemp (1978) explains, job competency analysis works in reverse. First, measures of job performance are established. Next, two samples of job holders are drawn – one whose performance is outstanding, the other whose performance is adequate. Lastly, the attributes (i.e., High Performance Competencies) which distinguish outstanding from adequate job performers are identified and validated. An example of this approach being applied to the job of school principal can be found in the Florida Council for Education Management study of Huff, Lake, and Schaalman (1982).

The attributes identified by job competency analysis are classified to form discrete dimensions which can be measured reliably (*see* RELIABILITY). Until recently, the very notion of competencies existing as relatively durable dimensions of behavior has had very little empirical support – see Robertson, Gratton, and Sharpley (1987) and Sackett and Dreher (1982). However, the factor analytic study of Cockerill, Schroder, and Hunt (1993) into the structure of the eleven HPMC dimensions and the confirmatory factor analysis of these data by Chorvat (1994) using the LISREL procedure show that the HPMCs are relatively stable dimensions of behavior. In the 1993 study, experienced managers performed general management roles in a simulated business organization and their behavior in a variety of settings was assessed by highly trained and experienced observers using the framework provided by the HPMC definitions and rating scales. In this study, considerable attention was placed on:

(a) the design of the competency definitions and rating scales;
(b) the design of the simulated business organization; and
(c) high levels of inter-rater reliability.

The study provides the first empirical support for the notion of competency and highlights the importance of both methodological clarity and rigor. It points to the need for a change in the way competency analysis and development is applied in practice.

Competencies are often clustered together by means of statistical analysis to form more general groups of attributes. For instance, when factor analysis is applied to the eleven HPMC, four groupings emerge – these are the *Cognitive* (Information Search, Concept Formation, and Conceptual Flexibility), the *Motivating* (Interpersonal Search, Managing Interaction, and Developmental Orientation), the *Directional* (Impact, Self Confidence, and Presentation) and the *Achieving* (Proactive Orientation and Achievement Orientation) groupings.

Job analysis shows that several competencies are needed to perform each activity, function or role contained within given job type. Furthermore, each competency will be applicable to several, if not all, of the various activities, functions or roles that makes up a given job type. For illustration, take the managerial roles proposed by Mintzberg (1973) (*see* MANAGERIAL BEHAVIOR). Each role requires the use of several HPMC – so the role of *Negotiating* highly demands the six HPMC included in the cognitive and directional groupings. At the same time, the cognitive and directional HPMC are demanded by several of the managerial roles.

A consequence of the HPC methodology is a shift in research away from simply describing what job holders do typically toward prescribing what job holders ought to do based on the behaviors which distinguish outstanding performers. A second consequence is the stimulus that has been given to the creation and application of new models and measures of job performance (*see* PERFORMANCE, INDIVIDUAL). A third consequence of the HPC approach has been the creation of models to explain how situational variables influences the relationship between behavior and performance. For example, it is clear that the rate of change (dynamism) of an organizational unit's environment significantly affects the relationship between the eleven HPMC and organizational unit performance. Essentially, the HPMC are associated with unit performance in a dynamic environment but not in a stable environment.

An alternative approach to competency which is receiving attention, has been provided by the U.K. Government Employment Department. Here, the definition of competency is wider than the attributes of job holders – in fact, these attributes are not the prime focus of attention. Instead, the approach identifies the outcomes expected from a job when it is performed adequately. Outcomes are divided into "units of competence" which are subdivided into "elements of competence." For example, a unit of competence for managers is, "Maintaining and improving service and product operations" which is subdivided into two elements: (1) "maintaining operations to meet quality standards"; and (2) "creating and maintaining the necessary conditions for productive work." The competence of individuals is judged by their capacity to produce the job outcomes specified by the relevant units and elements of competence.

To conclude, the word "competency" has currently a variety of meanings and no accepted consensus on its definition has emerged. It represents a new avenue of inquiry based on assumptions and methods different from those used traditionally and which stem from a concern for organizational performance rather than CAREER advancement, dynamic rather than stable environmental conditions, and normative rather than descriptive social science. The emergence of competency research and practice has been resisted and opposed vehemently by many individuals and groups. The approach has been described by many as the latest fad and it is often marginalized by commentators who put it into a restricted conceptual box that has not been integrated with any other aspect of ORGANIZATIONAL BEHAVIOR. In truth, much competency work has been conducted with these conceptual restrictions. The best work, however, perceives competency as one, yet a critical, part of an emerging organizational PARADIGM which challenges the economically based orthodoxies of management and organizations. The new paradigm is based on interconnected concepts which have emerged from the study of TOTAL QUALITY MANAGEMENT, organizational CORE COMPETENCE and ORGANIZATIONAL LEARNING (*see* LEARNING ORGANIZATION) and the stages of team and organizational development (*see* GROUP DEVELOPMENT). Its focus is on the organizational processes and behaviors which lead to superior performance in globally competitive environments. In this context, competencies are the relatively stable behaviors which create continuously the processes that enable the organizations to learn, adapt to new environmental demands, and change the environment so that it is better suited to the needs of STAKEHOLDERS (*see* ORGANIZATION AND ENVIRONMENT). The diversity of competency research and practice is to be expected at this point in its development. The continued application of relevance, reliability, and validity criteria will lead to consolidation without, it is to be hoped, constraining the creativity which has been the hallmark of the competency approach to date.

See also **Management development; Skills; Interpersonal skills; Transactional/transformational theory**

Bibliography

Boyatzis, R. E. (1982). *The competent manager*. New York: Wiley.

Chorvat, V. P. (1994). *Toward the construct validity of assessment centre leadership dimensions: A multitrait-multimethod investigation using confirmatory factor analysis*. University South Florida. Unpublished Doctoral Thesis.

Cockerill, A. P. (1989). *Managerial competence as a determinant of organisational performance*. University of London. Unpublished Doctoral Dissertation.

Cockerill, A. P., Schroder, H. M. & Hunt, J. W. (1993). *Validation study into the high performance managerial competencies*. London Business School: Centre for Organisational Research.

Huff, S., Lake, D. G. & Schaalman, M. L. (1982). *Principal differences: Excellence in school leadership and management*. Boston: McBer.

Klemp, G. O. (1978). *Job competence assessment*. Boston: McBer.

McClelland, D. C. (1973). Testing for competence rather than for "intelligence." *American Psychologist*, **28 (1)**, 1–40.

Mintzberg, H. (1973). *The nature of managerial work*. New York: Harper & Row.

Robertson, I., Gratton, L. & Sharpley, D. (1987). The psychometric properties and design of managerial assessment centres: Dimensions into exercises won't go. *Journal of Occupational Psychology*, **60**, 187–195.

Sackett, P. R. & Dreher, G. F. (1982). Constructs and assessment centre dimensions: Some troubling empirical findings. *Journal of Applied Psychology*, **67**, 401–410.

Schmitt, N., Gooding, R. Z., Noe, R. A. & Kirsch, M. (1984). Meta-analysis of validity studies published between 1964 and 1982 and the investigation of study characteristics. *Personnel Psychology*, **37**, 407–422.

Schroder, H. M. (1989). *Managerial competence: The key to excellence*. Iowa: Kendall Hunt.

Taylor, D. & McKie L. Final Report on Personal Competence Project, MCI, 1990.

A. P. COCKERILL

Competitiveness A company builds competitiveness through either timing, differentiation, or scope (Porter, 1980; Mintzberg, 1988). It competes through *timing* either by being first to develop and market new products or designs, or by quickly imitating an innovator (*see* INNOVATION). First-movers build advantage through technological leadership: They invest heavily to secure patents and then take aggressive action in setting up production and distribution arrangements that enable them to move quickly down the learning curve and stay ahead of rivals (Lieberman & Montgomery, 1988).

Imitators shy away from the complexities of maintaining a first-mover position. In many industries, patents and R&D offer only weak protection to innovating firms, and new products are easily imitated (*see* R&D MANAGEMENT; ENTREPRENEURSHIP). To quickly imitate pioneers and capture market share, astute followers develop proficient information gathering. By cultivating competitor intelligence, constantly scanning environments, and rapidly responding to opportunity, imitators often can capitalize on the large investments made by pioneers in R&D, buyer education, and personnel TRAINING. Because imitators rely on other firms to pioneer, they invest little in basic research and dwell more heavily on product development in related technologies. Competitive intelligence enables them to avoid the technological mistakes made by pioneers, and to incorporate into their product designs the timely FEEDBACK of the product's initial consumers (Porter, 1985).

Companies can gain advantage by *differentiating* their products and services. They achieve differentiation by offering either lower prices, better quality, or better service than rivals. Price leaders stress tight control of operating costs in order to achieve greater efficiency and PRODUCTIVITY. Successful price leaders constantly look for ways to standardize products and activities in order to capture a large component of the market with a basic configuration of their product.

Companies might also differentiate themselves by offering either better quality products and services, or unique features – making products of greater reliability, durability, or superior performance. Producing better quality products generally goes hand-in-hand with providing improved levels of support and service: They prop up a company's products by bundling valuable complementary characteristics into every sale. The most common means of gaining a service advantage involves providing credit terms, rapid delivery, user training, repairs, or instructional materials. A strategy of improving quality is generally costly, while a strategy of cost-reduction often drives down quality. Hence the recent surge of interest in "value-marketing" – a better ratio of quality to price to the consumer by bundling guarantees, 800 numbers, and frequent buyer plans – that is, service – as key product features.

Finally, companies can build competitiveness through *scope*: The decision to customize products for a narrow or broad market niche. Rather than standardize products for large markets, the company targets a niche with customized offerings that can better meet local needs. A narrow focus can be risky: Customizing is costly and requires specialized packaging, individualized marketing, and strong support. Insofar as rivals keep improving their standardized products, they can underprice the niche company.

Maintaining competitiveness is a top priority for companies in rapidly changing environments (Fombrun, 1992). It requires skill at deploying resources in ways that build mobility barriers against rivals and sustain advantage (Caves & Porter, 1977).

See also **Organizational effectiveness; Excellence; Reputation; Diversification; Total quality management; Strategic management; Strategic types**

Bibliography

Caves, R. & Porter, M. (1977). From entry barriers to mobility barriers. *Quarterly Journal of Economics*, **91**, 421–434.

Fombrun, C. J. (1992). *Turning points: Creating strategic change in corporations*. New York: McGraw Hill.

Lieberman, M. B. & Montgomery, D. B. (1988). First mover advantages. *Strategic Management Journal*, **9**, 41–58.

Mintzberg, H. (1988). Generic Strategies: Toward a comprehensive framework. *Advances in strategic Management*, **5**, 1–67.

Porter, M. E. (1980). *Competitive strategy*. New York: Free Press.

Porter, M. E. (1985). *Competitive advantage*. New York: Free Press.

CHARLES FOMBRUN

complexity The concept of complexity has been extremely important within organizational sociology although relatively ignored in the management literature. For many but not all organizational sociologists, complexity represents one of the most important structural properties of an organization because it is highly related to a number of other structural properties, the choice of coordination and CONTROL mechanisms, and the relative emphasis on the performance of product INNOVATION, that is, it has systemic effects.

The concept of complexity has several different names and alternative ways in which it can be measured. Hage (1965) was one of the first to emphasize the importance of complexity which he defined as the amount by which TRAINING lengthens as the tasks of an occupation become more complex. This definition is quite similar to that for the DIVISION OF LABOR. In subsequent research, Hage and Aiken (1970) broadened the definition to include the amount of professional activity as well as the level of training. This definition reflects the investment of knowledge in the organizational structure. In contrast, Blau (1970) and his students (Blau & Schoenherr, 1971) have stressed counts of job title and the number of departments and levels of the organization. When these measures are employed, they reflect the extent of structural DIFFERENTIATION that has occurred, that is how many distinct parts of the organizational structure are there (*see* ORGANIZATIONAL DESIGN). There is some relationship between the number of job titles in a professional organization such as a university and the variety of OCCUPATIONS but this relationship breaks down in organizations with large numbers of unskilled labor, e.g., where there is a job title for each distinct position on the assembly line. The idea of structural differentiation has also been used, however, to mean the distinctive differences between departments such as in the speed of FEEDBACK of information about the environment or the extent of FORMALIZATION in the department, as well as other characteristics (Lawrence & Lorsch, 1967). This line of research has also implicitly included number of departments because those organizations with, for example, both a basic research and a development department are considered to be more structurally differentiated (*see* DEPARTMENTALIZATION). Much more rarely, complexity is also defined in terms of spatial organization, for example, the number of physical units such as offices, plants, research sites, etc. (Hall, 1992).

During the late 1960s and the 1970s, a considerable amount of research was done on the relationship between ORGANIZATIONAL SIZE and the number of job titles, departments, and levels. Most of this research found a strong positive relationship: larger organizations are much more complex by these measures (for a review, *see* Hall, 1992).

In 1980, Hage advocated that complexity be defined as the proportion of the work force with extended training or who are recognized as distinct occupations, thus suggesting that the number of diverse occupations be standardized. The reasoning here is that a large organization such as Ford may have many workers but not many distinct occupations for which formal training is necessary, while a university can be quite small and yet have a much higher proportion of trained personnel. He called this idea the concentration of specialists so that it would not be confused with the earlier research on complexity, which was usually a raw count of either the number of different occupations or job titles.

In a review of a number of diverse studies including research by Blau and Schoenherr, the Aston group, and Azumi, the concentration of specialists was generally related to the amount of DECENTRALIZATION and STRATIFICATION of the organizational structure. One major exception was in Japan. Subsequent work suggests that length of training is more critical because many workers fill a large variety of jobs.

Complexity, simply defined as the variety of occupations and the amount of professional activity, is also related to the choice of coordination and control mechanisms, being associated with high COMMUNICATION rates and the absence of formalization (Hage, 1980). Finally, both complexity and the concentration of specialists appear to also be strongly related to the emphasis on either product or process INNOVATION.

More recently, complexity has been used to refer to the task complexity of networks of organizations that are working together to perform some quite complex goals (Alter & Hage, 1993) (*see* NETWORK ANALYSIS). In this context, the complexity of the interorganizational network is measured by the number of different kinds of organizations that are involved in the network (*see* INTERORGANIZATIONAL RELATIONS).

Finally, complexity, or the concentration of specialists, is a critical variable because the long-term tendency has been for organizational structures to become more complex as a response to the more complex environments in which they are located. This later dimension, the complexity of the environment (Mintzberg, 1979) has been somewhat more important in the management literature (*see* ORGANIZATION AND ENVIRONMENT).

See also **Bureaucracy; Matrix-organization; Job design**

Bibliography

Alter, C. & Hage, J. (1993). *Organizations working together*. Newbury Park, CA: Sage.

Blau, P. (1970). A formal theory of differentiation in organizations. *American Sociological Review*, **35**, 210–218.

Blau, P. & Schoenherr, R. (1971). *The structure of organizations*. New York: Basic Books.

Hage, J. (1965). An axiomatic theory of organizations. *Administrative Science Quarterly*, **10**, 289–320.

Hage, J. (1980). *Theories of organizations*. New York: Wiley–Interscience.

Hall, R. H. (1992). *Organizations: Structures, processes, and outcomes*, (5th edn). Englewood Cliffs, NJ: Prentice-Hall.

Lawrence, P. & Lorsch, J. (1967). *Organization and environment: Managing differentiation and integration*. Cambridge, MA: Harvard Graduate School of Business Administration.

Mintzberg, H. (1979). *The structuring of organizations*. Englewood Cliffs, NJ: Prentice-Hall.

JERALD HAGE

compliance This is the change in an individual's publicly stated attitudes and publicly observable behaviors which occurs under group pressure while the individual privately maintains his/her initially held beliefs (Nail, 1986; Festinger, 1953).

Like CONFORMITY and IDENTIFICATION, compliance is a response to social influence. However, unlike these other two responses, compliance reflects a major discontinuity between the individual's public and private personae. While compliant individuals change what they say or do in public, they maintain their initial beliefs and do not internalize or accept as valid the group's influence attempts. For example, lower POWER employees often comply with their supervisors' requests not out of true concurrence with those requests but out of fear of reprisal if they do not comply.

The term compliance also has connotations of coercion (Kelman, 1961). The compliant individual is seen as changing his/her publicly observable statements and behaviors to avoid PUNISHMENT from group members, to escape further interaction with INFLUENCE agents, to escape from an unpleasant situation, or to obtain REWARDS from those with whom the individual disagrees.

While compliance of individuals to social influence has often been seen as a desirable outcome of organizational activities like sales, bill collecting, and criminal investigations

(Rafaeli & Sutton, 1991), compliance in the context of GROUP DECISION MAKING has been seen as considerably more problematic (Kiesler & Kiesler, 1969; Janis, 1972). If individuals comply solely because of group pressure, they may be less likely to enthusiastically implement and execute a group's decision. Moreover, if multiple members publicly concur with a group decision while privately disagreeing with it, the group's decision-making effectiveness is likely to diminish in the long run as well (Hackman, 1976; Janis, 1972).

See also **Minority group influence; Group norms; Group culture; Conformity**

Bibliography

Festinger, L. (1953). An analysis of compliant behavior. In M. Sherif & M. O. Wilson (Eds), *Group relations at the crossroads* (pp. 232–256). New York: Harper.

Hackman, J. R. (1976). Group influences on individuals. In M. Dunnette (Ed.), *Handbook of industrial and organizational psychology* (pp. 1455–1525). Chicago: Rand McNally.

Janis, I. L. (1972). *Victims of groupthink: A psychological study of foreign-policy decisions and fiascos.* New York: Houghton Mifflin.

Kelman, H. C. (1961). Processes of opinion change. *Public Opinion Quarterly*, **25**, 57–78.

Kiesler, C. A. & Kiesler, S. B. (1969). *Conformity.* Reading, MA: Addison-Wesley.

Nail, P. R. (1986). Toward an integration of some models and theories of social response. *Psychological Bulletin*, **100**, 190–206.

Rafaeli, A. & Sutton, R. I. (1991). Emotional contrast strategies as means of social influence: Lessons from criminal interrogators and bill collectors. *Academy of Management Journal*, **34**, 749–775.

DANIEL C. FELDMAN

computer-aided design The term refers to the use of computers in the activity of design or redesign. Early systems date from the 1960s but the most rapid developments have been over the last decade. A typical CAD system comprises a graphics display terminal, a digitizing tablet (equivalent to a drawing board), an input device (such as a light pen), a keyboard, and a printer/plotter. Modern applications include the design of buildings, manufacturing processes, and commercial products.

CAD systems allow the user to undertake the conceptual design of an artifact on the computer screen, examining it from different perspectives in three dimensions. The user can then zoom in to parts of the design filling in more complete detail. Electronic storage enables rapid editing. Advanced systems facilitate an engineering analysis of the design. For example, when designing an aeroplane part, the system may incorporate an engineering database that allows the designer to analyze whether the new design is mechanically and structurally sound.

CAD systems have particular scope in small batch, complex, high quality engineering environments. There have been heavy investments in industrial sectors such as aerospace industries, and in many cases CAD workstations are replacing the use of traditional drawing boards. Potential benefits from the use of CAD include quicker design, enhanced designer PRODUCTIVITY, improved product quality, and fewer ERRORS (e.g., arising from transcription).

Increasing investments are being made linking CAD with computer-aided manufacture whereby the detailed drawings and geometric data are transmitted direct to the manufacturing engineers who use them to plan manufacturing processes. There is huge potential here for reducing overall lead times, for improving PRODUCTIVITY, and for improving integration between design and manufacture, two traditionally differentiated domains.

The introduction of CAD raises a number of individual and organizational issues (Barfield, Chang, Majchrzak, Eberts, & Salvendy, 1987). Designers may spend long periods of time working at their computers; ERGONOMIC and health and SAFETY considerations, along with the quality of HUMAN-COMPUTER-INTERACTION and decisions about the allocation of functions between designer and computer, may all influence user productivity and well being (*see* STRESS; QUALITY OF WORKING LIFE). Reduced use of drawing boards may be interpreted as JOB DESKILLING; on the other hand, new computer-based skills are required. There may also be repercussions for work organization, for example away from a traditional functional organization toward a product-based structure (*see* ORGANIZATIONAL DESIGN). The RECRUITMENT, SELECTION, and TRAIN-

ING of staff to operate and use CAD systems are of importance for organizations making such investments, as are the more general issues surrounding implementation and the management of change.

As with other forms of INFORMATION TECHNOLOGY, the list of individual and organizational issues arising from the introduction and use of CAD is extensive. Unfortunately, the evidence is that most of these implementations are dominated by technical concerns and this is held to be a key reason for their disappointing performance (Symon & Clegg, 1991). Regarding such new technologies as simply a change in medium may lead to improvements in local efficiency but fundamental reorganization (BUSINESS PROCESS RE-ENGINEERING) may be required to achieve significant improvements in effectiveness. A sociotechnical approach is required (Blackler & Brown, 1986) (*see* SOCIOTECHNICAL THEORY).

See also **Operations management; Advanced manufacturing technology; Software ergonomics; Total quality management**

Bibliography

Barfield, B., Chang, T., Majchrzak, A., Eberts, R. & Salvendy, G. (1987). Technical and human aspects of computer-aided design. In G. Salvendy (Ed.), *Handbook of human factors* (pp. 1617–1656). New York: Wiley.

Blackler, F. & Brown, C. A. (1986). Alternative models to guide the design and introduction of the new information technologies into work organizations. *Journal of Occupational Psychology*, **59**, 287–313.

Symon, G. J. & Clegg, C. W. (1991). Technology-led change: A study of the implementation of CADCAM. *Journal of Occupational Psychology*, **64**, 273–290.

CHRIS W. CLEGG

computer modeling Computer models of organizations are symbolic representations of organizations in executable computer code. They differ from discursive theories by the use of restricted, formal languages, and they can exploit the computational power that such languages make available. Computer models are helpful as a tool of analysis when the problem is too complex for thought experiments (*see* SIMULATION); also, they can simulate experimental designs when the domain resists real-life experiments. Computer models are at their best when they help to discover the counter-intuitive roots of an ordinary problem, and explain it as the result of systematic interaction effects.

The first methodology for computer modeling of organizations was proposed by Jay Forrester ("Industrial Dynamics", later: "System Dynamics") (*see* LEARNING ORGANIZATION). Other classical contributions to the field were made through Cyert and March's model of organizational decision making (1963), Cohen, March, and Olsen's GARBAGE-CAN MODEL (1972), and Burton and Obel's model of organizational forms (1984). All these models are based on numerical difference equations such that an equation describes the state of a variable at a given point in time as a function of the states of the same, or other, variables at previous points in time. The set of equations is solved iteratively along the time axis: a set of equations is initialized for t_0, and the outcomes for t_1, t_2, etc., are computed successively. More recently, techniques from Artificial Intelligence have become popular that can avoid the restriction of equational theories to numerical formulation and allow for computation with qualitative concepts. Masuch and LaPotin built an AI-version of the garbage-can model (1989), Baligh, Burton, and Obel synthesized mainstream ORGANIZATION THEORY as an Expert System (1990), and Carley used Newell's SOAR (a general-purpose program for solving problems) for simulations of ORGANIZATIONAL LEARNING (1992). In the new models, a logical inference machine drives the simulations, and one is no longer confined to assumptions in numerical terms. The latest trend is to treat discursive theories directly as computer models by representing them in a logical language and evaluating them by means-suitable applications ("theorem provers") (Péli, Bruggeman, Masuch, & Ó Nualláin, 1994).

Computer models are sometimes thought to have special properties that distinguish them from ordinary theories, a view which is based on the fact that the models "run" on a computer, and seem to represent reality more vividly than a written text or a mathematical formula. From an epistemological point of view, however, this view is ill-founded, since the computer code that embodies the model differs from other representations only in the choice of formal constraints on the description language. As a consequence, the VALIDITY of computer models remains as problematic as the validity of any other empirical THEORY.

See also **Research methods; Human–computer interaction; Information technology**

Bibliography

Baligh, H. H., Burton, R. M. & Obel, B. (1990). Devising expert systems in organization theory. In M. Masuch (Ed.), *Organization, management, and expert systems*. Berlin: De Gruyter.

Burton, R. M. & Obel, B. (1984). *Designing efficient organizations*. Amsterdam: North-Holland.

Carley, K., Kjaer-Hansen, J., Newell, A. & Prietula, M. (1992). Plural-SOAR: A prolegomenon to artificial agents and organizational behaviour. In M. Masuch & M. Warglien (Eds), *Artificial intelligence in organization and management theory* (pp. 87–118). Amsterdam: North-Holland.

Cohen, M. D., March, J. G. & Olsen, J. P. (1972). A garbage car model of organizational choice. *Administrative Science Quarterly*, **17**, 1–25.

Cyert, R. M. & March, J. G. (1963). *A behavioral theory of the firm*. Englewood Cliffs, NJ: Prentice-Hall.

Forrester, J. W. (1961). *Industrial dynamics*. Cambridge, MA: MIT Press.

Masuch, M. & LaPotin, P. (1989). Beyond garbage cans: An AI model of organizational choice. *Administrative Science Quarterly*, **34**, 38–69.

Péli, G., Bruggeman, J., Masuch, M. & Ó Nualláin, B. (1994). A logical approach to organizational ecology. *American Sociological Review*, **59**, 571–593.

MICHAEL MASUCH

conceptual frameworks *see* THEORY

conditioning Operant conditioning is the modification of some dimension of an operant behavior (e.g., topography, force, speed, accuracy, duration, and rate) by REINFORCEMENT, EXTINCTION, and SHAPING. The most direct representation of operant conditioning as a general model of behavior change due to experience involves the following procedures:

(a) specification of the behavior dimension(s) to be modified;
(b) observation of the behavior's occurrences; and
(c) scheduled administration of consequences [reinforcement(s)] contingent on occurrences of the behavior.

Operant behavior rate is one measure of the interaction between the person and the person's environment and typically serves as a dependent variable measuring learning as behavior (performance) change (*see* LEARNING, INDIVIDUAL). Consequences that increase the rate of the operant behavior they follow in a situation are called *reinforcers*. Reinforcers are defined as *positive reinforcers* when they appear and *negative reinforcers* when they disappear or cease to occur contingent upon an occurrence of the behavior. (Contingent and contingency here refer to conditional "if . . . then . . . " dependencies, i.e., "If x then y" denoted in symbols by "$x \rightarrow y$.")

An operant is defined as a class of behavior upon which a reinforcer is contingent. Operant behaviors typically occur in a situation at some rate greater than zero before operant conditioning procedures are employed to change the behavior's rate. This initial rate is called the *baseline rate* of operant responding and serves as a standard against which effects of subsequent operant procedures are evaluated, e.g., reinforcement.

See also **Influence; Feedback**

Bibliography

Mawhinney, T. C. & Mawhinney, R. R. (1982). Operant terms and concepts applied to industry. In R. M. O'Brien, A. M. Dickinson & M. Rosow (Eds), *Industrial behavior modification* (pp. 115–134). New York: Pergamon Press.

THOMAS C. MAWHINNEY

conflict Conflict is a common phenomenon in virtually all societies and organizations. Many definitions have been proposed. Some emphasize differences in perceptions or interests of the parties. Kolb and Putnam (1992), for example, argue that conflict exists "when there are real or perceived differences that arise in specific organizational circumstances and that engender EMOTION as a consequence" (1992: p. 312) (*see* EMOTIONS IN ORGANIZATIONS). Others define conflict in terms of actual behavior where parties interfere with each other's aims: Deutsch (1973) defines conflict as a phenomenon that "exists whenever incompatible activities occur" (1993: p. 10). There are many other definitions relating to the concerns and circumstances surrounding conflict.

Some definitions include both interest and behavior differences, as in the definition proposed here: "Conflict is incompatible behavior among parties whose interests differ" (Brown, 1983, p. 4). Incompatible behavior refers to intentional, purposeful behavior opposing the interests of the other party rather than accidental actions. Interests refer to stakes affected by an interaction between parties.

This definition focuses attention on conflicts experienced both behaviorally and psychologically. What of situations when one but not both elements are present? Sometimes the parties have different interests but do not display incompatible behavior. Potential conflicts may remain latent or covert when parties are unaware of or unable to express their differences in interest directly. Such hidden conflicts are quite common, for example, when large POWER differences between the parties hinder open expression of differences. It is common for subordinates to remain silent about disagreements with organizational superiors, even when it would be beneficial for the organization as a whole for those differences to be explicitly discussed.

In other situations, the parties may engage in incompatible behavior when their interests are not in conflict. Such mistaken conflicts are often grounded in misperceptions of the various interests involved by one or more of the parties (*see* PERCEPTION; ATTRIBUTION). It is quite common for parties with a history of conflict to assume that their interests conflict even when their interests are in fact similar. Union and management representatives, for example, may "assume the worst" and negotiate to impasse even when both parties have stronger interests in COOPERATION than in conflict (*see* COLLECTIVE BARGAINING; COLLECTIVE ACTION).

Paying attention to both interests and behavior in defining conflict clarifies the potential for future interaction. Hidden conflict may easily evolve into overt conflict if the parties come to understand their interests more clearly. Mistaken conflict may evaporate for the same reason.

The sources of conflict are legion. Among the most important are resource scarcities that lead to conflict among rival claimants, task differences that generate conflict over coordination and priorities, power inequalities that catalyze struggles over CONTROL and AUTHORITY, and CULTURE and VALUE differences that produce struggles over identity and respect. For organizational purposes the most explicit attention is often paid to resources, tasks, and power, though differences in less visible cultural factors may sometimes produce the most explosive results. Conflicts that combine multiple sources, such as tensions between individuals or groups that differ in power and cultural identity, may be extremely hard to resolve (Brown, 1983) (*see* INTERCULTURAL PROCESS). Organizations often have difficulty in coping with differences among ethnic groups that are unequal in social and organizational power (*see* DISCRIMINATION).

Is conflict a problem? Much of the early research on organizational conflict assumed that conflict was basically dysfunctional (*see* Pondy, 1967). It is clear that conflict sometimes fosters suppression or distortion of important information, strong feelings of hostility and antagonism, and behavior that is destructive to the purposes of organizations and their members. Regulating extremes of conflict escalation is important for ORGANIZATIONAL EFFECTIVENESS (*see* CONFLICT RESOLUTION).

On the other hand, many investigators have suggested that conflict in some situations can be constructive (e.g., Coser, 1956). In organizations, moderate levels of conflict encourage wide exchanges of information, energetic PARTICIPATION in problem-solving, and generation of creative alternatives for problem solving (*see* CREATIVITY; INNOVATION). Lack of conflict may in itself be a problem, as in GROUPTHINK, for example.

Whether conflict is desirable or problematic depends on the situation. Finding new ways to resolve differences among organizational subunits, such as maintenance and production units of a manufacturing firm, may be vital to improving organizational performance. Such solutions may be difficult to find if disagreements cannot be voiced. At the same time, managing conflict may require regulating such disagreements so they do not escalate. CONFLICT MANAGEMENT may require encouraging the expression of differences in some situations, and regulating that expression in others.

Conflict as a *process* is shaped by the perceptions of the parties, the GROUP COHESIVENESS within parties, the COMMUNICATIONS between parties, and their behavior in response to each other. When conflict is well managed, the parties regularly question their own assumptions to avoid STEREOTYPING and groupthink. They communicate freely, and act as joint problem solvers instead of adversaries. Too often, however, parties tend to develop stereotypes that favor themselves and denigrate other parties, mobilize strong LEADERSHIP and group CONFORMITY within parties, restrict their communications with others, and take pre-emptive action to counter expected aggression. This combination of tendencies can easily lead to self-reinforcing patterns of conflict escalation, in which parties can point to the other's behavior as justifying their own escalation. Thus initially constructive conflict can easily escalate into excessive conflict. A similar pattern can produce too little conflict: positive stereotypes that overemphasize common interests, high levels of cohesion across parties, reduced communication about differences, and actions to avoid or suppress conflict can combine in a self-reinforcing pattern.

Organizational conflict has been examined from several levels of analysis. Sheppard (1992) has argued that much of the confusion of present conflict theory can be understood in terms of the different LEVELS OF ANALYSIS and the perspectives associated with those levels. Much research has focused at the level of specific disputes, and examined the behavior, tactics, and consequences of conflict episodes. Analysis at this level produces ideas about the dynamics and tactics by which individuals deal with specific problems (*see* NEGOTIATION). Other researchers have examined conflicts at the level of the institutional context, and focused on the norms, rules, structures, and organizational interdependencies against which conflicts are evoked or controlled (*see* INDUSTRIAL RELATIONS; INTERORGANIZATIONAL RELATIONS). These investigations produce ideas about institutions and policies within which conflicts can be controlled. Between the levels of the specific dispute and the institutional context is the relationship level of analysis, which addresses the ongoing relations between parties over a series of conflicts. Relationship analysis also deals with systems and strategies that enable the management of conflict in an ongoing relationship. This level of analysis is affected by both institutional contexts and events of specific conflict episodes – but it has received less attention than the other two levels.

The study of conflict in organizations has evolved significantly over recent decades. Much research in the 1960s focused on the growing functional specialization in organizations and the conflicts inherent in the performance of organizational tasks carried out by diverse subunits. As organizations have reconfigured themselves to deal with increasing environmental UNCERTAINTY and competition, the importance of conflict among departments or project teams or interorganizational networks has focused increasing attention on conflict handling as a critical capacity.

Struggles over the allocation of organizational resources has also been the basis for increasing concern with conflict rooted in political differences (*see* POLITICS). In part these struggles reflect tensions over class differences in the larger society. They also reflect increased awareness of the dependence of organizations on external resources and the demands from external constituencies (*see* STAKEHOLDERS; RESOURCE DEPENDENCE). Conflict over power differences often generate more communication difficulties, asymmetrical mobilization, and more unpredicted explosions than conflicts over task differences (Brown, 1983).

More recently still, organizations have become concerned with conflicts produced by differences in cultural background or roles. Conflicts between "identity groups" that define the self-concepts of their members have become increasingly relevant to organizations that are recruiting a workforce diverse in cultural, GENDER, and ethnic identities (Alderfer, Alderfer, Tucker, & Tucker, 1980) (*see* MANAGEMENT OF DIVERSITY). Cultural differences are often value-laden and poorly understood, and so may be the basis for rapid and difficult-to-control conflict escalation, especially when they are closely correlated with power differences (Kanter, 1977). Tensions across GENDER and ethnic differences have produced serious misunderstandings and explosive conflicts in many organizations (*see* RACE).

Cultural differences also illustrate limitations to our existing understanding of conflict in organizations. Organizational conflict has been studied in some depth in Western industrialized countries, but much less is known about how it is experienced in other cultures. With increased interaction across national and cultural boundaries within and between organizations, there is more scope for conflicts across cultural divides. In cultures valuing competition and INDIVIDUALISM, like the United States (where much of the conflict research has been done), differences may produce overt conflict and distributive processes. In cultures that place a higher value on community welfare and COOPERATION, such as Japan, other ways of expressing differences and integrating diversity may be more common.

The changing demographics of the workforce in some industrialized countries are giving new impetus to the study of conflicts across gender and ethnic differences within societies (*see* ORGANIZATIONAL DEMOGRAPHY). Attention to such conflicts is an urgent need, especially where it is linked to gross discrepancies in wealth and power.

More attention is also needed for understanding conflicts that involve values, ideologies, (*see* IDEOLOGY) and emotional commitments that are not easily susceptible to "rational" analysis and resolution (Carnevale & Pruitt, 1992). Many of the most costly and intransigent organizational conflicts have roots in incom-patible values and ideologies which have been resistant to resolution. Such conflicts may not be resolvable – but they may be transformed to make their outcomes less destructive (Vayrynen, 1991).

Conflict theorists have infrequently spanned the levels of analysis necessary to integrate institutional and episodic perspectives to understand ongoing conflict that is rooted in systemic organizational relations. Often they have also failed to account for the variety of interests at stake in important conflicts. Many conflict theorists operate on the assumption that conflict is best understood in bilateral rather than multilateral terms, so their theories provide little help for understanding conflicts that involve many stakeholders, multiple interests, and complex forces operating at several levels of analysis. Learning more about such conflicts and their management is increasingly urgent as global interdependence expands. The most serious shortcoming of this definition is the restricted range of global experience represented in currently available theory and research about conflict and its organizational implications.

See also **Intergroup relations; Interorganizational relations; Commitment, dual; Organizational culture; Organizational effectiveness; Organizational neurosis**

Bibliography

Alderfer, C. P., Alderfer, C. J., Tucker, L. & Tucker, R. (1980). Diagnosing race relations in management. *Journal of Applied Behavioral Science*, **16**, 135–166.

Brown, L. D. (1983). *Managing conflict at organizational interfaces*. Reading, MA: Addison-Wesley.

Carnevale, P. J. and Pruitt, D. G. (1992). Negotiation and mediation. *Annual Review of Psychology*, **43**, 531–582.

Coser, L. (1956). *The functions of social conflict*. New York: Free Press.

Deutsch, M. (1973). *The resolution of conflict*. New Haven: Yale University Press.

Kanter, R. M. (1977). *Men and women of the corporation*. New York: Colophon.

Kolb, D. & Putnam, L. (1992). The multiple faces of conflict in organizations. *Journal of Organizational Behavior*, **13**, 311–324.

Pondy, L. R. (1967). Organizational conflict: Concepts and models. *Administrative Science Quarterly*, **12**, 296–320.

Sheppard, B. H. (1992). Conflict research as schizophrenia: The many faces of organizational conflict. *Journal of Organizational Behavior*, **13**, 205–207.

Vayrynen, R. (1991). To settle or to transform: Perspectives on the resolution of national and international conflict. In R. Vayrynen (Ed.), *New directions in conflict theory: Conflict resolution and conflict transformation*. (pp. 1–25). London: Sage.

L. DAVID BROWN and ANDREW E. CLARKSON

conflict, intergroup *see* INTERGROUP RELATIONS

conflict management CONFLICT is an ever-present fact of organizational life (*see* CONFLICT). Given the diversity of interests and concerns of organizational members and SUBUNITS and their interdependence for many purposes, it is not surprising that conflicts within and between organizations are common. Conflict management involves dealing with differences in interest and incompatibilities in behavior that might otherwise undermine the health and PRODUCTIVITY of organizations and their members.

Much of the early work on conflict management emphasized its role in reducing destructive conflict. This view of conflict management grew out of a conception of conflict as a fundamentally dysfunctional phenomena in organizations that required regulation or resolution (Deutsch, 1973; Thomas, 1976) (*see* CONFLICT RESOLUTION). More recently, investigators have recognized that too little conflict may be as problematic as too much in some situations (Brown, 1983).

From this perspective, conflict management is best understood as the encouraging of a level of conflict that is appropriate to the tasks and interests of the organization and its members. In some circumstances, when expression of differences and disagreement will enable better understanding and more effective solutions to complex problems, conflict management may require sharpening differences and promoting more direct challenges. In other situations, when shared decisions and cohesive action are important, conflict management may require emphasizing commonalities and regulating conflict escalation. Factors such as the nature of organizational tasks, the realities of resource interdependence, and the impacts of cultural diversity are all important factors in assessing the appropriateness of conflict levels and the relevance of conflict management strategies (*see* MANAGEMENT OF DIVERSITY)

Conflict management interventions may focus at different LEVELS OF ANALYSIS and utilize different kinds of leverage. Some interventions emphasize redirecting behavior and reframing the perspectives of individual parties to disputes. Examples include strategies and tactics for de-escalating conflicts, for determining fair outcomes, for avoiding the psychological traps involved in mutual STEREOTYPING, for focusing on interests rather than positions, and for being creative in competitive contexts (*see* Thomas, 1976; Fisher, Ury, & Patton, 1991).

Other strategies restructure the organizational and institutional contexts in which conflicts are embedded to make inappropriate levels of conflict less likely or to create procedures for dealing with conflicts when they occur. Examples include INDUSTRIAL RELATIONS systems in many countries that have been created to preserve industrial peace and productivity, or organizational structures like task forces, grievance systems, or MATRIX ORGANIZATIONS that are designed to deal with ongoing differences (*see* Ury, Brett, & Goldberg, 1988).

Still other interventions reallocate organizational resources to manage relationships shaped by important conflicts. Examples include redefining ROLES to encourage more attention to liaison problems, creating special interface organizations to manage conflict problems, or supporting the use of third parties to enable more effective conflict management (Sheppard, 1984; Brown, 1983).

Organizational conflict is grounded in differences and interdependence. The challenges of growing international competition, increasing global interdependence, and continuing social change and turbulence are likely to place increasing demands on organizations to deal effectively with conflict in many settings (*see* UNCERTAINTY).

See also **Collective action; Intergroup relations; Power**

Bibliography

Brown, L. D. (1983). *Managing conflict at organizational interfaces*. Reading, MA: Addison-Wesley.

Deutsch, M. (1973). *The resolution of conflict*. New Haven: Yale University Press.

Fisher, R., Ury, W. & Patton, B. (1991). *Getting to yes: Negotiating agreement without giving in*. New York: Penguin.

Sheppard, B. H. (1984). Third party intervention: A procedural framework. In B. M. Staw & L. L. Cummings (Eds), *Research in organizational behavior* (vol. 6, pp. 141–189). Greenwich, CT: JAI Press.

Thomas, K. (1976). Conflict and conflict management. In M. D. Dunnette (Ed.), *Handbook of industrial and organizational psychology*. Chicago: Rand-McNally.

Ury, W., Brett, J. M. & Goldberg, S. B. (1988). *Getting disputes resolved*. San Francisco: Jossey-Bass.

L. DAVID BROWN and
ANDREW E. CLARKSON

conflict resolution This is the process by which disputes occur and are resolved. A dispute begins when one party makes a demand or claim upon another who rejects it (Felstiner, Abel, & Sarat, 1980–1981). Dispute resolution implies turning the opposed positions toward a single outcome (Ury, Brett, & Goldberg, 1988).

This definition focuses on disputes as specific manifestations of CONFLICT, which can be defined as opposition or incompatibility in goals (or other concerns) of interdependent parties (Putnam & Poole, 1987). Disputes can be resolved, though they may not always be. Dispute resolution, however, should not be expected to resolve underlying fundamental conflicts of interest between, for example, labor and management, religious groups, functional areas within organizations, etc. (*see* INTEREST GROUPS; INDUSTRIAL RELATIONS). Fundamental differences in goals and means to achieve those goals will continue to create disputes between the parties. However, the procedures and systems that support the resolution of disputes provide the opportunity for parties to confront their differences and work together to find a state of equilibrium in which they can effectively coexist and be productive (*see* CONFLICT MANAGEMENT).

There are three fundamental processes for resolving disputes: reconciling interests; determining which party is right according to some standard of fairness, law, or contract; and determining which party is more powerful (Ury et al., 1988). *Interests* are needs, desires, hidden agendas – the reasoning underlying the position the party is taking. Reconciling interests may involve identifying creative solutions that meet all parties' interests (Fisher & Ury, 1981), trading off low priority interests in order to receive greater returns on higher priority interests (Neale & Bazerman, 1991), and making concessions. Procedures like NEGOTIATION and *mediation* (third party assisted negotiation) are appropriate for interest-based dispute resolution. Determining who is *right* is often difficult because different, sometimes contradictory, standards may apply to the dispute. Third parties – judges, arbitrators, or higher level managers are often called upon to provide either advisory or binding judgments as to which party is right. POWER is the ability to coerce the other party to do something it would not normally do. Power is typically exercised by imposing costs on the other party by acts of aggression or the withholding of benefits. Power may be exercised in negotiation by the exchange of threats or in power contests, for example, strikes or wars, in which parties take action to determine which one will prevail (*see* COLLECTIVE ACTION; COLLECTIVE BARGAINING).

Ury et al., (1988) argue that interests-based resolution of disputes generates lower transaction costs and higher benefits to the parties involved (*see* TRANSACTION COST THEORY), especially if they must continue to interact, than rights or power-based resolutions in which one party wins and the other loses. However, Ury et al., (1988) recognize that not all disputes can be resolved on the basis of interests. For ongoing relationships, in which some disputing is inevitable, they advocate designing a *dispute resolution system* in which interests-based procedures are backed up with advisory rights or power procedures and ultimately binding rights or power procedures. The advisory procedures allow for "looping back" to an interests-based resolution of the dispute.

Not all disputes will be resolved. The claiming party may decide to withdraw the claim, or the granting party decide to give in to the claim. This is called "lumping it." Alternatively, one or both parties may decide to withdraw from the relationship. These forms of avoidance may occur before the claim has ever been made. They may also result from interests-based negotiation, for example, if one party determines that it is no longer in its interests to interact with the other; or from a rights or power contest, for example, when one party learns that it has neither a likely legal claim nor the economic power to pursue the dispute.

Dispute resolution is not revolution. It provides a mechanism for a gradual shift in power. However, dispute systems design, in which disputing parties achieve recognition and LEGITIMACY, as well as regularized forums for making claims and bringing forward their interests, can be a powerful ORGANIZATIONAL CHANGE mechanism.

See also **Intergroup relations; Interorganizational relations; Justice, procedural; Justice, distributive; Decision making**

Bibliography

Felstiner, W. L. F., Abel, R. L. & Sarat, A. (1980–1981). The emergence and transformation of disputes: Naming, blaming, claiming. *Law and Society Review*, 15, 631–654.

Fisher, R. & Ury, W. (1981). *Getting to Yes*. Boston: Houghton Mifflin.

Neale, M. A. & Bazerman, M. H. (1991). *Cognition and rationality in negotiation*. New York: Free Press.

Putnam, L. L. & Poole, M. S. (1987). Conflict and negotiation. In K. H. Roberts & L. W. Porter (Eds), *Handbook of organizational communication* (pp. 549–599). Newbury Park, CA: Sage.

Ury, W. L., Brett, J. M. & Goldberg, S. B. (1988). *Getting disputes resolved: Designing systems to cut the costs of conflict*. San Francisco: Jossey-Bass.

JEANNE M. BRETT

conformity This is the shift of an individual's behaviors and attitudes toward the perceived standards of the group as a result of group pressure (Kelman, 1961; Asch, 1951; Sherif, 1936).

Substantial work has been conducted on distinguishing conformity from other responses to group pressure and social INFLUENCE (*see* COMPLIANCE and IDENTIFICATION). For conformity to exist, the following conditions should be present:

(a) the individual has a crystallized attitude or a regular behavior pattern before exposure to group influence;
(b) the individual's attitude or behavior changes as a result of group influence;
(c) the individual's attitude or behavior changes in the perceived desired direction of the group;
(d) the individual's attitude or behavior changes soon after exposure to group pressure; and
(e) the individual's private beliefs change as well as his/her publicly stated attitudes and publicly observable behaviors (Nail, 1986) (*see* MINORITY GROUP INFLUENCE).

There has been considerable research on the factors which predispose individuals to conform to group pressure. The classic Yale Obedience Study (Milgram, 1974) and Stanford Prison Study (Haney & Zimbardo, 1973) suggest that individuals are more likely to conform when the work environment is uncertain and individuals need the group for information, when individuals have low SELF-ESTEEM and need the group for affirmation, when the group is prestigious and individuals value group membership highly, when individuals have made a public COMMITMENT to the group, when individuals are new in the group or at lower levels of the organization, and when individuals are alone in their opposition to the group's position (Kiesler & Kiesler, 1969).

In general, the research suggests that situational factors have a greater impact on an individual's willingness to conform than individual PERSONALITY traits. For example, the Stanford Prison Study suggests that an individual's role demands can completely overwhelm other aspects of his or her self-identity under extreme social pressure (Haney & Zimbardo, 1973) (*see* ROLE-TAKING). Indeed, in studies of the conformity of individuals to immoral or unethical demands, it has been found that conformers are "ordinary people" who follow orders out of a sense of obligation to their leaders and not from any peculiarly aggressive tendencies (Milgram, 1974).

While individuals' conformity to group expectations may make daily functioning of the group more predictable and routine, there is substantial evidence that too much conformity can be detrimental to the quality of group decision making (Janis, 1972) (*see* GROUPTHINK). In organizational settings, too much conformity can result in the group's inattention to flaws in its planning and DECISION-MAKING activities as well as intolerance of, and lack of acceptance of, fresh perspectives of new group members (Feldman, 1984; Dentler & Erikson, 1959). For this reason, researchers and practitioners have been investigating group process interventions (*see* ORGANIZATIONAL DEVELOPMENT) and group decision-making heuristics (*see* GROUP DECISION MAKING) to help groups build in safeguards against overconformity.

See also **Group culture; Group dynamics; Affiliation, need for**

Bibliography

Asch, S. (1951). Effects of group pressure upon the modification and distortion of judgment. In M. H. Guetzkow (Ed.), *Groups, leadership, and men* (pp. 117–190). Pittsburgh: Carnegie Institute of Technology Press.

Dentler, R. A. & Erikson, K. T. (1959). The functions of deviance in groups. *Social Problems*, 7, 98–107.

Feldman, D. C. (1984). The development and enforcement of group norms. *Academy of Management Review*, **9**, 47–53.

Haney, C. & Zimbardo, P. G. (1973). Social roles and role-playing: Observations from the Stanford Prison Study. *Behavioral and Social Science Teacher*, **1**, 25–45.

Janis, I. L. (1972). *Victims of groupthink: A psychological study of foreign-policy decisions and fiascos*. New York: Houghton Mifflin.

Kelman, H. C. (1961). Processes of opinion change. *Public Opinion Quarterly*, **25**, 57–78.

Kiesler, C. A. & Kiesler, S. B. (1969). *Conformity*. Reading, MA: Addison-Wesley.

Milgram, S. (1974). *Obedience to authority*. New York: Harper & Row.

Nail, P. R. (1986). Toward an integration of some models and theories of social response. *Psychological Bulletin*, **100**, 190–206.

Sherif, M. (1936). *The psychology of social norms*. New York: Harper.

DANIEL C. FELDMAN

confrontation *see* INTERPERSONAL SKILLS; SENSITIVITY TRAINING

conglomerate diversification This refers both to the process of achieving a series of diversifications, usually by MERGERS AND ACQUISITIONS, which creates an organization with a wide variety of unrelated businesses in its portfolio, and to the results of that process. Most DIVERSIFICATION is related diversification, not conglomerate diversification.

The degree to which value can be added by having a portfolio of unrelated businesses under common ownership, compared with operating them as a series of independent businesses is limited. While financial and administrative synergies are possible, value creation through operating efficiencies or knowledge transfer amongst the unrelated businesses are not (*see* SYNERGY; TECHNOLOGY TRANSFER). It is therefore not surprising that research usually shows that conglomerates provide lower returns than other types of organizations, such as single businesses, dominant businesses, or related diversified organizations (*see* COMPETITIVENESS).

The very few high performing conglomerates which survive for long periods of time are characterized by effective financial control systems, which monitor the unrelated businesses through common financial measures, small head offices, which minimize the overhead cost per business, and DECENTRALIZATION of administrative and operational AUTONOMY to the operating businesses, coupled with a narrow range of tightly-defined corporate policies.

Conglomerates generally have high leverage ratios, meaning that their returns are financially risky. There have been two major waves of conglomerate diversification since World War II. The so-called "go–go" conglomerates of the 1960s and a major part of the 1980s acquisition activity were both facilitated by easy financing and rising stock markets which provided a cheap and plentiful supply of both debt and equity.

See also **Strategic management; Multinational corporations**

Bibliography

Porter, M. (1987). From competitive advantage to corporate strategy. *Harvard Business Review*, **67**, May–June, pp. 43–59.

GRAHAM HUBBARD

Congruence This term refers to a condition where two elements match, fit with, or are in harmony with one another. In ORGANIZATIONAL BEHAVIOR, congruence has been applied to at least two different phenomena – interpersonal COMMUNICATION and ORGANIZATION DESIGN. Congruence in interpersonal communication means that a person's message – i.e., the words spoken – match exactly the person's thoughts and feelings. Rogers (1961) claimed that the "fundamental law of interpersonal relationships" is centered on congruence: the more congruence in an interpersonal relationship, the stronger and more satisfying it is.

Congruence in organization design refers to consistency among various elements in an organization. Authors have focused on different organizational attributes, but the basic assumption is that when these elements are congruent, the organization is more effective (*see* Nadler & Tushman, 1980). The well-known "7-S FRAMEWORK," for example, proposes that effectiveness is enhanced when congruence exists among seven elements: strategy, structure, systems, staffing, SKILLS, style, and shared VALUES. This means that each element fits with, reinforces, or is consistent with all other elements. To attain high performance, organizations and teams must strive to develop congruence among these various elements.

See also **Group cohesiveness; Organizational effectiveness; Organization theory**

Bibliography

Nadler, D. A. & Tushman, M. L. (1980). A congruence model of organizational assessment. In E. E. Lawler, D. A. Nadler & C. Cammann (Eds), *Organizational assessment: Perspectives on the measurement of organizational behavior and the quality of work life* (pp. 261–278). New York: Wiley–Interscience.

Rogers, C. R. (1961). *On becoming a person*. Boston: Houghton Mifflin.

KIM S. CAMERON

consensus Consensus refers to an informal process that groups often use to make decisions (*see* GROUP DECISION MAKING). The typical pattern is for members to discuss various alternatives in an unstructured process until one person, often the group's chairperson, decides that the issues have been thoroughly aired and that one of the alternatives is clearly favored. This person then suggests that the group has reached a consensus and asks whether others agree. If no one dissents, the decision is made.

The benefits of consensus include the possibility of relatively strong commitment to the decision and strong GROUP COHESIVENESS (*see* COMMITMENT). The downside is that the process is so unstructured that a variety of problems can surface, including:

(1) relatively few, low quality alternatives or ideas;
(2) potentially strong social pressure within the group, especially when someone with POWER states the consensus and expects no dissent;
(3) low task orientation, when group members are motivated to spend more time interacting socially than attending to the task; and
(4) a high potential for CONFLICT if people disagree (Murnighan, 1981).

Nevertheless, consensus has such positive connotations, implying agreement and informal unanimity, that many organizational groups, even very large groups, use it for many if not all of their decisions.

See also **Group norms; Decision making; Groupthink**

Bibliography

Murnighan, J. K. (1981). Group decision making: What strategies should you use? *Management Review*, **70**, #2 55–62.

J. KEITH MURNIGHAN

consideration *see* INTERPERSONAL SKILLS; LEADERSHIP STYLE; MANAGERIAL STYLE

construct validity *see* PSYCHOLOGICAL TESTING; VALIDITY

consultancy The practice of consultancy has several distinguishing characteristics:

(a) it involves a voluntary relationship between a consultant and a client;
(b) it involves an attempt by the consultant to help the client; and,
(c) the relationship is perceived as temporary by both parties (Lippitt, 1969; Blake & Mouton, 1976).

Consultants may come from outside the client organization, or they may practice within the employing organization provided they are outside a hierarchical AUTHORITY relationship with the client.

Consultancy is a way of practicing a profession rather than a profession itself (Holtz, 1993) (*see* PROFESSIONALISM). Thus, one may be an engineer who does or does not practice consulting. Or, one may be a marketing expert who does or does not practice consulting. The consulting process (*see* CONSULTANCY INTERVENTION MODELS) may start with a diagnostic activity or it may begin with service delivery. Finally, the actions provided will sometimes be a one-time event (e.g., directing a reorganization) or may require a long-term recurrent service to the client (e.g., providing legal advice).

The extent to which the relationship between consultant and client is likely to be recurrent is influenced by the following:

1. Clarity of goals. The search and selection of a key executive is more likely to be a single project than a service goal defined as providing staffing services for key executives.
2. Depth of intervention. The installation of structure and systems is more likely to be a single project than an activity involving change in interpersonal or intrapersonal relationships.
3. Degree to which SKILLS shift to client. With such a shift, the consultant serves as a training source; without such a shift, the client must return when the skills are required.
4. The range of problems or skills covered by the consultant. Full service consultants are more likely to be recurrent than single service specialists.

Consulting Process

A typical consulting process is shown in Figure 1. The initial contact will occur either at the initiative of the potential client or the consultant, with the possible next step of a formal discussion about the consulting engagement, here called a "contract making" meeting. The "contract making" meeting is a major determinant of the success of a consulting engagement. In it decisions are made by both the consultant and the client about whether to work together, about what processes will be involved, and about mutual expectations regarding outcomes. The meeting is also a decision point for electing to use a diagnostic process to identify needs or electing to provide a service. Often, the client seeks a consultant to have the consultant provide a service: provide a solution to a problem which may or may not be defined. At the time of the "CONTRACT making" meeting, however, both parties may decide that service delivery is premature and that the client's needs will be better served with a problem identification (i.e., diagnostic) activity.

If the decision is made to engage in a diagnostic activity, the meeting is likely to cover details about the boundary of the client system to be included, the methods of data collection, time required, billing methods, personnel involvement, and reporting schedules. The outcome of the diagnostic activity is typically an identification of needs and their priority. The verbal agreements of this meeting will generally be restated in a letter of intent. Such documentation is recommended since it provides a clear and verifiable statement of mutual expectations.

Either at the end of the diagnostic activity or directly following the "contract making" meeting, decisions will be made between client and consultant about what will follow and who will

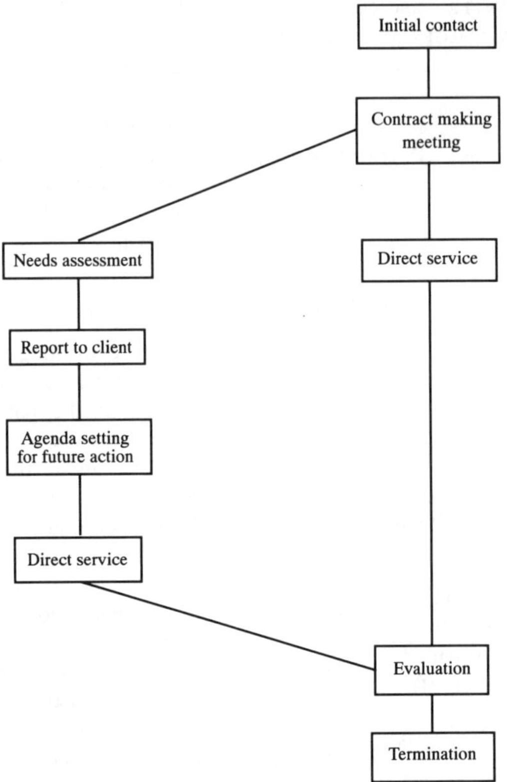

Figure 1 Consulting process

be responsible. For issues involving a substantial investment of time and resources, a formal proposal will often be prepared. As with the "contract making" meeting, the proposal is of major importance in determining whether or not the consultant will be considered a success when it is finished (Metzger, 1993).

Following the consultant's action, whether a simple advisory action or a complex project, there will be an evaluation and termination. Evaluation may take a number of forms, but an important element will be whether what was promised is what was accomplished and delivered. Beyond that, the evaluation may include the delivery of lasting skills or programs to the client, perceptions of positive change, and demonstrated accomplishment. Since client independence and commitment to change are considered to be important criteria for effective consulting (Argyris, 1973) the form and process of termination is, itself, an important element in the process.

Future Trends

A review of books and articles about consulting reveals the following trends:

1. With outsourcing and DOWNSIZING, more firms are relying on contract services rather than employing indirect labor themselves.
2. Management consulting services are increasingly differentiated by institution (e.g., schools, banks, insurance companies) or by specialty (e.g., accounting, recruiting, total quality).
3. There is an emerging literature on: (a) internal versus external consulting practice; (b) how to select a consultant; and (c) outplacement consulting.
4. It has become clear that training is not consulting; that is, the skills required for

training do not insure consulting skills as well.

See also **Double-loop learning; Organizational learning; Organizational development**

Bibliography

Argyris, C. (1973). *Intervention theory and method: A behavioral science view*. Reading, MA: Addison-Wesley.

Bermont, H. (1992). *How to become a successful consultant in your own field* (3rd edn). Rocklin, CA: Prima.

Blake, R. R. & Mouton, J. S. (1976). *Consultation*. Reading, MA: Addison-Wesley.

Greenbaum, T. L. (1990). *The consultant's manual: A complete guide to building a successful consulting practice*. New York: Wiley.

Greiner, L. E. & Metzger, R. O. (1983). *Consulting to management*. Englewood Cliffs, NJ: Prentice-Hall.

Holtz, H. (1993). *How to succeed as an independent consultant* (3rd edn). New York: Wiley.

Levinson, H., Molinari, J. & Spohn, A. G. (1972). *Organizational diagnosis*. Cambridge, MA: Harvard University Press.

Lippitt, G. L. (1969). *Organization renewal: Achieving viability in a changing world*. New York: Appleton-Century-Crofts.

Metzger, R. O. (1993). *Developing a consulting practice*. Newbury Park, CA: Sage.

ALAN C. FILLEY

consultancy intervention models CONSULTANCY intervention models are concerned with the style in which the consultant and client interact. If we consider consultancy in ORGANIZATIONAL BEHAVIOR or management, two dimensions are commonly involved:

(a) the extent to which the activity is primarily one of *diagnosis* versus that of *service delivery*; and
(b) the extent to which the activity is primarily one of *providing advice* versus that of *taking action*.

These dimensions are combined in Figure 1.

Consultancy which emphasizes diagnosis will emphasize problem identification while consultancy which emphasizes service delivery will emphasize providing solutions or services to solve problems. In contrast, consultancy which provides advice involves direction by the consultant to the client about proper action; consultancy which provides action involves the performance of activities for the benefit of the client.

I. *Diagnostic/advisory interventions*. Consulting methods of this type are primarily concerned with identifying problems through information gathering and analysis. An example of methods contained in this class is "PROCESS CONSULTATION" which is an identification of obstacles to organizational performance and JOB SATISFACTION obtained from organization members.
II. *Diagnostic/action interventions*. These methods combine problem identification with the development of a formal plan to meet those needs. An example of such action is the development of a strategic plan for a client based on an analysis of internal strengths and weaknesses as well as an analysis of external opportunities and threats.
III. *Service delivery/advisory interventions*. Consulting methods of this type are illustrated in providing prescriptive and expert advice by the consultant. Examples include directions to meet legislative or legal requirements as well as teaching theory and models which become the standard for decisions by the client.
IV. *Service delivery/action*. Consultations of this type require the consultant to act as a "pair of hands" (Block, 1981, p. 20) for the client. Examples could include the employment of a consultant charged with conducting a search and screen activity for a key position or employing a consultant to design a compensation system.

Combined Styles

The four consulting styles described may, in fact, be combined. One such combination is to balance responsibility for defining and solving problems between the consultant and the client. This is often labeled a "collaborative" (Block, 1981, p. 21) role, but it is also suggested in the "confrontational" style described by others (Blake & Mouton, 1976, p. 4). A second combination involves the staging or sequencing

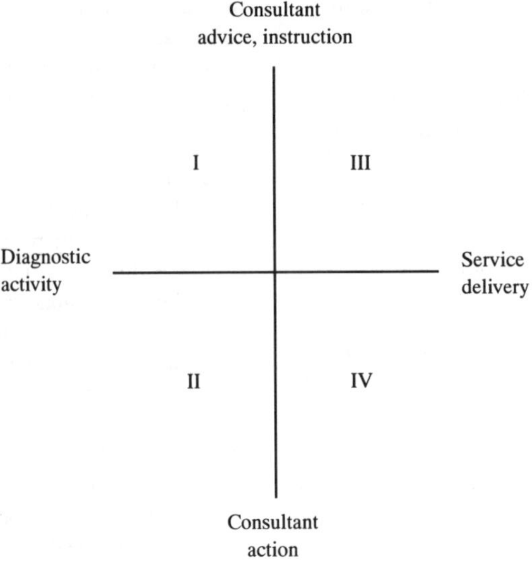

Figure 1 Consultancy intervention models

of styles, for example, process consulting followed by supervisory TRAINING if it is indicated.

Selection of Styles

The relative value of different consulting styles will depend upon the following:

1. The extent to which the consulting style generates valid information. Styles which spend relatively more effort at problem definition are likely to provide more reliable and valid information.
2. The extent to which the consulting style provides for client independence vis-à-vis the consultant. Independence is promoted by educating the client and by keeping responsibility of finding solutions with the client (Brickman, Rabinowitz, Karuza, Coates, & Kidder, 1982, pp. 368–384).
3. The extent to which the consulting style enhances internal COMMITMENT by the client. Styles which insure that actions by the client are based on his or her personal choice are more likely to promote internal commitment than actions which are dictated by others (Argyris, 1970, p. 20).
4. The extent to which emotional barriers interfere with rational choice by the client. Styles which provide for uncritical acceptance and support of clients may be needed before problem-solving actions are possible.
5. The extent to which the consulting style includes consultant support in problem solving. Consulting styles which insure that the consultant will help with problem solving as well as problem identification will meet this requirement, in contrast with styles which end responsibility with problem definition.

See also **Double loop learning; Organizational learning; Organization development**

Bibliography

Argyris, C. (1970). *Intervention theory and method: A behavioral science view*. Reading, MA: Addison-Wesley.

Blake, R. & Mouton, J. (1976). *Consultation*. Reading, MA: Addison-Wesley.

Block, P. (1981). *Flawless consulting*. Austin, TX: Learning Concepts.

Brickman, P., Rabinowitz, V., Karuza, J., Coates, D. & Kidder, L. (1982). Models of helping and coping. *American Psychologist*, 37, No. 4, 362–384.

Holtz, H. (1993). *How to succeed as an independent consultant*. New York: Wiley.

ALAN C. FILLEY

consultancy style *see* CONSULTANCY; CONSULTANCY INTERVENTION MODELS

contingency theory This denotes a body of literature that seeks to explain the structure of organizations by analyzing their adjustment to external factors, particularly changing circumstances that introduce UNCERTAINTY in DECISION MAKING.

Prior to the development of contingency theory, organizations were usually understood as closed systems (*see* SYSTEMS THEORY), with ORGANIZATIONAL DESIGN based primarily on maxims for organizing that emerged from literature on public BUREAUCRACY and military organization. Contingency theory drew attention to the organization's environment and to its TECHNOLOGY both of which were understood as outside the organization and as subjects of independent or exogenous causation; hence, the term OPEN SYSTEMS (*see* ORGANIZATION AND ENVIRONMENT). Contingency theory viewed organizations as reacting to the environments and technologies around and within them rather than to the effects of organizations on their environments. Conceptualization of these sources of contingency tended to be broad with frequent reference to "the environment" without specifying the sources of such effects. So while open systems perspectives continue to figure prominently in organizational research, most succeeding theory has focused on the reciprocal relationship between internal organization and its context. In addition, contingency theory often viewed organizations in a static way, assuming that adjustment to contingencies would happen in a straightforward, often rationally designed and managed way.

The primary argument of contingency theory is that when activity in the organization is routinized, bureaucratic organization prevails (*see* ROUTINIZATION). The fixed structure of bureaucracy is undermined when contingencies generate high levels of uncertainty. This happens either when technological factors or the environment is unstable, producing numerous unanticipated events requiring a response, or when the pattern of inputs to the organization is complex. In either case, structure becomes more complex with a finer DIVISION OF LABOR, more highly trained and skilled personnel, fewer written rules, and less direct vertical SUPERVISION. Organizations in unstable environments, or those using rapidly changing technologies, display patterns of interdependency that are characterized by large numbers of nonroutine problems whose solutions have implications for many parts of the organization. Because the parts affected by each problem differ, and the problems do not repeat themselves in precisely the same way, a customized response is required. This leads to a fluid mode of organization or an organic system as opposed to a mechanistic system (Burns & Stalker, 1961) (*see* MECHANISTIC/ORGANIC)

Contingency theory was undermined when its empirical base was called into question. Technology loomed less large to subsequent researchers when it was shown that research designs mixed partial organizations, such as factories owned by larger corporations, with free-standing organizations with a full complement of support functions (e.g., finance, marketing). Size seemed to matter as much as technology and many effects that appeared to emanate from the technology were as much a function of size (*see* ORGANIZATIONAL SIZE). In addition, the reactive nature of contingency theory drew criticism from those who saw many issues of TECHNOLOGY and environment as subject to managerial choice. Finally, the relatively undifferentiated conceptualization of the environment drew criticism as subsequent researchers focused attention on the flow of resources and the tendency for POWER in organizations to emanate from resource flows.

See also **Resource dependence; Leadership contingencies; Strategic types; Organization theory; Organizational change**

Bibliography

Burns, T. & Stalker, G. M. (1961). *The management of innovation*. London: Tavistock.

Lawrence, P. R. & Lorsch, J. W. (1967). *Organization and environment*. Cambridge, MA: Harvard University Press.

Pugh, D. S., Hickson, D. J., Hinings, C. R. & Turner, C. (1969). The context of organization structures. *Administrative Science Quarterly*, **14**, 91–114.

Thompson, J. D. (1967). *Organizations in action*. New York: McGraw-Hill.

JOHN FREEMAN

continuous improvement The view that organizations should strive ceaselessly to improve is a basic principle of TOTAL QUALITY MANAGEMENT. Continuous improvement has long been advocated by the two leading gurus of the quality movement, J. M. Juran and the late W. Edwards Deming. One of Deming's famous Fourteen Points was "improve constantly and forever the system of production and service."

Japanese students of Deming and Juran readily embraced the concept, translated as kaizen, decades ago. Continuous improvement today is a fundamental to the Japanese management style. Continuous improvement "is a pervasive concept linked to all Japanese manufacturing practices" (Young, 1992, p. 684).

The notion of continuous improvement is not obvious from the perspective of ORGANIZATION THEORY. For example, the concept of continuous improvement contrasts with the concept of dynamic homeostasis in OPEN SYSTEMS theories. Open systems theories treat changes to the system as disruptions or threats to survival. The system is seen as constantly striving to return to an equilibrium state that preserves its basic character. By contrast, the idea of continuous improvement suggests that there may be no state of dynamic equilibrium. Rather, organizational members consciously choose to keep the organization in a chronically unfrozen state.

A number of texts provide specific tools and techniques for the practice of continuous improvement (e.g., Imai, 1987; Robson, 1991; Schonberger, 1982). These tend to emphasize work analysis, production techniques, and group problem solving techniques.

Employees do not always embrace the concept of continuous improvement. Some in the labor movement characterize it as part of a pattern of "management by STRESS" (e.g., Parker & Slaughter, 1988), in which managers cajole employees into surrendering ideas that may eliminate their jobs. Without employment guarantees, the PRODUCTIVITY increases that result from continuous improvement may indeed threaten jobs (*see also* Job insecurity). Thus, Young (1992) hypothesized that continuous improvement will be adopted faster and will be more successful where there is a lower likelihood that workers will be laid off from their jobs. It is also possible to reward employees directly for offering suggestions leading to improvement. This is a common practice in Japan (Imai, 1987). Young (1992) hypothesized that the availability of monetary and nonmonetary REWARDS would enhance the adoption and effectiveness of continuous improvement efforts.

See also **Operations management; International management; Innovation; Employee involvement**

Bibliography

Imai, M. (1987). *Kaizen: The key to Japan's competitive success*. New York: Random House.

Parker, M. & Slaughter, J. (1988). *Choosing sides: Unions and the team concept*. Boston: South End Press.

Robson, G. D. (1991). *Continuous process improvement: Simplifying work flow systems*. New York: Free Press.

Schonberger, R. J. (1982). *Japanese manufacturing techniques: Nine hidden lessons in simplicity*. New York: Free Press.

Young, S. M. (1992). A framework for successful adoption and performance of Japanese manufacturing practices in the United States. *Academy of Management Review*, **17**, **(4)**, 677–700.

GERALD E. LEDFORD, JR.

contract Macneil (1980) in *The New Social Contract*, defines contract as "the relations among parties to the process of projecting exchange into the future." Stinchcombe argues that one can find in contract all the elements of HIERARCHY; that is, all the elements of organization. For example, in contracts you can find: command structures and AUTHORITY systems, incentive systems, administered pricing systems (costs, qualities, prices), a structure for the resolution of conflict and standard operating procedures, all elements of hierarchy. Clearly, an understanding of contract is essential to understanding organization, and organizational behavior.

Moreover, understanding what is meant by the concept of contract has taken on even greater importance in organizational literature in the light of increased reliance on economic-based theories of organization such as TRANSACTION COST THEORY and AGENCY THEORY. As contract's roots are embedded in law, a brief review of its legal elements will be helpful in understanding the varied ways in which it is being used in improving our understanding of organizations.

If they are to be legally enforceable, contracts must involve an agreement between *competent persons*. Whether the parties are competent may be evident from the COGNITIVE PROCESSES they employ and their cognitive styles. If they are not competent, their participation in the exchange governed by the contract is not voluntary.

One of the cornerstones of our definition of organizations, however, is that those who join them do so on a voluntary basis. Discussions of the JOINING-UP PROCESS frequently are built on explicit assumptions of voluntary action, but always voluntary behavior is an implicit assumption in research on relationships between organizations and their employees. For example, the reciprocal expectations and obligations that underlie the PSYCHOLOGICAL CONTRACTS between organizations and those who join them are premised on an unstated assumption of voluntariness. Thus, competence to contract is a necessary, but by itself, not sufficient condition of organization.

Legally enforceable contracts also require *consideration*, which can be defined as a right, interest, profit, or other form of benefit that accrues to one party; or, some detriment, disadvantage, responsibility, or loss assumed by the other party. Consideration reflects a promise (or a set of promises) to do or not to do something. To a large degree, the organizational literature describing psychological contracts focuses heavily on issues related to consideration. Needless to say, a substantial literature has evolved out of the need for consideration if a contract is to be legally enforceable. Theories regarding PAY and MOTIVATION, extrinsic REWARDS, or PERFORMANCE RELATED PAY, to name but three of the many cited elsewhere in this text, all stem from the need to provide consideration in employee contracts.

A case can also be made that consideration defines the minimal (if not the complete) authority and command system requirements of an organization. That is, all employees of an organization promise not to act in certain ways without consulting others, or cede the right to act independently to an individual (the CEO) or to some other governing group (the Board of Directors) (*see* GOVERNANCE AND OWNERSHIP).

The requirements of COMPETENCY and CONSIDERATION mean that legally enforceable contracts are reasoned and the products of free and rational agents; that is, the parties are possessed with AUTONOMY. These conditions are consistent with a third legal requirement in the design of a contract: it is essential that both parties agree to the same thing in the same sense and that they enjoy a meeting of the minds on the essential terms and conditions of the contract. This *mutual consent* must be evident in the language that the parties employ, or from their words or actions.

Obviously, good INTERPERSONAL SKILLS and bargaining ABILITY will be required of all parties to an exchange if a meeting of the minds is to result. Interpersonal CONFLICT must be dampened during the **ex ante contract** stages of a potential relationship.

Prior to commencing the **ex ante contract** stage of NEGOTIATION, the parties should have conducted their own GOAL SETTING so that they are clear on what are their own objectives for the exchange, and what they expect from their exchange partner(s).

Additionally, what parties promise must be *valid subject matter*. The goals pursued in voluntary PARTICIPATION, or the things which represent consideration, should not be contrary to public law, general policy, public justice, or violate provisions of federal or state constitutions, federal or state statutes, or the common law. This necessity for legal subject matter exists in both the **ex ante contract** and **ex post contract** stages of a relationship. In organizations, this explains the heavy emphasis on ACCOUNTABILITY, the need for public scrutiny, and the increasingly frequent reliance on CODES OF CONDUCT to facilitate ethical behavior (*see* BUSINESS ETHICS; CORPORATE SOCIAL RESPONSIBILITY).

Contracts can be classified in one of two forms: explicit or implicit. Explicit contracts are easily recognizable in classical or neoclassical contract law (Macneil, 1974; 1978). They are what we typically think about as we consider the concept of contract. For example, the partnership agreement, or the public corporation charter are explicit contracts. JOINT VENTURE agreements are explicit contracts, as are COLLECTIVE BARGAINING agreements.

Contracts may also be implicit. In organizational terms we think of them as psychological contracts, involving an "unwritten set of expectations operating at all times between every member of an organization" (Schein, 1970, p. 22). These expectations vary with the structure implied by explicit contracts defining organizational purpose. Expectations address areas such as norms, the nature of work, work ROLES, social relationships, or JOB SECURITY needs.

In frameworks based on the theory of transaction cost economics, contract thus contemplates a relationship between at least two parties, in which there is reliance on a law of contract, accompanied by an assumption that the parties will have access to institutions which John Commons has described as institutional guarantors. Institutional guarantors are creations of a state that permit private parties to employ the legitimized coercion of the state in the resolution of conflicts arising from transaction. The prior existence of "the state" thus facilitates, but is not required for contract (*see* GOVERNMENT AND BUSINESS).

In the economics literature, contract is the means through which transacting occurs under three types of governance structure; what Williamson describes as markets, hierarchies (or other authority based social structures), or so-called mixed modes of governance such as STRATEGIC ALLIANCES. A contract developed for use in any of these generic governance structures may (or may not) contain provisions that have been designed to protect the interests of the parties: safeguards. The general objective of these safeguards is to protect the parties from problems that arise out of two key behavioral assumptions made by many economists and organization theorists. First, parties to a contract are assumed to experience limited or BOUNDED RATIONALITY; that is, they cannot foresee (perfectly or otherwise) all possible states of nature and/or the performance obligations associated with each of those states of nature. Second, all parties to contracts are assumed to be capable of acting opportunistically (guilefully in their own self-interest), although they will do so in varying degrees. Contractual safeguards become more essential in cases in which the object(s) of exchange – assets – will be employed frequently under uncertain conditions and cannot easily be redeployed to equally productive (profitable) uses: the assets are idiosyncratic to the transaction.

The contract is also likely to say something about **how** the parties will design and manage their *production function* and its attendant costs. Alternative ways of defining these production costs are likely to be weighed by the parties with and against the costs of transacting within the design of the production function structure. Transaction costs economists assert that parties seeking economic efficiency in their dealings will employ a governance structure minimizing the combined affects of production and transaction costs, most of which are costs required to negotiate and agree to a contract that will be legally enforceable if need be.

Williamson (1985), one of the leading economic scholars involved in the development of a transactions approach to organization suggests that three forms of contract may be observed. First, nonidiosyncratic or general purpose assets may be employed by parties. Here, contracting approximates "classical market contracting." Classical market contract implies the existence of a legal contract and that the coercive force of a state is available to parties seeking remedies for breach. There may, however, be situations where the parties will need to exchange idiosyncratic assets. Two choices are open to the contracting parties here: they may contract (1) with, or (2) without, safeguards designed to protect those assets. An implicit assumption here is that all necessary safeguards will be created by the parties and thus will be endogenous to the contract.

Ring and Van de Ven (1989, 1992) offer an alternative perspective on contract, arguing that the different types of contract described by transaction costs economists constitute separate, and distinct, governance modes. They describe three types of contracting – discrete, recurrent, or relational – and the conditions under which each is likely to be employed. Discrete contracts are part of every day organizational life. Newspapers are purchased from vendors as employees enter the workplace. The "coffee vendor" provides reasonable food and beverage at reasonable prices; or, is replaced. Paper clips are exchanged for a "P.O." These exchanges tend to be simultaneous, the stakes are not high, and substitutes are plentiful.

Recurrent contracts involve repeated exchanges between the same organizations (or the same individuals) of assets that do not create great risks of opportunistic behavior. Parties using recurrent contracts tend to define terms related to consideration with some degree of specificity; but some contingencies may be left to future resolution when a complete meeting of the minds is not possible because of UNCERTAINTY or bounded rationality. Temporally, the duration of these contracts is relatively short term. The parties see themselves as autonomous, legally equal, but contemplating a more embedded relationship.

Recurrent contracting is frequently used to explore outcomes driven by motives other than efficiency, to experiment with safeguards, and with alternative methods for resolving conflict. Neoclassical contract law (Macneil, 1974) provides the legal framework within which these, predominantly, market-based transactions are governed, although as Macaulay observes, norms, more than law, governs much of this form of transacting.

In contrast, relational contracts tend to involve long-term investments, stemming from ground work laid by recurrent bargaining, in the production and transfer of property rights among these legally equal and autonomous parties. The property, products, or services jointly developed and exchanged in these transactions entail highly specific investments, in ventures that cannot be fully specified or controlled by the parties in advance of their execution. As a consequence, the parties to these relational contracts are exposed to a much broader variety of trading hazards than their counterparts employing either discrete or recurrent contracts. When inevitable disputes arise, they are resolved through internal mechanisms designed to preserve the relationship and insure that both the efficiency and equity outcomes sought in the long-term relationship are realized (*see* CONFLICT RESOLUTION). In contrast to the unified governance typically attributed to hierarchy, bilateral governance is employed in relational contracts.

A last type of contract relevant to organizations warrants a brief mention in closing. Implicit in relationships between organizations and the CULTURE or governmental system in which they are embedded, is the social contract. Changing societal expectations regarding the social contract have an enormous impact on organizations, the ways in which they contract, and the substance of their contracts with their stakeholders. The very recent interest in JUSTICE, PROCEDURAL and DISTRIBUTIVE, within organizational studies stems from an earlier awakening of its importance in the realm of social justice. Issues such as DISCRIMINATION, EQUAL OPPORTUNITIES, and corporate governance addressed elsewhere in this volume reflect redefinition of the nature of the social contract and have had a profound effect on organizations and their management. Issues related to COLLECTIVE BARGAINING and TRADE UNIONS reflect similar shifting societal views about the scope of the social contract.

See also **Intergroup relations; Interorganizational relations; Politics**

Bibliography

Alchian, A. A. & Demsetz, H. (1972). Production, information costs, and economic organization. *American Economic Review*, **62**, 727–795.

Cheung, S. (1983). The contractual nature of the firm. *Journal of Law and Economics*, **26**, 1–21.

Commons, J. R. (1950). *The economics of collective action*. Madison: University of Wisconsin Press.

Goldberg, V. (1980). Relational exchange: Economics and complex contracts. *American Behavioral Scientist*, **23**, 337–352.

Llewellyn, K. N. (1931). What price contract. *Yale Law Review*, **40**, 704–751.

Macaulay, S. (1963). Non-contractual relations in business. *American Sociological Review*, **28**, 55–70.

Macneil, I. R. (1974). The many futures of contract. *Southern California Law Review*, **47**, 691–816.

Macneil, I. R. (1978). Adjustments of long-term economic relationship under classical, neoclassical, and relational contract law. *Northwestern University Law Review*, **72**, 854–906.

Macneil, I. R. (1980). *The new social contract*. New Haven, CT: Yale University Press.

Ring P. S. & Van de Ven, A. H. (1989). Legal and managerial dimensions of transactions. In A. H. Van de Ven, H. Angle & M. S. Poole (Eds), *Research on the management of innovation: The Minnesota studies* (pp. 171–192). New York: Ballinger/Harper & Row.

Ring, P.S. & Van de Ven, A. H. (1992). Structuring cooperative relationships between organizations. *Strategic Management Journal*, **30**, 483–498.

Schein, E. (1970). *Organizational psychology*. New York: Prentice-Hall.

Stinchcombe, A. L. (1990). *Information and organizations*. Berkeley: University of California Press.

Williamson, O. E. (1985). *The economic institutions of capitalism*. New York: Free Press.

PETER SMITH RING

control The concept of control is of such wideranging significance and usage in almost all fields of inquiry, that it almost defies definition. The core of the concept is represented by the study of cybernetics as the application of an operator to effect an activity in relation to a standard. Note that this does not need to imply conformance to a standard – control can be effected to depart from as well as to maintain a standard. The essential notion is that some desired criterion exists or can be conceived, and that an agent or operator can effect an activity (behavior, mechanism, strategy, etc.) with reference to it.

In psychology, the basic cybernetic model was influentially employed by Miller, Galanter, and Pribram (1960) as a goal-oriented alternative to behaviorist models of human action (*see* LEARNING, INDIVIDUAL). In everyday tasks, it was argued, cognition and intent effect behaviors through TOTE cycles: Test-Operate-Test-Exit. The control sequence is exited when the results of behavior meet the test standard via FEEDBACK (e.g., PERCEPTION). This model has been widely adopted and elaborated to explain a variety of human functions, including learning, task behaviors, intention, and SELF-REGULATION. Control theory typically conceives of nested cycles from the most basic, and largely unconscious, perceptual-motor operations up to the most strategic or conceptual levels (*see* ACTION THEORY) (Lord & Levy, 1994). Applications of control theory are used to diagnose and correct dysfunctions in various contexts, such as ERRORS and SKILL acquisition (*see* HUMAN–COMPUTER INTERACTION).

Within ORGANIZATIONAL BEHAVIOR the concept of control has wide relevance. Feedback processes and feedback seeking are of particular importance (Ashford & Cummings, 1983), since both feedback and standards are required by organizational control systems. These concepts are especially important in the field of MOTIVATION, since goals and intentions mobilize control attempts. Of particular interest here are INDIVIDUAL DIFFERENCES in control-related motivation, such as achievement, power (*see* ACHIEVEMENT, NEED FOR; POWER, NEED FOR) (Heckhausen, 1991), and LOCUS OF CONTROL. Although the strength of need for control varies across individuals (*see* PERSONALITY) it has long been recognized that a drive for competence is a normal human characteristic. Indeed, so pervasive is this motive, coupled with the cognitive disposition to make causal attributions in chance situations, that it is commonplace for people to believe they have more scope for control than is actually feasible: the so-called "control illusion" (Langer, 1983). This is responsible for many typical errors of management and LEADERSHIP (*see* ATTRIBUTION; BEHAVIORAL DECISION RESEARCH; PERSISTENCE).

At the more general level of business operations, control theory can be of great practical value in understanding system failures and how to enhance management effectiveness (*see* ORGANIZATIONAL EFFECTIVENESS; SYSTEMS THEORY). The notion of a control loop (*see* Figure 1) can be applied to system performance at any level to inquire whether standards are appropriate, whether operations affect behavior, whether results meet standards, whether sensors are tuned to detect variances and whether they are positioned at appropriate positions in the system. The results of this analysis can be used to reform any of the elements, e.g., DECISION MAKING, environmental scanning, stategic goals, operating standards, measurement methods, REWARDS and disincentives, resourcing and sources of disturbance,

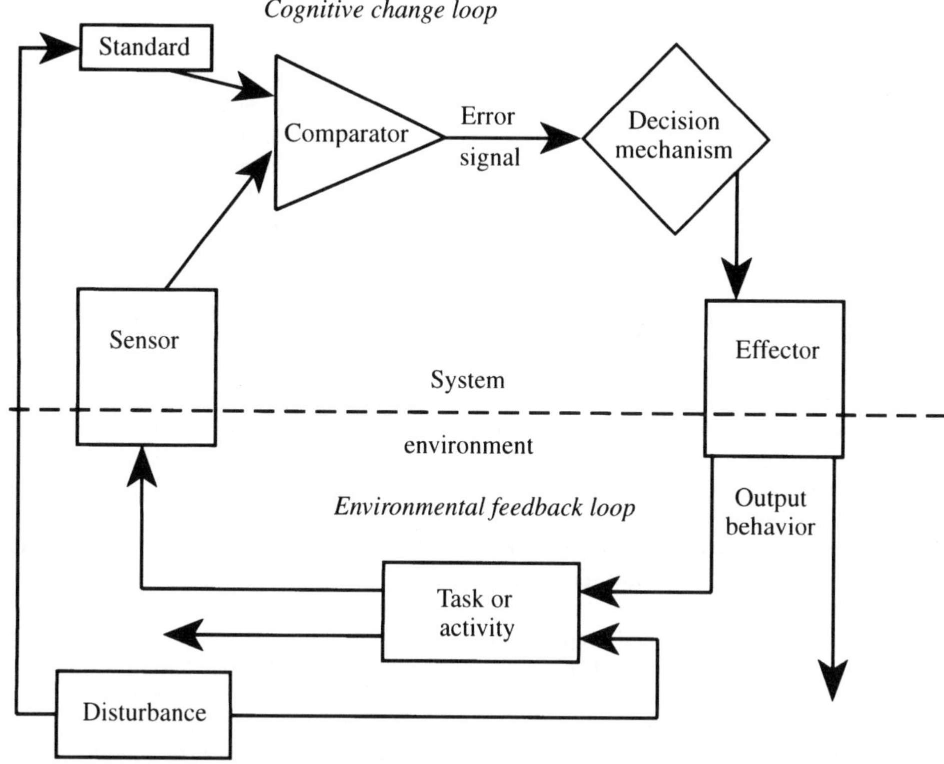

Figure 1 Basic negative feedback loop in a control system
Source: R. G. Lord and P. E. Levy (1994). Reprinted by permission of Lawrence Erlbaum Associates Ltd., Hove, UK.

or to question the constitution and focus of the control system overall (*see* DOUBLE LOOP LEARNING). The model is thus a powerful aid to managerial control at various levels – from the analysis and regulation of individual motivation (*see* VIE THEORY) to the STRATEGIC MANAGEMENT of the firm. The field has a potentially rich future, in which one can expect to see increasingly sophisticated COMPUTER MODELING of control systems as an aid to their analysis, design, and reform.

See also **Conditioning; Cognitive processes; Knowledge of results; Objectives, management by; Organizational learning**

Bibliography

Ashford, S. J. & Cummings, L. L. (1983). Feedback as an individual resource: Personal strategies of creating information. *Organizational Behavior and Human Performance*, **32**, 370–398.

Heckhausen, H. (1991). *Motivation and action.* New York: Springer-Verlag.

Langer, E. J. (1983). *The psychology of control.* Beverly Hills, CA: Sage.

Lord, R. G. & Levy, P. E. (1994). Moving from cognition to action: A control theory perspective. *Applied Psychology: An International Review*, **43**, 335–398.

Miller, G. A., Galanter, E. & Pribram, K. H. (1960). *Plans and the structure of behavior.* New York: Holt, Rinehart & Winston.

NIGEL NICHOLSON

control theory *see* PERSISTENCE; SELF-REGULATION

co-ownership *see* COOPERATIVES; DEMOCRACY; GOVERNANCE AND OWNERSHIP

cooperatives A convenient definition distinguishes cooperatives from other types of organization, primarily the conventional capitalist firm (CF), by requiring that:

(1) most services of a cooperative be provided or used by its members;
(2) the cooperative be the primary outlet for the provision or use of services by most members; and
(3) membership rights be held approximately equally.

Cooperatives may be organized by sellers of inputs or by buyers of outputs. The most prominent among sellers' cooperatives are those organized by workers, called worker or producer cooperatives (PCs). Other sellers' cooperatives include marketing cooperatives, especially in agriculture, where producers combine efforts to sell their produce. The most prominent among buyers' cooperatives are consumers cooperatives (CCs). Other buyers' cooperatives include, for example, purchasing cooperatives organized by farmers, and some nonprofit organizations. In many cooperatives membership is well defined and is related to the purchase of a certain number of shares. But members are rarely the only providers (in a PC) or users (in a CC) of a cooperative's services. For example, many PCs employ hired workers and many CCs allow nonmembers to purchase there.

In general, cooperatives come into existence when they can improve their members' welfare relative to what they could expect in CFs. For example, workers in PCs may be able to obtain a combination of better WORKING CONDITIONS and wages than they could in a CF in which management takes advantage of its bargaining power or if workers do not express their true preferences for the fear that this information will be exploited by management and will result in lower wages or worse conditions than otherwise. Similarly, consumers are not exposed to exploitation of asymmetric information in CCs as they may be in CFs. Effective and long lasting PCs and CCs therefore have mechanisms, such as democratic DECISION-MAKING mechanisms (*see* DEMOCRACY) that allow members to express their preferences, and limited trading of shares to prevent their concentration that may lead to transformation into CFs.

These and other traits express (or are intended to preserve) the unique features of cooperatives that distinguish them from CFs and provide their raison d'être in a market economy. The internal organization of cooperatives differs from that of CFs, reflecting their unique traits. Cooperatives have flatter hierarchies (*see* HIERARCHY), less formal monitoring of employees, considerable member PARTICIPATION in decision making, rely less on individual financial incentives, wages are more equal, and have more stable employment than comparable CFs. The little information about the economic performance of CCs is mixed: U.S. consumer-owned electric power companies seem to enjoy some advantage, whereas U.S. banking-like institutions owned by depositors appear to suffer some disadvantage, as compared to CFs. As for PCs, evidence suggests that they perform at least as well as CFs.

Nonetheless, various obstacles connected chiefly to problems of collective action, limit the formation of new cooperatives. The weight of PCs and CCs is most economies is quite limited, though related forms (mainly employee-owned firms and nonprofit organizations) are gaining prominence in many countries (*see* NOT-FOR-PROFIT ORGANIZATIONS). The economic weight of cooperatives as well as their structure and behavior differs markedly across countries. This is due to differences in national laws and CULTURE, and, probably more importantly, to the importance of national cooperative associations and the services they provide to member-organizations (*see* CULTURE, NATIONAL).

See also **Governance and ownership; Organizational citizenship; Cooperation**

Bibliography

Ben-Ner, A., Montias, J. M. & Neuberger, E. (1993). Basic issues in organizations: A comparative perspective. *Journal of Comparative Economics*, **17**, (2), 207–242.

Bonin, J., Jones, D. C. & Putterman, L. (1993). Theoretical and empirical studies of producer cooperatives: Will the twain ever meet? *Journal of Economic Literature*, **31**, 1290–1320.

Brazda, J. & Scheding, R. (Eds), (1990). *Consumer cooperatives in a changing world* International Cooperative Alliance.

Brown, L. (1985). Democracy in organizations: Membership participation and organizational characteristics in U.S. retail food cooperatives. *Organizational Studies*, **6**, (2), 313–334.

Cordell, L. R., MacDonald, G. & Wohar, M. (1993). Corporate ownership and the thrift crisis. *Journal of Law and Economics*, **36**, 719–756.

Peters, L. L. (1993). Non-profit and for-profit electric utilities in the United States: Pricing and Efficiency. *Annals of Public and Cooperative Economics*, **64**, (4), 575–604.

AVNER BEN-NER

core competence Prahalad and Hamel (1990) originated the term core competence. Without specifically defining it, they described core competencies as:

> the collective learning in the organization, especially how to coordinate diverse production skills and integrate multiple streams of technologies . . . (core competence) is also about the organization of work and the delivery of value . . . core competencies . . . spawn unanticipated products. The real sources of advantage are to be found in management's ability to consolidate corporate wide technologies and production skills into competencies that empower individual businesses to adapt quickly to changing opportunities (pp. 81–82).

As examples, Prahalad and Hamel suggested that Canon had core competence in optics, imaging and microprocessor controls, Philips in optical-media (laser disks), Honda in engines and powertrains, 3M in sticky tape, and Citicorp in systems.

Prahalad and Hamel considered that core competencies were analogous to the roots of a tree. The existence of core competencies could result in the development of core products (the tree's trunk) which could then create businesses (the tree's branches) and finally end products (the leaves on the tree).

Taking the optics example above, a core product that resulted from this was the laser printer engine, which created the business of computer printers with end products of laser printers, color video printers and bubble jet printers.

Prahalad and Hamel stated that a core competence must meet three tests. First, does it provide potential access to a wide variety of markets? Second, does it make a significant contribution to the perceived customer benefits of the end product? Third, is it difficult to imitate?

The concept of core competence is consistent with the RESOURCE-BASED THEORY of organizational success. Under this theory, resources – tangible and intangible assets – are combined through organizational routines (Nelson & Winter 1982), creating organizational capabilities. If any of these capabilities are valuable to the customer, difficult to acquire, difficult to replicate, difficult to be appropriated by other parties, and are durable, they provide the basis for sustainable competitive advantage and superior economic performance (*see* COMPETITIVENESS).

Selznick (1957) originated a similar term, "distinctive competence." This was defined as those things that an organization does especially well in comparison to its competitors. The difference between these terms is that a core competence is, necessarily, "core" to the organization whereas a distinctive competence need not be. However, it is unclear exactly how "core" should be determined. Since core competencies must be able to spawn products for a wide variety of markets, it seems that few competencies could be "core" for any particular organization. Further, for a core competence to be valuable, organizations would need to be diversified to use it. This need not be so for distinctive competencies or for the resource-based view in general (*see* DIVERSIFICATION).

There is little research available to demonstrate what core competencies are considered to exist in organizations, how they have been identified, how they have been used, or how their existence can be verified objectively. Nevertheless, in practice, the term "core competence" has become very common. It is being used for all types of organizations, not just diversified ones, to describe what might previously have been considered "distinctive competencies" or "capabilities."

All these terms emphasize the idea that business success can be built from within the organization. The popularity of the core competence concept and the emerging resource-based theory reflects a swing of concentration back to the organisation from the more externally-oriented industry analysis approach to strategy which dominated the 1980s (*see* FIVE FORCES FRAMEWORK). In fact, both must be addressed, if organizations are to exhibit superior performance.

See also **Strategic management; Organizational effectiveness; Excellence; Strategic types; Technology**

Bibliography

Grant, R. (1991). *Contemporary strategic analysis*. Oxford, UK: Blackwell.

Nelson, R. & Winter, S. (1982). *An evolutionary theory of economic change*. Cambridge, MA: Harvard University Press.

Prahalad, C. K. & Hamel, G. (1990). The core competence of the corporation. *Harvard Business Review*, **68**, May–June, 79–91.

Selznik, P. (1957). *Leadership in administration*. New York: Harper & Row.

Stalk, G., Evans, P. & Shulman, L. (1992). Competing on capabilities: The new rules of corporate strategy. *Harvard Business Review*, **70**, March–April, 57–69.

GRAHAM HUBBARD

corporate social performance Corporate social performance (CSP) is defined as a business organization's configuration of principles of social responsibility, processes of social responsiveness, and observable outcomes as they relate to the firm's societal relationships (Wood, 1991, p. 693). CSP theory is in part a response to neoclassical economics' narrow emphasis on maximizing shareholder wealth. CSP scholars envision societies as complex webs of interconnected cause and effect, and business as a social institution with both POWER and responsibility. CSP, then, has to do with the antecedents and outcomes of business organization operations.

In the CSP model, three principles of corporate social responsibility – institutional legitimacy, public responsibility, and managerial discretion – define structural relationships among society, the business institution, business organizations, and people.

The principle of institutional LEGITIMACY states that society grants legitimacy and power to business, and that business must use its power in a way that society considers responsible. General institutional expectations are made of any business organization, and organizational legitimacy is achieved and maintained by complying with these institutional expectations.

The principle of public responsibility states that business organizations are responsible for outcomes related to their primary (mission – or operations-derived) and secondary (related to, but not derived from, mission or operations) areas of societal involvement (Preston & Post, 1975). Each business *organization* has unique responsibilities because of the type of business it is – its size, industry, markets, product/service mix, etc.

The principle of managerial discretion states that managers are moral actors and are obligated to exercise all available discretion toward socially responsible outcomes (*see* MORAL DEVELOPMENT). This principle of individual responsibility emphasizes that within various domains of business activity (economic, legal, ethical, charitable; Carroll, 1979), managers are not completely constrained in their choices. This principle acknowledges the creative tension between a manager's DECISION-MAKING, autonomy and agency relationship.

Processes of corporate social responsiveness, the second dimension of CSP, represent characteristic BOUNDARY-SPANNING behaviors of businesses. These processes, linking social responsibility principles and behavioral outcomes, include:

(a) environmental assessment: gathering and assessing information about the external environment;
(b) STAKEHOLDER management: managing the organization's relationships with relevant persons, groups, and organizations; and
(c) issues management: tracking and developing responses to social issues that may affect the company.

In the neoclassical economic tradition, business outcomes are thought of as narrow financial measures such as profit, share value, and market share. In the stakeholder view of organizations, outcomes are defined as consequences to stakeholders, including persons, organizations, and societies; for example, product SAFETY, human rights, natural resource use, pollution, and effects on local communities.

Previous research has attempted to link corporate social and financial performance, but crude measures and the lack of adequate theory have precluded any consistent findings (Ullmann, 1985) (*see* ORGANIZATIONAL EFFECTIVENESS). Current scholarship instead considers financial performance to be only one dimension of social performance.

Current research focuses on linking CSP to theories of stakeholders, ethics, and organizations; systematizing the assumptions and theoretical implications of the CSP model; empirically testing ideas about how people perceive, interpret, and enact CSP; examining the validity of the CSP model in crosscultural and multinational settings; and critiques of existing CSP theory.

See also **Business ethics; Altruism; Values; Stakeholders; Reputation**

Bibliography

Carroll, A. B. (1979). A three-dimensional model of corporate performance. *Academy of Management Review*, **4**, (4), 497–505.

Preston, L. E. & Post, J. E. (1975). *Private management and public policy: The principle of public responsibility*. Englewood Cliffs, NJ: Prentice-Hall.

Ullmann, A. (1985). Data in search of a theory: A critical examination of the relationships among social performance, social disclosure, and economic performance. *Academy of Management Review*, **10**, 540–577.

Wartick, S. L. & Cochran, P. L. (1985). The evolution of the corporate social performance model. *Academy of Management Review*, **10**, (4), 758–769.

Wood, D. J. (1991). Corporate social performance revisited. *Academy of Management Review*, **16**, (4), 691–718.

DONNA J. WOOD

counseling in organizations There are a range of possible counseling activities in organizations, from those concerned with personnel selection to CAREER guidance to STRESS counseling at work (*see also* VOCATIONAL GUIDANCE). There is no clear-cut definition of counseling readily available, but it usually involves two fundamental activities; "advice giving" and "supporting and helping." Most counseling whether about careers or job stress is comprised of a number of SKILLS to achieve its objectives, as Dryden, Charles-Edwards, & Woolfe, (1989) suggest in their *Handbook of Counselling in Britain*, "such as listening actively to the other person's feelings, focussing on their problem rather than on our own immediate concerns, and being accepting and uncritical."

There are a number of different schools of counseling, from the psychoanalytic to the humanistic or experiential growth movement to the behavioral/cognitive therapies (Dryden et al., 1989). These range from exploring early childhood experiences in the former movement to cognitive re-appraisal or behaviorist approaches in the latter therapies.

In the workplace or organizational environment, the most common form of counseling is stress counseling. As the pace of economic, technological and social change grows, so employees are beginning to show increasing signs of job-related stress (Cartwright & Cooper, 1994). This is manifesting itself in sickness ABSENTEEISM, labor TURNOVER, "presenteeism" (being at work but not performing) and poorer organizational morale and PRODUCTIVITY (*see* WITHDRAWAL). One way in which organizations are trying to deal with this problem is through stress counseling. The movement toward organizational counseling has taken two forms; in-house stress counseling and Employee Assistance Programs (EAPs). In the former, counselors are employed within either the occupational health service or the human resource department. The counselors in this context make themselves available to all employees on a confidential basis and provide support and advice-giving on a range of problems, from personal to marital to CAREER DEVELOPMENT. Recent evidence indicates that these in-house programs are able to reduce sickness absence and improve the mental well-being of employees (Cooper & Sadri, 1991) (*see* MENTAL HEALTH). The downside is that some employees may feel inhibited from using them because they are "in-house", that is, not in essence, confidential, with personal information possibly ending up in their personnel records.

The other major form of counseling is the EAP. An EAP has been defined as: "A programatic intervention at the workplace, usually at the level of the individual employee, using behavioral science knowledge and methods for the control of certain work-related problems (notably alcoholism, drug abuse, and mental health) that adversely affect job performance, with the objective of enabling the individual to return to making her or his full contribution and to attaining full functioning in personal life" (Berridge & Cooper, 1993) (*see* ALCOHOL AND SUBSTANCE ABUSE). EAPs are out-house forms of counseling. Counseling, clinical psychology or psychiatric organizations provide the counseling for the private or public sector company on a consultancy basis. The organization may determine policies defining the goals of the counseling service, but contracts its delivery to an external EAP provider. Research in the United States shows them to be effective in reducing medical care costs. For example, Feldman (1991) reported that the General Motors program saved $37 million per year by assisting up to 100,000 employees. More detailed and systematic research needs to be done on both in-house and EAP programs to confirm their impact on the individual as well as on bottom-line costs.

See also **Quality of working life; Human resources management; Emotion; Performance, individual; Emotions in organizations; Consultancy intervention models**

Bibliography

Berridge, J. & Cooper, C. L. (1993). Stress and coping in US organisations; The role of the EAP. *Work and Stress*, 7, 89–102.

Cartwright, S. & Cooper, C. L. (1994). *No hassle: Taking the strain out of work*. London: Century.

Cooper, C. L. & Sadri, G. (1991). The impact of stress counselling at work. *Journal of Social Behavior and Personality*, **6**, 411–423.

Dryden, W., Charles-Edwards, D. & Woolfe, R. (1989). *Handbook of counselling in Britain*. London: Tavistock.

Feldman, S. (1991). Trust me: Earning employee confidence. *Personnel*, **68**, 7.

CARY L. COOPER

creativity Organizational researchers and high-level managers in organizations have displayed growing interest in creativity in recent years, perhaps because individual and team creativity is seen as the primary means by which organizations can maintain competitive advantage (*see* COMPETITIVENESS). Creativity is generally defined as the generation of ideas or products that are both novel and appropriate (correct, useful, valuable, or meaningful). However, theorists and researchers have a long history of disagreement over the definition of creativity. Gestalt psychologists and, more recently, cognitive psychologists have focused on the creative process (the thought processes and stages involved in creative activity). Other theorists have argued that creativity is best conceptualized in terms of the person (the distinguishing characteristics of creative individuals).

Although many contemporary theorists think of creativity as a process and look for evidence of it in persons, current definitions most frequently use characteristics of the product as the distinguishing signs of creativity. Most product definitions stipulate that a creative product or response must be both novel and appropriate. An additional criterion used by some researchers is that the task should be heuristic (open-ended) rather than algorithmic (having a clear path to solution). Although many researchers operationally define creativity as performance on creativity tests, most consider consensual product assessment by experts as more appropriate; a product or idea is deemed creative to the extent that appropriate observers agree it is creative. Similarly, in identifying particularly creative individuals in work organizations, most researchers rely on the consensual assessment of managers and peers.

Prior to about 1980, the field of creativity research was dominated by a PERSONALITY TRAIT approach that sought to identify reliable INDIVIDUAL DIFFERENCES between persons who consistently produce highly creative work and persons who do not. As a result, some areas of inquiry that are potentially important for organizational studies were virtually ignored. There was a concentration on the creative person to the neglect of creative situations; there was a narrow focus on intrapersonal determinants of creativity to the neglect of external determinants; and, within studies of intrapersonal determinants, there was an implicit concern with genetic influences to the neglect of contributions from learning and the social environment. Contemporary theorists have begun to argue that creativity is best conceptualized not as a personality trait or a general ABILITY but as a behavior resulting from particular constellations of personal characteristics, cognitive abilities, and environmental factors (e.g., Amabile, 1988).

Personal Characteristics

A cluster of personal characteristics has been repeatedly identified as important to high-level creative behavior:

(a) self-discipline in matters concerning work;
(b) an ability to delay gratification;
(c) perseverance in the face of FRUSTRATION;
(d) independence of judgment;
(e) a tolerance for ambiguity;
(f) a high degree of autonomy;
(g) an absence of SEX-ROLE stereotyping;
(h) an internal LOCUS OF CONTROL;
(i) an orientation toward RISK-TAKING; and
(j) a high level of self-initiated, task-oriented striving for excellence.

Recently, creativity theorists and researchers have also shown an interest in the role of MOTIVATION in creativity. Research suggests that INTRINSIC MOTIVATION (engaging in an activity because of interest, involvement, or personal challenge) is more conducive to creativity than EXTRINSIC MOTIVATION (engaging in an activity to achieve some external goal).

Although it is important for creative individuals to be skilled in their particular domain, several domain-independent features of cognitive style appear to be relevant to creativity:

(a) perceptual FLEXIBILITY;
(b) cognitive flexibility;
(c) understanding complexities;
(d) keeping response options open as long as possible;
(e) suspending judgment;
(f) using "wide" categories;
(g) remembering accurately;
(h) breaking out of performance scripts; and
(i) perceiving creatively.

Research on ENTREPRENEURSHIP has begun to examine the impact of the personality traits, motivational orientations, and cognitive style of entrepreneurs on their creative activity.

Work Environment Influences

Social–psychological experiments on the effect of particular factors on the creativity of adults and children have demonstrated that evaluative pressures, surveillance, contracted-for reward, competition, and restricted choice can undermine intrinsic motivation and creativity by focusing the individual on external reasons for doing the task (Amabile, 1988). Expanding beyond these experimental methods, research in work organizations has utilized the observational methods of interviews and questionnaires to examine the complex effects of work environment on individual and team creativity. Work environments most conducive to the fulfillment of creative potential appear to be characterized by: a high level of worker AUTONOMY in carrying out the work, encouragement to take risks from administrative superiors, work groups that are both diversely skilled and cooperative; COMMUNICATION and collaboration across WORK GROUPS, and a substantial degree of challenge in the work. There appear to be four "balance factors" handled effectively by managers who promote creativity: *goals* that are set clearly at the overall strategic level (*see* GOAL-SETTING), but left loose at the operational level; REWARDS that are neither ignored nor overly emphasized; *PERFORMANCE APPRAISAL systems* that provide constructive, frequent FEEDBACK on work without generating threatening negative criticism; and *pressure* arising from the challenging, urgent nature of the work rather than from arbitrary time pressure or intraorganizational competitive pressure.

Current research on work environments is directed toward identifying the links between individual or team creativity and overall organizational INNOVATION.

Creativity Enhancement in Organizations

Since the 1950s, a growing number of creativity-enhancement TRAINING programs have been offered to organizations. The oldest and most widely used program, and the source from which most such programs have been developed, is the Creative Problem Solving process. This process, developed during the 1950s and 1960s from the BRAINSTORMING technique, involves the use of checklists and forced relationships in addition to the brainstorming principles of deferred judgment and quantity of idea generation.

Synectics, a somewhat similar process, relies more heavily on the use of metaphor and analogy in the generation of novel ideas. The guiding principle of synectics is to "make the familiar strange and strange familiar" – to use cognitive techniques for distancing oneself from habitual thought patterns, and to also attempt to see connections between something new and something that is already understood. The prescribed cognitive techniques include personal analogy, direct analogy, symbolic analogy, and fantasy analogy.

Although research on the long-term effectiveness of creativity-training programs is limited, many managers and HUMAN RESOURCE MANAGEMENT professionals utilize such programs for employee development.

In order to gain a more comprehensive understanding of creativity in organizational contexts, contemporary theorists are attempting to integrate personality, cognitive, and work environment factors.

See also **Self-actualization; Self-regulation; Interactionism**

Bibliography

Amabile, T. M. (1988). A model of creativity and innovation in organizations. In B. M. Staw & L. L. Cummings (Eds), *Research in organizational behavior* (vol. 10). Greenwich, CT: JAI Press.

Isaksen, S. (Ed.), (1987). *Frontiers in creativity research: Beyond the basics*. Buffalo, NY: Bearly.

Runco, M. A. & Albert, R. S. (Eds), (1990). *Theories of creativity*. Newbury Park, CA: Sage.

Sternberg, R. J. (Ed.), (1988). *The nature of creativity*. New York: Cambridge University Press.

TERESA M. AMABILE and MARY ANN COLLINS

crises The terms crisis and disaster are frequently used but often not precisely defined. In common usage, a crisis refers to a radical change in status while a disaster characterizes a sudden, often unforeseen, misfortune. The terms evoke mixed interpretations concerning causality and intentions since crises and disasters stem from known and unknown uncontrollable causes as well as from carelessness, ignorance, and/or lack of due diligence.

Historically, analyses of crises and disasters have often attempted to isolate specific causal factors with deterministic models (e.g., from engineering as in the WASH-1400 a.k.a., the Rasmussen Report, 1975). Lists of separable causal factors include such categories as human error (*see* ERRORS), mechanical/electrical failure, external anomalies, design deficiencies (including systems, equipment, and component designs), and procedural inadequacies (including technical procedures, administrative protocols, and administrative controls). Analysts often attempt to isolate a proximate, primary cause as well as contributing factors.

OB research recognizes that increasing numbers of crises and disasters are embedded in organizations. Thus, Pauchant and Mitroff (1992) define a crisis in terms of disturbance to a whole system coupled with challenges to the basic assumptions of that system (*see* SYSTEMS THEORY). One can envision four severity levels of crises/disasters:

Level I: Dramatic reduction in financial and/or reputational well-being (*see* REPUTATION); substantial destruction of property; serious injury to persons and/or the physical environment (e.g., the 1993 Pepsi product tampering case and the 1979 Three Mile Island nuclear accident).

Level II: Death of involved individuals; injury to the general public or destruction of a habitat with disruption of an ecosystem (e.g., the 1989 Exxon Valdez oil spill).

Level III: Death in the general public, extinction of a species or destruction of an ecosystem (e.g., the 1982 Tylenol product tampering case and the 1986 Bophal chemical accident).

Level IV: Alteration of future generations such as by changes in the gene pool of a species (e.g., the 1986 Chernobyl nuclear disaster).

Collectively, the literature presents a rich series of concepts to isolate dynamics within organizations associated with dysfunctional outcomes. These concepts include both unintended and intended dynamic patterns of interaction among elements of a complex system. Perrow (1984) was among the first to emphasize a systems view in his analysis of "normal accidents." The concept of a normal ACCIDENT stresses that "given systems characteristics, multiple and unexpected interactions of failures are inevitable" (p. 5). Perrow emphasized the inherent inconsistencies among technical requirements in high-risk systems with their "tight coupling" and administrative capability (*see* LOOSE-COUPLING). Using Perrow's terminology, for example, plants that transform raw materials into marketable products may have numerous interactive "tight couplings" among technical systems, equipment, and components so that a small change in one part of the production process quickly alters another. To manage usual conditions, administrative systems are often rigid, procedural-driven mechanistic systems with sufficient detail to tell operators and supervisors what to do (*see* MECHANISTIC/ORGANIC). When an anomaly occurs, however, individual initiative, a keen sense of problem IDENTIFICATION, and other individualistic attributes fostered by more decentralized organic systems may be necessary (*see* DECENTRALIZATION). Since executives cannot now develop administrative systems that are simultaneously mechanistic and organic, Perrow recommends that high-risk transformation systems should be altered or abandoned if catastrophes are to be avoided.

Many scholars also stress the importance of multiple minor events and how they can quickly escalate into a catastrophe with high-risk technologies. This theme was a central feature of Starbuck and Milliken's (1988) analysis of the Challenger disaster (the 1986 explosion of a U.S. space shuttle). They introduced the concept of "fine-tuning to disaster." As with "normal accidents," "fine-tuning-to-disaster" attempts to explain a systems dynamic that underlies accidents. Starbuck and Milliken argued that engineers and managers are expected to improve technical and administrative systems. Unfortunately, these improvements may have unintended consequences because:

(a) specific improvements may be implemented in isolation but tightly coupled in operation; and
(b) the causal models linking prior success (failure) and future success (failure) are faulty.

Thus, partially contradictory attempts to improve different system features are continued even though the effects of the changes cannot be completely understood. "Improvements" are continued until the system mysteriously breaks. Both "normal accidents" and "fine-tuning-to disaster" emphasize unintended consequences arising from the complexities and limitations of modern organizations. Both are in the qualitative tradition of this literature where one or a few exemplary disasters are examined in detail.

In contrast, Osborn and Jackson (1988) suggest that high-risk systems may be prone to "purposeful unintended consequences." Here, it is assumed that executives have an influence on administrative systems. The concept of "purposeful unintended consequences" is based on a combination of PROSPECT THEORY, institutional inertia, and AGENCY THEORY. Although executives claim they make choices or at least modify recommendations by subordinates, they were found to purposively deny: (a) potential trade-offs among economic, executive, and social outcomes; (b) organizational inadequacies; and (c) their own risk biases (*see* RISK TAKING). Executives promulgated a series of myths suggesting that: (a) efficiency and safety are positively linked (e.g., a reliable plant is a safe plant); (b) their organizations are highly competent; and (c) they are risk neutral. Extensive data analyses concerning the safeness of all operating United States commercial nuclear power plants showed that not only were the myths inaccurate (e.g., safeness and efficiency measures were not related), but that executive risk biases and organizational inadequacies combined to yield a potentially serious pattern of safety deficiencies. While the risk bias and organizational inadequacies (e.g., Perrow, 1984; Starbuck & Milliken, 1986) are knowable, the threats to the public may continue because executives continue to perpetuate the criteria myth (e.g., a reliable plant is a safe plant).

Recent work by Pauchant and Mitroff (1992) also shows that mythology, in the form of rationalizations, can combine with "VICIOUS CYCLES" (*see* ORGANIZATIONAL LEARNING) to yield a crisis prone organization. A crisis prone organization is subject to vicious cycles because it has:

(1) too narrow a strategic focus;
(2) an inappropriately rigid structure with few provisions to deal with a crisis;
(3) a CULTURE replete with rationalizations and myths; and
(4) a collective psyche filled with defense mechanisms, among other factors.

Pauchant and Mitroff (1992) argue that by reversing identified strategic, structural, cultural, and psyche deficiencies, the firm can move toward becoming a crisis-prepared organization and be less subject to vicious cycles.

The concepts discussed here were developed to help understand and prevent some of the most deleterious consequences of organizational activity. However, these concepts also appear relevant to examining ORGANIZATIONAL CHANGE, ORGANIZATIONAL DESIGN and, of course, ACCIDENTS.

See also **Organizational culture; Learning organization; Safety; Risky shift; Dilemmas, organizational; Turnaround management**

Bibliography

Osborn, R. N. & Jackson, D. H. (1988). Leaders, riverboat gamblers, or purposeful unintended consequences in the management of complex dangerous technologies. *Academy of Management Journal*, **20 (4)**, 924–947.

Pauchant, T. C. & Mitroff, I. I. (1992). *Transforming the crisis-prone organization*. San Francisco: Jossey-Bass.

Perrow, C. (1984). *Normal accidents: Living with high-risk technologies*. New York: Basic.

Starbuck, W. H. & Milliken, F. J. (1988). Challenger: Fine-tuning the odds unit something breaks. *Journal of Management Studies*, **25**, (4), 319–340.

WASH-1400, a.k.a., the Rasmussen Report. (1975). *Reactor safety study: An assessment of accident risks in U.S. commercial nuclear power plants*. Washington, DC: U.S. Nuclear Regulatory Commission.

RICHARD N. OSBORN

critical theory Uncritical theory, from the perspective of critical theorists, characterizes most of management and ORGANIZATION THEORY. This is uncritical when it assumes that management and organizations, and their understanding in theory, are disinterested, rational, and technical activities, rather than specific instruments of domination (of employees, consumers, the ecology, etc.) that mask their POLITICS, VALUES, and effects through a rhetoric of technique, neutrality, and service. The inspiration for critical theory derives from the work of a number of influential scholars associated with the "Frankfurt School" (*see* Jay, 1973) who sought to practice a form of "emancipatory" scholarship that was not interested in sectional domination of one part of the social or natural world by another, but in the emancipation of all elements from domination by any others. The impetus initially derived from Western Marxism (Anderson, 1983).

Critical theory applied to management and organizations seeks to transcend the sectional limits of a "managerialist" perspective, by representing the interests of other, often suppressed or marginalized, voices. These interests may be many: women; the ecology; the workers; blacks (*see* GENDER; RACE). What they have in common is their nonrecognition in, and lack of interest for, conventional management theory, in terms that the repressed, marginalized, silenced, etc., interests, would find authentic.

One problem is immediately evident: critical theory must assume that it knows what these other interests "really" are better than conventional theory does. Not only must it know these interests better than conventional theory: it must have some representational role that enables it to speak for these other interests. Such an assumption, however, may be too much. To claim to speak on behalf of some category, like "women," the "environment," or "workers," is fraught with the danger of representing as an interest what is itself only another partial understanding, albeit one informed by a different theory to that of managerialism. It is not clear that the categories of social identity map easily on to the theoretical interests that are often assumed. Some critical theorists argue that this problem can be overcome through using a democratic method of enquiry that invites all interests to participate in the research process, opening up understanding so that a genuine consensus can emerge, rather than one that is achieved through technically rational claims to authority (Habermas, 1984; Forrester, 1988). Technically rational claims to AUTHORITY, based on expertise such as "management," can always be seen implicitly to require a "deauthorizing" or "delegitimation" of other views.

Critical theory seeks to ensure that these other views are heard. It does so from a radical and emancipatory interest. The implicit view is that the repressed have a critical and emancipatory role unfulfilled because of their oppression. It is assumed that they, and critical theory as their voice, are the bearers of authenticity. There is the possibility that one may be mistaken, however. There are no guarantees of the "correctness" of any political representation because all representations index a shifting, unstable, and dynamic political context. They do not map on to anything outside the form of their own practice and the effects that they produce. In which case, if there are no general interests being either repressed or represented by management, much of the force of critical theory lapses. The critique of it as a politics of knowledge that masquerades as technical, instrumental practice is correct. Whether it does so to serve some general interests in repression or to block one of emancipation is more debatable.

See also **Feminism; Social constructionism; Postmodernism; Theory**

Bibliography

Anderson, P. (1983). *In the tracks of historical materialism.* London: Verso.

Forrester, J. (1988). *Planning in the face of power.* Berkeley, CA: University of California Press.

Habermas, J. (1984). *The theory of communicative action: Reason and the rationalization of society.* Boston: Beacon.

Jay, M. (1973). *The dialectical imagination.* London: Heinemann.

STEWART CLEGG

culture Culture is a notoriously difficult concept to define. In what is still regarded as the seminal book on the topic, Krober and Kluckholn (1952) identified 164 different definitions of culture proposed by prominent anthropologists. Most organizational theorists employed the term "culture" only casually until the 1980s when ORGANIZATIONAL CULTURE became a topic of considerable interest and when scholars began to examine cross-national differences in organizational life (Hofstede 1980). No progress has been made since Krober and Kluckholn in either anthropology or organization studies toward standardizing the meaning of culture. Nor is any standardization likely to occur in the future. Nevertheless, one can identify several general notions of culture prominent in the ORGANIZATIONAL BEHAVIOR literature. The most common stipulates that culture consists of "shared meanings, values, attitudes, and beliefs." Equally cognitive is the claim that culture consists of "interpretive schemes." The distinction is best understood as the difference between a psychological and an anthropological conception of sense-making (*see* COGNITION IN ORGANIZATIONS). The former focuses on a distribution of individuals' cognitions and evaluations while the latter connotes an extra-individual phenomenon. All else being equal, those who adopt the former definition are more likely to operationalize culture as modal attitudes than are those who adopt the latter approach.

The weakness of cognitive definitions of culture is that they usually exclude behavior patterns and physical artifacts which differentiate social collectives. A third notion of culture therefore stipulates a broader definition: "the way of life of a people." This definition is most closely associated with traditional cultural anthropology and ETHNOGRAPHY.

Culture is frequently used in contrast with structure, as in the phase: "the culture and structure of an organization." The meaning of the contrast is unclear, since few scholars explicitly distinguish between what they count as structure and what they count as culture. Moreover, many anthropologists treat structural arrangements as culturally bound. In some usages, culture actually seems to subsume structure.

Ultimately, however, culture (like structure) is perhaps best treated as a "sensitizing" concept whose denotations and connotations are usefully ambiguous. Culture evokes any and all differences that distinguish life in one social collective from life in another. The relevant social collective might be a society, an organization, an occupation, a sect, or a group. From this perspective, defining culture is less important than detailing the salient aspects of a way of life, particularly those that contrast with ways of life found elsewhere.

See also **Culture, national; Organizational climate; Intercultural process; International management**

Bibliography

Hofstede, G. (1980). *Culture's consequences*. Beverly Hills, CA: Sage.

Kroeber, A. L. & Kluckholn, C. (1952). *Culture: A critical review of concepts and definitions*. New York: Vintage.

Martin, J. (1992). *Cultures in organizations: Three perspectives*. New York: Oxford University Press.

Schein, E. (1985). *Organizational culture and leadership*. San Francisco: Jossey-Bass.

STEPHEN R. BARLEY

culture, cross-cultural research Cross-cultural research is done with the intention of facilitating comparison, and by definition it normally includes the gathering of descriptions from two or more cultures. The issues studied comparatively have tended to focus on people's attitudes, VALUES, beliefs, sources of MOTIVATION, satisfaction, etc., and are commonly assumed to predict behavior. It is normal to discuss results in terms of mean scores and to assume that the average of a set of responses is an indicator of the position of a particular culture on a scale of such attitudes.

The literature contains much research of this nature and a number of comprehensive reviews have tracked its progress over time (Child, 1981; Boyacigiller & Adler, 1991; Redding, 1994). As a result of research, a great deal has been learnt which allows the description of national or ethnic differences in attitudes to, beliefs about, and values surrounding work, AUTHORITY, and COOPERATION. Not enough has been learnt about the societal origins of such differences, about their implications for organization, or about their interaction with other factors surrounding organizational behavior.

Although alternative categorizations exist (e.g., Trompenaars, 1993) the most commonly used description of cultural comparisons has been developed by Hofstede (1991). Derived from a very large sample of statements about people's values, this theory explains cross-cultural differences as lying along four dimensions. The two primary dimensions are: Power Distance, or a society's sense of HIERARCHY; and Individualism–Collectivism, or the sense a person has of being psychologically separate from and independent of others, or alternatively linked inextricably by bonds of obligation into a network of others. These are deep-seated formulas or mental programs running through any society which result from the universal needs for order.

The other two dimensions are called UNCERTAINTY Avoidance and Masculinity–Femininity. The former reveals the extent to which members of a CULTURE feel threatened by uncertain or unknown situations and tend to behave to reduce uncertainty. The latter separates "masculine" societies where GENDER roles are distinct from "feminine" societies where they overlap. More recently, a fifth dimension, long-term versus short-term orientation, has been added to the set.

A summary of the implications for organizations is given in Table 1. This shows contrasting attributes of the extreme poles of these dimensions, their organizational relevance, and which countries tend to score at either pole.

The use of dimensions such as these consolidates earlier work in sociology on the

Table 1

Small power distance e.g., *Israel, Austria, Denmark, New Zealand*	*Large power distance* e.g., *Malaysia, Philippines, Mexico, Indonesia*
• Hierarchy in organizations means an inequality of roles, established for convenience. • Decentralization is popular. • Narrow salary range between top and bottom of organization. • Subordinates expect to be consulted. • The ideal boss is a resourceful democrat. • Privileges and status symbols are frowned upon.	• Hierarchy in organizations reflects the existential inequality between higher-ups and lower-downs. • Centralization is popular. • Wide salary range between top and bottom of organization. • Subordinates expect to be told what to do. • The ideal boss is a benevolent autocrat or good father. • Privileges and status symbols for managers are both expected and popular.
Collectivist e.g., *Venezuela, Colombia, Pakistan, Taiwan*	*Individualist* e.g., *USA, Australia, UK, Canada*
• Relationship employer–employee is perceived in moral terms, like a family link. • Hiring and promotion decisions take employees' ingroup into account. • Management is management of groups. • Relationship prevails over task.	• Relationship employer–employee is a contract supposed to be based on mutual advantage. • Hiring and promotion decisions are supposed to be based on skills and rules only. • Management is management of individuals. • Task prevails over relationship.
Feminine e.g., *Sweden, Norway, Denmark, Netherlands*	*Masculine* e.g., *Japan, Austria, Switzerland, Germany*
• Work in order to live. • Managers use intuition and strive for consensus. • Stress on equality, solidarity, and quality of work life. • Resolution of conflicts by compromise and negotiation.	• Live in order to work. • Managers expected to be decisive and assertive. • Stress on equality, competition among colleagues, and performance. • Resolution of conflicts by fighting them out.
Weak uncertainty avoidance e.g., *Singapore, Hong Kong, UK, Denmark*	*Strong uncertainty avoidance* e.g., *Greece, Japan, Portugal, Uruguay*
• There should not be more rules than is strictly necessary. • Time is a framework for orientation. • Comfortable feeling when lazy; hard-working only when needed. • Precision and punctuality have to be learned. • Tolerance of deviant and innovative ideas and behavior. • Motivation by achievement and esteem or belongingness.	• Emotional need for rules, even if these will never work. • Time is money. • Emotional need to be busy; inner urge to work hard. • Precision and punctuality come naturally. • Suppression of deviant ideas and behavior; resistance to innovation. • Motivation by security and esteem or belongingness.

Source: Adapted from Hofstede (1991).

Note: The four principal dimensions identified in Hofstede's work are continual, and country scores do not necessarily cluster at the extremes. The above must therefore be taken only as indicators of tendencies rather than absolute positions. There is of course also great variety within societies and a wide distribution of any particular tendency.

basic components of societal or national culture (*see* CULTURE, NATIONAL). There remain, however, a number of major research questions, including: What are the ways in each society whereby cultural components become shaped, remain stable, and self-replicate; What are the processes whereby their influence is conveyed into organizations and affects ORGANIZATIONAL BEHAVIOR; Are those dimensions now commonly used reasonably valid for all cultures and is the list reasonably comprehensive? Surrounding those questions are many others about the interaction of such forces with elements such as TECHNOLOGY, political system, and economic policies.

See also **Stereotypes; International management; International human resources management**

Bibliography

Boyacigiller, N. & Adler, N. J. (1991). The parochial dinosaur: Organizational science in a global context. *Academy of Management Review*, **16**, (2), 262–290.

Child, J. (1981). Culture, contingency and capitalism in the cross-national study of organizations. In L. L. Cummings & B. M. Staw (Eds), *Research in organizational behaviour* (vol. 3), pp. 303–356. Greenwich, CT: JAI Press.

Hofstede, G. (1991). *Cultures and organizations*. London: McGraw-Hill.

Redding, S. G. (1994). Comparative management theory: Jungle, zoo or fossil bed? *Organization Studies*, **15**, 1.

Trompenaars, F. (1993). *Riding the waves of culture*. London: Brealey.

GORDON REDDING

culture, group The phenomenon of group culture is important to understand since it impacts the behaviors of individuals within the group and ultimately, organization. CULTURE may be defined as the basic, taken-for-granted assumptions and deep patterns of meaning shared by organizational participants and manifestations of these assumptions and patterns. Culture is manifested in many forms, including myths, rituals, symbolic artifacts, and structure (*see* RITUALS AND RITES). Group culture is defined as a set of shared meanings and VALUES that influence their members' behaviors. If individuals in a department, group or team do not share these beliefs and values, then there is no group culture. Therefore, shared assignment of meaning and values that are developed through social interactions and/or SOCIALIZATION practices are needed for a group culture to form. Group cultures arise to help their members interpret the formal structure and managerial folklore, reconcile individual differences, and cope with the uncertainty surrounding the performance of tasks. Often times, competing group cultures attempting to control the behaviors of their members coexist within the same department and/or organization. This then produces alternative viewpoints on the fundamental nature of members' relationships to their group and organization.

Group culture in organizations is manifested in two components. The *materials* component consists of tangible symbols (e.g., insignias, reward systems) that represent deeper layers of meaning. These tangible symbols are interpretable only in their relation to the hidden meaning with which they correspond. The material component of a group's culture is framed by structural components embedded within the larger organization. The search for a group's culture requires that the group's *ideational* component be understood. This leads to the study of shared beliefs about the organization's mission and desirable standards of behavior. Members' personal characteristics (e.g., RACE; GENDER; ETHNICITY), social histories (e.g., family background, social class membership), and their positional characteristics (e.g., departmental assignment, time of day worked) play a major role in the formation of a group's culture. A group's culture is also influenced by various contextual variables, such as a group's life cycle (*see* GROUP DEVELOPMENT), processes and size, organizational ecology, and technological interdependence, among others, affect shared parsimonious meanings that members assign to key events in their group. It is through understanding these ideational and material components that groups within organizations develop their own values, assumptions, and interpretations, and even their own perspectives on the organization's mission and appropriate patterns of conduct.

See also **Group dynamics; Group norms; Organizational culture**

Bibliography

Jermier, J. M., Slocum, J. W., Jr., Fry. L. W. & Gaines, J. (1991). Organizational subcultures in a soft bureaucracy: Resistance behind the myth and facade of an official culture. *Organization Science*, **2**, 170–194.

Kerr, J. & Slocum, J. W., Jr. (1987). Managing corporate culture through reward systems. *The Academy of Management Executive*, **1**, 99–109.

Martin, J. (1992). *Cultures in organizations*. New York: Oxford University Press.

Sheridan, J. E. (1992). Organizational culture and employee retention. *Academy of Management Journal*, **35**, 1036–1056.

Trice, H. M. & Beyer, J. M. (1993). *The cultures of work organizations*. Englewood Cliffs, NJ: Prentice-Hall.

JOHN W. SLOCUM JR.

culture, national One of the core problems in the study of national CULTURE has been the lack of agreement on a definition of what culture is. This is now becoming less of a problem as people come increasingly to accept Hofstede's (1980) definition of it as "the collective programing of the mind which distinguishes the members of one group or category of people from another," or his more graphic metaphor of it as the "software of the mind" (Hofstede, 1991; see also Keesing, 1974).

People grow up in strong or weak cultures. When the culture is strong, SOCIALIZATION will instill a set of guidelines about behavior and appropriate thinking, and a "civilized" or acculturated person conforms to those guidelines. The cost of deviance is exclusion and because human beings are instinctively gregarious, they conform as the price of membership (*see* CONFORMITY). Many strong culture societies, e.g., Japan, China, France, have worked out their particular combination of norms (*see* GROUP NORMS) and VALUES in relative isolation from alternatives and there is no reason why all such separate historical social processes should replicate each other: hence, cultural variety surrounding the universal requirements to have a society which can apportion power acceptably and establish means for cooperation.

In the context of organizational studies, the issues have been those of understanding:

(a) how culture affects the design and functioning of a society's organizations; and
(b) whether and how the culturally derived values contribute to organizational, and eventually national, performance.

The questions have been given impetus by the impact of Japanese management on Western markets and the knowledge that Japan has a very distinct culture (*see* INTERNATIONAL MANAGEMENT).

There is much rich material available describing national cultural differences, making a case out for an impact on ORGANIZATIONAL BEHAVIOR. There is less clarity in explaining how this process works, and even less on linking culture to national performance. This is because culture is one of a set of influences and operates alongside development policies, education levels, institutional structures, technological borrowing, trading patterns, etc., to affect national growth. It cannot be a sole determinant of national success, or of the character of an organization.

The main organizationally relevant ways in which national cultures vary lie in:

(a) the way power and AUTHORITY are legitimized (*see* LEGITIMACY); and
(b) the way systems of cooperation are structured.

These two dimensions can be said to account for much of the international variation in organizational behavior. Where a society has clear rules supporting HIERARCHY, its organizations tend to be paternalistic and familistic with power focused at the top. Egalitarianism, on the other hand, is associated with the pursuit of PARTICIPATION and the decentralizing of power (*see* DEMOCRACY). Where the rules for cooperation begin with a strong sense of identity with a subgroup, as, for instance, when an individual's identity is subsumed into that of a family, then those loyalties will condition how other loyalties, e.g., to an organization, are expressed. By contrast, where INDIVIDUALISM is strongly developed, as in most Western cultures, the rationalities of task performance and legal contractual relationships tend to drive out social obligations as rules for conduct.

See also **Culture; Cross-cultural research; Intercultural process; Organizational culture; International human resources management; Expatriates**

Bibliography

Hofstede, G. (1980). *Cultures consequences*. London: Sage.

Hofstede, G. (1991). *Cultures and organizations: Software of the mind*. London: McGraw-Hill.

Keesing, R. M. (1974). Theories of culture. *Annual Review of Anthropology*, **3**, 73–97.

GORDON REDDING

D

decentralization For both organizational sociologists and management specialists, the distribution of POWER is probably the single most important structural attribute. If most members of the organization participate in its decisions, then the organization can be considered to be decentralized. In contrast, if most of the decisions and especially the most important ones are made by one person, then the organization is categorized as centralized.

Essentially, the problem of decentralization is a problem of power or of CONTROL. And there are a variety of ways in which the organizational literature, this has been addressed including the topics of HIERARCHY of AUTHORITY, closeness of SUPERVISION and of control.

There is much less agreement on how best to measure this concept and the field has basically three different approaches. Tannenbaum (1968) pioneered in the structural study of power as distinct from the study of POWER BASES with what he called the control graph. This measure, a general survey of the members of the organization, reports how much influence, which he called control, each level in the hierarchy has over the others. He found generally there are about four or five levels. With particular shaped slopes, Tannenbaum could then define specific distributions of power as democratic (*see* DEMOCRACY). In contrast, the research of the Aston group (Pugh, Hickson, Hinings, & Turner, 1968) measured the level to which a decision was delegated (*see* DELEGATION) in a large battery of decisions based on information from five or six informants. Likewise, the Blau measures (Blau & Schoenherr, 1971) are essentially ones of delegation, although they did not include as many decision areas. A third way of measuring the distribution of power is by asking individual members of the organization how often they participate in decision-making (*see* PARTICIPATION), again where a number of different kinds of decisions are listed. This approach has not been prominent in the research of Hage and Aiken (1967).

All of the above research studies have tended to use averages either across decisions and informants or individuals who have been surveyed. This methodological procedure assumes that participation, influence, or delegation is approximately the same in all areas of decision-making and in addition assumes that as one moves from the top of the hierarchy to the bottom, there is a steady increase in the amount of centralization. The one exception has been the work of Tannenbaum, which did allow for nonlinear arrangements but his approach has been little employed in the field. There are three distinctive kinds of discontinuity that can be discerned.

First, work decisions might be delegated, providing workers with a considerable amount of AUTONOMY while strategic decisions are concentrated at the top. This is very common in traditional organizations where crafts people or semiprofessionals work (*see* PROFESSIONALS IN ORGANIZATIONS). These organizations are small and there is a strong sense of self-control (*see* SELF-MANAGEMENT).

Second, strategic decisions and work decisions might be decentralized in some parts of the organization and not in others. Most typically, research and development might be given considerable autonomy while production, marketing, and finance/accounting might be much more centralized. These organizations are sometimes called mixed MECHANISTIC/ORGANIC.

Third, strategic decisions might be decentralized to divisions heads within the same organization as in the famous studies of Chandler (1962) but then each of the divisions might be quite centralized. More recently there has been a further step in this same process, namely the decentralization of strategic decisions to what are called profit centers, that is SUBUNITS within divisions.

As yet, there has been little research on the patterns of decentralization across the levels of the hierarchy and particularly between headquarters and the various divisions or profit centers and its consequences for the performance of the organization. However, all of the evidence points to a steady movement toward greater autonomy being given to smaller and smaller units, first as cost centers then as profit centers. Another critical issue in this debate is the question of which functions if any are maintained at the central headquarters beyond investment decisions, and what consequences does this have. Again, there is wide variety of patterns, with marketing, research, and other functions in some large companies being maintained at the corporate headquarters. Again, there has been a tendency to gradually decentralize these functions.

It is quite another question whether or not decentralization really means effective sharing of power. There are two lines of attack on this assumption in the literature. First, some such as Blau and Schoenherr (1971) have argued that if the organization is highly formalized (*see* FORMALIZATION), then decisions can be easily delegated, giving people the sense of participating without the reality. This work has not, however, made much distinction between strategic decisions and work decisions. Second, others such as Pfeffer (1981) argue that if the top executive or power elite control the agenda and the criteria by which people are rewarded, then there may be the appearance of decentralization and participation but, in fact, the power elite effectively controls the organization (*see* TOP MANAGEMENT TEAMS).

Finally, we must conclude with a special comment about decentralization in Japanese organizations. Considerable job autonomy is provided for the worker. Furthermore, there is extended discussion of major decisions up and down the hierarchy. This pattern might be called a combination of centralization and decentralization. What distinguishes it from the American or European discussions is the heavy emphasis on delegation rather than a joint decision-making within the entire hierarchy (*see* INTERNATIONAL MANAGEMENT).

See also **Decision making; Multinational corporations; Differentiation; Organizational design**

Bibliography

Blau, P. & Schoenherr, R. (1971). *The structure of organizations*. New York: Basic.

Chandler, A. D. (1962). *Strategy and structure: Chapters in the history of industrial enterprise*. Cambridge, MA: MIT Press.

Hage, J. (1980). *Theories of organizations*. New York: Wiley–Interscience.

Hage, J. & Aiken, M. (1967). Relationship of centralization to other structural properties. *Administrative Science Quarterly*, **12**, 72–91.

Hall, R. H. (1992). *Organizations: Structures, processes, and outcomes* (5th edn). Englewood Cliffs, NJ: Prentice-Hall.

Mintzberg, H. (1979). *The structuring of organizations*. Englewood Cliffs, NJ: Prentice-Hall.

Pfeffer, J. (1981). *Power in organizations*. London: Pitman Press.

Pugh, D. S., Hickson, D. J., Hinings, C. R. & Turner, C. (1968). Dimensions of organization structure. *Administrative Science Quarterly*, **13**, 65–105.

Tannenbaum, A. S. (1968). *Control in organizations*. New York: McGraw-Hill.

JERALD HAGE

decision making Because the quality and the acceptance of organizational decisions is vital to a company's functioning, this topic has traditionally been a focus of attention in the management literature. Alongside these sources, with their often normative and typically rational approach, are more recent studies which tend to take a more descriptive, analytic viewpoint. These studies clearly show that organizational decisions generally take an entirely different course from the one recommended by the classical literature.

Depending on:

(1) various context factors;
(2) the topic of decision making; and
(3) the policy of management, organizational decision-making processes can assume very different shapes (Koopman & Pool, 1990).

Decision making can show much or little centralization, and much or little FORMALIZATION. Sometimes information plays an important role in the decision preparation, sometimes POWER processes determine the contents of the decision and information primarily serves the purpose of legitimating after the fact (*see* LEGITIMACY). On the whole, research results in this field show that decision-making processes can vary primarily on four dimensions:

1. Centralization. The amount of centralization is one of the most important parameters of decision making. Much research has been done of the manner in which decentralization and PARTICIPATION take place in decision making and of the question of how effective participation is.
2. Formalization. A second important dimension is the extent to which the decision making is formalized. Decisions can take place according to an established procedure set down in advance, or they can proceed more flexibly, according to informal considerations of what is required or desirable.
3. Information. The way in which the substance of a decision comes about is important. On the basis of what information is a decision made? What alternatives are developed or sought, and from where do they come? Have important possibilities or consequences been overlooked?
4. Confrontation. The extent to which there is confrontation and CONFLICT in the decision making process. This last dimension comes from models of decision making as a political process, in which parties try to achieve their own interests on the basis of their power positions (*see* POLITICS).

Theoretically, classification based on the four dimensions would yield sixteen different models. Koopman and Pool argued that, in practice, combination of these dimensions leads to a typology of four basic models of decision making which can reasonably accommodate most literature in this field (Koopman & Pool, 1990; see Figure 1). They distinguish in this order: the neo-rational model, the bureaucratic model, the arena model, and the open-end model, in order to encompass as much empirical research as possible, and models based upon it. For example, Hickson, Butler, Cray, Mallory, & Wilson (1986) distinguished sporadic, fluid, and limited processes. Schwenk (1988) discussed the rational choice perspective, the organizational perspective and the political perspective. Thompson and Tuden (1959) distinguished decisions through computation, majority judgment, compromise, and inspiration. Fahey (1981) reduced reality to two contrasting types of decision making: rational–analytical versus behavioral–political. McCall and Kaplan (1985) spoke of quick versus convoluted action. Shrivastava and Grant (1985) distinguished the managerial autocracy model, the systematic bureaucratic model, the political expediency model, and the adaptive planning model.

There is often a clear relationship between the various models and the context (organizational structure and culture, environment) in which the decision making takes place. These relations are summarized in Table 1.

The *neo-rational model* is characterized by strong centralization, combined with low formalization and confrontation, when fairly simple decision making processes are guided and controlled from one point: the top management. There is little power distribution in the organization. This is termed the *neo*-rational model because it takes account of some fundamental characteristics relating to human cognitions and emotions. Because of this the behavior of decision makers is characterized by "BOUNDED RATIONALITY" and "SATISFICING" (as opposed to maximal) goal achievement.

This type of decision-making process may primarily be expected in the organizational type that Mintzberg (1979) termed a "simple structure" or "autocracy." In terms of ORGANIZATIONAL CULTURE, Harrison's (1972) "power culture" would be most conducive to this type of decision-making process.

The model is rational in the sense that decision-making aims to maximize the goals of top management. Intuition and quick decisions

Table 1 The four decision-making models and their hypothetical relationships with various context factors.

	Neo-rational model	*Bureaucratic model*	*Arena model*	*Open-end model*
Context factors				
Environment:				
Complexity	low	low	high	high
dynamics	high	low	low	high
hostility	high	low	high	low/high
Organization:				
power distribution	low	low	high	high
type or org. (Mintzberg)	autocracy	machine bureaucracy	professional bureaucracy	adhocracy
type of culture (Harrison)	power culture	role culture	person culture	task culture
Characteristics of decision maker	proactive, intuitive	reactive, analytic	autonomous, intrapreneur	innovative, willing to take risks
Type of subject:				
complexity	low	high	low/high	high
dynamics	high/low	low	high	high

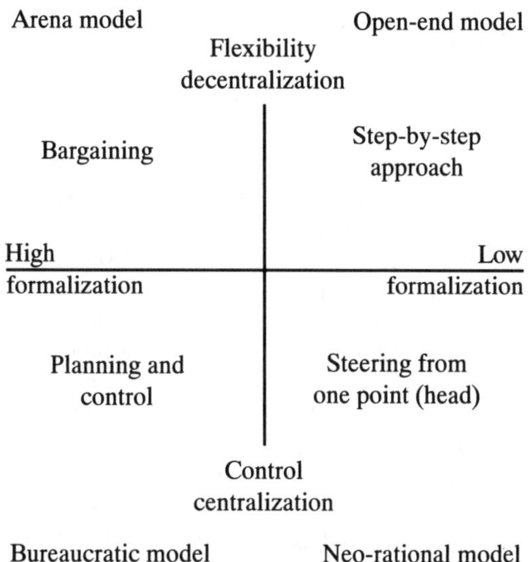

Figure 1 Four models of decision making
Source: P. L. Koopman and J. Pool (1990). Reprinted by permission of John Wiley & Sons, Ltd.

are more typical of this model than extensive analysis and study of alternatives. A dynamic and/or threatening environment can lead decision-making processes to follow the neo-rational model: they demand quick reaction.

Characteristic of the *bureaucratic model* is that decision making is "constricted" by rules and regulations. They may be rules of the organization itself, such as JOB DESCRIPTIONS, tasks and COMPETENCIES, meeting rules, etc., but also rules that are laid down outside the organization, as by legislation or by directives from the head office. Different actors or groups are expected to make their contribution at various stages, even if it merely means initialing a document. Various alternatives are explored and officially documented. The selection of the best solution is conducted by way of existing procedures. In contrast to the neo-rational model, the bureaucratic model usually involves fairly complex decision-making processes. Its counterpart in Mintzberg's structural typology is the "machine BUREAUCRACY" and in Harrison's culture typology the "ROLE culture." The environment is characterized by stability and predictability. When time pressure or external threats increase, decision making increasingly leans to the neo-rational model (temporary centralization). If innovation requirements are central, then characteristics of the open-end model gain the upper hand.

Decision making in the *arena model* is dominated by NEGOTIATIONS between various interested parties, which form coalitions around certain subinterests (*see* COALITION FORMATION). These groups defend a point of view or alternative as the only correct and legitimate view of reality. Power in the organization is distributed; power differences are small. There is no central machinery that can easily impose its will. Although there is a certain degree of coordination (primarily through professional training), the organization must constantly contend with the problem of acquiring sufficient consensus and acceptance for decisions. Mutual contention and lack of cooperation threaten the quality of the decision making. This type of decision making, over controversial topics, is primarily found in organizations composed of relatively independent units, such as universities or other "conglomerates." Decision making sometimes takes place at two levels: at the first level a small group of insiders arrives at the critical choices, which are subsequently legitimized for the constituency by the official bodies and by means of arguments which are accepted by these bodies. The natural counterpart in the structural typology of Mintzberg is the professional bureaucracy; in the culture typology of Harrison we should think of the "person culture."

Decision making in the *open-end model* is characterized by a limited view of the goals or of the means by which to achieve them. Chance circumstances and unpredictable events cross the path of this approach. Again and again, people must adapt to new demands and possibilities. This forces them to take a step-by-step approach (Quinn, 1980). Best known in this connection are the publications on the GARBAGE CAN MODEL, which were preceded by studies of the "Carnegie School" (Cyert & March, 1963).

A characteristic of the open-end model is that, depending on the problem in question, expertise of various types and locations must be gathered on a temporary basis (PROJECT MANAGEMENT). The message here is: organize flexibly (*see* FLEXIBILITY). Gradually, by way of iterations and recycling, the end product comes into view. Complex innovative decisions (e.g., automation) often take place in this way (*see* INNOVATION). Mintzberg's adhocracy forms the organizational structure conducive to this type of decision making. The environment is complex and dynamic. Such an organization generally has a "task culture" (Harrison, 1972).

Context and "Strategic Choice"

Decision making does not take place in a vacuum, but in a certain context, which can be described at various levels. From low to high aggregation levels, one can distinguish the decision maker(s), the group, the organization, and the environment. Each of these context levels makes up part of decision making and influences it. Furthermore, decision making is not a neutral exercise, but it is about something. Subjects of decision making can differ in complexity, in controversiality, in political import. Both of these factors (i.e., context and subject) are of importance for the manner in which the decision-making processes can be structured and controlled and for the course that they ultimately take.

In particular, the organization as the context in which decisions are made influences the manner in which decisions take place. The organizational context is, as Hickson et al. (1986) put it, "the rules of the game." Decision-making processes are largely determined by structural characteristics of the organization in which they take place (*see* ORGANISATIONAL DESIGN). Several researchers found a relationship between the type of organization and the dominant types of decision-making processes.

However, a decision-making process does not only come about as the result of interaction of several forces. Often one or more central actors (usually termed the "dominant coalition"), manage to give a strong personal accent to the decision-making process. This does not take place in complete freedom. A number of factors escape the control of management. No single party has complete control of the steering wheels, even if a coalition is dominant. Other actors or parties will also try to influence the direction the process takes. Nevertheless, a certain amount of leeway remains to give intentional form to decision-making processes, within the contingencies formed by the topic and the context.

A similar line of thought is used in the discussion of organizational structure as in Child's (1972) concept of "strategic choice." The presence of leeway for strategic choices implies that, in addition to the determining effects of environmental factors and TECHNOLOGY, opportunities still remain for personal accents. As opposed to a complete determinism, it is stated, there are opportunities for the management of a company to choose, without altering the determining influence of the contingency factors mentioned.

The same can be said of decision-making processes: although they are partly determined by their substance and the context in which they take place, the decision makers still have some discretion. The amount of discretion can vary by case and by organization, but how it is used largely determines how effective and efficient the decision-making process will be.

See also **Strategic management; Institutional theory; Organization and environ-**

ment; Top management teams; Group decision making

Bibliography

Child, J. (1972). Organization structure and strategies of control: A replication of the Aston study. *Administrative Science Quarterly*, **17**, 163–177.

Cyert, R. M. & March, J. G. (1963). *A behavioral theory of the firm*. Englewood Cliffs, NJ: Prentice-Hall.

Fahey, L. (1981). On strategic management decision processes. *Strategic Management Journal*, **2**, 43–60.

Harrison, R. (1972). Understanding your organizations character. *Harvard Business Review*, **50**, 119–128.

Hickson, D. J., Butler, R. J., Cray, D., Mallory, G. R. & Wilson, D. C. (1986). *Top decisions: Strategic decision-making in organizations*. Oxford, UK: Basil Blackwell.

Koopman, P. L. & Pool, J. (1990). Decision making in organizations. In C. L. Cooper & I. T. Robertson (Eds), *International review of industrial psychology*, (vol. 5), pp. 101–148. New York: Wiley.

McCall, M. W. & Kaplan, R. E. (1985). *Whatever it takes: Decision-makers at work*. Englewood Cliffs, NJ: Prentice-Hall.

Mintzberg, H. (1979). *The structuring of organizations: A synthesis of the research*. Englewood Cliffs, NJ: Prentice-Hall.

Pool, J. & Koopman, P. L. (1992). Strategic decision making in organizations: A research model and some initial findings. In D. Hosking & N. Anderson (Eds), *Organizational change and innovation: Psychological perspectives and practices in Europe* (pp. 71–98). London: Routledge.

Quinn, J. B. (1980). *Strategies for change: Logical incrementalism*. Homewood, IL: Irwin.

Schwenk, C. R. (1988). *The essence of strategic decision making*. Lexington, MA: Lexington Books.

Shrivastava, P. & Grant, J. H. (1985). Empirically derived models of strategic decision-making processes. *Strategic Management Journal*, **6**, 97–113.

Thompson, J. D. & Tuden, A. (1959). Strategies, structures and processes of organizational decision. In J. D. Thompson, P. B. Hammond, R. W. Hawkes, B. H. Junker & A. Tuden (Eds), *Comparative studies in administration*. Pittsburgh: Pittsburgh University Press.

PAUL KOOPMAN

decision modeling *see* COMPUTER MODELING

defence mechanisms *see* PROJECTION; ORGANIZATIONAL NEUROSIS

defenders *see* STRATEGIC TYPES

delayering *see* ORGANIZATIONAL RESTRUCTURING

delegation When a manager must depend on others to accomplish an objective, the notion of *delegation of authority* comes into play. Delegation means conferring of AUTHORITY from an executive to another to accomplish a particular assignment. Delegation gets the DECISION MAKING closer to the locus of where the decision is actually implemented. Typically, delegation refers to granting authority in a downward direction, although delegation can also be directed laterally or even upward. The idea of delegation has been well established in the historical management literature, and was a prominent part of the early principles of management (*see* Terry, 1972) (*see* MANAGEMENT, CLASSICAL THEORY).

Delegation is closely associated with the term PARTICIPATION, and *participative leadership*. Participation implies that the leader invites followers to participate actively in discussions, problem solving, and decision making, but retaining final decision-making authority. Delegation is somewhat stronger, implying the locus of decision making is in the hands of the follower.

Participation and delegation are points on a continuum, rather than discrete modes of leader behavior. But whatever the degree, delegation does not mean that a leader abdicates responsibility. A manager who delegates retains the overall responsibility, and must follow up to assure that the delegated task has been carried out.

One of the more widely known prescriptive models of delegation is the Vroom–Yetton (1974) model. The model attempts to answer the question of the conditions under which a leader should be directive versus participative. Vroom and Yetton propose a direction-participation continuum ranging from extreme leader decision making, through increasingly involving forms of participation, to pure delegation. The situational characteristics that define the conditions include such factors as: quality requirement, sufficiency of information, problem structure, and importance of subordinate acceptance (*see* GOAL-SETTING). Depending on the combination of these situational variables, the degree of decision-making participation and/or delegation is recommended.

Delegation is also related to the more contemporary concept of SUPERLEADERSHIP (Manz & Sims, 1989) which means "leading others to lead themselves." A Super Leader is one who develops followers to the point where they are capable of accepting a high degree of responsibility and decision-making discretion. Manz and Sims would describe a follower to whom a leader would delegate as empowered self-leaders. SuperLeadership is a more fine-grained and contemporary form of delegation. Also, today, one is more likely to find the popular use of the term "EMPOWERMENT" (rather than delegation) to represent a broad philosophy and practice of participation and delegation (*see* EMPLOYEE INVOLVEMENT).

Perhaps the most important contemporary form of real delegation are self-managing or self-directed teams (Manz & Sims, 1993) (*see* SELF-MANAGED TEAMS). After development and experimentation in the 1970s and 1980s, self-managing teams have become considerably more diffused in the early 1990s. Self-managing teams are a form of delegation where the WORK GROUP becomes empowered with a very high degree of decision-making discretion. In an important meta-analysis (*see* VALIDITY GENERALIZATION), Macy, Bliese and Norton (1991) have empirically shown the bottom line contribution of self-managing teams to organizational PRODUCTIVITY. Also, at the professional or middle level of organizations, empowered professional or KNOWLEDGE WORKER teams are becoming more important (*see* PROFESSIONALS IN ORGANIZATIONS). These include teams such as concurrent engineering teams, product improvement teams, office worker teams, and new venture teams.

See also **Self-management; Superleadership; Leadership; Path – goal theory; Power; Leadership contingencies**

Bibliography

Macy, B. M., Bliese, P. D. & Norton, J. J. (1991). Organizational change and work innovation: A meta-analysis of 131 North American field experiments—1961–1990. Working paper. Texas Technical University.

Manz, C. C. & Sims, H. P. Jr. (1989). *SuperLeadership*. New York: Berkley.

Manz, C. C. & Sims, H. P. Jr. (1993). *Business without bosses: How self-managing teams are producing high-performing companies*. New York: Wiley.

Terry, G. R. (1972). *Principles of management* (6th edn). Homewood, IL: Irwin.

Vroom, V. H. & Yetton, P. W. (1974). *Leadership and decision-making*. New York: Wiley.

HENRY P. SIMS JR.

Delphi The Delphi group format continues to be an important technique by which a wide array of expert opinion can be generated to maximize the range of alternative solutions to issues and problems. In the Delphi group format to DECISION MAKING, experts typically respond to questionnaires about issues and problems, which is then used to generate multiple expert opinions, without the need for face-to-face contact. Of course, the lack of face-to-face contact reduces the possibility of interactive discussion and challenge, but Delphi groups can be adapted to enable the experts to react to a second round of opinion, in response to the expert input from the first round.

The Delphi group technique for GROUP DECISION MAKING was originally developed by the Rand Corporation for the United States' Air Force in the 1950s. It has since been adapted in business organizations as an effective alternative to traditional methods of decision making, especially in relation to complex and long-term issues, problems, and concerns (Tompkins, 1985). An example would be to use the Delphi technique to gather the opinions of experts around the world about economic growth and political conditions over the next 10 years, with the aim being better prepared for conditions which might be substantially different from the present and require a substantially different organizational response.

The Delphi group technique for decision making continues to serve business and governmental organizations alike in a way that other similar techniques, such as the nominal group, are unable to. These other techniques, however, should be thought of not as competing alternatives, but rather complementary alternatives.

See also **Nominal group technique; Brainstorming; Creativity; Innovation**

Bibliography

Gustafson, D. H., Shukla, R. K., Delbecq, A. & Walster, E. H. (1973). A comparative study of differences in subjective likelihood estimates made by individuals in interacting groups, Delphi groups, and nominal groups. *Organizational Behavior and Human Performance*, **9**, 280–291.

Tompkins, C. J. (1985). Forecasting business conditions. In L. R. Bittel & J. E. Ramsey (Eds), *Handbook for professional managers* (pp. 337–367) McGraw-Hill. New York.

RANDALL S. SCHULER

democracy Within organizations democracy has the same general overtones as in POLITICS: the ability of members of the organization to voice their opinions and to exercise influence over policy (*see* EMPLOYEE INVOLVEMENT; EMPOWERMENT; PARTICIPATION). The means of expression are different: political democracy rests on the ability to vote leaders out of office whereas this is not the case in most organizations.

Various models of democracy have been proposed in the light of this. Some scholars (*see* COLLECTIVE BARGAINING) as the main democratic instrument in modern societies: through it, workers' representatives articulate interests and reach agreements with employers, and they can use COLLECTIVE ACTION if agreement cannot be reached. Others argue that this makes TRADE UNIONS an opposition that can never become a government and that bargaining covers only immediate issues of pay and conditions, not wider questions such as investment policy and business strategy (*see* Poole, 1978).

One alternative is a legally-required system of "works councils." Most Continental European countries have such a system, wherein managements are required to consult, and sometimes to share DECISION-MAKING POWER, with elected representatives (*see* GOVERNANCE AND OWNERSHIP). This approach is rare in Anglo-Saxon countries, with their traditional reliance on collective bargaining. Its most developed form is codetermination as practised in Germany (Turner, 1991). In this system, workers' representatives are appointed to company boards, while at establishment level there are works councils which are elected by all workers and which have a variety of rights of consultation (for example, on ACCIDENT prevention) and codecision (on hiring, dismissal, and TRAINING, for example) with management. This system has been found to require management to communicate more effectively and to strengthen strategic thinking. Thus the impossibility of dismissing workers without consulting the works council removes the simple "hire and fire" option from management (*see* REDUNDANCY). Some writers, however, believe that the system gives too little influence to the individual worker (*see* Lane, 1989, pp. 226–39).

A second alternative to collective bargaining is the workers' cooperative, in which managements are directly elected by members (*see* SELF-MANAGEMENT). Companies based on cooperative principles have existed for many years, and some grow quite large. Without institutional support, however, they are generally rare.

Other systems are more managerial in their initiative and operation. They include consultative councils and joint labour–management committees. Some companies have for many years had such committees alongside their collective bargaining arrangements. Evidence suggests that the committees could become powerless and focused on relatively trivial issues, and it was argued that they would be superseded by collective bargaining (Lane, 1989). In the 1980s, however, there was an upsurge in interest in COMMUNICATION, as part of a concern to promote worker COMMITMENT. Some writers see joint problem-solving as a means to promote genuine democracy (Heckscher, 1988). Research shows that the key is managerial commitment at all levels, and that it is often hard to maintain this. Other writers argue: that the sense of empowerment provided by a new experiment can fade away over time; and that the appearance of democracy can mask a weakening of trade unions and of autonomous organization which can effectively challenge managerial thinking (Wells, 1993).

See also **Decision making; Group decision making; Representation**

Bibliography

Heckscher, C. C. (1988). *The new unionism.* New York: Basic.
Lane, C. (1989). *Management and labour in Europe.* Aldershot, UK: Elgar.
Poole, M. (1978). *Workers' participation in industry.* London: Routledge & Kegan Paul.
Turner, L. (1991). *Democracy at work* (Ithaca, NY). Cornell University Press.
Wells, D. (1993). Are strong unions compatible with the new model of human resource management? *Relations Industrielles/Industrial Relations*, **48**, 56–83.

PAUL EDWARDS

density *see* POPULATION ECOLOGY

departmentalization One of the most critical tasks in ORGANIZATIONAL DESIGN is to decide which kinds of departments should be the focal point at the top of the organization. Typically the choices are between function (or process), product (or service), and area (or client). In manufacturing, this would mean either an organization with departments of manufacturing, marketing, research and development – the function choice; or departments of shavers, colognes, and shaving cream – the product choice; or departments of Britain, France, and Germany – the geographic area choice. Within public service, the parallel example from social welfare would be departments of intake, ASSESSMENT, treatment, and coordination – the process choice; or departments of foster care, domestic violence, or frail elderly – the service choice; or departments of acute, chronic or young chronic mental health services – the client choice (see Alter & Hage, 1993).

The design rule is that one starts at the top of the organization with the greatest single source of variety (static) or change (dynamic) relative to the goals of the organization. If there is more variety in the TECHNOLOGY of the products or in the distribution and marketing of the products or in the demands of the customer across geographical area, then one uses a function design, or a product design, or area design in choice of departments. At the next lower level, what some would call the sectional level, then the second greatest source of variety/change becomes the principle.

Closely related to the problem of departmentalization is the question of divisionalization. For one might ask what is the top of the organization? When companies manufacture 125,000 products as does General Electric, then one finds what Chandler (1962) in his classic study referred to as the divisional structure. Divisions represent distinct technological–market complexes that require separate organizations. For example, General Electric has one division (or organization) to produce jet engines, another to provide financial services, still another to make light bulbs, and still another to manufacture steam turbines. Within each of these divisions, quite divergent principles of departmentalization might be employed. Most countries have divided their military services into divisions called the army, the navy, and the air force, illustrating the same logic.

Chandler's (1962) reasoning was that separate divisions were necessary when the tacit knowledge and the rules of the game associated with the manufacturing of the product including customer service are so different that the same management can not operate the disparate divisions. This led to the idea of DECENTRALIZATION to the divisional level.

But while the principle of departmentalization on the basis of the greatest source of variation/change appears unambiguous, in practice, and increasingly so, companies find that there are considerable and equal amounts of variation in product technology and in customer demands. Given two equal sources of variation, the tendency has been to move toward what is called the matrix structure (*see* MATRIX ORGANIZATION), that is, where each individual belongs to two departments. Even more complex matrix structures are now being established in high-technology industries such as semiconductors.

See also **Loose-coupling; Division of labor; Multinational corporations**

Bibliography

Alter, C. & Hage, J. (1993). *Organizations Working Together*. Beverly Hills, C.A.: Sag.

Chandler, A. (1962). *Strategy and Structure*. Cambridge: M.I.T. Press.

Daft, R. (1989). *Organizational theory and design* (4th edn). St. Paul, MN: West.

Mintzberg, H. (1979). *The structuring of organizations*. Englewood Cliffs, N.J.: Prentice-Hall.

JERALD HAGE

deviance *see* CONFORMITY; EMPLOYEE THEFT; GROUP COHESIVENESS; GROUP DECISION MAKING; PUNISHMENT; SABOTAGE

dialectic *see* CONFLICT; LABOR PROCESS THEORY; THEORY

differentiation Perhaps the essential defining characteristic of what we mean by organization is that there is an internal structure differentiated in form and function. To be organized is, by definition, to be differentiated. In human work organizations differentiation can be defined as the horizontal and vertical DIVISION OF LABOR into specialized subunits and departments. Horizontal differentiation can be based on differences in task or function, or product, geography, or customer segment. Vertical differentiation is based on the number of levels in the organization and the decision-making responsibility each level has. Differentiation has also been defined as differences in underlying structural attributes such as FORMALIZATION and PROFESSIONALISM as well as differences in cognitive, cultural, and goal orientation.

Differentiation, paired with the concept of INTEGRATION, was made famous as a concept in organization theory by Lawrence and Lorsch (1969). They argued that as organizations grow in size and as their environments become more complex, the subunits of the organization would have to become more differentiated to deal with varying aspects of the environment (*see* ORGANIZATIONAL SIZE). They further argued that differentiation causes coordination problems and requires organizations to integrate their activities if they are to perform well.

See also **Organizational design; Contingency theory; Classical design theory organization and environment; Cooperation**

Bibliography

Lawrence, P. R. & Lorsch, J. W. (1969). *Organization and environment*. Cambridge, MA: Division of Research, Graduate School of Business, Harvard University.

ROBERT DRAZIN

dilemmas, ethical These can be defined as situations requiring the decision maker to choose between two unsatisfactory alternatives. They take on a moral dimension when the choices involve conflicting values (e.g., loyalty and promise-keeping). For example, in DOWNSIZING situations, managers may have to choose between keeping a promise of job security that could threaten the future of the firm and laying off valued, loyal workers.

See also **Business ethics; Decision making; values**

Bibliography

Toffler, B. L. (1986). *Tough choices: Managers talk ethics*. New York: Wiley.

LINDA TREVINO

dilemmas, organizational This term has its origins in the Greek word meaning "two propositions." The concept of dilemma, while new to organizational theory and analysis, has deep historical roots in Western and Eastern philosophy, as well as in other scientific disciplines. The basic concepts of personality theory, grounded in the work of Freud and Jung, were based on the analysis of the tensions between what they conceptualized as opposites in the psyche and personality of the individual.

While all organizations and individuals face dilemmas in the sense of the struggle to resolve opposites, some organizational scholars believe that dilemmas are a key to the understanding of complex social systems that must thrive in dynamic and turbulent environments (*see* ORGANIZATION AND ENVIRONMENT). They point out that organizations today are visibly besieged by such dilemmas, such as the opposing pulls of centralization (INTEGRATION) and of decentralization (DIFFERENTIATION), the short term and the long term, individuality (individual performance and ACCOUNTABILITY), and teamwork. There is a need to be organically loose for the purposes of INNOVATION and yet mechanistically tight for execution, the call for change and the need for continuity in implementation, the necessity for PLANNING and the desirability of FLEXIBILITY, the need for LEADERSHIP in the sense of doing the right things, and of management in the sense of doing things right.

These opposites are called *dilemmas* by Hampden-Turner (1990), *competing VALUES* by Quinn (1990), and *dualities* by Evans and Doz (1992), and the same concern is seen in studies of the paradoxical nature of organizational effectiveness (*see* PARADOX). One of the essential postulates of this emerging school of organizational analysis is that such opposites are not "either–or" choices but "and–and" contrasts that must be reconciled. These scholars are critical of CONTINGENCY THEORY, which has influenced traditional organizational analysis with its emphasis on fit, matching, and consistency. They argue that excessive concern with fit or consistency leads to pendulum or seesaw pathologies, alternating cycles of crisis/transformation, and complacency. A related idea is that positive qualities taken too far become negative or pathological, and an increasing number of case studies of corporations and individuals document this "failure of success" syndrome (*see* ORGANIZATIONAL NEUROSIS). One illustration is the limits of the prevailing concept of ORGANIZATIONAL CULTURE, traditionally formulated in terms of shared patterns of values, assumptions, and beliefs. If this sharing is taken too far and cultures become too strong, studies document that organizational rigidities and conformism can result and engender crisis (the paradox of the weakness of strong organizational culture) – (*see* CRISES).

Senior executives often talk about organizational leadership as a balancing act. For dilemma theorists, a key to ORGANIZATIONAL LEARNING and INNOVATION is constructively harnassing the tension between these opposites, a tension that can either lead to virtuous circles of development, or to VICIOUS CYCLES of CONFLICT and fragmentation. Indeed, dilemma theorists implicitly argue that change, learning, and innovation must be anchored into ORGANIZATIONAL THEORY rather than appendaged as a separate body of knowledge and know-how.

From this perspective, the dependent variable in organizational analysis is not so much profit, customer satisfaction, employee satisfaction, or the like. These are partial parameters of organizational effectiveness. The key dependent variable is tension, for example, the tension between short-term profitability and longer-term investment in customer satisfaction, or the tension between centralization and DECENTRALIZATION. An important question for research is under what conditions does tension become destructive or constructive. When does it lead to dysfunctional outcomes such as fragmentation, political infighting, conflict avoidance, or complacency, and under what conditions does tension lead to innovation and organizational renewal?

The analysis of dilemmas has been applied to MANAGEMENT STYLE, organizational diagnosis, and the conceptualization of ORGANIZATIONAL EFFECTIVENESS (Quinn, 1990), to STRATEGIC MANAGEMENT and the assessment of ORGANIZATIONAL CULTURE (Hampden-Turner, 1990), to ORGANIZATIONAL CHANGE and transformation (Pascale, 1990), and to the dynamics of the centralization–DECENTRALIZATION dilemma and its implications for HUMAN RESOURCE MANAGEMENT (Evans & Doz, 1992). However, it is implicit in much other current work in the field of ORGANIZATIONAL BEHAVIOR.

See also **Dilemmas, ethical; Decision making; Ideology**

Bibliography

Evans, P. A. L. & Doz, Y. (1992). Dualities: A paradigm for human resource and organizational development in complex multinationals. In V. Pucik, N. Tichy & C. Barnett (Eds), *Globalizing management: Creating and leading a competitive organization*. New York: Wiley.

Hampden-Turner, C. (1990). *Charting the corporate mind: From dilemma to strategy*. Oxford, UK: Blackwell.

Hedburg, B. L. T., Nystrom, P. C. & Starbuck, W. H. (1976). Camping on seesaws: Prescriptions for a self-designing organization. *Administrative Science Quarterly*, **21**, 41–65.

Pascale, R. T. (1990). *Managing on the edge: How successful companies use conflict to stay ahead*. New York: Viking.

Quinn, R. E. (1990). *Beyond rational management: Mastering the paradoxes and competing demands of high performance*. San Francisco: Jossey-Bass.

PAUL EVANS

disability This term, in general, refers to any physical, sensory, or mental impairment that substantially limits one or more of the major life activities of an individual. Specifically, the World Health Organization defines and distinguishes between three similar terms. Impairment is defined as an abnormality or loss of any physiological or anatomical structure or function. Disability is defined as the consequences of an impairment such as any restriction or lack of ability to perform an activity in the range considered appropriate for nonimpaired persons. Handicap refers to the social disadvantage that results from an impairment or disability.

The concept of disability has become very important to management disciplines (*see* HUMAN RESOURCES MANAGEMENT), at least in the United States, due to the passage of legislation, such as the Americans with Disabilities Act (ADA) of 1990, which outlaws DISCRIMINATION toward qualified persons with disabilities. The act also covers anyone with a record of impairment, and anyone regarded as having such an impairment. Qualified individuals with disabilities are defined as persons who, with or without reasonable accommodation, can perform the essential functions of the position in question, and reasonable accommodation is defined as making existing facilities used by employees readily accessible to and usable by individuals with disabilities. Although the ADA generally provides a definition of disability, the term is still used differently for different purposes such as employment, disability insurance, worker's compensation claims, etc.

Multidisciplinary research on persons with disabilities has a long history (Meyerson, 1988), however, the topic has been given relatively little attention by management scholars. Other fields which examine disability include social psychology, economics, law, sociology, rehabilitation psychology, and political science.

Research concerning persons with disabilities at work has followed several trends. Much thought in the area has been guided by Goffman's (1963) work on stigmas. Furthermore, persons with disabilities may be considered as a minority group (Fine & Asch, 1988), and thus, conceptual models applicable to other minority groups may be applied to research on persons with disabilities. However, application of other models may be complex or problematic due to variance in the nature of disability on such factors as self-concept of disability, functional impairments, degree of impairment, visibility, prognosis, aesthetic qualities, origin, and peril associated with the disability.

One line of research in this area has been to conduct surveys to determine in general how well persons with disabilities fare in the labor market. The results of this research indicate that persons with disabilities are often underemployed and underpaid (McNeil, 1983). However, Greenwood and Johnson (1987) reviewed the EVALUATION RESEARCH in this area and concluded that employees with disabilities have consistently high performance, do not demonstrate greater incidence of employee problems (e.g., ABSENTEEISM and poor SAFETY records), and do not place greater demands on supervisors than workers without disabilities. Thus, many of the problems facing employees with disabilities at work are thought to be the result of socially imposed discrimination (Stone, Stone, & Dipboye, 1992) (*see* SOCIAL CONSTRUCTIONISM).

Another line of research has been to examine the impact of disability on personnel decisions such as selection and performance ratings (*see* ASSESSMENT, SELECTION METHODS; PERFORMANCE APPRAISAL). A review of this literature is provided by Stone et al. (1992). The results of this line of research have been mixed. Some studies have found a bias against persons with disabilities. Others have found no effect for disability on personnel judgments. While yet other studies have found positive bias in favor of persons with disabilities. A related line of research has also examined whether or not different disability factors influence subsequent reactions to persons with disabilities. It is difficult to draw conclusions from these studies, primarily due to a lack of framework for categorizing disabilities along important dimensions (e.g., functional impairment or visibility).

A third line of research, relevant to management, has examined the attitudes and reactions of persons without disabilities toward persons with disabilities. This research has mainly been carried out by social and rehabilitation psychologists, and thus, has not focused on work settings. The results of this work point to several general findings. First, persons with disabilities may avoid interacting with or denigrate persons with disabilities (*see* STEREOTYPING). Second, this research also suggests the existence of a "norm to be kind" to persons with disabilities (*see* GROUP NORMS). Research which has attempted to integrate the norm to be kind with avoidance responses (e.g., Snyder, Kleck, Strenta, & Mentzer, 1979), found that people are more likely to interact with persons with disabilities when the cost of interacting with the person is low and/or the ability to conceal one's motive to avoid interaction is low. Finally, research examining attitudes and performance expectations toward persons with disabilities has found that:

(1) nondisabled people often do not know what to expect of persons with disabilities or how to communicate with them (e.g., Hastorf, Wildfogel, & Cassman, 1979);
(2) employers have low expectations regarding the ABILITY of persons with disabilities to advance and perform well in the organization (e.g., Krefting & Brief, 1976); and
(3) nondisabled persons may have unrealistically positive general expectations of persons with disabilities which included the perception of these individuals as "saints" (Makas, 1988).

Research concerning persons with disabilities has been criticized on many grounds, both conceptual and methodological. Some of the most commonly voiced concerns relate to the use of obtrusive manipulations of disability, poor external VALIDITY, lack of appropriate control groups, negative BIASES on the part of researchers, and a failure to examine the perspective and experience of persons with disabilities. Future research should address these concerns as well as the many fruitful avenues which have been relatively unaddressed. For example, research on social processes affecting employees with disabilities is needed, as well as research examining issues involved in accommodation. Theoretical and conceptual work is also called for which attempts to develop a taxonomy of disabilities based on factors likely to influence various employment issues, so that this framework can guide and integrate future research.

See also **Management development; Performance, individual; Attribution; Equal opportunities**

Bibliography

Fine, M. & Asch, A. (1988). Disability beyond stigma: Social interaction, discrimination, and activism. *Journal of Social Issues*, **44**, 3–21.

Goffman, E. (1963). *Stigma: Notes on the management of spoiled identity*. Englewood Cliffs, NJ: Prentice-Hall.

Greenwood, R. & Johnson, V. A. (1987). Employer perspectives on workers with disabilities. *Journal of Rehabilitation*, **53 (3)**, 37–45.

Hastorf, A. H., Wildfogel, J. & Cassman, T. (1979). Acknowledgement of handicap as a tactic in social interaction. *Journal of Personality and Social Psychology*, **37**, 1790–1797.

Krefting, L. A. & Brief, A. P. (1976). The impact of applicant disability on evaluation judgments. *Academy of Management Journal*, **19**, 675–680.

Makas, E. (1988). Positive attitudes toward disabled people: Disabled and nondisabled persons' perspectives. *Journal of Social Issues*, **44 (1)**, 49–61.

McNeil, J. (1983). *Labor force status and other characteristics of persons with a work disability: 1982.* U.S. Department of Commerce. Washington, DC: GPO.

Meyerson, L. (1988). The social psychology of physical disability: 1948 and 1998. *Journal of Social Issues*, **44**, 173–188.

Snyder, M. L., Kleck, R. E., Strenta, A. & Mentzer, S. J. (1979). Avoidance of the handicapped: An attributional ambiguity analysis. *Journal of Personality and Social Psychology*, **37**, 2297–2306.

Stone, E. F., Stone, D. L. & Dipboye, R. L. (1992). Stigmas in organizations: Race, handicaps, and physical unattractiveness. In K. Kelly (Ed.), *Issues, theory, and research in industrial and organizational psychology* (pp. 385–457). New York: Elsevier Science.

ADRIENNE COLELLA

disasters *see* CRISES

discretion *see* DECISION MAKING; JOB DESIGN; JOB ENRICHMENT

discrimination This concept can be generally defined as any behavior which denies persons certain rights because they belong to specific groups. It includes verbal and nonverbal acts, whether intended or unintended. Most theorists distinguish between discrimination at the individual level and institutional level (Katz & Taylor, 1988). The former refers to actions carried out by individuals based on negative attitudes. For example, a manager who will not hire women for middle management positions because of a belief that women are less competent than men. Institutional discrimination pertains to institutional norms, practices, and policies which help to create or perpetuate sets of advantages or privileges for dominant group members and to the exclusion or unequal access of subordinate groups (Rodriquez, 1987).

Institutions can produce discriminatory consequences intentionally or unintentionally. For example, job seniority practices implemented during a recession can yield negative consequences for minority employees who have lower seniority because of their historical exclusion from certain jobs. Institutional procedures such as hiring and promotion and evaluation are central features of institutional discrimination (Pettigrew & Martin, 1987). The distinction between institutional discrimination and individual discrimination is not unproblematic. First, it is important to point out that some scholars in the field argue that the term discrimination should not be used in lieu of terms like racism (*see* RACE) or sexism (*see* GENDER) because it underrates the significance of IDEOLOGY in the way systems of domination are structured in society (Essed, 1991). Second, the concept of individual discrimination detaches the individual from the institutions in which rules, procedures, and policies flourish.

Theories of discrimination are centered upon explaining its continued persistence. Most of these theories can be classified as order theories, person-centered theories, or POWER-CONFLICT and structural theories (Feagin, 1989). Order theories tend to accent assimilation and concentrate on the progressive assimilation of subordinate groups in to the dominant CULTURE. As groups are assimilated, they should experience less discrimination. Person-centered theories focus on the argument that there are real differences between majority group members and subordinate group members and these differences explain the differential treatment of each group. A corollary strand of person-centered theories is that discrimination is largely a function of prejudiced behavior of individuals (*see* PREJUDICE). In contrast, power-conflict theories place emphasis upon economic stratification, structural and power issues, and patriarchy in maintaining systems of domination (*see* CRITICAL THEORY). Prominent among these latter group of theories are class-based theories, feminist theories, and Marxist and neo-Marxist theories. These theories suggest the need to examine the policies and practices in social systems or in organizations which create and perpetuate systemic barriers for certain groups.

Since the passage of extensive civil rights legislation in many countries, the concept of institutional discrimination has developed largely as a technical notion, particularly in the United States. Two theories of discrimination growing out of this legislation, disparate impact and disparate treatment, have heavily informed the way discrimination has been studied in organizational behavior and personnel psychology. Disparate treatment theory holds that discrimination occurs when those belonging to a protected category (women, racial minorities, the disabled, etc.) are in some way intentionally treated differently regarding employment practices. For example, rejecting women applicants of childbearing age for certain jobs. Under disparate impact theory, facially neutral employment practices (e.g., standardized tests, height and weight requirements) which have an adverse impact on members of a protected group may constitute discrimination if they cannot be shown to be job related and essential to the organization's operations.

Much organizational research on discrimination has involved a search for objective and quantifiable evidence of discrimination in staffing, SELECTION predictors, performance evaluation ratings, compensation, and promotion (*see* ASSESSMENT, SELECTION METHODS). Race and sex discrimination have garnered the most attention, although more research is appearing on AGE and DISABILITY discrimination (Avolio & Barrett, 1987; Yuker, 1988). The results across studies on race and sex discrimination are often inconsistent with some studies reporting discriminatory effects and others finding none. The failure to find consistent results may be a function of methodological inadequacies, ranging from an overreliance on laboratory studies to underdeveloped theoretical frames and weak measures (*see* RESEARCH METHODS; RESEARCH DESIGN). Additionally, the subtle nature of modern discrimination may also contribute to the mixed results.

The literature on discrimination in organizations suggests that considerable progress has been made to address discriminatory barriers to job entry for women and minorities. Yet current research reports that subtle discrimination influences their chances for upward mobility where they encounter "glass ceiling" effects on their careers (Morrison & Von Glinow, 1990; Powell, 1993) (*see* WOMEN AT WORK; WOMEN MANAGERS; CAREER DEVELOPMENT). For instance, women and minorities have less access to many informal events in organizations and still suffer from the effects of solo and token status.

The persistence of discrimination in organizational settings, suggest that it is no longer adequate to study discrimination as though it were purely a technical question or the sole product of attitudes, stereotypes, or interpersonal relations (*see* STEREOTYPING). Some scholars have called for more attention to research that explores the phenomenology of discrimination in organizations. Understanding the process of discrimination and structural properties of exclusion are important toward changing organizational policies and practices operating to the detriment of some groups (Cockburn, 1991). An approach that combines micro and macro influences is needed. In the case of discrimination based on race, Essed (1991) introduced the concept of everyday racism to capture the structural–cultural properties of racial discrimination as well as the microinequities that perpetuate the system.

See also **Equal opportunities; Intergroup relations**

Bibliography

Avolio, B. J. & Barrett, G. V. (1987). Effects of age stereotyping in a simulated interview. *Psychology and Aging*, **2**, 56–63.

Cockburn, C. (1991). *In the way of women*. London: Macmillan.

Essed, P. (1991). *Everyday racism: An interdisciplinary theory*. Newbury Park, CA: Sage.

Feagin, J. (1989). *Race and ethnic relations*. Englewood Cliffs, NJ: Prentice-Hall.

Katz, P. & Taylor, D. (1988). *Eliminating racism: Profiles in controversy*. New York: Plenum Press.

Morrison, A. & Von Glinow, M. (1990). Women and minorities in management. *American Psychologist*, **45**, 200–208.

Pettigrew, T. & Martin, J. (1987). Shaping the organizational context for Black American inclusion. *Journal of Social Issues*, **43**, 41–87.

Powell, G. (1993). *Women and men in management*. Newbury Park, CA: Sage.

Rodriquez, A. M. (1987). Institutional racism in the organization setting: An action-research approach. In J. W. Shaw (Ed.), *Strategies for improving race relations: The Anglo-American Experience* (pp. 128–148). Manchester, UK: Manchester University Press.

Yuker, H. E. (Ed.) (1988). *Attitudes towards persons with disabilities*. New York: Springer-Verlag.

STELLA M. NKOMO

distributive justice *see* JUSTICE, DISTRIBUTIVE

diversification As organizations grow, they tend to increase both the range of products and markets which they serve and the range of businesses which they operate. The term "diversification" can be used for any of these situations. Diversification is often divided into related diversification and unrelated diversification (*see* CONGLOMERATE DIVERSIFICATION).

Related Diversification

Exactly what constitutes related diversification is one of the least clearly-understood areas in STRATEGIC MANAGEMENT. Abell (1980) argued that the relatedness of a particular product, market, or business diversification could be assessed using three criteria – the similarity of the customers, the functions served by the different products, and the technologies of production. However, it is unclear whether a diversification should be considered related if a new product, market expansion, or business is only similar on one or two of these dimensions.

Taking a different approach, Hatten and Hatten (1987) suggested that there are two general types of related diversification. In related-constrained diversification, each diversification is closely tied to a central core business, although diversifications themselves might be less closely connected with each other (*see* CORE COMPETENCE). In related-linked diversification, each diversification is linked to at least one other business in the group, but may have no direct or clear link to the center or main business activities of the organization. Thus, related-linked diversification allows for much more loosely-aligned groups, by comparison with related-constrained diversification.

These types of approaches to assessing the relatedness of a diversification can be performed by external observers, independent of the actual organization. There is, however, no guarantee that managers think about relatedness using these criteria.

Prahalad and Bettis (1986) suggested that, when managers think about the relatedness of a diversification, they have a "dominant logic" or pattern of thinking which they apply to the business, regardless of the apparent business-relatedness, as indicated by standard industrial classification codes, which exists. Thus, for instance, an organization which is built around strong financial systems, or one which specializes in strong consumer brand names may believe that diversification into an apparently unrelated business in SIC terms may be quite "related," because the management SKILLS needed to operate the new business are very similar to those needed for existing businesses.

Related diversification should create synergies from the combined activities of the existing business and the new business. In this way, the combined businesses can operate more efficiently than they could as independent operations. Synergies could occur from joint use of operating facilities, marketing skills and resources, distribution systems, research and development facilities, or spreading of central overheads. If diversification does not create shareholder value, there is little value in diversifying. It would be better to operate the two (or more) businesses separately.

In practice, most organizations describe most diverisification activity as being "related." However, research findings about the performance of related diversification have been quite mixed. The existence of these varying definitions of relatedness helps explain why this might be so.

Another form of related diversification is integration forward or backward in the business system (e.g., manufacturing, distribution, and retailing for a particular product range). This is usually referred to as VERTICAL INTEGRATION. It may be considered related diversification because of the product or service connection involved. However, the key success factors and important capabilities at different levels of the business system are quite different, so that it is quite difficult to create value through SYNERGY. The major reasons for this type of diversification are to capture the profit margin at another stage in the business system and/or to obtain strategic control of a key component of supply or access to distribution.

Unrelated Diversification

Unrelated diversification may be defined as diversification which does not qualify as related diversification. Since the products, markets, and technologies will be different, it is less clear what synergies can emerge. Administrative and financial synergies may be gained, but marketing and operating synergies, by definition, are not possible.

Unrelated diversification may occur because the organization's existing set of products, markets, or business(es) have unattractive futures and/or the organization wishes to move away from a particular business area. Those organizations which have many unrelated diversified businesses are known as conglomerates.

Diversification is often confused with merger or acquisition. Diversification is one of the possible goals of an organization's strategy of the organization. MERGERS AND ACQUISITIONS are the common methods of achieving business-level diversification, since it is often difficult and time-consuming to build a diversified business from within the organization. However, mergers and acquisitions do not always lead to diversification, since they may occur between two similar organizations. STRATEGIC ALLIANCES or JOINT VENTURES have emerged as alternatives to mergers and acquisitions in order to diversify.

See also **Organizational design; Organizational effectiveness; Competitiveness**

Bibliography

Abell, D. (1980). *Defining the Business: The starting point of strategic planning*. Englewood Cliffs, NJ: Prentice-Hall.

Goold, M. & Campbell, A. (1987). *Strategies and styles*. Oxford, UK: Blackwell.

Hatten, K. & Hatten, M. (1987). *Strategic management: Analysis and action*. Englewood Cliffs, NJ: Prentice-Hall.

Lubatkin, M. & Chatterjee, S. (1991). The strategy-shareholder relationship: Testing temporal stability across market cycles. *Strategic Management Journal*, **12**, 251–270.

Prahalad, C. & Bettis, R. (1986). The dominant logic: A new link between diversity and performance. *Strategic Management Journal*, **7**, No. 6, 485–501.

Ramanujam, V. & Varadarajan, P. (1989). Research on corporate diversification: A synthesis. *Strategic Management Journal*, **10**, 523–551.

Rumelt, R. (1982). Diversification strategy and profitability. *Strategic Management Journal*, **3**, 359–369.

GRAHAM HUBBARD

division of labor There are various ways in which the concept of the division of labor is relevant to the study of organizations. At the nation-state level, countries participate in a division of labor relative to which products and services that they produce most efficiently. This macro meaning of the concept involves such issues as comparative advantage, as in recent treatments of strategy (*see* STRATEGIC MANAGEMENT), utilizations of the concept beyond the scope of this discussion.

More relevant is a micro definition that focuses on the way in which activities are divided and combined into jobs (*see* JOB DESIGN). The history of industrial development has witnessed a general tendency, called Fordism, to break work into very small repeatable tasks, called task specialization, where there is a large volume of work and the tasks are relatively simple. The classic example is the assembly-line in the manufacturing of cars. More recently, this concept of dividing work into small tasks has been applied in the fast food industry by McDonalds. In contrast, when the volume of work associated with any particular task is small, and there are a variety of tasks, then these are added together in what is called person specialization. The typical illustrations are in the professions (*see* PROFESSIONALS IN ORGANIZATIONS).

But the real point is that within the same industry, the same work can be divided into quite distinct bundles of activities and aggregated into jobs in quite dissimilar ways. For example, in the United States and Britain, many manufacturing companies have relied upon task specialization. In contrast, in the same industries in Japan and Germany, many more activities have been combined into the same position. A particular striking illustration of how work can be divided is the issue of who does quality control. In the case of Japan and Germany, quality is frequently checked by the workers whereas in the United States and in Britain, until recently this has been traditionally assigned to a special department (see Womack, Jones, & Roos 1990). As yet, no one has studied what is the best constellation of activities within certain jobs.

Part of the answer of what might be the best way of combining activities into jobs and jobs into departments (*see* DEPARTMENTALIZATION) depends upon which performance criterion one wants to maximize. The emergence of Fordism was dictated by the maximization of PRODUCTIVITY and particularly in the short run where quality had little relevance. When quality becomes critical and when constant product change is needed, then the division of labor into more generalist, rather than specialist, jobs appears to be a better design principle. What has not been stressed, however, in available evidence, is that particular combinations of activities might depend upon the nature of the technical TRAINING that has been received. In other words, how one divides tasks presupposes how people have been trained (*see* Hage & Garnier, 1993).

A particularly dramatic illustration of the complexities of how work is divided and its consequences for performance is to be found in the studies of Pelz and Andrews (1979) (*see* COMPLEXITY). They demonstrated that those researcher who spent less than 100 percent of their time in research were more innovative and productive (*see* INNOVATION). Furthermore, whether the alternative activities involved administration or teaching did not make a difference.

Maximal performance in INNOVATION as distinct from PRODUCTIVITY was achieved at about 80 percent of the time. This study raises profound questions about the nature of the division of labor, questions that should be studied in the future.

See also **Organizational design; Differentiation; Classical design theory**

Bibliography

Hage, J. & Garnier, M. (1993). *The technical training advantages*. Center for Innovation, College Park: University of Maryland.

Pelz, D. & Andrews, F. (1979). *Scientists in Industry*, (2nd edn). New York: Wiley.

Womack, J., Jones, D. & Roos, D. (1990). *The lean machine*. New York: Rawsen.

JERALD HAGE

domain defenders, prospectors, analyzers, and reactors *see* STRATEGIC TYPES

dominance In STRATEGIC MANAGEMENT, the general term "dominance" refers specifically to market dominance. This denotes the situation where the leading firm in the industry has a market share much greater than any of its competitors, and which would remain greater, even if its competitors were to cooperate or merge. Thus, a market share of 50 percent or more would entail dominance, unless there were only one other major competitor, which might have close to 50 percent itself.

However, in more fragmented markets, the term "dominance" is often used where the leading firm's market share is simply much greater than that of any other firms, regardless of the absolute level. Thus, if the leading firm has a market share of 10 percent and its nearest competitors have only 2 percent, the firm is said to dominate its market. The term has also come to be used in situations where more than one firm is said to dominate the market. For instance, if the first two firms together have 60 percent of the market (say 30 percent each) and the next firm has only 10 percent, the first two firms are said to dominate the market. In these latter cases, the term is being used very loosely compared with its original intention.

The importance of a dominant market share came to prominence through two developments. The Boston Consulting Group market growth/relative market share matrix (a technique developed for the analysis of business portfolios) developed the concept of market share relative to competitors as being an important competitive variable (*see* COMPETITIVENESS). The evidence of the Profit Impact of Market Strategies (PIMS) studies showed a high correlation between profitability and relative market share in many industries, encouraging firms to seek to market dominance.

See also **Organizational effectiveness; Reputation; Strategic types**

Bibliography

Buzzell, R., Gale, B. & Sultan, R. (1975). Market share—a key to profitability. *Harvard Business Review*, 53, January-February, pp. 97–106.

GRAHAM HUBBARD

double-loop learning Learning occurs whenever ERRORS are detected and corrected. An error is any mismatch between intentions and actual consequences. Discovery of a mismatch is only a first step in learning. Additional steps occur when the error is corrected in such a way that the correction is maintained. Furthermore, there are at least two ways to correct errors. One is to change the behavior. This kind of correction requires single-loop learning. The second way to correct errors is to change the underlying program, or master program, that leads individuals to *believe as they do* about their error correction strategies.

Theories of action inform actors of the strategies they should use to achieve their intended consequences. Theories of action are governed by sets of VALUES which provide the framework for the action strategies chosen. Thus, human beings are designing beings. They create, store, and retrieve designs that advise them how to act if they are to achieve their intentions and act consistently with their governing values.

There are two types of theories of action. One is the theory that individuals espouse and that comprise their beliefs, attitudes, and values. The second is their *theory-in-use* – the theory that they actually employ.

Model I theory-in-use is the design we find throughout the world. It has four governing values: achieve your intended purpose; maximize winning and minimize losing; suppress negative feelings; and behave according to what you consider rational (*see* RATIONALITY). Model I tells individuals to craft their positions, evaluations, and attributions in ways that inhibit inquiries into them or tests of them with others' logic. The consequences of these Model I strategies are likely to be defensiveness, misunderstanding, and self-fulfilling, and self-sealing processes.

Organizations come alive through the thoughts and actions of individuals acting as organizational agents and creating the organizational behavioral world in which work gets done. If it is true that most individuals use Model I, then a consequence of this use will be the creation of organizational defensive routines (*see* ORGANIZATIONAL NEUROSIS)

An organizational defensive routine is any action, policy, or practice preventing organizational participants from experiencing embarrassment or threat and, at the same time, preventing them from discovering the causes of the embarrassment or threat. Organizational defensive routines, like Model I theories-in-use, inhibit double-loop learning and overprotect the individuals and the organizations.

Model II theories-in-use are hypothesized to produce double-loop learning. The governing values of Model II are valid information, informed choice, and vigilant monitoring of the implementation of the choice in order to detect and correct error. As in the case of Model I, the three most prominent behaviors are advocate, evaluate, and attribute. However, unlike Model I behaviors, Model II behaviors are crafted into action strategies which openly illustrate how the actors reach their evaluations or attributions and how they craft them to encourage inquiry and testing by others. As a consequence, defensive routines that are anti-learning are minimized and double-loop learning is facilitated. Embarrassment and threat are not bypassed and covered up; they are engaged. Model II action will interrupt organizational defensive routines and begin to create ORGANIZATIONAL LEARNING processes and systems that encourage double-loop learning in ways that persist.

For example, the director–owners of a professional firm wanted to reduce the destructive POLITICS at, and eventually below, their levels. Through observations and interviews a map was developed of the organizational defensive routines. Next, through the use of specially designed cases, the directors became aware of their Model I theories-in-use. Then, they learned to make Model II an additional theory-in-use. Five years of observations and tape recordings indicate that the dysfunctional politics have been reduced significantly, that issues that were considered undiscussable (e.g., financial ownership) have become discussable and alterable, and that the process is spreading at all levels of the organization (Argyris, 1993).

See also **Feedback; Evaluation research; Learning organization: Paradox**

Bibliography

Argyris, C. (1993). *Knowledge for action.* San Francisco: Jossey-Bass.

CHRIS ARGYRIS

downsizing This refers to a set of voluntary activities, undertaken on the part of the management of an organization, designed to reduce expenses. This is usually, but not exclusively, accomplished by shrinking the size of the workforce. However, downsizing is a term used to encompass a whole range of activities from personnel layoffs and hiring freezes to consolidations and mergers of organization units.

In the early 1980s organizational downsizing came into prominence as a topic of both practical and scholarly concern. Practically, this is because between one-third and one-half of all medium and large size firms in North America and Western Europe downsized during the 1980s and early 1990s. Two-thirds of the companies that engaged in downsizing did so more than once. The popularity of downsizing has brought into question the common assumptions that increased size, COMPLEXITY, and resources are inherently associated with ORGANIZATIONAL EFFECTIVENESS. Smaller and leaner have become associated with success, not largesse and over-abundance.

The concept of organizational downsizing has arisen out of popular usage, not precise theoretical construction. In fact, identifying the definition and conceptual boundaries of downsizing is more relevant for theoretical purposes than for practical ones. Cameron, Freeman, and Mishra (1993) found that the terminology used to describe downsizing strategies was quite unimportant to practicing managers, except for the negative connotations associated with decline (i.e., no manager wants to implement a decline). A wide array of terms were found by Cameron et al. to be used interchangably, even though each may have a different connotation.

For scholarly purposes, precise conceptual meaning is required in order for cumulative and comparative research to occur. For example, on the surface, downsizing can be interpreted as a mere reduction in ORGANIZATIONAL SIZE. When this is the case, downsizing is often confused with the concept of organizational decline, which also can be interpreted as mere reduction in organizational size. Yet important differences exist that make downsizing and decline separate phenomenon conceptually and empirically. Several important attributes of downsizing also make it distinct from other related concepts such as lay-offs, nonadaptation, or growth-in-reverse. These attributes of downsizing are; (1) *intent*; (2) *personnel*; (3) *efficiency*; and (4) *work processes*.

Intent. Downsizing is not something that happens *to* an organization, but it is something that managers and organization members undertake purposively as an *intentional* set of activities. This differentiates downsizing from loss of marketshare, loss of revenues, or the unwitting loss of human resources that are associated with organizational decline. Downsizing is distinct from mere encroachment by the environment on performance or resources because it implies organizational action.

Personnel. Second, downsizing usually involves *reductions in personnel*, although it is not limited solely to personnel reductions. A variety of personnel reduction strategies are associated with downsizing such as transfers, outplacement, RETIREMENT incentives, buyout packages, layoffs, attrition, and so on. These reductions in personnel may occur in one part of an organization but not in others, but can still be labeled organizational downsizing. Downsizing does not always involve reductions in personnel, however, because some instances occur in which new products are added, new sources of revenue opened up, or additional work acquired without a commensurate number of employees being added. Fewer numbers of workers are then employed per unit of output compared to some previous level of employment.

Efficiency. A third characteristic of downsizing, is that it is focused on improving the *efficiency* of the organization. Downsizing occurs either proactively or reactively in order to contain costs, to enhance revenue, or to bolster competitiveness. That is, downsizing may be implemented as a defensive reaction to decline or as a proactive strategy to enhance organizational performance. By and large, downsizing in most firms has been implemented as a defensive reaction to financial crisis, loss of COMPETITIVENESS, or inefficiency. Proactive and anticipatory downsizing has been rare.

Work Processes. Finally, downsizing affects *work processes*, wittingly or unwittingly. When the workforce contracts, for example, fewer employees are left to do the same amount of work, and this has an impact on what work gets done and how it gets done. Overload, BURNOUT, inefficiency, CONFLICT, and low morale are possible consequences, or more positive outcomes may occur such as improved productivity or speed (Cameron, 1994) (*see* ROLE). Moreover, some downsizing activities may include restructuring and eliminating work (such as discontinuing functions, abolishing hierarchical levels, merging units, or redesigning tasks) which lead, of course, to some kind of work redesign (*see* JOB DESIGN; ORGANIZATIONAL RESTRUCTURING). Regardless of whether the work is the focus of downsizing activities or not, work processes are always influenced one way or another by downsizing.

Note that the level of analysis is the organization itself, not the individual or the industry. For example, a substantial literature exists on the psychological reactions individuals have to layoffs and job loss (*see* JOB INSECURITY; REDUNDANCY). Impacts on financial well-being, health, personal attitudes, family relationships, and other personal factors have been investigated by a number of researchers (Kozlowski, Chao, Smith, & Hedlund, 1993). However, whereas laying off workers is by far the most common action taken in organizations engaging in downsizing, it entails a much broader set of actions and connotations. At the industry level of analysis, a large literature also exists on divestitures and organizational mergers (*see* MERGERS AND ACQUISITIONS). Market segmentation, divesting unrelated businesses, reinforcing CORE COMPETENCIES, and consolidating industry structures are among the topics addressed. The definition of organizational downsizing being described here, however, may or may not involve selling off, transferring out, merging businesses, or altering the industry structure. Much less research has investigated the organization level of analysis than the individual and industry LEVELS OF ANALYSIS. That is, strategies for approaching downsizing, processes for implementing downsizing, and impacts on organizational performance have been under-investigated in the scholarly literature.

To summarize, organizational downsizing refers to an intentionally instituted set of activities designed to improve organizational efficiency and performance which affects the size of the organization's workforce, costs, and work processes. It is implied that downsizing is usually undertaken in order to improve organizational performance. Downsizing, therefore, may be reactive and defensive or it may be proactive and anticipatory. Ineffectiveness or impending failure are the most common motivations for downsizing, but they are not prerequisites to downsizing. Downsizing may be undertaken when no threat or financial crisis exists at all (*see* CRISES).

Most research to date indicates that the impact of downsizing on organizational performance is negative. Cameron (1995) reported that two-thirds of companies that downsize end up doing it again a year later, and the stock prices of firms that downsized during the 1980s actually lagged the industry average at the beginning of the 1990s. More than 70 percent of senior managers in downsized companies said that morale, TRUST, and PRODUCTIVITY suffered after downsizing, and half of the 1,468 firms in another survey indicated that productivity deteriorated after downsizing. A majority of organizations that downsized in a third survey failed to achieved the desired results, with only 9 percent reporting an improvement in quality. These outcomes are not universal, of course, but organizations whose performance improves as a result of downsizing have managed the process as a renewal, revitalization, and culture change effort, not just as a strategy to reduce expenses or ORGANIZATION SIZE.

See also **Organizational design; Turnaround management; Unemployment**

Bibliography

Cameron, K. S. (1994). Strategies for successful organizational downsizing. *Human Resource Management Journal*, 33, 189–212.

Cameron, K. S. (1995). Strategic downsizing: The case of a U.S. Army Command. Working Paper, University of Michigan Business School.

Cameron, K. S., Freeman, S. J. & Mishra, A. K. (1993). Downsizing and redesigning organizations. In G. P. Huber & W. H. Glick (Eds), *Organiza-*

tional change and redesign (pp. 19–63). New York: Oxford University Press.

Kozlowski, S. W. J., Chao, G. T., Smith, E. M. & Hedlund, J. (1993). Organizational downsizing: Strategies, interventions, and research implications. In C. L. Cooper I. T. Robertson (eds) *International Review of Industrial and Organizational Psychology*, **Volume 8**, New York: Wiley.

KIM S. CAMERON

dual careers *see* CAREER DEVELOPMENT; NONWORK/WORK; WOMEN AT WORK

E

ecology *see* COMMUNITY ECOLOGY; POPULATION ECOLOGY

effectiveness *see* ORGANIZATIONAL EFFECTIVENESS

efficiency *see* ORGANIZATIONAL EFFECTIVENESS

elites *see* CEOS; STATUS; TOP MANAGEMENT TEAMS

emergent properties This term refers to characteristics of a collective that cannot be understood simply in terms of information about individual members. For example, an organization can be described by properties such as FORMALIZATION, social cohesion, or DIFFERENTIATION – characteristics that cannot be reduced to the properties of the individual members of the organization.

Similarly, a population of organizations has emergent properties that can be understood distinct from knowledge of its member organizations. For example, adaptiveness might be an emergent property of an organizational population, even when it is made up of individually-inert organizations. Such a population adapts when better-fitting (but inert) organizations are born, replacing outdated (and inert) organizations that die off. In this way, an emergent property can describe an organizational population apart from the properties of its members.

Research on emergent properties attempts to understand collectives, such as organizations or populations, as units in their own right (*see* LEVELS OF ANALYSIS).

See also **Community ecology; Population ecology**

Bibliography

Lazarsfeld, P. F. & Menzel, H. (1961). On the relation between individual and collective properties. In A. Etzioni (Ed.), *Complex organizations: A sociological reader* (pp. 422–440). New York: Holt, Rinehart, and Winston.

WILLIAM P. BARNETT

emotion This can be defined as a relatively intense feeling state which interrupts cognitive processes and/or behaviors (see AFFECT). As in the case of affective states in general, there are two broad-based dimensions of emotions, positive emotion and negative emotion. A positive emotional state is characterized by affect descriptors such as active, elated, enthusiastic, excited, peppy, and strong; a negative emotional state is characterized by descriptors such as distressed, fearful, hostile, jittery, nervous, and scornful (Watson & Tellegen, 1985). Within each of the two most general dimensions of emotion (e.g., negative emotion), distinctions between different types of emotions also can be made (e.g., ANXIETY and hostility). Emotions signify not only intense feeling states but also ways of thinking and relating to the environment.

Individuals differ in their propensity to experience positive and negative emotions. Individuals high on the PERSONALITY TRAIT of positive affectivity are more likely to experience positive emotions and individuals high on the PERSONALITY TRAIT of negative affectivity are more likely to experience negative emotions. Positive affectivity and negative affectivity correspond to the dimensions of extraversion and neuroticism, respectively, in the robust five-factor model of personality (*see* PERSONALITY TESTING).

A wide variety of situational factors at work have the potential to impact the emotions workers experience on the job, such as recognition for achievement acting as a cause of positive emotional states. Factors related to the economic instrumentality of work such as diminished job security (*see* JOB INSECURITY) and reductions in pay levels are pervasive causes of negative emotional states, since they affect workers' well-being both on and off the job (*see* NONWORK/WORK). Nonwork factors (e.g., marriage and divorce) also may impact emotions experienced on the job.

Self-report instruments are commonly used to assess emotional states, though care is needed in their use since emotions can be assessed as traits or states. Emotion as a trait (i.e., positive affectivity and negative affectivity) refers to a general tendency to experience a particular emotional state whereas emotion as a state refers to how an individual feels in the short run. Emotion as a state varies and fluctuates over time. Therefore the danger exists that researchers may think they are measuring emotions as states when actually they are assessing underlying traits.

Emotions can be seen as both significant causes of thought processes and behaviors at work and as consequences. As causes, for example, emotions impact the accessibility of material from memory, categorization processes, and DECISION MAKING. As consequences, emotions can result from attributions made about behaviors (*see* ATTRIBUTION). Additionally, attention has also been focused on the expression of emotion in organizations (as opposed to the experience of emotion). For example, research has explored how members of organizations use emotional expression to INFLUENCE others.

However, traditionally, emotion has not received that much attention from organizational behavior researchers and there are many fertile areas for future research on the causes and consequences of emotions in the workplace.

See also **Mental health; Stress; Burnout; Emotions in organizations**

Bibliography

George, J. M. (1992). The role of personality in organizational life: Issues and evidence. *Journal of Management*, **18**, 185–213.

Rafaeli, A. & Sutton, R. I. (1989). The expression of emotion in organizational life. In B. M. Staw & L. L. Cummings (Eds), *Research in organizational behavior* (Vol. 11, pp. 1–42). Greenwich, CT: JAI Press.

Simon, H. A. (1982). Comments. In M. S. Clark & S. T. Fiske (Eds), *Affect and cognition: The seventeenth annual Carnegie Symposium on Cognition* (pp. 333–342). Hillsdale, NJ: Erlbaum.

Tellegen, A. (1985). Structures of mood and personality and their relevance to assessing anxiety, with an emphasis on self-report. In A. H. Tuma & J. D. Maser (Eds), *Anxiety and the anxiety disorders* (pp. 681–706). Hillsdale, NJ: Erlbaum.

Watson, D. & Clark, L. A. (1984). Negative affectivity: The disposition to experience aversive emotional states. *Psychological Bulletin*, **96**, 465–490.

Watson, D. & Tellegen, A. (1985). Toward a consensual structure of mood. *Psychological Bulletin*, **98**, 219–235.

JENNIFER M. GEORGE

emotions in organizations The study of emotions in organizations stems from the acknowledgment that our experience of work is often essentially about feelings, such as of hate, joy, tedium, jealousy, pride, anger. While this might seem an obvious point, research in ORGANIZATIONAL BEHAVIOR has been slow to grasp the emotional complexity of work life, focusing more on attitudes toward work, such as JOB SATISFACTION, or extreme negative states relating to impaired performance, such as STRESS.

Although there is no strong consensus on the definitions of feelings and emotions, some useful distinctions can be drawn. A feeling is essentially a subjective experience, a personal awareness of some bodily state, perturbation or more diffuse psychological change. Some writers argue that certain feelings of working have a special status, a flow-related experience where the self is absorbed – such as getting "lost" in one's work of writing, painting, repairing, or negotiating. This form of acquaintance-knowledge is as yet unexplored in social science (Sandelands, 1988).

Importantly, emotions gain their significance and meaning from the social and cultural setting. We learn how to display our anger, love, shame, or embarrassment according to culturally and organizationally shared communicative signs – language, body movements, facial expressions (*see* CULTURE). Emotion episodes and private feeling do not always correspond – one can "be" angry without feeling angry. With dramatic skill, emotion display can be used strategically or politically in organizations to attract attention or influence decisions or relationships (*see* IMPRESSION MANAGEMENT). Emotions are also situationally/normatively defined – the "correct" emotions for an office party, boardroom, meeting a client, job interview, or redundancy announcement. The social constitution and construction of emotions suggests that people tacitly "negotiate" the form and boundaries of appropriate emotional display, and that feelings can change on personal reflection, telling, and through argument (*see* SOCIAL CONSTRUCTIONISM).

Traditionally, emotional processes have been separated from cognitive, thinking, ones. It has been claimed that RATIONALITY in organizations is achievable if interfering emotions can be controlled or obliterated. For example, psychoanalytic theorists contend that personal anxieties, often stemming from primitive, unconscious, vulnerabilities, are enacted in work life, and they hinder effective LEADERSHIP and group processes (*see* ORGANIZATIONAL NEUROSIS). People cope with these anxieties by producing protective individual and social defenses – which prevent rational thought and action (*see* ANXIETY). The task of the psychoanalytic consultant is to treat the organization like a diseased patient, and bring it to healthy rationality (Kets de Vries, 1991).

Other writers suggest optimal rationality is unattainable. Hunches, acts of faith, and feelings will unlock a problem or change the course of events. Feelings will steer us down some paths and guide us away from others. Processes of emotions and rationality are still relatively distinct, but the former serve the latter (Frank, 1993). A more radical approach goes a step further in insisting that emotions and rationality are in fact inseparable, as is thinking and feeling. We have feelings about what we want and what we want is infused with feelings; feelings are intrinsic, not residual to individual, interpersonal, and group functioning (Kemper, 1993).

Given that SELF-REGULATION is a very large part of what makes organization possible, emotions may be considered intrinsic to organizational order. They will influence a range of behaviors, from loyalty and honesty to COMMITMENT and care. In a sense, ORGANIZATIONAL CULTURE is the emotional order of the organization, features of which can be openly exploited, or engineered. Where a "strong" culture is desired, an atmosphere of excitement, enthusiasm, or passion for the task or company is orchestrated through social events, bonding rituals, and scripts reinforcing the company's "way" (Van Maanen and Kunda, 1989).

Company control of emotional performance can be seen to be relatively benign, even fun, "all about good acting." The enthusiasm, smiles, and "have a nice day," common to many corporate office encounters and service transactions, can be split off from private feeling – in order to sustain the organizational act or social game. But some writers have argued that this is not always the case. The "emotional labor" (i.e., being employed to smile, enthuse, be sincere, etc.) can be an onerous, identity-disturbing, form of ROLE TAKING (Hochschild, 1983; Wouters, 1989).

Emotional labor is, to a degree, built into many professional jobs, where presented image or demeanor has to be learned and sustained to maintain a proper role – such as nurse, doctor, lawyer, or banker (*see* PROFESSIONAL IN ORGANIZATIONS). If the emotional mask slips, the professional encounter is threatened. Emotional labor tends to be most onerous in jobs with low AUTONOMY, where one group can impose their valuation of emotionality on another group (especially men on women) and where people represent their companies to outsiders.

See also **Affect; Emotion; Personality; Organizational climate**

Bibliography

Fineman, S. (Ed.) (1993). *Emotion in organizations.* London: Sage.

Frank, R. H. (1993). The strategic role of the emotions. *Rationality and Society*, **5**, (3), 160–194.

Hochschild, A. (1983). *The managed heart.* Berkeley: University of California.

Kemper, T. D. (1993). Reasons in emotions or emotions in reason. *Rationality and Society*, **5**, (3), 275–282.

Kets de Vries, M. F. R. (Ed.) (1991). *Organizations on the Couch: Clinical perspectives on organizational behavior and change.* San Francisco: Jossey Bass.

Pekrun, R. & Frese, M. (1992). Emotions in work and achievement. In C. L. Cooper & I. T. Robertson (Eds), *International review of industrial and organizational psychology* (Vol. 7). Chichester, UK: Wiley.

Sandelands, L. E. (1988). The concept of work feeling. *Journal for the Theory of Social Behavior*, **18**, (4), 437–457.

Van Maanen, J. & Kunda, G. (1989). 'Real feelings': Emotional expression and organizational culture. *Research in Organizational Behavior*, **11**, 43–103.

Wouters, C. (1989). The sociology of emotions and flight attendants: Hochschild's 'Managed Heart'. *Theory, Culture and Society*, **6**, (1), 95–123.

STEPHEN FINEMAN

employee involvement The term Employee Involvement (EI) has been used to describe a wide range of practices in organizations. Common to all these practices, is the attention paid to increasing employee influence over how their work is carried out or over other areas of organizational policy and practice.

The most common practices that aim to increase employee involvement are: COMMUNICATION programmes (e.g., employee attitude SURVEYS), QUALITY CIRCLES, QUALITY OF WORKING LIFE programmes, consultative committees, GAINSHARING, JOB ENRICHMENT/work redesign, and SELF-MANAGED TEAMS.

Key dimensions on which EI efforts differ are:

individually based (e.g., job redesign) versus team based (e.g., quality circles, self-managing work teams), or organization based (e.g., gainsharing);

changes to core organization (e.g., self-managing work teams, job redesign) or COLLATERAL ORGANIZATION (e.g., quality circles, attitude surveys). The distinction here is whether the EI effort requires changes in the way the core work of the organization is carried out or whether the EI activities are "added on"; and

direct involvement versus indirect (i.e., through representatives).

Research evidence concerning the outcomes of EI is mixed. The most consistent finding is of successfully implemented EI leading to increased JOB SATISFACTION. Evidence for PRODUCTIVITY improvements is weak, although stronger for self-managed work teams and some forms of work redesign (*see* JOB DESIGN).

The most successful forms of EI are those that imply changes to the core work of the organization. Collateral or parallel organization forms of EI, such as quality circles, often have a limited lifespan. Their impact is often quickly absorbed by the more enduring organization structures and systems. There is some evidence that direct forms of EI have significantly greater impact on employee attitudes than indirect.

While many organizations have benefited considerably from the introduction of EI practices, in others EI efforts founder or deliver only minor benefits.

Several barriers to the successful application of EI are frequently cited. These include lack of clearly communicated COMMITMENT from top management, resistance from middle managers who see their interests threatened, opposition from unions, and failure to adapt organizational systems to new ways of working.

A frequent cause of EI failure is that organizational systems reinforce old ways of working rather than the goals of EI. In particular, managerial performance measurement and REWARDS often focus on short-term output measures of performance, and pay little attention to issues such as subordinate development, the management of linkages across the organization, or facilitating the effective performance of other organization members.

See also **Participation; Survey feedback; Democracy; Continuous improvement**

Bibliography

Cotton, J. L. (1993). *Employee involvement*. London: Sage.

Dachler, P. H. & Wilpert, B. (1978). Conceptual dimensions of boundaries of participation in organizations. *Administrative Science Quarterly*, **23**, 1–39.

Lawler, E. E. (1986). *High-involvement management*. San Francisco: Jossey-Bass.

MARK FENTON-O'CREEVY

employee participation *see* PARTICIPATION

employee theft This refers to any unauthorized appropriation of company property by employees either for their own use or for sale to another. It includes, but is not limited to, the removal of products, supplies, materials, funds, data, information, or intellectual property. This includes everything from pilfering a few pens from the office to selling proprietary information to a competitor. It has been estimated by the US Chamber of Commerce that employee theft, in its various forms, costs American businesses $40 billion annually, although unofficial estimates are considerably higher. In fact, approximately 20 percent of all US businesses fail because of excessive rates of internal theft (Greengard, 1993).

The causes of employee theft are numerous. At its core is temptation (i.e., human greed) coupled with opportunity, triggered by the motive to steal. In some cases, theft is motivated by financial pressure, making any employee a prospective target. However, employee theft is frequently triggered by conditions encountered on the job, such as an ORGANIZATIONAL CULTURE in which theft is perceived as condoned. For example, theft often occurs when employees witness others stealing while organizational officials turn a blind eye, failing to discipline the offenders (*see* PUNISHMENT).

Employee theft also occurs in conditions under which employees feel justified in retaliating against their employers. For example, employees steal from their employers when they feel exploited by them, such as when they are required to work too long, too hard, or under too harsh conditions (Hollinger & Clark, 1983). In such circumstances employees perceive that their theft behaviors are not deviant, but a morally justified form of RECIPROCITY – acts that not only "even the score," but that model the seemingly-deviant behavior of the employers themselves (for a review, see Greenberg, 1990).

In this vein, studies have applied EQUITY THEORY to understanding employee theft. For example, Greenberg (1990) reasoned that underpaid employees would steal more from their employers than equitably paid employees insofar as stealing would effectively raise the level of outcomes received. In a field experiment comparing the shrinkage rates (i.e., percentage of unaccounted for inventory) in manufacturing plants in which employees' PAY was cut 15 percent (the underpaid condition) to a comparable plant in which employees' pay was not cut (the equitably paid condition), shrinkage was found to be significantly higher in the underpaid condition. This study, and a follow-up laboratory investigation (Greenberg, 1993) found that theft among underpaid employees was reduced when employees were given a detailed and interpersonally sensitive explanation for the underpayment they faced.

Attempts to control employee theft have focused on several different tactics. First, the security industry attempts to tackle the problem by imposing procedures and devices (e.g., surveillance cameras) that deter theft by increasing the chances of getting caught (Bliss & Aoki, 1993). Second, personnel psychologists have attempted to develop employee screening procedures (e.g., tests and interviews) that can identify potentially dishonest employees before they are hired (Murphy, 1993). Third, human resources specialists have focused on ways of minimizing employees' MOTIVATION to steal, such as avoiding underpayment.

See also **Reinforcement; Human resources management; Payment systems; Justice, procedural**

Bibliography

Bliss, E. C. & Aoki, I. S. (1993). *Are your employees stealing you blind? San Diego, CA: Pfeiffer.*

Greenberg, J. (1990). Employee theft as a reaction to underpayment inequity: The hidden cost of pay cuts. *Journal of Applied Psychology*, **75**, 561–568.

Greenberg, J. (1993). Stealing in the name of justice: Informational and interpersonal moderators of theft reactions to underpayment inequity. *Organizational Behavior and Human Decision Processes*, **54**, 81–103.
Greengard, S. (1993 April). Theft control starts with HR strategies. *Personnel Journal*, pp. 81–87, 90–91.
Hollinger, R. D. & Clark, J. P. (1983). *Theft by employees*. Lexington, MA: Lexington Books.
Murphy, K. R. (1993). *Honesty in the workplace*. Pacific Grove, CA: Brooks/Cole.

JERALD GREENBERG

empowerment Prior to its adoption as a management term, the word empowerment was most often used, in fields such as politics, social work, feminist theory, and Third World aid (*see* FEMINISM). Writers in these fields have taken it to mean providing individuals (usually disadvantaged) with the tools and resources to further their own interests, *as they see them*. Within the field of management, empowerment is commonly used with a different meaning: providing employees with tools, resources, and discretion to further the interests of the organization (as seen by senior management).

Conger and Kanungo (1988) define empowerment as a psychological construct. They suggest that empowerment is the process of fostering SELF EFFICACY beliefs among employees. This implies both removing sources of powerlessness and providing employees with positive FEEDBACK and support (*see* ALIENATION).

Empowerment, in this sense of a psychological construct, is a principal goal of most forms of EMPLOYEE INVOLVEMENT.

See also **Participation; Decision making; Power: Influence**

Bibliography

Conger, J. A. & Kanugo, R. N. (1988). The empowerment process: Integrating theory and practice. *Academy of Management Review*, **13**, 471–482.

MARK FENTON-O'CREEVY

enactment The concept was first developed by Weick in his influential and innovative monograph, *The Social Psychology of Organizing* (1969), to connote an organism's adjustment to its environment by directly acting upon the environment to change it. Enactment thus has the capacity to create ecological change to which the organism may have subsequently to adjust, possibly by further enactment. Weick discusses this process in the context of active sense-making by the individual manager or employee, but also notes how one may enact "limitations," for example, by avoidance of disconfirming experience, or "charades," by acting-out in order to test understanding. Enactment is thus often a species of self-fulfilling prophesy. It may also be deviation amplifying, where consequences are successively multiplied by actions on the environment. Weick also identifies enactment as a form of SOCIAL CONSTRUCTIONISM, the reification of experience and environment through action.

Since Weick's origination of the concept, it has found most use in STRATEGIC MANAGEMENT, to capture the dynamics of relations between ORGANIZATION AND ENVIRONMENT. Child (1972) developed the analogous notion of STRATEGIC CHOICE with similar intent, i.e., to show how organizational adaptation should not be seen as entirely exogenously directed, but can be endogenous in origin and, in its effects, modify the contingencies bearing down upon the firm. This idea reinforces a model of organizations as "purposeful systems" (Ackoff & Emery, 1972), akin to willful actors, a construction which challenges the behaviorist PARADIGM of OPEN SYSTEMS' actions being determined by environmental CONDITIONING.

One can expect enactment processes to be most visible in large and powerful organizations which have market-making capacity, but they are no less relevant to the way smaller enterprises conceive their contexts and make choices about how they will act in relation to them. Enactment alternatives to accommodating environmental forces include creating buffers to diffuse impact, negotiating with STAKEHOLDERS, coopting influential agencies, and avoidance.

As an operational concept, enactment lacks precision and therefore cannot be expected to be much further elaborated in organizational analysis. However, it embodies an important recognition of how agency and constructive COGNITIVE PROCESSES are essential elements in our understanding of the behavior of individuals and organizations.

See also **Population ecology; Structuration**

Bibliography

Ackoff, R. L. & Emery, F. E. (1972). *On purposeful systems*. Chicago: Aldine.

Child, J. (1972). Organizational structure, environment and performance: The role of strategic choice. *Sociology*, **6**, 2–22.

Weick, K. E. (1969). *The social psychology of organizing*. Reading, MA: Addison-Wesley.

NIGEL NICHOLSON

entrainment This term means the adjustment of the pace, cycle, and rhythm of one activity to match that of another (Ancona & Chong, 1993). A cycle is a pattern of events over time and a rhythm is a recurrent cyclical pattern. Managers who shorten product development time or speed up their DECISION-MAKING processes to match accelerated INNOVATION cycles within an industry are exhibiting entrainment. Similarly, managers who consistently align ORGANIZATIONAL CHANGE with major technological discontinuities are entraining to their environment (*see* ORGANIZATION AND ENVIRONMENT).

Entrainment can be deliberate, as managers try to adjust pace, cycle, and rhythm to key environmental patterns, or unintentional, as dominant cycles and rhythms "capture" other cycles. An example of the latter is the coupling of PERFORMANCE APPRAISAL, budgeting, sales activity, and hiring practices to the fiscal year.

Entrainment to cycles in the workplace is very common. Shift workers' families often change meal times, leisure activities, and play patterns to accommodate sleep during the day (McGrath & Rotchford, 1983) (*see* HOURS OF WORK). Parents often sacrifice time with children to accommodate to intense work periods in their careers.

Entrainment appears to be inertial and initial entrainment appears to be the strongest. Once set, pace, cycles, and rhythm are hard to change. In a series of studies Kelly and McGrath (1985) showed that individuals and groups that were given 5, 10, and 20 minutes, respectively, to complete a task learned to work at decreasing rates of speed. The shorter the time limit, the higher the rate at which anagrams were solved. McGrath, Kelly, and Machatka (1984) argue "that groups and individuals attune their rates of work to fit the conditions of their work situations." Once established, this pace becomes inertial. The groups maintained their initial pace even when the time limits were subsequently changed to 20, 10, and 5 minutes, respectively.

Huygens was the first to write about entrainment in the seventeenth century (Minorsky, 1962). He observed that when two pendulum clocks that separately ran at different speeds were both hung on the same thin wooden board, they came to swing in perfect synchrony. The term entrainment is most commonly used in biology, whereby endogenous biological rhythms are modified in their phase and periodicity by powerful exogenous influences called external pacers. An example is the circadian (meaning about 1 day) rhythm where most bodily cycles are entrained to the external light-dark, 24-hour, cycle of the earth. Individuals who are isolated from these cycles revert back to their "natural" periodicities, which are usually an hour or so longer than 24 hours.

As the pace of organization change quickens, the cycles of time to market and product development shrink, and technological innovation accelerates, issues of speed and meshing of cycles become increasingly important. Similarly, organizations are subject to variant cycles, such as the quarterly and annual accounting cycles, the seasonal cycles of demand, and the roughly 4-year business cycle, and contain processes with intrinsic response times that vary substantially (order fulfillment may take seconds while capacity expansion may take years) (Sterman & Mosekilde, 1993). Organizations are filled with individuals going through various CAREER and life cycles, and teams that pace themselves to temporal milestones (*see* CAREER STAGES; LIFE STAGES). They exist in environments with technological, market, and business cycles in which pace seems to be ever quickening. These characteristics call for analysis through the entrainment lens.

Entrainment helps us to focus on how fast activities occur and the impact of how cycles and rhythms interact. It focuses on nonlinear patterns whereby you may have to act quickly, for if you wait too long the world will have changed and you have to do something different. It focuses on multilevel phenomena; examining how CEO, team, organizational, and environmental cycles interact over time. It also focuses on coordination by time rather than by activity; that is, rather than looking at whose activities are interdependent and finding appropriate coordination mechanisms, it specifies when activity must be completed, letting activities be reconfigured as necessary to meet deadlines.

Research on entrainment is just beginning. Many issues remain unresolved including the mechanisms that cause entrainment to occur, the methods that are best able to measure entrainment, and how entrainment differs from related concepts of coordination, scheduling, and time allocation. Nonetheless, society's increased obsession with speed and timing suggests an increasing role for entrainment in a theory of organizations.

See also **Cooperation: Organizational theory; Punctuated equilibrium; Vicious cycles**

Bibliography

Ancona, D. & Chong, C. (1993). Time and timing in top management teams. MIT Sloan School of Management Working Paper No. 3591–93-BPS.

Kelly, J. & McGrath, J. (1985). Effects of time limits and task types on task performance and interaction of four-person groups. *Journal of Personality and Social Psychology*, **49**, 395–407.

McGrath, J. E., Kelly, J. R. & Machatka, D. E. (1984). The social psychology of time: Entrainment of behavior in social and organizational settings. *Applied Social Psychology Annual*, **5**, 21–44.

McGrath, J. E. & Rotchford N. L. (1983). Time and behavior in organizations. In L.L. Cummings & B. M. Staw (Eds), *Research in organizational behavior* (vol. 5). Greenwich, CT: JAI press.

Minorsky, N. (1962). *Nonlinear oscillations*. Princeton, N.J.: Van Nostrand.

Sterman, J. D. & Mosekilde, E. (1993). Business cycles and long waves: A behavioral disequilibrium perspective. MIT Sloan School of Management Working Paper No. 3528–93-MSA.

DEBORAH ANCONA

entrepreneurship This a term which has been used in different ways. One usage views entrepreneurship as concerned with the processes leading to new venture creation, without regard to the type or potential of the organizations created. Another view sees entrepreneurship as primarily concerned with developing innovative ventures, whether these are independent or occur within already established organizations. Entrepreneurship inside organizations has sometimes been termed "corporate entrepreneurship" or "intrapreneurship." Both usages emphasize the role of the entrepreneur as one who organizes a venture and bears some degree of risk in return for rewards

Interest in entrepreneurship has increased for several reasons. As large organizations have "downsized," much of the net new job creation has occurred in new and small firms (*see* DOWNSIZING). (One study found that about 88 percent of the net new jobs created in the United States economy from 1981–1985 were in firms with less than 20 employees.) (Birch, 1987) New firms have served as centers of innovation, developing products or services attuned to a changing environment (*see* ORGANIZATION AND ENVIRONMENT). For many individuals, entrepreneurship has been the vehicle by which they pursue personal goals and achieve independence. In countries which have been moving from state-owned to private enterprise, entrepreneurship has been supported as a means to transform these economies. In regard to corporate entrepreneurship, managements of large organizations have recognized that one of their greatest challenges is to become more innovative and more responsive to changes in markets and TECHNOLOGY (*see* ORGANIZATIONAL SIZE).

The entrepreneur seeking to develop an independent venture must recognize an opportunity; in fact, some would regard the identification of opportunities as the essence of entrepreneurship. The entrepreneur must then develop a strategy or way of competing, investigate the venture's requirements and potential, assemble resources, and move forward to start and manage that organization. There is some evidence that, at any point in time, about 4 percent of the adult population are nascent entrepreneurs, but that only about 10 percent of these actually proceed to the point of creating new firms (Reynolds & White, 1993). The new organizations may differ widely in scale or potential as well as in the resources and technical or management sophistication required. Small scale ventures may be started with the financial resources, contacts, and "sweat equity" of the founder (*see* SMALL BUSINESSES). Large scale and high potential ventures often involve founding teams and the attraction of outside resources, sometimes provided by sophisticated investors. Although some FOUNDERS might be viewed as "habitual entrepreneurs," many engage in this process only once, and therefore must learn how to put a venture together and how to manage a particular line of business as they proceed.

New ventures start with ideas; the sources of these ideas are often previous jobs or personal interests, 43 percent and 18 percent, respectively, in one study (Cooper, Dunkelberg, Woo, & Dennis, 1990). Strategies must be developed which take into account the limited resources available to the start-up and the nature of existing competitors. The entrepreneur must then try to assemble resources, at a time when risks appear high to potential investors, customers, employees, and suppliers. Entrepreneurs often proceed sequentially – gathering information, revising plans, and making commitments in stages, with attempts to minimize exposure at each stage (Stevenson, Roberts, & Grousbeck 1989).

Corporate entrepreneurship can involve efforts to encourage INNOVATION and RISK-TAKING throughout the organization (*see* ORGANIZATIONAL CHANGE). It can also focus upon developing entirely new businesses, in which case it involves many of the same challenges that arise in starting independent ventures. Opportunities must be identified; strategies must be developed; and resources must be committed, all within the context of an existing organization. Important issues include whether ventures "fit" with corporate strategy and how resources not directly controlled by the corporate entrepreneurs can be accessed for the new venture. Other issues relate to how internal corporate entrepreneurs should be rewarded. Should they have the same prospects for wealth (and failure) that independent entrepreneurs experience, or should their REWARDS (and JOB SECURITY) be similar to those of other employees? The corporate strategy, including the extent to which the organization is expanding and diversifying, and the degree of personal sponsorship by influential senior executives are among the major influences which bear upon whether venture activities are supported (Fast, 1978) (*see* CEOS). It should be recognized that corporate entrepreneurship may take place in widely different contexts. Some venture activities occur within relatively separate subsidiaries or venture departments, which have control of their own assets and the freedom to depart from corporate policies. Others are embedded in the existing organization, and involve shared resources and sponsorship by existing departments.

One stream of research on independent venturing has emphasized traits of entrepreneurs, seeking to determine whether they are "different" in certain ways. Such PERSONALITY attributes as risk-taking propensity, internal LOCUS OF CONTROL, and ACHIEVEMENT MOTIVATION have been examined. There have been problems with this research stream, including lack of comparability of samples, inappropriate test instruments, and lack of consideration of contextual factors (Shaver & Scott, 1991). Demographic characteristics have also been considered, including AGE, whether there were entrepreneurial parents, and membership in particular subgroups. In general, some of the strongest findings reflect relationships between entrepreneurial activity and achievement motivation, as well as having had entrepreneurial parents. Some have urged that research should focus less upon traits and more upon COGNITIVE PROCESSES or the behaviors of entrepreneurs (Gartner, 1989).

Other research frameworks have considered how environmental influences and resource availability bear upon birth and survival (*see* POPULATION ECOLOGY). A considerable body of research has sought to determine how founding processes, initial firm characteristics, business strategies, and management methods influence later patterns of development. It appears that early venture characteristics may "imprint" the firm and shape its later strategy. Findings relating to performance have been mixed to date, but research suggests that higher performance is associated with ventures started by entrepreneurs who have a high need for achievement, who take explicit steps to manage risk, and who engage in relatively systematic planning. Furthermore, ventures may do better if they are closely related to the organizations which the entrepreneurs had left, if they are started by teams, entail larger amounts of capital, and involve industries in the growth stage (Cooper & Gimeno-Gascon, 1992).

See also **Competitiveness; Strategic management; Innovation adoption; Innovation diffusion**

Bibliography

Birch, D. L. (1987). *Job creation in America.* New York: Free Press.

Burgelman, R. A. (1984). Managing the internal corporate venturing process: Some recommendations for practice. *Sloan Management Review*, **25** (2), 33–48.

Cooper, A. C., Dunkelberg, W. C., Woo, C. Y. & Dennis, W. J., Jr. (1990). *New business in America: The firms and their owners.* Washington, DC: NFIB Foundation.

Cooper, A. C. & Gimeno-Gascon, J. (1992). Entrepreneurs, processes of founding, and new firm performance. In D. Sexton & J. Kasarda (Eds), *State of the art in entrepreneurship research* (pp. 301–340). Boston, MA: PWS–Kent.

Fast, N. D. (1978). *The rise and fall of corporate new venture divisions.* Ann Arbor, MI: UMI Research Press.

Gartner, W. B. (1989). "Who is an entrepreneur?" is the wrong question. *Entrepreneurship Theory and Practice*, **13** (4), 47–68.

Reynolds, P. D. & White, S. B. (1993). *Wisconsin's entrepreneurial climate study.* Madison, WI: Wisconsin Housing and Economic Development Authority. Final report.

Shaver, K. G. & Scott, L. R. (1991). Person, process, choice: The psychology of new venture creation. *Entrepreneurship Theory and Practice*, **16** (2), 23–45.

Stevenson, H. H., Roberts, M. J. & Grousbeck, H. I. (1989). *New business ventures and the entrepreneur* (3rd edn). Homewood, IL: Irwin.

ARNOLD C. COOPER

environment *see* CONTINGENCY THEORY; CORPORATE SOCIAL RESPONSIBILITY; STAKEHOLDERS

environmental dependence *see* ORGANIZATION AND ENVIRONMENT; RESOURCE BASED THEORY; RESOURCE DEPENDENCE

equal opportunity Legislation in most European countries is much less strict and proactive than in the United States. (European Community law tends to be more equality-promoting than does that of most individual member countries, and so may, in time, provide a significant force for change.) Many organizational employees are therefore less likely to be aware of equality issues or able to identify overt or covert discriminatory practices. Many companies do now have official Equal Opportunity Policies. These seem, however, to have limited impact unless supported by Chief Executive and senior management commitment (and understanding), major implementation effort, significant financial backing, appropriate monitoring activities, and cultural change; unfortunately most are not.

According to the stated goal of the United States Civil Rights legislation, DISCRIMINATION based on GENDER, RACE, color, religion, and national origin, has been illegal in the United States since the passage of the Civil Rights Act of 1964. Although various forms of discrimination were outlawed earlier, this legislation marked the first statement of unified policy of nondiscrimination, especially as it applied to work settings (Title VII of the Act). More recent legislation outlawed discrimination on the basis of DISABILITY or AGE. Furthermore, some states have passed laws forbidding discrimination on the basis of marital status or sexual orientation. The goal of all these laws was stated to be that all qualified persons would have the same access to jobs, and would be treated the same on those jobs, and the Equal Employment Opportunity Commission was established to enforce this legislation in work settings.

This legislation, and its stated goal has had a major impact on HUMAN RESOURCE MANAGEMENT because, once evidence was presented that a policy or action had a disproportionate effect on members of a given racial, sexual, etc., group (termed "adverse impact"), the burden of proof was on the employer that he or she was not guilty of discrimination. Employers found guilty of such discrimination could be liable for large financial damages, and could be required to hire greater numbers of members of affected groups. Charges of such discrimination led to the need for employers to demonstrate empirically that any procedure (such as a test or an interview) that was used in making a personnel decision, was valid for members of all affected groups (*see* VALIDITY). These cases resulted in a decreased reliance upon certain types of tests and even questions which appeared to discriminate against members of certain groups (*see* PSYCHOLOGICAL TESTING). It has even resulted in less reliance upon stating physical requirements for jobs (including height requirements), and educational requirements (such as a high-school diploma) unless they could be shown to be related to performance on the job.

The laws have also changed the way that individual employees are treated. Employees who could demonstrate that they were treated less favorably than other employees with similar qualifications or performance levels have thus proved discrimination, even if no direct evidence of an employer's discriminatory intent existed. In addition, the laws prohibit harassment of employees on the basis of race, sex, etc., and both employers and individual supervisors have been required to pay large financial damages when harassment has been proved (*see* SEXUAL HARASSMENT). These laws have convinced human resource management professionals that consistency in applying employer policies and thorough documentation of performance or discipline problems is essential to escape legal liability.

The legislation in question also led to a requirement (in some cases) for a policy of affirmative action, where employers were to take active steps to recruit and hire qualified women and members of minority groups. The policies established to promote equal opportunity have resulted in human resource management practices in the United States being closely tied to legal requirements, and in legal issues becoming a major factor in many decisions. These policies have also, however, led to a decreased reliance upon human resource practices that, intentionally or not, did discriminate against members of certain groups. Despite these efforts, however, most scholars would agree that true equal opportunity is still a goal that has not been realized in US human resource management practices.

See also **Assessment; Selection methods; Management of diversity; Corporate social responsibility; Business ethics**

Bibliography

Ledvinka, J. A. (1982). *Federal regulation of personnel and human resource management*. Boston, MA: PWS–Kent.

Kirp, D. L., Yudof, M. G. & Franks, M. S. (1986). *Gender justice*. Chicago: University of Chicago Press

"The New Civil Rights Act of 1991 and What It Means to Employers". *Employment Law Update*, **6**, (December 1991), 1–12.

Willborn, S. (1986). Theories of employment discrimination in the United Kingdom and the United States. *Boston College International and Comparative Law Review*, **9** (2), 243–256.

ANGELO DE NISI

equity theory Introduced by Adams (1965) as an extension of the distributive justice concept (*see* JUSTICE, DISTRIBUTIVE), equity theory proposes that people's attitudes and behavior are affected by their assessment of their work contributions (referred to as *inputs*) and the REWARDS they receive (referred to as *outcomes*). Inputs may include such contributions as effort, SKILL, and seniority. Outcomes may include such rewards as pay, STATUS, and recognition.

People are said to compare the ratios of their own perceived outcomes/inputs to the corresponding ratios of other people or groups. Reference comparisons may be made to such others as: coworkers on the job, industry standards, or oneself at an earlier point in time (*see* SOCIAL COMPARISON). The theory focuses on individuals' perceptions of their own and others' outcomes and inputs rather than actual states. When one's own outcome/input ratio is believed to be greater than another's, the individual is theorized to experience a state of *overpayment inequity*, causing feelings of guilt. In contrast, when one's own outcome/input ratio is believed to be less than another's, the individual is theorized to experience a state of *underpayment inequity*, causing feelings of anger.

When one's own outcome/input ratio is believed to match that of other persons or groups, a state of *equitable payment* is said to exist, resulting in feelings of satisfaction (*see* JOB SATISFACTION).

The negative emotions associated with inequitable states are undesirable, motivating people to alter – either behaviorally or cognitively – their own or the other's outcomes or inputs (if possible) so as to achieve an equitable state. For example, workers who feel underpaid may be motivated to lower their own outcomes (a behavioral reaction), or to convince themselves that their work contributions are not as great as another who is believed to receive higher outcomes (a cognitive reaction). Likewise, people may respond to overpayment by raising their own inputs, or by convincing themselves that relative to the comparison other, their own contributions are sufficiently great to merit the higher reward received. Research has generally supported these claims (for a review, see Greenberg, 1982). Researchers have used equity theory to explain a wide variety of work-related behaviors, such as reactions to job titles, office assignments, pay cuts, and layoffs. Although early tests of equity theory were conducted in the laboratory, more recent research has been successful in finding support for equity theory in a wide variety of work settings.

Attempting to refine equity theory and extend it to a wide variety of social situations (beyond the work context used by Adams), Walster, Walster, and Berscheid (1978) proposed equity theory as a general theory of social behavior. For example, they used equity theory to explain behavior in marriage and romantic relationships as well as parent–child relationships.

Equity theory has been criticized on several grounds, including the necessity of distress as a motivator of attempts to redress inequities, uncertainties regarding the choice of a comparison other, vagueness regarding the choice of a mode of inequity redress, and difficulties in quantifying inequities (see Adams & Freedman, 1976).

See also **Motivation and performance; Payment systems; Motivation**

Bibliography

Adams, J. S. (1965). Inequity in social exchange. In L. Berkowitz (Ed.), *Advances in experimental social psychology* (Vol. 2, pp. 267–299). New York: Academic Press.

Adams, J. S. & Freedman, S. (1976). Equity theory revisited: Comments and annotated bibliography. In L. Berkowitz & E. Walster (Eds), *Advances in experimental social psychology* (Vol. 9, pp. 43–90). New York: Academic Press.

Greenberg, J. (1982). Approaching equity and avoiding inequity in groups and organizations. In J. Greenberg & R. L. Cohen (Eds), *Equity and justice in social behavior* (pp. 389–435). New York: Academic Press.

Walster, E., Walster, G. W. & Berscheid, E. (1978). *Equity: Theory and research.* Boston, MA: Allyn & Bacon.

JERALD GREENBERG

ERG theory Formulated by Alderfer (1972) as an alternative to Maslow's need hierarchy (*see* NEED THEORY), ERG theory posits three categories of needs: existence, relatedness, and growth. All three needs can affect behavior simultaneously and lower-order needs are predicted to increase in motivational importance if higher-order needs are frustrated. The components of ERG theory are more amenable to empirical test than those of Maslow's theory. Although early research was generally supportive of the model, there has been little research interest in ERG theory since the mid-1970s, perhaps reflecting general disillusion in constructs like growth needs and SELF-ACTUALIZATION.

See also **Motivation; Growth need strength; Extrinsic/intrinsic motivation**

Bibliography

Alderfer, C. P. (1972). *Existence, relatedness, and growth: Human needs in organizational settings.* New York: Free Press.

SEYMOUR ADLER

ergonomics This body of knowledge is concerned with the study of the interaction of humans with TECHNOLOGY. Its aim is to maximize the safe and efficient utilization of technology for its designed purpose. It is a research discipline, drawing upon the sciences of psychology, physiology and anatomy. It is also a problem solving discipline, involved in the application of ergonomics principles to design. Initially, the topic was a multidisciplinary one, with individuals coming from different specialisms. University courses began in the 1960s and interdisciplinary-trained graduates began to emerge. The current situation has specialists and generalists working in both research and application.

The word ergonomics was coined by Hywel Murrell in the United Kingdom in 1949 to cover the field that emerged from the war-time activities of scientists who had come together to tackle the problems associated with the use of military equipment. These researchers were concerned to continue their multidisciplinary approach of studying humans in their working environments. Similar developments in the United States led to the adoption of the term human factors to cover much the same topics as ergonomics. Mention should also be made of Wojciech Jastrzebowski, who in 1857, in Poland, also put forward the term ergonomics to cover a science of labor. There are other related terms in current use. One is engineering psychology, which refers to the study of human INFORMATION PROCESSING in an applied context. Another term, COGNITIVE ERGONOMICS, has found favor in the human–computer world, and refers to the cognitive psychology implications of computer use. Also in the latter context, "usability" is rapidly replacing the ubiquitous "user-friendly" as a more meaningful term. The concept of "user-centred design" is also gaining wider acceptance, but is only another way of expressing ergonomics.

The definition of technology in this context is very broad. It ranges from something as simple as a warning symbol on a product's label to the complexity of the control room of a nuclear power station. Any object built for human use will benefit from ergonomics being an integral part of design. Too much emphasis was placed in the past on designers' intuitions or in design for the average person. In addition, reliance was placed on the adaptability of the human to poor design. A number of developments in the last 50 years have shaped where the emphasis has been in the subject. The immediate post-war concerns were in traditional production industries. The march of AUTOMATION in both civilian and military systems had led to the study of the ergonomics implications of new technology. Human ERRORS (*see* SAFETY) and the consequences of ACCIDENTS, most notably in aviation and in high-risk industries (e.g., nuclear power and petro-chemicals) have engendered interest in the subject. One contribution of ergonomics here is the improved layout of displays and controls to produce arrangements that are easy to understand and use and are not subject to confusion in stressful situations (*see* STRESS). This area has been given added impetus with the increasing use of visual display screens to replace conventional instruments. Unfortunately, established knowledge is still not always used, and human errors arising from poor design are still being implicated in accident investigations.

There has been a growing concern, marked by legislation, for health and well being at work and this has led to an increasing recognition of the role of ergonomics. The burgeoning use of computers in the workplace and elsewhere, has meant that there has been rising interest in studies of HUMAN–COMPUTER INTERACTION. Whilst the initial focus here has been on the design of the interface and its usability, the problems of upper limb disorders resulting from continued keyboard use, often with poorly designed and/or positioned equipment, is a current topic of ergonomics research.

Interesting issues have arisen with increasing female participation in traditional male jobs (*see* WOMEN AT WORK). Historically, the difference in average physical strength has led to females being debarred from some work. However, a close examination of the demands of the work and the capabilities of all the potential workers would show that stronger women might be capable of the work and that some weaker men might be physically harmed by doing it. A better solution would be to redesign the work in question, reducing its physical demands, to bring it within the capabilities of more workers.

Consumerism has placed emphasis on the safety and ease of use of consumer products. The need to involve the user in workplace design issues has given rise to participative ergonomics. The role of ergonomics in developing countries is also a topic of current interest. The design of manuals, other documentation, forms, symbols, and signs has also come under the scrutiny of ergonomics. In this latter area progress has been made across a range of issues from the legibility of signs to the intelligibility of forms.

Ergonomics has necessarily developed strong links with other disciplines. There is often a close working relationship with healthcare and safety experts. Similar links with the social sciences exist with topics like JOB SATISFACTION and the study of team situations (*see* WORK GROUPS). The latter topic has received renewed attention with the development of computer-supported cooperative work. The application of ergonomics principles to ORGANIZATIONAL DESIGN has emerged as a topic termed macroergonomics.

The central underlying concept of ergonomics could be said to be "compatibility." This term was first used in the context of making the response of a display (e.g., a dial) most naturally follow the movement of a control (e.g., a knob). In this case, naturalness would be a clockwise movement on the dial that followed a similar movement with the knob. However, the concept can be given a broader meaning and can encompass such things as the compatibility of a computer interface with the user's mental model, the compatibility of a car seat with the user's physical dimensions, and the compatibility of the physical force needed to turn a bottle top with the user's strength. Compatibility should be the goal of any design for human use, and in turn will depend on exact knowledge about the user population and about the way in which tasks will be carried out.

See also **Ability; Job design; Job analysis; Information technology; Hours of work; Working conditions**

Bibliography

Grandjean, E. (1988). *Fitting the task to the man: A textbook of occupational ergonomics* (4th edn). London: Taylor & Francis.

Kantowitz, B. H. & Sorkin, R. D. (1983). *Human factors: Understanding people-system relationships*. New York: Wiley.

Norman, D. A. & Draper, S. W. (Eds) (1986). *User centred system design*. Hillsdale, NJ: Erlbaum.

Oborne, D. J. (1995). *Ergonomics at work* (3rd edn). Chichester: Wiley.

Salvendy, G. (Ed.) (1987). *A handbook of human factors*. New York: Wiley.

Sanders, M. S. & McCormick, E. J. (1994). *Human factors in engineering and design* (7th edn). New York: McGraw-Hill.

Wickens, C. D. (1992). *Engineering psychology and human performance* (2nd edn). New York: Harper Collins.

Wilson, J. R. & Corlett, E. N. (Eds) (1995). *Evaluation of human work: A practical ergonomics methodology* (2nd edn). London: Taylor & Francis.

R. B. STAMMERS

error This term has two uses in statistics. In the first use, error is defined as any variation not assigned a cause. In other words, error is any deviation of an actual value from that predicted by the deterministic part of a statistical model. In experimental studies, of GOAL SETTING, for example, any variation, in individual performance from the average for all those in a common condition, such as level of FEEDBACK, is referred to as error. Similarly, in field studies of JOB DESIGN, the deviation of an individual's value on an outcome, such as INTRINSIC MOTIVATION, from that predicted for all those who share the same inputs, e.g., JOB CHARACTERISTICS, is also called error (*see* ERRORS).

The second use of the term occurs in hypothesis testing. In this sense, error is a logical condition in which an inference drawn from a statistical procedure is incongruent with what is actually true – though the latter may be unknown. There are two well-known kinds of error in hypothesis testing. An error of the first kind, often denoted as a Type I error, occurs when a researcher rejects a hypothesis that is true. The second kind, often denoted as Type II, happens if a researcher fails to reject a hypothesis when it is false. For example, a researcher who, on the basis of a particular sample, rejects the hypothesis that LOOSE-COUPLING increases INNOVATION, when it in fact does, would be making Type I error.

These kinds of errors in hypothesis testing can occur due to the probabilistic nature of statistical inference. The probability of making an error of the first kind is referred to as the size of a hypothesis test. The size can be chosen by the researcher. The probability of making an error of the second kind is called the power of a hypothesis test. Power is a property of a second hypothesis that is an alternative to the focal hypothesis. Due to the nature of hypothesis testing in organizational research, in which an alternative is often not well-explicated, power is usually indeterminate and subject to neither control nor scrutiny. Exceptions occur when concerns about sample sizes lead to considerations of power.

Many statisticians also admit to a third variety of error. Any statistical method requires a model. A model is a set of assumptions sufficient to specify a probability distribution for the statistic on which an inference is to be based. An incorrect model invalidates any inference or conclusions drawn from the associated method. This error propagates to mistakes in subsequent interpretation and use of the results. Errors of this kind may be the most problematic in organizational research, since issues of model selection and VALIDITY are often set aside in favor of convention and expediency. One criterion for evaluating statistical models is the minimization of errors – in the first use of the term, above.

See also **Reliability; Statistical methods; Bias; Research design; Research methods**

Bibliography

Gigerenzer, G., Swijtink, Z., Porter, T., Daston, L., Beattz, J. & Kruger, L. (1989). *The empire of chance: How probability changed science and everyday life*. New York: Cambridge University Press.

KENNETH W. KOPUT

errors Error research has a place in both technical systems (e.g., computers, nuclear power plants) and organizations. An error is defined as a goal not being reached and the erroneous behavior could have been potentially avoided (Zapf, Brodbeck, Frese, Peters, & Prüemper, 1992). Reason (1990) differentiates violations (doing something wrong on purpose) and unintentional behaviors (like spastic movements) from errors and further subdivides errors into mistakes (errors in conscious behaviors) and slips and lapses (errors in routinized behaviors).

An error taxonomy is presented in Figure 1. A major part of this taxonomy was empirically tested in the area of HUMAN COMPUTER INTERACTION (Zapf, Brodbeck, Frese, Peters, & Prümper, 1992). It differentiates errors according to where they appear in the action sequence (goal development, information integration, etc.) and at which level of regulation (heuristic, intellectual, etc. (*see* ACTION THEORY). The latter implies that errors are due to different cognitive processes. Errors appearing at the heuristic level are, for example, related to general heuristics (rules of thumb) pertaining to how one develops goals or plans. For example, an error may occur because one has misapplied a general heuristic of not planning one's future actions. Errors at the intellectual level imply conscious processing which results in errors because of limited processing capacity (e.g., not thinking about a plan of action because one has too many other things to do). Errors at the level of flexible action patterns relate to habits which are misapplied. In addition, there are knowledge errors shown in the Figure as a separate box. The knowledge base for regulation is treated separately because knowledge is not directly regulating actions but indirectly through goals, plans, etc.

In case of an error, people tend to assess who is at fault. This may be a "natural" response (*see* ATTRIBUTION) but it is not a useful approach in organizations. Rather organizations should allow their members to learn from errors. When designing systems (be they tools or organizations), one can maximize either error prevention or error management. *Error management* is defined as an "approach to errors with the goal of reducing future errors, of avoiding negative error consequences, and of dealing quickly with error consequences once they occur." (Frese, in press, p. 2). Thus, the emphasis of error management is to alleviate or avert negative error consequences. Error management means that a system supports early error detection (when an error is detected early, is it less likely to have severe negative consequences), learning from errors, which results in more error knowledge, better explanations for errors (without blaming), and the development and use of error correction strategies. The principle of "kaizen" is similar

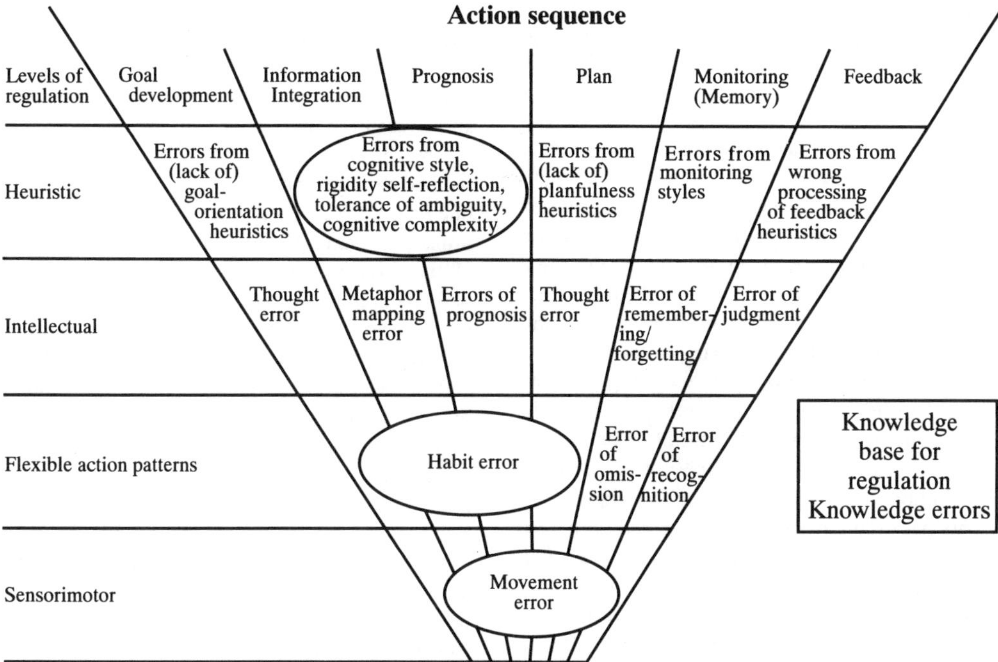

Figure 1 A taxonomy of action errors

Note: This taxonomy consists of two demensions – the action sequence and the levels of regulation – plus the knowledge base for regulation (important for knowledge errors). The reverse pyramid shape signifies that one cannot differentiate the action sequence on the lower levels of regulation.

to such an approach (*see* CONTINUOUS IMPROVEMENT).

Error prevention in organizations has the disadvantage of decreasing the expectation of errors, little use of systematic error detection strategies, concealment of errors because of negative sanctions, increase of "latent errors" in the sense of a resident pathogen (Reason, 1990), and once errors occur a higher chance of catastrophies (Perrow, 1984) (*see* CRISES).

Errors have expensive consequences. People working with computers spend 10 percent of their time dealing with errors (Zapf et al., 1992) and management errors may lead to the death of an organization (Hartley, 1991). Perrow (1984) specifies that errors lead to catastrophies in those organizations (or technical systems) that are complex and consist of tightly coupled subsystems (*see* LOOSE COUPLING). In terms of ORGANIZATIONAL DESIGN, uncoupling of subsystems is useful, e.g., with low-level DECISION MAKING or independence between subsystems (e.g., product divisions).

See also **Accidents; Persistence; Safety; Learning, individual; Cognitive processes**

Bibliography

Frese, M. (in press) Error management in training: Conceptual and empirical results. In S. Bagnara, C. Zucchermaglio & S. Stucky (Eds), *Organizational learning and technological change*. New York: Springer-Verlag.

Hartley, R. F. (1991). *Management mistakes and successes* (3rd edn). New York: Wiley.

Perrow, C. (1984). *Normal accidents: Living with high-risk technologies*. New York: Basic.

Reason, J. T. (1990). *Human error*. New York: Cambridge University Press.

Zapf, D., Brodbeck, F. C., Frese, M., Peters, H. & Prüemper, J. (1992). Errors in working with office computers: A first validation of a taxonomy for observed errors in a field setting. *International Journal of Human–Computer Interaction*, **4**, 311–339.

MICHAEL FRESE

ethics *see* BUSINESS ETHICS; CORPORATE SOCIAL RESPONSIBILITY; MORAL DEVELOPMENT

ethnicity This has been defined as belonging to and being perceived by others as belonging to an ethnic group. Social scientists have favored either a very broad or very narrow definition (Feagin, 1989). A central factor in these competing definitions is an attempt to make an absolute distinction between ethnic groups and racial groups. Those favoring a narrow view define ethnic groups as "a group socially distinguished or set apart, by others or by itself, primarily on the basis of cultural or nationality characteristics" (Feagin, 1989, p.9). Broader definitions also include RACE, religion, or national origin as distinguishing factors or race seen as a special case of ethnicity (van den Berghe, 1981). Still another view concludes that attempts to distinguish between racial and ethnic groups should be set aside in favor of a focus on the criteria that are used to construct and maintain social BOUNDARIES.

Despite these conflicting conceptions and the myriad of theories of ethnicity (*see* Thompson, 1989), there are fundamental elements. First, ethnicity like race is foremost a social construct determined by both outsiders' and groups' self-definitions. Second, ethnicity does not have independent explanatory power and should be understood within its historical, economic, political, and cultural context (*see* CULTURE, NATIONAL).

Ethnicity is particularly complex from an ORGANIZATIONAL BEHAVIOR point of view because it requires a multilevel perspective that simultaneously focuses on individual, group, intergroup, and societal dimensions (Ferdman, 1991). At the individual level, ethnicity is a central element in an individual's social identity and contributes to a person's sense of who they are and their feelings about their IDENTIFICATION. Group level analysis requires attention to both between group differences and within-group diversity (*see* INTERGROUP RELATIONS). Issues of POWER and STATUS differentials among groups become salient because of ethnic differences in CULTURE and history, stratification patterns, and the stereotypes and beliefs groups hold about each other (Feagin, 1989) (*see* STEREOTYPING). At the societal level, attention must be given to the kind of society in which the organization operates, prevalent attitudes regarding ethnicity, and overall ethnic relations (Ferdman, 1991).

For the most part, when ethnicity has been studied in organizations it is included as simply one of the many group-based variables that can impact organizational behavior (Ferdman, 1991). Research has followed two paths. One path focuses on social categorization and social identity and its implications for attitudes and behaviors. The other path focuses on culture and on between group cultural differences on a host of psychological processes and organizational behaviors including SOCIALIZATION, attitudes, MOTIVATION, JOB SATISFACTION, JOB DESIGN, LEADERSHIP STYLE, and GROUP DYNAMICS (e.g., *see* Hofstede, 1980). For example, ethnic differences in nonverbal COMMUNICATION and interpersonal styles seem to be well documented (*see* MANAGERIAL STYLE; INTERPERSONAL SKILLS). Differences in ethnic cultural traditions have been shown to be related to cooperative and competitive behavior in work teams (*see* CONFLICT). Some scholars have called for integrative paradigms that integrate both social categorization and cultural frameworks (Ferdman, 1991). In recent years, the growing heterogeneity of the workforce and continued globalization has spurred a new interest in how best to incorporate and manage ethnic diversity (*see* MANAGEMENT OF DIVERSITY) in organizations.

See also **Expatriation; International management; Intercultural process; Discrimination**

Bibliography

Feagin, J. (1989). *Racial and ethnic relations*. Englewood Cliffs, NJ: Prentice-Hall.

Ferdman, B. (1991). The dynamics of ethnic diversity in organizations: Toward integrative models. In K. Kelley (Ed.) (1992), *Issues, theory and research in industrial/organizational psychology* (pp. 339–384). Amsterdam: Elsevier Science.

Hofstede, G. (1980). *Culture's consequences: International differences in work-related values*. Newbury, CA: Sage.

Thompson, R. H. (1989). *Theories of ethnicity: A critical appraisal*. New York: Greenwood.

van den Berghe, P. (1981). *The ethnic phenomenon*. New York: Elsevier.

STELLA M. NKOMO

ethnography This has traditionally been the methodology of choice in cultural anthropology, although numerous sociologists and an increasing number of organizational theorists have pursued ethnographic research (*see* RESEARCH DESIGN; RESEARCH METHODS). The aim of ethnography is to comprehend and portray the CULTURE of a collective, or the activities that occur in a circumscribed setting from the point of view of an insider. Accordingly, ethnographers rely heavily on participation and observation as means of data collection. Doing ethnography requires a researcher to spend long periods of time observing, interviewing, and interacting with the people he or she studies. Ethnographers therefore measure periods of fieldwork in months and even years. Most ethnographers collect data in the form of fieldnotes – written records of the activities they have observed and the conversations in which they have engaged. Ethnographers may supplement their observations with data from surveys, archives, video tapes, audio tapes, and formal interviews. Although ethnography is frequently equated with "qualitative" research, the equation is misguided. Many forms of qualitative research, such as textual analysis, conversational analysis, and interpretive deconstruction (*see* POSTMODERNISM) do not qualify as ethnography because they have little to say about the way of life in a social collective. Moreover, numerous ethnographers make use of quantitative data. For instance, ethnographers were among the first social scientists to make extensive use of graph theory and NETWORK ANALYSIS (Hage & Harary 1983). The distinguishing marks of ethnography are therefore long periods of fieldwork and the intent to portray the culture of a group or setting from the inside.

As documents, ethnographies can be divided into two broad types: emic or etic. The terms derive from "phonetic" and "phonemic" and were coined by Pike (see Pike (1990) for a review of the history of and debate on the distinction). An emic ethnography attempts to communicate the "native's point of view," to portray a culture or setting entirely from the perspective of an insider. Emic ethnographies frequently organize information using the terminology and conceptual systems of a participant. In contrast, etic ethnographies organize information according to an analytic scheme developed by the researcher and tend to make more liberal use of concepts drawn from sociological or anthropological theory. In both cases, however, the analysis is presented in a discursive or narrative form. Van Maanen (1988) explicated several genres of ethnographic narrative that reflect ontological stances ranging from realism to interpretive relativism. The particular power of ethnography for organization studies is its ability to reveal processes and phenomena largely ignored by the field. Exemplary ethnographies in this regard are Kunda's (1991) study of the contradictions of life in a high-technology company and Jackall's (1988) investigation of how managers conceptualize and handle moral dilemmas (*see* DILEMMAS, ETHICAL).

See also **Organizational culture; Social constructionism; Symbolism**

Bibliography

Agar, M. H. (1980). *The professional stranger: An informal introduction to ethnography*. New York: Academic Press.

Hage, P. & Harary, F. (1983). *Structural models in anthropology*. Cambridge, UK: Cambridge University Press.

Jackall, R. (1988). *Moral mazes: The world of corporate managers*. New York: Oxford University Press.

Kunda, G. (1991). *Engineering culture: Control and commitment in a high-tech corporation*. Philadelphia: Temple University Press.

Pike, K. (1990). *Emics and etics: The insider–outsider debate*. Newbury Park, CA: Sage.

Van Maanen, J. (1988). *Tales of the field: On writing ethnography*. Chicago: University of Chicago Press.

STEPHEN R. BARLEY

ethnomethodolgy *see* SYMBOLIC INTERACTIONISM; RESEARCH METHODS

evaluation of training *see* TRAINING

evaluation research This involves the formal assessment against implicit or explicit criteria of the value of individuals, objects, situations, and outcomes, where choices have to be made "rationally" and decisions taken in a world of scarce resources (*see* DECISION MAKING; RATIONALITY). Traditionally, in the late 1960s and early 1970s, evaluation research was seen as having two defining characteristics: the use of scientific method to measure the impact/outcome of a change programme ("summative" evaluation), by professional evaluation researchers (*see* QUASI-EXPERIMENTAL DESIGN). It was recognized that evaluation research served a range of manifest and latent functions: informing decision making, facilitating learning and control, but also rallying support/opposition to a change programme, postponing a decision, evading responsibility, fulfilling grant requirements (*see* FUNCTIONALISM).

In the late 1970s and 1980s this model of evaluation research came under widespread criticism. Commentators argued that in practice its findings were not used, its favored RESEARCH METHODS did not produce "true" findings and that, far from facilitating change, evaluation research supported the status quo. Furthermore, the ethics of many of its practitioners were questionable. Criticisms about utilization focused on concerns about the irrelevancy and unresponsiveness of findings to those who might be in a position to use them (Patton, 1978). Disquiet about methods concerned the practicalities of using experimental and quasi-experimental methods in field settings, the tension between the requirements of internal and external VALIDITY in such designs (*see* RESEARCH DESIGN), and the legitimacy and appropriateness of a realist ontology and positivistic epistemology for uncovering truths about human action. Criticisms about values raised questions about the in-built conservatism and power-serving nature of evaluation research, particularly evident in the prevalence of evaluations focusing on goal achievement (whose goals?), using inherently conservative positivistic designs. Evaluation researchers' financial dependence on those with a vested interest in the "right" results was considered to have deleterious effects on their independence and, in extreme cases, their probity.

The "solutions" to these difficulties have resulted in a new orthodoxy. Some commentators suggest that no "real" utilization crisis exists because findings are used, but in subtle, climate-changing ways, rather than to achieve dramatic change. To have expected the latter was merely political naivety. Others recognize that a utilization crisis does exist but suggest that the answer lies in developing "utilization-focused" or "responsive" evaluations that serve the functions that STAKEHOLDERS in the evaluation wish them to serve. It is considered that if faith has been lost in positivistic evaluations the solution is to supplement them by the use of qualitative, interpretative methods, often embedded in a "formative" design, concentrating on providing programme designers and implementers with regular systematic FEEDBACK, in order that they might modify and develop the programme in an ongoing fashion. Such methods and designs are often easier to apply in field work settings as many of the control requirements of quasi-experimental approaches are no longer necessary. Furthermore, interpretative designs are claimed to be more democratic than the élitist experimental methods of positivism (*see* DEMOCRACY). Finally, if evaluation researchers are in the pay of, or likely to be subject to, undue influence from power holders in organizations, they can protect their independence and safeguard any liberal values they might possess through the development of professional associations and the collective adherence to ethical codes (*see* CODES OF CONDUCT).

Using the "deconstruction" analysis of POSTMODERNISM, Legge (1984) has called into question this new orthodoxy by identifying a series of paradoxes it contains (*see* PARADOX). For example,

- positivistic designs prosper largely through acting as a rhetoric for an evaluation ritual, whereby the lack of rationality of decision making and the ACCOUNTABILITY and responsibility demanded of the idealized decision maker are reconciled;
- interpretative designs may act as a rhetoric for an evaluation ritual whereby the appearance of democracy and non élitism serves to disguise greater room for manoeuvre accorded to powerful decision makers; and

• the call for ethical codes may serve as a vehicle for reformist aspirations and as both a justification and a mask for present conservative practice.

See also **Consultancy; Business ethics; Machiavellianism; Power; Professionalism; Consultancy; Intervention models; Ideology; Action research**

Bibliography

Annual handbook(s) of evaluation research. Beverly Hills, CA: Sage.

Guba, E. G. & Lincoln, Y. S. (1981). *Effective evaluation.* San Francisco: Jossey-Bass.

Legge, K. (1984). *Evaluating planned organizational change.* London: Academic Press.

Patton, M. Q. (1978). *Utilisation-focused evaluation.* Beverly Hills, CA: Sage.

Weiss, C. H. (1972). *Evaluation research.* Englewood Cliffs, NJ: Prentice-Hall.

KAREN LEGGE

evolution *see* COMMUNITY ECOLOGY; POPULATION ECOLOGY

excellence Companies are deemed *effective* when they meet the expectations of their key STAKEHOLDERS, namely their owners, customers, employees, and the local communities in which they operate (Cameron & Whetten, 1983). Companies are judged to be *excellent* when they exceed the minimum standards of effectiveness set by their rivals. Excellent companies develop internal practices and external relationships that demonstrate superior ability at fulfilling stakeholder demands. Over time, excellence brings REPUTATION – a company becomes highly regarded in its industry.

Excellent companies are high-performing companies: Economic performance indicates the merits of a company's strategy and is necessary to its survival (Peters & Waterman, 1982). Owners and creditors demand financial performance, either as a return on their investments or to service their loans. To achieve excellence therefore requires efficiency – the ability to transform inputs into outputs at minimum cost. It also requires COMPETITIVENESS – the ability to maintain financial performance over time (Porter, 1980).

In achieving efficiency, excellent companies rely on internal practices that attend to the human needs of employees. RECRUITMENT policies, PERFORMANCE APPRAISAL systems, REWARD programs, and TRAINING opportunities rely on merit as a discriminating criterion for judging individual contributions. And companies judge their own actions with a view, not only to improving the company's financial performance, but also to enhancing employee growth and fulfillment (Fombrun, Tichy, & Devanna, 1984).

Customers are also vital stakeholders. They expect a company's products to meet their expectations of quality, service, and reliability. Excellent companies show their commitment to fulfilling customer demands by initiating and enforcing internal practices that improve product quality and customer service (Hayes & Wheelwright, 1984).

Finally, companies rely heavily on the social, environmental, and educational infrastructure of local communities. Since they draw freely on many of those resources, excellent companies recognize a responsibility to meet the expectations of those communities that they will put back at least as much as they take out, and that their actions will conform to a community's moral standards (Etzioni, 1988) (*see* BUSINESS ETHICS; CORPORATE SOCIAL RESPONSIBILITY).

Jointly, it means that an excellent company acts to fulfill a broad mandate that recognizes the company's close involvement, not only with its owners, but also with its customers, employees, and the communities in which it operates. The excellent company achieves this mandate at least as well as its leading rivals.

See also **Learning organization; Organizational effectiveness; Total quality management**

Bibliography

Cameron, K. S. & Whetten D. A. (Eds) (1983). *Organizational effectiveness: A comparison of multiple models.* New York: Academic Press.

Etzioni, A. (1988). *The moral dimension.* New York: Free Press.

Fombrun, C., Tichy, N. & Devanna, M. A. (1984). *Strategic human resource management*. New York: Wiley.
Hayes, R. H. & Wheelwright, S. C. (1984). *Restoring our competitive edge: competing through manufacturing*. New York: Wiley.
Peters, T. & Waterman, R. (1982). *In search of excellence*. New York: Harper & Row.
Porter, M. E. (1980). *Competitive strategy*. New York: Free Press.

CHARLES FOMBRUM

exchange relations This refers to a theoretical perspective which provides formal analyses of interpersonal interactions by focusing on costs and benefits individuals may receive in their relationships. People's constant interactions with one another can be conceptualized as a series of exchanges, with all parties contributing and receiving something from their interaction. Their exchange relations can be analyzed to determine who has POWER over whom, and how much power they have.

Early exchange theorists (Homans, 1961; Thibaut & Kelley, 1961; Blau, 1964) assumed that people attempt to maximize their own utilities by weighing the potential outcomes of their various courses of action. Analysis included both sides of the exchange, i.e., the costs and benefits of both parties. The power in an exchange relationship can then be determined by the mutual interdependence of the involved parties. If person X, for instance, depends upon person Y for his/her positive outcomes, and person Y does not depend on X, then exchange theory would say that Y has considerable power over X (e.g., Cook & Emerson, 1978).

Organizationally, supervisors may not only control the financial outcomes of their employees (termed "fate control" by Thibaut and Kelley, 1961) but they can also influence employees' behavior ("behavior control"), by making one and only one set of behaviors most rewarding. At the same time, employees can organize and generate additional alternatives for themselves, and thereby control their employers' outcomes ("mutual fate control"; see Mechanic, 1962).

Thibaut and Kelley's (1961) analysis suggests that people use comparison levels (alternative states) to determine how happy or satisfied they are: They compare their current situation with alternative states, including their own past or their anticipated future (*see* SOCIAL COMPARISON). People also use what they called "a comparison level for alternatives," which determines how satisfied they might be if they changed (their job, their spouse, their home, etc.). When a person's comparison level for alternatives is so much better than his/her current state that a change will provide benefits that more than compensate for the costs of moving, then the person will move. Thus, people should only change jobs when an alternative is sufficiently better to cover the costs of changing (*see* COMMITMENT; TURNOVER). When employees do not have such alternatives (e.g., during poor economies or job scarcity), employers' fate and behavior control increases. The opposite is true when jobs are plentiful.

See also **Game theory; Prisoner's dilemma; Negotiation; Resource dependence**

Bibliography

Blau, P. M. (1964). *Exchange and power in social life*. New York: Wiley.
Cook, K. S. & Emerson, R. M. (1978). Power, equity, and commitment in exchange networks. *American Sociological Review*, **43**, 721–739.
Homans, G. C. (1961). *Social behavior: Its elementary forms*. New York: Harcourt, Brace, & World.
Mechanic, D. (1962). Sources of power of lower participants in complex organizations. *Administrative Science Quarterly*, **7**, 349–364.
Thibaut, J. & Kelley, H. H. (1961). *The social psychology of groups*. New York: Wiley.

J. KEITH MURNIGHAN

expatriates For organizations operating internationally, there is a need to recruit, select, and deploy individuals on a worldwide basis (*see* INTERNATIONAL HUMAN RESOURCES MANAGEMENT). Typically, these organizations utilize three types of international employees: expatriates, third country nationals, and local nationals or host country nationals. While there might be some exceptions, generally firms seeking global operations utilize these three types of employees in some typical ways. Thus, for example, utilizing Bartlett and Ghoshal's (1991) framework, as firms move from being international to multinational to transnational their need for employees operating internationally increases. As a consequence, their utilization of employees goes from predominately expatriate to predominately host country and third country nationals. With this perspective, one can describe each of these three categories of international employee.

Expatriates are staff recruited and selected in the country where the organization is headquartered and then sent abroad to work. These individuals are usually sent for a limited time period and with a specific duty to fulfill. While there is relatively minor variation in expatriate treatment by firms headquartered in different countries, there are differences by the type of assignment being given to the expatriate. For example, a technical specialist might be assigned to work on specific project for 6 months in another country and then return to headquarters (or at least the country in which the firm is headquartered). A manager, on the other hand, responsible for the operations of a regional facility, typically is given an assignment of between 3 and 5 years (Fontaine, 1989).

To make expatriate assignments attractive, firms typically remunerate individuals quite handsomely (*see* PAYMENT SYSTEMS). In addition to receiving normal remuneration, additional payments and benefits provided can include: allowances for food and housing; education allowances for the children; travel allowances for trips home; and hazardous duty pay if the location is particularly undesirable or poses dangerous or unsafe conditions. A major goal in developing remuneration schemes for expatriates is to keep the employee "whole," i.e., living in the style to which (s)he is living in the home country. This is very costly to the firm and may prove detrimental to the firm's operating success abroad. From the expatriate's viewpoint, assignments can be risky in one's career if "out of sight" means "out of mind," or entails one's suspension from the normal paths for promotion in the firm. There is also a risk that the firm will fail to utilize fully the skills and experiences of the expatriate upon repatriation to the home country. Firms seek to minimize these risks through the careful and preparation of expatriates and their families; MENTORING and providing buddy systems which reduce the difficulty of repatriation adjustment (*see* CAREER TRANSITIONS, SELECTION METHODS).

Research, while limited, suggests that expatriates are more likely to succeed in their assignments if they have a high tolerance for AMBIGUITY, low level of ethnocentric thinking, possess professional SKILLS to a high degree, and have the ability to translate, adapt to, and understand different CULTURES (Brewster, 1991). It is also the case that most expatriates are male and married, and one repeated finding is that spouse adjustment is the strongest and most reliable predictor of expatriate adjustment. However, surprisingly perhaps, prior years of expatriate experience is a poor predictor. *Quality* of prior experience is more important (Brett, Stroh & Reilly, 1992).

As alternatives to the use of expatriates (or home country nationals), international firms can employ individuals from the host country (local nationals) and other countries (third country nationals).

The use of third country nationals (TCNs) enables firms operating internationally to draw upon a much larger pool of potential employees than can be provided by just utilizing host country and expatriate employees. It also enables a firm to locate the most qualified individual to perform the tasks, regardless of location, and offers an environment which can be highly motivating to individuals who want to work in diverse environments yet for a single organization (*see* MANAGEMENT OF DIVERSITY).

A major issue associated with the use of third country nationals, as with host country nationals, is the development of a global-firm rather than just a regional or single country frame of thinking. As in the case of expatriates, there is the need for adequate preparation of the third country national for the international assignment and the carrer paths which may eventually lead back to headquarters.

In contrast to the use of expatriates, third country nationals are typically posted in foreign countries with far less costly remuneration schemes. This alone can make the use of third country nationals an invaluable part of the international firm's global labor force. Research indicates, however, that the firm then needs to devote more resources to developing the TCNs and integrating them into the global organization's scheme of operations and its unique culture (Pucik & Katz, 1986) (*see* ORGANIZATIONAL CULTURE).

Research also suggests that as firms utilize more TCNs, they develop greater diversity in their management teams. As with the use of host country nationals, the use of third country nationals makes it more functional for firms to offer MANAGEMENT DEVELOPMENT programs which include and span all groups of individuals, helping them to develop a common understanding of the firm and a common understanding of each other (*see* MANAGEMENT OF DIVERSITY). Research evidence indicates that this is more likely to occur the longer the firm's experience in international business operations.

By using host country nationals (HCNs), international firms obtain employees who know the local conditions, the language, the laws, and customs far better than expatriates. They are also able to remunerate them at levels which are consistent with the local conditions thereby avoiding the costly schemes required for expatriates. However, when the required skills and competencies are not available locally, use of expatriates is the most expedient remedy. Longer term, however, firms operating internationally may find it in their interests to identify and develop talent in the countries they are operating. This is particularly true in countries which insist upon foreign firms hiring a substantial portion of employees locally. This makes it particularly imperative for firms to develop local talent at all levels, professional and technical, nonmanagerial and managerial.

Major issues associated with using host country nationals include how to bring them into the operation of the international firm (*see* INTERNATIONAL MANAGEMENT). If the firm is truly international, it needs to develop a truly international labour force (especially at managerial, technical, and professional levels). When utilizing host country nationals then, the firm must design international CAREER paths and offer the means for host country nationals to remain in regular communication with one another. All this, of course, becomes more challenging as the firm expands the number of countries in which it operates. It is also problematic if the firm chooses to employ not only host country nationals but individuals from other countries to work in the host country.

Research thus far suggests that firms might best be able to integrate host country nationals into their global operation through management development programs (Evans, 1992). Increasingly these programs are being seen as an essential device for tying the various parts of the organization together. It achieves this objective by use of common experiences, such as discussing worldwide strategy at an international conference on a yearly basis. As the literature on social adjustment might suggest, the more frequently individuals are in contact, the more likely they will develop supportive bonds which facilitate subsequent communication once the conferences are over. Of course, these global management programs also prove effective to the extent that global (cross-business and cross-national) carrer paths are developed and utilized. As truly international management teams develop, organizations will increasingly acquire very diverse top management profiles (*see* TOP MANAGEMENT TEAMS). The growing literature on managing diversity and managing top teams will thus have major applicability in this area of host country nationals.

See also **Career transitions; Intercultural process; Management of high potential; Culture, national; Culture, cross-cultural research**

Bibliography

Bartlett, C. & Ghoshal, S. (1991). *Managing across boarders*. London: London Business School.

Brett, J. M., Stroh, L. K. & Reilly, A. H. (1992). Job transfer. In C. L. Cooper & I. T. Robertson (Eds), *International Review of Industrial and Organisational Psychology*. Chichester, UK: Wiley.

Brewster, C. (1991). *The management of expatriates*. London: Kogan Page.

Evans, P. (1992). Management development as glue technology. *Human Resource Planning*, **15**, 85–106.

Fontaine, G. (1989). Managing international assignments. *The strategy for success*. Englewood Cliffs, NJ: Prentice-Hall.

Pucik, V. & Katz, J. (1986). Information control of human resource management in multinational firms. *Human Resource Management*, **25**, 121–132.

RANDALL S. SCHULER

expectancy *see* VIE THEORY; MOTIVATION

expected utility theory *see* GAME THEORY: EXCHANGE RELATIONS; PROSPECT THEORY

extinction This refers to a procedure and its effect as a behavior change process. As a procedure, *extinction* is elimination of a contingency between a behavior and its previously reinforcing consequence(s). As a process, extinction refers to the time course of an operant behavior rate during nonreinforcement of the previously reinforced operant behavior. Sulzer-Azaroff and Mayer (1991) describe numerous alternatives to extinction as a behavior rate reduction method, e.g., DRO, differential reinforcement of other behavior.

See also **Conditioning; Learning, individual; Reinforcement; Punishment**

Bibliography

Sulzer-Azaroff, B. & Mayer, R. G. (1991). *Behavior analysis for lasting change*. London: Holt, Rinehart and Winston.

THOMAS C. MAWHINNEY

extraversion/introversion This personality trait reflects whether an individual is (extraversion) or is not (introversion) oriented toward interacting with others. Hans Eysenck identified extraversion/introversion as one of the central dimensions of personality, rooted in psychophysiological differences among people (Stelmack & Geen, 1992). Extraverts have lower levels of cortical stimulation and consequently seek arousal through external stimulation. Consequently, extraverts prefer and perform more effectively in jobs that are physically active, contain variety, and allow for more frequent social interaction, such as sales jobs. Correspondingly, given their relatively high level of cortical stimulation, introverts prefer and perform more effectively on routine tasks, executed alone, without social or other distractions. In particular, introversion is associated with performance on vigilance tasks (Koelega, 1992). Extraversion is on average moderately correlated with measures of job performance for managerial and sales populations (*see* PERFORMANCE, INDIVIDUAL). The strength of this relationship, however, varies a great deal across specific sales and management positions. Research also suggests that extraverts are more motivated by positive incentives (*see* REWARDS); introverts are more motivated by the threat of PUNISHMENT. Interestingly, extraversion is predictive of academic achievement early in life but from the teen years on, introversion is more predictive of academic success (Furnham, 1992).

See also **Personality; Individual differences; Personality testing; Assessment; Affiliation, need for**

Bibliography

Furnham, A. (1992). *Personality at work*. London: Routledge.

Koelega, H. S. (1992). Extraversion and vigilance performance: 30 years of inconsistencies. *Psychological Bulletin*, **112**, 239–258.

Stelmack, R. M. & Geen, R. G. (1992). The psychophysiology of extraversion. In A. Gale & M. W. Eysenck (Eds), *Handbook of individual differences: Biological perspectives*. Chichester, UK: Wiley.

SEYMOUR ADLER

extrinsic satisfaction *see* INTRINSIC/EXTRINSIC MOTIVATION; JOB SATISFACTION

F

family firms Although there is no generally agreed definition of what constitutes a family firm, two major criteria are:

(1) ownership (*see* GOVERNANCE AND OWNERSHIP) – the extent to which business assets are in the hands of an individual or several members of a single family; and
(2) control – the degree to which members or descendants of the founding family influence the running of the enterprise.

Cut off points vary and are, to some extent, arbitrary given differing and complex relationships between ownership and control. Families with relatively small ownership stakes and no direct managerial representation, for example, may nevertheless exercise significant influence over both assets and management. Influence can also be exercised via subtle and indirect mechanisms linked with factors such as MANAGERIAL STYLE and ORGANIZATIONAL CULTURE. Thus large, publicly owned corporations which inherit paternalistic management styles from FOUNDERS may often be described as family firms. Here the defining criterion is simply influence – by a family or family relationship.

Research on family firms focuses upon the manner in which two social systems – the family and the firm – overlap and interact. Three major issues have been addressed. First, the tensions between ownership, control, and organizational expansion. Family owners are often keen to retain extensive personal involvement in their businesses and may be unwilling to delegate control (*see* DELEGATION); growth and higher economic returns may be sacrificed as a result. Second, the management of succession (*see* SUCCESSION PLANNING). Founders must pass their businesses from one generation to another to ensure survival; but this form of delegation is difficult and often fatal. Third, the coexistence of affective and instrumental relationships. Family firms must balance the continuing involvement of kin with the need for business ability if they are to avoid charges of nepotism and to retain competent employees.

Most SMALL BUSINESSES as well as a number of very large enterprises remain owned and substantially controlled by private families. Indeed, the continuing reproduction of new family firms and the successful growth of a minority is a remarkable feature of modern economies. Significant sources of difference derive from structural, cultural, and family life cycle factors. The structuring of ROLES within families – the extent and interconnectedness of kinship networks, for example – will vary according to factors such as social class and ETHNICITY (*see* ROLE SET; NETWORKING). Similarly, cross-national cultural variations (*see* CULTURE, CROSS-CULTURAL RESEARCH) shape patterns of business startup and inheritance as well as the extent to which family and business networks overlap and intersect. In differing ways, such networks help to explain, for example, the remarkable vitality of family enterprises in economies such as Italy and Japan. Finally, patterned variations may occur across generations – second and third generation members typically having different priorities and motives to those of founders.

See also **Organizational change; CEOs; Leadership; Entrepreneurship**

Bibliography

Goffee, R. & Scase, R. (1985). Proprietorial control in family firms: Some functions of quasi-organic

management systems. *Journal of Management Studies*, **22**, 53–68.
Leach, P. (1991). *The family business*. London: Kogan Page
Organizational Dynamics, Special Issue on Family Firms, **12**, 1983.
Scott, J. P. (1986). *Capitalist property and financial power*. Brighton, UK: Wheatsheaf.

ROB GOFFEE

fast track development *see* MANAGEMENT OF HIGH POTENTIAL

fatigue In behavioral terms, this refers to the diminished capacity, PRODUCTIVITY, or ability of an organism to perform a given activity because of previously expended energy. Fatigue can be sensory, muscular, or psychological and is known to be a function of a number of variables including: energy intake–output, working temperature, fluid balance, and prolonged activity – physical or mental. Fatigue appears to affect performance in three main ways:

(1) simple decrement;
(2) performance disorganization; and,
(3) cumulative disruption of performance.

In the case of simple decrement, fatigue is characterized by a decrease in performance on particular aspects of activity on a task. This usually occurs more in REPETITIVE WORK than in more complex interlinked sequences of activity (*see* JOB DESIGN). In contrast performance disorganization caused by fatigue tends to affect those activities that involve highly complex behavioral and cognitive activity. The last type to affect performance is characterized by variation in one aspect of performance affecting another response further down the chain sequence, e.g., slowness affecting accuracy of responding where accuracy is speed-dependent. Fatigue is known to be related to arousal level, arousal duration, and to stress. It also impairs vigilance, information processing, decision making, and the quality of responding in general (*see* Singleton, 1989).

See also **Age; Cognitive processes; Performance, individual; Stress; Accidents; safety; Role overload/underload**

Bibliography

Singleton, W. T. (1989). *The mind at work: Psychological ergonomics*. Cambridge, UK: Cambridge University Press.

NOEL SHEEHY and A. GALLAGHER

feedback Information, provided to a person, which addresses the prior behavior of the person or the results of their behavior. If provided by another person, feedback is usually intended either to reinforce behavior or to suggest changes (*see* REINFORCEMENT).

The term may also be applied at the group or organizational level, although this use is less frequent. Examples include operational feedback on the total performance of an organization or its subunits (see Katz & Kahn, 1978, pp. 455–458), customer feedback to service organizations by means such as SURVEYS, or feedback to a WORK GROUP from quality inspections of products for which all members of the group are responsible.

The term "feedback" derives from engineering systems, where it refers to a signal indicating the status of one part of the system (such as the flow rate of a fuel line) which was "fed back" into another part of the system (such as the control on a fuel valve) in order that the system could maintain itself in some desired state (such as a constant rate of fuel supply) (*see* SYSTEMS THEORY).

The concept of feedback as applied to people in organizations is shown in the figure. The main difference is that, while in engineering systems feedback is generally used to maintain a particular state, in organizations it is often addressed toward the CONTINUOUS IMPROVEMENT of behaviors (and thus, effectiveness). The provision of feedback is considered by many to be a fundamental element in achieving positive work outcomes (*see* Hackman & Oldham, 1980). At the same time it is generally recognized to be one of the most difficult and poorly practised managerial SKILLS (*see* INTERPERSONAL SKILLS).

Key Dimensions

Feedback may be characterized by its source, its content, its frequency, its valence, and its subsequent use.

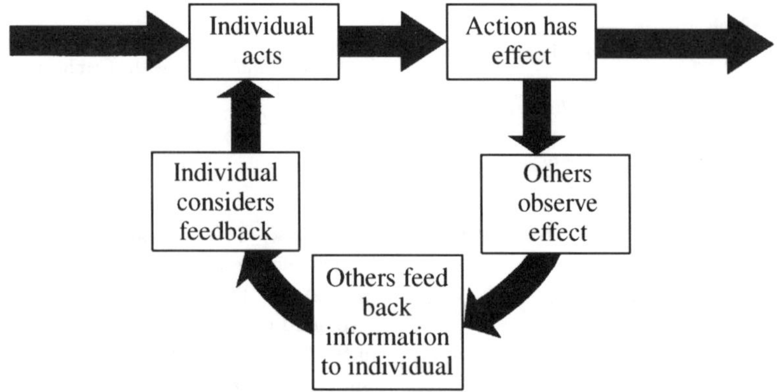

Figure 1 The feedback loop

Sources of feedback may include the individual actor him/herself, bosses, peers, subordinates, customers, and sometimes other people such as family and friends. Data-gathering machines (such as computers tracking rates or giving tests, simple gauges, or video cameras) are also potential sources of feedback. Multiple sources of feedback can add breadth and depth and increase the perceived VALIDITY of the information (the "360-degree feedback" described by London and Beatty (1993)). Although subordinate and in particular peer feedback can be highly valid, they are less common than traditional top-down methods (Bernardin & Beatty, 1984; Murphy & Cleveland, 1991).

Sources may provide feedback unbidden or only by request. Similarly, recipients may be constantly attempting to obtain feedback (*feedback-seeking*) or they may be uninterested in or averse to it. Some sources may be more willing than others to give feedback, which may not constitute the most appropriate set of sources. The systematic identification of potential feedback sources and the careful management of the process of feedback collection (who does it, how, and under what conditions) increases the likelihood of accuracy and acceptance.

Content of feedback may vary in level of specificity, relevance to the work or actions in question, and applicability (Is the individual able to apply the information to change their behavior?). Quality of feedback is generally considered to be higher the more specific, relevant, and applicable it is. The structured delivery of feedback is also important because of the psychological defense mechanisms which are often triggered when the recipient's self-concept is threatened. Skilled feedback-givers are sensitive to the recipient's level of defensiveness and often use a consultative approach, drawing out the recipient on the subject in question and making the feedback a conversational dialogue. However, when the information to be given is of a highly serious or immediate nature, more direct or confrontational approaches may be more appropriate.

Frequency. Most people in organizations believe that they should receive more feedback than they actually do. Feedback is most effective when it is given often and close in time to the observed behavior. However, feedback given constantly, or feedback given immediately after an unsettling event, may be less effective.

Valence. Feedback may be generally categorized as positive or negative; positive feedback is aimed at reinforcing desired behaviors while negative feedback is aimed at changing behavior. Positive feedback is also important to the maintenance of SELF-ESTEEM; it is often under-utilized as a tool for improving MOTIVATION. Negative feedback, even when presented constructively, usually presents a challenge to self-esteem. Experienced feedback-givers often precede negative feedback with specific, equally important positive feedback in order to effect a balance which allows recipients to remain secure and open to changing their behavior.

Use. Feedback information may be used purely as developmental information for the recipient, or it may be provided to others as input to formal PERFORMANCE APPRAISAL systems for determination of rewards and promotion. Studies have shown that givers and receivers of feedback react differently depending upon which of these is the case, but there is little consistency in the research as to which provides the better long-term result. The implied dichotomy may be partly considered a false distinction, if one takes the long-term view that what is aimed at in either case (whether or not rewards are involved) is a set of changes in behavior.

See also **Performance, individual; Motivation and performance; Management by objectives; Trust; Self-regulation; Goal-setting; Knowledge of results**

Bibliography

Bernardin, H. J. & Beatty, R. W. (1984). *Performance appraisal: Assessing human behavior at work*. Boston: Kent.

Hackman, J. R. & Oldham, G. R. (1980). *Work redesign*. Reading, MA: Addison-Wesley.

Katz, D. & Kahn, R. L. (1978). *The social psychology of organizations*. New York: Wiley.

London, M. & Beatty, R. W. (1993). 360-degree feedback as a competitive advantage. *Human Resource Management*, **32**, 353–372.

Murphy, K. R. & Cleveland, J. N. (1991). *Performance appraisal: An organization perspective*. Boston: Allyn and Bacon.

MAURY PEIPERL

feminism The label feminism covers many diverse perspectives linked by common themes. Feminists tend to believe that women are rendered invisible, stereotyped, or devalued in male-dominated societies (patriarchies), and want to change this situation to one of equality. They seek to value women's experiences and express their viewpoints. Types of feminism differ in how they explain women's devalued social position, how radically they critique current society, and what changes they seek. Feminism is as much a social movement and development of consciousness as it is a set of ideas. It is continually evolving.

Despite its social importance, feminism has not had much influence on mainstream ORGANIZATIONAL BEHAVIOR (OB). The potential significance of GENDER is ignored, for example, in most theories of LEADERSHIP, ORGANIZATIONAL CULTURE, POWER, COMMUNICATION (Marshall, 1993), and ORGANIZATIONAL CHANGE. Calas and Smircich (1992) suggest that there are taboos against mentioning "the F word."

The failure of mainstream OB to take more radical feminisms into account is not surprising, since they challenge the founding assumptions of the social and organizational order with which THEORY deals (Daly, 1979). They also critique how knowledge has been created in male-dominated societies, showing that women's experiences have often been systematically omitted or devalued relative to men's, and that research on men has been presented as theory about people generally. Taking radical feminisms seriously would require fundamental revision of many areas of OB.

Neither is it surprising that many women in organizations do not identify with feminism. Prevailing negative stereotypes of feminists may well discourage them. Ironically, the social unacceptability of being feminist proves the feminist critique. It suggests that for women to voice opinions considered disruptive by organizational power-holders, most of whom are men, involves great personal risk.

Some people, especially younger women, argue that we are in a post-feminist age, that full equality is achieved, and further debate unnecessary. This optimism seems premature and misguided. Whilst some changes have occurred, many deep structures of male-dominated society remain in place. There also appears to be some backlash, from both men and women, against recent change (Faludi, 1991).

Feminism offers a rich source of perspectives and potential insights from which OB could do more to benefit, although no easy integration of the two fields is appropriate at the moment. There is now a flourishing of different voices within feminism – for example, those of black women (Hooks, 1989 (*see* RACE), native peoples (Allen, 1992), lesbians and ecofeminists – which enrich its scope. In any organizational analysis it is, then, worth considering what feminists might attend to and how they would seek to interpret the behavior being studied.

See also **Women managers; Women at work; Management of diversity; Postmodernism; Critical theory**

Bibliography

Allen, P. G. (1992). *The sacred hoop: Recovering the feminine in American Indian traditions*. Boston: Beacon Press.

Calas, M. B. & Smircich, L. (1989). Using the F word: Feminist theories and the social consequences of organizational research. In A. Mills and P. Tancred (eds) *Gendering Organizational Analysis*. Newbury Park, CA Sage.

Daly, M. (1979). *Gyn/Ecology*. London: Women's Press.

Faludi, S. (1991). *Backlash: The undeclared war against women*. London: Chatto and Windus.

Hooks, B. (1989). *Talking back: Thinking feminist – thinking black*. London: Sheba.

Marshall, J. (1993). Viewing organizational communication from a feminist perspective: A critique and some offerings. In S. Deetz (Ed.), *Communication Yearbook* (Vol. 16 pp. 122–143). Newbury Park, CA: Sage.

JUDI MARSHALL

field-dependence *see* PERSONALITY

five forces framework Porter's (1980) five forces framework is designed to analyze the forces affecting the profitability of an industry. In particular, it is designed to explain why some industries are more profitable than others and what are the forces which sustain those differences in profitability.

The five forces framework revolutionized strategic thinking and has become the standard technique for basic industry analysis. It introduced a systematic way of thinking about and analyzing organizational relationships with competitors, suppliers, buyers, potential new entrants, and substitutes. Within each of these categories, the framework covered economic, technological, behavioral, financial, and psychological factors which could give POWER to each force.

Traditional industry analysis focused primarily on competitors of the organization (termed "industry rivalry" by Porter) in assessing an organization's competitive position within the industry. Porter noted that industry rivalry was affected by factors as diverse as the industry growth rate, the existence of intermittent overcapacity, product differences, brand identity, firm concentration, the perception of competitive balance within the industry, the diversity of competitors, and corporate commitment to the industry.

To the traditional focus on competitor analysis, Porter added four other forces. "Threat of new entrants" introduced the idea that industry rivalry was affected by the ease with which new entrants could enter the industry, as well as by the competitive position of existing organizations. BARRIERS TO ENTRY included economies of scale, the power of existing brands, the existence of switching costs from existing rivals, capital requirements, access to distribution, absolute cost advantages of existing rivals, government policy, and the likelihood of expected retaliation.

"Bargaining power of suppliers" suggested that suppliers to the industry can also be a potentially strong influence on industry profitability. The power of suppliers is determined by factors such as supplier concentration, the importance of the volume to the supplier and to the industry, the impact of a supplier's input on either the final cost or the extent of final product differentiation and the threat of forward integration by suppliers relative to the threat of backward integration by the industry.

"Bargaining power of buyers" (more commonly known as customers) indicated that buyers can also influence the profitability of the industry. Buyer concentration, buyer volume, buyer information, the ability of buyers to switch within the industry or to use substitute products, the power of brand identities, buyer profitability, product cost relative to buyer's total purchases, and decision-maker incentives were identified as determining buyer power.

Finally, the existence of "substitutes," their relative price and performance, the ease and likelihood of buyer substitution can also influence industry profitability.

Porter's five forces framework suggests that an industry should be very profitable if there are few rivals, which are content with their position within the industry, barriers to new entrants are high, both suppliers and buyers have little power and there are few acceptable substitutes. Industry profitability should be low if these characteristics are reversed.

Although Porter designed the five forces framework to analyze industry profitability, many organizations use it to analyze their own competitive position, in order to try to increase their own power relative to the other five forces.

While it has been extremely influential in the field of STRATEGIC MANAGEMENT, the five forces framework has been criticized for several reasons. It is a static analysis technique, assessing the existing position within the industry, when dynamic analysis is required to understand the evolving potential profitability of an industry and to develop strategy for the future. The framework also tends to understate the role of government as it affects competitive behavior, particularly in countries outside the United States (*see* GOVERNMENT AND BUSINESS). In addition, use of the framework requires a clear definition of "industry." Where TECHNOLOGY and regulatory changes are occurring, the definition of industry may be far from clear and it may not be agreed by firms which appear, on the surface, to be competitors.

More recent work by Porter (1990) has applied and expanded the concept to explain why successful organizations in a global industry seem to come from only one or two countries.

See also **Competitiveness; Dominance; Transaction cost theory**

Bibliography

Porter, M. (1980). *Competitive strategy*. New York: Free Press.

Porter, M. (1985). *Competitive advantage*. New York: Free Press.

Porter, M. (1990). *The competitive advantage of nations*. New York: Free Press.

GRAHAM HUBBARD

flexibility This concept denotes pliability, adaptability and a responsiveness to change. In recent years, added emphasis has been placed on the extent to which organizations can respond flexibly to a changing environment. Intensified competition, and particularly increased market UNCERTAINTY, together with the adaptive potential of new technologies, are commonly identified as key factors driving the search for greater flexibility (*see* COMPETITIVENESS; EXCELLENCE).

The notion of flexibility can be applied equally to the structure and processes of organizations (*see* ORGANIZATIONAL DESIGN). To date, however, most attention has been concentrated on workforce flexibility, and at the macro level, on LABOR MARKET flexibility. In turn, this focus reflects the greater attention given to flexibility on both sides of the Atlantic by INDUSTRIAL RELATIONS and labor market specialists, than by those with an ORGANIZATION BEHAVIOR perspective (*see*, in particular, Atkinson, 1984; Blyton & Morris, 1991, 1992; Laflamme, Murray, Berlanger, & Ferland, 1989.

Four principal sources of workforce flexibility have been identified: functional or task flexibility (relating to the mobility and adaptability of employees to undertake a broader range of functions); numerical flexibility (varying the volume of labor by such means as temporary contracts and the use of subcontractors); temporal flexibility (varying working hours patterns); and financial or wage flexibility (abandoning uniform pay structures in favor of more variable reward arrangements, more reflective of performance) (*see* PERFORMANCE-RELATED PAY). Atkinson (1984), in an early discussion of flexibility, put forward the notion of the "flexible firm" in which a "core" of skilled workers, operating with a high degree of functional flexibility, are supported by a "periphery" of semi- and unskilled workers some of whom are deployed in a numerically flexible way via temporary contracts or working variable hours.

The notion of flexibility continues to suffer from both conceptual and empirical problems. Conceptually, the diversity of work arrangements sheltering under the umbrella of flexibility raises doubts about whether a single concept can function as an index for such a wide range of developments. Discussion on flexibility has also been too ready to subscribe to a managerial perspective on the subject without taking sufficient account of employee interests regarding flexibility. There has also been a tendency for flexibility to be discussed only as a positive attribute. This is despite, for example, tensions which Blyton and Morris (1992) and others have identified between numerical flexibility and other management approaches to increasing COMPETITIVENESS, such as achieving increased levels of employee COMMITMENT and quality output. Standing (1986) has also noted that too great an emphasis on flexibility tends to understate the importance of organizational stability and continuity.

Empirically, flexibility remains problematic. There is little evidence of organizations strategically adopting the flexible firm model. Further, several of the elements discussed under flexibility, including temporary working, show little growth over the recent past.

Despite these problems, however, the factors identified as fueling the search for greater flexibility show little sign of abating; if anything they seem set to intensify in the coming period. In the future, however, the current discussion of workforce flexibility will hopefully be usefully augmented by significantly greater interest in other aspects of organizational flexibility.

See also **Flexitime; Hours of work; Organizational effectiveness; Skill; Competencies**

Bibliography

Atkinson, J. (1984). Manpower strategies for flexible organisations. *Personnel Management*, August 28–31.

Blyton, P. & Morris, J. (Eds) (1991). *A flexible future? Prospects for employment and organization*. Berlin: De Gruyter.

Blyton, P. & Morris, J. (1992). HRM and the limits of flexibility. In P. Blyton & P. Turnbull (Eds), *Reassessing human resource management*. London: Sage.

Laflamme, G., Murray, G., Belanger, J. & Ferland, G. (Eds) (1989). *Flexibility and labour markets in Canada and the United States*. Geneva: International Institute for Labour Studies.

Standing, G. (1986). *Unemployment and labour market flexibility: The United Kingdom*. Geneva: International Labour Organization.

PAUL BLYTON

flexitime This term refers to an arrangement whereby employees may vary their start and finish times provided they are present during a "core" period. Most flexitime schemes allow employees to vary (within limits) their quantity of daily work hours, provided contractual hours are worked over a preset period. Often, however, some carry-over of credit or debit hours from one settlement period to another is allowed. Besides formal flexitime systems, a significant minority of employees maintain informal arrangements for varying their starting and finishing times.

Flexitime has tended to be introduced during periods of labor shortage, with employers offering flexitime as an additional inducement to recruit and/or retain staff. Most flexitime systems involve white-collar staff only. Studies have generally identified positive employee attitudes toward flexitime. As Blyton (1985) points out, potential benefits for management include more positive employee attitudes, reductions in minor absence, and a reduced requirement to enforce punctuality (*see* ABSENTEEISM). Potential drawbacks for management include maintaining adequate cover in noncore periods, and, as a result of employees taking time off to balance previously accrued credit hours.

See also **Flexibility; Working conditions; Human resources planning; Labor markets; Hours of work**

Bibliography

Blyton, P. (1985). *Changes in working time: An international review*. London: Croom Helm.

PAUL BLYTON

force field analysis Force field analysis, attributable to Kurt Lewin (1951) as part of his general theory of change, is a technique for organizing and analyzing information about the forces maintaining a situation in its current state, such as a group's performance or an individual's relationship to his/her superior, and planning what might be done to move to a more desirable condition. The current condition is considered a quasi-stationery equilibrium, a changeable state maintained by a balance of dynamic (i.e., variable) forces, much like an aircraft in level flight. Force, in Lewin's model, is a psychological construct, a PERCEPTION of a factor and its influence. Forces have direction,

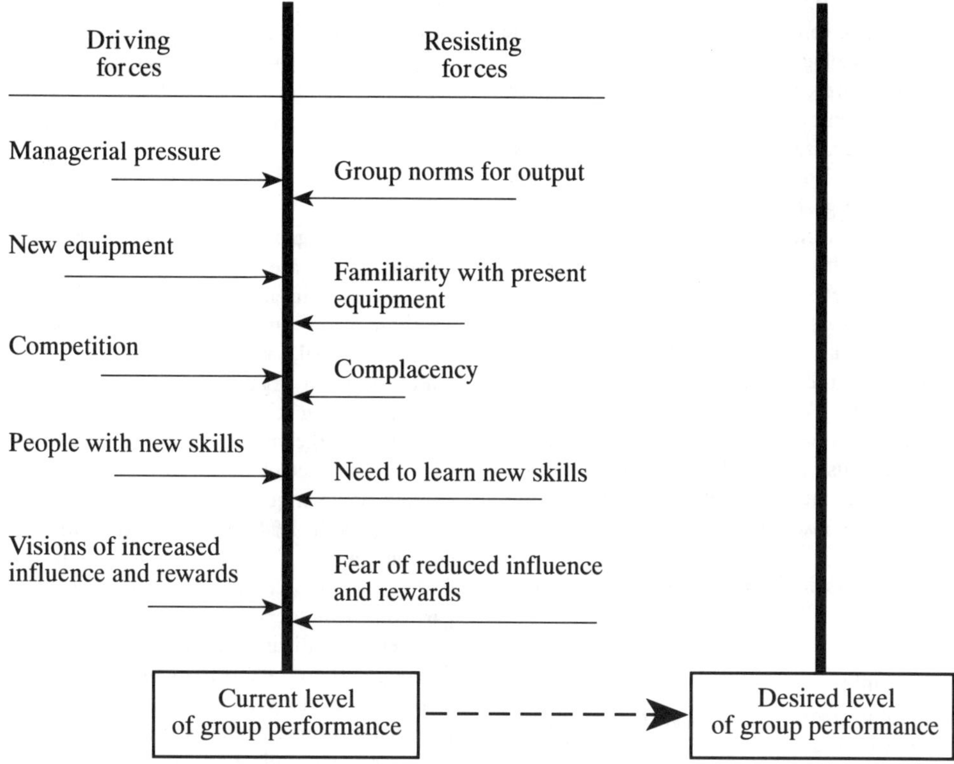

Figure 1 Force field diagram

driving or resisting movement toward the desired condition, and magnitude or intensity (*see* Figure 1). Lewin proposed three fundamental propositions about force fields and change, which subsequent research confirmed.

(1) Adding or increasing driving forces arouses an increase in resisting forces, the current equilibrium does not change but is maintained under increased tension.
(2) Reducing or removing resisting forces is preferable because it will allow movement without increasing tension.
(3) GROUP NORMS are an important force.

An individual with valued membership in a group will increase his/her RESISTANCE TO CHANGE to the degree that s/he must deviate from the group's norms. The group is critical in a change effort. If group norms can be changed, then this key source of individual resistance will be reduced.

See also **Organization development; Organizational change; Change methods; Stakeholders; Organization and environment; Power**

Bibliography

Burke, W. W. (1982). *Organization development: Principles and practices*. New York: Little, Brown.
Lewin, K. (1951) *Field Theory in Social Science*. New York: Harper.
—— (1958). Group decisions and social change. In E. E. Maccoby, T. M. Newcomb & E. L. Hartley (Eds), *Readings in social psychology* (pp. 197–211). New York: Holt, Rinehart, & Winston.

DALE E. ZAND

Fordism *see* CLASSICAL DESIGN THEORY; DIVISION OF LABOR; MASS PRODUCTION; ROUTINIZATION

formal organization This was developed as an alternative name for bureaucracies during the 1960s in sociology (*see* BUREAUCRACY). Both of these terms were used to distinguish a structural appraisal from the Human Relations idea of informal organization (*see* HUMAN RELATIONS MOVEMENT). Formal organizations are assumed to have high goal specificity and relatively high FORMALIZATION, and it is these qualities that make them highly rational. These properties should be seen as variables. Since the term formal organizations is not limited to just public sector organizations, it has the advantage of emphasizing the communalities across kinds of organizations. An alternative label is complex organizations (*see* COMPLEXITY). Today, few researchers use either adjective and instead the problem is to locate formal organizations as one type in some taxonomy.

See also **Classical design theory; Decision making**

Bibliography

Scott, W. R. (1991). *Organizations: Rational, natural, and open systems* (3rd edn). Englewood Cliffs, NJ: Prentice-Hall.

JERALD HAGE

formalization This is a property of the social structure of an organization and refers to the degree of specificity of ROLES in that structure (*see* ORGANIZATIONAL DESIGN). This aspect allows for work behavior to be defined independently of the personalities (*see* PERSONALITY) of the individuals who occupy the work roles and thus is a mechanism of social CONTROL. Furthermore, formalization, that is, detailed role descriptions (*see* JOB DESCRIPTION), rule manuals, or more generally programming are a way of coordinating the DIVISION OF LABOR. Although in recent years, formalization of the organizational structure has not been studied, it has reemerged in the study of CONTRACTS in interorganizational relationships such as JOINT VENTURES (*see* INTERORGANIZATIONAL RELATIONS).

See also **Bureaucracy; Classical design theory; Job design**

Bibliography

Hall, R. H. (1992). *Organizations: Structures, processes, and outcomes* (5th edn). Englewood Cliffs, NJ: Prentice-Hall.

JERALD HAGE

founders Organizations do not emerge spontaneously; they are set up at a distinct point in time in order to achieve a purpose. Founders are those who set up organizations of all kinds – political, social, religious, or work. Their INFLUENCE on organizations is typically profound, shaping the behavior, attitudes, and VALUES of other members. As such they have been the subject of much social, political, and organizational enquiry.

Along with leaders (*see* LEADERSHIP), in general, and – in a business context – entrepreneurs (*see* ENTREPRENEURSHIP), in particular, founders are often said to share a number of distinctive personal attributes. Although there are variations according to factors such as CULTURE and ETHNICITY, personal attributes typically include high levels of energy, determination, ambition, and self-confidence (*see* PERSONALITY). Founders can be further distinguished by their high achievement needs (*see* ACHIEVEMENT, NEED FOR) and clarity of purpose or vision; some may be said to have charisma. But these may be the attributes of the successful; founders who fail are less well researched and, plausibly, may look less distinctive.

Davis (1990) distinguishes three types of founders in FAMILY FIRMS:

(1) proprietors – who dominate the business on the basis of their ownership and allow little room for others to develop;
(2) conductors – who orchestrate the involvement of other family members but are reluctant to relinquish their paternalist role; and
(3) technicians – who build businesses on the basis of their creative or technical SKILLS and delegate administration often to non-family members.

Much contemporary interest is focused upon the manner in which founders may shape the evolution of ORGANIZATIONAL CULTURES.

According to Schein (1985) the process involves the following steps:

(1) the founder has an idea for a new enterprise;
(2) one or more other members are brought in to form a core group who commit to the founder's vision;
(3) this founding group act in concert to create an organization; and
(4) others are recruited and a common history begins to emerge.

The founders of family firms who wish to establish businesses which will survive them are thus engaged in a process which involves more than simply DELEGATION. Successful founders, in this sense, create and communicate a "workable" organizational culture which assists members in integrating their activities as well as adapting to the external environment.

How, then, do founders embed their own assumptions within the thoughts and actions of others? The process involves both conscious and deliberate action as well as that which is unconscious and possibly unintended. Again, according to Schein (1985), "primary mechanisms" include:

(1) what founders attend to, measure, and control;
(2) reactions to critical incidents and CRISES;
(3) role-modeling and coaching (*see* ROLE TAKING);
(4) criteria for allocation of REWARDS and STATUS; and
(5) criteria for RECRUITMENT, selection, promotion, RETIREMENT, and excommunication [pp. 224–5].

Through such actions founders establish "dynasties." Both founders and their creations may exhibit the characteristics of contemporary historical paradigms; they can be seen, in effect, as creatures of their times. But the process of establishing a dynasty may not be without conflict or risk. The example of Henry Ford is extreme but telling. His obsessive interference and desire for personal control almost bankrupted Ford by the 1940s; only the very different style of his successor, Henry Ford II, saved the business.

See also **Organizational change; CEO's**

Bibliography

Davis, P. (1990). Three types of founders – and their dark sides. *Family Business* [Feb] pp. 12–15.
Edwards, R. (1979). *Contested terrain*. London: Heinemann.
Pfeffer, J. (1992). *Managing with power: Politics and influence in organisations*. Boston, MA: Harvard Business School.
Scase, R. & Goffee, R. (1987). *The real world of the small business owner* (2nd edn). London: Routledge.
Schein, E. H. (1985). *Organizational culture and leadership*. San Francisco: Jossey Bass.

ROB GOFFEE

frustration Organizational frustration can be defined as any external interference with the individual's ability to carry out his day-to-day duties in his job effectively. It can take a variety of forms, including deliberate blocking by other people, petty and arbitrary rules, or simply lack of cooperation from work colleagues. Although the individual's reactions to frustration have been extensively studied by social psychologists, there is a dearth of studies on the causes and effects of frustration in organizational settings. The frustration–aggression hypothesis, which postulates that a characteristic response to frustration is aggression in one form or another, has had some support in social psychological studies. In line with this hypothesis one or two studies of frustration within an organizational context have found frustration to be associated with feelings of anger and latent hostility (e.g., Keenan & Newton, 1984). Since these anger/hostility reactions to the stressful effects of frustration would appear to be quite distinct from the anxiety reactions that are more typically investigated in STRESS research, future studies of organizational stress should be broadened to include these variables.

See also **Job satisfaction; Role conflict**

Bibliography

Keenan, A. & Newton, T. J. (1984). Frustration in organizations: Relationships to role stress, climate, and psychological strain. *Journal of Occupational Psychology*, **57**, 57–65.

TONY KEENAN

functional design This particular principle of ORGANIZATIONAL DESIGN divides work at the departmental level (*see* DEPARTMENTALIZATION) on the basis of the major areas of management. Typically, within manufacturing these include finance, production, marketing, and research and development. Although in any particular instance, other departments such as transportation or purchasing or personnel may be equally important, these three or four are considered to be the most critical. Since these divisions represents distinct stages in the process of generating a product and selling it on the market, design on this basis has been referred to as functional.

Within public service organizations, the process of providing services can have similar sounding names but quite different kinds of functions. For example, in child protection services, reporting, investigation and assessment, and service would be three major kinds of departments or functions that would have to be performed.

See also **Classical design theory; Differentiation; Technology**

Bibliography

Daft, R. (1989). *Organizational theory and design* (4th edn). St. Paul, MN: West Publishing.

JERALD HAGE

functionalism This concept, derived from sociology and social anthropology, applies an organic analogy to social institutions, conceptualizing elements of society as existing in a systemic interdependence, in which their function or "purpose" is the stability of society as a whole. It explains elements of society or subsystems in terms of their manifest (intended and recognized) and latent (unintended or unrecognized) functions or consequences for another part of the system or the system as a whole. Social activities or institutions are seen as having the function of satisfying basic social needs.

Criticism of functionalism center around the following issues. First, it cannot account for social CONFLICT, because it sees all social activities as interacting to stabilize society. Functionalists counter this criticism by arguing that: (a) conflict may have positive functions for social order; and (b) introducing the concept of dysfunction (i.e., that some of a social activity's consequences may impede the workings of another part of the system). Second, it cannot account for change, as there appears no mechanism to disturb existing functional relationships. Third, it is teleological, in that it explains the existence of a social activity or institution by its consequences. Fourth, it neglects the meanings individuals give to their actions by its concentration on the consequences of behavior. Essentially, it is a very conservative epistemology focusing as it does on regulation rather than radical change (*see* CRITICAL THEORY).

See also **Manifest and latent functions; Systems theory; Institutional theory; Organization theory; Organizational effectiveness**

Bibliography

Coser, L. A. (1956). *The functions of social conflict*. New York: Free Press.

Merton, R. K. (1957). *Social theory and social structure*. New York: Free Press.

KAREN LEGGE

fundamental attribution error The fundamental ATTRIBUTION error is the pervasive tendency of observers to underestimate the importance of situational factors and overestimate the influence of internal dispositions and traits (e.g., ABILITY, effort, intelligence, and hostility) as the cause of actor behavior and outcomes (*see* INDIVIDUAL DIFFERENCES; PERSONALITY). Thus, for example, in PERFORMANCE APPRAISAL situations, leaders often have a tendency to ignore the conditions surrounding the job and explain performance in terms of the characteristics and dispositions of employees. Moreover, in conditions of both success and failure, this bias suggests that supervisors tend to give their employees more credit and blame than they deserve.

Explanations of the fundamental attribution error suggest that this BIAS occurs because the focus of the observer's attention is on the actor rather than the situational constraints the actor may be experiencing. Thus, because the actor is the most salient aspect of the observer's attention, causation is attributed to the actor rather than less salient situational influences.

Research suggests that this bias is particularly critical in leader–member interactions where leaders often fulfill the role of observers. Performance appraisal processes and other evaluative situations such as TRAINING, selection, and placement processes are often influenced by fundamental attribution errors (*see* SELECTION METHODS).

See also **Selection Interviewing; Cognitive processes; Perception**

Bibliography

Ross, L. (1977). The intuitive psychologist and his shortcomings: Distortions in the attribution process. In L. Berkowitz (Ed.), *Advances in experimental social psychology* (Vol. 10). New York: Academic Press.

MARK J. MARTINKO

fuzzy sets The logic of fuzzy sets has yet to make an impact on the field of ORGANIZATIONAL BEHAVIOR, though it may be expected to do so in the future. It refers to the analytical methods emerging from applied science and mathematics to encompass the imprecision inherent in various natural phenomena, in much the same way as CHAOS THEORY has developed nonlinear modeling to represent the patterned change in naturally occurring systems. Fuzzy logic has developed to cope with qualitative distinctions, such as "very" and "few" which can be applied usefully to phenomena whose occurrence cannot be specified with numerical precision. It deliberately fudges the rules of logic which insist that categories are unambiguously applied and that there is an "excluded middle" between something being or not being the case. Its applications have to date been mainly in the analysis of control systems in engineering, greatly simplifying and improving their utility and predictive power. Its potential is also being realized in expert systems where it makes possible the incorporation of people's tacit knowledge (*see* PRACTICAL INTELLIGENCE) into their design.

See also **Statistical methods**

Bibliography

Alliger, G. M., Feinzig, S. L. & Janak, E. A. (1993). Fuzzy sets and personnel selection: Discussion and an application. *Journal of Occupational and Organizational Psychology*, **66**, 163–169.

Smithson, M. (1987). *Fuzzy set analysis for behavioral and social sciences*. New York: Springer-Verlag.

NIGEL NICHOLSON

G

Gainsharing This denotes an organization-wide involvement system that focuses attention on problem solving while sharing gains in cost reduction, improvements in quality, and/or PRODUCTIVITY in the form of a variable cash bonus (*see* BONUS PAYMENTS). Historically, its philosophy is one of industrial cooperation. In 1937, Joseph Scanlon, a local union president, was instrumental in helping the Empire Plate and Steel Company of Mansfield, Ohio, become more competitive by reducing costs via collaboration between workers and management. Minimally defined, gainsharing is just a financial formula paying broadly-based cash bonuses for increases in productivity.

Broadly-based bonuses are to be distinguished from individual bonuses (piece rate) in that most gainsharing bonuses are distributed as a percent of earned salaries and wages for a particular time period. As such, everyone receives the same percent which is then multiplied times individual earnings to equal the bonus amount. Individual high and low producers in the same wage grades receive the same bonus, if their earned hours are equal. Gainsharing philosophy reinforces cooperation and the sharing of information among workers rather than competition and the pursuit of narrow self-interest between workers.

Gainsharing is a generic term. However, it is known by a variety of proprietary and proprietary sounding names, e.g., Improshare(R), Rucker Plan, and Scanlon Plan. The key distinctions between any particular gainsharing plan are the type of financial formulas and the extent of the involvement systems (*see* Graham-Moore & Ross, 1990). For example, Scanlon Plans always have a system of production and screening committees to process suggestions. Rucker Plans may have suggestions systems. Originally, Improshare(R) plans did not have involvement systems since its financial formula reinforced quantity and not problem solving. However, contemporary organizations draw from any aspect of gainsharing to create their own programs. Indeed, there is no one gainsharing plan as empirical literature indicates that a successful gainsharing plan is adapted to fit a particular organization's culture and objectives (Doyle, 1983).

An estimated sixty (plus) years old, gainsharing has currently seen a rapid rise in interest and use. Much is known about successful and unsuccessful characteristics of gainsharing (*see* Graham-Moore & Ross, 1995; Bullock & Lawler, 1984). Experts agree that the first year represents the most critical period for learning new behaviors and the achievement of bonus opportunities. Most OB textbooks mention gainsharing in their discussions of variable and contingent reward systems. Academic and practitioner articles on gainsharing have increased in the last 10 years in part due to the growing interest in rewarding SELF-MANAGED TEAMS. Gainsharing has moved from manufacturing to service industries and even to the public sector. In the United States the states of North Carolina, Texas, and Washington have passed laws or have established procedures permitting gainsharing in state agencies (*see* GOVERNMENT AGENCIES). The federal government has permitted gainsharing since 1982. The American Compensation Association instituted a certification course in gainsharing in 1992.

Often confused with PROFIT SHARING, gainsharing's bonuses are paid out of the difference between expected costs and actual costs, not profits. If actual costs are lower during a given period of work because of problem solving, increased effort, and/or greater attention to quality, then the difference between expected costs and actual cost triggers a bonus. Beliefs about the relation between performance and outcomes are sharpened under gainsharing which, in turn, increases MOTIVATION (VIE THEORY).

See also **Democracy; Employee involvement; Payment systems; Rewards; Performance related pay**

Bibliography

Bullock, R. J. & Lawler, E. E. (1984). Gainsharing: A few questions and fewer answers. *Human Resource Management*, **23**, (1), 23–40.

Frost, C. F. (1982). The Scanlon plan at Herman Miller, Inc.: Managing and organization by innovation. In R. Zager & M. P. Rosow (Eds), *The innovative organization*. New York: Pergamon Press.

Doyle, R. J. (1983). *Gainsharing and productivity*. New York: AMACON.

Graham-Moore, B. & Ross, T. L. (1995). *Gainsharing and Employee Employment*. Washington, DC: BNA Books.

BRIAN GRAHAM-MOORE

game theory This theory analyzes how rational actors react to potentially conflictful interactions (*see* CONFLICT; CONFLICT RESOLUTION). In particular, game theory attempts to identify strategies for all parties such that each is optimal given the others' (*see* NEGOTIATION). Although such an endeavor seems immediately relevant for the study of cognitions and behavior both between and within organizations (*see* COGNITIVE PROCESSES), ORGANIZATIONAL BEHAVIOR has paid little or no attention to game theory, even though game theory is currently undergoing exciting expansion, both theoretically and empirically.

John von Neumann, an applied mathematician, and Osker Morgenstern, an economist, invented game theory in their ground-breaking and amazingly comprehensive, *Theory of Games and Economic Behavior* (1944). Since then, game theory has been used to analyze matters as weighty as international nuclear strategy, local and global environmental concerns, and global trade and monetary issues. Its models consider a variety of structural conflicts, ranging from cooperative to noncooperative games (*see* CO-OPERATION), from two- to n-party games (*see* COALITION FORMATION), from complete to incomplete information games, and from static to dynamic games (*see* GROUP DYNAMICS).

"Games" refer to strategic interactions where the parties' outcomes are interdependent (Rapoport, 1973). Game theory involves and has been defined as the problem of exchange (von Neumann and Morgenstern's original definition, 1947; *see* EXCHANGE RELATIONS), decisions in conflict situations (Rapoport, 1973), the interaction of rational decision makers (Myerson, 1991; *see* DECISION MAKING; RATIONALITY), or multiperson decision problems (Gibbons, 1992). "The essence of a 'game' . . . is that it involves decision makers with different goals or objectives whose fates are interwined" (Shubik, 1964, p. 8). Game-theoretic reasoning is "a mathematical shortcut" that theorists use to determine what intelligent, adaptive players will do (Camerer, 1991).

Although its potential applicability is far-reaching, game theory restricts its analytic approach to two overlapping domains: theoretical and empirical. A game theorist makes assumptions, considers their logical consequences, and proves theorems which, given the assumptions, are true. Theoretical game theorists: "examine what ultrasmart, impeccably rational, super-people *should* do in competitive, interactive situations" (Raiffa, 1982, p. 21).

Theoretical game theory is precise and clean. Like the physical sciences, it investigates human interaction as if it were in a vacuum. And also like the physical sciences, its greatest successes produce truly beautiful, elegant models. Game theory's theoretical domain is neither descriptive nor normative: It neither describes everyday people's actions nor does it tell them what to do. Instead, it is *analytic*: "game theorists analyze the formal implications of various levels of mutual rationality in strategic situations" (Aumann, 1991). By its very nature, theoretical game theory is not refutable: It analyzes limited problems in specifically bounded domains and solves them mathematically (*see* THEORY).

As an example, game theory makes a strong prediction in ultimatum bargaining. Say that one person receives an amount of money (say $50) and must offer some of it to another person. S/he can either accept or reject the offer. If the second person accepts, s/he receives the amount offered and the first person receives the remainder ($50 - the amount offered). If s/he rejects the offer, both people receive nothing. Game theory uses backward induction (i.e., starting at the end and working backward) to predict that, since something is better than nothing, the second person should accept any positive offer and, therefore, the offerer should make a small offer that is accepted. Not surprisingly, this strong theoretical prediction is upheld for few respondents and almost no offerers. (Research indicates that some people will accept offers as small as a penny and that many offers approach 50–50). Although game theory's prediction is not supported empirically, its logic is unassailable (given its assumptions).

This example shows how game theory's empirical domain tests its theoretical principles. The messy realities of everyday human interaction make the empirical domain (and most other social scientific endeavors) less deterministic than the theoretical domain. Nevertheless, researchers are investigating issues as diverse as bargaining, the efficiency of markets, fairness, preference formation and reversal, LEARNING, and a plethora of other theoretically grounded topics.

Unfortunately, game theory has suffered considerable criticism (*see* Murnighan, 1994). Some social scientists confuse the two game-theoretic domains; some are put off by game theory's difficult mathematics; others reject game theory's rational approach. Although game theory may not describe the behavior of the general public, its attention to sophisticated, experienced, knowledgeable, and strategic actors, and its recent attempts to accommodate nonequilibrium behavior, provide us with insights that are unattainable from more mundane strategists.

Current game theory is expanding its horizons to encompass the *general* analysis of potentially conflictual interactions. Models are now being developed to accommodate the foibles and psycho-logic of real, rather than strictly rational human actors (e.g., Raiffa, 1982). In addition, a number of easily read treatments make game theory understandable without sophisticated mathematics (e.g., Gibbons, 1992; McMillan, 1992).

Most business strategy decisions fit within the broader scope of game theory (Camerer, 1991). Dynamics, communication (*see* COMMUNICATIONS), and differential perceptions of the game are all now part of game-theoretic investigations – making it much more appropriate for applicability to research in organizational behavior and strategy. Game theorists' strong theory should provide researchers with potent tools for advancing understandings of conflict and POWER. Its influence is clearly evident in the frameworks it provides for analyzing the political dynamics of coalition behavior and the dilemma of volunteering (Murnighan, 1994). These are just two examples of areas where little progress has been achieved prior to the recent use of game-theoretic models.

Game theory has grown and become increasingly more useful throughout the social sciences. As Myerson (1992, p. 62) noted "Game theory provides a fundamental and systematic way of thinking about questions that concern all of the social sciences."

See also **Prisoner's dilemma; Behavioral decision research; Bounded rationality; Prospect theory; Risk-taking**

Bibliography

Aumann, R. (1991). Irrationality in game theory. In D. Gale & O. Hart (Eds), *Economic analysis of markets and games*. Cambridge, UK: Cambridge University Press.

Camerer, C. (1991). Does strategy research need game theory?. *Strategic Management Journal*, **12**, 137–152.

Gibbons, R. (1992). *Game theory for applied economists*. Princeton, NJ: Princeton University Press.

Murnighan, J. K. (1994). Game theory and organizational behavior. In L. Cummings & B. M. Staw (Eds), *Research on organizational behavior*. Greenwich, CT.: JAI Press.

Myerson, R. (1991). *Game theory: Analysis of conflict*. Cambridge, MA: Harvard University Press.

Myerson, R. (1992). On the value of game theory in social science. *Rationality and Society*, **4**, 62–73.

Raiffa, H. (1982). *The art and science of negotiation*. Cambridge, MA: Harvard University Press.

Rapoport, A. (1973). *Two-person game theory*. Ann Arbor, MI: University of Michigan Press.

Shubik, M. (1964). *Game theory and related approaches to social behavior*. New York: Wiley.

Von Neumann, J. & Morgenstern, O. (1947). *The theory of games and economic behavior*. Princeton, NJ: Princeton University Press.

J. KEITH MURNIGHAN

garbage can model In the literature on organizational DECISION MAKING the "garbage can" model denotes "organized anarchies" characterized by unclear or inconsistent goals, a TECHNOLOGY which is obscure and little understood by members and a highly variable member PARTICIPATION. Cohen, March and Olsen (1972) based their description of this model primarily on experiences with decision-making processes at universities. According to these authors, organizations can be viewed as collections of: (1) problems; (2) solutions; (3) participants; and (4) choice opportunities; situations in which participants are expected to link a problem to a solution, and thus make a decision. From this point of view, "an organization is a collection of choices looking for problems, issues and feelings looking for decision situations in which they might be aired, solutions looking for issues to which they might be the answer, and decision makers looking for work" (Cohen, March, & Olsen, 1972, p. 2).

These four elements are more or less randomly mixed together in the "garbage can." Combinations arise almost unpredictably. There is no a priori chronology. Solutions can precede problems, or problems and solutions can wait for a suitable opportunity for a decision. The traditionally assumed order: "identification and definition of the problem," "generation of decision alternatives," "examination of their consequences," "evaluation of those consequences in terms of objectives," and finally "selection" is thus often a poor description of what actually happens (March & Olsen, 1976).

Labels such as "garbage can model" and "anarchy" can be misleading. The authors certainly do not imply that no systematic decision making can be discovered in such organizations. On the contrary, the central message of these authors is that the seeming anarchy has a structure and an organization which form a reasonable, although not optimal, answer to the great environmental UNCERTAINTY in which the participants find themselves. In order for decision making to progress, it is essential that the organization manages to attract sufficient attention from the participants to solve the problems in question. However, participants generally have more on their minds. Thus, it is not unusual for decision making to take place without explicit attention to the problem, or by simply postponing the problem. The authors, however, see it as the task of management to coordinate and steer the required attention in a direction desired by the organization.

See also **Managerial behavior; Rationality; Group decision making; Social constructionism; Negotiated order**

Bibliography

Cohen, M. D., March, J. G. & Olsen, J. P. (1972). A garbage can model of organizational choice. *Administrative Science Quarterly*, **17**, 1–25.

Koopman, P. L., Broekhuysen, J. W. & Meijn, O. M. (1984). Complex decision making at the organizational level. In P. J. D. Drenth, H. Thierry, P. J. Willems & C. J. de Wolff (Eds), *Handbook of work and organizational psychology*. Chichester, UK: Wiley.

March, J. G. & Olsen, J. P. (1976). *Ambiguity and choice in organizations*. Bergen, Norway: Universitetsforlaget.

PAUL KOOPMAN

gatekeepers Like many concepts in organizational behavior, *gatekeepers* is metaphorical. When thinking literally of *gate*, one typically imagines a movable object that either stops or allows the flow of physical movement. Gatekeepers, a term originated by Lewin (1952), are persons who either facilitate or impede information flow between people. Gatekeepers are therefore at the nexus of exchange among individuals interpersonally, in groups, or within and across organizations.

Middle managers may occupy the most important gatekeeping roles in organizations. They pass or do not pass information up and down the HIERARCHY as well as horizontally in the organization. As gatekeepers they can determine whether and what kind of information flows throughout the organization.

The term has been used primarily in GROUP DYNAMICS. Gatekeepers are group members who either help the well being and maintenance of the group or hinder such processes. By seeking people's ideas and opinions and by asking members to participate (opening the gate for information flow and PARTICIPATION), gatekeepers effectively facilitate the group's work toward its objectives.

When compared with the more peripheral group members, research has shown that gatekeepers in small groups reported significantly higher feelings of participation, satisfaction, responsibility, and COMMITMENT to the final group product.

See also **Boundary spanning; Organizational boundaries; Organizational design; Managerial behavior**

Bibliography

Lewin, K. (1952). Group decision and social change. In E. E. Maccoby, T. M. Newcomb & E. L. Hartley (Eds), *Readings in social psychology* (3rd edn, pp. 197–211). New York: Holt, Rinehart and Winston.

W. WARNER BURKE

gender This term is used in a variety of ways to help people discuss aspects of interaction between women and men. It marks a changing field as thinking and practice develop. Much has been written from women's viewpoints, seeking to understand and change their previously devalued social position. How gender issues affect men is now receiving more attention. Gender constructions and relations vary greatly with culture, class, religion, and many other factors.

The question of whether women and men are "really" different, to which there is no definitive answer, often lurks in the background of discussions about gender (see SEX DIFFERENCES and SEX ROLES). Many scholars, particularly in the United States and United Kingdom, are unwilling to conclude that differences exist because interpretations of equality have required women to prove their likeness to men. Apparent differences have been viewed as faults or weaknesses on women's part, making them, for example, unsuitable for management jobs. This equality for similarity model still has much influence. However, an alternative view that women may be different from, as well as similar to, men **and** also equal, is gaining ground. This view opens the way to welcoming diversity (of many kinds) as potentially valuable to organizational life (*see* MANAGEMENT OF DIVERSITY).

Research does frequently seem to find one apparent difference between men and women, viewed as broad gender groups. Men often seem to operate from assumptions of hierarchy – for example, setting up social systems organized by this principle, asserting their status in conversation, or using POWER in competitive ways. Women, in contrast, seem more often to operate from notions of equality – favoring participative management styles, and encouraging equal contributions in discussion. In her analysis of conversation, Tannen (1991) depicts these tendencies as symmetrical, different but equal. Doing so avoids the paradox that, as operating frameworks, hierarchy and equality incorporate unequal assumptions about power. Someone working from an equality intent is vulnerable to the power moves of somone who frames the world according to hierarchy. This potentially gender-related tension has great significance for OB.

Many people now argue that women should be welcomed into organizations because of the potentially different contributions they may bring. For whatever reasons, women currently have a different cultural heritage from men, fostering different SKILLS and VALUES. It would therefore not only be equitable but exciting and effective to work in gender-equal environments (Marshall, 1984).

Differences and similarities are constructed and interpreted from value frameworks. Valuing, and the power to assign value, are therefore central issues in any consideration of gender. Until recently men have held the vast majority of positions of public power in Western societies. Characteristics, activities, and life patterns associated with men have been valued, and those associated with women devalued. Critiques of this situation, and the resulting principles of "male as norm" and "male positive–female negative," are now well established (Spender, 1980).

Much gender literature explores overt and covert processes through which unequal power relations between women and men have been maintained. This situation is only changing slowly. It is widely believed, for example, that "glass ceilings" still prevent many women reaching senior decision-making roles (Greenglass & Marshall, 1993). Despite equality legislation, at most 5 percent of senior managers in most Western countries are women, and corporate and governmental agendas continue to be shaped mainly by men.

The structures, norms of behavior, and values of most organizations are, then, still firmly male dominated. Some STRESS literature implicitly reveals the possible negative consequences for men of living in such environments. Gender stratification in employment remains prevalent, with women largely found in low-level, low-paid work and in a limited range of employment sectors. Women who escape these constraints by doing traditional men's jobs or by becoming managers are often judged by double standards. They must prove themselves against dominant, male, norms of behavior, but not offend stereotypes of femininity by being over-assertive or uncaring (*see* STEREOTYPING). A significant theme in gender research is the potential silence and invisibility of women when they encounter male-dominated cultures (Goldberger, Clinchy, Belenky, & Tarule 1987) (*see* ORGANIZATIONAL CULTURE).

Any discussion of gender therefore has power as an integral aspect. Attention can be paid, for example, to what NORMS are being used to judge behavior; whether some viewpoints are privileged and others excluded; and what processes of power are affecting the issue studied.

Female role stereotypes have been searchingly questioned since the 1960s resurgence of FEMINISM. Recently more men are criticizing their apparently advantaged social roles. For example, Keen (1992) argues that most men are tacitly socialized to become soldiers, encouraging them to compete, suppress emotions, and simplify issues to achieve action. He suggests this ideal-type has become a model for the corporate executive, constraining men's (and women's) behavior.

Many people argue that gender stereotypes are now breaking down, but they may be recreated in revised forms despite apparent change. For example, current advice to professional women about dress and image may create new ideals of physical appearance – designed to ensure that men take women seriously – to which women again have to conform (Wolf, 1991).

Some writers dismiss the idea of essential differences between women and men, concentrating instead on how gender and associated power differentials are constructed, maintained, or challenged in social interaction (Weedon, 1987). They make a valuable contribution to theory and considerations of action. For example, patterns of domination and subordination can be played out or changed in a particular social exchange. So, by controlling conversation, interrupting, ignoring the other party's contributions, making demands for support and attention, and using physical signals of dominance such as touching, a person can assert power. If individuals are aware of such processes they have more opportunity not to collude with traditional gender scripting and to resist, although not necessarily easily, power being used against them.

Taking only a social perspective on gender has limitations. Male and female can also be understood as complementary archetypal principles, akin to the Taoist concepts of yang and yin (Colegrave, 1991). In interaction, dynamically, these map a full range of potential qualities. Western society can be depicted as in transition from over-emphasizing the male principle to more appreciation of the female principle.

Various writers about gender critique mainstream OB for paying too little attention to the physical aspects of life in organizations. People are bodies too. It seems possible that women are more aware than men of themselves as physical beings, partly through the monthly rhythms of menstruation. But such topics are seldom broached in organizational literature (nor are pregnancy and the menopause), perhaps because any differences women exhibit may be interpreted as potential weaknesses until male-dominated frameworks are superseded.

Recently, the de-sexualized impression of corporate life given by most organizational theories has been strongly criticized (Hearn, Sheppard, Tancred-Sheriff, & Burrell, 1989). As a corrective, some attention is now being paid to topics such as SEXUAL HARASSMENT, affairs in the workplace, sexual attraction, sexual joking as intimidation, pressures on women managers to mask their sexuality, and the implications for lesbians and gay men of working in organizations which assume heterosexuality (Sims, Fineman, & Gabriel, 1993). Awareness of such themes is underdeveloped in OB.

Whilst some theories rightly focus on gender, the trend is for more organizational analyses to incorporate it as a potential theme. For example, any topic covered in this dictionary can be read through a gender-aware lens and its gender-power aspects explored. This could involve, for example, noticing if certain characteristics are assumed "natural" to people of a given gender, or those stereotyped as masculine or feminine are attributed more value.

But it is no easy matter to see beyond traditional gender value patterns, partly because these are so ingrained in the social fabric, and partly because doing so can be personally threatening, as gender is typically a foundational aspect of individual identity.

See also **Discrimination; Critical theory; Social constructionism; Women at work**

Bibliography

Colegrave, S. (1991). The unfolding feminine principle in human consciousness. In C. Zweig (Ed.), *To be a woman: The birth of the conscious feminine* (pp. 34–42). London: Mandala.

Goldberger, N. R., Clinchy, B. McV., Belenky, M. F. & Tarule, J. M. (1987). Women's ways of knowing: On gaining a voice. In P. Shaver & C. Hendrick (Eds), *Sex and culture* (pp. 201–228). Newbury Park, CA: Sage.

Greenglass, E. & Marshall, J. (1993). Special Issue: Women in Management, *Applied Psychology: An International Review*, **42 (4)**.

Hearn, J., Sheppard, D. L., Tancred-Sheriff, P. & Burrell, G. (Eds), (1989). *The sexuality of organization*. London: Sage.

Keen, S. (1992). *Fire in the belly: On being a man*. London: Piatkus.

Marshall, J. (1984). *Women managers: Travellers in a male world*. Chichester: Wiley.

Sims, D., Fineman, S. & Gabriel, Y. (1993). *Organizing and organizations: An introduction*. London: Sage.

Spender, D. (1980). *Man made language*. London: Routledge and Kegan Paul.

Tannen, D. (1991). *You just don't understand: Men and women in conversation*. London: Virago.

Weedon, C. (1987). *Feminist practice and poststructuralist theory*. Oxford, UK: Basil Blackwell.

Wolf, N. (1991). *The beauty myth: How images of beauty are used against women*. London: Vintage.

JUDI MARSHALL

generalization The goal of much of organizational science is generalization. Scholars (and reflective practitioners) wish to establish principles or theories of ORGANIZATIONAL BEHAVIOR (OB) that are usually correct for a class of cases (e.g., new workers, large organizations) or situations (e.g., during mergers). However, the evidence or data available from research or experience is often limited. What we know may derive from a single case, study, type of measure, investigator, even from a single nation. Thus writers in OB (especially textbook writers) are usually making a generalization when they assert (or teach) that a functional relationship exists between two factors, a practice will have a particular consequence or a particular business policy will have a specified impact (*see* THEORY). The correctness of any generalization will be a function of such factors as the: number and breadth of cases for which there is particularized knowledge; consistency of the findings across such cases; degree of Bias in the observer (*see* SOCIAL CONSTRUCTIONISM); quality of the research (*see* RESEARCH METHODS); or measures (*see* RELIABILITY); and degree of similarity between the instances on which the inferences are built and the individual, organization, or situation to which the generalization is being made (*see* VALIDITY).

See also **Research design; Error; Statistical methods; Case study research; Levels of analysis**

Bibliography

Cook, T. D., Campbell, D. T. & Peracchio, L. (1990). Quasi experimentation. In M. D. Dunnette & L. M. Hough (Eds), *Handbook of Industrial & Organizational Psychology* (pp. 491–576). Palo Alto, CA: Consulting Psychologists Press.

Schmitt, N. W. & Klimoski, R. J. (1991). *Research methods in human resources management*. Cincinnati, OH: South-Western.

RICHARD KLIMOSKI

goal setting This theory of MOTIVATION was originally developed by Locke (1968) to explain human action in specific work situations. The underlying assumptions of the theory are that goals and intentions are cognitive and volitional, and that they serve as the immediate regulators of human action. The two major findings of the theory are that specific goals lead to higher performance levels than general goals, and that difficult goals are positively and linearly related to performance. These effects are subject to two conditions – FEEDBACK, and the acceptance of goals by the performers. Goals regulate behavior through three mechanisms: choice/direction, intensity/effort/resource allocation, and duration/persistence. The effect of goal-setting in complex tasks is regulated by a fourth mechanism of strategy development, which is necessary for reaching the goal. The two unique characteristics of the goal-setting theory that make it more effective than any other theory of motivation to date are its strong empirical basis, and its continuous process of development.

The original goal-setting model (Locke, 1968) consisted of a sequential process of five steps: Environmental Stimuli → Cognition → Evaluation → Intentions/Goal-Setting → Performance. Goal-setting theory was developed by starting with goals and intentions as the two conscious motivational factors closest to the action. It then worked backward progressively to the preceding stages of evaluation, and cognition. The term *goal* refers to attaining a specific standard of proficiency on a given task, usually within a specified time limit. Goals have two main attributes: content and intensity. *Goal content* refers to the object or result being sought (e.g., producing 10 percent more units, reaching an executive position within 10 years). Goal difficulty specifies a certain level of standard of task proficiency. *Goal intensity* refers to the amount of physical and mental resources that goes into formulating the goal or a plan of action to realize it (Locke & Latham, 1990). It is expressed by goal COMMITMENT, effort, and attention. The parsimony of the early research paradigm which focused on the relationship between goals and performance allowed us to establish the strong empirical support to the effect of goal specificity and difficulty on performance. Once these basic relationships were established, the focus shifted backward to the *evaluation phase*, and the next step of theory development began. Four important variables that are evaluative by nature, serve to explain mediating and moderating effects on the goal–performance relationship: feedback KNOWLEDGE-OF-RESULTS, expectancies, SELF-EFFICACY, and goal commitment. *Feedback* pertains to performance evaluation relative to the goal, and it was identified as a necessary condition for goals to affect performance (Erez, 1977). Feedback may have negative effects on performance when it shifts resources to off-task processes of SELF-REGULATION, in particular, for individuals with low levels of self-efficacy (Kanfer, 1990). *Self-efficacy* is a judgment of one's capability to accomplish a certain level of performance (Bandura, 1986). Goal difficulty positively affects perceptions of self-efficacy, which further affect intentions, personal goals, and performance. In a cyclical process past performance affects self-efficacy, which further affects self-set goals and performance. *Expectancies* reflect the evaluations people make of their chance to obtain goals. For a given level of goal difficulty, individuals with high rather than low expectancies are more likely to attain their goals. Perceptions of self-efficacy, and expectancies determine the level of goal attractiveness which influences goal acceptance. *Goal acceptance* refers to initial agreement with the goal, whereas *goal commitment* refers to adherence to the goal, and resistance to changing the goal at a later point in time. Goal commitment both mediates and moderates the effect of goal difficulty on performance. A significant drop-off in performance is observed if and when goal commitment declines in response to increasingly difficult goals. Feedback and goal commitment were identified as the two necessary conditions for goals to affect performance. PARTICIPATION in goal setting was found to be one effective method for enhancing goal commitment (Latham, Erez, & Locke, 1988). Goal evaluation is guided by *values*, which determine what people consciously consider beneficial to their welfare. VALUES mediate between needs and goals which can be viewed as applications of values to specific situations (Locke, 1991). In parallel to the continuous research on the evaluation phase there is a growing interest in cognition which precedes evaluation. *Cognition* draws attention to paradigms of complex tasks, and multiple goals. The magnitude of goal effects on performance decreases as task COMPLEXITY increases. Goals of complex tasks affect performance to the extent that they lead to the development of effective plans and strategies. However, very often, goals generate pressure for immediate results and they become counterproductive when planning and strategy development is required. The negative effect of goals on the performance of complex tasks is mainly observed at initial stages of SKILL acquisition (Kanfer, 1990). The multiple goal PARADIGM is guided by the assumption that the human organism has a pool of limited resources. As a result, there is a trade-off relationship in the performance of multiple goals. More resources are shifted toward specific and difficult goals than general or easy goals, and to the attainment of performance goals which are supported by feedback.

It seems that the most recent phase of theory development is that of examining goals in different contextual levels – individual goals, group goals (Weldon & Gargano, 1988), visionary goals of leaders, and the effect of cultural values on goal choice and goal commitment (Erez & Earley, 1993). Monetary rewards is another situational factor which mediates, as well as moderates the effect of goals on performance. REWARDS increase goal commitment, but at the same time they inhibit the attainment of complementary goals which are not compensated for (Wright, George, Farnsworth, & McMahan, 1993). To summarize, the continuous development of the goal-setting theory integrates different motivational theories into one coherent model which contributes to our understanding of how goals affect the performance of multiple tasks, including performance quantity and quality, and at multiple levels of analysis – individuals, groups, organizations, and cultures. In its present development, the goal-setting theory is identified as a meta-cognitive theory of self-regulation, with a growing emphasis on the underlying cognitive resource allocation processes (Kanfer, 1990).

See also **Motivation and performance; Vie theory; Management by objectives**

Bibliography

Bandura, A. (1986). *Social foundations of thought and action: A social cognitive theory*. Englewood Cliffs, NJ: Prentice-Hall.

Erez, M. (1977). Feedback: A necessary condition for the goal setting-performance relationship. *Journal of Applied Psychology*, **62**, 624–627.

Erez, M. & Earley, P. C. (1993). *Culture, self-identity, and work*. New York: Oxford University Press.

Kanfer, R. (1990). Motivation theory and industrial and organizational psychology. In M. D. Dunnette & L. M. Hough (Eds), *Handbook of industrial and organizational psychology*. (Vol. 1, pp. 75–170). Palo Alto, CA: Consulting Psychology Press.

Latham, G. P., Erez, M. & Locke, E. A. (1988). Resolving scientific disputes by the joint design of crucial experiments: Application to the Erez–Latham dispute regarding participation in goal setting. *Journal of Applied Psychology (Monograph)*, **73**, 753–77.

Locke, E. A. (1968). Toward a theory of task motivation and incentives. *Organizational Behavior and Performance*, **3**, 157–189.

Locke, E. A. (1991). The motivation sequence, the motivation hub, and the motivation core. *Organizational Behavior and Human Decision Processes*, **50**, 288–299.

Locke, E. A. & Latham, G. P. (1990). *A theory of goal setting and task motivation*. Englewood Cliffs, NJ: Prentice-Hall.

Weldon, E. & Gargano, G. M. (1988). Cognitive loafing: The effects of accountability and shared responsibility on cognitive effort. *Personality & Social Psychology Bulletin*, **14**, 159–171.

Wright, P. M., George, J. M. Farnsworth S. R. & McMahan, G. C. (1993). Productivity and extra-role behavior: The effects of goals and incentives on spontaneous helping. *Journal of Applied Psychology*, **78**, 374–381.

MIRIAM EREZ

governance and ownership Organizational governance concerns how the organization's mission and objectives are defined in structures, policies, and procedures – "how a corporation is structured, what policies and objectives it seeks to fulfill, how it is managed, and which stakeholder interests it serves" (Wood, 1994). The term "includes specific issues arising from interactions among senior management, shareholders, boards of directors, and other corporate STAKEHOLDERS" (Cochran & Wartick, 1988, p. 4).

The basic questions of governance are of POWER, benefit, and ACCOUNTABILITY: Who controls the mission and actions of an organization? For what purposes, and to whose benefit, does the organization act? Who is held accountable for the consequences of an organization's actions? Governance issues are particularly salient in many large business organizations because the separation of stock ownership from management control (Berle & Means, 1932) changes the agent–principal relationship between managers and owners, granting much AUTONOMY to managers and little voice to owners. Managers can often avoid accountability for organizational actions, making it difficult for stakeholders (including owners/stockholders) or society at large to ensure that their legitimate interests are being met.

Reviewing the governance literature, Cochran and Wartick (1988, pp. 22–23, paraphrased) offer this list of board responsibilities:

- Strategic PLANNING – establishing long-range objectives and policies.
- Board renewal – nominating and orienting new board members.
- Supervision of the chief executive officer (CEO) – hiring, oversight, compensating, firing.
- Public image maintenance – guarding the firm's LEGITIMACY.
- Overseeing major organizational transformations such as divestments, MERGERS, AND ACQUISITIONS.
- Guarding corporate assets – maintaining fiduciary responsibility for appropriate use of assets and ensuring that controls and record-keeping practices do not allow for illegal acts.

Individual directors also have responsibilities:

(a) a duty of loyalty, expressed by placing the organization's interests above personal interests and avoiding conflicts of interest; and
(b) a duty of care, expressed by acting prudently, in good faith, with the organization's best interests in mind.

Current issues in governance have to do with changing definitions of who should control business organizations and for whose benefit they should function. Governance issues include business–government relationships (*see* BUSINESS AND GOVERNMENT), accommodation of stakeholder interests, executive compensation, the role of institutional investors, the balance and respective roles of executive versus outside or nonexecutive directors on boards, stakeholder representation on boards of directors, employee ownership, interlocking boards, proportions of external and internal directors, the board's role in linking the organization's mission with structures and incentive systems, and the board's role in monitoring CORPORATE SOCIAL PERFORMANCE and BUSINESS ETHICS (*see* MISSION STATEMENTS).

Stakeholder pressures to reform corporate governance are likely to change many things about how companies are run. For example, increased board oversight of the CEO, along with formalized stakeholder representation on boards, could alter executive succession patterns dramatically. Furthermore, many executives are accustomed to thinking of social responsibility as something to attend *after* meeting profit goals, but governance reforms could legitimize the relationship between social responsibility (or ORGANIZATIONAL CITIZENSHIP) and *day-to-day operating procedures*. A third example is found in the efforts of institutional investors such as large pension funds to gain a voice on corporate boards and in management decisions. Finally, international social and political issues may push closer coordination of governance and social performance in multinational business organizations (Windsor & Preston, 1988).

See also **Competitiveness; Trust; Organizational design**

Bibliography

Cochran, P. L. & Wartick, S. L. (1988). *Corporate governance: A review of the literature*. Morristown, NJ: Financial Executives Research Foundation.

Berle, A. A. & Means, G. C. (1932). *The modern corporation and private property*. New York: Macmillan.

Windsor, D. & Preston, L. E. (1988). Corporate governance and social performance in the multinational corporation. In L. E. Preston (Ed.), *Research in corporate social performance and policy* (Vol. 10, pp. 45–58). Greenwich, CT: JAI Press.

Wood, D. J. (1994). *Business and society* (2nd edn). New York: Harper Collins.

DONNA J. WOOD

government agencies These are public sector owned organizations which carry out the various functions of government, including fiscal and monetary policies and regulation (*see* GOVERNMENT AND BUSINESS). Until the beginning of the 1980s, a distinction was drawn between state-owned enterprises (SOEs) and government agencies. SOEs were defined as being owned by government in mixed economies, but could raise investment capital from private investors and earn revenues; government agencies were both publicly owned *and* publicly funded. Funds used by government agencies therefore had to be approved by a legislative assembly, raised through fiscal policy and spent in accordance with strict regulations. Government agencies fall into seven broad types (Dunleavy, 1991): delivery, regulatory, transfer, contracts, control, trading, and servicing.

A series of market-based and managerialist public sector reforms from 1980 onward, pursued by the governments of the major, developed, Western mixed economies, made these distinctions less relevant. Some government agencies still conform to the old model, but many are now also required to behave more like SOEs and raise funds through extra revenue-generating activities and may combine contracts, trading, and servicing elements. Even some regulatory agencies have been required to try and become self-funding. This has become an area of growing research interest for organizational theorists, raising questions about complex relationships between these new, hybrid organizational forms.

See also **Organization and environment; Organizational design; Stakeholders**

Bibliography

Dunleavy, P. (1991). *Democracy, bureaucracy and public choice*. London: Harvester Wheatsheaf.

ELIZABETH O. MELLON

government and business Government, through its agencies (*see* GOVERNMENT AGENCIES), manages the public sector of an economy; business, in the form of privately owned firms, manages the private sector of an economy. Another common phrase used is therefore "the public and private sectors" of an economy. Command economies, formerly typified by much of Eastern Europe, are socalled because all significant economic enterprise is run by government. Mixed economies, comprising most Western nations, are typified by a debate about how large the public sector should be, with some writers proposing normative limits (Rose, 1981). Ownership and funding are two key determinants of the allocation of organizations to the public or private sectors of an economy (Walmsley & Zald, 1973) (*see* GOVERNANCE AND OWNERSHIP). The boundary between the two sectors is not always clear (*see* NOT FOR PROFIT ORGANIZATIONS) and is considered by some to be a continuum (Dahl & Lindblom, 1953). For example, some organizations are publicly owned but privately funded, competing with other suppliers of competitive, or generic, services or goods, e.g., the United Kingdom and United States postal services. Some organizations are privately owned but publicly funded, e.g., defense firms funded primarily through government contracts. A definition of government based on budgets enacted by a political assembly has been proposed: "Public sector: Governmental consumption, investment and transfers" (Lane, 1993, p. 14). However, Government legislation and regulation also have a significant impact on society, omitted from a budget-based definition. For example, government is a significant environmental factor to be considered when trying to understand how business organizations adapt to changed circumstances, or may be an important stakeholder in a firm (*see* ORGANIZATION AND ENVIRONMENT; STAKEHOLDERS).

The main functions of government are to manage fiscal and monetary policies and regulation; to use fiscal revenues to provide goods and services not provided by privately owned businesses; to transfer payments from some individuals and organizations to others; and to regulate and control individuals and organizations based on legislation passed by a ruling assembly. Gujarah (1984, p. 4) offers a summary, shown in Figure 1.

Government policies therefore affect private sector business firms through all of these mechanisms. Welfare economics assumes that under ideal conditions the perfectly competitive market can ensure Pareto-optimal outcomes, i.e., no one becomes worse off because some-

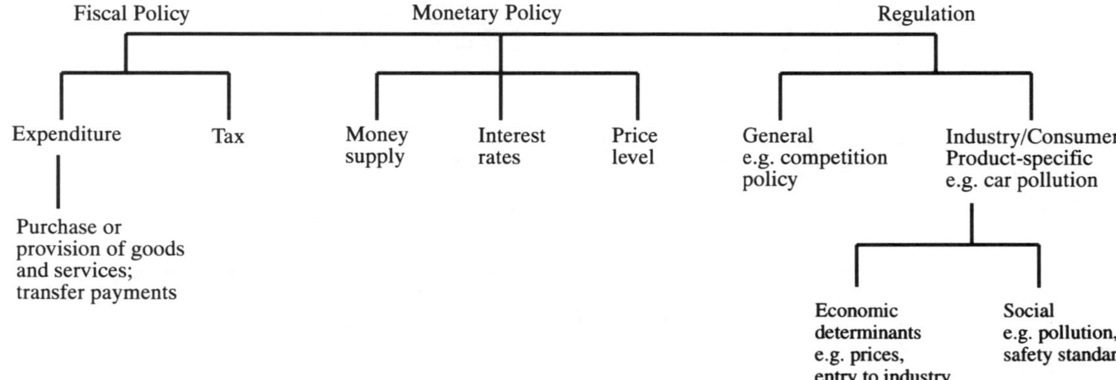

Figure 1 The main functions of government
Source: D. Gujarah (1984).

body else becomes better off. The public interest theory of regulation however holds that government must intervene in the market place to correct market failures which reduce Pareto optimality. Market failures may occur because of the need to regulate natural monopolies, externalities, e.g., pollution, inadequate information, erroneous decisions, the need to conserve natural resources, and an inadequate supply of public goods. Public goods and services by definition must be available to all, but certain recipients cannot pay (through taxes). This "free-rider" problem makes provision economically unattractive to private sector businesses, held to be driven primarily by the profit motive, so the government may intervene to ensure supply through wholly owned or controlled agencies.

The relationship a business firm has with government can therefore be multifaceted. A firm may routinely scan government monetary, fiscal, and industrial policy as part of its strategic planning processes and join pressure groups to attempt to change policies perceived to be deleterious to company operations. Private sector firms specializing in, for example, parliamentary lobbying, have grown to facilitate this interchange between government and business. A business which is privately owned but publicly funded may "shadow" the organizational structure of its funder and will often recruit ex-government employees to facilitate expert conversation. Firms which negotiate and win government contracts, where provision was formerly inhouse, may purchase the unsuccessful public sector supplier, or employ its staff, to aid efficient supply. Some government-owned natural monopolies, e.g., electricity, are being broken down (*see* PRIVATIZATION) with overall provision offered instead by a mix of, often competing, private and public sector companies. This involves complex interorganizational relationships (*see* INTERORGANIZATIONAL RELATIONS), with success for both the public and private sector companies highly dependent upon complementary systems, structures, and beliefs.

The range of options pursued is often ideologically determined by politicians. The period from 1980 onward was typified by a wave of strikingly similar reforms in the mixed economies of developed Western nations. These were intended to reduce the size of the public sector, through privatization and self-regulation, and to increase the efficiency of those elements remaining under public sector control through policies grounded in welfare economics, e.g., open competition. These reforms have further clouded the distinction between public and private enterprise. They have also increased the range and scope of possible relationships between the public and private sectors, as provision of public goods and services which transaction cost economics would have predicted should remain inhouse, were contracted out to private sector firms (*see* TRANSACTION COST THEORY). The reforms have also rendered the more "business-like" public sector suppliers of increasing interest in their own right to organizational theorists.

See also **Organization theory; Organizational economics; Corporate social responsibility**

Bibliography

Dahl, R. A. & Lindblom, C. E. (1953). *Politics, economics and welfare*. New York: Harper & Row.

Gujarah, D. (1984). *Government and business*. New York: McGraw-Hill.

Lane, J. E. (1993). *The public sector: Concepts, models, and approaches*. London: Sage.

Rose, R. (1981). What if anything is wrong with big government?. *Journal of Public Policy*, **1**, 5–36.

Walmsley, G. L. & Zald, M. N. (1973). *The political economy of public organizations*. Lexington, MA: Heath.

ELIZABETH O. MELLON

graph theory This is a branch of mathematics concerned with analyzing structural relationships depicted as a set of lines (or edges) mapped onto a set of points (or nodes). Such sets are known in mathematics as "graphs," although sociologists frequently use the term "network." Network analysis, which has become popular in organization studies, is based largely on graph theory.

Bibliography

Hage, P. & Harary, F. (1983). *Structural models in anthropology*. Cambridge, UK: Cambridge University Press.

Scott, J. (1991). *Social network analysis: A handbook.* Beverley Hills, CA: Sage.

STEPHEN R. BARLEY

graphology *see* SELECTION METHODS

group cohesiveness Cartwright (1968) defines group cohesiveness as how much its members want to stay in a group. The concept of group cohesiveness was a central element in the literature on group dynamics, which flourished in the 1950s and 1960s. McGrath (1984) observed that cohesiveness, COMMUNICATION, and CONFORMITY became the focal processes in the heyday of group dynamics research.

Highly cohesive group members may take much of their personal identity from the group and will want to contribute to its welfare. Thus, cohesiveness gives the group POWER to INFLUENCE its members (*see* EXCHANGE RELATIONS): cohesive groups that decide to be productive can influence their members to be more productive; conversely, cohesive groups that promote shirking tend to be relatively unproductive (e.g., Roy, 1960; *see* MOTIVATION AND PERFORMANCE; PERFORMANCE, INDIVIDUAL).

If people join groups to obtain positive outcomes, then joining and attraction to a group are driven by a person's needs, what the group can offer, whether positive outcomes are likely, and what other groups might offer. Once a group has formed, the internal forces that can increase cohesiveness include sharing common goals, having similar visions of how to achieve those goals, and needing each other's help (e.g., cooperative interdependence; *see* GROUP STRUCTURE). External forces that can increase cohesiveness include threats and competition with other groups (Sherif, 1977); internal forces include severe initiation and positive REINFORCEMENT. These forces are primarily perceptual: Staw (1975) showed that groups who were falsely told that they were successful concluded that they were cohesive, while comparable groups who were falsely told that they had failed concluded that they were not (*see* PERCEPTION).

Perceptions of cohesiveness help contribute to uniformity of action within groups, and increase the pressures directed toward and felt by dissenters to return to the fold. In addition, cohesive groups provide members with a stable base for social comparisons, allowing them to resolve their social or personal uncertainties by providing an attractive reference group of similar others. Thus, truly cohesive groups give their members safe social havens in what might otherwise be perceived to be a threatening external world.

Organizational groups can benefit from cohesiveness, particularly when their members are similar and attracted to one another, when they are small in size (*see* GROUP SIZE), when they have high entrance standards, relative isolation, and AUTONOMY, combined with supervisor support, prestige, PARTICIPATION, and REWARDS (*see* LEADERSHIP). Such forces can contribute to less tension and less pressure (*see* STRESS), less conflict, and less variation among group member PRODUCTIVITY.

See also **Group development; Group norms; Group culture**

Bibliography

Cartwright, D. (1968). The nature of group cohesiveness. In D. Cartwright & A. Zander (Eds), *Group dynamics* (2nd edn). New York: Harper & Row.

McGrath, J. E. (1984). *Groups: Interaction and performance*. Englewood Cliffs NJ: Prentice-Hall.

Roy, D. (1960). Banana time: Job satisfaction and informal interaction. *Human Organization*, **18.**

Staw, B. M. (1975). Attribution of the "causes" of performance: A general alternative interpretation of cross-sectional research on organizations. *Organizational Behavior and Human Performance*, **13**, 414–432.

Sherif, M. (1977). *Intergroup conflict and cooperation*. Norman, OK: University Book Exchange.

J. KEITH MURNIGHAN

group culture *see* CULTURE, GROUP

group decision making A principal assumption behind the structuring of organizational functioning into WORK GROUPS is that better decisions will be made than by group members working alone. However, a good deal of research has shown that groups are subject to social processes which undermine their DECI-

SION MAKING effectiveness. While they make better decisions than the average of decisions made by individual members, work groups consistently fall short of the quality of decisions made by the best individual member (Brown, 1988). The implications of this for the functioning of boards and TOP MANAGEMENT TEAMS are considerable. Organizational behaviorists and social psychologists have therefore devoted considerable effort to identifying the processes which give rise to deficiencies in group decision making:

1 PERSONALITY factors can affect social behavior such as shyness of individual members, who may be hesitant to offer their opinions and knowledge assertively, thereby failing to contribute fully to the group's store of knowledge.
2 Group members are subject to social CONFORMITY effects causing them to withhold opinions and information contrary to the majority view – especially an organizationally dominant view.
3 Group members may lack COMMUNICATION SKILLS and so be unable to present their views and knowledge successfully. The person who has mastered IMPRESSION MANAGEMENT within the organization may disproportionately influence group decisions even in the absence of expertise (*see* INTERPERSONAL SKILLS).
4 The group may be dominated by particular individuals who take up disproportionate "air time" and argue so vigorously with the opinion of others, that their own views prevail. It is noteworthy that "air time" and expertise are correlated in high performing groups and uncorrelated in groups that perform poorly.
5 Particular group members may be egocentric (such as senior organizational members whose egocentricity may have carried them to the top) and consequently unwilling to consider opinions and knowledge contrary to their own, offered by other group members.
6 STATUS and HIERARCHY effects can cause some members' contributions to be valued and attended to disproportionately. When a senior executive is present in a meeting his or her views are likely to have an undue influence on the outcome.
7 RISKY SHIFT is the tendency of work groups to make more extreme decisions than the average of members' decisions. Group decisions tend to be either more risky or more conservative than the average of individual members' opinions or decisions. Thus shifts in the extremity of decisions affecting the competitive strategy of an organization can occur simply as a result of group processes rather than for rational or well-judged reasons.
8 Janis (1982), in his study of policy decisions and fiascoes, identified the phenomenon of GROUPTHINK, whereby tightly knit groups may err in their decision making, as a result of being more concerned with achieving agreement than with the quality of group decision making. This can be especially threatening to organizational functioning where different departments see themselves as competing with one another, promoting "in-group" favoritism and groupthink.
9 The SOCIAL LOAFING effect is the tendency of individuals in group situations to work less hard than they do when individual contributions can be identified and evaluated. In organizations, individuals may put less effort into achieving quality decisions in meetings, as a result of the perception that their contribution is hidden in overall group performance.
10 Diffusion of responsibility can inhibit individuals from taking responsibility for action when in the presence of others. People seem to assume that responsibility will be shouldered by others who are present in a situation requiring action. In organizational settings, individuals may fail to act in a crisis involving the functioning of expensive technology, assessing that others in their team are taking responsibility for making the necessary decisions (*see* CRISES). Consequently, the overall quality of group decisions is threatened.
11 The study of BRAINSTORMING groups shows that quantity and often quality of ideas produced by individuals working separately, consistently exceed quality and quantity of ideas produced by a group working together. This is due to a "production-blocking" effect. Individuals are inhibited from both thinking of new ideas and

offering them aloud to the group by the competing verbalizations of others.

12 Another difficulty besetting group decision making is the tendency of groups to "satisfice" or make *minimally acceptable decisions* (*see* SATISFICING). Observations of group decision-making processes repeatedly show that groups tend to identify the first minimally acceptable solution or decision in a particular situation, and then spend time searching for reasons to accept that decision and reject other possible options. Groups tend not to generate a range of alternatives before selecting, on a rational basis, the most suitable option.

This catalogue of deficiencies in relation to group decision making indicates that the process is more complex and potentially more disastrous than is commonly understood within organizational settings. Recently researchers have begun to identify ways in which some of these deficiencies may be overcome. For example, research on groupthink suggests both that the phenomenon is most likely to occur in groups where a supervisor is particularly dominant, and that cohesiveness per se is not the crucial factor (*see* GROUP COHESIVENESS). Supervisors can therefore be trained to be facilitative, seeking the contributions of individual members before offering their own perceptions.

Rogelberg, Barnes-Farrell, & Lowe (1992), have offered a structured technique for overcoming some of these deficiencies called "the stepladder technique." In this procedure each group member has thinking time before proposing any decisions. Then pairs of group members present their ideas to each other and discuss their respective opinions before making any decisions. The process continues with each subgroup's presentation being followed by time for the group to discuss the problem and ideas proposed. A final decision is put off until the entire group has presented.

Initial evidence suggests that such procedures can enable groups to make decisions of a quality at least as good as those of their best individual members. This is consistent with the finding that fostering disagreement in a structured way in organizations leads to better decisions (Tjosvold & Deemer, 1980). Techniques such as this offer one solution to the problem that unless the most accurate group member is assertive and confident, he or she does not influence the ratings of quality of group decisions. Finally, there is some evidence that work groups which take time out to reflect upon and appropriately modify their decision-making processes are more effective than those which do not (Maier, 1970).

While organizational behaviorists have contributed a great deal to the understanding of how individual performance may be facilitated, research on the processes by which group decision making can be optimized is still in its infancy. The potential pay-off for organizations in improving decision-making quality throughout organizations is enormous.

See also **Nominal group technique; Group dynamics; Group norms; Group culture; Minority group influence**

Bibliography

Brown, R. (1988). *Group processes: Dynamics within and between groups*. Oxford, UK: Blackwell.

Janis, I. L. (1982). *Groupthink: Psychological studies of policy decisions and fiascoes*. Boston, MA: Houghton-Mifflin.

Maier, N. R. F. (1970). *Problem solving and creativity in individuals and groups*. Belmont, CA: Brooks Cole.

Rogelberg, S. G., Barnes-Farrell, J. L. & Lowe, C. A. (1992). The stepladder technique: An alternative group structure facilitating effective group decision making. *Journal of Applied Psychology*, **77**, 730–737.

Stasser, G., Kerr, N. L. & Davies, J. H. (1989). Influence processes and consensus models in decision-making groups. In P. B. Paulus (Ed.), *Psychology of group influence* (pp. 279–326). Hillsdale, NJ: Erlbaum.

Tjosvold, D. & Deemer, D. K. (1980). Effects of controversy within a cooperative or competitive context on organizational decision-making. *Journal of Applied Psychology*, **65**, 590–595.

MICHAEL A. WEST

group development This term expresses the assumption that group behavior changes systematically over time. That means a management committee will function differently after working together for a year than when first convened; a project group will face different challenges near its deadline than mid-way through a task. More importantly, it means that these changes can be understood and predicted through general theoretical concepts. Most group development research has sought to identify characteristic sequences of change, but efforts have also been made to understand how, why, and when developmental changes occur. Such knowledge helps us interpret team behavior accurately, and manage teams in ways that fit their needs.

Group development can be viewed in two ways. First, development can mean the path a group takes over its lifespan toward the accomplishment of its main tasks. This is important for understanding how temporary groups, with specific purposes to accomplish within time limits, progress from start to finish (*see* PROJECT MANAGEMENT). Such research traditionally examined either short-term problem-solving groups in the laboratory, or longer-term therapy or SENSITIVITY TRAINING groups. Most of these studies portray group development as a gradual forward evolution through a universal series of stages. For example, in their seminal work, Bales and Strodtbeck (1951) characterized group problem-solving as a progression from orientation (problem definition), to evaluation (assessment of alternatives), to control (solution construction). Tuckman's (1965) synthesis of group development literature is representative of subsequently proposed sequences: In the "forming" stage, this model suggests members explore and test task and social BOUNDARIES; in "storming," they battle over interpersonal and task issues; in the "norming" stage, groups resolve differences and establish social and work norms; finally "performing," members use the roles and norms they have built to carry out work (*see* GROUP NORMS).

Some recent research on task groups has questioned the PARADIGM of group development as a universal stage progression, and explored aspects of development other than those covered in traditional stage models. Poole (1983) showed there are many sequences through which decisions can develop in groups, not just one. Gersick (1988) found that project teams in organizations did not progress gradually, through uniform stages, but in PUNCTUATED EQUILIBRIUM – alternating periods of momentum and disjunctive change. Soon after convening, each team formed a unique set of behavior patterns and assumptions (largely implicit) about task, teammates, and outside STAKEHOLDERS. Teams worked within these patterns for long portions of their time, and made major changes in compact bursts, at temporal milestones – e.g., half way toward their deadlines. Groups' attention to time, pacing, and deadlines, not the completion of given stages of work, regulated their progress.

A second way to view group development is different from, but compatible with, the first. It concerns groups which last for significant periods of time, whether their life spans are temporary (as above) or open-ended. Here, group development concerns change over time in groups' abilities to work effectively. For example, research on therapy and Sensitivity Training groups examined the maturation of groups' capacities for productive work, as moderated by their developing abilities to deal with TRUST (openness and honesty of communication), CONTROL (competition for power), and dependency (seeking direction from authority figures versus making decisions within the group) (*see* GROUP DECISION MAKING).

Longitudinal studies of WORK GROUPS in organizations are unfortunately rare. The potential value of longitudinal research shows in such work as Katz' (1982) finding, based on cross-sectional study, that research-and-development team effectiveness rises, then declines over the years as intrateam COMMUNICATION waxes and wanes; or Hackman and Walton's (1986) observations on long-term changes in SELF-MANAGED TEAMS' needs for coaching versus independence.

See also **Consensus; Group dynamics; Socialization; Culture, Group**

Bibliography

Bales, R. F. & Strodtbeck, F. L. (1951). Phases in group problem solving. *Journal of Abnormal and Social Psychology*, **46**, 485–495.

Gersick, C. J. G. (1988). Time and transition in work teams: Toward a new model of group development. *Academy of Management Journal*, **31**, 9–41.

Hackman, J. R. & Walton, R. E. (1986). Leading groups in organizations. In P. S. Goodman (Ed.), *Designing effective work groups*. San Francisco: Jossey-Bass.

Katz, R. (1982). The effects of group longevity on project communication and performance. *Administrative Science Quarterly*, **27**, 81–104.

Poole, M. S. (1983). Decision development in small groups II: A study of multiple sequences of decision making. *Communication Monographs*, **48**, 1–24.

Tuckman, B. (1965). Developmental sequence in small groups. *Psychological Bulletin*, **63**, 384–399.

CONNIE J. G. GERSICK

group dynamics The term encompasses the processes that influence people when they interact in group situations. Group dynamics is also "a field of inquiry dedicated to advancing knowledge about the nature of groups, the laws of their development, and their interrelations with individuals, other groups, and larger institutions" (Cartwright & Zander, 1968, p. 7). The field of group dynamics is interdisciplinary in nature. Scholars with a sociological orientation are interested in how groups of people INFLUENCE and are influenced by societal forces. Those with a psychological orientation focus on how individual behavior is affected by a person's presence in and interaction with others in a group. Interest in group dynamics can be traced to seminal scholarship in each of these modern disciplines. Some of the first controlled studies of personal behavior, conducted by Norman Tripplett in 1897, examined how the presence of others affected an individual's performance of simple tasks. This started a stream of research, called SOCIAL FACILITATION, which continues to generate interest. Emile Durkheim and Georg Simmel, two founders of modern sociology, paid critical attention to small group dynamics, arguing that groups are the building blocks of society. Children learn society's norms, what is right and wrong, and even what they consider real in a process called SOCIALIZATION that takes place as they live in and interact with a variety of small groups, such as families, peer groups, school classes, and religious congregations (*see* GROUP NORMS).

Building on these early roots in psychology and sociology, the study of group dynamics in organizational settings began in earnest in the 1930s. Many of the ground-breaking works of ORGANIZATIONAL BEHAVIOR, such as Barnard's (1938) *The Functions of the Executive* and Elton Mayo's landmark studies of industrial behavior at Western Electric's Hawthorne Plant in suburban Chicago, Illinois, paid particular attention to the effects that groups and group membership have on employee behavior and organizational performance (*see* HUMAN RELATIONS MOVEMENT).

Kurt Lewin, another pioneer in the study of group processes, is generally credited with coining and popularizing the term "group dynamics," and is also widely viewed as the "father" of the field because of his extensive research addressing group processes in the 1930s and 1940s. Much of our current knowledge and understanding of group processes was fundamentally shaped by Lewin's research and theory.

Lewin, who once said, "nothing is so practical as a good theory," was a strong proponent of developing and testing THEORY by manipulating key elements of natural settings and carefully observing the behavior that resulted (*see* ACTION RESEARCH). He and his colleagues learned how to change people's attitudes and behaviors through the use of group discussion, LEADERSHIP, and PARTICIPATION. He is perhaps best known for developing the Field Theory of human behavior, which is based on the assumption that individual behavior is a function of a person's unique characteristics and characteristics of the environment, including features of the group, the group members, and the situation. Lewin's followers analyze personal and organizational change using a technique called FORCE FIELD ANALYSIS, in which the driving and restraining forces generated by these various characteristics are first identified and then acted upon to "unfreeze" the current situation. This allows behavior to change (during the "transformation" phase) and become reestablished and maintained by institutionalizing or "refreezing" the group dynamics present in the new situation. Many of the theories and techniques that comprise the modern practice of ORGANIZATION DEVELOPMENT are based on this orientation to ORGANIZATIONAL CHANGE.

Lewin initiated research on many of the central issues of group dynamics, such as interpersonal attraction, GROUP COHESIVENESS, CONFORMITY, and COMPLIANCE, INTERGROUP RELATIONS, LEADERSHIP, and MAN-

AGERIAL STYLE, GROUP DECISION MAKING, and RESISTANCE TO CHANGE. In addition to the areas pioneered by Lewin, group dynamics addresses issues of GROUP DEVELOPMENT and socialization, the dynamics associated with POWER and OBEDIENCE, and the effects of GROUP SIZE and GROUP STRUCTURE, that is, the ROLES, STATUS and AUTHORITY, POWER relations, and COMMUNICATION and interpersonal attraction patterns present among group members.

Group dynamics also examines how individual behavior changes in group situations. Two basic findings are:

(1) audiences tend to facilitate performance of simple, well-learned tasks but inhibit performance of complex, novel tasks (*see* SOCIAL FACILITATION); and
(2) groups make riskier decisions when social norms favor risk-taking and more conservative decisions in situations where risk is shunned (*see* RISKY SHIFT and RISK TAKING).

See also **Workgroups; Task and maintenance behavior; Interactionism; Theory**

Bibliography

Barnard, C. (1938). *The Functions of the Executive*. Cambridge, MA: Harvard University Press.

Cartwright, D. & Zander, A. (1968). *Group dynamics: Research and theory* (3rd edn). New York: Harper & Row.

Forsyth, D. R. (1990). *Group dynamics* (2nd edn). Pacific Grove, CA: Brooks/Cole.

McGrath, J. E. (1984). *Groups: Interaction and performance*. Englewood Cliffs, NJ: Prentice-Hall.

Shaw, M. E. (1981). *Group dynamics* (3rd edn). New York: McGraw-Hill.

KENNETH L. BETTENHAUSEN

group norms These are the informal rules which groups adopt to regulate and regularize group members' behaviors (Feldman, 1984). They are used as social influence mechanisms to move members' behaviors toward the group's preferred standards (*see* CONFORMITY and COMPLIANCE).

Norms are enforced to help the group more readily achieve its goals, to protect the group from potential external threats, to simplify and make predictable what behaviors are expected from group members, to help the group avoid embarrassing interpersonal problems, and to express and clarify what the central VALUES of the group are (Feldman, 1984). Individuals who repeatedly or flagrantly violate group norms are typically sanctioned by other group members.

Most norms develop gradually and informally over time as group members learn what behaviors are necessary for the group to function more effectively, although it is possible for norms to develop more quickly (Hackman, 1976; Bettenhausen & Murnighan, 1991) (*see* GROUP DEVELOPMENT). Groups often have norms of RECIPROCITY, for example, which pressure individuals to return favors given to them by other group members. Feldman (1984) suggests that the norm development process will be accelerated to the extent that supervisors and team members explicitly address group process issues and group members carry over shared behavior patterns from their previous work settings. The norm development process will also be accelerated when critical events early in the group's history establish important precedents and when initial behavior patterns prove effective and establish some primacy effects.

Several taxonomies of norms have been developed. Wallace and Szilagyi (1982) make a distinction between "behavior norms" and "performance norms"; behavior norms are rules that standardize how people act at work on a daily basis, while performance norms are rules that standardize employee output. March (1954) suggests there are three basic types of norms: preferred-value norms, unattainable-ideal norms, and attainable-ideal norms. In "preferred-value norms," the group specifies a range of acceptable behavior; both too little of the behavior and too much of the behavior are disapproved of by other group members. With "unattainable-ideal norms," group members receive increasing approval the more frequently and more intensely they exhibit desired behaviors. "Attainable-ideal norms" encourage members to engage in desired behaviors, but only up to a certain point; after a sufficient amount of the behavior is engaged in, the group will not continue rewarding its members for more of that behavior.

The structural characteristics of group norms have been most precisely specified by Jackson (1966) in his "Return Potential Model" (*see* GROUP STRUCTURE). Jackson's model allows researchers and observers to characterize group norms by five indices: the point of maximum approval; the range of tolerable behavior; the "potential return difference" (i.e., the amount of approval versus disapproval associated with a behavior); the intensity of the norm; and the crystallization of the norm (i.e., the degree of consensus among group members about the norm).

Empirical field research on how norms develop and are enforced has substantially lagged descriptive and theoretical work. In large part, this may be due to the methodological problems of measuring norms across time or across groups in organizational settings. Much more attention has been given as to how to change group norms (*see* ORGANIZATIONAL DEVELOPMENT), particularly in terms of unfreezing groups from their existing behavior patterns, facilitating groups examining their own interpersonal processes, and helping groups discover some of the dysfunctional consequences of their current set of norms.

See also **Group dynamics; Group cohesiveness; Group decision making; Resistance to change**

Bibliography

Bettenhausen, K. L. & Murnighan, J. K. (1991). The development of an intragroup norm and the effects of interpersonal and structural changes. *Administrative Science Quarterly*, **36**, 20–35.

Feldman, D. C. (1984). The development and enforcement of group norms. *Academy of Management Review*, **9**, 47–53.

Hackman, J. R. (1976). Group influences on individuals. In M. Dunnette (Ed.), *Handbook of industrial and organizational psychology*, (pp. 1455–1525). Chicago: Rand McNally.

Jackson, J. (1966). A conceptual and measurement model for norms and roles. *Pacific Sociological Review*, **9**, 35–47.

March, J. (1954). Group norms and the active minority. *American Sociological Review*, **19**, 733–741.

Wallace, M. J. & Szilagyi, A. D. (1982). *Managing behavior in organizations*. Glenview, IL: Scott Foresman.

DANIEL C. FELDMAN

group roles Within the study of GROUP DYNAMICS it has long been established that members may contribute in different ways to the effectiveness of DECISION MAKING and problem solving. The pioneering observational studies of Bales revealed that these could be principally broken down into task-related and socio-emotional behaviors (*see* TASK AND MAINTENANCE BEHAVIOR). A series of studies with managers led Meredith Belbin to elaborate the idea of group roles, developing a questionnaire measure to identify eight preferred styles of group participation: Chairman (coordinating effort), Shaper (directing activity), Plant (creating ideas), Team Worker (attending to group process); Monitor-Evaluator (critically assessing products and activities), Resource-Investigator (seeking information and resources), Company Worker (testing and implementing ideas) and Completer-Finisher (attending to detail and progress chasing). Belbin subsequently added a ninth Specialist preferred role. He also identified characteristic individual profiles from psychometric data associated with each preferred role.

The taxonomy has proved extremely popular in MANAGEMENT DEVELOPMENT and consulting, as a tool to aid TEAMBUILDING and to seek high performance through achieving a balance of essential group functions. This model has found little favor in academic writings, largely due to controversy about the robustness and factorial structure of the measurement model (Furnham, Stale, & Pendelton, 1993). A similar taxonomy has been developed by Margerison (1990) and colleagues, also more widely used in CONSULTANCY than in research.

The central idea clearly has intuitive appeal and practical utility, by helping groups to introspect about potential inbalances in their modes of conduct, and will probably continue to be used widely by practitioners for this purpose. However, a more solid body of impartial research evidence will be needed before the taxonomy is accepted as a valid and reliable characterization of INDIVIDUAL DIFFERENCES in preferred group roles and as a means of differentially predicting individual behavior in groups (*see* RELIABILITY; VALIDITY).

See also **Group decision making; Group structure; Groupthink; Role; Role taking**

Bibliography

Belbin, M. (1993). *Team roles at work: A strategy for human resource management.* Oxford, UK: Butterworth Heinemann.

Furnham, A., Steele, H. & Pendleton, D. (1993). A psychometric assessment of the Belbin team-role self-perception inventory. *Journal of Occupational and Organizational Psychology*, **66**, 245–258.

Margerison, C. & McCann, D. (1990). *Team management.* London: Mercury.

NIGEL NICHOLSON

group size The group's size is one of the most fundamental factors that shape GROUP STRUCTURE and GROUP DYNAMICS. Determining a group's size is not as straightforward as it first appears, especially in work settings. In almost every case, one could break a given group into smaller subgroups or combine it with other groups to form a larger entity that could also be considered a group. Research examining the effects of group size must, therefore, carefully consider which group boundary is appropriate for the theoretical issue being addressed.

In work and nonwork settings groups tend to be relatively small, ranging, on average, from two to seven members. Even when larger WORK GROUPS are created, most interaction occurs in groups of two or three. The dyad is unique in many ways. It is essentially stable and is, by definition, the only group that no longer exists with the loss of a single member. With the introduction of a third member, more intricate GROUP DYNAMICS emerge, especially those surrounding COALITION FORMATION, NEGOTIATION, and POWER. As size increases, groups tend to become more complex and more formally structured: ROLES, STATUS, and norms become more clearly defined and play a greater role in group interaction (*see* GROUP NORMS).

The relationship between group size and group performance depends largely on the group's composition and the type of task undertaken by the group. The number and diversity of group members affect the amount and range of resources, e.g., time, ability, knowledge, skill, range of opinion, etc., that can be brought to bear on the group task (*see* ORGANIZATIONAL DEMOGRAPHY). Thus, resources increase as the group gets larger. With increased size, however, come costs – coordination of effort becomes more difficult, attraction to the group, GROUP COHESIVENESS, morale, and member satisfaction tend to decline; COMMUNICATION among group members is more complex and less frequent, fewer people participate in group discussions, members' MOTIVATION is generally lower, and SOCIAL LOAFING increases.

See also **Group decision making; Minority group influence; Management of diversity; Organizational size**

Bibliography

Hare, A. P. (1976). *Handbook of small group research* (2nd edn). New York: Free Press.

KENNETH BETTENHAUSEN

group structure This is the stable pattern of relationships among the various unique positions occupied by members of the group. It is constantly generated by, and therefore can be observed in, the ongoing interaction of group members. It reflects the abilities and motivations of group members and the physical and social environments of the group. Because it reflects the pattern of relationships among *positions* in the group, group structure exists relatively independently of the individuals who occupy those positions. Group structure, therefore, provides a key to understanding behavior in groups that cannot be explained in terms of the traits, ATTITUDES, and personalities of individual group members (*see* PERSONALITY).

Group structure is defined along a number of interrelated dimensions, such as; the ROLES group members occupy, the STATUS and AUTHORITY of the different positions in the group, and the POWER relations, COMMUNICATION patterns and interpersonal attraction patterns present among the positions. Group structure is embodied in and maintained by

NORMS which prescribe accepted and expected behavior for people holding various positions in the group (*see* GROUP NORMS).

Any group which requires some DIVISION OF LABOR and coordination of effort establishes a structure to reduce uncertainty and facilitate task accomplishment and efficient group performance. Formal group structure is explicitly established and codified by the larger organization of which the group is a part. Informal structure may or may not be explicitly recognized by group members. Even when not explicitly stated, however, group members usually have little trouble identifying the roles and relationships that structure their behavior in the group.

Group structure emerges sometimes incrementally, sometimes abruptly as the group moves through successive stages of GROUP DEVELOPMENT. In mature groups a unique structure tends to persist even as it evolves with changes in GROUP SIZE or composition, task requirements, or contextual demands. This stability allows groups to function even as individual group members move in or out of the group, or in or out of various positions within the group.

While group structure encompasses all the elements described above, most research examines what is commonly called "single structures," that is, the effects of a single structural dimension, such as the authority structure, communication structure, or power structure. Each of these issues is addressed in greater detail elsewhere in this volume. A major managerial task is to establish formal group structures and then to codify them through written JOB DESCRIPTIONS which help reduce STRESS brought on by ROLE CONFLICT and ROLE AMBIGUITY. Newcomers learn their places in both the formal and informal group structures through REALISTIC JOB PREVIEWS, TRAINING, and SOCIALIZATION programs. The related issue of how individuals enact their ROLES within the group (*see* ROLE SET, ROLE TAKING) is the focus of ROLE THEORY.

Effective groups develop a good fit between their structure and their members' abilities and personalities (*see* ABILITY). For example, people with strong safety or security needs would more likely feel and perform better in groups with an authoritarian structure while people with strong SELF-ESTEEM needs would prefer groups with a more egalitarian structure. Likewise effective groups develop a good fit between their structure and task demands. A centralized communication structure facilitates the efficient performance of simple tasks. Complex tasks require a more decentralized and redundant structure with multiple communication links among members.

See also **Group decision making; Organizational design; Group culture**

Bibliography

Forsyth, D. R. (1990). *Group dynamics*. Belmont, CA: Brooks/Cole.

Shaw, M. E. (1981). *Group dynamics* (3rd edn). New York: McGraw-Hill.

KENNETH BETTENHAUSEN

groupthink This term was coined by scholars who were critical of the group dynamics movement in the 1960s and 1970s and it's impact on management theory, especially participative management (*see* PARTICIPATION).

Management theory was dominated in these years by the writings of Douglas McGregor, Rensis Likert, and Robert Blake and Jane Mouton (*see* MANAGERIAL GRID). All of these writers were influenced by the emphasis on group dynamics (especially the T group and the laboratory method) (*see* SENSITIVITY TRAINING) and a main focus of their analysis was that managers should involve people in the decisions, goals, and plans which affect them, and that decisions should be made by consensus (all members agreeing that the decision made sense and that they were willing to implement the decision.)

This CONSENSUS emphasis, according to some, makes it possible for some powerful members of a group to coerce less powerful group members to go along with a decision in public even though they may have private reservations. The earlier work of Sherif and Asch had clearly demonstrated that many naive subjects were willing to change their personal observations and judgments to agree with the majority in group experimental situations (*see* GROUP DECISION MAKING). This whole critical vein was ably summarized in a book by Janis

(1972) *Victims of Groupthink*. Janis pointed out, with cases from the current political scene, that decision makers with power may handle STRESS situations by demanding CONFORMITY from subordinates and isolating or threatening those who dare challenge the dominate position. Milgram (1974) at Yale had also shown in his research that many subjects were willing to capitulate to the demands of an AUTHORITY person and engage in behaviors that were in violation of some of their own VALUES.

Additionally, these criticisms were augmented by data coming out of the Korean War about the use of brainwashing techniques on American prisoners-of-war and other stories about the use of thought control methods, in groups, used by the Chinese Communists.

Thus it is clear that the groupthink criticism of the use of groups in organizations had some solid basis in fact from research and some emotional support from stories about the communists, the then most significant "enemy."

These criticisms had a positive impact on the whole group-centered, participative management movement. Almost all those who advocated participative approaches began to emphasize the importance of open discussion, disagreement, contrary opinions, diversity, and even controversy.

There is good evidence to indicate that suppressed controversy, or difference, with no allowance for open discussion and the sharing of contrary opinions was a major factor in the fiasco of the Bay of Pigs under President Kennedy, the Challenger disaster in 1986, and some commercial airplane crashes. It seems that all of these disasters could have been averted if all contrary ideas and information had been openly invited and explored (*see* CRISES, ACCIDENTS, ERRORS).

Tjosvold (1991) reviews some of the situations above and summarizes the current position on constructive controversy – the opposite view to groupthink – "Controversy, when discussed in a cooperative context, promotes elaboration of views, the search for new information and ideas, and the integration of apparently opposing positions."

See also **Group norms; Group culture; Group development; Team-building**

Bibliography

Janis, I. L. (1972). *Victims of groupthink*. Boston: Houghton Mifflin.

Milgram, S. (1974). *Obedience to authority: An experimental view*. New York: Harper & Row.

Tjosvold, D. (1991). *Team organization*. New York: Wiley.

WILLIAM G. DYER

growth need strength This refers to the strength of an individual's needs for personal growth and self-direction at work (Hackman & Oldham, 1976). Growth Need Strength (GNS) is a central part of JOB CHARACTERISTICS Theory and is expected to affect the way individuals respond to complex, challenging jobs characterized by high levels of AUTONOMY, variety, and personal DISCRETION at work. Specifically, employees with high GNS are expected to appreciate and respond enthusiastically to the opportunities for personal accomplishment provided by a complex, challenging job (*see* COMPLEXITY). On the other hand, individuals with relatively low GNS may not recognize the opportunities for growth provided by the job, or they may experience the complex job as threatening and balk at being stretched too far by the work.

Numerous empirical investigations have demonstrated that high GNS employees exhibit higher performance, attendance, and satisfaction on complex jobs than their low GNS counterparts (Kulik, Oldham, & Hackman, 1987). Moreover, research has demonstrated that GNS relates strongly to an employee's level of education – the more educated the employee, the higher the GNS (Hackman & Oldham, 1976). Unfortunately, the effects of the work environment on an employee's GNS remain unclear. That is, research has not yet established if individuals' growth needs are shaped by the complexity of their jobs or if these needs are stable characteristics of people that are relatively independent of work environments (*see* PERSONALITY).

See also **Job satisfaction, performance, job design, need theory, motivation; Self-actualization; ERG theory; Motivation and performance**

Bibliography

Hackman, J. R. & Oldham, G. R. (1976). Motivation through the design of work: Test of a theory. *Organizational Behavior and Human Performance*, **16**, 250–279.

Kulik, C. T., Oldham, G. R. & Hackman, J. R. (1987). Work design as an approach to person–environment fit. *Journal of Vocational Behavior*, **31**, 278–296.

GREG R. OLDHAM

— H —

halo effect This is said to occur when people are assigned the same or similar ratings on different characteristics, i.e., the ratings between the different characteristics are correlated. There is much research evidence to suggest that raters are prone to make ERRORS by allowing their general impressions of a person to influence ratings of specific qualities. If this happens during the completion of a rating form the separate characteristics rated will be given more similar ratings than they should be and halo error will be present. It is important to distinguish between the halo effect and halo error. One of the difficulties in doing this is that many human qualities are indeed related and accurate ratings of these qualities should correlate. Halo ERROR is present only when the observed correlations between the characteristics involved are bigger than the true correlations. Unfortunately, it is often impossible to tell whether the correlations between variables are a reflection of the true level of relationship between the variables or due to error on the part of the rater (*see* RESEARCH DESIGN). Probably the best way to avoid halo error is to train raters well and ensure that they are aware of the possibility of halo error, though this does not always work. Traditionally halo error has been seen as a widespread problem with ratings. More recent views suggest that this may not be so (Murphy, Jako, & Anhalt, 1993).

See also **Psychological testing; Selection methods; Selection interviewing; Bias**

Bibliography

Murphy, K. R., Jako, R. A. & Anhalt, R. L. (1993). Nature and consequences of halo error: A critical analysis. *Journal of Applied Psychology*, **78**, 218–225.

IVAN ROBERTSON

hardiness In attempting to discover a personality trait that might protect managers from the effects of STRESS Kobasa and Maddi proposed the concept of hardiness.

Hardy people were discovered to have three characteristics: a commitment to seeing stressful situations as meaningful and interesting, to seeing such situations as potentially in their own control; and as seeing change/threat as a *challenge* to be overcome. Many studies of hardiness have been carried out. Funk (1992) identifies a number of issues which bear on the main question – Do some personalities experience more or less strain under the same levels of stress?

One issue is measurement. Early measures used 6 scales – 71 items with two scales for each of the three subcomponents. Various shorter measures have been derived from these, some being reworded to eliminate the problem that the items were all phrased negatively. Some new measures have also been created.

Although the three subcomponents do not correlate very highly with each other it is normally the case that scores are added to give a hardiness score. This is inconsistent with the conceptual definition which assumes hardy people are high on COMMITMENT, control, and challenge. Many studies have shown hardiness to be correlated (modestly) with illness and psychological symptoms, but most other hypotheses (e.g., buffering) are not consistently found, and Funk shows that hardiness is correlated with neuroticism which confounds the relationship with illness. In sum,

RELIABILITY, VALIDITY, and even conceptual clarity, have not yet been convincingly demonstrated.

See also **Personality; Mental health; Burnout; Self-efficacy; Type-A**

Bibliography

Funk, S. C. (1992). Hardiness: A review of theory and research. *Health Psychology*, 11, (5), 335–345.

ROY L. PAYNE

Hawthorne effect This effect, observed in field experiments, occurs when:

(1) one or more changes or manipulations are made by researchers in a field setting;
(2) the persons in the target sample experiencing the change(s) are aware of the experimental manipulations; and
(3) the latter alter their behavior *not because of the specific variables manipulated* but because of the attention they receive.

As a result, the researchers may falsely attribute the observed effects on behavior to the variables manipulated rather than the attention. The effect gets its name from the research studies in which it was identified and labeled.

In the late 1920s and early 1930s, several studies were carried out at Western Electric's Hawthorne Works in Chicago, Illinois (*see* HUMAN RELATIONS MOVEMENT). The research, conducted by E. Mayo, F. J. Roethlisberger, W. J. Dickson, T. N. Whitehead, and others from the Graduate School of Business Administration at Harvard University, in cooperation with a number of persons at the Hawthorne Works, began as an investigation of the effects of illumination intensity on employees, particularly on employee performance. The goal of the research was to find the optimal level of illumination for work involving the assembly and inspection of relays used in telephone equipment. Therefore, the researchers simply varied the amount of illumination over time and measured changes in performance, among other things. The unanticipated finding was that performance did not covary with illumination but continued to improve over the course of the experiment, even when the level of illumination was reduced to very low levels. The post hoc explanation for the observed pattern of results was that the employees very much appreciated the attention that they received from the researchers, management, and others for being part of the experiment, and their improved performance was one way in which they expressed their appreciation. The explanation stuck, and the phenomenon has been known as the Hawthorne Effect ever since.

Ironically, the Hawthorne Effect was discovered only because, in the eyes of the researchers, their research had "failed." Had performance decreased as the amount of light decreased and vice versa, the Hawthorne Effect would not have been discovered. Since the effects on performance of illumination and those of attention were in opposite directions, the pattern of results fit one explanation, that of the Hawthorne Effect, and not the other.

Often in organizational behavior research in the field, the phenomenon of interest is manipulated in a way that leads to predicted changes in behavior that are in same direction as those that would result from the Hawthorne Effect. For example, interventions designed to empower workers, enrich jobs, increase SELF-EFFICACY, focus on quality, or in some other way impact positively on performance may be implemented in such a way that they create a Hawthorne Effect. In such cases, if performance changes as is predicted, based on the construct of interest (empowerment, increased self-efficacy, etc.), the tendency is to attribute the effect to the construct under investigation; the alternative explanation of a Hawthorne Effect is often ignored. At the very least, when the Hawthorne Effect is a possible cause of results that are found, it should be mentioned. Better yet, multiple studies and carefully designed research should be conducted to insure that effects attributed to constructs of interest are, most likely, caused by those constructs and not other common variables confounded with the constructs of interest, particularly those variables considered to cause the Hawthorne Effect.

See also **Performance, individual; Productivity; Research design; Research methods; Bias; Working conditions**

Bibliography

Roethlisberger, F. J. & Dickson, W. J. (1939). *Management and the worker*. Cambridge, MA: Harvard University Press.

DANIEL R. ILGEN

hierarchy This term is used in several different senses. One implies the STATUS differences that exist among various individuals in an organization, sometimes referred to as the status pyramid (*see* STRATIFICATION). This is commonly found in public sector organizations where ranks of individuals are distinguished upon the basis of particular kinds of prerogatives (*see* GOVERNMENT AGENCIES). More typically the term refers to the hierarchy of AUTHORITY, that is, the chain of command in an organization. In formal organizations, each position is arranged so that it reports to another, higher in the chain. Invested in each position is a set of rights and obligations, most of which refer to the ability to give orders to subordinates and supervise them. This arrangement is considered to be a formal one because the authority to give orders to others is based on the position that one occupies and not on any personal characteristics. Weber referred to this as the rational–legal basis of authority. It is quite different and not to be confused with informal sources of POWER that can accrue from control over information or personal characteristics (*see* POWER BASES).

The concept of hierarchy of authority has also been distinguished from DECENTRALIZATION, which is a more meso-level concept, concerned with PARTICIPATION of decision making or the DELEGATION of decisions to a particular level such as the divisional level (*see* DECISION MAKING). Hierarchy of authority, as has been interpreted in the literature, represents is more micro in focus.

During the 1960s, Hall (1992) developed scales for measuring the hierarchy of authority so that it could be distinguished from FORMALIZATION and kindred concepts associated with Weber's model of BUREAUCRACY. His measures were then used in a series of studies of welfare agencies (*see* Hage, 1980).

These studies indicated that strong hierarchies of authority were highly and positively associated with centralization of decision making POWER but equally strongly and negatively associated with morale as measured by JOB SATISFACTION scales. Generally, hierarchy of authority is a less important predictor of other organizational characteristics than centralization. And consistent with the more micro operationalization of the concept in Hall's scale, hierarchy of authority predicts better to other micro level concepts.

See also **Differentiation; Classical design theory; Span of control; Organizational design**

Bibliography

Hage, J. (1990). *Organizations: Form, process and transformation*. New York: Wiley.

Hall, R. H. (1992). *Organizations: Structures, processes, and outcomes* (5th edn). Englewood Cliffs, NJ: Prentice-Hall.

JERALD HAGE

home country national *see* EXPATRIATES

honesty testing This term refers to a broad category of tests, including polygraphs and paper-and-pencil "integrity" tests, that have been used primarily by U.S. employers to screen prospective employees (*see* SELECTION METHODS). Research has led to legislation restricting the use of the polygraph for employee screening in the United States (Saxe, Dougherty, & Cross, 1985) and to the development and increased use of paper-and-pencil examinations called integrity tests.

Integrity tests have been divided into two types (Sacket, Burris, & Callahan, 1989). The first type, "overt integrity tests" generally include a section on attitudes toward theft and a section that asks the individual to admit to theft. The second type, "personality-based measures," is more general and avoids explicit references to theft or other illegal activities.

Evaluations of integrity tests vary depending upon the tests studied and the criterion predicted. However, recent reviews acknowledge that:

(1) studies have improved;
(2) evidence supporting predictive VALIDITY is increasing (Ones, Viswesvaran, & Schmidt,

1993; Sackett, Burris, & Callahan, 1989); and

(3) integrity tests do not adversely impact protected groups (Sackett, Burris, & Callahan, 1989) (*see* DISCRIMINATION).

Some important remaining issues include ethics in honesty testing (e.g., questionable marketing tactics), the influence of faking and social desirability, the construct validity of integrity tests (Ones, Viswesvaran, & Schmidt, 1993; Sackett, Burris, & Callahan, 1989), and the relative influence of individual traits versus organizational influences on employee honesty and dishonesty. Finally, Ones et al. (1993) proposed that integrity tests tap a broader construct called conscientiousness, a potentially important determinant of overall job performance that has been missing in previous motivational research.

See also **Business ethics; Psychological testing; Recruitment Employee theft; Justice, procedural**

Bibliography

Ones, D. S. Viswesvaran, C. & Schmidt, F. (1993). Comprehensive meta-analysis of integrity test validities: Findings and implications for personnel selection and theories of job performance. *Journal of Applied Psychology*, **78**, 679–703.

Sackett, P. R., Burris, L. R. & Callahan, C. (1989). Integrity testing for personnel section: An update. *Personnel Psychology*, **42**, 491–529.

Saxe, L., Dougherty, D. & Cross, T. (1985). The validity of polygraph testing: Scientific evidence and public policy. *American Psychologist*, **40**, 355–356.

U.S. Congressional Office of Technology Assessment (1990). *The use of integrity tests for pre-employment screening* (Report No. OTA-SET-442), Washington, DC: U.S. Government Printing Office.

LINDA TREVINO

host country nationals *see* EXPATRIATES

hours of work Historically, most attention on working time has been paid to issues of duration and the effects of shiftworking. From World War One onward, psychologists have examined the effects of the length of the working period on fatigue and performance. More recently this has developed into a considerable body of research on the relationship between shiftwork and health (*see* Mott, Mann, McLoughlin, & Warwick, 1965; Folkard & Monk, 1985). It is widely agreed that individuals vary considerably in their ability to adapt to shiftwork, but to nightwork in particular, adjustment is at best only partial (*see* INDIVIDUAL DIFFERENCES). Circadian rhythms are slow to adjust and do so only partially, resulting in reduced physiological performance during night shifts. Rapid shift rotations and rest periods which reinstate normal diurnal living patterns generally impede the degree of any adjustment to nightwork (for a review of nightwork and its implications for social and physical well-being, *see* Carpentier and Cazamian (1977). The amount of shiftworking is generally increasing, due to factors such as the pursuit of increased capital utilization and changes in consumer behavior which impact upon the hours of operation of service activities. The proportion of nightwork in the total of shiftwork is, however, declining.

The average duration of weekly working time has fallen considerably over the twentieth century with many workers in Europe now working a basic workweek of 35–38 hours. Hours of work are somewhat longer in the United States and particularly South-East Asia (*see* INTERNATIONAL MANAGEMENT). In Japan for example, this longer working time is the result not only of somewhat longer weekly working hours but also of the tendency for many Japanese employees, particularly in non-manual jobs, not to take their full holiday entitlement (Blyton, 1989).

As the length of the working week has declined, there has been increased interest in compressed workweeks, whereby individual weekly hours are performed in fewer than the normal number of workdays. Employer interest in compression stems partly from a desire to maintain operating/opening hours as the duration of the working week falls. An extreme example of this has been some renewed interest in 12-hour shiftworking in a number of industries, including continuous process operations (Blyton, 1994). In some cases, these are linked to the calculation of hours on an annual rather than a weekly basis. Elsewhere, too, annual hours schemes appear to be spreading, not least in sectors which have a predictable seasonal variation in demand. By calculating hours on an annual rather than weekly basis, and by arranging working weeks to be longer at busier times and shorter during slacker periods, employers are potentially able to save on overtime costs and avoid over-production in nonpeak periods.

Reductions in working time are also focusing attention on the utilization of work hours. One common development in assembly line operations, for example, has been the introduction of stricter supervision of shift start and stop times (sometimes known as "bell-to-bell working"). If duration of the working week falls further (as can be expected toward a norm of 35 hours), employers are likely to look increasingly for offsetting gains in both the utilization and arrangement of hours of work.

See also **Flexitime; Working conditions; Productivity; Performance, individual; Psychological contract**

Bibliography

Blyton, P. (1989). Hours of work. In R. Bean (Ed.), *International Labour Statistics* (pp. 127–145). London: Routledge.

Blyton, P. (1994). Working hours. In K. Sisson (Ed.), *Personnel management: A comprehensive guide to theory and practice in Britain* (2nd edn, pp. 495–526). Oxford, UK: Blackwell.

Carpentier, J. & Cazamian, P. (1977). *Nightwork*. Geneva: International Labour Organisation.

Folkard, S. & Monk, T. H. (Eds) (1985). *Hours of work: Temporal factors in work-scheduling*. Chichester, UK: Wiley.

Mott, P. E., Mann, F. C., McLoughlin, Q. & Warwick, D. P. (1965). *Shiftwork: The social psychological and physical consequences*. Ann Arbor: University of Michigan Press.

PAUL BLYTON

human–computer interaction Human–computer interaction (HCI) is the descriptive and prescriptive study of how people use computer systems and how computer systems are integrated into organizations (Frese, 1987; Shackel, 1991). It should help in the design process (Card & Polson, 1990) (with SOFTWARE ERGONOMICS being one aspect of HCI).

Organizations may either design their technical systems with the workers in mind or they may attempt to optimize the technical system in isolation. The latter strategy often leads to badly designed work places, resistance by the workers, and jobs in which work has to be done that could not yet be automatized (e.g., data typists) (*see* SOCIOTECHNICAL THEORY; RESISTANCE TO CHANGE; ADVANCED MANUFACTURING TECHNOLOGY).

Studies of the impact of the introduction of new TECHNOLOGY at the work place (technology assessment, Björn-Anderson, Eason, & Robey, 1986; Kling, 1980) have shown that organizational changes are quite gradual and they are usually not planned to go along with new technology. However, POWER issues usually play an important role. Sometimes introducing new technology leads to increased Taylorization but they are also countervailing forces (*see* SCIENTIFIC MANAGEMENT). Clearly, the idea of technological determinism – the technology determining the organization – is wrong, since, for example, both higher and lower workers' control can accompany the introduction of computer systems (*see* INFORMATION TECHNOLOGY).

Introducing computers at the work place is smoother if PARTICIPATION in this process is used and if TRAINING is well done. The issue of training has been revitalized in HCI (Frese, 1987). Research has shown that training should be exploratory, allow the development of optimal mental models, and integrate work tasks to increase transfer; people should be encouraged to make ERRORS and learn from them (error training, *see* Frese, in press). Workers find handbooks difficult to use, therefore minimal manuals (Carroll, Smith-Kerker, Ford, & Mazur-Rimetz, 1987, "slash the verbiage") should be developed.

There has been some discussion of STRESS increasing with new technology. This depends on how computer work is organized. While there are dangers that introducing computers leads to higher time pressure, system response time, and breakdowns, the more important issue is whether or not the work situation allow operators control, the use of SKILLS, and leaves the social network intact (Frese, 1987) (*see* NETWORK ANALYSIS). In some jobs, for example, data typists, there is a correlation between hours of computer work and psychosomatic complaints (particularly eye and back strain) while in other jobs there is no relationship (e.g., computer programmers). The effects depend on the work content (*see* JOB DESIGN; JOB DESKILLING). If the job provides little AUTONOMY, FEEDBACK, and task significance, task identity, and task variety, there is a higher degree of strain with longer computer hours (*see* JOB CHARACTERISTICS).

However, a general danger may be that computer work is more abstract (e.g., blue collar workers do not know what really is happening in their computer driven tool and dye machine) and that this causes stress.

The issue of changes to COMMUNICATION patterns in computer mediated work has also been researched. In contrast to face-to-face communication, computer mediated communication reduces the impact of etiquette, power and STATUS differentials and is more democratic and participatory (Kiesler, Siegel, & McGuire, 1984). Furthermore, there is higher task focus and decision quality but longer decisions times, lower consensus, and lower satisfaction (McLeod, 1992).

Computers are tools in organizational and work design. Concepts that go beyond this and attempt to replace workers by machines (e.g., artificial intelligence, expert systems, etc.) have been shown to be impractical. While undoubtedly, computers and software will become more powerful, strategies to replace experts and workers have not been successful; rather computer systems should be used as tools to support experts.

See also **Information technology; Computer-aided design; Information processing; Cognitive processes**

Bibliography

Bjorn-Anderson, N., Eason, K. & Robey, D. (1986). *Managing computer impact: An international study of management and organization.* Norwood NJ: Ablex.

Card, S. K. & Polson, P. G. (1990). Special issue on foundations of human–computer interaction. *Human–Computer Interaction*, **5** (2), 3.

Carroll, J. M., Smith-Kerker, P. L., Ford, J. R. & Mazur-Rimetz, S. A. (1987–1988). The minimal manual. *Human–Computer Interaction*, **2**, 123–154.

Frese, M. (1987). Human–computer interaction in the office. In C. L. Cooper & I. T. Robertson (Eds), *International review of industrial and organizational psychology*. Chichester: Wiley.

Frese, M. (in press) Error management in training: Conceptual and empirical results. In S. Bagnara, C. E. Zucchermaglio & S. Stucky (Eds), *Organizational learning and technological change*. New York: Springer Verlag.

Kiesler, S. Siegel, J. & McGuire, T. W. (1984). Social psychological aspects of computer-mediated communication. *American Psychologist*, **39**, 1123–1134.

Kling, R. (1980). Social analyses of computing: Theoretical perspectives in recent empirical research. *Computing Surveys*, **12**, 61–110.

McLeod, P. L. (1992). An assessment of the experimental literature on electronic support of group work: Results of a meta-analysis. *Human Computer Interaction*, **7**, 257–280.

Shackel, B. (1991). Whence and where – a short history of human–computer interaction. In H.-J. Bullinger (Ed.), *Human aspects in computing* (pp. 4–18). Amsterdam: Elsevier.

MICHAEL FRESE

human relations movement This body of theory and practice is popularly associated with the sociologist Elton May (1880–1949) whose basic idea was that workers had strong social needs which they tried to satisfy through membership of informal social groups at the workplace. Managerial attempts to improve JOB SATISFACTION and work MOTIVATION had to take account of these needs and could not treat workers simply as economic individuals wanting to maximize pay and minimize effort (*see* SCIENTIFIC MANAGEMENT).

Human relations thinking emerged from a series of experiments conducted between 1924 and the early 1940s in Chicago which claimed to have found positive associations between workgroup cohesion (*see* GROUP COHESIVENESS), participative supervisory styles (*see* MANAGERIAL STYLE), job satisfaction, and job performance (*see* PERFORMANCE, INDIVIDUAL). These ideas led to a substantial body of research on WORKGROUPS, on supervisory style, and on worker attitudes (mostly in the 1950s and early 1960s) and the main impact of the movement in organizations was through programmes of supervisory TRAINING.

Many OB theorists are suspicious of the concept of social need; research on SUPERVISION has shown that a participative style does not always produce higher satisfaction and/or performance; and cohesive groups can promote low, as well as high, levels of performance: for these reasons the ideas of the movement have largely fallen out of favor.

See also **Motivation and performance; Management, classical theory; Participation; Theory x and y**

Bibliography

Rose, M. (1988). *Industrial behaviour: Theoretical development since Taylor* (3rd edn). Harmondsworth, UK: Penguin.

JOHN KELLY

human resource management Although the term has been used for many years, human resource management (HRM) came to prominence during the 1980s as pressure grew to give greater priority to the effective management of people at work. In considering this topic, we need to understand why it has come to prominence, to identify the distinctive characteristics of HRM, to assess its impact and, finally, to review its status some years after it first attracted widespread attention.

The pressures which led to greater interest in HRM in the early 1980s, some of which still persist, included growing market competition, changing expectations among the workforce, the growing complexity of the management process, the declining pressure from traditional INDUSTRIAL RELATIONS and availability of models of "EXCELLENCE." Competitive market pressures, demanding both fuller use of human resources and a higher quality of goods and services arguably provided the main pressure, while a key trigger was provided in accounts of successful companies (*see* COMPETITIVENESS). Analysis of Japanese companies appeared to demonstrate that they succeeded through a distinctive approach to management of human resources (*see* INTERNATIONAL HUMAN RESOURCES MANAGEMENT; INTERNATIONAL MANAGEMENT). The importance of human resources was reinforced, this time through a distinctively American perspective, by Peters and Waterman's (1982) book *In Search of Excellence*. This claimed that the best American companies succeeded by emphasizing the "soft" side of management, that is, the management of human resources. Reinforced by hyperbole and rhetoric, this message captured the popular imagination of industry, and, building on the optimistic spirit of the times, seemed to offer a counter to the growing competition from countries like Japan.

One of the distinctive features of human resource management (HRM), emphasized in particular by writers from Harvard (Beer, Spector, Lawrence, Quinn Mills, & Walton, 1985), is that as a critical success factor it is too important to be left to human resource specialists. What was needed was to present HRM as an approach which appealed to line managers. This meant that traditional PERSONNEL MANAGEMENT had to be repackaged and extended.

The Harvard approach identifies four generic human resource activities common to all organizations. These they term employee influence, human resource flow, reward systems, and work systems. Organizations have choices about how they want to pursue these according to the policy goals to which they give priority. By implication they, like their colleagues from MIT (Kochan, Katz, & McKersie, 1986) accept an OPEN SYSTEMS approach, indicating that a range of influences are likely to determine policy priorities. The Harvard team suggest four HR policy outcomes – COMMITMENT, COMPETENCE, congruence, and cost-effectiveness. Achievement of these should result in improvements in organizational performance and individual and societal wellbeing (*see* ORGANIZATIONAL EFFECTIVENESS). While this approach is plausible, it is not clear why it should hold particular appeal for line managers; nor is it distinctly different from what has been advocated over the years for personnel management.

While some writers have delineated the territory, the content and the policy choices in HRM, others (e.g., Fombrun, Tichy, & Devanna, 1984; Miles & Snow, 1984) have emphasized the role of HUMAN RESOURCE STRATEGY, suggesting that the distinctive feature of HRM is that it links HRM policy and HRM strategy to business strategy, shifting the emphasis from the traditional administrative, fire-fighting, and problem-solving activities of personnel management to a more proactive and strategically oriented role (*see* HUMAN RESOURCES PLANNING).

A third approach, reflected in the work of Walton (1985), presents HRM as an approach based on a distinctive set of VALUES. The starting point for this is the contrast between traditional management values which emphasize compliance and CONTROL of the workforce with HRM values based on employee commitment and workforce AUTONOMY. This implies a different kind of PSYCHOLOGICAL CONTRACT based on reciprocal commitment and high TRUST (*see* RECIPROCITY). Employees have interesting and challenging jobs but at the same time are fully utilized to the benefit of the company. Workers are encouraged to contribute to INNOVATION and change in return for implicit guarantees of job security (*see* JOB INSECURITY). The contrast between the more traditional values and those associated with this view of HRM are perhaps more marked in a country like the United Kingdom rather than the United States because of the stronger United Kingdom tradition of pluralist industrial relations with its heavy TRADE UNION influence. The HRM policies pursued most notably in the 1980s by a number of American high-technology companies such as IBM, Hewlett Packard, and DEC provided a vivid contrast and offered a distinctly different approach. Indeed HRM attracted the suspicion of trade union sympathizers since, by inducing employee commitment to the organization, it threatened to reduce commitment to the union and diminish the union role. This distinctive approach to HRM, built around commitment to the organization differs from the more pragmatic approach to HRM advocated by Beer and colleagues at Harvard and Kochan at MIT which emphasizes the need to give greater priority to human resource issues and acknowledges multiple STAKEHOLDER perspectives, including the possibility of DUAL COMMITMENT to both company and union (*see* COMMITMENT, DUAL).

The approach to HRM taken by American high-technology companies had the policy goals of securing a workforce highly committed to the company, highly flexible in skills and roles, and of high quality. These goals were achieved through careful attention to key policy levers such as selection, SOCIALIZATION, TRAINING and development, COMMUNICATION, EMPLOYEE INVOLVEMENT, and rewards systems. Success depended on achieving careful integration between corporate and human resource strategy; integration between the various human resource policies and practices; and integration of human resource and line management values. Line managers in these organizations had internalized the human resource values, were eager to own them and make them work. The question then arises as to whether these distinctive HRM values and the policy goals associated with them should be advocated for all organizations or only under specific conditions. Enthusiasts such as Walton believe that they should apply in all organizations. Others advocate generic strategies such as those of Porter (1985) and Miles and Snow (1984) as a basis for determining when this distinctive set of HRM goals might be appropriate (*see* STRATEGIC TYPES).

One further element in the development of HRM has been the emergence of a number of techniques with demonstrated benefits for performance. To take just a few illustrations, there has been major progress through application of utility analysis in demonstrating the benefits of the use of SELECTION TESTS; GOAL SETTING, when properly used, does appear, as its advocates suggest, to be an effective motivational technique; and careful JOB DESIGN has a demonstrated capacity to improve individual satisfaction and well-being (*see* JOB SATISFACTION). It is, of course, possible to apply the techniques without pursuing distinctive HRM policy goals. The HRM argument is that their impact will be greater if they are part of a coherent philosophy and strategy.

Given the powerful and enthusiastic case made for HRM by its advocates, what can be said about its impact? Evidence taken from the United States (Lawler, Mohrmann, & Ledford, 1992) and from the United Kingdom (Millward, Stevens, Smart, & Hawes, 1992) confirms that there has been a great deal of innovative activity. However there appears to be a risk that HRM becomes the umbrella under which a variety of techniques are tried and tested without ever achieving the strategic integration or congruence which the more sophisticated models call for. One context within which it might be expected that HRM would come into its own is in greenfield sites – newly built factories and offices – where managers have an opportunity to introduce the best contemporary practice with relative freedom for the constraints of custom and practice. Evidence from the United States (Lawler, 1990) suggests that where this opportunity is taken, it can result in sustained high performance over a long period. In the United Kingdom there are also well-known cases, usually of foreign-owned manufacturing plants, which have successfully applied HRM on greenfield sites. However, many managers still prefer the traditional approach, pursuing high performance through efficiency and tight control rather than by using HRM to ensure full utilization of human resources.

The impact of a number of techniques which might be expected to contribute to HRM policy goals has sometimes been disappointing. For example QUALITY CIRCLES have rarely made a sustained contribution and EMPLOYEE INVOLVEMENT initiatives have often failed to improve commitment to the organization. Explanations for failure can be found in the short-term, partial, and unenthusiastic application of these techniques. However a fuller explanation can be linked with the idea of strategic integration. The case, advanced by Lawler (1986), is that the positive impact will only arrive when there is real commitment to the philosophy of full utilization of human resources, to what he terms "total involvement management." This requires comprehensive strategic integration to the point where HRM is a core part of the business strategy. There is a critical mass of cohering and mutually supportive HRM policies, and top management displays full commitment and ownership to ensure the culture reinforces the application of HRM (*see* ORGANIZATIONAL CULTURE).

Lawler and others acknowledge that achieving success through a full utilization model of HRM is an extremely difficult long-term endeavor. The prizes are great but the organizations frequently cited as the models for the success of this approach, the high-technology companies, are currently experiencing huge problems in the marketplace. Any doubts this raises in the minds of some managers are likely to be reinforced by fashions such as BUSINESS PROCESS RE-ENGINEERING or lean management which place greater weight on efficiency. It may be that as the initial gloss wears off, it is time to reshape the concept of HRM to reflect changing circumstances, in which speed of response is a key to success. This requires a new kind of psychological contract. The bedrock of job security can no longer provide the ground on which to build HRM. This means greater weight needs to be given to the new forms of FLEXIBILITY and commitment as the basis for the future full utilization of human resources.

See also **Management development; Strategic management**

Bibliography

Beer, M., Spector, B., Lawrence, P., Quinn Mills, D. & Walton, R. (1985). *Human resource management: A general manager's perspective*. New York: Free Press.

Fombrun, C., Tichy, N. & Devanna, M. (1984). *Strategic human resource management*. New York: Wiley.

Kochan, T., Katz, H. & McKersie, R. (1986). *The transformation of American industrial relations*. New York: Basic Books.

Lawler, E. (1986). *High involvement management*. San Francisco: Jossey-Bass.

Lawler, E. (1990). The new plant revolution revisited. *Organizational Dynamics*, **19**, (2), 5–14.

Lawler, E., Mohrmann, S. & Ledford, G. (1992). *Employee involvement and total quality management*. San Francisco: Jossey Bass.

Ledford, G., Lawler, E. & Mohrmann, S. (1988). The quality circle and its variations. In J. Campbell & R. Campbell (Eds), *Productivity in organizations*. San Francisco: Jossey Bass.

Miles, R. & Snow, C. (1984). Designing strategic human resource systems. *Organizational Dynamics*, Summer, 36–52.

Millward, N., Stevens, M., Smart, D. & Hawes, W. (1992). *Workplace industrial relations in transition*. Aldershot, UK: Dartmouth.

Peters, T. J. & Waterman, R. H. (1982). *In Search of Excellence*. New York: Harper & Row.

Porter, M. (1985). *Competitive advantage: Creating and sustaining superior performance*. New York: Free Press.

Walton, R. (1985). From control to commitment in the workplace. *Harvard Business Review*, **63**, 76–84.

DAVID GUEST

human resource planning This is the process of developing strategies for the acquisition, utilization, improvement, and retention of an organization's human resources.

To understand the nature of human resource planning, we need to consider: the ways in which it is different from other approaches to analyzing human resources; the subject matter it addresses; methods of analysis employed; and the context in which it is used.

Human resource planning takes an essentially aggregate view of employees, grouping them according to various parameters (AGE, length of service, qualifications, GENDER, etc.) and to the types of jobs they perform (by level, function, location, etc.). This enables quantitative comparisons to be made between the demand for different types of employees now and in the future with the current and potential supply.

In addressing these central issues of supply and demand, human resource planning involves examining a number of key areas. The expression of demand itself is perhaps the most difficult for many organizations, as it requires assumptions both about the future of the business (involving huge uncertainties) and how this will be expressed in staffing terms (involving a second set of assumptions about ORGANIZATIONAL DESIGN, JOB DESIGN, etc.). On the supply side, human resource planning looks at the characteristics of the current workforce (*see* ORGANIZATIONAL DEMOGRAPHY), sometimes called the manpower "stock." It then considers the ways in which this stock will change over time as a result of the whole system of flows" into the organization (RECRUITMENT), between job groups (promotions, transfers) and out of the organization (retirements, natural wastage, or TURNOVER, other losses). In considering resourcing options, the balance of supply and demand in the relevant external LABOR MARKETS are also evaluated.

For each of these elements of human resource planning, data are often looked at over the recent past, and projected into the future. In its simplest form, human resource planning compares likely manpower demand over some forecast period with possible options for supply, both from internal and external labor markets. Strategies for the recruitment, retention, TRAINING, and career development of employees are the result of such comparisons. In its more sophisticated form, as developed in the United Kingdom and the United States in the early 1970s, operational research techniques were used to develop computerized models to simulate the interaction of demand and supply over time under various business scenarios (*see* COMPUTER MODELING, SIMULATION). The use of such techniques has mainly been restricted to large organizations with a specialized human resource planning function at the corporate centre, and with comprehensive personnel information systems.

Human resource planning is not confined to looking at the human resource implications of corporate business plans. The same approaches may be used, albeit more simply, by local line managers examining their departmental requirements. They may also be turned to the analysis and solution of specific issues or problems: poor retention rates, ABSENTEEISM, EQUAL OPPORTUNITIES monitoring, the requirements for MANAGEMENT DEVELOPMENT, and SUCCESSION PLANNING, DOWNSIZING, etc. In some organizations, issues of work organization and staff utilization are extremely complex, for example, in scheduling the movements of airline staff round the world, and may become a major focus of human resource planning activity.

See also **Human resources management; Human resources strategy**

Bibliography

Walker, J. W. (1980). *Human resource planning*. New York: McGraw-Hill.

Bramham, J. (1994). *Human Resource Planning*. London: Institute of Personnel Management.

WENDY HIRSH

human resource strategy The concept of Human Resource Strategy (HRS) integrates an organization's HUMAN RESOURCE MANAGEMENT (HRM) policies with a stable and strategic characteristic of organizational life, such as the corporate strategy, employment philosophies, core values, organizational competencies, or delivery of a value-added business process (*see* CORE COMPETENCE). It provides a "fixed point" toward which HRM policies may be targeted and developed and involves two processes of integration. Vertical integration identifies and shapes effective organizational behaviors across the hierarchy. Horizontal integration ensures that all activities felt to influence effective behaviors present a consistent and coherent picture, i.e., HRM policies send the same messages and shape a mutually reinforcing set of behaviors within the organization. Approaches to HRS differ in their LEVEL OF ANALYSIS (whether behaviors should be managed at the individual, role, or organizational level) and in the scope to which the term human resources is used (individuals, teams, key value-added skill groups, core versus peripheral employees, or the total pool of human capital).

An HRS requires a wide territory of control, including "... all those activities affecting the behavior of individuals in their efforts to formulate and implement the strategic needs of the business resulting from the organization's strategy" (Schuler, 1992). The list of "activities" to be coordinated lengthened as our understanding of organizational behavior developed. It includes traditional personnel activities; work design, organizational structure and culture; control systems; and underlying business processes. All send powerful signals to shape behavior. A single unifying theme is needed at some stage in the STRATEGIC MANAGEMENT process. Four perspectives dominate the field: linkage between strategic and HUMAN RESOURCE PLANNING (HRP) processes; contingency relationships between strategies and HRM practices (*see* CONTINGENCY THEORY); political and management of change processes; and the identification of organizational capabilities and competencies.

The first perspective considers the linkage between the HRP and the strategic plan. The HRS is articulated through a planned process that identifies strategic business needs, which may be redefined as organizations plan for survival, growth, adaptability, PRODUCTIVITY or profitability, and develop actionable objectives. HRS theorists focus on the extent to which the strategic plan and HRP are mutually developed and informed, seeing HRS as an umbrella concept created through strategic plans and articulated through the organization's philosophies, policies, programmes, and practices.

A second approach considers the connection between HRM and organizational strategy itself (Fombrun, Tichy, & Devanna, 1984; Lengnick-Hall & Lengnick-Hall, 1988; MacMillan & Schuler, 1985) from a "situational" perspective. The focus is on the translation of strategy into action, planning of resources, design of organizational structures and systems, and the matching of "appropriate" HRM practices to a specific organizational strategy (*see* ORGANIZATIONAL DESIGN). Managers make contingent choices about the content of HRM policies and practice. These have to be coherent, consistent, and linked to the strategy. Policies are aligned on the basis of "needed role behaviors" in order to channel behaviors and create a dominant value or culture in the organization. HRS becomes a social engineering process based on two relationships. In "contingent" relationships, triggers have a predictable, systematic influence on HRS (Schuler, 1992). Contingent relationships for HRS have been identified for: top management goals, values and strategic intent; the basis of competitive battles; industry or business life cycle; and the business sector. "Noncontingent" relationships trigger new developments in HRM, with an unpredictable, undiscriminating, or unknown effect across countries or organizations. The size of organizations, work flow layout, levels of profitability, structure and JOB DESIGN, socio-economic pressures, legislative environment, national CULTURE, LABOR MARKET or customer characteristics, and competitor behavior represent noncontingent factors. Contingency models have strengths and weaknesses (Boxall, 1991; Hendry & Pettigrew, 1990). They bring implementation issues into clear focus and demonstrate the importance of coherence and consistency across HRM policies, but they also lead to over-prescriptive theorizing and are highly culture-bound. HRS is cast in a reactive mode, serving efficient implementation of a preconceived and rational strategy but ignoring contributions to the formation of strategy. They underestimate CONFLICT and incremental processes of strategy-making and strategy-change.

A third perspective focuses on political and management of change processes within HRS. The contours of an HRS are unclear at the outset. Organizations follow different pathways to achieve the same results. Sensitivity to historical and change processes is required. Sustained inputs of energy and activity create a "critical mass" or point at which activity becomes self-reinforcing. Progress depends on highly political considerations and the sophistication, competence, and credibility of key actors (such as the HRM function) (*see* POLITICS). Corporate LEADERSHIP plays a significant role but business change is the primary driving force behind HRS. Transforming HRS is easier in times of a crisis (*see* CRISES), well-understood business performance gaps, charismatic leadership (*see* LEADERSHIP, CHARISMATIC), or strategic redirection articulated by diverse, intelligent, and proactive TOP MANAGEMENT TEAMS. HRS is the pursuit of board objectives realized through an imperfect, opportunistic, and learning-by-doing process.

A fourth perspective considers how human resources (and their competencies) become a source of competitive advantage. Theorists focus on COGNITION IN ORGANIZATIONS (the frames of reference, mental maps, and dominant logic of managers involved in the strategic management process) and the management of internal resources, capabilities, or competencies (Klein, Edge, & Kass, 1991; Sparrow, 1994; Whipp, 1991). The topic of ORGANIZATIONAL LEARNING – the ability to learn faster than the competition and reconstruct and adapt the organization's skills, structures, and values – links HRS to competitive advantage (*see* COMPETITIVENESS). HRS leads to competitive advantage under four conditions: value, rarity, inimitability, and nonsubstitutability (Wright & McMahan, 1992) (*see* RESOURCE DEPENDENCE). Value resides in organization-specific skills. When work designs build the system around the individual the best predictor of organization performance becomes the rarity of the individual's competencies. If competitors cannot identify the exact components of human capital associated with a competitive advantage and cannot duplicate the competencies (or conditions under which they are effective) then human resources become inimitable. Whilst employee behavior is the direct way through which strategies are implemented, employees must also have the competencies necessary to exhibit relevant behaviors. Human resources as individuals are distinguished from human resources as the total pool of human capital within the organization. The HRS focuses on the competency of the total pool of human capital within the organization (*see* COMPETENCIES).

Increasing theoretical sophistication will be sought in these four perspectives but practical questions will dominate the field in the future. What are the organizational performance criteria that an HRS should improve? Can positive links between HRS and organizational performance be demonstrated? Does the existence of an HRS make the organization more likely to achieve effective performance or do better-performing organizations simply have more opportunity to plan for the future? Is the HRS sufficiently future-orientated, flexible, and culture-free? How should highly measurable and focused approaches to HRS be balanced with the realities of facilitating change? As organization designs change, is it desirable to create more than one HRS? At what levels in the design should an HRS be developed, under whose ownership and at what stage in the business process? The field of HRS needs much development in theoretical and practical terms.

See also **Flexibility; Seven s's model; Organization and environment**

Bibliography

Boxall, P. F. (1991). Strategic human resource management: Beginnings of a new theoretical sophistication? *Human Resource Management Journal*, **2**, (3), 60–79.

Fombrun, C. J., Tichy, N. M. & Devanna, M. A. (1984). *Strategic human resource management*. New York: Wiley.

Hendry, C. & Pettigrew, A. M. (1990). Human resource management: An agenda for the 1990s. *International Journal of Human Resource Management*, **1**, (1), 17–43.

Klein, J., Edge, G. & Kass, T. (1991). Skill-based competition. *Journal of General Management*, **16**, (4), 1–15.

Lengnick-Hall, C. A. & Lengnick-Hall, M. L. (1988). Strategic human resources management: A review of the literature and a proposed typology. *Academy of Management Review*, **13**, 454–470.

MacMillan, I. C. & Schuler, R. S. (1985). Gaining a competitive edge through human resources. *Personnel*, **62**, (4), 24–29.

Schuler, R. S. (1992). Linking the people with the strategic needs of the business. *Organizational Dynamics*, **20**, 18–32.

Sparrow, P. R. (1994). Organizational competencies: Creating a strategic behavioural framework for selection and assessment. In N. Anderson & P.

Herriot (Eds), *Handbook of assessment and appraisal*. London: Wiley.

Whipp, R. (1991). Human resource management, strategic change and competition: The role of learning. *International Journal of Human Resource Management*, **2**, (2), 165–191.

Wright, P. M. & McMahan, G. C. (1992). Theoretical perspectives for strategic human resource management. *Journal of Management*, **18**, 295–320.

PAUL SPARROW

hygiene factors *see* MOTIVATOR/HYGIENE THEORY

— I —

identification This is the part of an individual's self-concept which derives from his or her membership in a social group (Tajfel, 1981). To the extent that individuals identify with a group, they experience the successes and failures of the group as their own and incorporate the dominant attitudes and VALUES of the group as their own (Ashforth & Mael, 1989). The term identification is also used to refer to the process by which this change in self-concept takes place (Kelman, 1961; Freud, 1949).

Traditionally, identification has been viewed as a voluntary response to group membership rather than as a coercive or instrumental response (*see* CONFORMITY and COMPLIANCE). Individuals who identify with their groups adjust to group expectations not out of fear of punishment or for instrumental reasons, but because they find relationships with other group members intrinsically satisfying and want to express attitudes that others in the group will find compatible. While identification has not been closely linked to productivity outcomes, it has been more consistently associated with altruistic behavior, cooperative behavior, and GROUP COHESIVENESS (Turner, 1984) (*see* ALTRUISM). For example, in organizational settings, individuals with high identification may be more likely to volunteer to work overtime, to recruit for the group, and to publicize the group in a positive way to outsiders.

Although there has been considerable theoretical speculation on the processes by which identification takes place, there has been relatively little empirical research on this topic. Organizational behavior research has concentrated on examining how identification results from escalating emotional investment in the group (Burke & Reitzes, 1991; Ashforth & Meal, 1989) (*see* COMMITMENT ESCALATION). In contrast, clinical and development psychology has focused on how identification results from the renunciation of the demands of competing groups and personal sacrifices for the group (Freud, 1949; Eysenck, 1960).

See also **Group norms; Group dynamics; Attitude theory; Groupthink; Group decision making; Group development**

Bibliography

Ashforth, B. E. & Mael, F. (1989). Social identity theory and the organization. *Academy of Management Review*, **14**, 20–39.

Burke, P. J. & Reitzes, D. C. (1991). An identity theory approach to commitment. *Social Psychology Quarterly*, **54**, 239–251.

Eysenck, H. J. (1960). The development of moral values in children: The contribution of learning theory. *British Journal of Educational Psychology*, **30**, 11–22.

Freud, S. (1949). *An outline of psychoanalysis*. New York: Norton.

Kelman, H. C. (1961). Processes of opinion change. *Public Opinion Quarterly*, **25**, 57–78.

Tajfel, H. (1981). *Human groups and social categories: Studies in social psychology*. Cambridge, UK: Cambridge University Press.

Turner, J. C. (1984). Social identification and psychological group formation. In H. Tajfel (Ed.), *The social dimension: European developments in social psychology* (vol. 2, pp. 518–538). Cambridge, UK: Cambridge University Press.

DANIEL C. FELDMAN

ideology This term typically refers to a reasonably coherent set of beliefs, attitudes, and opinions. The meaning is frequently prejorative, with a contrast drawn between ideology and science. The former deals in illusion, untruth, falsehood; the latter, with that which is real, correct, and true. Marxist thinkers initially developed this contrast in order to show how what people thought was real and objective and was the result of a "false consciousness," an understanding rooted in systematic error and illusion perpetrated by the "capitalist class." Such views have influenced some ORGANIZATION THEORY.

First, there is the suggestion that typical constructs, such as Weber's "ideal type" of rational BUREAUCRACY, crystalized a specific view of the world rather than a general analytical tool. Marxist critics deny the objective character of organization analysis. It has been seen as a projection of "managerialist" and "capitalist" ideology. Its function is to mask the exploitation of employees, particularly the working class, within organizations, by the owners of these organizations – the capitalists – and their appointed agents, the "managerial stratum." Critics such as Fergusson (1984) also have embraced a similar view, with a feminist twist, seeing the public, rational, and calculative world of the bureaucratic construct as a masculinist construct, against a more feminine world-view (*see* FEMINISM).

Marxist and feminist emphases share a common view. Ideology is instrumental in both the subordination of organization members and the partiality of organization theorists who mistake their perspectives (bourgeois, masculine) for reality.

Second, there is the "dominant ideology thesis" associated with the work of Abercrombie, Hill, and Turner (1980). The role of dominant ideology is not to subordinate lower strata, a role they believe exaggerated in view of the conflictual and pluralist nature of modern societies. Rather more, it is to organize dominant strata. From this perspective, organization and management theory are examples of ideology because they provide seemingly neutral and technical accounts of organization processes that dominant organization strata learn to apply in business schools. Using these tools, they are then able to justify political actions (restructuring, DOWNSIZING, layoffs, etc.) in technical terms that admit of no rational or alternative account. From this perspective there is little difference between Marxism as an ideological theory that admits of no truth other than its theory and management accounts that function in the same way. They merely articulate different interests.

Some writers influenced by the work of Michel Foucault suggest that ideology may be a meaningless concept. To know what is false and erroneous or illusionary we must know what is true and correct. Whereas once one might have thought that "science" could secure these conditions of knowledge, Foucault argues that concepts of "truth" and "falsity," "science" and "ideology," require understanding in terms of the social discourses that produce them. There are no absolutes, just provisional accounts. All that can be certain is that there are different ways of ceding "truth" and "falsity," that change historically and comparatively (Clegg, 1989).

From this perspective an opposition between truth and falsity, science and ideology, is insecure. The basis for a truth claim, as a judgment rooted in a particular THEORY, always will be susceptible to a charge of "ideology," opening up the possibility that any theory that claims to be able to provide true grounds for its analysis must of necessity be ideological, because it seeks to suppress the play of different perspectives.

Finally, from this perspective, the way is clear to an analysis of all organization theories as necessarily partial perspectives, such as those provided by Burrell and Morgan (1979) and Morgan (1985). No organization theory can be wholly true. Hence, all organization theories, given the way that their perspectives relate to different organizational interests, will always be partial. The best form of organization theory will be one that takes all perspectives seriously, that tries to incorporate a variety of viewpoints, because no one is adequate. The most adequate understanding will develop from the most plural use of perspectives rather than the endorsement of one over all the others. If this perspective is combined with some notion of empirical tests that can determine the relative strengths and weaknesses of competing theories, then we may conclude that some theories, by some tests, under some circumstances, may be more ideological than others. The problem remains, however, that there is no neutral theory of theory: which tests are used in what circumstances will always be tied up in the assumptions of the theory-in-use.

See also **Social constructionism; Critical theory; Values; Postmodernism; Double-loop learning**

Bibliography

Abercrombie, N., Hill, S. & Turner, B. S. (1980). *The dominant ideology thesis*. London: Allen and Unwin.

Burrell, G. & Morgan, G. (1979). *Sociological theory and organizational paradigms*. London: Heinemann.

Clegg, S. (1989). *Frameworks of power*. London: Sage.

Fergusson, K. (1984). *The feminist case against bureaucracy*. Philadelphia, PA: Temple University Press.

Morgan, G. (1985). *Images of organizations*. London: Sage.

STEWART CLEGG

impression management Organizational theorists, researchers, and practitioners have increasingly recognized the importance of *impression management* (also called *self-presentation*) as an explanatory model for a broad range of organizational phenomena. Impression management refers to the many ways that individuals attempt to control the impressions others have of them: their behavior, motivations, morality, and personal attributes like competence, trustworthiness, and future potential. Individuals may also attempt to control the impressions others form of entities besides themselves such as commercial products or a company (Schlenker & Weigold, 1992).

The impression management framework employs a "life as theater" or *dramaturgic* metaphor to describe social and organizational behavior. People are actors, taking many roles (e.g., parent, employee, supervisor), and are keenly aware of audience reactions to their behaviors (*see* ROLE TAKING). Thus, some actors' behavior is an attempt to control or modify the image that relevant audiences have of them and win audiences' moral, social, and financial support. The impression management framework assumes that a basic human motive, both inside and outside of organizations, is to be viewed by others in a favorable manner and to avoid being seen negatively. Individuals act as amateur publicity agents using enhancing impression management tactics (e.g. ingratiation, self-promotion) to look good and protective or defensive impression management (e.g., excuses, apologies) to minimize deficiencies and avoid looking bad.

Impression management has increasingly become a recognized part of organizational behavior theory, research, and practice. Two edited volumes (Giacalone & Rosenfeld 1989; 1991) have systematically applied an organizational impression management perspective to topics such as SELECTION INTERVIEWS, PERFORMANCE APPRAISAL, LEADERSHIP, CAREER strategies, exit interviews, organizational JUSTICE, and the MANAGEMENT OF DIVERSITY.

Impression management theory – so popular today in organizational settings – had its roots in the pioneering work of sociologist Erving Goffman. In his classic book, *The Presentation of Self in Everyday Life* (1959), Goffman systematically interpreted social behavior utilizing the terminology and methods of the theater. People were seen as social actors attempting to establish (in conjunction with those with whom they were interacting), a "working consensus" through their impression management behaviors. This reciprocal impression management served as a social lubricant: it allowed actors to know how to act and what actions to expect from others.

Beginning in the 1960s, experimental social psychologists (most notably Edward E. Jones' seminal studies of ingratiation) increasingly began utilizing impression management to explain a whole host of research areas including cognitive dissonance, reactance, ALTRUISM, and aggression. Rather than having independent theoretical status, however, impression management was often an alternative explanation for established social psychological laboratory phenomena (Baumeister, 1982).

The social psychological legacy of impression management theory also gave it a stigma that it still struggles to overcome. Impression management for many became synonymous with unscrupulous, nefarious, insincere, and deceptive actions. People who practiced impression management did not necessarily believe in the impressions they were claiming, but were saying and doing things to gain favor in the eyes of significant audiences as part of a general motive of manipulative social influence (Tedeschi, 1981; *see* MACHIAVELLIANISM, POLITICS).

This pessimistic view of impression management has gradually moderated during the last decade. The current thinking among most theorists is that impression management behaviors are often sincere components of social and organizational behavior. As Tetlock and Manstead (1985, pp. 61–62) noted, "although some writers have used the term *impression management* to refer to the self-conscious deception of others (e.g., Gaes, Kalle, & Tedeschi, 1978), there is no compelling psychological reason why impression management must be either duplicitous or under conscious control. Impression management may be the product of highly overlearned habits or scripts, the original functions of which people have long forgotten."

In an authoritative review, Schlenker and Weigold (1992) distinguished between *restrictive* and *expansive* views of impression management. The restrictive view sees impression management as a generally negative often deceptive set of behaviors aimed at illicitly gaining social POWER and approval. The now more accepted expansive view sees impression management as a fundamental aspect of social and organizational interactions. It is perhaps best to view impression management behaviors as falling on a continuum ranging from sincere, accurate presentations to conscious deception.

The popularity of impression management in organizational scholarship is a relatively recent phenomenon. While many of the concepts of impression management were utilized in areas such as organizational politics, there were few organizational investigations of impression management before the early 1980s. Not until the mid-1980s did the organizational impression management perspective begin to gain an identity theoretically distinct from the earlier literature on organizational politics and attain a degree of independent status. Thus, although popular in social psychology for over two decades, it is only relatively recently that the organizational impression management literature has expanded into the full range of organizational behavior topic areas. It seems fair to say that impression management now provides explanatory power for a wide range of topics across the organizational sciences.

A number of challenges remain for organizational impression management. Three of note are:

(1) *Can impression management be trained?* Although training in impression management performance and detection has been recommended (Giacalone, 1989), impression management has yet to have true empirically derived practitioner applications. A first step may require viewing impression management as a desirable set of skills rather than a deficit.

(2) *Are impression management motivation and tactics applicable to an increasingly diverse, multinational workforce?* As organizations grow increasingly diverse and multinational impression management may be crucial to members of racial/ethnic minority groups, women, immigrants, and expatriates who often need to please majority group members in positions of greater social power. Understanding how impression management behaviors are interpreted by others can also serve as the basis for smoother interactions and a means for solving potential communication problems among individuals from diverse backgrounds (Rosenfeld, Giacalone & Riordan, 1994).

(3) *Does impression management play a role in functional and dysfunctional interpersonal relationships?* Little impression management research has been done with individuals in ongoing personal and professional relationships. It would be of interest to know what types of impression management behaviors are associated with stable, long-lasting relationships. At the same time, organizations would benefit from understanding conditions that elicit impression management behaviors that are dysfunctional or destructive from the individual or organizational point of view (e.g., SUBSTANCE ABUSE, SABOTAGE, withholding of effort).

See also **Interpersonal skills; Minority group influence**

Bibliography

Baumeister, R. F. (1982). A self-presentational view of social phenomena. *Pcychological Bulletin*, **91**, 3–26.

Gaes, G. G., Kalle, R. J. & Tedeschi, J. T. (1978). Impression management in the forced compliance paradigm: Two studies using the bogus pipeline. *Journal of Experimental Social Psychology*, **14**, 493–510.

Giacalone, R. A. (1989, May). Image control: The strategies of impression management. *Personnel*, 52–55.

Giacalone R. A. & Rosenfeld, P. (Eds) (1989). *Impression management in the organization*. Hillsdale, NJ: Sage.

Giacalone, R. A. & Rosenfeld, P. (Eds) (1991). *Applied impression management: How image making affects managerial decisions*. Newbury Park, CA: Sage.

Goffman, E. (1959). *The presentation of self in everyday life*. Garden City, NY: Doubleday.

Rosenfeld, P., Giacalone, R. A. & Riordan, C. A. (1994). Impression management theory and diversity: Lessons for organizational behavior. *American Behavioral Scientist*, **37**, 601–607.

Schlenker, B. R. & Weigold, M. F. (1992). Interpersonal processes involving impression regulation and management. *Annual Review of Psychology*, **43**, 133–168.

Tedeschi, J. T. (1981). *Impression management and social psychological research*. New York: Academic Press.

Tetlock, P. E. & Manstead, A. S. R. (1985). Impression management versus intrapsychic explanations in social psychology: A useful dichotomy? *Psychological Review*, **92**, 59–77.

PAUL ROSENFELD
ROBERT A. GIACALONE
and CATHERINE A. RIORDAN

incentives *see* BONUS PAYMENTS; REWARDS; REINFORCEMENT

individual differences ORGANIZATIONAL BEHAVIOR is often conceptualized as focusing on three LEVELS OF ANALYSIS: individuals, groups, and organizations. Individual differences refers to the first level of analysis, and includes the study of personality, intelligence, attitudes, MOTIVATION, cognitions (such as memory, learning, and perception), and other "personal" variables. It is especially concerned with PERSONALITY and some would argue that personality embraces all the other aspects.

Differences associated with demography, such as AGE, education, GENDER, and CULTURE, are sometimes classed as group rather than individual differences. A more useful way of describing the role of these variables is as mediating variables, i.e., they directly impact on the relationship between individual differences and the organizational context. For example, most researchers have found a positive linear relation between age and JOB SATISFACTION (White & Spector, 1987). Similarly, research has shown that there are cultural differences in work motivation, with workers in Japan having a stronger COMMITMENT to work because of a stronger emphasis on this value in Japanese society (*see* CULTURE, NATIONAL; INTERCULTURAL PROCESS). In fact, some have argued that Western psychology's interest in individual differences is a cultural phenomenon. We define ourselves by our differences from other people. Guthrie (1980), among others, argues that not all peoples define the self in this way. Instead, we could define ourselves in terms of qualities, attitudes, customs, or history we share with our social group. Then the concern becomes "individual sameness" rather than individual difference. This notion encourages OB to research and compare work cultures in different parts of the world and challenges the Western emphasis on differences between people (*see* MANAGEMENT OF DIVERSITY).

While most people find the topic of how individuals differ or are similar to others to be interesting and important in everyday life, the question of whether individual differences matter in organizational life has been debated in OB for a long while. Some have argued that the influence personality and other individual difference factors have been greatly overstated in OB relative to situational effects (Davis-Blake & Pfeffer, 1989). Others have taken the opposite view, emphasising the role of internal, personal factors to the exclusion of external, contextual ones.

Much theory and research eschews these rather extreme positions. The increasingly influential interactionist perspective stresses that it is the interaction between one's disposition and the situation that determines behavior (Mischel, 1984) (*see* INTERACTIONISM). Pfeffer, who earlier maintained that organizations are situations that swamp individual personality variables, has recently written that individual factors such as energy, sensitivity, focus, and flexibility help people wield power effectively (Pfeffer, 1992). There is accumulating evidence that individual characteristics influence both reactions to environments and how environments are construed.

Aside from these broad issues concerning the importance of individual differences, there are many different approaches to the way individual differences are studied. The main ones are the psychoanalytic, phenomenological, social learning, social cognitive, and trait approaches. Each stresses the personal, situational, or interactionist view to a greater or lesser extent. The psychoanalytic, phenomenological, and trait approaches stress the dominance of internal factors as the major influence on behavior. In contrast, the social learning approach emphasizes external or situational influences and the social cognitive approach takes a more interactionist perspective.

Freud's psychoanalytic theory has had a great deal of influence on social scientists. He viewed human behavior as governed by instinctual forces, many of them not conscious to the individual. Although the psychoanalytic school is no longer as influential as it once was, the concepts continue to influence OB (*see* PROJECTION, ORGANIZATIONAL NEUROSIS).

Phenomenology contrasts sharply with traditional psychoanalytic views. It is concerned with how people experience their world. The self is the prominent concept. It focuses on cognition, freedom of choice, human values, and our capacity to construct meaning from our own experiences. Phenomenological approaches have not been widely adopted in OB. However, they have contributed to work in the areas of CAREER CHOICE, where counselors have made use of Kelly's concept of an individual construct system, and where self awareness on the part of the client is important. Similarly, CAREER DEVELOPMENT, theory, and practice, based on individuals' concerns at different stages of their lives, is often informed by phenomenological approaches.

The social Learning approach has its origins in behaviorism and traditional learning theory, which focus on observable behavior and the situations which elicit it, rather than inferring what is happening inside the organism, and are concerned with how REINFORCEMENT (reward) leads to learning (*see* LEARNING, INDIVIDUAL). Advocates of social learning have increasingly referred to their approach as social cognitive (e.g., Bandura, 1989). They stress that behavior can best be understood by considering it as a joint product of individual differences variables and environmental factors. Concepts from social learning and social cognitive approaches have wide applicability in OB. The use of REWARDS in TRAINING, learning by modeling the behavior of others. MENTORING, organizational BEHAVIOR MODIFICATION (where rewards are used to reinforce desired behavior by employees), and the concepts of LOCUS OF CONTROL and SELF EFFICACY are some of the contributions from this approach.

The trait approach describes people as characterized by sets of traits or dimensions along which they differ from others and is the approach most often associated with the term individual differences, especially in relation to studies of personality. It uses words such as tough minded, introverted, confident, and innovative to describe the basic factors of personality. It therefore comes closest of all to the approaches describing behavior in terms easily recognizable in organizations. Traits are viewed as reasonably stable over time, indicating a certain predictability of behavior. Well-known trait theorists are Eysenck (1970) and Cattell (1965) who have researched dimensions of personality and intelligence based on data from experimental studies subjected to statistical analysis. Although there are literally thousands of possible traits, recent research shows that five major factors (neuroticism, EXTRAVERSION, openness, agreeableness, and conscientiousness) have emerged from studies using different approaches (McCrae & Costa, 1987). Intelligence is sometimes added as a sixth major factor. The trait approach has been very influential in many areas of OB, notably PSYCHOLOGICAL TESTING, INTELLIGENCE-TESTING, VOCATIONAL GUIDANCE, and SELECTION METHODS.

See also **Person-job fit; Life stages; Managerial style; Assessment**

Bibliography

Bandura, A. (1989). Human agency in social cognitive theory. *American Psychologist*, **44**, 1175–1184.

Cattell, R. B. (1965). *The scientific analysis of personality*. Baltimore, MD: Penguin.

Davis-Blake, A. & Pfeffer, J. (1989). Just a mirage: The search for dispositional effects in organizational research. *Academy of Management Research*, **14**, 385–400.

Eysenck, H. J. (1970). *The structure of human personality* (3rd edn). London: Methuen.

Guthrie, R. (1980). The psychology of Black Americans: An historical perspective. In R. Jones (Ed.),

Black Psychology (2nd edn). London: Harper Collins.
McCrae, R. R. & Costa, P. T. (1987). Validation of the Five Factor model of personality across instruments and observers. *Journal of Personality and Social Psychology*, **52**, 81–90.
Mischel, W. (1984). Convergences and challenges in the search for consistency. *American Psychologist*, **39**, 351–364.
Pfeffer, J. (1992). *Managing with power*. Boston: Harvard Business School Press.
White, A. T. & Spector, P. E. (1987). An investigation of age-related factors in the age-job-satisfaction relationship. *Psychology and Aging*, **2**, (3), 261–265.

VIV SHACKLETON

industrial economics *see* ORGANIZATIONAL ECONOMICS; PROSPECT THEORY; TRANSACTION COST THEORY

industrial relations This term, in its broadest sense, is used to describe an interdisciplinary field concerned with all aspects of employment relations. Industrial relations researchers draw eclectically on the academic disciplines of economics, law, sociology, and, increasingly, psychology to describe, predict, and prescribe solutions to observed problems. The focus of interest is the institutions involved in employment relations. Two characteristics are present in much research. The first is that the prevailing assumption is that conflicts of interest between employer and employee are endemic and nonpathological (*see* COLLECTIVE ACTION). The second is that the analysis of TRADE UNIONS and COLLECTIVE BARGAINING is central; although industrial relations research focuses on nonunion firms, it is distinct from HUMAN RESOURCE MANAGEMENT in dealing primarily with collective organization and joint regulation of employment contracts.

Early research, for example, by Commons in the United States and the Webbs in the United Kingdom, embodied a collective focus, an atheoretical problem orientation and a tendency to prescribe policy solutions as part of a reaction to neoclassical approaches to labor as a commodity. Commons (1934, p. 162) defined industrial relations as the study of the "transactions and working rules of collective action." The Webbs (1907) focused on trade unions as remedies to inequalities of bargaining POWER between employer and employee. Both deliberately mixed empirical research with prescription – often involving advocacy of regulatory legislation – against the background of the emergence of high levels of trade unionism and widespread collective bargaining.

As Kochan notes (1980, pp. 1–22) the field of industrial relations emerged in isolation from contemporary developments in psychology and management theory. Where theory has emerged, it has tended to focus on trade unionism or collective bargaining (Poole, 1981; Clegg, 1976) rather than on industrial relations. A major exception is the work of Dunlop (1958) who developed the idea of an industrial relations system having certain active institutions, a context in which they operate, and certain outputs. The "web of rules" within this system governing relations between institutions is the dependant variable for the field of study. The rules are affected by:

(1) the environmental context;
(2) the IDEOLOGY of society; and
(3) the actors (labor, employers, and government) within the system. The approach was developed into a comparative study of industrial relations systems which was used to support convergence theory, i.e., the proposition that, because of an underlying "logic of industrialism," industrial relations systems in modern societies were becoming more alike (Kerr, Harbison, Dunlop, & Myers, 1960).

Although much criticized as a classification rather than an explanation, Dunlop's work was echoed in the United Kingdom by the work of Flanders (e.g., 1975) who defined industrial relations as the study of job regulation. However, with the rise of industrial CONFLICT and levels of union membership internationally from the mid-1960s, the idea of the field as a circumscribed subsystem of society became less appealing. Sociologists and economists concerned with strike activity, LABOR MARKETS and incomes policies became once more interested in the field and, particularly in Europe, industrial relations and industrial sociology converged around common concerns. Fox (1974) analyzed the relationship between the institutions of industrial relations and those findings from industrial sociology and psychology relevant to the employment relationship. He developed the distinction between:

(1) "unitary" (i.e., consensus based) theories of organization, typical of the classical management theorists (*see* MANAGEMENT, CLASSICAL THEORY);
(2) pluralist theories, typical of industrial relations approaches, which assumed conflict legitimate, endemic, but manageable (*see* LEGITIMACY); and
(3) radical theories, developed by Marxist writers such as Hyman (1971) for whom it was axiomatic that industrial conflict was a manifestation of wider potentially revolutionary class conflicts in society.

"Radical" industrial relations was sustained by the perceived links between union activity and wider social or political crises in the 1970s. The behavior of the institutions of industrial relations became central to analysis of corporatism and inflation. In addition, many Marxist theorists concerned with the labour process became concerned with the rules of job regulation (*see* LABOR PROCESS THEORY). However, in the 1980s, the decline in membership and influence of trade unions in many countries, together with the rise of individualistic human resource management caused a decline of interest in the institutions of job regulation. Traditional industrial relations research proved, because of its isolation from the wider behavioral sciences, poorly equipped to explain the managerial actions which might curtail the scope of unionism and collective regulation in favor of more individualistic approaches.

An exception was the emergence of the "new" institutional economics. The so-called "Harvard School" used Hirschman's exit-voice model to analyze union–management relations. The central measurable proposition was that one benefit of union organization was the establishment of a communicative and remedial "voice" mechanism which could improve organizational performance if used by management to outweigh the negative monopoly and featherbedding activities of unions (Hirschman, 1971; Freeman & Medoff, 1984].

A second strand of research with its origins in political economy focused on the relationship between the institutions of job regulation and comparative economic performance. This related performance to national level institutional differences (e.g., Maurice, Sellier, & Silvestre, 1986) or to differences in shop-floor relations (e.g., Lazonick, 1990). The emphasis was, unlike the earlier work of Kerr et al., on enduring national differences in evolutionary trajectories and performance, rather than in convergence. In addition, the focus was on outcome measures rather than description of the institutions alone.

In summary, industrial relations has emerged as an academic field in response to perceived policy problems emerging from union-management relations. Development of theory in the area has been stalled by the empirical tradition this has encouraged and by the eclecticism involved. Interest in the field has varied, both chronologically and internationally, in line with the perceived importance of collective employee behavior for wider social issues. In the 1980s, however, the field tends once more to support the institutional critique of neo-classical economics.

See also **Intergroup relations; Interorganizational relations; Representation; Trust**

Bibliography

Clegg, H. A. (1976). *Trade unionism under collective bargaining*. Oxford, UK: Blackwell.

Commons, J. (1934). *Institutional economics*. New York: Macmillan.

Dunlop, J. T. (1958). *Industrial relations systems*. New York: Holt, Rinehart, and Winston.

Flanders, A. (1975). *Management and unions*. London: Faber and Faber.

Fox, A. (1974). *Beyond contract; Work, power and trust relations*. London: Faber.

Freeman, R. & Medoff, J. (1984). *What do unions do?* New York: Basic Books.

Hirschman, A. (1970). *Exit, voice and loyalty*. Cambridge, MA: Harvard University Press.

Hyman, R. (1971). *Industrial relations; A Marxist introduction*. London: Hutchinson.

Kerr, C., Harbison, F., Dunlop, J. T and Myers, C. (1960). *Industrialism and Industrial Man*. Cambridge, MA: Harvard University Press.

Kochan, T. (1980). *Collective bargaining and industrial relations*. Homewood, IL: Irwin.

Lazonick, W. (1990). *Competitive advantage on the shop floor*. Cambridge, MA: Harvard University Press.

Maurice, M., Sellier, S. & Silvestre, J. J. (1986). *The social foundations of industrial power*. Cambridge, MA: MIT Press.
Webb, S. & Webb, B. (1907). *The history of trade unionism*. London: Longman, Green.

PAUL WILLMAN

influence This terms means any social process in which an individual's actions or attitudes are affected by the actual or implied presence of one or more others. It is essential to many features of group and organizational functioning, including LEADERSHIP, CONFORMITY, and ROLE-TAKING (*see also* MANAGEMENT DEVELOPMENT). Two-way influence is necessary in all of these to achieve mutual ends. Influence usually is distinguished from POWER (*see also* POWER BASES) by an emphasis on persuasion rather than coercion or CONTROL. As Bierstedt put it in a classic phrase, "Influence does not require power, and power may dispense with influence." In many ROLE relationships, power and influence may coexist and be brought to bear variably, as appropriate. Supervisory, managerial, administrative, and executive functions in organizations usually grant power based on authority (*see* AUTHORITY; LEGITIMACY).

However, these LEADERSHIP roles also require what Katz and Kahn (1978) refer to as "the influential increment over and above mechanical compliance with the routine directives of the organization," in the nature of a following (p. 528). A demand for compliance can limit individual initiative and CREATIVITY, with costs to individual satisfaction and the performance of the organization. Because individuals can interpret and learn from new experiences, they have resources to resist influence and to attempt means of counter-influence. This is exemplified by the upward influence (*see* UPWARD COMMUNICATION) tactics used within hierarchies. These tactics are contingent upon individual circumstances, such as one's level in the organization and years of experience (see, e.g., Kipnis, Schmidt, & Wilkinson, 1980).

Depending upon various situational factors, different tactics are suitable for the achievement of the influence objective within what is acceptable in the agent–target relationship. A questionnaire study of how 128 managers used nine influence tactics was conducted in the field with each manager's subordinates, peers, and boss (Yukl & Tracey, 1992). The results, regarding criteria of target task commitment and manager effectiveness, showed rational persuasion, inspirational appeal, and consultation to be most effective. Ingratiation and exchange were moderately effective with subordinates and peers but not with superiors. Least effective in this study were pressure, coalition, and legitimating.

Influence also may result from imitation, as in modeling, where one or more persons pattern their actions and attitudes on those of another. This process has utility in socializing newer members of an organization into appropriate ways of behaving (*see* SOCIALIZATION). Associated with it is the willingness of those in leadership roles to be influenced by followers through a recognition of mutual interdependence and the development of their leadership skills (see Hollander & Offermann, 1990, p. 185).

See also **Decision making; Interpersonal skills; Resistance to change**

Bibliography

Hollander, E. P. & Offermann, L. R. (1990). Power and leadership in organizations: Relationships in transition. *American Psychologist*, **45**, (2), 179–189.
Katz, D. & Kahn, R. L. (1978). *The social psychology of organizations* (2nd edn). New York: Wiley.
Kipnis, D., Schmidt, S. & Wilkinson, I. (1980). Intraorganizational influence tactics: Explorations in getting one's way. *Journal of Applied Psychology*, **65**, 440–452.
Yukl, G. & Tracey, J. B. (1992). Consequences of influence tactics used with subordinates, peers, and the boss. *Journal of Applied Psychology*, **77**, 525–535.

EDWIN P. HOLLANDER

information processing Originally used to describe the operation of INFORMATION TECHNOLOGY, information processing has served as a METAPHOR for both individuals and organizations. The basic components of an information processing system – devices for input, storage, operating on data, and output – describe a general model for an individual or social system which must interact with its environment (*see* SYSTEMS THEORY). The associated processes of representation, memory, transformation, and response model well corresponding individual and organizational processes.

The modeling of human cognition as an information processing system dates from the 1950s with the models of human problem solving by Newell, Simon, and others (*see* COGNITIVE PROCESSES). It has eventuated in a new branch of research, cognitive science. This approach involves study of the senses as input devices; exploration of the structure of human memory and knowledge representation; modeling of problem-solving, DECISION MAKING, and judgment; and study of the link between human action and information processing. It has led to advances in our understanding human decision making, artificial intelligence, and improvements in the design of information technology, particularly parallel processors and interfaces.

The information processing metaphor is also usefully applied to organizations. All organizations must deal with UNCERTAINTY, and they do this by acquiring and processing information. A key determinant of information processing effectiveness is ORGANIZATIONAL DESIGN. As Weber observed, a central purpose of the classical BUREAUCRACY is to manage the flow of information and related decisions in a rational manner. Rules and HIERARCHY were, in essence, substitutes for COMMUNICATION; they alleviated the need for consultation and left bureaucrats free to act in a standardized fashion that made coordination easy. Of course, the bureaucracy is not the only possible design, and other designs, such as the flat, organic organization, are appropriate for different information processing needs (*see* MECHANISTIC/ORGANIC). Additional design features, such as the temporary task force and lateral linkages, could also be incorporated to address information processing needs.

Galbraith (1977) developed an information processing contingency model for organizational design (*see* CONTINGENCY THEORY). It posits that design should depend on two factors, degree of uncertainty the organization faces and resource minimization. Uncertainty increases as a function of the organization's task, ORGANIZATIONAL SIZE, and speed of environmental change. In general, as uncertainty increases, more complex designs with more lateral communication linkages are needed to meet information processing demands. For low levels of uncertainty the traditional bureaucratic expedients of rules, hierarchy, and PLANNING will serve. As uncertainty increases, organizations must either:

(a) utilize SLACK RESOURCES;
(b) subdivide their work among units or divisions, each of which handles a self-contained part of the total information processing load;
(c) develop formalized organizational information systems; or
(d) develop lateral relations through mechanisms such as task forces, integrating roles, and in the extreme, the matrix and dynamic network designs (*see* MATRIX ORGANIZATION).

The particular mix of the four coping mechanisms an organization chooses determines its design. Generally, that mix which handles requisite uncertainty while minimizing resource utilization is most desirable.

Another method of adapting to uncertainty is choice of the appropriate communication medium. Media choice is discussed in the entry on COMMUNICATION.

See also **Cognition in organizations; Organization and environment, Communications technology; Perception; Attribution**

Bibliography

Galbraith, J. (1977). *Organizational design.* Reading, MA: Addison-Wesley.

Huber, G. P. & Draft, R. L. (1987). The information environments of organizations. In F. M. Jablin, L. L. Putnam, K. H. Roberts & L. W. Porter (Eds), *Handbook of organizational communication: An interdisciplinary perspective* (pp. 130–164). Beverly Hills, CA: Sage.

MARSHALL SCOTT POOLE

information technology Information technology (IT) refers to computer-based systems used in the management of an enterprise. IT is distinguished from ADVANCED MANUFACTURING TECHNOLOGY (AMT) in that the former applies computing to accounting, PLANNING,

DECISION MAKING, and COMMUNICATIONS activities, whereas the latter applies computing to the factory floor. (Increasingly, IT and AMT are merging, as managerial computing is integrated with manufacturing machinery.) IT can be viewed in terms of the target level of the organization which the TECHNOLOGY aims to support: transactions processing systems support ongoing exchanges between the organization and external parties, such as customers or suppliers; reporting systems and decision support systems support middle management; and executive information systems support upper management. Whereas early applications of IT largely benefitted accounting processes, newer applications aid in sophisticated decision analysis and global communication.

The impacts of IT can be assessed at organizational, group, or individual levels of analysis. Organizational impacts include the effects of IT on JOB SATISFACTION, PARTICIPATION, and centralization of management (*see* DECENTRALIZATION). At the group level, the impacts of IT on interpersonal communication and team decision making are studied (*see* GROUP DECISION MAKING). At the individual level, impacts of IT consider how use of a specific type or class of IT changes decision processes, attitudes, or behaviors. Rarely are the impacts of IT purely deterministic. More often, IT impacts are moderated by other organizational, group, or individual factors. For example, studies showing the effects of IT on organizational decision show both centralizing and decentralizing effects. Depending on a variety of factors, IT may lead to greater centralization or greater decentralization; similarly, IT may raise PRODUCTIVITY or lower it. Increasingly, IT impacts are considered to be multivariant and emergent. The effects of IT are a function of a range of organizational and environmental factors, and effects vary over time.

Important research issues include identifying contextual and other variables that account for positive and negative IT impacts; and describing the changes in IT impacts following adoption. HUMAN–COMPUTER INTERACTION research considers how IT might be designed to improve the likelihood of positive IT impacts. SOFTWARE ERGONOMICS research considers the design of IT to meet individual, group, or organizational needs. Diffusion of INNOVATION is also a key issue, as the adoption practices of organizations may influence the ultimate impacts of IT (*see* INNOVATION ADOPTION; INNOVATION DIFFUSION).

See also **Computer-aided-design; Automation; Information processing**

Bibliography

Dunlop, C. & Kling, R. (Eds) (1991). *Computerization and controversy: Value conflicts and social choices.* Boston: Academic Press.

Huber, G. P. (1990). A theory of the effects of advanced information technologies on organizational design, intelligence, and decision making. *Academy of Management Review*, **15**, (1), 47–71.

Huseman, R. C. & Miles, E. W. (1988). Organizational communication in the information age: Implications of computer-based systems. *Journal of Management*, **14**, (2), 181–204.

Orlikowski, W. J. (1992). The duality of technology: Rethinking the concept of technology in organizations. *Organization Science*, **3**, (3), 398–427.

Sage, A. P. (1981). Behavioral and organizational considerations in the design of information systems and processes for planning and decision support. *IEEE Transactions on Systems, Man, and Cybernetics*, **SMC-11**, no. 9, 640–678.

GERARDINE DESANCTIS

initiating structure *see* MANAGERIAL STYLE; LEADERSHIP STYLE

innovation Few subjects have received as much attention from social scientists, managers, and public policy makers as innovation. It is the engine for novel changes in social, economic, and political arrangements in organizations and society as a whole (*see* ORGANIZATIONAL CHANGE). An innovation is the creation and implementation of a new idea. The new idea may pertain to a technological innovation (new technical artifacts, devices, or products), a process innovation (new services, programs, or production procedures), or an administrative innovation (new institutional policies, structures, or systems). The idea may be a novel recombination of old ideas, a scheme that challenges the present order, or an unprecedented formula or approach (Zaltman, Duncan,

& Holbek, 1973). As long as the idea is perceived as new and entails a novel change for the actors involved, it is an innovation. When the actors who develop and implement the new idea are members or groups of an organization, the venture is considered an organizational innovation or an internal corporate venture, in contrast to efforts undertaken by independent individuals (ENTREPRENEURSHIP), or by organizations working collectively (*see* JOINT VENTURES).

Innovations can vary widely in novelty, size, and temporal duration. Some innovations involve small, quick, incremental, lone-worker efforts. Some are unplanned, and emerge by chance, accident, or afterthought. Although the majority of innovations in organizations may be of small scope, larger scale innovations have attracted most attention from practitioners and researches. In particular, the scope of innovations discussed below are those in which most managers and venture capitalists typically invest. They consist of planned, concentrated efforts to develop and implement a novel idea in a climate of substantial technical, organizational, and market UNCERTAINTY; entailing a collective effort of considerable duration; and requiring greater resources than are held by the people undertaking the effort.

Studies of organizational innovation tend to examine two kinds of questions:

(1) What are the antecedent factors that influence innovativeness? and
(2) How are innovations created, developed and implemented?

The first question usually entails study of the contextual factors (independent variables) which explain statistically variations in the number and kinds of organizational innovations introduced in a given period of time (the dependent variable). The second question involves processual study of the temporal order and sequence of events which unfold in the development of a given innovation. A brief overview of research on these two questions is described below.

Factors Influencing Organizational Innovativeness

Tornatsky and Fleischer (1990) point out that a positive bias pervades the study of innovation. Innovation is often viewed as a good thing because the new idea must be useful – profitable, constructive, or solve a problem. New ideas that are not perceived as useful are not normally called innovations; they are usually called mistakes (*see* ERRORS). Objectively, of course, the usefulness of an idea can only be determined after the innovation process is completed and implemented. Moreover, while many new ideas are proposed in organizations, only a very few receive serious consideration and developmental effort. Since it is not possible to determine at the outset which new ideas are "innovations" or "mistakes," it is important to understand what conditions motivate and enable organizational innovation.

Amabile (1983), Angle (1989), and Kanter (1983) and Tornatsky and Fleischer (1990) summarize a large body of research indicating that innovative behaviors are more likely to occur in organizational contexts that both enable and motivate innovation; it is less likely to occur where either enabling or motivating conditions are absent. The design of an organization's structure, systems, and practices influence the likelihood that innovation ideas will be surfaced, and that once surfaced they will be developed and nurtured toward realization (*see* ORGANIZATIONAL DESIGN; MECHANISTIC/ORGANIC).

Several organizational structural features are empirically related to innovative activities. The more complex and differentiated the organization, and the easier it is to cross boundaries, the greater the potential number of sources from which innovative ideas can spring. However, as Kanter (1983) discusses, organizational segmentation and bureaucratic procedures accompany increases in ORGANIZATIONAL SIZE and COMPLEXITY (*see* BUREAUCRACY). These often constrain innovation unless special systems are put in place to motivate and enable innovative behavior. Key motivating factors include providing a balance of intrinsic and extrinsic rewards for innovative behaviors (*see* EXTRINSIC/INTRINSIC MOTIVATION). While people work for pay to make a living, incentive pay (i.e., monetary rewards contingent on performance and in addition to base salary) seems to be a relatively weak motivator for innovation; it more often serves as a proxy for recognition (*see* PAYMENT SYSTEMS; BONUS PAYMENTS). Angle (1989) found that individualized rewards tend to increase idea generation and radical innovations; whereas group rewards tend to increase innovation implementation and incremental innovations.

In addition to these motivating factors, the following kinds of enabling conditions are equally necessary for innovative behavior:

- resources for innovation;
- frequent COMMUNICATIONS across departmental lines, among people with dissimilar viewpoints;
- moderate environmental uncertainty and mechanisms for focusing attention on changing conditions;
- cohesive WORK GROUPS with open CONFLICT RESOLUTION mechanisms that integrate creative personalities into the mainstream (*see* GROUP COHESIVENESS);
- structures that provide access to innovation ROLE models and mentors;
- moderately low personnel TURNOVER; and
- PSYCHOLOGICAL CONTRACTS that legitimate and solicit spontaneous innovative behavior.

Angle (1989) concludes that normal people have the capability and potential to be creative and innovative. The actualization of this potential depends on whether management structures an organizational context to not only motivate but also to enable individuals to innovate.

Many innovations transcend the BOUNDARIES of individual firms, industries, and populations or communities of organizations. As a result, economics and organizational researchers have examined innovation from an augmented industry LEVEL OF ANALYSIS (*see* Sahal, 1981). At this macro level, studies have focused on patterns of cooperation and competition among organizations developing similar, complementary or substitute innovations, as well as the roles of public and private sector actors in the development of an industrial infrastructure for innovation (*see* GOVERNMENT AND BUSINESS). This infrastructure includes:

(1) institutional arrangements that legitimate, regulate, and standardize a new innovation;
(2) public resource endowments of basic scientific knowledge, financing and insurance arrangements, and pools of competent labor; as well as
(3) proprietary R&D, testing, manufacturing, marketing, and distribution functions that are often required to develop and commercialize a technical or process innovation.

The development of this industry infrastructure significantly influences the odds of innovation success by individual organizations and entrepreneurs. This infrastructure does not emerge and change all at once through the actions of one or even a few organizational actors. Instead, it develops through an accretion of numerous events involving many public and private sector actors over an extended period of time.

The Process of Organizational Innovation

Perhaps the most widely known model of the innovation process is that proposed by Rogers (1983). It represents three decades of Rogers's own research and a synthesis of over 3100 published innovation studies. This model portrays the process of innovation as consisting of three basic stages:

(1) invention of novel idea, which comes from a recognition of market or user needs and advances in basic or applied research;
(2) its development, or the sequence of events in which the new idea is transformed from an abstract concept into an operational reality; and
(3) implementation, or the diffusion and adoption of the innovation by users.

Specialized fields of study have emerged to examine each innovation stage in greater detail. For the idea invention stage, an extensive literature has developed on individual and group CREATIVITY, primarily by psychologists (e.g., Amabile, 1983; Angle, 1989), and on "technology push" versus "demand pull" by economists (e.g., Sahal, 1981). Although less extensively studied than the other stages, the development stage is gaining more research attention from management scholars (e.g., Kanter, 1983; Tushman & Romanelli, 1985; Van de Ven, Angle, & Poole, 1989). Finally, Rogers (1983) notes that no area in the social sciences has perhaps received as much study as the implementation stage (*see* INNOVATION DIFFUSION and INNOVATION ADOPTION).

While a conducive organizational context sets the stage for innovation, the developmental process itself is highly uncertain, ambiguous, and risky (*see* AMBIGUITY; RISK-TAKING). Van de Ven, Angle, and Poole (1989) report recent studies showing that the sequence of events in developing innovations from invention to implementation do not unfold in a simple linear sequence of stages or phases. Instead, the innovation journey tends to unfold in the following ways. In the beginning, a set of seemingly coincidental events occur in an organization which set the stage for initiating an innovation. Some of these gestating events are sufficiently large to "shock" the action thresholds of organizational participants to launch an innovative venture. Soon after work begins to develop the venture, the process proliferates from a simple unitary sequence of activities into a divergent, parallel, and convergent progression. Some of these activities are related through a division of labor among functions, but many are unrelated in any noticeable form of functional interdependence. Many component ideas and paths that were perceived as being related at one time, are often reframed or rationalized as being independent and disjunctive at another time when the innovation idea or circumstances change. Problems, mistakes, and setbacks frequently occur as these developmental paths are pursued, and they provide opportunities either for learning or for terminating the developmental efforts. The innovation journey ends either when the innovation is adopted and implemented by an organization, when resources run out, or when political opposition prevails to terminate the developmental efforts (*see* POLITICS). These messy and complex processes that are being found in recent real-time studies of innovation development are leading researchers to reconceptualize the process of innovation, because the observed processes cannot be reduced to a simple sequence of stages or phases as most process models in the literature suggest.

We may never find one best way to innovate because the innovation process is inherently probabilistic and because there are myriad forms and kinds of innovations. In particular, the characteristics of the innovation processes described above are more pronounced or more complex in innovations of greater novelty, size, and duration.

Researchers have found the stages of the innovation process to be more disorderly for technically complex innovations than they are for technically simple innovations. Statistical relationships between the innovation processes and outcomes are much weaker for highly novel radical innovations than they are for less novel incremental innovations. Some organizations appear more successful in developing certain types of innovation. For example, an organization which values and rewards INDIVIDUALISM may have the advantage in radical innovation, while a more collectivist system may do better at an incremental one. However, across these organizations differences, studies show that transitions from innovation invention to development to adoption activities often entail shifts from radical to incremental and from divergent to convergent thinking. As innovations approach the culminating institutionalization step, they become more structured and stabilized in their patterns and less differentiated from other organizational arrangements.

The developmental pattern and eventual success of an innovation is also influenced by its temporal duration. Initial investments at the startup of an innovation represents an initial stock of assets that provides an innovation unit a "honeymoon" period to perform its work. These assets reduce the risk of terminating the innovation during its honeymoon period when setbacks arise and when initial outcomes are judged unfavorable. The likelihood of replenishing these assets is highly influenced by the duration of the developmental process. Interest and COMMITMENT wane with time. Thus, after the honeymoon period, innovations terminate at disproportionately higher rates, in proportion to the time needed for their implementation.

In terms of organization size, small organizations appear to have the advantage in starting up innovations, but larger organizations with more slack resources have the advantage of keeping an innovation alive until it is completed. Larger organizations can offer a more fertile ground for sustaining and nurturing spin-off innovations. Yet, as organizations grow in size they seem to rely increasingly on bureaucratic systems and procedures that may be efficient for managing ongoing operations, but may inhibit innovative behavior. So the message to managers of large organizations is to keep finding ways to remain flexible (*see* FLEXIBILITY), to permit sufficient attention and resources to concentrate on innovation, to build access to technical competence, and to listen attentively to the views of those directly responsible for implementation – factors which Nord and Tucker (1987) found were critical success factors for adopting innovations in large organizations.

See also **Organization development; Turnaround management; Open systems; Risk-taking; Technology transfer**

Bibliography

Amabile, T. M. (1983). *The social psychology of creativity*. New York: Springer-Verlag.

Angle, H. A. (1989). Psychology and Organizational Innovation. Chapter 5 in A. Van de Ven, H. Angle, M. S. Poole (Eds.) *Research on the management of innovation: The Minnesota studies*. New York: Ballinger/Harper & Row.

Kanter, R. M. (1983). *The change masters*. New York: Simon and Schuster.

Nord, W. R. & Tucker S. (1987). *Implementing Routine and Radical Innovations*. Lexington; MA: D. C. Heath.

Rogers, E. (1983). *Diffusion of innovations* (3rd edn). New York: Free Press.

Sahal, D. (1981). *Patterns of technological innovation*. Reading, MA: Addison-Wesley.

Tornatzky, L. G. & Fleischer M. (1990). *The processes of technological innovation*. Lexington, MA: D. C. Heath.

Tushman, M. & Romanelli, E. (1985). Organizational Evolution: A Metamorphosis Model of Convergence and Reorientation. In B. Staw & L. Cummings (Ed.), *Research in organizational behavior* (vol. 7). Greenwich, CT: JAI Press.

Van de Ven, A. H., H. Angle & M. S. Poole (eds.) (1989). *Research on the Management of Innovation: The Minnesota Studies*. New York: Ballinger/Harper & Row.

Zaltman, G. R., Duncan & J. Holbek (1973). *Innovations and organizations*. New York: Wiley.

ANDREW H. VAN DE VEN

innovation adoption The adoption of new ideas represents a major challenge for organizations since any INNOVATION represents a departure from standard practice. It is somewhat immaterial whether the new idea is indigenous to the organization or was imported from elsewhere. Innovation adoption, entails both a go/no go decision event as well as its subsequent implementation; it can be discussed from the standpoint of the adopter or from the object that is being adopted.

With some degree of exaggeration, it can be said that innovation amounts to a form of illegitimacy or non-CONFORMITY, because new ideas challenge current beliefs and practices (*see* LEGITIMACY). Four strands of work can be distinguished to alleviate the hurdles that innovations encounter before they might become adopted by the organization. (1) Sponsorship by the senior management of any new idea, whether a new production process, a new product, or new organizational arrangements will shield the innovation against SABOTAGE, resistance, or deprivation of critical resources. The innovation needs to be anchored in the strategic commitments, which are discernible from top managements deeds and words (*see* TOP MANAGEMENT TEAMS). Some authors (e.g., Burgelman, 1983), however, have argued that top management can be part of the conformity problem, and that in fact many successful adoptions occur in spite of top management's preferences and directions. Organizations which display room for (2) internal venturing will have a greater capacity for fledgling ideas to overcome their initial hurdles, and eventually to become an integral part of a firm's portfolio of product offerings. Such a view stresses the surreptitious role of individuals who operate from the organization's "trenches" and who create a context for new ideas to come to fruition (*see* ENTREPRENEURSHIP).

There is also a related view, which could be labeled the (3) "idea champion," which has strong political connotation. Idea champions are those organizational members, who are associated with a new idea, and who mobilize political support inside and outside the firm, are visible and often prominent political actors, whose *success* makes or breaks their CAREER. Finally, there is the view, probably most widely accepted, that an innovation adoption hinges on the presence of (4) collaborative relationships among the key parts of the organization – as a minimum production, service, marketing, and research and development (e.g., Cooper, 1986) – such that some degree of shared ownership emerges. Organizations accommodate several subcultures (*see* CULTURE, GROUP). The successful process of innovation adoption requires the pertinent subcultures to be merged so that their interaction resembles a rugby game rather than a relay race in which each department passes the baton to the next one. This meeting of the minds is widely practiced among Japanese organizations (*see* JUST-IN-TIME) and is indicated by such expressions as "concurrent engineering". The meeting of the minds is also crucial in linking the firm with external know-how. Boundary spanning activities facilitate the adoption of external know-how and have clear implications for the connection between adoption and diffusion (*see* INNOVATION DIFFUSION). Diffusion of innovation requires us to consider not only the communication NETWORKING between organizations, their suppliers, customers and others, but also the BOUNDARY SPANNING structures that channel external know-how into the core of the organization, and which induce the various above mentioned adoption behaviors.

Innovation adoption should not only be viewed from the perspective of the adopter, but also with respect to the attributes of the innovation itself. Those attributes include price, technical or administrative character, degree of discontinuity or radicalness. Radicalness will provoke problems of illegitimacy, but organizations differ with respect to their willingness to absorb new ideas. Normann (1971) was one of the first authors to link degree of novelty to the tolerance of organizations to adopt new and potentially upsetting ideas. Because pressures to conformity are strong, it is widely assumed that adoption of innovation will only succeed when the new idea is in the vicinity of current beliefs and practices. This accords with the notion that innovation amounts to creative destruction (of old ideas) and that organizations have the tendency to innovate incrementally. This view is well conceptualized in Nelson and Winter (1982) by stipulating that organizations are bundles of routines that govern the addition of new routines. The implication is that adoption of discontinuous ideas is more likely to fail.

See also **Creativity; Learning organization; Organizational change; Structuration**

Bibliography

Burgelman, R. A. (1983). A process model of internal corporate venturing in the diversified major firm. *Administrative Science Quarterly*, **28**, 223–244.

Cooper, R. G. (1986). *Winning at new products*. New York: Addison-Wesley.

Normann, R. (1971). Organizational innovativeness: Product variation and orientation. *Administrative Science Quarterly*, **16**, 203–215.

Nelson, R. R. & Winter S. G. (1982). *An evolutionary theory of economic change*. Cambridge, MA: Harvard University Press.

JOHANNES M. PENNINGS

innovation diffusion Innovations originate "somewhere" and may subsequently spread. Diffusion of INNOVATION entails the dispersion of a new idea, product, technology, or service. For example, Taylorism (*see* SCIENTIFIC MANAGEMENT) came to life in the United States and diffused to Europe, while JUST-IN-TIME went from Japan to the United States and firms in and EC countries. The diffusion can pertain to products or services, to production methods, or to organizational practices and is discernible among groups of individuals or organizations.

A variety of diffusion models has been developed. The most prominent among these have a marketing provenance, simply because marketing science tries to explain buyer behavior and has been foremost interested in the mechanisms that define the gradual acceptance of a new idea (e.g., Mahajan, Muller, & Bass, 1990). In the marketing view, diffusion is often described as a chain, for example, the product life cycle and the "s-curve". The curve shows the spread to have a slow beginning, then a "ramp-up" and a leveling off.

Organizationally, these models are not too useful, because unlike individuals, organizations are comprised of clusters of interdependent individuals, choices about adoption are very complex (*see* INNOVATION ADOPTION), and communication networks are more multiplex. An early contribution came from Rogers (1983) reviewing thousands of studies with mostly a sociological slant, and culminating in a "three-stage model" from invention, application to adoption and diffusion. The latter stage is subdivided into five "sub-stages": marketing, interest arousal, trial implementation, continued use, and full implementation. The stages are quite arbitrary and vague, which is probably the reason that others have adopted a more continuous approach to diffusion research. Among more recent organizational approaches to diffusion, social networks and institutionalization are interesting (*see* NETWORK ANALYSIS). Networks are prominent in research of innovation diffusion, because they appear to explain the pathways along which new ideas travel. The spreading of new ideas requires us to think in developmental terms, recognizing the idea here versus the same idea there presumes some linkage.

COMMUNICATION instills pressures toward conformity and is induced by the presence of networks (Burt, 1987). NETWORKING fosters the development of new norms and is therefore akin to institutionalization theory.

This latter theory holds that innovations spread to the extent that they are defined and approved by prevailing rationalized concepts of organizational conduct, are institutionalized in society (or in specific markets, industries, or populations), independent of the innovation's efficacy. Abrahamson (1991) is a clear exponent of this position and argues that most innovations find their way into organizations, not on the basis of some rational calculus, but because of the presence of fads and fashions, which reduce the uncertainty that surrounds a novel product, technology or practice (*see* GARBAGE CAN MODEL). Both network and INSTITUTIONAL THEORY adopt a multilevel framework, stressing the embeddedness of organizations. Unfortunately, they treat what happens inside the firm as a "black box," so that little is known about the propensity of organizations to become "contaminated" by innovations. Recent studies (e.g., Pennings & Harianto, 1992) seek to address aspects of that black box, for example, by treating the firm as set of CORE COMPETENCIES or skills to which new competencies are added (*see* ORGANIZATIONAL LEARNING). Further insights will emerge involving research being longitudinal and covering a multitude of industries or populations.

See also **Loose-coupling; Learning organization; Technology transfer**

Bibliography

Abrahamson, E. (1991). Managerial fads and fashion: The diffusion and rejection of innovations. *Academy of Management Review*, **16**, 586–612.

Burt, R. S. (1987). Social contagion and innovation: Cohesion versus structural equivalence. *American Journal of Sociology*, **92**, 1287–1335.

Mahajan, V., Muller, E. & Bass, F. M. (1990). New product diffusion models in marketing: A review and directions for research. *Journal of Marketing*, **54**, 1–26.

Pennings, J. M. & Harianto, F. (1992). Technological networking and innovation implementation. *Organization Science*, **III**, 1992, 356–382.

Rogers, E. (1983). *Diffusion of Innovation* (3rd edn). New York: Free Pres.

JOHANNES M. PENNINGS

institutional theory Much of the research on organizations since the 1970s focuses on the structure and composition of organizational environments (*see* ORGANIZATION AND ENVIRONMENT). In contrast to research in micro OB or corporate strategy, which stresses the efforts of individual organizations to adapt, most macro-level work maintains that ORGANIZATIONAL CHANGE is shaped largely by changes in the environment. The idea that organizations are deeply embedded in wider institutional environments suggests that organizational practices are often either direct reflections of, or responses to, rules and structures built into their larger environments. This line of institutional analysis traces its origins to research by John Meyer on the effects of education as an institution (Meyer, 1977; Meyer & Rowan, 1977); work by J. Meyer, W. R. Scott, and colleagues (Meyer & Scott, 1983) on the dependence of educational organizations on wider cultural and symbolic understandings about the nature of schooling (*see* SYMBOLISM); research by Zucker (1977; 1983) on the taken-for-granted aspects of organizational life; and work by DiMaggio and Powell (1983) on the social construction of organizational fields (*see* SOCIAL CONSTRUCTIONISM). In recent years, institutional theory and research have developed rapidly and it presently represents a significant strand of work in macro OB. Substantial collections of current research (Powell & DiMaggio, 1991; Scott & Meyer, 1994) present a wide range of applications of institutional analysis to topics as diverse as differences between public and private schools, internal LABOR MARKETS, art museums, the DIVERSIFICATION strategies of large corporations, and types of accounting systems.

Although ecological and institutional approaches differ markedly in the weight they assign to organization adaptation and managerial cognition, these approaches share a number of key insights. Both focus on the collective organization of the environment, insisting that the environment of organizations made up of other organizations and that processes of legitimation and competition shape ORGANIZATIONAL BEHAVIOR (*see* LEGITIMACY). But ecologists attend to demographic processes – organizational foundings, transformations, and deaths (*see* POPULATION ECOLOGY). Institutionalists, in contrast, analyze the diffusion of rules and procedures that organizations are rewarded for incorporating.

Institutional theory combines a rejection of the optimizing assumptions of rational actor models popular in economics with an interest in institutions as independent variables. The constant and repetitive quality of much of organizational life results not from the calculated actions of self-interested individuals but from the fact that practices come to be taken for granted. The model of behavior is one in which "actors associate certain actions with certain situations by rules of appropriateness" (March & Olsen, 1984, p. 741). Individuals in organizations face choices all the time, but in making decisions they seek guidance from the experiences of others in comparable situations and by reference to standards of obligation.

The unit of analysis in institutional research is the organizational field or societal sector. The assumption is that organizations exist in socially constructed communities composed of similar organizations that are responsible for a definable area of institutional life. An organizational field includes key suppliers, consumers, regulatory agencies, professional and labor associations, as well as other organizations that produce a similar service or product.

DiMaggio and Powell (1983) argue that the process by which a field comes to be organized consists of four stages:

(1) an increase in the amount of interaction among organizations within a field;
(2) the emergence of well-defined patterns of HIERARCHY and coalition;
(3) an upsurge in the information load with which members of a field must contend; and
(4) the development of a mutual awareness among participants that they are involved in a common enterprise.

Processes of Institutionalization

How do organizational practices and structures become institutionalized within a field? Scholars have posited several mechanisms that promote isomorphism, that is, structural similarities among organizations within a field. Some of these processes encourage homogenization within a field directly by leading to structural and behavioral changes in organizations themselves. Others work indirectly by shaping the assumptions and experiences of the individuals who staff organizations. DiMaggio and Powell (1983) posit three general types of institutional pressures:

(1) coercive forces that stem from political influence and problems of legitimacy;
(2) mimetic changes that are responses to uncertainty; and
(3) normative influences resulting from professionalization

These three mechanisms are likely to intermingle in specific empirical settings, but they tend to derive from different conditions and may lead to different outcomes. Indeed, institutional pressures may be cross-cutting and lead to CONFLICT.

Coercive influence results from both formal and informal pressures exerted on organizations by other organizations upon which they are dependent, as well as by strongly held cultural expectations in society at large (*see* CULTURE). In some circumstances, organizational change is a response to government mandate: manufacturers adopt new pollution control technologies to conform to environmental regulations, nonprofits maintain accounts and hire accountants to meet the requirements of the tax laws, restaurants maintain minimum health standards, and organizations hire affirmative action officers to fend off allegations of DISCRIMINATION.

UNCERTAINTY is a powerful force that encourages mimetic or imitative behavior among the members of an organizational field. When organizational technologies are poorly understand, that is, when managers are unclear about the relationship between means and ends, or when there is ambiguity regarding goals, or when the environment is highly uncertain, organizations often model themselves after other organizations. The modeled organization may be unaware of the modeling; it merely serves as a convenient source of organizational practices that the borrowing organization may use. Models may be diffused unintentionally, indirectly through employee transfer or TURNOVER, or explicitly by organizations such as consulting firms. In this view, the ubiquity of certain kinds of modern management practices is credited more to the universality of mimetic processes than to any concrete evidence that the adopted models enhance efficiency.

A third source of organizational change is normative and stems from the culture of PROFESSIONALISM. Two aspects of professionalism are particularly relevant. One is the growth of professional communities based on knowledge produced by university specialists and legitimated through academic credentials; the second is the spread of formal and informal professional networks that span organizations and across which innovations may diffuse rapidly (*see* INNOVATION DIFFUSION). Universities and professional training institutions are important centers for the development of organizational norms among professional managers and staff.

Empirical Results

Much of the initial research focused on public sector and nonprofit organizations in such areas as education, health care, mental health, and the arts (*see* NOT-FOR-PROFIT ORGANIZATIONS). The twentieth century has seen a large-scale expansion of the role of government and the professions in these fields (*see* GOVERNMENT AND BUSINESS). The more highly organized policy making has become, the more individual organizations focus on responding to the official categories and procedures specified by the larger environment. In order to be perceived as legitimate, organizations adapt their formal structures and routines to conform to institutional norms. Hence to the extent that pressures from the environment are exerted on all members of a field, these organizations will become more similar. But pressures for field-wide conformity may shape only an organization's formal structure (i.e., its organization chart and rules and reporting procedures), while backstage practices may be "decoupled" from official actions.

The concept of isomorphism has been utilized to describe the processes that encourage a unit in a population to resemble other units facing similar circumstances. Such pressures were theorized to be strongest in fields with a weak technical base (e.g., education, the arts, advertising, etc.), with ambiguous or conflicting goals (e.g., professional service firms), and that are buffered from market pressures (i.e., supported by endowment income or public funding, protected by government regulation, etc.). More recently, however, researchers have turned their attention to for-profit firms, examining the adoption of various employment practices, the utilization of different accounting standards, and the diffusion of management policies. This work has proven valuable in extending the reach of institutional analysis to some of the core firms in the U.S. economy, while at the same time showing that organizations do not passively conform to institutional pressures. Rather government or professional mandates can be contested, negotiated, or partially implemented. Work by Edelman (1992) on civil rights law illustrates that the diffusion of new legal practices is not unidirectional; instead a complex interaction emerges in which government compliance standards are shaped by the responses of organizations.

Most institutional studies have focused on organizational practices as responses to the actions of various governing bodies: legislatures, courts, regulatory agencies, certification and accreditation boards, and professional associations. The advantage of this research is that it permits specification of how the environment shapes organizations, allowing researchers to understand the effects of different types of CONTROL systems. These analyses also enhance our understanding of the relationship between environmental COMPLEXITY and internal organ-izational structure (*see* ORGANIZATIONAL DESIGN). For example, when environments contain multiple strong centers of authority and legitimacy, we find more levels of administration inside organizations, and greater differentiation across members of a field. When environments are more homogeneous, researchers find less elaborate internal organizational structures and less diversity across organizations.

Summary

Many of the prevailing approaches to ORGANIZATION THEORY assume implicitly that organizations are purposive and are progressing toward more efficient and adaptive forms. The institutional approach takes neither of these assumptions for granted, consequently it raises a different set of questions, asking how and from where do our notions of RATIONALITY emerge. This line of work seeks to treat the emergence of modern organizations and the laws and practices that govern them as the objects of study. Institutionalization, or the "process by which a given set of units and a pattern of activities come to be normatively and cognitively held in place, and practically taken for granted as lawful" (Meyer, Boli, & Thomas, 1987, p. 13) becomes the subject of inquiry.

See also **Exchange relations; Organizational learning**

Bibliography

DiMaggio, P. J. & Powell, W. W. (1983). The iron cage revisited: Institutional isomorphism and collective rationality in organizational fields. *American Sociological Review*, **48**, 147–60.

Edelman, L. (1992). Legal ambiguity and symbolic structures: Organizational mediation on civil rights law. *American Journal of Sociology*, **97**, 1531–1576.

March, J. G. & Olsen J. (1984). The new institutionalism: Organizational factors in political life. *American Political Science Review*, **78**, 734–49.

Meyer, J. W. (1977). The effects of education as an institution. *American Journal of Sociology*, **83**, 55–77.

Meyer, J. W., Boli, J. & Thomas, G. (1987). Ontology and rationalization in the Western cultural account. In G. Thomas, J.W. Meyer, F.O. Ramirez & J. Boli (Eds) *Institutional Structure*, pp. 12–37. Beverly Hills, CA: Sage.

Meyer, J. W. & Rowan, B. (1977). Institutionalized organizations: Formal structure as myth and ceremony. *American Journal of Sociology*, **83**, 340–63.

Meyer, J. W. & Scott, W. R. (Eds) (1983). *Organizational environments: Ritual and rationality*. Beverly Hills, CA: Sage.

Powell, W. W. & DiMaggio P. J. (Eds) (1991). *The new institutionalism in organizational analysis*. Chicago: University of Chicago Press.

Scott, W. R. & Meyer, J. W. (1994). *Institutional environments and organizations*. Thousand Oaks CA: Sage.

Zucker, L. G. (1977). The role of institutionalization in cultural persistence. *American Sociological Review*, **42**, 726–43.

Zucker, L. G. (1983). Organizations as institutions. In S. Bachrach (Ed), *Research in the Sociology of Organizations* (pp. 1–47). Greenwich, CT: JAI.

WALTER W. POWELL

institutions The study of institutions, long an area of interest in the social sciences, has burgeoned of late. The many diverse lines of current research display wide variation in key definitions and concepts. Two lines of research – the new institutional economics (Langlois, 1986; North, 1990) and the new institutionalism in organizational analysis (March & Olsen, 1989; Powell & DiMaggio, 1991) – are of most relevance to scholars of organizations. The economists treat institutions as regularities of behavior understandable in terms of rules and routines (*see* ORGANIZATIONAL ECONOMICS). They are "perfectly analogous to the rules of the game in a competitive team sport" (North, 1990, p. 4). Institutions reduce UNCERTAINTY by providing a stable, but not necessarily efficient, structure to everyday interaction.

Institutional economists do not assume that institutions represent optimal solutions to problems of exchange and production, but they do build their theory on the basis of individual choice (*see* EXCHANGE RELATIONS). Institutions are the products of human design. In contrast, research in sociology and ORGANIZATION THEORY views institutions as the result of human activity, but not necessarily the product of human design. In this view, "institutions are frameworks of programs or rules establishing identities and activity scripts for such identities" (Jepperson, p. 146, in Powell & DiMaggio, 1991). Viewed more broadly, institutions are meaning systems, based on symbolic representations and enforced by formal and informal regulatory processes, and provide models for organizational processes and structures. To say that a practice or model is institutionalized means that it has become a taken-for-granted assumption around which organizational activity is constructed. In contrast to the economist's view of institutions, the more sociological approach sees organizational action as less based on choice and design, and more on identifying the normatively appropriate behavior (March & Olsen, 1989).

See also **Institutional theory; Bureaucracy**

Bibliography

Langlois, R. N. (1986). The new institutional economics. In R. N. Langlois (Ed). *Economics as a process* (pp. 1–25). New York: Cambridge University Press.

March, J. G. & Olsen, J. (1989). *Rediscovering institutions*. New York: Free Press.

North, D. C. (1990). *Institutions, institutional change and economic performance*. New York: Cambridge University Press.

Powell, W. W. & DiMaggio, P. J. (Eds) (1991). *The new institutionalism in organizational analysis*. Chicago: University of Chicago Press.

WALTER W. POWELL

instrumentality This is one of the components of the VIE THEORY (expectancy theory) of MOTIVATION. Instrumentality, within these theories, is the perceived likelihood that the occurrence of one outcome will lead to another. The term "instrumentality" probably follows from behavioral approaches to motivation in which animal subjects learn to perform certain behaviors or at certain levels to receive a REWARD. Performance of the behavior or attainment at a particular level is "instrumental" for receiving the reward. Other things being equal, the stronger an individual's perception of the instrumentality of an outcome, the greater is motivation.

In employment, where the level and timing of pay rewards and their contingencies with employee accomplishment are determined by the employer, the PAYMENT SYSTEM'S design is expected to influence the direction and level of employee performance. For example, if increased pay follows from demonstrating higher abilities, then skill development is instrumental for higher pay. If the volume or quality of output is associated with bonuses or pay increases, then improving measures of these outcomes will be instrumental for higher pay. Randomness of rewards reduces instrumentality perceptions and bias in the measurement of organizationally relevant outcomes distorts chosen behaviors of individuals to attain rewards relevant to them.

See also **Performance, individual; Reinforcement**

JOHN A. FOSSUM

integration In their classic work, *Organization and Environment*, Lawrence and Lorsch (1969) introduced integration as one of the most important concepts in ORGANIZATION DESIGN. Integration refers to the behaviors and structures used by differentiated SUBUNITS in an organization to coordinate their work activities. As organizations become more differentiated, in order to deal with complexities in their environments, it becomes increasingly difficult for departments and units of the organization to coordinate effectively. Differences in goals, time horizons and other orientations of differentiated subunits create conflicts and make mutual DECISION MAKING for the welfare of the entire organization difficult to obtain. Effective integrating mechanisms aid in coordinating under these types of conditions.

Integrating mechanisms need to be matched to the degree of DIFFERENTIATION among subunits. Where differentiation is low simple integrating devices will suffice. Where differentiation is high more complex structures or behaviors need to be designed. Galbraith (1977) proposed a rough hierarchy of integrating mechanisms. He suggests that HIERARCHY (integration through the chain of command) and vertical information systems suffice in less demanding coordination environments. When coordination demands increase then more sophisticated forms are needed and these usually involve lateral relations such as: liaison roles, teams, task forces, and MATRIX ORGANIZATION. Other authors have suggested that effective integration can be created through behavioral as well as structural mechanisms.

Techniques discussed include the use of effective NEGOTIATION and problem solving techniques and the creation of cooperative rather than competitive cultures (*see* ORGANIZATIONAL CULTURE; ORGANIZATIONAL CLIMATE).

Much of the literature on integration revolves around INNOVATION and the development of new products. As in the original Lawrence and Lorsch study, current authors argue that Sales, Manufacturing, R&D, and Engineering must work closely and cooperatively to achieve timely, competitive product innovations. The importance of the integration concept has not diminished as product innovation has taken on increased emphasis through the 1980s and 1990s. Organizations today compete on the basis of the timely introduction of a series of new products and consistently attempt to reduce cycle time. This has required the development of even more sophisticated integration mechanisms that now include simultaneous engineering, and COMPUTER-AIDED DESIGN, engineering, and manufacturing (*see* ADVANCED MANUFACTURING TECHNOLOGY). The basic concept of a need for coordination among separate departments has not changed, only the COMPLEXITY and sophistication of the mechanisms has increased.

Little in the way of actual testing of the theory of integration has occurred after Lawrence and Lorsch's (1969) original study. It is as if integration has become accepted as a part of the background wisdom of ORGANIZATION THEORY. Possibilities for further theoretical and empirical development exist, particularly in practical areas that do not involve only product innovation, such as service organizations.

See also **Linking pin; Mutual adjustment; Contingency theory; Organization and environment; Classical design theory; Boundary spanning**

Bibliography

Lawrence, P. R. & Lorsch, J. W. (1969). *Organization and environment*. Cambridge, MA: Division of Research, Graduate School of Business, Harvard University.

Galbraith, J. R. (1977). *Organization design*. Reading, MA: Addison-Wesley.

ROBERT DRAZIN

intelligence, testing This construct reflects differences among individuals in the capacity for conscious, deliberative processing of information (*see* INFORMATION PROCESSING). It depends on the ABILITY to hold and manipulate information in working memory, a capacity cognitive psychologists now call computational ability. Intelligence is also associated with the ability to learn from conscious, deliberative processing.

Intelligence is a broad based capacity that supports many more specific abilities, hence it is often referred to as general intelligence or a g factor. Intelligence is strongly associated with verbal ability and academic performance. Most intelligence tests are validated against such criteria.

Early work tried to distinguish intelligence (g) from other more specific abilities. More recent work has focused on the information processing components that support intelligence. Intelligence is strongly related to working memory capacity. Thus, intelligence is most highly associated with effective performance when people are learning tasks. With practice, proceduralized knowledge PRACTICAL INTELLIGENCE becomes an increasingly important determinant of performance and computational capacity (general intelligence) becomes less critical.

Intelligence shows remarkable stability over time, due in part to consistencies in environments. However, large changes over time in intelligence for children can occur and typically reflect changes in parental or educational variables. In later life, large changes in intelligence are more closely related to health status than chronological AGE. Test users should be aware of this mutable aspect of intelligence.

The use of intelligence (general cognitive ability) tests for selection is widespread and can be justified by meta-analyses showing their ability to predict job performance (Hunter & Hunter, 1984) (*see* PERFORMANCE, INDIVIDUAL). However, intelligence tests may also produce adverse impact for minority groups, creating legal and/or ethical problems which limits their use as selection devices (*see* DISCRIMINATION).

Interestingly, sophisticated computer systems also can behave intelligently, and there is considerable interest in artificial intelligence. Both human and artificial intelligence were thought to depend on the capacity to process symbol structures, but recent research challenges this perspective showing that many aspects of intelligence (in both human and artificial) can be produced by subsymbolic, connectionist level processes.

See also **Assessment; Psychological testing; Cognitive processes; Selection methods**

Bibliography

Hunter, J. E. & Hunter, R. F. (1984). Validity and utility of alternative predictors of job performance. *Psychological Bulletin*, **96**, 72–98.

ROBERT G. LORD

interactionism This refers to the joint influence of the environment and PERSONALITY on the attitudes, behaviors, cognitions, and EMOTIONS of people (Endler & Magnusson, 1976). The interactionism perspective in the ORGANIZATIONAL BEHAVIOR domain attempts to deal with two difficulties that have been noted in research. First, not everyone responds the same to a given job situation. Some people, for example, may be satisfied with a particular job while others are not. Second, personality characteristics are at best only partial predictors of people's reactions to jobs. For example, while people with certain PERSONALITY TRAITS might tend to be more satisfied with their jobs than people with other traits, there is a job that will make almost anyone dissatisfied (*see* ATTITUDES, DISPOSITIONAL APPROACHES).

Interactionism can be seen in two lines of research in the organizational behavior domain. First, there have been studies in which personality was considered to moderate relations between job conditions and various employee outcomes, such as job performance or JOB SATISFACTION. Second, there have been PERSON–JOB FIT studies that have looked at the impact of matching people's characteristics with the conditions and demands of jobs. Much of this research has looked at the discrepancy between what people want in a job and what they get from the job (Edwards, 1991).

See also **Statistical methods; Research methods; Theory; Research design**

Bibliography

Edwards, J. R. (1991). Person-job fit: A conceptual integration, literature review, and methodological critique. In C. L. Cooper & I. T. Robertson (Eds), *International review of industrial and organizational psychology* (1991 pp. 283–357) Chichester: John Wiley.

Endler, N. S. & Magnusson, D. (Eds), (1976). *Interactional psychology and personality*. Washington, D.C.: Hemisphere (Halsted–Wiley).

PAUL E. SPECTOR

intercultural process Although certain universal human traits and social skills will normally foster a workable mutual accommodation when cultures mix, the extent of its expression will vary according to the compatibility of the ideals of the cultures concerned. Some mixtures are fertile due to mutual stimulus and more so than when ideas derive homogeneously from one CULTURE. Such SYNERGY is valuable to organizations if it can be released. Some mixtures can however lead to negative effects.

International processes affecting organizations occur in the following domains: EXPATRIATION; hosting outsiders; GROUP DYNAMICS; language learning; INTERNATIONAL HR MANAGEMENT; COMMUNICATIONS.

The expatriate who enters a new culture as a more or less isolated outsider commonly goes through a process which begins very positively due to anticipation, declines into cultural shock as alternative value systems and their related behaviors, poorly understood, are seen as threatening, and recovers towards equilibrium as learning increases understanding, and mutual accommodation (*see* CAREER TRANSITIONS). Failure rates are nevertheless high and are often connected to adjustment problems for family members not working directly with local colleagues.

When a culture hosts outsiders a similar process occurs in reverse with initial interested curiosity giving way to a defensive ethnocentrism, prior to gradual acceptance. In some cases an external culture perceived as attractive may result in xenophilia where one's own culture is partially abandoned in favor of a borrowed alternative. This is visible in, e.g., Japanese westernness or teenage pop culture.

When interaction occurs with either individuals or groups of an alternative culture, it is common for two effects to follow: enhanced identification with one's own group; and STEREOTYPING of non members. Ingroup/outgroup feelings tend to be stronger in collectivist cultures where group membership is also related to security needs.

Language learning is the clearest symbol of commitment to understanding an alternative culture, but it varies greatly in difficulty. Languages with common structures and source vocabularies will clearly be more accessible one to another than languages with different structures, scripts, grammars, and vocabularies. For effective interaction, however, language facility remains a universal ideal.

In international business the nature of the intercultural processes will vary with the kind of operations involved (*see* INTERNATIONAL MANAGEMENT) (Adler, 1982). Developing a new company slowly from scratch in another culture allows time for blending to occur. Taking over a foreign company may result in tensions from the absorption of both a new corporate and a new national culture. MERGERS, AND ACQUISITIONS across two cultures have a low success rate even though equality and partnership may be aimed at; they normally need strong integrative leadership. JOINT VENTURES with foreign partners based on pooled resources are better with one source of management than two, and may yield synergy. Specific limited co-operation agreements, such as projects, are generally less risky and foster learning (*see* COOPERATION).

The rules for effective communications interculturally are:

(a) awareness and respect for the alternative mind-set;
(b) knowledge and understanding of the sources of alternative values; and
(c) practice-based skill in interaction.

Bad risk personnel are those with inflated egos, a low tolerance of AMBIGUITY, emotional instability, racism or extreme left or right tendencies (*see* PERSONALITY).

See also **Intergroup relations; Prejudice; Socialization**

Bibliography

Hofstede, G. (1992). *Cultures and organizations: Software of the mind*. London: McGraw-Hill.

Adler, N. J. (1982). *International dimensions of organizational behaviour*. Belmont, CA: Kent.

GORDON REDDING

interest groups *see* POLITICS; SOCIAL COMPARISON

intergroup relations In organizational theory, the term "intergroup relations" refers to the collective behavior of groups in interaction with other groups, either within or between organizations. The classic definition of intergroup relations was provided by Sherif (1966) who suggested that, "Whenever individuals belonging to one group interact, collectively or individually, with another group or its members in terms of their group IDENTIFICATION, we have an instance of intergroup behavior" (p. 12).

Several important traditions distinguish how intergroup relations have been conceptualized in organizational theory. Sociological theory and research has generally focused on structural determinants of intergroup behavior. For example, organizational scholars in this tradition have emphasized how differences in goals, task structure, POWER, and STATUS affect intergroup relations. In addition, they have examined the impact of social processes such as COMMUNICATION patterns and social norms on intergroup behavior. In contrast, political perspectives on intergroup relations have focused on how strategic processes such as bargaining, COALITION FORMATION, and collective action influence intergroup relations. Finally, psychological theories have construed intergroup relations primarily in terms of intra-individualistic processes, such as interpersonal attraction, social PERCEPTION, and TRUST. These theories emphasize the importance of cognitive factors such as STEREOTYPING, as well as motivational underpinnings of intergroup behavior, including the presumed desire on the part of group members to maintain positive social group identities (Brewer & Kramer, 1985). According to these theories, such psychological processes influence intergroup behavior by affecting social judgment and behavior in intergroup contexts.

The major theories of intergroup relations illustrate these differing emphases. *Realistic Conflict Theory* posits that intergroup relations are influenced not so much by cognitive and motivational processes as they are by the inherent competition between groups for crucial but scarce resources (*see* SCARCITY). In this framework, interdependence is viewed as the basis of intergroup cooperation and CONFLICT. In contrast, other theories afford greater importance to the social and psychological processes that influence how individuals in social groups construe their interdependence with other groups. For example, *Social Categorization Theory* focuses on how social and organizational processes that categorize people into distinctive groups fosters competitive and conflictual orientations at the intergroup level. Research in this vein has shown that categorization results in a tendency for individuals to view members of their own group (the "ingroup") more positively than "outgroup" members. Along similar lines, it has been shown that, when allocating scarce resources such as REWARDS, individuals tend to confer more favorable treatment on members of their own group over those from other groups. A major presumption of this framework is that an understanding of COGNITIVE PROCESSES alone is sufficient to account for intergroup phenomenon such as stereotyping and DISCRIMINATION. In contrast, *Social Identity Theory* argues that a variety of motivational processes, such as the desire to maintain a positive social identity, also play a formative role in intergroup relations (Tajfel, 1982). According to this perspective, enhancement of the ingroup and derogation of the outgroup serve the important psychological function of bostering individual's SELF-ESTEEM and the collective esteem of the ingroup. Finally, *Relative Deprivation Theory* examines the role that SOCIAL COMPARISON processes play in understanding intergroup relations. This theory views intergroup relations as shaped by people's comparisons between what their own group has relative to other groups within an organization. When individuals feel that their group is receiving favorable treatment relative to other groups, satisfaction is likely to be high. In contrast, when they believe their own group is relatively deprived or disadvantaged, discontent is likely to result.

These perspectives are important because of the insight they provide with respect to two central concerns in the study of intergroup relations: intergroup conflict and cooperation. Theory and research on intergroup conflict has attempted to identify the origins and dynamics of conflict between various groups. For example, there exists a considerable literature pertaining to intergroup conflict in industrial settings (usually under the rubric of *labor–management conflict* (*see* COLLECTIVE ACTION). Much of this literature draws attention to the role perceptual and social processes – such as ethnocentrism and ingroup bias – play in the development and escalation of intergroup conflicts. As Blake and Mouton (1989) noted, "The striking conclusion from [this] research is that when groups are aware of one another's psychological presence, it is nature for them to feel competition . . . [suggesting] a very basic incipient hostility is operating at the point of contact between primary groups" (p. 192). These insights, in turn, suggest a number of perspectives on reducing intergroup competition and conflict (*see* CONFLICT MANAGEMENT). These perspectives generally take as given the pervasiveness of intergroup rivalry and conflict, and then attempt to address the problem of how to promote cooperation between groups. Several approaches to increasing intergroup cooperation have been proposed, and reasonable evidence is available to suggest the efficacy of each. First, introduction of superordinate (shared) goals to reduce competition has been shown to help attenuate or override competitive tendencies between groups. Second, certain forms of intergroup contact have been shown to enhance cooperation. Of particular importance is contact in which status differences and interaction patterns that reinforce negative stereotypes are minimized or controlled. In addition, the use of "boundary spanners" (individuals who have roles in both groups) can help correct misperceptions, improve communication and coordination, and reduce distrust between groups (*see* BOUNDARY SPANNING). Another important approach has emphasized the positive consequences of "recategorization" as a strategy for achieving intergroup cooperation. The recategorization approach is predicated on the assumption that the deleterious consequences associated with ingroup favoritism and outgroup derogation can be reduced by categorizing individuals in terms of shared or collective identities that draw attention to interpersonal similarities and that increase social attraction between individuals from different groups. Another major focus is on behavioral strategies designed to elicit cooperative interaction and build trust between groups, including the use of RECIPROCITY-based influence strategies, such as tit-for-tat. Finally, recent theory and research on the use of conflict resolution processes such as NEGOTIATION (*see* CONFLICT RESOLUTION). This includes the use of integrative bargaining involving the groups themselves, as well as various third-party interventions such as mediation and arbitration (*see* INFLUENCE). This is currently one of the most active and promising new directions in the study of intergroup relations.

See also **Industrial relations; Interorganizational relations; Group culture; Group cohesiveness; Group norms; Minority group influence**

Bibliography

Axelrod, R. (1984). *The evolution of cooperation*. New York: Basic Books.

Alderfer, C. P. & Smith, K. K. (1982). Studying intergroup relations embedded in organizations. *Administrative Science Quarterly*, **27**, 33–65.

Blake, R. & Mouton, J. (1989). Lateral conflict. In D. Tjosvold & D. Johnson (Eds), *Productive conflict management*. Edinia, MN: Interaction.

Brett, J. M. & Rognes, J. K. (1986). Intergroup relations in organizations. In P. Goodman (Ed.), *Work group effectiveness*. San Francisco: Jossey-Bass.

Brewer, M. B. & Kramer, R. M. (1985). The psychology of intergroup attitudes and behavior. *Annual Review of Psychology*, **36**, 219–243.

Kramer, R. M. (1991). Intergroup relations and organizational dilemmas: The role of categorization processes. In B. M. Staw & L. L. Cummings (Eds) *Research in organizational behavior* (vol. 13). Greenwich, CT: JAI Press.

Messick, D. M. & Mackie, D. (1989). Intergroup relations. *Annual Review of Psychology*, **40**, 45–81.

Sherif, M. (1966). *In common predicament: Social psychology of intergroup conflict and cooperation*. New York: Houghton & Mifflin.

Stephan, W. G. (1985). Intergroup relations. In G. Lindsey & E. A. Ronson (Eds), *The handbook of social psychology* (Vol. 2, 3rd edn). New York: Random House.

Tajfel, H. (1982). Social psychology of intergroup relations. *Annual Review of Psychology*, **33**, 1–39.

RODERICK M. KRAMER

interlocking directorships *see* INTERORGANIZATIONAL RELATIONS

international human resource management Former geographically bounded organizations, isolated across the globe have given way to a vast web of interconnected and boundaryless organizations that pay much less attention today to national and company borders. The transformation from domestic to international has been as much a cause of, as well as a result of, more competitive pressures, coupled with volatile changes, and environmental uncertainties (*see* UNCERTAINTY). As businesses have shifted from a purely domestic focus over the last decade, to a more international focus, competition has shifted away from the people "across the street" to the "people across the globe." Customers in Mexico City and Taipei demand quality jeans and television sets just as those in Tokyo and New York. The same goes for industrial products like steam turbines and locomotives. Yet, there are some products and services that must be accommodated to local customs, regulations and CULTURE, while they are simultaneously marketed and serviced worldwide. Thus, for many multinational enterprises (MNEs) (*see* MULTINATIONAL CORPORATIONS), the globalization of these competitive forces demands that their managers are simultaneously globally minded as well as locally sensitive. This is not an easy transition to make for most.

As companies become increasingly global in their operations, compensation, selection, TRAINING, and development, as well as a host of other HR practices that must be shared across borders, throughout industries, and between different organizational forms. As the movement of people across companies, business units, borders, and industries escalates (*see* CAREER TRANSITIONS), most MNEs will increasingly be tested by the need to bring multinational and multicultural perspectives to the practice of HUMAN RESOURCES MANAGEMENT (HRM), and deliver these perspectives in a highly integrated fashion so as to make practices seamlessly transferable on an international as well as an organizational basis. The challenge is real, since it is frequently the HR function that acts as a lightning rod for any number of problems. Supervising the shift from narrowly based specialists to global managers is a major strategic task facing the HR function in MNEs today. And it is within the domain of IHRM that these challenges now exist. IHRM is broader than HRM (see Human Resource Management), and is defined by Morgan (1986) as consisting of three broad human resource functions of procurement, allocation, and utilization, coupled with three national or country categories (home, host, and other), and finally three types of employees on an international enterprise: local/host country nationals (HCNs), EXPATRIATES/parent country nationals (PCNs), and finally third country nationals (TCNs). Dowling (1988) smoothes that definition and suggests factors that differentiate international from domestic HRM include more functions and activities, broader perspectives, more involvement in employees' personal lives, changes in emphasis as the workforce mix of expatriates and locals varies, risk exposure, and more external influences. These menus suggest that IHRM differs from HRM in the magnitude of different processes, and the complexity of execution of the practices. Dowling, Schuler, and DeCieri (1993, p. 422) define strategic international human resource management as "human resource management issues, functions, and policies and practices that result from the strategic activities of [MNEs] and that impact the international concerns and goals of those enterprises."

The challenge is for global MNEs to design IHRM systems and programs that are directly linked to the strategic direction of the firm, including its mission, vision, and shared objectives (*see* MISSION STATEMENTS). As such, all components of the HR system must in some way be meaningfully linked to all others, even in global arenas. To identify the integration among the different components is beyond the scope of this IHRM discussion, however, it is relevant to discuss a few of the systemic practices as they impact others.

Selection practices (see *SELECTION METHODS*)

As most of the industrialized countries of the world attempt to find the best and brightest employees to fill their organizational voids, selection processes become critical. Most United States and European firms favor interviews, as do many Asian MNEs, but approximately 90 percent of United States executives surveyed indicated that they have the most confidence in the interviewing process (*see* SELECTION INTERVIEWING). However, research (Von Glinow, 1993) suggests that the interview is the least valid predictor of subsequent performance. In Japan rotational performance is a tool frequently employed to give employees new challenges, in new settings, thereby enhancing overall performance not just in the short run, but in the long run as well (*see* JOB ROTATION). In Japan, as elsewhere in Asia, connections such as school, family, religious, and geographic area, are the most frequently employed selection criteria, and these may be augmented with rotational assignments in many different countries (*see* NETWORKING). Swedes indicated that while they do not use connections regularly, they would like to do more. In the Maquiladoras, the term for Mexico's off-shore manufacturing areas, connections are widely used to select employees, and nepotism is respected on the grounds that organizational connections now are part of the extended family. Many countries, including Mexico, employ selection tests which may be employment tests (used in Korea), personality tests (used in Germany, ranging from 16PF to the color pyramid test), to on-job tests (in Taiwan), and to graphology (in France) (*see* ASSESSMENT; PSYCHOLOGICAL TESTING).

Compensation and reward systems (see *PAYMENT SYSTEMS*)

Once people join an MNE, IHRM professionals face the challenge of compensating them in equitable ways. While pay has been viewed as the most attractive form of compensation in the United States, pay rarely correlates with ORGANIZATIONAL EFFECTIVENESS worldwide. Almost 70 percent of United States employees do not think pay is related to performance, however, large bonuses/incentive compensation, etc. totaling in excess of 20 percent of base pay seems to trigger greater satisfaction with pay (*see* BONUS PAYMENTS). Merit pay systems have been viewed as inadequate, barely covering cost of living increases, and generally, are not performance based. Merit pay seldom differentiates significantly between high performers and average performers, and there are few countries that even attempt to administer merit pay. The use of stock options can be used to align employees with shareholders and reinforce the MNEs vision, but these forms of compensation are not without problems (*see* SHARE/EQUITY OWNERSHIP). Compensation packages, negotiated freely in the home country are under strict scrutiny from multiple STAKEHOLDERS in the host country. For STRATEGIC ALLIANCES established abroad, compensation packages for expatriates would usually include the traditional base salary, benefits, plus allowances and tax equalization. In general, the proportion of base pay is decreasing while the portion of pay linked to long-term performance is increasing worldwide, however, for expatriate workers, the equation is more complex. The Japanese appear to be the most dissatisfied with their wages (and WORKING CONDITIONS), while the Singaporeans and Australians are the most satisfied (*see* JOB SATISFACTION). Two out of every three workers in Britain and Japan claimed to be underpaid. China's "iron rice bowl" is similar to Mexico's compensation/reward practices. Pay in Mexico is generally very low (thereby attractive to offshore production) since the government controls the minimum wage; benefits include holiday pay, meals, housing, childcare, and production incentives. In the late 1980s, bonuses and incentives averaged from a low of 2 percent in Italy, to a high of 22 percent in the United States. The United Kingdom averaged 15 percent, and Japan averages 40 percent of base pay paid to all employees as semiannual bonuses. Worldwide, bonuses tend to be viewed as shock absorbers, and removal of them becomes the first line of defense in troubled economic times (Von Glinow, 1993). In Germany, the MNE has little to say about bonuses, pay, or perquisites, since all basic pay determinations occur at the national level (*see* COLLECTIVE BARGAINING).

Appraising Performance

Most MNEs worry excessively about the PERFORMANCE APPRAISAL form. In truth, the form has little to do with success in the evaluation and performance appraisal process. Most employees tend to see themselves as above average, thus the form conflicts with their self-image (*see* SELF-ESTEEM). Usually, appraisal involves some element of traits, behaviors, or outcome related measures. In some cultures, traits (such as intelligence, dependability, integrity) are most important, and people who do not possess those traits will be negatively evaluated (*see* PERSONALITY). Traits in the United States tend not to be considered "bonafide occupational qualifications," however in many parts of Asia, traits are highly prized. While 360 degree performance appraisal has captured the attention of many scholars and practitioners alike, it has had enormous difficulties worldwide in implementation.

In summary, IHRM practices tend to vary worldwide, depending on the degree of integration of those practices with the core competencies of the MNE.

See also **International management; Culture, national; Intercultural process; Cross cultural research**

Bibliography

Dowling, P., Schuler, R. & DeCieri, H. (1993). An integrative framework of strategic international HRM. *Journal of Management*, **19**, no. 2, 419–459.

Dowling, P. (1988). International and domestic personnel/human resource management: Similarities and differences. In Schuler, R. Youngblood & Huber (Eds), *Readings in Personnel and Human Resource Management* (3rd edn). St. Paul, MN: West.

Morgan, V. P. (1986). International human resource management: Fact or fiction. *Personnel Administrator*, **31**, no. 9, 43–47.

Von Glinow, M. A. (1993). Diagnosing "Best Practice" in human resource management practices. *Research in Personnel and Human Resources Management*, Suppl. 3, 95–112.

MARY-ANN VON GLINOW

international management This denotes the ORGANIZATIONAL BEHAVIOR aspects of managing when the cultures of more than one country have to be taken into account (*see* CULTURE, NATIONAL). It is the OB element of international business – a wider concern which covers the geographic, economic, financial, political, cultural, and managerial environments in which world trade takes place and in which organizations produce and market their outputs globally. Its importance is growing as, increasingly, managers are becoming internationalists. They may export or import, work for MULTINATIONAL CORPORATIONS, invest abroad, or try to attract foreign capital into their home country, supply to or buy from, ethnic businesses. The list of international organizational interactions is endless.

In these situations, managers need to know the nature and dimensions of the differences in the workings of organizations in one CULTURE from those in another. If they are completely different, then knowledge of their home country organization and its functioning would not help them in dealing with those of other cultures. But if the structures and operations of organizations in different cultures are coming sufficiently closely together, then universally applicable approaches can be developed with the expectation of obtaining consistent outcomes. Clearly there are international differences, but the key issue is their importance for MANAGERIAL BEHAVIOR (cf. Hickson & Pugh, 1995).

For example, do the differences in organizational functioning between Britain and France and Germany matter? If they do then the influence of specific cultural factors must be understood and planned for. Some maintain that managing an organization in the developing Third World is fundamentally different and is likely to remain so. Others argue that the nature of operations in organizations all over the world is converging. Differences in national culture are reducing in importance, and increasingly becoming merely quaint. CROSS-CULTURAL RESEARCH examines these differences, and International management considers the degree to which organizations have already traveled along this convergent path (*see* CULTURE, CROSS-CULTURAL RESEARCH).

On the one hand the "convergers" in this debate base their arguments on the word-wide process of industrialization based on science and TECHNOLOGY, and the headlong rush toward an integrated global economy. Industrial technology spreads throughout the world through the normal channels of trade when developing countries buy new products and manufacturing facilities. The effects of economic aid, which involves the delivery of more advanced TECHNOLOGY and workforce TRAINING also further industrialization. So does international military confrontation which requires the training of workers to build bases, maintain vehicles and aircraft, etc. This forms the basis of the SKILLS necessary for continued industrialization. This world-wide diffusion of advanced technology creates a common range of tasks and problems which must be tackled no matter where the organization is located. The pressures toward efficient production will ensure that the most effective ways of tackling these will inevitably become adopted world-wide. As this process continues, organizations tackling the same tasks and problems in whatever culture will become more and more alike (Kerr, Dunlop, Harbison, & Myers, 1960).

At its strongest this thesis argues a long-term convergence of all cultures into the "global village." The vast impact of international communication networks means, for example, that jeans are everywhere becoming the preferred wear to any distinctive national costume. Multinational corporations typically wish to deliver the same product globally to gain economies of scale. If, in order to do so, they export their technology, working methods and management practices then the result will be the "McDonaldization of everything" (*see* TECHNOLOGY TRANSFER).

A weaker version of the thesis (Pugh, 1993) concentrates on the necessary convergence to a common global pattern of management functioning even if societies remain significantly different. For example, if a country anywhere in the world decided to go into the business of producing motor cars efficiently, there can immediately be spelled out some of the organizational characteristics which would be required of its production facility. There would have to be factories of considerable size – individual craftsmen would not do. They would have to have specialized machinery – hand tools or even general purpose presses would not be sufficient by themselves – and supplies of raw materials and components provided more efficiently through separate specialist technical processes and organizations. Then they would need trained staff, expert in their particular tasks to contribute a wide range of skills and effort, to be coordinated by professional managers with skills of production control, cost accounting, and so on. There would thus develop in this new motor car manufacturer's organization most, if not all, of the characteristics of the established motor car manufacturers in other countries. Since these operating strategies are shown to promote efficiency, they are adopted wherever new industries are set up. The South Korean motor industry, established since the 1960s, has trodden precisely this path.

The transfer of knowledge is not only one way from the older established to the newer industrial cultures. Japan was a late developer into industrialization, but the values and culture of the country enabled the process to become highly developed very quickly. Japanese management puts a heavier weight on training workers to produce parts and vehicles to highly reliable quality standards. This investment has paid off in terms of reliable products with a competitive edge in the market, together with lower rates of scrap and lower costs of reworking during manufacture (*see* COMPETITIVENESS). The Japanese have done so well out of this emphasis on quality that there is now a world-wide movement of TOTAL QUALITY MANAGEMENT, adopted by all motor car manufacturers in the world in an effort to reap the same benefits. The procedure has thus become part of the world-wide organizational convergence across cultures and many organizations in different cultures are looking for further ways of benefiting from the Japanese approach (Ouchi, 1981) (*see* THEORY Z).

One major series of studies (referred to as the Aston studies, Pugh (1993)) has shown that there is indeed considerable convergence across cultures in regard to organizational structures. For example, in all the many countries studied, increasing size of organization brings with it increasing formalization of procedures – and this is equally true of Japan as of Sweden. Similarly, increasing technological sophistication brings with it increasing specialization of tasks, as comparisons of engineering companies with retail shops in both Canada and Egypt equally show. Government ownership leads to centralizing of authority for decisions in both Poland and Britain.

At the behavioral level too there is evidence for convergence. For example, Luthans, Welsh, & Rosenkrantz (1993) carried out a detailed observational study of Russian managers comparable to a similar one they had previously carried out on United States managers. They found that the ordering of activity categories in terms of time spent to be the same in both countries, viz: first, PLANNING and controlling; second, communicating; third, motivating and managing conflict; fourth, NETWORKING.

On the other hand, the "culture-specific" theorists underline that while this convergence might apply to the formal management structures of organizations it does not apply to the actual behavior of organizational members in different cultures – even when the structure is the same. This is because the people are different. They have been exposed to different cultural processes from birth, and this "mental programming," as Hofstede (1980) puts it, means that they continually operate through the particular cultural interpretation which it gives. Hofstede shows, for example, considerable differences in work attitudes and VALUES across a large number of countries of employees of the same multinational company, IBM. The company's employees in France, for example, have very different views on the nature of AUTHORITY from those in the United States even though they are doing the same job in the same organization structure. Its employees in Greece have different views on the acceptable level of risk-taking for IBM, compared with those in Singapore. On the basis of these data and further studies Hofstede proposes characteristic dimensions of differences in work values and develops cultural maps of the world (*see* INTERCULTURAL PROCESS). His study is the most comprehensive of a whole range of studies which show differences in attitudes between mangers and workers in different countries.

Maurice (1979), however, did not study attitudes but investigated the relative STATUS and wage payments of workers and managers in comparable factories in France and Germany. He screened out factors such as size, industrial sector, and technology, by comparing only factories in equivalent industries (e.g., iron and steel, paper and cardboard products) who used the same technology and were comparable in size. The study was thus able to focus on national differences in HIERARCHY, job structures, and payments.

The results showed clear differences between the French and German firms. These included:

(1) There were considerably more staff not employed directly on shop floor manufacturing operations in French than in German firms. In addition, staff in these overhead functions were relatively better paid.
(2) The wage differential between the lowest and the highest paid of all employees (upper centile compared with lower decile) is much greater in French than German firms. Indeed, the difference was such that there was no overlap: the largest differential found in a German firm was still less than the smallest differential found in a French firm (2.7 times as against 3.7).
(3) The number of levels in the production hierarchy is greater in French than in German firms (5 compared with 3) because there are more middle level managers in French firms.

Maurice argues that these differences are not fortuitous but relate to differences in the educational systems of France and Germany. More top managers in France hold higher degrees, usually from the "grandes ecoles." These are very high status University Institutes which provide high-level technical and scientific education, and which by their very highly selective intake provide an elite of high status managers for French organizations. Graduates from them are recruited directly into upper levels of firms and are paid much greater comparative salaries than in Germany. This means that there is a group of less qualified supervisors and managers who can expect to be promoted only through the middle ranks of the organization. They can never realistically aspire to join the top management "cadre," or set.

In Germany, equivalent top managers are often promoted from within the firm which they join lower down with fewer general and more technical qualifications. Thus at the lower levels German supervisors are comparatively better qualified and better paid than their French equivalents. They can also take more technical decisions and are given more professional AUTONOMY.

In summary, the differences show French firms to be run more bureaucratically, with orders and procedures set from above, while German work organization relies more on the professional expertise which derives from the trained knowledge and skill of the more junior employees. Since these differences are well grounded in the educational systems of the two countries, their organizations are likely to be slow in converging, resisting pressures to become congruent even in a European Union.

International managers working in multinational corporations have to take account of existing national differences. In regard to INTERNATIONAL HUMAN RESOURCE MANAGEMENT, as well as to other aspects of their tasks, they have to strike a balance between extreme "ethnocentrism" (requiring each subsidiary to conform precisely to parent company ways regardless of the country in which it is operating) and extreme "polycentrism" (allowing each subsidiary to develop regardless of global activity). Both of these extremes will be inefficient; the former by not taking account of local factors which affect performance, and the latter by not gaining the benefits of global operations.

Even a decentralized multinational must have inputs from its home country head office (finance, technical know-how, etc.) which go to its subsidiaries in host countries to aid their performance (*see* DECENTRALIZATION). The usual method of attempting to coordinate parent–subsidiary relations is through the use of EXPATRIATES. These are experienced managers assigned to foreign subsidiaries who can retain the benefits of corporate knowledge while they gain insights into the local operation and the culture in which it is based. They aim to steer a viable path through the two sets of demands.

There are thus considerable cross-cultural differences existing between organizations. Are they moving toward convergence, and how fast? This is an important current debate and there is at present no clear-cut answer to it. The drive for industrial development on the part of developing countries, the impact of technological innovations, the ease and continually falling costs of international communications, the global operations of the multinational corporations, all push the convergence forward. The primacy of early established social norms and VALUES, family relationships and the societal position of women, educational systems and political ideologies, all hold the convergence back, perhaps permanently.

See also **Management of diversity; Management of high potential; Management development**

Bibliography

Adler, N. J. (1991). *International dimensions of organizational behaviour* (2nd edn). Boston, MA: PWS–Kent.

Hickson, D. J. & Pugh, D. S. (1995). *Managing worldwide*. London: Penguin.

Hofstede, G. (1980). *Culture's consequences: International differences in work related values*. Beverly Hills, CA: Sage.

Kerr, C., Dunlop, J. T., Harbison, F. H. & Myers, C. A. (1960). *Industrialism and industrial man*. Harvard: Harvard University Press.

Luthans, F., Welsh, D. H. B. & Rosenkrantz, S. A. (1993). What do Russian managers really do? An observational study with comparisons to U.S. managers. *Journal of International Business Studies*, **24**, 741–761.

Maurice, M. (1979). For a study of the societal effect: Universality and specificity in organization research. In C. J. Lammers & D. J. Hickson (Eds), *Organizations alike and unlike*. London: Routledge.

Ouchi, W. (1981). *Theory Z: How American business can meet the Japanese challenge*. Reading, MA: Addison Wesley.

Pugh, D. S. (1993). Organizational context and structure in various cultures. In T. Weinshall (Ed), *Societal culture and management* (pp. 425–435). Berlin: de Gruyter.

Ronen, S. (1986). *Comparative and international management*. New York: Wiley.

DEREK PUGH

interorganizational relations (IOR) This is a general term which directs attention to the sources, kinds, and consequences of linkages between and among organizations as social actors. Three general foci have animated studies of interorganizational relations: understanding the establishment and maintenance of dyadic cooperative interorganizational linkages; understanding the emergent processual dynamics (e.g., POWER, STATUS) in sets of these linkages; and understanding the properties of IOR networks and their effects across industries, organizational fields, and public policy domains (*see* NETWORK ANALYSIS).

The rise of OPEN SYSTEMS approaches in ORGANIZATIONAL THEORY provided the initial impetus for developing models of interorganizational relations. Scholars began focusing on the acquisition of needed inputs and the disposal of completed outputs as major determinants of ORGANIZATIONAL EFFECTIVENESS. This early work reflected prevailing research PARADIGMS: the legacy of structural–functionalism and its focus on efficient goal attainment processes, as well as the prevalence of SURVEY methods and case studies, and the emphasis on unit, or focal organization, analysis (Whetten, 1987) (*see* RESEARCH METHODS). Findings corroborated the recognition that linkages with other organizations served as the conduits for resource exchanges; this work stimulated inquiries that focused on ways to improve IOR coordination, particularly in task-focused multiorganizational units, referred to as action sets (e.g., service delivery systems or distribution channels). These studies of IORs provided systematic evidence of the ways organizations used purposeful linkages with other organizations to accomplish goals and to manage uncertain environments (*see* UNCERTAINTY). The role of BOUNDARY SPANNING actors and practices figured prominently in these studies – interorganizational linkages were viewed as extensions of relationships between organizational representatives (Aldrich & Whetten, 1981). The results tended to support the importance of awareness of common interests and organizational initiatives grounded in these perceptions for linkage formation.

A second area of research has focused on aggregates of dyadic linkages, comprising an "organization set" for a focal organization (analogous to a role set for individual actors). These studies focused on the structural properties of IORs, including the consequences of asymmetries of power and status, and on COMMUNICATION patterns and frequency. This widened conception of the forms and kinds of IORs redirected research to fundamental questions about the relations between structure and process in organizational dynamics, the focus on purposive organizational action, and the nature of organizational forms (*see* ORGANIZATIONAL DESIGN). These studies often maintained an organization set perspective, although the size and COMPLEXITY of the networks examined in these studies tended to increase over time. For example, in studies of the dispersion of INNOVATIONS or the flow of INFLUENCE between organization the "networks" examined consisted of aggregates of overlapping organization sets. This analysis yielded improved understanding of the relationship between such aggregate set attributes as size and diversity and focal organization members' perceptions of effective performance.

Subsequent analyses broadened the focus beyond cooperative activity, to examine more general patterns of relations within sets of organizations. For example, studies of the social network structure of economic activity describes the prevalence and persistence of various forms of linkage among business elites; these include a wider array of IOR types, including interlocks among boards of directors, alliances such as JOINT VENTURES, and flows of personnel between firms and between industries (Mizruchi & Galaskiewicz, 1993). Work in this area has examined the relationship between diverse measures of network centrality, REPUTATION, and the effects of vertical versus horizontal and local versus nonlocal linkages, to argue for the importance of these ties in coordinated action. The evidence provides support for familiar RESOURCE DEPENDENCE accounts of linkage dynamics, as well as for the effects of social and economic class interests on linkage patterns.

New lines of work on IORs examine the life cycle-processes of linkage development and their substantive content (Ring & Van de Ven, 1994) (*see* ORGANIZATIONAL CHANGE). The empirical results of these inquiries challenge static structural analyses, emphasizing coordination as a process over time, rather than as either a simple cause or effect of organizational and network properties. These inquiries also suggest the value of more attention to the substance of linkages. In general, the results here highlight the dynamic, situated character of many IOR arrangements and open up questions about the changing conditions that support diverse types of linkages. The attention to process represents one challenge to structural analysis. Other research directions provide further challenge, highlighting the emergence of new organizational forms that blur the distinctions between a focal organization and its network (Alter & Hage, 1993); evidence from emerging industries like biotechnology, from reinvigorated industrial regions, and from comparative studies of markets and states all provide evidence of the prevalence of new "hybrid" organizational forms (Powell, 1990).

The third stream of IOR research extends the work on organization–environment relations (*see* ORGANIZATION AND ENVIRONMENT), conceptualizing environments as structured networks that serve as both opportunities for and constraints upon ORGANIZATIONAL BEHAVIOR. Work in this area investigates the structuring processes within interorganizational fields, their determinants and their effects over time (Scott, 1983). The focus on the historical, cultural, and network elements of interorganizational fields provides an alternative to more abstract, dimension-based treatments of environments. DiMaggio (1986), for example, applies block-modeling techniques to partition these networks-as-environments into analyzable units; this kind of work redescribes complex fields of organizations in ways that combine earlier insights about asymmetries of POWER and STATUS with the attention to nonlocal and indirect ties in the structuring of organizational fields and networks. Other recent empirical studies trace the consequential mechanisms and the direct and indirect effects of state and other collective actors for embedded organizations (Fligstein, 1990; Hamilton & Biggart, 1988). The recognition that wider institutional arrangements matter for IOR dynamics is salutary (*see* INSTITUTIONAL THEORY).

Theory and empirical research on interorganizational relations have taken diverse avenues in recent years. On the one hand, core questions about the dynamics of cooperative linkages have persisted and have been recently reinvigorated by the interest in the business strategy literature on new organizational forms and on various types of corporate alliances (*see* STRATEGIC MANAGEMENT). On the other hand, broader currents in the study of social organization have reinforced and extended the early attention to cooperative linkages, such that interorganizational relations have come to include an increasingly expansive set of concerns, linked by common attention to extraorganizational LEVELS OF ANALYSIS. Much of the contemporary study draws from network imageries and methodologies, examining the consequences of social linkages for a broad range of organizational outcomes and drawing attention to the embeddedness of organized social and economic action.

See also **Intergroup relations; Coalition formation; Industrial relations**

Bibliography

Aldrich, H. & Whetten, D. A. (1981). Organization-sets, action-sets, and networks: making the most of simplicity. In W. H. Starbuck (Ed.), *Handbook of organizational design* (Vol. 1, pp. 385–408). Oxford: Oxford University Press.

Alter, C. & Hage, J. (1993). *Organizations working together*. Newbury Park CA: Sage.

DiMaggio, P. (1986). Structural analyses of organizational fields: A blockmodel approach. In B. Staw & L. L. Cummings (Eds), *Research in organizational behavior*, **8**, 335–370.

Fligstein, N. (1990). *The transformation of corporate control*. Cambridge, MA: Harvard University Press.

Hamilton, G. & Biggart, N. (1988). Market, culture, and authority: A comparative analysis of organization and management in the Far East. In C. Winship & S. Rosen (Eds), *Organizations and institutions, a supplement to American Journal of Sociology*, **94**, S52-S94.

Mizruchi, M. S. & Galaskiewicz, J. (1993). Networks of interorganizational relations, in *Sociological Methods & Research*, **22**, **(1)**, 46–70.

Powell, W. W. (1990). Neither market nor hierarchy: Network forms of organization. *Research in Organizational Behavior*, **12**, 295–336.

Ring, P. S. & Van de Ven, A. H. (1994). Developmental processes of cooperative interorganizational relationships. *Academy of Management Review*, **19**, **(1)**, 90–118.

Scott, W. R. (1983). The organization of environments: Network, cultural, and historical elements. In J. W. Meyer & W. R. Scott (Eds), *Organizational environments: Ritual and rationality* pp. 155–175. Beverly Hills, CA: Sage.

Whetten, D. A. (1987). Interorganizational relations. In J. Lorsch (Ed.), *Handbook of organizational behavior* (pp. 238–253). Englewood Cliffs, NJ: Prentice-Hall.

DAVID A. WHETTEN and MARC J. VENTRESCA

interpersonal skills Whereas the term "SKILLS" refers generally to an individual's capability for effective action, interpersonal skills refers to *the capability to accomplish individual and/or organizational goals through interaction with others*. In organizations, many types of goals are primarily accomplished through interaction, and each of these goal types corresponds to a certain type of interpersonal skill. For example, individuals in organizations must accomplish the goal of communicating effectively with others. The capability to accomplish this goal is referred to as "COMMUNICATION skill." As another example, individuals are sometimes in a position where they want to ensure the success of a group meeting. The capability to accomplish this goal may be referred to as skill in facilitating meetings. Goals may be stated broadly or specifically, and so may skills; e.g., "interpersonal" versus "reflective listening" skills.

Interpersonal skills are distinguished in principle from other types of skills which are also pertinent to organizational life. These include:

(1) *intrapersonal* skills, where goals involve self-change, such as self-awareness, TIME MANAGEMENT, or STRESS management;
(2) *learning* skills, where goals involve obtaining and using new information;
(3) *cognitive* skills, where goals are accomplished primarily through COGNITIVE PROCESSES; and
(4) *job* skills, where goals involve effective job performance (*see* PERFORMANCE, INDIVIDUAL).

Interpersonal skills are a type of "action" skill, wherein goal accomplishment requires significant exercise of behavior. While these skill types are conceptually distinct, they are typically used in concert in organizations.

Importance of Interpersonal Skills

Interpersonal skills are a uniquely important subset of the skills considered as valuable in organizations. Much of human intelligence is believed to have evolved to cope with the complexities of human interaction. Thus we would expect the exercise of interpersonal skills to involve a large part of intrinsic human capability. The importance of interpersonal skills is also underscored by its inclusion as one aspect of wisdom.

In understanding the relevance of interpersonal skills to organizations it is important first to understand the types of goals which may be accomplished through the exercise of interpersonal skills. These goals can generally be classified as "direct" and "indirect." Direct goals have to do with changes in others as a direct result of interaction; e.g., in others' orientation, COMMITMENT, TRUST, support, knowledge, MOTIVATION, etc. Indirect goals have to do with the larger impact of direct goal accomplishment. For example, interaction with another may result in the other's support for a policy (direct change), which in turn leads to a majority organizational vote to adopt the policy (indirect change).

Managers accomplish their work largely through the indirect effects of their interactions. Consequently, most of managerial time is spent in interpersonal interactions via phone, in meetings, and in face-to-face interactions with individuals (*see* MANAGERIAL BEHAVIOR; Mintzberg, 1975). Interpersonal skills, therefore, are critical for managerial effectiveness. Moreover, modern organizations have shifted toward more decentralized, interactive, and participatory designs (*see* DECENTRALIZATION; MATRIX ORGANIZATION; MECHANISTIC/ORGANIC; SOCIOTECHNICAL THEORY). In them, those doing the primary work of the organization are meeting more, doing more work in groups, and taking on greater managerial responsibilities (*see* AUTONOMOUS WORK GROUPS; PARTICIPATION; EMPOWERMENT NETWORKING; QUALITY CIRCLES; SELF-MANAGED TEAMS). For this reason interpersonal skills have become increasingly important for organizational members at all levels.

Skills and COMPETENCIES

Some authors have used the terms "COMPETENCY" and "skill" interchangeably. The two are similar, but by no means identical. To paraphrase Boyatzis (1982, p. 21), an interpersonal competency consists of an underlying characteristic of an individual which contributes to effective and/or superior performance in a given type of interpersonal setting. For example, "developing others," "use of unilateral power," and "spontaneity" are competencies which have been found to contribute to effectiveness in situations requiring "directing subordinates" (ibid, p. 230).

Skills and competencies are alike in that both are regarded as individual attributes which contribute to situational effectiveness. They differ, however, in two important ways. First, the relation between skills and situational effectiveness is closer: a skill has to do with effective action in relation to a particular goal. The relation between competencies and situational effectiveness, on the other hand, is less direct: many competencies may contribute to effectiveness toward particular goal, and a particular competency may contribute to effectiveness toward a variety of goals.

The second difference is that competencies include a wider variety of individual attributes than do skills. Whereas the concept of skill has only to do with the capability for effective action, competencies may also include motives (e.g., concern for impact), traits (e.g., self-control), and social roles (e.g., oral presentations).

Types of Interpersonal Skills and Their Relationships

Much of the study of interpersonal skills has centered around identifying skills which are important in organizations. At this point four major types of interpersonal skills can be distinguished, each centering around a basic type of goal, and each including one or more skills:

1. *COMMUNICATIONS*. Goal: Establishing effective communication between self and others, and among others. Skills include establishing a supportive climate, listening, NETWORKING, giving FEEDBACK, oral and written

communication, use of COMMUNICATIONS TECHNOLOGY, and language.

2. *INFLUENCE*. Goal: Effecting changes in others. Skills include persuading, asserting, MOTIVATION, PERFORMANCE APPRAISAL, MENTORING, COUNSELING, DELEGATION, and disciplining (*see* PUNISHMENT).
3. *NEGOTIATION* and CONFLICT MANAGEMENT. Goal: Developing beneficial agreement among parties. Skills include bargaining, diagnosing the other party, assessing negotiation sessions, mediation, and implementing negotiation tactics (*see* CONFLICT RESOLUTION; CONFLICT MANAGEMENT).
4. *FACILITATION*. Goal: Helping groups and organizations to operate effectively. Skills include conducting a meeting, TEAM BUILDING, participative problem solving, GROUP DECISION-MAKING, facilitation (*see* SOCIAL FACILITATION), ORGANIZATIONAL CHANGE, and LEADERSHIP.

The importance and expression of these skills can be expected to vary among organizations and over time. Remember that interpersonal skills are means of accomplishing certain types of goals. As organizations and their structures change, different kinds of goals may become more or less important. For example, as organizations become increasingly international, the ability to enter and establish effective work relationships in a culturally different organization may become increasingly important (*see* INTERNATIONAL MANAGEMENT; MANAGEMENT OF DIVERSITY). Thus, "entry" skills may eventually be added to our list of interpersonal skills. Moreover, as INFORMATION TECHNOLOGY develops, new methods of interpersonal interaction may become available. For example, the use of "groupware" may lessen the need for group facilitation skills, and increase the need for computer group session management, or "chauffeuring" skills.

Nature of Interpersonal skills

While the concept of skill has been in widespread use for many years, its primary users have been practitioners, such as educators, job trainers, and therapists working with the handicapped. Their interests have generally been in enabling their target groups to enact fairly straightforward behavioral routines. These practitioners have tended, often implicitly, to place skills in a behavioristic context (*see* LEARNING, INDIVIDUAL; BEHAVIOR MODIFICATION). A basic premise of this context is that behaviors are learned and maintained by a system of stimuli, which elicit a desired set of behaviors, or "skill" response, which are followed in turn by REINFORCEMENT.

Initial efforts to put interpersonal phenomena into a skills framework have tended to place them in a behavioristic context as well. Thus, interpersonal skills have been regarded as a set of fairly specific behavioral routines, and interpersonal skillfulness equated with the accurate demonstrations of these behaviors upon the appropriate cue. These early efforts have met with limited success, and this has led to a closer examination of the nature of interpersonal skills (Bigelow, 1993). The conclusion: the phenomenon of interpersonal skillfulness departs from behavioral premises in a number of ways:

1. *Response inspecificity*. Whereas a behavioristic approach requires clear descriptions of desired behaviors, skillful interaction is interactive and complex, often involving multiple, possibly conflicting goals and resulting DILEMMAS. It is usually not possible either to identify one best response or to describe desired responses behaviorally. Thus the set of possibly appropriate interpersonal behaviors is not closed, but open, requiring CREATIVITY and ongoing learning.
2. *Lack of cues*. Whereas a behavioristic approach requires cueing of behaviors, it is usually not possible to discern unambiguous cues for behavior in interpersonal situations (*see* AMBIGUITY). Thus, a part of interpersonal skillfulness consists of the ability to "cue" one's own behavior.
3. *Cognition*. Whereas a behavioristic approach does not include cognition, skilled interaction often requires significant cognition. For example, during an interaction a person may be weighing the implications of what the other said, vicariously projecting the impact of various tactics, assessing the success of a line of action, or considering modifying his/her goals for the interaction. Thus, a part of interpersonal skill learning

must include development of associated COGNITIVE PROCESSES (*see* COGNITION IN ORGANIZATIONS).

4. *Learning resistance*. Whereas a behavioristic approach assumes the skill learner is indifferent to the content of what is learned, interpersonal skill learners have already developed orientations and practice theories (i.e., implicit behavioral programs driving their behavior, *see* DOUBLE-LOOP LEARNING, Argyris & Schon, 1978) which already dominate their interactions. These prior learnings can strongly interfere with attempts to develop new behaviors. Thus, the learning of interpersonal skills must include the surfacing, examination, and reassessment of what the individual has already learned.

In sum, our picture of the interpersonally skilled practitioner is becoming much richer than that implied by behaviorism. Interpersonally skilled people are able to orient themselves to situations. They take into account not only the situation, but their prospective broader impact beyond the encounter itself. They have developed a repertoire of interaction tactics and are able to draw on them as needed, or may develop new tactics as the situation warrants. During interaction, they monitor their progress, and may change tactics or goals if necessary. They are able to learn on their own, both from their own encounters and from the encounters of others (*see* LEARNING ORGANIZATION).

Skill Learning

An increased reliance on interpersonal skills in organizations has led to concern as to where organizations will obtain interpersonally skilled participants. Many candidates for organizational positions are not very interpersonally skilled, by reason of youth and/or inexperience. This is particularly the case in individualistic cultures such as the United States (Adler, 1991, pp. 26–28), which do little to prepare individuals to operate effectively in group or organizational settings.

In response, many organizations have developed skill TRAINING programs for employees, and have attempted to enhance on-the-job learning. Moreover, some have suggested that colleges of business, which have traditionally emphasized cognitive skills, should also address interpersonal skills in their curriculum.

Currently a number of approaches to classroom learning are in use. These include:

(1) a *social learning* approach, based on Bandura's (1977) model, involving the steps of self-assessment, conceptual learning, skill modeling, application to cases and practice situations, and application to life situations;
(2) a *self-managed* learning approach, which empowers individuals to take responsibility for their own learning (*see* SELF-REGULATION & EMPOWERMENT); and
(3) a *situational learning* approach, which focuses on practice in holistic managerial situations and the development of "skillfulness," as opposed to development of separated skills.

These approaches are not entirely distinct in that each has elements which could be used in other approaches, and each has its own pros and cons (e.g., Bigelow, 1993).

Perhaps the thorniest problem faced in skill learning is the ASSESSMENT of results. Traditional assessment methods involving objective or essay exams are more geared toward assessing cognitive rather than skill accomplishment. Even when unbiased self-assessment can be obtained through self-administered instruments or portfolios, learners often do not have the insight to assess their own skills. The most promising approach appears to be the "action" or "performance" examination, in which learners are required to demonstrate their skill. Yet these require considerable investment in training of examiners, and are time-consuming to administer. Moreover, they measure skill capability only, and not disposition to actually use skills. Until viable and reasonably accurate measures of skill accomplishment are developed it will be difficult for educators to improve their pedagogy, and for institutions to make claims about the skillfulness of their graduates.

See also **Impression management; Trust; Psychological testing; Task and maintenance behavior**

Bibliography

Adler N. J. (1991). *International dimensions of organizational behavior*. Boston: PWS–Kent.

Argyris, C. & Schon, D. (1978). *Organizational learning: A theory of action perspective*. Reading, MA: Addison-Wesley.

Bandura, A. (1977). *Social learning theory*. Englewood Cliffs, NJ: Prentice-Hall.

Bigelow, J. D. (1993). *Teaching managerial skills: A critique and future directions*. Paper presented at the Organizational Behavior Teaching Conference, Bucknell University (June).

Boyatzis, R. R. (1982). *The competent manager: A model for effective performance*. New York: Wiley.

Mintzberg, H. (1975). The manager's job: Folklore and fact. *Harvard Business Review*, **53**, 49–71.

Porter, L. W. & McKibbin, L. E. (1988). *Management education and development: Drift or thrust into the 21st century?* New York: McGraw-Hill.

Bradford, D. L. (Issue Editor) (1983). Special issue on "Teaching managerial competencies." *The organizational behavior teaching Journal* (vol. 2). [A seminal issue, much of which continues to be relevant.]

Bigelow, J. D. (1991). *Managerial skills. Explorations in practical knowledge*. Newbury Park, CA: Sage. [Provides a variety of viewpoints on skills.]

JOHN D. BIGELOW

intervention studies *see* ACTION RESEARCH; ORGANIZATION DEVELOPMENT

interviewing *see* RESEARCH METHODS; RESEARCH DESIGN; SELECTION INTERVIEWING

in-tray/in-basket test *see* ASSESSMENT; SELECTION METHODS

intrinsic/extrinsic motivation Intrinsic REWARDS are found in work which allows employees to use valued SKILLS and feel competent (*see* JOB ENRICHMENT; CAREER DEVELOPMENT), and which allows them to determine to some degree how the work should be performed (*see* AUTONOMY; DECENTRALIZATION; PARTICIPATION; QUALITY CIRCLES). The most salient extrinsic reward is money, which is instrumental in obtaining other desired objects. Other extrinsic rewards include, employee benefits, physical work environment, and special privileges.

The economist, Adam Smith argued in 1750 that the highest profits could be achieved by simplifying work into elemental subtasks – Charlie Chaplin's 1929 film, *Modern Times* illustrates the dysfunctional effects of repetitive work when carried to extremes. Subsequently, writers such as Argyris (1964); Maslow, McClelland, and McGregor stressed the importance of an internal desire to succeed at challenging tasks and to seek responsibility (*see* THEORY X & Y). Herzberg argued that jobs should be redesigned so that the problems employees are expected to solve are sufficiently difficult, and so that they may develop their abilities (*see* MOTIVATOR/HYGIENE THEORY). Recent trends in organizational DOWNSIZING has required doing more with less and employees are being empowered to assume more responsibility at all levels (*see* EMPLOYEE INVOLVEMENT; EMPOWERMENT).

Intrinsically motivated behavior occurs in three ways (Bandura, 1986). Behavior may produce sensory effects which are a natural consequence of the behavior. These are either:

(1) external to the body such as in the musical and visual arts; or
(2) internal physiological effects such as athletic feats requiring high levels of physical coordination.

Few jobs, however, provide such opportunities. Behavior may also produce a level of accomplishment in an activity which;

(3) satisfies internal standards, whereby self-reactions to the accomplishment (e.g., feelings of pride) are the reward.

These rewards are internally generated, but because any activity may be the source of such rewards the contingency between behavior and effect is arbitrary, not natural (*see* SELF EFFICACY; SELF ACTUALIZATION).

Extrinsic (e.g., financial) rewards may be received contingent upon how well a job is performed (*see* PERFORMANCE RELATED PAY; BONUS PAYMENTS), on a noncontingent basis such as in wages and salary and in across-the-board-pay-raises, or upon a combination of the two. In 1911, Taylor advocated setting goals, providing performance FEEDBACK, and paying for performance (*see* SCIENTIFIC MANAGEMENT). Modern compensation policies must consider internal equity, in which jobs within a company are compensated based on value to the company; external equity, in which a company compensates according to the market value of a job; and individual equity, in which personal merit increases are perceived as fairly distributed among employees (*see* EQUITY THEORY; PERFORMANCE APPRAISAL).

Because people live within social systems, perceptions of how intrinsically motivating a job can be (e.g., amount of challenge, autonomy, and responsibility), and therefore internal standards, can be influenced by colleagues. Similarly, inspirational leaders infuse an organization with their values and affect internal standards of employees by providing a mission. This may explain why industrial psychologists have been unable to classify a number of job outcomes as intrinsic or extrinsic, and why the theoretical boundary between the two categories has not been clear (Dyer & Parker, 1975).

Some theorists argue that the combined effects of intrinsic, and contingently applied extrinsic, rewards on MOTIVATION are additive: interesting work and pay-for-performance together increase motivation. Others (Deci & Ryan, 1985) stress that contingently applied extrinsic rewards may, when perceived as outside pressure to achieve particular outcomes, decrease intrinsic motivation; therefore organizations should provide equitable salaries, unrelated to performance, and should rely on JOB DESIGN, PARTICIPATION, and TRAINING to improve performance. A review of the research findings (Wiersma, 1992) suggests that the additive model is more viable.

See also **Quality of working life; Gainsharing; Instrumentality; Payment systems; Motivation and performance; VIE theory**

Bibliography

Argyris, C. (1964). *Integrating the organization and the individual.* London: Wiley.

Bandura, A. (1986). *Social foundations of thought and action: A social cognitive theory.* Englewood Cliffs, NJ: Prentice-Hall.

Deci, E. & Ryan, R. (1985). *Intrinsic motivation and self-determination in human behaviour.* New York: Plenum.

Dyer, L. & Parker, D. (1975). Classifying outcomes in work motivation research: An examination of the intrinsic-extrinsic dichotomy. *Journal of Applied Psychology*, **60**, 455–458.

Wiersma, U. J. (1992). The effects of extrinsic rewards on intrinsic motivation: A meta-analysis. *Journal of Occupational and Organizational Psychology*, **65**, 101–114.

UCO J. WIERSMA

intrinsic satisfaction *see* INTRINSIC/EXTRINSIC MOTIVATION; JOB SATISFACTION

introversion *see* EXTRAVERSION; PERSONALITY TESTING

isomorphism A key principle in human ecology, developed by Hawley (1986), which holds that when the units of a social system are subjected to common environmental conditions, they acquire a similar form of organization. DiMaggio and Powell (1983) applied the idea in organizational studies, identifying three processes that encourage the members of an organizational field to become more alike. Coercive isomorphism results from pressures exerted on organizations by others upon whom they are dependent. Mimetic isomorphism, or imitative modeling, is a common response to uncertainty. Normative isomorphism reflects both the legitimacy and status associated with the modern professions and the growth and elaboration of professional networks that span organizations and encourage the diffusion of common organizational practices (*see* NETWORK ANALYSIS).

See also **Population ecology; Organizational change; Interorganizational relations**

Bibliography

DiMaggio, P. J. & Powell W. W. (1983). The iron cage revisited: Institutional isomorphism and collective rationality in organizational fields. *American Sociological Review*, **48**, 147–60.

Hawley, A. (1986). *Human ecology: A theoretical essay.* Chicago: University of Chicago Press.

WALTER W. POWELL

— J —

Japanese management *see* INTERNATIONAL MANAGEMENT

job analysis Job analysis is the process through which one derives a description of what an employee (usually referred to as the "job incumbent") does on his or her job. The outcome of the process usually (but not always) includes a JOB DESCRIPTION, as well as estimates of job requirements. Job analysis is often viewed as the building block for much of HUMAN RESOURCE MANAGEMENT since it provides the basis for identifying the knowledge, SKILLS, and ABILITIES required to carry out the job; the areas of responsibility for performance measurement; the identification of TRAINING needs; and the basis for identifying factors that should be compensated. In addition, jobs are sometimes described for very specific reasons, using instruments designed for those purposes. Probably most common among these are analyses performed to determine the extent to which the job can be redesigned to make it more "enriched" (*see* JOB DESIGN; JOB CHARACTERISTICS; JOB ENRICHMENT).

Job analysis was long regarded as a "given," in that job descriptions were generally assumed to reflect job requirements. Thus, the major research issues (Harvey, 1991) were concerned with the identification of the proper job analysis technique to be used, as well as the proper agent to conduct the job analysis. In relation to techniques, the major distinction has been between qualitative and quantitative job analysis. Qualitative approaches often have involved little more than the writing of a job description with few guidelines or rules to be followed. These techniques, although less costly and less time-consuming, provide little basis for making comparisons across jobs (which is critical for making compensation decisions), and little basis for establishing job requirements. For these reasons quantitative methods are generally preferred. An important exception to this, however, is the Critical Incidents Approach which focuses on the particular behaviors or incidents on the job which separate effective from ineffective performers. The technique has been used primarily for the development of PERFORMANCE APPRAISAL systems, rather than for other functions.

Quantitative methods allow jobs to be rated on scales, providing scores on various factors which allow comparisons across jobs, as well as a formal method for establishing job requirements. Although numerous techniques have been proposed, a few have emerged as the most popular and useful. The Task Inventory Approach has been used most widely in the United States military, and involves developing a checklist of tasks that an incumbent on a given job might perform. Subject Matter Experts (SMEs) develop the tasks, which can be a time-consuming process, and incumbents are then asked to indicate which tasks they actually perform and/or the relative time spent or relative importance of each. The information provided is generally seen as most useful for establishing TRAINING requirements for jobs, which makes it especially suitable for military applications. Functional Job Analysis allows all jobs to be described and rated relative to their involvement with People, Data, and Things. Scales have been developed for each of these areas, allowing jobs to be scored and directly compared. Functional Job Analysis is used as the partial basis for the classification of jobs in the Dictionary of Occupational Titles, and also provides guidelines for writing job descriptions and for establishing ability and trait requirements for jobs. The Position Analysis Questionnaire (PAQ) (McCormick, Jeanneret, & Mecham, 1972) is concerned with what workers do on jobs, rather than what gets done on jobs. Thus, the PAQ is considered a "worker oriented" technique, and was designed specifically to allow direct comparisons across jobs. The PAQ consists of 194 elements, or items, divided into six sections. Data can be used either at the level of the job elements, or at the level of "job dimensions" derived from factor analysis of individual items, which have been found empirically related to ABILITY requirements as well as to compensation levels.

Studies by Levine and his associates (e.g., Levine, Ash, Hall, & Sistrunk, 1983) have attempted to compare these quantitative methods to determine if there is one best technique. Their results have indicated that different methods can provide data leading to the identification of quite similar selection requirements, and therefore the choice of technique should be dependent upon the purpose of the job analysis.

Several studies have also examined the role of the job analyst, or Subject Matter Expect (SME) in the job analysis process. These studies have generally concluded that the RACE of the SME is not a critical factor, nor is education level, but the analyst must be experienced, to provide accurate job analysis information. The effects of GENDER, on the other hand, are somewhat inconsistent, and seem to depend on a number of other contextual factors (see review concerning SMEs by Landy (1993)).

More recently, questions have been raised about the extent to which job analysis information accurately reflects the content of the job. A study by Smith and Hakel (1979) raised the possibility that job analysts simply described commonly held stereotypes about jobs and what those jobs involved. Although subsequent studies suggested that this problem was not as serious as had been suggested, the authors of one of these studies (DeNisi, Cornelius, & Blencoe, 1987) proposed that, for more complex jobs, job analysis techniques may be limited in their utility. They point out that most job analysis techniques are not designed to describe adequately upper level managerial jobs (and few techniques to accomplish this have been proposed and tested) and so, in these cases, job descriptions may well be influenced by STEREOTYPING. Little is known about such stereotypes, their nature, or their prevalence, but it would seem that this provides a real challenge to job analysis in the future, and represents an area where research is needed.

See also **Payment systems; Person-job fit; Selection methods**

Bibliography

DeNisi, A. S., Cornelius, E. T. & Blencoe, A. G. (1987). A further investigation of common knowledge effects on job analysis ratings. *Journal of Applied Psychology*, **72**, 262–268.

Harvey, R. J. (1991). Job analysis. In M. D. Dunnette & L. M. Hough (Eds), *The handbook of industrial/organizational psychology* (2nd edn). Palo Alto, CA: Consulting Psychologists Press.

Landy, F. (1993). Job analysis and job evaluation: The respondent's perspective. In H. Schuler, J. L. Farr & M. Smith (Eds), *Personnel selection and assessment: Individual and organizational perspective*. Hillsdale, NJ: Lawrence Erlbaum.

Levine, E. L., Ash, R. A., Hall, H. & Sistrunk, F. (1983). Evaluation of job analysis methods by experienced job analysts. *Academy of Management Journal*, **26**, 339–347.

McCormick, E. J., Jeanneret, P. R. & Mecham, R. C. (1972). A study of the job dimensions as based on the Position Analysis Questionnaire. *Journal of Applied Psychology*, **36**, 347–368.

Smith, J. E. & Hakel, M. D. (1979). Convergence among data sources, response bias, and reliability and validity of a structured job analysis questionnaire. *Personnel Psychology*, **32**, 677–692.

ANGELO DE NISI

job characteristics These refer to objective properties of the work itself that are likely to contribute to the work effectiveness and satisfaction of employees. The characteristics that have received the most research attention have been suggested by Job Characteristics Theory (Hackman & Oldham, 1980). At its most basic level, the theory argues that the presence of five core job characteristics prompt a number of beneficial personal and work outcomes (e.g., high satisfaction, attendance and performance, and low turnover). The five characteristics are defined as follows:

SKILL variety. The degree to which a job requires a variety of different activities in carrying out the work, involving the use of a number of different skills and talents of the person.

Task identity. The degree to which the job requires completion of a whole, identifiable piece of work – that is, doing a job from beginning to end with a visible outcome.

Task significance. The degree to which the job has a substantial impact on the lives of other people, whether those people are in the immediate organization or the world at large.

AUTONOMY. The degree to which the job provides substantial freedom, independence and discretion to the individual in scheduling the work and in determining the procedures to be used in carrying it out.

Task FEEDBACK. The degree to which carrying out the work activities required by the job provides the individual with direct and clear information about the effectiveness of his or her performance.

The most frequently used measures of these characteristics are included in the Job Diagnostic Survey (JDS; Hackman & Oldham, 1975, 1980). The JDS asks individual jobholders to indicate the extent to which each of the five core characteristics is present in his or her job. In addition to the JDS, a companion instrument, the Job Rating Form (JRF; Hackman & Oldham, 1980) has been used to obtain measures of the job characteristics from individuals who do not themselves work on the focal job (e.g., supervisors or outside observers). Research has demonstrated that there is substantial agreement between the assessment of job characteristics made by jobholders and those made by outside observers (Kulik, Oldham, & Hackman, 1987).

In general, research has shown that measures of the core job characteristics are associated with the positive outcomes specified by Job Characteristics Theory (Fried & Ferris, 1987; Loher, Noe, Moeller, & Fitzgerald, 1985). For example, research has demonstrated that the higher the job scores on the five characteristics, the higher the employee's performance, JOB SATISFACTION, and attendance (*see* ABSENTEEISM). Moreover, employees who are strongly desirous of growth and development opportunities at work (*see* GROWTH NEED STRENGTH) respond even more positively to jobs high on the five characteristics than individuals who have little interest in growth opportunities at work.

These results have important implications for the redesign of jobs in organizations (*see* JOB DESIGN, JOB ENRICHMENT). Specifically, they suggest that boosting jobs on the five characteristics can result in substantial improvements in the effectiveness and well-being of employees. What remains unclear in this literature are the effects of job characteristics on other work and nonwork outcomes (*see* NONWORK/WORK). For example, we know little about the effects of job characteristics on employees' CREATIVITY at work or upon their relationships with family members.

See also **Job analysis; Sociotechnical theory; Motivation and performance**

Bibliography

Fried, Y. & Ferris, G. R. (1987). The validity of the job characteristics model: A review and meta-analysis. *Personnel Psychology*, **40**, 287–322.

Hackman, J. R. & Oldham, G. R. (1975). Development of the job diagnostic survey. *Journal of Applied Psychology*, **60**, 159–170.

Hackman, J. R. & Oldham, G. R. (1980). *Work redesign*. Reading, MA: Addison-Wesley.

Kulik, C. T., Oldham, G. R. & Hackman, J. R. (1987). Work design as an approach to person-environment fit. *Journal of Vocational Behavior*, **31**, 278–296.

Loher, B. T., Noe, R. A., Moeller, N. L. & Fitzgerald, M. P. (1985). A meta-analysis of the relation of job characteristics to job satisfaction. *Journal of Applied Psychology*, **70**, 280–289.

GREG R. OLDHAM

job description This is a written summary of the major tasks, duties, responsibilities, and work outcomes of a job as derived from JOB ANALYSIS. Job descriptions typically begin with a brief overview of job purpose, responsibilities, and outcomes, followed by a more specific listing of duties and tasks. Most descriptions also include PERSON SPECIFICATIONS: the knowledge, SKILLS, ABILITIES, and other characteristics (e.g., interests, PERSONALITY TRAITS) deemed necessary for satisfactory job performance.

A number of current issues surround job descriptions. One involves the relative merits of basing job descriptions on *qualitative* versus *quantitative* job analyses. Although quantitative analyses are generally preferred for their greater precision and comparability across dissimilar jobs, they also involve significant start-up and data-base management costs.

A second issue concerns the choice between descriptions based on *task-* versus *worker-*oriented job analyses. In general, worker-oriented approaches are more flexible for making comparisons across jobs (Harvey, 1991). However, task-oriented approaches may be more useful for assessing TRAINING needs.

A final issue involves whether to use a single, multipurpose description, or separate descriptions for different purposes (e.g., selection, training). Given the speed with which jobs are changing, flexible approaches that can be easily updated seem likely to increase in attractiveness, even if they involve higher start-up costs.

See also **Job design; Recruitment; Selection methods**

Bibliography

Harvey, R. J. (1991). Job analysis. In M. D. Dunnette & L. M. Hough (Eds), *Handbook of industrial and organizational psychology* (2nd edn, vol. 2, pp. 71–163). Palo Alto, CA: Consulting Psychologists Press.

SARA L. RYNES

job design Organizations have particular functions to accomplish if they are to meet their objectives. Those functions comprise a number of tasks, which are then grouped to form jobs undertaken by individuals. Job incumbents typically are trained to carry out their prescribed tasks, and given a certain degree of discretion over how they do so. The term "job design" refers to the outcome of this process and may be defined as the specification of the content and methods of jobs. Other terms often used as synonyms for job design include "work design" and "job" or "work structuring." "Work organization" is also frequently used to encompass job design, but usually signifies a broader perspective linking jobs more explicitly to their organizational context.

In principle, the concept of job design applies to all types of jobs and to the full range of possible job properties. Within OB, however, a more particular emphasis has developed, which has two aspects. First, with regard to types of work, attention has been directed mainly at lower level jobs within larger organizations, such as those involving clerical and especially shopfloor work. Second, with respect to job properties, the primary focus has been on generic JOB CHARACTERISTICS such as the variety of tasks in jobs, and the amount of discretion job incumbents have in completing those tasks. Interest in job design has centered on two main issues. One concerns the impact of job design on job attitudes and behavior; the other concerns the technological and organizational factors which influence the design of jobs. These emphases are best understood in the context of the historical development of shopfloor jobs and associated research.

Historical Context

From around the turn of the twentieth century, the trend in job design in manufacturing has been one of JOB DESKILLING or job simplification. The replacement of small craft-based enterprises with larger factories, the emergence of MASS PRODUCTION, and the application of the principles of SCIENTIFIC MANAGEMENT, are among the factors which encouraged organizations to design jobs so that they involved a narrow set of closely prescribed tasks. The rationale for this strategy was that simplifying jobs in this way would reduce costs, by making ERRORS less likely, enabling less skilled labor to be recruited and by shortening TRAINING times. The archetype of this process is the assembly line, where jobs can be so simplified that they entail the continuous repetition of a single operation with a short cycle time, minimal discretion over how to carry out the task, and no control over the pace of work.

The practice of job simplification gave rise to concerns about its psychological effects, and inspired some of the earliest research in OB. In the United Kingdom this was a focus of work conducted during the 1920s by the publicly funded Industrial Fatigue Research Board. That research, involving such jobs as tobacco weighing, cigarette making, cartridge case assembly, and bicycle chain assembly, was mainly formulated in terms of the psychological effects of the lack of task variety, that is, of REPETITIVE WORK. Not surprisingly, the evidence suggested that employees did indeed find repetitive jobs monotonous and boring. As this area of inquiry developed in the United Kingdom, the United States and elsewhere during the next few decades, evidence also began to emerge of a link between repetitive work and employee STRESS and MENTAL HEALTH. Research during the 1950s and 1960s began also to consider how the restriction of job discretion or AUTONOMY brought about by job simplification affected job incumbents, and showed similar and often stronger psychological effects. This is a key component of current approaches to job design as will be described later.

Job Redesign

Evidence of the undesirable effects of simplified job designs gave rise to various proposals for and initiatives in *job redesign*. This normative term, widely used in the literature instead of the more neutral "job design," reflects the historical background outlined above. Job simplification is cast as the traditional approach to job design, and job *re*design refers to deliberate attempts to reverse its effects by building into jobs greater task variety, autonomy, and associated characteristics. Suggestions for job redesign naturally reflect findings regarding simplified jobs. Thus one of the earliest proposals, focused on the reduction of repetitiveness by increasing task variety, was for JOB ROTATION, which involves individuals moving between different jobs at regular intervals. "Horizontal job enlargement" has the same objective, but increases task variety by incorporating into jobs a wider range of component tasks of a similar kind. Other proposals are more concerned with augmenting responsibility or autonomy. This is the thrust of both "vertical job enlargement" and JOB ENRICHMENT, which entail increasing the degree to which individuals can control the planning and execution of their work, usually including responsibilities and tasks which otherwise would be undertaken by specialist support or supervisory staff. Job enrichment is a term coined by Herzberg to denote the approach to job redesign based on his TWO-FACTOR THEORY (1966), but which is now used more generally (*see* MOTIVATOR-HYGIENE THEORY). A final type of proposal directed at enhancing the discretionary content of work, but which differs in taking the WORK GROUP rather than the job as the main unit of analysis, derives from SOCIOTECHNICAL THEORY (*see also* below), and is for the implementation of AUTONOMOUS WORK GROUPS or SELF-MANAGED TEAMS (*see* SELF-MANAGEMENT).

Major Theoretical Approaches

Current approaches to job design are more broadly based than the early work. Two theoretical frameworks have been particularly influential, and have yet to be superseded. The first of these is the JOB CHARACTERISTICS Model (Hackman & Oldham, 1976), which specifies five "core job dimensions" (namely autonomy, feedback, skill variety, task identity, and task significance) as predictors of WORK MOTIVATION, work performance, JOB SATISFACTION, labor TURNOVER and absence (*see* ABSENTEEISM; PERFORMANCE, INDIVIDUAL). The strength of the effects of the job characteristics on the outcomes is predicted to be affected by INDIVIDUAL DIFFERENCES, in particular, being stronger for employees with greater GROWTH NEED STRENGTH and (in later formulations of the model) for those with higher contextual satisfaction and more knowledge, SKILLS, and ABILITY.

The second main approach derives from SOCIOTECHNICAL THEORY. The emphasis in this case is on job design for groups of employees, the major proposal being for the implementation of autonomous work groups. Theorists identify six design criteria for promoting work effectiveness, individual well-being and the QUALITY OF WORKING LIFE more generally. These are that the work should: be reasonably demanding and provide variety; afford the opportunity to learn and to continue learning; include an area of decision making that employees can call their own; offer social support and recognition; be of wider social relevance; and lead to a desirable future (Cherns, 1976). There is no particular recognition of individual differences in this approach, but otherwise the specified variables are very similar to those of the Job Characteristics Model.

Examples

A series of studies by Wall, Clegg and colleagues illustrates empirical work in this area (Wall & Martin, 1994). For example, the redesign of work in a department in a confectionery factory led to the institution of two autonomous work groups, each taking responsibility for organizing their own work, within the constraints of meeting production targets and of normal health and SAFETY requirements. The groups set their own speed of work, allocated tasks amongst themselves, and took responsibility for daily operational decisions. The results were impressive and significant: levels of PRODUCTIVITY and job satisfaction increased, whilst reports of individual strain fell. A further study in a different organization compared the use of autonomous group work in a greenfield factory designed for such purposes, with a more traditional factory making similar products. This demonstrated that workers much preferred autonomous working, although interestingly the managers found it very challenging. Levels of operational efficiency were comparable across the two factories, although the indirect support costs were considerably lower in the new factory.

A series of studies in an electronics company substantiates the claim that people much prefer more enriched jobs. Furthermore, enriching individual's jobs led to substantial improvements in operational performance when there was uncertainty in the work system. Part of the improvement was "logistical," the operators were on hand to resolve difficulties as they arose. Part was also motivational, in the sense that the operators prefer to have and take responsibility. However, it is clear there was also a learning explanation to these improvements in performance. For example, operators learned to anticipate problems and acted to prevent them occurring (Wall & Jackson, 1994).

A further point should be stressed. Each of these studies revealed the importance of the surrounding organization within which jobs are designed or redesigned. Choices about the tasks for which individual operators or groups of operators take responsibility have a substantial impact on the work of others, most notably their supervisors (if there are any) and managers, and other staff in indirect support roles (e.g., in quality and engineering). The organizational context within which jobs are designed or redesigned is probably the major issue for people attempting practical changes in this area, and the failure to take this into account the main reason for lack of success.

Current Issues and Future Directions

Interest in job design which waxed during the 1970s, making it then one of the most prominent areas of inquiry within OB, waned during the 1980s. However, it is now resurfacing with renewed vigor, partly in response to the new strategies, practices, and technologies emerging in manufacturing and elsewhere. Organizations are placing increased emphasis on enhancing their COMPETITIVENESS through improved quality, FLEXIBILITY, and responsiveness to customer (or client) demand; and supporting this through the use of ADVANCED MANUFACTURING TECHNOLOGY, JUST-IN-TIME inventory control, TOTAL QUALITY MANAGEMENT, BUSINESS PROCESS REENGINEERING and other initiatives. It is widely recognized that these developments have implications for the nature of jobs, and that success depends on their being supported by appropriate job designs (e.g., Buchanan & McCalman, 1989; Lawler, 1992). This renewed emphasis on job design has highlighted the limitations of existing knowledge and thus clarified directions for further development.

One issue on which existing evidence is relatively conclusive is that of the effect of job design on attitudes. Evidence consistently supports the theoretically specified link between job design variables, especially autonomy, and job satisfaction. With regard to performance, in contrast, findings have been more variable. It is likely that this relationship varies according to unspecified contingencies, and those need to be determined. As in the examples described earlier, one such contingency, suggested by ORGANIZATIONAL THEORY, is UNCERTAINTY. It is possible that designing more autonomous jobs benefits performance under conditions of greater uncertainty, but that the effect declines as job requirements become more predictable. That is a particular issue that deserves serious attention. More importantly, however, it exemplifies the now apparent more general need in job design research for the development of a wider perspective and greater integration with cognate areas of inquiry (Wall & Jackson, 1994).

Four other areas of job design requiring such development are high on the agenda. The first concerns mental health. It is interesting that although this featured as a dependent variable in early studies it has subsequently been neglected by mainstream approaches. As if to rectify this neglect, there has emerged a separate area of inquiry on job stress, in which mental health is the focus and autonomy a key predictor variable (e.g., the Demands–Control Model, Karasek & Theorell, 1990). Those areas are ripe for integration. A second need is to broaden the range of job content variables taken into account within job design. Research on new technologies and work practices in particular has pointed to the potential relevance of such factors as cognitive demand and cost responsibility. This relates to a third need which is for the development of a stronger cognitive emphasis. At present job design is founded on motivational assumptions. Recent evidence suggests that at least some of the effects of job design operate through enhancing job incumbents' understanding of their tasks. The role of underlying cognitive mechanisms is worthy of investigation in its own right, and would benefit through being linked to developments in cognitive psychology. Finally, it is apparent the effect of TECHNOLOGY on job design has been neglected. Especially important in the context of new technology is the issue of prospective design, where social scientists and users work alongside development engineers in the design and implementation of systems to ensure that they are not specified in such a way as to preclude job design alternatives that would be of benefit (Clegg, Cooch, Hornby, Maclaren, Robson, Carey, & Symon, 1994). These and other developments are now underway.

See also **Information technology; Operations management; Human-computer interaction; Organizational design**

Bibliography

Buchanan, D. A. & McCalman, J. (1989). *High performance work systems: The Digital experience.* London: Routledge.

Cherns, A. (1976). The principles of sociotechnical design. *Human Relations*, **29**, 783–792.

Clegg, C. W. Cooch, P. Hornby, P. Maclaren, R. Robson, J. Carey, N. & Symon, G. (1995). Methods and tools to incorporate some psychological and organisational issues during the development of computer-based systems. SAPU memo 1435.

Hackman, J. R. & Oldham, G. R. (1976). Motivation through the design of work: Test of a theory. *Organizational Behavior and Human Performance*, **15**, 250–279.

Herzberg, F. (1966). *Work and the nature of man.* Cleveland, OH: World Publishing.

Karasek, R. & Theorell, T. (1990). *Healthy work: Stress, productivity and the reconstruction of working life.* New York: Basic Books.

Lawler, E. E. (1992). *The ultimate advantage: Creating the high involvement organization.* San Francisco: Jossey-Bass.

Wall, T. D. & Jackson, P. R. (1994). Changes in manufacturing and shopfloor job design. In A. Howard (Ed.), *The changing nature of work.* San Francisco: Jossey-Bass.

Wall, T. D. & Martin, R. (1994). Job and work design. In C. L. Cooper & I. T. Robertson (Eds.) *Key reviews in organizational behavior: Concepts, theory and practice.* Chichester: Wiley.

TOBY D. WALL and CHRIS W. CLEGG

job deskilling Deskilling is the process by which SKILL levels of either jobs or individuals are reduced. Particular attention in the social sciences has focused on the way in which, with the rise of modern industry, jobs were increasingly routinized, and devoid of any real skill content, i.e., they had become deskilled. The paradigm case of deskilled jobs are assembly line jobs which have very short (often well under a minute) job cycles and training times. Whilst technological developments such as Ford's moving assembly line and increased levels of automation are considered important causes of these, so also are methods of management and, in particular, Taylor's SCIENTIFIC MANAGEMENT.

Taylor's stricture that the conception of tasks should be divorced from their execution and, moreover, that management should have sole responsibility for conception implied that jobs would be deskilled and workers would have no autonomy or control over their work. In so far as Taylor's methods were being applied we would expect the number of deskilled jobs would increase. With the growth of MASS PRODUCTION methods, first in the United States in the 1920s and subsequently throughout the world, there has been, accordingly, a great concern about the deskilled nature of work. Certainly, the antagonistic INDUSTRIAL RELATIONS in industries such as automobile manufacture has part of its roots in such conditions; but low-skilled work should not automatically be associated with industrial CONFLICT, as many textile industries throughout the world, for example, despite being characterized by highly routinized work, are characterized by low levels of overt conflict.

As the levels of AUTOMATION and use of computers increased, largely from the Second World War onwards, a belief began to emerge that the number of deskilled jobs would reduce. Research by Blauner in the United States, for example, suggested that at higher levels of automation higher levels of skills would be demanded. Also jobs in the expanding service sector were widely thought to require higher levels of skills than the average factory job. These ideas prompted criticism – most notably from Braverman, also in the United States – who argued that deskilling was the dominant tendency in modern capitalism and that Taylorist principles would still apply at high levels of automation and would be increasingly applied in the growing service sector, as well as to conventional clerical work. Widespread deskilling arises because the DIVISION OF LABOR into narrow routinized tasks is cheaper and control of workers – a major objective of management within capitalism – is made easier. Accordingly, the initial pursuit of scientific management in the twentieth century was, for Braverman, very much about taking control from craft workers who previously were responsible for both conceiving and executing their tasks.

The deskilling thesis has been questioned most fundamentally on the grounds that control of labor need not become an end in itself for management and the achievement of their prime objective, profitability, may not always be furthered by deskilling work. The more fragmented the structure of tasks and the more limited the range of aptitudes possessed by individual workers, the greater the requirement for expensive managerial skills to co-ordinate the overall production system. More difficult also may be the problems of the organization in adjusting to fluctuating product market conditions. In the twentieth century the numbers of skilled workers has not, in fact, declined to the extent implied by the deskilling thesis, and the main consequence of mass production was a whole new set of semi-skilled OCCUPATIONS and not the substitution of craftwork by routinized labor. Such jobs are not devoid of skills, many of which may be tacit; and the degree of DISCRETION given to people may vary and not correlate perfectly with their skill level. Nor should the extent of the skills of the artisan be exaggerated. Relative to the nineteenth century, overall skill levels of individuals have increased, as the majority of workers then lacked basic skills such as literacy which are now, mistakenly perhaps, taken for granted.

Certainly taken over a long historical period, net changes in the skill levels will reflect the changing occupational and industrial composition in the economy more than changes within particular jobs. Analysis of industrial and occupational shifts in the twentieth century suggests that overall the direction of change has been toward higher-skilled industries and occupations, the opposite of deskilling. If we take the insurance industry as an example though technical change did take away certain skills, there was a net increase in skill levels, as these changes largely absorbed the skills of certain low level jobs, and as the industry itself expanded rapidly following the Second World War the numbers of higher-level jobs expanded disproportionately.

Nevertheless, much work in the twentieth century, as in the nineteenth, remains low skilled; there have been clear cases where TECHNOLOGY has reduced the skill level of and discretion required in particular jobs (e.g., in engineering); and many of the jobs created in the past 20 years with the great growth in the service sector are low skilled (e.g., work in fast-food chains). Though deskilled work may not be the current or emerging norm, there are sufficient numbers of jobs with low skill and/ or low discretion, to make for relatively low levels of MOTIVATION and COMMITMENT amongst a significant number of the working population. Several theories of motivation accord skill and autonomy a prime role (JOB CHARACTERISTICS, Herzberg's MOTIVATOR-HYGIENE THEORY), and Fox (1974) in particular has placed the low-skill content of jobs at the center of his explanation of the problems of industrial relations in post-war Western economies. There is little evidence of any widespread commitment of managements to genuinely enlarge the skills of jobs through conscious job redesign (*see* JOB ENRICHMENT) Nor is it clear that some of the latest developments in management such as TOTAL QUALITY MANAGEMENT or Japanese-style lean production significantly alter the skill or AUTONOMY attached to low-level jobs in organizations.

See also **Job design; Collective action; Repetitive work; Routinization; Motivation & Performance**

Bibliography

Attewell, P. (1987). The deskilling controversy. *Work and occupations*, **14**, 323–46.

Braverman, H. (1984). *Labor and monopoly capitalism.* New York: Monthly Review Press.

Fox, A. (1974). *Begond contract.* London: Faber & Faber.

Wood, S. (1982). *The degradation of work?* London: Hutchinson.

STEPHEN WOOD

job enrichment In its most general form, this involves expanding a job's content to provide increased opportunities for the individual employee to experience personal responsibility and meaning at work, and to obtain more information about the results of his or her work efforts. In practice, job enrichment programs often focus on improving a job's standing on JOB CHARACTERISTICS, specifically: AUTONOMY, task FEEDBACK, task significance, SKILL variety, and task identity. Several specific "implementing principles" have been identified (Hackman & Oldham, 1980; Hackman, Oldham, Janson, & Purdy, 1975) which can be used to boost a job on these characteristics and, therefore, to enrich the job itself. These are defined as follows:

Combining tasks. This refers to putting together existing, fractionalized tasks to form new and larger modules of work. When tasks are combined, all tasks required to complete a piece of work are performed by one person, rather than by a series of individuals who do separate small, parts of the job.

Forming natural work units. This involves giving employees continuing responsibility for work that has been arranged into logical or inherently meaningful groups. For example, an individual employee might be given responsibility for all work within a particular geographical area or for all work that originates in a particular department of a larger organization.

Establishing client relationships. This refers to putting the employee in direct contact with the "clients" of his or her work (e.g., customers or employees in other departments) and giving the employee personal responsibility for managing relationships with those clients.

Vertical loading. This involves giving the employee increased control over the work by "pushing down" responsibility and authority that were once reserved for higher levels of management (*see* SPAN OF CONTROL). Thus, vertical loading can involve giving the employee discretion in setting schedules, determining work methods, and deciding when and how to check the quality of work produced.

Opening feedback channels. This involves removing blocks that isolate the employee from naturally occurring data about his or her PERFORMANCE at work. Specifically, this may involve giving the employee the opportunity to inspect his or her own work and providing standard summaries of performance records directly to the employee.

The major objectives of job enrichment are to improve the JOB SATISFACTION, MOTIVATION, and work effectiveness of employees. Numerous studies have examined the effects of job enrichment on such outcomes, and the results have generally been positive (see Ford, 1969; Herzberg, 1976). For example, in a review of 32 empirical studies, Kopelman (1985) concludes that job enrichment programs typically result in a 17.2 percent increase in work quality, a 6.4 percent increase in work quantity, and a 14.5 percent decrease in ABSENTEEISM. Moreover, 80 percent of the studies that included measures of job satisfaction showed some improvement after job enrichment.

In addition, other research suggests that the outcomes of job enrichment will be even more positive when employees involved are strongly desirous of opportunities for growth and self-direction at work (*see* GROWTH NEED STRENGTH; SELF-REGULATION). Unfortunately, there remain a number of questions about the practice of job enrichment. One of the most serious of these concerns the durability of the effects of job enrichment interventions. Most empirical investigations have examined the effects of enrichment for periods of less than 12 months. Therefore, it is not yet clear that employees will find the enriched jobs stimulating and challenging after extended periods of time – or will find that the jobs provide insufficient opportunities for personal responsibility and continued growth.

See also **Job design; socio-technical theory; organizational design; Motivation & performance; Motivator-hygiene theory**

Bibliography

Ford, R. N. (1969). *Motivation through the work itself.* New York: American Management Association.

Hackman, J. R. & Oldham, G. R. (1980). *Work redesign*. Reading, MA: Addison-Wesley.

Hackman, J. R., Oldham, G. R., Janson, R. & Purdy, K. (1975). A new strategy for job enrichment. *California Management Review*, **17**, 57–71.

Herzberg, F. (1976). *The managerial choice*. Homewood, IL: Dow Jones-Irwin.

Kopelman, R. E. (1985). Job redesign and productivity: A review of the evidence. *National Productivity Review*, **4**, 237–255.

GREG R. OLDHAM

job evaluation *see* JOB ANALYSIS; PAYMENT SYSTEMS

job insecurity This is the concern an employee feels about the future of their employment. The discrepancy between experienced and desired security applies to several categories: secondary LABOR MARKET employees with poor terms of employment; some freelance and fixed-term contract employees; some new employees (for whom insecurity is temporary); those experiencing a *change* in their security beliefs due to perceived changes in the organizational or economic context; and those who are "survivors" after others are made redundant. Most interest has been focused on those employees undergoing change in their level of security, and this text relates to them. Further understanding is needed about other groups.

The population of insecure employees is larger than those who lose their jobs. Insecurity is an intrarole transition engendered by changes in individual assumptions concerning self, the organization, and its environment. It is not an event having a clear temporal onset and termination. There may be considerable variation in the experience of job insecurity within a given organization, though job insecurity is objective in that it varies between organizations.

The cognitive appraisal model of Lazarus and Folkman (1984) can be applied, including the primary appraisal of threat (to job continuity), and secondary appraisal (about coping with threat). Greenhalgh and Rosenblatt (1984) propose felt job insecurity consists of perceived severity of threat and perceived powerlessness to counteract threat. Hartley, Jacobson, Klandermans, and van Vuuren (1991) argue that powerlessness is more usefully conceptualized as an outcome. Some writers use a value-expectancy approach (*see* VIE THEORY) with insecurity a function of the perceived probability and perceived severity of losing one's job. Job insecurity is used to describe concern over the *loss* of the job (employment insecurity) but also concern about changing job content but this latter may weaken its conceptual value.

Antecedents include the organizational/industrial relations climate (TRUST in management; perceived strength of employee representation). Personal characteristics (personal capabilities, output, work experience) are believed by the insecure to be more important buffers against job loss than occupational characteristics (seniority, department). Factors perceived to reduce the severity of potential job loss (financial position, number of dependents, labor market opportunities) predict insecurity. Hartley et al. (1991) summarize the main findings.

Reactions to feelings of job insecurity vary. Jacobson (1985) argues that unconflicted inertia, unconflicted change, defensive avoidance, and vigilance are patterns of coping. Some research has pointed to the critical role of attributions (*see* ATTRIBUTION) influencing individual and collective behaviors.

Outcomes include individual effects (e.g. STRESS, psychological well-being, depression) (*see* MENTAL HEALTH), individual–organizational linkages (trust, company COMMITMENT, PSYCHOLOGICAL CONTRACT), and consequences for ORGANIZATIONAL EFFECTIVENESS (TURNOVER, job effort, acceptance of change). Consequences are largely negative for individuals. Individual–organization linkages, notably commitment, are weakened. Consequences for organizational effectiveness include: making employees less likely to quit, though they might suffer "presenteeism" (being psychologically absent from the job) (*see* WITHDRAWAL, ORGANIZATIONAL), less accepting of change; more resentful of imposed changes; and more secretive and competitive (Greenhalgh & Sutton, 1991). Greenhalgh (1991) indicates preventative, ameliorative, and restorative strategies for management.

See also **Redundancy; Unemployment; Job satisfaction; Motivation; Job deskilling; Agency restriction**

Bibliography

Greenhalgh, L. (1991). Organizational coping strategies. In J. F. Hartley, D. Jacobson, B. Klandermans & T. van Vuuren (Eds), *Job insecurity: Coping with jobs at risk*. London: Sage.

Greenhalgh, L. & Rosenblatt, Z. (1984). Job insecurity: Toward conceptual clarity. *Academy of Management Review*, **9**, 438–448.

Greenhalgh, L. & Sutton, R. (1991). Organizational effectiveness and job insecurity. In J. F. Hartley, D. Jacobsen, B. Klandermans & T. van Vuuren (Eds), *Job insecurity: Coping with jobs at risk*. London: Sage.

Hartley, J. F., Jacobsen, D., Klandermans, B. & van Vuuren, T. (Eds) (1991). *Job insecurity: Coping with jobs at risk*. London: Sage.

Jacobson, D. (1985). Determinants of job-at-risk behaviour. Paper presented to the West European Conference on the Psychology of Work and Organization. Aachen, Germany.

Lazarus, R. S. & Folkman, S. (1984). *Stress, appraisal, and coping*. New York: Springer.

JEAN HARTLEY

job redesign *see* JOB DESIGN; JOB ENRICHMENT; SOCIOTECHNICAL THEORY

job rotation This refers to systematically moving employees from one task assignment to another within a WORK GROUP or unit. Thus, in a seven-person work unit, each employee would be assigned initially to one of the seven identifiable tasks. In job rotation, the employee would work on that designated task for a specified period, and then would be reassigned for a period of time to one of the remaining tasks in the unit. This process would then be repeated until the employee rotated back to his or her original task assignment.

The major goals of job rotation are to enhance worker FLEXIBILITY and to reduce the boredom and dissatisfaction that often result from routinized, specialized tasks (*see* REPETITIVE WORK; ROUTINIZATION; JOB SATISFACTION). Although few studies have examined the effects of rotation programs on these outcomes, those that have been completed suggest that job rotation has few positive consequences (Griffin, 1982; Miller, Dhaliwal, & Magas, 1973).

These results are not altogether surprising given that job rotation does not necessarily involve changing the nature of the tasks in a work unit. That is, rotation may simply involve moving employees from one routinized task to another without any substantial increase in AUTONOMY, responsibility, or personal ACCOUNTABILITY for the outcomes of the work. As indicated elsewhere in this volume (*see* JOB ENRICHMENT and JOB CHARACTERISTICS), it is improvements in job attributes such as these that are likely to have beneficial effects on the well-being and effectiveness of employees (*see* MENTAL HEALTH).

See also **Job design; Motivation and performance**

Bibliography

Griffin, R. W. (1982). *Task design: An integrative approach*. Glenview, IL: Scott, Foresman.

Miller, F. G., Dhaliwal, T. S. & Magas, L. J. (1973). Job rotation raises productivity. *Industrial Engineering*, **5**, 24–36.

GREG R. OLDHAM

job satisfaction This is probably one of the most researched constructs in ORGANIZATIONAL BEHAVIOR. Literally thousands of articles have been written about its definition and meaning, its antecedents, and its consequences. Job satisfaction may be defined as the emotional state resulting from the appraisal of one's job and as such can be negative, positive, or neutral. A basic element in this definition is that job satisfaction has to do with an affective state or how one "feels" about one's job in contrast to simply describing a job (*see* AFFECT; EMOTION; EMOTIONS IN ORGANIZATIONS).

There are a variety of theories which help explain how job satisfaction comes about. One theoretical structure suggests that job satisfaction is a function of what one expects from a job compared to what is actually present in the job. Another theoretical structure suggests that job satisfaction is a function of the degree to which individual's needs are fulfilled; still another argues that satisfaction is a function of the degree to which a job fulfills important work values. All this connote reactions to some degree of fit or misfit between people and jobs (*see* WORK ADJUSTMENT).

Job satisfaction may be thought of as an "overall appraisal" of one's job, and be broken down in several different job facets such as achievement, working conditions, advancement opportunities, etc. Some controversy exists regarding whether an overall measure of job satisfaction has the same meaning as measuring satisfaction on different job facets and summing over these facets to obtain a composite measure. In addition, some research suggests that job satisfaction may be described along two relatively independent dimensions – intrinsic satisfaction which involves achievement, recognition, and other features associated with the work itself, and extrinsic satisfaction which involves working conditions, supervision, and other components of the environmental context in which the work is performed (*see* EXTRINSIC/INTRINSIC MOTIVATION). An important early framework was developed by Frederick Herzberg who argued that these two general independent types of events affected satisfaction and dissatisfaction differently. He argued that intrinsic factors (called "Motivators") could only enhance job satisfaction, and that extrinsic factors (called hygiene factors) would only operate to reduce or eliminate job dissatisfaction. This theory, known as the "two-factor" MOTIVATOR–HYGIENE THEORY was used as a starting point for JOB ENRICHMENT and enlargement efforts on the part of organizations. Subsequent research has shown that this model was perhaps too simplistic and that both intrinsic and extrinsic factors operate to influence both satisfaction and dissatisfaction.

There have been a variety of efforts to measure job satisfaction. Perhaps two of the best-known efforts are:

(1) the Minnesota Job Satisfaction Questionnaire (MSQ) which assesses job satisfaction along 20 separate job facets where separate composites are computed for Intrinsic, Extrinsic, and General Job Satisfaction; and
(2) the Job Description Index (JDI) where satisfaction is assessed along the following dimensions: work, pay, promotions, coworkers, and supervision.

Many factors have been hypothesized to contribute to job satisfaction. These may be broken roughly into two major categories: Individual or person factors and environmental factors. Individual or person factors include demographic variables such as AGE, RACE, GENDER, etc., as well as TRAIT factors associated with individuals (e.g., IQ, self-esteem, dominance, etc.). Research evidence has established that job satisfaction is significantly associated with general MENTAL HEALTH indices, with several PERSONALITY variables, age, and even genetic factors. Such personal variables are sometimes labeled dispositional factors referring to trait-like, stable, and reliable individual differences which correlate with satisfaction (*see* ATTITUDES, DISPOSITIONAL APPROACHES). Environmental variables are facets associated with the job and organization such as WORKING CONDITIONS, variety in the work, pay, AUTONOMY, interpersonal relations among coworkers. A voluminous body of research has established significant relationships between a variety of these environmental factors and job satisfaction. For example, skill variety in jobs, the degree of task or work significance, and the degree of FEEDBACK are significantly associated with job satisfaction. One of the ongoing debates today is how much independent and joint influence do these two broad factors have in determining job satisfaction.

There is also a sizable research base examining the consequences of job satisfaction. One of the more closely studied relationships has been between job satisfaction and job performance (*see* PERFORMANCE, INDIVIDUAL). While some have argued that high job satisfaction leads to higher levels of job performance, others have suggested that the relationship is reversed and that high performance leads to high satisfaction, but only if performance is rewarded. A sizeable number of research studies have been conducted to investigate the empirical relationship, and the findings indicate that the relationship is modest but generally significant (Iaffaldano & Muchinsky, 1992). The correlations generally range in the high teens to low 20's. Other research studies show a similarly modest relationship between satisfaction and ABSENTEEISM, but a more substantial relationship between satisfaction and TURNOVER. In addition, satisfaction has been shown to be significantly associated with the COMMITMENT individuals have with the organization, and overall CITIZENSHIP within the organization (*see* ORGANIZATIONAL CITIZENSHIP).

See also **Job design; Motivation and performance; Attitude theory**

Bibliography

Arvey, R. D., Carter, G. W. & Buerkley, D. K. (1991). Job satisfaction: Dispositional and situational influences. In C. L. Cooper & I. T. Robertson (Eds), *International review of industrial and organizational psychology* (vol. 6, pp. 359–383).

Cranny, C. J., Smith, P. C. & Stone, E. F. (1992). *Job satisfaction: How people feel about their jobs and how it affects their performance*. New York: Lexington Press.

Iaffaldano, M. T. & Muchinsky, P. M. (1992). Job satisfaction and job performance: A meta-analysis. *Psychological Bulletin*, **97**, 251–273.

Locke, E. A. (1985). The nature and causes of job satisfaction. In M. D. Dunnette (Ed.), *Handbook of industrial and organizational psychology* (pp. 1297–1349). Chicago, IL: Rand McNally.

RICHARD D. ARVEY

job simplification *see* JOB DESKILLING; REPETITIVE WORK

joining up process This refers to the entry and initial adjustment of newcomers into unfamiliar organizational settings (*see* WORK ADJUSTMENT). Although it is difficult to say just when it begins and ends, it is generally viewed as encompassing the earliest stages of the job transition cycle – the *preparation* process of expectation and anticipation of change, and the *encounter* phase of affect and sense-making during the first days or weeks of job tenure (*see* CAREER TRANSITIONS). Newcomers often discover that transitions are more disruptive and challenging than anticipated. They must cope with the STRESS of the REALITY SHOCK that their expectations do not fit their experiences and with the marginal status of being at once an insider and outsider (e.g., Louis (1980) has been at the forefront of research on how newcomers make sense of their experiences). They must begin the task of mastering new COMPETENCIES, building relationships with new co-workers, and learning the culture of their new organization (*see* ORGANIZATIONAL CULTURE).

Historically, the joining up process has been studied from three perspectives: TURNOVER, job stress, and ORGANIZATIONAL SOCIALIZATION. These perspectives are founded on disparate discipline and methodological bases: experimental and industrial psychology; PERSONALITY and social psychology; and organizational and occupational sociology, respectively. In the last decade, academics have attempted to link these points of view and thereby provide a richer appreciation of the entry phenomenon in particular, and job transitions in general (e.g., Hill (1992); Louis (1980); Nicholson & West (1988)). With the realization that work role transitions represent pivotal developmental opportunities for individuals and organizations, interest in these areas has grown. Researchers have studied the impact of initial employment in an organization in shaping employees' subsequent attitudes and behaviors, integration into the organization, and role as agents of change and INNOVATION.

A promising line of inquiry has addressed what organizations can do to help individuals effectively cope with their experiences and adapt to their new settings. Researchers have examined the relative efficacy of different socialization practices (e.g., formal orientation programs as compared to informal working relationships with superiors, peers, or mentors). The trend has been toward an INTERACTIONIST approach, that is, the interplay of organizational (e.g., ORGANIZATIONAL DEMOGRAPHY, and entry practices) and individual (e.g., PERSONALITY and CAREER history) factors on newcomers' experiences and subsequent outcomes (e.g, Wanous (1992)).

Although considerable progress has been made on the theoretical front in understanding the joining up process, there is much to be done empirically. Job transition has usually been studied as an event, rather than a process occurring over time. For example, most researchers have relied on retrospective and cross-sectional designs. To validate current conceptual frameworks of the newcomer experience, more longitudinal work is required.

See also **Career stages; Age; Career development; Realistic job previews; Selection methods**

Bibliography

Hill, L. A. (1992). *Becoming a manager: Mastery of a new identity*. Boston, MA: Harvard Business School Press.

Louis, M. R. (1980). Surprise and sense making: What newcomers experience in entering unfamiliar organizational settings. *Administrative Science Quarterly*, **23**, 226–251.

Nicholson, N. & West, M. A. (1988). *Managerial job change: Men and women in transition*. Cambridge, UK: Cambridge University Press.

Van Maanen, J. & Schein, E. H. (1979). Towards a theory of organizational socialization. *Research in Organizational Psychology*, **1**, 209–264.

Wanous, J. P. (1992). *Organizational entry: Recruitment, selection, orientation, and socialization of newcomers*. Reading, MA: Addison-Wesley.

LINDA A. HILL

joint ventures A joint venture is a form of COOPERATION, or a STRATEGIC ALLIANCE, typically defined as the pooling of separately owned resources by two or more firms to reduce competition, realize economies of scale, pool complementary resources, ease entry into foreign markets while reducing political risk, and leap over entry barriers to enter new markets (domestic or foreign). Researchers such as Killing (1983) and Berg, Duncan, and Friedman (1982) tend to define relationships in joint ventures using terms normally associated with families; e.g., parents, child, discretion, AUTONOMY. In creating a joint venture, the parents may, or may not, take equity interests in the venture until such time as its legal status is settled and the parents have agreed upon the name (an important consideration which can create immediate problems for the parents).

Typically, the equity position taken by parents is reflective of their respective contributions to the joint venture, and a matter over which they have exclusive control. However, in joint ventures involving MULTINATIONAL CORPORATIONS and firms (or state owned enterprises) in a number of host countries, law may limit the extent of the equity position taken by the MNC (see, e.g., Hennart (1988)). These laws are usually designed to ensure that control over the joint venture and its activities is retained by individuals assumed to represent the interests of the host country.

More often than not, a joint venture's legal status gives it the right to raise its own capital, to contract, and to conduct normal business activities: buying and selling, hiring and firing. Usually joint ventures take a corporate form, although it is legally possible to create limited partnership joint ventures. Unlike a "normal" firm, however, the management of a joint venture enjoying the legal status of a corporation usually does not have discretion to make unilateral decisions on important business matters. Rather, management must seek the approval of the parents of the joint venture. The parent firms, after all, created the joint venture a means of achieving *their* objectives.

Of course, this gives rise to one of the major "problems" with a joint venture as a governance structure: CONFLICT. Although the objectives of the parents of a joint venture may be congruent at the time of its formation, over time they are likely to diverge. These conflicts are likely to emerge over issues related to the allocation of costs and the distribution of profits, although they may also be related to the composition of the management team, representation on the joint venture's Board of Directors and other issues relating to management policies or business strategies of the joint venture. Where a limited partnership is employed as the legal basis for the joint venture, however, the silent partners usually will not have any say on matters of policy or strategy.

Because of the absence of unity of control, and the conflict that inevitably results, researchers studying joint ventures have concluded that managers will use them only as a matter of last resort. Where the assets that form the basis for a joint venture are tangible, other alternatives are available to the parties: MERGER OR ACQUISITION, licensing or other forms of technology transfer, and CONTRACT. In service settings, franchising can be employed as an alternative to a joint venture. Research conducted by transaction cost economists (*see* TRANSACTION COST THEORY) suggests that joint ventures are employed more effectively in cases involving tacit know-how, or so-called "invisible" assets, where protection against opportunistic behavior by one of the parties is more difficult to guard against outside a hierarchy (*see*, e.g., Kogut (1988)).

See also **Governance and ownership; Technology transfer; Collateral organization**

Bibliography

Berg, S. V., Duncan, J. & Friedman, P. (1982). *Joint venture strategies and corporate innovation*. Cambridge, MA: Oelgeschlager, Gunn, & Hain.

Gomes-Casseres, B. (1989). Joint ventures in the face of global competition. *Sloan Management Review*, **30**, (3), 17–26.

Harrigan, K. (1986). *Strategies for joint ventures*. Lexington, MA: Lexington Books.

Hennart, J. F. (1988). A transaction costs theory of equity joint ventures. *Strategic Management Journal*, **9**, 361–374.

Killing, J. P. (1983). *Strategies for joint venture success*. New York: Praeger.

Kogut, B. (1988). Joint ventures: Theoretical and empirical perspectives. *Strategic Management Journal*, **9**, 319–332.

PETER SMITH RING

just-in-time Just-in-time ("JIT") is a manufacturing strategy that minimizes finished goods inventory, work-in-process inventory, and inventory from suppliers (*see* OPERATIONS MANAGEMENT). Output is synchronized to customer orders, and orders "pull" material through the system from parts to finished goods. This contrasts with the Western "push" approach builds batches according to a production schedule, while maintaining inventory "just-in-case." Inventory is used to meet unexpected demand for finished goods, to decouple parts of the production process, and to protect against the disruption of vendors' deliveries.

In JIT, inventory is waste that permits quality problems to lurk unnoticed and uncorrected. Eliminating inventory quickly exposes production and quality problems, unbalanced operations, vendor quality problems, and so on.

JIT has gained prominence in recent years as a key to Japanese manufacturing strategy (*see* INTERNATIONAL MANAGEMENT). It is part of a TOTAL QUALITY MANAGEMENT approach. JIT represents a major Japanese contribution to management theory and practice. Some authors speculate that JIT arose first in Japan for cultural, economic, and social reasons (Eisenhardt & Westcott, 1988; Young, 1992).

JIT has profound organizational impacts because the entire system must change in order for JIT to work (Schonberger, 1982; Eisenhardt & Westcott, 1988; Young, 1992). The organization must fundamentally change quality control, purchasing, production control, accounting, capital equipment, and plant layouts. For example, inspection of incoming material is eliminated because the system cannot work without vendors who display near-perfect quality and dependably make frequent (perhaps daily or hourly) deliveries. JIT also transforms the production TECHNOLOGY, because eliminating inventory requires removing technical UNCERTAINTY and variability. MASS PRODUCTION comes to resemble PROCESS PRODUCTION, with material flowing steadily through a transformation process. However, mass production also comes to resemble BATCH PRODUCTION, with flexible production systems generating "mass customization" (*see* FLEXIBILITY).

In JIT systems, operators usually do their own inspection, maintenance, and setup, and may rotate among a number of work stations (*see* JOB ROTATION). Horizontal and vertical specialization are reduced. This greatly increases TRAINING needs. Compensation systems that reward employees for their flexibility, new responsibilities, and ideas for system improvement may be desirable. Employment stability may be needed to induce employees to cooperate with a system oriented toward the notion of CONTINUOUS IMPROVEMENT.

JIT has been adopted aggressively in the United States since its first implementation in the early 1980s (Schonberger, 1982). By 1990, 76 percent of *Fortune* 1000 firms used JIT (Lawler, Mohrman, & Ledford, 1992), although the depth of use still lags the Japanese considerably (Womack, Jones, & Roos, 1990). Most users are manufacturers, although some are in the service sector. For example, Seven-Eleven Japan restocks shelves in its small stores several times a day, emphasizing items appropriate to the time of day.

JIT is severely underresearched. The available evidence, although mostly anecdotal, suggests that JIT usually has very positive effects on organization performance (*see* ORGANIZATIONAL EFFECTIVENESS). The cost savings from inventory reduction can range into the billions of dollars for very large firms. Typically, organizations adopting JIT report reductions in quality defects of 30 to 60 percent, reduced production times of 50 to 90 percent, and reduced capital expenditures of 25 to 30 percent (Hall, 1989). Failures also have been reported, but factors that account for success and failure are not well researched.

Not all effects of JIT are positive. Employees may react negatively to the increased work pace that often accompanies JIT, as well as demands for flexibility, concentration, discipline, and constant suggestions for improvement (Young, 1992). Thus, some union leaders characterize JIT as "management by STRESS."

Some forms of EMPLOYEE INVOLVEMENT, particularly SELF-MANAGED TEAMS or AUTONOMOUS WORK GROUPS, may be difficult or impossible under JIT (Klein, 1991). Workers cannot choose which tasks to perform and which methods to use. The uninterrupted flow of material makes it imperative that standardized processes be followed. Through QUALITY CIRCLES or other PARTICIPATION groups, employees may exercise some control over task design (*see* JOB DESIGN). However, members of existing self-managed teams may resent their loss of autonomy under JIT.

JIT also increases the risk that natural disasters, union strife, or problems in one supplier or plant can disrupt an entire production system. For example, the United Auto Workers have discovered that they can strangle production throughout much of General Motors by staging strikes or slowdowns at a few key plants, increasing union POWER (*see* TRADE UNIONS).

A final question concerns how widely JIT can be applied. One barrier is geographic. Japan's small size and concentrated industrial areas make JIT practical. For example, Toyota locates most of its suppliers within a two-hour radius of Toyota City (Young, 1992). This makes hourly deliveries of parts and subassemblies practical. Whether anywhere near the same level of integration is possible or desirable in the West and elsewhere is unclear. Technology may represent a second barrier. The Japanese pioneered JIT in mass production industries such as autos, electronics, and cameras, where they set the world standard. It is uncertain that JIT is as meaningful in process technologies, such as chemicals, petroleum refining, and paper, where Western and especially American producers tend to set the world standard.

See also **Advanced manufacturing technology; Business process re-engineering**

Bibliography

Eisenhardt, K. M. & Westcott, B. J. (1988). Paradoxical demands and the creation of excellence: The case of just-in-time manufacturing. In R. E. Quinn & K. S. Cameron (Eds), *Pardox and transformation: Toward a theory of change in organization and management* (pp. 169–174). Cambridge, MA: Ballinger.

Hall, E. H. Jr. (1989). Just-in-time: A critical assessment. *Academy of Management Executive*, **3**, (4), 315–317.

Klein, J. A. (1991). A reexamination of autonomy in light of new manufacturing practices. *Human Relations*, **44**, (1), 21–38.

Lawler, E. E. III, Mohrman, S. A. & Ledford, G. E. Jr. (1992). *Employee involvement and total quality management: Practices and results in Fortune 1000 companies*. San Francisco: Jossey-Bass.

Womack, J. P., Jones, D. T. & Roos, D. (1990). *The machine that changed the world*. New York: Rawson.

Schonberger, R. J. (1982). *Japanese manufacturing techniques: Nine hidden lessons in simplicity*. New York: Free Press.

Young, S. M. (1992). A framework for successful adoption and performance of Japanese manufacturing practices in the United States. *Academy of Management Review*, 17, (4), 677–700.

GERALD E. LEDFORD, JR.

justice, distributive Based on Homans' (1961) seminal theory of social exchange, the concept of distributive justice refers to the perceived fairness of a distribution of REWARDS. Traditionally, a reward distribution is said to be distributively just to the extent that it reflects the proportional differences in STATUS or work contributions between the parties involved (*see* EQUITY THEORY). The study of distributive justice focuses on the decisions allocators make when distributing reward as well as the reactions of the recipients to the rewards received.

Allocators of organizational resources frequently distribute rewards in proportion to the parties' relative contributions (i.e., they follow an equity rule) - in large part because doing so is consistent with the prevailing norms of fair behavior that operate in most for-profit organizations (e.g., Leventhal, 1976) (*see* PAYMENT SYSTEMS). In work settings people usually expect to be rewarded differentially – that is, in proportion to their relative contributions – resulting in reward distributions recognized as distributively just. Theorists explain that equitable distributions of reward are not only followed because they are regarded as morally appropriate, but also because they are believed to be effective in attaining desired goals. As such, the decision to distribute rewards equitably may be instrumentally motivated. Insofar as equitable distributions reinforce the high contributions of more productive recipients, they are, in fact, generally effective in fostering PRODUCTIVITY (*see* PERFORMANCE RELATED PAY).

This is not to say that following the equity rule is the only practice considered distributively just. In some settings people also consider equal distributions of reward to be fair (i.e., they follow an *equality rule*). This is especially true in contexts in which promoting social harmony is the major concern of the reward allocator (see Deutsch, 1985). For example, when married couples or close friends divide resources between themselves, they tend to follow the equality rule, thereby precluding the need to distinguish between relative contributions. In such a context, equitable distributions would be potentially CONFLICT-arousing and inconsistent with the more harmonious, egalitarian expectations of the parties. Likewise, on the job, managers have been found to attempt to reduce conflict between subordinates by rewarding them equally rather than proportionally.

A third rule of distributive justice – the needs rule – dictates that fairness demands distributing rewards to parties based on their individual level of need (a Marxian notion of justice). Although needs-based distributive practices are often followed in some organizational contexts (e.g., making "triage" decisions in hospital emergency rooms), it is often considered inappropriate (at least in many Western cultures) to distribute rewards to employees based on their needs (i.e., to give more pay to employees with larger families than to those with smaller families regardless of any differences in their work performance (*see* CULTURE, NATIONAL).

In attempting to determine which norm of distributive justice is considered fairest, researchers have focused on such key variables as: the nature of the relationship between the parties (e.g., their level of intimacy and interdependence), INDIVIDUAL DIFFERENCES (e.g., GENDER and PERSONALITY differences), and their past history (e.g., the pattern of RECIPROCITY established in the relationship) (Greenberg, & Cohen, 1982).

See also **Business ethics; Justice, procedural; Legitimacy**

Bibliography

Deutsch, M. (1985). *Distributive justice*. New Haven, CT: Yale University Press.

Greenberg, J. & Cohen, R. L. (1982). Why justice? Normative and instrumental interpretations. In J. Greenberg & R. L. Cohen (Eds), *Equity and justice in social behavior* (pp. 437–469). New York: Academic Press.

Homans, G. C. (1961). *Social behavior: Its elementary forms*. New York: Harcourt, Brace, and World.

Leventhal, G. S. (1976). The distribution of rewards and resources in groups and organizations. In L. Berkowitz & E. Walster (Eds), *Advances in experimental social psychology* (Vol 9, pp. 91–131). New York: Academic Press.

JERALD GREENBERG

justice, procedural Procedural justice refers to the perceived fairness of policies and procedures used as the basis for making decisions. In contrast to distributive justice (*see* JUSTICE, DISTRIBUTIVE), which focuses on the perceived fairness of outcome distributions (i.e., "ends"), procedural justice focuses on the perceived fairness of the way those outcome distribution decisions are made (i.e., "means") (for more on this distinction, *see* Greenberg, (1987) (*see* DECISION MAKING).

The concept was first proposed by Thibaut and Walker (1975) in their comparative studies of legal dispute–resolution procedures. They found that the legal procedures recognized by disputants as being the fairest were ones that gave litigants control over the way their cases were handled (i.e., *process control*) although decisions regarding the outcomes, such as verdicts, were made by third parties, such as judges (i.e., *decision control*). Such procedures (known as *adversary procedures*) characterize the legal processes used in American and British courts, and offer litigants greater process control than the processes used in continental Europe (known as the *inquisitorial system*) in which judges not only control the legal decisions made, but also the collection and presentation of evidence.

Leventhal, Karuza, and Fry (1980) extended Thibaut and Walker's (1975) work by noting that procedural justice is also applicable outside dispute–resolution settings (*see* CONFLICT RESOLUTION). They identified six rules to identify the fairness of procedures: *consistency* (consistent use of procedures across people and over time), *bias suppression* (elimination of self-interest), *accuracy* (reliance on accurate information), *correctability* (opportunities to modify decisions as needed), *representativeness* (decisions that reflect the concern of all parties), and *ethicality* (decisions based on prevailing moral standards). Recently, theorists have added a social dimension to supplement these structural dimensions, noting that fair procedures also require the use of adequate explanations of procedures used as well as ostensible demonstrations of concern for parties adversely affected by the implementation of procedures.

Following from Folger and Greenberg (1985), researchers have applied procedural justice to organizational settings. It has been found, for example, that perceptions of fairness are enhanced by the use of procedures that give employees a voice in making decisions, such as the presentation of information about oneself to supervisors appraising their performance. Additionally, whereas satisfaction with outcomes (such as pay) is related to perceptions of distributive justice, satisfaction with the organization (such as organizational COMMITMENT) has been found to be related to perceptions of procedural justice. The use of fair procedures has been shown to facilitate employees' acceptance of such diverse practices as drug-testing programs, smoking bans, parental leave policies, and mass transit plans. It also has been found that informative and sensitive explanations of procedures tend to minimize negative reactions to adverse outcomes such as pay cuts, layoffs, and the rejection of budgets (for a review, see Greenberg 1990). Researchers continue to pose questions about the relationship between procedural justice and distributive justice, as well as the processes underlying the formation of judgments about procedural justice.

See also **Business ethics; Payment systems; Contract; Reciprocity**

Bibliography

Folger, R. & Greenberg, J. (1985). Procedural justice: An interpretive analysis of personnel systems. In K. Rowland & G. Ferris (Eds), *Research in personnel and human resources management* (vol. 3, pp. 141–183). Greenwich, CT: JAI Press.

Greenberg, J. (1987). A taxonomy of organizational justice theories. *Academy of Management Review*, **12**, 9–22.

Greenberg, J. (1990). Organizational justice: Yesterday, today, and tomorrow. *Journal of Management*, **16**, 399–432.

Leventhal, G. S., Karuza, J. & Fry, W. R. (1980). Beyond fairness: A theory of allocation preferences. In G. Mikula (Ed.), *Justice and social interaction* (pp. 167–218). New York: Springer-Verlag.

Thibaut, J. & Walker, L. (1975). *Procedural justice: A psychological analysis*. Hillsdale, NJ: Lawrence Erlbaum Associates.

JERALD GREENBERG

— K —

kaizen *see* CONTINUOUS IMPROVEMENT

knowledge of results The positive influence of knowledge of results are well documented and fundamental to models of work MOTIVATION and task performance (*see* MANAGEMENT BY OBJECTIVES; JOB DESIGN; REINFORCEMENT). Knowledge of results, or KOR, refers to information that a person receives concerning his or her work performance in terms of both quantity and quality. In a typical situation, an employee may receive FEEDBACK concerning work performance on a semi-annual basis during scheduled appraisal periods (*see* PERFORMANCE APPRAISAL). The importance of KOR to an individual's subsequent work performance is without question. People who receive timely and accurate KOR adjust their work activities along the lines indicated by the feedback that they receive. Some of the earliest work in management stressing the importance of KOR (feedback) is discussed by the Reinforcement theorists who describe it in terms of its role as an environmental consequence for an individual's actions. More recently, management researchers who stress the psychological aspects of managing describe the importance of KOR in terms of a person's self-regulatory processes (*see* SELF-REGULATION). Research has demonstrated that KOR alone is not likely to change a person's work habits, rather, it is KOR in conjunction with an individual's objectives or goals that act in concert to regulate activity. KOR varies along a number of key dimensions including: sign (positive versus negative), timeframe (short versus long-term), provider (self versus other generated), accuracy, clarity, among other dimensions.

See also **Goal-setting; Motivation and performance; Job characteristics**

Bibliography

Annett, J. (1969). *Feedback and human behavior.* Baltimore, MD. Penguin.

Ilgen, D. R., Fisher, C. D. & Taylor, M. S. (1979). Consequences of individual feedback on behavior in organizations. *Journal of Applied Psychology*, **64**, 349–371.

P. CHRISTOPHER EARLEY

knowledge workers A characteristic feature of post-industrial society is the growing number of employees who can be categorized as knowledge workers. Definitions of the term knowledge worker generally include:

(1) those concerned with production of intangible final outputs which embed expertise of differing degrees of FORMALIZATION; and
(2) those who are involved in intermediate production processes which embed expertise.

A distinction can be drawn between information-workers who process information without significant modification and knowledge workers who add value to the original information (Scott Morton, 1992). Knowledge work is often associated with relatively complex problem-solving activities linked to the development and application of INFORMATION TECHNOLOGY in products notably in the computer systems and telecommunications industries. Common occupational titles in these fields include software engineers and systems designers. Knowledge workers are also employed in sectors where the final product is not an IT application. The result is that the occupational categories covered by the term knowledge work are so wide, including lawyers, management consultants, and research scientists, as to limit the utility of the term for analytical purposes and render generalizations about work organization or employment conditions problematic. For instance, general propositions about changing SKILL patterns, pay structures, or MOTIVATIONS are almost meaningless.

Knowledge-work may be relatively formalized and codified as in organized professions such as accounting or less codified as in most of the areas of computer applications. This says less about differences in the quality of the underlying knowledge base of each occupation than the relative capacity to organize control of a jurisdiction (Abbott, 1988). Efforts to mobilize into an established profession may be hampered by the strong organizational specificity of much knowledge work and because applied problem solving progresses faster than formal theorizing. The strong experiential component of much knowledge work is often referred to as know-how (Sveiby & Lloyd, 1986).

The growth in the value to employers of knowledge which is held by individuals or teams, that is, the increasing importance of human capital relative to fixed capital as a source of comparative advantage, raises interesting management issues. First, definitions of the value of a firm are made more difficult and conventional accounting metrics do not do full justice to human capital valuation. Second, the development and appropriation of knowledge from individuals or teams becomes more critical. This has implications for the nature of employment CONTRACTS and styles of management. Third, knowledge work frequently appears to require fluid organizational structures such as the use of temporary project teams, in order to create close linkages with internal and external clients (*see* PROJECT MANAGEMENT). Each of these issues places strains on bureaucratic systems of control and orthodox methods of evaluation and ACCOUNTABILITY (*see* BUREAUCRACY).

See also **Professionals in organizations; Technology transfer; Labor markets; Occupations**

Bibliography

Abbott, A. (1988). *The system of professions.* Chicago: University of Chicago Press.

Sveiby, H. & Lloyd, T. (1986). *Managing knowhow.* London: Bloomsbury Press.

Scott, M. M. (1992). The effect of information technology on management and organization. In T. Kochen & M. Useem (Eds), *Transforming organizations.* New York: Oxford University Press.

TIM MORRIS

—— L ——

labor markets From an organization's perspective, the labor market is that space in which it encounters economically active individuals as a potential source of RECRUITMENT, and where it competes with other organizations for recruits. Individuals in the labor market are in work (whether employed or unemployed) or seeking work, and are distinguished from economically *inactive* individuals of working age, who are outside the labor market (*see* UNEMPLOYMENT).

In practice, an organization operates not in one labor market, but many. Distinct labor markets, between which there is little mobility, are defined both by OCCUPATIONS and location, and the two dimensions are related. A key concept in the labor market literature is the notion of a "local labor market", which is defined by commuting patterns. Organizations recruit to lower level occupations in a local labor market, whilst higher level (e.g., managerial and professional) occupations may be recruited in regional, national, or international labor markets; in these latter occupations it is common for new recruits to relocate to take up a new post (*see* CAREER TRANSITIONS). In practice, diverse commuting patterns usually make it impossible to define wholly self-contained local labor markets or "travel to work areas" (TTWAs), and some arbitrary cut-off is typically used. In the United Kingdom, for example, the country is divided into over 300 TTWAs, officially defined on the basis of 75 percent self-containment (similar approaches are found in other countries, including the United States, where the "Standard Metropolitan Area" is the relevant definition. The cut-off conventions vary between countries). Empirical research confirms that these generally correspond well to employers' and workers' notions of a local labor market, although defining workable TTWAs in large conurbations can be particularly difficult.

Even within a single labor market, there may be further subdivisions. The labor economics and INDUSTRIAL RELATIONS literature has long recognized that labor markets exhibit segmentation into "noncompeting groups" (Kerr 1954). These groups may be defined by GENDER, RACE, AGE, or other factors unrelated to the PRODUCTIVITY of the labor in question, and the existence of employer DISCRIMINATION has been a major challenge to the simple competitive labor market of neoclassical economic theory (a recent, largely American, overview of the economics of the labor market, and alternative theories can be found in Ashenfelter and Layard, 1986). Segmented labor market (SLM) theorists (Cain, 1976) have posited "primary" and "secondary" segments; in the former, firms offer high wages and stable employment to workers with certain favored characteristics; the latter are characterized by instability, poor wages and conditions, and are occupied by workers with less favored characteristics.

The "labor market" generally refers to something outside the organization, although the more recent literature distinguishes between *external* labor markets in this sense, and the labor market which is *internal* to a particular organization (Doeringer & Piore, 1971). The notion of an internal labor market (ILM), again contrary to competitive neoclassical theory, allows for the real world phenomena of ports of entry, internal career structures, and progressive earnings growth which insulate an organization's workforce from external competition. Firms with internal labor markets have typically been the "primary" firms of SLM theory. Arguably, however, following the emergence of the "flexible firm" (Atkinson & Meager 1986) (*see* FLEXIBILITY) and businesses exhibiting "flatter" structures and DECENTRALIZATION, many organizations with traditionally strong ILMs (government organizations and banks are often cited as examples) have begun to reduce the scope of the core ILM, and to supplement it with a flexible periphery of workers recruited from the external labor market at short notice.

See also **Human resource planning; Human resources strategy; Individual differences**

Bibliography

Ashenfelter, O. & Layard, R. (Eds) (1986). *Handbook of labor economics*. Amsterdam: North-Holland.

Atkinson, J. & Meager, N. (1986). Changing working patterns: How companies achieve flexibility to meet new needs. London: National Economic Development Office.

Cain, G. (1976). The challenge of segmented labor market theories to orthodox theory: A survey. *Journal of Economic Literature*, **14**, 1215–1257.

Doeringer, P. & Piore, M. (1971). *Internal labor markets and manpower analysis*. Lexington, MA: Heath.

Kerr, C. (1954). The balkanization of labor markets. In E. Wight Bakke (Ed.), *Labor mobility and economic opportunity*. Cambridge, MA: MIT Press.

NIGEL MEAGER

labor process theory Labor process is a term Marx used in Volume 1 of *Capital* to refer to creative, purposive labor activity that transforms nature into products human beings can use. All societies have labor processes. Labor process theory (LPT) is devoted to promoting understanding of the organization and control of human labor activity, particularly in capitalist societies, where wage laborers are persuaded to produce enough value to maintain themselves, the owners of capital, and the enterprise in which they are employed. According to classic Marxist theory, this extraction and appropriation of surplus value is exploitative, but, unlike feudal labor processes, the exploitation is obscured. Thus, relations between capital and labor tend to be antagonistic, but are not necessarily characterized by manifest CONFLICT at the point of production or throughout the capitalist political economy.

There were few Marxist studies of capitalist labor processes prior to publication of Harry Braverman's *Labor and Monopoly Capital* in 1974. Using the theme of the degradation of labor in the twentieth century, Braverman developed the idea that accumulation imperatives in monopoly capitalism led to widespread JOB DESKILLING and Taylorization of work (*see* SCIENTIFIC MANAGEMENT). During the past 20 years, a massive specialized literature stemming from Braverman's contribution and focused on building a more adequate framework for the critical analysis of work organization has been produced. Although critics have questioned the viability of LPT (Cohen, 1987), the debates concerning central themes and nuances remain vibrant and are likely to continue.

There have been three primary developments in LPT which grew out of criticisms of Marx and Braverman's analysis of labor process dynamics (*see* Knights & Willmott, 1990). First, the idea that capital accumulation necessitates managerial appropriation and control of craftworkers' and other laborers' production knowledge and skill (deskilling thesis) has been challenged. Researchers have argued that requisite job knowledge and SKILL, in most cases, has increased not decreased, or that even when management's strategy is aimed at deskilling work, a significant amount of tacit skill is retained by workers (*see* PRACTICAL INTELLIGENCE). Even more challenging to the deskilling thesis is the idea that management strategy tends not to be very coherent, but in following the paths of least resistance, more often involves bureaucratic forms of control, human relations manipulations, and even cultural programming and SELF-MANAGEMENT (e.g., Edwards, 1979).

Second, an ambitious critique of the objectivism in classical LPT has emerged. It focuses attention on the subjective content of class dynamics. Concepts of social identity have been at the center of LPTs' descriptions of the subject. For example, Burawoy (1979) focused on aspects of the development of consent among shopfloor factory workers engaged in the "game" of "making out" (maximising bonus pay in piece-rate work) (*see* BONUS PAYMENTS).

He was able to show how playing the game constituted workers in the labor process as competing individuals, reproducing class relations while undercutting the potential for class-conscious awareness. Contemporary LPTs have developed and are developing postmodern concepts of self-formation (*see* POSTMODERNISM). These concepts take into account the ANXIETY associated with identity formation problems in an age when traditional, collective schemas are being rejected. They present images of compound, shifting subjectivities as people attempt to understand themselves given new definitions of the meaning of work, leisure, class, POLITICS, GENDER, sexuality, RACE, ETHNICITY, religion, etc.

Third, following repeated calls to redress the neglect of resistance in LPT (and closely intertwined with concepts such as consciousness in the emerging CRITICAL THEORY of subjectivity in the labor process), attention is finally being paid to theorizing resistance in the labor process (*see* Jermier, Knights & Nord, 1994) (*see* RESISTANCE TO CHANGE). This work extends far beyond militant TRADE UNION activities practiced by male factory workers in response to capitalist exploitation and deskilling. It highlights everyday forms of resistance to local as well as macro circumstances, practiced by all employees, but often hidden in the crawlspaces and subterranean recesses of contemporary work organizations.

See also **Alienation; Power; Democracy; Intergroup relations; Legitimacy**

Bibliography

Burawoy, M. (1979). *Manufacturing consent*. Chicago: University of Chicago Press.

Cohen, S. (1987). A labour process to nowhere? *New Left Review*, **165**, 34–50.

Edwards, R. (1979). *Contested terrain*. New York: Basic Books.

Jermier, J., Knights, D. & Nord, W. (1994). *Resistance and power in organizations; Agency, subjectivity and the labour process*. London: Routledge.

Knights, D. & Willmott, H. (1990). *Labour process theory*. London: Macmillan.

JOHN M. JERMIER

labor turnover *see* TURNOVER

leadership Although systematic research into the topic of leadership is a product of the twentieth century, interest in identifying the properties that make leaders effective is almost as old as recorded history. Bass and Stogdill (Bass, 1990) noted that discussions relating to leadership and leadership effectiveness can be found in the Greek and Latin classics, the Old and New Testaments of the Bible, the writings of the ancient Chinese philosophers, and in the early Icelandic sagas. Bass (1990), in an exhaustive review of the present era's leadership literature, cites over 3000 empirical studies.

Despite the attention given to the topic there appear to be almost as many definitions of leadership as there are researchers in the field. Consider the following definitions found in the literature:

> Leadership is "the initiation and maintenance of structure in expectation and interaction" (Stogdill, 1974, cited in Yukl, 1994, p. 2).
>
> Leadership is ". . . the behavior of an individual when he is directing the activities of a group toward a shared goal." (Hemphill & Coons, 1957, cited in Yukl, 1994, p. 2).
>
> Leadership is ". . . interpersonal influence exercised in a situation, and directed through the communication process, toward the attainment of a specified goal or goals." (Tannenbaum, Weschler, & Massarik, 1964, cited in Yukl, 1994, p. 2).
>
> Leadership is ". . . the process of instilling in others shared vision, creating valued opportunities, and building confidence in the realization of the shared values and opportunities." (Berlew, 1974).
>
> "Leadership is leaders inducing followers to act for certain goals that represent the values and the motivations – of both leaders and followers." (Burns, 1978).
>
> "Leaders are those who consistently make effective contributions to social order, and who are expected and perceived to do so." (Hosking, 1988, cited in Yukl, 1994, p. 3).

> Leadership is "... a process of giving purpose (meaningful direction) to collective effort, and causing willing effort to be expended to achieve purpose." (Jacobs and Jaques, 1990, cited in Yukl, 1994, p. 3).
>
> Leadership is "a process by which members of a group are empowered to work together synergestically toward a common goal or vision, that will create change and transform institutions, and thus improve the quality of life. The leader is a catalytic force or facilitator who by virtue of position or opportunity empowers others to collective action toward accomplishing the goal or vision." (Astin, 1993).

Note that a rather significant shift occurred in the mid-1970s with the definitions offered by Berlew and Burns. Berlew was the first to introduce the concept of shared VALUES and follower confidence building. Berlew's discussion also emphasized the creation of organizational excitement, and emotional appeal of the leader into the managerially oriented leadership literature. In the definitions of leadership offered by Berlew (1974), Burns (1978), Hoskings (1988), Jacobs and Jacques (1990), and Astin (1993), we see the definition of leadership progressively broadened to include contributing to social order, introducing major change, giving meaning and purpose to work and to organizations, empowering followers, and infusing organizations with values and IDEOLOGY.

For analytic and expository purposes it is useful to distinguish between leadership, management, and SUPERVISION.

Leadership Contrasted with Management

Zaleznik (1977) has argued that there is a substantial difference between leadership and management. Zaleznik's position reflects the differences in the definitions listed above. Zaleznick reserves the term leadership for individuals who determine the major objectives and the strategic courses of organizations and introduce major change rather than individuals who transmit and enforce rules and policies, or implement goals and changes initiated by individuals at higher organizational levels.

Leadership is defined as behavior on the part of an individual which appeals to ideological values, motives, and self-perceptions of followers and results, in turn, in:

(1) unusual levels of effort on the part of followers above and beyond their normal role or position requirements; and
(2) follower willingness to forego self-interest, and make significant personal sacrifices in the interest of a collective vision, *willingly*.

Management is defined as rational–analytic behavior of a person in a position of formal authority directed toward the organization, coordination, and implementation of organizational strategies, tactics, and policies. The essential distinction between leader behaviors and MANAGERIAL BEHAVIORS is that managerial behaviors are rational–analytic and impersonal and leader behaviors appeal to follower motives and are interpersonally oriented. Leaders set the direction for organizations or collectivities. Managers provide the intellectual content necessary for organizations to perform effectively.

Examples of leader behaviors are articulation of a collective vision; infusing organizations and work with values by communicating and setting a personal example regarding the values inherent in the vision; making sacrifices and taking personal risks in the interest of the vision and the collective; motivating exceptional performance by appealing to the values, emotions, and self concepts of followers; inspiring followers by showing confidence, determination, PERSISTENCE, and pride in the collective; and by engaging in symbolic behavior such as serving as a spokesperson for the collective.

Examples of managerial behavior are PLANNING, organizing, and the establishment of administrative systems. These particular managerial behaviors are included because there is empirical evidence demonstrating that these behaviors distinguish effective managers from others, despite the fact that they are not interpersonal in nature.

Note that according to these definitions managers are individuals in positions of formal AUTHORITY. In contrast, leaders may or may not hold positions of formal authority. Leaders assert INFLUENCE by virtue of unique personal attributes and behaviors. Managers obtain

COMPLIANCE from subordinates on the basis of legitimate position influence and formal authority, and reward and coercive POWER (*see* LEGITIMACY). In contrast, leaders influence followers to internalize the values of the collective vision and identify with the collective on the basis of referent power rather than, or in addition to, positional authority (*see* POWER BASES). Leaders are followed willingly, and therefore those whom they motivate to action are referred to as followers rather than subordinates.

Subordinates of managers comply with the manager's directions only as long as the manager exercises formal authority and applies reward or coercive power. In contrast, followers of leaders continue to identify with the collective and internalize the values inherent in the collective vision in the absence of the leader.

Of course, some individuals in positions of authority may function as both managers and leaders. Such individuals will thus have some subordinates who minimally comply with normal levels of position requirements as well as some followers who go above and beyond the call of duty in the interest of a collective vision.

Leadership Contrasted with Supervision

Supervision is defined as behavior on the part of a person in a position of authority concerned with monitoring, guiding, and providing corrective FEEDBACK and support for subordinates or followers in their day-to-day activities. Examples of supervisory behaviors are showing individualized consideration, providing equitable recognition and REWARDS, scheduling and programming, problem solving, GOAL-SETTING, ROLE and goal clarification, coaching, direction, monitoring operations, PERFORMANCE APPRAISAL and feedback, providing guidance and on-the-job TRAINING, and the effective use of incentives to motivate followers.

The formal appointment of individuals to positions of authority in formal nonvoluntary organizations make followers dependent on leaders for their livelihood. Further, in formal organizations the leader–follower relationship is usually characterized by frequent face to face interaction between leaders and followers (Mintzberg, 1983).

The consequences of these two attributes of the leader–follower relationship – dependency and face-to-face interaction – are that leaders need to engage in instrumental management behaviors to organize, coordinate, and facilitate follower performance. These two attributes of the leader–follower relationship also require supportive behaviors to provide for followers a psychologically satisfying work environment. Consequently, effective leadership in formal organizations requires leaders to engage in not only strategic initiatives and the introduction of major changes, but also in the exercise of the management and supervisory behaviors described above.

Theories of Leadership

The vast number of empirical social scientific studies concerning leadership has yielded a small number of theories, which attempt to explain the PERSONALITY characteristics and behaviors distinguishing effective from ineffective leaders. While none of the theories are definitive, there is rather solid empirical evidence in support of each. Reviews of this evidence can be found in Bass (1990) and Yukl (1994).

These theories can be classified into three categories: instrumental theories, inspirational theories, and theories of informal leadership. Instrumental theories (House & Mitchell, 1974; Fiedler & Garcia, 1987; Wofford, 1982) are theories of supervision as defined above. These theories stress task and person oriented leader behaviors which facilitate, or are instrumental to, effective follower performance. They emphasize such task oriented leader behaviors as goal setting, coaching, direction, performance appraisal, and feedback, and the effective use of incentives to motivate followers. They also emphasize the use of such person oriented behaviors as showing consideration, joint PARTICIPATION, counseling, providing support, and empowering followers through delegation of authority and encouragement (*see* DELEGATION; EMPOWERMENT).

There are several inspirational theories as well: charismatic theory (House, 1977; Conger & Kanungo, 1987), transformational theory (Burns, 1978; Bass, 1990), and visionary theory (Bennis & Nanus, 1985) (*see* LEADERSHIP, CHARISMATIC; TRANSFORMATIONAL/TRANSACTIONAL LEADERSHIP). These are theories of leadership, as the term leadership is defined above, emphasizing ideological and emotional appeal by the infusion of values into work and organizations. This is accomplished by articulating an inspirational vision, values, and norms; communicating challenging performance expectations and confidence in followers; displaying exemplary behavior, and engaging in symbolic behaviors which encourage intrinsic motivation, COMMITMENT, and pride in work.

Theories of informal leadership (Hollander, 1964; Bowers & Seashore, 1966) emphasize the kinds of behavior associated with "emergent" or informal leadership by individuals who are not formally appointed to positions of authority. These theories stress individual contribution to group goals, facilitation of the work of others, and providing direction, collaboration, and support for coworkers.

There is a substantial amount of support for all three classes of theories (Bass, 1990; Yukl, 1994). This evidence demonstrates that task and person oriented behaviors described in the instrumental theories generally, but not always, differentiate effective supervisors and managers from others. The leader behaviors described by the inspirational theories generally, and quite consistently, differentiate outstanding or exceptionally effective leaders from others.

The leader behaviors described by the theories of informal leadership have also been shown to differentiate effective informal leaders from others, however the number of supporting studies remains small.

When tested individually, the behaviors specified in all of the above theories have been shown to have positive effects on follower psychological states such as follower satisfaction with, and commitment to leaders. However, the various combinations of leader behaviors remain to be tested empirically. In this context, scholars have raised the possibility that some instrumental behaviors, especially the exercise of contingent reward and PUNISHMENT behaviors, are incompatible with and undermine the effect of inspirational behaviors. This issue remains to be resolved in future research.

Conclusion

The considerable amount of empirical evidence and theory relevant to the practice of leadership is impressive. Despite this knowledge a substantial number of issues remain to be addressed. Available knowledge has not been brought to bear on such issues as management selection, the introduction of change, resolution of CONFLICT, the exercise of upward INFLUENCE in orgranizations. There is little theory or empirical evidence concerning how leaders exercise political influence in organizations. Further, a number of specific situational variables that enhance, constrain, or substitute for leadership have not been adequately researched.

The generality of prevailing theories remains to be specified and verified. Finally, it is noteworthy that the cultural constraints on what leader behaviors can be exercised and what leader behaviors are effective have not been explicated. Most prevailing theories of leadership have a definite North American cultural orientation: individualistic rather than collectivistic; oriented toward self-interest rather than duty; oriented toward rules and procedures rather than norms; emphasizing assumptions of RATIONALITY rather than asthetics, religion, or superstition; and assuming centrality of work and democratic value orientation (*see* CULTURE, NATIONAL).

A substantial body of cross cultural social psychological, sociological, and anthropological research informs us that there are many cultures that do not share the assumptions of North American leadership theories. As a result there is a need for empirically grounded theory to explain differential leader behavior and effectiveness across cultures (*see* CULTURE; CROSS-CULTURAL RESEARCH). In the past five years there has been an increase in the volume of cross cultural leadership research. This should, in a matter of only a few years, yield important insights concerning culture specific leadership and the generality of US based leadership theory.

Despite the limitations stated above it is safe to conclude that a there is a substantial amount of available knowledge concerning the exercise and effectiveness of leadership, and there are a sufficient number of remaining issues and questions to occupy the time of social scientists for a considerable, and indefinite duration.

Bibliography

Astin, H. & Leland, C. (1991). *Women of influence, Women of vision. A cross generations study of leaders and social change*. San Francisco: Jossey-Bass.

Bass, B. M. (1990). Bass & Stogdill's. *Handbook of leadership* (3rd edn). New York: The Free Press.

Bennis, W. & Nanus, B. (1985). Leaders: The strategies for taking charge. New York: Harper & Row.

Berlew, D. E. (1974). Leadership and organizational excitement. *California Management Review*, **17 (2)**.

Bowers D. G. & S. E. Seashore (1966). Predicting organizational effectiveness with a four-factor theory of leadership. *Administrative Science Quarterly*, **11**, 238–263.

Burns, J. M. (1978). *Leadership*. New York: Harper & Row.

Conger, J. A. & R. A. Kanungo (1987). Toward a behavioral theory of charismatic leadership in organizational settings. *Academy of Management Review*, **12**, 637–647.

Fiedler, F. E. & Garcia, J. E. (1987). *New approaches to leadership, cognitive resources and organizational performance*. New York: Wiley.

Hollander, E. P. (1964). *Leaders, groups, and influence*. New York: Oxford University Press.

House, R. J. (1977). A 1976 theory of charismatic leadership. In J. G. Hunt & L. L. Larson (Eds), *Leadership: The cutting edge*. Carbondale, IL: Southern Illinois University Press.

House, R. J. & Mitchell J. R. (1974). Path goal theory of leadership. *Journal of Contemporary Business*, **5**.

Mintzberg, H. (1983). *Power in and around organizations*. Englewood Cliffs, NJ: Prentice Hall.

Wofford, J. C. (1982). An integrative theory of leadership. *Journal of Management*, **8**, 27–47.

Yukl, G. (1994). *Leadership in organizations* (3rd edn). Englewood Cliffs, NJ: Prentice-Hall.

Zaleznik, A. (1977). Managers and leaders: Are they different? *Harvard Business Review* May–June, 47–60.

ROBERT J. HOUSE

leadership, charismatic Weber (1947) was the first to apply the term charisma to LEADERSHIP. According to Weber, charisma is a "divinely inspired gift" attributed to leaders by followers. Charismatic leaders as described by Weber are individuals who by force of their unique and powerful personalities, and their vision and convictions, are able to draw the attribution of charisma to command admiration, TRUST, loyalty, devotion, and COMMITMENT on the part of followers, and induce major social change. In the mid-1980s several psychologically oriented leadership scholars advanced theories to explain outstanding, exceptionally effective leadership. These theories were the 1976 Theory of Charismatic Leadership (House, 1977), the Attributional Theory of Charisma (Conger & Kanungo, 1987), and the Transformational (Bass, 1985) and Visionary Theories of Leadership (Bennis & Nanus, 1985; Sashkin, 1988) (*see* TRANSACTIONAL/TRANSFORMATIONAL THEORY). I refer to this genre of theory as the neocharismatic leadership paradigm.

The most recent definition of charismatic leadership is advanced by House and Shamir (1993) who argue that charismatic leadership is the ABILITY of an individual to gain intensive moral commitment of followers, and exceptionally strong IDENTIFICATION of followers with the charismatic vision and the collective. According to these authors charismatic leaders accomplish follower commitment and identification by appealing to follower cherished VALUES and nonconscious motives and by engaging follower self-perceived identities, enhancing follower SELF-EFFICACY and sense of consistency, and making follower self-worth contingent on their contribution to the charismatic mission and the collective. Theoretically, these effects are achieved by a select set of leader behaviors such as:

- Articulation of a vision of a better future for followers to which the followers are claimed to have a moral right (*see* MISSION STATEMENTS).
- Display of passion for the vision, and significant self-sacrifice in the interest of the vision and the collective.
- Display of self-confidence, confidence in the attainment of the vision, determination, and persistence in the interest of the vision.
- Behaviors that selectively arouse the nonconscious motives of followers that are of special relevance to the attainment of the vision.
- Extraordinary personal and organizational RISK-TAKING in the interest of the vision and the collective.
- Display of high performance expectations of followers and confidence in their ability to contribute to the collective effort.
- Concerted effort to assist followers in their professional development.
- Symbolic behaviors that emphasize the values inherent in the collective vision (*see* SYMBOLISM). Symbolic behavior is expressed in a number of forms: demonstration of integrity,

leader self-presentation in a positive manner, serving as a role model by setting a personal example of the values inherent in the vision, serving as a symbolic figurehead and spokesperson for the collective, and persuasiveness by oratorical COMMUNICATION (*see* IMPRESSION MANAGEMENT).
- Positive evaluation of followers and the collective by engaging in such behavior as stressing pride in the collective, expressing positive evaluation of followers, showing confidence in followers and in the eventual attainment of the collective vision.

It is, therefore, the central argument of the various theories of the neocharismatic leadership paradigm that the above common set of specifiable leader behaviors are generic to the leadership of individuals, small groups, formal or informal organizations, social or revolutionary movements, political parties, societies, or nation states. Theories of the neocharismatic leadership PARADIGM have been the subject of approximately 50 empirical studies. Bass and Avolio (1993) and House and Shamir (1993) present overviews of these studies. Considerable empirical evidence demonstrates that the theory has considerable predictive validity, with effect sizes in the range of 0.40 to 0.50, and generally above 0.50.

See also **CEOs; personality; Organizational culture; Leadership contingencies**

Bibliography

Bass, B. M. (1985). *Leadership and performance beyond expectations*. New York: Free Press.

Bass, B. M. & Avolio, B. J. (1993). Transformational leadership: A response to Critics. Academic Press, pp. 49–79.

Bennis, W. & Nanus, B. (1985). *Leaders: The strategies for taking charge*. New York: Harper & Row.

Conger, J. A. & R. A. Kanungo (1987). Toward a behavioral theory of charismatic leadership in organizational settings. *Academy of Management Review*, 12, 637–647.

House, R. J. (1977). A 1976 theory of charismatic leadership. In J. G. Hunt & L. L. Larson (Eds), *Leadership: The cutting edge*. Carbondale, IL: Southern Illinois University Press.

House, R. J. & Shamir, B. (1993). Toward the integration of transformational, charismatic, and visionary theories: Perspectives and Directions. In M. Chemmers & R. Aman (Eds). *Leadership: Theory, practice, perspectives and direction*. New York: Academic Press, pp. 81–105.

Sashkin, M. (1988). The visionary leader. In J. A. Conger & R. A. Kanungo (Eds), *Charismatic leadership: The elusive factor in organizational effectiveness*. San Francisco CA: Jossey-Bass.

ROBERT J. HOUSE

leadership contingencies Some of the emergence and effectiveness of leaders is due to their PERSONALITY but some is contingent on the situation. In Fiedler's contingency model, as assessed by their least preferred coworker (LPC), task-oriented leaders and relations-oriented leaders are most effective contingent on when they are either high or low in the power of their position, the task is high or low in structure and leader–member relations are very good or moderately poor.

In the Hersey–Blanchard situational test model, whether the leader should delegate, participate, sell, or tell the subordinate what to do is contingent on the psychological and job maturity of the subordinate.

In the Blake–Mouton grid (*see* MANAGERIAL GRID) not much room for exceptions is left for situational contingencies. Nevertheless, the high-task–high-relations leadership orientation (9, 9) is most likely to be effective when organizations are a mix of systems of hierarchies and groups. The task orientation fits with hierarchy; the relations orientation fits with groups (*see* WORK GROUPS). There is much empirical research evidence to support the Fiedler (1967) contingency model (*see also* COGNITIVE RESOURCE THEORY), somewhat less to support the Blake–Mouton grid, and least to support Hersey–Blanchard (1969) model (*see* MANAGERIAL STYLE).

Many societal, organizational, group, and task contingencies affect the emergence and effectiveness of LEADERSHIP. Some societal contingencies include the stability or turbulence of the environment and market, economic, political, social and legal circumstances, the sociopolitical ethos, regulatory agencies, socioeconomic status of the community, religious affiliation, nationality, ethnicity, reference groups and networks (*see* NETWORK ANALYSIS). Organizational constraints on leadership include the organization's philosophy, mission, policies, objectives, functions, service or production orientation size, structure, formalization, complexity, centralization, dispersion of authority, stability, unionization, and culture (Bass, 1990,) (*see* ORGANIZATIONAL CULTURE, ORGANIZATIONAL DESIGN). Whether leaders can be transactional or transformational depends on a number of these organizational constraints (Bass, 1985). At the group level, contingencies of consequence to the leadership include the status, esteem, and importance of the group, the maturity of the group, the stability of the group structure, group drive and cohesiveness, group size and group norms (Bass, 1990, Chap. 27) (*see* GROUP DYNAMICS; TEAM BUILDING; GROUP ROLES; TASK AND MAINTENANCE BEHAVIOR; GROUP DEVELOPMENT; GROUP NORMS).

See also **Leadership, Path-goal theory; Transformational/transactional theory**

Bibliography

Bass, B. M. (1985). *Leadership and performance beyond expectations*. New York: Free Press.

Bass, B. M. (1990). Bass & Stogdill's. *Handbook of leadership*. New York: Free Press Chapters 26 and 27.

Blake, R. R. & Mouton, J. C. (1964). *The managerial grid*. Houston, TX: Gulf Publishing.

Fiedler, F. E. (1967). *A theory of leadership effectiveness*. New York: McGraw-Hill.

Hersey, P. & Blanchard, K. H. (1969). *Management of organizational behavior*. Englewood Cliffs, NJ: Prentice-Hall.

BERNARD M. BASS

leadership style Leadership style refers to a consistent pattern of attitudes and/or behavior displayed by a leader. The style have been described and measured according to a variety of theories and models. Factor analytic studies at Ohio State University of surveys have yielded two-factor patterns of leader behavior: consideration and initiating structure. Consideration (for people) was more satisfying to followers and contributed to their performance. Initiating structure, at first, had coercive elements. After they were removed, initiating structure likewise contributed to PRODUCTIVITY.

Attitudinal patterns were implicated. Authoritarian managers believe people must be personally driven and controlled; equalitarian managers believe in the importance of democratic principles of governance (*see* AUTHORITARIAN PERSONALITY; DEMOCRACY). THEORY X managers believe workers were basically lazy and had to be directed, ordered, and controlled. Theory Y managers believe workers are basically internally motivated to do well, want AUTONOMY, and the opportunity to prove themselves. Theory Z managers believe in commitment, loyalty, and involvement in the organization and treating followers like members of a family.

A range of decision making results in still another way of looking at leaders' attitudinal and behavioral leadership styles. At one extreme, the leader "tells." Without his/her followers' contribution, the leader makes the decisions with or without giving reasons for them and expects them to be carried out. Or, the leader "sells" by making the decisions, then trying to persuade the followers to accept them. The leader may first consult with the follower, then decide, or the DECISION MAKING may be shared and consensus sought. Finally, the leader may delegate making the decisions to the followers (*see* DELEGATION). The leadership pattern in attitude and behavior may emphasize orientation toward the task of getting the work done, or orienting it may emphasize the leader–follower relationship. The former is directed at promoting productivity, the latter, at harmony, satisfaction, and good feelings (*see* MANAGERIAL GRID).

All of the above styles look at how much the leader emphasizes directive, task orientation, or quality relationships with followers. Remaining controversial is whether or not the best of leaders emphasize both in their ATTITUDES and behavior.

A new paradigm which cuts across the above stylistic dimensions looks at leaders as transactional or transformational (*see* LEADERSHIP; TRANSFORMATIONAL/TRANSACTIONAL THEORY). The transactional leader caters to the self-interests of the followers and fosters an exchange of promises of reward or threats of punishment for follower compliance or agreed-upon follower role enactment. The transformational leader moves followers to go beyond their self-interests for the good of the group, organization, or society and raises them to higher levels of MOTIVATION and morality (*see* MORAL DEVELOPMENT).

See also **Managerial behavior; Consultancy intervention models; Leadership contingencies**

Bibliography

Bass, B. M. (1990). Bass & Stogdill's. *Handbook of leadership: Theory, research & managerial applications*. New York: Free Press Chapters 21, 22, 23, and 24.

BERNARD M. BASS

lean production *see* BUSINESS PROCESS REENGINEERING; OPERATIONS MANAGEMENT

learned helplessness *see* ATTRIBUTION; PERSISTENCE; STRESS

learning, individual Learning, from a behavioral perspective, can be defined as an *unspecified* change within a person due to environmental experience that makes a change in observable behavior (performance) possible (Chance, 1979). *Behavior* is anything a person is observed to say or do (performances) (*see* PERFORMANCE, INDIVIDUAL). The following experiences capable of changing observed behavior (performance) are excluded from this view of learning: innate (unlearned or unconditioned) reflex responses, sensory adaptation (habituation), instincts, maturation (and old AGE), poor diet, motor fatigue, injury, disease, brain damage, and ingestion of drugs. Although classical (Pavlovian) conditioning processes describe experiences which affect the number and kind of environmental stimuli eliciting reflex responses from people, classical conditioning is not addressed in this and related entries. Rather, the focus is on operant CONDITIONING, REINFORCEMENT, EXTINCTION and SHAPING, These are fundamental and natural processes within which behavioral performance is known to change systematically with environmental experience.

The term operant response was adopted to denote a person's behavioral action on the environment in which the action takes place. Thus, operant behavior includes a person's actions (both corporal and verbal) that effect change(s) in behavior of other people; usually this occurs via symbolic or verbal behavior (Skinner, 1969). So reliably does operant conditioning change behavior (performance) that behavior scientists refer to operant based interventions as applications of scientific laws or principles of learning and reinforcement. As a naturally occurring learning process, however, operant conditioning can produce both dysfunctional and functional learned behaviors, evaluated relative to their effects on formal organizational goal achievement. To distinguish operant conditioning and reinforcement as a natural learning process from planned or contrived applications of operant principles during TRAINING and behavior modification, it can be called *learning per se*.

Cognitive models of learning per se are not developed here (*see* COGNITIVE PROCESSES). Cognitions can be seen as behavior, albeit covert behavior, inferred from combinations of observed experiences and, ultimately, observed behavior changes (performances). When the linkages among observed experience, covert cognitive behavior, and observed behavior change are well described, cognitions change in some orderly relation to experiences. Cognitions are not, therefore, explanations of observed behavior; rather, they are more behavior to be explained by observed experience (Skinner, 1974). Observational learning and imitative behaviors occur when a person observes a competent model perform some complex task and the observer is later, and perhaps under somewhat different conditions, able to perform the complex task observed. Theories have been introduced in attempts to *specify* what changes ("cognitions") within a person when this phenomenon occurs (Bandura, 1977). Ultimately, however, internal "cognitive" changes, if they are systematically related to observed experience and behavior, must be correlated with combinations of actual experiences and performances. From a practical standpoint, therefore, the utility of a cognitive construct arises from empirical evidence indicating how specific *observed* experiences have historically and reliably changed *unobserved* "cognitions" and *observed* behavior (performance). *Observational learning*, therefore, describes regularities among conditions under which experiences produce unobserved changes in a person that make future performances possible and the conditions under which a learner is likely to perform what was learned during the experienced observation of the model. For example, children learn both good and bad "habits" from observing parental behavior, e.g., cleanliness versus tobacco smoking or drinking to excess. Work "habits" can be learned in much the same way. Performance of what has been learned, however, depends critically on the consequences that typically follow performance in a given situation. Management of performance–consequence relationships in work settings is a major responsibility of organizational leaders and managers.

Training differs from learning per se in that training is the planned application of learning and conditioning principles to create experiences for trainees that insure, at least during training, they acquire basic knowledge and SKILLS needed to perform a particular job or class of jobs. The work situation a trainee graduates enter into is essentially another learning environment in which learning per se (operant conditioning) maintains or changes behavior (performance) learned during training. Work environments may further support [via reinforcement] what was learned during training or they may not [extinction]. Learning per se can actually produce dysfunctional behaviors (performances) within a work setting.

See also **Action theory; Influence; Motivation and performance**

Bibliography

Bandura, A. (1977). *Social learning theory*. Englewood Cliffs, NJ: Prentice-Hall.

Chance, P. (1979). *Learning and behavior*. Belmont, CA: Wadsworth.

Keller, F. S. & Shoenfeld, W. N. (1950). *Principles of psychology*. New York: Appleton-Century-Crofts.

Skinner, B. F. (1969). *Contingencies of reinforcement: A theoretical analysis*. New York: Appleton-Century-Crofts.

Skinner, B. F. (1974). *About behaviorism*. New York: Knopf.

THOMAS C. MAWHINNEY

learning organization The concept of organizations as dynamic systems having capacities of self-changing, and the ability to develop and more optimally satisfy the changing desires of STAKEHOLDERS. Learning organizations embody, probably as a result of deliberate management strategy, a high proportion of the processes of ORGANIZATIONAL LEARNING.

The concept achieved popularity in the 1990s as a follow on from the "EXCELLENCE" movement of the 1980s (*see* COMPETITIVENESS). "Excellent" organizations have not maintained this status. Failure of adaptation or learning has been the obvious explanation.

Theories and descriptions of the learning organization treat organizations as bounded systemic entities interacting with environments, having survival and growth as their main concerns (*see* SYSTEMS THEORY). Learning organization theories offer accounts of this process. Senge (1990) interprets organizational learning as overcoming systems patterns (archetypes) interfering with survival and development. Argyris and Schon (1978) suggest that a difficulty in changing fundamental purposes and visions (DOUBLE LOOP LEARNING) as well as operating procedures (single loop learning) is a major cause of organizational failure. Garratt (1987) advocates a "hands off, brains on" approach to the conduct of the roles of Directors, Presidents, and Vice-Presidents so that broad vision and strategic action is not sacrificed to reactive trouble shooting.

Pedler, Burgoyne, and Boydell (1991) describe organizational learning as depending on the balance and connection of the four processes of collective policy, group operations, individual action, and individual thought. This process is achieved through eleven organizational behaviors and features: experimental strategy moves, member PARTICIPATION in policy making, transparency of internal information through INFORMATION TECHNOLOGY, decision and FEEDBACK oriented accounting systems, internal coordination through lateral NEGOTIATION, REWARD for INNOVATION and problem solving, clear but flexible structures, information gathering by boundary workers (*see* BOUNDARY SPANNING), imitation of and experimentation with other organizations, cultures encouraging learning from mistakes, cultures and structures to encourage individual self-development (*see* SELF-REGULATION; ORGANIZATIONAL CULTURE).

A number of other theoretical issues link to the Learning Organization concept which offers a novel point of conceptual integration between them: questioning how firms achieve adaptation if hierarchical control is substituted for free market behavior in TRANSACTION COST THEORY. The consequent interest in the flexible firm appears in LABOR PROCESS THEORY as the source of new demands on labor (*see* FLEXIBILITY). New forms of HUMAN RESOURCE MANAGEMENT involving greater employee COMMITMENT, involvement, and incorporation into the performance and adaptation of corporate activity (*see* EMPLOYEE INVOLVEMENT). The POPULATION ECOLOGY theory of organizations raises the possibility that organizations change through variation at their foundation followed by natural selection, rather than an intrinsic ability to learn. Conventional approaches to corporate strategy see organizations as observing (*see* STRATEGIC MANAGEMENT), predicting, and reacting to their environments, but alternative formulations suggest a more proactive approach in which organizations create or enacting their contexts (*see* ENACTMENT; COGNITION IN ORGANIZATIONS); (Bougon, 1992) with minds that may be able to remember and learn.

The Learning Organization concept raises, when considered in conjunction with these other theoretical perspectives, questions of: the difference between learning and change; the entity that learns (individual, organization, industry sector, nation-state, society, or processes of ordering); the nature and problems of discontinuation in learning (*see* ORGANIZATIONAL CHANGE); the fundamental source of purpose and order in human activity.

See also **Organization and environment**

Bibliography

Argyris, C. & Schon, D. A. (1978). *Organizational learning: A theory in action perspective*. Reading, MA: Addison-Wesley.

Bougon, M. G. (1992). Congregate cognitive maps: A unified dynamic theory of organization and strategy. *Journal of Management Studies*, **29**, (3), 369–389.

Garratt, R. (1987). *The learning organisation*. London: Fontana/Collins.

Pedler, M., Burgoyne, J. G. & Boydell, T. (1991). *The learning company: A strategy for sustainable development*. London: McGraw-Hill.

Senge, P. (1990). *The fifth discipline: The art and practice of the learning organisation*. New York: Doubleday.

JOHN BURGOYNE

legitimacy This concept operates at multiple LEVELS OF ANALYSIS; it pertains to individuals, behaviors, organizations, industries, or institutions (in general, focal actor). Legitimacy is a relational concept created and maintained by other actors in the relevant social system. The essence of legitimacy is that a focal actor is *accepted* or *judged appropriate* by the social system in which the actor is embedded; a legitimate actor is one who is congruent with the beliefs and norms of a social system. This acceptance can be taken-for-granted, preconscious, and understood intuitively and unquestioningly. The institution of marriage and the structure of AUTHORITY based on rank in the military are examples of this type of acceptance. Alternatively, social actors confer legitimacy on a focal actor by deliberately evaluating them; for instance, the sale of shares of stock by a company to the general public requires regulatory approval in many countries. The process by which legitimacy is gained (or lost) is called (de)legitimation.

The standards which social actors use to judge legitimacy can exist at a societal level, within a group or organization, or at an intermediate social system such as an industry. In general, the standards for legitimacy are derived from formal laws and rules, legal norms, and social norms and VALUES (Katz & Kahn, 1978) (*see* GROUP NORMS; ORGANIZATIONAL CULTURE). The evaluation of legitimacy may result from attributes of the focal actor, from the characteristics of the focal actor's ROLE in a social system, or from a combination of the two (*see* STATUS).

Legitimacy most often has been examined as a base of POWER (*see* POWER BASES) and INFLUENCE within groups and organizations (French & Raven, 1968; Katz & Kahn, 1978; Michener & Burt, 1971; Zelditch & Walker, 1984). French and Raven (1968) proposed three structural foundations of legitimate power. The first is the cultural values of a social system, such as a respect for AGE or experience. The second is the acceptance of the structure of authority in a social system; for example, in bureaucratic organizations individuals accept the hierarchy of offices as legitimate (*see* BUREAUCRACY). Third, legitimate power may be exerted by a person designated by a legitimizing agent as having the right to exercise power; for instance, a company president may designate a vice president to form and lead a task force which will solve a particular company problem. Personal attributes also contribute to legitimacy; two such attributes are perceived competence and fairness (Michener & Burt, 1971) (*see* JUSTICE, PROCEDURAL; JUSTICE, DISTRIBUTIVE).

Organizational legitimacy refers to the appropriateness of an organization's goals and procedures. Much research examined organizational legitimation, and Galaskiewicz (1985) identified two ways organizations legitimated themselves. First, they identified with cultural symbols or legitimate figures in the environment through interlocking directorships or by obtaining endorsements. Second, business organizations enhance their legitimacy by donating to charitable organizations.

See also **Politics; Reputation; Representation**

Bibliography

French, J. R. P. Jr. & Raven, B. (1968). The bases of social power. In D. Cartwright & A. Zander (Eds), *Group dynamics* (3rd edn, pp. 259–269). New York: Harper & Row.

Galaskiewicz, J. (1985). Interorganizational relations. In R. H. Turner & J. F. Short, Jr. (Eds), *Annual review of sociology* (vol. 11, pp. 281–304).

Katz, D. & Kahn, R. L. (1978). *The social psychology of organizations* (2nd edn). New York: Wiley.

Michener, H. A. & Burt, M. A. (1971). Legitimacy as a base of social influence. In J. Tedeschi (Ed.), *Perspectives on social power* (pp. 311–348). Chicago: Aldine.

Zelditch, M. Jr. & Walker, H. A. (1984). Legitimacy and the stability of authority. In E. J. Lawler, Jr. (Ed.), *Advances in group processes* (vol. 1, pp. 1–25).

DAVID L. DEEPHOUSE

leisure *see* NONWORK/WORK

levels of analysis This term has at least two interrelated meanings as it is used in the discipline of ORGANIZATIONAL BEHAVIOR. The most concrete concerns the level at which research data are described or analyzed, where level refers to a HIERARCHY comprising, for example, individual employees, dyads, work groups, departments, organizations, and industries. For instance, at the lowest level of analysis, the individual, we might describe an employee as exhibiting a 3 percent absentee rate. This would mean that the person missed 3 percent of scheduled work days over some time period (*see* ABSENTEEISM). Alternatively, the absences of individuals might be averaged to express an absence rate at some higher level such as a work group, a department, or an organization as a whole.

More complexly, levels of analysis is often meant to refer to the theoretical or conceptual level at which some phenomenon is supposed to exist or operate. For example, in orthodox usage, PERSONALITY is an individual level construct, GROUP COHESIVENESS is a group level construct, and ORGANIZATIONAL CULTURE is an organizational level construct.

Level of analysis can be distinguished from level of measurement (Rousseau, 1985). The latter refers to the level at which data are collected, as opposed to the level at which they are summarized or analyzed. For example, in studying work group productivity, a researcher might add the PRODUCTIVITY of individual group members to produce an index for various groups. Here, the level of measurement is the individual, but the level of analysis is the group. As this example illustrates, the level of measurement need not always correspond to the level of analysis. However, there is general agreement that researchers need to justify very clearly the logical linkages between the chosen level of measurement, the mechanical level of analysis, and the theoretical level of analysis.

Organizations are inherently multilevel, and higher levels of analysis provide a potentially important context for processes at lower levels (Cappelli & Sherer, 1991). Also, a consideration of multiple levels often reveals how behavior is constrained or free to vary (Johns, 1991). Thus, we might expect to see much research that takes into account multiple levels of analysis. In fact, this is somewhat rare. Disciplinary isolation has led to a tendency for researchers with psychologically based training to concentrate on lower levels of analysis and those with sociologically based training to concentrate on higher levels of analysis (*see* THEORY; ORGANIZATION THEORY) (Roberts, Hulin, & Rousseau, 1978).

Critical Issues Concerning Levels of Analysis

Not all variables are easily assigned to a theoretical level of analysis. For example, there has been debate about whether MANAGERIAL STYLE is an individual characteristic, a dyadic variable (existing between a leader and an individual subordinate), or a group-level variable (in which all group members experience the same style) (Mossholder & Bedian, 1983). This issue frequently arises when individual responses are used to describe constructs that might exist at some higher level of analysis. For instance, is JOB DESIGN best represented as a property of the job (a higher level of analysis) or the perceptions of individual job holders (a lower level of analysis)? A related problem occurs when attempting to determine the degree of isomorphism between variables that differ in level of analysis. To what extent is individual learning similar to ORGANIZATIONAL LEARNING? How analogous is organizational culture to individual personality?

There has been longstanding concern about how to ensure that level of measurement is logically tied to level of analysis so that the measure fairly represents the variable under consideration. One approach is to match the level of measurement precisely to the level of analysis. For example, if TECHNOLOGY is viewed as an organization level variable, it might be measured by classifying firms according to the production process used in their operating core. This global measurement of technology corresponds to an organizational level of analysis. The alternative is to measure technology at some lower level of analysis and then aggregate these measures to represent the variable at a higher level of analysis (Roberts, Hulin, & Rousseau, 1978). Thus, individual perceptions of the degree of a firm's AUTOMATION might be averaged to represent its technology. For perceptual variables, there is considerable accord among researchers that there should be a high degree of agreement among research subjects before their responses are aggregated to represent a higher level construct. Thus, in a study of ORGANIZATION CLIMATE, there should be high within-firm agreement about a firm's climate and, by extension, detectable differences between firms (Glick, 1985). Unfortunately, there is much less accord about how to actually measure such agreement (James, Demaree, & Wolf, 1993).

It has long been recognized that relationships that hold at one level of analysis might not hold at another level of analysis, and that cross-level inferences are risky at best. For example, making inferences about the motives of individual consumers from aggregate economic data is questionable. Also, a correlation between JOB SATISFACTION and absenteeism at the individual level does not guarantee that work groups with lower morale will have higher absence rates. On the other hand, considerable interest has emerged about whether variables at one level of analysis can have a substantive impact at another level of analysis. For example, how can the behavior of an individual group member affect group cohesiveness? Does organizational technology or size influence the job satisfaction of individual employees? (*see* ORGANIZATIONAL SIZE). Can a group's "absence culture" affect the absence behavior of its individual members?

Several research tactics exist for examining potential cross-level effects when it is possible that variables at a higher level of analysis might have an impact at a lower level of analysis. One of the most straightforward cross-level designs uses hierarchical multiple regression in which the dependent variable is some variable of interest at the lower level of analysis (*see* STATISTICAL METHODS). Independent variables include any lower-level predictors of interest and, critically, higher level predictors in which subjects in natural units (such as work groups) at the higher level are all assigned the same value on that variable. This value might be a global measure or an aggregated measure of individual responses if within-group homogeneity can be demonstrated. If the higher level variables account for additional variance beyond that accounted for by lower level variables, a cross-level effect can be inferred (Mathieu, 1991; Mossholder & Bedian, 1983).

Another cross-level design is the varient approach (Dansereau, Alutto, & Yammarino, 1984; Markham, 1988). This approach uses within and between analysis to apportion the variance in multiple-level designs to its appropriate location.

Although considering multiple levels of analysis in research presents considerable methodological challenges, it also provides an important opportunity for truly understanding the systemic nature of organizations.

See also **Research design; Research methods; Systems theory**

Bibliography

Cappelli, P. & Sherer, P. D. (1991). The missing role of context in OB: The need for a meso-level approach. *Research in Organizational Behavior*, **13**, 55–110.

Dansereau, F., Alutto, J. A. & Yammarino, F. J. (1984). *Theory testing in organizational behavior: The varient approach*. Englewood Cliffs, NJ: Prentice-Hall.

Glick, W. H. (1985). Conceptualizing and measuring organizational and psychological climate: Pitfalls in multi-level research. *Academy of Management Review*, **10**, 601–616.

James, L. R., Demaree, R. G. & Wolf, G. (1993). r_{wg}: An assessment of within-group interrater agreement. *Journal of Applied Psychology*, **78**, 306–309.

Johns, G. (1991). Substantive and methodological constraints on behavior and attitudes in organizational research. *Organizational Behavior and Human Decision Processes*, **49**, 80–104.

Markham, S. E. (1988). Pay-for-performance revisited: Empirical example of the importance of group effects. *Journal of Applied Psychology*, **73**, 172–180.

Mathieu, J. E. (1991). A cross-level nonrecursive model of the antecedents of organizational commitment and satisfaction. *Journal of Applied Psychology*, **76**, 607–618.

Mossholder, K. W. & Bedian, A. G. (1983). Cross-level inference and organizational research: Perspectives on interpretation and application. *Academy of Management Review*, **8**, 547–558.

Roberts, K. H., Hulin, C. L. & Rousseau, D. M. (1978). Developing an interdisciplinary science of organizations. . San Francisco: Jossey-Bass.

Rousseau, D. M. (1985). Issues of level in organizational research: Multi-level and cross-level perspectives. *Research in Organizational Behavior*, **7**, 1–37.

GARY JOHNS

liability of newness/smallness etc. *see* POPULATION ECOLOGY

life cycle *see* CAREER STAGES; LIFE STAGES; ORGANIZATION CHANGE

life stage A life stage is a period of years during an individual's life-course distinguished from the periods before and after it by differences, usually identified by a researcher, in the individual's functioning and/or development.

Life stage theories describe individual change over the life course. In contrast to other developmental theories that conceive change as a continuous process, life stage theories propose that change occurs in relatively discrete time periods, dividing lives into segments, each with identifiable characteristics. For example, Erikson (1950) describes eight ages of man, each marked by specific developmental ego qualities. Levinson (1978) talks of life's "seasons" as "a series of periods or stages within the life cycle."

Several assumptions characterize life stage theories. First, the theories are psychological. Even though some mention external factors, their primary concern is describing change within the individual. Second, they view each stage as distinct from all others. Thus, a man in Levinson's "early adulthood" era is clearly distinguishable from a man in the "middle adult" era. Third, the theories define life stages as tied to specific AGE spans. Men falling in Levinson's "early adulthood" era, for instance, are between the ages of seventeen and forty-five. Finally, life stage theories assume that all individuals go through the same stages; so that, for example, a miner in England and a lawyer in Tokyo are expected to experience, during the same age span, the same stages, developmental issues, and changes in functioning (see Lawrence, 1980).

Although differences between childhood, adolescence, and old age have been recognized since the early 1900s, life stage theories that cover events throughout the life course are relatively new. Buehler (1933) and Erikson (1950) provide two of the earliest versions. Contemporary life stage theories focusing on men appeared in the late 1970s. Research suggesting that women's life stages differ from those of men appeared in the 1980s (*see* WOMEN AT WORK). Most life stage theories have emerged from research using cross-sectional, clinical interview data. Although widely cited, these theories are seldom tested or replicated because of data collection difficulties.

One critique of life stage theories is that they neglect the social and historical context in which they are embedded. The influence of context on age-related behavior and experiences has long been recognized by sociologists and anthropologists, and studies suggest that social systems influence patterns of aging. Moreover, because social systems change over time, through developments in medicine, transportation, communication and other technologies, population growth and decline, and other environmental factors, it seems likely that life stages change as well. Indeed, historical studies show that many life issues seen as widely shared today did not exist during earlier periods in history. For instance, today's "empty-nest" syndrome of middle age, when children leave the home, was not so common 200 years ago. Without modern contraceptives, many families had young children throughout the wife's childbearing years, unless she died or pregnancies were otherwise limited.

See also **Retirement; Individual differences; Nonwork/work; Career development**

Bibliography

Buehler, C. (1933). *Der menschliche lebenslauf als psychologisches problem*. Leipzig: Hertzel.

Erikson, E. H. (1950). *Childhood and society*. New York: Norton.

Hagestad, G. O. (1990). Social perspectives on the life course. In R. H. Binstock & L. K. George (Eds), *Handbook of aging and the social sciences* (3rd edn, pp. 151–168). San Diego: Academic Press.

Lawrence, B. S. (1980). The myth of the midlife crisis. *Sloan Management Review*, **21**, (4), 35–49.

Levinson, D. J. (1978). *The seasons of a man's life*. New York: Knopf.

BARBARA S. LAWRENCE

line/staff The distinction between line and staff members of an organization originates from the military – the line soldiers were those who did the fighting while the staff provided technical support. In civilian organizations the line has direct command over the final product or service (*see* ACCOUNTABILITY). Staff support the line through functions such as production control, marketing or information systems, and specialized advice. Because relatively highly educated young staff can give advice and instructions to experienced line people, conflicts can frequently arise. The terms have tended to fall into disuse due to the arbitrary nature of the distinction between line and staff which has been emphasized by structural changes in organizations, such as shifts toward team working and the desire to reduce managerial overheads by delayering and other changes.

See also **Classical design theory; Organizational design; Differentiation; Division of labor;**

Bibliography

Butler, R. (1991). *Designing organisations: A decision-making perspective*. London: Routledge.

RICHARD BUTLER

linking pin The term linking pin was introduced by Rensis Likert. As organizations become more horizontally and vertically differentiated, mechanisms must be developed to link these disparate parts together. Linking pins consist of the managers that participate in two levels of organizational involvement and thereby link these levels together. For example, work-unit supervisors are members of their own units and the departments they report to (*see* SUPERVISION).

The linking pin concept may have played an important role in the configuring of organizations in the 1960s and 1970s, however, references to the concept have almost disappeared from the literature in the 1980s and 1990s. Linking pins are only one mechanism for achieving coordination and INTEGRATION and are limited in meeting the higher demands for coordination that have appeared in the latter part of this century. Most organizations rely less on HIERARCHY today to achieve coordination and more on lateral relations that emphasize direct interdepartmental contact at lower levels of the organization. Additionally, most organizations have recently gone through an historical period of DELAYERING and of increasing SPANS OF CONTROL. As a consequence worker ROLES have expanded and they tend to be less removed from higher levels in the organization. While linking pin behavior will always be present in organizations, its central role in design may be less important today than when Likert introduced the concept.

See also **Classical design theory; Organizational design; Management, classical theory**

Bibliography

Likert, R. (1967). *The human organization: Its management and values*. New York: McGraw-Hill.

ROBERT DRAZIN

locus of control This is a personality construct denoting people's generalized expectancies for CONTROL of REINFORCEMENTS or REWARDS. People who believe that they can control reinforcements in their lives are termed internals. People who believe that fate, luck, or other people control reinforcements are termed externals. The locus of control concept is most frequently attributed to Rotter (1966). He also developed the most commonly used scale to assess the construct (Rotter, 1966).

Locus of control has been one of the most popularly studied PERSONALITY variables in the organizational behavior domain. In his review of organizational studies Spector (1982) noted that internality is associated with high levels of effort, MOTIVATION, job performance (*see* PERFORMANCE, INDIVIDUAL), and JOB SATISFACTION. Internals tend to exhibit initiative on the job and prefer participative supervisory styles (*see* MANAGERIAL STYLE). Externals, on the other hand, are more conforming to AUTHORITY and prefer directive supervisory styles. Research has found that externality (feeling that one has little control) is associated with counterproductive behavior in response to FRUSTRATION. Externals are more likely than internals to respond to frustrating events at work by engaging in aggression against others, SABOTAGE, starting arguments, and stealing (*see* Perlow & Latham, 1993) (*see* EMPLOYEE THEFT).

The higher performance of externals has been explained by the concept of expectancy from VIE THEORY. Internals tend to have greater expectancies than externals that they can be effective in task accomplishment. If they see the job as leading to desired rewards, internals should be more motivated to perform. Recent research has shown, however, that internals may not always be better performers. Blau (1993) found that internals did better at job tasks requiring initiative, but externals did better in highly structured routine tasks. Thus internals and externals may be suited for different kinds of jobs, depending upon their need for compliance or initiative.

Since Rotter's initial work scales have been developed to assess locus of control in specific domains relevant to organizations, including economic locus of control, health locus of control, SAFETY locus of control, and work locus of control (Spector, 1988). These specific scales tend to correlate more highly with variables within their domains than does the general Rotter scale. Spector (1988), for example, found that work locus of control had stronger correlations than general locus of control with work related variables, such as JOB SATISFACTION.

See also **Personality testing; Persistence; Interactionism; Self-efficacy**

Bibliography

Blau, G. (1993). Testing the relationship of locus of control to different performance dimensions. *Journal of Occupational and Organizational Psychology*, **66**, 125–138.

Perlow, R. & Latham, L. L. (1993). The relationship between client abuse, and locus of control and gender: A longitudinal study in mental retardation facilities. *Journal of Applied Psychology*, **78**, 831–834.

Rotter, J. B. (1966). Generalized expectancies for internal versus external control of reinforcement. *Psychological Monographs*, **80**, (1, Whole No. 609).

Spector, P. E. (1982). Behavior in organizations as a function of employees' locus of control. *Psychological Bulletin*, **91**, 482–497.

Spector, P. E. (1988). Development of the work locus of control scale. *Journal of Occupational Psychology*, **61**, 335–340.

PAUL E. SPECTOR

loose coupling Relationships that are not tightly specified or frequently monitored, but nevertheless persist, simultaneously characterized by responsiveness and AUTONOMY, are "loosely coupled." Loose coupling is a metaphoric description of association (and can be applied to links between or among individuals, units, hierarchical levels, ORGANIZATION AND ENVIRONMENT, intention and action, and cause and effect among others) rather than a precisely measured, unidimensional variable. Where linkages are carefully structured, well specified in advance, predictable, frequent and assiduously maintained, they can be characterized as "tightly coupled." Where relationships are less structured, the linked activities operate in partial independence from one another, and they may be characterized as "loosely coupled." Tight coupling implies less freedom to accomplish unit tasks autonomously and more careful coordination; loose coupling, more freedom. Yet the simple opposition of "loose" and "tight" coupling ignores important aspects of the idea.

Loose coupling highlights the apparent PARADOX of partial autonomy across links that endure, between individuals or units or items that do respond to one another; when the links break down or responsiveness ceases, the units may be said to be decoupled. Coordination between individuals or subunits that communicate or interact infrequently can be essential to effective organizational performance (*see* COMMUNICATIONS). Loose coupling enables such activities to diverge in detail yet to endure despite local disruption, whereas units tightly coupled to one another will all fall into disarray if any does, and decoupled units will not coordinate.

Loosely coupled activities can also be judged by different criteria–manufacturing efficiency in operations, and customer complaints in sales, for instance. Thus units can respond more effectively to local criteria and situations, while still retaining coordination. Units or activities are loosely linked to take advantage of the authonomy loose coupling permits, an especially useful feature for fragmented environments or conflicting demands. Loose coupling may also be used to describe relationships among organizations not formally dependent upon one another that nonetheless coordinate their activities, such as JOINT VENTURES, coalitions, federations, or intraorganizational systems (*see* COALITION FORMATION; INTERORGANIZATIONAL RELATIONS).

More properly, loosely coupled individuals, units, or activities may decouple if they lose sight of the larger goals their particular efforts are intended to further. When local goals assume primacy, local criteria and tasks are optimized at the expense of broader joint aims. Similarly, decoupling between individual incentives and group activities can lead to perverse outcomes when individual activities that undercut group activites are rewarded. In cause–effect linkages, loose coupling indicates ambiguous means–ends connections (which may be due to selective PERCEPTION, BOUNDED RATIONALITY, haste, uncertainty, or intangibility, among other sources), while decoupling indicates breakdown of links. Where the loose coupling fails, the units or activities decouple; where loose coupling endures, the paradox of simultaneous independence and responsiveness remains.

The chief benefit of the loose coupling concept is its potential for directing attention to the apparent contradiction of links that exist, but are not wholly determinate. This benefit requires users to resist simplifying the concept, however. For organization theorists or managers, the paradox of simultaneous connection and autonomy is among the most important of organizational facts.

See also **Network analysis; Organizational design; Stakeholders; Systems theory; Collateral organization**

Bibliography

Orton, J. D. & Weik, K. (1990). Loosely coupled systems: A reconceptualization. *Academy of Management Review*, **15**, (2), 203–223.

Weick, K. (1976). Educational organizations as loosely coupled systems. *Administrative Science Quarterly*, **21**, 1–19.

MARIANN JELINEK

loyalty *see* COMMITMENT

M

machiavellianism This construct denotes the disposition to view and treat others as objects to be manipulated for one's own ends. It derives its name from Nicolo Machiavelli who set forth principles for holding power in his 1532 book *The Prince*. Using his concepts, Jay (1967) presents a case for applying their insights to understand the operation of large corporations as parallels to empires. Christie and Geis (1970) developed a PERSONALITY measure based upon statements drawn from Machiavelli's work (*see* PERSONALITY TESTING). Respondents agree or disagree with such items as: "It is wise to flatter important people"; and, "Never tell anyone the real reason you did something unless it is useful to do so." Opposite items, reverse keyed, include "Honesty is the best policy in all cases." Those high on the resulting Mach Scale see the world in manipulative terms, with greater detachment from and cynicism about others. To study its relationship to LEADERSHIP, Gleason, Seaman, and Hollander (1978) conducted an experiment observing 16 four-man groups under structured or nonstructured task conditions. Each was composed of one High, one Low, and two Middle scorers on the Mach Scale. High Machs behaved most ascendantly, especially in the nonstructured condition. Middle Machs were chosen significantly more as a future leader than were those at either extreme.

See also **Influence; Legitimacy; Obedience; Power bases; Politics**

Bibliography

Christie, R. & Geis, F. L. (1970). *Studies in Machiavellianism*. New York: Academic Press.

Gleason, J. M., Seaman, F. J. & Hollander, E. P. (1978). Emergent leadership processes as a function of task structure and Machiavellianism. *Social Behavior and Personality*, **6**, 33–36.

Jay, A. (1967). *Management and Machiavelli*. New York: Bantam.

EDWIN P. HOLLANDER

machine bureaucracy *see* BUREAUCRACY; ORGANIZATIONAL DESIGN

macro/micro/meso theory *see* LEVELS OF ANALYSIS; THEORY

maintenance behavior *see* TASK AND MAINTENANCE BEHAVIOR

management, classical theory This body of thinking comes from the early development phase of management, in which initial efforts were made to formalize principles that might offer guidance to a growing class of professional managers. Classical theory sought rationality and order in work through what they called "the one best way," the most logical DIVISION OF LABOR, appropriate structure to relate the activities thus divided (in terms of the variety of activities and the levels of supervision), the correct SPAN OF CONTROL for directing activities, and the proper allocation of responsibility to a designated AUTHORITY. Classical theorists asserted their insights were universally applicable to all organizations. Specialized, subdivided labor, proper direction and coordination, and effective planning would insure efficiency.

Frederick W. Taylor's book, *Principles of Scientific Management* (1911) separated planning, coordination, and assessment from task accomplishment, and specified these as management responsibilities. Workers were to be provided with proper tools and specific tasks to perform; managers were to identify, plan, and coordinate the tasks, and to insure the work got done, as specified. Taylor's approach, stressing exhaustive time-and-motion studies, explicit instructions, and unquestioning obedience by workers, reflected both his engineering background and the prevalence of numerous semiliterate or illiterate immigrants, no less than the numerous laboring jobs in the American workforce of his time. Its underlying philosophy is clearly based on purely economic MOTIVATION, with fair pay for efficient work the aim (*see* EQUITY THEORY)

"Taylorism" was highly popular with some managers, who saw the approach as a rational and systematic form of management. Others, both advocates and critics, saw SCIENTIFIC MANAGEMENT as a means of gaining much tight control over workers. The controversy erupted into congressional investigation in 1912, and continues today. Critics attack Taylor's theory as unduly manipulative and exploitation of workers. Taylor himself is often portrayed as either exploitative or the dupe of greedy managers. Proponents down to the present day argue that Taylor saw himself as the champion of dignity and fair treatment for workers who were necessarily dependent upon managers for the coordination, instructions, and overall work design, an enlightened position for his time. Taylor's underlying assumptions of rationality and the importance of structure pervade much management theory still, as does his preference for the "scientific" study of organizations.

Henry Fayol, a French mining engineer, typified another thread of classical management insight distilled from personal experience. His book *Industrial and General Administration* (French edition 1916, first English edition 1930) was drawn from a lifetime of management experience. Fayol believed his principles could be taught, rather than merely learned on the job. Among Fayol's insights were important classical concepts such as unity of command (the principle that every person should have only one supervisor, and that all persons should be supervised in a consistent hierarchical structure), equity, and orderly division of work. Fayol identified the key management tasks as planning, coordination, and control.

Chester Barnard, another practising manager, was the author of *The Functions of the Executive* (1938). Barnard brought experience as President of New Jersey Bell Telephone and head of important government relief efforts during the American Depression, as well as the added sophistication of wide reading in the emerging science of sociology (including Vilfredo Pareto and Max Weber in their original French and German editions) to his task. Barnard's reflective insights moved well beyond the rigidities of rules and structures to emphasize the systemic, affective, and cooperative nature of how people accomplish organizational tasks. As a result, he is often distinguished from other classical management theorists.

German sociologist Max Weber, who coined the term "BUREAUCRACY" and first specified its characteristics, is also identified as a source for classical management theory. According to Weber, bureaucracy divided the work to define clearly the authority and responsibility of each member as legitimate, official duties. Positions and responsibilities were arranged in a hierarchy of authority constituting a chain of command, with those higher up superior to those below, and every member having a single direct superior. Members were selected on the basis of technical qualifications (not friendship, for instance), and leaders were appointed to their positions by superiors. Administrative officials worked for fixed salaries, and did not own their units. Strict rules controlled and disciplined members, setting limits to superiors' authority. Rules were impersonally applied to all. Because this description captures much of the sense and flavor of classical theory, Weber is typically cited as a classical theorist, although delays in translating his work into English assured that few outside Germany beyond scholarly circles were directly familiar with his ideas.

Others typically included in the classical management school are Mooney (1947) who had been an executive at General Motors; and Urwick, (see Fox and Urwick 1977) (1937). Classical theory provided a useful basis for later development, and, by its initial emphasis on division of work and organizational structure, profoundly colored later ORGANIZATION THEORY. One wing of classical theory emphasized time and motion study and engineering efficiency; representatives included Carl Barth and

H. L. Gantt, whose Gantt charts mapped out relationships over time between and among related tasks; and Frank and Lillian Gilbreth, who practiced widely as consultants on efficiency.

Classical management, even in its time, was complemented by approaches that gave less weight to structure and more to human interactions. Hugo Munsterberg, author of *Psychology and Industrial Efficiency* (1913) is counted as the father of industrial psychology. Munsterberg examined job demands to specify their requisite mental capabilities, in an effort to use PSYCHOLOGICAL TESTING to find the best candidate for a given job. This aim is quite similar to Taylor's, although the methods differ from Scientific Management. Mary Parker Follett, an important theorist of the 1920s, asserted the importance of the group as essential for full realization of individual development. Follett's thinking on integration, common purpose, and the importance of cooperation seem apropos today.

Classical Management was ultimately supplemented by theories like the Human Relations School (*see* HUMAN RELATIONS MOVEMENT) that turned increasingly to the emotional, nonstructural aspects of behavior in organizations, themes that continue to be reflected in ORGANIZATIONAL BEHAVIOR, ORGANIZATION DEVELOPMENT, and management theory. However, modern organization theory's emphasis on structure, rational arrangement of tasks and control, and its exclusion of topics like human EMOTION, interpretation, POWER, and CONFLICT, remains closer to classical management theory. Contemporary controversies include concern to find logically consistent bridges between these apparently contradictory emphases.

See also **Managerial behavior; Leadership; Organizational design; Classical design theory**

Bibliography

Barnard, C. I. (1938). *The functions of the executive*. Cambridge, MA: Harvard University Press.

Fox, E. M. & Urwick, L. (1977). *Dynamic administration: The collected papers of Mary Parker Follett*. New York: Hippocrene.

Mooney, J. D. (1947). *The principles of organization*. New York: Harper.

Munsterberg, H. (1913). *Psychology and industrial efficiency*. Boston, MA: Houghton Mifflin.

Taylor, F. W. (1911). *Principles of scientific management*. New York: Harper.

Urwick, L. (1943). *Elements of administration*. New York: Harper.

Wren, D. A. (1979). *The evolution of management thought*. New York: Wiley.

MARIANN JELINEK

management, information systems *see* COMMUNICATIONS; INFORMATION PROCESSING

management, international *see* INTERNATIONAL MANAGEMENT

management by objectives (MBO) One of the most fundamental aspects of the management process is called management by objectives, or MBO. This technique refers to the establishment of specific targets or goals for work activities in a variety of work contexts. MBO incorporates many important aspects of effective management including coordination of strategic with tactical and operational goals, individual accountability, clear and straightforward work objectives, and superior–subordinate interaction. The concept of MBO is most often credited to Peter Drucker in his management classic, *The Practice of Management* published in 1954, based on his extensive work with General Electric Company as well as industrialist Alfred Sloan. A typical MBO program consists of several stages including:

(1) define and clarify the desired strategic goals of a company or business unit;
(2) develop tactical goals to be implemented by specific personnel in order to determine the strategic goals (*see* STRATEGIC MANAGEMENT);
(3) determine the resources needed to accomplish these goals and make them available to key personnel;
(4) communicate strategic objectives with key personnel and solicit their input;
(5) implement work plans and monitor accordingly; and

(6) provide FEEDBACK at regular intervals concerning work performance (*see* KNOWLEDGE OF RESULTS).

More recently, Edwin Locke has refined the general concept of MBO in his GOAL-SETTING theory.

Research on the topic of MBO, and its more current manifestation, goal-setting, has been extensive and the results clearly support the proposition that people work more efficiently and effectively if they have challenging work objectives or goals with clearly defined time deadlines. MBO programs have been successfully implemented in a number of industries.

See also **Human resources management; Human resources strategy; Motivation; Decision making**

Bibliography

Carroll, S. J. & Tosi, H. L. (1973). *Management by objectives: Applications and research.* New York: Macmillan.

Odiorne, G. S. (1978). MBO: A backward glance. *Business Horizons* October 14–24.

P. CHRISTOPHER EARLEY

management development This term refers to experiences (both before and after management promotion, and both formal and informal) meant to enhance an individual's current and future effectiveness in a managerial position. Management is an art, requiring a mix of talents: technical, human, and conceptual. The relative importance of these SKILLS varies with the particular managerial assignment. These talents must be accompanied by the "psychological factors" of realistic self-appraisal, initiative, integrity, and, the ability to cope with STRESS. Finally, in response to today's rapidly changing business environment, LEADERSHIP and the capacity for continued LEARNING and growth have become requisites for effective management.

Estimates of the annual investment in development activities for managers fall in the tens of billions of dollars (Carnevale, Gainer, & Villet, 1990). Corporations have begun to ask themselves if these funds are being put to good use; despite considerable financial outlays, many believe they do not have cadres of managers capable of adapting to today's complex and dynamic business environment (e.g., Raskas & Hambrick, 1992). Moreover, they are concerned that too often management development is not closely aligned with business strategy and hence, often fails to contribute to key corporate objectives (*see* HUMAN RESOURCES STRATEGY).

Although countless books and articles had been written on how to develop managers, until recently, few had been based on empirical research. Most viewed management development from the single dimension of *task* learning: acquisition of necessary COMPETENCIES (the knowledge and skills necessary to fulfill managerial functions) and establishment of key relationships. Management development was treated largely as an intellectual exercise, admittedly a demanding one. Consistent with this conceptual foundation, a myopic perspective of management development evolved. Management development became synonymous with helping managers in a classroom setting develop the competencies of management.

In the last 5 years, the quantity and quality of research on management development have increased (Baldwin & Padgett, 1993, or Tannenbaum & Yukl, 1992, for recent reviews). This work has spawned both a more realistic and ambitious view of managerial development. Two themes have emerged. The first is that management development is not simply a matter of changing people's knowledge and skills (task learning); it also involves changing their attitudes and professional identity (personal learning). For instance, Hill (1992) found that it was the personal learning – the psychological transformation from "specialist and doer" to "agenda-setter and networkbuilder" – not the task learning, that first-time managers found more demanding and stressful.

The second theme of the growing body of research on management development is that it is largely a process of learning by doing. Researchers at the Center for Creative Leadership have been at the forefront of identifying the lessons managers can learn from different kinds of work experiences (e.g., McCall, Lombardo, & Morrison, 1988). As they and others have observed, the unsettling truth is that managers develop most effectively when faced with adversity, given "stretch" assignments, or the opportunity to make and implement tough decisions.

As we have come to understand how managers evolve and develop over time, the focus of management development has shifted from "teaching" managers in the classroom to helping managers learn how to capitalize on the developmental opportunities of their day-to-day work experiences (e.g., Manz & Manz, 1991). The fragmentary and reactive approaches to management development traditionally followed by organizations are being replaced by more deliberate and careful CAREER planning – making sure that individuals have the right kinds of developmental experiences at the right time (e.g., Hall & Foulkes, 1991) (*see* CAREER TRANSITIONS).

Research shows that individuals who successfully manage a particular organization in a particular industry usually have spent significant time in it. Going outside an organization to fill general management positions can be a risky proposition. Outsiders, even with exceptional track records, rarely have the detailed knowledge of the business and organization required to perform well. In response to these findings, companies have begun to link their management development initiatives with long-term business planning. Since it takes from 10 to 20 years to develop an effective general manager, companies are beginning to identify critical competencies executives will need in the future and cultivating them now in their highest potential managers (e.g., Baldwin & Padgett, 1993) (*see* MANAGEMENT OF HIGH POTENTIAL). In the current competitive and dynamic environment, it is not easy to adopt such a developmental perspective. The pressure for short-term results is intense. RESTRUCTURING and DOWNSIZING have reduced loyalty on the part of both companies and their employees; people no longer expect to stay with the same organization over the course of their careers (interestingly, some companies are using developmental assignments as incentives to retain high-potential employees).

Formal TRAINING, both corporate and university based, is being understood as simply one tool in the toolbox for management development. The content and pedagogy of formal training are being revisited, with attention paid to both task and personal learning and more emphasis placed on experiential and action-learning models. There is increasing investment in action learning in which managers work in small project teams on real problems in real companies (e.g., Mumford, 1987) (*see* TEAM BUILDING). Companies and academics alike are trying to figure out how to leverage and integrate formal training with on-the-job training. Consequently, there is a move toward apprenticeship models of management development, which focus on informal developmental tools like job rotation, coaching, and MENTORING.

Despite the proliferation of research related to managerial development, there is still much to be learned. We have just begun to identify the specific kinds of experiences important to developing managers and the specific lessons that each kind of experience can impart. However, providing such experiences does not guarantee that a person will learn anything, much less that he or she will learn what is intended. Some of the more intriguing research underway is trying to discover what can be done to enhance the learning that such experiences can offer and why it is that some individuals are better at learning from such experiences than others (e.g., Dechant, 1990). Finally, the emphasis of management development is shifting from individual development to achieving strategic goals or transforming ORGANIZATIONAL CULTURE. A promising area of inquiry in this regard is the research on the "LEARNING ORGANIZATION," organizations whose managers are self-directed learners and which are able to expeditiously respond and adapt to a forever changing business environment (*see* SELF-REGULATION).

See also **Joining-up process; Management education; Managerial behavior; Women managers**

Bibliography

Baldwin, T. T. & Padgett, M. Y. (1993). Management development: A review and commentary. *The International Review of Industrial and Organizational Psychology*, 8, 35–85.

Carnevale, A. P., Gainer, L. J. & Villet, J. (1990). *Training in America: The organization and strategic role of training*. San Francisco CA: Jossey-Bass.

Dechant, K. (1990). Knowing how to learn: The "neglected" management ability. *Journal of Management Development*, **9**, 40–49.

Hall, D. T. & Foulkes, F. K. (1990). Succession planning as a competitive advantage. In L. W. Foster (Ed). *Advances in applied business strategy*, vol. 2. Greenwich, CT: JAI Press.

Hill, L. A. (1992). *Becoming a manager: Mastery of a new identity*. Boston, MA: Harvard Business School Press.

Manz, C. C. & Manz, K. P. (1991). Strategies for facilitating self-directed learning: A process for enhancing human resource development. *Human Resource Development Quarterly*, **2**, 3–12.

McCall, M. W., Lombardo, M. M. & Morrison, A. M. (1988). *The lessons of experience*. Lexington, MA: Lexington Books.

Mumford, A. (1987). Action learning. *Journal of Management Development* [Special Issue], **6**, 1–70.

Raskas, D. F. & Hambrick, D. C. (1992). Multifunctional managerial development: A framework for evaluating the options. *Organizational Dynamics*, **21**, 5–17.

Tannenbaum, S. I. & Yukl, G. (1992). Training and development in work organizations. *Annual Review of Psychology*, **43**, 399–441.

LINDA A. HILL

management education In its modern sense, management education developed first in the United States in the early years of the twentieth century. Many of the early institutions of higher learning in management were funded directly by donations from prominent alumni and other successful businessmen. This trend has remained a feature of management education in the United States though, to a lesser extent, in the United Kingdom, Europe, and Japan with the Master of Business Administration (MBA) degree becoming established as the flagship program in management education after 1945. In a survey undertaken in the early 1970s, the British Science and Engineering Research Council stated "Only one radically new degree has become established at postgraduate level and that is the MBA." In the United Kingdom, two major reports undertaken to fathom the reasons for the continuing relative decline in British industrial and manufacturing success recommended that business schools "on the American pattern" should be established in the United Kingdom.

Developments in Europe have followed diverse paths, not all based on the American model and the MBA program. In France, the "Grandes Ecoles" on which traditionally entry to the professional and scientific elites had been based, expanded to include new institutions such as the Ecoles Superieurs de Commerce and the Hautes Ecoles de Commerce. Other schools such as INSEAD, IMEDE, IMI and IESE were based on looser variants of the American pattern, to cater for the emerging international market of managers in large multinational enterprises (*see* MULTINATIONAL CORPORATIONS). In Germany, business education was more normally subsumed within the traditional pattern of engineering formation and occurred under such guises as business economics of which marketing, for example, and finance were both perceived to be subdisciplines. In Japan, business and management education has typically been the province of corporate MANAGEMENT DEVELOPMENT, though latterly some attempts have been made to institute business schools of the conventional North American type.

The pedagogy of management education has been equally diverse but has traditionally emphasized learning in the functional disciplines of management such as marketing, production, personnel, HUMAN RESOURCE MANAGEMENT and finance, often based in a foundation program in economics, social science, quantitative methods and sometimes computer skills and study skills. Management education has not so far been characterized by a common core set of integrating theories. To some extent, management development loosely based on theories and practices in the organizational and individual social sciences has provided an integrating focus.

Management development as a practitioner-based area of activity coincided with the maturing development of the emerging concepts of behavioral and social sciences, in the 1970s moving from a focus on individuals as the object of TRAINING to encompass the organization itself as the basis for management learning. This has coincided with a growing emphasis on counseling, coaching, and career planning activities which emphasized the individual manager's responsibility for his or her own personal development. This period also saw the inception of action learning, project-based learning and live learning in more open-ended, TEAM BUILDING activities offered by independent training institutions.

The 1980s introduced theories of management learning which emphasized the three-way responsibility of individual, organization, and educational institutions for planning, individual learning, and ORGANIZATION DEVELOPMENT. The focus has therefore moved since the late 1940s when management was seen as an, albeit newly fledged, emerging, positive science in which predictability, planning, and deterministic models of behavior were the basis of understanding. More recently, theorists have characterized the essential unpredictability of organizational processes, seeing management education as an opportunity for the individual to acquire behavioral SKILLS, including the skills of learning. Current practice is embedded in an understanding that individuals present for a formal program of management education with a good deal of experience and some possibly quite specific expectations, and exit the formal stage of management education with an increased range of options for managing his or her own subsequent CAREER.

Parallel developments in the theory of organization have repositioned organization development in terms of the management of change. This has been based on a more subtle understanding of the nature of ORGANIZATIONAL CULTURE and ORGANIZATIONAL CLIMATE as looser and less systematic congeries of beliefs, attitudes, behaviors, and symptomatologies than totally structured patterns of belief and interpretation. The concept of the LEARNING ORGANIZATION has become significant as a function of this transition. Organization development theory, summarized in Burke (1994), offers a wider framework for the definition of management education. This approach reinforces a substantial broadening of knowledge and practice to include an emphasis on network structures, new forms of employer–employee contracts, and different approaches to the utilization of organizational POWER beyond those modalities relevant in hierarchical organizations. The identification of the opportunities available to an individual organization by means of a correct analysis of market segmentation, growth, and product development has been modified to incorporate new thinking about STRATEGIC ALLIANCES within and between organizations, and the role of cultural variables.

There has been a parallel shift in the orientation of professionals to the generation of new knowledge. Earlier models of management education located knowledge in university research faculties and identified the task of professional schools of management as that of disseminating knowledge which, in a sense, they "owned." It is now more generally presumed that knowledge is generated in the field at least as much as in the academy.

The changing structures of organizational power and the expectations of a more liberally educated labor force have refocused the emphasis on initiative, EMPOWERMENT, and entrepreneurial modes of behavior. The relationship between instructor and student is becoming much more of a partnership. A recent compilation which deals with these issues is *Mastering Management Education*, (Vance, 1994) which covers such topics as the art and power of asking questions, experiential learning, simulation, group-based learning, as well as the traditional topics as testing, ASSESSMENT, case-based learning, and microcomputer skills.

Increasingly, the focus in both management education and management development has moved to an emphasis on the acquisition of skills, conceptual models, and tools for the self-management of individual career paths within an essentially fast moving, unreliable, and unpredictable context.

All of these developments and the apparent decline in the attractiveness of some MBA programs, threaten the market position of the university business school. Many observers believe that the United States market for MBA education is saturated. There are some indications that the United Kingdom market may be becoming much more price competitive with only a few leading schools able to sustain the research basis which was the fundamental raison d'être of the earlier more traditional university model.

See also **International management; Career stages; Human resources planning**

Bibliography

Burke, W. W. (1994). *Organizational development*. Reading, MA: Addison-Wesley.
Cameron, S. (1994). *The MBA handbook*. London: Pitman.
Cunningham, I. (1994). *The wisdom of strategic learning*. New York: McGraw-Hill.
Lessem, R. (1990). *Developmental management*. Oxford, UK: Blackwell.
Peters, T. & Waterman, R. (1982). *In search of excellence*. New York: Harper & Row.
Senge, P. (1990). *The fifth discipline*. New York: Random House.
Vance, C. M. (1994). *Mastering management education*. Beverly Hills, CA: Sage.

DAVID T. H. WEIR

management of change *see* CONSULTANCY INTERVENTION MODELS; ORGANIZATIONAL CHANGE; ORGANIZATION DEVELOPMENT

management of diversity The phrase managing diversity has become widely accepted as a broad umbrella term that refers to management practices aimed at improving the effectiveness with which organizations utilize their diverse human resources. In the era when MASS PRODUCTION methods dominated business activity, many organizations managed diversity simply by avoiding it. Product specialization helped keep costs low, a function-based organizational form was almost universal, and the employees in most organizations all looked pretty much alike; often those employees who were different were segregated into one section of the company. Now many mass product markets have been replaced by smaller specialty markets, consumer markets are more precisely defined, and large businesses operate in multiple niches. Doing so often means that distinctly different business units – each with its own unique structure, strategy, management processes and organizational subculture – must synergistically coexist under one roof (DeLuca & McDowell, 1992). At the same time that business and organizational diversity is increasing, the diversity of human resources within organizations is increasing. Due to changing workforce demographics, globalization, and a desire to employ people who reflect their customer base, organizations in many countries are becoming more diverse in terms of GENDER, RACE, ETHNICITY, religion, national origin, AGE, area of expertise, and many other personal characteristics. Consequently, in modern organizations around the world, managers are finding that they must learn to embrace diversity and manage it effectively in order to ensure business success.

The nature of diversity in organizations

Demographic and cultural diversity are two important types of diversity in modern organizations. Throughout the world, women are entering the workforce in growing numbers. With the decline of gender-based segregation in the workplace, men and women are now more often found working side-by-side (*see* SEX DIFFERENCES; WOMEN MANAGERS; WOMEN AT WORK). In some countries, age diversity is also increasing, as declining rates of population growth push employers to hire both more youth and more older employees. Furthermore, as organizations allow the higher education of younger employees to substitute for the job experience that previous cohorts of employees had to accrue in order to be promoted, relatively young employees are found more often in higher-level jobs. Ethnic and cultural diversity also are increasingly important. For example, as the 1980s drew to a close, the U.S. Department of Labor projected that 22 percent of new entrants into the labor force would be immigrants and that an additional 20 percent would be ethnic minorities. In many European countries, ethnic and cultural diversity are increasing due to the consolidation of economic markets and related changes in immigration and employment policies. And, throughout the world, managing cultural diversity has become essential as corporations have expanded their operations into foreign countries and/or developed STRATEGIC ALLIANCES with foreign-owned firms (*see* INTERNATIONAL HUMAN RESOURCES MANAGEMENT and INTERNATIONAL MANAGEMENT).

The issue of managing diversity is important even in organizations where the workforce has not become more demographically and/or culturally diverse because many organizations are utilizing WORK GROUPS to pursue new business strategies. These often bring together employees from previously segregated areas of the company, creating occupational and knowl-

Table 1 Taxonomy of Primary Constructs in a Framework for Understanding Diversity.

1. Aspects of Diversity: Content and Structure	2. Mediating States and Processes	3. Short-term Behavioral Manifestations	4. Longer-term Consequences
Level of Analysis: Individual			
Readily detectable attributes: • Task-related: organizational tenure, team tenure, dep't./unit membership, memberships in task-relevant external networks, formal credentials, educational level • Relations-oriented: sex, culture (race, ethnicity, national origin), age, memberships in formal organizations (e.g., religious and political), physical features Underlying attributes: • Task-related knowledge, skills, abilities (cognitive and physical), experience • Relations-oriented: social status, attitudes, values, personality, behavioral style, extra-team social ties	Task-related: • Information processing (e.g., attention, recall) • Learning (e.g., discovery, creativity) • Task-based information • Power to control tangible resources • Power to control human resources Relations-oriented: • Social cognitive processes: operation of stereotypes and schema-based expectancies • Affective responses: attraction, anxiety, fear, guilt, frustration, discomfort	Task-related: • Seeking/offering/receiving work-related information, tangible resources, or human resources • Initiating/responding to influence attempts Relations-oriented: • Seeking/offering/receiving social information and/or support	Task-related: • Personal performance (speed, creativity, accuracy) • Satisfaction w/performance of self and team • Acquisition of knowledge and skills re: technical aspects of task managing human and tangible resources • Establishment of position in work communication networks Relations-oriented: • Acquisition of interpersonal knowledge and skills re: interpersonal aspects of task, • Establishment of position in social communication networks (within team and in external environment) • Satisfaction with social relationships

Level of Analysis: Interpersonal			
• Interpersonal (dis)similarity in terms of readily detectable and underlying attributes: Dyadic Individual-to-social group Individual-to-work team	Task-related: • Differences in task-based cognitions • Expertise-based status differentials • Differences in power over tangible and/or human resources Relations-oriented: • Social familiarity • Diffuse status differentials • Differences in social cognitions • Differences in affective responses	Task-related: • Exchanges/negotiations/consolidation of task-related information, tangible resources, or human resources Relations-oriented: • Exchanges/consolidation of social information and/or support	Task-related: • Power balance Relations-oriented: • Status hierarchy • Balance of interpersonal accounts (e.g., political debts and credits) • Solidification of friendship coalitions
Level of Analysis: Groups and Organizations			
• Composition: heterogeneity versus homogeneity of readily detectable and underlying attributes • Special configurations: Presence of "tokens" Presence of small minority faction Bipolar group composition	Task-related: • Shape of expertise-based status hierarchy • Patterns of task-based cognitions • Shape of power distributions for control of tangible and/or human resources Relations-oriented: • Stage of team socialization • Shape of diffuse social status hierarchy • Patterns of social cognitions • Patterns of affective responses among members	Task-related: • Task-related communication networks • Allocation and use of tangible and human resources • Influence networks Relations-oriented: • Friendship communication networks	Task-related: • Group/Organization performance (speed, accuracy, creativity) • Group/Organization satisfaction with performance • Group/Organization learning about technical aspects of task, and about the management of tangible and human resources Relations-oriented • Membership stability • Adoption of social structures (e.g., norms & roles, influence networks, friendship networks)

Adapted from S. E. Jackson, K. E. May, & K. Whitney (1994). Used with permission.

edge-based diversity. Teams may also bring together employees from two or more organizations. For example, manufacturers may include their suppliers and end users as part of a product design team. Such teams must develop a mode of operating that fits with the differing ORGANIZATIONAL CULTURES in which the subunits are embedded (Hofstede, 1991).

Table 1 illustrates the multitude of phenomena that are relevant to the topic of managing diversity. Within this framework, diversity is placed as a construct that appears early in the causal chain of events.

The Content and Structure of Diversity

Individual attributes reflect the *content* of diversity; in contrast, the configuration of attributes within a social unit reflects the *structure* of diversity. Terms for referring to the structure of diversity differ across levels of analysis, from interpersonal (dis)similarity to group and organizational composition. At the group and organizational levels, one of the most studied aspects of composition is *heterogeneity*. Along the continuum of homogeneity–heterogeneity, a few structural configurations have drawn special attention, including the demographic "token" or "solo" members, the presence of a small minority faction, and a bipolar team composition, with two equal-size coalitions present. Such configurations can be particularly influential in affecting GROUP DYNAMICS (*see also* COALITION FORMATION, MINORITY GROUP INFLUENCE, GROUP DECISION MAKING).

Consequences of Diversity

Diversity has many short-term and longer-term consequences. Detailed reviews of research examining these consequences (e.g., Jackson, May, & Whitney, 1995; Moreland & Levine, 1992) indicate that the consequences of diversity depend upon the precise nature of diversity being studied. For example, the amount and type of STEREOTYPING that people engage in can be influenced by the structure of diversity within a group but this is most likely to be true only for easily detected attributes such as sex, race, and age. Diversity in terms of task-related, underlying attributes is likely to reduce GROUPTHINK and improve the quality and CREATIVITY of a group's decision-making processes, but diversity in terms of relations-oriented attributes does not have clear consequences for group decision making. At the organizational level, diversity in terms of relations-oriented attributes appears to increase the amount of TURNOVER that occurs among employees – presumably because it causes interpersonal CONFLICT and interferes with COMMUNICATIONS (*see* NETWORK ANALYSIS). This sounds as if diversity may be detrimental, but there are good reasons and some evidence to believe diversity can be beneficial for organizations because it improves their ability to adapt quickly to a changing environment (*see* ORGANIZATIONAL DEMOGRAPHY; TOP MANAGEMENT TEAMS).

Practical Implications

No single theory explains the full set of beneficial and detrimental effects of diversity in work organizations and this makes it difficult for organizations confidently to develop effective means for managing diversity. Nevertheless, in recognition of the growing importance of diversity, many large and prominent firms began to implement "managing diversity" initiatives during the late 1980s. Such initiatives have proliferated since then and are now a major HUMAN RESOURCE MANAGEMENT activity. Examples of the approaches being used to effectively manage diversity include: nontraditional work arrangements such as job sharing, FLEXITIME, and telecommuting; education and TRAINING programs intended to reduce stereotyping, BIAS, and PREJUDICE, increase cultural sensitivity, and develop INTERPERSONAL SKILLS for working in multicultural environments; career management programs designed to promote constructive FEEDBACK to employees, MENTORING relationships, and access to informal networks; and new employee benefits, such as expanded parental leave and dependent care assistance. Such programs often are implemented in organizations that have already been proactive in their attempts to reduce DISCRIMINATION and provide EQUAL OPPORTUNITIES to a broad array of employees. They are also found in some organizations with large numbers of EXPATRIATES working abroad.

Ultimately, the best approach to managing diversity will depend on the types of diversity present in an organization and the outcomes of most concern to the organization. Therefore, those who wish to improve the ability of an organization to manage diversity effectively must be willing to develop a comprehensive approach tailored to their specific situation. It is impossible to prescribe interventions that will be universally acceptable, but organizations that have been successful in their efforts to effectively manage diversity appear to use the following principles to guide the process of ORGANIZATIONAL CHANGE (see Jackson & Associates, 1992, for several case descriptions; for more general discussions of how organizations are approaching the management of diversity, *see* Jamieson & O'Mara, 1991; Morrison, 1992).

Assess the organization's current state. Before launching new diversity initiatives, the organization's current human resource management practices should be analyzed to determine why things are the way they are and which things should stay the way they are. This includes evaluating whether current practices encourage or limit diversity, understanding the forces that support the use of the organization's present system of management, and assessing which aspects of the current system are consistent with the organization's current needs. Questions to be answered include: What are the backgrounds of people in the organization and how is diversity distributed throughout the organization? Do people with diverse backgrounds work closely together, or are they segregated into homogeneous subgroups based on occupations, hierarchical level, or geographic location? How do the backgrounds of people relate to their ATTITUDES and behaviors? Do subgroups of employees report different degrees of satisfaction with their coworkers or the supervision they receive? Are turnover patterns different among different groups of employees? Does CAREER mobility appear to differ across subgroups?

Set objectives. The next task is to set objectives and prioritize the dimensions of diversity that are important for the organization to address. These objectives might include: meeting social and legal responsibilities, attracting and retaining a qualified workforce, facilitating teamwork, creating synergy between dispersed and diverse work units, and spanning the boundary between the organization and its markets (*see* BOUNDARY SPANNING). Which objectives are top priorities for an organization will influence the types of diversity that must be managed and the types of initiatives likely to be most useful.

Design interventions that fit the situation. **The customers.** To be effective, new initiatives require buy-in from all relevant "customers." The customer metaphor emphasizes the importance of designing and delivering initiatives which customers see as valuable, are aware of, and evaluate positively. To achieve these objectives, close customer contact is essential. This includes contact with those who are targeted as the direct users (e.g., those attending a workshop) as well as those in a position to encourage or discourage the direct customers' use of a service.

The boundaries of the change effort. Many organizations are actively participating in new alliances with their suppliers, customers, and even their competitors. As interorganization alliances become more common, so do the pressures to extend human resources management practices beyond the organization's formal boundaries. Initiatives extending beyond organizational borders might include establishing relationships with schools (grade schools, high schools, and colleges) as well as community groups and other local businesses (*see* INTERORGANIZATIONAL RELATIONS).

Resources. Unrealistic expectations for quick and easy results may mean potentially useful change efforts are prematurely shut down. To avoid this, resources needed for new initiatives (e.g., time, money, people) should be analyzed carefully. Then a decision can be made about whether the resources are available to invest in order to capture the potential benefits of diversity and/or reduce its negative consequences.

Institutionalize New Learning

Initiatives for creating organizational changes are likely to involve many different people working on many different projects in many different places over a long period of time. A large amount of knowledge and information is likely to be generated. Recording systematically what is learned is an important first step, but this is not enough. Whereas standard operating procedures may ensure that systematically collected information is summarized and recorded in the form of a report, in order to institutionalize the ORGANIZATIONAL LEARNING, official policies and practices of the organization must change to reflect the new information.

Conclusion

Diversity is a complex and potentially "hot" issue with many facets. Although relatively little is known about what are the most effective ways to manage diversity within organizations, it is clear that almost all organizations must learn to manage diverse human resources. As is true for most strategic issues, the most effective approach to managing diversity differs from one organization to the next, so those who wish to improve an organization's effectiveness must be prepared to find and tailor solutions and approaches to fit their unique situation. This implies a learn-as-you-go approach. Inevitably, the learning process will be jolting at times, as change agents, supervisors, subordinates, and coworkers realize the need for changes within themselves, in their organization's culture, and in the basic human resources management systems of the organization. Some jolts may be beneficial for the change process, but too many jolts may bring the process to a screeching halt. To avoid this, managers are encouraged to diagnose carefully their own organization's situation and the types of diversity of most strategic importance, learn as much as possible about the potential costs and benefits of diversity and homogeneity before initiating change, work closely with the people who will be affected by any change process, monitor changes in individuals and the systems as a whole, and make adjustments as needed. This type of long-term, strategically oriented approach to managing diversity offers the greatest potential for success.

See also **Individual differences; Intercultural process; Culture, national; Culture, cross-cultural research**

Bibliography

Adler, N. J. (1991). *International dimensions of organizational behavior*. Boston, MA: Kent.

Cox, T. H. (1993). *Cultural diversity in organizations*. San Francisco, CA: Berrett-Koehler.

DeLuca, J. M. & McDowell, R. N. (1992). Managing diversity: A strategic "grass-roots" approach. In S. E. Jackson & Associates, *Diversity in the workplace: Human resources initiatives*. New York: Guilford.

Hofstede, G. (1991). *Cultures and organizations: Software of the mind*. London: McGraw-Hill.

Jackson, S. E. & Associates (1992). *Diversity in the workplace: Human resources initiatives*. New York: Guilford.

Jackson, S. E., May, K. E. & Whitney, K. (1995). Understanding the dynamics of diversity in decision making teams. In R. A. Guzzo & E. Salas (Eds), *Team effectiveness and decision making in organizations*. San Francisco, CA: Jossey-Bass.

Jamieson, D. & O'Mara, J. (1991). *Managing workforce 2000: Gaining the diversity advantage*. San Francisco CA: Jossey-Bass.

Moreland, R. L. & Levine, J. M. (1992). The composition of small groups. In E. J. Lawler, B. Markovsky, C. Ridgeway & H. Walker (Eds), *Advances in group processes* (vol. 9). Greenwich, CT: JAI Press.

Morrison, A. M. (1992). *The new leaders: Guidelines on diversity in America*. San Francisco CA: Jossey-Bass.

Thomas, R. R., Jr. (1991). *Beyond race and gender: Unleashing the power of your total workforce by managing diversity*. New York: AMACOM.

SUSAN E. JACKSON

management of high potential The term "high potential" (HIPO) refers to people who are believed to have the potential to reach senior levels in an organization. Generally, this belief is based upon their current and potential COMPETENCIES, MOTIVATION, and aspirations. The identification, development, and management of a high potential cadre differs somewhat across companies and nations.

The identification and development of high potential people is a critical factor for the long-term sustainability of many organizations, but the importance is particularly marked in those companies committed to "growing their own talent" through the use of the internal labor markets (the types of companies which Sonnenfeld and Peiperl (1988) refer to as Clubs and Academies). Systematic attempts to optimize the development of talented young people have in some companies resulted in *fast track* career management process.

Introduced some 30 years ago by a number of MULTINATIONAL CORPORATIONS, these fast track processes recreated the accelerated development of talent seen in the army and civil service. Talented people are identified at an early stage of their career and participate in a range of short cross-functional and international job assignments whilst receiving close senior management attention and MENTORING. These processes are created in part to establish and sustain a PSYCHOLOGICAL CONTRACT which enables the short-term inconvenience of mobility and job pressure experienced by the individual to be off set against the promise of longer-term POWER and resource gains. Fast track processes also serve to develop the breadth of vision and internal networks which some (e.g., Kotter, 1982) believe to be essential to senior management effectiveness (*see* NETWORKING). The facilitation of cross-functional and international assignments are underpinned by succession processes such as succession lists and senior management resource committees (*see* SUCCESSION PLANNING). The role of these processes is to ensure that those jobs deemed to have develop potential are assigned to nominated high potential people. Since their introduction, surveys in both Europe and North America show that fast track processes have become an increasingly familiar feature in large organizations (Derr, Jones, & Tommey, 1988; Thompson, Kirkham, & Dixon, 1985).

For companies which grow rapidly through acquisition or are highly decentralized into relatively autonomous business streams, fast track processes could be seen as overly bureaucratic, centrally controlled, inflexible with an overly long-term focus. In these acquisitive, bottom-line orientated companies a "JUST-IN-TIME" process of development and succession is more likely to be used. The emphasis is on significant and stretching job experiences, close management mentoring, and appraisal underpinned with highly performance orientated reward mechanisms (Gratton & Syrett, 1990). Talented individuals are "thrown in at the deep end" and expected to sink or swim. It is both short-term performance rather than long-term potential which is actively monitored and rewarded.

High potential management processes such as "fast tracks" can be found in companies across the world. However, researchers have described some fundamental cross-national differences in the identification, development, and management of high potential people (Evans, Doz, & Laurent, 1989; Pieper, 1990) (*see* INTERNATIONAL MANAGEMENT). The mapping of these cultural traditions has included the Japanese model, the Latin European approach, the Germanic tradition and the Anglo-Dutch model. The Japanese model is based on the recruitment of elite cohorts and a competitive tournament of elimination, leading the winners into executive positions (*see* TOURNAMENT PROMOTION). A rather similar process is found in French companies were the selection of top managers also takes place at entry, mostly on the basis of elite educational qualifications. The Germanic tradition is rather different, with a tradition of formal apprenticeship and more attachment to functional career paths. The generalist notion of high potential development is most rooted in the Anglo-Saxon culture. Entry is less elitist with graduates recruited for specific functional or technical jobs. Around their late 20s those individuals with potential are identified and enter the "fast track" described earlier.

Over the last decade, the issue of high potential development has received increasing attention. The debate has focused on the operationalizing of high potential identification and development, and the impact of future organizational forms and structures which affect managerial requirements.

The delivery of intensely structured, controlled, and centralized high potential development processes are presenting real challenges for organizations. From a supply perspective, dual CAREERS are limiting mobility , "one off" early identification can fail to build on the talents of late developers and women who have taken a CAREER BREAK (*see* WOMEN MANAGERS). Perhaps most importantly, the basis of the PSYCHOLOGICAL CONTRACT is under threat as even the most established organizations simultaneously delayer and recruit senior executives from the external labor market. As a consequence, they can no longer promise or deliver a life-time career. The demand perspective is just as bleak as early as 1988. Derr et al. reported that 28 percent of the companies they surveyed could no longer deliver a range of jobs and vertically accelerated job opportunities.

There is also a debate about whether structured and controlled processes are capable of identifying and developing executives capable of operating in the flat, matrix, team and project-based structures which will characterize an increasing number of companies (*see* MATRIX ORGANIZATION). It has been argued that individuals who have participated in accelerated vertical development do not develop open, empathic behaviors (Drath, 1990). This is supported by Luthans, Rosenkrantz, & Hennessy (1985) who report that those managers who have experienced most rapid promotion are observed to spend significantly more time networking, but less time giving credit, delegating and letting subordinates determine their own work. Clearly a challenge for the 1990s is how to develop high potential people to work comfortably and effectively in flatter, team-based structures.

See also **Career plateauing; Career transitions; Human resource planning; International human resource management; Management development; Performance appraisal**

Bibliography

Drath, W. H. (1990). Managerial strengths and weaknesses as functions of the development of personal meaning. *The Journal of Applied Behavioral Science*, **26**, (4), 483–499.

Derr, B., Jones, C. & Toomey, E. (1988). Managing high-potential employees: Current practices in thirty-three U.S. corporations. *Human Resource Management*, **27**, (3), 273–290.

Evans, P., Doz, Y. & Laurant, A. (1989). *Human resource management in international firms*. London: Macmillan.

Gratton, L. C. & Syrett, M. (1990). Heirs apparent: Succession strategies for the 90s. *Personnel Management*, 34–38

Kotter, J. P. (1982). *The general managers*. New York: Free Press.

Luthens, F., Rosenkrantz, S. & Hennessy, H. (1985). What successful managers really do? *Journal of Applied Behavioral Science*, **21**, 255–270.

Pieper, R. (1990). *Human resource management: An international comparison*. Berlin: Walter de Gruyter.

Sonnenfeld, J. & Peiperl, M. (1988). Staffing policy as a strategic response: A typology of career systems. *Academy of Management Review*, **13**, 588–600.

Thompson, P. H., Kirkham, K. & Dixon, J. (1985). Warning: The fast-track may be hazardous to organisational health. *Organizational Dynamics*, Spring, 21–33.

LYNDA GRATTON

managerial behavior The behavior of managers has been the subject of research since the 1950s. This research, prompted partly by an academic concern to examine how far management theory applied in practice and partly by a practical concern to furnish evidence on which MANAGEMENT EDUCATION, TRAINING/development, RECRUITMENT, and PERFORMANCE APPRAISAL might be based, has occurred in a variety of contexts and has employed a variety of methods.

Clearly, what constitutes "managerial behavior" depends on how "managers" and "behavior" are defined. Conventionally, managers have been regarded as those taking responsibility for the work of at least one other individual and designated as "managers" by their employing organization. However, with the diminution of HIERARCHY and the erosion of DEPARTMENTALIZATION and LINE-STAFF distinctions, together with the concomitant growth of SELF-MANAGED TEAMS, JOB ENRICHMENT and cross-functional projects, the boundaries between managers, professionals, and non-managers have become less clear-cut (*see* PROFESSIONALS IN ORGANIZATIONS). Distinguishing exclusively *managerial* behavior is increasingly difficult. Moreover, since "management," as a broad process, is not synonymous with what "managers," as an occupational category, do, the claim of some research on managerial behavior to have "disproved" CLASSICAL MANAGEMENT THEORY is questionable.

As for "behavior," research faces the problem of distinguishing among managerial *work*, *jobs* as clusters of work and *behavior* within jobs; between what managers are *expected* to do and what they *actually* do; and between the *ends* (tasks/responsibilities) and *means* (actions/behavior) of managerial work. In practice, studies of actual behavior in the context of jobs defined organizationally as "managerial" have predominated. From these have resulted conceptual models which seek to depict and explain managerial behavior and a set of empirical findings which shed light on its content and form.

Among the models which have been developed are: the conception of managers as subject to "demands," "constraints," and "choices" (Stewart, 1982; 1991); managerial work as a configuration of "interpersonal," "informational," and "decisional" roles (Mintzberg, 1973); the view of managers developing and pursuing "agendas" through "networks" of contacts (Kotter, 1982); analysis of the "expectations" surrounding managerial positions (Machin, 1982); and the notion of how different "managerial divisions of labor" impinge on managerial behavior (Hales, 1993). These models demonstrate a discernible shift over time away from viewing managerial behavior as an aggregate of static elements toward a greater appreciation of its dynamic and processual character.

Research findings demonstrate both commonalities and variations in managerial behavior. The *content* of managerial behavior (i.e., *what* managers do) commonly involves both specialist/professional and general managerial elements, with the latter including some combination of:

1. Acting as a figurehead, representative, and point of contact of a work unit or team.
2. Monitoring and disseminating information.
3. Negotiating with subordinates, superiors, colleagues, and those outside the organization.
4. Monitoring workflow, handling disturbances, and problem solving.
5. Allocating human, material, and financial resources.
6. Recruiting, training, directing, and controlling staff.
7. NETWORKING, forming contacts, and liaising with others.
8. Innovating, by seeking new objectives or methods of working.
9. PLANNING and scheduling work.
10. Engaging in "informal" activities such as instrumental socializing and organizational POLITICS.

The *form* of managerial behavior (*how* managers work) commonly exhibits the following characteristics:

(a) Fragmentation, with commuting between short, interrupted activities.
(b) Frequent reaction to, rather than initiation of, events and the requests of others.
(c) A concern with ad hoc, day-to-day exigencies.
(d) NEGOTIATION over the boundaries, content, and style of performance of the manager's job.
(e) Embeddedness, with decisions and plans developed in the course of other activities.
(f) A high level of interaction with others, often face-to-face.
(g) Pressure, CONFLICT, and contradictory demands.
(h) A degree of choice over what gets done and how.

Whilst these basic characteristics have remained fairly stable over time, a number of important developments and shifts in emphasis have taken place, stemming from increasingly fluid and ambiguous managerial job responsibilities. In particular, managers' behavior has become less focused on allocating and administering resources within a clearly defined work unit and more concerned with innovating, securing resources, and activities which span unit and organizational boundaries (*see* BOUNDARY-SPANNING). Consequently, it has become more fragmented, exigent, embedded, and interactive, concerned less with vertical relationships, involving the direction and CONTROL of subordinates, more with horizontal and external relationships, involving networking, and negotiation with a broad set of constituencies.

As well as these variations over time, there are also well-documented variations in managerial behavior by individual, position, function, organization, industry, and CULTURE. Variations in ROLE configurations, balance of work content, allocation of time, work patterns, contact patterns, interaction with others, and degree of choice have all been demonstrated (Stewart, 1991). One problem, however, is that some of this variation is as much an artefact of different research approaches as a reflection of substantive differences in managerial behavior. Consequently, studies reliant on single methods, such as diaries, observation or structured questionnaires, have given way to multimethod studies (*see* RESEARCH METHODS). The body of knowledge on managerial behavior remains somewhat disconnected, however.

Constructing a more integrated framework for analyzing managerial behavior is, therefore, one of a number of likely future developments in the field. Tackling the question of what constitutes *effective* managerial behavior is another, given the importance attached to managerial activity as a determinant of organizational performance. Only recently has research addressed this question directly (Luthans, Hodgetts, & Rosencrantz 1988), not least because of difficulties in establishing agreed criteria of effectiveness (*see* ORGANIZATIONAL EFFECTIVENESS). Thus, whether the reactive, fragmentary, and exigent nature of much managerial behavior indicates managerial ineffectiveness in applying rational planning and control or an effective way of handling the ambiguities of managing within complex organizations remains a matter of debate.

The connection between managerial behavior and its context requires further exploration and explanation in the light of current changes to that context. The link between BUREAUCRACY and managerial behavior is well documented (Hannaway, 1989; Jackall, 1989) but rapid organizational RESTRUCTURING means that the general relationship between forms of organization structure/culture and managerial behavior needs to be better understood. So too does the influence of national culture on managerial behavior, given the increasing internationalization of managerial relationships and careers (*see* INTERNATIONAL HUMAN RESOURCE MANAGEMENT; EXPATRIATES).

See also **Job design; Leadership; Managerial style; Management, classical theory; Management, international; Women managers**

Bibliography

Hales, C. P. (1986). What do managers do? A critical review of the evidence. *Journal of Management Studies*, **23**, (1), 88–115.

Hales, C. P. (1993). *Managing through organisation*. London: Routledge.

Hannaway, J. (1989). *Managers managing: The workings of an administrative system*. Oxford, UK: Oxford University Press.

Jackall, R. (1989). *Moral mazes: The world of corporate managers*. Oxford, UK: Oxford University Press.

Kotter, P. (1982). *The general managers*. New York: Free Press.

Luthans, F., Hodgetts, R. M. & Rosencrantz, S.A. (1988). *Real managers*. Cambridge, MA: Ballinger.

Machin, J. L. J. (1982). *The expectations approach*. Maidenhead, UK: McGraw-Hill.

Mintzberg, H. (1973). *The nature of managerial work*. New York: Harper & Row.

Stewart, R. (1982). *Choices for the manager*. Englewood Cliffs, NJ: Prentice-Hall.

Stewart, R. (1991). *Managing today and tomorrow*. Basingstoke, UK: Macmillan.

COLIN L. HALES

managerial grid The grid is formed by examining managerial behavior on two orthogonal dimensions: concern for people (the vertical axis of the grid) and concern for productivity (the horizontal axis). Managers indicate their endorsement or rejection of a set of assumptions and beliefs generating scores from 1 to 9 on each dimension. Managers are then typed in terms of their scores on the two axes:

9, 1 Authority–Obedience Management. The leader's maximum concern for production (9) is combined with a minimum concern for people (1). "Dictating to subordinates what they should do and how they should do it, the leader concentrates on maximizing production."

1, 9 "Country Club" Management. The leader shows a minimum concern for production (1) but a maximum concern for people (9). "Even at the expense of achieving results, fostering good feelings gets primary attention."

1, 1 Impoverished Management. The leader has a minimum concern for both production and people and puts forth only the least effort required to remain in the organization.

5, 5 "Organization Man" Management. The leader goes along to get along, which results in conformity to the status quo.

9, 9 Team Management. The leader integrates the concern for production and the concern for people at a high level; is goal centered; and seeks results through the participation, involvement, and commitment of all those who can contribute. The 9, 9 style is paternalistic if the leader fails to integrate the concerns of production and for people and keeps the two in logic-tight compartments. (Blake & Mouton, 1964, p. 10, in paraphrase.)

See also **Managerial style; Leadership; Managerial behavior; Leadership style**

Bibliography

Blake, R. R. & Mouton, J. S. (1964). *The managerial grid.* Houston, TX: Gulf Publishing.

BERNARD M. BASS

managerial style The pattern of managing varies with different managers in different settings. Many diverse theories provide alternative views of these styles. Classical management emphasized PLANNING, directing, and controlling subordinates. Some managers' styles emphasize one function rather than another. Increasingly, managers must see themselves as envisioning, enabling, and empowering their colleagues and as aligning the interests of their employees, management, owner–shareholders, suppliers, customers and clients, as well as their community and society (*see* STAKEHOLDERS).

See also **Theory X and Y; Theory Z; Management, classical theory; Leadership; Managerial behavior; Leadership style**

Bibliography

Kotter, J. P. (1987). *The leadership factor.* New York: Free Press.

BERNARD M. BASS

manifest and latent functions In an influential statement, Merton (1949) codified the issues and concepts that need to be considered in order to arrive at a fuller understanding of segments of social reality, such as organizations and institutions. The crux of his scheme is the distinction between manifest, intended and latent, unintended consequences of such items under analysis. Manifest functions (or consequences) are the implementation of an organization's purpose. But the complexity of the social context in which organizations are embedded, the rules and regulations required for their functioning, and the diversity of human actors needed for the implementation of these purposes have other, latent consequences which may advance or retard the basic purpose, or be unrelated to it. To inquire, for example, whether a business makes a profit from the provision of goods or services is to search for its manifest consequences; to ask whether it strengthens or undermines the health of its employees is to search for possible latent consequences.

Compared to the procedures involved in establishing manifest consequences, the identification of latent consequences is much more difficult and ambiguous. Not that it is always easy to trace the former, particularly not with patterns that have a long history – their original purposes may have become blurred or changed or be irrelevant to current conditions; in addition, many organizations have several purposes. But the logic of procedure for establishing manifest consequences is nevertheless straightforward: define the purpose or purposes and observe the extent of their implementation.

The discovery of latent consequences lacks such guidance through a defined purpose. By definition they can appear in unexpected quarters. Analytical imagination, chance observations, and vested interest in another intellectual issue are some guides to their discovery. In this manner, benefits to tourism or even to Kodak's sales volume can be identified as latent consequences of the British monarchy.

A somewhat more systematic way of identifying latent consequences consists in concentrating on explicit exclusions from the scope of an institution. Some differences between people or situations within the scope of the organization or outside it can be interpreted as the presence or absence of its latent consequences. A case in point is the situation of the unemployed, excluded from the institution of employment (*see* UNEMPLOYMENT). Many studies in several countries have conclusively demonstrated that financial STRESS is not the only consequence of job loss (*see* REDUNDANCY). Most of the unemployed carry in addition a psychological burden which they identify variously as boredom, social isolation, a sense of uselessness, uncertainty about their social identity, and enforced inactivity (*see* SELF-ESTEEM). By its manner of organization employment provides, incidental to the pursuit of its main purposes, time structure, an enlarged social network, PARTICIPATION in collective efforts, definition of social identity, and required regular activity. Experiences within some or all of these categories during employment are often unsatisfactory, but judging by the sense of psychological deprivation among the unemployed, the absence of the daily opportunity to have such experiences at all is worse. From this some latent consequences of employment have been inferred (Jahoda, 1982): they are the unintended daily provision of categories of experience which most people value and seem to need for their well-being (*see* MENTAL HEALTH).

The understanding of all organizations is enlarged by tracing both types of functions; in addition, the identification of latent functions, whether desirable or undesirable, can have significant policy implications.

See also **Agency restriction; Nonwork/work; Quality of working life**

Bibliography

Jahoda, M. (1982). *Employment and unemployment: A socialpsychological analysis.* Cambridge, MA: Cambridge University Press.

Merton, R. K. (1949). Manifest and latent functions. In R. K. Merton (Ed.), *Social theory and social structure* (pp. 21–81). Glencoe, IL: Free Press.

MARIE JAHODA

manpower planning *see* HUMAN RESOURCE PLANNING; SUCCESSION PLANNING

mass production This term refers to systems where inputs are transformed into high volumes of standardized outputs. Considered more complex than BATCH PRODUCTION, such systems are epitomized by the automobile assembly line.

Mass production is important in organizational research because many studies suggest that ORGANIZATIONAL DESIGN structure is linked to the PROCESS TECHNOLOGY the firm employs, and that high organizational performance requires matching TECHNOLOGY with structure (*see* CONTINGENCY THEORY). Mass production is generally very efficient, but inflexible. Consequently, organizational structures associated with such systems are often highly bureaucratic and mechanistic, employing elaborate rules and regulations, rigid HIERARCHY, and FUNCTIONAL DESIGN (*see* BUREAUCRACY; MECHANISTIC/ORGANIC).

Worker tasks under mass production are typically simple, standardized, repetitive, and monotonous (*see* REPETITIVE WORK). Consequently, assembly-line workers are frequently alienated from the organization and dissatisfied with their jobs (*see* ALIENATION; JOB SATISFACTION). This problem becomes exacerbated with more educated workers, since mass production was originally designed to provide relatively unskilled labor with uncomplicated tasks.

Mass production also tends to create a "PRODUCTIVITY DILEMMA" (Abernathy, 1978). The more specialized and highly integrated the assembly line becomes, the more difficult it becomes to introduce INNOVATION; for instance, little progress was made in automobile technology between 1950 and 1975 because minor model changes required shutting down assembly lines for several months to reorganize and retool.

See also **Automation; Advanced manufacturing technology; Technology**

Bibliography

Abernathy, W. J. (1978). *The productivity dilemma: Roadblock to innovation in the automobile industry.* Baltimore: Johns Hopkins University Press.

Hounshell, D. A. (1984). *From the American system to mass production 1900–1932: The development of manufacturing technology in the United States.* Baltimore: Johns Hopkins University Press.

Walker, C. R. & Guest, R. H. (1952). *The man on the assembly line.* Cambridge, MA: Harvard University Press.

Woodward, J. (1970). *Industrial organization: Theory and practice* (2nd edn). Oxford, UK: Oxford University Press.

PHILIP ANDERSON

matrix organization The distinctive feature of a matrix organization is that some individuals report to two (or even more) bosses. This form of organization, the only major type of ORGANIZATIONAL DESIGN with its origins in the twentieth century, violates the classic principle of unitary command ("one-person–one-boss") (*see also* CLASSICAL DESIGN THEORY; HIERARCHY; MECHANISTIC/ORGANIC). It is employed when firms must:

(i) tightly coordinate or balance two or more dimensions such as resources (e.g., functional expertise) and businesses (e.g., products or projects);
(ii) while facing uncertainties that require high information processing; and
(iii) strong constraints on financial and human resources.

The matrix can be viewed as a diamond with three roles: the top manager who heads up and balances the dual chains of command; two or more matrix bosses who share common subordinates, and the individuals who report to the two different matrix bosses. However, a point to be emphasized is that matrix organization is more than this matrix structure. The dual structure must be supported by matrixed processes such as joint GOAL-SETTING, dual evaluation systems, by matrix LEADERSHIP behavior and individual SKILLS, and by a matrix CULTURE that constructively resolves conflicts and balances POWER (Davis & Lawrence, 1977).

The origins of matrix organization are to be found in the US space program of the 1960s, where the challenge was to meet President Kennedy's target of putting man on the moon by 1970, requiring highly complex project coordination, while meeting Congressional cost constraints. The term was supposedly coined by mathematically training engineers to describe this evolution in PROJECT MANAGEMENT. Today, one recognizes that matrix organization takes different shapes on a continuum. Taking the continuum between function and project-oriented organization as an example, at each extreme are nonmatrix traditional organizations, where functional and project hierarchies are coordinated by general management at the top (*see* TOP MANAGEMENT TEAMS). Then there is the unbalanced matrix where one party is dominant (the secondary reporting lines are often denoted by dotted lines on organizational charts). In the full or balanced matrix, described above, the authority and responsibility of both project and functional managers is equal.

Matrix never applies to an entire organization. In balanced or unbalanced forms, it is applied to temporary projects, or it is an overlay on part of the organization. Almost all complex organizations, notably MULTINATIONAL CORPORATIONS, display some matrix overlays. A local personnel manager in Germany reports directly to his or her country manager but has a "dotted line" responsibility to coordinate certain issues with the regional or corporate vice president for human resources.

Matrix organization attracted much attention in the 1970s when the pioneering works on this form of organization were written. The purported advantages are an increase in lateral COMMUNICATION and the amount of information that the organization can handle, better deployment of and FLEXIBILITY in the use of human and other resources, increased MOTIVATION and personal development, and better achievement of technical excellence. But there are many disadvantages such as high levels of CONFLICT which may lead to power struggles between resource and business managers; ambiguity over resources, pay and assignments; difficulties in control ("passing the buck" and abdication of responsibility); the cost of support, information processes and meetings; slow DECISION MAKING; higher levels of STRESS (*see* ROLE CONFLICT). A number of organizations that introduced matrix in the 1970s reverted to traditional structures in the 1980s, leading some influential observers to comment that matrix organizations are so complex as to be virtually unmanageable. Davis and Lawrence (1977) argue that they are so difficult (because processes and culture must also be matrixed) that one should not consider this way of organizing unless there are no other alternatives.

In what settings and under what conditions is matrix management appropriate? The environment is one parameter (*see* CONTINGENCY THEORY). It may be considered when a high degree of both DIFFERENTIATION and INTEGRATION is required, coupled with strong resource and cost constraints. This is often true for complex projects in construction, aerospace, investment banking and consulting services. This applies also to organizations that draw upon a pool of common expertise to develop different products or services for segmented markets, especially when TECHNOLOGY and customer needs change frequently. The culture of the firm is another parameter (*see* ORGANIZATIONAL CULTURE). Matrix organization will not function well in bureaucratic or mechanistic cultures with strong vertical reporting lines, low competence in managing change, and minimal interdepartmental interaction (*see* BUREAUCRACY). There is also evidence that certain national cultures, those with a strong attachment to traditional AUTHORITY, are less receptive to matrix organization. And as a generalization, it appears that project or business oriented matrices are more effective than balanced matrices, while functional or resource matrices are least effective.

What are the internal requirements of a matrix organization for it to be effective? There is insufficient research to provide a clear answer. The list is endless, typically organized into a number of headings (e.g., matrix = matrix structure + matrix systems + matrix culture + matrix behavior (Davis & Lawrence, 1977)). The roles and responsibilities of the managers and individual contributors within the matrix must be spelt out, and the necessary COMPETENCIES provided through staffing and TRAINING. For example, the general manager at the apex of the matrix diamond must push responsibility down, maintain a certain distance, ensure clear goals, but be skilled at intervening in conflicts. Planning and control systems need to be tailored to the matrix organization. Unless a multidimensional measurement, reporting, and evaluation system is built, lack of clear accountability may lead to confusion and conflict escalation. Human resource systems must be adjusted, with implications for CAREER pathing, skill development (notably in TEAMWORK, negotiation, and conflict management), appraisal, and compensation (*see* HUMAN RESOURCE MANAGEMENT; MANAGEMENT DEVELOPMENT).

There has been surprisingly little research since the 1970s on matrix, partly because of the disillusionment and partly because of reduced interest in issues of organizational form and design. Both practitioners and researchers have turned their attention to how lateral relations (coordination and teamwork) can provide the flexibility of matrix without its disadvantages. Indeed, Ford and Randolph (1992) note that there are two dimensions of matrix management:

(i) the dual or multiple authority relationships (formal reporting lines); and
(ii) the horizontal communication linkages and teamwork that matrix organization intends to foster.

Reviewing the studies on matrix and project management, they suggest that most of the disadvantages appear to stem from the former, while most of the advantages originate from the latter.

Some organizations today appear to be moving "beyond matrix" in the sense of creating multidimensional management processes that provide flexibility to simple and unitary decision-making structures. Many multinational corporations exist in three- or four-dimensional matrix environments. Pressured by global competition, they must organize by product, geography, and function, often also having to satisfy customer segments that cut across product or geographic lines (e.g., global accounts) and to manage CORE COMPETENCIES embedded in different parts of the firm (*see* COMPETITIVENESS). However, formal three- or four-dimensional matrix structures might paralyze decision making.

Many of these firms believe in keeping the lines of the formal authority structure as simple as possible, typically focusing on business/product lines or geographic lines. Matrix organization and project groups are utilized on an *ad hoc* basis and "dotted reporting lines" are used to manage important independencies. But these dotted lines are complemented by other horizontal linkage mechanisms – coordination committees, councils, task forces, temporary project teams, workshops, and personal relationships. And while there is a unitary authority structure, the key managers in this formal line of authority have broad and balanced perspectives that allow them to take the appropriate decisions, fostered by formative experiences in both functional and business roles. From the point of view of decision-making authority, matrix management can be seen not as a structure but as a frame-of-mind (Bartlett & Ghoshal, 1990).

This emerging organization looks more like a network of relationships and perspectives, and "network" appears to be a more appropriate metaphor today than the matrix of the space agency engineers in the 1960s (*see* NETWORK ANALYSIS).

See also **Organization theory; Span of control**

Bibliography

Bartlett, C. A. & Ghoshal, S. (1990). Matrix management: Not a structure, a frame of mind. *Harvard Business Review*, **68**, (4), 138–145.

Davis, S. M. & Lawrence, P. R. (1977). *Matrix*. Reading, MA: Addison-Wesley.

Ford, R. C. & Randolph, W. A. (1992). Cross-functional structures: A review and integration of matrix organization and project management. *Journal of Management*, **18**, (2), 267–294.

Janger, A. R. (1979). Matrix organization of complex business. New York: Conference Board Report No. 763.

Kingdon, D. R. (1973). *Matrix organization*. London: Tavistock.

PAUL EVANS

mechanistic/organic The terms mechanistic and organic (sometimes organismic) organizations were introduced into the language of organizational behavior in a classic study of the development of the British electronics industry during and immediately after World War II. It was found that those firms which had most successfully adopted the new technology had flexible, nonbureaucratic structures, with minimal demarcation between positions, and people saw a connection between their jobs and the goals of the firm. In contrast, the mechanistic firms were bureaucratic with rigid hierarchies, communication was vertical rather than horizontal, and specialization divorced people from overall organizational goals (Burns & Stalker, 1961) (*see* BUREAUCRACY; SCIENTIFIC MANAGEMENT).

The terms gained a considerable currency and heralded an important step toward a CONTINGENCY THEORY of organizations. The mechanistic organization is not considered inappropriate for all conditions but is suitable for relatively stable environmental conditions and where the TECHNOLOGY is well understood, while organic organizations are more suitable for dynamic environments and new technologies. One limitation of the organic organization is size (*see* ORGANIZATIONAL SIZE). Since the intensity of coordination problems tends to rise steeply with the number of organizational members it becomes necessary to use a combination of mechanistic and organic principles. The mechanistic firm in trying to become more FLEXIBLE tends, according to the above perspective, to become pathological by creating more bureaucratic mechanisms such as committees and liaison roles.

See also **Organizational design; Organization theory; Organization and environment**

Bibliography

Burns, T. & Stalker, G. M. (1961). *The management of innovation* (2nd edn, 1968) . London: Tavistock.

RICHARD BUTLER

media *see* COMMUNICATIONS; COMMUNICATIONS TECHNOLOGY

mediation *see* CONFLICT RESOLUTION; CONFLICT MANAGEMENT

mental health "Mental health is an ascientific concept, and it is unlikely that present or future thinking or study in any of the behavioral or medical sciences is going to regularize its status." This comment by Freeman and Giovannoni (1969) indicates the presence of both complexity and controversy. Taking the lead from a definition of medical health suggests the existence of a total system which is made up of a number of functioning subsystems each of which is performing satisfactorily and all of which are in balance with each other, so that the whole functions as an integrated unity. The medical analogy is worth pursuing briefly because it highlights the difference between illness, health, and fitness. Health might be defined as the absence of illness, but fitness of the physiological system obviously entails much more than the absence of illness. Most writing on mental health makes the point even more strongly, defining mental health in terms of possessing high, rather than just adequate, levels of various psychological attributes and states.

Jahoda (1958) used the construct "Positive Mental Health" to emphasize this distinction. She suggested a number of criteria, supplemented by French et al. (1962) to guide their influential research program, subsequently leading to the concept of organizational STRESS and associated research on mental health in the workplace (Kahn, Quinn, Snoek, & Wolfe, 1964). The eleven criteria used included physiological indicators and the presence/absence of certain diseases, but clearly people can be physically diseased, yet have high levels of positive mental health, so these will be omitted. The psychological criteria are:

1. An accurate, realistic perception of the self which includes a positive evaluation strong enough to allow change in both self and mental health to occur.
2. The desire or motivation within the person to seek challenges leading to psychological growth and self-actualization.
3. Integration within the person of the various subidentities (roles) the person possesses, or in Freudian terms harmony of the Id, Ego, and Super-ego.
4. The capacity to be an autonomous person capable of self-direction.
5. The capacity to perceive reality accurately, to be free from unconscious biases and prejudices.
6. High interpersonal COMPETENCE enabling the person to establish and maintain mutually gratifying interpersonal relationships.
7. To be able to experience EMOTIONS of a wide range which are appropriate to the situation but which are also capable of being controlled by the person.
8. The ability to carry out work (and other roles) efficiently and effectively and to high standards.
9. The capacity to be well adjusted to environments but also to have high adjustability enabling the person to be effective in a wide range of different situations.

It is obvious enough that these criteria are not simple dichotomies where people are either healthy or unhealthy. They are all dimensions ranging from extremely healthy to extremely unhealthy, and some are likely to be more central to mental health than others. High levels of willpower may be less important than accurate and clear perception of reality. The existence of multiple dimensions indicates how complex the concept of mental health is. Warr (1987) offers a simpler list of five variables and relates them particularly to the literature on work and UNEMPLOYMENT. They are: Affective well-being; Competence; AUTONOMY; Aspiration (to improve, do better, etc.); Integrated functioning of the other four, leading to a sense of wholeness which is the origin of the word "health" itself.

A number of questionnaire measures exist which could be seen as measures of mental health, but as the list above indicates a wide range of measures is really needed. One of the simplest, and widely used in organizations, is Goldberg's General Health Questionnaire. The shortest version contains only twelve questions and can be shown to be quite a good predictor of more complex interview-based measures of mental health.

Empirical evidence shows mental health to be related to different jobs and levels within organizations, with lower level job occupants being the least mentally healthy, but as the comments on complexity imply, this oversimplifies the picture and ignores the influence of INDIVIDUAL DIFFERENCE variables such as ABILITY and PERSONALITY, as well as the degree of social support in the environment. Perrewe (1991) and Quick, Murphy, and Hunell (1992) contain examples of many different approaches to studying mental health in the workplace, and the role of the workplace in affecting mental health. Mental illness has considerable costs for employers through lost time and poor performance, though employment itself often helps to improve mental health (Warr, 1987).

See also **Affect; Burnout; Manifest and Latent functions; self-esteem**

Bibliography

Freeman, H. E. & Giovannoni, J. M. (1969). Social psychology of mental health. In E. Aronson & G. Lindzey (Eds.). *The handbook of social psychology* (pp. 660–702). Boston, MA: Addison-Welsey.

French, J. R. P., Kahn, R. L., Mann, F. C., Kasl, S. V., Quinn, R., Snoek, J., Williams, L. K. & Zaber, A. (1962). Work, health and satisfaction. *The Journal of Social Issues*, **XVIII**, No. 3.

Jahoda, M. (1958). *Current concepts of positive mental health*. New York: Basic Books.

Kahn, R. L., Quinn, R. P., Snoek, J. D. & Wolfe, D. M. (1964). *Organisational stress: Studies in role conflict and ambiguity*. New York: Wiley.

Perrewe, P. L. (Ed.), (1991). Handbook of job stress. *Journal of Social Behaviour and Personality*, **6**, (7) 463.

Quick, J., Murphy, L. & Hurrell, J. (Eds), (1992). *Work and well-being: Assessments and interventions for occupational mental health*. Washington, DC: American Psychological Association.

Warr, P. (1987). *Work, unemployment and mental health*. Oxford, UK: Clarendon Press.

ROY L. PAYNE

mentoring This refers to relationships between juniors and seniors (in terms of age or experience) that exist, primarily, to support the personal development and career advancement of the junior person. These relationships provide a wide range of developmental functions – including counseling, coaching, role modeling, sponsorship, exposure, protection, confirmation, and friendship – and they are characterized by considerable emotional intensity and involvement. Generally, mentoring relationships move through four predictable phases of *initiation*, *cultivation*, *separation*, and *redefinition*. The character and length of each phase are uniquely shaped by both individuals' needs and the surrounding organizational context.

Mentor relationships enable *both* individuals to build new SKILLS and COMPETENCIES, prepare for advancement and other growth opportunities, adapt to changing organizational circumstances, and/or build SELF-ESTEEM. The focus and quality of LEARNING that occurs within this kind of developmental relationship depends on the AGE and CAREER STAGE of each individual. For example, young newcomers are likely to learn the ropes and to establish their sense of occupational identity, and also develop self-esteem as they acquire new skills. More experienced protégés (in the advancement stage of their careers) are likely to broaden their range of skills and competencies and to learn how to balance increasing demands of more responsibility in both work and personal domains (*see* NONWORK/WORK). Similarly, relatively young mentors are likely to learn how to coach and to serve as a role model (*see* ROLE-TAKING). In contrast, mentors in the middle and later career stages learn how to pass on accumulated wisdom and to nurture the next generation of talent, while creating a personal legacy.

As the workforce becomes increasingly diverse, it has become evident that cross-racial and cross-gender relationships are more difficult to establish and maintain. For example, women and people of color find that senior white men can sponsor them, but not necessarily empathize, coach, and/or serve as role models due to fundamental differences in SOCIALIZATION and current work experiences (*see* WOMEN AT WORK, WOMEN MANAGERS and SEX DIFFERENCES). In addition, individuals need considerable self-awareness and INTERPERSONAL SKILL in order to build relationships with people who are different, that transcend powerful, yet subtle and undermining stereotypes (*see* MANAGEMENT OF DIVERSITY; INTERCULTURAL PROCESS; STEREOTYPING). Until these complex dynamics are better understood and more effectively managed, women and people of color are not likely to establish adequate mentoring alliances, and organizations will fail to fully utilize the diversity of available talent.

The critical role that mentoring plays in learning and MANAGEMENT DEVELOPMENT (*see also* HUMAN RESOURCES MANAGEMENT), is now readily acknowledged. However, scholars and practitioners regularly debate whether formalized mentoring (i.e., relationships that are arranged in the context of fast-track or management development programs) can be as effective as naturally occurring alliances (*see* MANAGEMENT OF HIGH POTENTIAL). In addition, other interventions – including education for potential mentors and protégés, changes in reward systems to encourage managers to mentor, and/or increased use of teams – can encourage mentoring by creating an environment more conducive to relationship building and development.

In most contexts, mentor relationships are relatively rare. Instead, individuals are more likely to find opportunities to build a variety of developmental relationships – those that provide some but not all of the functions outlined above – which are more limited in their involvement and support. Nonetheless, a network of developmental relationships is more realistic, generally more enriching, and also serves to compensate for the difficulties regularly encountered in cross-gender and cross-race relationships.

Current trends including rapid changes in TECHNOLOGY, globalization, RESTRUCTURING, DOWNSIZING, and an increasingly diverse workforce require individuals and organizations to regularly learn and adapt (*see* LEARNING ORGANIZATION). Thus mentoring – a relatively untapped development tool – is increasingly essential to survival and growth. Paradoxically, as the need for effective mentoring is on the rise, organizational turbulence and UNCERTAINTY may make it difficult for these critical developmental alliances to form and endure. Seeking mentor relationships outside the organization may be a necessary and effective strategy; alliances external to the firm are uniquely positioned to provide support, career advice, and much needed perspective.

See also **Supervision; Career plateauing; Career development**

Bibliography

Chao, G. T. & Gardner, P. D. (1992). Formal and informal mentorships: A comparison of mentoring functions and contrast with nonmentored counterparts. *Personnel Psychology*, 45, 1–16.

Kram, K. E. (1988). *Mentoring at work: Developmental relationships in organizational life*. Lanham, MD: University Press of America.

Kram, K. E. & Bragar, M. C. (1992). Development through mentoring: A strategic approach. In D. Montross & C. Shinkman (Eds), *Career development: Theory and practice* (pp. 221–254). Chicago: Charles C. Thomas Press.

Noe, R. A. (1988). Women and mentoring: A review and research agenda. *Academy of Management Review*, 13 (1), 65–78.

Thomas, D. A. (1993). Racial dynamics in cross-race developmental relationships. *Administrative Science Quarterly*, 38, 169–194.

KATHY E. KRAM

mergers and acquisitions An acquisition is the legal and accounting act of an investor buying more than 50 percent of a vendor's equity. A merger is a fusing together of two or more organizations. Mergers may occur between any form of organization (business, government, voluntary, religious) whereas acquisitions refer to legal purchases of equity within markets. In practice, the outcome of both a merger and an acquisition is some combination of the human, material, and financial assets of two or more organizations into a new legal and accounting entity.

In popular usage, a merger implies the acquiesence of those involved. An acquisition implies compulsion. In fact, this is not the case. Some firms do acquire the assets of others through hostile bids. However, these represent fewer than 10 percent of cases. Most acquisitions are mutually agreed bids between senior managers of the two firms. Through such deals small firms expand to become larger. Similarly, while a merger does suggest willing partners, and this is the most common case, there are mergers which are imposed by others (e.g., governments) on reluctant actors.

Research interest in acquisitions has reflected the growing use of these strategies to change organizations (*see* ORGANIZATIONAL CHANGE) and/or change the distribution of POWER within markets. However, merger and acquisition activity on the scale we know it now is a recent phenomenon. For most of this century, the majority of acquisitions and mergers occurred in the United States and Britain. Cycles of heightened activity occurred in periods of rapid growth: 1925–1931, 1967–1969, 1972–1973, and 1985–1988. More recently, other countries have adopted these strategies for change, making this phenomenon much more continuous, broad based, diverse, and global.

Early researchers classified mergers and acquisitions by the strategic objectives of the actors and by the degree of integration sought (*see* STRATEGIC MANAGEMENT). Classifications by the objectives include horizontal DIVERSIFICATION, vertical diversification, concentric marketing, concentric TECHNOLOGY, and conglomeration (*see* CONGLOMERATE DIVERSIFICATION).

Classifications of the intended integration proposed a continuum of CONTROL. At one end is the portfolio approach of autonomous units which maintain their corporate identities; control from the center is light. At the other extreme is the fully integrated firm in which the merged or acquired firm loses its identity, including its name, and the structures, VALUES, and systems of the dominant partner are imposed on the subordinate partner.

The most persistent research issue for both mergers and acquisitions is the rate of success. This raises difficult questions about how and when to assess success. A variety of research methods have addressed the "how" using accounting data, equity price movements, and assessments by the actors involved and/or externals (*see* ORGANIZATIONAL EFFECTIVENESS).

None of these methods on its own is very satisfactory even though they show remarkable consistency: the failure rate, using any of the above methods of assessment, is 50 percent. The second question of "when" to assess success is even more problematic. Accounting studies suggest the first year is not a sensible time to assess success (on the argument that funds from quick divestments are loaded into the first year's profits to maintain equity prices). However, the longer the assessment of success is delayed the higher the probability that accounting information will have been lost in the restructuring of the units, such that like cannot be compared with like.

The problems of assessment have not deterred investigators from attempting to establish why the failure rate is so high. Various factors such as bidding strategy, price, type of corporate control, lack of a plan, poor transfer of capability, the tone of negotiations, confused roles of negotiators, inexperienced actors, indecisive actions after closure, incompatible corporate cultures, excessive RESTRUCTURING, a failure to allow people to express their grief, poor COMMUNICATIONS post merger, imposing alien systems (especially HR systems), and a lack of LEADERSHIP have all been suggested as probable causes.

A related strategy literature focuses on the strategic fit of the two firms. An economic literature focuses on the affects of aggregation on economic performance and on communities. A moral, philosophical literature questions the ethics of certain types of acquisition and, in particular, the hostile type (*see* BUSINESS ETHICS).

Recent research sees the process as a behavioral one and argues that the causes of failure are behavioral. A popular, if simplistic, approach uses metaphors about two actors such as seduction, marriage, rape, plunder to classify relationships. In fact, members of organizations have varied experiences in both mergers and acquisitions. Some are highly affected by the process, undergoing all the emotions of surprise, shock, anger, withdrawal. Others are only marginally affected by the process. For yet others the process may mean loss of a job, for others it opens up new CAREER opportunities. For some, the acquiror is the predator, for others the liberator. Instead of a simple one-to-one relationship the processes involve a myriad of actors in a variety of relationships. Understanding the complexity and significance for success of these relationships and their contexts remains the central research challenge.

Human resource researchers reflect the behavioral approach and discuss which methods are more effective in absorbing actors' STRESS and how to communicate certainty despite UNCERTAINTY. Further, what rituals and events can be used for communication and improving cohesion in the merged firm (*see* RITUALS). At the macro LEVEL OF ANALYSIS, HR researchers review possible structures including the harmonization of recruitment, induction, ASSESSMENT, and REWARD systems.

Behavioral analysts have linked merger and acquisition activity to research on PRIVATIZATION, JOINT VENTURES, STRATEGIC ALLIANCES all of which involve the same wide range of micro and macro variables of any organizational transformation. However, in mergers and acquisitions there are two important conditions which are not always present in these other structural forms. First, inequality of power: one set of actors has enormous potential power to change the behavior of the less powerful. Second, readiness for change: the expectations of all actors is that change is inevitable. Given these two conditions Acquisitions and Mergers can exhibit major change within short periods of time raising important questions about the capacity of significant actors in organizations to learn (*see* ORGANIZATIONAL LEARNING).

See also **Coalition formation; Interorganizational relationships; Competitiveness;**

Bibliography

Ansoff, I. (1975). *Corporate strategy*. New York: McGraw-Hill.

Buono, A. F. & Bowditch, J. L. (1989). *The human side of mergers and acquisitions: Managing collisions between people and organizations*. San Francisco: Jossey-Bass.

Haspeslagh, P. C. & Jemison, D. B. (1991). *Managing acquisitions: Creating value through corporate renewal*. New York: Free Press.

Hunt, J. W., Less, S., Grumbar, J. & Vivian, P. D. (1987). *Acquisitions – The human factor*. London: London Business School/Egon Zehnder.

Kitching, J. (1976). Why do mergers miscarry? *Harvard Business Review* (November–December), 84–101.

Mirvis, P. H. & Marks, M. L. (1992). *Managing the merger*. Englewood Cliffs, NJ: Prentice-Hall.

Porter, M. E. (1985). *Competitive advantage*. New York: Free Press.

JOHN W. HUNT

meta-analysis *see* RESEARCH DESIGN; VALIDITY GENERALIZATION

metaphor A metaphor provides a way of seeing or representing one thing in terms of another. It is a ubiquitous figure of speech or master trope in which a word or phrase that typically denotes one kind of object or idea is used to replace another object or idea thus suggesting an analogy or likeness between them. A metaphor creates a figurative relationship between the two that is often unnoticed in everyday thought and speech. To say that "organizations are machines" is to claim merely that organizations are like machines for the purpose at hand in a given communicative context (*see* COMMUNICATIONS). The metaphor allows speakers and listeners to consider an organization *as if* it were a machine. By so doing, metaphor asserts similarity in differences and, less obviously perhaps, differences in similarity. Thus, by claiming similarity, a metaphor sets something apart from other things and establishes differences from them (e.g., as a machine, an organization does not live and die but is built and dismantled); but also, by taking an object in terms of the metaphor, the object is provided with selective but distinct characteristics associated with the term of similarity (e.g., as a machine, an organization is predictable, impersonal, functional, and occasionally in need of repair).

Metaphors should be held loosely for they may well conceal as much as they reveal. For example, the machine metaphor may mislead those who find it attractive by allowing them to read too little into an organization just as another metaphor such as a "CULTURE" or a "family" may allow its users to read too much into an organization. Popular metaphors are thus seductive. One of the central insights emerging from the study of metaphor and language use is that as a particular metaphor becomes conventionalized (widely communicated, accepted, and virtually taken for granted), users of the metaphor take the relationship it conveys between two objects or ideas to be the obvious, correct, or literal one. The use of other possible metaphors are thus obliterated and one way of seeing becomes a way of not seeing. Metaphors then are not merely linguistic or literary devices that decorate speech but are the conceptual building blocks by which we forge our understandings of the world. They provide the constructive force for representing experience and thus help shape what we know and how we think.

The analysis of metaphor is slowly penetrating organizational studies. Largely imported from the humanities – in particular, literary criticism and theory – a number of ORGANIZATIONAL BEHAVIOR scholars are finding the explication of metaphors quite useful for uncovering "deep" patterns or principles that appear to regulate organizational life. When metaphors are extended and generalized they become PARADIGMS – representing broad but relatively cohesive and coherent ways of seeing the world and interpreting situations of both a routine and novel sort. From this perspective, organizations operate in reasonably consistent ways because they provide their members (and customers, clients, suppliers, stockholders, and so on) with action-generating paradigms. Moreover, these paradigms are discoverable through intensive study. Stories, allegories, legends, uniqueness tales, and creation myths can be read by an analyst as organizing metaphors that incorporate histories, VALUES, purposes, and motives of individuals and groups. The epistemological strategy and perspective is structural and, when used to suggest that a given metaphor (or paradigm) is essentially arbitrary rather than "natural" or "real," it is akin to deconstruction. Ironically, the use of metaphor to explain organization behavior has probably been most powerful when applied to the organization behavior research community itself where it has been argued that most if not all of the research and theory groups in the field are more or less trapped by the metaphors that inform their practice including those who themselves study metaphors. Such is the state – and point – of metaphor analysis.

See also **Ideology; Organizational culture; Postmodernism; Symbolism; Paradox**

Bibliography

Burke, K. (1962). *A grammar of motives and a rhetoric of motives*. Cleveland, OH: Meridan.

Lakoff, G. & Johnson, M. (1980). *Metaphors we live by*. Chicago: University of Chicago Press.

Manning, P. K. (1979). Metaphors of the field. *Administrative Science Quarterly*, **24**, 660–71.

Morgan, G. (1986). *Images of organizations*. Newbury Park, CA: Sage.

Schon, D. (1979). Generative metaphor. In A. Ortony (Ed.), *Metaphor and thought* (pp. 254–283). Cambridge, UK: Cambridge University Press.

White, H. (1980). *Tropics of discourse*. Baltimore, MD: Johns Hopkins University Press.

JOHN VAN MAANEN

M-form organization *see* ORGANIZATIONAL DESIGN; MULTINATIONAL CORPORATION

minorities *see* DISCRIMINATION; EQUAL OPPORTUNITIES

minority group influence Minority group INFLUENCE is the process whereby a numerical or POWER minority within a group or society brings about enduring change in the attitudes and behavior of others. Exposure to minority influence appears to cause changes in attitudes in the direction of the deviant view, but also produces more creative thinking about the issue, as a result of the cognitive or social CONFLICT generated by the minority. Social psychological research on minority influence therefore has exciting implications for understanding organizational behavior. Many in large organizations believe that they cannot bring about changes which they see as necessary and valuable. Research on minority group influence suggests otherwise.

Traditionally, only majorities in groups and organizations have been assumed to achieve CONTROL, usually through CONFORMITY inducing processes. However, Moscovici (1976) has argued that *minorities* also have a significant impact upon the thinking and behavior of the majorities with whom they interact. Repeated exposure to a consistent minority view, leads to marked and internalized changes in attitudes and behaviors. When people conform to a majority view they generally comply publicly without necessarily changing their private beliefs. Minorities, in contrast, appear to produce a shift in private views rather than public compliance. Evidence further suggests that even if they do not cause the minority to adopt their viewpoints, minorities encourage greater CREATIVITY in thinking about the specific issues they raise. Moscovici cites the impact on public attitudes of the Green and Feminist Movements in the 1970s and 1980s as examples of the process.

An implication for organizations is that tolerating the expression of deviant views may be important if creativity and adaptability are not to be stifled. The conflict created by minorities can be seen as a valuable source of creative energy within organizations, counteracting the potentially soporific effects of conformity.

Research in social psychology and observation of organizational practice suggests that:

1. Minorities are most influential when they are persistent.
2. A lone deviant is dramatically less effective than a pair expressing minority opinions and, thereafter, the larger the minority group, the greater its influence.
3. The arguments presented by minorities must be coherent and convincing to be influential.

4. The minority must be seen to be acting out of principle, not for ulterior motives or out of self interest, if they are not to be dismissed.
5. Minorities have more influence to the extent that they are seen as making personal material sacrifices in order to achieve their aims.
6. Minorities which are seen as consistent but flexible are more powerful in changing opinions within groups and organizational settings than those which are seen as consistent but rigid.

This research is striking in suggesting that minority group influence can change attitudes and behavior more pervasively and enduringly than the conformity effects of majority influence. The considerable implications for understanding WORK GROUP behavior and organizational adaptation have only recently begun to be explored (Nemeth & Staw, 1989).

See also **Group development; Group decision making; Coalition formation; Politics; Intergroup relations; Groupthink; Group cohesiveness**

Bibliography

Moscovici, S. (1976). *Social influence and social change*. London: Academic Press.

Nemeth, C. J. (1986). Differential contributions of majority and minority influence. *Psychological Review*, **93**, 23–32.

Nemeth, C. & Staw, B. M. (1989). The trade-offs of social control and innovation within groups and organizations. In L. Berkowitz (Ed.), *Advances in experimental social psychology* (vol. 22, pp. 175–210). New York: Academic Press.

West, M. A. (1990). The social psychology of innovation in groups. In M. A. West (Ed.), *Innovation and creativity at work: Psychological and organizational strategies* (pp. 309–333). Chichester, UK: Wiley.

MICHAEL A. WEST

mission statements A mission statement is a formal summary (usually written) of what an organization seeks to become and accomplish. Mission statements are usually written by an organization's TOP MANAGEMENT TEAM, and describe, among other things, an organization's basic purpose, what is unique or distinctive about it, how it is likely to evolve in the long term, who are its principal STAKEHOLDERS (*see* ORGANIZATIONAL EFFECTIVENESS), what are its principle products or services, and its basic beliefs, VALUES, and aspirations (*see* ORGANIZATIONAL CULTURE).

Mission statements serve several purposes in a firm. First, the process of writing a mission statement can force an organization's managers to evaluate the fundamental attributes and characteristics of their organization (*see* RESOURCE BASED THEORY). Mission statements also establish BOUNDARIES to guide future strategy formulation, including specifying in which activities an organization will engage, as well as activities in which an organization will not engage (*see* STRATEGIC MANAGEMENT diversification). Third, mission statements set standards of organizational performance along multiple dimensions. Finally, mission statements can suggest standards for individual ethical behavior (*see* BUSINESS ETHICS; CORPORATE SOCIAL RESPONSIBILITY).

Mission statements are often part of the formal strategic PLANNING process in firms. Mission statements are used to define an organization's goals or objectives, which in turn can be used to define an organization's strategies and tactics.

See also **Communications; Reputation; Goal-setting**

Bibliography

Dess, G. & Miller, A. (1993). *Strategic management*. New York: McGraw-Hill.

Drucker, P. (1954). *The practice of management*. New York: Harper & Row.

Pearce, J. A. & David, F. (1987). Corporate mission statements: The bottom line. *Academy of Management Executive*, **1**, 109–115.

JAY B. BARNEY

modeling *see* COMPUTER MODELING; RESEARCH METHODS

monotony *see* JOB DESIGN; REPETITIVE WORK

mood *see* AFFECT

moral development This concept implies that people develop over time in the way that they think about moral issues. Kohlberg's (1969) theory of cognitive moral development (CMD) is the most widely cited theory of moral development although it has been criticized by both psychologists and philosophers. Psychologists have claimed that Kohlberg's theory is limited (e.g., in its cognitive emphasis or purported male GENDER bias), while philosophers have criticized it for being too wide-ranging in its attempt to integrate normative ethical theory and moral psychology (Gilligan, 1977; Modgil & Modgil, 1986). Despite these criticisms, Kohlberg's theory of moral development has been useful to organizational scholars trying to understand the moral judgments and actions of organizational members.

CMD theory focuses on the development, through childhood and young adulthood, of the cognitive processes involved in judging what is morally right. Kohlberg's research identified three levels of CMD, each composed of two stages. An individual's reasoning forms a coherent system that is best described by a single stage or by a combination of two adjacent stages. The stages are also hierarchical integrations, meaning that people comprehend reasoning at all stages below, but not more than one stage above their own.

Level one, termed preconventional, consists of the first two stages where moral decisions are explained and justified in terms of externally imposed REWARDS and PUNISHMENTS, and the exchange of favors. Stage one individuals think in terms of OBEDIENCE for its own sake and punishment avoidance. At stage two, fairness is judged in terms of a "you scratch my back, I'll scratch yours" RECIPROCITY (*see* EQUITY THEORY; JUSTICE, DISTRIBUTIVE).

At level two, termed conventional and consisting of stages three and four, the individual has internalized the shared moral norms of society or some group such as the family or peers (*see* GROUP NORMS). To stage three individuals, good behavior is that which pleases or helps relevant others (*see* IMPRESSION MANAGEMENT). At stage four, the individual's moral perspective broadens to consider society and the law, and fulfilling agreed upon duties and obligations in order to promote the common good. According to a number of studies most adults in industrialized societies are at the conventional level.

Level three (postconventional or principled – stages five and six) individuals are more inclined to look inward for guidance. At stage five, the emphasis is still on laws and rules because they represent the social contract, but stage five individuals would consider the possibility of changing the law for socially useful purposes. At stage six, the individual is guided by self-chosen ethical principles of justice and rights. Less than 20 percent of American adults reach stage five thinking and stage six remains a theoretical stage that very few individuals are expected to reach (Colby, Kohlberg, Gibbs, & Lieberman, 1983).

Research on CMD has generally supported the following findings, among others:

(1) Moral reasoning increases with AGE and education.
(2) Moral reasoning may be lower in hypothetical business situations than in more general ethical dilemma situations.
(3) Despite criticisms of gender-bias (noted above), trivial gender differences, if any, have been empirically supported.
(4) Moral judgment development is universal in that the underlying CMD-based conceptions and categories are common across cultures.
(5) Moral reasoning has a moderate statistical relationship with moral action.
(6) CMD stage can be increased through CMD-based educational interventions.

See also **Business ethics; Corporate social performance; Individual differences; Personality; Values**

Bibliography

Colby, A., Kohlberg, L., Gibbs, J. & Lieberman, M. (1983). *A longitudinal study of moral development. Monographs of the Society for Research in Child Development*, **48** (1,2), Series #200, pp. 1–107.

Gilligan, C. (1977). In a different voice: Women's conceptions of the self and morality. *Harvard Educational Review*, **49**, 431–446.

Kohlberg, L. (1969). Stage and sequence: The cognitive-developmental approach to socialization. In D. A. Goslin (Ed.), *Handbook of socialization theory and research*. Chicago: Rand McNally.

Modgil, S. & Modgil, C. (1986). *Lawrence Kohlberg; Consensus and controversy*. Philadelphia: Falmer Press.

Rest, J. (1986). *Moral development: Advances in research and theory*. New York: Praeger.

Trevino, L. K. (1992). Moral reasoning and business ethics: Implications for research, education, and management. *Journal of Business Ethics*, 11, 45–459.

LINDA TREVINO

morale *see* JOB INSECURITY; JOB SATISFACTION; ORGANIZATIONAL CLIMATE; QUALITY OF WORKING LIFE

motivation This term refers to the psychological mechanisms governing the direction, intensity, and persistence of actions *not* due solely to individual differences in ABILITY or to overwhelming environmental demands that coerce or force action (*see* Vroom, 1964). The field of motivation seeks to understand, explain, and predict:

(a) which of many possible goals an individual chooses to pursue (direction of action);
(b) how much effort an individual puts forth to accomplish salient goals (intensity of action); and
(c) how long an individual perseveres toward goal accomplishment, particularly in the face of difficulties (persistence of action).

The topic of motivation has a long history in the field of basic and applied psychology (*see*, e.g., Weiner, 1980). Work motivation represents a specialty area in the broader field of human motivation that focuses directly on theories, research, and practices that have implications for individual behavior in the context of work, and may be applied to a variety of HUMAN RESOURCE MANAGEMENT activities, including selection, TRAINING, and managerial practices.

In the organizational behavior domain, the term motivation often refers to a critical management activity; that is, to the techniques used by managers for the purpose of facilitating employee behaviors that accomplish organizational goals. Managerial practices designed to enhance employee performance are rarely straightforward applications of particular work motivation theories, but rather are uniquely tailored activities that incorporate motivational notions within the broader context of the organization's culture, dynamics, and practices (*see* ORGANIZATIONAL CULTURE). The tailoring of motivational techniques to the specific organizational context makes evaluation of the true validity of motivational approaches to organizational PRODUCTIVITY difficult. Nonetheless, in a review of 207 published experiments using psychologically based programs (including motivational programs such as GOAL-SETTING, MANAGEMENT BY OBJECTIVES, and other supervisory methods), Katzell and Guzzo (1983) found that over 80 percent of published studies showed evidence of productivity improvement on at least one measure. These results suggest that motivational techniques used by managers can have direct effects on organizational outcomes (*see* MOTIVATION AND PERFORMANCE).

Motivation tenets

Three assumptions guide contemporary thinking and research on human motivation. First, motivation is not directly observable. What is observed is a stream of behavior and the products of those behaviors. Motivation is *inferred* from a systematic analysis of how characteristics of the individual, task, and environment influence behavior and aspects of job performance. Second, motivation is not a fixed attribute of the individual. Unlike motives (which are often defined in terms of stable INDIVIDUAL DIFFERENCES in dispositional tendencies), motivation refers to a dynamic, internal state resulting from the independent and joint influences of personal and situational factors. As such, an individual's motivation for specific activities or tasks may change as a consequence of change in any part of the system. In other words, modern approaches do not view motivation as an individual trait (*see* PERSONALITY), but rather as an individual state affected by the continuous interplay of personal, social, and organizational factors (*see* INTERACTIONISM).

Third, motivation has its primary effect on behavior (covert and overt); that is, what an individual chooses to do and how intensely an individual works to accomplish his/her goal. The distinction between motivational effects on behavior versus job performance is of critical importance for understanding motivation effects in the work domain. In the workplace, changes in motivation may or may not affect job performance depending on how job performance is defined and evaluated. Programs designed to enhance job performance by increasing employee motivation may be unsuccessful if job performance is not immediately or substantially affected by an individual's on-task effort (*see* PERFORMANCE, INDIVIDUAL).

The processes by which motivation influences behavior and performance are best represented as comprised of two interrelated psychological systems; goal choice and goal striving (or SELF-REGULATION; see, e.g., Heckhausen, 1991; Kanfer & Hagerman, 1987; Kanfer, 1990). Cognitive theories of motivation describe goal choice as a DECISION-MAKING/COMMITMENT process in which choice is determined jointly by personal factors and the individual's perceptions of the situation. The product of this process, an individual's intentions or goals, provide a mental representation of a future situation that signifies a desired end-state. Relative to intentions, goals define more specific end-states. Commitment to a goal serves to direct the individual's attention, mobilize the individual's effort toward goal attainment, and encourage goal PERSISTENCE. Intentions and goals may relate to the individual's behavior (e.g., my goal is to work overtime for three hours today) or to an outcome the individual seeks to attain (e.g., my goal is to obtain a promotion). Person and situation characteristics influence goal choice as well as the specificity at which goals are articulated.

Theories that describe the decision-making process with respect to goal choice (e.g., Vroom, 1964) have frequently been used to successfully predict a variety of behaviors in which goals are readily attainable (e.g., choice among job offers). However, when goals involve difficult or prolonged tasks that require sustained effort in the face of difficulties, prediction of performance requires additional consideration of the individual's commitment to the goal as well as other motivational processes.

Goal striving refers to the motivational mechanisms set into motion by adoption of difficult goals for which accomplishment requires active self-regulation of one's cognitions, EMOTIONS, or actions. Goals, such as learning a complex new SKILL or earning a college degree require self-regulatory, or volitional processes by which the individual can develop subgoals, monitor his/her performance, and evaluate activities with respect to goal progress. Deficits in the goal striving system may thwart successful transition of a goal into action and obscure or weaken the effect of motivation on performance.

Work Motivation Overview

Numerous theories of work motivation have been proposed over the past 60 years. Comprehensive reviews by Campbell and Pritchard (1976) and Kanfer (1990) document major advances in work motivation through the mid-1970s and from the mid-1970s to 1990, respectively. Descriptions of major motivational approaches in the context of ORGANIZATIONAL BEHAVIOR are provided in Steers and Porter (1987). In concert with theoretical advances, a tremendous variety of programs and techniques have been developed for use in organizational settings. Although the popularity of particular motivation theories or techniques wax and wane, there is little evidence to indicate any decline in basic or applied interest in the topic over the past two decades. Motivation theories, research, and practices remain a topic of central importance in industrial/organizational psychology, organizational behavior, executive development, and managerial and job training programs (*see* MANAGEMENT DEVELOPMENT).

Historical Trends

The history of the application of scientific principles for enhancing work performance via changes in an individual's motivation corresponds closely to theoretical and empirical developments in the study of human behavior and the workplace. Early management theories, such as Taylor's SCIENTIFIC MANAGEMENT, made reference to the long-standing practice of using financial compensation to spur motivation and job performance. The emergence of personality and LEARNING theories in psychology during the early 1900s led to the development of motivational programs aimed at enhancing performance by creating organizational conditions that facilitated the match between employee need satisfaction and increased on-task effort. During the 1940s through the 1960s, explosive growth in theorizing and research on the determinants of choice led to the development of models aimed at enhancing prediction of individuals' workplace behaviors, such as TURNOVER. During this same period, results of the Hawthorne studies provided striking evidence for the influence of social norms and other nonfinancial incentives on work motivation and performance (*see* HUMAN RELATIONS MOVEMENT).

The rise of behaviorism during the mid-1900s stressed the importance of operant learning and REINFORCEMENT as a means of altering workplace behavior (*see* BEHAVIOR MODIFICATION). Organizational interventions using behavior modification techniques were developed to enhance performance on a variety of dimensions, such as SAFETY. At the same time, progress in the field of task characteristics led to greater consideration of the motivating potential of jobs. Integration of this work with intrinsic motivation theorizing led to the development of interventions aimed at enhancing motivation and performance through job redesign (*see* EXTRINSIC/INTRINSIC MOTIVATION). Similar in some respects to earlier work by Herzberg that focused on psychological determinants of JOB SATISFACTION (*see* MOTIVATOR-HYGIENE THEORY), job redesign efforts aimed to strengthen employee motivation by creating work environments that promoted a sense of achievement, perceptions of competence, and AUTONOMY (*see* JOB ENRICHMENT).

The past two decades have witnessed tremendous growth in the use of goal setting and management by objectives programs. These programs, based upon a view of human behavior that espouses goals as the immediate precursors of action, focus largely on the process of setting, establishing commitment to, and following-through on specific and challenging goals.

Goal-based approaches currently dominate the basic and applied literature. However, most organizational researchers and practitioners recognize that there is no one "best" theory or program. As a result, there has been a growing trend to develop broad formulations that subsume or complement major tenets of goal choice, behavioral, and goal striving theories of action (*see*, e.g., Naylor, Pritchard, & Ilgen, 1980; Kanfer & Ackerman, 1989; Locke & Latham, 1990). From a practical perspective, the broadening of theories has placed a greater burden on practitioners to conduct a careful analysis of the motivational problem in order to select an appropriate intervention perspective.

Key Perspectives

Modern approaches to motivation may be organized into three related clusters:

(1) personality-based views;
(2) cognitive choice/decision approaches (*see* VIE THEORY, INSTRUMENTALITY); and
(3) goal/self-regulation formulations.

The following section highlights major assumptions, theories, and findings from each perspective.

Personality-based views of motivation emphasize the influence of relatively enduring characteristics of persons as they affect goal choice and striving. Three types of personality-based work motivation perspectives may be distinguished. The first type pertains to models based upon broad theories of personality, such as Maslow's Need Hierarchy Theory (Maslow, 1954) (*see* SELF-ACTUALIZATION). In these approaches, workplace behavior and satisfaction are posited to be powerfully determined by an individual's current need state within a universal hierarchy of need categories. By understanding which needs were most salient to an individual (e.g., affiliation, self-actualization needs) (*see* AFFILIATION, NEED FOR), organizations could enhance work performance and satisfaction by creating environments that facilitated need satisfaction. Although this perspective is well known, scientific research has consistently failed to provide support for basic tenets of the model or to demonstrate that this model is useful in predicting workplace behaviors.

The second type of personality perspective derives from considering the influence of a single or small set of universal or psychologically based motives that may affect behavior and performance. A great deal of work in this perspective has focused on the role of individual differences in the strength of achievement motives (i.e., need for achievement) (*see* GROWTH NEED STRENGTH; ACHIEVEMENT, NEED FOR). Substantial research in this area indicates that individuals who score high on tests of achievement motivation are more likely to select appropriately challenging task goals and to persist longer than persons who score low on this trait (Heckhausen, 1991).

During the mid-1900s, attention also focused on the role of universal motives, such as the need for competence, self-determination, and fairness. In contrast to achievement motivation theories, motive theories such as Deci's Cognitive Evaluation Theory and Adam's EQUITY THEORY do not stress individual differences in the degree of the motive, but rather stress the conditions that arouse the motive and its influence on behavior. In equity theory, for example, arousal of the justice motive occurs when the individual perceives imbalance in the ratio of his/her inputs and outcomes relative to others (*see* JUSTICE, DISTRIBUTIVE).

Unlike broad personality theory formulations, motive-based theories more fully specify the organizational conditions that instigate motive-based behaviors, as well as the cognitive processes by which the motive affects behavior. Newer formulations of these motive-based approaches in the areas of intrinsic motivation (*see* EXTRINSIC/INTRINSIC MOTIVATION) and equity/fairness enjoy substantial popularity in the work motivation literature.

The third personality perspective on work motivation emerged in the early 1980s as a direct result of advances in basic research in personality. During the past two decades, personality researchers made significant progress in the identification and measurement of basic personality dimensions (*see* PERSONALITY TESTING; EXTROVERSION). The results of this work led to general agreement regarding the existence of five basic personality dimensions, or traits: (1) neuroticism; (2) extraversion; (3) openness to experience; (4) agreeableness; and (5) conscientiousness. Of the five factors, conscientiousness, also called will to achieve and dependability, represents the trait dimension most closely associated with motivation. Recent investigations of the association between personality dimensions and job performance indicate that conscientiousness shows consistent relations with several dimensions of job performance (*see*, e.g., Barrick & Mount, 1991). These results have led to renewed interest in delineating how individual differences on motivationally related traits might affect work behavior and performance, particularly in service sector jobs.

Cognitive choice/decision approaches emphasize two determinants of choice and action: (1) the individual's expectations (i.e., the individual's perception of the relationship between effort and performance level, as well as between performance level and salient outcomes); and (2) the individual's subjective valuation of the expected consequences associated with various alternative actions (i.e., the anticipated positive or negative effect associated with attainment of various outcomes). These formulations, known as Expectancy Value (ExV) theories (*see* VIE THEORY), are intended to predict an individual's choices or decisions, not necessarily subsequent performance. In most models, individuals are viewed as rational decision makers who make choices in line with the principle of maximizing the likelihood of positive outcomes. (Note, however, that ExV models predict choice behavior on the basis of the individual's perceptions; misperceptions of the environment or relationship between effort, performance, and outcomes may yield "poor" decisions.) In the motivational realm, choices may be made with regard to direction (goal choice), intensity (goal striving), or persistence of a specific course of action.

The popularity of these approaches reached a peak in the early 1980s. During the 1970s and 1980s, organizational research focused on testing key tenets of these models and investigating the predictive VALIDITY of various models. Results from this period indicated several limitations and difficulties associated with basic assumptions of the ExV models, and lower than expected levels of predictive validity for task and job performance criteria (though predictive validity for job choice has been substantially better; *see* Mitchell (1982) for a review). Limitations of ExV models in predicting ongoing workplace behaviors led to a general decline in the use of classic formulations in field research during the 1980s, and to the development of modern, integrative choice frameworks, such as Naylor, Pritchard, and Ilgen's (1980) theory of organizational behavior, and Beach and Mitchell's (1990) Image Theory. Both these theories incorporate several of the classic assumptions of ExV theorizing, but use a broader framework of decision making that includes individual differences in personality as well as other motivational processes, such as SELF-REGULATION.

Goal/Self-Regulation formulations of work motivation emphasize the factors that influence goal striving, or the translation of an individual's goals into action (*see* COGNITIVE PROCESSES). In organizational psychology, the most well-known goal setting model was developed by Locke and his colleagues (see Locke, Shaw, Saari, & Latham, 1981; Locke & Latham, 1990), and focuses on the relationship between goals and work behavior. Other broader formulations that specify the psychological processes involved in goal striving include cybernetic control theory (Lord & Kernan, 1989), resource allocation theory (Kanfer & Ackerman, 1989), and social-cognitive theory (Bandura, 1986).

Early organizational goal setting research examined the effects of explicit goal assignments that varied in difficulty. The majority of these studies indicated higher levels of performance among persons assigned difficult and specific goals (e.g., make six sales this week), compared to persons assigned "do your best" goals. Subsequent research has sought to more fully examine the boundary conditions of this robust effect. Results of this research indicate two critical preconditions for demonstration of the positive goal-performance relationship; namely, that the individual accept the goal assignment and that the individual be provided with performance FEEDBACK. Several studies further suggest that specific, difficult goal assignments may be more effective when used with relatively simple tasks (e.g., simple arithmetic tasks) than with complex tasks (e.g., SUPERVISION, programming).

More recently, cybernetic control, resource allocation, and social-cognitive theories have been used to more closely examine how particular attributes of the goal, the person, and the situation influence goal striving and performance. Studies from these theoretical perspectives indicate further conditions that mediate the effect of goals on task performance. Findings suggest that task demands, percepts of SELF-EFFICACY, goal commitment, and orientation toward task accomplishment are also important determinants of the effectiveness of goal setting methods.

Summary

The plethora of work motivation theories and motivational techniques underscores both the complexity of understanding and predicting individual behavior as well as the substantial progress that has been made in this domain. Older work motivation theories, such as Alderfer's adaptation of Maslow's Need Hierarchy Theory, Adams' Equity Theory, and Vroom's Expectancy Theory have given way to new approaches that build upon advances in cognitive psychology, INFORMATION PROCESSING, personality, and self-regulation. These newer perspectives, including for example, Locke and Latham's (1990) goal-setting model, Kanfer and Ackerman's (1989) integrative resource model of learning and performance, and Lord and Kernan's (1989) control theory, often incorporate elements of older theories, but do so in ways that reduce the sharp distinctions between various approaches. New approaches differ from older conceptualizations in other ways as well. For example, contemporary models of motivation place a central emphasis on the role of goals as the primary concept for linking individuals and organizations. In addition, these approaches typically focus on predicting specific job behaviors, rather than an overall job performance or satisfaction criterion.

Although there has been substantial progress in the theoretical field of work motivation, the dynamics of the modern workplace continue to raise important questions and challenges to the field. Two topics of particular relevance for the coming decade are indicated below.

(1) The social/cultural context of work. There is widespread agreement regarding the influence of the social context as an important determinant of work motivation and performance. This has led to the inclusion of broad "social factors" in several motivation models. But, until recently, little attention was paid to understanding the unique and dynamic motivational processes operative in WORKGROUP or team contexts. The growing use of team approaches to performance in organizations has renewed interest in this facet of motivation theory and research. In response, several ongoing programs of research, aimed at understanding workteam processes (*see*, e.g., Gersick, 1988; Swezey & Salas, 1992) (*see*

GROUP DYNAMICS), have begun to delineate how attributes of the team and the task affect the goals, motivation, and behaviors of individual team members.

In a related vein, results of cross-cultural research indicate that the use and effectiveness of motivational techniques depends in part on the congruence of the motivational approach with the cultural values of the society in which it is used (*see* CULTURE, CROSS-CULTURAL RESEARCH). Erez (1993) points out that motivational approaches consistent with collectivistic, group-oriented values (e.g., QUALITY CIRCLES, AUTONOMOUS WORK GROUPS, PARTICIPATION in goal setting) tend to be more effective when used in collectivistic cultures such as Japan, China, and Israel. In contrast, motivational programs consistent with individualistic values (e.g., individual job enrichment, individual goal setting, individual INCENTIVE plans) are used and reported more effective in individualistic cultures, such as the United States. Erez (1993) further argues that, with the growing internationalization of the workforce, the ultimate success of managerial techniques depends critically on their congruence with the cultural values of the particular organization and its social environment.

(2) Managing motivation. Traditional views of work motivation imply that employees are relatively passive recipients of managerial and organizational efforts to maximize work motivation by providing appropriate work conditions and incentives. However, this view is problematic for two reasons. First, theory and research over the past three decades clearly indicates that individuals are active agents in the motivation process. Employees interpret and respond to managerial practices in light of personal goals, schemas, and beliefs. Research in the areas of employee SOCIALIZATION, procedural justice (*see* JUSTICE, PROCEDURAL), and LEADERSHIP indicates that motivation is affected not only by what the manager and/or organization offers the individual, but by the way in which practices are implemented. Procedural justice research, for example, indicates that the process by which incentives are allocated or layoffs are realized exerts an important effect on employee attitudes and behavior, independent of the outcome.

Second, and perhaps more importantly, demographic, technological, and economic changes in the workplace, forecasted to continue through the end of this century, will likely continue to erode managerial control over employee motivation. Increasing workforce diversity, for example, is associated with growing diversity in employee goals and attitudes toward traditional motivational incentives, such as pay (*see* MANAGEMENT OF DIVERSITY). Similarly, the development of new technologies that permit employees to work in locations far removed from the manager makes traditional supervisory methods for increasing employee motivation more difficult to implement and raises new motivational issues, such as how to encourage work goal commitment and increased task effort in nontraditional work environments, such as the home.

For these reasons, further advances in work motivation theory and practice are most likely to come from integrative approaches that explicitly consider how the *employee* controls his/her motivation in response to managerial/organizational practices. In this goal-striving perspective, motivation may be represented as a job-related competency and employee resource (*see* COMPETENCIES); that is, a resource that organizations can help to develop and that managers and employees co-manage. Recent training programs, based on self-regulation principles aimed at cultivating employee skills in managing work-related goals and actions, for example, represent a promising avenue for potentially reducing substantial organizational costs associated with SUPERVISION, ABSENTEEISM, and poor performance.

See also **Attitude theory; ERG theory**

Bibliography

Bandura, A. (1986). *Social foundations of thought and action: A social cognitive theory*. Englewood Cliffs, NJ: Prentice-Hall.

Barrick, M. R. & Mount, M. K. (1991). The big five personality dimensions and job performance: A meta-analysis. *Personnel Psychology*, **44**, 1–26.

Beach, L. R. & Mitchell, T. R. (1990). Image theory: A behavioral theory of decision making in organizations. In B. Staw & L. L. Cummings (Eds), *Research in organizational behavior*, (Vol. 12, pp. 1–41). Greenwich, CT: JAI Press.

Campbell, J. P. & Pritchard, R. D. (1976). Motivation theory in industrial and organizational psychology. In M. D. Dunnette (Ed.), *Handbook of industrial and organizational psychology*, (pp. 63–130). Chicago: Rand McNally.

Cropanzano, R. (Ed.), (1993). *Justice in the workplace*. Hillsdale, NJ: Erlbaum.

Deci, E. L. & Ryan, R. M. (1980). The empirical exploration of intrinsic motivational processes. In L. Berkowitz (Ed.), *Advances in experimental social psychology*, (Vol. 13, pp. 39–80). New York: Academic Press.

Erez, M. (1993). Toward a model of cross-cultural industrial and organizational psychology. In M. D. Dunnette & H. Triandis (Eds), *Handbook of industrial and organizational psychology*, (Vol. 4). Palo Alto, CA: Consulting Psychologists Press.

Gersick, C. J. G. (1988). Time and transition in work teams: Toward a new model of group development. *Academy of Management Journal*, **31**, 9–41.

Heckhausen, H. (1991). *Motivation and action*. New York: Springer-Verlag.

Kanfer, R. (1990). Motivation theory and industrial/organizational psychology. In M. D. Dunnette & L. Hough (Eds), *Handbook of industrial and organizational psychology* Volume 1. *Theory in industrial and organizational psychology*, (pp. 75–170). Palo Alto, CA: Consulting Psychologists Press.

Kanfer, R. (1992). Work motivation: New directions in theory and research. In C. L. Cooper & I. T. Robertson (Eds), *International review of industrial and organizational psychology*, (vol. 7, pp. 1–53). London: Wiley.

Kanfer, R. & Ackerman, P. L. (1989). Motivation and cognitive abilities: An integrative/aptitude-treatment interaction approach to skill acquisition. *Journal of Applied Psychology – Monograph*, **74**, 657–690.

Kanfer, F. H. & Hagerman, S. M. (1987). A model of self-regulation. In F. Halisch & J. Kuhl (Eds), *Motivation, intention, and volition*, (pp. 293–307). New York: Springer-Verlag.

Katzell, R. A. & Guzzo, R. A. (1983). Psychological approaches to productivity improvement. *American Psychologist*, **38**, 468–472.

Katzell, R. A. & Thompson, D. E. (1990). Work motivation: Theory and practice. *American Psychologist*, **45**, 144–153.

Locke, E. A. & Latham, G. P. (1990). *A theory of goal setting and task performance*. New York: Prentice-Hall.

Locke, E. A., Shaw, K. N., Saari, L. M. & Latham, G. P. (1981). Goal setting and task performance: 1969–1980. *Psychological Bulletin*, **90**, 125–152.

Lord, R. G. & Kernan, M. C. (1989). Application of control theory to work settings. In W. A. Herschberger (Ed.), *Volitional action*, (pp. 493–514). Amsterdam: Elsevier Science, North-Holland.

Maslow, A. (1954). *Motivation and personality*. New York: Harper & Row.

Mitchell, T. R. (1982). Expectancy-value models in organizational psychology. In N. T. Feather (Ed.), *Expectations and actions: Expectancy-value models in psychology*, (pp. 293–312). Hillsdale, NJ: Erlbaum.

Naylor, J. C., Pritchard, R. D. & Ilgen, D. R. (1980). *A theory of behavior in organizations*. New York: Academic Press.

Steers, R. M. & Porter, L. W. (1987). *Motivation and work behavior*, (4th edn.). New York: McGraw-Hill.

Swezey, R. W. & Salas, E. (Eds), (1992). *Teams: Their training and performance*. Norwood, NJ: Ablex.

Vroom, V. H. (1964). *Work and motivation*. New York: Wiley.

Weiner, B. (1980). *Human motivation*. New York: Holt, Rinehart, & Winston.

RUTH KANFER

motivation and performance Motivation represents one of several major determinants of performance in work settings (*see* PERFORMANCE, INDIVIDUAL). The nature of the relationship between motivation and performance can be described by four major points. First, the two constructs are not synonymous. Motivation affects the direction, intensity, and PERSISTENCE of an individual's behavior. In contrast, job performance typically refers to the evaluation of job-related behaviors with respect to organizational objectives. Individuals may be motivated, yet perform poorly if the behaviors they enact do not correspond to the established performance criterion. The influence of motivation on work performance tends to be most often observed when performance is defined in terms of volitional behaviors (not outcomes or accomplishments) that are directly related to expenditures of time and effort, such as staying late at work.

Second, the nature of the task has a substantial influence on the extent to which motivation level may affect task or job performance. In habitual, well-learned tasks, such as driving a car or filing documents, increases in motivation level are not proportional to increases in performance. A minimal level of motivation is required for task performance, but small to moderate increases in motivation above this threshold may not substantially improve performance. Very substantial increases in motivation (to a maximal level), however, are likely to affect performance. In contrast, increases in motivation level are typically associated with proportional increases in performance in novel, complex, or prolonged tasks or jobs. In these tasks, higher levels of task motivation often enhance performance by encouraging task persistence in the face of difficulties or promoting the development of more effective work strategies.

Third, motivation and performance exert reciprocal influences on one another. Not only does motivation affect performance, but performance can affect motivation. Knowledge of how one has performed or is progressing on a task, may weaken or strengthen subsequent task motivation depending on performance level, attributions about the cause of performance, and motivational conditions (*see* KNOWLEDGE OF RESULTS). For example, obtaining a poor sales performance evaluation the first quarter may prompt an employee to devote more or less effort to this aspect of the job the next quarter, depending on the employee's commitment to the high performance goal and his/her perceptions about the most likely causes for the poor performance rating. For example, if the employee views performance as due to lack of effort, motivation is expected to be maintained or increased. In contrast, if the employee perceives the cause of performance to be due to circumstances completely beyond his/her control, motivation is expected to decline (*see* LOCUS OF CONTROL).

Fourth, an enduring issue in organizational behavior pertains to the question of when, for whom, and under what conditions motivation is most likely to influence performance. Clearly, motivation, or the allocation of one's time and effort to a job, represents only one determinant of job performance. In most jobs, the prediction of performance requires consideration of additional factors, including individual differences variables such as cognitive abilities (*see* ABILITY) and task comprehension, and environmental factors such as situational constraints and task demands. With respect to the question of when motivation is an important determinant of performance, most organizational scholars agree that motivation can have an effect on performance only in the *absence* of serious situational constraints. For example, among printing press operators, we would expect no differences in performance among persons who differ in motivation level if performance is limited by broken equipment or other factors that place an externally imposed limit on what the individual can accomplish.

The related issues of who benefits most (in terms of performance improvement) from high levels of job motivation, and under what conditions, is considerably more complex. For many jobs, INDIVIDUAL DIFFERENCES in cognitive abilities are powerful predictors of job performance. In 1964, Vroom proposed an interaction between motivation and ability as these factors affect performance (*see* INTERACTIONISM). Specifically, he suggested that at low levels of motivation, both lower and higher ability persons would perform similarly poorly. However, at high levels of motivation, performance of higher ability individuals would be greater than performance of lower ability individuals. That is, at high levels of motivation, persons with higher general cognitive ability typically outperform persons of lower general cognitive ability. The interaction proposed by Vroom (1964) implies that while organizations should strive to enhance motivation levels among all employees, the most serious threat to potential productivity stems from low levels of motivation among high ability employees (*see* INSTRUMENTALITY; COGNITIVE RESOURCE THEORY).

More recently, Kanfer and Ackerman (1989) suggested a complementary view of the ability–motivation interaction effect on performance in the context of complex SKILL training. They proposed that during TRAINING, motivation to perform is moderate to high and, consistent with Vroom's notion, higher ability trainees would be expected to perform better than lower ability trainees. However, they further predicted that during training, attempts to enhance performance through the use of motivational techniques, such as GOAL SETTING, would have larger effects on lower- rather than higher-ability trainees. In a series of experiments, Kanfer and Ackerman (1989) found that attempts to increase motivation via the goal-setting technique hindered performance among lower-ability persons when implemented early in training, but had a substantial positive effect when implemented later in training. In contrast, the motivational intervention had only negligible effects on performance of higher ability persons regardless of when implemented. From an organizational perspective, these findings suggest that specific motivational techniques may be differentially effective in enhancing performance, depending upon individuals' pre-existing motivational levels, individual differences in cognitive abilities, and the skill level at which the technique is implemented.

In summary, the relationship between motivation and job or task performance is dynamic and complex. The effects of motivation on performance depend on how performance is defined, the nature of the task, the APTITUDES of the individual, and the extent to which environmental factors may limit performance accomplishments. Two implications for HUMAN RESOURCE MANAGEMENT may be drawn from theory and research on the interaction between ability and motivation as it affects performance:

(1) substantial declines in motivation for job performance are likely to have a larger negative impact on performance among higher ability persons than lower ability persons; and
(2) attempts to enhance motivation (with techniques such as goal setting) during later phases of training appear to have a more positive impact on performance among lower ability persons than higher ability persons.

See also **Extrinsic/intrinsic motivation; Path-goal theory; Rewards; Feedback; Motivator–hygiene theory**

Bibliography

Kanfer, R. & Ackerman, P. L. (1989). Motivation and cognitive abilities: An integrative/aptitude-treatment interaction approach to skill acquisition. *Journal of Applied Psychology – Monograph*, **74**, 657–690.

Vroom, V. H. (1964). *Work and motivation*. New York: Wiley.

RUTH KANFER

motivator–hygiene theory This theory, also known as the Two-Factor Theory, was developed by Herzberg and colleagues (Herzberg, Mausner, Peterson, & Capwill, 1957) to answer the question: What do people want from their jobs? Herzberg, Mausner, and Snyderman (1959), interviewed 203 accountants and engineers, and asked them to tell "stories about times when they felt exceptionally good or bad about their jobs," so that the researchers could, "discover the kinds of situations leading to negative or positive attitudes toward the job..." (p. 17). They concluded that good WORKING CONDITIONS (hygiene) and good work (motivator) are needed to affect JOB SATISFACTION.

Hygienes (factor 1) refer to the context in which the job exists and includes: financial compensation, physical working conditions, relations with supervisors and peers, company policies and administration, benefits, and job security. These factors satisfy physiological, safety, and belongingness needs. Just as vaccinations, and personal cleanliness prevent disease, sufficient hygiene levels prevent dissatisfaction. But, they do not improve job satisfaction – for this, management must emphasize Motivators (factor 2), which are based primarily on job content. Jobs must be interesting enough to provide the opportunity for feelings of achievement, which, together with recognition for accomplishment, and advancement, serve to stimulate feelings of personal growth. In essence, Herzberg sought to extend Maslow's basic notion of SELF-ACTUALIZATION to the problem of job MOTIVATION. Just as physical hygiene prevents illness and exercising creates wellness; industrial hygiene prevents dissatisfaction, and performing a job that requires the use of valued skills creates psychological health and job satisfaction.

Empirical support for the theory is closely related to the "storytelling" method of collecting data, which has led to the criticism that findings which support the theory are attributable to methodological artifact (Behling, Labovitz, & Kosmo, 1968). This is because the storytelling technique does not control for a plausible alternative explanation: that people, in the process of maintaining their SELF-ESTEEM, attribute instances of dissatisfaction with factors beyond their control, whereas satisfying experiences are attributed to their own accomplishments (Farr, 1977) (*see* ATTRIBUTION). Subsequent research, with different methods, has failed to support the theory (Gardner, 1977). Furthermore, a theoretical confound is that job satisfaction and job motivation are not necessarily equivalent theoretical constructs – employees can be motivated but frustrated, lazy and satisfied, satisfied and motivated, or dissatisfied and unmotivated.

While most companies in the 1950s were attempting to motivate employees through wage-incentive systems and through training supervisors in human relations skills, Herzberg et al. suggested that a better approach would be to restructure the manner in which work was performed. Notwithstanding the methodological critique, a major contribution of motivator–hygiene theory is that it asks, and seeks to provide an answer to, the question: What features should we build into a job to increase its motivating potential?

See also **Human relations movement; Intrinsic/extrinsic motivation; Job design; Job enrichment**

Bibliography

Behling, O., Labovitz, G. & Kosmo, R. (1968). The Herzberg controversy: A critical appraisal. *Academy of Management Journal*, **11**, 99–108.

Farr, R. (1977). On the nature of attributional artifacts in qualitative research: Herzberg's two-factor theory of work motivation. *Journal of Occupational Psychology*, **50**, 3–14.

Gardner, G. (1977). Is there a valid test of Herzberg's two-factor theory? *Journal of Occupational Psychology*, **50**, 197–204.

Herzberg, F., Mausner, B., Peterson, R. & Capwill, D. (1957). *Job attitudes: Review of research and opinion*. Pittsburgh: Psychological Service of Pittsburgh.

Herzberg, F. Mausner, B. & Snyderman, B. (1959). *The motivation to work*. New York: Wiley.

UCO J. WIERSMA

multinational corporations There is no accepted definition of what constitutes a multinational corporation or MNC, a term that is loosely applied to firms with sizeable activities outside their mother countries. One widely used indicator is the extent of direct foreign investment or capital deployed outside the home country, thereby distinguishing modern MNCs from the European trading enterprises of the seventeenth and eighteenth centuries. By this measure, European firms in Britain, Holland, and Germany such as Unilever and Philips were the first MNCs, expanding beyond their limited home markets in the late nineteenth century, while most US firms focused on the immense national market with limited export operations until the opportunity to transfer their expertise pulled them abroad in the 1960s. Japanese firms multinationalized only in the 1980s.

Another definition of the MNC focuses on its structure. The two domains of differentiation that are typical of a complex national firm, function and product, are joined by a third, that of geography (and often by others such as customer accounts, that cut across products and areas). The most elaborate definition of "multinationalism" comes from Heenan and Perlmutter (1979), who include objective structural criteria such as the number of foreign operations and the form of organizational structure, objective performance criteria such as absolute and relative overseas sales, profits and employees, and subjective attitudinal criteria concerning the orientation of top management. This leads them to distinguish three orientations or cultures of MNCs. The first is the decentralized "polycentric" corporation where the assumption is that foreigners are different from the people at home, so they should be left alone as long as their work is profitable. The second is the "regiocentric" firm with strong regional headquarters focusing on managerial staffing and regional optimization of functions such as manufacturing. The third is the "geocentric" firm where both headquarters and subsidiaries see themselves as parts of a worldwide entity. Good ideas and good people may come from any country and go to any country within the corporation. Where the headquarters is located is simply a matter of history and convenience.

More recently, Bartlett and Ghoshal (1989) distinguish between four different types of international corporations with different heritages, each with a distinctive source of competitive advantage (*see* COMPETITIVENESS). The "multinational" firm is a decentralized federation of local firms linked together by a web of personal controls (EXPATRIATES from the mother firm who occupy key positions abroad).

Its strength is local responsiveness, and some European firms such as Unilever and Philips embody this model. The "global" firm is typified by US corporations such as Ford earlier this century and Japanese enterprises such as Matsushita. Worldwide facilities that are typically centralized in the mother country produce standardized products, while overseas operations are considered as delivery pipelines to access international markets. There is tight control of strategic decisions, resources, and information by the global hub. The competitive strength of the global firm is efficiencies of scale and cost. The competitive strength of the third type, the "international" firm, is its ability to transfer knowledge and expertise to less advanced overseas environments. It is a coordinated federation of local firms, controlled by sophisticated management systems and corporate staffs. The attitude of the parent company tends to be parochial, fostered by the superior know-how at the center. Many American and some European firms such as Ericsson fit this pattern.

Bartlett and Ghoshal argue that global competition is forcing many of these firms to shift to a fourth model, which they call the "transnational." This firm has to combine local responsiveness with efficiency and the ability to transfer know-how. The transnational corporation is a network of specialized or differentiated units, with integrative linkages between local firms as well as with the center. In the transnational, the subsidiary becomes a distinctive asset rather than simply an arm of the parent company. Manufacturing and TECHNOLOGY development are located wherever it makes sense, but local know-how is leveraged so as to exploit worldwide opportunities. The transnational is also described as a "heterarchy" rather than hierarchy by Hedlund (1986) and as a "multifocal organization" by Prahalad and Doz (1987).

Spurred by the multinationalization of American enterprises and the growth of business schools in Europe, Organizational Behavior and Strategy scholars first became interested in the phenomenon in the 1970s. A landmark study was that of Stopford and Wells (1972) who began to map out the stages in the development of the multinational firm. They pointed out that diversified MNCs were pulled in the direction of some form of MATRIX ORGANIZATION, and interest in this topic fueled research. The focus shifted in the early 1980s to HQ-subsidiary relations (How can the HQ control multinational operations?) (Prahalad & Doz, 1987). Interest is now turning to explore the patterns of relationships within and between subsidiaries and the ways in which these can be managed. The emerging metaphor for the transnational MNC is the "differentiated network" (Bartlett & Ghoshal, 1989), a network of relationships and mechanisms that link or glue differentiated subsidiaries. A network perspective is implicit in much recent work, and there is increasing interest in NETWORK ANALYSIS to understand intraorganizational and INTERORGANIZATIONAL RELATIONS within the same firm. If control was the predominant dependent variable in earlier MNC studies, with their parent company bias, INNOVATION is becoming that dependent variable today.

Given the increasing importance of such corporations in the economies of most countries, MNCs have in the last two decades become an important area of study. Such studies are contributing to our understanding of organizational processes (FLEXIBILITY, NETWORKING, ORGANIZATIONAL LEARNING, ORGANIZATIONAL CULTURE, INFORMATION PROCESSING, innovation processes, cultural differences in conceptions of organization, ENTREPRENEURSHIP, to name a few examples). The understanding of such complex organizations calls for interdisciplinary work between scholars of strategy, organization, HUMAN RESOURCE MANAGEMENT, network analysis, LEADERSHIP, change management, ORGANIZATIONAL CULTURE, and these studies are also contributing to breaking down barriers between traditional subfields of organizational analysis. In this sense, the interest in MNCs is having a significant impact on the field of Organizational Behavior itself.

See also **Collateral organization; Organizational design; International management; International human resource management**

Bibliography

Bartlett, C. A. & Ghoshal, S. (1989). *Managing across borders: The transnational solution*. Boston: Harvard Business School Press.

Hedlund, G. (1986). The hypermodern MNC: A hetararchy? *Human Resource Management*, **25**, (1) 9–35.

Heenan, D. A. & Perlmutter, H. V. (1979). *Multinational organization development: A social architecture perspective*. Reading, MA: Addison-Wesley.

Prahalad, C. K. & Doz, Y. L. (1897). *The multinational mission: Balancing local demands and global vision*. New York: Free Press.

Stopford, J. M. & Wells, L. T., Jr. (1972). *Managing the multinational enterprise*. New York: Basic Books.

PAUL EVANS

mutual adjustment This denotes those circumstances where DECISION MAKING requires individuals or work units to accommodate each other through reciprocal communication and action. The concept originates in the work of Thompson (1967) to denote the characteristic multidirectional flows of information and decision making between work units and actors under conditions of "reciprocal interdependence" in complex and "intensive" technologies (*see* TECHNOLOGY). This contrasts with "pooled interdependence" where information flows are bilateral and mainly unidirectional between atomized work stations and central authority, and with "sequential interdependence" where there is primarily one-way flow between linked work stations (as in assembly line technology). Mintzberg (1979) identifies mutual adjustment as one of the "prime coordinating mechanisms" in ORGANIZATIONAL DESIGN, and a characteristic mode within the "adhocracy."

See also **Complexity; Loose coupling; Uncertainty**

Bibliography

Mintzberg, H. (1979). *The structuring of organizations*. Englewood Cliffs, NJ: Prentice-Hall.

Thompson, J. D. (1967). *Organizations in action*. New York: McGraw-Hill.

NIGEL NICHOLSON

— N —

natural selection *see* POPULATION ECOLOGY

Naylor–Pritchard–Ilgen (NPI) theory *see* MOTIVATION

negotiated order This approach emphasizes NEGOTIATION as an ongoing process, usually tacit, in which participants create social order/organization "on line" so to speak. It is a variant of SYMBOLIC INTERACTIONISM. A study of the activities and relations of personnel in psychiatric hospitals provided considerable evidence of negotiated order. For example, ward aides negotiated for control over their conditions of work (e.g., with and for whom, what ward?), and negotiated with nurses (and indirectly with doctors) how particular patients should be handled. Negotiations between nurses and doctors achieved long term understandings such that little COMMUNICATION was needed concerning treatment programs. Patients negotiated with nurses and doctors over their treatment and for information and privileges, and with each other over conditions on the ward. General arguments for negotiated order include the following: formal rules and procedures require judgment concerning their applicability and do not cover all aspects of organizational work; organizational goals and values can only provide a "generalized mandate" and mean different things to different people; in order to work together, people have to agree and see as legitimate the terms and conditions of their interdependence (*see* LEGITIMACY); negotiation is needed to achieve order in the context of change. In sum, there are many reasons why order must more or less continuously be "worked at" and the "work" is negotiation.

See also **Organizational culture; Social constructionism; Decision making**

Bibliography

Strauss, A. (1978). *Negotiations: Varieties, contexts, processes and social order*. San Francisco: Free Press.

DIAN MARIE HOSKING

negotiation When two or more parties need to reach a joint decision but have different preferences, they negotiate. They may not be sitting around a bargaining table; they may not be making explicit offers and counteroffers; they may even not be making statements suggesting that they are on different sides. However, as long as their preferences concerning the joint decision are not identical, they have to negotiate to reach a mutually agreeable outcome.

Over the last decade, the topic of negotiation has captivated the field of ORGANIZATIONAL BEHAVIOR, and more broadly, business schools. It has grown to be one of the most popular topics of instruction, and the current state of research is very different as a result of the interest in this topic. This review will highlight the five dominant areas of research in negotiation:

(1) INDIVIDUAL DIFFERENCES;
(2) situational characteristics;
(3) GAME THEORY;
(4) asymmetrically prescriptive/descriptive; and
(5) cognitive.

More detailed reviews can be found elsewhere (Neale & Bazerman, 1991).

Individual differences

During the 1960s and early 1970s, the majority of psychological research conducted on negotiations emphasized dispositional variables (Rubin & Brown; 1975), or traits (*see* PERSONALITY TRAITS); individual attributes such as demographic characteristics, PERSONALITY variables, and motivated behavioral tendencies unique to individual negotiators. Demographic characteristics (e.g., AGE, GENDER, RACE, etc.), RISK-TAKING tendencies, LOCUS-OF-CONTROL, cognitive complexity, tolerance for AMBIGUITY, SELF-ESTEEM, AUTHORITARIANISM, and MACHIAVELLIANISM were all hot research topics in 1960s negotiation literature (Rubin & Brown, 1975).

Since bargaining is clearly an interpersonal activity, it seems logical that the participants' dispositions *should* exert significant influence on the process and outcomes of negotiations. Unfortunately, despite numerous studies, dispositional evidence is rarely convincing. When effects have been found, situational features imposed upon the negotiators often reduce or negate these effects. As a result, individual attributes typically do not account for significant variance in negotiator behavior.

A number of authors have reached the conclusion that individual differences offer little insight into predicting negotiator behavior and negotiation outcomes: ". . . there are few significant relationships between personality and negotiation outcomes" (Lewicki & Litterer, 1985).

In addition to the lack of predictability from individual differences research, this literature has also been criticized for its lack of relevance to practice. Bazerman and Carroll (1987) argue that individual differences are of limited value because of their fixed nature, i.e., they are not under the control of the negotiator. Furthermore, individuals, even so-called experts, are known to be poor at making clinical assessments about another person's personality in order to formulate accurately an opposing strategy (Bazerman, 1994).

In summary, the current literature on dispositional variables in negotiation offers few concrete findings. Future research in this direction requires clear evidence, rather than intuitive assertions, that dispositions are important to predicting the outcomes of negotiations.

Situational Characteristics

Situational characteristics are the relatively fixed, contextual components that define the negotiation. Situational research considers the impact of varying these contextual features on negotiated outcomes. Examples of situational variables include the presence or absence of a constituency, the form of COMMUNICATION between negotiators, the outcome payoffs available to the negotiators, the relative POWER of the parties, deadlines, the number of people representing each side, and the effects of third parties.

Research on situational variables has contributed much to our understanding of the negotiation process and has directed both practitioners and academics to consider important structural components. For example, situational research has found that the presence of observers in a negotiation can dramatically affect its outcome. This effect holds whether the observers are physically or only psychologically present. Further, whether the observers are an audience (i.e., those who do not have a vested interest in the outcome of the negotiation) or a constituency (i.e., those who will be affected by the negotiation) is of little importance in predicting the behavior of the negotiator (Rubin & Brown, 1975).

One of the main drawbacks of situational research is similar to that of individual differences research. Situational factors represent aspects of the negotiation that are usually external to the participants and beyond the individual's control. For example, in organizational settings, participants' control over third-party intervention is limited by their willingness to make the dispute visible and salient. If and when the participants do, their manager usually decides how he or she will intervene as a third party (Murnighan, 1987) (*see* CONFLICT RESOLUTION).

The same criticism holds true for other situational factors, such as the relative power of the negotiators or the prevailing deadlines. While negotiators can be advised to identify ways in which to manipulate their perceived power, obvious power disparities resulting from resource munificence, hierarchical LEGITI-

MACY, or expertise are less malleable. Negotiators are often best served by developing strategies for addressing these power differentials instead of trying to change them.

The Economic Study of Game Theory

The earliest attempts at providing prescriptive advice to negotiators were offered by economists. The most well-developed component of this economic school of thought is game theory. In game theory, mathematical models are developed to analyze the outcomes that will emerge in multiparty, DECISION MAKING contexts if all parties act rationally. To analyze a game, specific conditions are outlined which define how decisions are to be made; e.g., the order in which players get to choose their moves; and utility measures of outcomes for each player are attached to *every* possible combination of player moves. The actual analysis focuses on predicting whether or not an agreement will be reached, and if one is reached, what the specific nature of that agreement will be. The advantage of game theory is that, given absolute RATIONALITY, it provides the most precise prescriptive advice available to the negotiator. The disadvantages of game theory are two-fold. First, it relies upon being able to completely describe all options and associated outcomes for every possible combination of moves in a given situation – a tedious task at its best, infinitely complex at its worst. Second, it requires all players to act rationally at all times. In contrast, individuals often behave irrationally in systematically predictable ways that are not easily captured within rational analyses.

Asymmetrically Prescriptive/Descriptive

As an alternative to game-theoretic analyses of negotiation which take place in a world of "ultrasmart, impeccably rational, supersmart people," Howard Raiffa developed a *decision-analytic approach* to negotiations – an approach more appropriate to how "erring folks like you and me actually behave," rather than "how we should behave if we were smarter, thought harder, were more consistent, were all knowing" (Raiffa, 1982, p. 21). Raiffa's decision-analytic approach focuses on giving the best available advice to negotiators involved in real conflict with real people. His goal is to provide guidance for a focal negotiator given the most likely profile of the expected behavior of the other party. Thus, Raiffa's approach is prescriptive from the point of view of the party receiving advice, but descriptive from the point of view of the competing party. Raiffa's approach offers an excellent framework for approaching negotiations. However, it is limited in the insights that it provides concerning the behaviors that can be anticipated from the other party.

Raiffa's work represents a turning point in negotiation research for a number of reasons. First, in the context of developing a prescriptive model, he explicitly acknowledges the importance of developing accurate descriptions of opponents, rather than assuming they are fully rational. Second, by realizing that negotiators need advice, he recognizes that they do not intuitively follow purely rational strategies. Most importantly, he has initiated the groundwork for dialogue between prescriptive and descriptive researchers. His work demands descriptive models which allow the focal negotiator to anticipate the likely behavior of the opponent. In addition, we argue that decision analysts must acknowledge that negotiators have decision biases that limit their ability to follow such prescriptive advice.

Cognitive

The cognitive approach (Neale & Bazerman, 1991; Bazerman & Neale, 1992) addresses many of the questions that Raiffa's work leaves behind. If the negotiator and his or her opponent do not act rationally, what systematic departures from rationality can be predicted? Building on work in BEHAVIORAL DECISION RESEARCH, a number of deviations from rationality have been identified that can be expected in negotiations. Specifically, Neale and Bazerman's research on two-party negotiations suggests that negotiators tend to:

(1) be inappropriately affected by the positive or negative frame in which risks are viewed;
(2) anchor their number estimates in negotiations on irrelevant information;
(3) overrely on readily available information;
(4) be overconfident about the likelihood of attaining outcomes that favor them;
(5) assume that negotiation tasks are necessarily fixed-sum and thereby miss opportunities

for mutually beneficial trade-offs between the parties;

(6) escalate COMMITMENT to a previously selected course of action when it is no longer the most reasonable alternative (*see* COMMITMENT, ESCALATING);

(7) overlook the valuable information that is available by considering the opponent's cognitive perspective; and

(8) retroactively devalue *any* concession that is made by the opponent (Ross, 1994).

These tendencies seriously limit the usefulness of traditional prescriptive models' rationality assumption, i.e., the belief that negotiators are accurate and consistent decision makers. Further, these findings better inform Raiffa's prescriptive model by developing more detailed descriptions of negotiator behavior.

Collectively, these five prospectives provide a summary of the recent history and current state of knowledge of the topic of negotiation. Future research is moving in a cognitive direction, which will hopefully serve the need to better resolve disputes in personal, organizational, and societal affairs.

See also **Cognition in organizations; Collective bargaining; Negotiated order**

Bibliography

Bazerman, M. H. (1994). *Judgment in managerial decision making*, (3rd edn). New York: Wiley.

Bazerman, M. H. & Carroll, J. S. (1987). Negotiator cognition. In B. Staw & L. L. Cummings (Eds), *Research in organizational behavior*, (Vol. 9 pp. 247–288). Greenwich, CT: JAI Press.

Bazerman, M. H. & Neale, M. A. (1992). *Negotiating rationally*. New York: Free Press.

Lewicki, R. J. & Litterer, J. A. (1985). *Negotiation*. Homewood, IL: R.D. Irwin.

Murnighan, J. K. (1987). The structure of mediation and "intravention." *Negotiation Journal*, 2, (4), 351–356.

Neale, M. A. & Bazerman, M. H. (1991). *Cognition and rationality in negotiation*. New York: Free Press.

Raiffa, H. (1982). *The art and science of negotiation*. Cambridge, MA: Belknap.

Ross, L. (1994). Psychological barriers to dispute resolution. In K. Arrow, R. Mnookin, L. Ross, A. Tversky & R. Wilson (Eds), *Barriers to conflict resolution*. New York: Norton.

Rubin, J. Z. & Brown, B. R. (1975). *The social psychology of bargaining and negotiation*. New York: Academic Press.

MAX H. BAZERMAN

network analysis The study of ORGANIZATIONAL BEHAVIOR involves the analysis of social interaction and economic exchange among individuals and groups within organizations, and among organizations. As a consequence, all forms of coordination and DIVISION OF LABOR within and among organizations can be seen as specific patterns of roles and relationships, i.e., as forms of social networks (Baker, 1992) (*see* INTERORGANIZATIONAL RELATIONS).

Social network analysis offers a powerful analytical framework for describing and predicting organizational structures and processes in terms of relational patterns among actors in a system. Social network analysis provides a link between intuitive ideas about social relations and complex notions of ROLE, position, and STATUS in organizations.

Network models describe the structure of one or more networks of relations within a system of actors. The basic unit of observation of social network models is a relationship between two actors, but there is no inherent unit of analysis. Relations among pairs of actors can be:

(i) exploited to develop individual attributes;

(ii) analyzed at the dyadic level;

(iii) used to partition the network into subsets of actors; and

(iv) aggregated to analyze the resulting network as a whole.

Actors themselves can be defined at a micro or macro level: individuals or groups of individuals interacting within organizations, organizations competing and cooperating in economic or institutional sectors, and even nations participating in the international community.

Following Burt (1982) it is possible to identify two alternative and partially conflicting analytical approaches within social network analysis: relational and positional. Relational network models are concerned with the extent to which actors in a social network are connected within cohesive subgroups. The major analytical task of relational network models is clique identification. Positional network models are typically concerned with more sociological issues of role structure, status, AUTONOMY, and STRATIFICATION in organizations and organizational fields. The main goal of positional network models is to represent the structure of an (inter or intra) organizational system in terms of positions identified by an equivalence criterion. Such representations, referred to as blockmodels, assign to the same position actors who are similarly embedded in networks of relations and provide a model of roles as a system of relations among positions (Faust & Wasserman, 1992). Barley (1990) adopted the positional approach to analyze how technological change affected the organizational structure and work roles of radiologists and technologists in two Massachusetts hospitals. He found that technological INNOVATION in computerized image processing partitioned the organization of the radiology departments into distinct social entities.

Network data typically come in the form of one or more matrices containing information about the relational activity among actors in a system. Network data may take the form of joint involvement in events, or person-to-group affiliations. More frequently, network data are generated by binary or rank order sociometric choices, or by direct measures of relations. For example, Krackhardt (1990) used sociometric choice data to study the relationship between an individual's ability to reconstruct the networks of friendship and advice relations and reputational measures of power among the members of a small entrepreneurial firm. Burt (1992) used dollar flow data taken from the input–output tables to study the relationship between structural autonomy and profit margins in 77 US product markets.

See also **Group structure; Communication; Networking; Statistical methods**

Bibliography

Baker, W. (1992). The network organization in theory and practice. In N. Nohria & R. Eccles (Eds), *Networks and organizations: Structure form and action* (pp. 397–429). Boston: Harvard Business School Press.

Barley, S. (1990). The Alignment of technology and structure through roles and networks. *Administrative Science Quarterly*, **35**, 61–103.

Burt, R. (1982). Toward a structural theory of action. Network models of social structure perception and action. New York: Academic Press Quantitative Studies in Social Relations.

Burt, R (1992). Structural holes. The social structure of competition. Cambridge, MA: Harvard University Press.

Faust, K. & Wasserman, S. (1992). Blockmodels: Interpretation and evaluation. *Social Networks*, **14**, 5–61.

Krackhardt, D. (1990). Assessing the political landscape: Structure, cognition and power in organizations. *Administrative Science Quarterly*, **35**, 342–369.

ALESSANDRO LOMI

networking Research about networking and networks can be complicated. Understanding what networking is and the nature of networks is not complicated. Networking at its most basic is the process of contacting and being contacted by people in our social network and maintaining these linkages and relationships. A network, then, is a set of relations, linkages, or ties among people. A connection between people consists both of content (type of connection) and form (strength of the connection).

Content may include information exchange or simply friendship ties. The strength of the connection may be determined by the number of contacts made between people over time. Of course, strength can also be measured by the degree of intensity of the relationship, e.g., how long a singular contact is maintained, compared with the number of contacts made.

Like individuals, organizations are embedded in multiple networks, e.g., resource and information exchange. A domain of organization networks studied extensively is board of director interlock networks. Early research into these networks attempted to show collusion among competitors via their interlocking board members, but more recently Zajac (1988) has found little evidence to support this interpretation. Most researchers today view the interlock network as a way to exchange information rather than exert explicit control (Useem, 1984).

Much research has been conducted on networks. According to Davis and Powell (1992), the information content, maintenance, and mapping of network ties has received most attention whereas, for example, the consequences of an organization's position in various networks has hardly been studied. According to Burt (1980), methodological advances have been made, but theory is underdeveloped.

Fischer, Jackson, Stueve, Gerson, Jones, & Baldassare (1977) have contributed to the field by suggesting that networks can best be understood according to a choice-constraint approach, that is, a network is the result of individual choices made within certain social constraints. Social structures, such as class, determine whether and to what degree these choices can be made.

Tichy, Tushman, and Fombrun (1979) state that the study of networks can be traced to three broad schools of thought: sociology, anthropology, and ROLE THEORY. From these studies, the key properties of networks have been identified as:

(1) transactional content – what is exchanged between members, e.g., information;
(2) nature of the links – the strength and qualitative nature of the relationships, e.g., the degree to which members honor obligations or agree about appropriate behavior in their relationships; and
(3) structural characteristics – how members are linked, the number of clusters within the network, and certain individuals representing special nodes within the network; in other words, not all members are equally important; some, for example, are GATEKEEPERS.

Tichy et al. (1979) also describe ways of analyzing organizations according to a network framework. They conclude that the social network framework can be used to study and understand more effectively:

(a) INTER-ORGANIZATIONAL RELATIONS relationships;
(b) organizations and their Boundaries (*see* ORGANIZATIONAL BOUNDARIES; BOUNDARY SPANNING);
(c) career patterns and career succession (*see* CAREER SUCCESSION and CAREER TRANSITIONS);
(d) Organizational change (*see* ORGANIZATION DEVELOPMENT);
(e) ORGANIZATIONAL DESIGN configuration; and
(f) POWER and political processes (*see* POLITICS).

Networking in organizations is usually an informal process, that is, the contacts and interactions among people do not as a rule conform to the formal organization chart – which is usually in the form of a HIERARCHY. Today formal hierarchy is being viewed more as a hindrance than a help to ORGANIZATIONAL EFFECTIVENESS. The need to coordinate activities of organizational members is significantly greater today than in the past. Getting products to market more rapidly, providing quality service (which now is more dependent on numbers of people rather than a single individual), and partnering more with contractors, vendors and other organizational constituents are but a few of the many forces impinging on organizations to be more rapidly responsive. Some believe the "network organization" is a more effective alternative to hierarchy (Rockart & Short, 1991).

It would appear, then, that with the:

(a) need for more and faster responsiveness; and
(b) increasing reliance on INFORMATION TECHNOLOGY,

networking will be of growing importance in organizations.

Understanding and using networks can have practical outcomes, as illustrated by Granovetter (1973). Assume you are looking for a job. You are more likely to be successful via the weak ties in your social network than by the strong ones. Close friends are likely to have many of the same contacts and sources as yourself. More distant acquaintances travel in different circles and therefore provide a link to contacts you would not otherwise have. Thus, while certain kinds of networking may be frivolous, for example, a set of friends who share with you the same interest in, say, Stephen King novels, other networks in your life may provide highly useful information and assistance.

See also **Coalition formation; Network analysis; Intergroup relations**

Bibliography

Burt, R. S. (1980). Models of network structure. *Annual Review of Sociology*, **6**, 79–141.

Davis, G. F. & Powell, W. W. (1992). Organization-environment relations. In M. D. Dunnette & L. M. Hough (Eds), *Handbook of industrial and organizational psychology*, (2nd edn, vol. 3, pp. 316–375). Palo Alto, CA: Consulting Psychologists Press.

Fischer, C. S., Jackson, R. M., Stueve, C. A., Gerson, K., Jones, L. M. & Baldassare, M. (1977). *Networks and places: Social relations in the urban setting*. New York: Free Press.

Granovetter, M. (1973). The strength of weak ties. *American Journal of Sociology*, **78**, 1360–1380.

Rockart, J. F. & Short, J. E. (1991). The networked organization and the management of interdependence. In M. S. S. Morton (Ed.), *The corporation of the 1990s: Information technology and organizational transformation* (pp. 189–219). New York: Oxford University Press.

Tichy, N. M. Tushman, M. L. & Fombrun, C. (1979). Social network analysis for organizations. *Academy of Management Review*, **4**, 507–519.

Useem, M. (1984). *The inner circle: Large corporations and the rise of business political activity in the U.S. and U.K.* New York: Oxford University Press.

Zajac, E. S. (1988). Interlocking directorates as an interorganizational strategy: A test of critical assumptions. *Academy of Management Journal*, **31**, 428–438.

W. WARNER BURKE

neurosis *see* ORGANIZATIONAL NEUROSIS; ANXIETY

niche *see* POPULATION ECOLOGY; STRATEGIC MANAGEMENT

nominal group technique The nominal group format is a structured GROUP DECISION-MAKING technique used for the generation of a vast quantity of alternatives relevant to group issues, problems, and concerns (Gustafson, Shukla, Delbecq, & Walster, 1973). The nominal group technique allows for individual thinking and contribution in a group format. Ideas relevant to an issue, problem, or concern are solicited from group participants individually and silently. The group leader then systematically gathers this information from all participants before an open discussion commences. Ideas are discussed one at a time. Based upon the discussions, possible alternatives may be generated in and by the group. The group leader can then instruct the participants to vote on their preferred solutions. Once again, the leader gathers all this information systematically before commencing open discussion and deliberation. Eventually this group decision-making process may conclude with an acceptable solution.

The nominal group technique to group decision making generally consumes a substantial amount of time. However, individual PARTICIPATION is very high, allowing for understanding, involvement, and eventual COMMITMENT to the group's decision. Particularly, for immediate situations that directly affect the participants, the nominal group technique continues to be an effective DECISION MAKING method (Zimmerman, 1985; Murnighan, 1981). This technique, however, can also be used for the generation and evaluation of longer-term, and more strategic alternatives. Whether for short-term or longer-term goals, the nominal group technique is generally capable of generating a wider array of alternatives and options than other less systematic techniques. It is also capable of doing this more quickly than Delphi groups. Nevertheless, the nominal group technique need not be thought of as a competing model to other techniques, but rather a complementary alternative.

See also **Creativity; Innovation; Group decision making; Delphi; Brainstorming; Communications**

Bibliography

Gustafson, D. H., Shukla, R. K., Delbecq, A. & Walster, (1973). A comparative study of differences in subjective likelihood estimates made by individuals in interacting groups, Delphi groups and nominal groups. *Organizational Behavior and Human Performance*, **9**, 280–291.

Murnighan, J. K. (1981). Group decision making: What strategy should you use? Management Review, 56–60.

Zimmerman, D. K. (1985). Nominal group technique. In L. R. Bittle & J. E. Ramsey (Eds), *Handbook for professional managers*. New York: McGraw-Hill, pp. 604–624.

RANDALL S. SCHULER

nonprofit organizations *see* NOT FOR PROFIT ORGANIZATIONS

nonwork/work This refers to the relationship between one's work and nonwork life. Work generally refers to activities or attitudes undertaken in an employing organization. Nonwork has generally referred to activities and attitudes related to one's family, yet also includes what Zedeck (1992) considers, a personal sphere, where leisure activities, hobbies, and health-related activities occur. Zedeck (1992) further notes that the nonwork concept includes other spheres such as religion, community, and social. Yet, the most studied area of the nonwork/work literature has been the relationship between one's employing organization and one's family.

The need for research in the nonwork/work area became prevalent with the onset of the Industrial Revolution and the increasing separation of work from family life. In the past decade, interest in the nonwork/work field has continued to grow, as researchers recognize the interrelatedness of the nonwork/work spheres, and as the relationship between these two spheres becomes more diverse. For example, the definitions of nonwork/work have changed over time. Family no longer solely means a male headed household, but has become broadened to mean two or more people having influence over each other's lives, sharing a sense of identity and shared goals (Zedeck, 1992) (*see* SEX ROLES). This new definition encompasses both same and different sex partners. The definition of work has also evolved over time. Zedeck (1992) reminds us that work is something that is done, not only in the traditional work environment, but for many (e.g., homemakers, telecommunicators), work is something that is done within the home environment. With these changes in definitions, it becomes obvious that the way researchers view the nonwork/work relationship has evolved historically.

History of Findings

Research related to nonwork/work issues began in the 1930s (Voydanoff, 1989). Findings from this period consistently suggested that male *UN*EMPLOYMENT and female *em*ployment had negative effects on both children and the family (Voydanoff, 1989). While this era of research recognized a "relationship" between one's nonwork and work lives, the primary focus was on the negative effects of work on family. The notion that the family might also influence work life had not yet been considered.

Subsequently, the focus of the nonwork/work research slowly began to shift to a position of viewing nonwork and work lives as interdependent, and in the 1960s to increase attention to the dual-earner couple. Much of this research focused on the additional STRESS and tradeoffs of dual career couples in both their nonwork and work lives. Voydanoff (1989) notes that research during this era began to recognize the "unpaid contribution" of wives of professionals and managers to their husbands' careers. According to Voydanoff (1989) it was often the work of the wives that advantaged the husband's career, yet severely constrained the wife's career, due to geographic mobility, and demands on the wife's time.

Voydanoff (1989) notes that while earlier research examined primarily men's *un*employment, women's *em*ployment, and dual career couples, recent research has focused on the structural and psychological characteristics of work, and the relationship between JOB CHARACTERISTICS and JOB SATISFACTION. Nonwork/work research has also begun to investigate the relationship between job characteristics and stress and health. Structural aspects of the job, such as working hours, compressed work week schedules, and geographic mobility have been shown to affect family life. Weekend work is generally shown to be negatively related to quality of family life (Voydanoff, 1989), the compressed work week schedule is positively related to family satisfaction (Tippins & Stroh, 1991), and job-related geographic mobility has mixed results (Brett, Stroh, & Reilly, 1992a).

Models to Study Nonwork/work Issues

Combined with earlier research on nonwork/work issues, Kanter's (1977) influential review encouraged researchers to begin to think of the nonwork/work environment as an interface and theorists began to develop models to help explain the relationship.

The spillover theory suggests that work-related activities/satisfaction can affect nonwork life and nonwork responsibilities/satisfaction may also affect one's work life. For example, a person's marital satisfaction may affect their relationship to the work place (Brett, Stroh, & Reilly, 1992b).

Not all researchers accept the spillover theory. Other research argues in favor of a compensation theory. This theory suggests there is an inverse relationship between nonwork/work such that individuals compensate for shortcomings in one domain by satisfying needs in the other. For example, a person who is dissatisfied with their family or nonwork life may seek greater levels of satisfaction from their work life environment (Zedeck, 1992).

A third model explaining the relationship between nonwork/work is the segmentation theory, based on the premise that nonwork/work lives are distinct and one domain has no influence on the other. For example, family life satisfies needs for affection, intimacy, and relationships, while work life satisfies needs for competition and instrumental relationships (Zedeck, 1992).

In reality, all three models can be accepted insofar as they describe different relationships which may be obtained under particular circumstances.

Conclusion

The emphasis on the way one's family life can affect one's work life as well as one's work life affecting one's family life has given way to new, more applied research efforts on how to balance adequately the work/family interface. The practical implications of this research in terms of human resource policy and working arrangements are varied (*see* HUMAN RESOURCES MANAGEMENT). Economic and social pressures have forced many organizations to implement more progressive maternity, paternity, and child care related policies in efforts to attract and retain talented managers of both sexes who want to create more balance in their lives. FLEXITIME and job sharing are two examples of work restructuring that have been found to be useful in helping employees balance the work/family interface (*see* JOB DESIGN).

See also **Women at work; Management of diversity**

Bibliography

Brett, J. M., Stroh, L. K. & Reilly, A. H. (1992a). What is it like being a dual-career manager in the 1990s? In S. Zedick (Ed.), *Work and families, and organizations* (pp. 138–167). San Francisco: Jossey-Bass.

Brett, J. M., Stroh, L. K. & Reilly, A. H. (1992b). Job transfer. In C. L. Cooper & I. T Robinson (Eds), *International review of industrial and organizational psychology* (pp. 323–362). Chichester, UK: Wiley.

Kanter, R. M. (1977). *Work and family in the United States*. New York: Russell Sage Foundation.

Tippins, M. & Stroh, L. K. (1991). Shiftwork: Factors impacting workers biological and family well-being. *Journal of Applied Business Research*, 7, (4), 131–135.

Voydanoff, P. (1989). Work and family: A review and expanded conceptualization. In E. B. Goldsmith (Ed.), *Work and family* (pp. 1–22). London: Sage.

Zedeck, S. (1992). Exploring the domain of work and family concerns. In S. Zedick (Ed.), *Work and families, and organizations* (pp. 1–32). San Francisco: Jossey-Bass.

LINDA K. STROH

norms *see* CONFORMITY; GROUP CULTURE; GROUP NORMS; SOCIALIZATION

not-for-profit organizations These are organizations where management do not see profit as their primary goal. The term "nonprofit organization" is also used. The phrase "not-for-profit" first appeared during the 1950s and 1960s, when private sector organizations started to lose competitive bids to nonprofit organizations like universities (McLaughlin, 1986). These private firms wished to emphasize that, while profit might not be a primary objective, nonprofit organizations still make profits, not for distribution, but to be retained for salaries or reinvestment. They wished to dispense with the notion that "nonprofit" implied greater respectability or altruistic intent (*see* ALTRUISM). Advocates of nonprofit organizations also favored the term "not-for-profit" because they believed that such organizations could and should make profits.

Economists generally agree on four types of economic organization:

(1) decentralized, profit-oriented, private market organizations;

(2) Government and its agencies (*see* GOVERNMENT AGENCIES);
(3) households; and
(4) private or voluntary nonprofit organizations (Anthony & Young, 1984).

Some see the not-for-profit sector as a sort of garbage-can repository for all organizations not clearly belonging to the first three sectors. In fact, all categories contain a mixture of organizations and often lack clear boundaries (*see* ORGANIZATIONAL BOUNDARIES). For example, government is a complex of legislative, administrative, regulatory, and judicial institutions (*see* GOVERNMENT AND BUSINESS). Private sector organizations offer more or less differentiated goods and services, in circumstances of lesser and greater competition. In just the same way, the not-for-profit sector represents a cross-section of organizations: some small, some large; some staffed by volunteers, others by paid professionals; some funded by voluntary donations, others by government grants; some offering services, some campaigning; some operate as democratic self-help organizations, such as COOPERATIVES, others attempting to meet the service standards of different STAKEHOLDERS; and some have charitable status, while others do not (Leat, 1993).

The other definitive factor distinguishing not-for-profit organizations is that it is the service(s) offered to a defined constituency which is the primary aim of the organization. Unlike government or business, where provision of goods or services is instrumental in leading to a political or financial "bottom line," the service(s) itself is the most important factor (O'Neill & Young, 1988). Success is therefore not measured in profit, but in providing the best possible service (few not-for-profit organizations offer goods) within available resources. As not-for-profit organizations often have many stakeholders with differing needs, this can lead to disputes over both quality and the service mix. It can also lead to interesting theoretical questions as the expected organizational "rules" concerning, e.g., size and degree of structure or COMMITMENT levels fail to apply.

While writers define the not-for-profit sector by explaining how it is different from other sectors, management writers contend that these distinctions are unhelpful when trying to manage such organizations (Leat, 1993). For example, not-for-profit organizations *do* make profits, but retain them for internal use: objectives are just as multilayered and difficult to set for private sector firms, because "profit" is not a simple concept, and not-for-profit organizations *do* compete, mostly with other similar organizations, for attention and sponsorship.

See also **Business ethics; Corporate social responsibility; Organizational design**

Bibliography

Anthony, R. N. & Young, D. W. (1984). *Management control in nonprofit organizations*. Homewood, IL: Irwin.

Leat, D. (1993). *Managing across sectors: Similarities and differences between for profit and voluntary nonprofit organizations*. London: City University Business School.

McLaughlin, C. P. (1986). *The management of nonprofit organizations*. New York: Wiley.

O'Neill, M. & Young, D. R. (1988). Educating managers of nonprofit organizations. in M. O'Neill & D. R. Young (Eds), *Educating managers of nonprofit organizations*. New York: Praeger.

Weisbrod, B. A. (1980). Private goods, collective goods: "The role of the nonprofit sector?". In K. W. Clarkson & D. L. Martin (Eds), *The economics of non-proprietary organizations*. Greenwich CT: JAI Press.

ELIZABETH O. MELLON

— O —

obedience In the organizational context this refers broadly to the acceptance of AUTHORITY, usually with little question. However, insistence on uncritical obedience can stifle CREATIVITY and limit the information flow necessary to proper functioning. Behavior needs to go beyond minimal ROLE and rule specification to adapt to unanticipated conditions and problems (Katz & Kahn, 1978). Rigid rules that are supposed to be obeyed, especially when contradictory and nonconsensual, can needlessly ensnarl organizations. Some discretion is also necessary in dealing with orders, rather than simply obeying them. In his classic acceptance theory of authority, Barnard (1938) set forth conditions that permit a follower to judge whether an order is authoritative and to be obeyed, i.e., he or she understands it, believes it is consistent with organizational and personal goals, and is capable of being complied with. As an area of study, obedience has been particularly identified with the research of Milgram (1974) on the willingness to follow an experimenter's instruction to inflict evident pain on another person. Resistance to this demand was found to increase significantly in the presence of a mock subject who refused it. This finding fits the contextual point that obedience is qualified in part by situational factors, including the others present and prevailing norms.

See also **Compliance; Group norms; Influence; Legitimacy; Power**

Bibliography

Barnard, C. (1938). *The functions of the executive*. Cambridge, MA: Harvard University Press.

Katz, D. & Kahn, R. L. (1978). *The social psychology of organizations*, (2nd edn). New York: Wiley.

Milgram, S. (1974). *Obedience to authority*. New York: Harper & Row.

EDWIN P. HOLLANDER

objectives *see* MANAGEMENT BY OBJECTIVES

occupations These are shorthand descriptions of the nature of individuals' employment (*see also* JOB DESCRIPTION). In practice, however, there are many uses of the term "occupation" in the social science literature, embodying different conceptual approaches.

At a most basic level are approaches which see occupations simply as "coherent sets of work activities carried on by individuals" (*see* OPCS, 1991). This is the approach of governmental statistical offices in classifying occupations for population censuses and labor force surveys. Definitions commonly used by social scientists, however, go beyond this, to incorporate aspects of the personal characteristics of the individuals undertaking the jobs, defining occupations partly or wholly in terms of the SKILLS possessed or deployed, or the TRAINING and educational qualifications obtained by those individuals. Some definitions go further, implying a description of an individual's CAREER. Such definitions are close to a concept of a "profession" or "vocation."

To summarize, "occupations" can be used to define a job, an individual, or an individual's work history. What use is such a concept? At least five important general uses can be identified (see Thomas & Elias (1989)):

1. To provide an aggregate description of workforce structure, and how it is changing, either within an organization or across the whole economy. This is a basic requirement

of LABOR MARKET intelligence and HUMAN RESOURCE PLANNING. Typically such analyses show an ongoing shift in the occupational structure away from manual toward nonmanual occupations, and toward occupations embodying higher levels of skill and training. Recent developments incorporate GENDER, and the notion of occupational segregation, deriving from the empirical observation that women and men are occupationally concentrated (Blau & Hendricks, 1979; Dex, 1985). Such differences are typically explained by the interaction and mutual reinforcement of DISCRIMINATION in the labor market and RECRUITMENT on the one hand, and socially conditioned patterns of occupational and career choice by individuals on the other. Within organizations, data on the occupational structure by gender are essential for the monitoring of EQUAL OPPORTUNITIES policies.

2. To give an indication of the lifestyle, earnings, or social position of workers and their households, by reference to the type of work they do. A key use for occupational definitions has been in the analysis of the structure and distribution of earnings, income, and wealth (classic texts include Thurow and Lucas (1972), Atkinson (1975), and Phelps Brown (1977)).
3. In the analysis of social STATUS or class in a static sense, and social or occupational mobility in a dynamic sense (*see* STRATIFICATION). Many methods of socio-economic classification derive from the notion that occupation is a key indicator of an individual's position in society, whether conceived in terms of relation to the means of production, labor market position, or ranking according to prestige, status, or economic resources. Most definitions of social class or socio-economic status are, therefore, derived from occupational classifications, or from survey evidence of perceptions of different job categories (*see* Goldthorpe and Hope, 1972; 1974).
4. In vocational and career guidance, and job placement, as a basis for matching individuals' SKILLS and job aspirations to labor market opportunities.
5. In the analysis of occupational health, via the relationship between occupational data and data on disease, fertility, and mortality rates. Similar principles can be applied within an organization for examining patterns of ABSENTEEISM, sickness rates, and occupational health and SAFETY.

Finally, what do occupational classifications look like? There exist many such classifications, used for different purposes, at different levels of detail. Most share a number of common features, however, and a recent tendency is for such systems to converge on the International Standard Classification of Occupations (ISCO), produced by the International Labour Office. Debate on the relative merits of different classifications has concentrated on two issues in particular.

The first concerns their hierarchical structure, which is typically based on a mixture of skill/qualification and social status. A problem is that such hierarchies date rapidly, because new occupations emerge with changes in TECHNOLOGY and work organization, and traditional distinctions based largely on social status are breaking down (e.g., the divide between "white collar" and "blue collar," or between nonmanual and manual occupations). There has, therefore, been a tendency in recent years to place a greater emphasis on skill deployed, and the nature of the activity in question, in constructing such hierarchies. Thus, at a three-digit level ISCO has ten Major Groups, in a skill hierarchy ranging from "legislators, senior officials and managers" to unskilled "elementary occupations." Within each Major Group are Submajor Groups and Minor Groups, defined less in hierarchical skill terms and more in terms of the nature of the work. Thus "clerks" are subdivided into "office clerks" and "customer services clerks," and the former are further broken down into different areas of office clerical work.

A second issue is the overlap with other classification systems, particularly sectoral ones. In principle, an occupation (e.g., clerk) should be defined in terms of skill and work activity, independently of the sector in which the individual works. In practice, however, some occupational labor markets are "monopsonistic" with only one type of employer (in extreme cases – e.g., soldiers, or tax inspectors – only one employer) recruiting in that occupational labor market. In these cases the nature of the sector or employer becomes an integral part of the definition of the occupation, and most classifications used in practice are hybrid occupational–sectoral classifications.

See also **Division of labor; Professionals in organizations; Career theory**

Bibliography

Atkinson, A. (1975). *The economics of inequality*. Oxford, UK: Oxford University Press.

Blau, F. & Hendricks, W. (1979). Occupational segregation by sex: Trends and prospects. *Journal of Human Relations*, **14**, 197–210.

Dex, S. (1985). *The sexual division of work*. Brighton: Harvester Press.

Goldthorpe, J. & Hope, K. (1972). Occupational grading and occupational prestige. In K. Hope (Ed.), *The analysis of social mobility: Methods and approaches*. Oxford, UK: Oxford University Press.

Goldthorpe, J. & Hope, K. (1974). *The social gradings of occupations: A new approach and scale*. Oxford, UK: Oxford University Press

Office of Population Censuses and Surveys. (1991). *Standard occupational classification*, vol. 3, *Social classifications and coding methodology*. London: HMSO.

Phelps Brown, H. (1977). *The inequality of pay*. Oxford, UK: Oxford University Press.

Thomas, R. & Elias, P. (1989). Development of the standard occupational classification. *Population Trends*, **55**, 16–22.

Thurow, L. & Lucas, R. (1972). *The American distribution of income: A structural problem*. Washington, DC: Joint Economic Committee, US Congress.

NIGEL MEAGER

open systems When applying SYSTEMS THEORY to organizations, OB scholars conceptualize them as being open systems exchanging information and resources with their environment (*see* ORGANIZATION AND ENVIRONMENT; STAKEHOLDERS). This perspective draws attention to how organizations and their environments mutually influence each other. It seeks to explain how organizations maintain functional autonomy while adapting to external forces.

As open systems, organizations seek to sustain an input–output cycle of activities aimed at taking in inputs of information and resources from the environment, transforming them into outputs of goods and services, and exporting them back to the environment. This cycle enables organizations to replenish themselves continually so long as the environment provides sufficient inputs and the organization delivers valued outputs.

Considerable research has gone into understanding how organizations manage these information and resource flows (*see* INFORMATION PROCESSING). One perspective focuses on how organizations process information in order to discover how to relate to their environments. Another view concentrates on how organizations compete for resources through managing key resource dependencies (*see* RESOURCE DEPENDENCE). Still another perspective focuses on how organizations gain LEGITIMACY from environmental institutions so they can continue to function with external support (*see* INSTITUTIONAL THEORY).

In managing information and resource flows, organizations, like all open systems, seek to establish Boundaries around their activities. These ORGANIZATIONAL BOUNDARIES must be permeable enough to permit necessary environmental exchange, yet afford sufficient protection from external demands to allow for rational operation (*see* RATIONALITY).

Organizational scholars devote considerable attention to understanding the dual nature of organizational boundaries. They study various BOUNDARY SPANNING roles that relate the organization to its environment, such as sales, public relations, and purchasing. They examine how organizational members perceive and make sense out of environmental input (*see* ENACTMENT), and how organizational boundaries vary in sensitivity to external influences. Research is also aimed at identifying different strategies for protecting transformation processes from external disruptions while being responsive to suppliers and customers.

Viewed as open systems, organizations use information about how they are performing to modify future behaviors. This information FEEDBACK enables organizations to be self-regulating. It enables them to adjust their functioning to respond to deviations in expected performance. According to the system's law of requisite variety, however, organizations must have a sufficient diversity of responses to match the variety of disturbances encountered if self-regulation is to be successful.

Extensive research has been devoted to understanding how organizations control and regulate themselves. Using modern INFORMATION TECHNOLOGY, organizations develop a variety of methods for setting goals, obtaining information on goal achievement, and making necessary changes. They also devise different structures and processes for learning from this information about how to improve performance (*see* CONTINUOUS IMPROVEMENT; ORGANIZATIONAL LEARNING; LEARNING ORGANIZATION).

As open systems, organizations display the property of equifinality. They can achieve objectives with varying inputs and in different ways. Consequently, there is no one best way to design and manage organizations, but there are a variety of ways to achieve satisfactory performance (*see* SATISFICING).

Organizational scholars have devoted considerable attention to identifying different choices for designing and managing organizations (*see* STRATEGIC CHOICE). They have shown a range of ORGANIZATIONAL DESIGN options that can achieve success in particular situations (*see* CONTINGENCY THEORY).

See also **Organization theory; Organizational effectiveness; Population ecology**

Bibliography

Aldrich, H. (1979). *Organizations and environments.* New York: Prentice-Hall.

Galbraith, J. (1977). *Organization design.* Reading, MA: Addison-Wesley.

Pfeffer, J. & Salancik, G. (1978). *The external control of organizations: A resource dependence perspective.* New York: Harper & Row.

THOMAS G. CUMMINGS

operant conditioning *see* CONDITIONING; LEARNING, INDIVIDUAL

operationalization Organizational research or practice often deals with ideas or concepts that cannot be directly observed or measured (such as cooperation, dishonesty, work MOTIVATION, etc.). To facilitate observation, description, good measurement (*see* RELIABILITY) or policy, one frequently selects a specific, observable indicator to represent such concepts. An operationalization (or operational definition) then, is the publicly shared and reproducible operations necessary to define or measure a phenomenon. An operational definition may be inherent in the conceptualized property of interest (e.g., we may use "number of people" to operationalize the concept of "GROUP SIZE") or require a logical or inferential leap (e.g., "attendance behavior" used to infer "JOB SATISFACTION"). Moreover, because there may be many particular classes of operational definitions for a given concept, it is not unusual for people to use different ones to refer to the same thing (e.g., "ORGANIZATIONAL EFFECTIVENESS"). Thus it is always a good practice to closely examine an operationalization to see if it is appropriate. Alternatively, investigators may use more than one operationalization (multiple indicators) in order to pin down an important concept in their work. Good operationalizations are clearly defined, capture the essential qualities of a concept (*see* VALIDITY), and are found acceptable by people who are affected by its use (in either THEORY building or practice).

See also **Generalization; Research design; Research methods**

Bibliography

Runkel, P. J. & McGrath, J. E. (1972). *Research on human behavior. A systematic guide for method.* New York: Holt, Rinehart, & Winston.

RICHARD KLIMOSKI

operations management Also called "Production/Operations Management," "OM," or "P/OM." Operations Management is the deployment of the resources of an organization to deliver, effectively and efficiently, services and products to its customers. This involves practitioners in such issues as product and process design; resource utilization; capacity scheduling; quality management; on-time delivery and other elements of customer service. The operations function is typically concerned with a large proportion of the physical assets and employees of a company and hence with costs and PRODUCTIVITY. The academic study of operations management seeks to analyze and prescribe best practice in each of these areas. OM research has traditionally been linked with operations research and used quantitative methods. While these remain important, in recent years there have been increasing calls for, and use of, empirical methods derived from social science. This move recognizes that an operation is not only a physical system but also a social one. Process developments such as group technology (*see* SOCIOTECHNICAL THEORY) have revealed connections with OB, as have such Japanese-derived practices as CONTINUOUS IMPROVEMENT. Similarly, the importance of information management in operations links OM with INFORMATION TECHNOLOGY and the study of decision support systems.

Although much core OM thinking has its origins in Taylor's SCIENTIFIC MANAGEMENT and thus in manufacturing practice, the growth of service industries in advanced economies has led to greater study of nonmanufacturing situations. The study of manufacturing itself has broadened into a greater effort to understand the competitive role of production, a topic known as manufacturing strategy. In the late twentieth century then, while operations management itself continues to be recognized as a crucial aspect of business performance, the academic subject is at a crossroads. Scholars lament the lack of a rich theoretical base, and dispute the appropriate research methods. The relatively low profile of OM in the business schools seems to reflect the status of OM practitioners in organizations. Yet the boundaries of the subject seem likely to widen, with such topics as TOTAL QUALITY MANAGEMENT and BUSINESS PROCESS REENGINEERING taking researchers beyond both narrow definitions of the operations function and traditional research paradigms.

See also **Advanced manufacturing technology; Just-in-time; Technology**

Bibliography

Schmenner, R. W. (1993). *Production/Operations management: From the inside out*, (5th edn). New York: Macmillan.

ROY WESTBROOK

organization and environment The environment is a key concept in the study of organizations. Essentially, an organization's environment is everything that lies outside the organizational boundary (*see* ORGANIZATION BOUNDARIES). That is, other organizations, the society in which it operates, governmental agencies and institutions, the economic system, LABOR MARKETS, financial systems, and so on. These factors make up what is known as the "general environment." Organizations generally do not have to deal with the whole environment in its totality, particular parts of the environment will have special importance. These make up the "task environment" and include the organization's own customers, suppliers, shareholders, bankers, and so on (*see* STAKEHOLDERS). Within the organization, individual SUBUNITS will develop relationships with particular parts of this task environment. So, for example, the finance department will deal with external financial institutions and specific governmental agencies such as the Inland Revenue, while the purchasing department will deal with suppliers and their agents. Each department will therefore manage the interface between themselves and a segment of the total task environment, acting on behalf of the organization as a whole.

Although the environment is often discussed as though it is completely separate from the "focal" organization, in reality, organizational boundaries are not always easy to distinguish with absolute precision. For example, are contracted-in cleaners or catering staff, those working on temporary contracts, or consultancy and advisory staff really part of the organization or not? Furthermore, the organization only selectively accepts environmental inputs – it is not necessarily open to everything. For these reasons the organization may be said to be a "relatively" OPEN SYSTEM, with semipermeable boundaries.

An open systems view sets the organization in the context of the environment. It recognizes that in order to survive, the organization must interact with its environment, obtain resources from it, transform them into products or services and export them back into it.

The environment represents UNCERTAINTY for the organization. This is because organizations cannot exist without these resource exchanges and they therefore do not have complete control over everything they need. Other organizations are in a position to exert influence over the flow of critical inputs. Uncertainty can bring instability since what is uncertain is less predictable. Organizations therefore need to "buffer" themselves from the possibly damaging effects of the environment. BOUNDARY-SPANNING departments can help by "environmental scanning," monitoring what is going on outside the organization to try and forecast change. Part of the work of research and development departments, marketing, and the human resource function, for example, is to monitor the environment to predict changes in products and TECHNOLOGY, customer requirements, and labor markets. By doing this they hope to establish a secure supply of resources and take proactive decisions to ward off threats and take advantage of opportunities. Individuals such as the chief executive and senior managers also perform this function, developing networks and relationships outside the organization. Interlocking directorates are a specific way in which senior personnel form linkages across organizations, sitting as directors, often in a nonexecutive capacity, on the boards of a number of different organizations and influential agencies (*see* NETWORKING; INTERORGANIZATIONAL RELATIONS). In this way they can gather information, build alliances and promote their own organizational interests, or, as it is sometimes argued, the interests of their social sector or class (*see* COALITION FORMATION).

It is clear that organizations do not all face the same environment. Furthermore, the nature and characteristics of the environment may be different for different organizations. Environments differ in their degrees of *COMPLEXITY* and *turbulence*. Complexity refers to the number of environmental factors with which the organization has to deal. For example, particularly since deregulation, the banking industry now has to deal with a number of different competitors (insurance companies, building societies, credit companies) all seeking to offer financial services to customers. Banks are therefore facing an increasingly complex environment. In contrast, for many years universities faced a relatively simple environment. The turbulence of the environment refers to the degree of change that is present. A fashion company would be a good example of a firm operating within a fairly turbulent environment. Changes in fashion are rapid, continuous, and relatively unpredictable. In contrast, until the advent of lagers in the 1980s, the British beer industry faced a fairly stable environment. The market was growing, but growth was relatively constant and predictable.

The levels of complexity and turbulence are obviously linked to the degree of uncertainty faced by managers. The greater the rate of environmental change and the number of factors to be considered, the less predictable the environment becomes and the greater the uncertainty for managers having to make sense of it.

Theories of organization differ about what managers have to do to cope with this situation, and the degree to which they have the freedom to manage environmental demands.

CONTINGENCY THEORY takes as its central focus the way in which the organization needs to adapt to environmental constraints. In this view the successfulness of an organization is predicated on the "fit" between an organization and the environment in which it operates. A number of factors need to be taken into account in order to ensure congruency. For example, Burns and Stalker (1961) suggested that environmental features will influence the effectiveness of the structural arrangements that the organization adopts. When the environment is fairly simple and relatively stable a mechanistic structure will work reasonably well (*see* MECHANISTIC/ORGANIC). Hierarchical (*see* HIERARCHY) lines of COMMUNICATION that allow information to flow up and down the organization are sufficient, decisions are taken centrally, and precise job specifications and routinized procedures allow tasks to be performed in standardized ways that facilitate stability (*see* BUREAUCRACY; ROUTINIZATION). But where the environment is highly volatile, firms need to respond quickly to changing demands. This requires communication to be more free-flowing across the organization as well as through the usual hierarchical channels. Whoever has information about changes needs to be able to pass this on, and DECISION MAKING is more decentralized (*see* DECENTRALIZATION). Job specifications and procedures are more flexible in order to speed up decision making. Organic structures help firms to perform more effectively in this kind of environment.

Lawrence and Lorsch (1967) noted that with more dynamic environments there is a need for organizations to separate out activities to a greater extent to cope more directly with specific segments of the environment. This DIFFERENTIATION has to be complemented by a reciprocal degree of INTEGRATION – coordinating mechanisms that bring the differentiated parts together again for the effective working of the whole organization.

However, one comment in relation to this school of thought is that the environment is not defined with precision. This makes it difficult for managers to know which indicators are critical in signaling whether there is an appropriate or inappropriate environmental fit. And if there is not, there are few prescriptions about the actions they need to take to regain congruency.

Child (1972) responded to this early work in the contingency framework by arguing that much of this did not make enough provision for the concept of STRATEGIC CHOICE by managers. His argument was that managers often have a far greater range of options open to them than is generally allowed by more deterministic views. They are not always constrained by environmental demands but can sometimes shape their own environments by choosing to operate in certain markets and offer particular products. This is especially true in the case of larger organizations, or those operating in monopolistic situations. The power of multinational and global companies to influence their competitive environment and the policies of host governments is well documented. Certainly, the ability of managers to make strategic decisions should not be underestimated (*see* STRATEGIC MANAGEMENT). This suggests that the allocation of power in the organization and the use of influence by subunits has a greater part to play than the contingency approach allows.

A further point here is that the environment itself is mediated by the managers' own interpretations. The environment is not "given" but has to be experienced and made sense of. This ENACTMENT leaves room for differing interpretations and understandings. Selective PERCEPTION and biases may influence this process and so affect the actions which managers take (*see* BEHAVIORAL DECISION RESEARCH).

The RESOURCE DEPENDENCE approach (Pfeffer & Salancik, 1978) also subscribes to much of the above. In viewing organizations as resource exchanging entities, this perspective sees the environment as playing a central part in any study of organizations. Organizations need to obtain external resources in order to survive, and since these are located in the environment it has a central role to play in organizational functioning. The resource dependence approach holds that a key function for managers is to manage this interface, as well as managing the internal organizational processes. For Pfeffer and Salancik, organizations can either try to change their environments or form interorganizational relationships to control or absorb uncertainty. Methods of changing the environment would include political lobbying to secure favorable trading or competitive conditions and choosing to operate in different market sectors. The development of interorganizational relationships can be accomplished in a number of ways. For example, by contracting arrangements, JOINT VENTURES, interlocking directorates, MERGERS, AND ACQUISITIONS. All these measures seek to reduce the dependence the organization has on its environment by securing access to external resources, including information.

The POPULATION ECOLOGY approach goes further than this. It too places the environment at the center of organizational analysis, but it is rather more pessimistic about the ability of managers to influence their situation. The view is that organizations do not so much adapt to their environment, but need to be selected by it if they are to survive. This is very similar to the Darwinian model of evolution. Organizations are subject to a process of natural selection, whereby the "fittest" survive, the rest do not. To survive, organizations need to find a niche where the environmental resources they require are available.

In the population ecology view, the environment is seen to have a number of dimensions in addition to the ideas of complexity and turbulence discussed above. The "capacity" of the environment refers to how rich or lean its stock of resources is. Rich environments provide more resources for growth but also attract more organizations so competition is fiercer. Environmental "concentration" describes a situation where environmental elements (such as customers, or clients) are relatively concentrated, whereas "dispersion" indicates they are scattered. Organizations will generally find it easier to operate within a more concentrated environment. Finally, the dimension of "domain consensus–dissensus" refers to the degree to which there is agreement about the area of operation of an organization. If claims to a domain or market are contested then domain dissensus will result.

This perspective goes beyond the analysis of individual organizations to study organizations as populations and tries to provide a general explanation for growth and death (*see* ORGANIZATIONAL CHANGE). Growth, if it happens at all, happens in stages. The first stage is when organizational forms begin to vary. Some of these forms are then selected and survive – others do not. This is the second stage. The final stage is retention, when those that are selected are duplicated or reproduced.

From the above discussion it will be seen that the environment occupies a central place in the analysis of organizations. But, as has been shown, the concept is much debated. A great deal of discussion focuses on the degree to which organizational actors are constrained by externalities or how far they have a measure of strategic choice. A central theme here is the discourse surrounding the free-will – determinism dialectic. Certainly, the environment is not always all-powerful and the ability of larger organizations to control external forces should not be overlooked.

The environment is a complex concept and definitions of its constituent parts are offered with varying degrees of precision and specificity. However, one significant point is that environments are perceived and interpreted by organizational actors. In this way, managers can and do shape their own environments.

See also **Competitiveness; Five forces framework; Organization theory; Organizational effectiveness; Resource based theory; Systems theory**

Bibliography

Aldrich, H. (1979). *Organizations and environments.* Englewood Cliffs, NJ: Prentice Hall.

Burns, T. & Stalker, G. M. (1961). *The management of innovation.* London: Tavistock.

Child, J. (1972). Organizational structure, environment and performance: The role of strategic choice. *Sociology*, (6), 1–22.

Lawrence, P. R. & Lorsch, J. W. (1967). *Organization and environment.* Cambridge, MA: Harvard University Press.

Pfeffer, J. & Salancik, G. R. (1978). *The external control of organizations: A resource dependence perspective.* New York: Harper & Row.

SUSAN MILLER

organization development This is a field of applied behavioral science focused on understanding and managing ORGANIZATIONAL CHANGE. As such, organization development (OD) is both a field of social and managerial action and a field of scientific inquiry (Cummings & Worley, 1993; Woodman, 1989). As a field of applied behavioral science, OD draws heavily from psychology and sociology, and, to a lesser extent, from anthropology. In terms of organizational behavior topics, OD relies on information from MOTIVATION theory, PERSONALITY theory, and LEARNING theory, as well as research on GROUP DYNAMICS, LEADERSHIP, POWER, and ORGANIZATION DESIGN, among others. The field is truly an interdisciplinary one, and many theoretical perspectives may inform the investigation and management of organizational change processes.

Representative Definitions of OD

Some representative definitions help to frame the boundaries and identify the focus of the field.

> [Organization development is] "a system-wide application of behavioral science knowledge to the planned development and reinforcement of organizational strategies, structures, and processes for improving an organization's effectiveness" (Cummings & Worley, 1993, p. 2).

> "Organization development is a top-management-supported, long-range effort to improve an organization's problem solving and renewal processes,

particularly through a more effective and collaborative diagnosis and management of ORGANIZATIONAL CULTURE – with special emphasis on a formal work team, temporary team, and intergroup culture – with the assistance of a consultant–facilitator and the use of the theory and technology of applied behavioral science, including action research" (French & Bell, 1990, p. 17).

"Organization development is a set of behavioral science-based theories, VALUES, strategies, and techniques aimed at the planned change of the organizational work setting for the purpose of enhancing individual development and improving organizational performance, through the alteration of organizational members' on-the-job behaviors" (Porras & Robertson, 1992, p. 722).

"Organization development means creating adaptive organizations capable of repeatedly transforming and reinventing themselves as needed to remain effective" (Woodman, 1993, p. 73).

These and other definitions emphasize OD's focus on planful, systematic change, its knowledge base in the behavioral sciences, and the ultimate goal of improving performance or effectiveness. Indeed, at some level of abstraction, ORGANIZATIONAL EFFECTIVENESS is the goal of all planned change interventions (*see* PLANNING).

Further Defining Characteristics

In addition to the themes appearing in the above definitions of the field, there are basic characteristics that distinguish OD from other approaches to understanding and changing organizations (Beer, 1980, p. 10).

(1) OD seeks to create self-directed change to which people are committed. The problems and issues to be solved are those identified by the organization members directly involved.
(2) OD is most typically a systemwide change effort. Making lasting changes that create a more effective organization requires an understanding of the entire organization. It is not possible to change part of the organization without changing the whole organization in some sense. Emphasizing this characteristic, Burke (1994) defines OD as essentially a process of fundamental change in an organization's culture.
(3) OD typically places equal emphasis on solving immediate problems and on the long-term development of an adaptive organization (*see* LEARNING ORGANIZATION). The most effective change program is not just one that solves present problems but one that also prepares employees to solve future problems.
(4) OD places more emphasis than do other change approaches on action research – a collaborative process of data collection, diagnosis, and action planning designed to create widely supported solutions to organizational problems.
(5) OD has a dual emphasis on organizational effectiveness and human fulfillment through the work experience.

The emphasis on human fulfillment gives the field a reputation for a humanistic orientation which has sometimes contributed to an unfavorable view of OD as being both a "soft" science and an equally "soft" approach to managing human resources. However, the current trends toward TOTAL QUALITY MANAGEMENT (TQM) and CONTINUOUS IMPROVEMENT philosophies have reaffirmed the crucial role of committed human actors in organizational performance (Woodman, 1993). Organizational effectiveness and employee well-being and development often go hand-in-hand – something the field of management seems to relearn about every 20 years.

Development of the Field

Historically, OD has been more micro than macro in orientation, more focused on individual and group behaviors than on organizational processes, perhaps more concerned with the tactics of intervention design and conduct than with the strategy of changing whole systems. Organization development grew out of early laboratory training methods (*see* SENSITIVITY TRAINING) and survey research and feedback methodologies in the United States and SOCIOTECHNICAL THEORY developments in the United Kingdom and Sweden. However, the field has moved well beyond these early conceptualizations. OD has been broadening its focus considerably – from a focus on interpersonal and group processes to a greater focus on structure and strategy; from a focus exclusively at the individual and group level to a focus which encompasses the organization as a system. In fact, the somewhat longer-term "organizational change and development" is becoming increasingly popular in place of the traditional OD label as a way of recognizing the expanding boundaries of the field. The reader is referred to Cummings and Worley (1993, pp. 6–15) or French and Bell (1990, pp. 24–43) for an overview of the early history of the field. For an understanding of the evolution of OD, *see* the encyclopedic chapters by Mirvis (1988; 1990).

Organization Development Theory and Issues

A notable characteristic of the field of OD is the rich diversity of theories that have been employed in attempts to explain organizational change. Porras and Robertson (1987; 1992) have identified two types of organization development theory: change PROCESS THEORY and implementation theory. Change process theory focuses on explaining the dynamics through which organizations change. Implementation theory, most closely related to OD practice, focuses on specific interventions and procedures that can be used to actually change organizations. This dichotomy of theories reflects the dual nature of the field as one encompassing both scientific inquiry and organizational action. In general, implementation theory is more fully developed than change process theory in OD (Porras & Robertson, 1992).

The future of OD would seem bright, if for no other reason than the fact that the challenge and necessity of managing change in complex organizations continues to be among the key issues that organizations must address in order to be effective. However, as with many other applied sciences, the field suffers from tensions between theory and practice. The schism between the science of organizational change and the art of changing organizations perhaps represents the single greatest impediment to progress in OD.

See also **Consultancy intervention models; Group dynamics; Management development; Organizational restructuring; Process consultation**

Bibliography

Beer, M. (1980). *Organization change and development: A systems view*. Santa Monica, CA: Goodyear.

Burke, W. W. (1994). *Organization development: A process of learning and changing*, (2nd edn). Reading, MA: Addison-Wesley.

Cummings, T. G. & Worley, C. G. (1993). *Organization development and change*, (5th edn). Minneapolis/St. Paul, MN: West.

French, W. L. & Bell, C. H. (1990). *Organization development: Behavioral science interventions for organization improvement* (4th edn). Englewood Cliffs, NJ: Prentice-Hall.

Mirvis, P. H. (1988). Organization development: Part I – An evolutionary perspective. In W. A. Pasmore & R. W. Woodman (Eds), *Research in organizational change and development*, (vol. 2, pp. 1–57). Greenwich, CT: JAI Press.

Mirvis, P. H. (1990). Organization development: Part II – A revolutionary perspective. In W. A. Pasmore & R. W. Woodman (Eds), *Research in organizational change and development*, (vol. 4, pp. 1–66). Greenwich, CT: JAI Press.

Porras, J. I. & Robertson, P. J. (1987). Organization development theory: A typology and evaluation. In R. W. Woodman & W. A. Pasmore (Eds), *Research in organizational change and development*, (vol. 1, pp. 1–57). Greenwich, CT: JAI Press.

Porras, J. I. & Robertson, P. J. (1992). Organizational development: Theory, practice, and research. In M. D. Dunnette & L. M. Hough (Eds), *Handbook of industrial and organizational psychology*, (2nd edn, vol. 3, pp. 719–822). Palo Alto, CA: Consulting Psychologists Press.

Woodman, R. W. (1989). Organizational change and development: New arenas for inquiry and action. *Journal of Management*, **15**, 205–228.

Woodman, R. W. (1993). Observations on the field of organizational change and development from the lunatic fringe. *Organization Development Journal*, **11**, 71–74.

RICHARD W. WOODMAN

organization theory This is a body of scholarship that attempts to explain variations in the structure and operating processes of organizations. Its unit of analysis is the organization itself, or SUBUNITS of the organization, not individual people, the units of analysis to which ORGANIZATIONAL BEHAVIOR refers (*see* LEVELS OF ANALYSIS). The term "organization theory" is a misnomer because this body of scholarship includes empirical research and prescriptive analyses of managerial problems as well as theory.

The field of organizational behavior emerged as industrial psychologists entered business schools in the United States and sought a term to distinguish their positivistic research from the more normative field of PERSONNEL MANAGEMENT. When other kinds of social scientists followed, organizational research began to find a broader audience in business schools and other professional schools (*see* MANAGEMENT EDUCATION). People already in the field sought a term to distinguish this new way of looking at organizations from the previous focus on individual behavior. Since this new style of research seemed quite abstract, it came to be known as "organization theory" as a complement to "organizational behavior."

There is, however, a fundamental difference between how these two groups thought about human behavior in organizations. Industrial psychologists generally have not believed human beings think differently when they are in an organizational context. Consequently, their approach has applied theories and methods developed for other purposes to understanding human behavior in organizations. Organizational sociology, in particular, is not an application of some other theory to organizations. Rather, sociologists believe that organizations are units of social organization manifesting phenomena to be explained in ways that differ fundamentally from the explanations offered to account for phenomena manifested by other units of social organization such as families or residential communities.

Organization theory began almost simultaneously in two places in the United States shortly after World War II. In New York City, at Columbia University's Department of Sociology, people began to study organizations as units of analysis, not simply as bureaucracies that were the instruments of political process (*see* BUREAUCRACY). The inspiration for such a new interest was structural–functional analysis in which social organization develops to satisfy functional requisites or "needs" of society. Formal organizations are important units through which this is done. The other locus of organizational research was the Carnegie Institute in Pittsburgh where the psychologist Herbert Simon, the political scientist James G. March, and the economist Richard Cyert began to develop a different approach to the study of organizations.

Philip Selznick, trained at Columbia, published *The TVA and the Grass Roots* (1949) and *Leadership in Administration* (1957). They appeared at almost precisely the same time as Herbert Simon's *Administrative Behavior* (1948) and March and Simon's *Organizations* (1958).

The Columbia sociology department produced doctoral students who spread out across the United States to develop organizational sociology. While Selznick went to Berkeley, Peter Blau eventually took a job at Chicago where he trained a series of doctoral students including W. Richard Scott. Their book *Formal Organizations* (1962) was the first textbook devoted exclusively to organization theory. Scott moved to the Stanford sociology department where he teamed up with another Columbia graduate, John Meyer, to found modern INSTITUTIONAL THEORY. Students from Carnegie-Mellon, as it ultimately came to be called, include Oliver Williamson and Jeffrey Pfeffer (who received an undergraduate degree and MBA from Carnegie).

Organizational theory penetrated business schools in the United States as CONTINGENCY THEORY drew a new audience for learning about organizations. This audience was higher level managers and students who aspired to such high positions. While organizational psychology and its normative cousin, PERSONNEL MANAGEMENT, were principally about individuals and small groups, with emphasis on the factory work settings, organization theory and its normative cousin, ORGANIZATIONAL DESIGN, were principally about the organization as a whole. This new audience grew as a transition toward more theoretically-based material gained impetus in US business schools. As the social sciences invaded business schools and other professional schools as well, social science contributions to organizational studies broadened and became more theoretical. So organizational theory grew rapidly through the 1970s and 1980s.

At about the same time contingency theory emerged as the body of scholarship pushing organization theory itself into the mainstream, SYSTEMS THEORY emerged from engineering and rapidly gained a presence in the field of management science. Systems theory drew attention to the organization as a unit of analysis, and thus was consistent with other strands of organization theory. Furthermore, it treated organizations dynamically, with a focus on operating processes that linked organization with its environment (*see* ORGANIZATION AND ENVIRONMENT). It also stressed the problems associated with self-regulating systems (sometimes called cybernetic systems), which are the properties of organizations describing their tolerance for and adjustment to environmental and technical change. Systems theory did not penetrate the mainstream of organizational theory very deeply, however. While virtually all organization theorists adopted the metaphors of systems theory, including using the term "system" itself, systems theory never developed a strong empirical base. Many of its more interesting ideas were difficult to render observable in real organizations. In addition, the dynamic nature of the systems conceptualization proved daunting to capture in formal mathematical models. This problem proved a major weakness at the core of systems theory and it ceased to be a major PARADIGM, in management science and operations research as well as in organization theory.

Interest by sociologists in the relationship between ORGANIZATION SIZE and structure developed a literature that made small impact on organization theory as a whole. The main tenet of this work was that larger organizations have more complex structures: more levels in the HIERARCHY of AUTHORITY, more departments and sections on the horizontal dimension (*see* DEPARTMENTALIZATION). Probably the most important and lasting contribution of the size and structure literature was to encourage empirical quantitative research on organizations in which large, systematically drawn samples of organizations were used to generate data. This in turn encouraged the use of statistical methods and formalized theories. Organization theory developed methodological sophistication at the same time other branches of scholarship in the social science and professional schools developed such methods. This had the effect of keeping the field current with developments elsewhere. It also had the effect of focusing interest on things that were measurable, diverting attention from issues of great interest and importance to many scholars and students of organizations.

In the early 1970s two new branches of organization theory developed, both emanating from the Carnegie school. Pfeffer and Salancik (*see* Pfeffer & Salancik (1978) for a summary) began a series of studies drawing attention to the RESOURCE DEPENDENCE of organizations. While contingency theorists wrote about uncertainties imposed on organizations by their environments, resource dependence developed the argument first appearing in Cyert and March (1963) that organizations developed their structures around access to resources. These resources are controlled by other powerful actors whose preferences and practices constrain the organization under study. Control over resources is the primary subject of dispute within organizations and thus conditions POWER structures (*see* RESOURCE BASED THEORY).

At about the same time Oliver Williamson was combining the organizational theories of the Carnegie school with the institutional economics of John R. Commons and Ronald Coase to develop a new version of TRANSACTION COST THEORY. While neoclassical economists treated organizations as single, unified actors with clearly evident and consistent preferences, Williamson argued that their internal structures mattered. People in organizations have their own agendas and will pursue them when they can, sometimes to the detriment of the organization as a whole. Organizations are built as attempts to create efficient structures where markets fail to do so.

Each of the strands of theory described thus far, with the exception of systems theory, took it as axiomatic that organizations were to be understood as the purposeful creations of some recognizable individual or group. They were treated as tools to be used to achieve specific purposes. Failure to cooperate, then, is at least implicitly a form of subversion. The inherent conservatism of structural–functional analysis continued in organization theory long after it disappeared in other branches of sociology, political science, and anthropology. The research of the 1960s and 1970s, however, showed the organizational goals are often more apparent than real. Much of what makes an organization organized is the informal system that springs up spontaneously among the people. This organization is often barely recognized and usually misunderstood by higher level managers. By definition, it is not designed by them. So organizations can be seen as having lives of their own. If this is true, how do we understand their structure and operations?

Two branches of organization theory appeared in the late 1970s as an explicit attempt to answer this question. Both grew out of sociological studies of organizations: POPULATION ECOLOGY of organizations and sociological institutional theory.

Population ecology focuses on the tendency of organizations to cluster together in social categories. Observable variations in organizations do not blend smoothly and continuously so that it makes little sense to refer to a "bank" as compared with a "hospital." The former do not blend seemlessly with the latter so that in common parlance one is forced to refer to a "more or less bank." The variables on whose dimensions we can distinguish banks from hospitals come distributed in discrete chunks called organizational forms. The organizations manifesting a form are populations of organizations. Among the features these population members share is a common dependence on resources and a common dependence on other organizations for support. In this sense, the members of a population have a shared fate. As resources, cooperation, and opposition from other organizations rise and fall, the population as a whole is advantaged or disadvantaged. The rates of foundings and failure for that population rise and fall. Members of these populations have the odds increasingly with them or against them in consequence. As these populations expand, creating opportunity for organization founders and for existing firms, and contract, signifying tough times for members of those populations, distributions of interesting organizational variables shift. For example, as populations of locally owned and managed banks decline, and nation-wide chains of banks expand, the employment opportunities, WORKING CONDITIONS and services offered all change.

Population ecology focuses on the typical case, what population members have in common. As such it provides context against which to gauge the behavior of individuals and single organizations, particularly those that are chosen for study because of their unusual features.

While population ecologists tend to stress the resource environments of organizations, institutional theorists stress the cultural and political environments. For them, the societies in which organizations operate impose expectations about structure and operating procedures on the individual organization and its participants. So even if a bank is owned by a single individual, he or she is not perfectly free to organize in any manner that might be possible. A body of social norms, including those formalized in laws and banking regulations, constrains the bank organizer. Further, these patterned expectations include more subtle constraints such as architecture, modes of dress, and styles of interaction. Institutional theorists generally argue that operating efficiency is only one criterion affecting the mode of organization. And efficiency itself is culturally defined (*see* SOCIAL CONSTRUCTIONISM). Population ecologists and institutional theorists agree that environmental factors limit the choices available to those who organize and that such decisions are only some of the factors that generate observed organizational patterns.

As population ecology and institutional theory developed in the 1980s, a growing interest in culture and its effects on organization produced related streams of theory and research. Some of this work on CULTURE blended with institutional theory but some focused more on differences between national cultures and the challenges of organizing across such boundaries (*see* CULTURE, NATIONAL). Such issues loom larger in the imagination of many European scholars who can see the political boundaries between societies evaporating, marking the cultural distinctions even more clearly. As European organizations expand across those boundaries, often by constructing JOINT VENTURE or by effecting mergers (*see* MERGERS AND ACQUSITIONS), attempts to understand the consequences have burgeoned. The gropings to understand "Japanese management" and "corporate culture" often missed the point that culture is no more an option to be chosen and designed by chief executives than being Japanese or French is a matter of choice for individuals (*see* ORGANIZATIONAL CULTURE).

Finally, throughout this period interest in DECISION MAKING has continued. The Carnegie school began with the assumption of BOUNDED RATIONALITY. This evolved into a critique of organizations as tools designed by rational managers (*see* RATIONALITY). Organizations face continuing ambiguity as decision makers face vague COMMUNICATIONS about how imprecise TECHNOLOGY are being used or abused in pursuit of more or less understood goals. All of this leads to a view of organizations as groping through time and space, muddling through rather than conquering strategically chosen obstacles (*see* GARBAGE CAN model).

See also **Critical theory; Postmodernism; Theory**

Bibliography

Cyert, R. & March, J. (1963). *A behavioral theory of the firm*. Englewood Cliffs, NJ: Prentice-Hall.

March, J. G. & Simon, H. A. (1958). *Organizations*. New York: Wiley.

Mouzelis, N. P. (1968). *Organization and bureaucracy: An analysis of modern theories*. Chicago: Aldine.

Pfeffer, J. & Salancik, G. (1978). *The external control of organizations: A resource dependence perspective*. New York: Harper & Row.

Scott, W. R. (1981). *Organizations: Rational, natural, and open systems*. Englewood Cliffs, NJ: Prentice-Hall.

Selznick, P. (1949). *TVA and the grass roots*. Berkeley, CA: University of California Press.

Selznick, P. (1957). *Leadership in administration*. New York: Harper & Row.

Simon, H. A. (1948). *Administrative behavior*. New York: Macmillan.

JOHN FREEMAN

organizational adaptation *see* POPULATION ECOLOGY

organizational behavior Commonly referred to under its acronym "OB" by practitioners and students, and scholars in the field, it is the study of human agency in organizations of all types. This means an interest in the behavior *of* organizations as well as behavior *in* organizations, since the actions, cognitions, and motives of human agents affect the structure, strategy, and functioning of organizations, as well as vice versa. Therefore, OB seeks to explain and predict the experience and behavior at four LEVELS OF ANALYSIS:

(1) the individual actor: owners, managers, and staff at all levels;
(2) the group: WORK GROUPS, teams, and other organizational subunits, and the relations between them;
(3) interest groups: occupational, professional, and representative groups such as TRADE UNIONS; and
(4) organizations: public institutions and private firms, voluntary and NOT-FOR-PROFIT ORGANIZATIONS.

At all these levels OB scholars are engaged in THEORY building and testing, methodological advance, and practical applications for the benefit of organizations and their members. This breadth of scope makes OB a multidisciplinary social science enterprise, rooted primarily in applied psychology and sociology, but also drawing upon anthropology and economics (*see* ORGANIZATIONAL ECONOMICS). The field also embraces applications including, HUMAN RESOURCES MANAGEMENT and business strategy at the level of the firm or institution (*see* STRATEGIC MANAGEMENT). OB represents one of the major subject areas or departmental subdivisions of the modern business school (typical others being finance, accounting, economics, marketing, OPERATIONS MANAGEMENT, and decision science). As such it is a recent creation, of American origin, from the post-war growth of business administration and management as substantive fields in higher education (*see* MANAGEMENT EDUCATION). In the last 30 years it has become the principal pedagogic and research focus for fields such as industrial sociology and industrial–organizational (I/O) psychology, which formerly were located in the departments of their parent disciplines, but which increasingly are centered on the OB departments of business schools. This development is more advanced in

North America than in Europe and elsewhere, but is a visibly continuing trend.

See also **Industrial relations; Organization theory; Personnel management; Research methods; Research design**

NIGEL NICHOLSON

organizational birth and death *see* ORGANIZATIONAL DEATH AND DECLINE; POPULATION ECOLOGY; FOUNDERS

organizational boundaries These are perimeters that by convention are said to define an organization, with members designated as "within" the boundary, and clients, customers, suppliers, and regulators, for instance, as "outside." Transactions occur at the interface. Boundaries signify a distinction between the organization and its environment, with members having particular rights and obligations not recognized in others (*see* ORGANIZATION AND ENVIRONMENT). Physical bounds, such as gates, fences, or doors, are complemented by imagined boundaries, such as initiation or hiring, or the interaction (between a salesperson and a customer, for instance). Members who interact regularly with outsiders are responsible for BOUNDARY SPANNING.

Traditional ideas about organizational boundaries assume a clear distinction between those "inside" and those "outside," but contemporary trends toward highly responsive organizations, close attention to the customer, interorganizational collaboration, and information sharing dilute the concept of boundary substantially (*see* INTERORGANIZATIONAL RELATIONS). Computer links can further diffuse boundaries, as when a customer's computer executes a purchase by automatically scheduling production on a vendor's computer, or customers and vendors jointly participate in product design. Such arrangements suggest highly porous boundaries or overlap between the firms. STRATEGIC ALLIANCES, JOINT VENTURES licensing agreements, and similar arrangements also diminish the sharpness of boundaries, creating forms of LOOSE COUPLING.

See also **Population ecology; Systems theory; Stakeholders; Open systems**

Bibliography

Aldrich, H. & Herker, D. (1977). Boundary spanning roles and organization structure. *Academy of Management Review*, **2**, 217–230.

MARIANN JELINEK

organizational change The study of organizational change is at the very core of management and ORGANIZATIONAL BEHAVIOR. Organizational change is a difference in form, quality, or state over time in an organizational entity. The entity may be an individual's job, a WORK GROUP, an organizational subunit, strategy, or product, or the overall design of an organization (*see* ORGANIZATIONAL DESIGN). Change in any of these entities can be calculated by measuring the same entity at two or more points in time on a set of dimensions, and then calculating the differences over time in these dimensions. If the difference is greater than zero (assuming no measurement ERROR), we can say that the organizational entity has changed. Much of the voluminous literature on organizational change focuses on the nature of this difference, what produced it, and what are its consequences. Change can take many forms; it can be: planned or unplanned, incremental or radical, and recurrent or unprecedented. Trends in the process or sequence of changes can be observed over time. These trends can be accelerating or decelerating in time, and move toward equilibrium, oscillation, chaos, or randomness in the behavior of the organizational entity being examined (*see* CHAOS THEORY; PUNCTUATED EQUILIBRIUM). Thus, the basic concept of organization change involves three ideas:

(1) difference;
(2) at different temporal moments; and
(3) between states of the same organizational unit or system.

As this definition suggests, changes in an organizational system can occur at various LEVELS OF ANALYSIS, including the individual, group, organization, population or networks of organizations (*see* NETWORK ANALYSIS), and even larger communities or societies of organizations (*see* SYSTEMS THEORY). Understanding organizational change therefore requires careful focus on what level of analysis is being examined if one is to understand how changes occurring at these various levels interrelate. Organizational change is often mediated through individual actors. Therefore, Van de Ven and Poole (1988) argue that theories of organizational change should show how macro variables affect individual motives and choices and how these choices in turn change the macro-organization.

The topic of change depends on what events or variables are used to measure differences in an organizational entity over time. If an organization is viewed as a social system, the changes observed may include the following issues:

- changes in composition (e.g., personnel mobility, RECRUITMENT, promotion, or layoffs, and shifts in resource allocations among organizational units);
- changes in structure (e.g., alterations of the organization's governance structure, centralization of decision making, formalization of rules, monitoring and control systems, and inequalities of STATUS or POWER among units or positions);
- changes in functions (e.g., organizational or subunit strategies, goals, mandates, products, or services);
- changes in boundaries (as brought about by MERGERS AND ACQUISITIONS, or divestitures of organizational units, establishing JOINT VENTURES or STRATEGIC ALLIANCES, modifying membership admission criteria, organizational expansions or contractions in regions, markets, products/services, and political domains) (*see* ORGANIZATIONAL BOUNDARIES);
- changes in relationships among organizational levels and units (e.g., increases or decreases in resource dependencies, work flows, COMMUNICATIONS, CONFLICT, cooperation, competition, CONTROL, or CULTURE among organizational entities) (*see* RESOURCE DEPENDENCE);
- changes in performance, including effectiveness (degree of goal attainment), efficiency (cost per unit of output), and morale of participants (e.g., JOB SATISFACTION or QUALITY of WORKING LIFE (*see* ORGANIZATIONAL EFFECTIVENESS)); and
- changes in the environment (ecological munificence or scarcity, turbulence, UNCERTAINTY, COMPLEXITY, or heterogeneity) (*see* ORGANIZATION AND ENVIRONMENT).

Changes in any of these substantive areas can be planned or unplanned. In the late 1960s and 1970s, much attention to planned organizational change came from scholars and practitioners identified with ORGANIZATIONAL DEVELOPMENT (OD). Beckhard (1969, p. 9) defined OD as "an effort (1) *planned*, (2) *organization-wide*, and (3) *managed* from the top to (4) increase *organization effectiveness* and *health* through (5) *planned interventions* in the organization's processes using *behavioral science* knowledge" (italics in original). While Beckhard's definition implies a relatively conservative change strategy, Bartunek (1993) discusses other OD views that are more revolutionary in purpose and focus on bottom-up rather than top-down strategies for change. OD encompasses a variety of behavioral science interventions and action research methods (*see* ACTION/INTERVENTION RESEARCH) that may help organizational participants make decisions, solve problems, overcome resistance, resolve conflicts, and play roles as needed to implement a planned change (*see* RESISTANCE TO CHANGE). OD takes a normative and interventionist orientation that is useful to management consultants and change agents who are frequently called upon to help undertake a variety of changes that are planned and desired by organizational executives (*see* CONSULTANCY).

Other management and organizational scholars have taken a more descriptive and positive approach to organizational change. Recognizing that varying degrees of change and stability are facts of any organization over time, much of the literature has distinguished between two modes of change:

(1) incremental (first-order) change which channels an organizational entity in the direction of adapting its basic structure and maintaining its identity in a stable and predictable way as it changes; and
(2) radical (second-order) change, which creates novel forms that are discontinuous and unpredictable departures from the past (*see* review by Meyer, Brooks, & Goes, 1990).

Typically, observed changes represent small, incremental, convergent, or continuous differences in localized parts of the organization, without major repercussions to other parts of the system. The organization as a whole remains intact, and no overall change of its former state occurs in spite of the incremental changes going on inside. While first-order changes may represent radical transformations *of* organizational subunits, they typically represent only incremental or continuous changes *in* the overall organizational system. Indeed, system stability often requires these kinds of incremental changes. Occasionally, large differences may occur in all (or at least the core) components of the system, producing a radical transformation or mutation *of* the overall organization. These second-order changes lead us to treat the new organizational system as fundamentally different from the old one.

The borderline between these extremes is somewhat fluid. Incremental changes in organizational units may accumulate and affect the core of the system, producing a radical change *of* the overall organization. Path dependencies or positive FEEDBACK may exist among incremental change events so that the timing of the changes may lead to major transformations. These incremental and radical changes in organizations may also alternate over time. For example, in Tushman and Romanelli's (1985) PUNCTUATED EQUILIBRIUM model, organizational metamorphosis is explained by long periods of incremental, first-order changes that refine an organization's operations, products, and services. These convergent periods are occasionally punctuated by short periods of technological ferment, which may produce radical and discontinuous second-order changes in the organization.

Theories Explaining Organizational Change Processes

Explaining how and why organizations change is a central and enduring quest of scholars in management and many other social science disciplines (*see* reviews in Sztompka, 1993; and Van de Ven & Poole, 1994). The processes or sequences of events that unfold in these changes are very difficult to explain, let alone to manage. Van de Ven and Poole (1994) identify four different theories that are often used to explain how and why organizational changes unfold: life cycle, teleology, dialectics, and evolution. These four theories will be reviewed here, for they represent fundamentally different explanations of organizational change in any of the substantive areas or topics listed before. Each theory focuses attention on a different set of generating mechanisms and causal cycles to explain what triggers change and what follows what in a sequence of organizational changes (*see* VICIOUS CYCLES).

Life cycle theory. Many OB scholars have adopted the metaphor of organic growth as a heuristic device to explain changes in an organizational entity from its initiation to its termination (*see* applications in Huber and Glick, 1993) (*see* MECHANISTIC/ORGANIC). Witness, for example, often-used references to the life cycles of organizations, products, and ventures, as well as stages in the development of individual CAREERS, groups, and organizations: startup births, adolescent growth, maturity, and decline or death (*see* ORGANIZATIONAL DECLINE AND DEATH). Life cycle theory assumes that change is immanent; that is, the developing entity has within it an underlying form, logic, program, or code that regulates the process of change and moves the entity from a given point of departure toward a subsequent end that is already prefigured in the present state. What lies latent, rudimentary, or homogeneous in the embryo or primitive state becomes progressively more realized, mature, and differentiated. External environmental events and processes can influence how the immanent form expresses itself, but they are always mediated by the immanent logic, rules, or programs that govern development.

The typical progression of events in a life cycle model is a unitary sequence (it follows a single sequence of stages or phases), which is cumulative (characteristics acquired in earlier stages are retained in later stages) and conjunctive (the stages are related such that they derive from a common underlying process). This is because the trajectory to the final end state is prefigured and requires a specific historical sequence of events. Each of these events contributes a certain piece to the final product, and they must occur in a certain order, because each piece sets the stage for the next.

Each stage of development can be seen as a necessary precursor of succeeding stages.

Life cycle theory is rooted in the approach of the gross anatomist in biology who observes a sequence of developing fetuses, concluding that each successive stage evolved from the previous one. From this perspective, change is driven by some genetic code or prefigured program within the developing entity. This view can be extended to include a number of historically driven processes of cognitive development in which each stage logically presupposes the next, such as when the development of manipulative skills precedes writing (*see* MORAL DEVELOPMENT). There is no reason to suppose organizational systems could not have such processes as well.

Life cycle theories of organizations often explain development in terms of institutional rules or programs that require developmental activities to progress in a prescribed sequence. For example, a legislative bill enacting state educational reform cannot be passed until it has been drafted and gone through the necessary House and Senate committees. Other life cycle theories rely on logical or natural properties of organizations. For example, Rogers' (1983) theory posits five stages of INNOVATION: need recognition; research on the problem; development of an idea into useful form; commercialization; and diffusion and adoption (*see* INNOVATION ADOPTION; INNOVATION DIFFUSION). The order among these stages is necessitated both by logic and by the natural order of Western business practices.

Teleological theory. Another family of process theories uses teleology to explain development. This approach underlies many organizational theories of change, including functionalism, DECISION MAKING, adaptive LEARNING, and most models of STRATEGIC CHOICE and GOAL SETTING. A teleological theory is based on the assumption that change proceeds toward a goal or end state. It assumes that the organization is populated by purposeful and adaptive individuals. By themselves or in interaction with others they construct an envisioned end state, take action to reach it, and monitor their progress. Thus, this theory views development as a cycle of goal formulation, implementation, evaluation, and modification of goals based on what was learned or intended (*see* RATIONALITY). The theory can operate in a single individual or among a group of cooperating individuals or organizations who are sufficiently like-minded to act as a single collective entity (*see* GROUP CULTURE). Since the individual or cooperating entities have the freedom to set whatever goals they like, teleological theory inherently accommodates CREATIVITY; there are no necessary constraints or forms that mandate reproduction of the current entity or state.

Unlike life cycle theory, teleology does not presume a necessary sequence of events or specify which trajectory development will follow. However, it does imply a standard by which development can be judged: development is that which moves the entity toward its final state. There is no prefigured rule, logically necessary direction, or set sequence of stages in a teleological process. Instead, these theories focus on the prerequisites for attaining the goal or end-state: the functions that must be fulfilled, the accomplishments that must be achieved, or the components that must be built or obtained for the end-state to be realized. These prerequisites can be used to assess when an entity is developing; it is growing more complex, it is growing more integrated, or it is filling out a necessary set of functions. This assessment can be made because teleological theories posit an envisioned end state or design for an entity and it is possible to observe movement toward the end state vis-à-vis this standard.

Teleological models of development incorporate the systems theory assumption of equifinality; i.e., there are several equally effective ways to achieve a given goal. There is no assumption about historical necessity. Rather, these models rely on voluntarism as the explanatory principle. They posit a set of functions or goals desired by an organizational unit, which it must acquire in order to "realize" its aspirations. Changes in organizations are viewed as movements toward attaining a desired purpose, goal, function, or desired end state. There is no hard and fast order in which the organization must acquire the means and resources to achieve this goal.

While teleology stresses the purposiveness of the individual as the generating force for change, it also recognizes limits on action. The organization's environment and its resources of knowledge, time, money, etc., constrain what it can accomplish. Some of these constraints are embodied in the prerequisites, which are to some extent defined by institutions and other actors in the entity's environment. Individuals do not override natural laws or environmental constraints, but make use of them in accomplishing their purposes.

Once an entity attains this end state does not mean it stays in permanent equilibrium. Influences in the external environment or within the entity itself may create instabilities that push it to a new developmental path or trajectory. Theories that rely on a teleological process cannot specify what trajectory development will follow. They can at best list a set of possible paths, and rely on norms of rationality to prescribe certain paths (*see* ORGANIZATION AND ENVIRONMENT).

Dialectical theory. A third family, dialectical theories, is rooted in the assumption that the organization exists in a pluralistic world of colliding events, forces, or contradictory values that compete with each other for domination and control. These oppositions may be internal to an organization because it may have several conflicting goals or interest groups competing for priority. Oppositions may also arise external to the organization as it pursues directions that collide with those of others (*see* Burawoy & Skocpol (1982)).

Dialectical process theories explain stability and change by reference to the relative balance of POWER between opposing entities (*see* CONFLICT). Stability is produced through struggles and accommodations that maintain the status quo between oppositions. Change occurs when these opposing VALUES, forces, or events gain sufficient power to confront and engage the status quo. The relative power of an opposing PARADIGM or antithesis may mobilize to a sufficient degree to challenge the current thesis or state of affairs and set the stage for producing a synthesis. More precisely, the status quo subscribing to a thesis (A) may be challenged by an opposing entity with an antithesis (Not-A), and the resolution of the conflict produces a synthesis (which is Not Not-A). Over time, this synthesis can become the new thesis as the dialectical process recyles and continues. By its very nature, the synthesis is something created new, discontinuous with thesis and antithesis.

Creative syntheses to dialectical conflicts are often not assured. Sometimes an opposition group mobilizes sufficient power to simply overthrow and replace the status quo, just as many organizational regimes persist by maintaining sufficient power to suppress and prevent the mobilization of opposition groups. In the bargaining and CONFLICT RESOLUTION literature the desired creative synthesis is one that represents a win–win solution, while either the maintenance of the status quo or its replacement with an antithesis are often treated as win–lose outcomes of a CONFLICT engagement (*see* CONFLICT MANAGEMENT). In terms of organizational change, maintenance of the status quo represents stability, while its replacement with either the antithesis or the synthesis represents a change, for the better or worse.

In general, a PROCESS THEORY that focuses on the intercourse of opposites can explain organizational changes that move toward:

(1) equilibrium;
(2) oscillation; and
(3) chaos.

First, organizational stability and inertia result when the routines, goals, or values of the status quo are sufficiently dominant to suppress opposing minority positions, and thereby produce incremental adaptations flowing toward equilibrium (*see* MINORITY GROUP INFLUENCE). For example, an existing ORGANIZATIONAL CULTURE, structure, or system can remain intact by undertaking incremental adaptations that appease or diffuse opposing minority positions. Such equilibrium-maintaining adaptations underlie many structural–functional theories of exchange, power, and order (*see* EXCHANGE RELATIONS). Second, organizational business cycles, fads, or pendulum swings occur when opposing interest groups, business regimes, or political parties alternate in power and push the organization somewhat farther from a stable equilibrium. Such cycles explain recurrent periods of organizational feast and famine, partisan MUTUAL ADJUSTMENT among political parties, and alternating organizational priorities on efficiency and innovation. Third, seemingly-random organizational behaviors are produced when strong oscillations or shifts occur between opposing forces that push the organization out of a single periodic equilibrium orbit and produce multiple equilibria and bifurcations, each bounded by different strange attractors. Currently there is growing interest in recent advances in catastrophe theory and CHAOS THEORY to explain such seemingly random behavior in organizations. Thus, different patterns for resolving dialectical oppositions can push an organization to flow toward equilibrium, to oscillate in cycles between opposites, or to bifurcate far from equilibrium and spontaneously create revolutionary changes.

Evolutionary theory. Although evolution is sometimes equated with change, evolution is used here in a restrictive sense to focus on cumulative and probabilistic changes in structural forms of populations of organizations (*see* POPULATION ECOLOGY). As in biological evolution, change proceeds through a continuous cycle of variation, selection, and retention. Variations, the creation of novel forms, are often viewed to emerge by blind or random chance; they just happen. Selection occurs principally through the competition among forms, and the environment selects those forms that optimize or are best suited to the resource base of an environmental niche. Retention involves the forces (including inertia and persistence) that perpetuate and maintain certain organizational forms. Retention serves to counteract the self-reinforcing loop between variations and selection (Aldrich, 1979). Thus, evolutionary theory explains changes as a recurrent, cumulative, and probabilistic progression of variation, selection, and retention of organizational entities.

Alternative theories of social evolution can be distinguished in terms of how traits can be inherited, whether change proceeds gradually and incrementally or rapidly and radically, and whether the unit of analysis focuses on populations of organisms or species. A Darwinian perspective argues that traits can be inherited only through intergenerational processes, whereas a Lamarkian argues that traits can be acquired within a generation through learning and imitation. A Lamarkian view on the acquisition of traits appears more appropriate than strict Darwinism for organization and management applications of social evolution theory. As McKelvey (1982) discusses, to date no adequate solutions have been developed to identify operationally an organizational generation and an intergenerational transmission vehicle.

Social Darwinian theorists emphasize a continuous and gradual process of evolution. In *The Origin of Species*, Darwin wrote, "as natural selection acts solely by accumulating slight, successive, favourable variations, it can produce no great or sudden modifications; it can act only by short and slow steps." Other evolutionists posit a saltational theory of evolution, such as punctuated equilibrium, which Tushman and Romanelli (1985) introduced to the management literature. Whether an evolutionary change proceeds at gradual versus saltational rates is an empirical matter, for the rate of change does not fundamentally alter the theory of evolution – at least as it has been adopted thus far by organization and management scholars.

The paleontologist, Gould (1989), argues that another basic distinction between Darwinian evolution and his punctuated equilibrium theory is hierarchical level. This distinction has not yet been incorporated in the management literature, but ought to be. Gould points out that classical Darwinism locates the sorting of evolutionary change at a single level of objects. This sorting is natural selection operating through the differential births and deaths of organisms, as exemplified in many population ecology studies of organizational birth and death rates (*see* reviews in Hannan & Freeman (1989). Gould's punctuated equilibrium model adds a hierarchical dimension to evolutionary theory by distinguishing this sorting (a description of differential birth and death) from speciation (a causal claim about the basis of sorting). "Speciation is a property of populations (organisms do not speciate), while extinction [a sorting process] is often a simple concatenation of deaths among organisms" (Gould, 1989, p. 122). This multilevel view of evolution is important for understanding how organizational adaptation and selection can occur at multiple levels (both the species and organism levels). Adaptation is the class of heritable characters that have a positive influence on the fitness of an organism within a constraining situation. Selection focuses on the evolutionary process of choosing new situations (i.e., variations). So selection assumes variation, while adaptation assumes fitting within a selected environment.

Conclusion

Life cycle, teleology, dialectics, and evolutionary theories provide four useful ways to think about and study processes of change in organizations. The relevance of the four theories will differ depending upon the conditions surrounding the organizational change in question. Specifically, Van de Ven and Poole (1994) propose that the four theories explain processes of organizational change and development under the following conditions:

- Life cycle theory explains change processes within an entity when natural, logical, or institutional rules exist to regulate the process.
- Teleological theory explains change processes within an entity or among a cooperating set of entities when a new desired end-state is socially constructed and consensus emerges on the means and resources to reach the desired end-state.
- Dialectical theory explains change processes between conflicting entities when the aggressor entities are sufficiently powerful and choose to engage the opposition through direct confrontation, bargaining, or partisan mutual adjustment.
- Evolutionary theory explains change processes between a population of entities when they compete for similar scarce resources in an environmental niche.

Thus, to explain organizational change in any content area, one applies the theory that best fits the specific conditions. Of course, changes in organizations are often more complex than these propositions suggest. Conditions may exist to trigger interplays between several change theories and produce interdependent cycles of change. While each of these types has its own internal logic or generating mechanism, confusion and complexity arise when these logics interact. To deal with some of these complexities, it is helpful to distinguish the myriad ongoing changes in organizational life into those that are routine versus novel and the level of analysis at which they occur.

To stay in business, most organizations follow routines to reproduce a wide variety of recurring changes, such as adapting to economic cycles, periodic revisions in products and services, and ongoing instances of personnel TURNOVER and executive succession (*see* SUCCESSION PLANNING).

These commonplace changes within organizations are typically programmed by preestablished rules or institutional routines, and can be analyzed and explained using a life cycle theory of change. At the industry or population level, competitive or environmental selection for shifts in resources typically govern the rates of reproduction (and resulting size and number) of various forms of organizations. Evolutionary theory is useful for explaining these population-level changes as the probabilistic workings of variation, selection, and retention processes.

Occasionally, organizations also experience unprecedented changes for which no established routines or procedures exist. They include many planned (as well as unplanned) changes in organizational creation, innovation, turnaround, reengineering, cultural transformation, merger, divestiture, and many other issues the organization may not have experienced (*see* TURNAROUND MANAGEMENT; BUSINESS PROCESS REENGINEERING; MERGERS AND ACQUISITIONS). These kinds of novel changes can be usefully analyzed and explained with a teleological theory if they are triggered by a reframing or frame-breaking goal of powerful people in control of the organization. Alternatively, a dialectical theory might better explain the novel change process when conflicts and confrontations between opposing groups occur to produce a synthesis out of the ashes of the conflict engagements.

The processes through which these novel changes unfold are far more complex and unpredictable than routine changes because the former require developing and implementing new change routines, while the latter entail implementing tried-and-tested routines. Novel changes entail the creation of originals, whereas routine changes involve the reproduction of copies. Novel changes are organizational innovations, whereas routine changes are business as usual.

An important concluding caveat is to recognize that existing theories of organizational change are explanatory, but not predictive. Statistically, we should expect most incremental, convergent, and continuous changes to be explained by either life cycle or evolutionary theories, and most radical, divergent, and discontinuous changes to be explained by teleological or dialectical theories. But these actuarial relationships may not be causal. For example, the infrequent statistical occurrence of a discontinuous and radical mutation may be caused by a glitch in the operation of a life cycle model of change. So also, the scale-up of a teleological process to create a planned strategic reorientation for a company may fizzle, resulting only in incremental change.

See also **Organization theory; Strategic management; Organizational learning**

Bibliography

Aldrich, H. (1979). *Organizations and environments*. Englewood Cliffs, NJ: Prentice-Hall.

Bartunek, J. M. (1993). The multiple cognitions and conflicts associated with second order organizational change. In J. K. Murningham (Ed.), *Social psychology in organizations: Advances in theory and research* (Chapter 15). Englewood Cliffs, NJ: Prentice Hall.

Beckhard, R. (1969). *Organization development: Strategies and models*. Reading, MA: Addison-Wesley.

Burawoy, M. & Skocpol, T. (1982). *Marxist inquiries: Studies of labor, class, and states*. Chicago: University of Chicago Press.

French, W. L. & Bell, C. H. Jr. (1978). *Organization development: Behavior science interventions for organization improvement*. Englewood Cliffs, NJ: Prentice Hall.

Gould, S. J. (1989). Punctuated equilibrium in fact and theory. *Journal of Social and Biological Structures*, **12**, 117–136.

Hannan, M. T. & Freeman, J. (1989). *Organizational ecology*. Cambridge, MA: Harvard University Press.

Huber, G. P. & Glick, W. H. (1993). *Organizational change and redesign: Ideas and insights for improving performance*. Oxford, UK: Oxford University Press.

McKelvey, B. (1982). *Organizational systematics: Taxonomy, evolution, classification*. Berkeley, CA: University of California Press.

Meyer, A. D., Brooks, G. R. & Goes, J. B. (1990). Environmental jolts and industry revolutions: Organizational responses to discontinuous change. *Strategic Management Journal*, **11**, 93–110.

Rogers, E. (1983). *Diffusion of innovations*, (3rd edn). New York: Free Press.

Sztompka, P. (1993). *The sociology of social change*. London: Blackwell.

Tushman, M. L. & Romanelli, E. (1985). Organizational evolution: A metamorphosis model of convergence and reorientation. In B. Staw & L. Cummings (Eds), *Research in organizational behavior*, (vol. 7). Greenwich, CT: JAI Press.

Van de Ven, A. H. & Poole, M. S. (1988). Paradoxical requirements for a theory of organizational change. In R. Quinn & K. Cameron (Eds), *Paradox and transformation: Toward a theory of change in organization and management*. New York: Harper Collins, Ballinger Division

——— (1994). Explaining development and change in organizations. Minneapolis, MN: University of Minnesota Strategic Management Research Center, Discussion Paper #189.

ANDREW H. VAN DE VEN

organizational citizenship The concept of organizational citizenship connotes membership in a polity that grants rights and enforces responsibilities. It is related to the idea of corporate, or organizational, social responsibility. In any society, major institutions and organizations constitute "interpenetrating systems," interrelated but not completely overlapping sets (*see* INSTITUTIONAL THEORY). Rights and privileges of organizations protect their independence in society; responsibilities acknowledge their interdependence.

In the United States, corporations are legally considered as persons, having many rights and duties as though they were individual citizens. Other rights and duties devolve to organizations because of their collective characteristics and their importance to societal welfare. In nations without legal organizational citizenship, organizations may still be accorded citizen-like rights and be expected to fulfill socially-defined responsibilities.

Responsibilities of business organizations as citizens include:

(a) economic duties such as providing jobs, creating wealth, and paying taxes;
(b) legal and regulatory compliance;
(c) responsiveness to ethical norms and principles; and

(d) discretionary social welfare or cultural contributions (Carroll, 1979) (*see* EQUAL OPPORTUNITIES).

In addition, business organizations may have responsibilities as "world citizens," such as compliance with international agreements governing commerce, human rights, or natural environment protection.

Scholarly debates over whether, or the degree to which, business organizations have social responsibilities, or citizenship duties, have largely been supplanted by analysis of CORPORATE SOCIAL PERFORMANCE (Wood, 1991), focusing on the consequences of business operations for persons, groups, societies, and the natural environment. Business's economic responsibilities are only part of the set of organizational responsibilities.

See also **Governance and ownership; Stakeholders; Business ethics; Psychological contract; Contract**

Bibliography

Carroll, A. B. (1979). A three-dimensional model of corporate performance. *Academy of Management Review*, **4**, (4), 497–505.

Wood, D. J. (1991). Corporate social performance revisited. *Academy of Management Review*, **16**, (4), 691–718.

DONNA J. WOOD

organizational climate The concept of climate is clearly metaphorical implying that organizations, groups, teams, and other collectives possess the equivalent of "prevailing atmospheric phenomena such as temperature, humidity, wind, and clearness, etc." (OED). Definitions range from the shared perceptions of "the way things are around here" (Schneider, 1990), to Payne's, "a molar concept reflecting the content and strength of the prevalent VALUES, norms, attitudes, feelings, and behaviors of the members of a social system which can be operationally measured through the perceptions of system members or observational and other objective means."

One of its earliest uses was by Lewin, Lippitt, and White (1939) who used it to describe the effects of different LEADERSHIP STYLES on groups of young boys whose leaders were required to act in a democratic, autocratic, or laissez-faire manner (*see* MANAGERIAL STYLE). This manipulation produced climates which were, respectively, busy, co-operative, productive, enjoyable (democratic); less busy, hostile, less productive, and unenjoyable (autocratic); and anarchic, less productive, less cohesive, and less satisfying (laissez-faire). These descriptions were based largely on the observations of the researchers/observers, but climate research really burgeoned when researchers developed questionnaire measures which asked the members of the social groups themselves to describe how they saw their environment. These early studies were carried out in organizations, leading to the most widely used concept – organizational climate.

Large-scale comparative studies of organizational climate were first carried out in educational organizations by Pace and Stern, though during the next decade Stern (1970) developed the work both conceptually and empirically, and designed measures for industrial organizations. Both authors raised fundamental problems with the concept which are still highly relevant today. Stern was concerned with the relationship between PERSONALITY and PERCEPTIONS of the climate, and Pace with the question: "What proportion of the population has to agree/disagree with a particular description of the climate to justify describing the climate in that way?" This is the *aggregation issue*.

Pace had set 66 percent as the criterion, but others have argued that it should be much closer to 100 percent. In practice, most other researchers avoided the issue by using multi-item scales and taking the mean score to represent the organization's climate. It was obvious from the standard deviations that this cloaked wide variations in perceptions amongst members of organizations. This VALIDITY problem became even clearer when studies showed mean scores differed by hierarchical level, and by functions/departments. One possible response to this is to accept the existence of subclimates, but unfortunately the aggregation problem also exists within levels and departments – there are still wide variations in perceptions. It was then suggested that cluster analysis might be a technique for revealing groups of people who see the climate in the same way (*see* STATISTICAL METHODS).

This has recently been tested empirically and the clusters labeled collective climates, but Payne (1990) has argued that this approach is only justified if the collectives had some other meaningful socio-psychological identity (e.g., were in the same department, clique, etc.) (*see* GROUP CULTURE). To date this approach has rarely revealed clusters with such an identity.

In parallel with this activity researchers tackled the aggregation issue by calculating the degree of agreement amongst the members of the organization, department, or team. The interrater RELIABILITY coefficient has been used as well as versions of the intraclass correlation coefficient. There is ongoing debate about the advantages and disadvantages of these various coefficients (Kozlowski & Hattrup, 1992). Whatever their respective merits, the empirical fact is that the degree of agreement shown is often not high enough to justify the claim that the mean is an accurate score of the climate. In one study of 334 colleges Zammuto and Krakower (1991) report that only 25 percent of the colleges studied had intraclass correlations better than 0.66. It should be noted that the number of raters in each organization only varied from 10 to 19 and all were associated with the top of the organization which should have optimized the chances of gaining agreement. This lack of agreement about the organizational climate raises serious problems about the validity of the concept of collective climate.

One reason for the existence of variations in perceptions of environment is, of course, personality, attitudes, values, etc., which returns us to Stern's work. He was able to test whether having a particular need (e.g., achievement) influenced one's perceptions of the demand for achievement in the organizational environment (*see* ACHIEVEMENT, NEED FOR). Correlations up to about 0.3 were found. JOB SATISFACTION is also positively correlated with perceptions of climate, the more satisfied people tending to report a more positive climate.

These sorts of findings, and the problem of the aggregation issue, led to the distinction of psychological climate from organizational climate. Conceptually, however, this assumes that the individual is the unit of analysis but many measures still asked the individual to describe the climate of the organization (*see* LEVELS OF ANALYSIS). Because of the aggregation issue some argue that using the individual as the unit of analysis is the only valid use of climate measures, but it is worth noting some conceptual confusion. Would it not be more conceptually consistent to develop measures of the *psychological* climate by exploring the person's immediate environment? Why should the climate of the chief executive contain the same dimensions as that of the shop-floor worker? Sadly, the climate literature contains a number of examples of such conceptual slippage.

Another type of conceptual slippage occurs in the *content* of climate measures. Many measures contain items which really measure ORGANIZATIONAL DESIGN such as centralization of AUTHORITY, amount of rules, and structuring of processes and activities. Since most models of organization propose that mechanistic structures produce different cultures/climates than organismic structures (*see* MECHANISTIC/ORGANIC), it is surely sensible to keep the concepts separate. This does not mean one cannot have perceptual measures of structure, of course, as long as people agree about the structure.

Many measures of climate were developed in the 1960s and 1970s and changes in organizations continue to lead to the developments of new dimensions (e.g., to do with attitudes and values toward information technology, customer service, quality, etc.), but the following dimensions regularly appear as independent dimensions of climate and give an idea of its content, as well as emphasizing that it is multidimensional: interpersonal warmth and support; concern for conforming versus personal autonomy; concern for being progressive and innovative; rewarding versus punishing orientation; concern for results or achievement. Specialized measures of climate have also been produced (e.g., Service Climate and Safety Climate).

The content of climate measures overlap a lot with descriptions of organizational CULTURE. Schneider (1990) edited a book *Organizational Climate and Culture*, which discusses the two concepts without coming to definitive conclusions except that they are similar, but different in their approach to measurement, and that climate is unlikely to reveal the deeper, taken-for-granted aspects of culture that might be revealed by anthropological investigation.

Despite the measurement difficulties that exist for both culture and climate, empirical studies have regularly demonstrated that the performance and survival of companies is affected by their climate/culture (e.g., Dennison, 1990). Climate measures are also used with great practical benefits in survey-feedback situations where they help to diagnose what the climate is like, prompt strategic thinking about what a better climate would be like, and aid in monitoring progress toward the vision.

As a practical concept both social scientists and lay persons find it easy to grasp the idea of a social climate and it is undoubtedly a useful thinking tool – as a scientific concept it continues to encounter stormy weather.

See also **Organizational culture; Attitude theory; Group norms**

Bibliography

Dennison, D. R. (1990). *Corporate culture and organizational effectiveness*. New York: Wiley.

Kozlowski, S. W. J. & Hattrup, K. (1992). A disagreement about within group agreement; disentangling issues of consistency versus consensus. *Journal of Applied Psychology*, **77**, (2), 161–167.

Lewin, K., Lippitt, R. & White, R. K. (1939). Patterns of aggressive behaviour in experimentally created social climates. *Journal of Social Psychology*, **10**, 271–299.

Payne, R. L. (1990). Method in our madness: A reply to Jackofsky and Slocum. *Journal of Organizational Behaviour*, **11**, 77–80.

Schneider, B. (Ed.), (1990). *Organizational climate and culture*. San Francisco: Jossey-Bass.

Stern, G. G. (1970). *People in context*. New York: Wiley.

Zammuto, R. F. & Krakower, J. Y. (1991). Quantitative and qualitative studies of organizational culture. In R. W. Woodman & W. A. Pasmore (Eds), *Research in organizational change and development*, (vol. 5, pp. 83–114). Greenwich, CN: JAI Press.

ROY L. PAYNE

organizational commitment *see* COMMITMENT

organizational culture The surface manifestations of a CULTURE must be distinguished from culture itself. Manifestations of cultures in organizations include formal practices (such as pay levels, structure of the HIERARCHY, JOB DESCRIPTIONS), informal practices (such as norms), espoused VALUES, RITUALS, organizational stories, jargon, humor, and physical environment (including office/work spaces, dress norms, architecture). These manifestations are interpreted, evaluated, and enacted in varying ways because cultural members have differing interests, experiences, responsibilities, and values. The underlying patterns or configurations of these interpretations, and the ways they are enacted, constitute culture. Culture is not simply the espoused values of managers, supposedly shared by all or most employees. Rather, culture is embedded in the everyday working lives of all cultural members. Therefore, subcultural differentiation and the ambiguities that pervade organizational life are essential features of any organization's culture.

The 1980s brought a renaissance of interest in organizational culture. The resulting proliferation of research was accompanied by fundamental and fruitful disagreements about what culture is, how it should be studied, if its content can be controlled by management, and whether a particular kind of culture can result in stronger organizational performance. This dissension among cultural researchers, regarding such fundamental issues, makes it difficult to define culture and summarize the results of this growing literature.

Theoretical Hairsplitting or Differences of Consequence?

Given this dissension, it is reasonable to ask why applied researchers and practitioners should care about cultural research. One reason is financial. Organizations have spent considerable amounts of money in response to seductive promises of easy cultural change. Some managers have sought to replicate the supposedly "strong" cultures of profitable companies, while others have tried "engineering values" to generate COMMITMENT to a philosophy of management, in the hopes of increasing loyalty, PRODUCTIVITY, or profitability. Some FOUNDERS or top executives have sought to create a culture cast in their own image, to perpetuate their own personal values and achieve an organizational form of immortality (*see* CEOs). Usually practitioners respond to promises of easy solutions and quick fixes with well-deserved skepticism, but organizational culture, at first, seemed immune from such skepticism. Later, disillusionment set in and many dismissed culture as yesterday's fad. For some organizations, both responses have been expensive mistakes.

This seesaw between credulity and disillusionment has caused considerable waste of time, money, and emotional effort. Practitioners need to know enough to judge – with appropriate skepticism – what researchers and strategic advisors are focusing on and what they are ignoring. Without some understanding of why researchers come to different conclusions about how cultures change and whether these transitions can be managed, it is impossible to judge whether the results of a particular study are in some sense valid and whether they have practical applications in a given context. For all these reasons, theoretical differences of opinion are not just hairsplitting debates of interest only to ivory-tower scholars.

Overview

One way to make sense of this growing body of literature is to distinguish three traditions of cultural research: the Integration, Differentiation, and Fragmentation perspectives (Martin, 1992). Below, this essay defines the premises of each perspective, summarizes results of representative studies, identifies problems inherent in each viewpoint, and outlines a three-perspective resolution of some of these difficulties.

Integration Perspective

Of the three perspectives that have come to dominate organizational culture research, the Integration perspective is the most popular and the least well supported empirically. Integration studies of culture implicitly assume that a "strong" culture is characterized by consistency, organization-wide consensus, and clarity. According to Integration studies, consistency occurs because people at the higher levels of an organization articulate a set of espoused values, sometimes in the form of a philosophy of management or MISSION STATEMENT; these values are then reinforced by a variety of cultural manifestations which presumably generate organization-wide value consensus. In Integration studies, there is clarity concerning what the organizational values are and should be, what behaviors are preferable, and what a particular story or ritual means. Organizational members apparently know what they are to do and they agree why it is worthwhile to do it. In the few instances when ambiguity is acknowledged, it is described as "not part of the culture" or as a evidence of a failure to achieve a "strong" culture.

For example, MacDonald (in Frost, Moore, Louis, Lundberg, & Martin, 1991) studied the Los Angeles Olympic Organizing Committee, as its employees and volunteers rallied to perform at their peak during the Olympic games. According to MacDonald, attractive uniforms, elaborate rituals, brightly colored stadium decorations, an intense working pace, and stories about a charismatic leader consistently reinforced organization-wide commitment around a set of shared values (*see* LEADERSHIP, CHARISMATIC). Schein (1985) focused attention on individual corporate leaders who attempt to generate company-wide consensus regarding their personal values and corporate goals through a wide range of consistent corporate policies and practices. Barley (in Frost et al., 1991) described how Funeral Directors use a series of practices and rituals (e.g., putting make-up on a corpse, changing sheets on a death bed, etc.) to reinforce the idea that death can be life-like.

In most but not all Integration studies, culture supposedly originates in the values articulated by a leader or top management (*see* TOP MANAGEMENT TEAMS); these values are then reinforced by selectively hiring people with similar priorities and by attempting to socialize new employees thoroughly (*see* SOCIALIZATION). The Integration perspective conceptualizes cultural change as an organization-wide cultural transformation, whereby an old unity is replaced – hopefully – by a new one. In the interim, conflict and ambiguity may occur, but these are interpreted as evidence of the deterioration of culture before a new unity is established. Much of the research that has generated the renaissance of interest in culture, particularly in the United States, falls within the Integration perspective. This view of culture has gained wide acceptance, in part because such a harmonious and clear environment is attractive, particularly to managers who would like to think that they could create a vision and enact a culture that would inspire such consensus.

Although all cultural manifestations mentioned in a given Integration study may be consistent with each other, it is likely that inconsistent or ambiguous elements have simply been excluded from the account as not part of the culture. Often an Integration study will cite just a few manifestations, for example, the espoused values of top management or a collection of organizational stories – and claim that this subset of cultural manifestations is characteristic of the entire culture. Most Integration studies rely primarily on the views of managerial and professional employees, although it cannot be assumed that the view of this minority of powerful individuals are shared by all employees, particularly given the likelihood of conflicts of interest between different functional groups and among levels of a hierarchy. In addition, employees' behavioral COMPLIANCE to top management's preferences or policies cannot be taken as evidence of shared values or interpretations.

Given the absence of systematic studies which provide comparative data from a large number of companies, claims that "strong" cultures are a key to improved organizational effectiveness, should be regarded as, at best, unproved (Siehl & Martin, 1990). Many studies make a stronger claim: that it is highly unlikely that any organizational culture, studied in depth, would exhibit the consistency, organization-wide consensus, and clarity that Integration studies have claimed to find (e.g., Alvesson & Berg, 1992; Martin, 1992; Turner, 1986; Van Maanen & Barley, in Frost, Moore, Louis, Lundberg, & Martin, 1985). Thus, Integration studies offer managers and researchers a seductive promise of harmony and value homogeneity that is empirically unmerited and unlikely to be fulfilled.

Differentiation Perspective

Differentiation studies see the origins of culture in the fact that organizational members have different interests, task responsibilities, backgrounds, experiences, and expertise. The material conditions of their work, and the pay they receive for it, differ. In addition, individuals bring differing group identities (such as class, GENDER, or ETHNICITY), and differing interpretations of the meanings of those identities, to the workplace (Alvesson & Berg, 1992; Martin, 1992; Van Maanen & Barley, in Frost et al., 1985). For these reasons, Differentiation studies describe organizations as composed of overlapping, nested subcultures that coexist in relationships of intergroup harmony, CONFLICT, or indifference.

For example, in a Differentiation study, Bartunek and Moch (in Frost et al., 1991) show how five subcultures in a food production firm reacted differently to management's imposition of a QUALITY OF WORKING LIFE intervention. Top management was primarily concerned with control. In-house consulting staff were cooperative. The management of the local plants where the program was implemented were paternalistic, using imagery of employees as "children" to managerial "parents." Line employees exhibited a dependent reaction, following management's preferences. Machinists, historically an active, independent, and comparatively well-paid group, actively resisted the intervention.

A hierarchical alignment of subcultures is also evident in Van Maanen's (in Frost et al., 1991) study of ride operators at Disneyland. Food vendors were allocated to the bottom of the STATUS ranking and operators of yellow submarines and jungle boats share high status. Tension between ride operators, customers, and supervisors was evident, as ride operators arranged for obnoxious customers to be soaked with water when submarine hatches open and supervisors are foiled in their constant attempts to catch operators breaking rules. In Young's (in Frost et al., 1991) study of "bag ladies" in a British manufacturing plant, tensions between management and labor were evident, as were fissions within the worker subculture between the younger and older workers who did different sewing jobs. As these examples indicate, subcultures often appear along lines of functional and hierarchical DIFFERENTIATION. Also evident in these studies is a subtext: many of these subcultural differences also reflect class, RACE, ethnic, AGE, and gender differences, in part due to occupational segregation (Cox, 1993) (*see* OCCUPATIONS).

Inconsistency across cultural manifestations is evident in Differentiation studies. For example, top management in the bakery says one thing to employees, and does something different. At Disneyland, ride operators appear to conform to management's rules, while doing what they please. In a particularly detailed examination of the effects of such inconsistencies on an individual, Kunda (1991) studied engineers' reactions as they conformed to a company ritual (designed to exhibit commitment to supposedly shared company values) while "off stage" they expressed, through humor and sarcastic side remarks, their internal ambivalence.

To summarize, a Differentiation study includes evidence of inconsistency between one cultural manifestation and another. Consensus is evident, but only within the boundaries of a subculture. Within a subculture all is clear, but ambiguities do appear at the interstices where one subculture meets another. When viewed from the Differentiation perspective, the organization is no longer seen as a cultural monolith; instead, it is a collection of subcultures (Christensen & Kreiner, 1984; Turner, 1986) (*see* SUBUNITS). Some of these subcultures enthusiastically reinforce the views of the top management coalition or operate cooperatively with each other. Others become pockets of ignorance or resistance to top management initiatives. From the Differentiation perspective, change is localized within one or more subcultures, alterations tend to be incremental, and change is triggered (if not determined) by pressures from an organization's environment (*see* ORGANIZATION AND ENVIRONMENT). That environment is likely to be segmented, so different subcultures within the same organization experience different kinds and rates of change.

Of the three perspectives, the Differentiation viewpoint is most congruent with research that emphasizes environmental determinants of organizational behavior. The subcultures within an organization can reflect, and be partially determined by, cultural groupings in the larger society (*see* CULTURE, NATIONAL). For example, functional subcultures within a firm can reflect occupational subcultures that cross firm boundaries, as when accountants appear to be the "same everywhere" or when programmers change organizational affiliations, only to find the programming subculture at their new job to be quite familiar (e.g., Trice & Beyer, 1993) (*see* ORGANIZATIONAL BOUNDARIES).

Thus, an organization is a *nexus* where a variety of societal cultural influences come together within an organization's permeable boundaries (Martin, 1992). A few of the cultural elements within that boundary will be truly unique to the organization. Other elements (some of which will be erroneously believed to be unique) will reflect cultural influences external to the organization. What is unique and "organizational" about a culture, then, is the way a particular mix of cultural influences combines and interacts within a given organization's boundary. This nexus approach to the study of culture posits that we cannot understand what goes on inside an organizational culture without understanding what exists outside the boundary. The nexus approach brings environmental concerns into the domain of cultural studies, complicating what is meant by the term organizational culture or, more precisely, cultures in organizations.

As is the case with Integration research, the methodological choices made in Differentiation studies partially determine what results are found. For example, as can be seen in the Disneyland and "bag lady" studies, there is a tendency for Differentiation research to focus on relatively low-ranking employees or first-line supervisors – people who are less likely to share the views of top management. And within any subculture, there is a tendency to focus on the ways subcultural members share the same views, rather than the ways they differ or what they find ambiguous. As a result, Differentiation studies do not distance themselves far enough from the oversimplifications and distortions of the Integration view; within a subculture, consistency, consensus, and clarity still predominate.

Fragmentation Perspective

The Fragmentation perspective offers a quite different alternative. Rather than banning ambiguity from the cultural stage (the Integration view) or relegating ambiguity to the interstices between subcultures (the Differentiation view), Fragmentation studies see ambiguity as *the* defining feature of cultures in organizations. Ambiguity pervades all but the most routine and trivial aspects of organizational functioning. The meanings that different cultural members attach to particular cultural manifestations are neither clearly consistent nor clearly in conflict. There are many plausible interpretations of any one issue or event, making the idea of a single clear, shared cultural reality highly unlikely. To the extent that consensus exists, it is issue-specific and transient – problems or issues get activated, generate positive and negative reactions, and then fade from attention as other issues take center stage.

For example, Meyerson (in Frost et al., 1991) studied the ambiguities of social work. Goals were unclear; there was no consensus regarding the appropriate means to achieve those goals; success was hard to define and even harder to assess. For social workers, ambiguity is the salient feature of working life and any cultural description that excludes ambiguity from the realm that is considered cultural, would be dramatically incomplete. Similarly, Feldman (in Frost et al., 1991) studied federal policy analysts who analyze policy options, write reports that may never get read, and if they are read, probably never will impact policy decisions. In such a context, ambiguities which cloud and undermine claims of consistency, consensus, and clarity, are protective; cultural members might otherwise be forced to confront directly the issue of the meaning (lessness) of their work (*see* ALIENATION).

Weick (in Frost et al., 1991) has worked within the Fragmentation perspective in a context where the effects of ambiguities can be less benign: a foggy airport in Tenerife where one jet was attempting to land while another waits to take off. Weick focused on the ambiguities of COMMUNICATION among pilots, cockpit crews, and air traffic controllers, as they coped with the complexities of making themselves understood across barriers created by differences in native language, prestige, and incompletely shared knowledge. Hundreds of passengers died in the ensuing crash, making this study a powerful illustration of the conclusion that most Fragmentation studies draw: that an understanding of ambiguities should be a central component of any cultural study that claims to encompass the full range of cultural members' working lives.

From the Fragmentation perspective, claims of clarity, consistency, and consensus are shown to be idealized oversimplifications that fail to capture the confusing complexity of contemporary organizational functioning. In a Fragmentation account, POWER is diffused broadly at all levels of the hierarchy and throughout the organization's environment. Culture has no specific point of origin; fleeting affinities are issue-specific. Change is a constant flux, rather than an intermittent interruption in an otherwise stable state. Change is largely triggered by the environment or other forces beyond an individual's control, so that Fragmentation studies of change offer few guidelines for those who would normatively control the change process.

The methodological choices made in Fragmentation research enable these kinds of conclusions to be drawn. For example, Fragmentation studies tend to focus on highly ambiguous occupations (i.e., social worker, policy analyst) and contexts (e.g., cross-national communication under STRESS, literally in the fog). As noted regarding research conducted from the other two perspectives, Fragmentation studies exhibit a form of methodological tautology: these researchers define culture in a particular way and then find what they are looking for.

Advantages of Using all Three Perspectives

These problems of methodological tautology, and the theoretical blind spots associated with any single perspective, can be avoided if a single cultural context is studied from each of the three perspectives, permitting a more complete understanding to emerge. While most studies utilize only one of the three perspectives, more recent research indicates that *any* organizational culture contains elements congruent with all three viewpoints (e.g., Pettigrew, 1985). If any organization is studied in enough depth, some issues, values, and objectives will be seen to generate organization-wide consensus, consistency, and clarity (an Integration view). At the same time, other aspects of an organization's culture will coalesce into subcultures that hold conflicting opinions about what is important, what should happen, and why (a Differentiation view). Finally, some problems and issues will be ambiguous, in a state of constant flux, generating multiple, plausible interpretations (a Fragmentation view).

Thus, a three-perspective approach to the study of an organization's culture(s) yields a deeper understanding than if only a single theoretical perspective had been used (Martin, 1992). A wide range of organizational contexts have been examined using the three-perspective framework, including studies of a temporary educational organization for unemployed women in England, a newly privatized bank in Turkey, the problem of truancy in an urban high school in the United States, and changing organizational cultures in the Peace Corps/Africa.

A Subjective Approach

Sometimes the three perspective framework is mistakenly taken to mean that some organizations will be correctly described by an Integration viewpoint, while other contexts may better fit the Differentiation or Fragmentation perspectives. This is a misunderstanding. The three perspectives are theoretical viewpoints developed by organizational culture researchers. Although these perspectives are empirically derived from the perspectives of cultural members, they are not objective representations of the views of cultural members. Different researchers bring different sensitivities and preconceptions to a cultural context. Who a researcher is affects what he or she sees and what questions she or he seeks to address. And the identity of a cultural member also affects what information is shared, because of HALO EFFECTS related to overall JOB SATISFACTION, social desirability of particular responses, and IMPRESSION MANAGEMENT considerations. The measurement, collection, and interpretation of cultural data are inevitably affected by subjective factors, whether quantitative or qualitative methods are used (*see* RESEARCH METHODS).

Thus, none of the three perspectives is an objective description of empirical facts. Instead, it is an interpretative framework that is subjectively imposed on the process of collecting and analyzing cultural data. To say that a particular organization has an Integrated or Differentiated culture would be mistaken; any cross-sectional (single time period) study of an organization, if thorough and deep enough, will produce evidence congruent with all three cultural perspectives.

This subjective orientation is counter-intuitive for many. Often one perspective, labeled the "home" viewpoint, is easy for cultural members and researchers to see, while the other two perspectives can be more difficult to access. The harder it is to see applicability of a particular perspective, the more likely it is that, in changed circumstances, insights from that perspective may be crucial for organizational survival. Thus, the three perspective framework is particularly useful for understanding the process of cultural change. For example, if most cultural members would like to see their organization as strongly Integrated, perhaps around the personal values of a well-respected leader, they may repress, or avoid seeing, evidence of any kind of subgroup conflict. If then that leader were to leave the organization, subcultural conflicts might surface in a totally unanticipated way. As this example illustrates, awareness of the perspectives that are less easily seen may provide a key to anticipating, or at least understanding, organizational change.

This brief review has explained why and how many cultural researchers have disagreed about such fundamental ideas as to what culture is, how it should be studied, and whether it generates (and reflects) harmony, conflict, and/or confusion. These disagreements may ultimately be fruitful if cultural research enables us, through the utilization of all three perspectives, to understand organizations more thoroughly, deeply, and holistically. Alternatively, as post-structural cultural theorists have argued (e.g., Alvesson & Berg, 1992; Calas & Smircich, 1987; Jeffcutt, in press; Wilmott, in press) (*see* POSTMODERNISM), cultural studies may reveal the hidden biases and the silenced voices in organizational accounts, broadening the scope of our inquiries to include a wider range of contradictory theories and a greater number of cultural members' viewpoints, without coming to any single conclusion about the superiority or predominance of any of these views.

See also **Organization development; Organizational change; Organization theory; Symbolism; Group culture**

Bibliography

Alvesson, M. & Berg, P. (1992). *Corporate culture and organizational symbolism*. Berlin: de Gruyter.

Calas, M. & Smircich, L. (1987). Post-culture: Is the organizational culture literature dominant but dead? Paper presented at the International Conference on Organizational Symbolism and Corporate Culture. Milan Italy.

Christensen, S. & Kreiner, K. (1984). On the origins of organizational culture. Paper presented at the International Conference on Organizational Symbolism and Corporate Culture. Lund, Sweden.

Cox, T. (1993). *Cultural diversity in organizations: Theory, research, and practice*. San Francisco: Berrit-Koehler.

Frost, P., Moore, L., Louis, M., Lundberg, C. & Martin, J. (Eds), (1985). *Organizational culture* (pp. 31–54). Beverly Hills, CA: Sage.

Frost, P., Moore, L., Louis, M., Lundberg, C. & Martin, J. (Eds) (1991). *Reframing organizational culture*. Newbury Park, CA: Sage.

Jeffcutt, P. (1995). *Culture and symbolism in organizational analysis*. Newbury Park, CA: Sage.

Kunda, G. (1991). *Engineering culture: Control and commitment in a high-tech corporation*. Philadelphia: Temple University Press.

Martin, J. (1992). *Cultures in organizations: Three perspectives*. New York: Oxford University Press.

Pettigrew, A. (1985). *The awakening giant: Continuity and change*. Oxford, UK: Blackwell.

Schein, E. (1985). *Organizational culture and leadership*. San Francisco, CA: Jossey-Bass.

Siehl, C. & Martin, J. (1990). Organizational culture: The key to financial performance? In B. Schneider (Ed.), *Organizational climate and culture* (pp. 241–281). San Francisco: Jossey-Bass.

Trice, H. & Beyer, J. (1993). *The cultures of work organizations*. Englewood Cliffs, NJ: Prentice-Hall.

Turner, B. (1986). Sociological aspects of organizational symbolism. *Organizational Studies*, 7, 101–115.

Wilmott, H. (In press) Postmodernism and excellence: The de-differentiation of economy and culture. *Journal of Organizational Change Management*.

JOANNE MARTIN

Organizational decline and death Much research on organizational decline and death was published in the 1980s and 1990s, largely in response to economic downturns in North America and Europe. Decline is a two-step process in which deteriorating environmental adaptation leads to reduced internal financial resources (Cameron, Sutton, & Whetten, 1988). An organization has environmental support when it has favorable EXCHANGE RELATIONS with groups and individuals that hold critical resources and when its actions are endorsed by powerful external groups and individuals (*see* RESOURCE-BASED THEORY; RESOURCE DEPENDENCE). Lost environmental support results from the intertwined deterioration of an organization's image and its resource base.

Following writings on sociobiology, deterioration in environmental support can be "k-type" or "r-type." Deterioration of the k-type occurs when an organization is part of an industry, or population, with a shrinking resource base and a decaying image; such deterioration threatens all organizations in the niche. Conversely, r-type deterioration occurs when an organization is in a stable or growing niche, but takes action that causes deterioration of its specific external resource base and image.

Both kinds of deterioration lead to reduced financial resources in the organization. Decline results in pressure to reduce costs through means including workforce reduction, or "DOWNSIZING" (*see* ORGANIZATIONAL RESTRUCTURING). Although sometimes used interchangeably, downsizing is distinct from decline (Sutton, 1990). Workforce reduction may reflect increased technical efficiency or be used to please external constituencies rather than in response to shrinking financial resources. Downsizing is also best viewed as a symptom rather than a cure for decline. At best, downsizing reduces the need for internal resources. At worst, it hastens decline. Departures of key personnel can harm an organization's image or its ability to produce quality products or services. Downsizing may also increase costs when displaced employees are replaced with more expensive external contractors.

If decline persists, then organizational death may occur because there are not enough resources to support core activities. Organizational death has, however, proved difficult to define and operationalize. The disappearance of an organization's name from a population is often used as the measure of death (or "mortality") in POPULATION ECOLOGY research. But it is debatable whether an organization that has "disappeared" because of a name change or merger, but otherwise continues operating, is dead. Furthermore, an organization may halt operations, but not disappear from the listed population, because it persists as a legal entity (Hannan & Freeman, 1989).

Organizational death is unambiguous to the extent that two conditions are met (Sutton, 1987). First, past participants agree that the organization has disappeared. Second, the activities once accomplished by the organization have stopped or been transferred to two or more organizations. This second condition is necessary for an unambiguous death because an organization's activities may continue intact even though it is widely construed to have disappeared as a result of a merger or name change. Unambiguous deaths often unfold through a process where the organization is first construed as a permanent entity that can live indefinitely, then as a temporary entity that is disbanding the people, things, and activities that compose it, and finally as a defunct entity.

See also **Organizational change; Organization and environment; Redundancy**

Bibliography

Cameron, K. S., Sutton, R. I. & Whetten, D. A. (1988). *Readings in organizational decline: Frameworks, research, and prescriptions.* Boston: Ballinger.

Hannan, M. T. & Freeman, J. (1989). *Organizational ecology*. Cambridge, MA: Harvard University Press.

Sutton, R. I. (1987). The process of organizational death: Disbanding and reconnecting. *Administrative Science Quarterly*, **32**, 542–569.

Sutton, R. I. (1990). Organizational decline processes: A social psychological perspective. In B. M. Staw & L. L. Cummings (Eds), *Research in Organizational Behavior*, (vol. 12, pp. 205–253). Greenwich, CT: JAI Press.

ROBERT I. SUTTON

organizational demography The demography of an organization is the composition of its workforce on variables such as AGE, GENDER, ETHNICITY, length of service, and education (Pfeffer, 1985). The diversity or homogeneity of this composition has important implications for ORGANIZATIONAL BEHAVIOR at a number of levels. Homogeneity is generally associated with cohesiveness, on the principle established within social psychology that similarity is associated with COMMUNICATION frequency, interpersonal attraction, and social integration (*see* GROUP COHESIVENESS). Demographic homogeneity is therefore associated with "strong" ORGANIZATIONAL CULTURE. This may also apply to organizational, SUBUNITS, such as the highly cohesive nature of certain professional or STATUS defined subcultures within organizations (*see* PROFESSIONALS IN ORGANIZATIONS). It is also apparent that homogeneity can have dysfunctional properties if it leads to excessive CONFORMITY, such as the phenomenon of GROUPTHINK in decision making. A SYSTEMS THEORY perspective would suggest that insufficient internal diversity in complex environments constitutes a breach of the law of "requisite variety."

Diversity also has its costs. Not least is the extra management effort required to coordinate employees and engender COOPERATION. Success in doing so, however, has the claimed benefit of SYNERGY, especially in volatile, uncertain, and international operating environments (*see* INTERNATIONAL MANAGEMENT; ORGANIZATION AND ENVIRONMENT; UNCERTAINTY).

A primary focus of research on organizational demography has been the increased risk of TURNOVER under conditions of diversity (Wagner, Pfeffer, & O'Reilly, 1984). Cohorts or similar age and other characteristics entering an organization at the same time develop common attitudes via shared experience and NETWORKING, especially when cohorts are small in size. Employees, who, through difference from the cohort norms, distance themselves from the group and are more likely to quit (O'Reilly, Caldwell, & Barnett, 1989). The management of demography, either via hiring policies or by placement and rotation strategies, is therefore a potentially powerful instrument for building COMMITMENT and ORGANIZATIONAL EFFECTIVENESS.

Internal demography is, of course, heavily dependent upon the external demography of LABOR MARKETS, and organizations have to adapt their MANAGEMENT OF DIVERSITY according to the circumstances they currently face, or which they have accommodated in the past. Thus companies with homogeneous ageing workforces, due to past expansion on the back of a demographic bulge, face special problems in trying to create dynamic CAREER systems. The COMPETITIVENESS of businesses in different national cultures (*see* CULTURE, NATIONAL) may owe much to their current demographic profiles and projected future trends, and is likely to be an increasing focus of research and management attention as the demography of societies shift and migration of labor compensates for deficits in the availability of key groups.

See also **Individual differences; Organizational change; Group decision making; Minority group influence**

Bibliography

O'Reilly, C. A., Caldwell, D. & Barnett, W. P. (1989). Work group demography, social integration and turnover. *Administrative Science Quarterly*, **34**, 21–37.

Pfeffer, J. (1985). Organizational demography: Implications for management. *California Management Review*, **XXXVIII**, 67–81.

Wagner, W. G., Pfeffer, J. & O'Reilly, C. A. (1984). Work group demography and turnover in top management groups. *Administrative Science Quarterly*, **29**, 74–92.

NIGEL NICHOLSON

organizational design This term is used rather loosely to refer to the choosing of structures and associated managerial processes to enable an organization to operate effectively. The term, therefore, includes at least five interconnected concepts:

1 *Organization* can be taken to cover a wide range of types such as business, NOT-FOR-PROFIT, private, public, service, or manufacturing organizations. The extent to which societies have a capacity to organize, Stinchcombe (1965) argues, will be dependent upon a number of factors such as the literacy rate, degree of communication, existence of a money economy, political revolution, and the density of social life. As most of these factors are on the increase around the world, the rate of increase of organizational formation can be expected to be maintained and hence the need to design them more effectively to be ever more urgent.
2 *Design* implies a deliberate attempt to find an effective organizational form and, therefore, a managerial AUTHORITY to put into effect such structures, usually seen as a fundamental responsibility of top management (*see* TOP MANAGEMENT TEAMS). In democratic organizations design would be more likely to also involve the total membership (*see* COOPERATIVES).
3 *Structure* (*see* STRUCTURATION) can be seen as rules for making decisions. ORGANIZATION THEORY has developed many variables and dimensions of structure concerning variables such as the degree of specialization, FORMALIZATION, or centralization (*see* DECENTRALIZATION).
4 *Effectiveness* (*see* ORGANIZATIONAL EFFECTIVENESS) refers to the performance of an organization as measured against a range of norms. Organizations generally have to satisfy heterogeneous and variable norms coming from a wide constituency of supporters (or STAKEHOLDERS). Following the principle of BOUNDED RATIONALITY organizations, when faced with contradictory norms of performance, tend to concentrate upon a relatively small number of norms demanded by their most powerful constituency.
5 *Choice* in the particular pattern of structures and processes adopted exists. If there was no choice and all organizations were designed the same, the notion of organizational design would be meaningless. The notion of choice also indicates that specific decisions about structures can be made in organizations.

Although it could be said that traditional organizations such as the church were "designed," the earliest organizational design principles that may be recognized as belonging to modern management theory came from a group of practicing managers and engineers who wrote eruditely about their work (*see* CLASSICAL DESIGN THEORY; SCIENTIFIC MANAGEMENT). Interest in organizational theory developed in the post-World War II period as a result of the increasing complexity of organizational and managerial problems, and in appreciation of the need to adapt designs to the contingencies of the environment and technology (*see* CONTINGENCY THEORY; ORGANIZATION AND ENVIRONMENT)

Under the heading of sociotechnical systems (*see* SOCIOTECHNICAL THEORY) a number of far-reaching studies conducted by researchers at the Tavistock Institute immediately post-World War II on organizational change in British coal mines and in an Indian textile factory can be seen as concerned with organizational design. Mention of organizational design in the American organizational literature appears around 1960 (Rubenstein & Haberstroh, 1965) and in March's edited *Handbook of Organizations* (1965). It was the era of large-scale American military and quasi-military organizations, the style that of systems analysis, simulations, and various optimizing methods. The American space agency NASA and the RAND Corporation were major sponsors of such work.

The four editions of Daft's (1992) book *Organization Theory and Design*, and Nystrom and Starbuck's (1981) *Handbook of Organizational Design* point to the sustained interest in this topic. In particular, these books draw together a number of themes which were previously left to relatively separate management subjects such as strategic management, marketing, production, and the like.

Some Principles

Attempts have been made to develop systematic theoretical underpinnings to organizational design issues by drawing upon a growing body of literature on organizational information systems and DECISION MAKING. Ashby's (1956) Law of Requisite Variety provides one such basis. This law states that informational variety is needed to cope with variety. Hence, if a production process is highly variable in the quality of its output, informational variety is needed to solve the coordination problem.

Building upon Ashby's Law is a tradition of treating organizational design as a problem of an optimal control theory of decision making. A decision-based theory of organizational design (Huber, 1990) draws attention to developments management information systems design (*see* COMMUNICATIONS).

Thompson's book (1967) *Organizations in Action* provides a framework for thinking about organizational design which still has an immense influence. Building upon the work of Simon, March, and Cyert with their view of organizations as indeterminate behavioral systems (*see* SATISFICING), Thompson's propositions show how an organization can cope with the often conflicting demands of technical and organizational RATIONALITY.

Many of Thompson's ideas were taken up by later writers on organizational design, particularly the three types of coordination methods (rules, plans, and mutual adjustment) and the three types of interdependencies for which each is most suited, respectively, pooled, sequential, and reciprocal interdependency. Galbraith (1977) developed detailed propositions regarding organizational design, in particular, concerning the need for horizontal and vertical communication in organizations (*see* INTEGRATION).

The theory of BUREAUCRACY has also been a major source of influence upon principles of organizational design, particularly by those principles which emphasize the need to specify job descriptions and formal hierarchical reporting relationships. It has been shown (Pugh and Hickson 1989) that an organization tends to increase centralization of decision making as its dependency in the environment increases (*see* RESOURCE DEPENDENCE); a highly dependent organization is one that relies for a high percentage of its inputs upon a small number of sources, or which sends a high percentage of its output to a small number of outlets. An alternative more horizontal coordination mechanism is structuring of activities, meaning that control resides in the standardized procedures that are set up. Once set up, structuring allows a high degree of DELEGATION although writing the rules in the first place and dealing with exceptions will require centralization.

Galbraith (1977) devised a typology of vertical and horizontal linkage mechanisms according to the degree of coordination and the information capacity needed. Vertical linking providing the least information capacity is hierarchical referral, with rules and plans, adding levels in the HIERARCHY and finally vertical information systems providing increasing degrees of information capacity (*see* INFORMATION PROCESSING). Horizontal linking mechanisms, in order of increasing information capacity, are paperwork, direct contact, liaison roles, task forces, and teams. These proposed linkage mechanisms are basically similar to the coordinating mechanisms suggested by Thompson and illustrate the underlying accepted organizational design PARADIGM.

The transactions costs approach to organizations (Williamson 1975) also reflects attempts to see the coordination problem of organization in terms of the type of information, and the cost of acquiring that information for effective decisions to be made (*see* TRANSACTION COST THEORY). What has become known as institutional economics (*see* ORGANIZATIONAL ECONOMICS) proposes that markets are replaced by hierarchies when informational variety is insufficiently high to match the complexity of the transactions being conducted.

OPEN SYSTEMS theory of organization design emphasizes the relationship between task environment and structure. Organizations create boundary structures (*see* ORGANIZATIONAL BOUNDARIES) to cope with environmental uncertainties and interdependencies. As environments get more complex, organizations tend to differentiate (*see* DIFFERENTIATION) their structures more indicating the need for more integration, that is, coordination effort.

Related to an open-systems perspective are theories that more specifically link organizational structure and business strategy. Chandler (1962) noted how the American corporation tended to develop divisionalized or m-form organization structures in response to increasing size and diversified markets. Miles and Snow (1978) developed four types of strategy (*see* STRATEGIC TYPES) (the defender, prospector, analyzer, and reactor) and argued that, for effectiveness, firms need to find the right match between environment, structure, and technology.

Due to the development of greater interorganizational linkages there has been increasing emphasis upon cooperative strategies and the need to manage boundary transactions more effectively (*see* INTERORGANIZATIONAL RELATIONS). Designs for this purpose include JUST-IN-TIME management, JOINT VENTURES, use of CONTRACTS, and coopting. Increasing attention has also turned to the issue of corporate governance and the need to ensure an appropriate membership of governing bodies (*see* GOVERNANCE AND OWNERSHIP).

Determinants and Outcomes

Organizational design principles attempt to determine relationships between independent and dependent variables in order to achieve effectiveness. DEPARTMENTALIZATION (who is grouped with whom) is a major dependent variable of organizational design. Four principal ways of departmentalizing have been outlined, namely, by function (or process), by product (or service), by area, or by client. Functional departmentalization puts people of a similar skill together in groups representing different stages in the production of a product or service (*see* FUNCTIONAL DESIGN). The advantages of a functional organization are that they allow development of professional SKILLS; the disadvantages are that workers lose contact with the overall product and its associated customers.

Product departmentalization puts people of a similar product (or service) together in groups. This arrangement provides the advantage of greater commitment to matching the product to customer need but with the disadvantage of losing professional skill development (*see* PROFESSIONALS IN ORGANIZATIONS).

Functional and product departmentalizations are therefore the inverse of each other but these are not mutually exclusive types, however, and most organizations are hybrids. The MATRIX ORGANIZATION is an attempt to provide the benefits of both functional and product types without the disadvantages of each, although this can be difficult in practice. The project form of organization is similar to the matrix except that projects have a definite life (Knight, 1976) (*see* PROJECT MANAGEMENT).

Another approach to determining relationships between variables is to define "bundles" of variables which occur together in particular configurations. Some configurations are empirically defined, such as that of Pugh and Hickson (1989) who identify four types of bureaucracy according to the two dimensions of degree of structuring of activities and concentration of authority:

(1) Full bureaucracy occurs when structuring of activities and concentration of authority is high.
(2) Workflow bureaucracy occurs when structuring is high but concentration of authority is low: in this type, control of the work is so

precisely programmed into instructions that little direct decision making by management is needed.

(3) Personnel bureaucracy occurs when structuring is low but authority is concentrated: formal procedures are now replaced by direct intervention by top management, or by outside fiat.

(4) Nonbureaucracy occurs when neither direct authority nor structuring is used: under these conditions a number of things can happen, one of which is for a more collective form of organization based upon TRUST to take over whereby participants come to control their own work more closely.

Markets and hierarchies represent two broad contrasting organizational types which are able to cope with different types of transactions, the hierarchy being more costly but better able to cope with more complex information (*see* COMPLEXITY). A third generic collective type of institutional arrangement for managing transactions (Butler, 1991) has also been suggested. In the collective, the coordination of transactions is governed by means of trust and MUTUAL ADJUSTMENT. The collective is therefore the most suitable form of organization when complexity is very high since it allows the development of trust and the use of special languages and a generally highly rich informational environment.

Mintzberg (1983) combined Thompson's propositions of coordination with a general SYSTEMS THEORY defining the subsystems needed by an organization to produce five organizational configurations. These are: the simple structure, machine bureaucracy, professional bureaucracy, divisionalized form, and the adhocracy. Each configuration displays a prime coordinating mechanism, a key part of the organization, a number of design parameters concerning especially the type of decentralization used, and the situational factors to which each is most suited. For example, the simple structure uses direct SUPERVISION for coordination, the key part of the organization is the strategic apex, the main design parameters are centralization combined with an organic structure, and the situational factors pertain to small size, youth, and a homogeneous dynamic environment (*see* MECHANISTIC/ORGANIC).

The configurational approach to organizational design has produced a large number of typologies and the problem is finding some underlying logic to these configurations. The relationship between TECHNOLOGY and organizational design has received a lot of attention. Woodward (1965) classified manufacturing technology on a continuum from craft through batch to process production. It was found that craft and process technologies shared small SPANS OF CONTROL and a high ratio of skilled to unskilled workers while MASS PRODUCTION was high on these features. Other structural features, such as the proportion of support staff, showed a linear increase from craft to process production.

Perrow's (1970) four types of technology is posited in terms of task analyzability and variability. The routine type requires the most structuring of activities whilst the nonroutine requires a very flexible structure; craft and engineering types can be seen as possessing intermediate structures. More recent theories about the connection between technology and structure emphasize the need for flexibility. The use of AUTOMATION, COMPUTER-AIDED DESIGN (CAD), computer-aided manufacturing (CAM), and ADVANCED MANUFACTURING TECHNOLOGY have tended to emphasize the ability to introduce product design more rapidly with a vision, as yet not widely realized, of designs being transferred directly to manufacturing instructions without many intermediate steps (Dudley & Hassard, 1990).

A fundamental variable is ORGANIZATIONAL SIZE which can be both an independent and a dependent variable of organizational design. As an independent variable increase in size leads to an exponential rise in management costs, in return the organization can gain economies of scale. In order to cope with the complexities of increased size, organizations tend to routinize their activities or break them down into autonomous units.

From a strategic viewpoint size can be used as a means of gaining advantage in the task environment. Organizations can grow organically by going through a certain life cycle (*see* ORGANIZATIONAL CHANGE). To grow can also be a deliberate strategy since by extending the domain of customers and suppliers a firm can gain more secure support for itself. Growth can also occur by means of acquisition (*see* MERGERS AND ACQUISITIONS) and can include a deliberate attempt to move out of a local market to national, international, and global markets. Although the principles of organizational design should remain the same, the main difference would be the requirement to take into account a wider range of cultures and to cope with extensive communication problems over long distances. Reductions in size, or DOWNSIZING, is not necessarily a completely reversible process. Recent research is showing that downsizing can also be accompanied by increases in ROUTINIZATION.

Ideological Aspects

Ideological (*see* IDEOLOGY) and cultural aspects of organizational design have received increasing attention. The distinction between the two terms is somewhat blurred but there appears general agreement that variables capturing the underlying beliefs and VALUES of organizational members and of the wider society need to be in a model of organizational design. These beliefs and values provide a kind of organizational lens through which the context, ways of making decisions, and appropriate structures are viewed.

There is, however, also a feedback link from structure to ideology. Particular types of structure will tend to foster particular types of ideology. For example, if structure sets rules emphasizing highly individualistic profit based pay (*see* PERFORMANCE RELATED PAY), it would be surprising if such an organization managed to develop a robust ideology, that is, an ideology which encourages team work and concern for overall organizational objectives.

We might expect connections between cultural symbols (*see* CULTURE; SYMBOLISM) and structures since structures themselves can become symbolic of the intentions of management. For example, reward systems indicate what kinds of behaviors are approved; executive pay can therefore become very indicative of the key contingencies at any one time (*see* PAYMENT SYSTEMS). As with ideology, culture provides a repertoire of managerial recipes which are used in organizational design.

Critiques and Syntheses

A critique of a coordination and decision cost paradigm of organizational design comes from the POSTMODERNISM position which denies the notion of organizational rationality by arguing that theories of organization are in themselves self-fulfilling and deny the essential chaos of social life. However, chaotic as the post-modern world may be, the goods and services consumed in that society can only be produced by means of high levels of intended RATIONALITY even though that rationality may be, at some later point, found to rest upon an illusion. It seems unlikely, therefore, that interest in organizational design will diminish. Developments within organizational theory which may impact upon organizational theory design practice, such as FUZZY SETS analysis and CHAOS THEORY, may give mathematical tools that can be used to make sense out of the inherent indeterminacy of complex situations.

A more specific current concern in this direction is seen in the interest in ORGANIZATIONAL LEARNING as a major dimension of organizational effectiveness (*see also* LEARNING ORGANIZATION). The notion of an organization as an error-coping and learning device shifts attention from rationality to the need for developing new knowledge. Organizational design, therefore, needs to create the conditions for learning to take place. Argyris and Schon (1978) have elaborated two types of learning which link with the two types of error outlined above. Errors of under-capacity only allow single loop learning, that is, learning to do better what is already being done. DOUBLE LOOP LEARNING involves learning to do new things to enable the organization to adapt to complexity.

INSTITUTIONAL THEORY provides a critique of the dominant paradigm of organizational design which focuses upon the need to minimize coordination costs. The institutional view sees organizational structures as strongly determined by their institutional settings and that the dominant organizational design PARADIGM as too rationalistic, a view which is particularly appropriate to professional, educational and public service types of organizations (*see* GOVERNMENT AGENCIES). Organizations, therefore, attempt to increase their legitimacy by adopting structures which are institutionalized in society rather than structures which are the most efficient for the task of producing products and services. This search for LEGITIMACY means that structures can take on a ritualistic role in order to satisfy institutionalized norms.

A critical omission in much of the organizational design literature concerns the issue of how to achieve change. Organizational design has tended to concentrate upon providing propositions connecting variables on how to improve effectiveness, but change is a technical, political, and cultural problem, although more recent books on organizational design now include sections on achieving change (Butler, 1991; Daft, 1992). A number of structural ideas have been suggested to allow organizations to make changes which can, in general terms, be seen as ways of managing the tension between organizational rigidity and FLEXIBILITY. The ambidextrous organization would incorporate both crisp and fuzzy structures simultaneously. When, for example, introducing a new technology a fuzzy structure would be used but as learning develops a more crisp structure would be needed. The use of venture teams, idea champions, and ENTREPRENEURSHIP are ways of introducing change.

An attempt has been made to bring together these related approaches to the problem of organizational coordination through an institutional model of organizational design (Butler, 1991). This model divides the environment of an organization into the task and institutional environments. The task environment is where the competitive exchange resources (with suppliers, customers, and the like) occur and here the main problem is managing resource dependence (*see* EXCHANGE RELATIONS). The institutional environment sets norms of performance for an organization and here the main problem is that of gaining legitimacy. Legitimacy can be acquired in a number of ways, for instance, by performing well in the task environment or by adopting appropriate structures. Achieving legitimacy by satisfying minimum performance norms becomes the first objective of organizational design and, in order to achieve this, attention needs to be paid to the interrelationship between four sets of variables:

(1) the technical and task context within which an organization operates, of which the notion of complexity is the key descriptor;
(2) the structures adopted;
(3) the ideologies held by organizational participants; and
(4) the DECISION MAKING processes.

Underlying the model is the notion that organizational design should be aimed at error coping and learning rather than output optimizing (*see* LEARNING ORGANIZATION). In coping with complexity errors will be made. If structures are too rigid and ideologies too narrowly focused for the degree of complexity, errors of decision under-capacity are made; the problem becomes lack of organizational adaptability. If structures are too fuzzy and ideologies too robust, errors of decision over-capacity are made; the organization here achieves high adaptability but at the expense of efficiency. The institutional model sees organizational design as a dialectic between conflicting features and alerts designers to how a wide range of aspects of the institutional environment can impact upon design parameters. In particular, changes in the political, social and cultural, and economic segments of the environment can radically alter the performance norms to which an organization has to attend.

The Future

Until the 1980s the general trend was for organizations to grow and organizational theory was generally built upon this premise. Since then reductions in size have become common. Reducing the number of people does not necessarily mean a reduction in output, turnover, or capital employed. Number of people employed has been the usual measure of size in organizational theory since the subject is most concerned with organization as a social rather than as a financial or a technical phenomenon. Whether size increases or decreases makes no difference to the principles of an intendedly rational organizational design but will make a difference to the process of change.

The availability of networks of low-cost personal computers combined with the enormous information processing capacity of larger computers means that networks of organizations can be created; airline booking and bank telling systems are archetypes (*see* NETWORK ANALYSIS; NETWORKING). This is allowing organizations to develop flatter, less centralized, but probably more routinized, structures. Research continues to show, however, that formal executive information systems are not used much by senior managers since, in making the more complex higher-level decisions, they prefer to rely less upon formal and more upon informal information (*see* CEOs).

In most Western economies there has been an increase in the number of small firms and it is increasingly being observed that organizations do not need to employ people but can buy in goods and services from a network of small suppliers. Taken to the limit the proposition of downsizing poses an interesting paradox for organizational design since it would mean the replacement of large organizations in the formal sense by transactions contract governance. Manufacturing a motor car, for instance, would be a matter of buying in sufficient goods and services and managing a vast network of contracts. Such an image suggests that some of the conventional variables of structure will have to change. However, the underlying principles of transaction costs, requisite informational variety, and requisite decision capacity should still hold.

See also **Group structure; Formal organization; Loose coupling; Collateral organization**

Bibliography

Argyris, C. & Schon, D. A. (1978). *Organizational learning: A theory of action perspective*. Reading, MA: Addison-Wesley.

Ashby, W. R. (1956). Self-regulation and requisite variety. In F. E. Emery (Ed.), *Systems thinking*. Harmondsworth, UK: Penguin (1969), Ch. 6. Originally in W. R. Ashby *Introduction to Cybernetics*. New York: Wiley (1956), Ch. 11.

Butler, R. J. (1991). *Designing organizations: A decision-making perspective*. London: Routledge.

Chandler, A. D. (1962). *Strategy and structure: Chapters in the history of the industrial enterprise*. Cambridge, MA: MIT Press.

Daft, R. L. (1992). *Organization theory and design*, (4th edn). St Paul: MN. West.

Dudley, G. & Hassard J. (1990). Design issues in the development of computer integrated manufacturing (CIM). *Journal of General Management*, **16**, 43–53.

Galbraith, J. R. (1977). *Organization design*. Reading, MA: Addison-Wesley.

Huber G. P. (1990). A theory of the effects of advanced information technologies on organizational design, intelligence and decision making. *Academy of Management Review*, **15**, 1.

Knight, K. (1976). Matrix organization: A review. *Journal of Management Studies*, **13**, 11–130.

March, J. G. (Ed.), (1965). *Handbook of organizations*. Chicago: Rand McNally.

Miles, R. E. & C. C. Snow (1978). *Organizational Strategy, Structure and Process*. New York: McGraw-Hill.

Mintzberg, H. (1983). *Structures in fives: Designing effective organizations*. Englewood Cliffs, NJ: Prentice-Hall.

Nystrom, P. C. & Starbuck, W. H. (Eds), (1981). *Handbook of organizational design*, (vols. I & II). Oxford, UK: Oxford University Press.

Perrow, C. (1970). *Organizational analysis: A sociological view*. London: Tavistock.

Pugh, D. S. & Hickson, D. J. (1989). *Writers on organizations*. Newburg Park, CA: Sage.

Rubenstein, A. H. & Haberstroh, C. J. (Eds), (1966). *Some theories of organization*. Homewood, IL: Irwin & Dorsey.

Stinchcombe, A. (1965). Social structure and organizations. In J. G. March (Ed.), *Handbook of organizations*, (Ch. 4). Chicago: Rand McNally.

Thompson, J. D. (1967). *Organizations in action*. New York: McGraw-Hill.

Trist E. L., Higgin G. W., Murray H. & Pollack A. B. (1963). *Organizational choice*. London: Tavistock.

Williamson O. E. (1975). *Markets and hierarchies: Analysis and Anti-Trust Implications: A Study in the Economics of Internal Organization*. New York: Free Press.

Woodward, J. (1965). *Industrial organization: Theory and practice*. Oxford, UK: Oxford University Press.

RICHARD BUTLER

organizational economics There is little doubt that organizations are profoundly affected by the competitive environments within which they operate. There is also little doubt that economics, and especially micro-economics, has a great deal to say about competition and its implications. However, until the early 1980s, micro-economic concepts were not included in most organizational research. Since that time, several important economic models of organizational phenomena have been developed and applied by scholars. These models, including transaction cost economics (Williamson, 1975) (*see* TRANSACTION COST THEORY; AGENCY THEORY) (Jensen & Meckling, 1976); the evolutionary theory of the firm (Nelson & Winter, 1982) (*see* POPULATION ECOLOGY); the STRUCTURE–CONDUCT–PERFORMANCE paradigm (Bain, 1956); and, more recently, the resource-based view of the firm (Barney, 1991) (*see* RESOURCE BASED THEORY); constitute what is known as Organizational Economics (Barney & Ouchi, 1986).

These organizational economic models differ from traditional economics in two important ways. First, the dependent variable in most organizational economic models is firm behavior, or even the behavior of individuals and groups within a firm. In traditional economics, the dependent variable more often than not is industry structure or social welfare. Second, organization economic models tend to relax one or more of the strong assumptions underlying traditional economic analyses. For example, transaction cost economics and agency theory replace the perfect information assumption of traditional economics with the assumption of BOUNDED RATIONALITY. Evolutionary economics replaces traditional equilibrium analyses with more dynamic analyses of firm behavior. The structure–conduct–performance paradigm replaces perfect competition assumptions with imperfect competition assumptions. Finally, the resource-based view replaces traditional assumptions of firm homogeneity and resource mobility with assumptions of firm heterogeneity and resource immobility.

Organization economic models can be applied in the analysis of a wide range of organizational phenomena from firm strategy and competitive advantage, to JOINT VENTURES and organizational structure, to the analysis of internal compensation systems and the development of ORGANIZATIONAL CULTURE (Barney & Ouchi, 1986).

See also **Competitiveness; Organization theory; Prospect theory**

Bibliography

Bain, J. (1956). *Barriers to new competition*. Cambridge, MA: Harvard University Press.

Barney, J. (1991). Firm resources and sustained competitive advantage. *Journal of Management*, **17**, 99–120.

Barney, J. & Ouchi, W. (1986). *Organizational economics*. San Francisco: Jossey-Bass.

Jensen, M. & Meckling, W. (1976). Theory of the firm: Managerial behavior, agency costs, and ownership structure. *Journal of Financial Economics*, **3**, 305–360.

Nelson, R. & Winter, S. (1982). *An evolutionary theory of economic change*. Cambridge, MA: Harvard University Press.

Williamson, O. (1975). *Markets and hierarchies*. New York: Free Press.

JAY B. BARNEY

organizational effectiveness This has been defined in a variety of ways but no single definition has been accepted universally (Cameron & Whetten, 1983). This is because organizational effectiveness is inherently tied to the definition of what an organization is. As the conceptualization of an organization changes, so does the definition of effectiveness, the criteria used to measure effectiveness, and frameworks and theories used to explain and predict it. For example, if an organization is defined as a goal seeking entity, effectiveness is likely to be defined in terms of the extent to which goals are accomplished. If an organization is defined as the central focus of a social CONTRACT among constituencies, effectiveness is likely to be defined in terms of constituency satisfaction. To understand what is generally agreed upon about organizational effectiveness, it is helpful to discuss several of its important attributes. In particular, effectiveness:

(1) is a *construct*,
(2) it is grounded in the *VALUES* and *preferences* of constituencies; and
(3) it must be *bounded* to be measured.

As a *construct*, effectiveness cannot be observed directly. This is because constructs are abstractions "constructed" to give meaning to an idea (*see* SOCIAL CONSTRUCTIONISM). In other words, organizational effectiveness cannot be pinpointed, counted, or objectively manipulated. It is an idea rather than an objective reality. In addition, effectiveness is reflective of the *values and preferences* of various constituencies. What one group may prefer or label as effective may not be the same as that of another group. Moreover, preferences may knowingly or unknowingly change, sometimes dramatically, over time among individuals. The attachment of effectiveness to goodness or to excellence makes judgments of effectiveness inherently subjective and valued-based. This helps explain why no single definition of effectiveness is universal. Different constituencies have different preferences, different values, and different evaluation criteria.

This does not mean, of course, that effectiveness cannot be measured. But in order for acceptable criteria of effectiveness to be identified, the *boundaries* of the construct must be clearly delineated. This means that the answers to seven questions must be answered which specify the construct boundaries:

(1) From whose perspective is effectiveness being judged (e.g., customers, stockholders, employees)?
(2) On what domain of activity is the judgment focused (e.g., service delivery, new product design, production processes)?
(3) What level of analysis is being used (e.g., individual satisfaction, organizational profitability, industry COMPETITIVENESS)?
(4) What is the purpose for judging effectiveness (e.g., to recognize achievements, to identify weaknesses, to eliminate waste)?
(5) What time frame is employed (e.g., immediate snap-shot indicators versus long-term trend lines)?
(6) What type of data are being used for judgments (e.g., employee perceptions, financial results, customer satisfaction)?
(7) What is the referent against which effectiveness is judged (e.g., effectiveness compared to an ideal standard, compared to past improvement, compared to stated goals)?

Every judgment of effectiveness must answer these seven questions, either explicitly or implicitly, in order to reach a conclusion. When the answer to each question is clearly specified, then acceptable criteria of effectiveness can be clearly identified. Unfortunately, in the organizational behavior literature few writers have been careful enough to specify their answers to each of these questions, so comparable measurements of effectiveness have been difficult to find (see Whetten & Cameron 1994).

Certain common approaches to the definition and measurement of organizational effectiveness have emerged over time; each "era" with its own underlying definition of effectiveness. For example, the earliest models of organizational effectiveness emphasized "ideal types," that is, forms of organization that maximized certain attributes. Max Weber's characterization of BUREAUCRACY as the ideal form of organization is an obvious and well-known example. The most common criterion of effectiveness under this model was efficiency (maximum output with minimum input). The more nearly an organization approached the ideal bureaucratic characteristics – which were designed to produce maximum efficiency – the more effective it was. In other words, the more specialized, formalized, and centralized, the better.

Subsequent models of organizing challenged this bureaucratic model, however, suggesting that many effective organizations were actually nonbureaucratic. The most effective organizations, they argued, were cooperative and participative. Effective organizations satisfied the needs of their members by providing adequate inducements to sustain required contributions. They controlled employee activities via goals, PARTICIPATION, or decision processes, not rules. They became legitimated by linking their role in society to social values (e.g., Likert, 1967) (*see* HUMAN RELATIONS MOVEMENT).

Over the years, several ideal type approaches have been widely used. The most common model used organizational goal accomplishment as the ideal indicator of effectiveness. If stated goals are achieved, the organization is effective. Advocates of a "natural systems" view of organizations, however, argued that effectiveness ultimately depends on obtaining critical resources (*see* SYSTEMS THEORY; OPEN SYSTEMS). The more resources acquired (e.g., revenues, personnel, recognition), the more effective. Others emphasized the organization's COMMUNICATION and "interpretation" systems, the satisfaction of organizational members, the achievement of profitability, and the consistency of activities with principles of social equity (see Pfeffer & Salancik, 1978; Scott, 1992). The common ingredient among all these models was an advocacy of one definitive, universalistic definition and set of criteria for assessing organizational effectiveness. Organizations are effective if they are characterized by the ideal criteria.

Challenges to this universalistic approach to effectiveness, coupled with mounting frustration over the truth of the claims of the competing models, gave rise to the"CONTINGENCY THEORY" approach to effectiveness (e.g., Lawrence & Lorsch, 1967). This approach argued that effectiveness is not a function of the extent to which an organization reflects the qualities of an ideal profile, instead, it depends on the match between an organization's profile and environmental conditions. Definitions of effectiveness were built on the idea of "fit" between certain environmental characteristics and certain organizational characteristics, such as between mechanistic organizational forms and stable, simple environments, and organic forms with rapidly changing, complex environments (*see* MECHANISTIC/ORGANIC).

The critical difference between the ideal type and the contingency theory approaches to effectiveness is that the former assumes that "one size fits all." Effective organizations are distinguished by a universal set of attributes. In contrast, contingency approaches argue that organizations are effective only to the extent to which they match the conditions of their environments (*see* ORGANIZATION AND ENVIRONMENT).

A third approach to effectiveness arose when the focus shifted away from the abstract *constructs* (i.e., dimensions) associated with the organization itself and began to focus on the expectations of the organization's constituencies. Effective organizations were defined as those that had accurate information about the expectations of strategically critical constituents and that had adapted internal processes, goals, and values to meet those expectations. Proponents of the "strategic constituencies" perspective viewed organizations as highly elastic entities in a dynamic force field of constituencies that manipulated organizational form and performance (*see* Connolly, Conlon, & Deutsch, 1980) (*see* RESOURCE DEPENDENCE; STAKEHOLDERS). The organization was molded to the demands of powerful interest groups such as stockholders, unions, regulators, customers, and top management. Effectiveness became linked, therefore, to concepts such as customer satisfaction, learning, adaptability, and LEGITIMACY. The assumption was that organizations are effective if they satisfy their customers, or if they are learning systems, or if they are adaptable to constituency demands, or if they acquire legitimacy with their publics (*see* LEARNING ORGANIZATION).

When the expectations of these various constituencies diverged from or contradicted one another, however, organizations were faced with a dilemma. Which constituencies should the organization satisfy and which criteria should be emphasized? Four alternatives emerged in the organizational behavior literature (see Zammuto, 1984):

(1) strive to provide as much as possible to each constituency without harming any other constituency;
(2) strive to satisfy the most powerful or dominant constituency first;
(3) favor the least advantaged constituencies who are most likely to be harmed; and
(4) adapt to the changing set of constituency expectations and respond as rapidly as possible to all of them.

In other words, conscious choices were required under this approach regarding which constituency or set of demands received priority.

This strategic constituencies approach to effectiveness, then, differs from the previous two approaches – ideal type and contingency theory – by emphasizing dynamic criteria of effectiveness. Rather than relying on ideal attributes or on appropriate fit to define effectiveness, this approach relies on key constituencies to determine the most appropriate criteria.

An especially visible manifestation of this strategic-constituencies approach is the current quality movement (*see* TOTAL QUALITY MANAGEMENT). The term quality has overtaken effectiveness, in fact, as the construct of choice in describing and assessing desirable performance in the organizational behavior literature. This represents a significant change in the ORGANIZATIONAL BEHAVIOR literature because prior to the late 1980s, quality was treated as a predictor of effectiveness, not a substitution for it. Quality referred to the rate of errors or defects in goods-producing organizations, to institutional REPUTATION in educational organizations, to ambiance and talent in arts organizations, to recovery rates in health care organizations, and to customer satisfaction levels in service organizations. In every case quality was *one* of the desired attributes organizations wanted to pursue, and a qualifier in describing a product or service, i.e., high-quality products, high-quality education, high-quality art, high-quality health care.

However, with the increased visibility achieved by several quality gurus (e.g., Edwards Derning, Joseph Juran, Philip Crosby, Kaoru Ishikawa), quality became an ultimate objective, something of a *summum bonum*, for organizations. "Quality is defined by the customer" was a commonly accepted definition, through which organizational processes, attributes, behavior, and achievements were relevant only if they helped achieve customer satisfaction. At the present time, this perspective, and the strategic constituencies approach it represents, is currently the most frequently utilized approach to effectiveness.

However, the recognition that tensions exist among the demands placed on organizations, that different customers may possess different expectations, and that focusing exclusively on customer satisfaction implies a reactive orientation gave rise to a fourth approach to effectiveness – a PARADOX approach (Cameron, 1986a). This approach emphasized the paradoxical nature of effective organizational performance. It incorporated elements of each of the three previous models in defining effectiveness as, for example, both fitting with and enacting the external environment, being both responsive to external constituencies (e.g., customers) and being independent of them, being both short- and long-term focused, being both flexible and rigid, being both centralized and decentralized, and being both efficient and malleable. Organizational behavior that is most highly effective, it was argued, is that which is characterized by seemingly paradoxical attributes.

One study concluded, for example, that the presence of simultaneous opposites in organizations created the highest levels of effectiveness, as well as improvements in effectiveness over time, particularly under conditions of environmental turbulence (Cameron, 1986b). Another pointed out that "it is not just the presence of mutually exclusive opposites that makes for effectiveness, but it is the creative leaps, the flexibility, and the unity made possible by them that leads to excellence . . . the presence of creative tension arising from paradoxical attributes helps foster organizational effectiveness" (Cameron, 1986a).

In other words, proponents of this definition of effectiveness argued that effectiveness refers not just to matching an ideal profile, nor matching environmental conditions, nor responding to constituency expectations. Instead, they emphasized that effectiveness is inherently tied to organizations that are Simultaneously defensive and aggressive, entrepreneurial and conservative, consistent and inconsistent, reinforcing and destroying traditions, growing and declining, tightly coupled and loosely coupled (*see* LOOSE COUPLING).

This paradoxical approach to effectiveness also had impact on the definition of quality. Among some (especially the Japanese), quality began to focus on more than the mere pursuit of customer satisfaction, by encompassing attributes of process, structure, and employee behavior as well as the production of products and services. It has taken on the broader meaning and more encompassing label of total quality management.

Despite the fact that organizational effectiveness lies at the center of all theories of organizations (i.e., all theories of organization ultimately rely on the fact that some way to organize or behave is *more effective* than others) despite the fact that organizational effectiveness is an ultimate dependent variable in organizational behavior (i.e., all relationships among organizational elements assume that achieving effectiveness is an ultimate objective), and despite that fact that individuals and organizations are constantly required to maintain accountability for effectiveness (i.e., individuals and organizations are regularly appraised on their performance, which assumes that one kind of performance is more effective than another), one common definition of effectiveness has remained elusive. However, at least four approaches to effectiveness are currently available, each of which has legitimacy and value.

See also **Organization theory; Seven s's framework; Structure-conduct-performance model**

Bibliography

Cameron, K. (1986a). Effectiveness as paradox: Consensus and conflict in conceptualizations of organizational effectiveness. *Management Science*, **32**, 539–553.

Cameron, K. (1986b). A study of organizational effectiveness and its predictors. *Management Science*, **32**, 87–112.

Cameron, K. & Whetten, D. A. (1983). *Organizational effectiveness: A comparison of multiple models.* New York: Academic Press.

Connolly, T., Conlon, E. & Deutsch, S. (1980). Organizational effectiveness: A multiple-constituency view. *Academy of Management Review*, **5**, 211–217.

Lawrence, P. & Lorsch, J. (1967). *Organization and environment.* Cambridge, MA: Harvard University Press.

Likert, R. (1967). *The human organization.* New York: McGraw-Hill.

Pfeffer, J. & Salancik, J. (1978). *The external control of organizations.* New York: Harper & Row.

Scott, R. (1992). *Organizations: Rational, natural, and open systems.* Englewood Cliffs, NJ: Prentice-Hall.

Whetten, D. & Cameron, K. (1994). Organizational effectiveness: Old models and new constructs. In J. Greenberg (Ed.), *Organizational behavior: The state of the science.* Northvale, NJ: Lawrence Earlbaum.

Zammuto, R. (1984). A comparison of multiple constituency models of organizational effectiveness. *Academy of Management Review*, **9**, 606–616.

KIM S. CAMERON

organizational learning Work in the behavioral tradition of organization level learning since then is summarized well by Levitt and March (1988, p. 319), who describe organizations as experiential learning systems that are ". . . routine-based, history-dependent, and target-oriented." A brief exposition of these three characteristics summarizes the key points of the organizational learning perspective.

The first characteristic is that organizations are routine-based systems that respond to experience. Models of organizations as experiential learning systems typically focus on three categories of routines: search, performance, and change (Mezias & Glynn, 1993):

Search Routines. Models of search routines address the process by which organizations attempt to discover adaptive opportunities in an ambiguous world via a costly and routinized process of search.

Performance Routines. Models of performance routines suggest that organizations compare actual outcomes against a moving target: an aspired level of performance that changes over time in response to experience. The functional forms guiding the adaption of aspiration levels and empirical evidence for these different forms is presented in some detail by Lant (1992).

Change Routines. Models of change routines suggest that ORGANIZATIONAL CHANGE, whether an attempt to refine current capabilities or to implement new and different capabilities, is a stochastic response to experience.

The second characteristic of models of organizations as experiential learning systems is an emphasis on the fact that the learning process is history-dependent; there are no unique equilibria or closed form solutions. Past behavior constrains the path that future behavior by organizations can take in a way that is difficult to specify a priori. The prime example of this is the effect of increasing competence with current routines, e.g., the well-known learning curve (*see* CORE COMPETENCE). It is well established that over time, organizations improve their performance with new TECHNOLOGY but at a decreasing rate. This is one reason why organizations may be reluctant to innovate: They will lose the competencies they have built using the status quo (*see* INNOVATION). As a result, inferior alternatives with which the organization has competence might be preferred to superior alternatives with which the organization lacks competence. Indeed, this notion is at the heart of concepts like the competency trap (Levitt & March, 1988) and the distinction between competence-enhancing and competence-destroying technological change (Tushman & Anderson, 1986).

The third and final characteristic of models of organizations as experiential learning systems is an emphasis on the importance of aspiration levels in mediating the execution of change routines. Organizations are more likely to persist in activities associated with success and desist activities associated with failure. The importance of aspiration level is in determining whether a particular level of performance is defined as success and failure: Performance above aspiration level is defined as success while that below aspiration level is defined as failure. Thus, organizational change will be more likely under conditions of failure than under conditions of success.

See also **Community ecology; Exchange relations; Learning organization; Population ecology**

Bibliography

Cyert, R. M. & March, J. G. (1963). *A behavioral theory of the firm*. Englewood Cliffs, NJ: Prentice-Hall.

Lant, T. K. (1992). Aspiration level updating: An empirical exploration. *Management Science*, **38**, 623–644.

Levitt, B. & March, J. G. (1988). Organizational learning. *Annual Review of Sociology*, **14**, 319–340.

Mezias, S. J. & Glynn, M. A. (1993). The three faces of corporate renewal: Institution, Revolution, and Evolution. *Strategic Management Journal*, **14**, 77–101.

Tushman, M. T. & Anderson, P. (1986). Technological discontinuities and organizational environments. *Administrative Science Quarterly*, **31**, 439–65.

STEPHEN J. MEZIAS

organizational life cycles *see* POPULATION ECOLOGY; ORGANIZATIONAL CHANGE

organizational neurosis Organizational research has traditionally focused on telling executives how to do things correctly by creating models for rational analysis. However, the reality of the situation often requires a radically different approach. Organizations are not immune to neurotic behavior patterns, disturbing interpersonal interactions, and rigid defensive mechanisms. An organization cannot perform successfully if the quirks and irrational processes that are part and parcel of individual behavior are ignored. Many observers and practitioners of organizational life have come to understand that the "irrational" PERSONALITY traits of the principal decision makers can seriously affect the management process. There is a substantive body of evidence to support the contention that organizational leaders are not necessarily rational, logical, sensible, and dependable human beings, but, in fact, are prone to a fair amount of irrational behavior (*see* CEOs). Organizations are not spared the impact leaders have on their environment. Clinical investigation demonstrates that many organizational problems originate in the private, inner world of an organization's senior executives – in the way they act out their conflicts, desires, fantasies, and defensive structures (*see* TOP MANAGEMENT TEAMS).

In most individuals, we can discern the predominance of one particular style of functioning or character pattern that consistently typifies many aspects of their behavior. Extreme manifestations of a single style or a lack of adaptive behavior, however, can eventually lead to psychopathology and serious functional impairment. Not surprisingly, the clinical study of organizations shows that parallels can be drawn between individual pathology – excessive use of one "neurotic style" – and organizational pathology, the latter resulting in poorly functioning organizations. Particularly, in dysfunctional, centralized firms, the rigid neurotic styles of the top executives will be strongly mirrored in the nature of inappropriate strategies, structures, and ORGANIZATIONAL CULTURES of their firms.

For example, the former CEO of ITT, Harold Geneen, is a good illustration of how the personality of a leader can affect an organization. His suspicious outlook toward the world transformed ITT into a corporation where paranoid thinking became rampant. Geneen became infamous for his search for "unshakable facts" leading to elaborate information processing systems which eventually became a serious burden to organizational functioning. DECISION MAKING became overly sluggish, strategic, and too reactive, and capable executives started to leave.

Neurotic organizations are troubled firms whose symptoms and dysfunctions may combine to form an integrated "syndrome" of pathology. Just as numerous symptoms combine to form a human disorder, similar patterns of

Table 1 The characteristics of "Neurotic" Organizations.

Type	Organization	Executive	Culture	Strategy	Guiding theme
Dramatic	Too primitive for its many products and broad market; overcentralization obstructs the development of effective information systems; second-tier executives retain too little influence in policy-making	Needs attention, excitement, activity, and stimulation; feels a sense of entitlement; has a tendency toward extremes	Dependency needs of subordinates complement "strong leader" tendencies of chief executive; leader is idealized by "mirroring" subordinates; leader is catalyst for subordinates; initiative and morale	Hyperactive, impulsive, venturesome, dangerously uninhibited; executive prerogative to initiate bold ventures; diversifications and growth rarely consistent or integrated; action for action's sake; nonparticipative decision-making	Grandiosity: "I want to get attention from and impress the people who count in my life"
Suspicious	Elaborate information-processing; abundant analysis of external trends; centralization of power	Vigilantly prepared to counter any and all attacks and personal threats; hypersensitive; cold and lacks emotional expression; suspicious, distrustful, and insists on loyalty; overinvolved in rules and details to secure complete control; craves information; sometimes vindictive	"Fight-or-flight" culture, including dependency, fear of attack, emphasis on the power of information, intimidation, uniformity, lack of trust	Reactive, conservative; overly analytical; diversified; secretive	"Some menacing force is out to get me; I had better be on my guard. I cannot really trust anybody"

Table 1 continued

Type	Organization	Executive	Culture	Strategy	Guiding theme
Detached	Internal focus, insufficient scanning of external environment, self-imposed barriers to free flow of information	Withdrawn and not involved; lacks interest in present or future; sometimes indifferent to praise or criticism	Lack of warmth or emotions; conflicts, jockeying for power; insecurity	Vacillating, indecisive, inconsistent; the product of narrow, parochial perspectives	"Reality does not offer satisfaction; interactions with others will fail; it is safer to remain distant"
Depressive	Ritualistic; bureaucratic; inflexible; hierarchical; poor internal communications; resistant to change; impersonal	Lacks self-confidence, self-esteem, or initiative; fears success and tolerates mediocrity or failure; depends on messiahs	Lack of initiative; passivity; negativity; lack of motivation; ignorance of markets; leadership vacuum	"Decidiphobia"; attention focused inward; lack of vigilance over changing market conditions; drifting with no sense of direction; confinement to antiquated "mature" markets	"It is hopeless to change the course of events; I am just not good enough"
Compulsive	Rigid formal codes; elaborate information systems; ritualized evaluation procedures; thoroughness, exactness; a hierarchy in which individual managers' status derives directly from specific positions	Tends to dominate organization from top to bottom; insists that others conform to tightly prescribed procedures and rules; dogmatic or obstinate personality; perfectionist or is obsessed with detail, routine, rituals, efficiency, and lockstep organization	Rigid, inward directed, insular; subordinates are submissive, uncreative, insecure	Tightly calculated and focused, exhaustive evaulation; slow, unadaptive; reliance on a narrow established theme; obsession with a single aspect of strategy, e.g., cost-cutting or quality, the exclusion of other factors	"I don't want to be at the mercy of events: I have to master and control all the things affecting me"

Reproduced from 'Unstable At The Top'.

strategic and structural defects often point to an integrated organizational pathology.

Kets de Vries and Miller (1984) have extrapolated findings from the psychoanalytic and psychiatric literature to identify five very common neurotic types of organizations: dramatic, suspicious, compulsive, detached, and depressive. Each type has its specific characteristics: structure, executive style, culture, strategy, and predominating guiding theme. (See table 1 for a summary of the five organizational types.)

See also **Emotions in organizations; Organizational effectiveness; Mental health; Managerial behavior**

Bibliography

Hirschhorn, L. (1988). *The workplace within: Psychodynamics of organizational life*. Cambridge, MA: MIT Press

Kets de Vries, M. F. R. (1993). *Leaders, fools and impostors*. San Francisco: Jossey-Bass.

Kets de Vries, M. F. R. & Associates (1991). *Organizations on the couch*. San Francisco: Jossey-Bass.

Kets de Vries, M. F. R. & Miller, D. (1984). *The neurotic organization*. San Francisco: Jossey-Bass.

Levinson, H. (1981). *Executive: The guide to responsive management*. Cambridge, MA: Harvard University Press.

Zaleznik, A. (1989). *The management mystique*. New York: Harper Collins.

MANFRED KETS DE VRIES

organizational performance *see* COMPETITIVENESS; ORGANIZATIONAL EFFECTIVENESS

organizational size The way that organizational size has been defined is mostly in terms of its OPERATIONALIZATION. Organizational size has been measured as: the number of employees (full-time equivalents); the sales revenue of the firm; the number of product lines offered; or, more generally, the scale of operations most relevant to the industry being studied (i.e., patients in hospitals, assets in mutual funds). Despite some early controversy over which measures for size were best, most studies showed high correlations between multiple measures when a single industry was being analyzed.

The apparent simplicity of the concept masks the fact that size has been perhaps the single best predictor of organizational structure and behavior in the history of the field (*see* ORGANIZATIONAL DESIGN). Studies conducted by Blau and associates and by the Aston group in Great Britain in the late 1960s and early 1970s, showed that the size of an organization is consistently and uniformly related to its DIFFERENTIATION, specialization, SPAN OF CONTROL, centralization, and stage of growth or development. Other authors argue that these relationships may be driven by contextual factors other than size alone, or that size may merely be causally difficult to untangle when other factors are present. Because of the almost universal impact of size on ORGANIZATIONAL BEHAVIOR it is often included as a control variable in empirical studies. The inclusion of size as a control often obliterates or reduces the magnitude of effect of an alternative independent variable.

Change in size, in terms of growth or retrenchment also influences organizational behavior. A large literature has developed around the organizational life cycle concept with many researchers suggesting that as growth occurs organizations go through a series of predictable set of gestalts of strategy and structure that can best be thought of as stages. Organizational DOWNSIZING and ORGANIZATIONAL DECLINE AND DEATH also have been shown to have regular effects on organization behavior.

It is almost impossible to summarize the literature on size because of its frequent use as an independent variable. Size has been used as a contextual factor in CONTINGENCY THEORY where size and structure interact to predict organizational performance (*see* ORGANIZATIONAL EFFECTIVENESS). In the POPULATION ECOLOGY literature size has been used as a predictor of survival. Small, new organizations are predicted to be more susceptible to failure than larger older organizations. INSTITUTIONAL THEORY argues that large organizations often adopt innovations and legitimize them and then smaller organizations imitate the larger organization's behavior.

Where size is not used explicitly it is implied through the choice of organizations researchers choose to study. Samples of organizations often fall into three categories. Small entrepreneurial business or family run operations, moderate size corporations or GOVERNMENT AGENCIES, and, monolithic, often international conglomerates (*see* MULTINATIONAL CORPORATIONS). The choice of problem to study, the theories generated and the methods of data collection all depend on the size of the organization being studied. Size then is indirectly included in the analysis of these organizations because the phenomena being observed are, in great part, due to size.

See also **Organization theory; Organization and environment; Organizational change**

Bibliography

Hall, R. H. (1977). *Organizations: Structure and process*. Englewood Cliffs, NJ: Prentice-Hall.

ROBERT DRAZIN

organizational structure *see* ORGANIZATIONAL DESIGN; RESTRUCTURING

— P —

paradigm Confusion over the meaning of the term is not just related to its wide-spread use, and thus vulgarization, but because Kuhn (1970), the originator of the idea in his celebrated book *Scientific Revolutions*, implied a variety of definitions as well. This multiplicity flows from two critical characteristics of the use of THEORY in science:

(1) there are many definitions of what is theory; and
(2) there is a wide range of styles across various disciplines.

For example, theory can mean either formal deductive laws or mathematical models or geometric representations or empirical GENERALIZATIONS (such as in statistical analysis) or iconographic models. Furthermore, what distinguishes the disparate disciplines is their particular emphasis on one or another of these ways of representing reality. Finally, there is even some disagreement as to whether or not theory, regardless of how this is defined, and paradigm can be equated. This is because of Kuhn's emphasis on the consensual aspects of the set of ideas and problems that represent the focus of a particular discipline.

However, despite this diversity in the interpretation of the meaning of the word paradigm, Kuhn's central idea, namely, that a paradigm is the single consensual model of the discipline that most members accept, suggests that it may have limited application to the organizational sciences. Even within the social sciences, it would appear that only economics has achieved a wide-consensus on the theoretical ideas and problems associated with the micro-economic model of supply and demand (*see* ORGANIZATIONAL ECONOMICS). This is a discipline that emphasizes formal deductive reasoning and mathematical models (*see* COMPUTER MODELING), much as does physics. No other social science has the same degree of unity. In particular, the organizational sciences are distinguished by the wide variety of theoretical models and perspectives as is illustrated in this dictionary. Examples are the headings: CLASSICAL DESIGN THEORY, INSTITUTIONAL THEORY, POPULATION ECOLOGY theory, SYSTEMS THEORY, and CONTINGENCY THEORY among others.

Kuhn's particular interest was in the problems of changing the paradigm once it is widely accepted, hence the title scientific revolutions. But an equally important question which may be raised is whether there will be any development or codification of knowledge so long as the field or speciality is divided into a multitude of perspectives.

See also **Process theory; Critical theory; Punctuated equilibrium**

Bibliography

Kuhn, T. (1970). *The structure of scientific revolutions*. Chicago: University of Chicago Press.

JERALD HAGE

paradox During the 1980s a number of studies of ORGANIZATIONAL EFFECTIVENESS have suggested that this concept is inherently paradoxical in the sense that to be effective, an organization must possess attributes that are simultaneously contradictory. Thus Peters and Waterman (1982) suggested that excellent companies have learned how to manage paradox, possessing both loose and tight properties, a "soft" concern for people and a "hard" bias for action, both ENTREPRENEURSHIP and focus (*see*

EXCELLENCE). There is growing evidence that organizations in dynamic and competitive environments require such opposite yet complementary attributes – high specialization of ROLES and broad generalist perspective, continuity of LEADERSHIP and the infusion of new blood, deviation amplifying processes associated with INNOVATION and deviation reduction processes linked to efficiency.

Cameron (1986) summarizes evidence for the paradoxical nature of effectiveness, arguing that extremity in any criterion of effectiveness creates dysfunctions. A good illustration is the study by Miller (1990) on the failure of successful companies. Cameron also argues that while reconciliation or synthesis of opposites may be desirable, paradox need not be resolved to enhance effectiveness. The mere recognition that two contradictory elements are simultaneously true may create a constructive tension that facilitaties ORGANIZATIONAL DEVELOPMENT (Pascale, 1990).

The paradoxical perspective has also significant implications for research methodology (*see* RESEARCH METHODS), particularly if the dependent variable is some form of effectiveness. For example, conventional statistical analysis based on means, linear trends, and assumptions of normal distributions masks the presence of paradox (*see* STATISTICAL METHODS). The absence of an attribute does not necessarily indicate the presence of its opposite; both complementary qualities need to be measured. The phenomenon of paradox is also seen in the study of dilemmas or dualities (*see* DILEMMAS, ORGANIZATIONAL) for a more extended discussion).

See also **Theory; Metaphor; Punctuated equilibrium; Rationality; Critical theory**

Bibliography

Cameron, K. S. (1986). Effectiveness as paradox: Consensus and conflict in conceptions of organizational effectiveness. *Management Science*, 32, 539–553.

Miller, D. (1990). *The Icarus paradox: How exceptional companies bring about their own downfall*. New York: Harper Business.

Pascale, R. T. (1990). *Managing on the edge: How successful companies use conflict to stay ahead*. New York: Viking.

Peters, T. J. & Waterman, R. H. (1982). *In search of Excellence: Lessons from America's best run companies*. New York: Harper & Row.

PAUL EVANS

participant observation *see* RESEARCH DESIGN; RESEARCH METHODS

participation In an OB context, the term participation usually refers to EMPLOYEE INVOLVEMENT in decision making within enterprises. This distinguishes it from other forms of participation, such as financial participation (e.g., GAINSHARING or employee stock ownership). There is no universally agreed definition of participation, though the concept of INFLUENCE is regarded as central by most researchers and practitioners (Hollander & Offerman, 1990). Thus, participation may be said to increase as the degree of subordinate influence over decisions increases from no influence (decision is made by management, with no advanced warning to employees) through consultative decision making (employees are asked for their opinion, before management decides) to joint decision making (where the influence of parties to the DECISION MAKING process is equally balanced). For some the continuum of influence extends to a situation where the employee or group of employees make the decision alone. Others argue that the process used reaching a decision is important, suggesting that true participation is characterized by an absence of the exercise of coercive power.

In addition to the degree and nature of influence, employee participation may also be characterized by the degree of formality of the process. Formal participation involves set rules and procedures directing the process of decision making (e.g., formally constituted QUALITY CIRCLES). However, participation may also merely reflect an informal consensus reached between managers and subordinates, and as such can be viewed as a function of a particular LEADERSHIP STYLE. Participation may also be direct or indirect, depending on the extent to which employees are personally and actively involved in making the decision. Programs of JOB ENRICHMENT and structures such as AUTONOMOUS WORK GROUPS typically lead to employees personally participating in the decision-making process. However, this form of participation is to be distinguished from the many which involve some form of collective representation of employee interests, leading to more "distant" involvement of most employees (e.g., an elected worker representative on a company board or a consultative committee). Participative mechanisms may also be distinguished from each other in terms of their time span. Some are relatively transient (e.g., a temporary task force or a SOCIOTECHNICAL SYSTEMS design team) and some long-term (e.g., a permanent work team). Finally, there is the issue of what decisions employees are allowed to participate in. These potentially include decisions about technical matters and the work itself, employment and personnel matters, as well as company strategic, economic, and policy matters.

Participation is a central concept within the "human relations" tradition of management theorists and, by extension, the QUALITY OF WORKING LIFE movement (*see* HUMAN RELATIONS MOVEMENT). Within this view, participation is related to JOB SATISFACTION and thence to PERFORMANCE by virtue of facilitating the satisfaction of various "higher-order" needs, such as SELF-ACTUALIZATION and GROWTH NEED STRENGTH. This "affective" model may be contrasted with "cognitive" frameworks, in which the causal mechanism for participation's effect on PRODUCTIVITY is seen in terms of better information flow and knowledge generation (Miller & Monge, 1986). Both frameworks would predict a range of positive outcomes for participation, including job satisfaction and organizational COMMITMENT, positive MENTAL HEALTH, increased MOTIVATION AND PERFORMANCE, reduced turnover and ABSENTEEISM as well as reduced incidence of industrial CONFLICT (*see* COLLECTIVE ACTION). However, Vroom and Yetton (1973) have developed a normative contingency model of the effects of participation in which situational factors (*see* LEADERSHIP CONTINGENCIES), such as the requirements for a quality solution or for employee commitment, critically define the effectiveness of varying degrees of employee influence within the decision-making process.

Given the number of dimensions on which particular forms of participation may vary (influence, content of decisions, direct/indirect, formal/informal, short-term/long-term), it is not surprising that studies of the impact of participation on employee attitudes and performance have produced extremely varied results, an outcome also influenced by the poor design of many studies (Wagner & Gooding, 1987) (*see* RESEARCH DESIGN). Reviews of participation research generally conclude that it has a moderate positive correlation with positive work attitudes and a small positive effect on performance. However, even in well-designed studies, the specific form and context of participation does appear to determine its impact (Cotton, Vollrath, Froggatt, Lengnick-Hall & Jennings, 1988). For example, in a longitudinal quasi-experimental field study (*see* QUASI-EXPERIMENTAL DESIGN), Wall, Kemp, Jackson and Clegg (1986) found that employees in autonomous work groups (which may be characterized as formal, immediate, long-term participation involving a high level of influence in task-related and routine personnel decisions) reported increased job satisfaction, though not increased MOTIVATION, performance, organizational commitment or mental health. On the other hand, Griffin's (1988) longitudinal study of quality circles found that employee attitudes and performance both improved significantly over an 18-month period following implementation. Both sets of outcome variables then declined to pre-intervention levels, suggesting that duration of participation is also a factor. Certainly, tests of the Vroom–Yetton model have generally supported the model's contention that there are situations where a relatively low level of employee involvement in decision making will be associated with optimum outcomes, and others where a relatively high level of involvement is called for (Vroom & Jago, 1988) (*see* PATH-GOAL THEORY).

Participation in enterprise decision making, whatever the form, is a key component of organizational DEMOCRACY. Programs of employee participation in work-related decisions also feature strongly in strategic approaches to HUMAN RESOURCE MANAGEMENT aimed at enhancing quality and INNOVATION, where employee COMMITMENT to the organization is seen as a source of competitive advantage (Beaumont, 1992) (*see* COMPETITIVENESS). Whether such programs actually enhance democracy has been questioned, however, on the grounds that in practice they may subtly strengthen managerial control over employees, whilst proscribing the degree of real influence employees have over the operation of the enterprise as a whole (e.g., limiting the domain of participation to task-related matters and the degree of influence to consultation) and weakening attachment to the structures and institutions of COLLECTIVE BARGAINING (Guest, 1990).

See also **Trust; Employee involvement; Empowerment; Self-managing teams; Self-management**

Bibliography

Beaumont, P. B. (1992). The U.S. human resource management literature. In G. Salaman (Ed.), *Human resource strategies*. London: Sage.

Cotton, J. L., Vollrath, D. A., Froggatt, K. L., Lengnick-Hall, M. L. & Jennings, K. R. (1988). Employee participation: Diverse forms and different outcomes. *Academy of Management Review*, **13**, 8–22.

Dachler, H. P. & Wilpert, B. (1978). Conceptual dimensions and boundaries of participation in organizations: A critical evaluation. *Administrative Science Quarterly*, **23**, 1–39.

Griffin, R. W. (1988). Consequences of quality circles in an industrial setting: A longitudinal assessment. *Academy of Management Journal*, **31**, 338–358.

Guest, D. E. (1990). Human resource management and the American dream. *Journal of Management Studies*, **27**, 399–416.

Hollander, E. P. & Offerman, L. R. (1990). Power and leadership in organizations: Relationships in transition. *American Psychologist*, **45**, 179–189.

Miller, K. I. & Monge, P. R. (1986). Participation, satisfaction & productivity: A meta-analytic review. *Academy of Management Journal*, **29**, 727–793.

Vroom, V. H. & Jago, A. G. (1988). *The new leadership: Managing participation in organizations*. Englewood Cliffs, N.J.: Prentice-Hall.

Vroom, V. H & Yetton, P. W. (1973). *Leadership and decision-making*. Pittsburgh: University of Pittsburgh Press.

Wagner, J. A. & Gooding, R. Z. (1987). Shared influence and organizational behaviour: A meta-analysis of situational variables expected to moderate participation-outcome relationships. *Academy of Management Journal*, **30**, 524–541.

Wall, T. D., Kemp, N. J., Jackson, P. R. & Clegg, C. W. (1986). Outcomes of autonomous work groups: A long-term field experiment. *Academy of Management Journal*, **29**, 280–304.

JOHN CORDERY

path–goal theory The Path-Goal Theory of Leader Effectiveness (House, 1971; House & Mitchell, 1974) was developed to explain how leaders influence subordinates' MOTIVATION, satisfaction, and performance (*see* MOTIVATION AND PERFORMANCE). In the initial version of the theory it was asserted that

> "The motivational function of the leader consists of increasing personal payoffs to subordinates for work-goal attainment and making the path to these payoffs easier to travel by clarifying it, reducing roadblocks and pitfalls, and increasing the opportunities for personal satisfaction en-route." (House, 1971, p. 324).

The theory assumes that individuals choose the level of effort they will devote to their tasks on the basis of the degree to which they expect to receive, or experience, valued outcomes as a result of their effort (*see* VIE THEORY). Thus the theory makes a strong RATIONALITY assumption about the nature of subordinate's work motivation. The theory further assumes that the experience of ROLE AMBIGUITY is stressful and unpleasant and that reducing ambiguity will lead to subordinate satisfaction and effective performance (*see* JOB SATISFACTION). Finally, the theory assumes that when leaders reduce subordinate dissatisfaction or increase subordinate ROLE clarity, subordinate self-confidence and motivation will be increased.

The central propositions of the theory are:

Directive-role and goal clarifying leader behavior, when enacted in a nonauthoritarian manner, will clarify subordinates' perceptions of relationships concerning the degree to which their efforts will result in successful performance (goal attainment) and the degree to which performance will be extrinsically rewarded with recognition by the leader, pay, advancement, job security, and the like.

Supportive-subordinate oriented leader behavior will be a source of follower social satisfaction and confidence, especially when followers perform dissatisfying tasks or work under dissatisfying conditions.

Participative-consultative leader behavior will be motivational when subordinates have a high need for independence and/or knowledge that can contribute to effective DECISION MAKING by the leader.

Achievement-improvement oriented leader behavior will add challenge to subordinate's jobs and thus increase the instrinsic satisfaction subordinates experienced as a result of goal accomplishment (*see* EXTRINSIC/INTRINSIC MOTIVATION).

When the task demands of followers are satisfying but ambiguous, leader-directive behavior will be a source of clarification.

Subordinates whose jobs are satisfying, but which have ambiguous performance demands will view leader-directive behavior as satisfying and instrumental for performance.

Subordinates whose jobs are dissatisfying, but impose unambiguous performance demands, will view leader-directive behavior as over-controlling and dissatisfying.

When subordinates' tasks or work environment are dangerous, monotonous, stressful, or frustrating, supportive-leader behavior will lead to increased subordinate effort and satisfaction by increasing self-confidence, lowering ANXIETY, and unpleasant aspects of the work.

When tasks are interesting and enjoyable, and subordinates are confident, leader consideration will have little effect on follower satisfaction, motivation, or performance.

Unfortunately, as Yukl (1994) has noted, the theory has not been adequately tested to date. Overall, the findings provide more support for the predicted effects of supportive-leader behavior than for directive-leader behavior. The findings suggest that leader-directive leader behavior does not always have the role clarifying and performance enhancing effects predicted by the theory.

Because of the strong rationality assumptions of the theory it is most likely invalid when subordinates are under conditions of substantial STRESS or UNCERTAINTY. Such conditions make it impossible to formulate accurate and rational expectations of REWARDS contingent on effort expended. It is most likely that the theory holds under conditions of certainty or risk, and when subordinates are not highly stressed. Under such conditions probabilities can be assessed rationally. Therefore these conditions satisfy the underlying rationality assumptions of the theory.

See also **Goal-setting; Leadership; Leadership contingencies; Performance, individual**

Bibliography

House, R. J. (1971). A path-goal theory of leader effectiveness. *Administrative Science Quarterly*, **16**, 321–338.

House, R. J. (1977). A 1976 theory of charismatic leadership. In J. G. Hunt & L. L. Larson (Eds), *Leadership: The cutting edge*. Carbondale, IL: Southern Illinois University Press.

House, R. J. & Mitchell, J. R. (1974). Path goal theory of leadership. *Journal of Contemporary Business*, **3**, 81–97.

Yukl, G. (1994). *Leadership in organizations* (3rd edn). Englewood Cliffs, NJ: Prentice-Hall.

ROBERT J. HOUSE

pay and performance *see* MOTIVATION AND PERFORMANCE; MOTIVATOR/HYGIENE THEORY; PAYMENT SYSTEMS; PERFORMANCE RELATED PAY

payment systems The employment relationship is a social exchange where both the employee and the organization must receive something of value to enter into and continue to participate in the relationship (*see* EXCHANGE RELATIONS). For most employees, pay is a significant reward that influences their decisions about employment. In return for such payments, which are often the single largest operating cost, the organization expects employees to lend their effort to achieving the goals of the organization.

Payment systems, broadly defined, differ across employment units (organizations, business units, and facilities) in several ways. The focus of the employee compensation literature has been on defining these dimensions, understanding why organizations differ on them (determinants), and whether such differences have consequences for employee attitudes and behaviors, and ORGANIZATIONAL EFFECTIVENESS. The following discussion is organized accordingly around payment dimensions, determinants, and consequences.

Payment System Dimensions and Pay Programs

Payment systems vary significantly across employing units and to some degree, across jobs. We discuss the form, level, structure, mix, and administration of payment systems (Heneman & Schwab, 1979; Milkovich & Newman, 1990).

First, pay can be in the form of cash or benefits (e.g., health care, retirement, paid vacation). On average, about 70 percent of payments to US employees are in the form of cash, leaving 30 percent in the form of noncash benefits.

Second, cash compensation can be described in terms of its level (how much). Most organizations use one or more market pay surveys to determine what other organizations pay for specific jobs in making their own pay level decisions. Both cash and benefits need to be compared. Moreover, comparisons of labor costs need to consider PRODUCTIVITY differences by comparing, for example, the number of employees doing various types of work.

Third, the structure refers to the nature of pay differentials within an employing unit. How many steps or grades are in the structure? How big are the pay differentials between different levels in the structure? Large organizations often have over 20 such levels, although a number of organizations have recently reduced the number of steps ("delayered") (*see* RESTRUCTURING). Are employees at the same hierarchical level in different parts of the organization (e.g., different product sectors or different occupational groups) paid the same? Yet another aspect of structure is the timing of payment over employees' careers. Some organizations may bring entry level people in at a relatively high rate of pay, but then provide relatively slow pay growth, while another organization may bring employees in relatively low but offer greater opportunities for promotion and pay growth over time.

For better or worse, much of the effort in the structure area has focused on job evaluation, a tool for measuring the relative internal value of jobs to the organization. Job evaluation is used in conjunction with pay surveys to set rates of pay for jobs. Critics, however, suggest that job evaluation is associated with several drawbacks such as too much BUREAUCRACY, employees only doing what is in their JOB DESCRIPTION, and a lack of focus on market comparisons, which are critical for COMPETITIVENESS. Indeed, some organizations are moving away from linking pay to job content through job evaluation and instead paying workers for the SKILLS they possess. Skill-based pay links pay to the breadth or depth of employee skill. The goal is to encourage learning, which in turn facilitates FLEXIBILITY in work assignments and encourages learning as a way of life to help with future ORGANIZATION CHANGE.

Fourth, payment systems differ in their mix (how and when cash compensation is disbursed). Some organizations pay virtually all employees a base salary that is adjusted once per year (almost always upward, very rarely downward unless times are very tough). Other organizations use so-called variable pay or pay at risk, which means that some portion of employees' pay is uncertain and depends on future profits, stock performance, or productivity. Specific pay programs that influence pay mix are merit pay, incentive pay, GAINSHARING, profit sharing, and stock plans (e.g., stock options) (*see* BONUS PAYMENTS; PERFORMANCE RELATED PAY).

Fifth, payment systems are administered differently in different organizations. The design of pay policies differs, for example, in terms of who is involved in the process. The roles of human resource departments, line managers, and rank and file employees differ across situations (*see* HUMAN RESOURCE MANAGEMENT). Line managers may design plans, often with assistance from human resources. In other cases, human resources takes the lead. Less frequently, employees to be covered by a payment system are involved, and in some cases, may actually design plans for themselves.

COMMUNICATION is another aspect of administration. EQUITY THEORY suggests that employee perceptions of what they contribute to the organization, what they get in return, and how their return–contribution ratio compares to others inside and outside the organization, determine how fair they feel their employment relationship is. The most technically sophisticated payment plan can generate desired employee reactions or exactly the opposite, depending on whether the rationale for the payment plan is understood and accepted and whether employees' perceptions of the facts (e.g., the company's financial health, the pay of employees in other jobs or organizations) are the same as the perceptions of those charged with seeing that the payment plan has the intended effects.

Determinants

Four general factors determine pay level, pay mix, and the cash–benefits tradeoff. First, pay decisions are influenced by personal characteristics. Economists speak of education and other TRAINING as investments in human capital (Becker, 1975). The more a person invests in him- or herself, the higher their expected productivity and thus the higher their expected lifetime earnings (i.e., returns on their investment). Other individual factors such as cognitive ABILITY, MOTIVATION, and possibly personality characteristics also contribute to pay through their impact on productivity.

Second, the job or type of work influences pay. Managers and professionals are paid more than production workers, presumably because more human capital is required and because incentives are needed for employees to take more complex and demanding jobs. Higher job levels also tend to have a higher percentage of pay at risk. The rationale is twofold. The lower the pay, the less an employee can afford to have his or her pay fluctuate because a greater portion of his or her pay likely goes to cover relatively fixed living costs (e.g., housing, utilities). Also, any individual employee in the hourly ranks is usually thought to have less opportunity to influence organization performance than top managers (*see* CEOS).

Third, different employers have different pay policies and practices. Industry, life cycle stage (e.g., growth versus maintenance), organization strategy (e.g., cost leadership versus DIFFERENTIATION through INNOVATION or quality), union status, and size are examples of organization characteristics that influence pay decisions. Industry effects, for example, reflect the fact that each company faces similar cost pressures that limit the level of pay. If Ford pays its employees much more than General Motors or Toyota pay theirs, it will have more expensive cars that are more difficult to sell, unless its employees can offset the higher labor costs with higher productivity.

Employees covered under COLLECTIVE BARGAINING contracts are often paid differently than those not covered. In the United States, for example, many union employees work under single rate systems, under which all employees in a particular type of job are paid an identical amount. Individual differences in performance are not compensated (*see* PERFORMANCE, INDIVIDUAL). Union-represented employees promotions are also more formally based on seniority (often in conjunction with performance) than is the case for nonunion employees where promotion based almost solely on performance is usually the stated policy.

Fourth, in a global market, differences between countries are increasingly relevant in determining pay (*see* INTERNATIONAL HUMAN RESOURCE MANAGEMENT). Even limiting comparison to the two largest economies, the United States and Japan, reveals significant differences in pay practices. For example, relative to US employers, Japanese organizations tend to link pay more closely to seniority and less closely to individual performance. Japanese production employees also receive a large share of their cash compensation in the form of semiannual bonuses, whereas US production employees are more likely to be paid a straight base salary.

Perhaps the most interesting question under determinants is to what extent do different organizations have different pay strategies and why? Also, on what dimensions of pay do organizations differ most?

Organizations have some flexibility in how much they pay, but there are limits, because if they pay too much, their product will be more expensive than that of their competitors, making it difficult for them to compete in the product market. If they pay too little, they will have difficulty competing in the LABOR MARKET for quality employees.

Organizations may have the most flexibility in the mix of cash compensation – how they pay (Gerhart & Milkovich, 1990). For example, two organizations that each pay new MBAs an average of $50,000 per year can differ significantly in the basis for that amount of pay. The first organization could pay all the $50,000 in the form of base pay. In contrast, the second organization could pay $45,000 in base pay, with the potential for an additional $5,000 to $15,000 coming from a short-term bonus plan (e.g., linked to quarterly profits) and a stock ownership plan that pays out only if the stock price increases. The portion of pay that does not come in base salary is not guaranteed and thus is sometimes referred to as variable pay or pay at risk. It may not be paid at all or the amount paid may result in earnings that are higher than would have been the case if pay was based only on base salary. The payment varies, depending on stock price, production, and quality goals, or some other measure of individual, group, or organization performance. In any case, if the expected value of the bonus in the second organization is $5,000, its pay level (and labor cost) is the same as in the first organization, but its pay mix may send a very different message to prospective employees.

As with pay mix, the structure, form, and administration of pay can be designed in a variety of ways without necessarily having significant consequences for overall cost. Therefore, although there is little empirical evidence to tell us the degree to which organizations differ on these dimensions (but, *see* Gerhart, Milkovich, & Murray, 1992), there should be considerable discretion in such decisions.

Consequences

From a policy perspective, we need to know what types of payments systems are most effective and how their effectiveness differs according to contingency factors such as business strategy, national culture, competitive environment, and employee characteristics. Effectiveness is a multifaceted concept that could include cost, productivity, innovation, quality, financial, and attitudinal dimensions (Gerhart & Milkovich, 1992).

Most research on payment system consequences has examined payment system influences on individual employee attitudes and behaviors and has been in the context of behavioral theories such as AGENCY THEORY, Expectancy Theory (*see* VIE THEORY), REINFORCEMENT Theory, and Equity Theory.

Although the theories differ in important ways, there are some fundamental areas of agreement. First, each theory (particularly the first three) as it has been applied to payment systems suggests that making pay contingent on particular objectives (e.g., performance measures) makes attainment of those objectives more likely. So, quite simply, pay can be a powerful motivator. Second, each theory suggests that pay influences employees in two general ways. Most obviously, it influences the attitudes and behaviors of current employees. In addition, however, pay can influence which employees are attracted to the organization and which employees decide to stay or leave (*see* TURNOVER). The level of pay may influence the quality of employees and the other dimensions of pay may influence the types of employees (e.g., VALUES, goals, PERSONALITY traits, such as individualism, RISK-TAKING propensity, and so forth). So, payment systems help determine whether the types of employees fit with the CULTURE and strategy of the organization (*see* ORGANIZATIONAL CULTURE).

Much of the research on consequences has been in the context of studying specific types of payment programs such as incentive pay, gainsharing, profit sharing, and so forth. Some of the conceptual underpinnings of these plans is discussed in PERFORMANCE RELATED PAY.

More recently, economic theories of efficiency wages, TRANSACTION COST THEORY, and rank-order tournament models have also been proposed (*see* TOURNAMENT PROMOTION). Strategy concepts are also now being applied to the payment literature with a focus on determining what types of payment strategies fit different types of business strategies (e.g., cost leadership, differentiation, or STRATEGIC TYPES) and whether a better fit contributes to better ORGANIZATIONAL EFFECTIVENESS. The initial evidence suggests the answer to both questions is "yes" (Gomez-Mejia & Balkin, 1992).

See also **Rewards; Assessment; Performance appraisal**

Bibliography

Becker, G. (1975). *Human capital: A theoretical and empirical analysis, with special reference to education* (2nd edn). Chicago: University of Chicago Press.

Gerhart, B. & Milkovich, G. T. (1990). Organizational differences in managerial compensation and financial performance. *Academy of Management Journal*, 33, 663–691.

Gerhart, B. & Milkovich, G. T. (1992). Employee compensation: Research and practice. In M. D. Dunnette & L. M. Hough (Eds), *Handbook of industrial and organizational psychology*, (2nd edn, Vol. 3). Palo Alto, CA: Consulting Psychologists Press.

Gerhart, B., Milkovich, G. T. & Murray, B. (1992). Pay, performance, and participation. In D. Lewin et al. (Eds), *Research frontiers in industrial relations and human resources*. Madison, WI: Industrial Relations Research Association.

Gomez-Mejia, L. R. & Balkin, D. B. (1992). *Compensation, organizational strategy, and firm performance*. Cincinatti, OH: South-Western.

Heneman, H. G., III & Schwab, D. P. (1979). Work and rewards theory. In D. Yoder & H. G. Heneman, Jr. (Eds), *ASPA handbook of personnel and industrial relations*. Washington, DC: Bureau of National Affairs.

Milkovich, G. T. & Newman, J. (1990). *Compensation*. Homewood, IL: BPI/Irwin.

BARRY GERHART

perception This can be defined as the psychological process by which individuals select, organize, and interpret sensory information. Perception is distinguished from sensation in that sensation is the physiological process by which stimuli are received through the five senses. Perception begins with sensory registration and is the active cognitive process of selecting, organizing, and interpreting the multitude of stimuli that are received.

Perception is of key importance to ORGANIZATIONAL BEHAVIOR because people's behavior is a function of their perceived as opposed to their objective world. Although individuals may occupy nearly identical objective realities and receive similar sensory information, their perceptions of reality may differ markedly. These differences in perceptions are important determinants of behavior. Thus although two individuals may attend the same meeting and receive essentially the same information, they may have very different interpretations and reactions to the information.

Several topics are commonly included in discussions of perception within organizational contexts. Perceptual selectivity addresses the issue of why certain stimuli are perceived and processed whereas others are apparently ignored. Thus it has been found that environmental factors such as size, repetition, familiarity, and contrast increase the probability that individuals will attend to a stimulus. Internal personal factors are also viewed as influencing selection as well as interpretation. These factors include the PERSONALITY of the perceiver (e.g., thinking versus feeling oriented); LEARNING (i.e., prior experience); MOTIVATION (e.g., the effects of needs such as the need for power, mastery, and affiliation) (*see* AFFILIATION, NEED FOR; POWER, NEED FOR); and expectations. Thus, an individual who identifies with an organization's culture, has extensive experience with the culture, and has aspirations for promotion within the organization is likely to view organizational actions more positively than an outsider who has no affiliation with or interest in the organization.

Principles of perceptual organization are concerned with how the information is developed into cohesive patterns and impressions. Principles of perceptual organization include figure-ground relationships, closure, proximity, and similarity.

Recent work has emphasized social perception which is concerned with the issue of how people form impressions of each other. This area includes the process of social categorization and addresses how information is organized into schemata and stereotypes which provide cognitive "short-cuts" for developing impressions and making decisions about other people. A key aspect of social perception is the ATTRIBUTION process. These causal interpretations about the behavior of others form an important part of people's perceptions of each other. In addition, research on IMPRESSION MANAGEMENT has described how people create and manage specific impressions thereby enhancing their image to others or reducing their responsibility for poor performance. There is also a fairly extensive literature which describes the development and impact of perceptual ERRORS such as STEREOTYPING and HALO EFFECTS on HUMAN RESOURCE MANAGEMENT processes such as SELECTION METHODS and PERFORMANCE APPRAISAL.

See also **Cognitive processes; Projection; Role**

Bibliography

Arvey, R. & Campion, J. (1984). Person perception in the employment interview. In M. Cook (Ed.), *Issues in person perception*. London: Methuen.

Bierhoff, H.-W. (1989). *Person perception and attribution*. Berlin: Springer-Verlag.

Gardner, W. L. & Martinko, M. J. (1988). Impression management in organizations. *Journal of Management*, **14**, (2), 321–338.

Jones, E. E. (1990). *Interpersonal perception*. New York: W. H. Freeman.

Luthans, F. (1992). *Organizational behavior*, (6th edn), New York: McGraw-Hill.

MARK J. MARTINKO

performance, individual The performance of an individual at work is one of the most fundamental and central constructs in all of ORGANIZATIONAL BEHAVIOR. It exists at the intersection of three major systems in the work setting – the physical/task system, the human system represented by the person himself or herself, and the social system in which the performance takes place. Thus, individual performance serves as a link and a potential integrating construct among many diverse areas.

Two major clusters of work capture how organizational behavior has addressed individual performance. The first is descriptive. It involves defining and measuring individual performance. Performance is typically defined in reference to a person's job. Dimensions capturing the domain of what is meant by performance are identified and standards established on those dimensions. The units of the standards depend upon the nature of the job, but should reflect the quality and quantity of the work accomplished.

Descriptions of performance dimensions and the establishment of standards on those dimensions are necessary but not sufficient for describing individual performance. Missing is the measurement of an individual's behavior in terms of the performance dimensions and standards. Although measurement may seem simple, often it is not. There are a number of reasons for this. First, since individual performance often occurs in interaction with other people, it can be difficult, if not impossible, to separate any one person's performance from that of others. Second, even when this is possible, differences in the TECHNOLOGY used to do the job (e.g., a word processor versus a typewriter) or other unique conditions not under the control of the person (e.g., the ease or difficulty of the district to which a salesperson is assigned) may be inextricably entangled with the person's observed behavior, making it very difficult to decide what can be attributed to the *individual's* performance.

Finally, to evaluate performance requires the use of some measuring instrument. If the performance dimension is simple, allowing easily recognized outputs to be counted, then the instrument is straightforward; it consists of whatever is used to count and record the units produced. However, for many jobs, such simple measures of performance are rarely available. In their absence, subjective judgments of supervisors or others are often used. The person using some rating scale or PERFORMANCE APPRAISAL in effect serves as the measuring instrument.

Years of research have focused on developing good rating scales for this purpose. From this work has emerged a number of ways to reduce UNRELIABILITY and improve the VALIDITY of individual performance measures. However, in spite of the gains, the reliability and validity of performance ratings are limited by the very nature of the rating process, since it must be conducted in a social system where TRUST, COOPERATION, and many other variables intervene in ways which cannot be fully anticipated or controlled. Measuring individual performance with rating scales will remain an imperfect exercise.

Some of the more promising recent attempts to measure individual performance are those that have expanded the number and types of jobs on which performance is measured by means other than ratings. This has been done for a number of military occupational specialities in a large-scale study conducted during most of the 1980s in the US Army (Campbell, 1990).

The second major domain of research activity takes definition and measurement for granted and focuses upon why individuals perform as they do. The goal is understanding individual performance, with performance often viewed as a function of three major sets of variables.

The first domain contains variables external to the individual. Here the focus is on how to design the job so that people perform it well. Practitioners in the fields of ERGONOMICS (human factors) and industrial engineering approach individual performance from this perspective, but, unfortunately, this work is rarely cited in the organizational behavior literature, where attention is concentrated almost exclusively on the effects of JOB DESIGN on work MOTIVATION (*see* MOTIVATION AND PERFORMANCE).

The other two foci are internal to the person. Both view individual performance as a function of a person's ABILITY and motivation, but each focuses on one subdomain or the other. The ability focus sees individual performance as the criterion to be predicted from stable characteristics of people (*see* INDIVIDUAL DIFFERENCES). This model is the backbone of HUMAN RESOURCE MANAGEMENT practice associated with SELECTION METHODS, placement and TRAINING.

The third approach is that of searching for motivational influences on performance. It tends to be more dynamic in the sense that it relies less on stable traits or abilities for explanations of performance and more on temporary states in the work environment or the person. It incorporates work place mechanisms designed to influence individual performance. FEEDBACK, GOAL SETTING, and PERFORMANCE RELATED PAY are a few of the ways that an individual's performance at one point in time is used to attempt to influence their performance at some time in the future.

Two implicit assumptions underlie almost all interest in individual performance. The first is that policies and practices can be developed which increase the likelihood of good individual performance and decrease the likelihood of poor individual performance. The validity of this assumption is well supported. Cases too numerous to mention have demonstrated that through the design of jobs, proper selection, placement and training of job holders, effective REWARD systems, and good supervisory practices, individual performance can be influenced in a positive way.

The second assumption is so basic that it rarely is recognized. It is the assumption that individual performance in organizations is positively correlated with ORGANIZATIONAL EFFECTIVENESS. It is assumed that, if we improve the effectiveness of individuals who populate organizations, the performance of organizations will improve. Yet, given the complex mix of technical, social, and individual system outputs affecting individual and organizational performance, it should be clear that this assumption may not always hold. The fact that it may not, has only recently been confronted as researchers have become more sensitive to interactions across LEVELS OF ANALYSIS.

Although there is no reason to doubt that in many instances positive relationships between individual and organizational performance do exist, sensitivity to possible exceptions to the assumptions and discovery of their boundary conditions will be important themes in future work.

See also **Productivity; Competitiveness; Learning, individual**

Bibliography

Campbell, J. P., McCloy, R. A., Oppler, S. H. & Sager, C. E. (1993). A theory of performance. In N. Schmitt & W. C. Borman (Eds), *Personnel selection in organizations* (pp. 35–70). San Francisco: Jossey-Bass.

Campbell, J. P., McHenry, J. J. & Wise, L. L. (1990). Modeling job performance in a population of jobs. *Personnel Psychology*, **43**, 313–333.

Wigdor, A. K. & Greene, B. F. Jr. (1991). *Performance assessment for the workforce*, (vols. I & II). Washington D.C.: National Academy Press.

DANIEL R. ILGEN

performance appraisal This term refers to organizational practices whereby the performances of individuals in the organization are formally appraised by others for a number of purposes. Usually, the appraisers are direct supervisors of the employees. Usually, the appraisal is in the form of a subjective judgment by the appraiser. Performance appraisal (PA) is usually classified as a HUMAN RESOURCE MANAGEMENT practice.

Purposes

PA practices have arisen to serve a number of purposes. PA results are used as inputs into pay determinations as part of PERFORMANCE RELATED PAY. PA processes are used as mechanisms for FEEDBACK from the appraiser to the appraisee. PA results are often used to determine developmental and TRAINING needs of employees (*see* MANAGEMENT DEVELOPMENT). PA results sometimes have been used as convenient data for input into layoff decisions. PA results sometimes are used as inputs into promotion decisions. Frequently, PA results become part of employees' personnel files and are accessible for various personnel decisions. They are also often reduced to summary ratings and stored in computer human resource data files. PA results can be used to inform human resource planning endeavors and to evaluate such practices as SELECTION METHODS and training programs.

Approaches

A number of approaches are used to appraise performance. Most involve methods by which appraisers record their judgments or ratings of the appraisee's performance on paper-based instruments (increasingly these are electronic forms for use with personal computers and computer networks). These instruments are partly determined by the aspects of performance to be measured. Some measures focus on the end results of performance such as the units produced, profit realized, value of goods sold, quality of service, PRODUCTIVITY, dollars saved, patents awarded, and publications. Sometimes the desired results are predetermined as part of the job, such as in the form of standards that must be met and sometimes they are predetermined through GOAL-SETTING processes. Performance is then evaluated, perhaps in terms of whether goals were accomplished or surpassed, how difficult the goals were, or whether standards were met or surpassed. When goal-setting practices are coupled with appraisals that measure the degree to which the set goals are attained, the resulting process has most commonly been known as MANAGEMENT BY OBJECTIVES.

Another set of approaches focus on the behaviors that the performer exhibits during performance. The behavioral focus is often adopted because end results are considered to be inadequate measures of a person's performance since they are subject to contextual influence. For instance, goals might not be met because some aspect of the performer's environment prevented it, such as a system breakdown. Furthermore, the way an employee behaves may be as important to an organization as the achievement of results. Behavioral approaches describe the actions of the performer. Appraisal is accomplished by different behaviors being mapped onto valuations of performance in various ways.

The core elements of all behavioral approaches are the behavioral descriptions of performance. Differences arise as to how the behavioral descriptions are generated and how they are used to value performance. Critical incident approaches to behavioral appraisals focus on describing the performer's behavior during specific incidents that in the opinion of the appraiser represent various good or poor levels of performance. Other approaches use generic descriptions of behavior. A common approach is to present the appraiser with a number of behavioral descriptions that each represent good or poor performance on some dimension and to then ask the appraiser to rate the degree to which the appraisee tends to exhibit the behavior described in each. Sometimes several behavioral statements, each describing a different level of performance on some dimension, are arranged along a continuum from poor to good performance. The appraiser then selects the single behavioral description on the continuum that best describes the behavior of the appraisee. The evaluation of the appraisee's performance is represented by the position of the selected behavioral statement on the poor–good continuum of the dimension. Such a continuum is called a Behaviorally Anchored Rating Scale. There are a number of other variations on behavioral measures.

Other approaches to appraisal try to measure qualities of the performer. The most dominant example of this approach is the measurement of performer traits. In this approach the appraiser is presented with some word or phrase such as "honesty" or "initiative" and asked to rate the person on that trait according to some rating scale supplied on the appraisal form. The trait approach has fallen out of favor since it heightens the appearance of subjectiveness because there are usually no concrete behaviors or results to point to that exemplify the trait. More recently, some appraisal approaches have tried to measure the skills of the performer by looking at whether or not the person can behave in a way that represents the presence of the skills (*see* COMPETENCIES).

Most contemporary examples of appraisal practices are eclectic combinations of several appraisal approaches. In addition, the actual appraisal is usually embedded in a system of related practices, such as goal setting, work PLANNING, feedback of appraisal to the appraisee, determination of developmental needs, planning for development, CAREER planning, and determination of compensation changes or bonuses based directly or indirectly on the appraisal (*see* BONUS PAYMENTS). These more extensive systems may go by such names as performance planning and review, PERFORMANCE MANAGEMENT, and performance related pay to signify a scope broader than just performance appraisal. Because of multiple approaches to appraisal and because appraisals are embedded in a system of related practices, appraisal forms can become fairly complex. It is not uncommon to find forms that have space for writing down the goals set, adjoining space for recording and describing the degrees to which goals have been attained, a section with predefined dimensions of performance that may be more or less behaviorally worded and are responded to on some rating scale, a section that is filled in with job responsibilities idiosyncratic to the performer, each of which are to be rated on how well the performer accomplishes it, a section for listing development needs, a section for specifying developmental plans, a section in which the appraisee is rated for promotability, and a section with a summary rating scale meant to sum up all the component measures of performance in preceding sections. The summary rating is often used as input for pay or bonus decisions.

Processes

Feedback to the appraisee is a formal part of almost all PA systems. Most systems require some type of face-to-face discussion between the appraiser and the appraisee. This can be solely a discussion of the supervisor's rating or in more complex systems it can include such things as goal-setting, work planning, developmental planning, career advice, and discussions of how the appraisal might affect pay decisions and bonuses. In many cases these various processes can stretch across several sessions. Each of these discussion topics and tasks can require skills and knowledge on the part of the appraiser and the appraisee.

Appraisals vary in the ways practices are carried out. Appraisals can be done in an extremely one-sided hierarchical fashion, in which the appraiser/supervisor fills out the forms and submits them to his or her manager before telling the subordinate the results of the appraisal. On the other hand, appraisals can be highly participative with all phases jointly carried out by appraiser and appraisee. For instance, manager and employee might each fill out the appraisal forms independently then come together and mutually agree on what the final version of the forms should be. In other systems the performer is expected to compile the bulk of the forms and/or materials illustrating performance, with the manager commenting and perhaps making a summary judgment of the performance as shown by the materials provided. Research in appraisal has strongly suggested that PARTICIPATION in the appraisal process (whatever it entails) by the performer will result in higher acceptance of the appraisal, increased satisfaction, and improved performance. Research also shows that process dimensions of appraisal are probably much more important to successful appraisal than the forms used.

Issues

The multiple purposes of appraisal systems are often at cross purposes. For instance, a common practice in the United States is to use appraisals as the basis for salary increases. These same organizations usually require that employees receive feedback about their performances with the purpose of helping them improve their performance and identify developmental needs. Each purpose drives a different approach to measuring performance: salary decisions require that individual performances be ranked relative to one another since they involve the distribution of a fixed budgeted amount, feedback requires that employees receive specific information about their work relative to their job-based criteria. This state of affairs leads to the following dilemma. It is possible, indeed likely, that an individual may perform well in terms of the job criteria but when ranked against others who also performed well fall in the bottom half of the ranking. Management is then faced with the problem of telling people they performed well but are going to receive a below average salary increase. This conflict is often resolved by giving everyone a similar pay raise or by making salary actions secret, both of which compromise pay for performance. Sometimes organizations choose to start with the ranking process and then write the appraisals to be fed back so that they reflect the ranking. The result is that some employees are told that they are performing lower on job criteria than either they or their appraisers feel they actually are. This sacrifices accurate feedback.

Different purposes demand different ways of measuring performance. For example, ranking employees to determine who should be promoted will often result in a different ranking than when the same employees are ranked to determine who should be laid off.

Much of established PA practice developed within the dominant organizational forms of the 1950s, 1960s, and 1970s. New organizational forms have begun to emerge in the 1980s and 1990s. Two emergent directions bring new issues for appraisal:

(1) New organizational forms bring change with them; not just the change associated with transitioning from the old to the new, but change as a continuing aspect of organizations that must be managed. In particular change will constantly undermine appraisal practices and demand their adaptation to new realities.
(2) New organizations also accentuate the lateral or horizontal dimensions of form in addition to the vertical or hierarchical. Within lateral settings others in addition to the supervising manager have a direct stake in and access to the performance of an employee, such as customers and coworkers.

The definition of performance is relatively problematic (*see* PERFORMANCE, INDIVIDUAL). As long as organizations are relatively stable and based on a hierarchical breakdown of jobs and tasks, then the performance definition problem can start with some description of duties, accountabilities, and responsibilities and proceed to describing the performance in whatever ways are appropriate given the purpose of the appraisal.

In contemporary organizations that are frequently changing and in which performers are embedded in a lateral network as well as a hierarchical system the definition of what an individual's performance should be is heavily tied up in the processes of aligning and realigning performances of individuals with the performance needs of the organization, the business unit, the team, customers, and coworkers. Such alignment is the result of vertical and horizontal NEGOTIATION processes between the performers and their STAKEHOLDERS.

Definitions of what performance should be are, at best, imperfect momentary alignments of what is expected of a performer from those that have a stake in the person's performance. A person's performance will tend to be differently appraised depending on the stakeholder's perspective. Under this set of circumstances performance appraisal is obviously not a cut-and-dried affair. It needs to involve a process by which multiple stakeholder viewpoints are surfaced and balanced. This highlights the need for processes for negotiating and balancing among multiple stakeholders. An emerging approach to appraisal is called 360° feedback and involves input from managers, subordinates, coworkers, customers, and the appraisee.

See also **Knowledge of results; Human resources planning; Succession planning; Management of high potential**

Bibliography

Anderson, G. C. (1993). *Managing performance appraisal systems*. Oxford, UK: Blackwell.

Bernardin, H. J. & Beatty, R. W. (1984). *Performance appraisal: assessing human behavior at work*. Boston, MA: Kent.

DeVries, D. L., Morrison, A. M., Shullman, S. L. & Gerlach, M. L. (1986). *Performance appraisal on the line*. Greensboro, NC: Center for Creative Leadership.

Latham, G. P. & Wexley, K. N. (1981). *Increasing productivity through performance management*. Reading, MA: Addison-Wesley.

Mohrman, A. M. Jr., Resnick-West, S. M. & Lawler, E. E. III (1989). *Designing performance appraisal systems: Aligning appraisals and organizational Realities*. San Francisco: Jossey-Bass.

Murphy, K. R. & Cleveland, J. N. (1991). *Performance appraisal: An organizational perspective.* Boston, MA: Allyn & Bacon.

ALLAN M. MOHRMAN JR.

performance management There is no universally accepted definition of performance management, and it is sometimes used simply to refer to PERFORMANCE APPRAISAL or to PERFORMANCE RELATED PAY. However, it is increasingly coming to mean a general, integrated HUMAN RESOURCES STRATEGY that seeks to create a shared vision of the purpose, aims, and values of the organization, to help each individual employee understand and recognize their part in contributing to them, and in so-doing to manage and enhance the performance of both individuals and the organization. Typically, elements of such a strategy will include developing the MISSION STATEMENT and business plan, objective setting, and other methods of performance measurement, appraisal, performance related pay, and various approaches to enhancing internal COMMUNICATIONS. Two of the attributes that differentiates performance management from other systems (such as MANAGEMENT BY OBJECTIVES or appraisal) are:

(1) that it is supposed to be line management-owned and driven; personnel departments have a mainly facilitative role; and
(2) that it seeks to combine and integrate the various elements into a coherent set of procedures.

See also **Human resource management; Performance, individual; Payment systems**

Bibliography

IPM (1992). *Performance management in the UK: An analysis of the issues.* London: Institute of Personnel Management.

Fletcher, C. (1993). *Appraisal: Routes to improved performance.* London: Institute of Personnel Management.

Spencer, L. M. (1991). Performance management systems. In M. L. Rock & L. A. Berger (Eds), *The compensation handbook.* New York: McGraw-Hill.

CLIVE FLETCHER

performance related pay Pay for performance is a term that typically refers to a host of pay programs that seek to link pay to the individual, group, and organization level performance measures. Merit pay continues to be widely used, but organizations are also increasingly using other pay for performance programs, at least in parts of their organizations as several surveys and case studies can attest (Conference Board, 1990). Human resource executives, academics, and consultants expect this trend to continue for all employee groups, with much of the new emphasis being on programs linking pay to group and organization performance (Dyer & Blancero, 1993).

Milkovich and Wigdor (1991) classify pay for performance programs according to whether payments are linked to group/organization versus individual performance and whether payments become part of base pay or are variable (e.g., bonuses) and must always be re-earned. Lawler (1989) offers a similar classification, adding payout frequency and typical employee groups covered by the programs. The basic features of some of the most common pay for performance programs are summarized in Table 1.

In analyzing the potential consequences of these pay programs, we can look at both cost and behavioral objectives. On the cost dimension, an organization will, all else equal, prefer a pay program where labor costs move in the same direction as ability to pay. A profit-sharing plan, for example, pays a bonus only when the organization hits a particular profit target (*see* BONUS PAYMENTS). Therefore, labor costs are higher when the ability to pay (e.g., profit) is higher and when ability to pay is low (low or negative profit), labor costs are lower because no bonus is paid. In contrast, merit pay and GAINSHARING payments are not necessarily dependent on profits, so an organization can encounter a situation where its labor costs remain high despite a lack of profits.

On the other hand, programs that do well on the cost dimension may have drawbacks in achieving behavioral objectives. According to expectancy theory (*see* VIE THEORY), MOTIVATION is higher to the extent that employees see a clear link between their effort and REWARDS. This so-called line of sight, however, may be poor under profit sharing plans because profits

Table 1 Features of pay for performance programs.

	Individual Incentives	*Merit Pay*	*Merit Bonus*	*Gainsharing*	*Profit Sharing*	*Ownership*	*Skill Based Pay*
Payment Method	Bonus	Changes in base pay	Bonus	Bonus	Bonus	Equity Changes	Changes in base pay
Payout Frequency	Weekly	Annually	Annually	Monthly or quarterly	Semiannually or annually	When stock sold	When skill acquired
Performance Measure	Output, productivity, sales	Performance rating	Performance rating	Production or controllable costs	Profit	Stock value	Skill Acquisition
Coverage	Direct labor	All employees	All employees	Production or service unit	Total organization	Total organization	All employees

Source: Adapted from Milkovich & Wigdor; Lawler.

depend on so many factors beyond the control of most employees (aside from the higher-level managers). In addition, AGENCY THEORY suggests that employees are typically risk averse (*see* RISK TAKING). Consequently, sharing business risk with employees by placing some portion of their pay at risk (e.g., linking bonuses to profit levels) is not a costless decision for the organization because employees are hypothesized to require a compensating premium for risk, otherwise they would choose other employment. Programs that link pay more closely to individual performance are likely to provide for a better line of sight and thus, stronger motivation. In addition, strong individual contributors may be more likely to gravitate toward and remain in situations that recognize and reward their individual achievements. Of course, individual contributions are not always sufficient for ORGANIZATIONAL EFFECTIVENESS, and programs that direct employees efforts toward purely individual objectives may be ill-suited for settings where teamwork and cooperation are also important. Therefore, organizations may find that a mix of pay for performance programs is needed to help achieve a balance in the various and sometimes partially conflicting goals that employees are expected to work toward.

See also **Payment systems; Performance, individual; Extrinsic/intrinsic motivation; Feedback**

Bibliography

Bureau of National Affairs (1988). *Changing pay practices: New developments in employee compensation*. Washington DC.

Bureau of National Affairs (1991). *Non-traditional incentive pay programs*. Personnel Policies Forum Survey, No. 148. Washington, DC:.

Conference Board (1990). *Variable pay: New performance rewards*. Research Bulletin No. 246.

Dyer, L. & Blancero, D. (1993). Workplace 2000. Working paper, Center for Advanced Human Resource Studies, Cornell.

Milkovich, G. T. & Wigdor, A. K. (1991). *Pay for performance*. Washington, DC: National Academy Press.

Lawler, E. E. III (1989). Pay for performance: A strategic analysis. In L. R. Gomez-Mejia (Ed.), *Compensation and benefits*. Washington, DC: Bureau of National Affairs.

BARRY GERHART

persistence This is defined by psychologists as the phenomenon of increased or persistent effort after failing in a task. Although this quality is often highly valued in Western CULTURE – "if at first you don't succeed; try, try again" – it is also often irrational and costly behavior in organizations. Unreasonable persistence can be seen to underlie major problems at both corporate and individual levels in organizations, such as CRISES and STRESS, where investments of time and effort continue to be sunk into failing projects and improbable causes.

Persistence as a dysfunction can be seen as the opposite of "learned helplessness," where failure on a task leads to lack of persistence on subsequent tasks, a phenomenon associated with depressive conditions (*see* MENTAL HEALTH). Persistence often closely resembles escalating commitment (*see* COMMITMENT, ESCALATING), where continued investment in a failing project is due to the desire to recoup sunk costs or to justify past expenditure. It differs in being more due to psychological than material investments, amounting to a disorder in SELF-REGULATION. In these terms researchers have explained it as caused by highly self-focused attention in situations where the individual has expectations of control and high standards to do well – the triumph of hope over experience where SELF-ESTEEM is at stake.

Research also indicates that persistence is encouraged by task difficulty, since failure may be attributed to the task rather than personal qualities such as ABILITY (*see* ATTRIBUTION). Experimental studies have also shown that individuals with high self-esteem persist longer and perform worse following failure FEEDBACK on a task than people with lower self-esteem. They may also actually ignore or reject helpful information about when to persist – rejecting advice for the sake of the chance to enhance their self-credit. There is also evidence of SEX DIFFERENCES in persistence – males being more likely to engage in unreasonable persistence.

The phenomenon has only recently attracted the attention of psychological research, and remains largely unexamined within ORGANIZATIONAL BEHAVIOR, though it is clearly highly relevant to many of the failings in individual performance (*see* PERFORMANCE, INDIVIDUAL), GROUP DECISION MAKING, STRATEGIC MANAGEMENT, and ORGANIZATIONAL EFFECTIVENESS.

See also **Locus of control; Knowledge of results; Self-efficacy**

Bibliography

Kernis, M. H., Zuckerman, M., Cohen, A. & Spadafora, S. (1982). Persistence following failure: The interactive role of self-awareness and the attributional basis for negative expectancies. *Journal of Personality and Social Psychology*, **43**, 1184–1191.

Miller, A. & Klein, J. S. (1989). Individual differences in ego value of academic performance and persistence after failure. *Contemporary Educational Psychology*, **14**, 124–132.

NIGEL NICHOLSON

person specification The knowledge, SKILLS, ABILITIES, and other person characteristics (often referred to as "KSAOs") deemed necessary for satisfactory job performance. Usually included as part of a JOB DESCRIPTION, and used for various HUMAN RESOURCE MANAGEMENT activities, particularly selection (*see* SELECTION METHODS).

Harvey (1991) makes a distinction between KS- versus AO-based specifications. He argues that knowledge ("a body of information applied directly to the performance of a function") and skills ("a present, observable competence to perform a learned act") (*see* COMPETENCIES) can be *directly* linked to job activities, whereas abilities and other characteristics (e.g., PERSONALITY TRAITS) are constructs ("*theoretical* concepts . . . that have been *constructed* to explain *observable* behavior patterns") that can be linked only *indirectly* to job requirements (Harvey, 1991, pp. 75–79).

In the United States, litigation has decidedly favored human resource DECISION MAKING based on directly observable knowledge and skills (KS). However, this preference for narrow, observable decision criteria has been challenged on a number of fronts, particularly by findings that constructs such as ability and conscientiousness (a personality trait) are valid predictors across a wide range of settings (Schmidt, Hunter, & Pearlman, 1981). Concerns have also been expressed that KS-based specifications are too inflexible for today's rapidly-changing work environments.

Whether or not there is a substantial shift toward AO-based specifications in future practice will depend on additional research findings, as well as continued developments in litigation and social constructions of such constructs as "fairness" and "efficiency" (*see* EQUAL OPPORTUNITIES).

See also **Job analysis; Recruitment; Assessment; Succession planning**

Bibliography

Harvey, R. J. (1991). Job analysis. In M. D. Dunnette & L. M. Hough (Eds), *Handbook of industrial and organizational psychology*, (2nd edn, vol. 2, pp. 71–163). Palo Alto, CA: Consulting Psychologists Press.

Schmidt, F. L., Hunter, J. & Pearlman, K. (1981). Task differences as moderators of aptitude test validity in selection: A red herring. *Journal of Applied Psychology*, **66**, 166–185.

SARA L. RYNES

person–job fit This refers to the extent to which the dispositions, abilities, expectations, and performance contributions of an individual worker match the job demands, situational demands, expectations, and available REWARDS of a particular job. Individuals bring to their respective jobs a set of dispositions and expectations about what they can and want to accomplish at work and what they expect in return. They also contribute their effort, talents, SKILL, ABILITY, education, and experience. In return, they expect certain outcomes, including (but not limited to) financial compensation, security, stimulation, and opportunities for growth, development, and advancement.

At the same time, individual jobs require certain things of the people who perform them. In particular, job incumbents must have the physical, cognitive, and emotional skills and abilities necessary to meet minimum performance requirements, as well as the MOTIVATION to perform at an adequate level. At a more general level, organizations also expect certain levels of attendance, various forms of "citizenship behaviors," and other contributions (*see* ORGANIZATIONAL CITIZENSHIP). In exchange, the organization provides direct and indirect compensation and other forms of inducement (*see* EXCHANGE RELATIONS; EQUITY THEORY).

The higher the level of congruence between what an individual provides to and expects from the organization and what the organization expects from and provides to the individual, the greater the degree of person–job fit. When the person–job fit is poor, several outcomes are possible. Individual STRESS, FRUSTRATION, ANXIETY, job dissatisfaction, and low performance are all likely outcomes (*see* JOB SATISFACTION; PERFORMANCE, INDIVIDUAL). As a consequence, the organization may find it necessary to replace the worker and/or to invest heavily in additional TRAINING or to seek a new job assignment for the individual.

It is also important to recognize that person–job fit is likely to change over time. For example, a job that seems exciting, motivating, and stimulating to an organizational newcomer may seem boring and tedious after a longer time. Similarly, as such contributors to person–job fit as job demands, salary, ability, and motivation change, the overall level of congruence may also change.

See also **Personality; Age; Individual differences; Job design; Psychological contract; Quality of working life; Work adjustment**

Bibliography

Brousseau, K. R. (1983). Toward a dynamic model of job–person relationships: Findings, research questions, and implications for work system design. *Academy of Management Review*, 8, 33–45.

RICKY W. GRIFFIN

personality As far back as 1937, Gordon Allport identified fifty different definitions for the term personality. The most widely used scientific definition identifies personality as that set of nonphysical and nonintellectual psychological qualities which make a person distinct from other people.

Status within OB

Within the field of ORGANIZATIONAL BEHAVIOR, personality has been defined, measured, and studied in vastly different ways. Moreover, the very value of personality constructs in understanding organizational behavior has itself been a matter of much controversy over the decades and has been questioned on both conceptual and empirical grounds. Conceptual criticism has come from both ends of the theoretical spectrum. On the one hand, radical humanists see the use of personality dimensions as reductionist, as breaking apart the essential uniqueness of each individual. On the other end of the theoretical spectrum, radical behaviorists see the study of personality as attempting to measure variables not directly observable, an incursion into the "black box" which falls beyond the scope of scientific inquiry.

On empirical grounds, the proved contributions of personality variables to our understanding of work behavior have been limited. Positive findings, when they appear, are often of marginal significance and personality effects within a given research area are often inconsistent. These disappointing results within OB are consistent with empirical findings in other areas of personality research. Best known is Mischel's (1968) famous critique of personality research in which he claimed, after reviewing the literature, that behavior is inconsistent across situations, and that rarely do personality variables account for more than 10 percent of the variance in criterion behaviors of interest. Mischel argued that behavior is largely determined by situational factors.

Many scholars within OB, following Mischel (1968), have made the same argument, that behavior in work organizations is largely situationally determined. Accordingly, the thrust of research on JOB ENRICHMENT, expectancy, VIE THEORY of work MOTIVATION, job attitudes and many other areas has emphasized situational determinants. The approach recommended to organizations for creating a motivated work force, for example, is not necessarily to hire people who are dispositionally high in motivation, but rather to expand job scope, alter reward contingencies, and empower the work force.

Weiss and Adler (1984) questioned this bias against personality, arguing that the potential for personality in theory, research, and practice within OB has, in fact, scarcely been explored. In area after area, research typically does not adequately test for personality effects. Often personality is of secondary interest to the researcher and is accordingly treated marginally, given little thought, and studied in inappropriate settings using inappropriate designs. A conservative evaluation of the role of personality within OB, conclude Weiss and Adler, is that this role has simply not yet been adequately examined.

The negative view of personality was so widely accepted within OB for so long that there are whole areas of personality research which once were productive and then almost completely abandoned. Selection testing (*see* PERSONALITY TESTING), the study of work attitudes, and LEADERSHIP all were areas in which decades of interest in personality were followed by decades of uninterest. Only very recently have researchers in these areas begun reexamining the value of personality. The past few years indeed have generally seen some increased interest in personality within OB, marked by the publication of several important summaries of theory and research on this topic (e.g., Barrick & Mount, 1991; Brockner, 1988; Furnham, 1992; Hogan, 1991).

Personality Traits

OB researchers and practitioners have studied a wide range of personality constructs. Among the more widely studied are SELF-ESTEEM, SELF-EFFICACY, achievement motivation (*see* ACHIEVEMENT, NEED FOR), LOCUS OF CONTROL, and EXTROVERSION. These constructs all reflect a particular conception, which describes personality in terms of traits. There have been other approaches to conceptualizing personality, the most prominent being psychoanalytic approaches. These nontrait approaches have contributed insightful analyses of important aspects of behavior in organizations (*see* e.g., ORGANIZATIONAL NEUROSIS). Psychodynamic approaches have also been used in clinical applications to human resources management, such as in treating psychopathology that impacts on work behavior or in screening out high-risk candidates for positions that involve potential danger to the public (e.g., police officers and airline pilots). However, the overwhelming preponderance of empirical personality research in OB has adopted traits as the unit of analysis.

Personality traits are seen as internal psychological structures or properties that relate to regularities in behavior. For example, people scoring high on a measure of the trait of conscientiousness are more likely than those scoring low in that trait to attend to details when performing a task, to double-check calculations before submitting financial projections to their manager, and to exert a high level of energy to achieve an assigned objective.

A somewhat different conception of traits has been advanced by Hogan (1991) who has suggested that personality traits can better be understood as dimensions of a person's social reputation. That is, if your behavior leads others to see and describe you as conscientious, then you are high in the trait of conscientiousness, whether or not this trait really exists internally.

Personality traits are generally thought of as dimensions or continuous variables. People are seen as being arrayed on a continuum with respect to the attribute in question, being low, medium, or high in self-esteem, for instance. Thinking of personality traits as continuous variables corresponds to how ABILITY attributes (e.g., intelligence, *see also* INDIVIDUAL DIFFERENCES) are generally conceptualized. Continuous trait measures are also amenable to the correlation-based statistical techniques that have been the primary tools of organizational researchers (*see* STATISTICAL METHODS). There is some evidence, though, that a few personality traits may be more fruitfully conceptualized as typologies or class variables. The extent to which people are or are not disposed to adapt their behaviors and attitudes to environmental cues, entitled Self-Monitoring, is one such typology. Programmatic research (Gangestad & Snyder, 1985) supports the notion that high- and low- self-monitors are really two different types of people, and not merely opposite ends of a single continuum. There is similar evidence that the trait of STRESS-proneness is a class variable yielding two distinct types of people, TYPE A and Type B.

Rather than developing their own models of personality, OB researchers almost always draw on personality constructs and measures from existing personality models, although unfortunately without always examining in-depth the theoretical and empirical base from which these constructs and measures are drawn. Some OB researchers, though, have both drawn on and contributed to basic personality theory. For example, Brockner (1988) has developed a model of self-esteem and behavioral plasticity, defined as the susceptibility of people low in self-esteem to social influence. Brockner has systematically examined that influence on the expectations, motivations, and attributions of those high and low in self-esteem before, during and after task performance (*see* ATTRIBUTION). This work has contributed to both OB and basic self-esteem theory.

OB researchers have similarly developed an appreciation of work in personality theory identifying dispositional differences in emotionality and have applied these developments to better understand the causes and consequences of JOB SATISFACTION. Staw and his colleagues (*see* Judge, 1992, for a summary of this area) first demonstrated the surprisingly strong consistency of job attitudes over relatively long periods of time (3–5 years), even as respondents change jobs and organizations. Later research showed that general tendencies toward a positive or negative evaluation of life evidenced as early as the teen years can predict specific job attitudes decades later. People with optimistic, emotionally positive, dispositions are consistently more satisfied on the job than those with more negative, anxious, pessimistic, and cynical dispositions. Subsequent research demonstrated the role of these differences in affective disposition in the complex linkages between job satisfaction, other work attitudes and stress. Recent evidence from studies of identical twins reared apart suggests that these dispositional differences in positive and negative emotionality may actually be reflected in genetic effects on job attitudes, though the linkage remains controversial (*see* ATTITUDES, DISPOSITIONAL APPROACHES).

These two examples represent a trend toward the more serious consideration of basic personality theory when its constructs are incorporated into OB models.

Role in OB Models

There are essentially four ways that personality has been treated in models of work behavior:

1. *As Simple Predictors.* In these models a single personality trait is hypothesized to have a direct effect on some relevant criterion variable. For example, a measure of Extraversion is expected to predict sales performance. These simplistic bivariate models are conceptually limited; most complex behaviors of interest to organizations cannot be adequately explained by isolated personality traits. Indeed, these models have also proved to be empirically limited; rarely does a single trait explain more than a small proportion of variance in work-relevant criteria. Moreover, although much of the OB research fitting this model is actually cross-sectional in design – that is, both the personality trait and the criterion are measured at the same point in time – significant correlations between traits and criteria are too often interpreted in terms of the personality variable having had a causal effect on the criterion in question. It is a well-known principle that correlation is not necessarily proof of causality.

2. *Interacting with Other Factors.* In this more sophisticated conceptualization, the effects of a personality variable on a criterion are considered at least partially dependent on another factor, most commonly a situational factor. For example, people high in Achievement Motivation will show more effort than those low in Achievement Motivation only in competitive situations. In noncompetitive situations, no significant difference in task effort is expected between those high and low in Achievement Motivation. This kind of interaction model underlies work on PERSON–JOB FIT, the notion that people will be most content and productive in work situations that provide REWARDS and challenges suited to the individual's ability and personality dispositions. Correspondingly, some interaction models posit that the effects of a situational factor on behavior depend on a personality factor. For instance, high-pressure work environments are more likely to produce symptoms of stress in those with Type A rather than Type B personalities. The interactive effect of two or more personality constructs on behavior can and has been studied in the same way. As an example of this configural approach, McClel-

land's Leadership Motive Pattern (*see* LEADERSHIP STYLE) predicts that the most effective leaders will be those who are high in need for power, low in need for affiliation, and high in Activity Inhibition (*see* POWER, NEED FOR; AFFILIATION, NEED FOR). In contrast with models focused on single personality predictors, interactive models can be used to investigate more complex multivariate relationships.

3. *As Impacted by Situations*. In both the simple and complex models described above, personality is seen as a causal factor. It is possible to treat personality as a dependent variable, impacted by situational factors. Longitudinal research has shown, for instance, that long-term assignment to simple, REPETITIVE WORK results in a decrease in an individual's cognitive complexity and flexibility. Personality has been conceptualized as the dependent variable in studies on the effects of rural versus urban upbringing on adult work needs and of job mobility on LOCUS OF CONTROL. The Management Progress Study (Howard & Bray, 1988) conducted over a 20-year period at AT&T similarly showed how certain personality traits can change as a function of CAREER advancement (*see* CAREER DEVELOPMENT). Obviously, research on how work experiences affect personality are of immense theoretical and practical interest, especially since most people spend such a large portion of their waking hours in the work place. However, it is important to remember that adult personality traits are likely to change slowly and only with prolonged exposure to psychologically salient environmental factors. Testing models of this type requires carefully planned longitudinal research.

4. *In Dynamic Interplay with Situational Factors*. Even more rare are those dynamic models which describe some process in which personality, behavior and situations are seen as continuously influencing each other. The following model serves as an illustration. More Dogmatic individuals, if given a choice, will prefer to interact with people whose opinions are likely to be similar to their own. Prolonged exposure to like-minded others will subsequently strengthen the confidence that Dogmatic people have in the veracity of their own opinions, making their thinking become more rigid over time. This type of polarization of traits over time, in fact, was noted for several of the personality factors studied in the AT&T longitudinal study (Howard & Bray, 1988). New managers who were initially high in achievement orientation were more likely to advance up the managerial hierarchy than those low in achievement orientation. As a consequence of having advanced, achievement orientation grew stronger over time. The opposite was true for those who failed to advance. These dynamic models suggest that the most important role for personality may be through the influence of personality traits on the choices people make about which situations to enter. Once in a particular situation, indeed situational forces may have the dominant role in shaping how people behave, as Mischel (1968) and others have argued. It should also be noted that in any given study based on dynamic models of the reciprocal influences of personality and on personality, the personality construct of interest may be treated as either the dependent or independent variable. Sophisticated multivariate techniques are now available for untangling the effects of personality and situational factors on each other.

Whatever the role assigned to personality in OB models, these models also vary in the extent to which the links between the personality construct and the criterion of interest are specified. Brockner's (1988) Behavioral Plasticity Model very clearly specifies how self-esteem is ultimately linked to plasticity. Those low in self-esteem are more concerned with securing social approval. Consequently, they are more attentive than those high in self-esteem to social cues relevant to approval, such as negative FEEDBACK or INFLUENCE attempts. When these cues occur, people low in self-esteem are more likely to notice and respond with CONFORMITY, a strategy more likely to bring the desired approval from others.

In contrast, Fiedler's CONTINGENCY THEORY of leadership, for example, hypothesizes that leaders with a relations-oriented personality are most effective in certain leadership situations and least effective in other situations. However, the theory does not specify the mediating processes which link the leader's personality to work group performance. Several reviews of the literature have shown that carefully thinking through the potential linkages of personality and job performance (e.g., by first conducting a JOB

ANALYSIS to identify tasks that might be impacted by a particular trait) enhances the chances of finding significant validities for measures of personality in predicting performance criteria (*see* VALIDITY).

Although there are various ways, then, that personality could potentially be incorporated within OB models, it is clear that most existing models have either ignored personality altogether or have assigned to it a conceptually limited role. Many of the models that do incorporate personality variables fail to adequately specify how those variables are linked to criteria of interest. Few studies have employed longitudinal designs; the emphasis has been on correlational designs or relatively short-term experimentation (*see* RESEARCH DESIGN). Consequently, it has not been possible within OB to adequately study the effects of work on personality or the dynamic interplay of personality and situations. Hopefully, the future will see the emergence of more elaborate, conceptually rich treatments of personality in OB theory to guide productive research and application.

Predictive Power

The availability of multiscaled inventories widely used in organizations to measure personality has been partially responsible for atheoretical approaches to studying personality in OB. These inventories yield scores on 10–30 different traits, allowing researchers to take a "shotgun" approach: since it is probable that a few of these traits will significantly correlate with a criterion. Not surprisingly, this body of research produced little by way of consistent and meaningful findings.

One of the major developments in personality psychology has been the consolidation of this assortment of individual, particularistic traits into a more coherent taxonomy, the Big Five Model (Barrick & Mount, 1991; McCrae & Costa, 1987). The Model proposes five broad dimensions of personality: Extraversion (or Surgency), Stability (or Neuroticism), Agreeableness (or Likeability), Conscientiousness (comprising achievement-orientation and Dependability), and Openness. Several personality inventories have been developed around the structure of the Big Five Model and specifically validated for use in employment settings (e.g., the NEO Personality Inventory, McCrae & Costa, 1987). These inventories have demonstrated a high degree of stability over time, perhaps because they measure fewer, more abstracted, personality dimensions than did the earlier inventories.

Using the Big Five model to statistically summarize previous research, Barrick and Mount (1991) found that Conscientiousness is moderately predictive of a range of performance criteria across a range of occupational categories (*see* PERFORMANCE, INDIVIDUAL). Some of the other Big Five dimensions were specifically related to particular criterion categories for particular occupational groups. For example, Openness was moderately predictive of training proficiency across occupational groups. The analysis by Barrick and Mount (1991) as well as other statistical reviews make it very clear that, at best, within simple predictive models, individual Big Five dimensions will have only moderate power in predicting job performance criteria. However, it is important to note that these broad personality dimensions have little or no relationship to the mental ability dimensions so often used to predict performance criteria. Consequently, measures of the Big Five may well significantly enhance the predictive power of existing ability-focused models of individual performance.

Although the Big Five Model has brought some coherence to the study and measurement of traits, there is still controversy about whether five broad dimensions is adequate to describe individual differences in personality. Different scholars, and various inventories, break the Big Five down into a list of anywhere from 6 to 11 somewhat more narrowly defined dimensions. For example, Hogan (1991) distinguishes between two aspects of Extraversion, Sociability, and Ambition. Those proposing a longer list of dimensions argue that the Big Five do not allow for fine-tuned analyses of personality profiles, especially needed when diagnosing the suitability of job candidates. On the other hand, it should be noted that one of the earliest, most sophisticated and enduring of trait taxonomies, that developed by Hans Eysenck (*see* Furnham, 1992), consists of just three broad dimensions: Neuroticism, Extraversion, and Psychoticism.

Attempts to enhance the predictive power of personality variables go beyond consideration of how those constructs are categorized and address the organizational context in which personality-criteria relationships are examined. One critical contextual factor is situational strength. Strong situations are those which provide people with: salient and clear cues, a high degree of structure, uniform expectancies about what will or will not happen, and incentives for the performance of a particular response pattern. Strong situations, then, constrain the range of behaviors that people are likely to exhibit and consequently minimize the impact of individual differences. Weak situations are ambiguous, low in structure, and allow for a wide range of behaviors. It is in weak situations that personality factors are most likely to make a difference.

One relatively unstructured context in which personality has been shown to have an impact is NEGOTIATION. For example, people high in the trait of MACHIAVELLIANISM are more effective in novel bargaining situations and, based on past success in such situations, also set higher negotiating goals relative to those low on this trait (*see* GOAL-SETTING). In stronger, more structured situations within organizations, personality is unlikely to predict criterion behaviors.

Also, it should be clear that a trait is unlikely to predict any criterion if the population under study shows little range on the trait. For example, since it is unlikely that shy, retiring types would apply for a high-pressure commission sales position, there is little reason to expect Surgency to predict sales performance within this particular population of sales applicants. Relative homogeneity on organizationally relevant traits may be the rule, rather than the exception, within work environments. Organizations tend to create homogeneity with respect to particular personality traits by differentially attracting people of a certain type, selecting those who most closely fit the desired type, and causing relatively high rates of attrition among those not fitting in (*see* ORGANIZATIONAL DEMOGRAPHY). Thus, the personality traits most likely to predict behavioral criteria are those criterion-relevant traits on which people in the sample vary widely, a relatively uncommon set of circumstances within a single organization (*see* WORK ADJUSTMENT).

Serious consideration of the relevance of personality to behavior in a particular context can also enhance the predictive power of personality variables. As an illustration, Field Independent individuals have consistently been found to be more instrumentally oriented and effective on group tasks than Field Dependent people. However, research on these relationships has almost always employed structured tasks in a mechanistic group environment (*see* MECHANISTIC/ORGANIC). In performing unstructured tasks in an organic T-group type setting (*see* SENSITIVITY TRAINING), Field Dependents are actually more task-oriented and effective than Field Independents. In such contexts, the self-focused, autonomous, individualistic style of Field Independent types tends to place psychological distance between themselves and other group members and to minimize their contributions to the more emotion-centered group process (Gruenfeld & Lin, 1984). By analyzing critical contextual factors and developing a clear, theory guided understanding of how linkages between personality and behavior are affected by these contextual factors, researchers can arrive at creative interactive hypotheses and more accurate predictions of behavior.

Criteria

There are three critical facets of criteria that are likely to impact on predictor–criterion relationships. These facets are: (a) criterion type; (b) criterion level; and (c) time of criterion measurement.

(a) *Type*. As noted above, individual personality traits typically have at best a moderate relationship with mean, total, or typical job performance criteria. However, personality traits may relate to the reliability or consistency of an individual's performance across tasks, situations, or time. Similarly, personality traits are only weakly related to the effectiveness of an appointed group leader, but are related to an individual's informal emergence as a group's leader. The key here, as noted above, is to carefully analyze the criterion to identify personality-sensitive elements.

(b) *Level*. Virtually all personality research in OB has focused on the prediction of individual-level criteria. In contrast, Staw and Sutton (1993) have proposed an approach they entitle "macro organizational psychology," using individual-level personality traits to explain organizational-level criteria. For example, there is some evidence that the personality of the organization's leader may influence organizational structure. In one study, CEOs who were high in need for achievement were found to create more centralized structures, establish more individual organizational units so that concrete results could be more clearly monitored, and engage in more planning activity requiring integration across units. As expected, these effects of CEO personality on organizational structure were stronger in newer and smaller firms. Similarly, the personality of those organizational members with high visibility to the organization's exchange partners may impact on organizational-level exchange behaviors.

(c) *Time*. Another criterion-relevant issue concerns the period of time over which criterion measures are aggregated. Low correlations typically found in personality research may be due to poor RELIABILITY in behavioral criterion measures. When criterion measures are collected over several occasions and aggregated into composite scores, their stability increases and their correlations with personality predictors increase as well. Thus, personality is more likely to predict employee lateness aggregated over a year's time than lateness during any given week of that year.

In addition, the effects of personality on criterion measures may vary over the course of time. Specifically, basic ability factors, and most importantly general mental ability, seem to account for much of the variance in performance early on, when the employee is learning the job. Personality comes to play a more significant role once this SKILL acquisition phase is over. In a sample of airline reservation agents, for instance, correlations of personality measures with performance over the first 3 months after the completion of training were not significant. Personality measures were significantly correlated with reservationist performance when criterion measures were collected after 6 months and 8 months on the job.

In sum, developments within basic personality theory and research and within OB have created an intellectual climate that is more conducive than in the recent past to a serious consideration of the role of personality and organizational behavior.

See also **Authoritarian personality; Learning, individual; Attitude theory; Role; Managerial style; Leadership, charismatic**

Bibliography

Barrick, M. R. & Mount, M. K. (1991). The big five dimensions and job performance: A meta-analysis. *Personnel Psychology*, **44**, 1–26.

Brockner, J. (1988). *Self-esteem at work*. Lexington, MA: Lexington Books.

Furnham, A. (1992). *Personality at work*. London: Routledge.

Gangestad, S. & Snyder, M. (1985). To carve nature at its joints: On the existence of discrete classes in personality. *Psychological Review*, **92**, 317–349.

Gruenfeld, L. W. & Lin, T. R. (1984). Social behavior of field independents and dependents in an organic group. *Human Relations*, **37**, 721–741.

Hogan, R. (1991). Personality and personality measurement. In M. D. Dunnette & L. M. Hough (Eds), *Handbook of industrial and organizational psychology*. Palo Alto, CA: Consulting Psychologist Press.

Howard, A. & Bray, D. W. (1988). *Managerial lives in transition*. New York: Guilford.

Judge, T. A. (1992). The dispositional perspective in human resources research. In G. R. Ferris & K. M. Rowland (Eds), *Research in personnel and human resource management*. Greenwich, CT: JAI Press.

McCrae, R. R. & Costa, P. T. Jr. (1987). Validation of the five-factor model of personality across instruments and observers. *Journal of Personality and Social Psychology*, **52**, 81–90.

Mischel, W. (1968). *Personality and assessment*. New York: Wiley.

Staw, B. M. & Sutton, R. (1993). Macro-organizational psychology. In J. K. Murnighan (Ed.), *Social psychology in organizations*. Englewood Cliffs, NJ: Prentice-Hall.

Weiss, H. M. & Adler, S. (1984). Personality and organizational behavior. In B. M. Staw & L. L. Cummings (Eds), *Research in organizational behavior*. Greenwich, CT: JAI Press.

SEYMOUR ADLER

personality development *see* LIFE STAGES; CAREER STAGES; PERSONALITY

personality testing Although this is the term in general use, it is not one liked by psychologists, on the grounds that measures of PERSONALITY are not tests because they do not have answers that are right or wrong. The concept of personality is complex, and measures of personality attributes tend to reflect particular theoretical approaches to explaining personality. For example, projective tests of personality (*see* PROJECTION) are based on Freudian and psychodynamic theories which emphasise unconscious processes as determinants of behavior. These tests present individuals with a vague stimulus, such as an ink-blot, and ask them to say what they see in it; on the assumption that they unconsciously "project" aspects of their personality in making their interpretations. These tests are what many of the public have in mind when they think of personality testing, but they are, in fact, seldom used as most lack any VALIDITY (*see* PSYCHOLOGICAL TESTING).

In organizational settings, the most commonly encountered form of personality ASSESSMENT is the questionnaire method, yielding scores on various personality characteristics, usually based on the work of trait theorists. They may, however, also focus on MOTIVATION (*see* MOTIVATION AND PERFORMANCE; NEED THEORY), cognitive styles, interests or other aspects of personality. Personality questionnaires may be administered on paper or, increasingly, by computer. Like other forms of psychological testing, their use in employment selection has grown greatly in recent years. In the United Kingdom, it tripled in the period of 1984–1989, and there are indications of a similar trend in other parts of Europe (Shackleton & Newell, 1991), though personality measures are still not as widely used as tests of cognitive (intellectual) ability (*see* INTELLIGENCE TESTING). Amongst the most popular are the Cattell 16PF, the Myers Briggs Type Inventory (MBTI), the Occupational Personality Inventory (OPQ), and the California Psychological Inventory (CPI). All of these measure a range of psychological characteristics, but there are many others with more limited aims, assessing just one or two attributes.

There are two broad ways in which personality inventories can be used (Toplis, Dulewicz & Fletcher, 1991). The first is in a holistic fashion, trying to secure an overall picture of the individual by looking at their pattern of scores and examining the interrelationships between the different traits. So, for example, a manager given a personality questionnaire may have produced a profile indicating high levels of emotionality and aggression. This does not necessarily mean, however, that the individual concerned will frequently display these dispositions in an overt way. Other scores may suggest that the person is actually very restrained, exercises firm self-control, and has a high level of objectivity and insight, indicating that the subject is unlikely to be someone who is easily offended. Only by taking account of the wider pattern of personality scores can the implications for behavior be inferred. This approach to interpreting personality data is sometimes called the clinical method, since it reflects the way a psychologist might use the information to try to gain a deeper understanding of the personality of a particular individual. To be effective, it calls for considerable skill and experience, coupled with an underlying knowledge of the psychology of personality. The alternative to this, which is generally used in organizations, is to take a more statistical and mechanistic approach. Here, the objective is not to focus on interpretation of individual personality scores, but to be guided by the established empirical relationships between the scores and various criteria of job success. The aim is to select people who have the kind of personality questionnaire scores associated with effective performance – irrespective of any possible interrelationships there might be between individual dimension scores.

The value of personality measures is a contentious subject, amongst academics and practitioners alike. Many organizations are willing to use tests of congnitive ability but not personality. A key question is about their VALIDITY – the relationship between personality scores and performance measures. The most recent and thorough reviews of the evidence on this indicate that modern personality questionnaires do predict job performance (Jackson & Rothstein, 1993; Tett, Jackson, & Rothstein, 1991), with correlations averaging around 0.25–0.40 (*see* PERFORMANCE, INDIVIDUAL). However, this does not mean that they automatically achieve success. Poorly constructed tests, or even good ones applied inappropriately, will not be effective. Also, personality questionnaires are not as predictive as cognitive tests or ASSESSMENT CENTERS (they are often used in conjunction with both of these).

Another issue is honesty. Do candidates simply dissimulate and present an image of their personality they think will get them the job (Anastasi, 1990)? The evidence on this is mixed. Certainly, people can simulate certain personality characteristics if briefed to, but it is not always easy to know exactly what the selecting organisation is looking for. Also, some inventories have "motivational distortion" (lie) scales to detect deliberate IMPRESSION MANAGEMENT. Giving FEEDBACK, sharing the results with the candidate, seems to reduce defensiveness and increase openness. The other point is that most other SELECTION METHODS are just as open to dissimulation as are personality questionnaires.

Finally, what are the most important personality attributes to measure? In one sense, the answer to this question depends on the analysis of the job in question (*see* JOB ANALYSIS), but it can also be interpreted in terms of the most stable and well-established personality characteristics. Attention is increasingly focused on what are known as the "big 5" – extraversion, neuroticism, openness, conscientiousness, and agreeableness – which have repeatedly come through in analyses of personality data and which show consistent correlations with other behavioral measures (Barrick & Mount, 1991). One of the most commonly used measures of these is the NEO-PI-R inventory (*see* Costa & McCrae, 1985). However, it is unlikely that organizational selection needs will be met by these five traits alone; usually, a more detailed analysis and assessment of the personal qualities – including APTITUDES and ABILITIES, as well as a wider range of personality dimensions – for successful performance in the job is required.

See also **Individual differences; Recruitment; Human resource management**

Bibliography

Anastasi, A. (1990). *Psychological testing* (6th edn). New York: Macmillan.

Barrick, M. R. & Mount, M. K. (1991). The big five personality dimensions and job performance: A field study. *Personnel Psychology*, **44**, 1–26.

Costa, P. T. & McCrae, R. R. (1985). *Manual for the NEO personality inventory*. Odessa, FL: Psychological Assessment Resources.

Jackson, D. & Rothstein, M. (1993). Evaluating personality testing in personnel selection. *The Psychologist*, **6**, 8–11.

Shackleton, V. J. & Newell, S. (1991). Management selection: A comparative survey of methods used in top British and French companies. *Journal of Occupational Psychology*, **64**, 23–36.

Tett, R. P., Jackson, D. & Rothstein, M. (1991). Personality measures as predictors of job performance: A meta-analytic review. *Personnel Psychology*, **44**, 703–742.

Toplis, J., Dulewicz, V. & Fletcher, C. (1991). *Psychological testing: A manager's guide*, (2nd edn). London: Institute of Personnel Management.

CLIVE FLETCHER

personality traits *see* ASSESSMENT; PERSONALITY; PERSONALITY TESTING

personnel management This is the traditional term applied to the specialist function responsible for the development and administration of policies and practices concerned with the management of employees. Chief among its areas of coverage are SELECTION METHODS, TRAINING, and REWARDS.

Personnel management grew as a specialist function in response to the need to solve problems such as labor shortages and poor employee relations, to deal with the increasing amount of employment legislation, and the growing complexity of organizations in general and the specific body of knowledge about management of employees in particular. Personnel managers are the managers most likely to have studied and remained interested in organizational behavior and can be important GATEKEEPERS for its application in industry.

Although many people make a career as professional personnel specialists, every manager is, in some respects, a personnel manager, responsible, for example, for motivating and communicating with their own employees. This has led to analysis of the ambiguities in the personnel role over allocation of responsibility between the specialist and line manager, the blurring of boundaries, and the consequent difficulty of attributing credit or blame for outcomes.

Concern with the sometimes excessive emphasis on administration and problem solving by personnel managers has helped to foster interest in HUMAN RESOURCE MANAGEMENT, which places greater emphasis on a more strategic, integrated management of people at work.

See also **Human resource strategy; Professionals in organizations**

Bibliography

Sisson, K. (Ed.), (1993). *Personnel management in Britain* (2nd edn). Oxford, UK: Blackwell.

DAVID GUEST

planning An important idea central to the early study of management was the "principles of management" – planning, organizing, and control (e.g., Koontz & O'Donnell, 1968). Indeed, in his classical book on management, Terry (1972) included four separate chapters on planning. According to Terry, planning is a fundamental function of management. He defines planning as ". . . the visualization and formulation of proposed activities believed necessary to achieve desired results" (Terry, 1972, p. 192).

In more recent years, planning has also become integrated with the notion of goals and objectives. Donnelly, Gibson, and Ivancevich (1987) define planning as " . . . those managerial activities that determine objectives for the future and the appropriate means for achieving those objectives" (p. 92). The outcome of the planning process is a written document that articulates alternative courses of action. According to Donnelly et al., (1987) planning consists of the following elements: (1) objectives; (2) actions; (3) resources; and (4) implementation.

Planning has also become more closely associated with the notion of "strategic planning," or, just plain "strategy." Strategic planning entails the analysis of the environment and a definition and formulation of a mission and strategies for the organization (*see* STRATEGIC MANAGEMENT).

See also **Management, classical theory; Managerial behavior; Decision making; Rationality; Management by objectives**

Bibliography

Donnelly, J. H. Jr., Gibson, J. L. & Ivancevich, J. M. (1987). *Fundamentals of management*. Plano, TX: Business Publications.

Koontz, H. & O'Donnell, C. (1968). *Principles of management*, (4th edn). (New York). McGraw-Hill.

Terry, G. R. (1972). *Principles of management* (6th edn). Homewood, II: R. D. Irwin.

HENRY P. SIMS JR.

politics Politics in organizations may be defined as POWER in action. Specifically, this refers to behaviors designed to INFLUENCE others to reach an outcome one favors. Such behaviors usually reflect competing individual (CAREER) and collective (SUBUNIT) interests that must somehow be managed for an organization to be effective. Politics exist in varying degrees in all organizations, as the article will indicate.

Old Paradigms: Politics is Bad

Virtually every major management scholar writing on politics, including Kanter, Kotter, and Pfeffer, has emphasized that it was a neglected subject until the mid-1970s, and it still lags relative to other specialties. They argue that politics was seen traditionally as representing the nonrational, underside of organizational life, deflecting people away from task performance, emphasizing instead devious, Machiavellian maneuverings for personal career or group (e.g., department, division) advantage. Politics, as Bennis was quoted to have said, "is the organization's last dirty secret."

A dichotomy was often posed between "rational," "businesslike" organizations and "political" ones. In the former, decisions regarding strategy, organization design, and personnel, for example, were presumably made "on their merits." Managers were seen as using "objective" (financial, economic, organizational, and behavioral) approaches, e.g., optimization models, SWOT analysis, motivational theory. Political organizations, by contrast, were seen as making decisions by manipulation, logrolling, and compromise, reflecting mainly turf and personal career interests.

New Paradigms: Power and Politics are Universal and Can Be Good

Since the early 1960s, several streams of writing have converged, arguing for the universality of politics in organizations. They also argue that politics may well be functional for individual and ORGANIZATIONAL EFFECTIVENESS, holding organizations together, aligning them with their environments, and distinguishing successful from unsuccessful managers (*see* ORGANIZATION AND ENVIRONMENT).

One stream from Simon, Cyert, and March emphasizes the cognitive limits to rationality in DECISION MAKING, given managers' limited information, noting that many decisions ultimately involve matters of judgment and are made and implemented by shifting coalitions, depending on their importance to different groups.

Sociologist James Thompson argued that many important organizational decisions – e.g., on strategy – involve matters on which there is no consensus regarding goals and no clearly established or agreed on programs or means. The result, again, is an intrusion of politics, with decisions emerging as resultants from negotiations among various coalitions, rather than as rationally planned through the use of sophisticated analytic techniques or models (*see* COALITION FORMATION; NEGOTIATION).

Lawrence and Lorsch (1967) observed that all organizations differentiate into various subunits, as they adapt to their environments, with these subunits establishing separate functions, interests, and tendencies toward territoriality – e.g., across departments, divisions, and levels. A critical problem is then one of INTEGRATION, usually through bargaining and, again, that involves politics.

Political scientists added their perspective in the 1960s and 1970s, arguing that organizations may be seen as collections of interest groups or stakeholders. One of the main tasks of the manager, so they argue, is to negotiate agreements with these STAKEHOLDERS in establishing organizational goals. This theme is picked up in Pfeffer and Salancik's work (1978) on RESOURCE DEPENDENCY.

A particularly relevant contribution in this regard is David Hickson and Derek Pugh's strategic contingencies theory of power. It posits that power gravitates to those individuals and subunits whose expertise enables them to control for the organization's critical uncertainties. Effective organizations, from this perspective, are those whose dominant coalition have the SKILLS most relevant to the dominant issues those organizations are facing.

John Kotter argues that the manager must negotiate with more and more individuals and groups who fall outside the chain of command, as organizations become less hierarchical and more horizontal, and as more decisions are made in cross-functional teams. He writes of the "power gap" that managers increasingly face, as they attempt to manage these stakeholders. Managing dependency, then, is a central task of all managers, particularly those at higher levels.

An underlying theme from all these writings is that organizations are not just tools for rational action whose decisions may be systematically programmed and implemented. They have both increased in COMPLEXITY – with many more stakeholders than before – and in environmental uncertainty – faced with much more change that is harder to read and predict. For both reasons, managing effectively under such circumstances is incredibly challenging. The recent emphasis on politics as a central feature of organizational life takes up an important component of that challenge.

Key Substantive Issues in Politics

There are many ways of conceptualizing key issues in organizational politics. Pfeffer's is particularly useful, dividing the field into four broad questions:

(1) assessing politics by developing a map indicating the key players, their goals and resources, and how they play the game;
(2) developing a power base;
(3) using it through various tactics; and
(4) the role of politics in shaping organizational change.

This framework is particularly useful for practicing managers. Thus, for a manager to be effective in getting decisions implemented, it is critical to gain the support of key players with stakes in the decision. Gaining that support requires building a political base and then applying it in various influence tactics, e.g., framing or defining the issue, timing, using data and analysis to legitimate one's positions, exercising interpersonal influence, and using the appropriate SYMBOLISM (the manager as "evangelist") necessary to get others to collaborate (*see* LEGITIMACY). This is not, of course, a linear process, and effective managers are engaged constantly in various political resource building activities and power tactics.

Ultimately, politics is only important as it shapes how things get done in organizations, particularly how organizations adapt (*see* ORGANIZATIONAL CHANGE). This last issue on the consequences of politics for organizational performance is critical.

Still another way of conceptualizing the field is in terms of the politics of key relationships and career stages for managers. This is Kotter's approach, as he characterizes the relational and life cycle contexts of managers.

Some Illustrative Propositions

This field is a long way from being easily codified. It is possible, however, to indicate some propositions. One set relates to the following conditions under which organizational decisions are more likely to be political: in highly differentiated organizations, where subunits are very interdependent, where there is considerable resource SCARCITY, on high stakes decisions whose outcomes are important for several participants, and where AUTHORITY and power are widely dispersed. In addition, the larger the organization, the more uncertain its environment, the more it is dependent on outside groups, the more ambitious its goals, the more complex and sophisticated its TECHNOLOGY, the more consolidated it is geographically, the less its measurement systems clearly measure individual performance, and the less the reward system rewards individual performance, the more political the organization is likely to be (*see* ORGANIZATIONAL SIZE).

Taking a more micro perspective, those managerial positions that have more responsibilities, more direct and indirect reports, and more formal authority will be more political by virtue of having in each instance more job related dependence. In general, those decisions where discretion is high, where there is much AMBIGUITY, and where it is difficult to apply techno-economic criteria, are more likely to be political. This would include strategic decisions at high levels, decisions around interdepartmental or interdivisional coordination, those relating to budgets, resource allocation across subunits, and purchasing, ORGANIZATION DESIGN, and many personnel decisions – e.g., promotions and transfers.

Finally, from Pfeffer, power is likely to be most effectively exercised when it is done so in unobtrusive ways, when it makes decisions and processes stemming from its exercise look rational, and when it involves much coalition building. Given industrialized societies' cultural emphasis on RATIONALITY and objectivity, any appearance of manipulation or MACHIAVELLIANISM may lead to a manager being seen as unethical and losing coalition support.

Examples of political behavior that reflect this rationalistic bias include the selective use of objective criteria, the use of outside consultants, controlling the agenda (which issues get discussed and in what order), selective hiring and promotions, and coopting potential opponents, often through committees. Each of these tactics often involves managing appearances and may be represented as appealing to objective criteria in making decisions. In actual fact, it is a way of breaking a deadlock on highly complex decisions where there are no clear, objective solutions, where power is widely dispersed among multiple players with different interests, where the stakes for the organization and these players are high, and where the costs of a continuing stalemate are too great to allow it to continue. Such political tactics thus become the means of generating a consensus enabling the organization to make and implement decisions that are vital to its future and on which it had been unable to act in the past.

Future Directions

Even though the new emphasis on politics is a significant advance over traditional writings, one main objective from past paradigms still prevails: Make organizations more effective. The only difference is that politics is a new tool in such an effort.

Little attention is given in this new politics literature, however, to what is meant by effectiveness or to the question of effectiveness for whom. In particular, there is little emphasis on how politics may contribute to inequality in organizations, to "unfair treatment" of particular categories of employees (women, blacks, other minorities), or to social harm that organizations may incur on the communities and society in which they are located (*see* DISCRIMINATION). Following from that, little attention has been given to how politics might be used within organizations to effect social change in humanistic ways in relation to these issues.

European academics have been ahead of Americans in recognizing how formal organizations are often the arenas in which class and ethnic struggles are enacted. Organizations may be seen from this perspective as tools through which elites maintain their dominance by controlling their employees and by preventing noncompliance with organization goals and policies (*see* CEOs). A distinction may be made, between *power to* and *power over*. In the former, the emphasis is on how politics may be harnessed for career mobility for managers and for organizational adaptation, narrowly defined by the senior managers of organizations (*see* TOP MANAGEMENT TEAMS). In the latter, it is on domination and control.

An alternative research agenda that might well flow from these points would be to look more critically at the ways senior managers use politics to control stakeholder demands. The larger context of such research might be to devise ways of enabling dispossessed stakeholders to use political skills and analysis to effect more organizational responsiveness to their concerns. This might be a way of promoting social change by developing the countervailing power of an underclass who may well be victimized by the top down decisions of senior managers. While such decisions may be defined in existing paradigms as contributing to organizational effectiveness, that may be a narrow definition, reflecting the interests of those senior managers who make the decisions. A more humanistic and social change oriented politics, driven by such perspectives as CRITICAL THEORY in the organizations field, might well move it in such intriguing new directions.

Another agenda for politics research would take as its starting point new trends and organizational forms in the 1980s and 1990s. One is MERGERS AND ACQUISITIONS. Though the conglomerate craze of the 1970s and 1980s has passed, growth through mergers is still common throughout industrialized nations. The political problems of postmerger integration – e.g., who will gain control, over what functions and levels – are major issues for managers. A second is the politics of DOWNSIZING, an experience many corporations are going through, though with few guidelines on how to manage it (*see* ORGANIZATIONAL RESTRUCTURING).

Still a third trend is for corporations to form STRATEGIC ALLIANCES and JOINT VENTURES to stabilize their market position in globally competitive industries. The large US auto companies – GM with Toyota or Ford with Nissan – are examples. Managing the power struggles involved in these ventures is a critical issue.

Finally, such new forms as the "horizontal corporation" and the "virtual corporation" generate their own politics. With regard to the former, the interest in the politics of managing cross-functional teams was mentioned earlier. We need to know much more about that process. The virtual corporation involves the out-sourcing that many corporations have engaged in, to shed nonessential businesses in an era of down-sizing. Working out the political dynamics of such relationships with subcontractors requires major political skills.

In conclusion, between the humanistic politics of the dispossessed in organizations and the politics of emerging organizational forms, a rich agenda of future research should generate new knowledge – both for managers and for academics. This is a field with a promising future.

See also **Collective action; Collective bargaining; Democracy; Consultancy intervention models; Organizational culture**

Bibliography

Cyert, R. M. & March, J. G. (1963). *A behavioral theory of the firm*. Englewood Cliffs, NJ: Prentice-Hall.

Gandz, J. & Murray, V. V. (1980). The experience of workplace politics. *Academy of Management Journal*, **23**, 237–251.

Hickson, D. et al. (1971). A strategic contingencies' theory of intraorganizational power. *Administrative Science Quarterly*, **16**, 216–229.
Kanter, R. (1977). *Men and women of the corporation*. New York: Basic Books.
Kotter, J. (1979). *Power in management*. New York: Amacom.
Kotter, J. (1985). *Power and influence*. New York: Free Press.
Lawrence, P. R. & Lorsch, J. W. (1967). *Organization and environment*. Cambridge, MA: Harvard University Press.
Pfeffer, J. (1981). *Power in organizations*. Marshfield, MA: Pitman.
Pfeffer, J. (1992). *Managing with power*. Boston: Harvard Business School Press.
Pfeffer, J. & Salancik, G. R. (1978). *The external control of organizations: A resource dependence perspective*. New York: Harper & Row.
Thompson, J. (1967). *Organizations in action*. New York: McGraw-Hill.

DAVID ROGERS

pooled interdependence *see* TECHNOLOGY

population ecology This theoretical perspective attempts to explain organizational diversity as resulting from natural selection processes. The perspective was introduced in 1977 by Michael Hannan and John Freeman, who proposed that the organizations we see around us can be understood as the survivors of past processes of organizational founding and dissolution (Hannan & Freeman, 1989) (*see* FOUNDERS). The theory and methods of organizational ecology attempt to explain the empirical record of these processes, and have expanded in scope to include the study of organizational aging, growth, change, and performance (*see* ORGANIZATIONAL CHANGE).

Environmental Selection

The primary unit of analysis is the "organizational form", the various "blueprints" that guide organization building. A basic ecological principle is that selection processes favor one organizational form over all others in a given niche, or segment of the organizational environment (*see* ORGANIZATION AND ENVIRONMENT). Based on this idea, studies typically model how conditions of the organizational environment select among organizational forms. The estimates of these models can then be used to determine an environment's "carrying capacity" for a particular organizational form – the number of a particular form that can be supported in a given environment.

The initial Hannan and Freeman paper (1977) discussed the survival prospects of specialist and generalist organizational forms. They predicted, and later found, that specialist organizations are favored over generalists under most conditions. Only when resource availability is highly variable and the time between variations is long did they predict an advantage for generalists.

Other work has extended the study of environmental selection processes to include political and social forces (*see* POLITICS). Work in this vein finds that political upheaval tends to increase both failure and founding rates – jeopardizing existing forms while freeing up resources for the founding of new organizations. Carroll and Huo (1986) looked at the effects of both the task and institutional environments on newspaper organizations, finding that institutional factors were most important for predicting vital rates while aspects of the task environment most strongly predicted organizational performance (*see* ORGANIZATIONAL EFFECTIVENESS).

Formal government policies and regulations have become standard variables explaining the vital rates of organizations. In most cases these variables are found to have their expected effects, but under some conditions public policies have had unintended consequences due to ecological dynamics. Other work has looked at how organizational viability is affected by institutional affiliations.

Resource partitioning. While most research has treated the structure of environmental niches as given, Carroll (1985) proposed a model that accounts for the evolution of niche structure over time. In his resource partitioning model, Carroll argued that the availability of niches for specialists changes when an organizational population becomes more concentrated. As concentration increases, generalists become more suited to the "mass market" but less tailored to particular specializations. Consequently, his model predicts that increasing concentration actually increases the niches available to specialists, making them more viable. Carroll found evidence in support of this prediction in his study of newspaper publishing organizations, and recent work on other populations also supports the model.

Ecological Interdependence

A growing body of research looks at selection forces endogenous to organizational populations – where organizations affect one another's life chances.

Density dependence. Interest in ecological interdependence has sky-rocketed since Hannan developed the so-called "density dependence" model (Hannan & Carroll, 1992). The model is based on the idea that both LEGITIMACY and competition increase with the density (number) of organizations in a population (*see* COMPETITIVENESS). When an organizational population is new it lacks legitimacy. At this point increases in numbers enhance legitimacy considerably but intensify competition only a little. At high levels of density, however, additional increases in density add little to the legitimacy of the form but increase competition significantly due to overcrowding. Together, these arguments predict that increases in density at low levels increase founding rates and decrease failure rates, while increases in density at high levels should drive founding rates down and failure rates up. A sizeable empirical record mostly supports these predictions (Singh & Lumsden, 1990).

Other work has sought to specify the geographic levels of analysis where competition and legitimation occur, under the idea that legitimation may develop more broadly across societies while competition is more localized. Results do not break into this neat pattern, however, but suggest:

(1) that higher-level patterns may conceal important differences between rural and urban areas; and
(2) that ENTREPRENEURSHIP may be driven more by local factors while the ultimate fates of these organizations may depend on broader regional competition.

Carroll and Hannan extended the density-dependence model to include "density delay" – a reduction in an organization's viability experienced over its lifetime due to competition at the time it was founded. Two ideas combine for density delay. First, organizations are thought to be made more frail when they are founded under crowded, high-density conditions. Second, this initial frailty is argued to be permanent since it effects the characteristics "imprinted" into an organization at its time of founding. Other generalizations of the density model look at how competition depends on ORGANIZATIONAL SIZE and experience.

Multiform models. Why do different forms of organizations sometimes coexist in the same domain? Ecologists typically answer this question by proposing that the environment is segregated into distinct niches were the conditions are right for different organizational forms (*see* STRATEGIC TYPES). The more that these niches are segregated by institutional boundaries, technological barriers, and the like, the less "overlap" will exist between them and so the less their organizational forms will compete (*see* ORGANIZATIONAL BOUNDARIES). With competition attenuated, different organizational forms can coexist in equilibrium.

Empirical tests have searched for such differentiation in several ways. The most widely used approach is to apply the density-dependence model, specifying density effects between forms. McPherson (1983) developed a different approach by conceiving of competition among particular organizations, and then directly measuring the extent to which they depend on common resources.

Extending the idea of segregated niches, Hannan, Ranger-Moore, and Banaszak-Holl (1990) proposed that competition is "size-localized", so that similar-sized organizations compete more strongly than organizations of different sizes. The idea is that size typically co-varies with many other aspects of an organization's form. If organizations of similar forms tend to occupy the same niche, and so compete more strongly, then we should see greater competition among organizations when they are more similar in size. Baum and Mezias (1992) find support for this prediction and extend the model.

A new application of multiform competition models was developed by Carroll and Swaminathan (1992), who argue that the concept of organizational form is essentially the same as the idea of strategic group developed in the strategy literature (*see* STRATEGIC MANAGEMENT). With this in mind, multiform competition models have been used to test hypotheses about strategic behavior and its effects on competition.

Population dynamics. The evolution of organizational populations is also shaped by the effects of foundings and failures at one point in time on ensuing foundings and failures, so-called population dynamics. Failures are followed by foundings, since they free-up resources – although periods of extremely high failure rates act to lower founding rates by dissuading potential entrepreneurs. By contrast, observed foundings in one period encourage potential entrepreneurs and so increase the ensuing founding rate. However, this effect is reversed at high levels since very large numbers of foundings deplete resources for further organizing.

Organization-level Processes

Ecological theory can be applied to the evolution of individual organizations (Aldrich, 1979), and ecological processes are often modeled using data where individual organizations are the units of analysis (*see* LEVELS OF ANALYSIS). Consequently, researchers have investigated regularities that vary from organization to organization – especially age- and size-dependent failure, organizational change, and organizational growth.

Age- and size-dependent failure. Researchers have argued that organizations are more likely to fail when they are young, since the internal roles and routines as well as the external position, legitimacy, and relations of a new organization are not yet well developed. Researchers in organizational ecology have usually found support for this so-called "liability of newness."

More recently, some have questioned the ubiquity of this effect. Halliday, Powell, and Granfors (1987) studied US state bar associations. They described these organizations as "minimalist" in that they incur low costs and are supported by other organizations, and did not find that they suffer a liability of newness (although they do suffer from a liability of smallness). Others have found that the liability of newness does not start immediately when an organization is born, but only after an initial period when a new organization can survive on its initial resource endowment.

Barron, West, and Hannan (1994) argue that the finding of negative age-dependent failure rates reflects only an uncontrolled "liability of smallness". In a study of credit unions, they find that controlling for organizational size, organizations are more likely to fail as they get older – evidence of internal problems that become worse over time (senescence) and obsolescence (*see* ORGANIZATIONAL DECLINE AND DEATH).

Organizational change. A controversial tenant of the ecological perspective is that organizations are unlikely to change in dramatic ways, and are likely to fail when they do try to change. In what is known as Structural Inertia Theory, Hannan and Freeman laid out the logic behind this tennet. Their central argument is that selection processes favor inert organizations. Organizations are rewarded for performing reliably, and for being able to account rationally for their behavior. Such reliability and accountability are greater for organizations with stable routines that resist change. Thus selection forces tend to favor the creation of inert organizations.

This theory has testable implications for the study of change in "core" organizational characteristics. With respect to the likelihood of change, it implies that organizations become more stable as they age and grow. ROLES, political coalitions, routines, and ties to other social actors in the environment (among other factors) tend to resist change. Furthermore, these forces become well established – and so more resistant to change – as time passes and as organizations grow in size. This implies that organizations become less likely to change as they age and grow. Should change occur, however, this stabilizing process is restarted. The newly changed organization has not yet had time for new internal processes, structures, and external ties to stabilize. Consequently, change rachets up the likelihood of additional change – an effect that again falls away as time passes (*see* PUNCTUATED EQUILIBRIUM).

When change does occur it is predicted to be hazardous, since organizational action often generates unanticipated consequences. Furthermore, even when organizations do change as planned, this is not sufficient for success. The question is whether an organization can change fast enough to match its environment – which typically also is changing. For these reasons, dramatic organizational change is predicted to make organizations again as likely to fail as a new organization – essentially "resetting" the liability of newness clock. As time passes, however, organizations are predicted to recover from the shock of having changed, as internal processes and routines develop and external legitimacy and ties are again secured. Thus the hazard associated with change should wear off over time – if the organization does not die first.

Amburgey, Kelly, and Barnett (1993) found support for the predictions of structural inertia theory in a thorough test on the Finnish newspaper industry, and Barnett (1994) found that technological change increased failure rates among telephone companies. By contrast, Haveman (1992) found that change enhanced viability among savings and loans during a period when not changing implied nearly certain failure. Other studies have shown mixed effects, probably because they analyzed changes in peripheral as well as core characteristics.

Organizational Growth

Organizations differ dramatically in size, and several studies attempt to explain these differences from an ecological perspective. Researchers typically start with the null hypothesis that proportionate organizational growth is random and independent of current size – so-called "Gibrat's law." Studies then test whether ecological dynamics can account for deviations from this baseline model. In most cases, researchers have applied theoretical propositions developed in studies of vital rates to explain organizational growth. For instance, Barron, West, and Hannan (1994) find support for the density-dependence model in their analysis of credit union growth.

See also **Interorganizational relations; Institutional theory; Organizational design; Organization theory**

Bibliography

Aldrich, H. E. (1979). *Organizations and environments.* Englewood Cliffs, NJ: Prentice-Hall.

Amburgey, T. L., Kelly, D. & Barnett, W. P. (1993). Resetting the clock: The dynamics of organizational change and failure. *Administrative Science Quarterly*, **38**, 51–73.

Barnett, W. P. (1994). The liability of collective action: Growth and change among early American telephone companies. In J. Baum & J. Singh (Eds), *Evolutionary Dynamics of Organizations.* New York: Oxford University Press.

Barron, D. N., West, E. & Hannan, M. T. (1994). A time to grow and a time to die: Growth and mortality of credits 1914–1990. *American Journal of Sociology*, **100**, 381–421.

Baum, J. A. C. & Mezias, S. J. (1992). Localized competition and organizational failure in the Manhattan hotel industry, 1898–1990. *Administrative Science Quarterly*, **37**, 580–604.

Carroll, G. R. (1985). Concentration and specialization: Dynamics of niche width in populations of organizations. *American Journal of Sociology*, **90**, 1262–1283.

Carroll, G. R. & Huo, Y. P. (1986). Organizational task and institutional environments in ecological perspective: findings from the local newspaper industry. *American Journal of Sociology*, **91**, 838–873.

Carroll, G. R. & Swaminathan, A. (1992). The organizational ecology of strategic groups in the American brewing industry from 1975–1990. *Industrial and Corporate Change*, **1**, 65–97.

Halliday, T., Powell, M. J. & Granfors, M. W. (1987). Minimalist organizations: Vital events in state bar associations: 1870–1930. *American Sociological Review*, **52**, 456–471.

Hannan, M. T. & Carroll, G. R. (1992). *Dynamics of organizational populations: density, competition, and legitimation.* New York: Oxford University Press.

Hannan, M. T. & Freeman, J. (1977). The population ecology of organizations. *American Journal of Sociology*, **83**, 929–984.

Hannan, M. T. & Freeman, J. (1989). Organizational ecology. Cambridge, MA: Harvard University Press.

Hannan, M. T., Ranger-Moore, J. & Banaszak-Holl, J. (1990). Competition and the evolution of organizational size distributions. In J. V. Singh (Ed.), *Organizational evolution: New directions* (pp. 246–268). Newbury Park, CA: Sage.

Haveman, H. A. (1992). Between a rock and a hard place: Organizational change and performance under conditions of fundamental environmental transformation. *Administrative Science Quarterly*, **37**, 48–75.

McPherson, J. M. (1983). An ecology of affiliation. *American Sociological Review*, **83**, 340–363.
Singh, J. V. & Lumsden, C. J. (1990). Theory and research in organizational ecology. *Annual Review of Sociology*, **16**, 161–195. Palo Alto, CA: Annual Reviews.

WILLIAM P. BARNETT

positivism *see* CRITICAL THEORY; POSTMODERNISM

postmodernism This is a cultural movement of the late twentieth century, which may be defined in opposition to modernism. Modernism is characterized by a rationalistic, positivistic technological knowledge base which, allied to a belief in metanarratives (large-scale theoretical interpretations of purportedly universal truth and application, e.g., marxism, capitalism), promised linear progress through rational planning and development, aimed at mass producing standardized goods and private and public services for mass markets/citizens. Modernism is typified by authoritarianism and élitism, through a belief in bureaucratic and hierarchical systems as instruments and guarantors of order, control, and efficiency (*see* BUREAUCRACY; HIERARCHY; RATIONALITY; SCIENTIFIC MANAGEMENT) and in "art for art's sake," divorced from popular culture, reserved for the appreciation of an artistic establishment. The institutions of modernity are industrialism, capitalism, the nation state, and surveillance (*see* INSTITUTIONAL THEORY). The individual finds a coherent, if often alienated, identity as a productive worker (*see* ALIENATION).

Postmodernism, often seen as a reflection of "disorganized" (i.e., deregulated) capitalism and time–space compression consequent on electronic media, rejects positivism's tenet of absolute truths in favor of relativism. This is reflected in a rejection of metanarratives in favor of a plurality of "language games," in which the medium is the message, and both may vary depending on situation and which image of our fragmented selves we wish to project (*see* IDEOLOGY; SYMBOLISM). Postmodernists suggest that our shifting identities are defined by our patterns of consumption, rather than by our roles as productive workers, but, as postmodernists would assert, it is images we consume rather than purely the use value of products and services. The images are created and transmitted by a new middle class of KNOWLEDGE WORKERS in the media (e.g., in advertising, PR and TV). Postmodernists suggest that our tastes, erasing distinctions between high and popular culture (e.g., Pavarotti mingling opera with the football World Cup) are eclectic, playful, and transient, focusing on style rather than substance and on immediate gratification rather than long-term aspiration. Further, that time–space compression disrupts any sense of linear continuity or spatial boundaries (e.g., use of video, global village). Hence history becomes a repository of images to be mined by politicians, leisure industry and advertisers, which are more readily consumed when presented through shock tactics, such as pastiche or collage forms, or as spectacle (e.g., Spielberg films, Disneyland). Truth and fiction, fact and artefact are confounded, as the "real" world looks a pale copy of a media created world (e.g., UK royal family as soap stars, virtual reality). In this fragmented world postmodernists believe that relationships tend to be temporary and that many boundaries are blurred.

Postmodernism provides several insights into OB/OT. It suggests the end of rationalistic planning, based on extrapolation from the past, and points to emergent strategy formation, concerned with scenario painting of future shocks. It recognizes an enacted rather than discovered environment (*see* ENACTMENT). It suggests that the popularity of "EXCELLENCE" gurus lies not in the substance of their messages so much as in the images they project of the US transformational leader as hero (*see* LEADERSHIP, SEVEN S MODEL). It proposes that in managing corporate cultures (*see* ORGANIZATIONAL CULTURE) such leaders engage in stylish media-based performances to sell a vision – often about customer awareness, including the employee as customer – that legitimize decision making based on hunch rather than rationality (*see* COMPETITIVENESS; DECISION MAKING; JUST-IN-TIME; MISSION STATEMENTS). This is necessary because postmodernism's relativism calls into question AUTHORITY based on bureaucratic hierarchies while recognizing that pure rationality is impossible in a world characterized by UNCERTAINTY and accelerating rates of change (*see* ORGANIZATIONAL CHANGE). Postmodernism would consider that new loosely coupled organizational forms such as teams, partnerships, alliances, joint ventures, as well as moves to functional flexibility and flexible specialization, reflect the blurring of boundaries. It regards such phenomena as delayering, downsizing, CAREER BREAKS, and numerical flexibility as expressions of the increasing temporariness of relationships (*see* CAREER; FLEXIBILITY; ORGANIZATIONAL RESTRUCTURING). In blurring boundaries and confounding "truth" and fiction postmodernism is comfortable with the contradictions embedded in organizations (*see* PARADOX). For example, that relationships with "outsiders," such as partners, may be more permanent than those with "insiders," such as employees; that TOTAL QUALITY MANAGEMENT may represent labor intensification rather than EMPOWERMENT (*see* EMPLOYEE INVOLVEMENT; CONTINUOUS IMPROVEMENT).

See also **Critical theory; Social constuctionism; Theory**

Bibliography

Clegg, S. (1990). *Modern organizations, organization studies in the postmodern world.* London: Sage.

Cooper, R. & Burrell, G. (1988). Modernism, postmodernism and organizational analysis: An introduction. *Organization Studies*, **9**, 91–112.

Harvey, D. (1989). *The condition of postmodernity.* Oxford, UK: Basil Blackwell.

Lash, S. & Urry, J. (1987). *The end of organised capitalism.* Oxford, UK: Polity.

Lyotard, J. F. (1984). *The postmodern condition.* Manchester, UK: Manchester University Press.

Parker, M. (1992). Postmodern organizations or postmodern organization theory? *Organization Studies*, **13**, 1–17.

KAREN LEGGE

power This can be defined as the probability of carrying out one's own will despite resistance (Weber, 1947). It is neither all-or-none, nor generalizable across situations. To have power is relative, not absolute, since it relies on the specifics of the context and the relationships there.

Power and INFLUENCE are not the same. Although the terms are sometimes used as if synonymous, behaviors associated with them have been found to be distinctive from one another (e.g., Hinkin & Schriesheim, 1990). Influence is usually more dependent upon persuasion than upon explicit or implicit coercion. However, in given circumstances, power and influence may be intertwined. This is seen when those in AUTHORITY employ persuasion rather than power, since restraint in its use saves unnecessary costs in resistance and negative feelings.

Power need not be exercised to get results. It holds a potential for gaining intended effects. An evident instance occurs when a person cannot be forced to do something, but is aware of the negative later consequences of failing to comply. This is seen, for example, if a person is concerned about a needed letter of recommendation (*see* OBEDIENCE). Furthermore, power implies various psychological states, i.e., motivational, perceptual, as well as behavioral. McClelland (1975) has investigated the motive to exert power over others (*see* POWER, NEED FOR), which he finds has many implications, interpersonally and organizationally. For example, people with a strong power motive may present themselves well when seeking a post but prove to be disastrous choices once selected. They may also perceive situations in power terms, and act accordingly, as exemplified in MACHIAVELLIANISM.

Organizational power is basically structural insofar as it comes from imposed authority (*see* BASES OF POWER). Pfeffer (1981) observes that most studies of power in organizations focus on hierarchical power, i.e., the power of supervisors, or bosses over employees. There are, however, at least two other forms that power may take, in addition to power over. These are power to and power from, represented respectively by power sharing or empowerment (*see* EMPLOYEE INVOLVEMENT), and the ability to fend off the unwanted power demands of others (Hollander & Offermann, 1990).

The "power and POLITICS" view of organizations considers such realities by looking at the ways individuals and groups in organizations contend for resources and other desired ends. This affords a more reality-based picture of the organizational world than is presented by seeing only formal structures, or accepting images of common purposes being sought with little CONFLICT.

Special attention is given to resources and REWARDS, including promotions, pay, and other career goals, sought by individuals and units within the organization. Control of these is illustrative of position-based *legitimate power* that comes with authority, but can be accorded by the acceptance of others (*see* LEGITIMACY). Higher status as a leader usually equates with having more benefits to allocate at one's discretion, which represents *reward power* in the short and long range.

Though power is imputed to an organizational role, actualizing it depends upon who occupies it and how that person is perceived by others, and relates to them. In short, power becomes a reality when others perceive it and respond accordingly. Some power still depends more on personal qualities, such as relevant knowledge and expertise than on position, and is designated *expert power*.

Power and LEADERSHIP

Power is not the same as leadership, but is a feature of it. Analyses of leadership and power usually begin with the basis on which one person, a leader, is able to exert power over others. In organizations the most fundamental sources of power are structural and personal. These refer to position or place and to individual qualities, respectively, including "RESOURCE DEPENDENCY" (Pfeffer, 1981). Excessive reliance on power can have negative effects, but the reverse is also true. A failure to employ power can be limiting. As Gardner (1990) says, "Leaders who hold high rank in organized systems have power stemming from their institutional position, and they do not hesitate to use that power to further their purposes. They may be very persuasive, but they do not live by persuasion alone – rather by persuasion interwoven with the exercise of power" (p. 56).

Holding and wielding power have unintended effects, as Kipnis (1976) details in *The Powerholders*. It is not the fate of the powerholder that concerns Kipnis so much as it is the destructive effects of excessive power on relationships. He presents a set of concepts about the "metamorphic effect of power," going beyond Lord Acton's famous adage that "Power tends to corrupt; absolute power corrupts absolutely," and analyzing its redounding effects. Four corrupting influences of power are seen to operate:

(1) the desire to have power becomes an end in itself, with implications for the means–end relationship;
(2) access to power tempts the individual to use institutional resources for illegitimate self-benefit;
(3) false FEEDBACK is elicited from others, with an exalted sense of self-worth; and
(4) others' worth is devalued with a desire to avoid having close social contacts with them.

Uses and Abuses of Power

The uses of power come from its perception as well as its reality. In the process of NEGOTIATION, for example, the perception of power is important both for one's self and others. Bargainers who perceive themselves as more powerful will delay concessions, while those who perceive themselves as less powerful may be encouraged to try to build their power, or make unilateral concessions. The self-definition of relative power therefore can be consequential to the outcome.

Similarly, in exercising "legitimate power" it is still necessary to have the "endorsement" of followers, who must perceive its appropriateness (Hollander, 1992). Granting the effect of position, a leader's acquiescence to group pressure may depend upon a sense of that affirmation. A leader experiencing low endorsement from followers accordingly may feel it necessary to use coercive power on them so that it becomes a response to weakness and a sense of threat.

Even in a clear social exchange, power does play a part, though Blau (1964) accentuated the distinction between a noncoercive social exchange relationship versus one characterized by power. Coercive power may operate in various subtle ways so that the idea of having noncoercive choice is illusory. In such cases, dependence is made more prominent. This occurs for instance when discontent produces a desire to resign from an organization, but one is reminded of what would be lost by such a course of action.

Harassment, sexual or otherwise, exemplifies the power-dependence connection which underlies organizational relationships. Throughout one's CAREER, there is the continuing need to have the approval of superiors, not least for later recommendations. It is therefore understandable that the less powerful are seen to be more vulnerable and open to exploitation by the more powerful. SEXUAL HARASSMENT is one variant of the coercive use of power as it applies to GENDER distinction.

Another instance of it is seen in *negative power*, which is saying no to a request, a proposal, program, or whatever, to substantiate the greater power of the rejector, independently of the merits of the case at hand. It may be designed to keep down younger, threatening members of the organization. This tactic sometimes takes the form of asking questions to trivialize and dismiss the points being raised.

Lukes (1974) has considered overt and covert conflicts in power relations. In the overt case, both parties are aware of a manifest conflict of interest. However, one party may see benefits in obscuring the conflict, and keeping it covert, lest others look behind the scenes to see who in fact is "pulling the strings."

Sharing Power

Whatever the leader's source of power, the quantitative variable of how much power is of fundamental importance, as the social psychologist Mark Mulder noted in the 1950s. He said, for example, that power differences can act as an impediment to authentic worker PARTICIPATION in organizations. A good part of this effect may be due to variations in available information and expertise related to STATUS in organizations. Accordingly, low status participants may feel even more FRUSTRATION when exposed to a supposed participation situation where they are not equipped with these resources. Hence his conclusion that no participation is preferable to sham participation.

There also may be informal as well as formal power in organizations. These can be highly dispersed, with people of both lower and higher status having access to power. Informal power may be exercised by people who are relatively low on the status ladder – such as secretaries, bookkeepers, and hospital attendants – but who are structurally well placed. Such positions provide for opportunities to control others, not because of a grant of authority or personal qualities, but by their location in the organization.

An emphasis on power over others has tended to obscure the important place of power to, as well as power from (Hollander & Offermann, 1990). Among other things considered are the benefits of, and sources of resistance to, delegation and empowerment of followers. On balance, by sharing power and allowing followers to influence them, leaders foster leadership skills in others, as well as achieving other gains through their greater participation and involvement.

Delegation comes out of a cognitive growth approach to job enrichment, and represents distibuting power beyond traditional participation. Self-managed work teams exemplify groups to whom such authority has been successfully delegated (Goodman, Devadas, & Hughson, 1988). Despite such evidence, there are clear barriers to extending a process of power sharing in organizations.

The largest barrier to employee empowerment is the commonplace belief that the amount of power is fixed in an organization. This zero-sum conception supports the fear that power granted to others is lost to one's self or unit. Banas (1988) reported the difficulties in introducing an employee involvement program at the Ford Motor Company, until supervisor concerns were allayed about losing their authority and jobs (*see* RESISTANCE TO CHANGE).

Finally, there is the reality of ACCOUNTABILITY. In many organizational settings, even with assurances to the contrary, supervisors are ultimately held responsible for decisions made in their units. This source of resistance to power sharing needs to be understood and addressed, given the sensitivities and concerns that power generates about one's strengths and vulnerabilities in the organization.

See also **Decision making; Conformity; Leadership; Leadership contingencies**

Bibliography

Banas, P. A. (1988). Employee involvement: A sustained labor/management initiative at the Ford Motor Company. In J. P. Campbell & R. J.

Campbell (Eds), *Productivity in organizations* (pp. 388–416). San Francisco: Jossey-Bass.
Blau, P. M. (1964). *Exchange and power in social life*. New York: Wiley.
Gardner, J. W. (1990). *On leadership*. New York: Free Press.
Goodman, P. S., Devadas, R. & Hughson, T. L. (1988). Groups and productivity: Analyzing the effectiveness of self-managing teams. In J. P. Campbell & R. J. Campbell (Eds), *Productivity in organizations* (pp. 295–327). San Francisco: Jossey-Bass.
Hinkin, T. R. & Schriesheim, C. A. (1990). Relationships between subordinate perceptions of supervisory influence tactics and attributed bases of supervisory power. *Human Relations*, **43**, 221–237.
Hollander, E. P. (1992). Legitimacy, power, and influence: A perspective on relational features of leadership. In M. M. Chemers & R. Ayman (Eds), *Leadership theory and research: Perspectives and directions*. San Diego: Academic Press.
Hollander, E. P. & Offermann, L. (1990). Power and leadership in organizations: Relationships in transition. *American Psychologist*, **45**, 179–189.
Kipnis, D. (1976). *The powerholders*. Chicago: University of Chicago Press.
Lukes, S. (1974). *Power: A radical view*. London: Macmillan.
McClelland, D. (1975). *Power: The inner experience*. New York: Irvington.
Pfeffer, J. (1981). *Power in organizations*. Marshfield, MA: Pitman.
Weber, M. (1947). *The theory of social and economic organization*. (Translated and edited by T. Parsons & A. M. Henderson.) New York: Oxford University Press.

EDWIN P. HOLLANDER

power, need for INDIVIDUAL DIFFERENCES in this motivational disposition to seek positions of INFLUENCE are commonly measured by content coding responses to a projective instrument such as the Thematic Apperception Test (*see* PERSONALITY TESTING; PROJECTION). Those high in npow have stronger impulses toward aggressive acts, although the likelihood that they will actually act in an aggressive manner is also a function of SOCIALIZATION and maturity. There is evidence that those high in n pow tend to gravitate toward CAREERS in which they can influence but not necessarily dominate others, such as teaching or the ministry. Those who develop high n pow were more likely to have been raised in an environment that was permissive toward aggressive acts. Npow appears to have strong physiological correlates. Compared to those low in npow, those high in npow have higher rates of hypertension, cardiac disease, and stress-related symptoms (*see* STRESS; MENTAL HEALTH; TYPE-A). High npow combined with low impulse control is also associated with relatively high rates of alcoholism (*see* ALCOHOL AND SUBSTANCE ABUSE). The relationship between npow and LEADERSHIP is more complex than originally thought. Effective leaders appear to channel their POWER needs into more socially beneficial, rather than personally beneficial or egotistical, activities. The combination of high n pow combined with high activity inhibition and, in bureaucratic organizations (*see* BUREAUCRACY) also low-to-moderate levels of need for affiliation produces a PERSONALITY profile that McClelland has labeled the Leadership Motive Pattern. This profile has been found to strongly predict managerial advancement over a 20-year period. In addition, n pow is a significant determinant of the charisma attributed to political leaders (*see* TRANSACTIONAL/TRANSFORMATIONAL LEADERSHIP; LEADERSHIP, CHARISMATIC).

See also **Politics; Machiavellianism; Achievement, need for; Affiliation, need for**

Bibliography

House, R. J. (1988). Power and personality in complex organizations. *Research in Organizational Behavior*, **10**, 305–357.
McClelland, D. C. & Boyatzis, R. E. (1982). The leadership motive pattern and long term success in management. *Journal of Applied Psychology*, **67**, 737–743.
McClelland D. C. & Burnham, D. H. (1976). Power is the great motivator. *Harvard Business Review*, **54**, 100–110, 159–166.
Winter, D. G. (1972). *The power motive*. New York: Free Press.

SEYMOUR ADLER

power bases POWER as conventionally used is the ability to bring about a desired effect despite opposing forces. Power is relative, not absolute, since it depends upon the context and the relationships there. In organizations, power derives from two fundamental sources. These are structural and personal, as a function of position or place, and individual qualities. Illustrating the former, Pfeffer (1981) contends that power is "first and foremost a structural phenomenon" based on holding a position of AUTHORITY, as in appointed LEADERSHIP.

Counterposed to this structural view is attention to individual personal qualities, such as knowledge and expertise, on which others rely. Kanter (1979) extends these to include the ability to get cooperation in doing what is necessary, as in securing organizational resources. Such dependence creates power, with dependence of the less powerful person on the more powerful one presenting an imbalance in their relationship, which can make for discomfort for both. However, even lower-level organization members have means by which to gain power through others' dependence on them. Included in these means are their personal attributes of COMMITMENT, effort, interest, willingness to use power, SKILLS, and attractiveness. Other factors making for dependence are such structural elements as one's irreplaceability and position location, e.g., a secretary who serves as a "gatekeeper" outside the door to a major executive (*see* RESOURCE DEPENDENCE).

The well-known formulation of "bases of power" proposed by French and Raven (1959) identifies many of these, including expert power and legitimate power. The latter requires an acceptable mode of legitimation of a person in an authority position, as in leadership (*see* LEGITIMACY). This can be achieved through appointment by the upper levels in organizations, or by an electorate in the political realm (*see* POLITICS). Reward and coercive power, as the terms indicate, are based upon gains or losses for compliance or noncompliance with a person in authority. Referent power extends reward power through a process of IDENTIFICATION with that person. Once such identification has occurred, it is no longer necessary for the person in authority to monitor the less powerful person's behavior continuously. Expert power, as already suggested, comes from specialized knowledge or distinctive competence (*see* COMPETENCIES).

These bases of power are not likely to be so categorically discrete, but rather to overlap and be intermingled, depending upon the particular people involved and their circumstances. Among the issues this consideration raises are the effects of a sense of powerlessness (Kanter, 1979), and of the "power distance" between leader and led regarding access to benefits and information.

See also **Influence; Leadership contingencies; Obedience**

Bibliography

French, J. R. P., Jr. & Raven, B. H. (1959). The bases of social power. In D. Cartwright (Ed.), *Studies in social power* (pp. 118–149). Ann Arbor: University of Michigan Press.

Kanter, R. M. (1979). Power failure in management circuits. *Harvard Business Review* July–August.

Pfeffer, J. (1981). *Power in organizations*. Marshfield, MA: Pitman.

EDWIN P. HOLLANDER

power distance The power distance between two people in a social system is the degree of inequality of POWER between the dyad. In general, the less powerful person will tend to reduce the power distance while the more powerful person tries to increase it. These efforts equilibrate at some level, which varies for each dyad based on the characteristics of the individuals and the social system in which they are members.

Within organizations, power distance is commonly examined in the relationship between superior and subordinate. In relationships with larger power distances, the subordinate is more likely to accept the close supervision and autocratic behavior of a superior. Consultative decision-making processes increase satisfaction in relationships with smaller power distances (*see* PARTICIPATION; DEMOCRACY; EMPLOYEE INVOLVEMENT).

Power distance norms among people in an organization or society are related to ORGANIZATIONAL DESIGN and ORGANIZATIONAL BEHAVIOR (*see* GROUP NORMS). In the latter case, employees are more cooperative and perceive a strong work ethic in social systems which have smaller power distance norms. In the context of organizational design, countries with lower power distance norms have flatter organizational structures, less centralization, and smaller wage differentials.

See also **Reciprocity; Equity theory; Role distancing**

Bibliography

Hofstede, G. (1980). *Culture's consequences.* Beverly Hills, CA: Sage.

DAVID L. DEEPHOUSE

practical intelligence This construct pertains to differences among individuals in the ABILITY to manage mental capacities in achieving desired ends in real-world environments. It is distinct from general intelligence in that it is not highly related to a general *g* factor, academic ability, or working memory capacity. Practical intelligence is better conceptualized as the mental functions used to adapt to and shape real-world environments. It is developed through experience, but also depends on executive processes that plan and monitor activities, and performance components through which one executes plans (Sternberg, 1985). Practical intelligence is important because effective performance on many organizational tasks depends on practical rather than academic intelligence.

Three research traditions relate to practical intelligence. First, Sternberg's triarchic (1985) theory of intelligence provides a political model of mental self-government based on executive processes, performance components, and knowledge acquisition components. Second, research on expertise shows that as SKILL develops, people do tasks in different ways. Experts rely more on organized knowledge, recognizing rather than creating appropriate responses. Experts also have exceptional meta-monitoring capacities. Third, research distinguishing among implicit and explicit processing shows these two constructs are neurologically and behaviorally distinct. Implicit (or tacit) knowledge is often used without conscious awareness in the performance of tasks, whereas explicit processes demand attention. Practical intelligence may depend more on implicit processes, whereas academic intelligence emphasizes explicit processing capacities.

See also **Intelligence, testing; Performance, individual; Knowledge workers; Individual differences; Training**

Bibliography

Sternberg, R. J. (1985). Human intelligence: The model is the message. *Science*, **230**, 1111–1118.

ROBERT G. LORD

prejudice This can be defined as a negative attitude toward a social group and members of that group, usually based upon a faulty and inflexible generalization or stereotype (Van Oudenhoven & Willemsen, 1989) (*see* STEREOTYPING).

Modern social psychology theories for explaining prejudice include social identity theory, social categorization theory, ATTRIBUTION THEORY, and the contact hypothesis. These theories assume that prejudice underlies racism and DISCRIMINATION and focus on explaining the origins, functioning, and reduction of intergroup conflict (Van Oudenhoven & Willemsen, 1989) (*see* INTERGROUP RELATIONS).

The phenomenological approach of social identity and social categorization theory postulates that individuals depend on social group (e.g., men, women, blacks, whites, etc.) membership for their identity, and they tend to strive for a positively valued social identity (Tajfel, 1981). The evaluation of one's own group is determined with reference to specific other groups through social comparisons in terms of value laden-attributes and characteristics. Categorization and cognitive biases result in stereotypes and the mere categorization of persons into ingroup and outgroup membership is sufficient to affect interpersonal PERCEPTIONS of behavior. The solution to prejudice is a reduction in the salience of group boundaries.

Social attribution theory refers to how members of different social groups explain the behavior, outcomes of behavior, and the social conditions that characterize members of their own group (ingroup) and other (the outgroup) social groups (Hewstone, 1989, p. 25) (*see* FUNDAMENTAL ATTRIBUTION ERROR).

The contact hypothesis suggests that an increase in intergroup interaction will result in a reduction in prejudice under certain conditions. While its VALIDITY has been partially established in laboratory studies, there has been less support in field studies (Van Oudenhoven & Willemsen, 1989).

Theoretical controversy centers around the dominance of cognitive approaches to the neglect of structural and institutional influences (Van Oudenhoven & Willemsen, 1989). Pettigrew and Martin (1987) offer an approach that combines cognitive and structural elements of prejudice. Research also suggests that there are contradictions in the way individuals hold prejudiced attitudes and their subsequent behavior. Some scholars have proposed constructs that capture new forms of racism and the persistence of prejudice (*see* RACE). These constructs include symbolic racism, modern racism, and aversive racism, and identify a new form of racial prejudice composed of a blend of antiblack affect and the traditional moral values embodied in the Protestant ethic and egalitarian beliefs (Dovidio & Gaertner, 1986).

Much of the research on racial prejudice in organization settings can be found under the literature on discrimination. Additionally, there is a substantial body of literature that has demonstrated the relationship between social categorization and prejudiced behavior. The simple creation of group boundaries resulting in ingroup and outgroups can create prejudiced attitudes and behaviors. Individuals who are members of the ingroup tend to see outgroup members as more similar to one another and may think of them in stereotyped terms or evaluate them negatively.

See also **Attitude theory; Cognitive processes; Group norms.**

Bibliography

Dovidio, J. F. & Gaertner, S. L. (1986). *Prejudice, discrimination, and racism*. Orlando, FL: Academic Press.

Hewstone, M. (1989). Intergroup attribution: Some implications for the study of ethnic prejudice. In J. Van Oudenhoven & T. Willemsen (Eds), *Ethnic minorities: Social psychological perspectives* (pp. 25–42). Amsterdam: Swets & Zeitlinger.

Pettigrew, T. & Martin, J. (1987). Shaping the organizational context for Black American inclusion. *Journal of Social Issues*, **43**, 41–87.

Tajfel, H. (1981). *Human groups and social categories*. Cambridge, MA: Cambridge University Press.

Van Oudenhoven, J. P. & Willemsen, T. M. (Eds), (1989). *Ethnic minorities: Social psychological perspectives*. Amsterdam: Swets & Zeitlinger.

STELLA M. NKOMO

prisoners' dilemma This is a strategic interaction originally based on the story of two burglars who were caught, separated by the police, and offered the opportunity to confess and receive a reduced sentence – if their partner did not confess. This story provided the basic model for any number of situations where two (or more) parties' mutually cooperative payoffs exceed their mutually noncooperative payoffs but where each is tempted by larger, short-term individual outcomes if they do not cooperate. Argyris (1957) framed this problem organizationally as the CONFLICT between the person working for self versus working for the organization. If everyone works for the organization, it thrives. "Free riders," who work more for themselves, take advantage of others' organizational contributions and do not incur the costs of contributing (*see* SOCIAL LOAFING). With many free riders, organizations struggle and/or die. The basic prisoners' dilemma is inherent in most group interactions (*see* GROUP DYNAMICS), and explains the interest shown by researchers and theorists throughout the social sciences (anthropology, economics, political science, psychology, sociology, etc). The prisoners' dilemma can act as a model for competitive strategy (Porter, 1980), romance (Murnighan, 1991), energy conservation (Dawes, 1980), international politics (Poundstone, 1992), or many other interactions.

Axelrod has shown that the tit-for-tat strategy (*see* RECIPROCITY) can be a particularly effective response in repeated prisoners' dilemmas. By starting cooperatively and responding as one's counterpart has, this strategy *trains* others to be cooperative, so that all can benefit, by being both retaliatory and forgiving. Difficulties arise when others' choices are not easily identified as cooperative: Then more relaxed strategies (e.g., a tit for two tats) become necessary, even though they increase risk.

Research has shown that other factors can also increase cooperative solutions, including diminishing the temptation to defect (via payoff changes), information about the consequences of noncooperation (which may deter all but the most competitive party), cooperative personal VALUES (some people have strong drives toward cooperation), constant and effective COMMUNICATION (e.g., stressing morality), and the establishment of a group identity (by promoting the ingroup and its mutually cooperative benefits; Murnighan, 1991).

See also **Coalition formation; Game theory; Group norms; Cooperation; Risk taking**

Bibliography

Argyris, C. (1957). *Personality and organization*. New York: Harper.

Dawes, R. (1980). Social dilemmas. *Annual Review of Psychology*, **31**, 169–193.

Murnighan, J. K. (1991). *The dynamics of bargaining games*. Englewood Cliffs, NJ: Prentice-Hall.

Porter, M. (1980). *Competitive strategy*. Boston: Free Press.

Poundstone, W. (1992). *Prisoner's dilemma*. New York: Doubleday.

J. KEITH MURNIGHAN

privatization This is the sale of government-owned firms to private entities or cessation of provision of certain services by government in favor of their provision by private entities. The government may retain some control rights through general regulation of the firm's activities (e.g., in the privatization of utility companies), or by concluding individual contracts with private suppliers (e.g., to fund provision of certain social welfare services by private entities, often nonprofit organizations (*see* NOT-FOR-PROFIT ORGANIZATIONS).

Privatization occurs for a number of reasons. Where nationalization was motivated by the desire to expropriate owners of firms who collaborated with the Nazis during World War II, the motive for government ownership has expired. In economies that underwent transformation from plan to market, the need to control firms through direct ownership has evidently expired. In several industries critical to national security or which supplied services and products under conditions of nearly natural monopoly, technological changes in production and marketing, the increase in the size of markets due to improved communication and the lowering of barriers to trade, and the improved ability of governments to regulate private entities have combined to reduce the advantages of government ownership of firms (*see* GOVERNMENT AND BUSINESS). The extent to which these changes should call for privatization in various industries and countries is difficult to evaluate, but the belief that this may be so has gained widespread support among the governing parties in many countries.

The importance of the "belief factor" is particularly salient in the case of the evaluation of the relative performance of government-owned firms (GOFs) and conventional capitalist firms (CFs). Whereas during the period around World War II the main debate was on the role of markets versus plan as key determinants of economic performance, developments in economic and management theory called for increased emphasis on the organization of firms and their ownership. In particular, the development in the early 1970s of agency (or principal-agent) theory (*see* AGENCY THEORY), in combination with public choice theory, lead to the consolidation of the argument that GOFs are less efficient than CFs. The argument concerns the absence of an adequate principal in GOFs and proceeds as follows. Citizens have no interest in becoming experts in the affairs of GOFs because their individual returns are likely to be too low to merit the bother, and because their ability to influence matters is diluted by the multitude of voters. This leaves sufficient scope for politicians to pursue their interests related to GOFs, resulting in the exercise of insufficient control over management of these firms. As a result, management will be more lax, pursuing in turn their own objectives, taking it more easily in managing firms and in bargaining with their employees or getting them to work efficiently, thus generally running firms less in the interests of their owners – the citizenry – than they should or would if they were privately owned. The absence of tradable shares prevents the external control mechanism embedded in the stock exchange – the takeover threat – from working and disciplining management and compensating for the insufficient control by citizens and politicians. In addition, governments tend to employ GOFs for purposes that sometimes can be accomplished better through other policy means, such as increasing inefficiently the number of employees to achieve higher national employment levels, or employing individuals who cannot find gainful employment in the private sector.

There are those who doubt the general validity of this argument. They claim that GOFs will be less efficient than closely-held CFs where the owners are actively involved in control, and than publicly-traded CFs that operate in financially sophisticated environments where shares are traded on efficient stock exchanges. However, the stock markets of even most developed economies do not operate as effective arenas for control over the management of firms. Further, it is suggested that shareholders have their own incentives to free-ride and therefore may not exercise adequate control over management. Hence, all things considered, CFs may perform better or worse as compared with GOFs, especially if those selected to positions of management are well-trained management and are committed to the effective running of the GOFs. Such commitment may stem from IDEOLOGY, ordinary decency, or from perceived prospects of promotion in government and the private sector, and may be enhanced if the politicians behind them are substantially honest, are accountable to the citizenry, and exercise control over management.

The two opposing arguments have merit, and their relative weight cannot be determined in general. The evidence on comparative performance by GOFs is mixed: in samples that contain firms in multiple industries and several countries the efficiency of GOFs is often (but not always) lower than that of CFs, whereas in samples that include firms that produce a similar product (railway transport, cement, electric power) the differences mostly disappear and GOFs are found at times to be more efficient than their private counterparts.

In GOFs that produce marketable outputs, many organizational practices are similar to those employed in CFs, with the important exception of various incentive schemes connected to the distribution of shares to management or employees (*see* SHARE/EQUITY OWNERSHIP). In GOFs that earn a large share of their revenue from subsidies or government transfers or have significant nonfinancial goals, the feasibility of financial incentives is further weakened, and even tying part of remuneration to output may not be feasible. This places added importance on the selection of upper management. In addition, as compared with CFs, there is a tendency in GOFs to rely on administrative–bureaucratic means that substitute for profit-related measures. This manifests itself in greater incidence of rules, promotion ladders, monitoring, and HIERARCHY in general (*see* BUREAUCRACY).

See also **Governance and ownership; Government agencies; Organizational change**

Bibliography

Aharoni, Y. (1981). State and enterprise: An agent without principal. In L. P. Jones (Ed.), *Public enterprise in less developed countries*. Cambridge, UK: Cambridge University Press.

Ben-Ner A., Montias J. M. & Neuberger, E. (1993). Basic issues in organizations: A comparative perspective. *Journal of Comparative Economics*, **17**, no. 2, 207–242.

Boardman, A. & Vining, A. (1989). Ownership and performance in competitive environments: A comparison of the performance of private, mixed and state-owned enterprises. *Journal of Law and Economics*, **32**, 1–33.

Cakmak, E. H. & Zaim, O. (1992). Privatization and comparative efficiency of public and private enterprise in Turkey: The cement industry. *Annals of Public and Cooperative Economics*, **63**, no. 2, 271–284.

Rathgeb Smith, S. & Lipsky, M. (1993). *Nonprofits for hire: The welfare state in the age of contracting*. Cambridge, MA: Harvard University Press.

Vickers, J. & Yarrow, G. (1991). Economic perspectives on privatization. *Journal of Economic Perspectives*, **5**, no. 2, 111–132.

AVNER BEN-NER

problem solving *see* ACTION THEORY; DECISION MAKING

procedural justice *see* JUSTICE, PROCEDURAL

process consultation There is a subtle but important difference between process and content which is fundamental to process consultation (*see* PROCESS THEORY; CONTENT THEORY). Process refers to how something is done by an individual, a group, or an organization. For example, how goals are set or how conflicts are managed – who is involved, when, how, their actions, beliefs, and attitudes, their power, their influence, whom they represent, and so on. Content, on the other hand, is subject matter, the specifics, for example, of goals such as a market share target, or conflicts such as which of three marketing plans should be followed to reach a target. Process consultation posits that how something is done, process, determines the content, quality, and implementation of decisions. For example, a work group with a poor CONFLICT MANAGEMENT process will have difficulty confronting and solving its serious, work problems.

Process consultation consists of efforts to increase an organization's effectiveness (*see* ORGANIZATIONAL EFFECTIVENESS), with the aid of a process analysis consultant, by identifying faulty processes and then analyzing and improving them. Processes which may be diagnosed as faulty and which become targets of learning and change include COMMUNICATION – who communicates with whom, about what, when, arousing what EMOTIONS, who is ignored, who is interrupted – and other processes such as GOAL SETTING, task ROLES, maintenance roles (*see* TASK AND MAINTENANCE), problem solving, DECISION MAKING, LEADERSHIP styles (*see* MANAGERIAL STYLE), trust, conflict management, norms (*see* GROUP NORMS), interaction patterns, GROUP COHESIVENESS, ROLE CONFLICT, intergroup conflict (*see* INTERGROUP RELATIONS), SOCIALIZATION, CULTURE, POWER, INFLUENCE, and REWARD systems. Process consultation is used most often with individuals and groups although it applies to larger organizational units as well.

A primary goal of process consultation is to increase the client's process awareness and skills so that with coworkers s/he can analyze and improve processes and become less dependent on the consultant. The transfer of process analysis SKILLS to a client is best accomplished by using the joint-diagnosis consulting model. The client learns to see and solve process problems him/herself by participating in diagnosing process difficulties and generating a solution. In the joint diagnosis model, the client and consultant jointly gather data, diagnose the situation, define change goals, and design and implement change. This contrasts with the expert model of consulting, such as the conventional purchased services or doctor–patient relationship, in which the hired expert unilaterally gathers data, diagnoses the situation, and generates a solution and the client is expected to accept and use the hired expert's conclusions.

The knowledge and skills used in process consultation primarily come from the areas of GROUP DYNAMICS, SENSITIVITY TRAINING, leadership, ACTION RESEARCH, and ORGANIZATION DEVELOPMENT. Methods to describe and analyze a current process include observation of behavior in meetings, interviews, and other forms of data gathering, FEEDBACK, joint diagnosis, FORCE FIELD ANALYSIS, and sociotechnical analysis (*see* SOCIOTECHNICAL THEORY). Methods to facilitate change include modeling, in which the consultant or group leader exhibits the desired new behavior, simulations, exercises, COUNSELING, coaching, TEAM BUILDING, confrontation meetings, TRAINING, and OPEN SYSTEMS analysis.

Process consulting depends on a voluntary relationship between client and consultant. A manager who feels forced into process analysis becomes defensive and strongly resists learning because s/he is not prepared to examine his/her leadership or relationships with coworkers, subordinates, or superiors. The consulting relationship itself is a critical, changing process which client and consultant must continually review as goals and methods change and as the client's process skills increase. Client and consultant must develop a mutually trusting relationship which will facilitate the client's process learning and increased self-sufficiency.

See also **Change methods; Consultancy; Consultancy intervention methods; Interpersonal skills**

Bibliography

Schein, E. H. (1987). *Process consultation: Lessons for managers and consultants*. Reading, MA: Addison-Wesley.

Schein, E. H. (1988). *Process consultation: Its role in organization development*, (2nd edn). Reading, MA: Addison-Wesley.

DALE E. ZAND

process technology This refers to the TECHNOLOGY used to transform material inputs into outputs in an organization. It is usually contrasted with product technology, which refers to the knowhow embedded in a product or service, and administrative technology, which refers to the knowledge embedded in a firm's administrative routines. Often, these are intertwined; for example, an iron steamship represents a different product technology than does a wooden ship, and is made with different process technology (e.g., welding instead of carpentry).

Process technology has assumed importance in organizational research principally because a firm's process technology is thought to influence its structure (*see* CONTINGENCY THEORY). Woodward (1970), for example, showed that critical factors such as number of levels in a HIERARCHY, SPAN OF CONTROL, and the ratio of administrative to other employees systematically differed depending on whether a firm employed BATCH PRODUCTION, MASS PRODUCTION, or continuous production. Although evidence is mixed, achieving fit between process technology and ORGANIZATIONAL DESIGN structure may be one key to high performance (*see* ORGANIZATIONAL EFFECTIVENESS).

Many scholars suggest that ADVANCED MANUFACTURING TECHNOLOGY may revolutionize industry by permitting batch-like production in lots of one with the same economies found in mass production. This might allow most products to be customized for each different user, perhaps revolutionizing organizational structure and strategy.

See also **Automation; Organization and environment; Operations management; Business process re-engineering**

Bibliography

Piore, M. J. & Sabel C. F. (1984). *The second industrial divide: Possibilities for prosperity*. New York: Basic Books.

Woodward, J. (1970). *Industrial organization: Theory and practice*, (2nd edn). Oxford, UK: Oxford University Press.

PHILIP ANDERSON

process theory The term "process" is ubiquitous throughout social science; it has long been clear that processes have great potential as basic elements of the conceptualization and understanding of social life, at least equal to "events."

Mohr (1982) drew a distinction between "process theory" and "variance theory." A variance theory, typified by a regression equation, explains variance in one dimension with variance in others, so that scores on some outcome variable Y are a function of scores on a set of explanatory variables {X} (*see* STATISTICAL METHODS). For example, the degree of innovativeness is hypothesized to be explainable by variables indicating the degree of MOTIVATION to innovate and the resources available for INNOVATION.

The target of explanation in process theory is not a score on a variable but rather an encounter between two or more elements. It therefore demands a different kind of theorizing, one that is not as well understood. Perhaps the best-known process theory is Darwin's theory of the origin of species by natural selection. The THEORY consists primarily in illuminating that what is required to produce viable individuals and species is a probabilistic fit between characteristics of the individual and of the environment. The GARBAGE CAN MODEL of organizational choice (Cohen, March, & Olsen, 1963) is in the same genre, since it portrays the making of a decision as the probabilistic encounter of choice opportunities, problems, participants, and energy in certain balance (*see* DECISION MAKING). Any theory of success or failure would have to be similar, as would theories of a large number of other events of great interest.

Mohr (1982) also pointed out the category of "descriptive quasi-theory." The description involved is one of a process, taking place in identifiable stages over time, such as a process of organizational innovation or decision making. The idea of "theory" comes in with the claim that the particular description captures the essence of how the phenomenon generally proceeds or unfolds. Here, the target of explanation is not an event, as in the case of scores on variables or encounters between two or more elements, but a process itself.

What is critical is that variance theory and the two sorts of theory involving processes are quite distinct; they are not easily mixed together without muddle and confusion, although the tendency to combine them is common.

See also **Levels of analysis; Research design; Systems theory**

Bibliography

Cohen, M. D., March, J. G. & Olsen, J. P. (1972). A garbage can model of organizational choice. *Administrative Science Quarterly*, 17, (no. 1), 1–25.

Mohr, L. B. (1982). *Explaining organizational behavior: The limits and possibilities of theory and research*. San Francisco: Jossey-Bass.

LAWRENCE B. MOHR

productivity This term was originally used in the early 1900s by labor economists. By the 1970s, the term had come into much broader use and the issue of productivity became much more important, especially in the United States. American superiority in productivity was being threatened by other countries and this was seen as a major contributor to serious long-range economic problems. Continued productivity improvement/growth was seen as the solution to national economies and as having a positive impact either directly or indirectly on everyone's quality of life (*see* QUALITY OF WORKING LIFE). Because of this, productivity growth has become an issue of great social and political importance in all industrialized nations.

Defining "productivity" is a difficult task. Since the 1970s, behavioral scientists of many types have done a great deal of work in this area. One result has been a proliferation of definitions of "productivity." The term has been used to refer to individuals, groups, organizational units, entire organizations, industries, and nations. It has been used as a synonym for output, efficiency, MOTIVATION, individual performance (*see* PERFORMANCE, INDIVIDUAL), ORGANIZATIONAL EFFECTIVENESS, production, profitability, cost/effectiveness, COMPETITIVENESS, and work quality. Productivity measurement has been used interchangeably with PERFORMANCE APPRAISAL, management information systems, production capability assessment, quality control measurement, and the engineering throughput of a system.

However, the vast majority of definitions of "productivity" fall into three categories. The first is that productivity is a measure of outputs divided by inputs. Thus, the number of outputs generated such as refrigerators, potatoes, or university graduates are divided by the inputs used. Such inputs usually include raw materials, labor, energy, etc. Typically, both outputs and inputs are measured in terms of cost so that the two can be divided to form a ratio that is interpretable across different settings. This definition is used by most economists and by some behavioral scientists.

When all the input and output factors are included in the ratio, the resulting measure is termed "total factor productivity." When selected measures are used, the result is termed "partial factor productivity." The most common type of partial factor productivity measure is labor productivity where monetary value of outputs is divided by cost of labor used to produce the outputs.

The second definition is that productivity is a combination of efficiency and effectiveness. Efficiency in the productivity literature is the output/input measure used in the first definition. Effectiveness is the ratio of outputs relative to some standard or objective. For example, the number of trucks produced relative to a specific, quantitative goal is an effectiveness measure. Those taking the approach that productivity should include both efficiency and effectiveness argue that both are necessary for a complete definition of productivity.

The third type of definition is the most broad and essentially includes any characteristic that makes the organization function better. This approach includes efficiency and effectiveness, but also includes such factors as quality of output, work disruptions, ABSENTEEISM, TURNOVER, customer satisfaction, etc. It is important that anyone working in the area of productivity be aware that these different definitions exist. Some researchers and practitioners are very rigid in their choice of one of these definitions and do not accept that the other definitions are "productivity." Thus, for effective communication, it would be well to make sure that the same definition of "productivity" is being used by all.

There have been two major approaches to improving productivity. The first is through a change in TECHNOLOGY. Some economists argue that most or all major improvements in productivity can be traced to technology improvements. Behavioral scientists argue that the investment in new technology can only generate a reasonable return on investment if organizational personnel use it effectively.

In order to improve productivity, it is important to measure it, and measure it well. Productivity measurement is a very complex issue. The first step is to decide on the purpose of the measurement since that decision will affect how the measurement is done. One purpose in measuring productivity is to compare large aggregations of organizations to each other. Comparing national economies such as the United Kingdom with Japan or comparing the electronics industry to the automobile industry are examples of this purpose. Another purpose is to evaluate the overall productivity of individual organizations for comparison with each other or with some standard. A third purpose is as a management information system or CONTROL system. Here the focus is on a single organization and the measurement deals with the functioning of the human/technological system (*see* SOCIOTECHNICAL THEORY; SYSTEMS THEORY). Finally, productivity could be measured for use as a motivational tool. This is the typical purpose of the organizational behavior specialist. The objective is to improve productivity, and the assumption is that if individuals change their behavior appropriately, productivity will increase. Personnel are typically given FEEDBACK on the productivity measures with the assumption that such feedback will help produce the behaviors that will increase productivity. Research has indicated that such feedback can be very effective in improving productivity.

There are a large number of specific issues that must be considered in measuring productivity by the ORGANIZATIONAL BEHAVIOR specialist. These include insuring that all important aspects of the work are measured, having reliable and valid measures, using measures that the personnel have control over, and developing a measurement system that will be accepted by both managers and the people doing the actual work. These are more fully discussed in Campbell and Campbell (1988), Muckler (1982), Pritchard (1990), (1992), and Sink (1985).

A number of specific techniques for measuring productivity have been proposed. Those which focus on using productivity measures to help personnel improve their productivity are summarized by Pritchard (1992).

See also **Advanced manufacturing technology; Information technology; Total quality management; Automation**

Bibliography

Brief, A. P. (Ed.), (1984). *Productivity research in the behavioral and social sciences.* New York: Praeger.

Campbell, J. P. & Campbell, R. J. (Eds), (1988). *Productivity in organizations.* San Francisco: Jossey-Bass.

Kendrick, J. W. (1984). *Improving company productivity.* Baltimore: Johns Hopkins University Press.

Muckler, F. A. (1982). Evaluating productivity. In M. D. Dunnette & E. A. Fleishman (Eds), *Human performance and productivity*, (Vol. 1), *Human capability assessment* (pp. 13–47). Hillsdale, NJ: Erlbaum.

Pritchard, R. D. (1990). *Measuring and improving organizational productivity: A practical guide* (p. 248). New York: Praeger.

Pritchard, R. D. (1992). Organizational productivity. In M. D. Dunnette & L. M. Hough (Eds), *Handbook of Industrial/Organizational Psychology*, (2nd edn, vol. 3). Palo Alto, CA: Consulting Psychologists Press.

Sink, D. S. (1985). *Productivity management: Planning, measurement and evaluation, control and improvement.* New York: Wiley.

ROBERT D. PRITCHARD

professional bureaucracy *see* BUREAUCRACY; ORGANIZATIONAL DESIGN; PROFESSIONALS IN ORGANIZATIONS

professionalism In its everyday sense professionalism is used broadly to convey notions of technical competence, a concern to meet high standards of quality in the product or service and high ethical standards of behavior (*see* COMPETENCIES). It also has a more specialized meaning to refer to the behavior of occupational groups with the STATUS or aspirations of the established professions. Current dilemmas which raise doubts about how meaningful the concept of professionalism is include:

(i) a general decline in the social status of professions and semiprofessions and a reduction in the degree of deference accorded to them by clients, probably because of the wider access to knowledge through education systems and increased social mobility;
(ii) publicized failures to maintain appropriate ethical and technical standards (*see* BUSINESS ETHICS);
(iii) professionalism and commercial or cost efficiency pressures, particularly a problem for public (nonprofit) sector professionals resulting in efforts to control their decision-making autonomy through the introduction of tighter budgetary systems and resource allocation; and
(iv) the persistence of competition for professional jurisdictions among disparate occupational groups.

Notwithstanding these issues, professional projects continue because of the material and prestige benefits professional status bestows (Larson, 1977). Professionalism is arguably evolving from a term which connotes attention to client interests above material gain to one which refers to high technical expertise in solving certain types of client problem.

See also **Not-for-profit organizations; Occupations; Knowledge workers; Labor markets; Professionals in organizations**

Bibliography

Larson M. (1977). *The rise of professionalism: A sociological analysis*. Berkeley: University of California Press.

TIM MORRIS

professionals in organizations A common trend in the employment patterns of professionals has been the move away from self-employment to the STATUS of salaried employees in organizations. This has raised questions about the influence of bureaucratic controls on professional AUTHORITY, and the effects of organizational goals on professionals' CAREER paths, work goals, and sources of satisfaction and COMMITMENT. Latterly, it has also led to theorizing about the effects of increasing numbers of professional employees on the structures and goals of employing organizations.

From the professional's point of view, subordination to the organization's goals and CONTROL by a management HIERARCHY raise questions about goal congruency and career paths. Some professionals (e.g., engineers; city planners) have to confront the problem that their expertise on its own offers limited scope for career progression and that the adoption of managerial responsibilities is necessary to acquire higher-organizational status and REWARDS. This, in turn, leads to the risk that expertise becomes outdated because it is not applied to contemporary problems.

Certain professions have found the integration with managerial functions much less problematic. The classic contrast between "cosmopolitan" professionals and "local" nonprofessionals (Gouldner, 1957) has to be tempered to the extent that some professional groups have developed within large bureaucratic organizations (*see* BUREAUCRACY), for instance, management accountants, personnel, and purchasing specialists. These occupations are likely to see less distinction between organizational and professional interests and would expect to practice their profession within an organizational context. Indeed, their professional status complements their managerial authority: the dominance of accounting in many areas of business in the United Kingdom and North America is a case in point (Armstrong, 1993).

Nonetheless, the notion of a distinction between professional and organizational interests has prompted a stream of research on professionals' work satisfaction (*see* JOB SATISFACTION) and commitment. Although professionals' alienation from their organizations and their work is cited as a frequent managerial problem, other work has concluded that professionals are able to reconcile organizational and professional interests (Morrow & Wirth, 1989).

Research has also been concerned with the ways in which features of bureaucratic organization impinge upon professional authority. At issue here is the compatibility of a bureaucratic system where authority is derived from hierarchical position and control is exerted through procedures and rules, with the self-regulating aspects of the professional's work, the importance of authority based on expertise and the emphasis of collegial decision making (*see* SELF-REGULATION). While the assumption of Parsons and others was that the bureaucratic model was incompatible with professional norms, empirical research suggests that organizations have rather successfully combined the two systems in the hybrid organization form, the professional bureaucracy, in which control is relatively decentralized and is balanced between powerful groups of professionals (Montagna, 1968; Smigel, 1964) (*see* DECENTRALIZATION). Empirical work has also shown how different forms of professional bureaucracy may evolve within a single organizational field and that these differences in structure may have important influences upon the process of STRATEGIC MANAGEMENT (Hardy, 1990).

Nonetheless, CONFLICT between professionals and managers does seem to be an endemic feature of the professional bureaucracy, particularly where managers have the POWER to impose bureaucratic goals on professionals, supervise their activities, and evaluate their performance. A common form of CONFLICT RESOLUTION is to promote professionals to senior managerial roles but as this does not dissolve the structural differences underlying the professional/managerial conflict, success depends upon considerable personal competence on the part of the professional-cum-manager.

An associated area of debate about the influence of bureaucracy on professionals concerns the issue of deprofessionalization. The line of argument has been that professions are deskilled in forfeiting the rights to determine the objectives, methods, and evaluative criteria applying to their work, but on empirical grounds a generalized deprofessionalization thesis is unsustainable: historical analysis would show much greater variation in the experience of specific professions and professional subgroups (*see* JOB DESKILLING).

Much of the foregoing discussion has reflected the concern with the influence of bureaucracy on professionals. More recently, this relationship has been examined from the other direction, asking how professionals may influence organizations. In particular, the work of the neoinstitutional school of sociology has argued that professionals are an important source of isomorphism or organizational homogeneity (*see* INSTITUTIONAL THEORY). Isomorphism refers to the adoption of similar structures and systems by organizations operating in a particular field. Neoinstitutionalists argue that isomorphism occurs because of custom and taken-for-granted assumptions about appropriate structures or through imposition of externally derived standards and values rather than competitive pressures. The adoption of similar "professional" personnel systems of RECRUITMENT or reward by different organizations would be examples of such isomorphic influences (DiMaggio & Powell, 1991). While there is some empirical work examining how isomorphism occurs (*see*, e.g., the work of Tolbert (1983) on the recruitment practices of law firms) this is an area which requires further enquiry.

See also **Managerial behavior; Organizational design; Knowledge-workers; Occupations; Labor markets**

Bibliography

Armstrong, P. (1993). Professional knowledge and social mobility: Postwar changes in the knowledge base of management accounting. *Work Employment and Society*, 7, no. 1, 1–21.

DiMaggio, P. & Powell, W. (1991). The iron cage revisited: Institutional isomorphism and collective rationality in organizational fields. In W. Powell & P. DiMaggio (Eds), *The new institutionalism and organizational analysis* (pp. 63–82). Chicago: University of Chicago Press.

Gouldner, A. (1957). Cosmopolitans and locals: Towards an analysis of latent social roles. *Administrative Science Quarterly*, 2, 281–306; 444–480.

Hardy, C. (1990). Strategy and context: Retrenchment in Canadian universities. *Organization Studies*, **11**, no. 12, 207–237.

Montagna, P. (1968). Professionalization and bureaucratization in large professional organizations. *American Journal of Sociology*, **74**, 138–145.

Morrow P. & Wirth, R. (1989). Work commitment among salaried professionals. *Journal of Vocational Behaviour*, **34**, 40–56.

Smigel, E. (1964). *The Wall Street lawyer: Professional organization man?*. New York: Free Press.

Tolbert, P. (1983). Institutional sources of organizational culture in major law firms. In L. G. Zucker (Ed.), *Institutional patterns and organizations:*

Culture and environment (pp. 101–113). Cambridge, MA: Ballinger.

TIM MORRIS

profit sharing This is a formal plan to share a portion of a corporation's profits with most, if not all the employees. In the United States actual registration of profit-sharing plans takes place via the Securities and Exchange Commission (SEC) and special tax laws have been written to cover profit sharing as a defined benefit if it is used as deferred compensation for RETIREMENT purposes. Often confused, profit sharing and GAINSHARING are not the same. While both contribute to income, they are not similar. For the most part, profit sharing is a financial plan. Almost always, it pays annually. It is a measure of financial profitability and not necessarily performance PRODUCTIVITY. Thus, gainsharing could have deficits all year long and profit sharing could pay huge dividends if a financial windfall befell a corporation (yet employees neither worked harder nor increased their skills).

See also **Bonus payments; Payment systems; Rewards; Performance related pay**

Bibliography

Kruse, D. (1993). *Profit sharing: Does it make a difference?* Kalamazoo, MI: Upjohn Institute for Employment Research.

BRIAN GRAHAM-MOORE

project management Some kinds of tasks are completed in a short period of time, making permanent organizational units unwieldy and unnecessary. Examples include film making and commercial construction. In these instances, managers rely on project structures, where individuals and resources are assembled temporarily, their task is completed, then the unit is disbanded. They are important to managers who must deal with nonroutine tasks where people work together on a temporary basis (*see* MATRIX ORGANIZATION). A project's entire duration is by definition short compared with an organization's traditional activities. Success therefore depends on managers' SKILLS over a compressed life-cycle of venturing, learning, administering, and disassembling the project upon completion (Ford & Randolf, 1992).

Project management requires recognition that tasks are temporary and rather unique. Where managers see the contrasts with permanent organizations, they can solve operational issues effectively. Venturing calls for managers to champion their projects, acquire resources, and assemble them into a structure. In venturing, top-echelon support and focused but flexible management are key factors (*see* JOINT VENTURES).

The agenda for project administration is influenced by time pressures and by ambiguity concerning AUTHORITY relationships (Boal & Bryson, 1987). First, even for companies with extensive experience, each project is unique. Without the continuity that defines permanent organizations, managers must be attuned to an extraordinary amount of learning (*see* ORGANIZATIONAL LEARNING). Success begins with managers whose needs and abilities are suited to unique, temporary situations (*see* PERSONALITY). With care, familiar methods might be used in new situations: both differences and similarities must be understood. Specialization in a function or market helps, so does recognizing and responding to new conditions. Finally, if settings and parties change over different projects, then issues associated with one-time contracting may arise. Managers might anticipate opportunism and asymmetric information since contracts are not repeated (*see* AGENCY THEORY) (Harrison & Harrell, 1993). REPUTATION is therefore important in project management. Contractual precautions (e.g., bonding or completion bonuses) can also be taken. Additionally, projects are typically time-sensitive. So long as they are not yet complete, opportunity costs are absorbed, and benefits may be deferred. Scheduling key events and maintaining time-lines are familiar problems, and established techniques can help. Many are available in the form of software applications. PERT and Gantt charts are examples.

Authority and responsibility lines are complicated since projects are typically staffed with individuals who have different organizational homes, incentives, and orientations. Among the responses found in the project management literature are that project managers can take the role of facilitator. They must identify means to cooperate, formally or otherwise, with functional managers. Awareness, anticipation, and NEGOTIATION are all components of managing COOPERATION (Bryson & Bromiley, 1993; Pinto, Pinto, & Prescott, 1993).

Natural consequences of even successful projects – disestablishing the project structure and detaching personnel – call for careful implementation. Contracting is more complex, since future transactions are not the incentive they are in permanent relationships, for example with personnel and procurement. For instance, performance and morale suffer where personnel leave early, anticipating a project's end. Disestablishing a project starts before the task is complete. Incentives and sanctions, outplacement assistance, diligence around contract completion, and managing contingencies all increase chances for success.

See also **Collateral organization; Contract; Organizational design; Innovation**

Bibliography

Boal, K. & Bryson, J. (1987). Representation, testing, and policy implications of planning processes. *Strategic Management Journal*, **8**, 211–231.

Bryson, H. & Bromiley, P. (1993). Critical factors affecting the planning and implementation of major projects. *Strategic Management Journal*, **14**, (5), 319–337.

Ford, R. & Randolph, W. (1992). Cross-functional structures: A review and integration of matrix organization and project management. *Journal of Management*, **18**, (2), 267–294.

Harrison, P. & Harrell, A. (1993). Impact of adverse selection on managers' project evaluation decisions. *Academy of Management Journal*, **36**, (3), 635–643.

Pinto, M., Pinto, J. & Prescott, J. (1993). Antecedents and consequences of project team cross-functional cooperation. *Management Science*, **39**, (10), 1281–1297.

MICHAEL LAWLESS

projection The process of ascribing to someone else one's own impulses, wishes, desires, or dispositions. Projection is often an individual's unconscious strategy for expelling undesirable impulses or personal failures and attributing these to others. This primitive defense mechanism accomplishes the avoidance of personal responsibility. It is a way of denying that one possesses these undesirable tendencies oneself. Projective processes are commonly a part of paranoid delusions whereby individuals, through blaming others, convince themselves that people are plotting against them.

For example, the director of the sales department of a robotics firm was accusing the head of marketing of trying to eliminate his job. As could be predicted his accusations led to a serious deterioration in the atmosphere between the two departments. The truth of the matter was, however, quite different. It was the sales director who had been responsible for starting the process. Somewhat less than a year before he had lobbied the president of the firm to put him in charge for both sales and marketing. But his effort to push this kind of change through had failed. Now, it seemed, he was taking a defensive stand, projecting what he had wanted to do himself. He blamed the head of marketing for doing the same thing to him.

See also **Organizational neurosis; Personality; Mental health; Trust**

Bibliography

Kets de Vries, M. F. R. & Miller, D. (1984). *The neurotic organization*. New York: Harper Business.

MANFRED KETS DE VRIES

promotion *see* CAREER TRANSITIONS; SUCCESSION PLANNING; TOURNAMENT PROMOTION

prospectors *see* STRATEGIC TYPES

prospect theory This modification of expected utility theory was developed to predict and explain patterns of choices that appear to be incompatible with the theory. One such pattern occurs when managers persist in committing resources to a risky and questionable project in an attempt to recoup prior invested costs. This tendency to consider "sunk costs" as relevant violates the expected utility theory principle that prior losses should be ignored in risky DECISION MAKING (*see* RISK TAKING).

According to prospect theory, choice among risky alternatives, or prospects, is influenced by the magnitudes as well as the probabilities of outcomes. Outcomes are defined and evaluated as positive or negative deviations (gains or losses) from a neutral reference point (normally the status quo). Gains and losses are typically evaluated according to an S-shaped value function that is concave above the reference point and convex below it. This value function implies that the displeasure of losing a given amount of a resource (e.g., money) is greater than the pleasure associated with winning the same amount (*see* REWARDS). The function also implies contrasting preferences in situations of gains versus losses. Individuals will tend to prefer a sure gain over a probabilistic gain of equal expected value, but will prefer a probabilistic loss over a sure loss of equal expected value. Thus, in general, a sure gain of $10,000 is preferred to a 0.5 chance to win $20,000, but a 0.5 chance of losing $20,000 is preferred to a sure loss of $10,000.

Prospect theory distinguishes two phases in the choice process: editing and evaluation. In the editing phase, the individual cognitively organizes and reformulates the prospects to simplify choice. In the evaluation phase, the individual evaluates the edited prospects by, in effect, multiplying the value of their outcomes by their respective decision weights. The prospect with the highest overall subjective value is then chosen.

Prospect theory has several implications for decision making under risk. The most important of these follow from the notion that because gains and losses are evaluated relative to a neutral reference point, any factors that affect the placement of that point can influence risky choice (*see* RISKY-SHIFT). For example, the way in which prospects are presented, or "framed," can influence the reference point an individual adopts, and therefore his or her choices. A set of prospects framed in terms of losses will elicit risk-taking, whereas the identical set of prospects framed in terms of gains will elicit risk-aversion. Thus a proposed 3 percent raise in wages may be framed as a gain, if the current wage rate is used as the reference point, or as a loss, if the projected inflation rate of 5 percent is used as the reference point. A labor union member will be more inclined to reject the proposed raise and support the risky alternative of striking for higher wages if the proposed 3 percent raise is framed as a loss. Numerous factors can influence the placement of the reference point, including prior losses or gains, social norms, comparison with other individuals, and goals or aspiration levels (*see* SOCIAL COMPARISON).

In organizations, observed patterns of decision making under risk are consistent with prospect theory predictions. For example, firms with returns above a target level tend to be risk-averse; those with returns below a target level tend to be risk-seeking. The aforementioned "sunk cost" effect, in which the decision maker risks additional resources in order to recoup prior losses, is likely to occur when the decision maker retains his or her initial aspiration level as a reference point. For example, consider a brand manager who has set a high target return for a new product that has been developed at great cost. If he retains this target level in the face of a poor reception of the product by consumers, the manager will prefer to risk additional resources (e.g., in advertising) on the product, rather than withdraw the product from the market and thereby accept the prior costs as a loss. In sum, although some aspects of prospect theory remain to be investigated, the theory appears able to account for a wide range of individual and organizational choice behavior under risk.

See also **Organizational economics; Strategic management; Negotiation; Game theory; Prisoners' dilemma; Behavioral decision research**

Bibliography

Bazerman, M. H. (1994). *Judgment in managerial decision making*, (3rd edn). New York: Wiley.

Fiegenbaum, A. (1990). Prospect theory and the risk-return association: An empirical examination in 85 industries. *Journal of Economic Behavior and Organization*, **14**, 187–204.

Kahneman, D. & Tversky, A. (1979). Prospect theory: An analysis of decision under risk. *Econometrica*, **47**, 263–291.

Osborn, R. N. & Jackson, D. H. (1988). Leaders, riverboat gamblers, and purposeful unintended consequences in the management of complex, dangerous technologies. *Academy of Management Journal*, **31**, 924–947.

Tversky, A. & Kahneman, D. (1981). The framing of decisions and the psychology of choice. *Science*, **211**, 453–458.

Whyte, G. (1986). Escalating commitment to a course of action: A reinterpretation. *Academy of Management Review*, 11, 311–321.

ARIEL S. LEVI

psychoanalysis/psychodynamics *see* INDIVIDUAL DIFFERENCES; ORGANIZATIONAL NEUROSIS; PERSONALITY

psychological contract As with any other form of CONTRACT, the concept of the psychological contract implies an agreement between parties whereby each commits to future actions. These actions are seen as a form of exchange between the parties: if you do this, I will do that. The word "psychological" is used in contrast with formal legal contracts, especially in employment. The psychological contract has thus come to mean those aspects of the employment relationship between organization and employee over and above the legal requirements. However, "psychological" in this context also carries the connotation of perception. Psychological contracts are in the eye of the beholder.

The concept was first used by Argyris (1960), who emphasized that many psychological contracts were implicit in nature, and that considerable benefits were to be gained for both parties if they were made explicit. For Argyris, the employment relationship as a whole was interpretable as a psychological contract.

The parties to the psychological contract may differ in their perceptions of its terms. There may be ambiguity about what each has agreed to do or when and how they will do it. There may even be ambiguity about whether a psychblogical contract exists in the first place; for example, a temporary worker employed on strictly formal terms of employment might believe a CAREER was on offer. Moreover, this ambiguity may not itself be perceived; each party may believe that the other shares exactly the same view of the contract as they hold themselves. This may even be true if the psychological contract has been made verbally explicit: "We will develop you further if you stay with us for a reasonable period after initial training." What does "develop" imply? What is a "reasonable period?"

The scope for disagreement about the nature and the fulfillment of the psychological contract is therefore considerable. There are, perhaps, three mitigating factors. First, custom and practice in the organization or sector; for example, in the banking and finance sector until 10 years ago, the universal assumption was of a security-for-loyalty contract. Second, general social NORMS, such as keeping agreements and RECIPROCITY, can support the contract. Third, there is evidence that there is considerable agreement among reasonable third parties as to what the contract is and whether it is fair.

Why is the concept of current importance? As the social, economic, political, and business environments change ever more rapidly, so do organizations in their efforts to keep pace. Changes in ORGANIZATIONAL DESIGN, processes, and personnel imply changes in the nature of the psychological contracts operating (*see* ORGANIZATIONAL RESTRUCTURING). Partly as a consequence of environmental change, organizations are determined to optimize the use of their so-called human resources to achieve business objectives (*see* HUMAN RESOURCES MANAGEMENT). In an effort to achieve such optimization, they expect more and more from their employees. They even try to alter the fundamental VALUES and assumptions of their workforce by means of culture change programs (*see* ORGANIZATION DEVELOPMENT; ORGANIZATIONAL CHANGE; ORGANIZATIONAL CULTURE). Furthermore, especially during the recent global recession, demanning, delayering, and casualization of labor have increased. By way of response, individuals have increasingly seen their employment and their careers as entirely their own affair, and their employability as their main asset.

If employment becomes more an organizational career than a job, a contract becomes more *relational* than *transactional*. In other words, specific agreements of exchange (e.g., wage rates for overtime) give way to more general exchanges based on TRUST and reliance. Where there is a long delay between formation and fulfillment of the psychological contract (as, e.g., with the promise of CAREER DEVELOPMENT by the organization) then trust that the bargain will be fulfilled is of the essence. In relational contracts, the elements of the bargain are not agreed independently of each other. Rather, there is a general exchange of support, the social and emotional nature of which has often been likened to family or ORGANIZATIONAL CITIZENSHIP. The good family member and the good citizen will go the extra mile, beyond the call of duty.

The corollary is clear. Just as both parties invest much in a relational contract, so the costs are greater when that relationship breaks up. When promised promotion is withheld or JOB SECURITY shattered by compulsory REDUNDANCY, strong emotional reactions to the perceived violation of trust may result. If the relational contract is broken but the individual remains in employment, they may contribute less than before. It is not merely that the perceived terms of the contract have been broken, it also is *how* they are broken that concerns. People made redundant often express more anger about how they were told than about the redundancy itself. In theoretical terms, they feel that procedural as well as distributive injustice has been done them (*see* JUSTICE, DISTRIBUTIVE; JUSTICE, PROCEDURAL).

While the concept of the psychological contract and its implications appears to be relevant and powerful, there is relatively little empirical research directly aimed at testing its predictions. What research there is has been well summarized by Rousseau. It is mostly concerned with demonstrating that expectations of reciprocal exchange of both a transactional and a relational nature do exist in employees' minds; and that external observers are capable of agreeing what the contract is, and how equitable it appears (*see* EQUITY THEORY).

While the concept of the psychological contract is fruitful, there remain at least two issues which need to be addressed. First, if the contract is between the individual and the organization, who exactly is "the organization?" A recruiter might promise training for which the recruit's line manager will not release them. A professional mentor offers technical development, while the HR Director expects cross-functional job change. Different people representing "the organization" have different expectations regarding the terms of the contract. A response is to argue that this is all part of the AMBIGUITY inherent in the contract. However, this still leaves the identity of the parties incompletely determined.

The second issue relates to POWER. For the idea of contract to have any validity, the parties have to be reasonably commensurate in the power that each wields. Otherwise, there is a degree of dependency which prevents bargaining between free and equal partners. In particular, where there is mainly a buyer's labor market, as during recession, power is clearly with the organization. Unequal contracts may result, with the organization expecting more and more COMMITMENT for less and less security or prospects.

See also **Career theory; Organizational culture; Exchange relations; Joining-up process; Socialization**

Bibliography

Argyris, C. (1960). *Understanding organizational behavior*. Homewood, IL: Dorsey.

Greenberg, J. (1990). Organizational justice: Yesterday, today, and tomorrow. *Journal of Management*, **16**, 399–432.

Handy, C. (1985). *The future of work*. Oxford, UK: Basil Blackwell.

Herriot, P. (1992). *The career management challenge*. London: Sage.

Kanter, R. M. (1989). *When giants learn to dance*. New York: Simon & Schuster.

Rousseau, D. M. & Anton, R. (1991). Fairness and implied contract obligations in job terminations: The role of contributions, promises and performance. *Journal of Organisational Behavior*, **12**, 287–299.

Rousseau, D. M. & Parks, J. M. (1993). The contracts of individuals and organizations. In L. L. Cummings & B. M. Staw (Eds), *Research in organizational behaviour*, (vol. 15, pp. 1–43). Greenwich, CT: JAI Press.

Weick, K. E. & Berlinger, L. A. (1988). Career improvisations in self-designing organisations. In M. B. Arthur, D. T. Hall & B. S. Lawrence (Eds), *Handbook of Career Theory*. New York: Cambridge University Press.

PETER HERRIOT

psychological testing A psychological test is a procedure for the evaluation of psychological functions. The distinction is sometimes made between tests of maximum performance and tests of habitual performance; the former refer to tests of intellectual abilities, the latter to personality measures (*see* PERSONALITY TEST-

ING). People may display their maximum performance on intellectual tests, but whether they will achieve equivalent levels on a day-to-day basis may depend on PERSONALITY factors, which may tell us more about their habitual performance. Within the category of intellectual measures (also referred to as Cognitive tests), a differentiation is sometimes made between tests of Ability and of Aptitude; the former assessing existing capabilities, the latter assessing the individual's potential to acquire specific SKILLS and knowledge needed to perform particular kinds of work (Anastasi, 1990).

An effective psychological test (also called Psychometric Tests) must possess five key attributes (Toplis, Dulewicz, & Fletcher, 1991):

RELIABILITY. This means that it is consistent in the results that it gives. Most tests are seeking to measure stable characteristics of the individual, and a test of, for example, reasoning ability would be of no value if it gave widely differing scores for the same group of people from one week to the next.

Reliability is not sufficient; a test might be consistent in the scores it yields, but still not measure what it claims to – which means the concept of VALIDITY.

Validity. This is the most fundamental attribute of a sound test. A test has validity if it measures what it purports to measure, but to establish validity is a complex matter. Because a test has Face Validity, i.e., it looks as if it measures what it sets out to, does not prove anything. Normally, validity evidence is expressed in terms of empirically established relationships with external criteria, for example, showing that scores on a test of numerical reasoning correlate with success in accountancy examinations. Such evidence can be obtained by correlating test scores with existing measures of performance (Concurrent Validation) or with measures of performance taken at a future date (Predictive Validation).

Objective Scoring. Tests are scored by machine or hand according to a fixed marking system. In other words, the feelings or judgments of the person doing the scoring do not affect the results (in contrast, say, to examinations).

Standardized Administration. This ensures that all candidates receive the same instructions and take the tests in as near identical conditions as possible.

Appropriate Norms. A person's score on a test is only meaningful when interpreted against a spread of scores and norms for a particular group. For the comparison and interpretation to be sound, the group against which the individual's score is viewed must be appropriate; graduates compared with graduates, senior managers with other senior managers, and so on.

These attributes are not easily established, and the development of new psychological tests is a slow, methodical, and quite scientific process. Tests may take many forms, but the most common are essentially paper-and-pencil tests (or their equivalent administered on a computer). The use of tests has become increasingly popular for selection and ASSESSMENT in employment settings (*see* SELECTION METHODS). One reason for this is evidence of their validity (*see* Robertson & Kinder (1993), for a discussion of this topic); for cognitive tests, correlations with external criteria average around 0.50–0.60, for modern personality measures around 0.25–0.40, compared to the average interview correlation of 0.10–0.20 (where 0 equates with no relationship between assessment and criterion, and 1.0 with perfect prediction). In the United States, where tests were first used on a wide scale, EQUAL OPPORTUNITIES legislation temporarily put a brake on their application, though the problems in this context do seem largely to have been overcome. In the United Kingdom and the rest of Europe, their popularity has been a more recent phenomenon, but deployment of tests is clearly growing (Shackleton & Newell, 1991). They are used in initial screening of candidates, as part of ASSESSMENT CENTERS, in promotion assessment, for in-depth assessment of senior management candidates, and for individual development and TEAM BUILDING purposes.

There are many issues that surround test use, and it is a topic which often engenders strong feelings, not least because people are often poorly informed on what is quite a complex topic. Some of the main issues fall under four headings:

(1) *Conceptual Basis*. The nature of human personality and intelligence (*see* INTELLIGENCE TESTING; INDIVIDUAL DIFFERENCES) is open to

analysis from differing perspectives, and their conceptualization in psychological testing is not universally accepted; hence the accusation that intelligence tests simply measure the ability to do intelligence tests.

(2) *Test Quality*. There are literally thousands of psychological tests available, and new ones appear frequently, often marketed with considerable sophistication, which is not necessarily matched by the quality of the test itself. Tests which appear quick, cheap, and easy to use generally offer illusory benefits. Any test should be evaluated against the five attributes listed above; in particular, it should have documented evidence of its reliability and validity. Its relevance to the organization's needs, should be assessed against alternatives tests or other assessment methods.

(3) *Misuse of Tests*. Even where a test is well constructed, there is no guarantee that it will be applied correctly. The TRAINING and competence of those using tests is difficult to control, and different countries have adopted different solutions, though none is perfect. In some European countries, attempts are made to restrict tests to qualified psychologists, whereas in the United Kingdom and the United States, tests are more widely available to anyone who has gone through an approved course. Incompetent use of tests is still common, however.

(4) *Ethical Considerations*. These range from issues about candidate FEEDBACK (should they get it, what is the best way to give it) on test results to the danger of GENDER and ethnic bias in test scores.

See also **Human resource management; Performance appraisal; Recruitment**

Bibliography

Anasatasi, A. (1990). *Psychological testing* (6th edn). New York: Macmillan.

Robertson, I. T. & Kinder, A. (1993). Personality and job competences: The criterion-related validity of some personality variables. *Journal of Occupational and Organizational Psychology*, **66**, 225–244.

Shackleton, V. J. & Newell, S. (1991). Management selection: A comparative survey of methods used in top British and French companies. *Journal of Occupational Psychology*, **64**, 23–36.

Toplis, J., Dulewicz, V. & Fletcher, C. (1991). *Psychological testing: A manager's guide*, (2nd edn). London: Institute of Personnel Management.

CLIVE FLETCHER

public scrutiny Research on public scrutiny considers the consequences enjoyed or suffered by people and organizations that try to operate under the bright, and sometimes harsh, spotlight of public attention. Unchecked scrutiny is present when a person or organization encounters constant:

(1) attention from others;
(2) performance evaluation by others;
(3) interruptions from others;
(4) questions about past, current, and future actions, along with pressure to explain the reasons for these actions; and
(5) advice, especially unsolicited advice.

Little research has explicitly examined scrutiny in organizations explicitly, but related psychological studies suggest that, if unchecked, consequences include less CREATIVITY and learning, more perseverance at planned and ongoing activities, frequent setbacks in ongoing tasks, and devoting more resources to managing impressions (*see* IMPRESSION MANAGEMENT) about plans and actions and less resources to other aspects of planning and acting.

People and organizations facing intense public scrutiny often develop defenses to reduce its negative consequences. Individual defenses include limiting interactions with purveyors of scrutiny, using vague and innocuous platitudes when answering questions, and being boring. Structural defenses implied by INSTITUTIONAL THEORY include decoupling people in visible symbolic roles from people who accomplish the organization's primary tasks and adopting visible and socially desirable procedures and structures that have little effect on the organization's core activities. Other defenses include using gatekeepers to screen purveyors of scrutiny and ostracizing those who ask about or reveal unflattering organizational or individual actions.

See also **Social facilitation; Corporate social responsibility; Stakeholders; Organization and environment**

Bibliography

Sutton, R. I. & Galunic, D. C. (1994). *The consequences of intense public scrutiny for leaders and organizations*. Dallas, TX: Academy of Management Meetings.

Tetlock, P. (1991). The impact of accountability on judgment and choice: Toward a social contingency model. *Advances in Experimental Social Psychology*, **25**, 331–376.

ROBERT I. SUTTON

punctuated equilibrium This phrase expresses a view of change as an alternation between relatively long periods when things stay basically the same (equilibrium), with relatively short periods of metamorphic change (punctuation). The term "punctuated equilibrium" comes from the field of biological evolution. Eldredge and Gould (1972) proposed the concept as an alternative to the dominant, Darwinian "gradualist" view that new species emerge through the smooth, gradual accumulation of insensibly small changes. Without disputing Darwin's central evolutionary mechanisms, variation, and selection, Eldredge and Gould argued that the punctuated equilibrium concept better fits the fossil record, where life forms are stable for long periods, and change appears abruptly, not gradually. Taken more broadly, the punctuational and gradualist views constitute contrasting PARADIGMS, with different implications for studying, interpreting, predicting, and planning change.

To understand this concept, and how it differs from gradualism, it is important to appreciate the close link between equilibrium and punctuation. Each derives from the same central feature of systems that exhibit punctuated equilibrium: deep structure. Entities with deep structure (e.g., a living cell versus a pile of sand, or a gymnastics class versus random playground activity) share two characteristics:

(1) they have differentiated parts; and
(2) the parts exchange resources with the environment in ways that both maintain, and are controlled by, this differentiation (*see* Prigogine & Stengers, 1984, pp. 154 and 287).

Punctuated equilibriums occur because such interdependence of parts and working mechanisms makes a system tenaciously self-reinforcing. Deep structure persists and actively limits change during equilibrium periods; in punctuational periods, deep structure disassembles, reconfigures, and enforces wholesale transformation.

Sport provides an illustrative METAPHOR. The deep structure of a sport, for example basketball, is its interdependent system of basic rules and court design. Equilibrium is like a game in play. The term indicates neither lack of variation nor tranquility. Each match is unique; teams play well or disastrously; their memberships change; they play in different cities. Much incremental change and activity can occur, yet the sport, its deep structure intact, will still be basketball. If the baskets were to be removed, however, the rules and court would stop working as an internally coherent system. Such an action would dismantle the game's deep structure, triggering punctuational change. If a central element of a system's deep structure is altered, the ramifications cascade to affect everything depending on that element.

Punctuated Equilibrium in Organizational Theories

Punctuational theories pertinent to ORGANIZATIONAL BEHAVIOR have appeared in several fields and LEVELS OF ANALYSIS. Examples range from Kuhn's (1970) distinction between normal science and scientific revolution, to Levinson's (1978) theory of adult development (*see* LIFE STAGES) as an alternation between periods of stability and transition (*see* CAREER TRANSITIONS). Within organizational literature, Abernathy and Utterback (1982) have contrasted evolutionary and radical innovation in industry, and Gersick (1988) has modeled momentum and transitions in GROUP DEVELOPMENT.

Tushman and Romanelli's (1985) work on convergence and reorientation in organizational evolution provides a good example of punctuated equilibrium in organizations. They describe deep structure ("strategic orientation") in organizations in terms of five attributes or sets of choices (1985, p. 176):

(1) core beliefs and values regarding the organization, its employees, and its environment;

(2) products, markets, technology, and competitive timing;
(3) the distribution of POWER;
(4) the organization's structure; and
(5) the nature, type, and pervasiveness of control systems.

During "convergent" periods, these attributes become increasingly consistent with one another. The organization's resources and repertoire of SKILLS, its members' interests, its operating routines, and its very perceptions of reality become intertwined, and deeply tied to the existing system. Without equilibrium, organizations could not learn from experience or increase their efficiency and effectiveness. However, the kinds of change that can occur in an equilibrium period are limited. Organizations have trouble recognizing problems or inventing solutions that fall outside accustomed boundaries; vested interests resist threats to existing POWER structures; INNOVATIONS that don't "fit" tend to wither or get rejected. Especially when convergence periods have been long and successful, it is hard for organizations to adapt to radical shifts in their situations or environments. They are used to problem solving by playing harder at their own game, not by switching to a whole new sport.

Tushman and Romanelli (1985) propose that performance CRISES (experienced or anticipated) are required to break convergence periods, and that in most – but not all – cases it takes new top management from outside the organization to mount a "reorientation." Gersick (1991) outlines this and other circumstances that trigger punctuations in human systems. Nadler and Tushman (1989) discuss the challenges of steering through the difficult process of punctuational change.

Implications for Theory, Research and Intervention

In the gradualist paradigm, almost any type of change is possible if it is small enough. Large, dramatic shifts are expected to occur through incremental changes over very long time periods; there is no postulated deep structure maintaining a system's basic configuration. Gradualist theories permit the assumption that the distant future can be predicted by extrapolation from past trajectories. In contrast, punctuational models assume that systems' deep structures normally restrict the type and degree of change accepted. However, special circumstances (such as system failure, radical environmental change, or recognized resource limits) can disrupt the equilibrium, triggering wholesale change in relatively short time periods. These models caution against distant future predictions, because trajectories can change fundamentally during punctuations.

The two paradigms foster different research approaches. Traditional theorists of system evolution have assumed that organizations, groups, individual careers, etc., move gradually from one stage to another; they have sought to identify universal stage sequences. Punctuational theorists, arguing that systems evolve through alternating momentum and metamorphosis, have been more interested in explicating mechanisms that enforce equilibrium and catalyze punctuation, and are more likely to portray systems' evolutionary pathways as varied than as universal.

Finally, the contrasts between the two paradigms raise questions about planned change intervention. Gradual (or incremental) change may be achievable through small, relatively manageable steps. While there is a place for such change in punctuational models, they also portray a second, radical type of change process which cannot be accomplished so easily. They portray major change as faster, riskier, and more difficult than it appears in traditional models.

See also **Organizational change; Organization theory; Group decision making; Population ecology**

Bibliography

Abernathy, W. & Utterback, J. (1982). Patterns of industrial innovation. In M. Tushman & W. Moore (Eds), *Readings in the management of innovations* (pp. 97–108). Boston: Pitman.

Eldredge, N. & Gould, S. J. (1972). Punctuated equilibria: An alternative to phyletic gradualism. In T. J. Schopf (Ed.), *Models in paleobiology* (pp. 82–115). San Francisco: Freeman, Cooper.

Gersick, C. J. G. (1988). Time and transition in work teams: Toward a new model of group development. *Academy of Management Journal*, **31**, 9–41.

Gersick, C. J. G. (1991). Revolutionary change theories: A multilevel exploration of the punctuated equilibrium paradigm. *Academy of Management Review*, **16**, 10–36.

Kuhn, T. S. (1970). *The structure of scientific revolution*. Chicago: University of Chicago Press.

Levinson, D. J. (1978). *The seasons of a man's life*. New York: Knopf.

Nadler, D. A. & Tushman, M. L. (1989). Leadership for organizational change. In A. M. Mohrman, Jr., S. A. Mohrman, G. E. Ledford, Jr., T. G. Cummings and E. E. Lawler III (Eds), *Large scale organizational change*. San Francisco: Jossey-Bass.

Prigogine, I. & Stengers, I. (1984). *Order out of chaos: Man's new dialogue with nature*. New York: Bantam.

Tushman, M. & Romanelli, E. (1985). Organizational evolution: A metamorphosis model of convergence and reorientation. In L. L. Cummings & B. M. Staw (Eds), *Research in organizational behavior*, (vol. 7, pp. 171–222). Greenwich, CT: JAI Press.

CONNIE J. G. GERSICK

punishment The concept of punishment in organizations has to do with the delivery of some aversive event to an employee (or employees) contingent on behavior, or the withdrawal of some valued work outcome as a result of behavior which has violated organizational rules, policies, and practices, as well as sometimes unstated norms. Two elements are central here. First, there are the kinds and types of sanctions and aversive events delivered as punishment. Second, is the process by which aversive sanctions are delivered. While punishment, and the related concept of discipline, is generally thought of as a formal procedure involving such sanctions as formal warnings, dismissal, and oral warnings by management, it can also be informal, such as supervisors withholding information, delaying actions on requests, and shouting at employees.

Punishment and discipline have received surprisingly little research attention compared to positive reward systems. While there is a good deal of speculation, little solid research evidence exists establishing the empirical correlates of punishment, even when "everybody knows" punishment exists in organizations and has some kind of impact. On the other hand, there is a large body of information based on labor law and arbitration hearings establishing principles of fair treatment in the delivery of and penalties associated with discipline in organizations.

Punishment and discipline in organizations may serve several different functions. It may serve as a direct behavior control system by which employees learn through their experiences not to violate specific policies, practices, and procedures, as set out by the organization. Disciplinary systems, formal and informal, also serve to provide indirect cues and signals to employees concerning what is acceptable and what is unacceptable, through social-learning processes from observing other employees. The process of punishment involves several related steps. First, there must be a perception by a disciplinary agent of a rule infraction. Research has developed taxonomies of the kinds of behaviors likely to trigger punishment (Arvey & Jones, 1985). The most common are ABSENTEEISM, tardiness, dishonesty, incompetence, violation of SAFETY rules, intoxication, fighting, horseplay, trouble-making, insubordination, and disputes with supervisors. Most disciplinary policy manuals in organizations set out the major classes of behaviors which constitute violations. Second, there must be a decision to take some punitive action. Studies have identified a number of variables which influence the decision to take action. Punitive action is more likely to be taken when infractions involve high cost and/or risk to the organization, when the employee has a history of poor job performance and/or disciplinary history, when there is a poor relationship with the supervisor, and when the infraction is thought to be volitional and under the control of the employee. Third, there is the choice of what kind of punishment is to be administered, such as whether formal sanctions are applied or more informal tactics chosen to control behavior. Finally, there is the manner in which the punishment is administered. Research and theory suggests that punishment which is applied soon after an infraction, is administered consistently, is accompanied by a clear explanation for the punishment, and is not unduly harsh, will be more effective than punishment administered haphazardly, with little explanation, or a long delay after the infraction (Arvey, Davis, & Nelson, 1984).

There is conflicting research evidence concerning the impact and effect of punishment in organizational settings. The literature generally supports the proposition that when punishment is administered contingently, a relationship develops or exists between punishment and satisfaction and/or performance. However, when punishment is viewed as random or noncontingent, there is no relationship. Perhaps when punishment is noncontingent employees turn to other mechanisms to escape, avoid, or gain retribution and it is these conditions which lead to FRUSTRATION, apathy, SABOTAGE, or EMPLOYEE THEFT (*see* WITHDRAWAL, ORGANIZATIONAL). However, research has tended not directly to examine the impact of punishment on the specific behaviors associated with rule violations, but instead on more broad band job performance criterion measures (e.g., overall job performance). Punishment and disciplinary systems in organizations will also affect perceptions of employees regarding the fairness and justice of such systems. Recent research has discussed the role of procedural justice (how punishment is carried out) and outcome justice (the relative fairness of the sanctions) on these perceptions (*see* JUSTICE, PROCEDURAL). In addition, labor arbitration cases and principles also emphasize procedural and outcome issues in relation to the fairness of specific disciplinary acts and systems. Generally speaking, disciplinary systems are perceived as just when there appears to have been good cause, when prior notice has been given, when the sanctions are not unduly harsh, when proper investigative procedures are employed, and when consistent and equal treatment is applied (Koven & Smith, 1982).

See also **Feedback; Learning, individual; Reinforcement; Human resources management**

Bibliography

Arvey, R. D., Davis, G. A. & Nelson, S. M. (1984). Use of discipline in an organization: A field study. *Journal of Applied Psychology*, **69**, 448–460.

Arvey, R. D. & Jones, A. P. (1985). The use of discipline in organizational settings: A framework for future research. In L. L. Cummings & B. M. Staw (Eds), *Research in organizational behavior*, (vol. 7, pp. 367–408). Greenwich, CT: JAI Press.

Koven, A. M. & Smith, S. L. (1992). *Just cause: The seven tests*, (2nd edn). Revised by D. F. Farwell. Washington, DC: Bureau of National Affairs.

Podsakoff, P. M. (1982). Determinants of a supervisor's use of rewards and punishments: A literature review and suggestions for further research. *Organizational Behavior and Human Performance*, **29**, 58–83.

RICHARD D. ARVEY

Q

quality *see* TOTAL QUALITY MANAGEMENT; QUALITY CIRCLES

quality circles A quality circle (QC) is a small group of employees from a common work area who meet regularly to solve problems they encounter in their work. Specific characteristics include the following (Ledford, Lawler, & Mohrman, 1988; Van Fleet & Griffin, 1989).

Membership typically is voluntary, although often only nominally so in Japan. Usually only some employees in a work area are QC members. The group is responsible for *making suggestions* to management, and does not have the POWER to decide about implementation. The *goals* of QCs in Japan focus almost exclusively on quality, but also focus on PRODUCTIVITY and costs in the United States. *Meetings* usually are held on company time in the United States, on personal time in Japan. A typical circle meets for 1 hour per week. QC members receive 1 to 5 days of *training* in GROUP DECISION MAKING techniques. A staff of *facilitators* conducts TRAINING, assists with group process, provides communication links to the organization, and administers the program. The organization usually offers no financial REWARDS for group suggestions, except normal suggestion awards, although there may be extensive nonfinancial recognition. The circle typically receives *information* specifically relevant to its problem.

QCs belong to a class of employee PARTICIPATION groups that provide employees with *suggestion involvement*. Such groups are special COLLATERAL ORGANIZATION structures that are dependent on the FORMAL ORGANIZATION for the implementation of changes. Other types of suggestion involvement groups may differ from QCs along one or more of the design dimensions listed above. Suggestion involvement is more limited than *job involvement*, which builds employee DECISION-MAKING power into the job through JOB DESIGN. It is also more limited than a *high involvement* design, which systematically reinforces EMPLOYEE INVOLVEMENT through various human resource practices (Lawler, 1988) (*see* EMPOWERMENT).

By the early 1980s, several million Japanese were QC members. Western firms began borrowing QC designs from successful Japanese competitors in the late 1970s. By 1990, two-thirds of *Fortune* 1000 firms reported using QCs, and more than 20 percent of employees were members in about one-third of the firms (Lawler, Mohrman, & Ledford, 1992). By this time, however, QCs had become less common than other types of employee participation groups. Other designs were being used by 85 percent of the sample.

Several key questions remain about QCs (Ledford et al., 1988; Van Fleet & Griffin, 1989). First, how effective are they? The practitioner literature on QCs is much larger and more positive than the research literature. Research indicates that quality circles sometimes improve organizational performance, but tend not to have strong effects on employee attitudes such as JOB SATISFACTION. Second, how sustainable are QCs? QC programs typically survive only a few years in the United States. QC designs appear to generate self-destructive forces even when they succeed. Third, what organizational conditions and types of employees are conducive to QC effectiveness? Not enough research has been conducted to answer these questions definitively, although existing research provides a number of models and suggestions.

For example, some research supports the particulars of the QC model. However, volunteerism and limited participation opportunities, which are more characteristic of QCs in the United States than Japan, are negatively related to success (Ledford et al., 1988). A large literature examines societal and cultural factors. For example, Cole (1985) argues that the use of small groups such as QCs depends on LABOR MARKET conditions, an infrastructure of supportive associations and other organizations, and the orientation of organized labor (*see* INDUSTRIAL RELATIONS). Others contend that cultural factors such as INDIVIDUALISM, worker attitudes and skills, and management style make Western societies less hospitable to QCs than Japan. The available research does not permit resolution of these issues.

See also **Team building; Total quality management; Continuous improvement; Group culture**

Bibliography

Cole, R. E. (1985). The macropolitics of organizational change: A comparative analysis of the spread of small-group activities. *Administrative Science Quarterly*, **30**, 560–585.

Lawler, E. E. III (1988). Choosing an involvement strategy. *Academy of Management Executive*, **2**, (3), 197–204.

Lawler, E. E. III, Mohrman, S. A. & Ledford, G. E. Jr. (1992). *Employee involvement and total quality management: Practices and results in Fortune 1000 companies*. San Francisco: Jossey-Bass.

Ledford, G. E. Jr., Lawler, E. E. III. & Mohrman, S. A. (1988). The quality circle and its variations. In J. P. Campbell & R. J. Campbell (Eds), *Productivity in organizations: New perspectives from industrial and organizational psychology* (pp. 255–294). San Francisco: Jossey-Bass.

Van Fleet, D. D. & Griffin, R. W. (1989). Quality circles: A review and suggested future directions. In C. L. Cooper & I. Robertson (Eds), *International review of industrial and organization psychology 1989* (pp. 213–233). New York: Wiley.

GERALD E. LEDFORD, JR.

quality of working life The term "quality of working life" (QWL) refers to people's reactions to work, particularly personal outcomes related to JOB SATISFACTION, MENTAL HEALTH, and SAFETY. Attention to QWL issues started initially in Scandinavia and Europe in the 1960s and spread to North America in the 1970s. The major impetus was the growing concern among industrialized nations for the health, safety, and satisfaction of workers. In Norway and Sweden, QWL has become a national movement fostered by cultural and political forces advocating employee rights to meaningful work and PARTICIPATION in work decisions. In the United States and Canada, QWL has been more pragmatic and localized, often limited to work situations where unions and management have a strong commitment to improving WORKING CONDITIONS.

QWL research has focused on three major issues:

(1) identification of work conditions that contribute to QWL;
(2) development of methods and techniques for enhancing those conditions; and
(3) understanding how QWL affects PRODUCTIVITY.

Researchers have discovered a number of conditions that affect whether employees experience work as satisfying, psychologically healthy, and safe. These include: challenging jobs, development of human capacities, safe and healthy work environment, adequate and fair compensation, and opportunity for balancing work and home life (*see* NONWORK/WORK). Considerable attention has been directed at developing methods for improving these conditions. Among the QWL innovations that have been implemented successfully in modern organizations are JOB ENRICHMENT, AUTONOMOUS WORK GROUPS, FLEXITIME, and EMPLOYEE INVOLVEMENT. A key finding of this applied research is that the success of these QWL interventions depends on a variety of contingencies in the work setting having to do with INDIVIDUAL DIFFERENCES, TECHNOLOGY, and task environment (*see* CONTINGENCY THEORY).

An assumption underlying QWL research is that there is a positive linkage between QWL and productivity. This derives from the idea that increased satisfaction with work will motivate employees to perform at higher levels (*see* MOTIVATION AND PERFORMANCE). Research has shown, however, that the satisfaction-causes-productivity premise is too simplistic and sometimes wrong. A more realistic explanation for how QWL can affect productivity is that QWL innovations, such as job enrichment and participative management, can improve employee COMMUNICATION, coordination, and capability. These improvements, in turn, can enhance work performance (*see* PERFORMANCE, INDIVIDUAL). QWL innovations can also improve the well-being and satisfaction of employees by providing a better work environment and more fulfilling jobs. These positive work conditions can indirectly increase productivity by enabling the organization to attract and retain better workers (*see* RECRUITMENT; TURNOVER).

Over the past two decades, both the term QWL and the meaning attributed to it have undergone considerable change and development. Concerns about employee well-being and satisfaction have expanded to include greater attention to ORGANIZATION EFFECTIVENESS, particularly in today's highly competitive, global environment. QWL research and practice have given rise to current attention to employee involvement and EMPOWERMENT, reflecting the need to make organizations more decentralized (*see* DECENTRALIZATION) and responsive to customer demands. Today, QWL finds expression primarily in union–management cooperative projects in both the public and private sectors. These involve committees, comprised of employees and managers, that seek to address common workplace issues falling outside COLLECTIVE BARGAINING, such as safety, quality, TECHNOLOGY management, and job satisfaction.

See also **Industrial relations; Democracy; Job characteristics; Job design; Manifest and latent functions**

Bibliography

Cummings, T. & Molloy, E. (1977). *Improving productivity and the quality of work life*. New York: Praeger.

Davis, L. & Cherns, A. (Eds), (1975). *The quality of working life*. New York: Free Press.

THOMAS G. CUMMINGS

quasi-experimental design Quasi-experiments usually test the causal consequences of long-lasting treatments outside of the laboratory. But unlike "true" experiments where treatment assignment is at random, assignment in quasi-experiments is by self-selection or administrator judgment. All experiments seek to identify whether a treatment made a difference in a particular outcome rather than to explain why the difference occurred. Experiments can be made more explanatory by selecting theory-relevant treatment and outcome variables or by adding measures of potential moderator or mediator variables. Yet the structure of all experiments, including quasi-experiments, implies a more important goal for causal description than causal explanation.

Campbell and Stanley (1966) explicated some of the VALIDITY threats that random assignment rules out but that have to be explicitly probed in quasi-experiments to ensure they were not artifically responsible for results. Cook and Campbell (1979) added more validity threats, arguing they should be ruled out by experimental design rather than through measuring them and then statistically manipulating the data to purge their influence from the treatment–outcome relationship. As Cook, Campbell and Peracchio (1990) illustrate with many examples from ORGANIZATIONAL BEHAVIOR, quasi-experimental designs are stronger for descriptive causal inference:

(1) the more pretreatment (and posttreatment) measures they have on the dependent variables under examination so as to estimate the most immediate time trends;
(2) the better matched are comparison groups so as to minimize the initial difference from treatment groups; and
(3) the more instances there are of a treatment that has been implemented at different times on different sets of respondents.

Some scholars within econometrics (Heckman & Hotz, 1989) still maintain it is possible to adjust statistically for all the initial differences between nonequivalent treatment groups. But empirical research on the selection adjustment techniques they prefer has shown them to be fallible. Statisticians prefer direct measurement of the selection process whereby different kinds of persons come to be in different treatments groups, since there is no doubt that a *fully known* selection model can lead to unbiased treatment effects. Indeed, the randomized experiment is effective, not because it creates initially comparable groups, but because the differences between these groups are fully known. The regression discontinuity design – where a quantitative score on a scale (say, of individual PRODUCTIVITY) is used to determine which members of an organization deserve special treatment because of their exceptionally high level of merit (or need) – is another instance where selection into treatment is therefore completely known. Hence, unbiased treatment effect estimation is also potentially possible in this case (*see* BIAS). However, in all other contexts it is not easy to assume that the selection model is completely known and that unbiased treatment estimates are possible.

Over the last 25 years (Cook, 1991), we have come to see that causal inferences are superior under two conditions. First, when obtained data patterns corroborate causal predictions that are point-specific, i.e., the outcome is predicted to change either at a predicted time point (as with the interrupted time series design) or at a predicted point along the continuous variable used for determining treatment assignment (as with regression discontinuity). Second, causal inferences are generally superior when the causal hypothesis under test has multiple empirical implications. This happens when a quasi-experimental design has multiple comparison groups, multiple pretreatment time points, multiple introductions of the treatment at different times, or some dependent variables which theory says should change because of the treatment and other dependent variables which theory says should not change. It will be rare for an alternative interpretation to predict the specific data patterns associated either with interventions at a specific time or point or with interventions that have multiple causal implications. But it will not be impossible.

See also **Research design; Reserch methods; Statistical methods; Generalization**

Bibliography

Campbell, D. T. & Stanley, J. C. (1966). *Experimental and quasi-experimental design for research.* Chicago: Rand McNally.

Cook, T. D. (1991). Clarifying the warrant for generalized causal inferences in quasi-experimentation. In M. W. McLaughlin & D. Phillips (Eds), *Evaluation and education at quarter century.* Chicago: National Society for the Study of Education 1991 Yearbook.

Cook, T. D. & Campbell, D. T. (1979). *Quasi-experimentation: Design and analysis issues for field settings.* Boston: Houghton-Mifflin.

Cook, T. D., Campbell, D. T. & Peracchio, L. (1990). Quasi-experimentation. In M. D. Dunnette & L. M. Hough (Eds), *Handbook of industrial & organizational psychology* (2nd edn). Palo Alto, CA: Consulting Psychologists Press.

Heckman, J. J. & Hotz, J. (1989). Choosing among alternative nonexperimental methods for estimating the impact of social programs: The case of manpower training. *Journal of the American Statistical Association*, **84**, 862–874.

THOMAS D. COOK

R

race Prior to the eighteenth century in Europe, race referred to descendants of a common ancestor with an emphasis on kinship ties and not biological or physical characteristics. It was in the late-eighteenth century that race gradually came to signify an inherent physical quality and there was a hierarchy of races. This biological view was advanced by a number of scientists in Western Europe and the United States who proposed that phenotypical features (e.g., skin color, hair texture) explain differences in mental and cultural behavior of racial groups (Banton, 1987). Modern genetic science dislodged the biological meaning of race and contributed to its reconceptualization as a social construct. Although, race is without a scientific basis in biological terms, in everyday discourse, the vast majority of people believe that "races" exist. Their beliefs about race affect their behavior. Thus, race denotes the particular way in which phenotypical differences among people come to be constructed or understood. Race in this sense is not natural or immutable. Racial categories are unstable and fundamentally social in nature. Their meanings are determined by political, social, and cultural systems (Omi & Winant, 1986) (*see* CULTURE).

Much of the research on race in organizations lies along the PREJUDICE–DISCRIMINATION axes with an emphasis on discovering objective evidence of racial discrimination and racial differences in behavior, primarily between blacks and whites (Cox & Nkomo, 1993; Nkomo, 1992). The results of the studies are mixed. Studies using obtrusive methods have shown no effects, effects of low magnitude, or counterintuitive effects for race (Stone, Stone, & Dipboye, 1992). Results yielding no effects often lead scholars to conclude that race is not an important explanatory variable. Unobtrusive studies in social psychology, however, show clear effects of race on such variables as helping, aggression, and other variables. When studies have been performed in organizational settings, there are clear effects of race on such variables as performance ratings, upward mobility, ratings of LEADERSHIP or managerial potential, JOB SATISFACTION, and interview-based ratings of job suitability (Cox & Nkomo, 1993). For instance, the accumulated evidence on the effects of race on performance ratings suggest that ratees receive higher ratings from raters of the same race (*see* ASSESSMENT; PERFORMANCE APPRAISAL). Similarly, research has demonstrated the effects of race on upward mobility with nonwhites experiencing lower upward mobility compared to whites.

The fact that much of this research fails to provide an understanding of the social construction of race in organizations has led some organizational scholars to call for a rethinking of race (*see* SOCIAL CONSTRUCTIONISM). This reconceptualization would not treat race as a demographic variable but one that views it as a necessary and productive analytical category for theorizing about and understanding organizations (Nkomo, 1992). This view implies a move toward phenomenological and historical RESEARCH METHODS. Such methods would help to foster understanding of how rules, policies, practices, and POWER relations tend to reproduce race in everyday organizational life and how it is a core feature of organizations. Race should also be understood as just one part of the more complicated web of socially constructed elements of identity such as GENDER and class that influence social relations in organizations.

See also **Equal opportunities; Stereotyping; Culture; Intercultural process**

Bibliography

Banton, M. (1987). *Racial theories*. Cambridge, UK: Cambridge University Press.

Cox, T. Jr. & Nkomo, S. M. (1993). Race and ethnicity. In R. T. Golembiewski (Ed.), *Handbook of organizational behavior* (pp. 205–229). New York: Marcel Dekker.

Omi, M. & Winant, H. (1986). *Racial formation in the United States: From the 1960s to 1980s*. New York: Routledge & Kegan Paul.

Nkomo, S. M. (1992). The emperor has no clothes: Rewriting race in organizations. *Academy of Management Review*, **17**, 487–513.

Stone, E., Stone, D. & Dipboye, R. (1992). Stigmas in organizations: Race, handicaps, and physical attractiveness. In K. Kelley (Ed.), *Issues, theory and research in industrial/organizational psychology* (pp. 385–456). Amsterdam: Elsevier Science.

STELLA M. NKOMO

rationality This denotes the selection of preferred behavioral alternatives in terms of systems of values through which the consequences of behavior can be evaluated. Especially in the disciplines of economics and statistics, rational behavior is defined as making a decision that, after a review of all the alternatives, promises to maximize satisfaction or utility. Herbert Simon argued that it is not feasible to attempt a search for each and every alternative. Because of their limited cognitive capacities, decision makers use only part of the relevant information. Time and money considerations also play a role in determining if there will be a search for more information and how long it will last. The search process generally stops when a "SATISFICING solution" has been found: alternatives are not studied exhaustively. This is implied by Simon's concept of BOUNDED RATIONALITY.

In other words, rational behavior in the DECISION MAKING process simply involves the evaluation and selection of some relevant alternatives which offer a perceived advantage to the decision maker. All that is necessary to make a choice a rational one is that an objective exists and that the decision maker perceives and selects some alternative which promises to meet the objective (Harrison, 1987, p. 107).

See also **Garbage can model; Paradox; Postmodernism; Social constructionism**

Bibliography

Harrison, E. F. (1987). *The managerial decision-making process*, (3rd edn). Boston: Houghton-Mifflin.

PAUL KOOPMAN

realistic job previews The realistic job preview (RJP) is a RECRUITMENT technique in HUMAN RESOURCES MANAGEMENT designed to facilitate the JOINING UP PROCESS for new organization members. The RJP contains accurate information about job duties, and especially about the major sources of JOB SATISFACTION and dissatisfaction, that is given to recruits prior to organizational entry. The RJP is focused on inflated expectations of high importance to most recruits. The RJP can be presented during the interview, in a booklet or video, during a job visit (which may include meeting future coworkers), or in a combination of methods (*see* SELECTION INTERVIEWING; SELECTION METHODS).

The RJP is designed to increase the degree of PERSON–JOB FIT and WORK ADJUSTMENT of new recruits by allowing them to make better job choices (which are typically made as predicted by VIE theory) based on much more information than is typically available. The primary effects of RJPs are to increase newcomer job satisfaction and COMMITMENT, resulting in lower TURNOVER rates because the RJP is one type of ANTICIPATORY SOCIALIZATION. The most recent review (Wanous, 1992, pp. 78–82) calculated the average amount of increase in job survival from RJPs as 10 percent for business versus 3 percent for military recruits. For example, if a business retains 50 percent of new hires over a 1 year period without an RJP, then using the RJP will increase this survival rate up to 55 percent.

There are several explanations for the effects of RJPs on turnover. First, because the RJP makes more informed job choices possible, those who actually accept a job offer are likely to have better person–job fit. Second, the RJP is also viewed as a "vaccination" against disappointment after organizational entry, because the most important dissatisfying job factors are already anticipated. Thus, newcomer expectations are lowered and are thus more likely to be fulfilled. Third, the information contained in an RJP may also help newcomers to cope more effectively with both job duties as well as newcomer STRESS. Because of more effective coping, newcomer performance is enhanced, thus decreasing turnover.

Research continues to specify the possible limitations of RJPs. First, the severity of an organization's turnover problem among newcomers is one limiting factor. If turnover is extremely high, the RJP may have no effect because the job may be so undesirable that accurate expectations are irrelevant to the decision to quit. One year job survival rates among newcomers of 50–85 percent seem to be where RJPs increase survival (Wanous, 1992, p. 82). In very low turnover organizations, the RJP may still improve the PSYCHOLOGICAL CONTRACT via expectations clarification. Second, in "tight" LABOR MARKETS where the recruit has only one job offer, the possibility of increased person–job fit via informed job choices is eliminated. Third, the earlier the RJP is presented in recruitment, the better. Those which are given after a job offer has been accepted are less effective because the information cannot be used to make an informed job choice (*see* CAREER CHOICE; VOCATIONAL GUIDANCE).

See also **Job description; Person specification; Career transitions**

Bibliography

Dawis, R. V. & Lofquist, L. H. (1984). *A psychological theory of work adjustment*. Minneapolis: University of Minnesota Press.

Premack, S. L. & Wanous, J. P. (1985). A meta-analysis of realistic job preview experiments. *Journal of Applied Psychology*, **70**, 706–719.

Wanous, J. P. (1992). *Organizational entry: Recruitment, selection, orientation, and socialization of newcomers*. Reading, MA: Addison-Wesley.

Wanous, J. P., Poland, T. D., Premack, S. L. & Davis, K. S. (1992). The effects of met expectations on newcomer attitudes and behavior: A review and meta-analysis. *Journal of Applied Psychology*, **77**, 288–297.

Weitz, J. (1956). Job expectancy and survival. *Journal of Applied Psychology*, **40**, 245–247.

JOHN P. WANOUS

reality shock This term refers to the phenomenon that the expectations of new job incumbents are often inconsistent with their experiences in a new setting. Studies of reality shock have identified three important and distinct entry features: change, contrast, and surprise (*see* JOINING UP PROCESS). Unfortunately, companies often contribute to prospective employees' unrealistic expectations in their effort to convey a positive image of themselves.

Reality shock poses considerable affective and cognitive challenges. For instance, first-time managers are often caught off-guard by the starkness of the transition from an individual contributor to managerial ROLE and the associated stress (*see* CAREER TRANSITIONS). New managers may have to make decisions and act before they understand what they are supposed to do. Only through on-the-job experience do they discover what their new responsibilities are. Reality shock is associated with dysfunctional outcomes including newcomer dissatisfaction, poor subsequent adjustment, and TURNOVER (*see* Wanous (1992) for a literature review) (*see* WORK ADJUSTMENT).

Much of the research has focused on what organizations can do to reduce reality shock and/or facilitate the sense-making process. A number of organizational entry tools have been identified – REALISTIC JOB PREVIEWS, formal orientation programs, and informal SOCIALIZATION practices such as peer MENTORING.

See also **Expatriates; Role ambiguity; Role taking; Management development**

Bibliography

Wanous, J. P. (1992). *Organizational entry: Recruitment, selection, orientation, and socialization of newcomers*. Reading, MA: Addison-Wesley.

LINDA A. HILL

reciprocal interdependence *see* TECHNOLOGY; MUTUAL ADJUSTMENT

reciprocity This is a strong, pervasive, ancient norm that can be represented by three sayings: one negative ("An eye for an eye; a tooth for a tooth."), one positive ("You scratch my back, I'll scratch yours."), and one general ("Do unto others as you would have others do unto you.") (*see* GROUP NORMS). The positive and general sides of reciprocity have considerable social value: if people fulfill each others' expectations, everyone is well served. Ignoring negative reciprocity, however, provides the basis for unfulfilled expectations and interpersonal CONFLICT.

Cialdini (1985) notes that all societies subscribe to the norm of reciprocity. Organizationally, reciprocity is most obvious during COLLECTIVE BARGAINING, where reciprocating concessions is an almost immutable norm that contributes toward the resolution of labor–management conflict (*see* CONFLICT RESOLUTION; MANAGEMENT OF CONFLICT).

But reciprocity's positive side can be turned around and used manipulatively (*see* INFLUENCE): having received a favor, an individual may feel obligated to reciprocate. Thus, a subordinate who flatters the boss can establish subtle pressures for the boss to reciprocate. Differentiating between a favor (positive reciprocity) and a sales strategy (manipulative reciprocity), then, becomes an important interpersonal and organizational skill (*see* INTERPERSONAL SKILLS). Unfortunately, most people's needs for social affirmation also encourage flattery. Thus, while reciprocity provides the potential for enormous interpersonal good, it also can tempt people toward ingratiation rather than actual work performance (*see* IMPRESSION MANAGEMENT).

See also **Exchange relations; Moral development; Game theory**

Bibliography

Cialdini, Robert B. (1985). *Influence: Science and practice* (2nd edn). Glenview, IL: Scott Foresman.

J. KEITH MURNIGHAN

recruitment Traditionally, recruitment has been conceptualized as the organizational process that precedes selection. More specifically, recruitment has been described as the process of generating pools of applicants for job vacancies; selection as the process of choosing from among those applicants. Recruitment has been regarded as an *attraction* activity, selection as a *screening* or winnowing activity.

More recently, recruitment and selection have come to be regarded as less distinct activities. For example, because recruitment decisions (e.g., where to advertise) inevitably affect the characteristics of the applicants generated, recruitment is in a very real sense the first stage in selection. Furthermore, recruitment and selection often take place simultaneously and thus are difficult to disentangle in practice (as when applicants are both enticed and evaluated in pre-employment interviews) (*see* SELECTION INTERVIEWING).

Following a thorough review of the literature, Breaugh (1992) offered the following definition: "Recruitment involves those organizational activities that:

(1) influence the number and/or the types of applicants who apply for a position; and/or
(2) affect whether a job offer is accepted" (p. 4).

However, a close examination of the recruitment literature reveals that only a small subset of the potentially large number of organizational decisions that influence application and acceptance behaviors have historically been considered part of the recruitment domain. This point is elaborated below.

Three topics have heavily dominated discussions of recruitment. They are recruiters, recruitment sources (e.g., employment agencies, newspaper advertising), and recruitment messages (realistic versus inflated). Although these variables clearly are capable of influencing application or job choice behaviors, other variables that may have similar (or even greater) effects on applicants have been largely ignored. For example, although PERSON SPECIFICATIONS, starting salaries, and hours of work clearly affect application and choice behaviors, they have rarely been included as part of the recruitment domain (*see* Rynes, 1991).

A number of factors probably account for this pattern. First, discussions of recruitment may focus primarily on recruiters, sources, and messages because those topics are largely *unique* to the prehire phase of employment. In contrast, JOB DESIGN, person specifications, and

PAYMENT SYSTEMS are believed to influence a variety of outcomes in addition to job acceptance, such as performance and TURNOVER. These multiple roles have probably caused some of these variables to be regarded as *less manipulable* solely for recruitment purposes. Finally, there has been a high degree of *fragmentation* in the recruitment literature, with each main topic being considered in isolation from the others. This fragmentation has made it difficult to get a holistic view of recruitment, its antecedents, and its consequences.

For example, research on *recruiters* has tended to use field surveys to assess what applicants like or dislike about recruiters, and how much it matters to their job choice intentions. Note that these are all prechoice, prehire outcomes. In contrast, research on recruitment *sources* has used archival data to link source of entry (e.g., campus placement) with posthire outcomes (performance, length of service). *Recruitment realism* research has also looked primarily at posthire outcomes, employing field experiments to do so (*see* REALISTIC JOB PREVIEWS).

In summary, there is some (perhaps unavoidable) confusion over the boundaries between recruitment and selection, the range of activities that comprise recruitment, and the variety of factors that influence recruiting success. These distinctions are important operationally, because taking an overly narrow view of recruitment can result in ineffective staffing practices. For example, taking the traditional perspective, an organization wishing to improve its recruiting outcomes would modify its sources, replace its recruiters, or revise its recruiting messages. However, a broader view of recruitment would suggest that solutions are equally likely to be found by such means as job redesign or the tailoring of inducements.

Additional progress in the recruitment area will require that future studies examine recruitment in a broader context (e.g., tight versus loose LABOR MARKETS; desirable versus undesirable organizations). This is critical because strategies effective under certain conditions are unlikely to succeed in others (Rynes & Barber, 1990). For example, minor refinements of traditional recruitment practices may suffice for organizations with positive reputations, while a much broader set of tactics (changes in job design, person specifications, or payment systems) may be required in poor-image environments.

Research is also needed that jointly examines recruitment and selection as interactive, longitudinal processes. Recruitment and selection have long been conceptualized as semiconflicting activities (with the purported purpose of recruitment being to attract applicants; selection, to screen them out). However, this conceptualization tends to obscure emerging evidence that there may multiple opportunities for "win–win" strategies with respect to both objectives. For example, it appears to be possible to construct SELECTION METHODS that are both valid and impressive to applicants (*see* Rynes, 1992). Additionally, failure to conceptualize recruitment and selection as two-way decision processes can cause organizations to lose candidates by being unduly complacent about prompt follow-up between stages (Rynes, Bretz, & Gerhart, 1991).

A third area in need of increased attention concerns applicant *quality*. Because most vacancies are eventually filled with *some*body, the most critical questions regarding recruitment effectiveness involve the longterm performance and work adjustment of new hires, relative to those who rejected offers or who never applied. To date, most investigations of INDIVIDUAL DIFFERENCES in reactions to recruitment have focused on gross, observable characteristics such as race or sex. Examination of characteristics that are more closely aligned with WORK ADJUSTMENT and performance (e.g., cognitive ability, conscientiousness) would be highly desirable.

Finally, both researchers and practitioners need to be more aware of possible methodological biases in reported results. For example, conclusions about the importance of recruiters (or pay) in applicants' job choices appear to depend on the method used to generate the results (Rynes, 1991; Rynes, Bretz, & Gerhart, 1991). More generally, applicant responses to questions about job choice (as well as interviewer responses to questions about applicant selection) seem to be fraught with social desirability biases and lack of self-insight. These findings prescribe caution with respect to reliance upon the results of any single study, and argue for a broader range of methodological approaches to major questions in this area.

See also **Joining-up process; Job description; Human resources management; Human resources planning; Vocational guidance**

Bibliography

Breaugh, J. A. (1992). *Recruitment: Science and practice*. Boston: PWS-Kent.

Rynes, S. L. (1991). Recruitment, job choice, and post-hire consequences: A call for new research directions. In M. D. Dunnette & L. Hough (Eds), *Handbook of industrial and organizational psychology*, (2nd edn, vol. 2, pp. 399–444). Palo Alto, CA: Consulting Psychologists Press.

Rynes, S. L. (1992). Who's selecting whom? Effects of selection practices on applicant attitudes and behaviors. In W. C. Borman & N. W. Schmitt (Eds), *Personnel selection* (pp. 240–274). San Francisco: Jossey-Bass.

Rynes, S. L. & Barber, A. E. (1990). Applicant attraction strategies: An organizational perspective. *Academy of Management Review*, **15**, 286–310.

Rynes, S. L., Bretz, R. D. & Gerhart, B. (1991). The importance of recruitment in job choice: A different way of looking. *Personnel Psychology*, **44**, 487–521.

Wanous, J. P. (1980). *Organizational entry: Recruitment, selection, and socialization of newcomers*. Reading, MA: Addison-Wesley.

SARA L. RYNES

redundancy This denotes loss of employment where the job is no longer required. Redundancy may occur in: organizational "DOWNSIZING"; PRODUCTIVITY enhancement; SKILLS obsolescence; externalization of services. It is sometimes used to avoid invoking the disciplinary procedure. Many writers treat redundancy and UNEMPLOYMENT as interchangeable concepts but this is misleading. Employees may be redundant but move to other jobs without unemployment. Some unemployed are not redundant.

Redundancy has been compared with bereavement, with early stages of shock and disbelief and later, acceptance. However, this implies the employee preferred to stay in the job and did not foresee its loss. Some employees volunteer for redundancy. The bereavement model may be useful for some but not all employees.

Redundancy involves the loss of financial income and probably prestige, STATUS, and social identity. Psychological well-being is reduced upon announcement of redundancies (*see* AFFECT). ATTRIBUTION theory is used to explain:

(1) scapegoating of redundant employees;
(2) redundancy as less difficult psychologically where the experience involves large numbers; and
(3) adjustment easier for those with external attributions for redundancy and internal attributions for regaining employment (*see* LOCUS OF CONTROL).

Some outplacement counseling has built on attribution theory (*see* COUNSELING IN ORGANIZATIONS).

Longer-term effects, especially when followed by unemployment, include re-employment often at a lower level, and the employee more vulnerable to future redundancies (Daniel, 1972). The PSYCHOLOGICAL CONTRACT may change, though some recover their COMMITMENT upon re-employment.

"Survivors" (colleagues remaining employed) feel guilty and are willing to work harder: explained by EQUITY THEORY. However, JOB INSECURITY research suggests survivors become insecure. The perception of procedural justice mitigates some negative effects (*see* JUSTICE, PROCEDURAL).

See also **Mental health; Organizational decline and death; Career transitions**

Bibliography

Daniel, W. W. (1972). *The unemployment flow*. London: Policy Studies Institute.

JEAN HARTLEY

reference group *see* SOCIAL COMPARISON; JUSTICE, DISTRIBUTIVE

referent power *see* POWER BASES

regulation *see* GOVERNMENT AND BUSINESS; INDUSTRIAL RELATIONS; CORPORATE SOCIAL RESPONSIBILITY

regulations *see* BUREAUCRACY; MANAGEMENT, CLASSICAL THEORY

reinforcement Operant reinforcement refers to a procedure, a behavior change process, and a single event. As a procedure, *reinforcement* is the creation of a contingency between an operant behavior and a known reinforcer. As a process, *reinforcement* is the increased rate of an operant behavior above its naturally occurring base-line rate when occurrences of the behavior are followed by occurrences of a known reinforcer. As a single event, *reinforcement* refers to an instance in which a reinforcer follows an operant behavior, i.e., "the response produced a reinforcement" or each time the student correctly imitated the model's behavior a reinforcement was delivered. Operant behavior rates and patterns of rates during both reinforcement and EXTINCTION, at least under laboratory conditions, depend on the schedule of reinforcement experienced during a person's exposure to operant reinforcement procedures. *Schedules of reinforcement* are rules specifying conditions under which a reinforcer will follow a behavior. A *fixed ratio* (FR-N) schedule specifies that every N^{th} response will be followed by a reinforcement. When $N = 1$ the FR-N schedule is called a *continuous reinforcement schedule*, or CRF. A *variable ratio* (VR-N) schedule specifies that the N between reinforced behaviors vary randomly within some range so that on average every N^{th} behavior is followed by reinforcement. Slot machines or one armed bandits exemplify VR-N schedules that exert powerful (sometimes addictive) control over operant behaviors. The following equation is a feedback function for ratio schedules: $R = B/N$, where R is rate of reinforcement received, B is rate of behavior performances, and N is the ratio schedule value. It clearly indicates that, if performance occurs on ratio schedules, a virtually perfect correlation between performance rate, B, and reinforcement rate, R, will occur regardless of values taken by N. In part, this functional relationship accounts for the fact that ratio schedules support very high performance rates. *Fixed interval* (FI-t) schedules specify that the first response to occur after passage of t time units since the last reinforcement occurred will be followed by reinforcement. *Variable interval* (VI-t) schedules specify that the interval of time that must elapse between one reinforcement and the next reinforcement vary over some range so that the average time between reinforcements will be t. Empirical evidence indicates that in general (i.e., except for exceedingly small values of t, and large values of N, respectively, for interval and ratio schedules), ratio schedules virtually always support higher behavior rates than do interval schedules. The *fixed time* (FT-t) schedule specifies that a reinforcement be delivered every t time units contingent only upon the person being in a specific location when the reinforcement is delivered. *Concurrent reinforcement schedules* (e.g., conFR/VI = concurrent FR and VI) specify that two or more alternative schedules be continually available so the person can continually choose between them.

Applications of operant CONDITIONING procedures in organizations resemble applications of the law of gravity in everyday affairs in that both applications represent analogue of the processes originally described and quantified under controlled laboratory conditions. In organizations reinforcements can be contingent on performance but follow with too long a delay to be isomorphic with reinforcement as it occurs under laboratory conditions (Malott, 1992). Nevertheless, effective use has been made of laboratory based operant learning concepts in the design of field interventions, and the process can be described in terms of recently refined operant concepts (*see* Agnew & Redmon, in Mawhinney, 1992b). Field interventions typically involve procedures of behavior specification, observation (measurement), and scheduling consequences contingent on performances, e.g., constructing ratio-like schedules of incentives and bonus pay (*see* BONUS PAYMENTS; PAYMENT SYSTEMS; REWARDS). For example, Latham and Dossett (*see* Latham & Huber, in Hopkins & Mawhinney, 1992) constructed continuous (CRF) and variable ratio four (VR-4) schedules of monetary pay contingencies among 14 beaver trappers who were randomly assigned to either the CRF or VR-4 schedule of bonus pay added to their normal wages. The amount of bonus pay per occasion of "reinforcement" was, respectively, \$1.00 and \$4.00 contingent on each beaver trapped and the reinforcement schedule. Note that the feedback functions for the two schedules are as follows: CRF: R = \$1 • B/1 and VR-4: R = \$4 • B/4; thus, net value of reinforcements received (rate times amount) was equal across the two schedules for equal performance rates. The number of beavers trapped per trapper hours worked was 0.44 prior to the intervention and 0.63 during the intervention. During the intervention, trapper hours per beaver trapped were 0.67 under the CRF and 0.58 under the VR-4 schedule. A reinforcement schedule-by-experience level of the trappers was observed; inexperienced trappers performed at a higher rate on the CRF and experienced trappers performed at a higher rate on the VR-4 schedule. This interaction conforms with operant-based laboratory results that suggest SKILL learning occurs more rapidly on CRF schedules while maintenance can be achieved with VR schedules of partial reinforcement. The cost per beaver caught fell from \$16.75 prior to the intervention to \$12.86 during the intervention. Verbal reports indicated high satisfaction with the intervention among the unionized trappers and their supervisors. Performance increases in the classic Hawthorne Experiments (*see* HAWTHORNE EFFECT) have been related to operant conditioning (*see* Parsons, in Hopkins & Mawhinney, 1992) and the pay and cultural practices of the highest paid and most productive work force in the United States, and perhaps the world, within the Lincoln Electric Company can be considered applied principles of operant conditioning whether the formal principles guided development of that work environment or not (*see* Handlin, in Hopkins & Mawhinney, 1992). Verbal praise and other forms of social recognition from one's superiors, when properly scheduled, can be powerful reinforcements often rivaling monetary reinforcement in their effects on behavior.

PREE refers to Partial Reinforcement Extinction Effect, in which partial reinforcement (number and random order of reinforced and unreinforced occurrences of B during reinforcement) results in greater *resistance to extinction* (number of responses occurring before responding ceases) during an extinction procedure (Capaldi, 1966). Researchers have provided experimental subjects with histories of continuous and partial (and irregular) reinforcement of their decisions to allocate limited resources among alternative investments or industrial projects and then exposed them to extinction procedures. As predicted by PREE, subjects with histories of partial irregular reinforcement were more resistant to extinction and allocated more resources to failing investments and projects (*see* PERSISTENCE), than subjects who provided a history of regular (more predictable) partial or simply continuous reinforcement (Hantula & Crowell, 1994). These results may well have implications for executive level DECISION MAKING.

Recent develops in the literature include analyses of linkages between operant learning (*see* LEARNING, INDIVIDUAL) processes and the role they may play in understanding and dealing with practical issues such as ORGANIZATIONAL CULTURE analysis and change (Mawhinney, 1992b), pay-for-performance (*see* PERFORMANCE RELATED PAY) (Hopkins & Mawhinney, 1992), and quality improvement (Mawhinney, 1992a) (*see* TOTAL QUALITY MANAGEMENT). For current accounts of social learning theory, SAFETY, ethics, and other topics viewed from an operant stand point, *see Organizational performance: Behavior analysis and management* (Johnson, Redmon, & Mawhinney, 1995).

See also **Feedback; Knowledge of results; Punishment**

Bibliography

Capaldi, E. J. (1966). Partial reinforcement: A hypothesis of sequential effects. *Psychological Review*, **11**, 459–477.

Hantula, D. A. & Crowell, C. R. (1994). Intermittent reinforcement and escalation processes in sequential decision making: A replication and theoretical analysis. *Journal of Organizational Behavior Management*, **14**, (2), 7–36.

Hopkins, B. L. & Mawhinney, T. C. (Eds), (1992). *Pay for performance: History, controversies, and evidence*. New York: Haworth Press.

Johnson, M., Redmon, W. K. & Mawhinney, T. C. (Eds), (1995). *Organizational performance: Behavior analysis and management*. New York: Springer-Verlag.

Malott, R. W. (1992). A theory of rule-governed behavior and organizational behavior management. *Journal of Organizational Behavior Management*, **12**, (2), 45–65.

Mawhinney, T. C. (1992a). Total quality management and organizational behavior management: An integration for continual improvement. *Journal of Applied Behavior Analysis*, **25**, 225–243.

Mawhinney, T. C. (Ed.), (1992b). *Organizational culture, rule-governed behavior and organizational behavior management: Theoretical foundations and implications for research and practice*. New York: Haworth Press.

THOMAS C. MAWHINNEY

reliability In the context of organizational research, reliability refers to the degree of self-consistency among the scores earned by an individual on a measure or the degree of consistency that exists among observations made (e.g., of service quality) over repeated attempts to do so. More technically, it is the extent that a set of scores, quantitative descriptions, or observations is free from unsystematic (ERROR variation, when some aspect of an individual, organization, or a phenomenon is measured more than once. Reliability is usually estimated from statistical evidence of covariation among a set of items, scores, or observations (*see* STATISTICAL METHODS). Good reliability is a necessary condition for a useful measure or procedure. Evidence of poor or low reliability is a clue that it would be unwise to accept the information, "facts" or data in question at face value (e.g., we should not try to generalize from what we have (*see* GENERALIZATION)). Moreover, low reliability sets limits to the order of magnitude and stability of statistical relationships that we can expect in research. High reliability can be promoted by using appropriate operational definitions (*see* OPERATIONALIZATION), standardized measurement procedures, careful training of observers/recorders, or by choosing to measure phenomena that are not too subtle or elusive.

See also **Research methods; Psychological testing; Research design; Validity; Bias**

Bibliography

Ghiselli, E. E., Campbell, J. P. & Zedeck, S. (1981). *Measurement theory for the behavioral sciences*. San Francisco: W. H. Freeman.

Schmitt, N. W. & Klimoski, R. J. (1991). *Research methods in human resources management*. Cincinnati, OH: South-Western.

RICHARD KLIMOSKI

repetitive work This term refers to the repeating of some act or chain of acts in the completion of tasks at work. It is commonly assumed that repetitive and monotonous work can have detrimental effects on psychological and physical well-being (*see* MENTAL HEALTH; STRESS). However, this view is simplistic and challenged by psychological evidence that some workers may prefer repetitive tasks. Some types of repetitive work can have severe psychological and physical consequences: repetitive strain injury (RSI) or repetitive trauma disorder (RTD) are examples. RSI is a label given to a variety of painful, debilitating conditions believed to be caused by rapid repetitive movements of the hands, wrists, or arms when awkwardly positioned. RSI was traditionally associated with manual work (e.g., carpentry) but a significant new group of affected workers has been identified – computer keyboard operators. Exacerbating factors for these individuals appeared to be the static load imposed on certain parts of their body (e.g., keeping wrists and shoulders in the same position for lengthy periods). Other occupational risk factors which may cause, contribute to, or aggravate RSI or RTD can be reduced or eliminated through careful JOB DESIGN: repetitive or sustained exertions, certain postures, vibration, low temperatures, and mechanical stress on the palmer side of the hands or on the sides of the fingers.

See also **Ergonomics; Job satisfaction; Scientific management; Quality of working life; Technology; Role**

Bibliography

Philips, C. R., Bedeian, A. G. & Molstad, C. (1991). Repetitive work: Contrast and conflict. *Journal of Socio Economics*, **20**, 73–82.

NOEL SHEEHY and A. GALLAGHER

representation This involves the articulation and expression of the interests of employees to the management of an organization. It differs from PARTICIPATION, which is the active involvement in organizational activities. In practice, the distinction is often blurred as representative structures allow some participation in DECISION MAKING. Representation can be achieved on an individual or collective basis. Individual mechanisms include single-issue means, such as grievance procedures and "open door" policies, and multiple-issue methods such as opinion surveys (*see* SURVEY FEEDBACK). The former permit responses to specific concerns but are not designed to cover more general issues. The latter collect wider sets of views but do not allow direct NEGOTIATION between managers and workers. Collective systems, allowing the aggregation of the interests of workers as a group, involve elected committees, which may cover specific issues such as health and safety or the whole of an organization's activities. Representation can occur through special-purpose bodies such as works councils (*see* DEMOCRACY) or as part of the wider system of COLLECTIVE BARGAINING. Representation systems operate at various levels, from the immediate work place to the corporate head office, though representation at the highest levels is rare except in countries where it is legally required.

See also **Trade unions; Decision making; Industrial relations; Collective action**

Bibliography

Fox, A. (1985). *Man mismanagement* (2nd edn). London: Hutchinson.

PAUL EDWARDS

reputation Companies rely on both tangible and intangible resources to gain competitive advantage against rivals (*see* COMPETITIVENESS). Chief among intangible resources is a company's "reputation" – the salient characteristics that external observers ascribe to the company (Fombrun & Shanley, 1990). When surveyed, senior managers point to a company's reputation as among the most important success drivers and ponder how to induce and maintain favorable assessments of their companies by outside observers. Efforts to understand how corporate reputations develop draw on the perspectives of either economics, STRATEGIC MANAGEMENT, or sociology.

The Economic View

Economists adhere to a view of reputation as either a trait or a signal. Game theorists regard reputations as character traits that distinguish among "types" of companies and can explain their strategic behavior (*see* GAME THEORY). Signalling theorists emphasize the informational content of reputations. Both recognize that reputations are perceptions of companies held by external observers.

Weigelt and Camerer (1988, p. 443) point out that ". . . in game theory the reputation of a player is the perception others have of the player's values . . . which determine his/her choice of strategies." Information asymmetry forces external observers to look for proxies to describe the preferences of rivals and their likely courses of action. Consumers rely on a company's reputation because they have less information than managers do about the company's commitment to delivering desirable product features (Stiglitz, 1989). Similarly, since outside investors are less informed than managers about a company's future actions, a favorable reputation increases investor confidence that managers will act in ways that are reputation-consistent. For game theorists, reputations are therefore functional: they generate perceptions among employees, customers, investors, competitors, and the general public about what a company is, what it does, and what it stands for.

Signaling theorists concur: reputations derive from the prior resource allocations managers make to first-order activities likely to create a perception of reliability and predictability to outside observers. Since many features of a company and its products are hidden from view, reputations are information signals which increase an observer's confidence in the company's products and services.

Managers can make *strategic* use of their company's reputation to signal its attractiveness. When the quality of a company's products and services is not directly observable, high-quality producers may invest in reputation-building in order to signal the greater quality of their products and services (Shapiro, 1983). Their initial investments in building reputation allows them to charge premium prices and earn rents from the repeat purchases that their reputations generate. In contrast, low-quality producers avoid investing in reputation-building because they do not expect repeat purchases.

Similar dynamics may operate in the capital and labor markets. In the capital markets, managers routinely try to signal investors about their company's economic performance. Since investors are more favorably disposed to companies with high and stable earnings, managers often try to smooth quarterly earnings and keep dividend pay-out ratios high and fixed, despite earnings fluctuations. In the labor market, sometimes companies will also pay a premium price to hire high-reputation auditors and outside counsel. They rent the reputations of their agents in order to signal investors, regulators, and other publics about their company's probity and credibility (Wilson, 1983).

The Strategic View

When viewed strategically, reputations are mobility barriers (Caves & Porter, 1977) that produce returns to companies because they are difficult to imitate. By circumscribing companies' actions and rivals' reactions, reputations act as a distinct source of industry-level structure.

In part, reputations are barriers to competition because they derive from unique internal features of companies that are difficult to duplicate. They describe the history of a company's past interactions with STAKEHOLDERS and so suggest to observers what the company stands for (Dutton & Dukerich, 1991). Reputations are also difficult to replicate because they are *externally* perceived, and therefore difficult to manipulate. Rivals cannot generate the performance results of their better-regarded rivals because, other things being equal, all stakeholders favor the products and services of the more reputable companies. After all, it takes time for a reputation to congeal in observers' minds, and empirical studies show that even when confronted with negative information, observers resist changing their reputational assessments.

Like economists, then, strategists call attention to the competitive benefits of acquiring favorable reputations and support a focus on the longitudinal resource allocations that companies must make to erect reputational barriers to the mobility of rivals. Since primary resource allocations also stand to directly improve organizational performance, however, it proves difficult to isolate their unique impact on performance and reputation. That's why empirical studies have had difficulty untangling a causal ordering: Both are produced by the same underlying initiatives (Chakravarthy, 1986).

Although most strategists dwell on the economic and competitive aspects of managerial decision making, a subset call attention to the social aspects of these decisions. Social performance theorists tend to take the moral high-ground to suggest principles and practices that managers should adhere to in order to induce ethically sound strategic decisions (*see* CORPORATE SOCIAL RESPONSIBILITY). However, current approaches now emphasize that companies have diverse stakeholders with valid claims on the strategies that companies pursue, and so advise politically savvy managers to address social concerns in order to secure external LEGITIMACY (Cameron & Whetten, 1983). Implictly, they suggest that corporate reputations may well gauge the legitimacy of companies' strategic initiatives (Fombrun & Shanley, 1990).

The Sociological View

Sociologists suggest that economic and strategic models both distort the socio-cognitive process which actually generates reputational rankings (Granovetter, 1985). To them, rankings are social constructions that come into being through the relationships that a focal company establishes with its stakeholders within an institutional field (*see* SOCIAL CONSTRUCTIONISM). Companies have multiple evaluators, each of whom apply different criteria in assessing companies. Reputations come into being as individuals struggle to make sense of a company's past and present actions. So that reputational rankings represent aggregated assessments of institutional prestige and describe the stratification of the social system surrounding companies and industries (Shapiro, 1987).

Faced with incomplete information about a company's actions, observers not only interpret the signals that a company routinely broadcasts, but also rely on the evaluative signals refracted by key intermediaries such as market analysts, professional investors, public interest monitors, and media reporters. These intermediaries are key nodes in an intercompany network that transmits and refracts information among companies and their stakeholders (*see* NETWORK ANALYSIS). An empirical study of companies involved in nuclear-waste disposal and photovoltaic cell development demonstrated how in both these industries reputational status depended, not only on structural factors like company size and economic performance, but also on a company's position in the interaction networks linking companies in each institutional field (Shrum & Wuthnow, 1988).

An Integrative View

Jointly, these three perspectives suggest that reputations constitute subjective, collective assessments of the credibility and reliability of companies, with the following characteristics:

Reputations are *derivative, second-order* characteristics of an industrial social system that crystallize the emergent status of companies in the field.

Reputations develop from companies' prior resource allocations and histories and *constitute mobility* barriers that constrain companies' actions and rivals' reactions.

Reputations crystallize from the *bottom-up constructions of diverse evaluators*, each applying a combination of economic and social, selfish and altruistic criteria.

Reputations reconcile the multiple images of companies among *all of their stakeholders*, and signal their *overall attractiveness* to employees, consumers, investors, and local communities.

Reputations embody two key dimensions of companies' effectiveness: An *appraisal of companies' economic performance*, and *an appraisal of companies' success in fulfilling social responsibilities* (Etzioni, 1988).

So that a corporate reputation is a collective representation of a company's past actions and results that describes the company's *overall* attractiveness to its diverse stakeholders.

See also **Organizational effectiveness; Trust; Organization and environment; Structure-conduct-performance model**

Bibliography

Cameron, K. S. & Whetten, D. A. (Eds), (1983). *Organizational effectiveness: A comparison of multiple models*. New York: Academic Press.

Caves, R. E. & Porter, M. E. (1977). From entry barriers to mobility barriers. *Quarterly Journal of Economics*, **91**, 421–434.

Chakravarthy, B. (1986). Measuring strategic performance. *Strategic Management Journal*, **7**, 437–458.

Dutton, J. E. & Dukerich, J. M. (1991). Keeping an eye on the mirror: Image and identity in organizational adaptation. *Academy of Management Journal*, **34**, 517–554.

Etzioni, A. (1988). *The moral dimension*. New York: Free Press.

Fombrun, C. J. & Shanley, M. (1990). What's in a name? Reputation-building and corporate strategy. *Academy of Management Journal*, **33**, 233–258.

Granovetter, M. (1985). Economic action and social structure: The problem of embeddedness. *American Journal of Sociology*, **91**, 481–510.

Shapiro, C. (1983). Premiums for high-quality products as returns to reputations. *Quarterly Journal of Economics*, **98**, 659–681.

Shapiro, S. P. (1987). The social control of impersonal trust. *American Journal of Sociology*, **93**, 623–658.

Shrum, W. & Wuthnow, R. (1988). Reputational status of organizations in technical systems. *American Journal of Sociology*, **93**, 882–912.

Stiglitz, J. E. (1989). Imperfect information in the product market. In R. Schmalensee & R. Willig (Eds), *Handbook of industrial organization* (Chap. 13, pp. 769–847). Amsterdam: North-Holland.

Weigelt, K. & Camerer, C. (1988). Reputation and corporate strategy: A review of recent theory and applications. *Strategic Management Journal*, **9**, 443–454.

Wilson, R. (1983). Auditing: Perspectives from multiperson decision theory. *Accounting Review*, **58**, 305–318.

CHARLES FOMBRUN

requisite variety *see* OPEN SYSTEMS; SYSTEMS THEORY

research and development management Research and development (R&D) are sources of profits from new products and services that raise a distinctive set of issues for managers. In simple terms, research leads to the discovery of new knowledge or technology, and development is taking them to market as a product or service.

R&D brings both high potential for profits and high UNCERTAINTY, introducing several groups of management issues: investment under uncertainty, interfaces with marketing and production, R&D alliances, and managing scientific professionals (Pearson, 1989) (*see* PROFESSIONALS IN ORGANIZATIONS).

Managers are likely never to face as much uncertainty as when they select R&D projects to fund. Where new technologies are involved, technical performance, production feasibility, and market response are all poorly understood. Still, the short market life of many TECHNOLOGY products makes these decisions recurring – although not routine (*see* DECISION MAKING). Managers can reduce some uncertainty with technology forecasting and market analysis. However, the research on innovation management indicates that intangibles, for instance, the effectiveness of project champions, are also important (Cohen & Levanthal, 1990).

The more critical is INNOVATION to firms' performance, the greater the demands to effectively manage the R&D/Marketing interface. Marketing is often cited as a weak spot for technology companies. However, customers' acceptance of new products is the ultimate test of the value of R&D. New products sometimes represent a discontinuous break with the familiar. It is likely that customers perceive no need for such products, technical superiority notwithstanding. Companies can gain advantages with the proper balance of technology push-and-market pull. R&D and marketing personnel jointly identify needs, assess market response, design products, and develop a product presentation. Organizational structures, like cross-functional teams, have been recommended (*see* MATRIX ORGANIZATION). New information and COMMUNICATION TECHNOLOGIES also have potential to improve coordination in unprecedented ways (Ancona, 1990; Keller, 1994).

A second important interface is with PRODUCTION SYSTEMS. Speed to market and reduced cycle times may both lead to competitive advantage (*see* COMPETITIVENESS). Customers also value high reliability, even in new products. Relations between R&D and production are important to each. Products can be designed for manufacturability, to minimize the number of components, automate assembly, simplify handling, and promote quality (*see* TOTAL QUALITY MANAGEMENT). Coordination and proper balance of influence between the two functions are key functions. As in the case of marketing, champions, organizational structures like teams, and COMMUNICATIONS are some of the solutions from organizational research (Katz & Allen, 1985).

STRATEGIC ALLIANCES involving R&D are an outgrowth of firms specialization. Companies can realize the benefits of R&D even though they are not vertically integrated (*see* VERTICAL INTEGRATION). Instead, managers may choose to specialize in activities where they are best, and leave other tasks to other companies. Advantages of specialization are an incentive behind alliances. They can efficiently carry out R&D transactions, and concentrate on their advantages. However, managing PARTICIPATION in alliances presents a different challenge from managing activities in-house. Differences occur in the needs to evaluate partners, contract for contingencies, assess costs and benefits, and control the flow of proprietary information (*see* TECHNOLOGY TRANSFER).

Finally, cultures and values can conflict between engineers and scientists and their managers. Some sources are alignment of professional orientation with organizational goals, individual versus team INCENTIVES, advancement, and information sharing. Responses include cross-TRAINING of technical and management people and communication.

See also **Knowledge-workers; Professionalism; Project management; Innovation adoption; Innovation diffusion**

Bibliography

Ancona, D. (1990). Outward bound: Strategies for team survival in an organization. *Organization Science*, 3, 321–341.

Cohen, W. & Levinthal, D. (1990). Absorptive capacity: A new perspective on learning and innovation. *Administrative Science Quarterly*, 35, 128–152.

Katz, R. & Allen, T. (1985). Project performance and the locus of influence in the R&D matrix. *Academy of Management Journal*, **28**, 67–87.

Keller, R. (1994). Technology-information processing fit and the performance of R&D project groups: A test of contingency theory. *Academy of Management Journal*, **37**, (1), 167–179.

Pearson, A. (1989). Twenty-one years of research into the management of R&D. *R&D Management*, **19**, (2), 99–101.

MICHAEL W. LAWLESS

research design This can be defined as the methodological strategy employed by empirical investigators in order to contribute to knowledge in a field of inquiry. It is the lynch-pin between ideas and data, and the adequacy of research design determines whether THEORY is tested, whether concepts are applied (*see* OPERATIONALIZATION), whether data are analyzable, whether measures are reliable (*see* RELIABILITY), whether results are generalizable (*see* GENERALIZATION), and whether inferences are valid (*see* VALIDITY).

Research design involves a number of choices:

1. *Strategy/Procedure*. The overall research strategy can be seen as embodying the investigator's implicit model of the relationship between ideas and data. Four main types of approach can be distinguished:

(a) Deductive – the design constrains and manipulates variables in order to test hypotheses, usually about causal relations or other associations among them, e.g., whether A is consistently linked with B;
(b) Inductive – the design seeks to accumulate data to add to an existing corpus, or build "grounded theory" (Glaser & Strauss, 1967) by accretion for empirical or ecological generalization, e.g., whether all As are Bs;
(c) Interpretive – the design explores the interior dynamics of a phenomenon by observation and description at close hand within an interpretive frame, e.g., how A works; and
(d) Interventionist – the design involves the recording of the results of controlled intervention in a social setting, e.g., how B changes as a result of action on A.

These approaches are not mutually exclusive, and a researcher may adopt more than one of them within the compass of a single study. It is termed "methodological triangulation" when different approaches are used to converge and cross-validate each other.

2. *Measurement*. Measurement is defined here as any systematically applied method of data gathering and classifying. Within ORGANIZATIONAL BEHAVIOR (OB) a wide variety of measurement methods are to be found, broadly divided into qualitative and quantitative types (*see* RESEARCH METHODS). These include records of observational data, archival analysis, paper and pencil measures (e.g., questionnaires), diary methods, and individual and group interviews. Each has strengths and weaknesses, as summarized in various sources (Nachmias & Nachmias, 1982; Bryman, 1989; Gill & Johnson, 1991).

3. *Control*. The essence of research design is what kinds of controls are applied to data gathering. Thus how the design is structured determines both the form of data to be analyzed and what range of data analytic techniques could be applied. The most common forms of research design to be found in OB are:

(a) Experiments – Control is applied by the assignment of subjects to groups, either randomly or selectively by a specified criterion. In the "experimental" (or "treatment") group, potentially explanatory variables are manipulated. In the control group these factors are held constant, or, in some variations, a treatment is applied which is expected not to generate equivalent effects (e.g., a "placebo" treatment). Thus the differential effects on one or more dependent variables can be observed and interpreted. Additionally, to eliminate unconscious experimenter BIAS, "blind" and "double blind" controls are often applied, keeping experimenters and subjects in ignorance during the experiment about whom has been assigned to which group. Areas where experimental methods are commonly used include laboratory studies of NEGOTIATION, COGNITIVE PROCESSES, and ERGONOMICS.
(b) Quasi-experiments – Design parameters follow the above as closely as possible but

in naturalistic settings where controls are generally more partial or incomplete (*see* QUASI-EXPERIMENTAL DESIGN). Examples of this approach are to be found in such areas as JOB DESIGN, PARTICIPATION, and GROUP DECISION MAKING.

(c) Natural experiments – As above, but the treatment is some naturally occurring event whose effects are measured. Examples of this design are typically found in areas where interest is mainly focused on the incidence of a dependent variable, such as ACCIDENTS, PRODUCTIVITY, and TURNOVER.

(d) SURVEYS – Responses to questions are gathered in a standardized form, often subject to scaling to allow valid comparison across individuals and groups, and for relationships between variables to be quantified by statistical analysis (*see* STATISTICAL METHODS). Surveys have designs which are either cross-sectional (one-shot) or longitudinal (repeated). In both, causal relationships must be inferred from correlational or difference-testing statistics, but can be done more confidently from longitudinal designs. Surveys are very extensively used at both the micro and macro levels of OB, to gather data from populations of employees, workgroups, or firms. Most of the research on JOB SATISFACTION, MOTIVATION, PERSONALITY, and LEADERSHIP relies heavily upon standardized questionnaire scales.

(e) Case method (*see* CASE STUDY RESEARCH) – Data are gathered from one or more cases, usually by more than a single method, such as observation, interview, and archives. Where a single or small number of cases is examined the method is usually termed clinical, idiographic or ethnographic (*see* ETHNOGRAPHY). Larger numbers of cases are studied for inductive, taxonomic, or comparative purposes. Cases may also be longitudinal or cross-sectional in design. Case method has made key contributions in many areas of OB, including the study of MANAGERIAL BEHAVIOR, ORGANIZATIONAL CULTURE, COMPETITIVENESS, organizational CRISES, and research into such areas as POWER, POLITICS, and CONFLICT.

(f) Other – Various other approaches can be found including SIMULATIONS, where models are tested either by observing human performance in simulated environments (*see* COGNITIVE ERGONOMICS) or by means of artificially generated inputs (*see* COMPUTER MODELING). Data from various kinds of sources can also be subject to NETWORK ANALYSIS, to map relational properties within defined populations. Archival data are used in many studies, for example, by event-history analysis, to study how populations change over time, e.g., in POPULATION ECOLOGY studies of the birth and death of firms. Finally are various secondary analytical methods, where data from previous studies are recombined inductively. The most common in current use is meta-analysis (*see* VALIDITY GENERALIZATION), where the extant studies on a small number of variables are accumulated by strict statistical criteria to take account of sample and effect sizes, measurement ERROR, and covariates to estimate the true relationship among the variables (e.g., the magnitude of the link between ABSENTEEISM and JOB SATISFACTION; Hackett & Guion, 1985).

Schaubroeck and Kuehn (1992) recently surveyed design strengths and weaknesses in Industrial/Organizational Psychology research by examining 199 studies published during 1989 and 1990. The analysis was conducted in the nomothetic tradition, i.e., assessing studies' adherence to scientific methodology. The criteria applied were

(a) construct validity, the extent to which operations represented the theoretical construct in question;
(b) internal validity, the extent to which causal relationships could be reasonably inferred; and
(c) external validity, the extent to which results could be expected to generalize to different settings.

The study found research into job attitudes and selection/staffing tended to be the most exploratory; selection/staffing and MOTIVATION studies made most use of occupational (as opposed to student) samples; selection/staffing and PERFORMANCE APPRAISAL studies tended to be more multioperational. Overall, motivation and leadership studies appeared to have the most design strengths, i.e., they more often used a strong inference methodology, testing theories against one another and using results to establish new hypotheses.

The study concluded that a general strength of the field was the large volume of work conducted in the field. Experimental studies were generally quite sophisticated in terms of measurement and treatment conditions. At the same time, much research was cross-sectional, with infrequent use of objective measures and little cross-validation of exploratory findings. Very few studies combined design strengths such as longitudinal observations and multiple data sources.

Schaubroeck and Kuehn's review focused on journals representing psychological or micro level approaches (*see* LEVELS OF ANALYSIS), in which it appears there are fairly strong attempts to adhere to scientific methodology, whilst indicating considerable room for improvement in meeting this criterion. It may be wondered whether a similar review of more macro or sociological approaches would yield a different array of strengths and weaknesses – with greater attention to contextual realism and methodological triangulation, but less refinement of measurement and more limited scope for quantifiable generalization. This is plausible, but empirically untested (Gummesson, 1988).

As the field of OB matures we may find two developments occurring. On the one hand, there may be less polarization between the contrasting extremes represented by different disciplinary PARADIGMS, and more integrative approaches to organizational issues. On the other hand, we may find more subject-specific methods emerging from the rapidly increasing sophistication of methodological and analytical tools, such as electronic event-recording or interactive software designs.

See also **Action research; Interactionism; Theory**

Bibliography

Burrell, G. & Morgan, G. (1979). *Sociological paradigms and organizational analysis*. London: Heinemann.

Bryman, A. (1989). *Research methods and organization studies*. London: Unwin Hyman.

Gill, J. & Johnson, P. (1991). *Research methods for managers*. London: Paul Chapman.

Glaser, D. G. & Strauss, A. L. (1967). *The discovery of grounded theory: Strategies for qualitative research*. New York: Aldine.

Gummesson, E. (1988). *Qualitative research in management*. Bromley, UK: Chartwell-Bratt.

Hackett, R. D. & Guion, R. M. (1985). A reevaluation of the absenteeism–job satisfaction relationship. *Organizational Behavior and Human Decision Processes*, **35**, 340–381.

Nachmias, C. & Nachmias, D. (1982). *Research methods in the social sciences*. London: Arnold.

Schaubroeck, J. & Kuehn, K. (1992). Research design in industrial and organizational psychology. In C. L. Cooper & I. T. Robertson (Eds), *International review of industrial and organizational psychology*, (vol. 7). Chichester, UK: Wiley.

NIGEL NICHOLSON and JOHN SCHAUBROECK

research methods These can be classified into two main types – qualitative and quantitative. Both have been used extensively in ORGANIZATIONAL BEHAVIOR research.

Choice of method is usually justified by the argument that qualitative approaches provides depth and quantitative ones breadth. The former are said to be useful in concept and THEORY generation, the latter for testing specific theories and hypothesized relationships between variables. But this distinction does not fully hold. Many quantitative studies have led to major conceptual and/or theoretical development and a number of qualitative studies involve the collection of some quantitative data to test hypotheses.

There are numerous texts on organizational research methods, though some are written for those researching from within a more general social science perspective and others for those with a management research perspective. An example of the former is Miller (1991), and of the latter is Easterby Smith, Thorpe, and Lowe (1991).

A key issue for quantitative researchers is how innovative to be in the use of concepts, variables, and research questions. INNOVATION in theory, conceptualization, and method, simultaneously, is best avoided. A major strength of the classic Aston studies (Pugh & Hickson, 1976), for example, was their innovativeness in generating variables and questionnaire items but developing these as measures of well-established Weberian concepts of bureaucratization (*see* BUREAUCRACY). Subsequent studies in the Aston tradition used the same measures and variables but innovated in the way they have been applied. Though psychologists have several well-established and tested standard questionnaires which they can use in novel circumstances there are rather few other examples in organizational research of standard protocols of this kind (*see* SURVEYS). More are needed and those that there are should be used more systematically and intensively. Too much methodological innovation vitiates the RELIABILITY of organizational behavior research and does not help build up a cumulative body of reliable knowledge in the field.

Qualitative research usually means the case study, the classic methodology text for this being Yin (1984) (*see* CASE STUDY RESEARCH). He distinguishes the case study from ETHNOGRAPHY and participant observation, both the latter implying a much greater degree of involvement by the researcher in the organization than for normal case study research. There is a tendency for the case study method to be associated with the use of grounded theory along the lines developed by Glaser and Strauss (1967) but this is by no means necessary. Case study research usually requires good access to the organization under investigation, though a number of insightful case studies have relied on interviews with informants outside the working context or on historical sources.

A further dimension to the research process is the position of the researcher. Choice of method, and the nature and quality of the results obtained, depend substantially on the seniority of the researcher, and whether, if junior, they are working under the direction of a more senior colleague, perhaps as part of a research team. Junior staff are usually more free to use time-intensive research methods. Senior staff may have less time but more power to command larger research funds and higher-level organizational access. Choice of methods may also be constrained if one is a member of a research team. Such practical factors may dictate research methods more than the theoretical posture of the researcher or the topic under investigation.

What trends might be discerned for the future direction of organizational research methods? As economists increasingly interest themselves in organizational issues will their tendency to conceptual simplification for the sake of operational measures shift the field further in the direction of more quantitative studies? Or will changes in the nature of organizations toward more flexible, small-scale forms operating in increasingly mobile and fluid LABOR MARKETS shift the field further toward qualitative studies generating holistic explanations of organizational behavior? Organizational research is to some extent a political activity and methods reflect the politics. To what extent will, and should, organizational researchers increasingly adopt methods such as action/intervention research in order to work in partnership with organizational members to generate results that they judge relevant and useful? How much funds, and access, will there be in the future for organizational research methods that reflect a more critical perspective and are for an audience outside the organization, engaged perhaps in policy formulation?

See also **Research design; Evaluation research; Statistical methods**

Bibliography

Easterby-Smith, M., Thorpe, R. & Lowe, A. (1991). *Management research: An introduction*. London: Sage.

Glaser, D. G. & Strauss, A. L. (1967). *The discovery of grounded theory: Strategies for qualitative research*. New York: Aldine.

Miller, D. C. (1991). *Handbook of research design and social measurement* (5th edn). Newbury Park, CA: Sage.

Pugh, D. S. & Hickson, D. J. (Eds), (1976). *Organizational structure in its context: The Aston programme I*. Aldershot, UK: Gower.

Yin, R. K. (1984). *Case study research: Design and methods*. Beverly Hills, CA: Sage.

ARTHUR FRANCIS

resistance to change Change is basic to life. Whether compelled by circumstances or intentionally planned, it is often essential to survival. But organizations and individuals vary widely in the way they deal with the necessity to adapt to new conditions. Such adaptation may take various forms: redesigning jobs; altering organizational structure; adding and/or removing members; and modifying prevailing norms and relationships that are part of the ORGANIZATIONAL CULTURE.

Among the major sources of resistance to change are the protection of material interests, fear of the unknown, and mistrust based upon bad past experience. There also may be an underlying concern about upsetting comfortable social arrangements represented in GROUP NORMS, STATUS, HIERARCHY, and REWARD systems. Exemplifying this, Miller and Rice (1967) reported that organizational groups may defend an outmoded task procedure because of such concerns. Yet, organizations require adaptative change to overcome their rigidities, including conformism, the rejection of new ideas, territoriality, favoritism, and other dysfunctional practices.

Introducing change requires a multistep process. A pioneer in developing a GROUP DYNAMICS approach to creating social change, psychologist Kurt Lewin in the 1940s emphasized a three-step group process:

(1) introducing an innovation with information aimed to satisfy a need;
(2) overcoming resistance by group discussion and DECISION MAKING; and
(3) establishing a new practice.

Prevailing practices are seen to be in a "quasi-stationary equilibrium," i.e., a steady though impermanent balance, that must be "unfrozen" before new practices can be introduced through a group process. Nadler and Tushman (1989) have advanced these points with regard to MOTIVATION for change, the transition state to be managed during and after, and the political dynamics of the situation needed for its support. As a general matter, those likely to be affected by a change should be informed and have a stake in the process shaping it.

The process of overcoming resistance is especially furthered by problem recognition when a need becomes manifest, as with scarcity in time of war, depression, or other calamity. The sheer availability of new information also contributes to the possibility of change, particularly with the widespread presence of instantaneous media. Among other things, information gives awareness of more alternatives for action. However, these are perceived within the frames provided by the conceptual models held by organization members, especially leaders. Resistance to change may therefore be based on a limited conception of organizational functioning, as with strict reliance on a hierarchical mechanical structure rather than a more adaptable organic one (Burns & Stalker, 1968).

On pragmatic grounds, however, a rational basis may exist for resistance to change. This is evident in the case of managers who see themselves being displaced by such organizational practices as SELF-MANAGED TEAMS, DELAYERING, and DOWNSIZING. The understandable concerns of those affected need to be recognized and addressed by such means as an information-based group process. It is also essential to see resistance as part of a system of relationships, as Miller and Rice (1967) have observed.

At the macro level, this system is embedded in the organization's culture, represented in the prevailing norms, VALUES, and beliefs underpinning the structures, COMMITMENTS, and actions there (Kilmann, Saxton, & Serpa, 1985). While it may make for comfortable stability, CULTURE also presents rigidity in the face of needed change, unless an effective LEADERSHIP process can be instituted. This is one of the major contributions which can be made through techniques of ORGANIZATIONAL DEVELOPMENT (OD), to encourage organization renewal and change. This process may need to cope with a reluctance to air disagreements, because of an avoidance of emotional conflict.

Other conceptual models have emphasized such factors as "momentum" (Miller & Friesen, 1980) in describing an organization's evolution toward a structure that provides coherence in a single interpretive scheme, an archetype. To change it, rather than simply make incremental changes within it, has been called "frame-breaking" versus "frame-bending" by Nadler and Tushman (1989). In bringing about strategic change, such structural elements as these need to be recognized, understood, and dealt with, as part of overcoming resistance to it (*see*, e.g., Greenwood & Hinings, 1993).

See also **Collective action; Conflict; Employee involvement; Group norms;**

Obedience; Organizational change; Politics

Bibliography

Burns, T. & Stalker, G. M. (1968). *The management of innovation*, (2nd edn). London: Tavistock.

Greenwood, R. & Hinings, C. R. (1993). Understanding strategic change: The contribution of archetypes. *Academy of Management Journal*, **36**, 1052–1081.

Kilmann, R., Saxton, M. & Serpa, R. (Eds), (1985). *Gaining control of the corporate culture*. San Francisco: Jossey-Bass.

Miller, D. & Friesen, P. (1980). Momentum and revolution in organization adaptation. *Academy of Management Journal*, **23**, 591–614.

Miller, E. J. & Rice, R. K. (1967). *Systems of organization*. London: Tavistock.

Nadler, D. A. & Tushman, M. (1989). Organizational framebending: Principles for managing reorientation. *Academy of Management Executive*, **1**, 194–204.

Robertson, P. J., Roberts, D. R. & Porras, J. I. (1993). Dynamics of planned organizational change: Assessing empirical support for a theoretical model. *academy of Management Journal*, **36**, 619–634.

EDWIN P. HOLLANDER

resource based theory One approach for describing the strategy formulation process in organizations focuses on matching an organization's internal strengths and weaknesses with its external opportunities and threats. Several models have been developed for analyzing an organization's external opportunities and threats (*see* FIVE FORCES MODEL). Most of these models build on insights from industrial ORGANIZATIONAL ECONOMICS (*see* STRUCTURE–CONDUCT–PERFORMANCE MODEL). Resource based theory provides an approach for analyzing an organization's internal strengths and weaknesses.

Resource based theory builds on a variety of research traditions in organization science and economics. For example, Ricardo's analysis of the economic consequences of land and other fixed factors of production is very much in the spirit of resource based theory, as is traditional research on the impact of general managers in organizations, and Selznick's analysis of institutional LEADERSHIP (*see* INSTITUTIONAL THEORY). Perhaps the most obvious precursor to resource based theory is Penrose's work on the limits of firm growth (*see* ORGANIZATIONAL SIZE).

The concept of resources, in resource based theory, should be understood broadly and includes physical resources (e.g., land, machines), financial resources (e.g., money), human resources (e.g., individual experience, individual training), and organizational resources (e.g., teamwork among individuals, organizational REPUTATIONS, ORGANIZATIONAL CULTURE (*see* TRAINING, HUMAN RESOURCES STRATEGY, ORGANIZATIONAL DESIGN). Different authors have used different terms to describe these resources. While distinctions are subtle, resources are often described as the fundamental attributes of organizations, capabilities as those attributes of organizations enabling them to take advantage of their resources, and COMPETENCIES are those attributes of organizations particularly relevant in managing DIVERSIFICATION strategies (*see* CORE COMPETENCE). Agreement about these distinctions is still emerging.

Two assumptions underpin resource based theory:

(1) that different organizations, even if they are in the same industry, may have different resources and capabilities; and

(2) these differences are stable over time.

Thus, in contrast to traditional economic models, the resources and capabilities of different organizations are thought to reflect an organization's unique history, its unique geographic location(s), the unique relations among its managers, the unique relations it has with suppliers and customers, its unique culture, traditions, and so forth.

Resources and capabilities become strategically relevant to the extent that they enable an organization to respond to external threats and opportunities in ways that organizations without these resources and capabilities cannot respond. They become sources of sustained competitive advantage to the extent that they are also costly for other firms to imitate (*see* COMPETITIVENESS). High cost imitation may reflect a variety of attributes of a firm's resources and capabilities, including:

(1) that these resources and capabilities are only developed over long periods of time (path dependence);
(2) that they may be tacit and taken for granted; and
(3) that they may be socially complex and relatively immune from direct managerial action.

Resource based theory provides a direct conceptual link between an organization's more behavioral and social attributes and its ability to gain a competitive advantage, since behavioral and social organizational attributes are often costly to imitate. In this sense, resource based theory provides an economic rationale for the study of behavioral and social attributes of organizations.

See also **Resource dependence; Organization and environment; Population ecology; Strategic management**

Bibliography

Barney, J. B. (1986). Strategic factor markets: Expectations, luck, and the theory of business strategy. *Management Science*, **42**, 1231–1241.

Barney, J. B. (1986). Organizational culture: Can it be a source of sustained competitive advantage? *Academy of Management Review*, **11**, 656–665.

Barney, J. B. (1991). Firm resources and sustained competitive advantage. *Journal of Management*, **17**, 99–120.

Conner, K. (1991). A historical comparison of resource-based theory and five schools of thought within industrial organization economics: Do we have a new theory of the firm? *Journal of Management*, **17**, 121–154.

Wernerfelt, B. (1984). A resource-based view of the firm. *Strategic Management Journal*, **5**, 171–180.

JAY B. BARNEY

resource dependence This perspective views organizations as needing to exchange resources in order to survive and looks at the way in which organizations can cope with the environmental dependencies thereby created.

Using an OPEN SYSTEMS framework, the approach emphasizes that organizations must interact with their environments (*see* ORGANIZATION AND ENVIRONMENT). Organizations need to take in resources such as materials, finance and personnel and transform these into products and services. These processes necessitate interactions that must be managed effectively. A key job for managers is to manage the relationships with these externalities as well as overseeing internal organizational processes.

Because the environment provides resources, organizations do not have complete control over the inputs they need. This is a source of UNCERTAINTY. Some of these resources will be more critical than others and some will be under the control of more dominant organizations (*see* DOMINANCE). These factors affect how dependent the organization is. Dependence is therefore a function of:

(1) the importance of the resource in terms of how much of it is required and how critical it is to the organization;
(2) how much discretion the provider of the resource has over its use and allocation; and
(3) how far those who control it are in a monopoly situation.

Organizations can take a number of actions to cope with dependence. They can either form INTERORGANIZATIONAL RELATIONSHIPS or change the environment (*see* INTERORGANIZATIONAL RELATIONS).

Interorganizational relationships are cooperative alliances formed with other organizations to try and control uncertainty or absorb it. For example, firms can CONTRACT with each other, enter into JOINT VENTURE agreements, or merge with or acquire other organizations (*see* STRATEGIC ALLIANCES). Interlocking directorates are a means of gaining information about the environment and forging networks within it (*see* NETWORKING).

Firms can try and change their environments by forming trade associations with other companies. Political lobbying can be used to secure a favorable competitive environment. Ultimately organizations also have some choice about the kind of environment in which they want to compete, by making decisions about the products they produce and the markets they serve (*see* COMPETITIVENESS).

This view of organizations shares some similarities with the POPULATION ECOLOGY approach. Both perspectives see the environment as centrally important in influencing ORGANIZATIONAL EFFECTIVENESS. But the resource dependence approach is less deterministic, seeing a crucial role for managers. Building on Child's (1972) concept of STRATEGIC CHOICE (1978), Pfeffer and Salancik acknowledge that managers have some AUTONOMY over what happens. There is *interdependence* between the organization and its environment and organizations, especially larger ones, can influence their environments. Managers can be proactive about the coping mechanisms they adopt. But internal POWER relationships will affect the choices that are made about how the organization will manage its dependencies, and this accounts for the variation in organizational forms and arrangements (*see* ORGANIZATIONAL DESIGN).

It is also recognized that the environment is not "given" to managers. It is "enacted" (*see* ENACTMENT), interpreted and made sense of by individuals. Thus even firms facing similar environments may respond in different ways because of their individual interpretations.

The resource dependence perspective places great emphasis on understanding the dependencies and exchange relationships between organizations (*see* EXCHANGE RELATIONS). In this view, the key DILEMMA for organizations is how to absorb uncertainty by forming relationships with other organizations, without losing too much control over their self-determination.

See also **Resource based theory; Five forces framework; Stakeholders; Systems theory**

Bibliography

Child, J. (1972). Organizational structure, environment and performance: The role of strategic choice. *Sociology* (6), 1–22.

Pfeffer, J. & Salancik, G. R. (1978). *The external control of organizations: A resource dependence perspective*. New York: Harper & Row.

SUSAN MILLER

resource partitioning *see* POPULATION ECOLOGY

restructuring This is the deliberate modification of formal relationships among organizational components. Three concepts are fused together in the word restructuring: *re* meaning to do again, *structure* referring to the formal arrangements among organizational components, and *ing* implying a process. Hence, restructuring refers to a process of changing already existing relationships among organizational elements (*see* ORGANIZATIONAL DESIGN). There are two ways to restructure: by changing actual organizational components or by changing the relationships among components. An organization can restructure, in other words, by adding, eliminating, splitting, or merging components within a structure; or it can restructure by strengthening, weakening, reversing, or redefining the relationships among components.

In its most common form, organizational restructuring usually involves actions such as delayering (removing hierarchical layers from the organization); redesigning work processes (mapping processes and removing the non-value-added steps or redundancies); and eliminating structural elements (outsourcing, selling off, or dismissing units, activities, or jobs within the organization). However, restructuring can involve much more than just the manipulation of organizational components. Organizations have a wide variety of structural elements that can be reconfigured, such as financial structures, market structures, technological structures, information structures, and organizational structures. These various types of structures are reconfigured in different ways. Financial restructuring can be accomplished, for example, by renegotiating loan agreements, changing the investment portfolio, selling off unproductive divisions, or outsourcing products or services to an external provider (as illustrated by several major airlines that restructured their financial debt in the last decade in order to remain viable and to begin anew in the industry). Market restructuring can be accomplished by reconfiguring the product portfolio or by moving the competitive market position of an organization so that it competes in a different market niche (as illustrated, for example, by a major retailer which changed from competing on the basis of price with lower-end merchandise to competing on the basis of quality and image with upper-end merchandise) (*see* COMPETITIVENESS). Technological and informational restructurings are generally accomplished through the application of new technologies, including AUTOMATION, computerization, and NETWORKING (*see* INFORMATION TECHNOLOGY; ADVANCED MANUFACTURING TECHNOLOGY). Despite the obvious importance of these various types of restructuring, organizational restructuring – the alteration of arrangements among internal organizational components, including SUBUNITS, hierarchical relationships, and work processes – is the phenomenon of most interest to students of ORGANIZATIONAL BEHAVIOR (*see* HIERARCHY).

Recently, two terms have been used so often in the popular literature as substitutes for restructuring that they deserve special mention. One is the concept of DOWNSIZING, and the other is the concept of re-engineering (*see* BUSINESS PROCESS REENGINEERING). In other words, restructuring, downsizing, and re-engineering have been used as synonyms by many writers even though they have clearly distinctive meanings. Restructuring is used as a substitute for downsizing, for example, in order to avoid the negative connotations associated with job loss or contracting ORGANIZATIONAL SIZE. However, when organizations have experienced pressure to reduce redundancy or waste, to eliminate headcount, or to increase efficiency through downsizing, few actually engage in restructuring. Past research has shown that downsizing has mainly involved personnel reductions, not the restructuring of organizational elements. Similarly, re-engineering refers to a zero-based redesign of an organization's processes, structures, or relationships. Restructuring does not assume that the entire old way of doing things or of structuring relationships is abandoned and recreated. It assumes remodeling rather than new construction. Consequently, restructuring is not an appropriate synonym for downsizing or for re-engineering.

At least two different orientations are prominent in the theory and practice of organizational restructuring. The two approaches can be arranged on a continuum, anchored on one end by an assumption that managers have complete control over the process of restructuring, and anchored on the other end by the assumption that managers have no control over the process of restructuring. The scholarly and popular literature, thus far, have been dominated by the assumptions represented by the managerial Control end of the continuum.

On the one hand, for example, restructuring can be assumed to be the prerogative and responsibility of an organization's management. It is an activity designed to improve the efficiency, PRODUCTIVITY, or effectiveness of the organization, and so is an important part of the managers' role (*see* ORGANIZATIONAL EFFECTIVENESS). Restructuring is motivated by maladaptation or nonalignment with the environment or by competitive opportunities or pressures. For example, Miller and Friesen (1980) found that organizations are restructured in a limited number of archetypical forms when faced with competitive pressures, among which they labeled consolidation, DECENTRALIZATION, professionalization, and entrepreneurial revitalization. Miles and Cameron (1982) found that the firms in the US tobacco industry restructured in three dominant ways in reaction to a hostile and turbulent external environment – defending current practices and incremental restructuring (domain defense), aggressive changes and redesigned forms of organization (domain offense), and completely new structures and original competitive activities (domain creation). Meyer (1992) identified four types of restructuring in hyperturbulent environments:

(1) incremental change within the organization;
(2) framebreaking change within the organization;
(3) incremental change in the organization's relationship to its environment; and
(4) transformation and creation of new relationships and structures in the external environment (*see* ORGANIZATION AND ENVIRONMENT).

Freeman and Cameron (1993) found that organizations facing financial pressures adopted either a reorientation approach to restructuring or a convergence approach to restructuring. A reorientation approach involves major, strategic changes in hierarchical arrangements and the nature of the work. Restructuring entire units and clusters of subunits in an organization characterizes reorientation. A convergence approach involves minor, tactical changes in work and working relationships. Restructuring the tasks and job relationships in a firm is typical of a convergence approach. A reorientation approach to restructuring has been associated with higher levels of effectiveness over time when organizations face threatening conditions.

The other end of this continuum reflects an assumption that restructuring is outside the purview of management action and is a product of uncontrolled circumstances. Restructuring occurs not because of planned managerial action but because of evolutionary processes and environmental inertia. Theoretical perspectives represented by the POPULATION ECOLOGY or natural selection models, or by the evolutionary life cycles models, exemplify the most common form of unmanaged restructuring. For example, several theorists who represent the population ecology perspective (e.g., Hannan & Freeman, 1977) argue that a variety of organizational and environmental constraints inhibit managers' impact on an organization's structure. The structures, processes, and COMPETENCIES of surviving organizations are almost entirely determined by the demands of the external environment, according to this view. Organizational restructuring that does not match the requirements of the environment results in organizational demise. Hence, if one looks at organizations over time, successful restructuring is a product of environmental selection or environmental determinism rather than managerial choice. The environmental dictates what restructuring will occur and that restructuring will usually occur in slow, evolutionary patterns, although it may also be experienced on rare occasions in revolutionary spurts. Another variation on this deterministic theme is represented by writers on organizational life cycles. One representative study, for example, was conducted by Quinn and Cameron (1983), who found that new organizations restructure in predictable ways over their early life cycles. These stages of restructuring are similar to the progression of group stage development (*see* GROUP DEVELOPMENT). The initial structures of organizations, they found, are generally characterized by loosely coupled elements and an entrepreneurial orientation (*see* LOOSE COUPLING). Subsequent sequential restructurings include a change to teamwork and integration, then a change to hierarchical structures and a focus on control, and finally a restructuring which emphasizes and is aimed at optimizing external relationships and competitive market success.

The challenge for future research on restructuring is to reconcile the two ends of the continuum. For example, Orton (1994) studied the 1976 reorganization of the U.S. intelligence community. By studying original memos, notices, notes of conversations, and minutes, Orton created a six-stage model of reorganizing processes. First, organization members confronted limitless frontiers of actions, statements, influences, and ideas. Second, organization members pulled out of that frontier – through action, perception, discussion, and discovery – small brackets or boundaries on which they focused attention. Third, organization members generated mental maps that made sense of the frontiers, brackets, or boundaries. Fourth, organization members combined their individual-level mental maps to build an overall, agreed-upon organization-level foundation for a restructuring. Fifth, organization members decided upon a set of restructuring initiatives which were presented together as a deliberate organization design. Sixth, the restructuring alternatives were absorbed into and, consequently, changed the existing structure. Over time, Orton argued, emergent restructuring becomes deliberate restructuring.

In sum, organizational restructuring may involve many aspects of an organization, and it may take many forms. What is common about restructuring in all its forms, however, is that it is a process in which already existing elements and their interrelationships are permanently altered. Restructuring is currently a popular way in which organizations are trying to make themselves more effective.

See also **Organizational change; Mergers and acquisitions; Job design**

Bibliography

Freeman, S. J. & Cameron, K. S. (1993). Organizational downsizing: A convergence and reorientation perspective. *Organization Science*, **4**, 10–29.

Hannan, M. & Freeman, J. (1977). The population ecology of organizations. *American Journal of Sociology*, **82**, 929.

Meyer, A. D. (1992). Adapting to environmental jolts. *Administrative Science Quarterly*, **27**, 515–537.

Miles, R. & Cameron, K. S. (1982). *Coffin nails and corporate strategies*. Englewood Cliffs, NJ: Prentice-Hall.

Miller, D. & Friesen, P. (1980). Archetypes of organizational transition. *Administrative Science Quarterly*, **25**, 268–299.

Orton, J. D. (1994). Reorganizing: An analysis of the 1976 reorganization of the US Intelligence Community. Unpublished doctoral dissertation. University of Michigan.

Quinn, R. E. & Cameron, K. S. (1983). Organizational life cycles and shifting criteria of effectiveness: Some preliminary evidence. *Management Science*, **29**, 33–51.

KIM S. CAMERON and J. DOUGLAS ORTON

retirement This is typically associated with the phase of life individuals experience at the end of their careers working for an employer for primary income (*see* LIFE STAGES). Retirement, however, does not imply inactivity, but a different type of activity. Many individuals continue to be active in retirement by part-time or flexible employment, engaging in leisure activities, or volunteer work; these are often related to attitudes from their working years.

The meaning of retirement has changed drastically in the last 100 years from rarely being experienced by individuals because they did not live long enough to many workers currently retiring between the ages of 55 and 67 with acceptable health conditions in advanced industrial countries. Retirement AGE regulations vary by country and in the United States, the Amendments to the Age Discrimination in Employment Act (1986) removed mandatory retirement for most workers; in Japan, large companies require workers to retire between the ages of 55 and 60 (Forteza & Prieto, 1994). Although there is evidence that social security systems and legislation are promoting a later age of retirement for employees, the average age of retirement is decreasing. In addition, because of the aging of the world population, many individuals who retire at age 65 will likely spend 15 to 20 years in retirement (Woodruff-Pak, 1988).

Individuals' transition (*see* CAREER TRANSITIONS) from work to retirement may require substantial adaptation because of the previously imposed structure by work on their time and activities. Work is a central aspect of many individuals' lives; the work ethic has dominated the leisure ethic for most individuals. Retirement experiences, however, are a continuity of individuals' experiences in their working phase of life (*see* NONWORK/WORK).

Two recent approaches to the transition from work to retirement have been discussed including early retirement as a voluntary organizational WITHDRAWAL behavior similar and related to correlates of other withdrawal behaviors such as quitting, choosing to be laid off, and being absent from work (Hanisch & Hulin, 1990) (*see* ABSENTEEISM; TURNOVER). This classification of early retirement as a withdrawal behavior was related to organizational attitudes. The difference between individuals' satisfaction with work and their anticipated satisfaction with retirement predicted early retirement decisions; income and health were not significant predictors (*see* JOB SATISFACTION). These findings have implications for retaining older individuals in the workforce by focusing on employee attitudes.

Second, Hanisch (1994) examined the relation between work, personal, and health reasons for retiring and their impact on individuals' attitudes and behaviors in retirement. Individuals who retired for personal reasons planned more events, participated in more activities, and were more satisfied with their retirement than either those who retired for work or health reasons. Implications of this research include encouraging individuals prior to retirement to plan activities and events; this should help in their adjustment to retirement (Gibson & Brown, 1992).

Retirement is an extension of individuals' working lives. The previous lifestyle or past behaviors of individuals will be the best predictor of their behaviors in retirement. The smooth transition from work to retirement is a function of financial resources, health, activities, attitudes, and social networks.

See also **Career stages**

Bibliography

Forteza, J. A. & Prieto, J. M. (1994). Aging and work behavior. In H. C. Triandis, M. D. Dunnette & L. M. Hough (Eds), *Handbook of industrial and organizational psychology* (pp. 447–483). Palo Alto, CA: Consulting Psychologists Press (discusses retirement statistics across countries).

Gibson, J. & Brown, S. D. (1992). Counseling adults for life transitions. In S. D. Brown & R. W. Lent (Eds), *Handbook of counseling psychology* (pp. 285–313). New York: Wiley.

Hanisch, K. A. (1994). Reasons people retire and their relations to attitudinal and behavioral correlates in retirement. *Journal of Vocational Behavior*, **45**, 1–16.

Hanisch, K. A. & Hulin, C. L. (1990). Job attitudes and organizational withdrawal: An examination of retirement and other voluntary withdrawal behaviors. *Journal of Vocational Behavior*, **37**, 60–78.

Woodruff-Pak, D. S. (1988). *Psychology and aging*. Englewood Cliffs, NJ: Prentice-Hall.

KATHY A. HANISCH

rewards Theories of MOTIVATION seek to explain and predict the direction, intensity, and persistence of behavior (Kanfer, 1990). In other words, what does a person choose to do, how hard does s/he work at it, and for how long? These motivational outcomes are typically thought (e.g., VIE THEORY) to be a function of both the person (e.g., values) and the environment (e.g., perceived rewards and their perceived liklihood), and whether an aspect of the environment is perceived as a reward depends on the person's VALUES. Therefore, it is somewhat difficult (perhaps even misleading) to speak in terms of general taxonomies of rewards because they tell us only what people, on average, find rewarding, and may not be terribly accurate for understanding what different individuals find rewarding.

Many different literatures have something to say about what people generally find rewarding. Content theories of motivation such as Maslow's need hierarchy theory (*see* SELF-ACTUALIZATION) and Alderfer's existence, relatedness, and growth theory (*see* ERG THEORY) identify hierarchies of needs ranging from physiological and safety up through esteem and self-actualization. Herzberg's MOTIVATION–HYGIENE THEORY focuses on identifying factors that either contribute to satisfaction or help avoid dissatisfaction.

The literature on JOB SATISFACTION and its measurement has built on such theories to identify a number of specific reward areas. The Job Descriptive Index (JDI; Smith, Kendall, & Hulin, 1969) asks about the work itself (e.g., routine, satisfying), pay, promotion opportunities, SUPERVISION, and coworkers. The Minnesota Satisfaction Questionnaire (MSQ; Weiss, Dawis, England, & Lofquist, 1967) asks about these and other facets of satisfaction. The pay dimension has been further broken down by Heneman and Schwab (1985) in the Pay Satisfaction Questionnaire, which measures satisfaction with pay level, pay raises, pay structure–administration, and benefits.

A good deal of work has also gone into developing instruments to measure work-related values for use in predicting occupational choice (*see* CAREER CHOICE), job satisfaction, and worker satisfactoriness (i.e., performance). Dawis (1991) summarizes five such scales, including the Minnesota Importance Questionnaire (MIQ). The MIQ measures the value attached to ability utilization, achievement, activity, advancement, AUTHORITY, company policies and practices, compensation, coworkers, CREATIVITY, independence, moral VALUES, recognition, responsibility, security, social service, social STATUS, supervision – human relations, supervision – technical, variety, and WORKING CONDITIONS.

Finally, studies of job choice and job preferences suggest at least two factors that influence the rank ordering of importance people attach to rewards. First, self-reports of reward preference often yield different results than less direct assessments methods such as policy-capturing (e.g., Zedeck, 1977). For example, money is typically found to be very important when a policy-capturing methodology is used, but less important when self-reports are used. One explanation is that self-reports are more subject to social desirability bias (Schwab, Rynes, & Aldag, 1987) and money tends to be seen as a more pedestrian, less noble sounding value than are some others (e.g., challenge). Another finding from the job choice and preference literature is that the measured importance of a reward depends on its variability (Rynes, Schwab, & Heneman, 1983). Therefore, if companies all have the same pay, but have different advancement opportunities, pay will not be an important factor in job choice, but advancement opportunities will matter in such choices. Pay is not unimportant, but its importance in the decision only comes to light if there is sufficient variance in pay.

Although it is difficult to take these diverse and rich literatures and boil their findings down into a short list of key rewards, one such list is as follows (Noe, Hollenbeck, Gerhart, & Wright, 1994):

Pay level – A person's job is typicially the primary source of his or her income.

Challenge and responsibility – For many people, work plays an important role in establishing their self-concepts.

Job security (*see* JOB INSECURITY) – Work force reductions in the United States have become commonplace, making this an increasingly important concern among employees.

Advancement opportunities – The opportunity to advance one's career and move on to new challenges is attractive to most people.

Geographic location – Dual career and other family issues often mean that choice and flexibility with respect to work location is important (*see* NONWORK/WORK).

Benefits – Heath care, retirement income, and so forth, are major factors in ensuring employee health and income security.

Additional rewards – This preceding list obviously excludes a great many factors that are likely to be important to significant segments of the population. Some of these were discussed previously.

See also **Motivation and performance; Payment systems; Extrinsic/intrinsic motivation; Performance, individual**

Bibliography

Dawis, R. V. (1991). Vocational interests, values, and preferences. In M. D. Dunnette & L. M. Hough (Eds), *Handbook of industrial and organizational psychology*, (2nd edn, vol. 2). Palo Alto, CA: Consulting Psychologists Press.

Heneman, H. G. III & Schwab, D. P. (1985). Pay satisfaction: Its multidimensional nature and measurement. *International Journal of Psychology*, **20**, 129–141.

Kanfer, R. (1990). Motivation theory and industrial and organizational psychology. In M. D. Dunnette & L. M. Hough (Eds), *Handbook of industrial and organizational psychology*, (2nd edn, vol. 1). Palo Alto, CA: Consulting Psychologists Press.

Noe, R. A., Hollenbeck, J. R., Gerhart, B. & Wright, P. M. (1994). *Human resource management: Gaining a competitive advantage*. Burr Ridge, IL: Austen Press/Irwin.

Rynes, S. L., Schwab, D. P. & Heneman, H. G. III (1983). The role of pay and market pay variability in job application decisions. *Organizational Behavior and Human Performance*, **31**, 353–364.

Schwab, D. P., Rynes, S. L. & Aldag, R. J. (1987). Theories and research on job search and job choice. In K. Rowland & G. Ferris (Eds), *Research in personnel and human resources management*, (vol. 5, pp. 129–166). Greenwich, CT: JAI Press.

Smith, P. C., Kendall, L. & Hulin, C. L. (1969). *The measurement of satisfaction in work and retirement*. Chicago: Rand McNally.

Weiss, D. J., Dawis, R. V., England, G. W. & Lofquist, L. H. (1967). *Manual for the Minnesota satisfaction questionnaire* (Bulletin No. 22). Minneapolis: University of Minnesota, Minnesota Studies in Vocational Rehabilitation.

Zedeck, S. (1977). An information processing model and approach to the study of motivation. *Organizational Behavior and Human Performance*, **18**, 47–77.

BARRY GERHART

risk-taking The terms risk, risk-taking, UNCERTAINTY, and AMBIGUITY have been used in a variety of ways. In the most common usage, a decision maker must choose between two alternatives (A1 and A2). If A1 is chosen, then one of a set of outcomes will occur (say $O_{1,1}$ or $O_{1,2}$). If all the alternatives and outcomes, and the outcomes' probabilities of occurrence given a specific choice are known, then the decision is under risk. Alternatively, in many cases the outcomes and/or their probabilities of occurrence cannot be specified leading to uncertainty or ambiguity. Several literatures have been centrally concerned with issues of risk-taking.

Decision theorists develop rational procedures for choices under risk often based on expected utility theory although GAME THEORY analyses have also begun to address some such issues. Decision theory techniques address decisions under risk, but have less success under uncertainty or ambiguity.

BEHAVIORAL DECISION RESEARCH (or theory), a branch of psychology, considers risk-taking by individuals largely in experimental situations although often with monetary REWARDS. Behavioral decision theorists began by exploring how actual decision makers differ from the assumptions of expected utility. The field has progressed rapidly. Numerous studies demonstrate experimentally instances where decision makers differ from prescriptive models in either assessment of probabilities or choices. To summarize the general thrust of this field, people in many instances are extremely poor intuitive statisticians and do not act as utility maximizers.

Economics and finance theorists use risk as the primary explanation for differential returns in capital markets. A smaller group considers how capital structure influences the risk of bankruptcy. In explaining market returns, risk generally means the risk to stockholders that they cannot eliminate by holding a well-diversified portfolio (systematic risk or beta). Although systematic risk remains widely used in finance, recent research questions of role of beta and has sparked efforts to find alternative measures and models of risk.

Organizational psychologists studying the RISKY SHIFT phenomenon find that groups make decisions with different apparent risk preferences than their members. In situations where all members of a group may find a given alternative overly risky, the group as a whole may choose that alternative.

Finally, STRATEGIC MANAGEMENT researchers consider corporate-level risk and performance issues defining risk and performance in both capital market and accounting returns terms. Strategic management research on risk has examined numerous topics including DIVERSIFICATION, mergers, and performance effects (*see* MERGERS AND ACQUISITIONS). Whereas risk and return appear positively related in capital market models, both positive and negative associations between risk and return have been found when risk is measured by income stream uncertainty. These associations appear to vary over business cycles and across industries.

Overall, these differing approaches have made significant progress but have generated confusion by using the term risk to mean quite different constructs. MacCrimmon and Wehrung (1986) demonstrate that differing measures of risk-taking gathered from the same individuals at the same time exhibit almost no association. Furthermore, both psychological and organizational research indicates risk-related behaviors are quite sensitive to contextual factors. These findings pose serious problems for the development of integrated approaches to risk.

See also **Decision making; Prisoner's dilemma; Satisficing**

Bibliography

Yates, J. F. (1992). *Risk-taking behavior*. New York: Wiley.

MacCrimmon, K. R. & Wehrung, D. A. (1986). *Taking risks: The management of uncertainty*. New York: Free Press.

PHILIP BROMILEY

risky shift/group polarization Social psychological research in the 1960s suggested that individual group member decisions in a potentially risky situation were, on average, less risky than the final decision of the group as a whole. The risky shift phenomenon attracted much research interest since it suggested that GROUP DECISION MAKING might produce dangerous decisions at all organizational levels (e.g., within the nuclear power or defence industries) as a result of unconscious group processes. Subsequent research has indicated that the shift to risk is, in fact, a shift to extremity. Groups shift away from a neutral point beyond the average of the decisions initially favored by individuals in the group; in other words, shifts to caution as well as risk occur. This phenomenon, more accurately called *group polarization*, influences attitudes as well as decisions.

When individuals discover the position of others they tend to move along the scale partly because of a "majority rule" influence – the largest subgroup tends to determine the group decision. Moreover a process of SOCIAL COMPARISON may take place, whereby information about a socially preferred way of behaving leads to polarization. When we compare ourselves with those immediately around us in the organization we tend to locate our position closer to theirs rather than retaining the integrity of our initial position (Myers & Lamm, 1976).

In organizations the dangers of polarization are most likely when the group has just been formed or when the group is confronted with an unusual (often a crisis) situation (*see* CRISES).

See also **Minority group influence; Risk taking; Decision making**

Bibliography

Myers, D. G. & Lamm, H. (1976). The group polarization phenomenon. *Psychological Bulletin*, 83, 602–627.

MICHAEL A. WEST

rituals An organizational ritual is a rule-governed, structured, and preplanned activity of a symbolic character, collectively produced and enacted in a social context, face-to-face with an audience (*see* SYMBOLISM). It is a dramatic occasion, with beginnings and endings are clearly demarcated. Participants have well-defined roles to be performed, like parts in a play (*see* ROLE; ROLE-TAKING). Participants enact what members in good standing are supposed to think, feel, and do.

Cultural researchers sometimes, but not always, distinguish among rituals, rites, and ceremonies. When these terms are used interchangeably, or when researchers use different definitions of the same term, conceptual confusion can be a problem. Trice and Beyer (1984), for example, define a ritual in a restricted manner, as a relatively rote, clearly specified, set of repetitive behaviors. Unlike most other researchers, Trice and Beyer reserve the term "rite" for the more complex sets of behaviors defined above as a ritual; ceremonies then are defined as complex collections of rites that are enacted only once, at a special occasion. Alternatively, Alvesson and Berg (1992) reserve the term rituals for activities which reinforce existing POWER relations in a HIERARCHY, seeing rites as less formal activities serving a broader variety of functions. Such fine distinctions are difficult to maintain. For example, power can be enhanced in informal collective activities; both rites and rituals can be relatively short, specified sets of behavior; and some ceremony-like activities are repeated periodically. For the purposes of this short essay, with apologies, such fine distinctions cannot be usefully maintained.

A wide range of organizational rituals have been studied, usually drawing on anthropological theory and using ethnographic methods (*see* ETHNOGRAPHY). Trice and Beyer (1984) offer a typology of the most commonly studied rituals. Initiation rituals have been examined in a variety of organizations, including banks, police academies, and military organizations (*see* SOCIALIZATION). These studies draw attention to "liminality," a vulnerable state in which an individual's old identity has been stripped away and a new identity not yet established (e.g., Louis, 1980; Turner, 1969; Van Maanen, 1973) (*see* JOINING-UP PROCESS). Enhancement rituals bring recognition to exceptional performers, such as top sales people and recipients of promotions (e.g., Rosen, 1991) (*see* MANAGEMENT OF HIGH POTENTIAL). Degradation rituals celebrate the opposite – the defamation and removal of supposedly poor performers, particularly those in LEADERSHIP positions (e.g., Gephart, 1978). Renewal rituals seek to strengthen group functioning, temporarily resolving some problems while drawing attention away from others – a description that, Trice and Beyer observe, bears a striking resemblance to most ORGANIZATIONAL DEVELOPMENT interventions. Other kinds of rituals celebrate conflict reduction, integration, and endings (*see* CONFLICT RESOLUTION). For example, Harris and Sutton (1986) describe the content of organizational "wakes," held to recognize the sadness caused when a firm goes out of business (*see* ORGANIZATIONAL DECLINE AND DEATH).

Kunda (1992, p. 93) observes that most researchers see ritual "as a crucial link between ideologies that provide the framework for collective life and the associated forms of individual experience" (*see* IDEOLOGY). This approach encompasses several conflicting schools of thought: functionalist, critical, dramatalurgical. Functionalist interpretations describe rituals in Durkheimian terms, as enhancing group solidarity (*see* GROUP COHESIVENESS), serving an integrative function that reinforces the power of the powerful, intensifying collectivity members' satisfaction, COMMITMENT, and loyalty. For example, Trice and Beyer (1984) describe rituals serving manifest and latent, instrumental and expressive functions – all of which are congruent with managerial interests.

In contrast, Kunda notes, critical students of rituals emphasize conflict and power, describing how rituals help dominant groups achieve and maintain dominance (e.g., Van Maanen & Kunda, 1989). Some critical studies, for example, have documented the existence of rituals of countercultural resistance by lower level or competing, managerial-level groups. For example, Young (1991) described rituals that different groups of assembly line workers use to preserve, strengthen, and differentiate their various, overlapping collective identities.

Finally, research in a dramaturgical tradition (e.g., Turner, 1969) has attempted to transcend both functional and critical perspectives by attending to the ways rituals are like dramas, with scripted roles, hidden meanings, and latent functions. Rosen (1991), for example, describes an annual business breakfast meeting as a partially successful integration ritual, where varying subgroups (reflecting functional divisions, the promoted and the unpromoted, insiders and outsiders) react quite differently to the activities scripted by management, some withdrawing, others actively resisting, and still others eagerly (apparently) embracing prescribed VALUES and behaviors.

When a ritual is successful, participants are emotionally affected; they embrace the role they have portrayed. However, as Kunda notes, rituals have transition moments, when participants can self-consciously and skillfully, or semiconsciously and awkwardly, distance themselves from the good-member role they have been asked to play. Often such ROLE DISTANCING activities take the form of humor, irony, or self-deprecating remarks. Thus, by framing a ritual as a link between the collective and the individual, the possibility of less-than-perfect role embracement emerges. Furthermore, Kunda illustrates moments within a ritual where a deviant may step out of scripted interaction by challenging a participant who represents the powers whose authority is being legitimized. Such deviant challenges can be highly dramatic and, if resolved to the satisfaction of those who are attempting to orchestrate the ritual, may actually reinforce its desired effect by silencing or punishing dissenting interpretations.

As in other areas of ORGANIZATIONAL CULTURE research, studies of rituals have focused more often on the functionalist, managerial, power-reinforcing aspects of rituals, rather than on the deeper, more complex conflict, power, and dissent issues highlighted in careful enthnographies by scholars as Kunda, Van Maanen, Rosen, and Alvesson and Berg. Studies of ROLE AMBIGUITIES in ritual activities are relatively rare, offering a fruitful avenue for future research.

See also **Critical theory; Emotions in organizations; Social constructionism; Symbolic interactionism**

Bibliography

Alvesson, M. & Berg, P. O. (1992). *Corporate culture and organizational symbolism*. Berlin: De Gruyter.

Gephart, R. (1978). Status degradation and organizational succession: An ethnomethodological approach. *Administrative Science Quarterly*, **23**, 553–581.

Harris, S. & Sutton, R. (1986). Functions of parting ceremonies in dying organizations. *Administrative Science Quarterly*, **29**, 5–30.

Kunda, G. (1992). *Engineering culture: Control and commitment in a high-tech corporation*. Philadelphia, PA: Temple University Press.

Louis, M. (1980). Surprise and sense making: What newcomers experience in entering unfamiliar organizational settings. *Administrative Science Quarterly*, **25**, 226–251.

Rosen, M. (1991). Breakfast at Spiro's: Dramaturgy and dominance. In P. Frost, L. Moore, M. Louis, C. Lundberg & J. Martin (Eds), *Reframing organizational culture* (pp. 77–89). Newbury Park, CA: Sage.

Trice, H. & Beyer, J. (1984). Studying organizational cultures through rites and ceremonials. *Academy of Management Review*, **9**, 653–669.

Turner, V. (1969). *The ritual progress*. Chicago: Aldine.

Van Maanen, J. (1973). Observations on the making of policemen. *Human Organization*, **32**, 407–417.

Van Maanen, J. & Kunda, G. (1989). Real feelings: Emotional expression and organizational culture. *Research in Organizational Behavior*, **11**, 43–103.

Young, E. (1991). On the naming of the rose: Interests and multiple meanings as elements of organizational culture. In P. Frost, L. Moore, M. Louis, C. Lundberg & J. Martin (Eds), *Reframing organizational culture* (pp. 90–103). Newbury Park, CA: Sage.

JOANNE MARTIN

role A role is a delineation of the set of recurrent behaviors appropriate to a particular position in a social system (*see* SYSTEMS THEORY). The social system may range from an informal group to a formal organization. Every social system consists of multiple interdependent positions, each defined by a role. Roles specify many aspects of these relationships, including the AUTHORITY and STATUS relationships within the system. As with social systems, roles can be informal or formal. Informal roles may evolve or be negotiated as a social system such as a group develops. In work organizations, formal roles are often specified by JOB DESCRIPTIONS.

Roles help us to determine what we should do in order to meet others' expectations, as well as what to expect from others. They are specific to particular positions within particular social systems. Although a person may belong to many different groups and organizations, the role an individual occupies in one social system may be completely different from the role that same individual occupies in other social systems. Furthermore, an individual may occupy more than one role within the same social system.

There are many examples of relatively generic roles that exist in most organizations. The role of boss (i.e., superior, supervisor, manager, etc.) delineates many recurrent behaviors such as evaluating, rewarding, correcting, disciplining, and generally overseeing the work of subordinates in an assertive manner. Likewise, subordinates are expected to behave respectfully and responsively toward their bosses. A person in the role of mentor is expected to be nurturing, patient, and helpful (*see* MENTORING). A secretary's role includes behaving courteously and in a businesslike manner. While these general roles are fairly universal, many organizational roles delineate much more specific behaviors. However, the exact content of specific role behaviors depends on the particular organization in which the roles are located. For example, a manager in the marketing department of a particular organization may be expected to communicate weekly with a particular production manager, send a summary report to the vice-president of marketing every other week, oversee and evaluate the work of six marketing assistant managers, and entertain certain customers of the company once a month. These specific expectations are unique to the role occupied by the marketing manager in this particular organization.

Because people occupy multiple roles within their social systems, they frequently experience ROLE CONFLICT, when the expectations specified by a person's multiple roles are incompatible. PROFESSIONALS IN ORGANIZATIONS often experience role conflict. For example, a corporate lawyer may feel pressures to behave in differing ways from her dual roles as member of the legal profession and employee of the corporation. This latter case is an example of interrole conflict in which there exist incongruent expectations from members of two different role sets. This is distinct from intrarole conflict, which occurs when incongruent expectations are present within a single role set.

Role conflict is one of several role-related concepts that facilitate an understanding of the phenomenon of performing a role. Closely related to role conflict is ROLE AMBIGUITY, which is uncertainty about what is expected regarding role performance. Role ambiguity is minimized when role differentiation occurs. Role differentiation refers to the establishment of clear definitions for group members of their specific duties and responsibilities to the group, and how these duties and responsibilities contribute to the realization of the group's goals. Ideally, organizations will go beyond simply making sure that each member have a role and know what it entails. The roles assigned to group members should also maximize each individual's opportunities to contribute to the objectives of the individual and the social system.

Kahn, Wolfe, Quinn, Snoek, and Rosenthal (1964; *see also* Katz & Kahn, 1966) constructed a comprehensive theoretical development of roles. In this conceptualization, each role is surrounded by a ROLE SET which is the collection of people who are concerned with the performance of the occupant of the role. Role episodes consist of role sending, role receiving, and role expectations. When the expectations associated with a particular role are overwhelming to the occupant of the role, ROLE OVERLOAD occurs. Alternatively, role underload results when there are too few role demands (*see also* ROLE OVERLOAD/UNDERLOAD.

Together these role-related concepts from ROLE THEORY. Role theory is closely related to situated identity theory, which posits that people learn about their role by taking the perspective of others in their role set (Mead, 1934). Because everyone undertakes this process, a mutual understanding develops about what each person's role is (*see* ROLE TAKING). This perspective emphasizes the interpersonal nature of roles; because roles are defined by the expectations of others, conceptually they are in interpersonal phenomenon (Gerth & Mills, 1967). This is true even though roles are often studied with the individual as the unit of analysis.

The concept of role has been very useful to researchers theoretically, but formulating hypotheses about roles requires a specification of which conditions surrounding the role are to be tested. A role is difficult to operationalize without narrowing the inquiry to specific types of role conditions. Thus, research on roles has generally taken the form of looking for correlates of role conditions. Role conditions refer to the role conflict or role ambiguity associated with the role, role overload and role underload, and the other specific concepts discussed above. Research in several domains of ORGANIZATIONAL BEHAVIOR are relevant to roles, for example, research on PERCEPTION, COMMUNICATIONS, and expectancies. Even though research on these latter topics is not necessarily couched in terms of roles, there are clear connections between these phenomena and role theory.

There are several directions in which research on role conditions could usefully progress. Surprisingly, even after hundreds of studies on various role conditions, there is still debate about the definition of constructs and how best to measure them (King & King, 1990). It is promising that several researchers have been working on conceptually and operationally disentangling these role conditions. As convergence is reached on how to define accurately and measure these constructs, the findings from previous research on correlates of role conditions can be pooled together to determine the robustness of these findings (Jackson & Schuler, 1985). As relationships between role conditions and personal and organizational characteristics are determined to be robust, it will be useful to investigate factors that moderate and mediate these relationships to further specify the boundary conditions under which these effects are strongest (*see* Pierce, Gardner, Dunham, & Cummings (1993) for an example of this type of research).

Because of the interpersonal nature of roles and role conditions, integrating the study of networks with the study of roles may increase our understanding of roles within the broader social system. For example, early theorizing on roles suggested that there are objective role conditions and subjective (or perceived) role conditions, but little empirical research investigates the match between objective and subjective role conditions. NETWORK ANALYSIS could shed light on how expectations from other people in the role set match the perceived expectations of the person occupying the role. Similarly, network methods could be used to determine how formal organizational roles (defined by JOB DESCRIPTIONS, for example) match the informal roles that develop in organizations.

Several current organizational trends may dramatically affect the expectations, and thus the role conditions, of organizational members. For example, how does ORGANIZATIONAL DEMOGRAPHY affect role conditions in an increasingly diverse workforce? How does TECHNOLOGY, especially regarding communication, affect how role expectations are sent and received? New roles are beginning to emerge in many organizations for people who are technologically proficient. An example of a behavior that is expected from someone in this type of role is to disseminate information about new technologies to less proficient members of the organization. These emerging roles are especially important because surprising degrees of status and power may accompany them. Another important question is how ORGANIZATIONAL RESTRUCTURING and the increased use of temporary employees affect the expectations of employees and the patterns of role relationships within organizations. Decreased loyalty to the organization may result in people attaching more importance to their roles outside the organization, especially when role conflict occurs. These issues highlight the importance of furthering our understanding of how roles affect behavior in organizations.

See also **Attribution; Managerial behavior; Stress**

Bibliography

Gerth, H. & Mills, C. (1967). Institutions and persons. In J. G. Manis & B. N. Meltzer (Eds), *Symbolic interaction: A reader in social psychology*. Boston: Allyn & Bacon.

Jackson, S. & Schuler, R. (1985). A meta-analysis and conceptual critique of research on role ambiguity and role conflict in work settings. *Organizational Behavior and Human Decision Processes*, **49**, 8–104.

Kahn, R., Wolfe, D., Quinn, R., Snoek, J. & Rosenthal, R. (1964). *Organizational stress: Studies in role conflict and ambiguity*. New York: Wiley.

Katz, D. & Kahn, R. (1966). *The social psychology of organizations*. New York: Wiley.

King, L. & King, D. (1990). Role conflict and role ambiguity: A critical assessment of construct validity. *Psychological Bulletin*, **107**, 48–64.

Mead, G. (1934). *Mind, self and society*. Chicago: University of Chicago Press.

Pierce, J., Gardner, D., Dunham, R. & Cummings, L. (1993). Moderation by organization based self-esteem of role condition-employee response relationships. *Academy of Management Journal*, **36**, 271–288.

JEFFREY T. POLZER

role ambiguity This denotes uncertainty about the expectations, behaviors, and consequences associated with a particular ROLE. Specifically, a person has a need to know others' expectations of the rights, duties, and responsibilities of the role, the behaviors that will lead to fulfillment of these expectations, and the likely consequences of these role behaviors. Role ambiguity results when these three types of information are nonexistent or inadequately communicated. Organizational factors (e.g., rapidly changing organizational structures, job FEEDBACK systems) and individual factors (e.g., INFORMATION PROCESSING biases) may cause role ambiguity. Consequences of role ambiguity may include tension, job dissatisfaction, and TURNOVER. It is useful to distinguish objective role ambiguity from the subjective role ambiguity experienced by the person in the role. A JOB DESCRIPTION is an example of a formal organizational mechanism that may alleviate role ambiguity. Kahn, Wolfe, Quinn, Snoek, and Rosenthal (1964), were the first to extensively develop these elements of role ambiguity within an organizational context. Research indicates that role ambiguity is positively correlated with both ANXIETY and propensity to leave (the role) and negatively correlated with several factors such as organizational COMMITMENT, WORK INVOLVEMENT, and JOB SATISFACTION

See also **Job characteristics; Stress: Uncertainty**

Bibliography

Kahn, R., Wolfe, D., Quinn, R., Snoek, J. & Rosenthal, R. (1964). *Organizational stress: Studies in role conflict and ambiguity*. New York: Wiley.

JEFFREY T. POLZER

role conflict This is the experience of contradictory, incompatible, or competing role expectations. It occurs when an individual has two or more salient roles in a situation which include expectations to act in incompatible ways (inter-role conflict), or when expectations within one role are incompatible with each other (intra-role conflict). CONFLICT between a role and an individual's values or beliefs is also referred to as role conflict. Role conflict is often assumed to be an uncomfortable state that individuals are motivated to change.

Current research focuses on characteristic role conflicts like those between family and work, union member and family breadwinner, and foreign and native cultures; situations that evoke role conflict; the resolution of role conflict; and the evolution of roles within an individual's life. Meta-analyses (*see* VALIDITY GENERALIZATION) have shown role conflict to be "moderately" ($r = 0.30$) related to dissatisfaction with job content and coworkers (*see* JOB SATISFACTION) and with TURNOVER.

Many studies rely on an eight-item scale, *The Role Conflict Scale*, developed by Rizzo, House, and Lirtzman (1970). Studies of its construct VALIDITY have concluded it has adequate validity.

See also **Job design; Role; Stress**

Bibliography

Rizzo, J. R., House, R. J. & Lirtzman, S. I. (1970). Role conflict and ambiguity in complex organizations. *Administrative Science Quarterly*, **15**, 150–163.

CATHERINE A. RIORDAN

role distancing This is behavior (e.g., explanations, apologies, or joking) undertaken by the occupant of a ROLE with the intent of communicating to others that the individual's actions should be attributed to the role rather than to the individual. The person's intention is to create or maintain separateness between herself and the role. The individual is not denying her occupancy of the role; instead, the individual is denying that she would act the same way if it were not for the role. The most likely cause of role distancing is the pressure exerted from another role to act inconsistently from the expectations of the first role (i.e., ROLE CONFLICT). Role distancing behaviors suggest that the individual has some resistance to the role. An example of role distancing is when a teacher explains to students that his disciplinary actions for the student's inappropriate behaviors are not due to him being a mean person, but instead are due to his role as a teacher. The concept of role distancing is embedded in the field of sociology and is most comprehensively developed in Erving Goffman's book *Encounters* (1961).

See also **Attribution; Projection; Fundamental attribution error**

Bibliography

Goffman, E. (1961). *Encounters: Two studies in the sociology of interaction*. Indianapolis: Bobbs-Merrill.

JEFFREY T. POLZER

role modeling *see* TRAINING

role over/underload Role overload occurs when an individual experiences excessive role demands. *Quantitative* overload is when there is too much to do. *Qualitative* overload is when the individual does not have the experience or ability to carry out role demands. Having more than one demanding role at the same time, like parent and professional, or a job position which includes many weighty responsibilities, are two frequently researched examples. Role underload is the opposite condition in which the individual has very few role demands, or the demands are very easily accomplished. Underload can also be quantitative or qualitative.

Both overload and underload are job stressors. They, in conjunction with other job stressors and the amount of control individuals feel they have over job demands, have been found to be predictive of STRESS-related illness. Anecdotal accounts of death from overwork ("karoshi") have come from Japan. The relationship of overload and underload to organizational variables like ABSENTEEISM, JOB SATISFACTION and ACCIDENTS is inconsistent, probably affected by other moderating variables. BURNOUT and "rustout" are believed to be potential consequences of overload and underload, respectively. TIME MANAGEMENT techniques are used to deal with problems of quantitative overload.

See also **Mental health; Role theory; Role**

Bibliography

Lazarus, R. S. & Folkman, S. (1984). *Stress, appraisal and coping*. New York: Springer-Verlag.

CATHERINE A. RIORDAN

role set This is the set of people who influence or are concerned with the behavior of the person in a ROLE. A role set typically consists of the people in organizational roles that are directly associated with the focal role, such as those that are adjacent in the work-flow structure or the organizational HIERARCHY. Members of the role set do not have to be in the same organization as the person in the focal role, however (e.g., customer or salespersons from other organizations can be in the role set).

Role episodes, which include role-sending, role-receiving, role expectations, and role behavior, occur within the role set. Role expectations are beliefs and attitudes held by members of the role set regarding what behaviors are appropriate for the person in the role. Role-sending is the COMMUNICATION of role expectations by members of the role set. Role-receiving refers to the perceptions and cognitions by the person in the role of the expectations that are sent by members of the role set. Finally, role behavior refers to the role occupant's recurring actions that are attributable to the role (*see* Katz & Kahn, 1966).

See also **Group structure; Systems theory; Boundary spanning**

Bibliography

Katz, D. & Kahn, R. (1966). *The social psychology of organizations*. New York: Wiley.

JEFFREY T. POLZER

role taking ROLE taking, or "taking the role of the other," is a process in which an individual develops an empathetic understanding of other people's roles as the result of observing their behavior. George Herbert Mead (*see* SYMBOLIC INTERACTIONISM), stated role taking is an essential process in developing our own roles. In this sense, roles develop in relation to other people. It is presumed that for interactions to be smooth, people must achieve a rough agreement about their relative roles, but the research evidence is not consistent.

Often situations imply specific roles, which may explain why people familiar with a situation sometimes can predict other people's behaviors. Individuals too can become identified with the roles they take consistently (e.g., a leader). Sarbin (1954) and others have suggested some individuals have an aptitude for "role taking."

Two related concepts are worthy of note. *Altercasting* refers to one individual's attempt to define or influence the role another assumes. Role taking is an attempt to understand, not influence. Reflexive role taking is when an individual reflects on another's role in order to evaluate how his or her own behavior seems to the other person. Role taking does not include self evaluation.

See also **Role theory; Social constructionism; Negotiated order**

Bibliography

Sarbin, T. R. (1954). Role theory. In G. Lindzey (Ed.), *Handbook of social psychology*, (vol. 1, pp. 223–258). Cambridge, MA: Addison-Wesley.

CATHERINE A. RIORDAN

role theory This term specifies the conceptual relationships among several distinct role conditions (*see* ROLE for an extended discussion of these role conditions). Role theory is concerned with the general question of how an individual's behavior is connected to his or her social environment. One of the earlier contemporary conceptions of role theory was enumerated by Kahn, Wolfe, Quinn, Snoek, and Rosenthal (1964). This theory posits that, in most social situations, and especially within organizations, the role that a person takes is "the central fact for understanding the behavior of the individual" (Katz & Kahn, 1966; *see* ROLE TAKING). The organization is conceptualized as a system of roles, with the ROLE SET of a particular position in an organization consisting of role episodes, which include role-sending, role-receiving, role expectations, and role behavior.

The greatest contribution of this theory is probably its detailed conceptual description of how people are affected by their social situation, particularly the expectations of the social actors to whom they are connected. Most research related to this theory tests relationships among specific role conditions, organizational and individual characteristics (e.g., hierarchical structure, individual SELF ESTEEM), and organizational and personal outcomes (e.g., performance, JOB SATISFACTION).

See also **Network analysis; Managerial behavior; Systems theory**

Bibliography

Kahn, R., Wolfe, D., Quinn, R., Snoek, J. & Rosenthal, R. (1964). *Organizational stress: Studies in role conflict and ambiguity*. New York: Wiley.

Katz, D. & Kahn, R. (1966). *The social psychology of organizations*. New York: Wiley.

JEFFREY T. POLZER

routinization This term represents the process of rationalization and standardization of the work of the organization. Routinization can occur via several different kinds of processes. First, work might be routinized via the integration of machines as in an assemble line. In this context, it is sometimes called work-flow INTEGRATION. More recently this has been called Fordism. Second, work might be routinized via FORMALIZATION, that is the standardization of roles via rules, JOB DESCRIPTION and the like.

The concept of routinization was developed by Perrow (1967) as the basis of a four-fold classification of types of organizations. He called this routine versus nonroutine technology. In his work, he made the further distinction between whether or not the work was analyzable or not and whether there many or few exceptions. Routine work, that is work that could be readily rationalized and standardized, exists when the problems are analyzable and there are few exceptions.

Routinized work flows tend to be highly associated with the centralization of decisions (*see* DECENTRALIZATION). Bureaucracies are one example of this kind of organization (*see* BUREAUCRACY).

See also **Organizational design; Repetitive work; Mechanistic/organic; Functional design; Strategic types**

Bibliography

Hage, J. (1980). *Theories of organizations*. New York: Wiley–Interscience.

Perrow, C. (1967). A framework for the comparative analysis of organizations. *American Sociological Review*, 32, 194–209.

JERALD HAGE

rules *see* BUREAUCRACY; MANAGEMENT, CLASSICAL THEORY

— S —

sabotage This may be conceptualized as a form of resistance to capital interests. It may be defined as any deliberate action or inaction directed to lower the quantity or quality of production (Dubois, 1979). It has as its intent the destruction, disruption, or damage of some aspect of the work environment, including the setting and machinery of production and/or the good or service produced itself (Taylor & Walton, 1971). Contrary to popular images of the "mad saboteur," sabotage is often a rational and highly symbolic act (*see* RATIONALITY; SYMBOLISM). Usually, it is social in nature, conspiratorial and restrained. Most often, it occurs underground, obscured from public view and does not signify an anti-machine mentality (Jermier, 1988).

Dialectical ORGANIZATION THEORY offers a view of workers as engaged in CONFLICT at the point of production (Edwards & Scullion, 1982). The struggle between workers and owner–managers over control of the labor process reflects the fundamentally political nature of production in organizations (*see* LABOR PROCESS THEORY). Sabotage is central to these struggles and has the potential to alter POWER dynamics substantially as it challenges the LEGITIMACY of unlimited rights of capitalists and other elites.

Several typologies of sabotage have been advanced. One study delineates a four-fold classification of sabotage that includes violent and illegal actions, labor methods (*see* COLLECTIVE ACTION), information sabotage (*see* INFORMATION TECHNOLOGY), and acts directed at profit/production (Giacalone & Knouse, 1990). It is manifested in varied forms that may include maintaining an absolute adherence to rules, disabling equipment or machinery, adulterating products, doing personal work on company time with company supplies, and creating downtime.

Acts of sabotage have been classified as comprising two aims: one being instrumental (*see* INSTRUMENTALITY), directed toward shifting the balance of POWER or achieving certain limited demands; the other intended to serve a demonstrative function as a protest against injustice (*see* JUSTICE PROCEDURAL and JUSTICE DISTRIBUTIVE) or as a rejection of organizational VALUES (Dubois, 1979). Sabotage may result from performing boring, monotonous, tedious, or hazardous work (*see* REPETITIVE WORK) and from a diminished sense of control over some aspect of the work environment, especially control of time, work practices, or output quality. It may also stem more directly from negative AFFECT or FRUSTRATION (LaNuez & Jermier, 1994).

Commonly held assumptions of sabotage as a form of resistance exclusive to blue-collar workers are largely inaccurate. Recent literature reflects its prevalence among managers and technical and professional workers as well (LaNuez & Jermier, 1994) (*see* PROFESSIONALS IN ORGANIZATIONS). This is attributable to the transmuted nature of MANAGERIAL WORK (*see* JOB DESKILLING), increased monitoring and measurement of employees, and rapid technological changes such that workplace COMMUNICATION patterns have been radically altered, minimizing human interaction. These forces heighten the incentive of managerial and technocratic groups to engage in acts of sabotage as loyalties wane from the interests of owners and other elites, and as social identities assume an orientation that is more closely aligned with collegial/professional interests, a concern with the larger public good, or even with working class interests (*see* IDENTIFICATION).

Forms of sabotage adopted by managers and technical employees may differ from that of unskilled laborers, and may include sabotage by circumvention (e.g., non-cooperation, open-mouth sabotage, data falsification) or sabotage by direct action, encompassing physical damage to property, data or product/service (LaNuez & Jermier, 1994). These forms of sabotage are no less pernicious than those adopted by laborers. They may, in fact, have more wide-ranging implications for the firm given the specialized knowledge base and understanding of organizational systems among high status employees, and their easy accessibility to records and data. Perhaps most notable are those forms of sabotage associated with computer technologies, illustrated by popular press attention to system crashes and computer viruses.

See also **Stress; Alienation; Withdrawal, organizational**

Bibliography

Dubois, P. (1979). *Sabotage in industry*. Middlesex, UK: Penguin.

Edwards, P. K. & Scullion, H. (1982). *The social organization of industrial conflict: Control and resistance in the workplace*. Oxford, UK: Basil Blackwell.

Giacalone, R. A. & Knouse, S.B. (1990). Justifying wrongful employee behavior: The role of personality in organizational sabotage. *Journal of Business Ethics*, **9**, 55–61.

Jermier, J. M. (1988). Sabotage at work: The rational view. *Research in the Sociology of Organizations*, **6**, 101–134.

LaNuez, D. & Jermier, J. M. (1994). Sabotage by managers and technocrats: Neglected patterns of resistance at work. In J. M. Jermier, D. Knights & W. Nord (Eds), *Resistance and power in organizations*. London: Routledge.

Taylor, L. & Walton, P. (1971). Industrial sabotage: Motives and meanings. In S. Cohen (Ed.), *Images of deviance* (pp. 219–245). Harmondsworth, UK: Penguin.

THERESA DOMAGALSKI
and JOHN M. JERMIER

safety The management of safety in organizations involves the development and implementation of measures for hazard identification, assessment, and control, and the maintenance, measurement, and adaptation of control standards and procedures. It embraces the mechanisms for ensuring that employers and employees remain committed to safety objectives and motivated to ensure they are maintained (Petersen, 1978; Dawson, Willman, Bamford, & Clinton, 1988). Although the maintenance of safety might be assumed to be a shared, objective interest, much academic interest has focused on the sources of failure in safety management and how they may be counteracted.

Several authors have focused on the extent to which certain "tightly coupled" or "finely tuned" highly complex technical systems might be intrinsically accident prone (*see* ACCIDENTS). Changes occurring to particular elements within complex systems can generate multiple outcomes and interactions whose end result is system failure (Perrow, 1984; Starbuck & Milliken, 1988) (*see* SYSTEMS THEORY). Other writers have focused on managerial willingness to incur costs in the interests of hazard control. Cost–benefit analysis provides one tool for risk assessment and cost estimation, but there are differences between businesses and even within sectors in management *capability* and willingness to generate effective safety resources. These differences were examined by Dawson et al. (1988) for the United Kingdom. They argued that small organizations may lack capability through lack of resources or expertise. In addition, firms characterized by high levels of subcontracting experience problems of both hazard control and regulation. Third, unionized firms where safety representation is established are more capable of effective safety management than those where no such representation structure exists. Pauchant and Mitroff (1992) have argued that managers may systematically misperceive dangers and risks. Grunberg (1983) suggests there is a direct relationship between productivity and accident rates. Nichols (1986) has argued for the United Kingdom that cycles of economic activity may influence safety provision and thus accident rates, through the variable of capacity utilisation. Higher per capita accident rates may follow from higher levels of utilization during the upturn in the economic cycle. The effect is argued to be lagged rather than direct.

Another key variable affecting safety provision is ease of detection. This has spawned an interest in the institutions of safety regulation both in the United States and the United Kingdom and their effectiveness in monitoring safety management. The bargaining style of OSHA in the United States has been contrasted with the consensus-seeking style of the HSE in the United Kingdom. The latter organization seeks education rather than enforcement and is reluctant to prosecute detected safety failures. However, estimates of regulatory effectiveness are difficult to obtain because of the inadequacy of accident statistics in both the United States and the United Kingdom, and because it is difficult to assess, for example, from the number of enforcement activities, what would be the accident rate in the absence of regulation (Bacow, 1981; Dawson et al. 1988). Wilson (1985) has argued that, in both countries, political rather than safety considerations have become important, so that regulators are pressured by the need for cooperation from employees into relatively noninterventionist stances on safety management within firms. Dawson et al. (1988) have argued in the United Kingdom context that deregulation of the labor market and the decline of trade union representation are likely to exert a negative impact on safety provision, when reduced inspection levels lead to a reduction in detection probabilities.

A further consideration is employee involvement. Employees' interest in their own safety is not unproblematic. Viscusi (1979) has shown that, although workers accurately perceive the magnitude of hazards involved in their jobs, the existence of hazard-compensating wage differentials reduces quit rates: employees will tolerate unsafe conditions for some time. He found some evidence that unions were disposed toward wage compensation rather than hazard elimination. In the United Kingdom, Guest, Peccei, and Thomas (1993) have shown that safety rules may be disregarded by employees where they are seen to be managerial in origin and controlling in intent. They fall victim to a wider disaffection which has its origins in reactions to other managerial policies.

As risk assessment techniques and cost–benefit approaches become more sophisticated and widely used by firms it is likely that future research will focus on their implications for safety rules and procedures. However, a second broad area of interest is the effects of organizational culture and climate on employee perceptions of safety rules and the implications of those perceptions for rule observance.

Bibliography

Bacow, L. (1981). *Bargaining for job safety and health.* Cambridge, MA: MIT Press.

Dawson, S., Willman, P., Bamford, M. & Clinton, A. (1988). *Safety at work: The limits of self regulation.* Cambridge, UK: Cambridge University Press.

Grunberg, L. (1983). The effect of social relations of production on productivity and workers' safety. *International Journal of Health Studies*, **13**, (4), 621–634.

Guest, D., Peccei, R. & Thomas, A. (1993). The impact of employee involvement on organisational commitment and "them and us" attitudes. *Industrial Relations Journal*, **24**, (3), 191–201.

Nichols, T. (1986). Industrial injuries in British manufacturing in the 1980's. *Sociological Review*, **34**, 290–306.

Pauchant, T. & Mitroff, I. (1992). *Transforming the crisis prone organisation.* San Francisco: Jossey-Bass.

Perrow, C. (1984). *Normal accidents: Living with high risk technologies.* New York: Basic Books.

Peterson, P. (1978). *Techniques of safety management.* New York: McGraw-Hill.

Starbuck, W. H. & Milliken, F. J. (1988). Challenger; Fine tuning the odds until something breaks. *Journal of Management Studies*, **25**, 320–40.

Viscusi, W. K. (1979). *Employment hazards: And investigation of market performance.* Cambridge MA: Harvard University Press.

Wilson, G. K. (1985). *The politics of safety and health.* Oxford, UK: Clarendon Press.

PAUL WILLMAN

satisfaction *see* ATTITUDE THEORY; JOB SATISFACTION; MOTIVATOR/HYGIENE THEORY

satisficing This refers to a choice situation in which the final decision is one that only minimally satisfies the necessary requirements. The decision satisfies and suffices rather than optimizes.

Classical theories of DECISION MAKING see the decision maker as an economic individual ("economic man") who rationally diagnoses a problem, draws up a complete range of alternative solutions, evaluates each against explicit criteria, and is therefore able to make a choice which maximizes outcomes.

BEHAVIORAL DECISION RESEARCH acknowledges that decision makers often operate in complex environments where there is much UNCERTAINTY (*see* COMPLEXITY). The issue for decision cannot be easily defined, there are many alternative solutions, and criteria are unclear and may conflict. This is especially likely when decisions are made in an organizational setting, and when they are about strategic issues for which there are few tried and tested problem-solving routines.

So "administrative man" (Simon, 1976) has to simplify, and the limitations of human cognitive capacities and constraints of time mean that not every aspect of the situation can be examined in full. The analogy often given is that the decision maker does not search for the sharpest needle in the haystack, only one sharp enough to sew with. Decision makers therefore operate within a BOUNDED RATIONALITY and satisficing solutions are the result.

See also **Cognitive processes; Group decision making; Persistence; Risk taking**

Bibliography

March, J. G. & Simon, H. A. (1958). *Organizations*. New York: Wiley (2nd edn, 1993; Oxford: Blackwell).

Simon, H. A. (1976). *Administrative behavior* (3rd edn). New York: Free Press.

SUSAN MILLER

scarcity A condition of scarcity exists whenever demand for a product or resource is less than the supply of that product or resource. Of course, scarcity is usually not constant over time. Under conditions of scarcity, organizations usually begin producing more of the undersupplied product or resource, up to the point that aggregate supply approximately equals aggregate demand.

At least two exceptions to this dynamic attribute of scarcity exist. First, governments, cartels, or other external agents can act to artificially restrict supply, thereby creating the condition of scarcity. Second, the supply of certain resources or products may be fixed by nature. Thus, for example, the total supply of nonrenewable raw materials is fixed. This suggests that, sooner or later, the demand for these raw materials may be greater than the supply, and thus a condition of scarcity may develop.

However, even in these settings, scarcity can still vary. In particular, substitute products or resources are often developed in response to either anticipated or actual conditions of scarcity. Thus, when OPEC, acting as a cartel, created artificial scarcity in the crude oil market, a variety of substitutes for crude oil, including conservation, emerged. As the finite supply of certain raw materials drops below demand, it is often the case that substitute materials are developed.

Overall, the existence of scarcity can be seen as a major driver of economic activity. Scarcity creates the need for economic exchange, as well as the opportunity for economic profit, as organizations act to either exploit a condition of scarcity (by selling scarce products or resources for high prices) or reduce a condition of scarcity (by introducing substitute products or resources).

See also **Exchange relations; Resource-based theory; Resource dependence; Organization and environment**

Bibliography

Samuelson, P. (1942). *Foundations of economic analysis*. Cambridge, MA: Harvard University Press.

JAY B. BARNEY

scientific management This term refers to the theory and practice of management originated by Frederick Winslow Taylor (1856–1915), an American engineer best known for his development of time and motion study. Taylor became concerned about the collective controls over output levels exercised by skilled workers and reinforced by strong social norms (*see* GROUP NORMS). He attributed management's inability to tackle these problems to its lack of scientific knowledge of the production process and therefore proposed to measure the time required for each element of a job in order to establish the "one best way" of performing that job, and the level of output that was possible. Management would then be able to reassert its control over production and prescribe work methods and output goals. Taylor also believed that jobs should be divided up into small units; workers should be motivated with financial incentives linked to performance (*see* MOTIVATION AND PERFORMANCE); they should be allocated a daily work quota (*see* GOAL SETTING); they should be subject to close supervision; and factory departments should be reorganized to permit the most efficient flow of work and materials (Kelly, 1982; Littler, 1982; Rose, 1988).

Underlying Taylor's ideas was a set of assumptions now referred to as THEORY X (*see* THEORY X AND Y): workers are alienated from their work, wish to avoid high levels of effort, are motivated solely or largely by pay, and distrust management. The worker–management relationship is therefore based on low TRUST, although Taylor believed co-operation was possible given high wages, high PRODUCTIVITY, and positive attitudes by both parties.

Taylor and his associates measured a wide range of jobs in a range of industries – engineering, construction, transportation – and often raised labor productivity, although the more spectacular claims – 100 percent productivity increases for instance – were probably exaggerated. At the same time, Taylor's practices and his authoritarian way of implementing them produced intense hostility from unionized workers, and the use of time and motion study became the focus of bitter conflict until well into the 1960s. TRADE UNIONS objected to the deskilling of work (*see* JOB DESKILLING), to increased managerial CONTROL and to the "speed-up" or intensification of effort levels.

Many of Taylor's principles were still popular in post-war American industry, where jobs were designed to minimize SKILL, costs, and training time, and subject to close SUPERVISION. Henry Ford combined these ideas with a moving assembly line to establish even tighter control of work levels. Even today many scientific management principles and practices are still widespread: work measurement, individual PERFORMANCE-RELATED PAY, performance targets and close supervision. Despite their progressive reputation many Japanese manufacturing plants display similar features (Fucini & Fucini, 1990).

Some of his ideas and practices have been questioned. There is a growing trend toward multiskilling of work since it became clear from the 1950s that assembly-line work was not always efficient and produced strong dissatisfacton amongst its workers. Moreover, a growing number of companies have sought to acquire the production knowledge of their workers in a co-operative way, through means such as QUALITY CIRCLES. Taylor's ideas on financial MOTIVATION and his belief that workers hold antagonistic attitudes toward management are unfashionable but valid insights that should not be lost sight of.

See also **Human relations movement; Flexibility; Performance, individual; Quality of working life; Management, classical theory; Alienation**

Bibliography

Fucini, J. & Fucini, S. (1990). *Working for the Japanese: Inside Mazda's American auto plant*. New York: Free Press.

Kelly, J. E. (1982). *Scientific management, job redesign and work performance*. London: Academic Press.

Littler, C. (1982). *The development of the labour process in capitalist societies*. London: Heinemann.

Rose, M. (1988). *Industrial behaviour: Theoretical development since Taylor*, (3rd edn). Harmondsworth, UK: Penguin.

JOHN KELLY

selection interviewing Interviews take a variety of forms and are carried out for a wide range of different purposes. Perhaps the most common use of the interview is for selection. Because of its ubiquitous use in selection, and because of the practical consequences of employment interview decisions, it is this type of interview which has received by far the most attention by researchers and practitioners in the field of Organizational Behavior.

Due to the fact that interviews differ greatly in length, form, content, and structure, it is not possible to give a single comprehensive definition of what constitutes a selection interview. However, broadly speaking, the typical selection interview is characterized by face-to-face contact of limited duration between two or more people who are strangers. Its purpose is to attract and select from the available pool of applicants those individuals who will perform the job in question most effectively.

The single issue which has attracted the most attention of researchers over almost three-quarters of a century, and which has resulted in a large number of published studies (Eder & Ferris, 1989; Keenan, 1989), is the degree to which the interview is reliable and valid (*see* RELIABILITY; VALIDITY). The question is, can interviewers make consistent judgments about candidates and to what extent do these judgments predict subsequent job performance? Early reviews (e.g., Mayfield, 1964; Ulrich & Trumbo, 1965), concluded that the interview was seriously lacking in validity, with correlations between interview scores and subsequent job performance regularly turning out to be very low or zero (*see* PERFORMANCE, INDIVIDUAL). These reviews had considerable impact on academic researchers and led many to advocate a much reduced role for the interview in selection. However, it is probably true to say that this research had a minimal effect on practicing managers who, as far as one can tell, continued to put their faith in the interview in much the same way as they had always done.

One consequence of recruiters' continued reliance on the traditional interview, despite the research evidence, was a number of attempts on the part of researchers to devise improved interview techniques. The most important development here was the advent in the 1980s of structured interview methods such as the situational interview (Latham & Saari, 1984) and the patterned behavior description interview (Janz, 1982). There would appear to be four main distinguishing features of structured interviews. These are:

(1) The interview is preceded by a systematic JOB ANALYSIS, the purpose of which is to identify the essential behavioral requirements for successful job performance.
(2) All questions asked in the interview are job related and are consistently applied across all interviews.
(3) Scoring guides and rating scales are derived from the job analysis and provided for interviewers.
(4) Ratings of specific abilities are combined to arrive at an overall rating for each candidate.

The Latham and Janz approaches have much in common, insofar as they both take the structured approach described above. However, they differ markedly in terms of question content. In the situational interview, applicants are invited to describe how they think they *would* deal with a predetermined set of job-related hypothetical situations. All applicants are asked the same questions and it is assumed that their actual behavior would correspond to their intended behavior as described to the interviewer. The patterned behavior description interview (PBDI), on the other hand, requires candidates to describe their *past* job behavior in detail. In this case the questions vary to some extent from one candidate to another, reflecting each person's unique past experiences. The basic assumption here is that past behavior predicts future behavior.

Coinciding with the advent of these structured interview techniques was the development of improved methods of estimating validity in the form of meta analysis (*see* VALIDITY GENERALIZATION). Recent meta-analytic studies of the interview have shown much improved validity coefficients, especially for structured interviews (Wiesner & Cronshaw, 1988; Wright, Lichtenfels, & Pursell, 1989). These have quoted average validity coefficients similar to or approaching those typically obtained using cognitive tests, which are generally regarded as amongst the most valid predictors of job performance (*see* PSYCHOLOGICAL TESTING).

These recent results are very encouraging since they suggest that the selection interview can have respectable validity. However, many unresolved issues remain in relation to the selection interview. For example, there is a need for a systematic comparison of the situational and PBDI approaches to establish which is more effective generally, and under what circumstances each works best. So far these techniques have only been applied to a narrow range of jobs, and the extent to which they have wide applicability remains to be seen. There is also the question of the abilities actually being assessed by these structured approaches (*see* ABILITY). There is some evidence suggesting that highly structured interviews may be largely measuring cognitive abilities (Campion, Pursell, & Brown, 1988). Apart from the fact that perfectly adequate pencil and paper tests of cognitive abilities already exist, does this mean that the interview cannot be used to assess any of the other qualities that are relevant for job performance such as, for example, interpersonal and motivational factors? This, in turn, begs the question as to the appropriate content of the interview in terms of the range and type of questions that can sensibly be asked. Everyday experience suggests that questions about opinions, MOTIVATION, job knowledge, and preferences, and the like are frequently used in an effort to obtain information about just such interpersonal and motivational factors. Notwithstanding this everyday observation, it is a fact that, despite many decades of research endeavor, we know hardly anything about interview content in terms of the range and type of questions interviewers ask and their relationship to the overall effectiveness of the interview. This should undoubtedly be on the research agenda for the future. Last, but by no means least, despite the received wisdom that some managers make much better interviewers than others, to-date we know little about individual differences in interviewer effectiveness. The interested reader is referred to Graves (1993) for a detailed discussion of this important issue.

See also **Assessment; Selection methods; Research methods; Realistic job previews; Recruitment**

Bibliography

Campion, M. A., Pursell, E. D. & Brown, B. K. (1988). Structured interviewing: Raising the psychometric properties of the employment interview. *Personnel Psychology*, **41**, 25–42.

Eder, R. W. & Ferris, G. R. (1989). *The employment interview: Theory, research, and practice*. Newbury Park, CA: Sage.

Graves, L. M. (1993). Sources of individual differences in interviewer effectiveness: A model and implications for future research. *Journal of Organizational Behavior*, **14**, 349–370.

Janz, J. T. (1982). Initial comparisons of patterned behavior description interviews versus unstructured interviews. *Journal of Applied Psychology*, **67**, 577–580.

Keenan, A. (1989). Selection interviewing. In C. L. Cooper & I. Robertson (Eds), *International review of industrial and organizational psychology*. New York: Wiley.

Latham, G. P. & Saari, L. M. (1984). Do people do what they say? Further studies on the situational interview. *Journal of Applied Psychology*, **69**, 569–573.

Mayfield, E. C. (1964). The selection interview: A re-evaluation of published research. *Personnel Psychology*, **17**, 239–260.

Ulrich, L. & Trumbo, D. (1965). The selection interview since 1949. *Psychological Bulletin*, **63**, 100–116.

Wiesner, W. H. & Cronshaw, S. F. (1988). A meta-analytic investigation of the impact of interview format and degree of structure on the validity of the employment interview. *Journal of Occupational Psychology*, **61**, 275–290.

Wright, P. M., Lichtenfels, P. A. & Pursell, E. D. (1989). The structured interview: Additional studies and a meta-analysis. *Journal of Occupational Psychology*, **62**, 191–199.

TONY KEENAN

selection methods Personnel selection methods are procedures for identifying the most suitable person for a job from a field of candidates. There is an extensive literature available giving detailed information on the development, design and usage of personnel selection methods and personnel selection has been one of the central areas of research and practice for psychologists and human resource professionals for many years (*see* PERSONNEL MANAGEMENT; HUMAN RESOURCES MANAGEMENT). Personnel selection is based on the view that there are stable INDIVIDUAL DIFFERENCES between people which can be measured and are, at least partly, responsible for determining peoples' job performance and other aspects of work-related behavior.

A traditional procedure for designing personnel selection systems exists and several comprehensive texts, available in the United States, Europe, and elsewhere give details of this (Schneider & Schmitt, 1986; Herriot, 1989; Smith & Robertson, 1993). The process begins with a JOB ANALYSIS to identify the essential components of the job. This information is then used to prepare a JOB DESCRIPTION which, in turn provides a basis for assessing the key qualities that an effective performer in the job will need. These are usually expressed in the form of a PERSON SPECIFICATION. Selection methods are then used to assess candidates and evaluate the extent to which they meet the requirements of the job. For example, if it became clear that to perform well in the job candidates would need good numerical ability, a psychological test of numerical ability could then be incorporated into the selection procedure (*see* PSYCHOLOGICAL TESTING).

Although this traditional approach is widely used there are variations. One of the major variations concerns the use to which job analysis information is put and the type of selection method that is used. Job analysis information may be used to identify the major task elements in the job. These may then be incorporated into a selection exercise which literally samples the elements of the job and requires candidates to perform a work sample. In the case of executive positions this could involve working through the contents of a typical in tray (in basket). This "sampling approach" does not focus so heavily on identifying the key personal qualities that candidates will need but concentrates on ensuring that the key elements of the job are embodied in the selection exercise.

The major personnel selection procedures in common usage are outlined below.

Interviews (panel or individual). The most important features of an interview are the extent to which a preplanned structure is followed and the use of questions that are directly job-related (*see* SELECTION INTERVIEWING).

References. Usually obtained from previous employers, often in the final stages of the selection process. The information requested may be specific or general and open-ended.

Psychological Tests. Standardized samples of behavior including tests of cognitive ability and self-report measures of personality.

BIODATA. Specifications of biographical information about a candidate's life history. Some biodata inventories may contain many (e.g., 150 plus) questions.

Work Sample Tests. Such tests use samples of the job in question (e.g., the contents of an in-tray for a managerial post or specific kinds of typing for a secretarial position). The applicant is given instructions and a specific amount of time to complete the tasks.

Handwriting Analysis (Graphology). Inferences are made about a candidates' characteristics by examining specific features of their handwriting (e.g., slant, letter shapes). Although not widely used in many countries, in some parts of the world (e.g., France and Israel) handwriting analysis is a common selection procedure.

ASSESSMENT CENTERS. A combination of several of the other techniques. Often used for executive positions.

To be of use selection methods need to show good levels of criterion-related VALIDITY. This may be assessed quantitatively by computing correlations between scores on the selection method and scores on criterion measures (such as supervisors' ratings of work performance). A great deal of research work has concentrated on exploring the criterion-related validity of various personnel selection methods. Until recently, it was difficult to obtain maximum benefit from this work since many studies were conducted with small samples and appeared to give conflicting conclusions. One of the major advances in the 1980s was the development of procedures (meta-analysis) for quantitatively cumulating the results from many independent validation studies (Hunter & Schmidt, 1990) (*see* VALIDITY GENERALIZATION). The statistical procedures of meta-analysis give methods for estimating the amount of sampling error in a set of studies and hence calculating a more accurate estimate of the likely upper and lower limits of validity. Meta-analytic investigations of the available studies on most of the major selection methods have been conducted and psychological testing (general INTELLIGENCE TESTING and tests of specific cognitive abilities), work sample tests, assessment centres, biodata questionnaires, PERSONALITY TESTING and structured, job-related, interviews have all been shown to display useful criterion-related validities (see Muchinsky, 1986; Smith & George, 1992).

Although, as a result of this meta-analytic research, personnel selection specialists have some confidence in the criterion-related validity of many selection methods, there are still many unresolved and important practical and research issues. Other types of validity (such as construct validity i.e., what psychological constructs are measured by a particular method) are relatively under-researched. There is uncertainty about the constructs measured by many selection methods, including assessment centers and interviews; this results in corresponding uncertainty about how methods may best be combined to form a battery of procedures for any given selection process, without producing unnecessary overlap or omissions (*see* RELIABILITY).

As well as displaying good criterion-related validity selection methods need other important properties including the capacity to discriminate between candidates in a way that is not biased by factors that are irrelevant to job success (e.g, GENDER or ethnic origin) (*see* RACE) but may influence assessors' judgments. EQUAL OPPORTUNITIES issues are of crucial importance in personnel selection. Adverse impact occurs when members of a particular subgroup are rejected by a selection system in disproportionately high numbers (*see* BIAS; DISCRIMINATION). Although it may be socially undesirable, adverse impact alone is not conclusive evidence that a selection method is unfair. The precise legal definitions of unfairness vary from country to country but most selection specialists would accept that a method is unfair and (depending on the precise setting and country involved) probably illegal if errors of prediction are more frequent for members of any specific subgroup, i.e., if differential validity is shown. This definition provides a basis for an unambiguous assessment of the fairness of selection methods but it can be adopted only when sufficient data are available.

In general, research into the bias of personnel selection methods has revealed little evidence of differential validity. This does not mean that unfair discrimination does not take place in practice. There is good evidence that it does and any method can be corrupted to provide support for unfair decision making. Using methods with good criterion-related validity helps to safeguard against unfairness. Unfortunately, the available evidence shows that the usage of methods is not in line with research evidence concerning their validity (e.g., Smith & Abrahamsen, 1992). Unstructured interviews and reference checks are widely used whereas methods with much better validity such as work sample tests and some forms of psychological testing are not used as much.

See also **Assessment; Ability**

Bibliography

Herriot, P. (1989). *Assessment and selection in organizations*. Chichester, UK: Wiley.

Hunter, J. E. & Schmidt, F. L. (1990). *Methods of meta-analysis*. Newbury, CA: Sage.

Muchinsky, P. M. (1986). Personnel selection methods. In C. L. Cooper & I. T. Robertson (Eds), *International review of industrial and organizational psychology, 1986*. Chichester, UK: Wiley.

Schneider, B. & Schmitt, N. (1986). *Staffing organizations*. Glenview, IL: Scott-Foresman.

Smith, J. M. & Abrahamsen, M. (1992). Patterns of selection in six countries. *The Psychologist*, **5**, 205–207.

Smith, M. & George, D. (1992). Selection methods. In C. L. Cooper & I. T. Robertson (Eds), *International review of industrial and organizational psychology*, (vol. 7). Chichester, UK: Wiley.

Smith, M. & Robertson, I. T. (1993). *Systematic personnel selection*. London: Macmillan.

IVAN ROBERTSON

self-actualization This is the fifth and highest level need of Maslow's (1943) need hierarchy (*see* MOTIVATION). It is the fulfillment of a person's life goals and potential. Maslow defined it as, ". . . the desire to become . . . everything that one is capable of becoming" (Maslow, 1943, p. 382). According to theory, self-actualization is a need that motivates people's behavior (*see* MOTIVATION AND PERFORMANCE). A person whose self-actualization need is met, is said to be self-actualized, but few are thought to achieve this state in their lifetime. Many famous people in the arts and sciences have been presumed to have achieved self-actualization.

Self-actualization is somewhat akin to the GROWTH NEED STRENGTH component of Hackman and Oldham's (1976) JOB CHARACTERISTICS theory. Both these concepts share the idea that people have a need for continual development throughout their life. Growth need strength, however, is a PERSONALITY characteristic that varies among people.

See also **Creativity; Self-regulation; Job satisfaction; Human relations movement**

Bibliography

Hackman, J. R. & Oldham, G. R. (1976). Motivation through the design of work: Test of a theory.

Organizational Behavior and Human Performance, **16**, 250–279.
Maslow, A. H. (1943). A theory of human motivation. *Psychological Review*, **50**, 370–396.

PAUL E. SPECTOR

self-efficacy This can be defined as the extent to which a person feels capable and effective in accomplishing a particular task. It is task specific and a person can have different levels of self-efficacy for various tasks. Self-efficacy theory (Bandura, 1982) says that self-efficacy is a major motivational factor that contributes to successful task performance (*see* MOTIVATION AND PERFORMANCE). People who believe that they are good at a task (high self-efficacy) should put forth more effort and persist longer at a task than individuals who have low self-efficacy.

The concept of self-efficacy is somewhat like the expectancy theory concept of expectancy (*see* VIE THEORY). The difference is that expectancy concerns people's beliefs about their ABILITY to accomplish a task at a given point in time in a specific situation. Self-efficacy concerns a person's belief about how good they are at a task in general across time and situations.

Research on self-efficacy theory has supported its predictions for task performance in a number of situations (Locke & Latham, 1990). The theory has useful implications for organizations as it suggests that employee performance can be improved by enhancing self-efficacy. This can be accomplished by assigning tasks to employees that maximizes their likelihood of success.

See also **Competencies; Self-Esteem; Self-regulation; Persistence; Locus of control; Personality**

Bibliography

Bandura, A. (1982). Self-efficacy mechanisms in human agency. *American Psychologist*, **37**, 122–147.
Locke, E. A. & Latham G. P. (1990). *A theory of goal setting & task performance*. Englewood Cliffs, NJ: Prentice-Hall.

PAUL E. SPECTOR

self-esteem This condition is the attitude that a person has about himself or herself, as a good or bad person and the extent to which people like themselves. Self-esteem has been considered a PERSONALITY TRAIT, a stable INDIVIDUAL DIFFERENCE in the extent to which people hold positive or negative views of themselves. People who are high in self-esteem have been found to be psychologically better adjusted, to perform better in school, to handle criticism more appropriately, and to cope better with failure (Baron & Byrne, 1991).

Tharenou (1979) summarized the research on self-esteem in the work domain. She found that high esteem was positively associated with JOB SATISFACTION and intention to stay on the job (*see* TURNOVER). Low esteem was associated with poor employee health, but it is not clear whether esteem is the cause of health (*see* MENTAL HEALTH). Tharenou suggests that both low self-esteem and poor health may be responses to STRESS on the job. Research has failed to find relations of esteem with job performance in field settings (*see* PERFORMANCE, INDIVIDUAL). The more task specific variable of SELF-EFFICACY seems to have more promise in explaining and predicting task performance.

See also **Personality; Affect; Persistence**

Bibliography

Baron, R. A. & Byrne, D. (1991). *Social psychology*. Needham Heights, MA: Allyn & Bacon.
Tharenou, P. (1979). Employee self-esteem: A review of the literature. *Journal of Vocational Behavior*, **15**, 316–346.

PAUL E. SPECTOR

self-managed teams A self-managed team is:

(a) a real group (i.e., an intact social system with boundaries, interdependence among members, and differentiated roles (Alderfer, 1977));
(b) that has one or more group tasks to perform for which members are collectively accountable (*see* ACCOUNTABILITY AND),
(c) whose members are responsible not only for executing the work but also for monitoring and managing their own work and inter-

personal processes (*see* SELF-MANAGEMENT).

See also **Employee involvement; Delegation; Group decision making; Democracy; Superleadership**

Bibliography

Alderfer, C. P. (1977). Group and intergroup relations. In J. R. Hackman & J. L. Suttle (Eds), *Improving life at work*. Santa Monica, CA: Goodyear.

Hackman, J. R. (1987). The design of work teams. In J. Lorsch (Ed.), *Handbook of organizational behavior*. Englewood Cliffs, NJ: Prentice-Hall.

J. RICHARD HACKMAN

self-management When work is done in an organization, four functions must be fulfilled. One, someone must actually *execute* the work – applying personal energy (physical or mental) to accomplish tasks. Two, someone must *monitor* and manage the work process – collecting and interpreting data about how the work is proceeding and initiating corrective action as needed. Three, someone must *design* the performing unit and arrange for needed organizational supports for the work – structuring tasks, deciding who will perform them, establishing core norms of conduct in the work setting, and making sure people have the resources and supports they need to carry out the work. Four, someone must set direction for the organizational unit, determining the collective objectives and aspirations that spawn the myriad of smaller tasks that pervade any organization.

Four types of performing units can be distinguished in terms how AUTHORITY for these four functions are distributed. (The term *performing unit* refers to the people who have been assigned responsibility for accomplishing some specified task. A performing unit can be a single individual, a team (*see* SELF-MANAGED TEAM), or an entire organizational unit whose members share responsibility for a major piece of organizational work.)

Manager-led units: Members have authority only for actually executing the task; managers monitor and manage performance processes, structure the unit and its context, and set overall directions. This type of unit has been common in US industry since the "scientific management" ideas of Taylor (1911) took hold early in the century (*see* SCIENTIFIC MANAGEMENT). In this view, managers manage, workers work, and the two functions are kept distinct.

Self-managing units: Members have responsibility not only for executing the task but also for monitoring and managing their own performance. This type of unit is often seen in new plants designed in accord with what has been termed the "COMMITMENT model" of management (Walton, 1985). Self-managing units are commonplace in managerial and professional work (e.g., a team of research assistants who share responsibility for collecting a set of data) (*see* MANAGERIAL BEHAVIOR).

Self-designing units: Members have the authority to modify the design of the unit itself or aspects of the organizational context in which the unit operates (*see* SUB-UNITS). Managers set the direction for such units but assign to members full authority to do what needs to be done to get the work accomplished. Top management task forces often are self-designing units (e.g., a team created to develop a new program and given free reign in determining how the work will be structured, supported, and carried out).

Self-governing units: Members have responsibility for all four of the major functions listed above: They decide what is to be done, structure the unit and its context, manage their own performance, and actually carry out the work. Examples of self-governing units include certain legislative bodies, some corporate boards of directors, advisory councils of community service agencies, worker COOPERATIVES, and sole proprietorships.

Although the four types of units are described above as if they are distinct, that is merely a convenience. In practice, units often fall on the boundaries of the self-management categories.

See also **Self regulation; Superleadership; Employee involvement; Participation; Empowerment**

Bibliography

Hackman, J. R. (1986). The psychology of self-management in organizations. In M. S. Pallack &

R. O. Perloff (Eds), *Psychology and work: Productivity, change, and employment*. Washington, DC: American Psychological Association.

Manz, C. E. & Sims, H. P. Jr. (1989). *Superleadership: Leading others to lead themselves*. Englewood Cliffs, NJ: Prentice-Hall.

Taylor, F. W. (1911). *The principles of scientific management*. New York: Harper.

Walton, R. E. (1985). From control to commitment: Transformation of workforce management strategies in the United States. In K. B. Clark, R. H. Hayes & C. Lorenz (Eds), *The uneasy alliance: Managing the productivity-technology dilemma*. Boston: Harvard Business School Press.

J. RICHARD HACKMAN

self-monitoring *see* PERSONALITY; SELF-REGULATION

self-regulation This cybernetic phenomena refers to a dynamic process by which key criteria (AFFECT, job performance, SELF-EFFICACY) are kept within an acceptable range through behavioral and cognitive adjustments. Early work emphasized the self-corrective aspects of self-regulatory processes. Subsequent work emphasized that standards can also change over time, producing a slower acting, cognitive means to reduce discrepancies (Lord & Hanges, 1987). Self-regulatory processes are important in social perceptions, social learning theory, motivational processes, STRESS, and MENTAL HEALTH, and many other phenomena because self-regulatory processes are crucial in explaining the interaction between an individual and his or her environment (internal or external) (Lord & Levy, 1994).

Essentially, self-regulation involves a negative FEEDBACK processes by which environmentally produced deviations from standards are opposed and precisely counterbalanced by self-corrective behaviors (Powers, 1973). For example, deviations from a self-relevant standard such as being a good employee, might be counteracted by behavior such as being more diligent at work. Research by Carver and Scheier (1981) demonstrated that people adhered more closely to standards under conditions that produced self-focus.

Self-regulatory systems involve five dynamically related components: a sensor that register information from relevant environments; a *standard or referent* to which information is compared; a *comparator* which detects sensed discrepancies from standards; a *decision mechanism* that selects appropriate responses such as adjusting behavior or changing standards, and an effector that operates on an external task environment. Such control systems are usually applied to individual behavior, although Lord and Hanges (1987) note that control systems can also characterize group processes if different individuals correspond to the different components of control systems.

Many critical interventions in organizations involve changing components of self-regulatory systems. For example, GOAL SETTING interventions can be conceptualized as attempts to change the standards used in motivational control systems. Similarly, frame of reference training involves changing the standards used to control social perceptions. Interventions oriented toward feedback processes in organizations pertain to another important components of cybernetic systems.

One area of research on self-regulation, control theory, also emphasized that discrepancy reducing behaviors occur within a more general hierarchical organization of control loops. In such hierarchies, the means to reduce higher level discrepancies often involve *creating* discrepancies at lower levels. Importantly, such hierarchical organization can explain both discrepancy reduction and the production of discrepancies, thereby providing a powerful mechanisms for explaining both stability and change in behavior (Lord & Levy, 1994). Stability occurs because higher level, abstract standards change fairly slowly, producing consistent patterns in behavior. On the other hand, lower level standards change continually in response to the demands of environments and the requirements of higher level control loops.

More recent work also addresses the regulation of thought processes such as retrieval of information from memory, allocating attentional resources, and sequencing mental operations (Lord & Levy, 1994). Such work emphasizes the role of very fast, unconscious processes (priming and negative priming) that control the activation of goals and goal relevant information needed to produce coherent actions. Such processes are crucial in understanding how current intentions are protected from competing tendencies while actions are executed (Kuhl, 1992). Factors that reduce the capacity of individuals to protect intentions while behavior is being executed (aging, FATIGUE, stress, or disease) produces more disorganized and less action oriented systems (*see* AGE).

See also **Motivation; Performance, individual; Motivation and performance**

Bibliography

Carver, C. S. & Scheier, M. F. (1981). *Attention and self-regulation: A control theory approach to human behavior*. New York: Springer-Verlag.

Kuhl, J. (1992). A theory of self regulation: Action versus state orientation, self-discrimination, and some applications. *Applied Psychology: An International Review*, **41**, 97–129.

Lord, R. G. & Hanges, P. J. (1987). A control systems model of organizational motivation: Theoretical development and applied implications. *Behavioral Science*, **32**, 161–178.

Lord, R. G. & Levy, P. E. (1994). Moving from cognition to action: A control theory perspective. *Applied Psychology: An International Review*, **43**, 335–398.

Powers, W. T. (1973). Feedback: Beyond behaviorism. *Science*, **179**, 351–356.

ROBERT G. LORD

self-serving bias This denotes the tendency to take credit for successful outcomes and to deny responsibility for failures.

See also **Attribution; Bias**

sensitivity training This is a method of facilitator-led small group activities intended to foster changes in attitudes and behaviors necessary to improve participants' interpersonal skills by increasing their awareness of others' reactions to them (*see* GROUP DYNAMICS). Small groups of participants (originally, 10 to 12 persons in "stranger groups" unknown to one another previously) met without an agenda; their own behaviors with one another became the "laboratory data" for group discussion under the leader's direction. Seeing themselves through others' eyes by virtue of direct and open "FEEDBACK" was expected to "unfreeze" participants' long-held assumptions, attitudes, and behaviors. Through discussion in the group with the aid of the leader, participants would "change" to more effective, more rewarding interpersonal behaviors and the new patterns would be reinforced or "refrozen," according to Kurt Lewin's model of change.

Sensitivity training gave rise to the highly influential "T-group" (for training group) activities in numerous settings (including teachers and counselors, recovery groups for drug addicts, and self-improvement groups for the general public), and to the ORGANIZATIONAL DEVELOPMENT movement which followed (but focused on improving relational skills for WORK GROUP effectiveness and ORGANIZATIONAL CHANGE, rather than INTERPERSONAL SKILLS per se). Critics charged that sensitivity training and T-groups manipulated participants' basic attitudes and self-concept, that they might be so powerful as to cause harm or, alternatively, so impotent as to be ineffective upon participants' return to ordinary settings. Nevertheless, these ideas continue to have broad impact, especially in the United States.

See also **Team building; Training; Group cohesiveness**

Bibliography

Bradford, L. P., Gibb, J. R. & Benne, K. D. (Eds), (1964). T-Group theory & laboratory method: Innovation in re-education. New York: Wiley.

Golembiewski, R. T. & Blumberg, A. (Eds), (1973). Sensitivity training and the laboratory approach, (2nd edn). Itasca, IL: Peacock.

MARIANN JELINEK

seven s model McKinsey consultants developed this model to explain how successful companies integrated strategic analysis and strategy formulation with implementation processes, in order to achieve their success.

Peters and Waterman (1982) popularized the model, arguing that the development of an analytically brilliant strategy was not sufficient for organizational success. To succeed, the implementation process was also crucial. It had to be consistent with the strategy, as well as the elements of the implementation process being internally consistent.

The seven S's of the model are strategy, structure (information, operating, administrative, and financial) systems, (LEADERSHIP and management) style, staff (abilities, SKILLS, attitudes, and MOTIVATION), (organizational and individual) skills and shared VALUES (*see* ORGANIZATIONAL CULTURE). Strategy, structure and systems are sometimes referred to as the "hard" S's and the others as the "soft" S's, reflecting the perceived differences required in analyzing and managing the two groups. All the S's are interconnected with each other. Therefore, each of the S's should be consistent with the strategy and with each other S. Further, change in any one of the S's could potentially lead to or require a change in other S's.

At the time the model was developed, most of the concentration in the strategy field was in strategic analysis (*see* STRATEGIC MANAGEMENT). The seven S model focused attention on process and implementation issues, a shift which has been maintained since that time. The seven S model is rarely seen in its original form because each of the elements has effectively been expanded into whole areas of strategy implementation. All its elements are separately considered to be very important in the process of ensuring that the strategy which is formulated is the strategy which is actually implemented.

See also **Organizational effectiveness; Five forces framework; Excellence; Organizational design**

Bibliography

Peters, T. & Waterman, R. (1982). *In search of excellence.* New York: Harper & Row.

GRAHAM HUBBARD

sex differences The study of sex differences has a long history and is a topic of enduring interest to social and organizational scientists, and to almost everyone else from philosophers and novelists to readers of newspapers and popular magazines. A significant difference between mean scores of men and women on some variable is generally assumed to constitute a sex difference considered publishable. Traits, states, attitude, behavior, experience, treatment, and others' beliefs about differences are all quite different types of sex differences and they are not equally the subject of research (*see* WOMEN AT WORK for examples of topics studied by researchers interested in sex differences).

Most of the research on sex differences is a subset of research on INDIVIDUAL DIFFERENCES and focuses on differences in traits – assumed to be relatively long-lasting and not easily changed (*see* PERSONALITY). For example, which sex is more aggressive or do men and women manage differently? But at least three other strands can be detected in sex difference research:

(1) Some research focuses on beliefs about the way men and women behave, e.g., Do people believe that women managers behave differently from male managers or use a different style of leading? (*see* MANAGERIAL STYLE)
(2) Research also focuses on sex differences in actual behavior including verbal reports, e.g., Do male managers behave differently from women managers or hold different work-related VALUES?
(3) Other research focuses on differential treatment of the two sexes, e.g., Are women and men equally likely to be promoted or are they equally compensated for their work? (*see* DISCRIMINATION)

Research on sex differences highlights differences in the mean scores of men and women in all of these areas, focusing on between-sex rather than within-sex variation, typically controlling other variables through the use of random assignment or through regression models of analysis (*see* STATISTICAL METHODS).

The study of sex differences is problematic: because significance levels vary with sample size, many widely known sex differences are small in magnitude, but are used to justify social and organizational policy. Only recently have researchers studying sex differences started to report effect sizes. Even when they do, there is disagreement about interpreting the importance of an effect size of, say, 2 percent or 6 percent. Another common problem is the confounding of types of sex difference, e.g., beliefs about differences between men and women assumed to reflect real but unmeasured differences, or confounding sex differences with other variables associated with sex or gender. Because women and men tend to hold different kind of jobs and have different life experiences (*see* WOMEN AT WORK, GENDER, WOMEN MANAGERS), it is difficult to infer trait differences between the sexes from field studies, although this is often done, e.g., a report of differences in WORK INVOLVEMENT of men and women may be confounded if the women are largely in clerical positions while the men are mostly engineers or managers.

See also **Feminism; Sex roles**

Bibliography

Eagly, A. & Johnson, B. T. (1990). Gender and leadership style: A meta-analysis. *Psychological Bulletin*, **108**, (2), 233–256.

Tavris, C. (1992). *The mismeasure of woman*. New York: Simon & Schuster.

BARBARA A. GUTEK

sex roles Also known as GENDER roles, these refer to shared expectations about appropriate qualities and behaviors associated with being a man or woman in any given society. The term, gender roles, is preferred by some scholars, in keeping with the distinction between gender (referring to socially constructed sex-linked characteristics or behavior) and sex (referring to biologically based sex-linked characteristics or behavior, such as pregnancy). Sex role is a general ROLE that one occupies along with other roles such as a work role, parent role, or LEADERSHIP role. Sex roles can change over time and may vary somewhat from one society to another. Because sex roles are society-wide, they affect ORGANIZATIONAL BEHAVIOR in a variety of ways, e.g., in the way men and women behave, the way they believe they should behave, the way others expect them to behave, the way others treat men and women. Sex roles can either conflict or enhance the enactment of roles. For example, sex role may enhance a man's enactment of the managerial role but conflict with a woman's efforts to occupy the role of manager. More specifically, WOMEN MANAGERS typically face a conflict in trying to meet expectations associated with being a manager (such as being forceful) and expectations associated with being a woman (such as being nurturing) (*see* ROLE CONFLICT).

See also **Women at work; Role-taking**

Bibliography

Deaux, K. (1985). Sex and gender. *Annual Review of Psychology*, **36**, 49–81.

BARBARA A. GUTEK

sexual harassment Sexual harassment is illegal in many countries and its conceptual definition often parallels a legal definition. It is generally defined as unwelcome verbal or physical sexual overtures that may be made a condition of employment or otherwise affect one's job or CAREER and/or create a hostile or intimidating work environment that can affect the one's work or work performance. Sexual harassment is treatment based on GENDER, constitutes a form of STRESS for victims, is an impediment to EQUAL OPPORTUNITY, and thus is a HUMAN RESOURCE MANAGEMENT issue for organizations. Most of the research conducted thus far focuses on two complementary questions: (1) How common is it? (2) How do people define it? In general, in several countries where extensive research has been done, it is estimated that from 25–50 percent of women have been sexually harassed sometime in their worklife. Women who work in nontraditional jobs are more likely than other women to be sexually harassed, in part because of the amount of contact they have with men in their work. While men can be and are harassed by both sexes, the probability that a man will be sexually harassed is very small relative to a woman's chances.

Although there is much discussion of the "subjective nature" of sexual harassment, recent research suggests that there is a fair amount of consensus on definition of harassment. Most people agree that behavior like rape, fondling, and sexual overtures accompanied by job threats are sexual harassment, but there is disagreement about the less severe behavior and many researchers have examined the factors which affect the definition of sexual harassment. Notable among these is a consistent difference between the sexes in the definition of harassment. Although the effect appears to be small, it is widely discussed as evidence that sexual harassment is subjective and appears to have influenced the adoption of a "reasonable woman" standard by some courts in the United States.

See also **Stereotyping; Women at work**

Bibliography

Gutek, B. A. (1985). *Sex and the workplace*. San Francisco: Jossey-Bass.

Tinsley, H. E. A. & Stockdale, M. (1993). Special issue on sexual harassment. *Journal of Vocational Behavior*, **42**, (1).

BARBARA A. GUTEK

Shaping This refers to the differential REINFORCEMENT of all behavior or its results (e.g., a unit of work resulting from a chain of behaviors) that meet or exceed some temporary criterion that is shifted toward an ultimate criterion as behavior shifts in the direction of the ultimate criterion. Suppose a typist's number of ERRORS initially range from 10 to 30 per hundred words typed with a mean of 15 errors per hundred typed. Praise or some other reinforcer is administered each time work is turned in with fewer than 15 errors per hundred. Suppose the distribution then shifts so the range is from 5 to 25 and the mean 10. Finally, only work with 10 or fewer errors per hundred are followed by reinforcement and the distribution shifts to a range from zero to 15 errors per hundred. The performance distribution now contains some errorless work which was never the case before the shaping procedure began. Thus shaping behaviors that share some dimension with a desired behavior that is not currently within a person's repertoire can be created by successive approximations that shift behavior to the ultimate criterion.

See also **Conditioning; Learning, individual; Management by objectives**

Bibliography

Honig, W. K. & Staddon, J. E. R. (1977). *Handbook of operant behavior*. Englewood Cliffs, NJ: Prentice-Hall.

THOMAS C. MAWHINNEY

share/equity ownership share/equity represents the phenomenon of employee ownership. Not to be confused with a cooperative, share/equity refers primarily to Employee Stock Ownership Plans or ESOPS. Also, Employee Stock Ownership Trusts (ESOTS) are variations of this ownership structure. Not to be confused with stock purchase plans which, ironically, accomplish the same purpose, ESOPS have a specific legislative history in the United States (Blasi, 1988).

See also **Democracy; Participation; Payment systems; Gainsharing; Employee involvement; Profit-sharing**

Bibliography

Blasi, J. (1988). *Employee ownership: Revolution or ripoff?* Cambridge, MA: Ballinger.

BRIAN GRAHAM-MOORE

shiftwork *see* HOURS OF WORK; WORKING CONDITIONS

simulation, computer A computer simulation takes a complex set of assumptions, simulates a set of organizational processes, and represents the outcomes of these processes. Five elements comprise a computer simulation:

(1) researcher-specified assumptions;
(2) parameters, i.e., the fixed values or control variables;
(3) inputs, or independent variables;
(4) algorithms, or process decision rules that convert input values into outputs; and
(5) outputs, or dependent variables (Whicker & Sigelman, 1991, p. 7).

The purpose of a computer simulation is to simplify and clarify ideas about a system, e.g., an organization, and to see how premises based on these ideas may lead to outcomes, both intended and unintended. By manipulating simulation parameters, including whether the system in question is modeled as stochastic or deterministic, the researcher attempts to control for a variety of factors that may impact the processes under study. Computer simulations are particularly appropriate when the system under study is complex, when the researcher wants to test the sensitivity of outcomes to different assumptions, and when performance assessment lends itself to quantitative measurement. Computer simulations have been used in organizational research to study models of organizations as experiential learning systems, adaptation to complex environments, organizational search behavior, longitudinal decision processes, and the impact of structure and TURNOVER on organizational outcomes.

See also **Research design; Research methods; Information processing; Cognitive processes; Human-computer interaction**

Bibliography

Whicker, M. L. & Sigelman, L. (1991). *Computer simulation applications: An introduction*. Newbury Park, CA: Sage.

STEPHEN J. MEZIAS

skill This is proficiency on a specific task. The definition includes an evaluation of the level of proficiency (e.g., highly skilled) and the task to be accomplished (e.g., drive a car). Skills are acquired through learning and experience (*see* COMPETENCIES). Perceptual and motor skill requires voluntary coordinated movement to execute a task. Cognitive and social skill requires interpreting and controlling COMMUNICATIONS and then responding. In the workplace, basic skills include reading, writing, arithmetic, mathematics, listening, and speaking. Thinking skills include creative thinking, DECISION MAKING, problem solving, and reasoning (*see* CREATIVITY). INTERPERSONAL SKILLS at work include communicating, solving interpersonal problems, meeting people, maintaining relationships, directing others, upholding NORMS, and handling pressure.

Skill builds from an ability (talent) foundation of basic COMPETENCY and extends performance proficiency to specific activities. Basic ABILITY is a prerequisite for skill; skill cannot develop in the absence of basic ability (Welford, 1976). Skills are learned through education, training, and experience. They develop through practice and performance FEEDBACK. Measurement of skill is specific to the task under consideration and content valid tests provide accurate assessments. Examples of such evaluations are ASSESSMENT CENTER exercises, typing tests, and vehicle driving tests. Skill tests, supported by content validity evidence, are used widely for CAREER counseling, job referral, apprentice TRAINING, and personnel SELECTION (*see* SELECTION METHOD).

See also **Individual differences; Assessment; Performance, individual; Aptitude**

Bibliography

Welford, A. T. (1976). *Skilled performance: Perceptual and motor skills*. Glenview, IL: Scott, Foresman.

JOYCE C. HOGAN

slack resources These include any resources owned or controlled by a firm in excess of what is required to engage in current organizational activities (*see* RESOURCE BASED THEORY). Slack resources can be tangible (i.e., product inventory in excess of current market demand, raw material supplies in excess of current production demand) or intangible (i.e., unused debt capacity, management talent in excess of current operations).

Slack resources can accumulate in an organization for any of a variety of reasons. First, slack resources may reflect an organization's very high level of success. Thus, for example, an organization's success in the market may enable it to have very large cash reserves that are greater than what is required to support current operations. Second, slack resources can reflect management's efforts to buffer an organization from uncertain environmental events (*see* RESOURCE DEPENDENCE). For example, in this uncertain setting, stock piles of raw materials may enable an organization to continue production while organizations without these stock piles may not be able to continue. Third, slack resources may accumulate in an organization when managers overestimate the resources needed to succeed in their activities, are overcautious in pursuing new business opportunities, or unwilling to distribute slack resources to an organization's owners in the form of dividends or other payments. Indeed, some research suggests that excess slack resources may encourage unfriendly takeover efforts (*see* MERGERS AND ACQUISITIONS).

See also **Organizational effectiveness; Scarcity; Strategic management; Innovation**

Bibliography

Bourgeois, L. J. (1981). On the measurement of organizational slack. *Academy of Management Review*, 6, 29–39.

Cyert, R. M. & March, J. G. (1963). *A behavioral theory of the firm*. Englewood Cliffs, NJ: Prentice Hall.

Pfeffer, J. & Salancik, G. (1978). The external control of organizations: A resource dependence perspective. New York: Harper & Row.

JAY B. BARNEY

small businesses Until recently small businesses have been relatively neglected in studies of ORGANIZATIONAL BEHAVIOR. Yet it remains the case that the overwhelming majority of business enterprises are small and that together they account for a substantial share of output and employment within all the industrialized and developing economies.

Quantitative definitions of what constitutes a small firm vary between economic sectors. "Small" within capital intensive manufacturing (e.g., up to 200 employees) may be considered large in more labor intensive service sectors. However, small firms are typically seen as those which:

(1) have a relatively small market share;
(2) are independent; and
(3) are directly managed by their owners (*see* GOVERNANCE AND OWNERSHIP).

The widespread increase in levels of small business activity from the early 1980s onward may be linked to broader patterns of economic and social change. Increasing levels of unemployment, corporate DOWNSIZING through outsourcing, and the resurgence of free market political ideologies – "the enterprise culture" – are the context within which self-employment and small firms have attracted more attention.

Studies of those who start small businesses (*see* ENTREPRENEURSHIP) suggest a variety of motives including:

(1) the need to simply make a living (traditionally important for marginalized social groups – ethnic minorities and migrants, for example – who may be disadvantaged in the labor market);
(2) the desire for independence and AUTONOMY; and
(3) the drive to apply SKILLS and talents which may be under-utilized in employment – an important motive for increasing numbers of women (*see* WOMEN AT WORK).

Most small businesses remain very small or else are liquidated; only a small minority grow. Evidence suggests many owner-FOUNDERS do not seek growth – their material ambitions may be modest and they value the informality of a small team. Those who do attempt growth are often reluctant to delegate control or to develop more formalized organizational structures and systems (*see* FAMILY FIRMS). Long after the emergence of a managerial HIERARCHY then, many small firms retain both informal yet highly centralized – often very personal – control systems.

See also **Cooperatives; Organizational design; Organizational size; Stakeholders**

Bibliography

Scase, R. & Goffee, R. (1987). *The Real world of the Small Business Owner*. London: Routledge.

ROB GOFFEE

social comparison This theory, developed by Leon Festinger in 1954, comprises a set of hypotheses, corollaries, and derivations concerned with why, with whom, and to what effect people compare themselves with other people. Festinger (1954b) assumed a motive to know that one's opinions are correct and to know what one is and is not capable of doing. This leads to "derivations" about the conditions under which social comparison processes arise and about their nature. For example: A process of social comparison arises when a person cannot directly evaluate his or her opinions or abilities by objective nonsocial evidence. When that occurs, individuals use other persons as points of comparison, preferably others who are similar to themselves. One ceases comparison with another person when that person becomes very divergent from one's self.

There have been many recent developments, for example, a focus on the process of downward comparison, that is, comparison with a person who is less well-off, rather than the upward comparison (comparison with a person who is better-off). Festinger (1954a) believed that under certain conditions one would compare oneself with persons of slightly better ability.

The theory has a long history and has resulted in a significant body of research (a fine recent summary can be found in Suls and Wills (1991). Although many aspects of the theory have been questioned (e.g., there may be other motives for social comparison) – we may be more interested in establishing that our opinions are correct and that our abilities are exceptional than in learning the truth about them – social comparison theory remains a classic formulation of social comparison processes.

Temporal Comparison Theory, Albert (1977), derived from social comparison theory, was a set of propositions about when, with whom, and for what reasons one would compare one's self at one point in time with one's self at another point in time. The theory argues, for example, that such comparisons are particularly likely during periods of rapid change as a way to maintain a coherent sense of personal identity. For example, exiting an organization (which is usually viewed as a large and significant change) may evoke memories of the time when the individual first joined the organization. Much less empirical research has been devoted to temporal comparison theory than social comparison theory. (For references to relevant work, *see* Suls and Wills (1991)).

Processes of social and temporal comparison, that is, comparisons with other persons in the light of one's own past and projected future are highly relevant to judgments of perceived equity and fairness (*see* EQUITY THEORY; JUSTICE, DISTRIBUTIVE). For example, the pain of inequity may be tempered by the fact that all parties are experiencing rapid improvement.

See also **Attribution; Social facilitation; Role; Cognitive dissonance**

Bibliography

Albert, S. (1977). Temporal comparison theory. *Psychological Review*, **84**, (6), 485–503.

Festinger, L. (1954a). A theory of social comparison processes. *Human Relations*, **7**, 117–140.

Festinger, L. (1954b). Motivation leading to social behavior. In M. R. Jones (Ed.), *Nebraska symposium on motivation*. Lincoln, NE: University of Nebraska Press.

Suls, J. & Wills, T. A. (Eds), (1991). *Social comparison: Comtemporary theory and research*. Hillsdale, NJ: Lawrence Erlbaum.

STUART ALBERT

social constructionism (SC) This perspective argues that apparently concrete realities such as our own qualities and the characteristics of our contexts, including other people, are created through discourse and are less "concrete," that is more mutable and arbitrary, than actors assume. What is understood as real is not concrete but relational, constructed through processes in which a linguistic statement or "text" is related to preexisting referents. Reality is experienced as concrete because the referents are implicit, taken for granted, their role in meaning making going unrecognized. Through language, understood as a public, communal, social performance, actors construct meanings and reconstruct particular meanings in their social practices. This means that SC is interested in "texts," both written and spoken, as a means to explore the referents by which actors make some particular meaning rather than another. A person's referents produce and are produced by their own career of constructing their self understandings and understandings of their contexts, including other people and their relations with them. A person's referents are neither their own, nor entirely idiosyncratic, as they embrace wider local and national cultural narratives (*see* CULTURE, NATIONAL). So, for example, the recent western narrative of individualism may provide the wider relational context within which particular "organizational" narratives such as success and LEADERSHIP make sense, these meanings being reflected and (re)constructed in the social relational processes of participants. When compared with related approaches, explicit SC contributions have most often been in the form of social critiques. Of potential relevance to OB are existing critiques which examine common constructions, for example, of GENDER, EMOTION, and motives, showing how they are socially constructed and socially warrented, created and sustained by social institutions and processes. The central concerns of OB also may be examined to identify existing and alternative referents and so open-up the possibility to change current practices. For example, critiques of management and leadership reveal the implicit referents in relation to which their meaning is constructed: the implicit references which make meaningful, for example, talk of "subordinates," and the assumption that "subordinates" need "motivating" and "leading" (e.g., Dachler, 1991). Critiques of "organization" expose the implicit references which make meaningful the common emphasis on formalized (static) structures and obscure ongoing processes of construction (Hosking & Morley, 1991). Recent interests in women and in EQUAL OPPORTUNITIES could benefit from attention to the many implicit referents in relation to which the meaning of "male" and "female" are constructed. A final example is that of personnel ASSESSMENT. The meaning and practice of this activity will radically be changed when traits are recognized as social constructions, and furthermore, as constructions whose meaning and significance varies with the wider context of referents implicit in the culture of the employing organization (*see* ORGANIZATIONAL CULTURE). Finally, apart from critique, SC offers a relatively novel perspective of organisations: not separate from persons, but as an ongoing production of persons in relation (e.g., Hosking & Morley, 1991; Weick, 1979); at this point SC shades into NEGOTIATED ORDER, SYMBOLIC INTERACTIONISM, and interpretive sociology.

See also **Critical theory; Metaphor; Postmodernism, symbolism**

Bibliography

Dachler, H. P. (1991). Management and leadership as relational phenomena. In M. von. Cranach, W. Doise & G. Mugny (Eds), *Social representations and the social bases of knowledge*. Bern: Haupt.

Gergen, K. (1985). The social constructionist movement in modern psychology. *American Psychologist*, **40**, (3), 266–275.

Harre, R. (1992). What is real in psychology. *Theory and Psychology*, **2**, (2), 153–158.

Hosking, D. M. & Morley, I. E. (1991). *A social psychology of organising*. London: Harvester Wheatsheaf.

Weick, K. (1979). *The social psychology of organising*. London: Addison-Wesley.

DIAN MARIE HOSKING

social desirability *see* RECRUITMENT; HONESTY TESTING; RESEARCH DESIGN

social facilitation This denotes how the presence of others can significantly enhance performance. Working with others doing the same task, for example, on a production line performing a simple procedure, generally produces better performance than working alone. Interpersonal competition has been ruled out as an explanation for this effect; rather, the "mere presence of others" seems to be responsible. The presence of others has also been shown to inhibit performance, as in the case of public speaking, through a process called *social inhibition*.

Three principal explanations have been offered for these effects. Zajonc (1965) argued that the presence of others increases arousal in all higher mammals which may facilitate greater effort and therefore greater effectiveness in task performance. The second explanation proposes that the presence of others is cognitively distracting on complex tasks and leads to performance decrement. A third suggests that evaluation apprehension may interfere with task performance.

These explanations have been integrated with the notion of task COMPLEXITY to suggest that social facilitation occurs consistently with simple or routine tasks. Where tasks are more complex and cognitively demanding, such as responding to difficult questions, the presence of others, as a result of evaluation apprehension and distraction leads to social inhibition and performance decrement.

See also **Performance, individual; Group dynamics; Cognitive dissonance; Social comparison**

Bibliography

Zajonc, R. B. (1965). Social facilitation. *Science*, **149**, 269–274.

MICHAEL A. WEST

social identity theory *see* ETHNICITY; INTERGROUP RELATIONS; MANIFEST AND LATENT FUNCTIONS; PREJUDICE

social learning theory *see* INDIVIDUAL DIFFERENCES; INTERPERSONAL SKILLS

social loafing This occurs when members of a group context do not make as much effort as they would had they performed alone. Although there are a number of benefits to group-based work activities, these also incur costs. For instance, social psychological work has demonstrated that individuals who think that they are working along with others may reduce their efforts and hence, their performance, independent of any potential loss attributable to distraction or lack of coordination during actual group performance. Such a lowered performance is referred to as *social loafing* and it was first identified by Latane, Williams, and Harkins (1979).

Individuals may "loaf" because they assume that the actions of others will ensure the attainment of the collective good, freeing individuals to redirect their efforts toward additional personal gains and personal outcomes. This tendency of people to rely on the efforts of others is related to the so-called "free-rider" problem in economics, in which an individual enjoys a collective good (e.g., national defense) while foregoing a personal contribution. Although much of the research concerning social loafing has been conducted using university students in laboratory experiments, recent applications to organizational settings demonstrate that the phenomenon also occurs in work settings.

Perhaps the most immediate application of this phenomenon concerns the establishment of WORK GROUPS or SELF-MANAGED TEAMS. In North America and Europe, a number of writers on management have called for the establishment of AUTONOMOUS WORK GROUPS as a means of humanizing the workplace. The phenomenon of social loafing, however, suggests that such advocacy needs to be tempered by a more complex understanding of social processes.

An important, and related, question concerns social loafing and its universality across international borders (*see* CULTURE; VALUES). Do people from various cultures exhibit this Western tendency to "loaf" in a group context? Several international and intercultural studies of social loafing have been conducted. For example, Gabrenya, Latane, and Wang (1985) reported loafing in one study of Taiwanese school children although the same researchers found a *facilitation* effect of group-based performance in two other research studies (*see* SOCIAL FACILITATION). Matsui, Kakugama, and Onglatco (1987) looked at the impact of individual and group responsibility for work performance and argued that the superiority of group-based over individual-based performance in their results may have been related to the collectivistic cultural values of their subjects (Japanese students). Earley (1989) directly tested the idea that social loafing would be moderated by individualistic–collectivistic beliefs using samples of Chinese, and American managers. His results found loafing effects in the individualistic (e.g., primarily the American managers) but not the collectivistic (e.g., primarily the Chinese managers) samples. It was concluded that people from collective cultures will "loaf" if they are working with strangers, or people not in their ingroup, but they will not if they are working with ingroup members. People from individualistic cultures appear to "loaf" when in the presence of others if they are not held accountable for their individual contributions.

See also **Intercultural process; Group dynamics; Group norms; Social comparison**

Bibliography

Earley, P. C. (1989). Social loafing and collectivism: A comparison of the United States with the People's Republic of China. *Administrative Science Quarterly*, **34**, 565–581.

Gabrenya, W. K. Jr., Latane, B. & Wang, Y. (1985). Social loafing on an optimizing task: Cross-cultural

differences among Chinese and Americans. *Journal of Cross-Cultural Psychology*, **16**, 223–242.
Latane, B., Williams, K. D. & Harkins, S. G. (1979). Many hands make light the work: The causes and consequences of social loafing. *Journal of Personality and Social Psychology*, **37**, 822–832.
Metsui, T., Kakugama, T. & Onglatco, M. L. (1987). Effects of goals and feedback on performance in groups. *Journal of Applied Psychology*, **72**, 407–415.
Triandis, H. C. (1989). The self and social behavior in differing cultural contexts. *Psychological Review*, **96**, 506–520.

P. CHRISTOPHER EARLEY

socialization This is a process of ROLE TAKING frequently referred to as "learning the ropes." It has been applied in several different OB contexts, such as career entry, the JOINING-UP PROCESS, entering WORK GROUPS, and the entry/re-entry of EXPATRIATES. As discussed here, however, socialization will refer to new organization members, i.e., organizational socialization.

While almost all scholars agree that socialization is "learning the ropes," there is less agreement as to what this actually means. Van Maanen and Schein (1979, pp. 226–227) say that it involves three elements:

(1) learning new knowledge important for both one's own job performance and for general functioning in the organization;
(2) acquiring a strategic base, which is a set of decision rules for solving problems/making decisions; and
(3) learning the organization's mission, purpose, or mandate.

These three areas of learning are acknowledged to be closely related to each other. Other students of socialization go even further to include changes in newcomer attitudes and VALUES (*see* ATTITUDE THEORY). These are different from the acquisition of knowledge, a strategic base, or organizational mission. When attitudes and values are changed, the newcomer as a person is also changed, and a deeper attachment to the organization is achieved.

Organizational socialization is a process not a specific event, in contrast to job interviews or PSYCHOLOGICAL TESTING, for example. This is probably the main reason why experts have had difficulty specifying both the content and process of socialization. One popular view is that socialization is directly associated with boundary transitions, such as crossing from outside to inside, moving functionally within the organization, and moving up in the HIERARCHY (Van Maanen & Schein, 1979, pp. 217–226) (*see* CAREER TRANSITIONS). According to this view, socialization efforts by members of the organization peak just prior to an individual's movement across one of these boundaries.

Organizational socialization refers to the changes in newcomers, rather than changes in the organization itself – a process sometimes referred to as "personalization." As such socialization is a specific example of general psychological processes as attitude change, COMPLIANCE, CONFORMITY, INFLUENCE, RECIPROCITY, and the development of both loyalty and COMMITMENT (*see* IDENTIFICATION). Clarifying the PSYCHOLOGICAL CONTRACT and MENTORING are components of socialization. Because socialization is primarily accomplished via social learning, the newcomer's peers, coworkers, and boss all provide elements of that which is learned, as well as different types of conformity pressure. For example, one's boss is a source of AUTHORITY, as well as both REWARD and PUNISHMENT. Peers can influence newcomers by being desirable as friends, as well as through their informal ability to reward and punish (*see* Hackman, 1992, for a review of group influences on individuals (*see* GROUP DEVELOPMENT).

Most of the efforts at a THEORY of socialization has been paid to developing "stage models," which purport to describe the typical experiences of newcomers as they make the transition to "insider" status (*see* Wanous, 1992, pp. 200–214, for a review and comparison among these models). Most of the models that have been suggested have some or all of these stages:

(1) confronting and accepting organizational reality (which also includes ANTICIPATORY SOCIALIZATION;
(2) achieving role clarity;
(3) locating oneself in the organizational context; and
(4) detecting signposts of successful socialization.

In contrast, relatively little attention has been paid to the actual psychological processes of both the newcomer and the socializing agents. One noteworthy exception is the articulation of how newcomers can be "seduced" by an organization (Lewicki, 1981), although this is just one facet of socialization in general. The central tenet of organizational seduction is the assumption that newcomers are motivated by reciprocity, so that their loyalty results from the various rewards that are provided by the organization.

Rather than specifying the exact psychology of socialization, some have taken instead to describing the "tactics" that can be used on newcomers. These tactics have been divided into six dimensions:

(1) collective versus individual;
(2) formal versus informal;
(3) sequential versus random;
(4) fixed versus variable;
(5) serial versus disjunctive; and
(6) investiture versus divestiture (Van Maanen & Schein, 1979, pp. 230–254).

Early research on the effects of these six tactics indicates that newcomers are more likely to conform to the organization when their socializing experiences are like the first half of each pair (i.e., collective, formal, sequential, etc.), rather than the latter half of the pair (i.e., individual, informal, random, etc.).

Research on socialization has been plagued by a number of problems. As a result, what is actually known from empirical research is much less than one might suppose from reading all of the writings on socialization. The most difficult problem facing the researcher is designing and executing a study that will lead to valid conclusions (*see* VALIDITY). Because organizational socialization unfolds over a period of time with many possible socializing agents and a variety of specific foci, it is virtually impossible for any single study to address more than just one facet of this process. It is frequently the case that researchers will rely on cross-sectional data, rather than using a longitudinal design (*see* RESEARCH DESIGN). This leads to problems of data interpretation, because cross-sectional designs do not include those individuals who left the organization – a group of important "socialization failures."

The two most common research designs, individual case study and survey research, both have important flaws that make their conclusions somewhat suspect. (*see* CASE STUDY RESEARCH; RESEARCH METHODS; SURVEYS). Those who conduct a case study in a particular organization often generate interesting, "rich" accounts of a newcomer's experiences. However, the extent to which these accounts apply to other contexts is questionable. On the other hand, those who survey newcomers across a broad range of organizations only have the perceptions of the newcomers as data; they have no data from the socializing agents in each of the organizations that could be compared to what is reported by the newcomers themselves.

One review concluded that research has not yet supported the popular idea that socialization can be represented as a set of common stages. This is important because stage models are at the heart of most writing on socialization. Furthermore, the same review found that one of the most frequently cited research results about socialization has never been replicated, i.e., that newcomers should be given as much job challenge as possible (Wanous & Colella, 1989). The belief that job challenge is an effective socialization tactic is based on one sample of AT&T employees (all men) hired in the early 1960s.

Future research and thinking about socialization should proceed in two directions. First, the role of COGNITIVE PROCESSES should be given more attention. Although Louis (1980) called attention to this some time ago, little or no research has been produced. Second, Schneider (1987) has suggested that socialization has been dominated by a search for situational influences, rather than PERSONALITY TRAITS. He has called for a more balanced view, i.e., INTERACTIONISM.

See also **Learning organization; Career stages; Training**

Bibliography

Hackman, J. R. (1992). Group influences on individuals in organizations. In M. D. Dunnette & L. M. Hough (Eds), *Handbook of industrial & organizational psychology*, (vol. 3, pp. 199–267). Palo Alto, CA: Consulting Psychologists Press.

Lewicki, R. J. (1981). Organizational seduction: Building commitment to organizations. *Organizational Dynamics*, Autumn, 5–21.

Louis, M. R. (1980). Surprise and sense-making: What newcomers experience in entering unfamiliar organizational settings. *Administrative Science Quarterly*, **25**, 226–251
Schneider, B. (1987). The people make the place. *Personnel Psychology*, 40, 437–453.
Van Maanen, J. & Schein, E. H. (1979). Toward a theory of organizational socialization. In B. Staw (Ed.), *Research in organizational behavior*, (vol. 1, pp. 209–266). Greenwich, CT: JAI Press.
Wanous, J. P. (1992). *Organizational entry: Recruitment, selection, orientation, and socialization of newcomers*. Reading, MA: Addison-Wesley.
Wanous, J. P. & Colella, A. (1989). Organizational entry research: Current status and future directions. In G. Ferris & K. Rowland (Eds), *Research in personnel and human resources management*, (vol. 7, pp. 59–120). Greenwich, CT: JAI Press.

JOHN P. WANOUS

sociotechnical theory The theory is concerned with the analysis and design of work organizations and proposes the need for the joint optimisation and parallel design of its social and technical subsystems. The theory rejects the dominant, longstanding Tayloristic (*see* SCIENTIFIC MANAGEMENT) view of JOB DESIGN and the prevailing practice of TECHNOLOGY-led change.

The origins of the work were at the Tavistock Institute in London during the 1950s and 1960s. Trist and Bamforth's (1951) study of coal mining methods is seminal. They compared the impact of a new mechanized method of mining with the group-based method it replaced. The old system incorporated a number of features such as small group working, SUPERVISION internal to the group, a sense of responsible AUTONOMY, a complete work cycle, multiskilling and self-selection. The new system, based on MASS PRODUCTION principles, involved a radical change in work organization that effectively destroyed the previous social structure and led to a catalogue of individual, organizational, and performance problems (*see* QUALITY OF WORKING LIFE).

Sociotechnical Theory is best known for its general proposition (as above), for its underlying design principles as articulated by Cherns (1976, 1987), for the innovation of AUTONOMOUS WORK GROUPS, and for its criteria on job design. It has been applied in a wide range of research and development studies.

Cherns (1976, updated in 1987) articulated the meaning of sociotechnical design theory in the form of a set of principles. He argued that:

(1) design processes should be compatible with desired design outcomes (i.e., they should be highly participative);
(2) methods of working should be minimally specified;
(3) variances in work processes should be handled at source;
(4) ORGANIZATIONAL BOUNDARIES should not be drawn to impede the sharing of information, learning, and knowledge;
(5) information should support those who need to take action;
(6) those who need resources should have access to, and authority over, them;
(7) ROLES should be multifunctional and multiskilled;
(8) other systems supporting the focal group should be congruent in their design (e.g., planning, PAYMENT SYSTEMS and CAREER systems);
(9) transitional arrangements between an existing and a new system should be planned and designed in their own right;
(10) redesign should be continuous, with regular review and evaluation.

One of the key innovative practices to emerge from the sociotechnical approach has been the autonomous work group. The essential feature of such groups is that they are self-managing (*see* SELF-MANAGED TEAMS), although their autonomy is constrained by the need to meet agreed targets and standards of performance and by prevailing SAFETY and disciplinary requirements. To support such working practices the role of SUPERVISION and management becomes that of managing the boundaries and supporting the group in achieving its goals.

So far as the individual working within a sociotechnical system is concerned, Emery (1964) identified six desirable characteristics for job design. These are that:

a job should be reasonably demanding (in terms other than sheer endurance);
there should be opportunities to learn and continue learning;
there should be an area of decision making the individual can call his or her own;

there should be a degree of social support and recognition;
it should be possible to relate what one does and what one produces to wider life; and
the work should have some desirable future.

These criteria are very similar to those emerging from the empirical tradition in the United States (Hackman & Lawler, 1971).

The current status of sociotechnical thinking is mixed. It is widely taught; its central proposition is accepted, at least by social scientists; the principles are widely cited, and indeed some of them have wide currency, for example that variances should be handled at source; and the job design criteria remain relevant in the 1990s. But nevertheless a number of trenchant criticisms exist (Mumford, 1987; Pasmore, Francis & Haldeman, 1982).

The major criticisms of the theory are that, in practice, most of those attempting sociotechnical initiatives have identified the same (one best way) solutions to problems of work organization, stressing need for employee PARTICIPATION and autonomous work groups. Furthermore, almost all the intervention work in this area has taken the technology as given, redesigning the social systems around an existing technology. The design principles themselves are largely social in content; there is little to guide the design of the technical subsystem. Indeed it is possible to redesign the social system alone and satisfy Cherns' principles. There is also little support, for example, in the form of methods or tools, for those people who wish to engage in sociotechnical design. Whilst there are some exceptions to this (e.g., Mumford, 1986), these criticisms hold for the new technologies. There is a danger that sociotechnical theory is ignored by the vast majority of innovations occurring in ADVANCED MANUFACTURING TECHNOLOGY and office AUTOMATION. There is also a criticism that the theory is too managerial and entails too unitaristic a view of work organization and ORGANIZATIONAL CHANGE (i.e., based on an assumption of shared objectives and interests). Finally, the theory has proved disappointing in its long-term practical impact. The application of these ideas over several decades has proved to be limited, especially when compared with fashionable ideas such as TOTAL QUALITY MANAGEMENT and JUST-IN-TIME. Many of these criticisms can be interpreted as problems of application; and yet they reflect underlying theoretical weaknesses, most especially concerning the lack of attention to technical issues.

Sociotechnical theory is at something of a crossroads. Under the banner of human-centered technology, other social scientists and engineers are working hard to influence the design of new technologies with similar goals but within a different intellectual tradition (Rosenbrock, 1989). Under the rubric of BUSINESS PROCESS REENGINEERING, the engineering community is addressing the need for redesigning wider organizational systems when undertaking technical change, although this remains technology-led in emphasis. It is not clear what will be the future role and contribution of sociotechnical theory. To remain salient and become influential much work needs to be done addressing the issues identified above, for example by developing new principles and new methods of change that are much more technically sophisticated and can be applied to the new INFORMATION TECHNOLOGIES. However, it is not evident that work is underway that will achieve this; furthermore, some believe that there are many powerful social forces that militate against the widespread adoption of such ideas (Clegg, 1993).

See also **Systems theory; Human-computer interaction; Ergonomics; Software ergonomics; Productivity; Performance, individual**

Bibliography

Cherns, A. (1976). The principles of sociotechnical design. *Human Relations*, **29**, 783–792.

Cherns, A. (1987). Principles of sociotechnical design revisited. *Human Relations*, **40**, 153–162.

Clegg, C. W. (1993). Social systems that marginalize the psychological and organizational aspects of information technology. *Behaviour and Information Technology*, **12**, 261–266.

Emery, F. (1964). *Report on the Hunsfoss Project*. London: Tavistock Documents Series.

Hackman, J. R. & Lawler, E. E. (1971). Employee reactions to job characteristics. *Journal of Applied Psychology*, **55**, 259–286.

Mumford, E. (1986). *Using computers for business success*. Manchester, UK: Manchester Business School.

Mumford, E. (1987). Sociotechnical systems design: Evolving theory and practice. In G. Bjerknes, P. Ehn & M. Kyng (Eds), *Computers and democracy: A Scandinavian challenge*, (pp. 59–76). Aldershot, UK: Avebury.

Pasmore, W., Francis, C. & Haldeman, J. (1982). Sociotechnical systems: A North American reflection on empirical studies of the seventies. *Human Relations*, **35**, 1179–1204.

Rosenbrock, H. H. (1989). *Designing human-centred technology: A cross-disciplinary project in computer-aided manufacture*. Berlin: Springer-Verlag.

Trist, E. L. & Bamforth, K. W. (1951). Some social and psychological consequences of the longwall method of coal-getting. *Human Relations*, **14**, 3–38.

CHRIS W. CLEGG

software ergonomics This field of study develops criteria-based standards and methods for the design and evaluation of software to enhance effectiveness, efficiency, and satisfaction of use. Its current trends are presented in two conference series (Interact, CHI), and in a number of journals (e.g., Human–Computer Interaction, International Journal of Human–Computer Interaction, Behavior, and Information Technology). Under the heading of CSCW (Computer Supported Collaborative Work) the framework was widened to collaborative work.

Human–computer interaction modes include command entry, as in programming languages, menu selection, and direct manipulation (*see* Shneiderman, 1992). In general, menu systems are easier to learn and to use than are command languages. In direct manipulation the person handles representations of objects rather than working on an abstract representation. An example is the desk top metaphor used in the Apple systems. The metaphoric character of these systems has several advantages (*see* Shneiderman, 1992). However, there is no one best interaction mode for every application and for every user. For example, command languages give more control to experienced users and in abstract application areas.

Functionality (how well is task performance supported) and usability (ease of using the software) are illustrated in Figure 1. Both functionality and usability should be incorporated into the organization by providing work places with few stressors, good developmental opportunities (i.e., the chance to develop one's

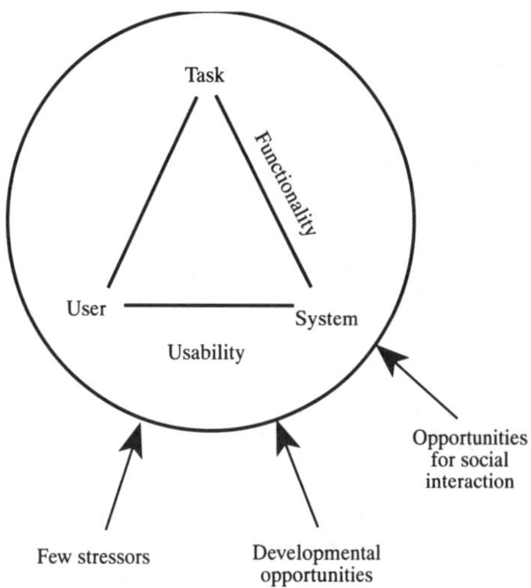

Figure 1 Relationship between organizational contingencies and software ergonomic critera

COMPETENCIES and opportunities for social interactions (Frese, Ulich, & Dzida, 1987) (*see* JOB DESIGN, QUALITY OF WORKING LIFE). In cases of doubt, functionality is more important because people are task driven.

To help software designers to develop usable and functional software, guidelines, and style guides provide detailed rules and recommendations for concrete design decisions such as screen layout (e.g., Smith & Mosier 1986, compare also Apple's Human Interface Guidelines or IBM's Common User Access).

The International Standardization Organization developed criteria for the design of the human–computer interface (ISO 9241, Part 10) with regard to suitability for the task (system support of the task), self-descriptiveness (a comprehensible system through FEEDBACK and explanation), controllability (users ability to direct the interaction), conformity with user expectations (system corresponds with user expectations, knowledge etc.), ERROR tolerance (little error handling is necessary), suitability for individualization (system modification to individual needs and SKILLS is possible), and suitability for learning (system support for learning) (*see* ERRORS).

In contrast to the rational orientation of the criteria approach, the prototyping approach (Budde, Kautz, Kuhlenkamp, & Züllighoven,

1992) is empirical: An iterative design involving future system users in repeated tests of prototypes should be used to improve software. Users' task solving behaviors are studied to identify and remedy software ergonomic problems.

To use prototyping the software must be evaluated. The following methods have been developed: questionnaires, observation of users solving benchmark tasks (sometimes combined with thinking aloud or logfile protocols), error analyses, and a combination of methods to evaluate ISO standards (Reiterer & Oppermann, 1993).

Ill-designed user interfaces lead to inefficient use, low acceptance, high error rates, and STRESS. The European Community demands, by law, that software conforms to new ergonomic standards. Moreover, software design is related to work design issue (work processes prescribed by the software frequently lead to a problems of meeting the design criteria for humane work).

See also **Performance, individual; Self-regulation; Information processing; Information technology**

Bibliography

Budde, R., Kautz, K., Kuhlenkamp, K. & Zullighoven, H. (1992). *Prototyping: An approach to evolutionary system development*. New York: Springer-Verlag.

Frese, M., Ulich, E. & Dzida, W. (Eds), (1987). *Psychological issues of human–computer interaction in the workplace*. Amsterdam: North-Holland.

Reiterer, H. & Oppermann, R. (1993). Evaluation of user interfaces: Evadis II. A comprehensive evaluation approach. *Behaviour and Information Technology*, **12**, (3), 137–148.

Shneiderman, B. (1992). *Designing the user interface: Strategies for effective human computer interaction*. Reading, MA: Addison-Wesley.

Smith, S. L. & Mosier, J. N. (1986). *Guidelines for designing user interface software*. Bedford, MA: Mitre.

MICHAEL FRESE
and TORSTEN HEINBOKEL

span of control This is defined as the number of persons reporting directly to an individual supervisor, who is responsible for their direction. A "wide" span of control is a large number of persons who would be less closely supervised than the smaller number of direct reports in a "narrow" span of control, with whom the supervisor could interact more closely. CLASSICAL MANAGEMENT THEORY, emphasizing structure in a HIERARCHY of AUTHORITY, advised that the span of control be limited (one authority, Graicunas (1937), suggested a limit of six direct reports) to insure adequate oversight. Span of control is a central feature of the hierarchical SUPERVISION deemed essential to maintain good organizational order and insure that tasks are properly performed. This assumption made more sense in the context of mass manufacturing operations with numerous identical or highly similar tasks that might be grouped together under a single supervisor.

The spans of control of supervisors at any level were structured to include all organization members the next level down; each supervisor fell in turn within the span of control of a single superior. All organization members would thus be ultimately linked beneath the command of the most senior officer of the organization (*see* LINKING PIN). Such inclusive, rigid hierarchies assume clear distinctions between levels and between tasks, as well as static organizational needs – assumptions that have become increasingly questionable.

While hierarchy and direct supervision remain important, especially in more traditionally organized firms, contemporary trends in management have increasingly tended toward much broader spans of control, with far less direct supervision. Indeed, the term span of control is less used as emphasis has shifted away from direct supervision. In place of direct supervision of functionally similar workers who know only a small segment of the overall task, employees are now often organized into cross-functional teams responsible for substantial fractions of activity (design of a new product, for instance). Such teams often manage themselves (*see* MANAGEMENT, CLASSICAL THEORY; and SELF-MANAGED TEAMS).

See also **Managerial behavior; Organizational design; Communications; Group size; Group structure**

Bibliography

Urwick, L. F. (1974). V. A. Graicunas and the span of control. *Academy of Management Journal*, 17, June 349–354.

MARIANN JELINEK

speciation *see* POPULATION ECOLOGY; ORGANIZATIONAL CHANGE

stakeholders A stakeholder is "any group or individual who can affect or is affected by the achievement of [an organization's] objectives" (Freeman, 1984, p. 24), i.e., those who have or could have a *stake* or interest in the organization's activities.

The stakeholder concept originates in ROLE THEORY, which posits a complex interdependent network of relationships for every person, marked by differing interests and expectations for each role relationship (*see* ROLE SET). Similarly, stakeholders constitute a complex relational environment for organizations (*see* ORGANIZATION AND ENVIRONMENT).

An organization's core stakeholders – those with ongoing, intensely interdependent relationships – depend to some extent on the nature of the organization and its activities. Most organizations have the following types of core stakeholders:

(a) *constituents* on whose behalf the organization exists and operates, e.g., business owners or voluntary association members;
(b) *employees* who conduct the organization's affairs;
(c) *customers* who receive the goods or services the organization produces;
(d) *suppliers* who provide the input materials for the organization's activities; and
(e) *government* that guarantees an organization's rights and privileges, enforces its responsibilities, and regulates its behaviors through political processes (*see* GOVERNMENT AND BUSINESS).

In addition, some scholars are now adding the *natural environment* as a core organizational stakeholder.

Organizations have many other stakeholders, including local communities, competitors, media, financial analysts and markets, financial institutions, voluntary organizations, environmental and consumer protection groups, religious organizations, military groups, political parties or factions, etc. Depending on the cultural context, any of these stakeholders can be very important to an organization. Furthermore, an organization's stakeholder-set changes over time, as stakeholders enter and exit the environment, and as stakeholder interests and interdependencies change.

International business organizations experience a much more complex stakeholder environment than do single-country organizations (*see* INTERNATIONAL MANAGEMENT).

An international company will have a different stakeholder set in every country in which it operates. Furthermore, some stakeholders will themselves be international, not tied to a particular country.

Understanding stakeholder relationships gives managers a more realistic view of the organization's environment. An organization's social performance is evaluated with respect to stakeholder expectations; organizational governance occurs in the context of stakeholder interests. Stakeholder analysis and management begins with identifying the stakeholders in an organization's environment. Next, relationships *between* the organization and each stakeholder are examined, assessing the nature of each stakeholder's interest in the organization, and determining other characteristics of the relationship (e.g., the direction, strength, and immediacy of effect; types of POWER held; single- or multiple-issue orientation; shared values or problems). Then, relationships *among* stakeholders are mapped. Finally, organizational strategies for managing stakeholder relationships are developed and implemented (Wood, 1994).

Current research in stakeholder management concerns questions such as the relationship between stakeholders' interests and POWER BASES (Freeman & Reed, 1983); processes by which stakeholder expectations are established, communicated, understood, and acted upon; the value bases of differing stakeholder expectations; cross-cultural differences in organizational stakeholder environments; collaboration as a means of resolving stakeholder conflicts (Gray, 1989); and the relevance of the stakeholder concept for theories of agency (*see*

AGENCY THEORY), transaction costs (*see* TRANSACTION COST THEORY), moral behavior, RESOURCE DEPENDENCE, institutional isomorphism, and behavioral or economic explanations of organizational behavior. Eventually stakeholder research may result in a new, more comprehensive theory of the firm.

See also **Institutional theory; Business ethics; Corporate social performance; Governance and ownership; Interorganizational relations; Organizational citizenship**

Bibliography

Freeman, R. E. (1984). *Strategic management: A stakeholder approach*. Boston: Ballinger (now New York: Harper Collins).

Freeman, R. E. & Reed, D. L. (1983). Stockholders and stakeholders: A new perspective on corporate governance. *California Management Review*, **25**, (3), 93–94.

Gray, B. (1989). *Collaborating*. San Francisco: Jossey-Bass.

Wood, D. J. (1994). *Business and society* (2nd edn). New York: Harper Collins.

DONNA J. WOOD

statistical methods The defining feature of techniques known as statistical methods is that they are designed to sort out what appears as chance in individual units (be they persons, groups, firms, industries, or otherwise) into collective regularities and frequencies. There are two branches into which statistical methods are classified, having developed some what separately: descriptive and inferential.

The term statistics dates from the early eighteenth century, being "that which statists do." Mostly, statists engaged in describing their states. Accordingly, methods within this original domain now fall under the heading of descriptive statistics, whose range extends beyond states to all manner of populations, whether concrete (e.g., blue-collar employees) or abstract (e.g., all possible realizations of a stochastic founding process). Such methods seek to organize large amounts of raw data on individual units into more readily assimilated, population-level summary measures. Descriptive statistical methods are used in organizational research to help researches get a grasp of what goes on in a population – establishing the existence of phenomena for study. These methods have been used to answer such questions as what are typical levels of TURNOVER, how widely dispersed are values of JOB SATISFACTION, how values of ORGANIZATIONAL SIZE are distributed, and what are the characteristics of Japanese management.

Inferential statistics, the second branch, did not begin to develop until the turn of the nineteenth century. Inferential statistical methods use probability theory to draw conclusions about a population from a sample, or subset, of the individuals comprising the population. We first formulate an hypothesis about the descriptive properties of or relationships between variables characterizing the individuals in the population, then we observe data from a sample. We are uncertain about the hypothesis, but we do know that the data have occurred. Hence, if obtaining the sample data actually observed is a high probability event under some hypothesis, we are inclined to accept that hypothesis; else, we are inclined to favor some alternative.

Many statistical methods are well established in organizational research. The choice of method is determined by the nature of the variables (continuous, discrete) and the hypothesized relationships (cross-sectional, time-series, etc.). Analysis of variance, regression and contingency tables are the most widely used for "static" studies, where the relationship under study is between variables measured concurrently (at the same time). Uses of such methods range from studying the effects of INDIVIDUAL DIFFERENCES on MOTIVATION AND PERFORMANCE to testing predictions of CONTINGENCY THEORY about the fit between ORGANIZATIONAL DESIGN variables such as FORMALIZATION, and such key dimensions of the environment as UNCERTAINTY. Where social dynamics are of interest, event history analysis has become a popular to study discrete dependent variables, as in CAREER TRANSITION or organizational birth and death. Time series regression is typically used for longitudinal studies where the dependent variables is continuous, as in ORGANIZATIONAL ECONOMICS. Limitations of the data or OPERATIONALIZATIONS (e.g., level of measurement available) can also influence the choice of technique. Multivariate methods, such as factor or cluster analyses, have been used to infer the existence of unobservable constructs, especially in studies of PERSONALITY or STRATEGIC GROUPS. Choice of a statistical method that is not suited to the characteristics of a study can lead to BIAS.

Despite the mathematical foundation on which inferential statistics is built, which gives the appearance of objectivity, there are four approaches to formalizing the process of inference which have and continue to be the subject of some debate: Fisherian significance testing, Neyman–Pearson hypothesis testing, Bayesian analysis, and a hybrid of the Fisherian and Neyman–Pearson approaches. The hybrid, in which a researcher sets a level of significance against which the probability of the data occurring under a single hypothesis is compared and on the basis of which a clear decision to accept or reject the hypothesis as truth is made, has been dominant in organizational research. The reason is straightforward: it simplifies the process of evaluating research, making editorial decisions, and defining researcher's careers.

However, this "objectification of subjectivity" also has some negative consequences. Some hypotheses die premature deaths – even though there may be no well-explicated alternative, while others are born without paying due respect to a stream of prior research to the contrary (*see* ERROR). Neyman and Pearson railed against the first sin, while Bayesians promise salvation from the latter. As for Fisher, he maintained that a hypothesis could never be shown plausible – only implausible – and that the demonstration of a natural phenomenon requires "that we know how to conduct an experiment that will rarely fail to give us a statistically significant result." Attention needs to be paid not only to the choice of statistical methods for particular studies, but also to the way we use the results of these methods in accumulating knowledge across studies.

See also **International management; Organizational decline and death; Research methods, simulation; Research design; Quasi-experimental design; Reliability; Validity**

Bibliography

Fisher, R. A. (1990). *Statistical methods; Experimental design and scientific inference*. Oxford, UK: Oxford University Press.

Gigerenzer, G. et al. (1989). *The empire of chance; How probability changed science and everyday life*. New York: Cambridge University Press.

Oakes, M. W. (1986). *Statistical inference: A commentary for the social and behavioral sciences*. New York: Wiley.

KENNETH W. KOPUT

status This is a concept with descriptive and evaluative connotations. Descriptively, status is the position of a social entity in a social system based on a set of relevant dimensions (*see* SYSTEMS THEORY). For instance, a person may be the president of an organization. Associated with statuses are ROLES. Evaluatively, status refers to a ranking of a social entity in terms of the values of a social system. These judgments often are formed without conscious deliberation. For instance, the president of an organization is deemed important in both the organization and society. Status evaluations help determine HIERARCHY and maintain the LEGITIMACY of AUTHORITY. Together, descriptive and evaluative status enhance the predictability of social interaction.

The general term status can be separated into three types (Mitchell, 1982). Social status is the standing of a person in general society. Occupational prestige is the importance of an occupation to society. Organizational status is the position one holds in an organizational setting.

For descriptive and analytic purposes, status dimensions can be partitioned. One partition is based on the amount of control the social actor has over them. Ascriptive dimensions are those which the social actor cannot control; for individuals, these include AGE and RACE. Achieved dimensions are those a social actor partially can control, such as educational attainment or job performance. A useful application of this division occurs in employment law; DISCRIMINATION by a number of ascriptive dimensions is prohibited in some countries.

Evaluations of status require either global judgments or the evaluation of each of the descriptive dimensions of status. In the former case, status can be determined by asking organizational members to state the status of others. This reputational measure is similar to that used for prestige (see Wegener, 1992) and risks confounding the two. Alternatively, a dimensionalized approach requires the weighing of dimensions from the perspective of either organizational members (a realist strategy) or researchers (a nominalist strategy). Theoretically, evaluative status is multidimensional, not equivalent with a single status dimension such as prestige or economic position. For instance, a young engineer may have higher status than an older, more highly paid accountant.

In task groups, the formation of status hierarchies and its effects have been examined in depth, especially in laboratory studies. A well-established theory in this area involves a social psychological process which Webster and Foschi (1988) called status generalization. Group members form cognitive performance expectations based on status characteristics, including those called diffuse status characteristics which exist outside setting the group setting, such as GENDER and AGE. The performance expectations then lead to differences in behaviors, such as deference, LEADERSHIP, and effort. The status characteristics on which performance expectations are formed may be irrelevant to actual task performance, however. Thus, status in WORK GROUPS may be dysfunctional to task performance.

Recently, researchers examining organizational status tended to focus on specific dimensions in their studies. Ibarra (1993, p. 474) acknowledged that she was using status dimensions such as experience and education as indicators of POWER in an examination of INNOVATION involvement. Messé, Kerr, and Sattler (1992) focused on formal authority in a study of supervisory privileges.

See also **Group structure; Occupations; Professionals in organizations**

Bibliography

Ibarra, H. (1993). Network centrality, power, and innovation involvement: Determinants of technical and administrative roles. *Academy of Management Journal*, **36**, 471–501.

Messé, L. A., Kerr, N. L. & Sattler, D. N. (1992). But some animals are more equal than others: The supervisor as a privileged status in group contexts. In S. Worchel, W. Wood & J. A. Simpson (Eds), *Group process and productivity*, (pp. 203–223). Newbury Park, CA: Sage.

Mitchell, T. R. (1982). *People in organizations* (2nd edn). New York: McGraw-Hill.

Webster, M. Jr. & Foschi, M. (1988). *Status generalization: New theory and research*. Stanford, CA: Stanford University Press.

Wegener, B. (1992). Concepts and measurement of prestige. In J. Blake & J. Hagan (Eds), *Annual review of sociology*, (vol. 18, pp. 253–280.)

DAVID L. DEEPHOUSE

status incongruence This state occurs in two ways. First, a person may be ranked high on some evaluative STATUS dimensions but low on others. A quintessential example is the person with a doctoral degree driving a taxicab; this person has high educational attainment but low occupational prestige. A second type of status incongruence occurs when a person's status characteristics appear inappropriate for the person's position or ROLE. For instance, a marketing person may be put in charge of a production.

Status incongruence can affect the particular person and the person's coworkers. In the first case, status incongruence may engender cognitive dissonance. This, in turn, may influence JOB SATISFACTION and performance (*see* PERFORMANCE, INDIVIDUAL). In the second case, the person's coworkers may question the fairness of the person's status. EQUITY THEORY suggests that coworkers may alter their behavior and attitudes in this situation.

See also **Self-esteem; Role theory; Cognitive dissonance**

Bibliography

Mitchell, T. R. (1982). *People in organizations* (2nd edn). New York: McGraw-Hill.

DAVID L. DEEPHOUSE

stereotyping This is the process of categorizing an individual as a member of a particular social group (e.g., females or Hispanics) and assuming that the characteristics attributed to the group apply to the individual. Thus, stereotyping can be viewed as an error of overgeneralization. For example, stereotyping a person as a black female manager implies that the manager will exhibit the set of characteristics that the observer attributes to black female managers as a group. Thus, a stereotype is an oversimplified picture of a social group which is generalized to perceptions of specific individuals. Stereotypes often develop for a social groupings relating to GENDER, geographic location, socioeconomic STATUS, ETHNICITY, AGE, organizational level, and nature and type of work.

Stereotyping may be viewed as a subcategory of PERCEPTION and ATTRIBUTION. Because of the enormous amount of information people must process in complex social and organizational situations, people have a high need to process information quickly and efficiently. Stereotypes can be viewed as cognitive short-cuts or schemata which enable individuals to make judgments about individuals and their characteristics quickly. Stereotyping often results in perceptual and attributional errors (*see* FUNDAMENTAL ATTRIBUTION ERROR) because the complete set of characteristics of a complex individual cannot be accurately inferred from the characteristics of a social group. Nevertheless, stereotyping may also be viewed positively in that it increases efficiency in making judgments and decisions about others. Although the impact of stereotyping on individuals may be negative, the impact can also be positive. Thus, because of the positive stereotype an employee holds about union officials, a union steward may be able to work more effectively with an employee to resolve her grievances.

Stereotypes have been found to be relatively stable and persistent over time. Once a stereotype develops, it appears that selective attention and perception operate such that data which confirms the stereotype become more salient. On the other hand, data which contradict the stereotype tend to be viewed as atypical and disregarded. Thus it appears that a disproportionate amount of disconfirming evidence is needed to change well established stereotypes.

The organizational literature has documented that stereotypes often result in negative impacts on the selection, placement, and HUMAN RESOURCE MANAGEMENT practices relating to minorities (Falkenberg, 1990). The literature on gender DISCRIMINATION suggests that discrimination is most acute when the perceiver lacks information. Thus, if a manager is asked to make a decision about an individual and only has information relating to the employee's social class, BIAS is likely to occur because the decision maker will tend to rely on the information derived from the stereotype. On the other hand, when more complete information regarding the specific characteristics of an individual is available, in addition to social categorization information, bias is less evident (Gardner & Martinko, 1988). Thus, more specific information regarding the characteristics of individuals appears to be an important strategy for reducing the negative impact of stereotypes.

See also **Decision making; Conflict; Race; Group norms; Communication; Cognitive processes**

Bibliography

Arvey, R. & Campion, J. (1984). Person perception in the employment interview. In M. Cook (Ed.), *Issues in person perception*. London: Methuen.

Bierhoff, H. W. (1989). *Person perception and attribution*. Berlin: Springer-Verlag.

Falkenberg, L. (1990). Improving the accuracy of stereotypes in the workplace. *Journal of Management*, **16**, 107–118.

Gardner, W. L. & Martinko, M. J. (1988). Impression management in organizations. *Journal of Management*, **14**, (2), 321–338.

Jones, E. E. (1990). *Interpersonal perception*. New York: W. H. Freeman.

Luthans, F. (1992). *Organizational behavior*, (6th edn). New York: McGraw-Hill.

MARK J. MARTINKO

strain *see* MENTAL HEALTH; STRESS

strategic alliances Managers and scholars, such as Ken-ici Ohmae (1989), continue to demonstrate interest in the increasingly complex array of collaborations observable in the global economy of the mid-1990s. These CONTRACT based governance forms have been described by researchers as strategic alliances, partnerships, coalitions, research consortia, and various forms of network organizations (*see*

JOINT VENTURES). The term "strategic alliance," however, is generally used in the popular press and seems on its way to becoming the dominant construct in the discussion of these kinds of collaborative agreements among firms.

These new forms seem so pervasive that they are likely to become a permanent part of the business scene. Lodge and Walton (1989) assert that if US firms (and, arguably, other nations' firms) are to stay at home, yet compete in a global environment they will have to alter the way they think about relationships with other organizations from those that are "adversarial, arm's length, short term, contractual, and rigid . . . towards ones which are more cooperative, intimate, long-term, consensual, and flexible" (p. 9).

Beyond the rich description provided by numerous cases studies, there are a number of theoretical bases for predicting when an organization should pursue a strategic alliance. For example, working within TRANSACTIONS COST THEORY or AGENCY THEORY, much scholarly attention has focused on comparing alternative transaction governance structures (e.g., markets, hierarchies, and mixed modes) by institutional economists, organizational sociologists, and management and organizational theorists (*see*, e.g., Barney & Ouchi, 1986) (*see* GOVERNANCE AND OWNERSHIP) (1986). In a related vein, an extensive stream of research, principally by organizational sociologists, has examined the environmental conditions and contingent factors that can be employed to explain the formation and structure of the cooperative INTERORGANIZATIONAL RELATIONS that are the essence of a strategic alliance. The newly emerging RESOURCE BASED THEORY view of the firm provides yet another lens through which strategic alliances are being studied.

Why do strategic alliances form? Powell (1990) offers researchers and managers the following potential motivations. The firms that frequently employ strategic alliances are pursuing a diverse set of business objectives requiring COOPERATION because they involve reciprocal dependencies. These business objectives include: access to technologies that are state-of-the-art or beyond the capacity of a single firm to develop; access to markets the firm cannot enter by itself; benefits which economies of scale can provide in value chain activities such as joint research, production, or marketing; the acquisition of complementary assets such as know-how located outside the boundaries of the firm; the spreading of risk in activities beyond the scope or the capabilities of one business firm; or achieving SYNERGY by combining the strengths and overcoming the weaknesses of the firms making up a strategic alliance designed to be something more than a traditional supplier relationship or technology licensing arrangement. Strategic alliances also appear to be employed by managers hollowing out the corporation by contracting out. These re-engineering or DOWNSIZING actions also are being used by GOVERNMENT AGENCIES and their managers engaged in the PRIVATIZATION of public services.

Rigorous empirical investigations of the performance of strategic alliances have only recently begun. Results are mixed. Factors that appear to be associated with more successful alliances include environments in which the ability to rely on TRUST is present, common norms, embedding alliances in a single national CULTURE, and a history of successful transacting between the parties in the past.

See also **Mergers and acquisitions; Strategic management; Collateral organization; Resource dependence**

Bibliography

Barney, J. B. & Ouchi, W. G. (1986). *Organizational economics*. San Francisco: Jossey-Bass.

Borys, B. & Jemison, D. (1989). Hybrid arrangements as strategic alliances: Theoretical issues in organizational combinations. *Academy of Management Review*, **14**, 234–249.

Contractor, F. & Lorange, P. (Eds), (1988). *Cooperative strategies in international business*. Lexington, MA: Lexington Books.

James, B. G. (1985). Alliance, the new strategic focus. *Long Range Planning*, **18**, 76–81.

Kanter, R. (1988). The new alliances: How strategic partnerships are reshaping American business. In H. L. Sawyer (Ed.), *Business in the contemporary world* (pp. 59–83). Lanham, MD: University Press of America.

Lodge, G. & Walton, R. (1989). The new American corporation and its new relationships. *California Management Review*, **29**, (3), 9–23.

Mowery, D. (Ed.), (1988). *International collaborative ventures in U.S. manufacturing*. Cambridge, MA: Ballinger.

Ohmae, K. (1989). The global logic of strategic alliances. *Harvard Business Review* (March-April) 143–154.

Powell, W. W. (1990). Neither market nor hierarchy: Network forms of organization. In L. L. Cummings & B. M. Staw (Eds), *Research in organizational behavior*, (Vol. 12, pp. 295–336). Greenwich, CT: JAI Press.

Ring, P. S. & Van de Ven A. H. (1992). Structuring cooperative relationships between organizations. *Strategic Management Journal*, 13, 483–498.

PETER SMITH RING

strategic choice *see* STRATEGIC MANAGEMENT

strategic contingencies theory *see* RESOURCE DEPENDENCE; UNCERTAINTY

strategic groups *see* POPULATION ECOLOGY; STRATEGIC MANAGEMENT

strategic management Although scholars differ on how to define strategic management, most definitions include the major objectives, policies, and programmatic activities of the organization and how they come to be determined. Some authors assume that such factors necessarily reflect conscious and deliberate managerial choices while others argue that the pattern of these items constitutes the firm's strategy-in-operation whether or not its managers have consciously thought through such a strategy.

Most strategic management researchers implicitly assume that strategic management constitutes an applied science. Research which does not in any way suggest it might lead to prescriptions for corporate actions is generally seen as belonging more in a base discipline such as organizational sociology or economics rather than strategic management. Reflecting this applied concern, a high percentage of strategy research attempts to relate corporate characteristics to performance, although a large variety of performance measures have been employed (*see* ORGANIZATIONAL EFFECTIVENESS).

Andrews (1980) argued that corporate performance depends not simply on achieving high performance on a set of independent corporate characteristics (e.g., good marketing, good production, good R&D), but rather on the interaction of a variety of characteristics both internal and external (i.e., good marketing, R&D, and production can only be defined in the context of a strategy for competing in a given market). Strategic management assumes that the interaction of business environment, the way in which the organization attempts to compete in that environment, and internal management determines performance. (The SEVEN S'S MODEL is a practitioner tool to address such interrelations.)

Research on strategy often divides into work on content of strategy or process of strategy. Strategy content generally addresses what markets the corporation will compete in and how it will compete in those markets. Strategy process examines the processes and mechanisms which result in choices to compete in certain ways in certain markets, and the way the organization attempts to implement such choices. Both process and content work address issues of business-level strategy (how a firm competes in a given industry or market) and corporate-level strategy (how the firm competes in whatever set of markets it is in and how it chooses to be in those markets). The present overview emphasizes process issues. Although any subdivision of the field is inherently arbitrary, this discussion of strategy process will consider: the Harvard approach; formal planning systems; strategy types; contingency studies; DECISION-MAKING; TOP MANAGEMENT TEAMS and strategic human relations management; cognitive approaches; and emergent and incremental approaches.

Harvard approach. Following Andrews (1980) and other faculty at the Harvard Business School, this approach emphasizes the need to manage the complex interactions among the differing parts of the corporation. Harvard approach researchers tend to take a top management perspective where the objective is to advise top management, ascribing much corporate action to strategic decisions of top management. Given the approach's concern for COMPLEXITY, most research in this tradition relies on multiple case studies in which the researcher examines several instances of a given phenomenon, describes these in rich detail, and then generates explanations of the behaviors observed and prescriptions for action (*see* e.g., Bower's (1970) study of capital investment decision processes).

Most of the other approaches to strategic management research adopt social science approaches that emphasize numerical data whether from surveys or historical sources, or emphasize qualitative data in studies of highly specific processes.

Formal planning. Early research on strategic management focussed heavily on formal long-range planning (indeed the field was often called long-range planning), often with prescriptive intent. Much of the empirical work in the area tried to show that firms which plan perform better than those which do not. The emphasis on formal planning declined when mixed results on planning and performance persisted. Furthermore, researchers recognized that most major strategic choices did not occur in the planning system, because the system's schedule does not necessarily correspond to the development of major strategic issues. The study of planning systems as part of the strategic management process and information network of the corporation makes sense, but such systems cannot hold the central place in strategic management once given them.

Strategic types. This perspective emphasized the development of typologies of strategies and then related them to corporate management processes. Porter argued that firms following one of his generic strategies (low cost, differentiation, segment or niche) should adopt consistent organizational procedures (*see* FIVE FORCES MODEL). For example, low-cost firms need to avoid costly staffing policies, though such policies might form the basis of a differentiation strategy. Miles and Snow (1978) categorized firms as prospectors, analyzers, defenders, and reactors and subsequent research associated organizational characteristics with these strategic types. These two typologies have been widely used, along with measures of industry growth/decline and stability to identify contingencies within which other strategy processes occur.

Contingency studies. A very large and diverse set of studies consider contingencies framing relations among strategy, corporate structure, and human relations management systems. Miller (1986) and his colleagues, in a series of studies on small business managers in Quebec, found strong relations among business strategy, structure and performance. Gupta and Govindarajan (1984) identified links among business unit strategies, managerial characteristics, and business unit effectiveness. Although these complex results cannot be summarized simply, the literature strongly supports the position that particular patterns of market and internal policies lead to higher performance (*see* ORGANIZATIONAL EFFECTIVENESS).

Decision making. This approach examines how the characteristics of managerial decision processes influence corporate performance (*see* Eisenhardt & Zbaracki, 1992, for a review). Current research suggests effective decision processes vary depending on the firm's industry environment (*see* ORGANIZATION AND ENVIRONMENT). Fredrickson (1989) has defined decision processes in terms of comprehensiveness, which is associated with high performance in a stable industry but low performance in an unstable one. Eisenhardt and Bourgeois (1992) used an exploratory approach to examine decision processes in small firms in "high velocity" environments. They found that effective firms had balanced power among the top management teams, used quick numerical analysis on many options, made decisions by consensus but with a decision by the top manager if consensus did not occur, and made decisions more quickly than low-performance teams.

Top management. A large variety of studies have examined the influence of CEOS and top management teams on corporate performance. Their focus has included stock market reactions to CEO turnover, determinants of CEO and top management team turnover, and the influence of top management team characteristics on corporate performance. These studies demonstrate significant influences of top management team composition and changes in composition on performance.

Cognitive approaches. A rapidly growing area has examined managerial beliefs as explanations for corporate behavior. For example, in some industries managers define the firms in their industry in ways that differ significantly from how an outsider might define the industry. Other studies show positive associations with performance of characteristics of managers' beliefs about their industry and what determines their firm's performance and their willingness to change their beliefs (*see* COGNITION IN ORGANIZATIONS).

Emergent and incremental strategies. Most strategy research assumes planned actions and choices influence outcomes but another set of studies emphasize strategic management as a far less direct process. Mintzberg and his associates have examined change processes and argue that strategic changes occur infrequently in most organizations and that many strategic changes emerge spontaneously from the operation of the organization rather than as a preconceived change in direction. Quinn argues that major changes often involve such high levels of UNCERTAINTY that detailed programmatic planning of such change is futile. Rather, he prescribes a course of channeling and directing organizational processes and activities around a general area of concern so as to move incrementally (hence the name, logical incrementalism).

Strategy Content

A significant portion of early strategy content research derived from close ties to applied strategy consulting. Widely used tools for analyzing a corporation's portfolio of businesses include the Boston Consulting Group Matrix (which categorized businesses within a corporation on their relative market share and growth rate), and the GE Matrix (which used a wider variety of measures to evaluate desirability of a market and the business' competitive strength. These derived from research within corporations or from consultants, but some subsequent academic studies have attempted to validate them. In recent years, the area has become increasingly associated with research rooted in economics research on industrial organization.

Research on the content of business strategy has relied heavily but by no means exclusively on related work in Industrial economics (also known as industrial ORGANIZATIONAL ECONOMICS). Industrial economics attempts to explain profitability differentials across industries largely within the STRUCTURE–CONDUCT–PERFORMANCE paradigm. This paradigm argues that the structure of the industry (defined in terms of things like the number of firms in the industry and BARRIERS TO ENTRY into the industry) influences how firms will compete and consequently determines the profitability of firms in the industry. Such content work has emphasized the study of strategic groups (portions of an industry that appear to compete most directly with one another) and generic strategies such as cost leadership strategy (being the low-cost producer/seller), product differentiation strategy (producing a product customers perceive as different from others available), and niche or focus strategy (emphasizing a small market where either cost or differentiation advantages can be gained).

At the corporate level, strategy content research has examined DIVERSIFICATION (the mix of businesses in which a corporation competes), VERTICAL INTEGRATION (the mix of stages of the production process incorporated in a given company), and MERGERS AND ACQUISITIONS (one mechanism by which diversification or vertical integration can be implemented). Although much of the research in these areas draws heavily on economics, other researchers approach these same topics with explicitly behavioral theories and interests.

In recent years, an important connection between strategy process and content has been re-established. Early Harvard work on strategy emphasized the need to align internal management and market-oriented strategy. Although some work continued to emphasize this alignment, much strategy content research, based on the industried economics approach, tended to ignore complex differences in corporations. It was often assumed knowledge and know-how were readily available, with differences among firms being limited and of limited kind (e.g., differences in a conventional production function). Yet these homogeneity assumptions make it hard to explain why firms within industries differ as greatly as they do in profitability.

Writings under the label of CORE COMPETENCE and RESOURCE BASED THEORY have, in recent years, re-emphasized the connection between the content of strategy and corporate capabilities. Although the concept of "resources" may also include some nonorganizational items, the idea that the organization's abilities constitute a major explanation for corporate performance underlie both core competence and resource-based approaches. Since organizational abilities can be very hard to purchase or imitate, these approaches are quite consistent with heterogeneity in performance within industries.

To summarize, strategic management takes a corporate standpoint in generally addressing questions associated with selection and implementation of the major goals, policies, and activities (including products, markets, etc.) leading to high corporate performance. It generally assumes that coherence among various policies and activities determines performance.

See also **Competitiveness; Reputation**

Bibliography

Andrews, K. R. (1980). *The concept of corporate strategy*, (2nd edn). Homewood, IL: Irwin.

Bower, J. L. (1970). *Managing the resource allocation process*. Cambridge, MA: Harvard Business School.

Eisenhardt, K. M. & Zbaracki, M. J. (1992). Strategic decision making. *Strategic Management Journal*, **13**, 17–37.

Eisenhardt, K. M. & Bourgeois, L. J. (1988). Politics of strategic decision making in high velocity environments: Toward a midrange theory. *Academy of Management Journal*, **31**, 737–770.

Fredrickson, J. W. & Iaquinto, A. L. (1989). Inertia and creeping rationality in strategic decision processes. *Academy of Management Journal*, **32**, 516–542.

Gupta, A. & Govindarajan, V. (1984). Business unit strategy, managerial characteristics, and business unit effectiveness at strategy implementation. *Academy of Management Journal*, **27**, 25–42.

Miles, R. E. & Snow, C. C. (1978). *Organizational strategy, structure, and process*. New York: McGraw-Hill.

Miller, D. (1986). Configurations of strategy and structure: Towards a synthesis. *Strategic Management Journal*, **7**, 233–249.

PHILIP BROMILEY

strategic types Defenders, Prospectors, Analyzers, and Reactors are four types of strategies defined by Miles and Snow (1978) in a model which matches organizational strategy, structure, and process. This typology is based on the idea that organizations discover and develop relatively enduring patterns of strategic behavior which actively coalign the organization and the environment (*see* ORGANIZATION AND ENVIRONMENT).

Defenders are organizations which have narrow product-market domains and do not tend to search outside of their domains for new opportunities. A defender strategy is to offer a relatively stable set of products or services to existing, well-defined, stable markets, concentrating on doing the best job possible in its area of expertise. Growth is normally slow and incremental. The emphasis is on tight internal controls, operating efficiencies, and a cost orientation.

Prospectors are organizations which are constantly seeking new product and market opportunities. The key elements in a prospector strategy include being enterpreneurial (*see* ENTREPRENEURSHIP) in attitude, developing and maintaining the capacity to monitor a wide range of environmental signals, obtaining and remaining on the leading edge of technological developments in the industry, and being flexible in internal structures and processes, so that necessary changes to meet new opportunities can be made quickly and easily (*see* FLEXIBILITY). Prospectors and defenders are at opposite extremes. Whereas defenders are internally oriented on efficiency and controls, prospectors are externally oriented on new developments and market needs.

Analyzers represent a balanced compromise strategy somewhere between the extremes of defenders and prospectors. An analyzer strategy will be to have a balance of products and markets, some of which are stable and provide relatively certain returns, which can be used to allow the development of other products and markets, which are new and/or changing. An analyzer is likely to follow prospectors into new products and markets, rather than lead. Analyzers will have a dual focus. That part of the organization which resembles the defender strategy will be more efficiency- and control-oriented, while that part which is more concerned with new developments will be more externally oriented. Since the products and markets may be closely related, this duality of orientation will be difficult to manage. Miles and Snow suggest that a matrix structure is most appropriate (*see* MATRIX ORGANIZATION).

By contrast with the first three strategies, reactors are organizations which lack a consistent strategy, simply reacting to isolated events as they unfold. This may occur because the organizational strategy is not clearly articulated, because the structure is inappropriate for the strategy, or because the strategy has not kept up with changing external conditions. Miles and Snow see the reactor strategy as an unstable strategy, since it is not internally or externally consistent. It is also a residual strategy type, for those organisations which do not fit into one of the three other more stable strategies.

This typology has supported a steady stream of research, because it incorporates a managerial attitudinal orientation within the classification of alternative business strategies. However, this is also the great difficulty for using this typology, because assessing these attitudes is difficult in practice.

See also **Mechanistic/organic; Strategic management; Structure-conduct-performance model**

Bibliography

Miles, R. & Snow, C. (1978). *Organizational strategy, structure, and process*. New York: McGraw-Hill.

GRAHAM HUBBARD

strategy *see* STRATEGIC MANAGEMENT

stratification Seldom studied, stratification is another structural property. Stratification is defied as the distribution of rewards such as income and fringe benefits and/or prestige (sometimes called STATUS) across either jobs or pay levels in an organization. The most typical measure is the ratio between the amount remuneration of the top executives or administrators and the workers. There is an enormous variation in the degree of stratification not only between countries as evidenced in executive benefits but also within countries across kinds of organizations.

See also **Organizational design; Differentiation**

Bibliography

Hage, J. (1980). *Theories of organizations*. New York: Wiley–Interscience.

JERALD HAGE

stress There are at least three uses of the word "stress" in OB. It is used as a *cause* (my job is inherently stressful); as a *consequence* (I feel stressed when I'm at work); as a *process* (this is happening when I am are under stress). In its broadest sense "stress" has come to refer to a field of study which encompasses all the above meanings, and in OB to be concerned with organizational or occupational stress, though this has also come to include stress arising from UNEMPLOYMENT.

In keeping with this broad usage, the word is probably most usefully applied to stress as a process because the major organizational and personal consequences of stress occur over time. The process approach fits most closely with the definition of stress provided by Selye (1951). Selye was one of the founders of stress research and his medical training led him to an interest in the physiological, and disease consequences of exposure to physical and emotional stresses. Selye concluded that when faced with demands our psycho-physiological systems respond with a nonspecific, uniform response which he labeled the General Adaptation Syndrome (GAS). The main components of this response are that digestion slows to release blood for muscles, breathing increases for extra oxygen supply to muscles, heart rate accelerates, blood pressure rises, perspiration increases to cool the body, muscles tense for action. All of these effects are under the influence of the hormonal system with cortisol, adrenaline, and nonadrenaline being the main biochemical agents (*see* MENTAL HEALTH).

According to Selye these nonspecific responses vary in intensity over time but if stress continues they produce the following pattern:

Alarm (in preparation for flight or fight); *Resistance* (sustained psycho-physiological mobilization at a lower level of intensity); *Exhaustion* (resulting from depletion of the body's stores of vitamins, sugars, proteins, and immune defenses). It is clear that this process can encompass all three uses of the word stress.

Cox and Ferguson (1991) claim that different approaches to stress have focused on different parts of the process corresponding to the main uses identified above. The causal approach is described by them as the "engineering" approach. Stress here defines the cause which produces the reaction strain. Many writers use the word strain to describe the psycho-physiological response to stress and it can include two of the uses described above (the current state of feeling strain and the more enduring state which occurs in Selye's Resistance phase). Following the medical literature these two states of strain can be acute or chronic. This is also true of the exposure to stress and the terms acute stress and chronic stress make the same distinction.

The engineering or stimulus oriented approach has led to a search for the causes of occupational stress and a well-known classification is:

- Factors intrinsic to the job (tasks, WORKING CONDITIONS, shift work, dangers, etc.).
- ROLE factors (ROLE OVER/UNDERLOAD, ROLE AMBIGUITY, CONFLICT, etc.).
- Relationships at work (support from boss, colleagues, subordinates, etc.).
- CAREER (success, failure, JOB SECURITY, REWARDS, etc.).
- ORGANIZATIONAL DESIGN and climate (control versus DISCRETION, openness, HIERARCHY, etc.) (*see* ORGANIZATIONAL CLIMATE).
- Home-work interface (effects of travel, work-family conflicts, women's roles) (*see* NON-WORK/WORK).

Recent studies of many of these variables and their relationship to measures of psychological and physiological strain can be found in Quick, Murphy, and Hurrell (1992). Any one of these variables has relatively small correlations (0.1–0.3) with measures of strain, though in combination they may account for 25 percent of the variance.

Cox and Ferguson describe a second theoretical stress focus as the medico-physiological or response approach. This approach has led to techniques for measuring both physiological and psychological reactions to stressful stimuli/situations. Many of these are self-report questionnaires and include symptoms from categories such as the following:

- AFFECT (ANXIETY, worry, panic, depressed mood).
- Cognition (failures, errors, inability to think logically, forgetting) (*see* ERRORS).
- Behavior (ABSENTEEISM; aggression; SABOTAGE; ALCOHOL AND SUBSTANCE ABUSE).
- Symptoms (sleep loss, headaches, vomiting, sweating, impotence).

It is perhaps worth noting about the above four categories of strain that only the person themselves has priveleged access to information/experience about them all. The outsider (manager or supervisor) only has access to observable behavior (unless the person confides in them). Since the mere presence of many of these symptoms does not necessarily indicate the presence of stress and strain (e.g., heavy smoking and drinking are ways of life for many people), the manager needs to be sensitive to *changes* in behavior as much as anything else. Not surprisingly, there are moderate correlations amongst the different symptom groups (e.g., psychological strain correlates about 0.45 with measures of physical ill health).

These studies have their difficulties and the association between self-report measures of strain and physiological evidence of strain is by no means compelling. The difficulties of conclusive research in organizations are described in Fried (1988).

Although the use of physiological markers of strain provide more objectives indices, a more fundamental question is how chronic stress might link to disease. Stress is hypothesized to be linked to hypertension, coronary heart disease (CHD), skin and other disorders though causal proof is surprisingly difficult to demonstrate. The link to CHD in particular has been associated with TYPE A Behaviour Pattern (TABP).

The third approach to modeling stress, and the most effective according to Cox and

Ferguson, is the transactional approach. It is a processual approach as it assumes that a person is strained only if he/she appraises a situation to be a threat (Primary Appraisal), and resources, capacities, knowledge, etc., are unable to cope with the threat successfully (Secondary Appraisal). This model has been much influenced by the work of Folkman and Lazarus (1986). This model brings the person much more into the process so INDIVIDUAL DIFFERENCES become important determinants of whether situations are stressful or not, though the outcome is always a function of the interaction of the person and the environment. Person-Environment fit models of stress have many similarities to the Folkman and Lazarus approach (*see* PERSON-JOB FIT).

Individual differences are important here because they can influence all stages of the process. At the primary appraisal stage the neurotic PERSONALITY is more likely to see threat than the person high in HARDINESS. At the secondary appraisal stage, more intelligent, problem-solving, self-confident people are less likely to see their resources as unable to cope, even if there is threat (*see* SELF-EFFICACY). This concern with coping capacities has led to another active area of stress research: the measurement of coping or coping styles. Lazarus and his coworkers have been at the center of this development. Several authors have produced measures of coping, with similar dimensions. The three major ones are: Problem Focused coping (getting information, looking for solutions, trying out solutions, etc.); Emotion Focused coping (denial, wishful thinking, pretending it will go away); Appraisal Focused coping (redefining the situation, comparing self with others). Problem-focused styles seem more effective in work settings.

Programmes to help people improve their coping have grown in the last 30 years. Many of them are outside the work context, but organizations have also developed stress management programmes for their employees (*see* COUNSELING IN ORGANIZATIONS). As well as providing information and advice about coping strategies, programmes also include advice about diet, physical fitness, alcohol and substance abuse, health practices, counseling techniques including self-help groups, and techniques such as relaxation and meditation. Charlesworth and Nathan (1988) provide an excellent guide to stress management and Theorell (1993) has provided an evaluative review of stress management programmes in the workplace.

The literature also contains research on improving/changing the workplace to reduce stress through job redesign, ORGANIZATIONAL RESTRUCTURING, and CULTURE management. Karasek's (1979) highly influential paper on the causes of work stress demonstrated that the most stressful jobs were those combining high demands (workload, difficult tasks) with low discretion or AUTONOMY. Low discretion is often associated with low levels of PARTICIPATION in decision making and this condition has been shown to be associated with higher levels of strain. An associated literature has grown up around the concept of social support and its role in helping to protect people from the effects of stress (Payne & Jones, 1987). Leaders and managers are, therefore, potential sources of stress, as well as sources of support, and responsibility for people has itself been shown to be a principal managerial stressor.

Although the popular literature emphasizes the stress of the modern executive, Karasek's model implies that their level of strain is buffered by their high levels of discretion. The epidemiological literature on work stress supports this analysis. Fletcher (1988) has shown that elevated levels of strain and poor health are more prevalent in lower level jobs. He also shows that at any one time about 15 percent of the workforce report levels of strain high enough to affect their attendance at work and their performance at work if they do attend. Whilst it is difficult to calculate the costs of stress at work, it has been estimated that stress may account for half of absenteeism, and that the total stress bill might be as much as 6 percent of sales in a company with an average absenteeism rate of 4 percent Practically, theoretically, and methodologically stress continues to present a major challenge.

See also **Job design; Quality of working life; Repetitive work; Role theory; Emotions in organizations**

Bibliography

Charlesworth, E. A. & Nathan, R. G. (1988). *Stress management: A comprehensive guide to your well-being*. Guernsey, Channel Islands: Guernsey Press.

Cox, T. & Ferguson, E. (1991). Individual differences, stress and coping. In C. L. Cooper & R. Payne (Eds), *Personality and stress: Individual differences in the stress process*. Chichester, UK: Wiley.

Fletcher, B. C. (1988). The epidemiology of occupational stress. In C. L. Cooper & R. Payne (Eds), *Causes, coping and consequences of stress at work*. Chichester, UK: Wiley.

Folkman, S. & Lazarus, R. (1986). Stress process and depressive symptomology. *Journal of Abnormal Psychology*, **95**, 107–13.

Fried, Y. (1988). The future of physiological assessments in work situations. In C. L. Cooper & R. Payne (Eds), *Causes, coping and consequences of stress at work*. Chichester, UK: Wiley.

Karasek, R. A. (1979). Job demands, job decision latitude, and mental strain: implications for job redesign. *Administrative Science Quarterly*, **24**, 285–308.

Payne, R. L. & Jones, J. G. (1987). Measurement and methodological issues in social support. In S. Kasl & C. L. Cooper (Eds), *Stress and health*. Chichester, UK: Wiley.

Quick, J., Murphy, L. & Hurrell, J. (Eds), (1992). *Work and well-being Assessments and interventions for occupational mental health*. Washington, DC: American Psychological Association.

Selye, H. (1951). The general adaptation syndrome and the gastrointestinal diseases of adaptation. *American Journal of Proctology*, **2**, 167.

Theorell, T. (1993). Medical and physiological aspects of job interventions. In C. L. Cooper & I. T. Robertson (Eds), *International review of industrial and organisational psychology*, (Vol. 8, pp. 173–192). Chichester, UK: Wiley.

ROY L. PAYNE

structuration This term was coined by Giddens (1984) to refer to the dynamic articulation between structure and action (which Gidden's called "agency"). Traditionally, sociologists and organizational theorists have treated structure as an exogenous constraint on action. In turn, they have viewed action as independent of structure and, in many instances, as a phenomenon that exists at "lower" LEVEL OF ANALYSIS. In organization studies, the implicit gulf between structure and action is reflected in the distinction between micro- and macro-organizational behavior. Giddens argued that action and structure are inextricably linked, that action both "constitutes and is constituted by" structure. From this perspective human action always instantiates structures. Actions may replicate, but they may also alter existing structural patterns. The relationship between action and structure is therefore a process that can best be understood when studied over time. The importance of structuration for organization studies is that is provides a theoretical and empirical base for bridging the longstanding gulf between studies of organizational structure and studies of everyday action within organizations (*see* ORGANIZATION DESIGN). Gidden's notion of structuration bears similarities to Strauss's (1978) concept of a "NEGOTIATED ORDER," the rules, roles, rights and obligations that individuals and other types of actors establish as they interact with each other over time.

See also **Enactment; Interactionism; Organization and environment; Social constuctionism; Theory**

Bibliography

Giddens, A. (1984). *The constitution of society*. Berkeley, CA: University of California Press.

Strauss, A. (1978). *Negotiations*. San Francisco: Jossey Bass.

STEPHEN R. BARLEY

structure–conduct–performance model The structure–conduct–performance model (SCP) is one of several approaches to understanding the determinants of organizational performance in industrial organization economics. This perspective is based primarily on the work of R. Mason and J. Bain, and takes the industry as the primary unit of analysis (*see* FIVE FORCES MODEL; RESOURCE BASED THEORY). Structure, in the SCP model, means industry structure, and is measured by industry concentration, BARRIERS TO ENTRY, the level of product differentiation in an industry, and other industry characteristics (*see* ORGANIZATION AND ENVIRONMENT). Conduct, in the SCP model, means organizational conduct, and includes an organization's strategies, policies, and tactics (*see* STRATEGIC MANAGEMENT).

Performance, in the SCP model, means industry performance, measured by average firm profitability in an industry (*see* ORGANIZATIONAL EFFECTIVENESS).

Three versions of SCP logic have developed over the years. In strong-form SCP, industry structure is assumed to determine totally both organizational conduct and average industry performance. Indeed, strong-form SCP logic suggests that analysts can safely ignore organizational conduct, since it is determined by industry structure (*see* STRATEGIC CHOICE).

A second, more popular, form of this model is weak-form SCP. Here industry structure is assumed to determine a range of possible activities an organization might engage in. Thus, in this version, organization conduct is not totally determined by industry structure, and remains an important component in explaining industry performance.

A third form of SCP logic is strategic SCP. The original objective of both strong- and weak-form SCP was to specify industry attributes preventing perfect competition dynamics in an industry from emerging, so that GOVERNMENT AGENCIES could remove these impediments. In strategic SCP these objectives are reversed, and SCP logic is used to describe those industries within which perfect competition is not likely to develop, and thus where firms may earn greater than competitive levels of performance (*see* COMPETITIVENESS). Two of the major proponents of strategic SCP have been R. Caves and M. Porter.

See also **Organizational design; Reputation; Resource dependence**

Bibliography

Barney, J. B. (1986). Types of competition and the theory of strategy: Toward an integrative framework. *Academy of Management Review*, **11**, 791–800.

Conner, K. (1991). A historical comparison of resource-based theory and five schools of thought within industrial organization economics: Do we have a new theory of the firm? *Journal of Management*, **17**, 121–154.

Porter, M. (1980). *Competitive strategy*. New York: Free Press.

Porter, M. (1981). The contributions of industrial organization to strategic management. *Academy of Management Review*, **6**, 609–620.

JAY B. BARNEY

substance abuse *see* ALCOHOL AND SUBSTANCE ABUSE

substitutes for leadership These are the characteristics of tasks, organizational design, or interpersonal arrangements which reduce or obviate the need for leadership to be enacted by an individual.

See also **Bureaucracy; Leadership**

subunits A subunit is defined as a supervisor and all subordinates who report to that supervisor. Subunits form an intermediate LEVEL OF ANALYSIS, falling between individuals and the total organization, and are the building blocks of more complex organizations. The configuring of subunits into larger entities is referred to as ORGANIZATION DESIGN. According to various principles of design subunits can be combined to form functional, geographic, product, or MATRIX ORGANIZATIONS.

Some authors consider subunits as more or less permanent and enduring features of organization that should be distinguished from temporary teams and group structures. Others consider any WORK GROUP to be a subunit, including managerial level teams. Subunits play a vital role in the functioning of any organization because they are the level at which the day-to-day work of the organization is carried out.

One of the largest programs of research on subunits has been carried out by Van de Ven and colleagues (Van de Ven & Ferry 1980), who developed measures for subunit context, structure, and performance and conducted successful tests of CONTINGENCY THEORY at the subunit level. Other researchers have investigated subunits in terms of: their own performance and design as distinguishable entities; how they fit into the larger configuration of the organization; and, as relationships among subunits. The relative ease and precision with which data can be collected at the subunit level has resulted in a tendency for researchers to confirm a theory at this level of analysis and then generalize their findings to the total organizational level. The context of subunits is sufficiently different than the context of organizations and such generalizations may not be supportable.

See also **Differentiation; Formal organization**

Bibliography

Van de Ven, A. H. & Ferry, D. L. (1980). *Measuring and assessing organizations*. New York: Wiley–Interscience.

ROBERT DRAZIN

succession planning This is the systematic attempt to identify possible future holders of particular positions ahead of time. It is a device used, mainly by large organizations, to assist in identifying suitable internal candidates for job vacancies and to encourage the proactive development of employees. Formal succession planning has normally been restricted to senior management posts. The successors considered for such posts are usually already well established in their management CAREERS or regarded as having high potential (*see* MANAGEMENT OF HIGH POTENTIAL; MANAGEMENT DEVELOPMENT).

By no means all organizations use formal succession planning to address the issue of succession to managerial jobs. Small organizations may develop their own staff to future management positions, but are likely to accomplish this task in a more informal way. Many large organizations still take a short term view of managerial resourcing and are willing to take a gamble on the external LABOR MARKET if they are short of management talent.

Succession planning has been most highly developed in large companies with strong corporate cultures (*see* ORGANIZATIONAL CULTURE), especially those with an international dimension (e.g., oil companies, major electronics companies, international banks, etc.). Such companies see succession planning as one way in which they can develop a pool of highly experienced managers, whom they would see as a "corporate resource." Large public sector organizations have also practiced formal succession planning. The approach to succession planning needs to be consistent with the wider managerial resourcing strategy of the organization (*see* HUMAN RESOURCE STRATEGY; HUMAN RESOURCE PLANNING).

Succession plans themselves record the names of one or more possible successors for each of the positions included in the process. They may also contain summary information on positions, job holders, and successors. Successors of three different kinds may be identified. Emergency successors are people who can "stand-in" for a job holder on a temporary basis if sudden and unforeseen circumstances arise. They may be identified for both senior management and other key positions, and often this is done locally by the manager concerned. Most corporate effort goes on the other two types of successors – short- and longer-term successors.

Short-term successors are individuals who would be suitable candidates to consider for the position if it became vacant in the near future. The benefit in identifying a number of short-term successors lies in ensuring a wide candidate search which is not always possible when there is a hurry to fill a vacant position. It may also forewarn the organization of particular positions where there is no pool of candidates available. Organizations practising succession planning do not necessarily expect to fill every senior vacancy with one of its listed successors. Some use other parallel processes (including internal advertisement) to generate other candidates who then compete alongside the planned successors (*see* RECRUITMENT). So succession planning also has to fit in with the appointment processes of the organization.

Longer-term successors are individuals who would be able to fill the position in time (perhaps 2–5 years ahead), but for whom it would not be the next job. One or two other jobs are likely to intervene. It is these longer-term successors who are classified as high potential staff or on a fast-track development programme. Succession planning is often the process by which job moves are planned and engineered for high potential individuals. Such developmental job movement is often aimed at giving cross-functional, cross-country, or cross-divisional experience (*see* CAREER TRANSITIONS; CAREER DEVELOPMENT).

Succession planning processes range from the very simple to the elaborate. The simplest form of succession planning involves individual managers looking at possible successors for the positions for which they are responsible and agreeing these plans with the HR function and/or their own managers. This process has the disadvantage of not identifying successors in other departments or units because they are not known to the manager concerned. In more elaborate processes, groups of senior managers meet together, with the HR function acting in a support role. Such succession planning committees or management development forums look at senior posts right across the organization and agree possible short- and longer-term successors for each position. They often also agree individual career plans for the longer-term successors to broaden their experience.

Effective succession planning requires consistent and up-to-date information to be available to managers to help in identifying successors, to record the plans themselves and to monitor the delivery of developmental activities. The laborious process of keeping succession plans by hand on organization chart diagrams has been replaced by computer systems. These maintain summary information on posts and people, as well as the lists of successors and possible job options. Such databases become very useful for a wide variety of applications.

This type of formal corporate succession planning is now being adapted as a result of several pressures. The more devolved business structures of the 1990s are pushing succession planning for all but the very top jobs out to operating divisions or down to unit level (*see* DECENTRALIZATION). This can lead to a multilevel model for succession planning with ownership of the process lying at different levels in the organization for different levels of management. The process for identifying longer-term candidates is also coming under scrutiny as the self-fulfilling nature of many fast track schemes has been criticized. The tendency for senior management to "clone" a new generation in their own image also raises important equal opportunity issues. Such concerns are placing more emphasis on the quality of ASSESSMENT data looked at in choosing successors, and on entry to and exit from the high potential pool. The need for a flexible pool of successors is also increased as career patterns become more variable, and managers do not spend their whole career with one company. Succession planning is also under pressure to become less secretive in response to employee expectations about access to information and personal CAREER CHOICE. Employee career preferences may form part of the input to succession planning, and discussion of possible types of job move may also take place with the employee. However, there is a tension between a general willingness to be more open, and a natural reserve about seeming to "promise" an individual their next job.

See also **Job analysis; Person specification; Career plateauing**

Bibliography

Friedman, S. D. (1986). Succession systems in large corporations: Characteristics and correlates of performance. *Human Resource Management*, **25**, (2), 191–213.

Gratton, L. & Syrett, M. (1990). Heirs apparent: Succession strategies for the future. *Personnel Management*, January, 34–38.

Hirsh, W. (1991). Succession planning: Current practice and future issues. *International Journal of Career Management*, 3, (2), 17–28.

Mayo, A. (1991). *Managing careers: Strategies for organizations*. London: Institute of Personnel Management.

Peterson, R. B. (1985). Latest trends in succession planning. *Personnel*, August 47–54.

Sarch, Y. (1993). Nothing succeeds like succession planning. *Human Resources*, Spring, 90–94.

WENDY HIRSH

SuperLeadership This is a contemporary form of participatory or empowering LEADERSHIP originated by Manz and Sims. SuperLeadership is defined as "leading others to lead themselves," providing a special focus on the role and behavior of the follower. The object of the SuperLeader is to cultivate and develop independent selfleadership capabilities of followers.

More recently, Manz and Sims (1991) articulated a typology of historical leadership archetypes from which the theory of SuperLeadership is drawn:

(1) the *Strong man* who depends on direction, instruction, command, and reprimand;
(2) the *Transactor* who depends on contingent reward and reprimand;
(3) the *Visionary Hero*, a type of transformational or charismatic leader who depends on vision, inspiration, and challenge to the status quo; and
(4) the *SuperLeader*, who encourages selfleadership from the follower. (*see also* LEADERSHIP CHARISMATIC; TRANSFORMATIONAL/TRANSACTIONAL LEADERSHIP).

SuperLeadership theory is inspired by previous theories of participative leadership, but is much more specific about the independent role of the follower, and what the leader must do to develop followers to be capable selfleaders. Subordinate independence, initiative, self-responsibility, and selfcontrol are encouraged by behaviors such as self GOAL SETTING, initiative, positive thought patterns, and teamwork. While SuperLeadership is intended to be a pragmatic applied mode of leadership, it is rooted in psychological theory, including REINFORCEMENT theory, social cognition, behavioral SELF-MANAGEMENT, SELF-REGULATION theory, social learning theory, and cognitive BEHAVIOR MODIFICATION.

To understand SuperLeadership, one must first comprehend selfleadership, which is both a philosophy and a systematic set of behavioral and cognitive strategies for leading one's self to higher performance and effectiveness (Manz & Sims, 1990, 1991). Self-leadership actions, such as self-set goals, rehearsal, self-observation and evaluation, and self-administered REWARDS, can powerfully enhance personal performance if applied in a systematic manner. Self-leadership also consists of building natural rewards into one's own tasks, so that the performance of the task itself becomes a source of performance MOTIVATION (*see* MOTIVATION AND PERFORMANCE). Cognitive self-leadership strategies such as constructive thought patterns, opportunity thinking, mental imagery, and cognitive self-talk can also enhance performance.

SuperLeadership is a challenge to the traditional fundamental assumptions about leadership practices and AUTHORITY relationships. While transformational leadership seems to be appropriate to the top of the organizational HIERARCHY, SuperLeadership is a type of empowering leadership that is appropriate at all levels of the organization, including the so-called first-line supervisor (*see* SUPERVISION). In it's most sophisticated form, SuperLeadership is expressed through the implementation of SELF-MANAGED TEAMS (Manz & Sims, 1987, 1993), which completely change the role and nature of the leader. In fact, under this system, the traditional directing and controlling supervisor disappears, replaced by leadership roles typically called coordinator, facilitator, coach, and (elected) team leader.

Finally, the essence of SuperLeadership was captured in a poem by the ancient Taoist philosopher, Lao-tzu, as follows:-

A leader is best
When people barely know he exists,
Not so good when people obey and acclaim him.
Worse when they despise him.
But of a good leader, who talks little,
When his work is done, his aim fulfilled,
They will say:
We did it ourselves.

See also **Influence; Group decision making; Empowerment; Employee involvement; Participation; Self-management**

Bibliography

Manz, C. C. & Sims, H. P. Jr. (1987). Leading workers to lead themselves: The external leadership of self-managing teams. *Administrative Science Quarterly*, **32**, 106–28.

Manz, C. C. & Sims, H. P. Jr. (1990). *SuperLeadership*. New York: Berkley.

Manz, C. C. & Sims, H. P. Jr. (1991). SuperLeadership: Beyond the myth of heroic leadership. *Organizational Dynamics*. Spring 18–35.

Manz, C. C. & Sims, H. P. Jr. (1993). *Business without bosses: How self-managing teams are building high-performing companies*. New York: Wiley.

HENRY P. SIMS, JR.

supervision This term refers to LEADERSHIP at a particular level in an organizational hierarchy: the "first-line" or lowest level of management/leadership. A supervisor typically leads employees who actually do the work. Over the years, viewpoints of supervision, or more specifically, supervisory behavior, have changed dramatically. As first conceived, the supervisor was one charged with directing and controlling the behavior of subordinates. Today, this concept of supervision has virtually become obsolete, now replaced by hierarchical ROLES designed to empower lower-level employees through facilitation and coaching (Manz & Sims, 1987).

One cannot discuss theories of "supervision" without an inextricable linkage to leadership. In fact, most of the early leadership research used supervisors as subjects. In the broadest sense, the role of supervisors is to influence the behavior and performance of subordinate employees, and this INFLUENCE process is a form of leadership. Most of the earliest theories of supervisory behavior were simplistic, usually characterizing supervisors as "authoritarian" versus "democratic," or "concern for task" versus "concern for people" (*see* MANAGERIAL STYLE).

Early attempts to measure leadership emphasized the supervisory behaviors of "consideration" and "initiating structure" (*see* LEADERSHIP STYLE). *Consideration* describes the extent to which a supervisor shows concern for members of the work group. This dimension relates to friendship trust, interpersonal warmth, and relationships. In contrast, *initiating structure* describes the extent to which a supervisor initiates and organizes task activity toward followers, and defines the way work is to be done. For many years, through the 1960s and into the early 1980s, the dimensions of consideration and initiating structure virtually defined the study of supervision.

While initiating structure and consideration received the most attention, Stogdill (1959) also proposed the following supervisory behaviors: (1) REPRESENTATION; (2) reconciliation; (3) tolerance of UNCERTAINTY; (4) persuasiveness; (5), tolerance of freedom; (6) role retention; (7) production emphasis; (8) predictive accuracy; (9) integration; and (10) influence with supervisors. Also, an empirically grounded study of first-line supervision from Dowell and Wexley (1978) analyzed the structure of 89 work activities. They found the following seven dimensions of supervisory activities: (1) working with subordinates; (2) organizing the work of subordinates; (3) work planning and scheduling; (4) maintaining efficient and high-quality production; (5) maintaining safe/clean work areas; (6) maintaining equipment and machinery; and (7) compiling records and reports.

A careful examination of this earlier view of supervision reveals that the generic emphasis was mainly on the traditional role of the supervisors as director and controller; that is, one who uses direction, instruction, command, goals, and occasionally reprimand to influence worker behavior and performance (*see* PERFORMANCE, INDIVIDUAL).

Later study defined the supervisor as one who administers REWARDS and PUNISHMENTS. (see Podsakoff & Schriesheim, 1985; Sims, 1980). Many studies have shown that leaders who use rewards contingent upon subordinate performance can positively influence performance. Also, several studies have probed the supervisory use of punishment. These results have been mixed, sometimes producing negative correlations with performance, but other times producing no correlation or positive correlation with subordinate performance. Supervisory punishment almost always relates negatively to subordinate satisfaction (*see* JOB SATISFACTION). Another area of research related to GOAL SETTING, although this work is not often directly linked with leadership (Locke & Latham, 1990).

Recent leadership theory has drifted away from supervisors as target subjects, but deserves mention. Prominent theories include transformational leadership (Bass, 1988), charismatic leadership (House, 1977), and SUPERLEADERSHIP (Manz & Sims, 1990) (*see* LEADERSHIP, CHARISMATIC; TRANSFORMATIONAL/TRANSACTIONAL THEORY). These views of leadership also articulated a distinction between "the manager" versus "the leader." While attracting substantial attention to the issue of leadership, these theoretical perspectives seem more fitting to leadership at the top (*see* CEOs), but less appropriate to first line supervision.

Today, the role of the supervisor is changing at a most dramatic rate. In its most sophisticated form, this new role is expressed through self-managed teams (Manz & Sims, 1987, 1993), which completely change the role and nature of the supervisor. In fact, under this system, the old concept of "supervision" disappears, replaced by leadership roles typically called coordinator, facilitator, coach, and (elected) team leader. Despite new roles, supervisors have always been subjects of high STRESS as "persons in the middle." With the implementation of TOTAL QUALITY MANAGEMENT, delayering and DOWNSIZING, and global emphasis on PRODUCTIVITY, the stress level of supervisors is higher than ever.

In summary, in today's organization, the original concept of supervision (direction and control) seems to be obsolete. Indeed, the behaviors of those who occupy the role of "supervisor" have changed dramatically over the past 25 years, so that now coaching and facilitation skills are the most valued supervisory SKILLS (*see also* INTERPERSONAL SKILLS).

See also **Self-management; SuperLeadership; Job design; Organizational design; Managerial behavior**

Bibliography

Bass, B. M. (1988). The inspirational process of leadership. *Journal of Management Development*, **7–5**, 21–31.

Dowell, B. E. & Wexley, K. N. (1978). Development of a work behavior taxonomy for first-line supervisors. *Journal of Applied Psychology*, **63**, 563–572.

House, R. J. (1977). A 1976 theory of charismatic leadership. In J. G. Hunt & L. L. Larson (Eds), *Leadership: The cutting edge*. Carbondale: Southern Illinois University Press.

Locke, E. A. & Latham, G. P. (1990). *A theory of goal setting and task performance*. Englewood Cliffs, NJ: Prentice-Hall.

Manz, C. C. & Sims, H. P. Jr. (1987). Leading workers to lead themselves: The external leadership of self-managing teams. *Administrative Science Quarterly*, **32**, 106–28.

Manz, C. C. & Sims, H. P. Jr. (1990). *SuperLeadership*. New York: Berkley.

Manz, C. C. & Sims, H. P. Jr. (1993). *Business without bosses: How self-managing teams are building high-performing companies*. New York: Wiley.

Podsakoff, P. A. & Schriesheim, C. A. (1985). Leader reward and punishment behavior: A methodological and substantive review. In B. Staw & L. L. Cummings (Eds), *Research in organizational behavior*. San Francisco: Jossey-Bass.

Sims, H. P. Jr. (1980). Further thoughts on punishment in organizations. *Academy of Management Review*, **5**, 133–138.

Stogdill, R. M. (1959). *Individual behavior and group achievement*. New York: Oxford University Press.

HENRY P. SIMS JR.

surveys A survey is a method used to gather self-reported descriptive information about the attitudes, behaviors, or other characteristics of some population. The information can be obtained by administering a questionnaire (via paper-and-pencil, computer, personal, or telephone interviews, etc.) to an entire population or some defined subset of that population called a sample (*see* STATISTICAL METHODS). More formally, surveys "consist of relatively systematic, standardized approaches to the collection of information . . . through the questioning of systematically identified samples of individuals" (Rossi, Wright, & Anderson, 1983, p. 1).

Although surveys of voting preferences or social attitudes may receive most of the media attention, surveys have long been used in organizational settings including private and public businesses, universities, and medical centers. Surveys are popular in organizations because they can provide accurate information about major organizational issues. One reason for their widespread use stems from their adaptability. Because of this feature, organizational surveys can be utilized for diverse purposes such as assessing employee needs and attitudes toward the workplace; measuring employee morale, MOTIVATION, JOB SATISFACTION, and intentions to remain with or leave an organization (*see* TURNOVER); and determining consumers' opinions and preferences about the goods and services they receive. Surveys can also establish baselines, benchmarks, or norms at the time of an organizational intervention (*see* ACTION RESEARCH). These standards can be used in future evaluations to determine the effectiveness of new programs and policies.

In addition to providing organizations with useful information, surveys can be a powerful motivational device. Surveys allow employees to feel that they are a part of the decision process – their views are important to management (*see* SURVEYS, FEEDBACK). This sense of EMPOWERMENT may enhance employee motivation, organizational COMMUNICATION, and PRODUCTIVITY (*see* EMPLOYEE INVOLVEMENT).

Given the widespread role of organizational surveys, it is surprising that few treatments have simultaneously addressed both methodological concerns and practical applications – the science and the practice – of organizational surveys. To address this deficit, Rosenfeld, Edwards, and Thomas (1993) recently edited a book encompassing topics such as question writing; measurement ERRORS; sensitive questions; consortium surveys; exit surveys; and surveys about pregnancy, parenthood, SEXUAL HARASSMENT, QUALITY OF WORKING LIFE, and EQUAL OPPORTUNITY climate.

Although conducting a well-written, well-administered organizational survey can be costly, challenging, and a labor-intensive enterprise, the survey process is also very rewarding. Managers have the satisfaction of seeing a need for information turn into survey items. The items return as data, which when are analyzed and interpreted, and provide an empirical basis for answering organizationally important questions. For respondents, organizational surveys provide a vehicle that allows employees to communicate their concerns and questions to management.

While the benefits of surveys are many, they also entail dangers and difficulties. These include raising unfulfilled expectations, inadequate follow-up communications, and suggesting unattainable outcomes. Surveys are not a panacea for all organizational ills; expectations of what a survey can do may need to be tempered with the realities of what it cannot accomplish. These potential pitfalls often can be avoided through careful design and administration and an awareness of the organization's culture and interpersonal politics.

See also **Research design; Research methods; Statistical analysis**

Bibliography

Bradburn, N. & Sudman, S. (1988). *Polls and surveys: Understanding what they tell us*. San Francisco, CA: Jossey-Bass.

Rosenfeld, P., Edwards, J. E. & Thomas, M. D. (Eds), (1993). *Improving organizational surveys: New directions, methods, and applications*. Newbury Park, CA: Sage.

Rossi, P. H., Wright, J. D. & Anderson, A. B. (1983). Sample surveys: History, current practice, and future prospects. In P. H. Rossi, J. D. Wright & A. B. Anderson (Eds), *Handbook of survey research* (pp. 1–20). Orlando, FL: Academic Press.

PAUL ROSENFELD, JACK E. EDWARDS and MARIE D. THOMAS

surveys, feedback Organizations use SURVEYS to gather information on the attitudes, behaviors, and characteristics of employees. Once this information has been gathered and analyzed, the process of informing STAKEHOLDERS (e.g., top management, respondents) of the findings begins. Preliminary to this step is the determination of who will receive the survey FEEDBACK and the methods that will be used to provide it. Survey feedback will work best when it is tailored to the audience having a need or desire to know. Typical methods for feeding back information include briefings to top management, small group or organization-wide presentations, short written synopses for distribution in organizational mail, and technical reports containing in-depth information.

Studies indicate that survey feedback is highly valued by employees. Thus, one positive outcome resulting from survey feedback may be improved two-way COMMUNICATION between management and workers. Through feedback, surveys can become a way to generate employee COMMITMENT, enthusiasm, and involvement in ORGANIZATIONAL CHANGE initiatives that often follow the survey effort (*see* EMPLOYEE INVOLVEMENT).

Survey feedback has long been an integral component of ORGANIZATION DEVELOPMENT (OD) method and practice. In a typical OD survey, employees and researchers collaborate in the design, administration, and follow-on actions as part of an overall organizational change strategy.

See also **Consultancy intervention models; Action research; Learning organization**

Bibliography

Edwards, J. E. & Thomas, M. D. (1993). The organizational survey process: General steps and practical considerations. In P. Rosenfeld, J. E. Edwards & M. D. Thomas (Eds), *Improving organizational surveys: New directions, methods, and applications* (pp. 3–28). Newbury Park, CA: Sage.

PAUL ROSENFELD, MARIE D. THOMAS and JACK E. EDWARDS

symbiosis *see* COMMUNITY ECOLOGY; STRATEGIC MANAGEMENT

symbolic interactionism This is a broad perspective which views "interaction" as a social process involving two or more persons communicating on the basis of language – and therefore symbols – hence "symbolic interactionism" (SI). Symbolic interactions constitute the locus for the social construction of both person and social organization or "social order" (*see* SOCIAL CONSTRUCTIONISM). The latter has received most attention in the literatures of OB. From an SI perspective, "organization" is found in the social processes in which participants merge lines of action with reference to one another, drawing upon and creating conventional understandings and practices; organization is viewed as an ongoing practical accomplishment. Manning (1982) applied this approach to police work, describing conventional "practices" in which, for example, the officer constructed an order of speaking and controlled the movements of participants in some incident. Such practices were shown to be linked with taken-for-granteds, such as "formal rules . . . are not to be trusted," and conventional understandings, for example, concerning what constituted good policework. The core themes of SI are differently developed and emphasized in variants such as "dramaturgy," "ethnomethodology" and NEGOTIATED ORDER. In OB, SI is becoming more evident with increasing recognition of the importance of social processes and meanings.

See also **Interactionism; Self-regulation; Symbolism; Ethnography**

Bibliography

Manning, P. K. (1982). Organizational work: Structuration of environments. *The British Journal of Sociology*, **33**, (1), 118–134.

DIAN MARIE HOSKING

symbolism Refers to the manipulation of meaning through the use of symbols. It involves the linking of a sign to a content or referent by some ordering principle. This is a process of coding/decoding which is a mental and therefore cultural activity. Symbols work to organize experience. In semiotic terms, they are signs that stand for something else. A symbol such as a corporate logo or a political slogan may stand for a particular company or ideological stance. They may also invoke notions of IDENTIFICATION, fealty and honor or alienation, disgust, and fear. They often carry denotative and connotative meanings. Denotative meanings refer to the direct, instrumental uses of a symbol – the flag as standing for a given country. Connotative meanings refer to the expressive, more general, and broader uses of a symbol – the flag as standing for law and order. To study symbolism is to learn how the meanings on which people base actions are created, communicated, contested, and sometimes changed.

There are at least four interelated domains to be explored if the workings of a given symbol are to be understood. First, symbols are cultural objects whose form, appearance, logic, and type can be categorized (although category systems differ and some differ spectacularly). Second, symbols are produced and used by specific people and groups for certain purposes and thus the intentions of symbol creators and users must be understood. Third, symbols are always displayed within particular social contexts and these contexts severely shape (and limit) the possible meanings a symbol may assume. Finally, symbols typically mean different things to different groups of people so the receptive competences and expectations of those who come into contact with given symbols must be examined. Since each domain plays off the others, the interpretation of symbols – even simple ones – can be quite complex.

Take, for example, the Big Mac as a symbol of interest. Consider the audience first. To some McDonald's patrons, the Big Mac is the quintessential American meal, a popular and desirable hamburger served up in a timely and tasty fashion. To others, the Big Mac is food without nourishment, a travesty of a meal served up in a most sterile and unappetizing way. But social context is of considerable importance also. A Big Mac in Tel Aviv is simply not the same cultural object as a Big Mac in Boston. Nor is the history of the Big Mac itself irrelevant to symbolism for this more or less edible symbol has been around for some time and comes packed with consumer myths, production rules, social standing, snappy advertising, and associated symbols all cross-referenced to an uncountable number of life's little pleasures – "you deserve a break today." Some of this is by design, some accidental and some circumstantial and fleeting. Symbolism is about how context helps shape meaning; how symbols are created, packaged and, in a variety of ways, understood; how connotative meanings grow from denotative ones and vice versa; and, most critically, how various audiences receive and decode symbols and then act on the basis of the meaning the symbols hold for them.

Symbolism is of great importance when cultural perspectives are used to describe and explain ORGANIZATIONAL BEHAVIOR. The interpretation of symbols is at the heart of any cultural analysis whether the culture being represented is a small and relatively autonomous workgroup within an organization or a huge multinational firm operating in diverse social, linguistic, and political contexts around the world. Symbolism is also central to studies of virtually all forms of organizational COMMUNICATION since communication itself rests on a socially constructed coding framework that is shared by at least some if not all organizational members. From this perspective, symbolism reaches into all aspects of organizational behavior because it is the process by which all organizational activities, ceremonies, objects, products, stories, services, roles, goals, strategies, and so on are made sensible and hence logical and perhaps desirable to given audiences both inside and outside recognized ORGANIZATIONAL BOUNDARIES. LEADERSHIP can therefore be seen as symbolic action as can other organizational influence attempts such as selection, SOCIALIZATION, and reward practices. Broadly conceived, symbolism is an elementary or fundamental process that makes organizational behavior both possible and meaningful.

See also **Culture; Metaphor; Organizational culture; Rituals and rites; Symbolic interactionism**

Bibliography

Blumer, H. (1969). *Symbolic interactionism*. Englewood Cliffs, NJ: Prentice-Hall.

Feldman, M. S. & March, J. G. (1981). Information in in organizations as symbol and signal. *Administrative Science Quarterly*, **34**, 171–86.

Geertz, C. (1973). *The interpretation of culture*. New York: Basic Books.

Griswold, W. (1992). *Cultures and Societies in a Changing World*. Thousand Oaks, CA: Pine Forge Press.

Manning, P. K. (1992). *Organizational communication*. New York: de Gruyter.

Pfeffer, J. (1981). Management as symbolic action. In L. L. Cummings & B. M. Staw (Eds), *Research in organizational behavior*, (vol. 3, pp. 1–52). Greenwich, CT: JAI Press.

Swidler, A. (1986). Culture in action: Symbols and strategems. *American Sociological Review*, **51**, 273–86.

JOHN VAN MAANEN

synectics *see* CREATIVITY

synergy All organizations are made up of subsystems or components such as strategy, structure, CULTURE, reward systems, staffing, and LEADERSHIP. Synergy occurs when these components work together to create high performance. A more precise way to think of synergy is as an interaction effect, where certain combinations of effects yield significantly higher performance than would be expected from main effects alone.

See also **Group dynamics; Excellence; Strategic management; Organizational effectiveness**

ROBERT DRAZIN

systems dynamics *see* COMPUTER MODELING; LEARNING ORGANIZATION; SYSTEMS THEORY

systems theory This denotes broad metatheory for describing the structure and behavior of complex wholes called systems. Drawn from diverse work in the physical, biological, and social sciences, systems theory seeks to discover laws and principals which apply to all levels of systems from single cells to societies. ORGAN-

IZATIONAL BEHAVIOR scholars use this cross-level perspective to describe the general properties of organizational systems, such as groups and organizations. These characteristics have a profound impact on how we view modern organizations.

One key feature has to do with the notion of system itself and how it forms an organized whole. A system is composed of parts and relationships among them. The system provides the framework or organizing principal for structuring the parts and relationships into an organized whole capable of behaving in a way that is greater than merely the sum of the behaviors of its parts.

In organizational systems, this draws attention to identifying the constituent members or SUBUNITS of the system and examining relationships among them. Equally important, it forces us to go beyond members and relations to assess the organizing principal through which they are arranged into a coherent whole. GROUP DYNAMICS scholars, for example, have spent considerable time addressing issues of group membership and member interaction. They have discovered different ways of organizing members and relations for performing tasks that members could not achieve working alone, such as SELF-MANAGED TEAMS and QUALITY CIRCLES. Similarly, organization theorists have expended effort identifying the different components of organizations and examining relations among them. They have found different ways to organize the components and relationships for competitive advantage (*see* COMPETITIVENESS), such as the M-form organization, the BUREAUCRACY, and the MATRIX ORGANIZATION.

A second important feature of systems has to do with whether they are relatively closed or open to their environment. Closed systems do not interact with the environment, and consequently their behavior depends largely on the internal dynamics of their parts. OPEN SYSTEMS, on the other hand, exchange with the environment, and thus their behavior is influenced by external forces (*see* ORGANIZATION AND ENVIRONMENT).

Early conceptions of organizational systems tended to employ a closed-system perspective. Attention was directed mainly at the internal dynamics of groups and organizations, for example, and at how their behaviors could be controlled internally. This led to knowledge of a variety of internal control mechanisms, such as HIERARCHY, rules/procedures, and FUNCTIONAL DESIGN. In the late 1960s, OB scholars began to broaden their focus to external forces affecting organizational systems. This open systems view was fueled by growing applications of it to the social sciences, and by realization that the behavior of organizational systems could not be adequately explained without examining environmental relationships and their effects on the system. It has led to considerable research and theory about organizational environments, their dynamics and effects, and how organizational systems interact with them. Moreover, open systems theory has provided a number of powerful concepts for understanding how organizations maintain themselves while adapting to external forces.

A third characteristic of systems has to do with their viability. In order to survive and prosper, open systems need to perform at least four critical functions:

(1) transformation of inputs of energy and information to produce useful outputs;
(2) transaction with the environment to gain needed inputs and to dispose of outputs;
(3) REGULATION of system behavior to achieve stable performance; and
(4) adaptation to changing conditions.

Because these different functions often place conflicting demands and tension on the system, system viability depends on maintaining a dynamic balance among them.

In organizational systems, considerable research is devoted to identifying and explaining how these four functions operate and contribute to ORGANIZATIONAL EFFECTIVENESS and survival. This has led to knowledge about how organizations and groups produce products and services through acquiring, operating, and developing different technologies (*see* TECHNOLOGY; TECHNOLOGY TRANSFER); how they protect their technologies from external disruptions while acquiring raw materials and marketing finished products; how they regulate themselves for stable performance while initiating and implementing innovation and change (*see* INNOVATION; ORGANIZATIONAL CHANGE; ORGANIZATION DEVELOPMENT). This research defines a key role of management in organizational systems as sustaining a dynamic balance among these functions; one that allows the organization or group sufficient stability to operate rationally (*see* RATIONALITY) yet requisite FLEXIBILITY to adapt to changing conditions (*see* ORGANIZATION THEORY; POPULATION ECOLOGY).

A fourth key feature of systems that has influenced our conceptions of organizational systems has to do with their multilevel nature. Systems exist at different levels. The levels display a hierarchical ordering, with each higher level of system being composed of systems at lower levels. For example, societies are composed of organizations; organizations are composed of groups; groups are composed of individuals; and so on. Because systems are embedded in other systems, it is necessary to look both upward and downward when describing a system and explaining its behavior. Higher-level systems provide constraints and opportunities for how a system organizes its parts, and the nature of those parts affects the system's organizing possibilities.

This multilevel perspective has led OB scholars to identify different levels of organizational systems, and to focus on understanding them and how they interact with each other. Considerable attention is directed at specifying appropriate LEVELS OF ANALYSIS, both for conceptualizing about organizational systems and for aggregating and disaggregating data that apply to different levels. As researchers have developed more extensive theories and more powerful analytical methods, they have made finer distinctions among levels of organizational systems, particularly above the organization level. Today scholars focus on at least six levels of organizational systems:

(1) individual member (*see* INDIVIDUAL DIFFERENCES);
(2) group (*see* WORK GROUPS);
(3) organization (*see* ORGANIZATIONAL DESIGN);
(4) population of organizations and/or alliance among organizations (*see* INTERORGANIZATIONAL RELATIONS; JOINT VENTURES);
(5) community of populations and/or community of alliances (*see* COMMUNITY ECOLOGY); and
(6) nation (*see* CULTURE, NATIONAL; CULTURE, CROSS-CULTURAL RESEARCH).

See also **Theory; Collateral organization; Organizational boundaries**

Bibliography

Buckley, W. (1968). *Modern systems research for the behavioral scientist*. Chicago: Aldine.
Cummings, T. (1980). *Systems theory for organization development*. Chichester, UK: Wiley.
Sutherland, J. (1973). *A general systems philosophy for the social and behavioral sciences*. New York: Braziller.

THOMAS G. CUMMINGS

T

taboos Organizational or societal ROLE expectations delineate what people are expected to think, feel, and do. When these expectations are broken, and cause reactions of disgust and strong disapproval, a taboo has been broken.

Taboos, in a sense, are a kind of norm, RITUAL, and/or role expectation that specifies thoughts, feelings, and actions that are forbidden (*see* GROUP NORMS). Goffman (1967) showed that even in situations that appear to be trivial or inconsequential, role violations can cause severe disapproval.

Organizational studies which focus on taboos are relatively rare. Most such studies focus on the breaking of behavioral norms in working contexts, as when the frame of a quiet discussion is broken by an overt expression of anger or when a company used to consensual management encounters an autocratic executive prone to making decisions on his or her own. Other studies have focused on sexuality as an organizational taboo (e.g., Hearn, Sheppard, Tancred-Sheriff, & Burrell, 1989). In this regard, postmodern theory (*see* POSTMODERNISM) and deconstruction have proved useful in showing how even bland and mundane, apparently taboo-respecting language can break organizational sexual taboos in subtle and unexpected ways that work to the disadvantage of women (*see* WOMEN AT WORK). What is forbidden has a lure that is difficult to evade.

See also **Culture; Gender; Group decision making; Emotions in organizations; Organizational culture; Punishment**

Bibliography

Goffman, E. (1967). *Interaction ritual.* New York: Doubleday Anchor.

Hearn, J., Sheppard, D., Trancred-Sheriff, P. & Burrell, G. (1989). *The sexuality of organization.* London: Sage.

JOANNE MARTIN

tacit knowledge *see* PRACTICAL INTELLIGENCE; TECHNOLOGY TRANSFER

task analysis *see* JOB ANALYSIS; ACTION THEORY

task and maintenance behavior The distinction is widely used to differentiate behaviors in small groups and organizations which focus on getting the work done, from those which concentrate on building and sustaining the team or organization. Task behaviors include: initiating activity, seeking and giving information and opinions, elaborating, summarizing, testing for feasibility, evaluating, and diagnosis. Maintenance behaviors include: encouraging, gatekeeping, standard setting, expressing feelings, consensus-testing, harmonizing, and reducing tensions (Benne & Sheats, 1948). An integration of adequate frequencies of task and maintenance behavior are required if the team or organization is to become and remain effective. With shared LEADERSHIP, all members need to see themselves displaying both kinds of behavior when both are needed by the team or organization. Where responsibility and AUTHORITY for leadership is lodged in an appointee or electee, he or she must exhibit both kinds of behavior, as needed by those being led. The two-fold classification is replicated in many theories of organization behavior. Misumi's Performance (P) & Maintenance (M) is illustrative (Misumi & Peterson, 1985).

See also **Group dynamics; Team building; Group roles; Managerial grid; Group decision making**

Bibliography

Benne, K. D. & Sheats, P. (1948). Functional roles of group members. *Journal of Social Issues*, **4**, 41–49.
Misumi, J. & Peterson, M. F. (1985). The performance–maintenance (PM) theory of leadership. Review of a Japanese research program. *Administrative Science Quarterly*, **30**, 198–223.

BERNARD M. BASS

TAT (thematic apperception test) *see* ACHIEVEMENT, NEED FOR; AFFILIATION, NEED FOR; POWER, NEED FOR

taylorism *see* MANAGEMENT, CLASSICAL THEORY; SCIENTIFIC MANAGEMENT

team building In the general field of ORGANIZATION DEVELOPMENT (OD), the title given to the grandfather process of intervening in organizations to improve PRODUCTIVITY and morale has been called team building. It was probably the first innovation historically in the OD movement, advancing the basic premise, that before any group of people can begin to improve their performance, group members must be able to work together effectively and collaboratively. Team building, then, is a planned, systematic process designed to improve the collaborative efforts of people who must work together to achieve goals.

Team building methods grew out of an earlier invention called the Training Group (or T group) (*see* SENSITIVITY TRAINING). This learning process, developed in the late 1940s and 1950s, featured an unstructured group, usually for a collection of strangers, for the purpose of allowing interaction to occur without predetermined directions. Out of this interaction participants were trained to observe the dynamics and structure of a group emerge (*see* GROUP STRUCTURE), and to gain insights into their own and other members' interaction style. Emphasis was also placed on giving personal FEEDBACK to all group members, and as the T group movement developed this latter emphasis began to predominate, subordinating GROUP DYNAMICS analysis to the detriment of team building activities.

Participants in early T groups were captivated by the impact the group had on the members in terms of increased TRUST, openness, and cohesiveness (*see* GROUP COHESIVENESS). In an attempt to transfer these same conditions back to their organizational settings, T group trainers we asked to come and conduct the T group for working staff. These early practitioners used the T group methodology at first but soon found that the method, appropriate for a focus on how a group forms and giving feedback with stranger groups, was less suited to groups of employees with specific assignments, common work goals, and long-standing knowledge of each other. The T group methodology had to be altered to take into account the conditions found in WORK GROUPS of common goals, specific assignments, deadlines, allocation of important rewards such as salary and advancements, and often high task interdependence within an organization context where there was a given structure and on-going culture.

In his early analysis of organizations, Likert (1961) clearly pointed out that despite most organization charts showing individuals reporting to other individuals, the true nature of organization structure is a set of interlocking groups or teams variously called departments, divisions, sections, councils, or committees (*see* ORGANIZATIONAL DESIGN). Managers are not only reponsible for individual performance, but must be able to coordinate the efforts of these several individuals where cooperation and interdependence of effort is necessary. The modified T group approach, now called Team Building, became the new tool for building collaboration into a work unit.

The goals of almost all team building efforts were to help group members develop a sense of trust among themselves, open up channels of COMMUNICATION so all relevant issues could be discussed, make sure everyone understood the goals and the interlocking of assignments, make decisions with the real commitment of all members, prevent the leader from dominating the group, openly examine and resolve conflicts, carry out assignments and regularly review and critique work activities to improve processes.

While it was recognized early on that groups differed along a series of important dimensions: size, composition, length of life, nature of the task, degree of interconnectedness of individual tasks or assignments, sophistication of members in group performance, time frames and deadlines, management patterns, and organization culture, there has been a tendency to consider all groups (or teams) as being similar and team building methods were commonly applied to all types of groups (*see* GROUP CULTURE). Practitioners began to consider that different actions needed to be taken if one was working with a new team, a team rife with CONFLICT, an apathetic team, a team dominated by a boss, or split into cliques. An expanded set of actions and skills were developed to meet these various conditions and a repertoire of team building models emerged.

In recent years, the most dramatic difference in team building methods has been between decision teams and work teams. A decision team such as a management executive committee or a university academic department, or a collection of doctors or lawyers in a clinic or firm, must function as a team primarily to make decisions. These team members do not have to coordinate their daily tasks to accomplish a goal. They do have to made decisions which people can accept and implement with real commitment. In contrast, a work team (a hospital operating unit, a police SWAT team, a NASA space crew and some production units, must coordinate their efforts constantly every day (*see* MUTUAL ADJUSTMENT). This has lead to a new set of methodologies around building the autonomous or semiautonomous work team (*see* AUTONOMOUS WORK GROUPS). It is apparent that work teams must also make a range of decisions, so effective decision making is a central activity.

Dyer (1994) found that many companies said they believed in team building but few (only 22 percent) actually engaged in any on-going team building.

When asked why team building programs were not being used, the companies listed the following:

(1) Managers did not know how to do team building.
(2) They did not understand the payoff or rewards for spending the time.
(3) They thought it would take too much time.
(4) Team building efforts were not really rewarded in the company.
(5) People felt their teams were all right – they did not need team building.
(6) People felt it was not supported by their superiors.

The simple designs for team building ask team members to come and be prepared to talk about the following kinds of matters:

(1) What keeps our work group from being an effective team?
(2) What changes would help us become a better team?
(3) What are we currently doing that helps us work together as a team?

All group members share their responses to the above questions, a list of issues is developed specifiying changes needed and change actions are agreed on and taken.

Another common design (Role Clarification Model) asks each person in the work group to describe his/her work or job assignment, obtain clarification from others and then agreements from every other person about what is needed from them in order for the person in question to get the job accomplished. This is especially useful when work roles are not clear.

A fundamental principle of team building is that it is a process, not an event. Too many companies have a one-time team building event and then wonder why the organization's teams do not improve.

See also **Group decision making; Group development**

Bibliography

Dyer, W. (1994). *Team building: Issues and alternatives*. Reading, MA: Addison-Wesley.

Fisher, K. (1993). *Leading self-directed work teams*. New York: McGraw-Hill.

Likert, R. (1961). *New patterns of management*. New York: McGraw-Hill.

Zenger, J. H., Musselwhite, E. & Hurson, K. (1994). *Leading teams*. Homewood, IL: Business One Irwin.

WILLIAM G. DYER

team roles *see* GROUP ROLES; TASK AND MAINTENANCE BEHAVIOR

technology Although technology is a central construct in organizational research, it is defined and employed in different ways by different scholars, a fact which has caused considerable confusion. Most fundamentally, technology is a human activity undertaken by those whose efforts produce material objects (unlike activities such as religion or sports). Derived from the Greek word *techne*, meaning art or skill, technology is a collection of techniques, ways of fabricating things with a useful purpose in mind.

Typically, technology involves the making and using of artifacts. Yet tools or objects are not technology themselves – they embody technology, which is the knowhow that underlies making and using them. The body of knowledge and SKILLS required to produce useful artifacts is the technology, and it may reside in people, things, or processes. In essence, technology mediates between man and the objective world.

Technology is a central construct in organizational research because an organization's technology is the means through which work gets accomplished. Technology provides an organization's means of transforming raw materials (human, symbolic, or material) into desirable goods and services. As a result, the technology that an organization adopts, and the technology adopted by other organizations with which it interacts, can hardly be divorced from its strategy, structure, CULTURE, or characteristic pattern of social relations (*see* CONTINGENCY THEORY).

Until quite recently, economists defined technology simply, in terms of production possibility frontiers. A curve could be drawn showing the trade-off inherent in the production of any two goods – for any set of inputs, such an "isoquant" showed all the different combinations of the two goods that could be affected. Technological progress consisted of moving this curve outward, so that with the same inputs, more of either or both outputs could be produced.

Organizational research has adopted a more complex view of technology. Because technology is a human activity and a body of knowledge, it is not treated as a force purely external to the firm; technology both shapes and is shaped by human VALUES. Orlikowski (1992) summarizes the prevailing view that technology is an external force impacting the organization, but these effects are moderated by human actors and the organizational contexts within which they act. Technology is to some extent autonomous of the firm, but its meaning is socially constructed (*see* SOCIAL CONSTRUCTIONISM).

Several fine distinctions appear in the organizational literature, although they are not applied consistently. Technology is treated as distinct from science in that technology is oriented toward producing useful artifacts, while science is oriented toward producing new THEORY and empirical tests of theory. However, the line between the two is not sharp.

Commonly, at least three different types of technology are distinguished. Product technology is the know-how embedded in an artifact, the blueprint of an object. PROCESS TECHNOLOGY is the know-how embedded in the sequence of tasks that creates artifacts. Clearly the distinction depends on the firm's position in a value chain; to a machine tool maker, the skill embodied in a tool is product technology, but to the firm employing the tool to make things, the same skill is process technology. The third form is administrative technology, which is the set of skills underlying the process of coordinating economic production and exchange of goods (*see* PRODUCTIVITY).

Occasionally, organizational research focuses on industries termed "high technology." There is no formal definition that distinguishes high-technology settings from any other type of setting. Generally, however, high technology industries employ highly advanced or specialized systems or devices, and the degree of technical UNCERTAINTY surrounding these elements is typically very high.

Technology and Organizational Environments

To some extent, the set of technologies available to an organization is external and autonomous, and thus is a critical part of the organizational environment (*see* ORGANIZATION AND ENVIRONMENT). For example, an organization wishing to produce and sell a wrench has a variety of cutting, forming, and assembly technologies available to it, and their technical characteristics are to a great extent independent of the organization's interpretation of them. In the OPEN SYSTEMS models which prevail in organization theory, the organization must adapt to its environment; hence, it must adapt to the pattern of technology adoption it observes and to changes in technology over time.

Technological change appears to behave like an evolutionary system in PUNCTUATED EQUILIBRIUM. This is to say that technological development is typically characterized by long eras of incremental change, occasionally interrupted by breakthrough technologies (*see* INNOVATION). Such discontinuous advances typically inaugurate an era of ferment and flux, in which the new technology displaces the old while various versions of the new technology compete for marketplace acceptance. Eventually, a standard, or "dominant design," typically emerges in response to organizational avoidance of uncertainty. The emergence of a standard creates conditions under which incremental change, focused on improving one general design, can resume. Technological standards have assumed increasing importance in recent times, as the increased interconnection of products into systems, particularly systems interconnected by digital INFORMATION TECHNOLOGY, creates pressure for products to be compatible with one another and able to communicate.

Almost all technologies are brought to economic use by organizations. As a result, technical communities form, and institutional factors often govern the trajectory of a technology's development (*see* COMMUNITY ECOLOGY; INSTITUTIONAL THEORY; POPULATION ECOLOGY). Technologies seldom achieve widespread use due to technical superiority alone. The evolution of a technology is not driven by sheer engineering performance; the development of an institutionalized social framework around a technology plays a critical role. It is more accurate to say that technologies and organizations coevolve than it is to say that technology is solely an autonomous environmental force.

Additionally, technologies both help to shape and are shaped by cultural forces. The same technologies may have different social consequences in different countries, depending on institutional relationships and national sets of values. Although some scholars contend that technology imposes its own value system on humans, the weight of the evidence suggests that all technologies undergo different interpretations in different settings, and thus are socially constructed within a cultural context (Bijker, Hughes, & Pinch, 1987).

Technology and Organizational Strategy

Since technology is central to the organizational environment, scholars examining the strategies firms use to adapt to their environments (*see* STRATEGIC MANAGEMENT). frequently examine the impact of technology, particularly technological change, upon strategic choices and outcomes (*see* ORGANIZATIONAL CHANGE). The effects of INNOVATION ADOPTION is the most widely studied topic in this area. Because much know-how is tacit, firms often find it difficult to adjust to technological change, especially when it is rapid and unpredictable (*see* PRACTICAL INTELLIGENCE). Thus technology can be a powerful force in reshaping and overturning industry structure. The foundation of most research in this vein is the economist Josef Schumpeter's vision of "creative destruction" – the replacement of a set of dominant firms by another group of rivals employing a radically new technology – as the fundamental engine of capitalist progress.

As technical systems grow more complex and interconnected – due largely to innovations in COMMUNICATIONS TECHNOLOGY and information technology that embed intelligence in different products which must communicate – technological systems and networks assume increasing importance. As a consequence, more technological development is taking place through interorganizational ventures than appears to have been the case in the past (*see* JOINT VENTURES). Competitive success via technology may depend more and more on the firm's ability to build alliances and partnership networks, not simply on the firm's individual technological prowess, and consequently, the study of technology-based alliances is one of the most vibrant areas in modern strategy research (*see* INTERORGANIZATIONAL RELATIONS).

Technology and Organizational Structure

The way in which a firm gets work done is a fundamental determinant of ORGANIZATIONAL DESIGN structure. Firms devising technically complex and advanced products typically require a combination of a flexible structure with close coordination to manage the COMPLEXITY (*see* FLEXIBILITY).

Firms also tend to develop a higher ratio of supervisors to other employees as the range and technical difficulty of their tasks increases (*see* SPAN OF CONTROL).

The nature of a firm's process technology may also influence its organizational structure. The more a firm relies on mass production to achieve high PRODUCTIVITY, the more mechanistic it tends to be. The more it relies on flexible, low-volume batch production, the more organic it tends to be (*see* MECHANISTIC/ORGANIC). However, ADVANCED MANUFACTURING TECHNOLOGY may be changing these historical relationships. Computer-integrated manufacture may make possible customized, batch production that is as economical as is mass production (*see* AUTOMATION). A good deal of scholarly research is aimed at discerning the effect of advanced manufacturing technology on the organizational structures of the future, so far without conclusive results.

The idea that firms face a "technological imperative" in organization design is much less popular now than it was in the past. Research in the 1960s tended to suggest that there was one best way to organize, given a firm's technology, and that high performance resulted from the achievement of good fit between the organization's technology and its structure (*see* CONTINGENCY THEORY). The weight of empirical evidence suggests that different structures may be used to implement the same technology successfully; technology still influences organization design, but it does not appear to determine in and of itself the relationship between structure and performance.

SOCIOTECHNICAL THEORY dates back to the early 1950s, and continues to produce useful insights. The fundamental idea is that interrelationships between technological subsystems and social subsystems determine the overall effectiveness of organizational arrangements. For example, in a classic study of new coal-mining technology, Trist and Bamforth demonstrated that a new, mechanized production technology disrupted the equilibrium of traditional work methods without substituting a new, viable social structure. A social system in which a team of six workers developed strong norms and coordinated routines collapsed when new, automated methods broke up the teams and substituted a specialized, hierarchical, 50-person unit as the basic production organization.

The influence of technology on organizational structure generally appears to be far from deterministic. Different organizations may respond differently to the implementation of very similar technologies because of their distinctive histories and patterns of social relations. This is not to say that technology has no orderly, regular influence on organizational structure. Rather, it is to say that organizations have considerable latitude in constructing the meaning of new technologies they adopt, and the structural responses they generate depend in large part on the way in which different interpretations structure behavior (Orlikowski, 1992).

Technology and the Nature of Work

Technology has played a very large part in organizational research on the sociology of work and INDUSTRIAL RELATIONS. The key idea underlying much of this research is that technology is not simply a neutral instrument by which knowledge is put to useful purposes. Rather, a firm's choice of technology may well influence the relationship between workers and their work, and between workers and the organizations to which they belong.

One aspect of Karl Marx's materialism is the assertion that the organization of the means of production determines the other features of a society. In the Marxist tradition, Blauner (1964) describes a specific relationship between dominant production technology, organizational structure, worker attitudes, and worker consciousness. In Blauner's view, the relationship between the worker and his or her job tasks is one of ALIENATION under modern production technology because technology is an instrument of domination, wielded by managers who possess POWER. Other studies suggest that relations between workers and their companies is also significantly affected by the type of production technology employed.

One way in which managers achieve control over people and things is by substituting technical RATIONALITY for human interpretation (Berting, 1993). Thus the contemporary dominance of technology is connected to the rise of universal instrumental rationality as a value. Managing for technical efficiency appears to be rational, and society generally demands from organizations the appearance of rationality. In some industries and societies, pressure to display dispassionate, instrumental rationality had led to the formation of a "technocratic" class of managers, whose control and authority stem from their mastery of a distinctive body of technical knowhow (*see* PROFESSIONALS IN ORGANIZATIONS). However, technology choices may well hinge on the manager's desire to maintain dominance and avoid dependence on worker idiosyncrasies, not on purely technical considerations (Noble, 1984).

More recent developments in the relationship between technology and WORKING CONDITIONS include a greater emphasis on designing work systems to achieve more satisfactory ERGONOMICS, and design systems that can achieve high quality, through vehicles such as CONTINUOUS IMPROVEMENT and QUALITY CIRCLES (*see* TOTAL QUALITY MANAGEMENT). In these efforts, technology is intimately linked with HUMAN RESOURCE MANAGEMENT, particularly in the area of JOB DESIGN. The area of HUMAN-COMPUTER INTERACTION has also received considerable attention. Underlying these outgrowths is the realization – perhaps spurred by insights from Japanese management – that technology, as a knowledge-based human activity, is increasingly becoming embodied in workers who possess flexible knowledge and skills.

See also **Knowledge workers; Organization theory; Technology transfer**

Bibliography

Adler, P. S. (1989). Technology strategy: A guide to the literatures. In R. S. Rosenbloom & R. A. Burgelman (Eds), *Research on technological innovation, management and policy* (pp. 25–151). Greenwich, CT: JAI Press.

Berting, J. (1993). Organization studies and the ideology of technological determinism. In S. Lindenberg & H. Schreuder (Eds), *Interdisciplinary perspectives on organization studies* (pp. 183–194). Oxford UK: Pergamon Press.

Bijker, W. E., Hughes, T. P. & Pinch, T. J. (1987). *The social construction of technological systems: New directions in the sociology and history of technology*. Cambridge, MA: MIT Press.

Blauner, R. (1964). *Alienation and freedom: The factory worker and his industry*. Chicago: University of Chicago Press.

McGinn, R. E. (1978). What is technology? In P. T. Durbin (Ed.), *Research in philosophy and technology* (pp. 179–197). Greenwich, CT: JAI Press.

Noble, D. (1984). *Forces of production: A social history of industrial automation*. New York: Knopf.

Orlikowski, W. J. (1989). The duality of technology: Rethinking the concept of technology in organizations. *Organization Science*, 3, 398–427.

Trist, E. L. & Bamforth, K. W. (1951). Some social and psychological consequences of the longwall method of coal getting. *Human Relations*, **4**, 3–38.

Usher, A. P. (1954). *A history of mechanical inventions*. Oxford, UK: Oxford University Press.

PHILIP ANDERSON

technology transfer This refers to the process whereby TECHNOLOGY (embodying knowledge, ideas, devices, artefacts, and software) which has been invented, developed, or used in one organizational setting, is transferred so that it is developed and used in another, where hitherto it was probably unknown and certainly unused. The concept covers a wide range of activities.

The originating base for the technology may be within a university, independent, or industrial research organization, profit or nonprofit making, process, manufacturing, or service organization. The transfer process may be entirely within the originating organization, for example, the marketing and production of a new product developed by an in-house R&D group. It may involve crossing ORGANIZATIONAL BOUNDARIES, for example, the development of an IT system for handling patient records in a hospital on the basis of a client services system in the leisure industry, or the development of a new procedure for testing color fastness in garment manufacture as a result of sponsored university-based research. It may also involve crossing national as well as organizational boundaries, for example, with the development of a "low tech" water treatment process by a European company and its provision through the World Bank to a region in India.

Successful Technology Transfer is a significant contributor to economic performance at three levels: for organizations, industrial sectors, and national economies. Companies may secure significant competitive advantage if they have the capacity to manage technology transfer (*see* COMPETITIVENESS). For example, it may allow them to increase profitability or market share by cutting down the time it takes to get a new product from conceptual design to the market place. Lessons learnt about increasing efficiency or quality in one set of operations may be translated to others, and their capacity to attract and retain appropriately skilled staff may be increased. At sectoral and national levels, benefits are accrued from sets of competing organizations being successful in securing effective product or process developments. Governments and international agencies (*see* GOVERNMENT AGENCIES) play important parts in determining policy on technology transfer between nations, and thereby influencing global economic development.

Whilst products can be defined in terms of volume, cost, and quality, and the process of making products (whether in manufacturing or service) in engineering terms of mass, flows, density, or information systems, it is important to remember that products and processes also embody knowledge. Concepts, theories and SKILLS, may be formally and openly documented or held "tacitly" in the minds and senses of inventors or users (*see* PRACTICAL INTELLIGENCE). Technology transfer can involve unlocking tacit knowledge, codifying it and thereby facilitating its transfer to other settings. Tacit knowledge is evidenced in all sorts of technologies, from the traditional crafts like weaving, to heavy industry, like foundry operations, to highly advanced software applications. The developers and users of these products and processes build up a knowledge of how they can "sense" – through touch, smell, or intellectual insight – progress and performance. It is often these aspects of tacit knowledge which are most difficult to transfer from one location and CULTURE to another, and which account for some failure in Technology Transfer.

The bulk of relevant empirical work is concerned with studies which examine organizational and individual factors which facilitate or inhibit effective technology transfer within single large, complex organizations. This work can provide a base for looking beyond single company studies in order to understand what is involved in seeking to transfer technology across organizational as well as departmental and professional boundaries (*see* ORGANIZATIONAL BOUNDARIES). Early work in the 1960s and 1970s tended to view Technology Transfer as a linear process from idea generation, through development, into production. Subsequent work drew attention to the importance of FEEDBACK between participants and stages and today the iterative, nonlinear, complexities of Technology Transfer are regarded as crucially important.

There are common themes between the literature on technology transfer and that concerned with COMMUNICATION, innovation, and diffusion (*see* INNOVATION ADOPTION; INNOVATION DIFFUSION). There are structural barriers deriving from functional and hierarchical boundaries which may be reinforced by methods of resource allocation and REWARD structures. For example, if development and production departments are treated as self-contained organizations with tight budgets and a resource allocation process which does not encourage people to seek to improve their performance through utilizing the fruits of others' endeavors, little effective technology transfer will take place. Structural barriers interact with cultural barriers, particularly, the assumptive worlds of participants, which derive from their particular (and often professionally or vocationally specific) TRAINING and experience.

Attempts to remove such barriers require structural INNOVATION and cultural change (*see* ORGANIZATIONAL CHANGE). Structurally, one can encourage secondments between departments, multidepartmental task forces, flatter organizations, project focused teams, and the requirement that research projects have to secure "sponsorship" from a party who is sufficiently interested in the subject to contribute toward its finance (*see* INTEGRATION). To secure these changes clear messages have to be given through appraisal, promotion, and reward, which show, for example, that cross disciplinary team working is positively regarded. Furthermore, to facilitate a willingness to learn from and with others, the strategic vision of the organization needs to reflect a commitment to CONTINUOUS IMPROVEMENT. This is the sort of approach which is advanced to secure effective ORGANIZATIONAL LEARNING.

Allen's work was particularly important in identifying the barriers to communication between R&D and other departments. He stressed the importance of encouraging informal linking networks and has investigated the effects of STATUS, HIERARCHY, and physical distance in inhibiting communication (*see* NETWORKING). Receptivity to new ideas was found to decrease as the life cycle of any project progressed, with a tendency to avoid critical information in the later stages in an effort to reduce UNCERTAINTY and increase predictability.

In moving away from a linear view of Technology Transfer in which significant barriers have to be "overcome" to secure the "delivery" of the technology to its end user, there is now more emphasis on joint problem solving between all those involved in development, adaptation, and use. It is now recognized that organizations or departments do not generally have a "wish list" of technological developments which they hope to be able to resource. Instead they have an awareness of problems, for example, falling market share, global competition, or poor morale. They want solutions to their problems. In order for Technology Transfer to be "effective" there needs to be a willingness to engage with others in working out problem definitions and solutions and in learning lessons. Success in technology transfer is now therefore seen as less associated with clear views on what technology "can do" and more focused on the benefits which may accrue and how they will be achieved. This places emphasis on activities such as scanning for new ideas and joint working on problem definition as well as solutions. There also needs to be a willingness to invest in new ventures and a culture which is supportive of failure as well as success.

In addition to work on managing Technology Transfer by and within organizations, there is also literature on the role of government and sectoral organizations in facilitating Technology Transfer (*see* GOVERNMENT AND BUSINESS). Different mechanisms are used. They include the provision of databases and networks to increase access to information about available technologies, the establishment of quasi governmental agencies to seek out potentially useful innovations and through licensing, to make them more widely available, the development of Science Parks to provide infrastructure and "incubation" for emergent companies based on new technologies, and lastly, the encouragement of Technology Transfer Companies within the scientific community to help researchers put forward their ideas and protect their commercial ownership whilst facilitating wide dissemination.

See also **Information technology; Learning organization; Sociotechnical theory; Strategic alliances**

Bibliography

Allen, T. (1977). *Managing the flow of technology*. Cambridge, MA: MIT Press.

Coombs, R., Saviotti, P. & Walsh, V. (Eds), (1992). *Technological change & company strategies*. London: Harcourt Brace Jovanovich.

Ettlie, J. E. & Reza, E. M. (1992). Organizational integration and process innovation. *Academy of Management Journal*, **35**, (4), 795–827.

Frosch, R. A. (1984). R&D choices & technology transfer. *Research Management*, May–June, 11–14.

Gupta, A. K. & Wileman, D. (1990). Improving R&D/marketing relations from the R&D perspective. *R&D Management*, **20**, no. 4. 277.

Hamel, G. (1991). Competition for competence and inter-partner learning within international strategic alliances. *Strategic Management Journal*, **12**, 83–103.

Massey, D., Quintas, P. & Wield, D. (1992). *High tech fantasies – Science parks in society, science & space*. London: Routledge.

Rothwell, R. & Zegweld, W. (1985). *Reindustrialisation & technology*. London: Longman.

Seaton, R. A. F. & Cordey-Hayes, M. (1993). The development and application of interactive models of industrial technology transfer. *Technovation*, **13**, no. 1, 45–53.

Souder, W. E. & Padmanabhan (1989). Transferring new technologies from R&D to manufacturing. *Research Technology Management*, **32**, 38–43.

Williams, R. & Gibson, D. V. (1990). *Technology transfer: A communications perspective*. London: Sage.

SANDRA DAWSON

teleology *see* ORGANIZATIONAL CHANGE

theft *see* EMPLOYEE THEFT

theory Theory, which is about suppositions that are general, idealized, and abstract, can easily be misunderstood in a field like ORGANIZATIONAL BEHAVIOR where pragmatists, practitioners, and positivists worry about practice, profits, and precision. To forestall such misunderstanding, this entry discusses theory in general, what it is, how people approximate it, and the consequences of these approximations.

Definition of Theory

If theory is equated with knowledge claims preserved in statements involving concepts, then its nature and importance are captured as well by Kant as anyone: "Perception without conception is blind; conception without perception is empty." For comparison, here are two descriptions that are more prosaic but less elliptical.

(1) Theory is "an ordered set of assertions about a generic behavior or structure assumed to hold throughout a significantly broad range of specific instances" (Sutherland, 1975, p. 9).
(2) Theory is "a collection of assertions, both verbal and symbolic, that identifies what variables are important for what reasons, specifies how they are interrelated and why, and identifies the conditions under which they should be related or not related" (Campbell, 1990, p. 65).

What is common among these descriptions is the idea that theories refer to "specific instances," which provides the perceptions that keep conceptions from becoming empty, and the idea that these references are abstract, general simplifications, which provides labels for perceptions and keeps them from becoming blind. But not all theories are equally successful at removing emptiness and blindness. The reason is that they vary in the degree to which their assertions facilitate sensemaking, move beyond common sense, and approximate the properties of a fully developed theory. Variation in these three dimensions affects the extent to which the theory is able to explain, predict, and delight. We review these dimensions briefly to create a more nuanced understanding of theory.

Theory and Sensemaking

If sensemaking is defined as "the reciprocal interaction of information seeking, meaning ascription, and action" (Thomas, Clark, & Gioia, 1993, p. 240), then the affinity between it and theorizing is apparent. Dubin (1976) says as much in his statement that "a theory tries to make sense out of the observable world by ordering the relationships among elements that constitute the theorist's focus of attention in the real world" (p. 26). To think more clearly about theory is to take this correspondence seriously.

Blumer (1969) took it seriously in his extended gloss of Kant's aphorism about perception and conception. Blumer argued that conception comes into play when an activity, driven by perception, becomes blocked or frustrated. "A concept always arises as an individual experience, to bridge a gap or insufficiency in perception" (p. 160). This bridging, in the form of a new orientation that reshapes perception and guides action, unfolds similarly in the mind of the theorist and the lay person. Concepts give blocked experience an "understandable character" (p. 156) by referring to something whose existence is presumed, isolated through abstraction, labeled, and shared, even though its character is not fully understood. Perhaps most important, the conception is instrumental. It releases and allows completion of activity, whether that activity be Pasteur solving the problem of anthrax (p. 163), or practitioners solving problems of DOWNSIZING or identity.

To make sense by means of conception is to invent, to bring things into existence. Theorists do this by means of sentences that make knowledge claims. That is less innocent than it sounds. The tipoff is the word "claims." Van Maanen (1993) captures the issues: "Theorizing is a social practice that represents the construction of reality via the only method at our disposal – language . . . . Theorists produce discourse whose purpose is to persuade readers that they've got it right, have something to say" (pp. 6, 8). Theories do not mirror reality. Instead, they create a sense of what is real and unreal, which means they are rhetorical rather than foundational (Mailloux, 1990, p. 133).

Theorists have no choice but to use sentences if they want to communicate knowledge for purposes of evaluation. Furthermore, only sentences can be evaluated as true or false. There is no such thing as a "true" or "false" experience. Therefore, what is said becomes what we know, which means that how we formulate what we say, determines how systematic and shared the things will be that we claim to know. Thus, ways of writing theory influence what can be done with it.

Theory and Discovery

Perception remains relatively blind unless theories tell us something we do not already know. To do this, theorists often deliberately move away from collective social wisdom so that they can gain access to knowledge with a low a priori probability of ever being known. Common knowledge is suspended temporarily when people invoke possible worlds such as those created in SIMULATIONS, laboratories, formal models, and thought experiments involving imagination (Weick, 1990). Possible worlds are tools of rhetoric that create a unique sense of what is real and unreal. Nevertheless, their content can be given an empirical interpretation at any time, which means their departures from common knowledge are transient and instrumental. Theorists and practitioners sometimes forget this.

Theory and its Approximations

Theory in organizational behavior is a dimension rather than an all-or-none activity and it ranges from "guess" to "explanatory system." Merton (1967) suggests possible points along this dimension, all of which represent distinct interim struggles, but none of which represent a final product. To "compare" theories for their usefulness is often a misleading exercise since what is actually being compared are approximations that have developed different parts of a theory.

Theory work is sometimes approximated by *general orientations* to materials. Broad frameworks specify types of variables that people should take into account, but determinate relationships between specific variables are not set forth. References in the organizational behavior literature to "lenses," "images," "perspectives," and "frameworks" typically signal work of this kind. Scott's (1987, p. 29) three organizational perspectives – rational, natural, and OPEN SYSTEMS – are advanced general orientations since they also embody elaborated concepts and empirical GENERALIZATIONS.

As we saw earlier, much theory work is language work or, as Merton calls it, *analysis of concepts* (p. 143). As the label suggests, conceptual analysis consists of specification and clarification of key concepts. But, a list of concepts and definitions is not a theory. "It is only when such concepts are interrelated in the form of a scheme that a theory begins to emerge" (p. 143). Perrow's (1984) development of the idea of a "normal accident" exemplifies conceptual analysis. And his elaboration of this idea in terms of coupling and complexity represents steps toward interrelating variables associated with the concept.

Post-factum interpretation often passes as theory work in organizational behavior because so much of the database is case histories (*see* CASE STUDY RESEARCH). These interpretations have a spurious adequacy because they are often ad hoc hypotheses, selected because they fit observations, with no systematic exploration of alternative interpretations that are also consistent with the data and no tests of the ad hoc fit with new observations. Weick's (1990) analysis of the Tenerife air disaster as stress-induced regression illustrates this tactic, and in doing so is just that, an illustration rather than a test of claims about stress.

Finally, *empirical generalization*, the raw material for theory, may be misidentified as theory itself. However, since the generalization is "an isolated proposition summarizing observed uniformities of relationships between two or more variables" (Merton, 1967, p. 149), it lacks the crucial property of an interrelated set of propositions. The idea that power flows toward those who reduce significant uncertainties (Salancik & Pfeffer, 1977) represents an empirical generalization in search of related propositions.

By way of conclusion, readers should understand that approximations are the bulk of theory in organizational behavior. Approximations can still supply "substantive ideas about what things mean, how things work, or what the serious problems are" (Campbell, 1990, p. 67). Those approximations that do so, persuasively, in uncommon ways, that are susceptible to further elaboration, hold the future of the field.

See also **Critical theory; Process theory; Paradigm; Systems theory**

Bibliography

Blumer, H. (1969). *Symbolic interactionism*. Englewood-Cliffs, NJ: Prentice-Hall.

Campbell, J. P. (1990). The role of theory in industrial and organizational psychology. In M. D. Dunnette & L. M. Hough (Eds), *Handbook of industrial and organizational psychology* (2nd edn, vol. 1, pp. 40–73). Palo Alto, CA: Consulting Psychologists.

Dubin, R. (1976). Theory building in applied areas. In M. D. Dunnette (Ed.), *Handbook of industrial and organizational psychology* (pp. 17–39). Chicago: Rand McNally.

Mailloux, S. (1990). Interpretation. In F. Lentricchia & T. McLaughlin (Eds), *Critical terms for literary study* (pp. 121–134). Chicago: University of Chicago.

Merton, R. K. (1967). *On theoretical sociology*. New York: Free Press.

Perrow, C. (1984). *Normal accidents*. New York: Basic Books.

Salancik, G. R. & Pfeffer, J. (1977). Who gets power – and how they hold on to it: A strategic-contingency model of power. *Organizational Dynamics*, **5**, 3–21.

Scott, W. R. (1987). *Organizations* (2nd edn). Englewood Cliffs, NJ: Prentice-Hall.

Sutherland, J. W. (1975). *Systems: Analysis, administration, and architecture*. New York: Van Nostrand.

Thomas, J. B., Clark, S. M. & Gioia, D. A. (1993). Strategic sense making and organizational performance: Linkages among scanning, interpretation, action, and outcomes. *Academy of Management Journal*, **36**, 239–270.

Van Maanen, J. (1993). Theory as style: The uses, abuses and pleasures of organizational theory. Talk presented at Academy of Management. August 10, 1993.

Weick, K. E. (1989). Theory construction as disciplined imagination. *Academy of Management Review*, **14**, 516–531.

Weick, K. E. (1990). The vulnerable system: Analysis of the Tenerife air disaster. *Journal of Management*, **16**, 571–593.

KARL E. WEICK

theory x & y According to McGregor (1960), traditional management believed implicitly in Theory X, which postulates that employees are inherently lazy, indifferent to the needs of the organization, and uninterested in doing a good job. Employees should not be expected to do any more than absolutely necessary. As a consequence, management has to direct, motivate, and control the workforces, as if they were immature children. Control systems are essential, and assignments must be specific. Close monitoring and correction of performance by supervisors is essential. Thinking should be left to superiors. Discipline and fear of PUNISHMENT should be used to maintain standards of performance. Employees should be motivated primarily by "carrots" for good performance and "sticks" for poor performance. Opposite to belief in Theory X is Theory Y, which postulates that employees essentially want to do a good job. They have ego needs as well as needs for material benefits. They respond positively to being treated like adults and given responsibilities commensurate with their capabilities. Their involvement, loyalty, and COMMITMENT to the organization are important motivators of their performance. Wherever possible, they should be able to participate in decisions affecting their performance (*see* PARTICIPATION).

The two theories are predicated on distinctive assumptions about human behavior. Theory X assumes workers must be persuaded, rewarded, punished, controlled, and directed if the coordination of effort is to be achieved. In fact, no work at all will get done unless there is active intervention by management. This is because employees are naturally lazy and will work as little as possible. They lack ambition, dislike accepting responsibility, and prefer to be led. They are only concerned with their own needs and not with the goals of their organization. They resist change (*see* RESISTANCE TO CHANGE). They are not good decision makers. As much as possible, all decisions within the organization should be routinized so that under all circumstances, the individual will require a minimum of thought without alternatives. Indeed, they must be told in detail what to do or they will not be able to do their job. They must be prodded with external incentives and close surveillance. While management is responsible for organizing the elements of productive enterprise – money, materials, equipment, people – in the interest of economic ends, employees develop passivity and resistance to organizational needs as a result of their experience in organizations (*see* RESISTANCE TO CHANGE).

Theory Y says that workers have the potential for development, the capacity for assuming responsibility, and the readiness to work for organizational goals. Management makes it possible for workers to recognize and develop these traits. Therefore, management is responsible for arranging organizational processes and conditions so that employees can achieve their own goals by directing their efforts toward organizational objectives. Management creates opportunities, releases potential, removes obstacles, encourages growth and provides guidance. Belief in Theory Y promotes decentralization, delegation, job enlargement, empowerment, participation, and self-management.

See also **Values; Employee involvement, Human relations movement; Self actualization; Theory Z; Scientific management; Managerial behavior; Managerial style**

Bibliography

McGregor, D. M. (1960). *The human side of enterprise*. New York: McGraw-Hill.

BERNARD M. BASS

Theory z Ouchi (1981) introduced the idea of Theory Z, to represent the beliefs underlying Japanese management, in contrast to THEORY X & THEORY Y. The management of Theory Z firms is characterized by long-term employment and intensive SOCIALIZATION of their workforce. Objectives and VALUES emphasize cooperation and teamwork. There is slow promotion from within the firm and jobs are rotated. Employees are expected to be generalists rather than specialists. PERFORMANCE APPRAISAL systems are complex. Emphasis is on WORK GROUPS rather than individuals, open COMMUNICATION, consultative DECISION MAKING, and a relations-oriented concern for employees. In comparison to Theory X organizations, Theory Z organizations are more decentralized and have fewer levels of management. Subordinates exercise more upward influence in dealing with their bosses in the Type Z than in the Type X organizations.

See also **Organizational culture; Group, cohesiveness; Group dynamics; International management**

Bibliography

Ouchi, W. G. (1981). *Theory Z: How American business can meet the Japanese challenge*. Reading, MA: Addison-Wesley.

BERNARD M. BASS

third country national *see* EXPATRIATES

time and motion *see* JOB ANALYSIS; OPERATIONS MANAGEMENT; SCIENTIFIC MANAGEMENT

time management The method of time management is predominantly aimed at making more effective use of time, mainly at the individual level within organizations, forming part of TRAINING for example, in the management of change and managerial development and effectiveness (*see* MANAGEMENT DEVELOPMENT). It is also usual for time management to be implemented within a package, alongside an assortment of other STRESS management techniques (i.e., relaxation, assertiveness training, and lifestyle audits). In defining time management it is necessary to examine the problems it attempts to resolve, its methods and techniques, and its limitations.

At the individual level, poor time management has been found to be a source of negative health outcomes (e.g., reduced MENTAL HEALTH), and so it is mainly used in the area of stress management with an emphasis on SELF-MANAGEMENT. From an organizational and managerial perspective, one of the main problems to be acknowledged in managing time is that time is a finite resource like other organizational resources such as money and equipment, except that we cannot manufacture more time when we need it.

Time management should focus upon both work and nonwork activities (*see* NONWORK/WORK) and involve identifying the key areas in one's life, recognizing time wasters, and developing and identifying priorities. The most popular techniques used in time management TRAINING are identifying time wasters, prioritization, GOAL SETTING and PLANNING, "Eating the Elephant" (i.e., How do you eat an elephant? – one bite at a time!), effective meetings, and the use of schedules and diaries.

There are, however, a number of limitations to the approach to time management which are less to do with the methods employed and more to do with the conceptual framework within which it is founded. A major criticism of time management is that it often entails even more work, when what is required is for more time to be liberated for alternative stress management techniques such as the pursuit of leisure activities, often neglected under conditions of excessive work load and stress (*see* ROLE OVER/UNDERLOAD).

A more crucial drawback to current approaches and practice of time management is the disregard of INDIVIDUAL DIFFERENCES (e.g., the PERSONALITY and behavioral style of the individual), which may underlie way they manage time (e.g., *see* TYPE A). To illustrate, individuals high on Type A behavior have a tendency to take on ever more work, coupled with an inability to delegate to others. For time management to be effective, individuals need to have the right MOTIVATION and frame of mind as well as the right techniques.

See also **Performance, individual; Role; Self-regulation**

Bibliography

Bliss, E. C. (1985). *Getting things done: The ABC's of time management*. New York: Futura.

Ferner, J. D. (1980). *Successful time management*. New York: Wiley.

Fontana, D. (1993). *Managing time*. Leicester, UK: British Psychological Society.

Januz, L. R. (1981). *Time management for executives*. New York: Scribner.

CHERYL J. TRAVERS

top management teams The term "top management team" (TMT) has been adopted by organization and strategy theorists to refer to the relatively small group of most influential executives at the apex of an organization – usually the general manager (*see* CEOS) and his or her direct reports. The term does not necessarily imply a formalized management-by-committee arrangement, but rather simply the constellation of, say, the top three to ten executives. As such, many top management "teams" may have few genuine team properties (interaction, shared purpose, collaboration) and might more accurately be referred to merely as top management groups.

A scholarly interest in top management teams emerged in the early 1980s and has been pervasive ever since. Realizing that top management typically is a shared activity, researchers have moved beyond an examination of singular leaders, to a wider focus on the top LEADERSHIP group.

The underlying assumption is that the collective dispositions and interactions of top managers affect the choices they make. The limited empirical evidence as to whether the characteristics of the top executive or of the entire top team are better predictors of organizational outcomes clearly supports the conclusion that the top team has greater effect. For example, the VALUES of top teams have been found to be more strongly related to INNOVATION strategies than are the values of chief executives alone. Similarly, major strategic change is more likely to occur following major changes in the composition of the TMT than when only the CEO changes (*see* ORGANIZATIONAL CHANGE).

The vast majority of research on TMTs has focused primarily on the composition of teams as predictors of organizational outcomes. Unfortunately, other team characteristics have not received as much attention, probably because they are more difficult for researchers to observe and measure. A complete portrayal of a TMT would include not only composition, but also team structure (e.g., GROUP SIZE and roles), incentives (e.g., financial and succession prospects) (*see* SUCCESSION PLANNING), processes (e.g., COMMUNICATION flows and sociopolitical dynamics) (*see* GROUP DYNAMICS), as well as the characteristics and behaviors of the group leader.

Complementing the larger body of work on the effects of TMTs, some research has examined the determinants of TMT characteristics. In this vein, both external factors (such as industry age, growth rate, and munificence) and organizational characteristics (including strategic profile, size, and financial resources) have been found to explain in part the characteristics of TMTs. One of the major limitations of many studies on TMTs is that the direction of causality has been imputed but not verified. It is most plausible to believe that firms select and promote executives who fit certain critical contingencies and, in turn, those executives make choices in line with their particular predispositions and COMPETENCIES. Over time, a reinforcing spiral probably occurs; hence establishing definitive causality will be difficult.

Available research does allow us to conclude that the biases, blind spots, experiences, and interactions of top executives greatly affect what happens to companies. Thus, CEOs or general managers who wish to improve the performance and fitness of their organizations are well advised to focus attention on the characteristics and qualities of their top teams.

See also **Culture, group; Team building; Group decision making; Organizational effectiveness**

Bibliography

Hambrick, D. C. (1994). Top management groups: A conceptual integration and reconsideration of the team label. In B. M. Staw & L. L. Cummings (Eds), *Research in organizational behavior*, (vol. 16). Greenwich, CT: JAI Press.

Hambrick, D. C. & Mason, P. A. (1984). Upper echelons: The organization as a reflection of its top managers. *Academy of Management Review*, **9**, 195–206.

Jackson, S. E. (1991). Consequences of group processing for the interpersonal dynamics of strategic issue processing. In P. Shrivastava, A. Hugg & J. Dutton (Eds), *Advances in strategic management*, (vol. 8, pp. 345–382). Greenwich, CT: JAI Press.

Katzenbach, J. R. & Smith, D. K. (1991). *The wisdom of teams*. Boston: Harvard Business School.

DONALD C. HAMBRICK

total quality management Total quality management, (TQM) is a management philosophy and business strategy intended to embed quality improvement practices deeply into the fabric of the organization. It is also a social movement that has become partly institutionalized in many countries.

No single authority speaks for the entire movement. Rather, TQM is a collection of related ideas from different sources. One source is American quality consultants, especially Juran (1988), Deming (1986), and Crosby (1984). Despite similarities, each authority differs from the others in important respects. Second, the Japanese have made vital contributions to TQM (Ishikawa, 1985; Young, 1992). Third, some have attempted to integrate management theory and research and TQM (Dean & Bowen, 1994; Sashkin & Kiser, 1993).

Major themes in TQM include the following. First, the entire organization becomes focused on quality, defined as *satisfying customer requirements*. Conventional wisdom holds that quality or customer satisfaction is only one outcome, subject to trade-offs with other outcomes. TQM proponents argue that quality is paramount because improving it improves PRODUCTIVITY, decreases costs, and increases speed to market. Quality experts typically estimate that the "cost of quality," including inspection, defects, scrap, rework, warranty cost, and so on, is usually 10 to 25 percent of product cost. Decreasing this cost is a major objective of TQM. Some trade-offs between organizational outcomes do exist, however, and these are not well specified in TQM thinking.

TQM efforts also attempt to create a CULTURE of *CONTINUOUS IMPROVEMENT* in which improving quality and meeting customer needs better is part of the responsibility of every employee. This requires *LEADERSHIP* by top management. The overwhelming majority of quality problems are viewed as system problems, not worker MOTIVATION problem (*see* SYSTEMS THEORY). A TQM culture requires new VALUES, perspectives, and tools, and these are unlikely to be developed without the active involvement of senior management. *PLANNING* to integrate a quality focus in all operations receives a heavy emphasis. Thus, TQM has a "top-down" flavor.

Teamwork receives considerable stress. QUALITY CIRCLES and JOB DESIGN may enhance teamwork within work units (*see* TEAM BUILDING). Cross-functional cooperation helps address system problems. Strong collaborative relationships with a relatively small number of quality-oriented vendors are encouraged.

A major contribution of the quality movement is the development of specific tools for quality analysis and GROUP DECISION-MAKING. These include BENCHMARKING statistical process control, measurement of the "cost of quality," process analysis, Pareto charts, fish bone cause-and-effect diagrams, control charts, and other tools.

A critical part of Japanese management, especially in manufacturing firms using MASS PRODUCTION technologies, is JUST-IN-TIME. JIT requires many organizational changes to be successful (*see* INTERNATIONAL MANAGEMENT).

Finally, certain human resource practices are characteristic of TQM efforts. Jobs are designed so that employees are responsible inspecting their own work and correcting their own ERRORS. However, work simplification and standardization mean that employees do not necessarily gain self-management responsibility in TQM systems (*see* JOB DESKILLING). Employees typically receive considerable quality information. Monetary REWARD systems are de-emphasized in TQM theory in favor of recognition systems.

TQM has become widely accepted. For example, over three-fourths of US *Fortune* 1000 companies cover at least some employees with a TQM effort (Lawler, Mohrman, & Ledford, 1992). On average, they cover 41 percent of their employees, and about one in six companies covers 100 percent of its employees under TQM. More than 75 percent make at least some use of such practices as cost of quality monitoring, work simplification, self-inspection, and just-in-time inventory systems. It appears that Japanese companies make even deeper use of these practices.

Formal standards and prizes recognize firms with exemplary quality practices in many countries. The Union of Japanese Scientists and Engineers annually awards the Deming Prize to firms passing rigorous examinations. The US Department of Commerce sponsors the annual Malcolm Baldridge National Quality Award. Over 60 countries, including all members of the European Union and the United States, have adopted ISO 9000 standards to certify that companies are using standardized procedures to insure high quality. Finally, many large manufacturers operate demanding vendor certification programs.

Practice has led research in TQM (Dean & Bowen, 1994). TQM does not fit conveniently into existing research domains, and has been neglected by academics. Many research questions cannot be answered satisfactorily at this point. These include the degree of TQM effectiveness and the determinants of success, diffusion, and institutionalization.

Most of the evidence of TQM effectiveness is anecdotal. Many positive stories are dramatic, telling of drastic reductions in quality problems, millions of dollars of costs eliminated, markets and profits regained, and so on. For example, Xerox was failing but regained lost market share from Japanese competitors through TQM. However, many anecdotes and nonacademic studies point to a high failure rate. Studies by consulting firms such as Arthur D. Little and Rath & Strong indicate that more than half the firms adopting TQM are disappointed with the results (Port, 1992).

What organizational factors account for the degree to which TQM practices yield benefits? Despite claims of universal benefits, it is doubtful that all quality practices will benefit all organizations (Dean & Bowen, 1994). For example, a study by Ernst & Young and the American Quality Foundation found that the effects of specific quality practices depended on the maturity of the TQM effort (Port, 1992).

A related issue concerns the degree to which familiar human resource practices are compatible with TQM philosophies and practices. Some established practices, such as employee selection testing, are advantageous but ignored in the quality literature. In other cases, there may be serious conflicts. Lawler (1994) points out that familiar employee involvement practices aimed at self-management and the use of rewards for group and organizational performance may be incompatible with TQM philosophies and principles.

TQM practices appear to offer a promising arena for the study of INSTITUTIONAL THEORY, since an explicit goal of TQM proponents is to create a permanent shift toward a quality philosophy in contemporary organizations. Institutions taking part in these efforts include consulting firms and organizations granting quality certifications and awards. This would be an interesting time to study such institutions because some observers are criticizing them as excessively bureaucratic and too costly. These complaints have been fueled by the well-publicized struggles of some winners of the Baldridge Award (one went bankrupt) and Deming Prize (the first American winner dismantled its quality bureaucracy after winning the prize).

See also **Business process reengineering; Operations management; Competitiveness; Organizational effectiveness; Employee involvement**

Bibliography

Crosby, P. B. (1984). *Quality without tears: The art of hassle-free management*. New York: New American Library.

Dean, J. W. & Bowen, D. E. (1994). Management theory and total quality: Improving research and practice through theory development. *Academy of Management Review*, **19**, (3), 392–418.

Deming, W. E. (1986). *Out of the crisis*. Cambridge, MA: MIT Press.

Ishikawa, K. (1985). *What is total quality control? The Japanese way*. Englewood Cliffs, NJ: Prentice-Hall.

Juran, J. M. (1988). *Juran on planning for quality*. New York: Free Press.

Lawler, E. E. III (1994). Total quality management and employee involvement: Are they compatible? *Academy of Management Executive*, 8, (1), 68–76.

Lawler, E. E. III Mohrman, S. A. & Ledford, G. E. Jr. (1992). *Employee involvement and total quality management: Practices and results in Fortune 1000 companies*. San Francisco: Jossey-Bass.

Port, O. (1992). Quality. *Business Week*, November 30, 66–72.

Sashkin, M. & Kiser, K. J. (1993). *Putting total quality management to work*. San Francisco: Berrett-Koehler.

Young, S. M. (1992). A framework for successful adoption and performance of Japanese manufacturing practices in the United States. *Academy of Management Review*, 17, (4) 677–700.

GERALD E. LEDFORD, JR.

tournament promotion Tournament mobility is a model to describe the promotion system in organizations (Rosenbaum, 1984, 1989). In this model, promotions operate like sports tournaments in which new employees compete in a sequence of implicit competitions. Winners compete among themselves for further advancements, and losers of early competitions are eliminated from the tournament for top positions. While competitions are usually invisible, the model predicts certain career mobility patterns: early winners, though not assured of advancements, are in an advantaged position compared to others who lost early competitions, even if the late starters seem to catch up.

Tournaments arise because promotion committees use past successes as easily interpreted signals of potential, which is otherwise hard to judge. Tournaments assume that the losers at any stage are less able than the winners.

Rosenbaum showed that the career moves of a corporation's entry cohort over a 13-year span fit tournament hypotheses. Employees getting an early promotion were significantly more likely to get another promotion in the next 4 years than employees who were not initially promoted. Among those at the same level after 7 years, those who got there first advanced further than those arriving later. Early jobs affect later jobs, even after controlling for intervening jobs and personal attributes.

These findings are supported by Veiga's (1983) study of managers in three organizations, Sheridan, Slocum, Buda, and Thompson (1990) confirmed tournament hypotheses, showing that early experiences (traineeships or high-power departments) had lasting effects on career advancements. While Forbes (1987) distinguished among three kinds of tournament (single elimination; round robin; horse race), his study also finds significant effects of early jobs (technical entry jobs, number of moves) on later jobs, even after controlling for intervening positions.

One implication, older employees in a job are considered as competition losers, so AGE reduces promotion chances, even after controlling for company experience and other attributes. This age effect is so durable that it increases during economic contraction (although promotions decrease), and it is unaffected by a strong affirmative action program (which failed to help older women or to hurt older males, while strongly affecting younger employees; Rosenbaum, 1984, Chap. 6). Age effects have been shown by other studies, and their social and psychological impact has been suggested (Lawrence, 1988).

The tournament model has practical implications. Firms using the tournament model will limit late bloomers' advancement and may overlook talent. Employees who get off to a bad start or who have competing commitments to child-care will be penalized, with lasting effects. "Mommy track" programs to reduce job demands in early careers of mothers will create long-term disadvantages unless tournament assumptions are explicitly relinquished (*see* DISCRIMINATION; WOMEN AT WORK). The tournament model also describes the structure of psychological incentives in a career system, with implications for mid-career motivation crises. By viewing CAREER systems as a whole, the model suggests precautions to avoid inadvertently restricting the development of talent and MOTIVATION.

See also **Career transitions; Career plateauing; Human resources planning; Succession planning**

Bibliography

Forbes, J. B. (1987). Early intraorganizational mobility: Patterns and influences. *Academy of Management Journal*, **30**, 110–125.

Lawrence, B. S. (1988). New wrinkles in the theory of age: Demography, norms, and performance rating. *Academy of Management Journal*, **31**, 309–337.

Rosenbaum, J. E. (1984). *Career mobility in a corporate hierarchy*. New York: Academic Press

——(1989). Organization career systems and employee misperceptions. In M. B. Arthur, D. T. Hall & B. S. Lawrence (Eds), *Handbook of career theory* (pp 329–354). Cambridge, UK: Cambridge University Press.

Sheridan, J. E., Slocum, J. W., Buda, R. & Thompson, R. C. (1990). Effects of corporate sponsorship and departmental power on career tournaments. *Academy of Management Journal*, **33**, 578–602.

Veiga, J. F. (1983). Mobility influences during managerial career stages. *Academy of Management Journal*, **26**, 64–85.

JAMES E. ROSENBAUM

trade unions Although trade unions' behavior may, in some important respects, vary according to the society in which they organize (Martin, 1989) the classical definition provided by Sidney and Beatrice Webb (1907) of a trade union as ". . . a continuous association of wage earners for the purpose of maintaining or improving the conditions of their working lives" is still a useful starting point for the analysis of unions in market economies. It can be improved by substituting the term employees for wage earners, so as to include salaried staff, and by adding a reference to COLLECTIVE BARGAINING as the main means of achieving their purpose. Hence, trade unions seek to create, and exploit, the greater power which collective employee strength offers, compared to that of the individual employee, in order to exercise INFLUENCE over work-related decisions which would otherwise be made unilaterally by employers and managers. Thus, unions are concerned with the political process of decision making as well as the economic outcomes (*see* POLITICS).

Studies of trade unions, as complex organizations, tend to focus on their objectives and means, external structure and growth/decline, and government (internal organization) and democracy (*see* ORGANIZATIONAL DESIGN).

Union Objectives and Means

Unions may be categorized (following Hoxie, summarized in Dabscheck & Niland, 1981) in terms of the following ideal types: Revolutionary, Reformist or Uplift, and Business unions. Revolutionary unions have generally been associated historically with class conscious movements and, in some cases, have acted as the industrial arm of the Communist Party. Their ultimate objective has been to overthrow the existing social and political system. Reformist or Uplift unions, may also be organized on a class basis, or they may organize occupationally or industrially specific groups of workers. They do not seek to overthrow the existing system, but strive, long-term, to reform it from within, while bargaining for immediate gains. Business unions are essentially sectional organizations representing a particular group, or groups, of workers. They want "more" for their members and bargain for it collectively without seeking to change radically society's social or political system. In practice, many unions tend to combine elements of reformist and business unionism.

The means unions use to achieve their objectives, and the adversarial or co-operative stance adopted vis-à-vis management, may differ according to the contexts in which they organize. Nevertheless, collective bargaining is the method most commonly used to influence PAY and conditions of employment (*see* WORKING CONDITIONS). Unions may also seek to exercise a degree of unilateral control over some aspects of work allocation and organization. At higher levels of management DECISION MAKING union representatives, e.g., shop stewards, may also try to influence, and be consulted on, policy questions, such as capital investment. In addition, unions will petition governments to protect their legal right to organize and negotiate. This pressure group activity may be performed by federations of unions. The American Federation of Labor and Congress of Industrial Organizations (AFL–CIO) in the United States and the Trades Union Congress (TUC) in the United Kingdom perform this and other functions. Reformist unions may also affiliate to a political party of a socialist or social democratic nature, for example, the Labour Party in Britain, for wider social purposes. Unions, or their federation, may also provide members with training, insurance, legal and financial services.

Union External Structure, Growth, and Decline, in Membership

Union structure is conventionally defined as the coverage of a union's membership i.e., the union's job territory or jurisdiction. Traditionally, it has been categorized as craft, industrial, or general. Industrial unionism, e.g., in Germany (and company unionism, e.g., in Japan), results in employers dealing with a single union and may be preferred by management. In the United States and Britain union structure is more complex, and subject to change, largely because of union mergers (*see* Lipset, 1986; McCarthy, 1985) (*see* MERGERS AND ACQUISITIONS).

Union membership in many parts of Europe and the United States declined throughout the 1980s and early 1990s, following growth in some countries in the 1970s (see OECD, 1991, Chap. 4). Controversy continues concerning the causes of these changes. Theories divide broadly into those that explain it in terms of factors external to the unions, e.g., decline is rooted in the hostile economic (including level, location, and composition of employment), political (legislation) and social environment, and the growth of HUMAN RESOURCE MANAGEMENT. Other researchers stress internal factors, i.e., the role of unions themselves in attracting, recruiting, and retaining members (Mason & Bain, 1993). It is likely that different combinations of external and internal factors operate at different points in the growth and decline cycles.

Union Government and Democracy

Union government is composed of the decision-making processes and internal structures of unions. Michel's (1962) aphorism "who says organizations says oligarchy" has been taken by some authorities to apply to trade unions. In contrast, other researchers, while accepting that unions have the potential for oligarchy, because of the internal differences between the full-time officials (bureaucrats), activists (e.g., shop stewards), and ordinary members, argue that unions are more or less democratic, according to one or more of the following five criteria: the level of participation in decision-making and competition for office; checks and balances on the official's powers; the existence and role of factions and parties; bargaining between members and leaders; and the degree to which decisions are decentralized (Undy & Martin, 1984).

Unions, in terms of the above organizational characteristics, are also dynamic. Research shows that they respond to changes in their environment and that the national leadership has important choices to make concerning the most effective form of union government and union structure (*see* ORGANIZATION AND ENVIRONMENT). Further, they have scope to shape the means which unions employ to achieve their objectives. Nevertheless, over the past decade, a hostile environment, particularly in the United States and the United Kingdom, has made it difficult for unions to sustain a significant role and, indeed, a substantial presence, in some companies and industries. In particular, their collectivist values have been undermined by the rise of INDIVIDUALISM and human resource management. Research is continuing into how unions may effectively respond to this challenge.

See also **Negotiation; Collective action; Psychological contract; Democracy; Participation**

Bibliography

Dabscheck, B. & Niland, J. (1981). *Industrial relations in Australia* (Chap. 4). Sydney, Australia: Allen & Unwin.

Lipset, S. M. (Ed.), (1986). *Unions in transition.* San Fransisco, CA: Institute for Contemporary Studies.

Martin, R. M. (1989). *Trade unionism: Purposes and forms.* Oxford, UK: Oxford University Press.

Mason, B. & Bain, P. (1993). The determinants of trade union membership in Britain: A survey of the literature. *Industrial and Labour Relations Review*, **46**, no. 2, 332–351.

McCarthy, W. E. J. (Ed.), (1985). *Trade unions.* Harmondsworth, UK: Penguin.

Michels, R. (1962). *Political parties.* Glencoe, IL: Free Press.

OECD (1991). Trends in Trade Union Membership. *OECD Employment Outlook*, 97–134.

Undy, R. & Martin, R. (1984). *Ballots & trade union democracy.* Oxford, UK: Blackwell.

Webb, S. & Webb, B. (1907). *History of trade unionism.* London: Longmans.

ROGER UNDY

trainability testing *see* TRAINING

training When learning events are planned in a systematic fashion and are related to events in the work environment, they are called training programs. From this point of view, the training process is defined as the systematic acquisition of SKILLS, rules, concepts, or attitudes that result in improved performance in the work environment (Goldstein, 1993) (*see* PERFORMANCE, INDIVIDUAL). Thus, training programs can be planned to result in a more considerate supervisor or a more consistent technician. In some cases, such as on-the-job training, the instructional environment is almost identical to the actual job environment. In other instances, such as a classroom lecture on electronics theory for technicians, the learning environment is removed from the job situation. However, in either situation, effective training stems from a systematically designed learning atmosphere based upon a careful ASSESSMENT of job requirements and the capabilities of the trainees.

Training represents a positive hope for persons first entering the world of work or those individuals changing their work environment (*see* JOINING UP PROCESS). When training is designed well, it gives individuals opportunities to enter the job market with needed skills, to perform in new functions, and to be promoted into new situations (*see* SELECTION METHODS). Therefore, it should not be a surprise that labor unions (*see* TRADE UNIONS) often include training opportunities as parts of a CONTRACT during bargaining negotiations or that large companies have designed multimillion dollar facilities to annually train thousands of craftspersons in new technological innovations. Saari, Johnson, McLaughlin, and Zimmerle (1988) reported about the most frequent reasons for sending managers to training programs. Their data were based upon a comprehensive survey of over 600 US companies with each having more than 1000 employees. The primary reasons for sending managers to MANAGEMENT EDUCATION and training programs were to broaden the individual, and to provide knowledge and skills such as job specific and state of the art knowledge. As far as the use of the different types of training settings, they reported that 90 percent, of the over 600 companies responding, reported using external short course programs, 75 percent report using company specific programs, 31 percent university residential programs, and 25 percent executive MBA programs. Also, there is an indication that the larger the company in terms of number of employees, the more likely they were to use formal management training and education programs. Considering the extensive amount of training that is being offered, it should not be surprising to learn that many different disciplines contribute to research and

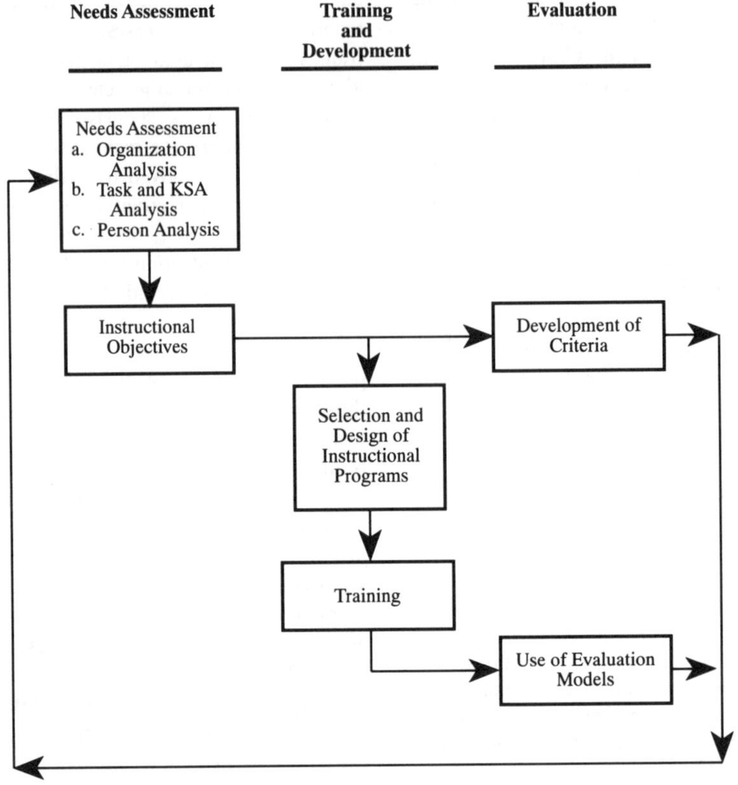

Figure 1 An instructional system
Source: Adapted from I. L. Goldstein (1993) *Training in Organizations*

development. This includes disciplines from adult education, industrial and organizational psychology, HUMAN RESOURCES MANAGEMENT, instructional technology, and ORGANIZATIONAL BEHAVIOR.

A model is presented here (see Figure 1) to provide a context for understanding the interactions between training system components as well as training research issues. Following the presentation of the training systems model, material on work force issues which are particularly relevant to training concerns will be presented. The model presented in Figure 1 emphasizes careful needs assessment, precisely controlled learning experiences designed to achieve instructional objectives, and use of performance criteria and evaluation information.

Needs Assessment

Needs assessment consists of a series of analyses which assess the organization, the job, and the persons performing the job in order to provide input for the design and evaluation of training systems. There are a number of different steps in the needs assessment process. Organizational analysis involves a macro level analysis of the role of training which includes an examination of the system-wide components of the organization that affect a training program's design and development. This phase includes an examination of the organizational goals and ORGANIZATIONAL CLIMATE for training. For example, in this stage, it is determined whether training is the appropriate strategy to use in resolving the human resources issues facing the organization. In addition, it is determined whether there are organizational system constraints that will make it difficult for training to be successfully transferred onto the job. An example of such a constraint could be supervisors who do not support the objectives of the training systems being employed. Recent research by Rouillier and Goldstein (1993) have identified many of the organizational facilitators and inhibitors which help determine whether what is learned in training will actually be eventually used by trainees when they arrive on the job. Based upon the assessment obtained as a result of the organizational analysis, decisions are then made as to whether the organization should or is ready to provide training.

As presented in Figure 1, another phase of the needs assessment is the determination of which tasks are required on the job and which knowledge, skills, and abilities (KSAs) are necessary to learn to perform those tasks (*see* ABILITY; INDIVIDUAL DIFFERENCES). In this phase, the researcher determines which KSAs are critical in the sense that they make a difference in the performance of the important task components of the job. This is a complex process which involves the collection of data identifying tasks and KSAs as well as determining the answers to questions such as which KSAs should be learned in training as compared to which should be learned on the job.

Another component of the needs assessment is person analysis which involves specifying the trainees' capabilities. This involves determining the target population for the training program which can include persons already in the organization or individuals who are not yet part of the organization. By determining the capabilities of these target populations on the required KSAs for the job, it becomes possible to focus the training program on critical KSAs which are not in the repertoire of the target population.

From the information obtained in the needs assessment, a blueprint emerges that describes the objectives to be achieved upon completion of the training program. This provides input for the design of the training program as well as for the measures of success (criteria) that will be used to judge the program's adequacy. Thus, objectives communicate the goals of the program to both the learner and the training designer.

Training Environment

Once the tasks, KSAs, and objectives have been specified, the next step is designing the environment to achieve the objectives. Training is a delicate process that requires a supportive learning environment. The training process must be designed to facilitate the learning of the KSAs required to perform the tasks that the trainee needs for successful job performance. The analysis of job tasks and required KSAs and the design of a matching training environment requires very careful analyses (*see* JOB ANALYSIS). As Gagné (1984) describes it, this is a process in choosing the most powerful learning environment for what the trainee needs to acquire. Thus, providing FEEDBACK to the learner concerning their performance is very helpful in some situations but the choice of the type of feedback (and even whether feedback will always be helpful) depends on what needs to be learned (*see* KNOWLEDGE OF RESULTS). Similar choices need to be made about the entire training situation. For example, most golfers would agree that instructing them to correct a flaw in their golf swing by reading a text description is not nearly as useful as video tapes which allow the instructor to point to the exact flaws in their swing. Similarly, simulators have been found to be very effective in teaching pilots to fly airplanes. Some of the advances in modern technology have resulted in a vast array of very complex training simulation systems (*see* COMPUTER SIMULATION). For example, the Federal Aviation Agency in the United States decided that flight simulators had become so sophisticated that business jet pilots could use the simulator to meet many of their training requirements, thereby not always requiring actual flying time in the plane.

Another interesting technological INNOVATION is the development of interactive videodiscs. As described by Pursell and Russell (1990), the hardware components of videodisc systems consist of computers, videodisc players, monitors, and connecting equipment (*see* INFORMATION TECHNOLOGY). These instruments present information in many different forms including motion pictures, stills, text, and graphics along with sound tracks. The most sophisticated of these systems is called interactive videodisc and it permits the student and system to interact providing a large number of individualized learning experiences. Several companies are now employing this technology to provide employees with workstations that have the capability to respond to changes in manufacturing processes. The system is often used to provide what is called "JUST-IN-TIME" TRAINING as manufacturing systems driven by computer technology shift from one operation to another. Indeed, simulations built around work situations have been found to be very effective in teaching many skills including helping managers to develop COMMUNICATION skills (*see* INTERPERSONAL SKILLS). These later simulations include techniques known as behavioral role modeling (*see* ROLE TAKING). A good example of their effective use is presented by Latham and Saari (1979) who demonstrated the value of the approach in training managers in a extremely well-controlled study. But again, that does not mean that the use of behavioral role modeling or an interactive videodisc will always be the most effective training system to teach learners for all situations. A critical point is that the fanciest gadget does not make for a training system unless it is designed properly on the basis of a proper needs assessment and it is evaluated to make sure that it performs its functions. There are literally dozens (perhaps hundreds) of different types of training methods. Goldstein (1993) presents detailed information about a variety of training approaches ranging from classroom instruction to complex simulators.

Cognitive and instructional theorists have progressed to a stage of development where information is emerging concerning the choice of training environments. Tannenbaum and Yukl (1992) have summarized recent advances concerning our understanding of important LEARNING variables that contribute to the enhancement of the training process. For example, they note that learners do best when given the opportunity to actively produce the capability; that FEEDBACK should be accurate, credible, timely, and constructive; and that the instructional process should enhance trainee SELF-EFFICACY and expectations that training will be successful and lead to valued outcomes. Obviously, it is also the case that training systems that can be designed to utilize these variables are more likely to produce better learning. Excellent discussion of this work on learning and instructional theory can be found in Campbell (1988), Baldwin and Ford (1988), and Howell and Cooke (1989).

Training Evaluation

The number of different types of objectives that organizations hope training programs can achieve vary widely but could, for example, include: producing quality goods in a shorter time period; reducing ACCIDENTS with a corresponding decrease in insurance premiums; implementing a management system which is more service oriented toward its customers; and increasing a health oriented approach to life styles as a way of reducing time away from work due to illness and STRESS. The potential number of goals is unlimited. While training is not a panacea for all the ills of society, well-conceived training programs have achieved beneficial results. There certainly appears to be an increasing number of thoughtfully developed programs. However, it would be unrealistic to pretend that all programs are either based upon appropriate needs assessment, or that these programs are even examined to determine the degree to which they achieve their objectives. Unfortunately, many organizations do not collect the information to determine the utility of their own instructional programs. Thus, their techniques remain unevaluated, except for the high esteem with which they may be regarded by training personnel. For example, a survey by Ralphs and Stephan (1986) of the *Fortune* 500 firms provides information about evaluation methods which indicates that most evaluations (86 percent) consist of trainee reactions which are written up at the end of the course. While positive reactions are important, there is evidence which indicates that positive feelings do not necessarily mean that the appropriate level of learning has occurred. Relatively few efforts are made to collect information concerning performance changes by means of follow-up on the job, which is when both the trainee and the organization could find out whether the programs are achieving the desired results, and when the evaluation could provide clues to the modifications necessary to enable the program to work. This is very short-sighted because evaluations can provide information which can lead to meaningful revisions that can result in programs meeting important organizational goals.

The evaluation process centers around two procedures – establishing measures of success (criteria) and using RESEARCH DESIGNS to determine what changes have occurred during the training and transfer process. Criteria must be established for both the evaluation of trainees at the conclusion of the training program and the evaluation of on-the-job performance. One classification for this purpose suggests that several different measures are necessary, including reactions of participants, learning of participants in the training program, behavior changes on the job, and final utility of the total program (Kirkpatrick, 1959, 1960).

In addition to criterion development, the evaluation phase must also focus on the necessary design to assess the training program. There are a number of different designs which can be used to evaluate training programs and to some extent the choice of a design depends on the questions you want to answer. Some examples of questions (from Goldstein, 1993) are as follows:

1 Do you wish to determine whether the trainees learn during training?
2 Do you wish to determine whether what has been learned in training transfers as enhanced performance in the work organization?
3 Do you wish to determine whether the performance for a new group of trainees in your organization is consistent with the performance of the original training group?
4 Do you wish to determine whether a training program evaluated as being effective in another organization can be used successfully in your organization (*see* PERFORMANCE INDIVIDUAL).

An answer to these different questions helps to determine the components of your evaluation model (*see* QUASI-EXPERIMENTAL DESIGN). For example, the answers to these questions help determine when you should collect information and how you can use control groups as a way of accounting for extraneous effects. A number of writers have written material to help in the effective design of evaluation programs (e.g., Cook, Campbell, & Peracchio, 1990; Goldstein, 1993).

Training and Selection Systems

Training interventions are just one component within a larger set of interacting organizational and societal systems (*see* HUMAN RESOURCE PLANNING). Thus, the need for training systems often is determined by other factors such as, when new technology will be introduced, or when groups of persons will retire thus requiring others to be trained to take their place (*see* RETIREMENT). However, it is clear that there is a continuing interaction between training and selection systems both at the entry level and promotion level (*see* SELECTION METHODS). Both training and selection systems stem from a JOB ANALYSIS or needs assessment which helps an organization determine both the basis for selection and also what needs to be trained at what point in time. Often, the organization needs to decide whether they wish to select (or even find) persons with particular capabilities or whether training needs to be provided. Of course, usually both selection and training are required to ensure the most capable work force. But, the level of training, and at what capability level training needs to begin, is determined by the types of individuals who have been selected. This point is also discussed above in the section on person analysis in the needs assessment section

The interactions between training and selection system often go even further and sometimes, the differences between the uses of selection and training systems are hard to distinguish. For example, ASSESSMENT CENTERS are a standardized set of simulated activities often used as a way of testing and selecting managers. It is also the case that these simulated activities can be designed to provide information to the candidates about which skills need to be developed further in order for them to qualify as future managers. Further, it is possible to design these exercises so the candidate has the opportunity to practice (or be trained) in performing assessment center simulations requiring these various skills and abilities. Sometimes the assessment has to be designed in a slightly different way so that helpful feedback can be given to the candidate. However, much of the simulations and procedures used are very similar. In this later case, it is clear that the same instrument can essentially serve both selection and training purposes.

Another example of the overlap between training and selection devices is known as trainability testing. Investigators interested in predicting performance suggest that a person who can demonstrate proficiency in learning to perform on a small job sample will also learn better in the actual training program and perform better on the job. Thus, the measure has been named a trainability test. This is not an entire training program but rather a sample of tasks that call forth some of the knowledge, skills, and abilities needed on the job. Note that in order to have a good trainability test, it necessarily requires a careful needs assessment to determine the tasks and knowledge, skills, and abilities required for the job. As one might guess, this emphasis on good needs assessment as the basis of the measure often leads to successful efforts. Research by Robertson and Downs (1989) over a 20-year period of time reports on a considerable number of trainability tests that successfully predict later performance for jobs such as carpentry, bricklaying, dentistry, and sewing.

The Training Scene Tomorrow

As noted above, training is a big business with both organizations and employees having high expectations about what can be accomplished. Many conditions make it likely that expectations concerning what training needs to accomplish in the future will be even greater (Goldstein & Gilliam, 1990). Some of the reasons for this are described next.

Advances in technology. Already, a significant portion of our lives is spent in educational and training programs. Prognosticators would predict that instructional technology is likely to have an even greater impact. There are a number of reasons for such a prediction including the startling effects resulting from developments in TECHNOLOGY. There is a clear trend toward more highly automated systems. Klein and Hall (1988) point to technological developments such as programmable AUTOMATION which includes the use of robots that are reprogrammable, multifunctional machines that will manipulate materials, and various forms of COMPUTER-AIDED-DESIGN and computer assisted manufacturing (*see* ADVANCED MANUFACTURING TECHNOLOGY). It is clear that many countries are investing in technology in the hope that automation will result in increased PRODUCTIVITY and product quality and as a result will permit them to gain a competitive edge in global market competition. Paradoxically, the increases in technology and machine responsibility increase the demands on the human being. As noted by Howell and Cooke (1989), instead of simple procedural and predictive tasks, the demands of operating extremely sophisticated computer systems requires the human operator to become responsible for inferences, diagnoses, judgments, and decision making, often under severe time pressure (*see* HUMAN-COMPUTER INTERACTION). All of these types of developments in automation and computer technology place even greater demands on training systems to produce a highly sophisticated work force. The training needs that are likely to affect the future of organizations are clearly stated by a description of the expectations of executives at a Mazda car manufacturing plant. "They want employees to be able to work in teams, to rotate through various jobs, to understand how their tasks fit into the entire process, to spot problems in production, to trouble shoot, articulate the problems to others, suggest improvements and write detail charts and memos that serve as a road map in the assembly of the car" (Vobejda, 1987, p. A14). The effects of failing to provide adequate training was sadly demonstrated in the nuclear power plant ACCIDENT at Three Mile Island. A major finding of that investigation was that key maintenance personnel did not have adequate training for their jobs.

Interestingly, as discussed in the section above on the training environment, advances in technology have led to increasingly sophisticated training systems. It is also clear that these advanced systems will only work to the degree that the individual is capable of mastering the technology needed to operate the learning system. Thus, an additional feature to designing the learning program on the basis of a thorough needs assessment is also making sure that the workers are capable of operating the system. In a sense, an environment is being created where some of the advanced training systems will take training for a person to learn to operate it. This all becomes another reason for making sure that all training is evaluated to ensure that it functions as well as possible.

Organizations and global markets. A future look at jobs and organizations makes increasingly fluid world market arrangements appear even more likely than is already obvious. Many novel strategies are being explored. For example, Klein & Hall (1988) note that some firms are exploring pilot projects involving data entry in countries outside the home of the host organization because the advantages of low wages and surplus workers outweigh the disadvantages of long-distance electronic data transmission. Most consumers now realize that it is not unusual for a manufacturer to produce a product (e.g., an automobile) which is manufactured in a number of different countries. Sometimes, these involve arrangements between liaison teams directing the overall efforts between different employees in different organizations in different countries all contributing to the production of a single final product (*see* JOINT VENTURE). In these situations, managers will be expected to understand and manage the processes for achieving quality as well as managing team efforts across individuals who have different values and come from different CULTURES (*see* EXPATRIATES; INTERNATIONAL HUMAN RESOURCE MANAGEMENT). In discussing the enormous training implications, Ronen notes that the manager given an assignment in a foreign country must possess the "patience of a diplomat, the zeal of a missionary, and the linguistic skill of a UN interpreter" (1989, p. 418). Ronen is correct, but the issue is likely to become just as complicated for managers working in their own countries because the workplace will need to incorporate individuals who come from environments with very diverse cultures and values (*see* MANAGEMENT DEVELOPMENT). That issue becomes more obvious in discussing workplace demographics.

Changing Demographics. Projections clearly indicate that the work force is changing and thus will impact HUMAN RESOURCE MANAGEMENT in a way never experienced before. In some countries in Europe, such as Sweden, the small number of workers available have made it difficult to even employ selection systems because everyone is needed in the market place. In other countries such as the United States, data (Cascio & Zammuto, 1987) clearly indicate that the rate of increase in the population available for the work force will decrease significantly in the upcoming decades and new entrants or those primarily between the ages of 16 and 24 will decrease substantially. In addition, demographics indicate that a large number of individuals who will be available for entry into the work force will be under-educated youth lacking basic literacy skills. The impact of this problem is made more dramatic by the corresponding developments in advanced technology which increase the need for technical skills to enter the job market. In addition, significant numbers of the under-educated youth are members of racial minority groups that society has not completely integrated into the work force (*see* RACE). While many members of these groups have successfully entered professional and technical careers, it is also true that many of the hard core unemployed are racial minorities.

In addition to the problem of under-educated youth, there are other serious demographic issues. There are a number of different groups including women, racial minorities, and older persons who have faced problems of substantial UNEMPLOYMENT as well as job DISCRIMINATION related to promotional opportunities. With this focus, the question of training programs and their fairness to these groups has become a serious legal issue in some countries such as the United States (*see* PREJUDICE; CONFLICT). Training techniques that have not been validated and that are discriminatory in promotional and job opportunities are being struck down by the courts in the United States (*see* EQUAL OPPORTUNITIES). Settlements often result in millions of dollars in back pay to current employees as well as requiring training to enable the employees to qualify for better jobs.

The design and implementation of these programs require a special sensitivity to the needs of the applicant population and the job requirements. For example, an analysis by Sterns and Doverspike suggests that training programs for older trainees can be more successful by following certain principles (*see* AGE). Their review indicates that older workers are often highly motivated to learn but sometimes fear failure in competition with younger workers especially where high technology needs to be utilized in performing the job. They suggest that training should be organized so that materials are organized to ensure complete mastery of previous components before moving ahead and where possible training should build on elements that are familiar to trainees from past learning. In addition, systems should be organized to minimize memory requirements and to avoid paced or time pressured situation. Finally, the materials should be as job relevant as possible, provide positive feedback and encourage the self-confidence of the trainee. Of course, it is possible to point out that many of these principles are important for any type of training program but they appear to be particularly pertinent to ensure the success of the older worker. In these situations, an additional training issue is the degree to which the organization is itself willing to make a commitment rather than assuming all of the change necessary must come from the trainee. Organizations which are likely to be successful in integrating persons from diverse groups will need to provide MENTORING and training for individuals already in their organization as well as the entry level trainee.

It almost seems unnecessary to suggest that the training implications of all of the issues discussed above are enormous, especially for training managers who will be working with a very culturally and racially diverse workforce. Managers will need to provide on the job training to integrate unskilled youth into the work force, while also at the same time working with job incumbents and other managers who may not have previously been a traditional part of the work force. Supervisors will need to perform these activities at a time when jobs have become increasingly complex, and national and international competition more intense. All of this will make training in areas such as INTERPERSONAL SKILLS even more important in the future workplace. A related impact for training is that there is an increasing emphasis on quality for both service oriented jobs and manufacturing oriented jobs. This has important training implications in that more employees will need to be trained in quality techniques and processes. However, for the manager, the training implications for being able to manage such emphases are dramatic. Managers will be expected to understand and manage the processes for achieving quality as well as learning to manage team efforts which are likely to be emphasized as a way of achieving success. Clearly, training can be a positive force for both the individual and organization. To meet those expectations, it should be clear that the training agenda for the next decade will provide quite a challenge.

See also **Learning organization; Organizational learning; Management education**

Bibliography

Baldwin, T. T. & Ford, J. K. (1988). Transfer of training: A review and directions for future research. *Personnel Psychology*, **41**, 63–105.

Campbell, J. P. (1988). Training design for performance improvement. In J. P. Campbell & R. J. Campbell (Eds), *Productivity in organizations*. San Francisco: Jossey-Bass.

Cascio, W. F. & Zammuto, R. F. (1987). *Societal trends and staffing policies*. Denver: University of Colorado Press.

Cook, T. D., Campbell, D. T. & Peracchio, L. (1990). Quasi-experimentation. In M. D. Dunnette & L. M. Hough (Eds), *Handbook of Industrial and organizational psychology*. Palo Alto, CA: Consulting Psychologists Press.

Gagné, R. M. (1984). Learning outcomes and their effects: Useful categories of human performance. *American Psychologist*, **39**, 377–385.

Goldstein, I. L. (1993). *Training in organizations: Needs assessment, development and evaluation* (3rd edn). Pacific Grove, CA: Brooks/Cole.

Goldstein, I. L. & Gilliam, P. (1990). Training system issues in the year 2000. *American Psychologist*, **45**, 134–143.

Howell, W. C. & Cooke, N. J. (1989). Training the human information processor: A review of cognitive models. In I. L. Goldstein (Ed.), *Training in development and organizations*. San Francisco: Jossey-Bass.

Kirkpatrick, D. L. (1959–1960). Techniques for evaluating training programs. *Journal of the American Society of Training Directors*, **13**, 3–9, 21–26; 14, 13–18, 28–32.

Klein, K. J. & Hall, R. J. (1988). Innovations in human resource management: Strategies for the future. In J. Hage (ed.) *Journal of Organizational Behavioral Management*, **1**, (1) 53–77.

Latham, G. P. & Saari, L. M. (1979). The application of social learning theory to training supervisors through behavioral modeling. *Journal of Applied Psychology*, **64**, 239–246.

Pursell, E. D. & Russell, J. S. (1990). Employee development. In K. N. Wexley (Ed.), *Developing human resources*. Washington, DC: BNA Books.

Ralphs, L. T. & Stephan, E. (1986). HRD in the Fortune 500. *Training and Development Journal*, **40**, 69–76.

Robertson, I. T. & Downs, S. (1989). Work sample test of trainability: A meta-analysis. *Journal of Applied Psychology*, **74**, 402–410.

Ronen, S. (1989). Training the international assignee. In I. L. Goldstein (Ed.), *Training and development in organizations*. San Francisco: Jossey-Bass.

Rouillier, J. Z. & Goldstein, I. L. (1993). The relationship between organizational transfer climate and positive transfer of training. *Human Resource Development Quarterly*, **4**, 377–390.

Saari, L. M., Johnson, T. R., McLaughlin, S. D. & Zimmerle, D. M. (1988). A survey of management training and education practices in U.S. companies. *Personnel Psychology*, **41**, 731–743.

Tannenbaum, S. I. & Yukl, G. (1992). Training and development in work organizations. *Annual Review of Psychology*, **43**, 399–441.

Vobejda, B. (1987). The new cutting edge in factories. *Washington Post* April 14, A14.

IRWIN L. GOLDSTEIN

training needs evaluation *see* TRAINING

traits *see* PERSONALITY; PERSONALITY TESTING

transaction cost economics This has become one of the most influential (and somewhat controversial) theoretical perspectives in organizational and strategy research (Coase, 1937; Williamson, 1975, 1985) (*see* STRATEGIC MANAGEMENT). Transaction cost economics (TCE) and AGENCY THEORY represent the two major economics-based theories of organizational governance and contracting, and like agency theory, TCE has a broad reach, seeking to explain phenomena across levels of organizational analysis, such as employer–employee relations, the choice of functional versus divisional organization forms, and the boundaries of the firm. It is in the arena of firm boundaries, however, that TCE has had its greatest influence, such as in discussions of topics such as VERTICAL INTEGRATION (*see* ORGANIZATIONAL BOUNDARIES).

Williamson's pathbreaking 1975 book on "Markets and Hierarchies" discusses the organization of economic activity as a decision between markets or hierarchy. He explains vertical integration as the efficient solution to a transaction cost minimization problem, where the costs of market exchange compare unfavorably with the costs of controlling production hierarchically through ownership. Transaction costs are those costs of negotiating, monitoring, and enforcing contractual exchange relationships (*see* EXCHANGE RELATIONS). Thus, TCE is a perspective that examines the efficiency of alternative mechanisms for minimizing the risk of being exploited by one's exchange partner. Transaction costs may be significant, given Williamson's (1975, pp. 9–10) root assumptions regarding two human factors (BOUNDED RATIONALITY and opportunism) and two environmental factors (UNCERTAINTY and small numbers).

It is the intensity of the small numbers (of exchange partners) problem that substantively defines the intensity of a transaction cost problem (the other three factors are actually assumptional conditions that do not vary in Williamson's framework). This can be seen in Williamson's (1975, p. 104) discussion of vertical integration, where he observes that it is "favored in situations where small numbers bargaining would otherwise obtain." It may appear that this emphasis on small numbers has been replaced in Williamson (1985, p. 56) by an emphasis on asset specificity, which refers to the investments an exchange partner makes that are highly specialized and can be redeployed only by sacrificing productive value (Williamson calls this the "big locomotive to which transaction cost economics owes much of its predictive content"). Asset specificity, however, is central only to the extent that it creates what Williamson (1985, p. 12) refers to as the "Fundamental Transformation – whereby a large-numbers condition . . . is transformed into a small-numbers condition during contract execution. . .". In other words, the structural dimension of small numbers (i.e., limited exchange partner alternatives) is therefore still of critical importance to Williamson's (1985) transaction cost analysis.

Much of the recent controversy surrounding TCE relates to the inordinate weight placed on transaction cost economizing as underlying organizations' decisions regarding firm boundaries (as typified by Williamson's (1985, p. 17) claim that the "economic institutions of capitalism have the main purpose and effect of economizing on transaction costs"). Zajac and Olsen (1993), for example, are critical of TCE explanations of formal INTERORGANIZATIONAL RELATIONS, such as JOINT VENTURES, and argue instead that the recent proliferation of such interorganizational relations is typically more a function of anticipated value gains, rather than anticipated losses due to opportunism. In addition, Zajac and Olsen (1993) suggest that Williamson's (1985, p. 61) notion of a "fundamental transformation" is in fact a *process* that is never fully specified in the structural perspective of transaction cost analysis. Rather than dwelling on the problems of one-time structural changes (large numbers to small numbers condition) in interorganizational strategies, Zajac and Olsen (1993) stress how many interorganizational processes can result in a transformation that leads to greater expected net benefits for both parties, rather than a transformation that leads to greater expected losses for one party due to an increased risk of costly exploitation (as would be predicted in a TCE framework).

See also **Organizational economics; Diversification; Organizational effectiveness; Competitiveness; Trust**

Bibliography

Coase, R. H. (1937). The nature of the firm. *Economica*, **4**, 386–405.

Williamson, O. E. (1975). *Markets and hierarchies: Analysis and antitrust implications*. New York: Free Press.

Williamson, O. E. (1985). *The economic institutions of capitalism: Firms, markets, relational contracting*. New York: Free Press.

Zajac, E. J. & Olsen C. (1993). From transaction costs to transaction value analysis: Implications for the study of interorganizational strategies. *Journal of Management Studies*, **30**, 131–145.

EDWARD J. ZAJAC

transformational/transactional theory Before 1980, social and organizational behavior research on LEADERSHIP focused on observable, short-term, leader – follower relations – relations on the micro level. Leadership on the macro level (heads of organizations) and meta levels (leaders of society) was generally ignored. Autocratic versus democratic leadership, task versus relations, orientation, direction versus participation, and initiation versus consideration remained the paradigms of consequence for research and education (*see* MANAGERIAL STYLE). In all these paradigms, leadership was conceived as an exchange process. A *transaction* occurs in which followers' needs are met if their performance is as contracted with their leader. Transactional leadership depends on the leader's POWER to reinforce subordinates for their successful completion of the CONTRACT. But a higher order of change in followers is also possible. The *transformational* leader motivates followers to work for transcendental goals for the good of the group, the organization, the community of society as a whole, for achievement and SELF-ACTUALIZATION, and for higher level needs of the collectivity rather than immediate personal self-interests.

Traditional transactional paradigms and exchange theories of leadership failed to account for the effects on leader–follower relations of vision, SYMBOLISM, and imaging. The transactional leader adapts to the ORGANIZATIONAL CULTURE; the transformational leader changes it. As conceived by Burns (1978), transformational leaders motivate followers to do more than they originally expected to do as they strive for higher-order outcomes (*see* GROWTH NEED STRENGTH).

In one study, 70 South African senior executives were asked if any had experienced a transformational leader in their career, everyone was able to describe such a leader. Their leaders motivated them to extend themselves, to develop, and become more innovative. The executives were motivated to emulate their transformational leader. They were led to higher levels of COMMITMENT to the organization as a consequence of belief in the leader and in themselves. They exerted extra effort for their leader (Bass, 1985).

The executives' statements and those from the literature on charisma and managerial leadership, after refinement and validation studies, formed the basis of the Multifactor Leadership Questionnaire (MLQ). This measures four interrelated factors (the 4 I's):

Idealized Influence – leaders become a source of admiration often functioning as role models for their followers. They enhance follower pride, loyalty, and confidence and align followers through identification with the leaders around a common purpose or vision.

Inspirational Motivation – leaders articulate in simple ways an appealing vision and provide meaning and a sense of purpose in what needs to be done.

Intellectual Stimulation – leaders stimulate their followers to view the world from new perspectives; that is, to question old assumptions, values, and beliefs, and move toward new perspectives.

Individualized Consideration – leaders diagnose and elevate the needs of each of their followers. They promote the development of their followers, emphasize equity, and treat each follower as an individual.

Transactional leadership, which involves a reinforcing exchange of reward or punishment by the leader for follower compliance, yields the factors of:

Contingent Reward (CR) – leader clarifies what needs to be done and exchanges psychological and material rewards for services rendered.

Active Management-by-Exception (MBE-A) – leader arranges to monitor follower performance and takes corrective action when deviations from standards occur.

Passive Management-by-Exception (MBE-P) – leader only intervenes when standards are not met.

Laissez-Faire Leadership (LF) – leader avoids intervening or accepting responsibility for follower actions.

Factor analysis orders the eight factors from lowest to highest in activity (4I's, CR, MBE-A, MBE-P, LF) (Avolio & Bass, 1990). The eight factors can also be ordered on a second dimension – effectiveness. The 4I's are most effective; then, in order are contingent reward, active management-by-exception, passive management-by-exception, and laissez-faire leadership.

A leader has a pattern of frequencies of behavior which is optimally effective, when the 4I's for the leader are highest in frequency and laissez-faire leadership lowest in frequency. An inactive and ineffective leader's highest frequencies are for laissez-faire leadership and passively managing-by-exception, and the lowest frequencies are for the 4I's (Avolio & Bass, 1990).

Furthermore, there is a hierarchy of relations among the full range of leadership styles and outcomes in effectiveness, effort, and satisfaction. Transformational leaders are more effective than those leaders practicing contingent reward; contingent reward is somewhat more effective than active management-by-exception which in turn is more effective than passive management-by-exception. Laissez-faire leadership is least effective. Research also supports the conclusion that there is a one-way augmentation effect. Transformational leadership adds to transactional leadership in predicting outcomes, but not vice versa. Transformational augments transactional leadership but it does not replace it.

Studies already completed in at least a dozen countries, suggest that whatever the country, when people think about leadership, their prototypes and ideals are transformational. In training efforts in the United States, Canada, Sweden, Italy, and elsewhere in Europe, in an exercise conducted with over 800 participants in the Full Range of Leadership Training Program (Avolio & Bass, 1990), participants are asked to describe the ideal of a leader they have experienced. Invariably, most of the traits which emerge are transformational, not transactional.

See also **Superleadership; Leadership, charismatic; Leadership contingencies**

Bibliography

Avolio, B. J. & Bass, B. M. (1990). *The full range of leadership*, Manual. Binghamton, NY: Center for Leadership Studies.

Bass, B. M. (1985). *Leadership and performance beyond expectations*. New York: Free Press.

Burns, J. M. (1978). *Leadership*. New York: Harper & Row.

BERNARD M. BASS

transitions *see* CAREER TRANSITIONS

trust When trust is used in the organizational literature, two significantly different definitions are usually found. The first defines trust between parties to a transaction or exchange as an expression of confidence or predictability in their expectations that they will not be harmed, or put at risk, by the actions of the other party (Zucker, 1986). In the second definition, the confidence of the parties rests in the other's goodwill (Ring & Van de Ven, 1992). Dealing with the concept of trust now appears to be essential in efforts to define the nature of relationships among individuals and between organizations. There is substantial evidence to support the inclusion of trust as a critical factor in the design and management of business organizations. Indeed, the philosopher Sissela Bok views trust as something that needs protection "just as much as the air we breathe or the water we drink. When [trust is] damaged, the community as a whole suffers;. . . when . . . destroyed, societies falter and collapse." The evidence of the importance of trust in economic (as well as social) exchange comes from economists, lawyers, sociologists, psychologists, ethicists, management, and organization scholars. In general, trust is a situational feature: reliance on trust, or trustworthy behavior by economic actors, is only necessary under conditions involving interdependence, UNCERTAINTY (where the actors on one economic actor hinge on choices made by others) and consequentiality, i.e., if an economic actor relies on trust, and it is not reciprocated, she will suffer substantial harm (*see* RECIPROCITY). In short, where one acts on faith alone, trust is not necessary. The same appears to be the case in situations involving perfect information. Thus, the conditions under which trust seems most likely to be a factor in organizational behaviors where alternative choices involve "exit, betrayal, defection," and "bad outcomes would make you regret your actions."

In the first definition above, trust is frequently equated with risk, or the predictability that future outcomes will be successful. TRANSACTION COST THEORY and AGENCY THEORY discuss how this risk-view of trust can be secured through a variety of impersonal institutional means, such as guarantees, insurance mechanisms, hostages, laws, and organizational HIERARCHY. These exogenous safeguards are needed because, standing alone, trust is not a sufficient condition for the effective social control of business behavior. The prevailing view of economic theory is that economic actors are self-interested and will pursue their interests opportunistically (with guile) if conditions under which exchange is to take place are right: frequent transactions, uncertainty, transaction specific assets, and small numbers of parties. This definition focuses, however, on outcomes and is principally relevant to analysis of the *ex post contract* stages of a business relationship.

In the second definition, connoting goodwill, trust is viewed as necessary for stable social relationships, and functions to reduce complexity in social worlds. It is a "lubricant" facilitating exchange on a continuing basis (Barber, 1983). Research flowing from the sociological literature provides organizational scholars with insights into the role that institutions play in creating trust, or dealing with its absence. The results of this research suggest that when trust is low, other control mechanisms are employed (Shapiro, 1987). Typically, legalistic remedies (e.g., accrediting organizations, insurance, bonds, guarantees, etc.) are used either to compensate for the lack of trust in exchange restore trust, or to create conditions under which trust might be restored. However, the results of research investigating the effectiveness of these kinds of mechanisms also suggest that they can lead to higher levels of mistrust.

Effective or not, these remedies are costly and one consequence of the absence of trust in economic relationships is higher cost. When trust is present within organizations, or in relationships between economic actors, the cost of transacting appears to be lower. Fewer controls are needed to measure and monitor performance. Forecasts of future events are more realistic, as are budget projections. COOPERATION improves along the value chain, PRODUCTIVITY improves, and profitability is enhanced, all other things remaining equal.

When economic actors perceive that those with whom they are dealing are trustworthy, they tend to reciprocate that trust. The effectiveness of COMMUNICATION between economic actors is frequently a factor in determining the level of trust that exists between them. Another factor associated with the existence of, or reliance on, trust between economic actors is cooperation. The results of research exploring associations between trust and cooperation suggest that preexisting cooperation may be required if trust is to develop; other findings suggest that cooperation is an outcome of preexisting trust between economic actors (Gambetta, 1988).

Trust appears to flow from a variety of sources. When economic actors share important VALUES and norms trust seems more likely (*see* GROUP NORMS). Trust may also result from, or be supported by, institutional sources such as law (Luhmann, 1979). Finally, the processes that economic actors employ in their dealings can be a source of trust (Ring & Van de Ven, 1992).

Results of research suggest that trust evolves slowly, from on-going social or economic exchanges between parties. Two possible explanations for the emergence of trust can be found in the ORGANIZATIONAL BEHAVIOR literature. The first is based on the norms of EQUITY which define the degree to which one party judges that another party will fulfill its commitments and that the relationship is equitable (*see* EQUITY THEORY). The concept of equity is developed in exchange theory (*see* EXCHANGE RELATIONS), which argues that participants in a relationship desire:

(1) reciprocity, by which one is morally obligated to give something in return for something received;
(2) fair rates of exchange between utilitarian costs and benefits; and
(3) distributive justice, through which all parties receive benefits that are proportional to their investments (*see* JUSTICE, DISTRIBUTIVE).

Alternatively, the emergence of trust can be based on more direct utilitarian reasoning. First, there are many nonlegal sanctions which make it expedient for individuals and organizations to fulfill commitments. Repeated personal interactions across firms encourages some minimum level of courtesy and consideration, and the prospect of ostracism among peers attenuate individual opportunism. At the organizational level, the prospect of repeat business discourages attempts to seek a narrow, short-term advantage.

Trust is also an individual attribute. Here the focus of the research is on individual characteristics associated with being perceived as trustworthy. Among those characteristics employed most frequently in survey instruments are items measuring the COMPETENCIES of the individual (technical SKILLS, levels of knowledge); the ability to keep confidences; fairness; integrity (honesty, moral character); loyalty; sincerity; openness; reliability; empathy; patience; stamina; self-assurance; and ingenuity (Sitkin & Roth, 1993).

Individuals evidencing high levels of trust seem less likely to lie, cheat, or steal. It also appears that they are more inclined to give others a second chance and to generally respect the rights of others. In so doing, they do not appear to be any more gullible than individuals who are classified as low trusters. Low trusters in situations involving economic exchange can be characterized as having a short-term focus, seek monetarized returns, and require a great deal of specificity in defining the terms of exchange. When "problems" arise, low trusters will attribute them to the bad faith of their partners, or to negligence. They will seek to resolve these "problems" by resort to coerced bargaining. Low trusters tend to play a "zero-sum" game (*see* GAME THEORY; PRISONERS' DILEMMA). High trusters, on the other hand, engage in economic exchange that is interwoven with social exchange. Their perspectives are longer term in nature, they accept "problems" are part of economic life, and they seek integrative solutions: those involving so-called "win–win" outcomes. These kinds of relational trust behaviors tend to spiral upward if reciprocated; downward if not (Husted, 1989).

See also **Interorganizational relations; Industrial relations; Negotiation; Conflict; Business ethics; Altruism**

Bibliography

Anderson, E. & Weitz, B. (1989). Determinants of continuity in conventional industrial channel dyads. *Marketing Science*, 8, 310–323.

Baier, A. (1986). Trust and antitrust. *Ethics*, **96**, 231–260.

Barber, B. (1983). *The logic and limits of trust*. New Brunswick: NJ: Rutgers University.

Bhide, A. & Stevenson, H. (1992). Trust, uncertainty, and profits. *Journal of Socio-Economics*, **21**, 91–208.

Butler, J. K. (1991). Toward understanding and measuring conditions of trust: Evolution of a conditions of trust inventory. *Journal of Management*, **17**, 643–663.

Fox, A. (1974). *Beyond contract: Work, power and trust relations*. London: Faber & Faber.

Gambetta, D. (Ed.), (1988). *Trust: Making and breaking cooperative relations*. London: Basil Blackwell.

Husted, B. W. (1989). Trust in business relations: Directions for empirical research. *Business and Professional Ethics Journal*, **8**, 23–40.

Luhmann, N. (1979). *Trust and power*. New York: Wiley.

Moorman, C., Zaltman, G. & Deshpande, R. (1992). Relationships between providers and users of market research: The dynamics of trust within and between organizations. *Journal of Marketing Research*, **29**, 314–328.

Ring, P. S. & Van de Ven, A. H. (1992). Structuring cooperative relationships between organizations. *Strategies Management Journal*, **3**, 483–498.

Shapiro, S. P. (1987). The social control of interpersonal trust. *American Journal of Sociology*, **93**, 623–658.

Sitkin, S. & Roth, N. L. (1993). Explaining the limited effectiveness of legalistic remedies for trust/distrust. *Organization Science*, **4**, 367–392.

Zucker, L. G. (1986). Production of trust: Institutional sources of economic structure, 1984–1990. In B. M. Staw & L. L. Cummings (Eds), *Research in organizational behavior*, (vol. 8, pp. 53–122). Greenwich, CT: JAI Press.

PETER SMITH RING

turnaround management This is the active process of managing a company through a period of crisis sufficiently serious to threaten the company's survival as a participant in its major industry (*see* CRISES). It involves an amalgam of managerial SKILLS, systems, procedures, value systems, individual character traits, and actions taken to achieve a recovery. Turnaround is not the same as RESTRUCTURING – the rearrangement of company businesses, assets, and liabilities. Turnaround management is more operational where actual improvements in products, operations, marketing, and overhead functions result in a stronger competitive position for the company (*see* COMPETITIVENESS).

Crisis situations frequently go unrecognized by company managers who fail to detect the need for the decisive action required for the firm's survival. Quite often, gradual drift takes place until the threatened firm deteriorates beyond the point where reasonable action can save it. The resulting catastrophe takes a cruel toll on employees, creditors, suppliers, stockholders, customers, and members of the local community. These problems are avoidable.

The signs of decline, or warning signals, frequently occur in the form of liquidity problems, collection problems, profit problems, quality problems, the attrition of high-caliber people, low morale, high rates of ABSENTEEISM, low PRODUCTIVITY, organizational problems, and ethical problems. However, it is not always true that managerial incompetencies are rampant throughout troubled organizations. Economic and market conditions also stress corporate resources and cause revenues, cashflows, and declining profits. These misfortunes affect capable as well as incapable firms, and it cannot be assumed that because a company is in trouble it has no competent managers and no distinctive competencies (*see* CORE COMPETENCE).

Successful turnaround management usually involves three principal strategies; improving the firm's effectiveness as a low-cost operator, improving the firm's effectiveness as a provider of increasingly differentiated products and capable, and experienced LEADERSHIP well distributed throughout the organization.

The tactical dimensions of turnaround management fit within the framework of the strategies employed. Low-cost operation involves the design of products for low-cost delivery, high rates of efficiency, and the containment of overhead costs to below industry levels. Product differentiation involves distinguishing product or service features, high reliability and performance, exceptional product quality, and continuity with the markets being served. Turnaround leadership involves experience in the industry being served, technical experience and a major propensity to focus on operational issues such as manufacturing, product development, and sales. Successful turnaround agents tend to have longer-term associations with their companies, enjoy generally favorable personal reputations, and employ a sense of fair play in dealing with employees, creditors, suppliers, and customers.

Well-executed turnarounds quite often take several years, rather than months, because of the time it takes to develop new products, achieve low-cost status, and mobilize the involvement of the entire organization. Turnarounds are only part managerial, they are also technical involving breakthrough new processes and landmark product designs.

In the troubled company, well-trained, dedicated, competent people are interspersed with people of limited training and dedication. Turnaround management requires the ability to nurture, encourage, and reinforce what is good as well as root out what is unsatisfactory. The turnaround practitioner is well advised to proceed cautiously. Many potentially successful turnarounds have been ruined by newly appointed top managers operating with the assumption that everything needed changing when everything did not. Turnaround managers must be quick, but not cavalier, and must appreciate the limitations of the information supplied – which is often misleading and occasionally quite false.

Recovery should be a lasting event – covering at least several years and resulting in a measurably better situation for the company in terms of profits, market position, technical contribution, and general contribution to the economy. This is only possible by people throughout the organization learning to do things in new, less costly, ways (*see* ORGANIZATIONAL LEARNING). Turnarounds involve a great many variables – some managerial, some technical. Some lend themselves to quantitative analysis while others are more organic. The entire process is holistic. Every variable impacts every other variable.

Companies that ultimately succeed in turnarounds are quite often more severely affected initially. Successful companies experience more pronounced downturns and respond more quickly. Unsuccessful companies often tolerate conditions lethal to their survival long before actions are taken.

The research on turnaround management includes some findings useful for practitioners.

- Large dominant firms fail as well as smaller producers. Size appears not to be a factor in turnaround success (*see* ORGANIZATIONAL SIZE).
- During the early years of crisis, successful turnarounds often experience steeper business declines and deeper loss rates than unsuccessful firms. Improved performance may not appear for 2 or 3 years.
- Successful companies are noticeably more efficient in operations than the unsuccessful firms. Operational efficiency can account for 70 percent of the profitability difference.
- Successful companies stay with their cost-reduction programs longer and make deeper cuts, bringing costs down to the level of revenue. Unsuccessful companies often attempt to increase revenue to cover existing costs, either by selling into new markets or by making acquisitions (*see* MERGERS AND ACQUISITIONS).
- Management often plays an exemplary role in the cost reduction programs of successful firms by accepting less pay.
- Successful companies handle money conservatively on an ongoing basis by spending less money on overhead expenses, corporate image and pointless expansion.
- Successful companies make small, constant, incremental improvements to produce differentiated products and occasionally deliver major new product breakthroughs. Unsuccessful firms often fail to improve existing products even when product shortcomings are widely perceived.
- Unsuccessful companies often make significant and abrupt changes in the positioning of their products in the market, a practice avoided by successful firms.
- Successful firms more accurately gauge their ability to implement fully their strategic plans. Unsuccessful firms often have strategic plans that are inconsistent with their resources.

Both successful and unsuccessful turnarounds have both high points and low points. No turnaround goes perfectly in all respects and firms do not fail in all respects. But sharp contrasts do exist in the strategies selected, the procedures used, in managerial emphasis, and in the strengths and styles of the management (*see*

MANAGERIAL STYLE). Turnaround management is being practiced widely in many countries, and was the principal methodology employed in the resurgence of such companies as Chrysler, Pentair, and Ford.

See also **Commitment; Innovation; Organization effectiveness; Trust; Organization development; Organizational change**

Bibliography

Argenti, J. (1976). *Corporate collapse: Causes and symptoms*. New York: Wiley.

Goodman, S. (1982). *How to manage a turnaround*. New York: Free Press.

Hall, W. K. (1983). Survival strategies in a hostile environment. In *Survival strategies for American industry*. New York: Wiley.

Hambrick, D. C. & D'Aveni, R. A. (1988). Large corporate failures as downward spirals. *Administrative Science Quarterly*, **33**, 1–23.

Lorange, P. & Nelson, R. T. (1987). How to recognize – and avoid – organizational decline. *Sloan Management Review*, **28**, Spring, 41–48.

Miller, D. (1977). Common syndromes of business failure. *Business Horizons*, **20**, December, 43–53.

Nueno, P. (1992). *Reflotando la emprese: Corporate turnaround*. Madrid: Ediciones Deusto S.A.

O'Neill, H. M. (1986). Turnaround and recovery: What strategy do you need. *Long Range Planning*, **19**, (1), 80–88.

Schendel, D. & Patton, G. R. (1976). Corporate stagnation and turnaround. *Journal of Economics and Business*, **28**, no. 3, 236–241.

Slatter, S. (1984). *Corporate recovery: Successful turnaround strategies and their implementation*. London: Penguin.

Zimmerman, F. M. (1986). Turnaround – A painful learning process. *Long Range Planning*, **19**, (4), 104–114.

Zimmerman, F. M. (1991). *The turnaround experience: Real world lessons in corporate revitalization*. New York: McGraw-Hill.

FREDERICK M. ZIMMERMAN

turnover This is defined as voluntary cessation of membership in an organization, and is one of several forms of organizational withdrawal (*see* WITHDRAWAL ORGANIZATIONAL) such as ABSENTEEISM and tardiness (Mitra, Jenkins, & Gupta, 1992). Understanding why employees leave is important because that information can be used to reduce turnover.

Ease and Desirability of Movement

Turnover decisions are a function of two factors, ease of movement, how easy it is to find another job, and desirability of movement, whether employees experience enough dissatisfaction to want a different job (March & Simon, 1958).

Economists focus primarily on LABOR MARKET determinants of the ease of movement. Firm turnover (quit) rates are best predicted by general economic activity. When the economy is healthy or unemployment is low and jobs plentiful, turnover rates will increase. When economic activity and job growth are slow, turnover rates will generally decline. Economists have also found that most but not all who leave do so for better paying jobs.

Desirability of movement is typically measured by asking workers to report their level of JOB SATISFACTION, which has a small, negative relationship with turnover. Raising levels of job satisfaction, however, can substantially decrease turnover. For example, Hulin (1968) found that pay and promotional opportunities were negatively related to turnover for clerical employees. These findings were translated into specific steps for reducing turnover (i.e., regular salary reviews, consistent pay policies across departments, and job transfers for those wanting advancement). Results one year later indicated sizable increases in satisfaction with pay and promotions and a decrease in turnover to 18 percent from 30 percent.

Research also shows that ease of movement and desirability of movement can jointly affect workers' turnover decisions. When jobs are scarce, many dissatisfied employees who want to leave cannot leave, thus yielding smaller correlations between job satisfaction and turnover (Carsten & Spector, 1987). When jobs are plentiful, however, many dissatisfied employees will leave, and the relationship between satisfaction and turnover increases.

Psychological Process of Leaving

The psychological process of leaving involves a simple, five-factor causal model that begins with job satisfaction. Dissatisfied employees start to have thoughts about quitting, then decide to search for other jobs, and then formalize specific intentions to quit their jobs (Mobley, 1982;

Mowday, Porter, & Steers, 1982). However, strong intentions to quit do not always result in turnover. When alternative jobs (i.e., UNEMPLOYMENT levels) are scarce, dissatisfied employees, as well as employees with clear intentions to quit, find other, acceptable jobs harder to locate. REALISTIC JOB PREVIEWS and JOB ENRICHMENT can also modestly reduce employee turnover by improving job satisfaction (McEvoy & Cascio, 1985).

Investment Model of Turnover

Another approach to understanding turnover is the investment model, suggesting that turnover increases when employee COMMITMENT decreases (Rusbult & Farrell, 1983). Commitment decreases when job REWARDS worsen (e.g., pay, satisfying work, supervision), when job costs increase (e.g., high work load, inadequate resources), when investment decreases (e.g., tenure, organization-specific SKILLS, nontransferable retirement plans, friends at work), and when attractive, alternative jobs are available.

Rusbult and Farrell's model (1983, p. 437) suggests several ways to reduce turnover:

(a) increase pay relative to competing firms (rewards);
(b) provide workers with realistic job previews, redesign jobs, and eliminate aversive elements of work (costs);
(c) promote employee–firm linkages through home loan assistance, employ spouses (investments); and
(d) offer unique advantages such as job sharing that are not available elsewhere (alternatives).

Interaction Between Workers and Working Environment

Yet another approach to understanding turnover is to examine the interaction between workers and their environments. In general, workers who fit better into their work environments should be less likely to quit (e.g., Schneider's attraction–selection–attrition model, Taylor & Giannantonio, 1993).

For example, demographic models (*see* ORGANIZATIONAL DEMOGRAPHY) predict that executives who differ significantly from their peers in terms of AGE, education, or experience, etc., are more likely to quit. Employee fit with ORGANIZATIONAL CULTURES also affects turnover. Military cadets are more likely to complete their education if they are assertive, and motivated to influence others and perform routine duties. Thus, in contrast to the psychological process and investment models, the interaction/fit models propose turnover reduction at the point of hire (*see* PERSON-JOB FIT; CAREER CHOICE). That is, firms can reduce turnover by hiring workers who are similar to existing workers and who have values consistent with the organizational culture.

Consequences of Turnover

All of the previous approaches assume that employee turnover is inherently bad, expensive, and should be reduced whenever possible. Yet, some kinds and levels of turnover, for example, when poor performers leave, are beneficial for companies. Dalton, Krackhardt, and Porter (1981) believe that the traditional stay/quit definition overstates the negative consequences of employee turnover and ignores its positive consequences. They defined two kinds of turnover, dysfunctional turnover, where someone valued by the organization leaves, and functional turnover, where a person not valued leaves.

In their study, Dalton et al. (1981) determined that turnover was functional if the supervisor would not rehire the person who quit, or if that person was a poor performer, or if it would be easy (inexpensive) to replace them. Consistent with their prediction, they found that the rate of voluntary turnover (32 percent) overstated the negative consequences of turnover. In comparison, on two of these measures (quality and replaceability), the rate of dysfunctional turnover was only 18.4 percent for the quality measure and only 8.8 percent for the replaceability measure. The marginal cost implication for employers is to target turnover reduction strategies to prevent only the loss of good performers.

In summary, the causes of voluntary turnover are numerous and reside in the individual, the organization, and the interaction between them (*see* INTERACTIONISM). Narrative and quantitative (meta-analytic) (*see* VALIDITY GENERALIZATION) reviews of the literature suggest that organizational efforts to reduce turnover can be directed at multiple levels and sources. Psychological process models of turnover provide a diagnostic tool for assessing probable causes of turnover. From a staffing perspective, screening based on skill, attitude, APTITUDE, PERSONALITY, interests, expectations, education can reduce turnover likelihood. Similarly, TRAINING and orientation programs that invest in aligning employee attitudes and skills with job and organizational demands can further lessen turnover propensity. Firms may also seek a better fit between a redesigned (restructured) organization and their employees (*see* RESTRUCTURING). Such organizations become flatter, more flexible, and more responsive by using staffing, training, and CAREER management strategies to enhance retention. Finally, appraisal and reward systems can be designed to measure and reward organizational, division, team, and individual level contributions to organizational PRODUCTIVITY and effectiveness. Performance based reward systems (those that put a greater proportion of pay at risk) thus become tools to attract, motivate, and retain valued employees (*see* PAYMENT SYSTEMS; PERFORMANCE RELATED PAY).

See also **Career transitions; Job design; Performance, individual; Motivation and performance; Organizational effectiveness**

Bibliography

Carsten, J. M. & Spector, P. E. (1987). Unemployment, job satisfaction, and turnover: A meta-analytic test of the Muchinsky model. *Journal of Applied Psychology*, **72**, 374–381.

Dalton, D. R., Krackhardt, D. M. & Porter, L. W. (1981). Functional turnover: An empirical assessment. *Journal of Applied Psychology*, **66**, 716–721.

Hulin, C. L. (1968). Effects of changes in job satisfaction levels on employee turnover. *Journal of Applied Psychology*, **52**, 122–126.

March, J. G. & Simon, H. A. (1958). *Organizations*. New York: Wiley.

McEvoy, G. M. & Cascio, W. F. (1985). Strategies for reducing employee turnover: A meta-analysis. *Journal of Applied Psychology*, **70**, 342–353.

Mitra, A., Jenkins, D., Jr. & Gupta, N. (1992). A meta-analytic review of the relationship between absence and turnover. *Journal of Applied Psychology*, **77**, 879–889.

Mobley, W. H. (1982). *Employee turnover: Causes, consequences, and control*. Reading, MA: Addison-Wesley.

Mowday, R. T., Porter, L. W. & Steers, R. M. (1982). *Employee organization linkages*. San Francisco: Academic Press.

Rusbelt, C. E. & Farrell, D. (1983). A longitudinal test of the investment model: The impact of job satisfaction, job commitment, and turnover of variations in rewards, costs, alternatives, and investments. *Journal of Applied Psychology*, **68**, 429–438.

Taylor, M. S. & Giannantonio, C. M. (1993). Forming, adapting, and terminating the employment relationship: A review of the literature from individual, organizational, & interactionist perspectives. *Journal of Management*, **19**, 461–515.

STUART A. YOUNGBLOOD and
CHARLES R. WILLIAMS

two-factor theory *see* MOTIVATOR/HYGIENE THEORY

type A The Type A/B distinction has come to be viewed as a typology which distinguishes individual susceptibility to STRESS and stress outcomes. Research has suggested that INDIVIDUAL DIFFERENCES can affect the way people respond to adverse pressure and the Type-A behavior pattern (TABP), identified by Friedman and Rosenman, is the most researched stress related behavioral style. In a number of studies, individuals manifesting particular behavioral traits were found to be significantly more at risk of coronary heart disease (CHD). Hence these behaviors collectively are referred to as the "coronary-prone behavior pattern Type A" as distinct from Type B (i.e., the opposite of these characteristic behaviors and at low risk to CHD). The concept is now more commonly used to indicate PERSONALITY types, which persist over time and make individuals more or less vulnerable to stress. Though many of these early studies examined men, more recent work by these researchers has found a link between TABP and CHD in both men and women. Research has also revealed that extreme Type A's report more stress symptoms, higher blood pressure, higher cholesterol, and triglyceride levels, are more likely to smoke, and take less exercise – all criteria in the etiology and onset of CHD.

Individuals exhibiting TABP are those who, in contrast to their Type B counterparts, work long, hard hours under constant deadline pressures and conditions for overload; often take work home at night or on weekends, and are unable to relax; constantly compete with themselves, setting high standards of PRODUCTIVITY that they seem driven to maintain; tend to become frustrated by the work situation (*see* FRUSTRATION), to be irritated with the work efforts of others, feel misunderstood by superiors, seek more work and nonwork challenges and prefer more difficult problems. They may be so involved in their work that they tend to neglect other aspects of their life and at work they tend to like to function by themselves rather than with others (*see* NONWORK/WORK). They lose their tempers more frequently, and are more likely to lash out at others for slight provocations, and have consistently been shown to obtain significantly higher scores on life events stress inventories. Type B's, on the other hand, tend to exhibit the opposite of these characteristics.

Though there has been a general consensus in the importance of TABP in the development of CHD, attempts to uncover its exact meaning and measurement have been fraught with difficulties. In the early studies, individuals were designated as being Type A or Type B on the basis of clinical judgments of doctors and psychologists, or by peer ratings and by interview. Due to the need for large-scale research, self-report measurement scales have been designed (e.g., Bortner scale, 1969; Jenkins Activity Survey (JAS), Jenkins et al. 1967). More recent investigations of TABP have attempted to unravel and understand the more specific components of the phenomenon and its relationship to stress (e.g., hostile behavior, or doing too many things at once), as opposed to the global concept of overall Type A (*see* Edwards and others). More appropriate management of particular stress related behavioral responses may result, as more specific problems are targeted (e.g., with TIME MANAGEMENT, relaxation, DELEGATION, and improved social support).

Those displaying TABP have been found to be more prominent amongst those of higher socioeconomic status and education, who tend to occupy more demanding jobs, i.e., with more responsibility, larger supervisory SPAN OF CONTROL, higher workload (*see* ROLE OVER/UNDERLOAD), and involving more difficult tasks (*see* Payne, 1988). One of the major difficulties in interpreting the findings regarding TABP is whether these individuals are more exposed to stress, more likely to perceive stress, or are more likely to select stressful environments in which to work.

See also **Mental health; Perception; Role; Hardiness; Alcohol and substance abuse; Counseling in organizations; Burnout**

Bibliography

Bortner, R. W. (1969). A short rating scale as a potential measure of pattern A behaviour. *Journal of Chronic Diseases*, **22**, 87–91.

Edward, J. R. (1991). The Measurement of Type A Behavior Pattern: Assessment of Criterion-oriented Validity, Content Validity, and Construct Validity. In Cooper, C. L. and Payne, R. (Eds), *Personality and Stress: Individual Differences in the Stress Process*. (1991), pp. 151–181.

Friedman, M. & Rosenman, R. H. (1974). *Type A behaviour and your heart*. New York: Knopf.

Jenkins, C. D., Rosenman, R. H. & Friedman, M. (1967). The development of an objective psychological test for the determination of the coronary-prone patterns in employed men. *Journal of Chronic Disease*, **20**, 371–379.

Payne, R. (1988). Individual differences in the study of occupational stress. In C. L. Cooper & R. Payne (Eds), *Causes, coping and consequences of stress at work*. Chichester, UK: Wiley.

CHERYL J. TRAVERS

— U —

uncertainty This is a key concept in relation to a number of organizational areas. From an OPEN SYSTEM perspective, the environment is a key source of uncertainty since all organizations need to interact with, and are in some measure dependent on, their environments (*see* ORGANIZATION AND ENVIRONMENT). The more turbulent and complex the environment, the more difficult it is for organizations to control and predict events.

Thompson (1967) has suggested that the technical core of an organization (the transformational or production process) needs to be "buffered" from uncertainty. "BOUNDARY-SPANNING" departments can perform this function, helping to shield the heart of the organization from damaging shocks and providing a measure of stability and continuity. In recent years, the trend has been for some companies to adopt JUST-IN-TIME techniques and flexible working practices as alternative ways of coping with the uncertainty of the competitive environment.

CONTINGENCY THEORY suggests a number of ways in which the organization can cope with environmental uncertainty, particularly by altering its structural arrangements. To be successful, firms need to adapt to uncertainty by adopting appropriate mechanisms of DIFFERENTIATION and INTEGRATION.

TECHNOLOGY also plays a part in influencing how uncertainty can be managed. The more uncertainty there is in the nature of the work (task uncertainty), the better INFORMATION-PROCESSING must be.

Control over uncertainty can be a source of POWER. Hickson, Hinings, Lee, Schneck & Pennings (1971) put forward their "strategic contingencies theory," suggesting that *coping* with uncertainty is an important way of securing power for SUBUNITS in the organization, especially if the uncertainty affects a critical and central part of the organization's functioning.

Uncertainty is a key problem in DECISION MAKING as assumptions have to be made about the future, which is inherently uncertain. This is one reason why BOUNDED RATIONALITY often prevails. "Uncertainty absorption" is also a factor. This is where information loses its uncertainty as it is passed through the organization – gradually appearing to be more precise and reliable than it actually is.

"Uncertainty avoidance" is one of the concepts used by Hofstede (1980) in his examination of national cultures (*see* INTERCULTURAL PROCESS; CULTURE, NATIONAL). It is used to denote the degree to which different cultures cope with novelty, either accepting the attendant uncertainty or seeking to reduce it.

The concept of uncertainty has a long history in the study of organizations as well as a number of particular meanings in specialist areas. Given that most organizations and individuals are faced with uncertainty, the pressure to understand its nature and origins, and the need to develop coping mechanisms is still of great current interest.

See also **Resource dependence; Organizational effectiveness; Resource based theory; Mechanistic/organic**

Bibliography

Hickson, D. J., Hinings, C. R., Lee, C. A., Schneck R. E. & Pennings, J. M. (1971). A strategic contingencies theory of intraorganizational power. *Administrative Science Quarterly*, **16**, (2), 216–229.

Hofstede, G. (1980). *Culture's consequences: International differences in work-related values.* Beverly Hills, CA: Sage.
Thompson, J. D. (1967). *Organizations in action.* New York: McGraw-Hill.

SUSAN MILLER

unemployment During the 1930s social scientists concluded, largely from qualitative research, that unemployment was associated with: hopelessness regarding the future; low SELF-ESTEEM; low self-confidence; social isolation; ANXIETY; depression; and impaired physical health. Unemployment, it was concluded, affected not only men but also women on both social and financial grounds, exacerbated family problems and put at risk the MENTAL HEALTH of children in families with unemployed parents.

Contemporary research, dominated by quantitative methods, has consistently shown that the unemployed have poorer mental health than otherwise comparable employed people. Group mean scores on well-validated measures of anxiety, depression, dissatisfaction with one's present life, experienced strain, negative self-esteem, hopelessness regarding the future, and other negative states have been repeatedly demonstrated to be higher in groups of unemployed people than in matched samples of employed people. Unemployed people are also disproportionately likely to report social isolation and relatively low levels of daily activity. The physical, as well as mental, health of unemployed people has also been shown to be generally poorer.

Recent longitudinal studies have demonstrated that experience of particular labor market transitions (gaining or losing employment, leaving school, entry to government training schemes, etc.) causes, rather than results from, changes in mental health (*see* CAREER TRANSITIONS). For example, the average psychological well-being of school leavers who become unemployed diverges negatively from those who become satisfactorily employed, and people moving from unemployment to satisfactory employment exhibit improvements in average mental health compared with continuously unemployed groups. These findings have been replicated across studies, research groups, countries, and time periods.

Most of these studies deal with the average mental health of large groups of people. Within groups there are wide variations in mental health consequences. Some people are affected very badly, some hardly at all and the psychological health of a very small minority actually improves when they become unemployed. One cannot infer from the fact that an individual has been made unemployed that the particular individual's mental health will actually suffer, though the risk of their mental health deterioration has substantially increased.

Specific factors have been identified as likely to determine the psychological distress of unemployment. Pre-unemployment jobs vary in the extent to which they promote psychological health (*see* STRESS; JOB SATISFACTION). People also vary widely in their employment-related and other VALUES. Unemployed people who are particularly committed to paid employment – the vast majority according to research – are harder hit by unemployment (*see* JOB INVOLVEMENT). People also vary in the social support they receive from others and in their capacity to cope with stressors (*see* HARDINESS). An unemployed person's AGE is relevant, with the middle aged more affected than younger or older unemployed (*see* LIFE STAGES). Availability of adequate economic resources are also important, with people who are under more financial strain tending to be more psychologically affected by unemployment. Length of unemployment is also a factor. Mean levels of psychological distress generally increase steeply with unemployment then level out or even decline slightly – though still on average registering significantly more distress than comparison employed groups.

Contrary to conventional wisdom, there is little persuasive evidence that the experience of unemployment follows a series of distinct stages or phases.

The psychological consequences of unemployment also extend beyond actual job losers to partners and other members of their families. Classic studies of whole villages suggest that the corrosive impact of unemployment eats into the whole community. Empirical research is increasingly converging on the similarity in the psychological consequences of unemployment, JOB INSECURITY, and unsatisfactory employment.

What is responsible for the psychological consequences of unemployment?

Employment is a social relationship in which work, mental or physical activity for a purpose beyond the pleasure of the activity in itself (*see* NONWORK/WORK), determined by one agent is carried out in exchange for payment by another agent within the context of a PSYCHOLOGICAL CONTRACT of rights and obligations, in a relationship constituted and regulated by powerful social forces.

People who are made redundant (*see* REDUNDANCY), therefore, might be expected to experience psychological repercussions of both the loss of the social relationship and the loss of the work they performed within that relationship, as research bears out (*see* MANIFEST AND LATENT FUNCTIONS).

However, it is also necessary to consider what is structurally common to both unemployment and employment. Work, in the sense of the definition offered above, takes place both inside and outside the employment relationships. Unemployed people should not, therefore, be assumed to be without work. Indeed, within the unemployment relationship, specific work is often required as a condition of receiving income from the State, quite apart from the self-initiated unemployment-related work performed by most unemployed people and the domestic and other work carried out by both employed and unemployed people.

Psychological consequences of unemployment relate to implications of particular forms of the social relationships described above, of the work done within them, and of transitions between them in a complex interaction of individual, social, organizational, and social institutional forces over time. More specifically, negative psychological consequences of unemployment might be expected to occur because unemployed people are party to labor market relationships within which they are required to perform unsatisfactory tasks, such as futile job search, exposing them to potential psychological stressors, such as repeated rejection and experienced humiliation, in poor working conditions for subsistence-level pay within grossly unequal, institutionally constituted, and regulated psychological contracts, within which they have severely limited collective and individual rights, all within a culture replete with powerful social norms regarding the unacceptability of the unemployed role. Research bears this out as a contributory factor (*see* AGENCY RESTRICTION).

See also **Affect; Labor markets; Quality of working life**

Bibliography

Eisenberg, P. & Lazarsfeld, P. F. (1938). The psychological effects of unemployment. *Psychological Bulletin*, **35**, 356–390.

Fryer, D. (1990). The mental health costs of unemployment: Towards a social psychology of poverty. *British Journal of Clinical and Social Psychiatry*, 7, (4), 164–176.

Fryer, D. (Guest Ed.) (1992). Marienthal and beyond: 20th century research on unemployment and mental health. *Journal of Occupational and Organizational Psychology*, **65**, (4), 257–358.

Fryer, D. & Ullah, P. (1987). *Unemployed people: Social and psychological perspectives*. Milton Keynes, UK: Open University Press.

Jahoda, M., Lazarsfeld, P. F. & Zeisel, H. (1972). *Marienthal: The sociography of an unemployed community*. London: Tavistock.

Warr, P. B. (1987). *Work, unemployment and mental health*. Oxford, UK: Clarendon Press.

Winefield, A. H., Tiggemann, M., Winefield, H. R. & Goldney, R. D. (1993). *Growing up with unemployment: A longitudinal study of its psychological impact*. London: Routledge.

DAVID FRYER

unions *see* TRADE UNIONS

upward communication COMMUNICATION upward conveys important information regarding work and personnel-related problems, FEEDBACK, suggestions for work and quality improvements, and subordinate attitudes (*see* CONTINUOUS IMPROVEMENT). It also enables subordinates to INFLUENCE their task effectiveness, WORKING CONDITIONS, and CAREER advancement. Evidence suggests that most organizations have difficulty encouraging upward communication. Superiors and subordinates typically demonstrate significant information gaps, and the gaps grow larger as messages are filtered and distorted by intervening hierarchical levels (*see* INFORMATION PRO-

CESSING). Several factors increase the likelihood of distortion or miscommunication. There is a general tendency for communicators to exaggerate information favorable to themselves and to minimize or not pass on unfavorable information. This is stronger if the superior has influence over subordinate promotion or REWARDS, if the subordinate does not TRUST the superior, if the subordinate knows the superior withholds information, and if the subordinate has mobility aspirations. Whether subordinates communicate upward is strongly dependent on their perceptions of superior openness. Openness is signaled by the superior's willingness to listen, exhibited trust in the subordinate, willingness to approach the subordinate, warmth, and question asking. Introduction of INFORMATION TECHNOLOGIES such as electronic mail generally also result in increases in upward communication.

See also **Employee involvement; Participation; Decision making**

Bibliography

Jablin, F. M., Putnam, L. L., Roberts, K. H. & Porter, L. W. (1987). *Handbook of organizational communication*. Newbury Park, CA: Sage.

MARSHALL SCOTT POOLE

utility *see* GAME THEORY; EXCHANGE RELATIONS; ORGANIZATIONAL ECONOMICS; PROSPECT THEORY

— V —

valence *see* VIE THEORY

validity In the context of organizational research, validity is defined as the appropriateness of the inferences drawn from an observation, test score(s), a study, or a set of studies.

Issues of validity relate to measures, to RESEARCH DESIGNS or to data. The validity of a *measure* has been further interpreted in terms of its content, relationship to external variables (criteria) or to the constructs it is designed to get at. (A construct is a concept that has been created or adopted for a scientific purpose.) Thus "Content" validity is the degree to which responses required by the items of a test or measure are representative of the behaviors or knowledge to be exhibited in the domain of interest. A job knowledge test would be content valid if it fairly assessed the knowledge needed for a job. A measure would have "criterion-related" validity if scores received by individuals (groups or organizations) covary with scores on some external standard (criterion). A cognitive ABILITY test might have criterion-related validity of its scores correlated with a measure of job performance. A measure would have "construct" validity to the extent that an underlying explanatory concept (e.g., honesty) can account for the scores obtained (i.e., truly honest individuals receive high scores and dishonest individuals receive low scores). Construct validity can be established through careful operational definitions (*see* OPERATIONALIZATION) and through the statistical analysis of accumulated empirical evidence regarding the pattern of scores yielded by the measure vis-à-vis scores from other, well-known or trusted measures.

The validity of *research designs* refers to the extent that the plan for a study and the methods employed allow for accurate inferences or conclusions from the data (*see* CASE METHOD; QUASI-EXPERIMENTAL DESIGN; RESEARCH METHODS). Usually, this means that the plan deals with (rules out) plausible, rival explanations for the results. If research is designed satisfactorily, one can speak of "internal" validity, the capacity to infer causal relationships, and "external validity," the capacity to generalize (*see* GENERALIZATION) to other studies or cases. Common threats to the validity of a research design include small or inappropriate samples of subjects (e.g., number of employees or business units), unstandardized research conditions, inappropriate methods, or the failure to recognize the impact of unmeasured factors. Assessing the validity of a research design is usually done through a critical analysis by a competent researcher who is also a subject matter expert.

The validity of *data* is related to both the validity of measures and designs. Thus, we cannot make correct inferences (descriptions or predictions), from data that are derived from poor measures or weak designs. In particular, if scores are derived from unreliable measures (*see* RELIABILITY) with questionable construct validity, obtained from a set of people who are unrepresentative of those who we are really interested in, and/or were gathered in atypical situations, there is little basis on which to claim that we have valid data. Assessing of the validity of data is both a statistical and logical/analytical process.

See also **Selection methods; Assessment; Psychological testing**

Bibliography

Cook, T. D., Campbell, D. T. & Peracchio, L. (1990). Quasi experimentation. In M. D. Dunnette & L. M. Hough (Eds), *Handbook of industrial & organizational psychology* (pp. 491–576). Palo Alto, CA: Consulting Psychologists Press.

Ghiselli, E. E., Campbell, J. P. & Zedeck, S. (1981). *Measurement theory for the behavioral sciences.* San Francisco: W. H. Freeman.

Landy, F. J. & Schmitt, N. (1993). The concept of validity. In N. Schmitt and W. C. Borman (Eds) *Personnel selection in organizations* (pp. 275–309). San Francisco: Jossey-Bass.

Runkel, P. J. & McGrath, J. E. (1972). *Research on human behavior. A systematic guide for method.* New York: Holt, Rinehart, & Winston.

Schmitt, N. W. & Klimoski, R. J. (1991). *Research methods in human resources management.* Cincinnati, OH: South-Western.

RICHARD KLIMOSKI

validity generalization This is an approach to summarizing what is known about a key characteristic (usually predictive validity) of a test or test type (*see* STATISTICAL METHODS). It is one of a class of meta-analytic techniques which treats the validation study as the unit of analysis. It is based on the assumption that the results from any one study might be misleading, given the potential impact of one or more factors in a piece of research which are known to artificially raise or lower computed correlations.

After a frequency distribution of the results (e.g., VALIDITY coefficients) found in published and unpublished studies is developed, various statistical procedures are applied. Thus the steps in a validity GENERALIZATION study are as follows:

(1) Identify a set of studies from the research domain of interest. Investigators usually attempt to be as complete as possible in this step.
(2) Code key information from each study in a way that would allow one to compute an estimate of effect size.
(3) Record any additional information that could plausibly be a factor in affecting the results (e.g., whether it was a study in one type of industry or another, one type of employee, etc).
(4) Correct the frequency distribution and/or individual effect size estimates for sources of artifactual variance. Such sources have traditionally included such things as lack of predictor (test) RELIABILITY and size of the sample respondents in the study.
(5) If necessary or desired regress the corrected effect sizes upon those study characteristics coded in order to help to explain the effect sizes (e.g., one might find higher validity for the test in one type of industry).

The end product of the procedure becomes a quantitative index ("a corrected or estimated 'true' correlation") rather that a traditional narrative summary of findings (e.g., "significant correlations were found for the test in most of the studies"). Using this approach permits one to reach a conclusion regarding, for example, whether a particular (employment) test established as useful in one setting (company) would be appropriate to use in another (called transportability). Validity generalization analyses are also helpful in resolving ambiguities that exist if one were only to attend to the results of individual studies. An instance of this relates to the usefulness of what are called integrity tests. The authors of a meta-analysis (Ones, Viswesvaran, & Schmidt, 1993) based on 665 (often contradictory) individual validity studies were suprised to find that, collectively, integrity tests do predict a broad range of organizationally disruptive behaviors (including rule breaking incidents and EMPLOYEE THEFT). Hence they would appear to be useful in employee selection (*see* SELECTION METHODS).

One caveat: despite the apparent statistical control of the subjectivity typically found in a narrative summary, numerous judgment calls are involved in conducting a validity generalization study (e.g., just which studies should be included or excluded in the analysis?).

See also **Assessment; Psychological testing; Research design; Research methods**

Bibliography

Hunter, J. E., Schmidt, F. L. (1990). *Methods of meta-analysis.* Newbury Park, CA: Sage.

Ones, D. S., Viswesvaran, C. & Schmidt, F. L. (1993). Comprehensive meta-analysis of integrity test validities: Findings and implications for personnel selection and theories of job performance. *Journal of Applied Psychology*, **78**, 679–703.

Schmidt, F. L. & Hunter, J. E. (1977). Development of a general solution to the problem of validity generalization. *Journal of Applied Psychology*, **62**, 529–540.

Wanous, J. P., Sullivan, S. E. & Malinak, J. (1989). The role of judgement calls in meta-analysis. *Journal of Applied Psychology*, **74**, 259–264.

RICHARD KLIMOSKI

values These are a set of core beliefs held by individuals concerning how they should or ought to behave over broad ranges of situations. These values are generalized beliefs about modes of conduct (Rokeach, 1972) that form a primary component of the self-schema, the "ought" self (as compared to the "actual" or "desired" self). Because beliefs about the self tend to be the most deeply held and influential of cognitions, values are stable and central, and are pervasive in their influence on other cognitions, PERCEPTION, and behavior.

This conceptualization differs from the interpretation of values as preferences for objects, which in turn affect responses to those objects (Locke, 1976; (*see* ATTITUDE THEORY). Values, as generalized, core beliefs, provide the standard that individuals use to determine whether an object has value or is to be preferred. Values as defined here act as a primary organizing structure for much of the rest of our belief system, including cognitions commonly perceived to be "facts," rather than simply acting as evaluative responses.

Values also act as motivational elements (*see* MOTIVATION) in that they indicate which behaviors are more desirable to perform than others from an ideal perspective, all other things (such as INSTRUMENTALITY) being equal. Acting on values may fulfill innate needs, however, there is no necessary correspondence between the two.

People typically will endorse value-oriented statements; therefore, INDIVIDUAL DIFFERENCES in values lie not so much in the specific values that individuals hold, but in their order of importance. Thus values are hierarchical in nature. Because of this systemic quality, and because of their high social desirability, values are difficult to measure adequately outside of a forced choice or ranking format (Ravlin & Meglino, 1987).

Values are acquired from societal institutions (family, economic, and political systems) and their cultural context. They are initially learned in isolation, in an absolute fashion. As an individual matures, he/she integrates them into a hierarchical system, also based in part on PERSONALITY factors (Rokeach, 1973). A relatively small number of value dimensions seems to generalize across NATIONAL CULTURES (Hofstede, 1980); thus the role of values is pivotal in understanding cultural differences in ORGANIZATIONAL BEHAVIOR.

Because values are learned early in life, and occupy a central position in cognitive structure, they are difficult to change during adulthood (*see* COGNITIVE PROCESSES). Such a change requires a change in the self-schema and the network of beliefs, attitudes, and perceptions that the individual acquires over a lifetime (*see* LIFE STAGES). Pitting two conflicting values against one another may produce change. It is also possible that having violated a value once, individuals find it progressively easier to violate that value until it has lost its level of priority. Finally, repeated functional failure of value-related behavior may produce change. These latter propositions seem more likely to explain long-term, cross-situational change in the values of adults (*see* SELF-REGULATION).

Organizational SOCIALIZATION is one avenue by which values are conveyed to adults. Myths, stories, repetition, and formal socialization processes are often cited as sources of work values. Organizational leaders may set the values of the organization and propagate them among employees. To be acquired, however, a value must serve some sort of function for the individual, or be presented as the only possible interpretation of the situation. Values may also eventually lose their priority if organizational reward systems facilitate their frequent violation (*see* REWARDS; PAYMENT SYSTEMS). Employees bring values to the organization with them, so under some circumstances, their values may influence those of the organization rather than the reverse.

Values act as a perceptual screening device to influence what we see in our environment, and as a channel to influence behavioral decisions (England, 1967) (*see* BEHAVIORAL DECISION RESEARCH). Goals may mediate the relationship between values and behavior, and potential moderators, such as personal discretion and the labeling of a behavior as value-relevant, may act to determine when values will be predictive of behavior. Specific values play important roles in influencing certain behaviors. In the context of ethics, a dominant honesty value produces more ethical decisions (*see* BUSINESS ETHICS). ALTRUISM facilitates personal adjustment because it predisposes individuals to respond to information from their environments, and to adapt to it (Simon, 1993). These relationships between specific values and behavior typically are expected to be small at any one point in time, but stronger over time, as with other individual differences.

In some instances, individuals use value statements (espoused values) to provide some justification for behavior that has already occurred (*see* LEGITIMACY). However, empirical evidence shows that these justification effects are not the only process underlying values–behavior relationships.

Shared value systems (value congruence) also have been shown to have important effects. The sharing of values within an organization may positively influence internal processes (integration; Schein, 1985) such that common cognitive processing leads to less CONFLICT, less UNCERTAINTY, shared goals, and more predictability, interpersonal TRUST, and satisfaction (*see* JOB SATISFACTION). This view is consistent with the Attraction–Selection–Attrition (ASA) framework of Schneider (1987), which holds that organizations tend to attract and retain people with similar views, and thus become more homogeneous over time (*see* ORGANIZATIONAL CLIMATE).

Alternative views of ORGANIZATIONAL CULTURE and value sharing within organizations include differentiation perspectives, which focus on the differences in beliefs that exist between groups within organizations, and fragmentation perspectives, which note that shared beliefs are temporary because of a multiplicity of societal beliefs and the innate ambiguity of complex systems (Martin, 1992) (*see* SYSTEMS THEORY). Each of these views is probably descriptive of part of the organization's value system at any given time. These differing perspectives have important implications for how and what research is conducted. Thus far, value congruence has been explored at multiple levels (individual–organization, supervisor–subordinate, between coworkers) in studies which primarily reflect either integration or differentiation perspectives.

Although evidence shows that value congruence does result in more positive attitudes, the relationship between the sharing of values and performance is unclear. The integration perspective tends to suggest that the existence of value congruence will lead to higher performance. Other points of view, in particular, the GROUP DECISION MAKING and ASA literatures, suggest that too much homogeneity of belief systems should hinder performance in nonroutine, changing situations. Recent research suggests that while routine task performance may be facilitated by value congruence, performance on nonroutine tasks is not. Clearly, many issues regarding this relationship are left unresolved.

See also **VIE theory; Corporate social responsibility; Rituals and rites; Motivation and performance**

Bibliography

England, G. W. (1967). Organizational goals and expected behavior of American managers. *Academy of Management Journal*, **10**, 107–117.

Hofstede, G. (1980). *Culture's consequences: International differences in work related values*. Beverly Hills, CA: Sage.

Locke, E. A. (1976). The nature and consequences of job satisfaction. In M. D. Dunnette (Ed.), *Handbook of industrial psychology* (pp. 1297–1349). Chicago: Rand-McNally.

Martin, J. (1992). *Cultures in organizations*. New York: Oxford University Press.

Ravlin, E. C. & Meglino, B. M. (1987). Effect of values on perception and decision making: A study of alternative work values measures. *Journal of Applied Psychology*, **72**, 666–673.

Rokeach, M. (1973). *The nature of human values*. New York: Free Press.

Schein, E. H. (1985). *Organizational culture and leadership*. San Francisco: Jossey-Bass.

Schneider, B. (1987). The people make the place. *Personnel Psychology*, **40**, 437–453.

Simon, H. (1993). Altruism and economics. *American Economic Review*, **83**, 156–161.

ELIZABETH C. RAVLIN

vertical integration The production of an organization's products or services generally involves several discreet stages. To the extent that one or more of these stages provides supplies, subassemblies, or other inputs to other stages, they are said to form a vertical production chain. The number of different stages of production within which an organization directly operates determines that organization's level of vertical integration.

An organization's level of vertical integration is not constant. When an organization includes more early stages in the vertical production chain by, for example, purchasing its former suppliers, it is said to be engaging in backward vertical integration. When late stages are incorporated into the vertical production chain by, for example, developing its own distribution network, the organization is said to be engaging in forward vertical integration.

Several theories have been proposed to explain the extent of an organization's vertical integration. The three most often applied models are:

(1) RESOURCE DEPENDENCE theory (*see* RESOURCE BASED THEORY);
(2) TRANSACTION COST THEORY (*see* M-FORM ORGANIZATION); and
(3) AGENCY THEORY.

See also **Integration; Strategic management; Collateral organization**

Bibliography

Jensen, M. C. & Meckling, W. H. (1976). The theory of the firm: Managerial behavior, agency costs and ownership structure. *Journal of Financial Economics*, 3, 305–360.

Pfeffer, J. & Salancik, G. (1978). *The external control of organizations: A resource dependence perspective*. New York: Harper & Row.

Williamson, O. (1975). *Markets and hierarchies*. New York: Free Press.

JAY B. BARNEY

viability *see* COMPETITIVENESS; POPULATION ECOLOGY

vicious cycles These cycles (or circles) in organizations are circular chains of activities that induce undesired trends. They are best understood in cybernetic terms, where the basic distinction is between positive and negative FEEDBACK. Vicious cycles evolve:

(1) when stability is the goal but change results (undesired positive feedback: *spiral*); or
(2) when change is the goal but stability results (undesired negative feedback or *stasis*).

Spirals ultimately cause collapse, stasis causes stagnation. Spirals – spectacular as they are – capture the imagination (*see* ORGANIZATIONAL CHANGE; ORGANIZATIONAL DECLINE AND DEATH), but stagnating vicious cycles, in their silent, unobtrusive way, may occur more frequently, because they are difficult to detect. Every vicious cycle is based on the (partial) ignorance of the participants, since they ought to act differently, were they aware of the true consequences of their actions. Persistent ignorance of vicious cycles is often based on psychological bias (e.g., attribution errors) or pathological conditions (*see* ORGANIZATIONAL NEUROSIS; ATTRIBUTION).

Implicitly, vicious cycles are already present in Machiavelli's analysis of POLITICS and Weber's analysis of organization. Robert K. Merton made them famous in his study of the vicious circle of BUREAUCRACY ("rigidity," as a side-effect of bureaucratic formality causes partial bureaucratic failure; in turn, psychological mechanisms induces more rigidity). Other important contributions are due to Chris Argyris (whose analysis of organizations failing to learn exposes many stagnating cycles (*see* DOUBLE LOOP LEARNING) and Manfred Kets de Vries.

See also **Learning organization; Systems theory; Open systems**

Bibliography

Masuch, M. (1985). Vicious circles in organizations. *Administrative Science Quarterly*, **30**, 14–33.

MICHAEL MASUCH

VIE theory This theory (also known as expectancy theory) is a cognitive process model of MOTIVATION. The theory explains three components of rational behavioral choice and predicts behavior without making assumptions about the general types of outcomes individuals seek. Because the theory assumes behavior results from rational decisions, the primary use of the theory is in predicting or explaining the behaviors individuals employ to attain valued outcomes (*see* RATIONALITY).

There are three components contained within VIE theory: valence, INSTRUMENTALITY, and expectancy. Valence is the perceived value of an outcome. Valence is personally determined, thus several individuals may perceive different valences for the same outcome. Occupational choice is partially based on differences between outcomes for occupations and the preferences of individuals for these outcomes (*see* CAREER CHOICE). Valence takes on positive (attractive) or negative (repellant) values depending on the outcome and the individual.

Instrumentality is the perceived likelihood one outcome will lead to another (e.g., performance → reward). Instrumentality perceptions vary between -1 and +1. Negative values predict certain subsequent outcomes will be avoided if this first-level outcome occurs, while positive values predict other outcomes will likely follow. Instrumentality is very important in the design of PAYMENT SYSTEMS. To enhance motivation, employers tie pay changes to performance measures of which the individual is aware (*see* PERFORMANCE RELATED PAY). Piece rate pay plans, merit pay plans, gain- and profit-sharing plans are all examples in which the employer defines and communicates a linkage between performance outcome and pay outcomes (*see* GAINSHARING).

Expectancy is the perceived likelihood that a behavior (e.g., effort) will lead to an instrumental outcome (e.g., performance). Expectancy is assumed to take values between 0 and 1. Expectancies close to zero indicate the behavior is perceived to be unlikely to lead to a specific outcome, while expectancies close to one assume the behavior will almost certainly lead to the outcome. In employment, selection and TRAINING to increase employee ABILITY are likely to increase expectancies of attaining organizationally relevant outcomes.

In deciding among alternative behaviors, the theory assumes individuals first consider the valence of relevant second-level outcomes, then the likelihoods that these outcomes will follow from other first-level outcomes (instrumentalities), and finally the likelihood that first-level outcomes will follow from specific behaviors. The chosen behavior is expected to be the one yielding the highest expected value to the individual.

Example: In an employment setting an individual perceives the following outcome valences: pay increase, +1, friendly coworkers, +2, longer hours, -1. Instrumentalities of performance rating levels of excellent (E), average (A), and poor (P) for attaining the three outcomes, respectively, are: pay, E=0.8, A=0.3, P=0.5; friendly coworkers, E=0.6, A=0.8, P=0.3; and longer hours, E=0.8, A=0.5, P=0.1. The valence of receiving an E performance rating is 0.8 × 1 + 0.6 × 2, + 0.8 × (-1) = 1.2; an A, 0.3 × 1 + 0.8 × 2 + 0.5 × -1 = 1.4; a P, 0.05 × 1 + 0.3 × 2 + 0.1 × -1 = 0.55. Expectancies of high (H), moderate (M), and low (L) effort for attaining E, A, and P ratings are: H, 0.7(E), 0.2(A), 0.1(P); M, 0.1(E), 0.7(A), 0.2(P); L, 0.1(E), 0.5(A), 0.4(P). The force to perform (or motivation) level for H is 0.7 × 1.2 (the valence of an E rating) + 0.2 × 1.4 (valence of an A rating) + 0.1 × 0.55 (valence of a P rating) = 1.175; for M, 0.1 × 1.2 + 0.7 × 1.4 + 0.2 × 0.55 = 1.21; and for L effort, 0.1 × 1.2 + 0.5 × 1.4 + 0.4 × 0.55 = 1.04. The individual would be expected to choose moderate effort.

Because different individuals attach different valences to second-level outcomes and have varied perceptions of instrumentalities and expectancies, expectancy theory makes predictions of individual behaviors, not decisions of groups of people.

The predictions made by expectancy theory are supported in studies where the measures have been faithful to the model. At this point the theory is relatively mature. Motivation researchers are currently involved with exploring the effects of GOAL-SETTING and various INDIVIDUAL DIFFERENCES on behavior, in addition to rational DECISION-MAKING in specific situations. Expectancy theory is widely adopted by HUMAN RESOURCE MANAGEMENT practitioners in designing work and reward systems and continues to be a mainstream theory of motivation for organizational behavior researchers.

See also **Motivation and performance; Performance, individual; Reinforcement**

Bibliography

Kanfer, R. (1990). Motivation theory and industrial and organizational psychology. In M. D. Dunnette & L. M. Hough (Eds), *Handbook of Industrial and Organizational Psychology*, (vol. 2, pp. 75–170). Palo Alto, CA: Consulting Psychologists Press.

Kennedy, C. W., Fossum, J. A. & White, B. J. (1983). An empirical comparison of within-subjects and between-subjects expectancy theory predictions. *Organizational Behavior and Human Performance*, **32**, 124–143.

Lawler, E. E., III (1973). *Motivation in work organizations*. Monterey, CA: Brooks/Cole.

Vroom, V. H. (1964). *Work and motivation*. New York: Wiley.

JOHN A. FOSSUM

virtual organization *see* COMMUNICATIONS; INFORMATIONAL TECHNOLOGY; POLITICS

vocational guidance This term covers a range of systems, interventions and activities aimed at helping people make and implement CAREER related decisions. It deals with people's preferences for areas of work, their preparation for and entry into OCCUPATIONS, changes in occupation or development within an occupation, and the associated use of nonwork time for leisure activities that may draw on similar interests, SKILLS or ABILITIES. The term has its roots in the notion of a religious vocation or task in life to which one is "called." Despite the much broader emphasis in the current use of the term, a major aim of vocational guidance remains helping people find meaningful work outlets for their interests. Increasingly, however, descriptors such as career planning, CAREER DEVELOPMENT planning, and career counseling are being used in place of vocational guidance (Lea & Leibowitz, 1992; Arthur, Hall, & Lawrence, 1989).

Historically, the emphasis of vocational guidance was on late adolescence with assistance being given in acquiring self-knowledge, knowledge about opportunities, and, in Parson's terms, "true reasoning on the relation between these two sets of facts" (Crites, 1969). To assist this process vocational guidance typically involved administering psychological tests covering domains such as interests, abilities, and PERSONALITY and relating the results to job requirements. The "trait-and-factor" approach, as it was known, foreshadowed much of what is currently referred to as person–environment fit (Edwards, 1991) in organizational psychology (*see* PERSON-JOB FIT). Increasingly vocational guidance is undertaken within a developmental perspective with help being extended to the full spectrum of the life-span, from early career awareness programs in primary schools to organizational career development and retirement planning later in life (Lea & Leibowitz, 1992) (*see* AGE).

The traditional approaches to vocational guidance in educational institutions and in organizations was one of an expert giving advice, or of managers making decisions about the best career moves for their staff. More recently, vocational guidance or career development systems aim to equip people with the knowledge and skills to make and implement their own decisions throughout life (Hesketh & Bochner, 1993). In an organizational context this involves offering employees career development programs to help clarify skills, interests, COMPETENCIES and VALUES, through PSYCHOLOGICAL TESTING, ASSESSMENT CENTERS or as part of a traditional PERFORMANCE APPRAISAL and staff development system. The programs also include information about the variety of opportunities within the organization for TRAINING, JOB ROTATIONS, promotions, or other skill development activities. Finally, programs include a component on personal GOAL SETTING and DECISION MAKING, aimed at giving employees the skills to manage and implement their own career plans (*see* SELF-REGULATION). In light of the changes to the nature of many work contracts, a current trend in organizations is to integrate training and career or vocational guidance systems and to help employees identify the sequence of training and job moves needed to take advantage of different career opportunities (Hesketh & Bochner, 1993) (*see* CAREER TRANSITIONS). These programs raise the issue of compatibility or conflict between individual and organizational career goals.

See also **Career choice; Individual differences; Personality testing; Realistic job previews; Career anchors; Anticipatory socialization; Counseling in organizations**

Bibliography

Arthur, M. B., Hall, D. T. & Lawrence, B. S. (Eds), (1989). *Handbook of career theory*. Cambridge, UK: Cambridge University Press.

Crites, J. O. (1969). *Vocational psychology*. New York: McGraw-Hill.

Edwards, J. R. (1991). Person-job fit: A conceptual integration, literature review and methodological critique. In C. Cooper & I. Robertson (Eds), *International review of industrial and organizational psychology* 1991. Chichester, UK: Wiley.

Hesketh, B. & Bochner, S. (1993). Technological changes in a multi-cultural context: Implications for training and career planning. In M. D. Dunnette, L. Hough & H. Triandis (Eds), *Handbook of industrial and organizational psychology*, (vol. IV). Palo Alto, CA: Consulting Psychologists Press.

Lea, D. & Leibowitz, Z. (1992). *Adult career development: Concepts issues and practices*. Alexandria, USA: The National Career Development Association.

BERYL HESKETH

— W —

withdrawal, organizational This is a construct denoting various behaviors employees engage in to remove themselves from their job or avoid their work. Two behavioral families of organizational withdrawal have been empirically identified. *Work Withdrawal* includes behaviors employees engage in to avoid their work tasks while retaining organizational membership; it is composed of, for example, tardiness, ABSENTEEISM, taking long breaks, and missing meetings. *Job Withdrawal* comprises behaviors employees engage in to remove themselves from their job with a specific organization; TURNOVER, retiring early (*see* RETIREMENT), and choosing to be laid off are examples of its behaviors. These behavioral families have been empirically related to organizational attitudes. Studying aggregates of behaviors (i.e., behavioral families) is theoretically, psychometrically, and practically appropriate because employees engage in multiple, patterned behaviors as responses to multiple antecedents (e.g., JOB SATISFACTION; STRESS). Behaviors in a behavioral family may serve similar functions for individuals; the selection of a specific or multiple behaviors may vary based on organizational constraints, personal convictions, REINFORCEMENT histories, and social pressures. Although organizational withdrawal is a relatively new construct and departs from the past research focus on specific behaviors, assessing multiple outcomes from behavioral families may provide greater generalizability of findings than has been possible by studying individual behaviors (*see* GENERALIZATION). However, for some individuals, behaviors may be context or cause specific and insufficiently correlated to justify the application of the withdrawal construct.

See also **Motivation and performance; Performance, individual**

Bibliography

Hanisch, K. A. (In Press) Behavioral families and multiple causes: Matching the complexity of responses to the complexity of antecedents. *Current Directions in Psychological Science*.

KATHY A. HANISCH

women at work Most women have always worked, of course, but traditionally, fewer women than men have engaged in *paid* work. In 1890, for example, women made up only 17 percent of the US labor force; by 1980, women were 44 percent of the US labor force. In 1985, 54.5 percent of the US women 16 years of age an older and 64.7 percent of the women between the ages of 25 and 64 were employed (Statistical Abstract of the United States, 1988, Table No. 627). In the Scandinavian countries, typically 75 percent or more of adult women are in the labor force. The same was true in many countries of the former Soviet Union, but the current situation is unstable, changing rapidly, and UNEMPLOYMENT among women is high in many of these countries. During the 1970s and 1980s in particular, women increased their share of the labor force in almost every country of the world (United Nations, 1991). Furthermore, in all areas of the world today, women in the prime child-bearing years (25–44) are more likely to be employed than women either younger or older in age (United Nations, 1991, Table 6.8).

The topic of "women at work" as a coherent subfield is less than 20 years old (e.g., Nieva & Gutek, 1981), and it tends to be interdisciplinary, involving researchers from many fields, e.g., management, psychology, sociology, economics, anthropology. While the field is not bereft of theory, so far, much of the research has been descriptive, a necessary step because the topic is fraught with misperceptions and misinformation. In all of the research, GENDER figures prominently, and women and their experiences are either overtly or covertly compared with men: Jobs are "sex-segregated" and in the job choice literature, women choose and work in either "male-dominated" or "female-dominated jobs." "SEX DIFFERENCES" is a common theme in the research and encompasses both differences between men and women and differences in treatment of men and women.

Women tend to work in "women's jobs," jobs defined in a particular time and place as appropriate for women. Although there are some consistencies across countries, cultures, and organizations (e.g., jobs involving children tend to be labeled women's jobs), there are also many examples of one job being a "man's job" in one country, culture, or organization, and a "woman's job" in another (e.g., medicine, sales, clerical work).

Women's work is characterized by horizontal and vertical segregation. Horizontal segregation means that women tend to have different occupations and career choices than men and they tend to work with other women. In 1970 in the United States about 55 percent of women worked in the 20 most female-dominated occupations (Jacobs, 1989, Table 2.4). Sex-segregation is measured by several statistics (*see* Jacobs, 1989), notably the index of segregation (also known as the index of dissimilarity, D) which tells the percentage of one sex who would have to change jobs so that they would be distributed across jobs the same as the other sex. In the United States, sex-segregation has declined from about 76 in 1910 to 62 in 1981 (Jacobs, 1989), and it has done so, not because more men are working in jobs traditionally held by women (they are not), but because women have moved into traditionally male jobs, especially professional and managerial jobs such as law, medicine, management, and the professorate. During the 1970s, in the United States a number of jobs that were male-dominated prior to the 1970s became sex-integrated or female-dominated between 1970 and 1980, including bartending, residential real estate, baking, accounting, editing, public relations, and pharmacy (Reskin & Roos, 1990). Reskin and Roos (1990) concluded that women made inroads into these male-dominated fields because either the jobs were rapidly growing so that not enough men were available to fill them and/or these jobs tended to have fewer attractions to men (e.g., declining pay, fewer fringe benefits, fewer opportunities for AUTONOMY or entrepreneurial activity) who shifted their career attention to more attractive alternatives. Jacobs (1989) concluded that for every 11 women who enter a nontraditional job, 10 leave, yielding a net decrease in sex-segregation of jobs, but not as much change as might be expected given women's interest in the jobs. An extensive literature on women's career aspirations, CAREER CHOICES, and CAREER DEVELOPMENT document the processes by which work maintains a sex-segregated character and the experiences of individual women (*see*, e.g., Betz & Fitzgerald, 1987; Gutek & Larwood, 1987).

Vertical segregation means that men and women are located at different places in the hierarchy in their work. Women tend to be located in lower level positions in their occupations and in their organizations whereas men are found in jobs throughout the hierarchy. Women are said to face a "glass ceiling" in that they are rarely found above certain hierarchical levels. Like horizontal segregation, vertical segregation is also decreasing, although women have made little headway at the top (*see* WOMEN MANAGERS).

It is worth noting that the research tends to focus disproportionately on women in nontraditional jobs (i.e., management and the male-dominated professions) and women at higher organizational ranks (managers and executives). Likewise, the research focuses disproportionately on white women and middle and upper class women. These features are characteristic of ORGANIZATIONAL BEHAVIOR as a whole, not just women at work.

In general, the research on women at work fits into one of three categories: sex-differences, problem-focused, and changes initiated to alleviate problems (e.g., Firth-Cozens & West, 1991).

One type of research focuses on differences and similarities between the sexes. Among the topics covered, and some of the researchers exploring each topic, are the following: differences in masculinity and femininity and their implications (Powell); differences or similarities in LEADERSHIP or MANAGERIAL STYLE or LEADERSHIP STYLE (Eagly; Dobbins); sex differences in CAREER CHOICES and career interests (Betz; Astin); and differences and similarities in achieving (Tangri; Lipman-Blumen). Early research focused on traits or characteristics believed to be associated with women more than men such as fear of success (Horner). A few areas are notable for the lack of expected sex differences. For example, while there is an active debate about whether men and women exhibit different leadership styles, the extant research suggests that men and women in leadership positions exhibit few differences (Eagly; Dobbins). And despite the fact that women's and men's job experiences tend to differ, they tend to report similar levels of JOB SATISFACTION, and in recent years, job COMMITMENT.

A large body of research on women at work focuses on problems faced by women. These topics include the following, listed with some researchers and theorists in each field: biases in selection, placement, PERFORMANCE APPRAISAL, and promotion (Nieva & Gutek; Swim et al.); SEXUAL HARASSMENT (Fitzgerald; Gutek; Powell; Pryor; Terpstra & Baker); obstacles to achievement, advancement, and attainment of positions of leadership (Larwood; Morrison); lack of MENTORING (Ragins; Fagenson); sex DISCRIMINATION (Heilman; Crosby; Larwood); the pay gap (England; Olson; Konrad; Langton); stereotyping (Fiske); lack of job mobility (Brett); conflict between work and family responsibilities (Pleck; Brett; Burke; Davidson; Cooper); reproductive hazards at work; conflict between work role and gender role (Nieva & Gutek) (see "SEX ROLES"). Other researchers have noted the problems faced by tokens (women who are numerically rare) (Kanter; Laws), the "double whammy" of being minority and female in nontraditional jobs (Nkomo), and the problems faced by women when there are few women in top management positions in the organization (Ely).

A third type of research focuses on the success or failure of attempts to alleviate problems faced by working women (*see* e.g., Sekaran, 1992), including the impacts of laws and other programs aimed at providing EQUAL OPPORTUNITY, addressing affirmative action, establishing the comparable worth of jobs, and eliminating sexual harassment. But laws are not the only approach to alleviating problems faced by working women. In general, the type of solution sought depends on the way the problem is defined. Nieva and Gutek (1981; *see also* Gutek, 1993) listed four models of problem definition and some problem-solving strategies that follow from them. They are: the individual deficit model, i.e., the problem is defined as problem people; the structural model, i.e., organizational structures and policies hamper women (see Kanter, 1977); the sex-role model, i.e., social roles and ROLE expectations and role stereotypes hamper women; and the intergroup model wherein men and women are viewed as opposing groups fighting over a limited amount of desirable jobs, POWER, and INFLUENCE. They conclude that the most commonly proposed solutions fit the individual-deficit model. Women are given training and opportunities to overcome their "deficits" through courses and self-help materials targeted at them. Examples include dressing for success, assertiveness training, how to write a business plan or obtain venture capital. Increasingly, men too are targets of training aimed at sensitizing them to issues like sexual harassment and sex discrimination.

See also **Stereotyping; Management of diversity**

Bibliography

Betz, N. & Fitzgerald, L. (1987). *The career psychology of women*. New York: Academic Press.

Firth-Cozens, J. & West, M. (Eds), (1991). *Women at work; Psychological and organizational perspectives*. Buckingham, UK: Open University Press.

Gutek, B. A. (1993). Changing the status of women in management. *Applied Psychology: An International Review*, **43**, (4), 301–311.

Gutek, B. A. & Larwood, L. (Eds), (1987). *Women's career development*. Newbury Park, CA: Sage.

Jacobs, J. (1989). *Revolving doors; Sex segregation and women's careers*. Stanford, CA: Stanford University Press.

Kanter, R. M. (1977). *Men and women of the corporation*. New York: Basic Books.

Nieva, V. F. & Gutek, B. A. (1981). *Women and work: A psychological perspective*. New York: Praeger.

Reskin, B. & Roos, P. A. (1990). *Job queues, gender queues*. Philadelphia, PA: Temple University Press.

Sekaran, U. (Ed.), (1992). *Womanpower*. Newbury Park, CA: Sage

Statistical Abstract of the United States. (1988). Washington, DC: U.S. Government Printing Office

United Nations. (1991). *The world's women: Trends and statistics, 1970–1990*. Social Statistics and Indicators, Series K, No. 8. New York: The United Nations.

BARBARA A. GUTEK

women managers Today women hold a larger share of managerial positions than ever and the subfield of women in management, though only about 20 years old (*see* Larwood & Wood, 1977), has grown as well (*see* Powell, 1993; Fagenson, 1993). Women have made the greatest inroads into management in those countries in which an academic degree (MBA, bachelor's degree in commerce) is used as criterion for obtaining the position of manager. The United States, where about 12 percent of all employees hold the position of manager, leads in moving women into management. In 1900, women were 4.4 percent of all US managers; in 1950, 13.6 percent; in 1980, 26.1 percent, and by 1992, women constituted 42 percent of all US managers (Fagenson, 1993). About 34.5 percent of Canadian managers are women, compared to 20 percent in (the former West) Germany, 23 percent in the United Kingdom, 15 percent in Israel, 9 percent in France and Ireland, and 7.5 percent in Japan (Antal & Izraeli in Fagenson, 1993). In countries that do not rely much on formal educational programs to prepare people for management, the percentage of women is lower.

Although the numbers of women managers have increased, women are virtually unrepresented in the highest ranking DECISION MAKING positions in business and government in almost every country in the world. Women occupy less than 5 percent of high ranking positions in the United States and only one woman heads a *Fortune* 500 corporation. A study of the 1000 most valuable publicly held companies in the United States in 1989 showed only two women among CEOS (up from one in 1988). The $3.3 trillion in annual sales of these companies underscores the minuscule influence of women in big business in the United States. Over the past 10 years, the number of women at the senior management level of the United States' top corporations has increased by less than 2 percent. Currently, there is a lively debate over whether the gender gap between the lower and higher ranks of management is a temporary or more-or-less permanent phenomenon. Some scholars believe that insufficient time has passed for women to move into the top ranks whereas others disagree (*see* Gutek, 1993; Northcraft & Gutek in Fagenson, 1993); both sides are able to marshall some evidence for their position.

Another lively debate in the field addresses the issue of MANAGERIAL STYLE: do women have a unique management style or a style that differs from that typically used by men? Although those who argue that they do rely on people's experiences and "common sense" observations (Rosener, 1990), the bulk of the research evidence suggests that men and women who are in management do not differ in management style (Powell, 1993; *see also* meta-analysis (*see* VALIDITY GENERALIZATION) on leadership style by Eagly and Johnson, 1990). There is more intra- than between-sex variation in management style.

Management represents a "nontraditional" job choice for women and has traditionally been viewed as more appropriate for men than women (*see* WOMEN AT WORK). A series of studies by V. Schein and colleagues (Brenner, Tomkiewicz, & Schein, 1989) showed that in the mid-1970s both sexes associated the traits of successful managers with stereotypically male traits but they were independent of stereotypes of female traits (*see* STEREOTYPING). Recent research by Schein suggests that this finding is generalizable to many different countries, although by the late 1980s in the United States, women but not men, were somewhat more likely to associate the traits of successful managers with traits associated with both men and women (*see* PERSONALITY).

See also **Equal opportunities; Gender; Discrimination; Women at work; Management development; Management of diversity**

Bibliography

Brenner, O. C., Tomkiewicz, J. & Schein, V. E. (1989). The relationship between sex role stereotype and requisite management characteristics revisited. *Academy of Management Journal*, **32**, 662–669.

Fagenson, E. A. (ed.) (1993). *Women in management: Trends, issues, and challenges in managerial diversity*, (vol. 4 in the Women and Work series). Newbury Park, CA: Sage.

Gutek, B. A. (1993). Changing the status of women in management. In E. Greenglass & J. Marshall (Editors of a special issue: Women in management) *Applied Psychology: An International Review*, **43**, (4) 301–311.

Larwood, L. & Wood, M. (1977). *Women in management*. Lexington, MA: Lexington Books.

Powell, G. (1993). *Women in management*, (2nd edn). Newbury Park, CA: Sage.

Rosener, J. B. (1990). Ways women lead. *Harvard Business Review*, **68**, (6) 119–125.

BARBARA A. GUTEK

work adjustment The term "adjustment" is used in a variety of ways to connote employees' adaptation to jobs, typically following career entry, mobility, job redesign, or other changes of employment experience. The concept of adjustment is widely used in the STRESS literature, and in connection with SOCIALIZATION processes. The term "work adjustment" is especially associated with the work of Lofquist, Dawis, and colleagues who have used it to connote the fit between measurable characteristics of OCCUPATIONS and individuals, especially at career entry. Their studies, in similar fashion to the work of Holland, have confirmed that low work adjustment is a predictor of TURNOVER and other CAREER TRANSITIONS.

See also **Career choice; Job satisfaction; Joining-up process; Person-job fit; Vocational guidance**

Bibliography

Dawis, R. V. & Lofquist, L. H. (1984). *A psychological theory of work adjustment*. Minneapolis: University of Minnesota Press.

Holland, J. L. (1973). *Making vocational choices: A theory of careers*. Englewood Cliffs, NJ: Prantice-Hall.

NIGEL NICHOLSON

work and nonwork *see* NONWORK/WORK

work flow This refers to the sequence of tasks through which work is performed as inputs are transformed into outputs.

Work flow is an important concept in organizational research because the sequencing of tasks is one key source of interdependence among people and among organizational units. For example, if unit A is strictly "upstream" of unit B in a work flow, B may depend on A much more heavily than A depends on B.

Thompson (1967) set forth an extremely well-known distinction between three types of work flows: pooled interdependence, where units do not interact directly but their joint output is threatened if any unit fails; sequential interdependence, where the sequence of tasks is linear, and uniform; and reciprocal interdependence, in which the sequence of tasks "downstream" depends on feedback from operations performed earlier, instead of being predetermined. Each tends to be associated with a different type of TECHNOLOGY, different way of coordinating work, and means of compensating for UNCERTAINTY.

Work flow has assumed great importance recently with the rise of BUSINESS PROCESS REENGINEERING, which strives to simplify work flows by taking advantage of INFORMATION TECHNOLOGY to eliminate unnecessary steps and combine steps to produce the smoothest, shortest work flow path possible.

See also **Organizational design; Productivity; Operations management**

Bibliography

Hammer, M. & Champy, J. (1993). *Reengineering the corporation: A manifesto for business revolution*. New York: Harper Business.

Hickson, D. J, Pugh, D. S. & Pheysey, D. (1969). Operations technology and organizational structure: An empirical appraisal. *Administrative Science Quarterly*, **14**, 378–397.

Reimann, B. (1980). Organization structure and technology in manufacturing: Systems versus work flow level perspectives. *Academy of Management Journal*, **23**, 61–77.

Thompson, J. D. (1967). *Organizations in action: Social science bases of administrative theory*. New York: McGraw-Hill.

PHILIP ANDERSON

work groups These are both formal and informal collectives of individuals within organizations. Formal groups are those designated as work groups by the organization and whose members usually have shared task objectives. Informal groups are those not defined by the organization as functional units, but which nevertheless have an impact upon organizational behavior. Examples include friendship and pressure groups.

From early in the study of organizational behavior it became clear that work groups influenced individual behavior in a variety of ways. The Hawthorne studies established how group influences can have a major impact on work group behavior (*see* HUMAN RELATIONS MOVEMENT; HAWTHORNE EFFECT). They have effects on group member well-being, attitudes, and individual performance through SOCIALIZATION, social support, MINORITY GROUP INFLUENCE, and CONFORMITY processes.

The concept of the work team is becoming increasingly important in organizations. Sundstrom, De Meuse, and Futrell (1990), have distinguished four main types: *advice/involvement teams* such as committees, review panels, boards, QUALITY CIRCLES, EMPLOYEE INVOLVEMENT groups, and advisory councils; *production/service groups* such as assembly teams, manufacturing crews; *project/development groups* such as research groups, planning teams, specialist functional teams, development teams, and task forces; and finally *action/negotiation groups* such as entertainment groups, expeditions, negotiating teams, surgery teams, and cockpit crews.

In some organizations, groups as a whole may be hired, fired, trained, rewarded, and promoted. This trend has developed as organizations have grown and become increasingly complex, demanding that shared experiences and complementary SKILLS are constantly utilized in DECISION-MAKING processes. Another reason for the dominance of the work team is the belief that the combined efforts of individuals may be better than the aggregate of individual contributions, i.e., the principle of synergy.

In recent years, the influence of work groups on individual behavior has come to be considered as less important than their activity as collectively performing units (Guzzo & Shea, 1992). Studies of work groups have focused particularly on their effectiveness and have revealed important deficiencies in GROUP DECISION MAKING, such as GROUPTHINK, RISKY SHIFT, group polarization, and SOCIAL LOAFING – collectively called "process losses." A distinction has also been made between groups performing disjunctive, conjunctive, and additive tasks. On disjunctive tasks performance depends on the best individual (e.g., in a research team); on conjunctive tasks, such as an assembly line, performance is a function of the weakest individual; finally, on additive tasks (e.g., a group shoveling snow) all member activities added together determine performance.

A good deal of effort is now directed toward understanding the factors which promote group effectiveness, including organizational context, group composition, GROUP STRUCTURE, decision-making processes, and group resources. This suggests that ideally:

1 Groups should have intrinsically interesting tasks to perform.
2 Each individual's role should be essential and unique.
3 Each individual should be subject to evaluation and receive clear performance FEEDBACK.
4 The group as a whole should have clear objectives, be subject to evaluation, and receive performance feedback.
5 The group should frequently reflect upon and appropriately modify their task objectives, strategies, and processes.

In relation to social functioning, a positive social climate, constructive conflict resolution strategies, support for individual development, and social support for dealing with STRESS, all contribute significantly to group member well-being. However, GROUP COHESIVENESS appears to contribute little directly to task performance.

See also **Group dynamics; Group culture; Division of labor; Organizational design**

Bibliography

Brown, R. (1988). *Group processes: Dynamics with and between groups*. Oxford, UK: Blackwell.

Goodman, P. S. & Associates (1990). *Designing effective work groups*. San Francisco: Jossey-Bass.

Guzzo, R. A. & Shea, G. P. (1992). Group performance and intergroup relations in organizations. In M. D. Dunnette & L. M. Hough (Eds), *Handbook of industrial and organizational psychology*, (vol. 3 pp. 269–313). Palo Alto, CA: Consultant Psychologists Press.

Sundstrom, E., De Meuse, K. P. & Futrell, D. (1990). Work teams: Applications and effectiveness. *American Psychologist*, **45**, 120–133.

West, M. A. (1994). *Effective Teamwork*. Leicester, UK: BPS Books.

MICHAEL A WEST

work involvement This concept refers to the degree to which work is important in the psychological make-up of the individual. It refers to an orientation toward work activities in general, rather than toward a particular organization (*see* COMMITMENT). Two dimensions of work involvement have been identified. First, it has been described as the extent to which work plays a central role in a person's life (Kanungo, 1981). Alternatively, involvement has been defined as the degree to which a person's feelings of SELF-ESTEEM are derived from his or her performance at work. How these two dimensions are related is currently an unresolved issue.

Work involvement has been found to be related to important aspects of individual attitudes and behavior. For example, it has been shown to be associated with JOB SATISFACTION and ABSENTEEISM. The origin of a person's level of work involvement is unclear at present. Some have argued that it is a personal characteristic which is little affected by the work environment (*see* PERSONALITY). Others have suggested that it is primarily a reaction to psychological stimulation (or lack of it) in the job. Research to date suggests that both factors contribute to an individual's level of work involvement.

See also **Job design; Job characteristics; Motivation**

Bibliography

Kanungo, R. N. (1981). Work alienation and involvement: Problems and prospects. *International Review of Applied Psychology*, **30**, 1–15.

TONY KEENAN

working conditions The study of the effects of working conditions is an area of both ERGONOMICS and the health and SAFETY professions. The way in which conditions can affect the physical and psychological well-being of workers has been a long-standing concern. Similarly, the relationship between conditions and work efficiency, in terms of PRODUCTIVITY and ERRORS, has been researched for some time. It is also clear that attitudes and JOB SATISFACTION can be influenced by conditions in the work context.

The term working conditions can be taken to include; the ambient environment in the workplace (e.g., temperature, noise), the physical design of the workplace and the working positions and postures that have to be adopted (e.g., seating, keyboard positions), and the pattern of work/rest cycles required (e.g., shift systems, rest breaks).

A number of aspects of the ambient environment have been studied. The harmful effects of substances present in raw materials, in the work environment, or in products, has been the subject of toxicology research. These studies have led to the strict imposition of controls and the need for the protection of workers. The once benign office environment has also come under scrutiny following concern over sick-building syndrome (apparently resulting from recycled air in sealed office buildings) and the seemingly unfounded fears over radiation emissions from computer terminals. Noise in the workplace has strict legal limits in most developed countries in order to minimize hearing damage. The thermal environment has also been studied, one example would be the extreme conditions where protective clothing, to heat or to cool individuals, may be needed. The contrast between preferred and acceptable levels of room temperature is another example, here energy conservation is a key factor. Lighting conditions for different tasks have also been studied in some detail, with international standards being set. The problems of lighting and computer use is an example of recent work, with one finding being the advantages of replacing direct lighting sources above screens with indirect lighting to avoid reflectance problems.

Work methods and postures have also been researched. Legislation can be used to regulate such things as the maximum weight that workers can be asked to lift, but little is laid down over other aspects of physical work. The prevalence of upper limb disorders, following repetitive manual work, is now causing concern. The size of legal settlements has focused attention on the need for preventative measures. The optimization of the workplace layout, together with frequent changes in activity, appear to be the best solution.

The study of shiftwork continues to be of importance (*see* HOURS OF WORK), with the search for an ideal system being set against evidence on what constitutes the "natural" sleep/waking patterns for people (*see* FATIGUE). Solutions are not straightforward as rapidly changing shifts are the most disruptive to the body's natural rhythms, but permanent shifts, whilst they enable new rhythms to be established, are not generally socially acceptable. The disruptive effect of long air journeys, the jet-lag phenomenon, has also been studied in detail.

See also **Job analysis; Job design; Motivator-hygiene theory**

Bibliography

Parsons, K. C. (1993). *Human thermal environments.* London: Taylor & Francis.

Monk, T. H. & Folkard, S. (1992). *Making shiftwork tolerable.* London: Taylor & Francis.

Osborne, D. J. (Ed.), (1983). *The physical environment at work.* Chichester, UK: Wiley.

Singleton, W. T. (Ed.), (1982). *The body at work: Biological ergonomics.* Cambridge, UK: Cambridge University Press.

Wilson, J. R. & Corlett, E. N. (Eds), (1995). *Evaluation of human work: A practical ergonomics methodology.* (2nd edn). London: Taylor & Francis.

R. B. STAMMERS

work measurement *see* JOB ANALYSIS

work role transitions *see* CAREER TRANSITIONS

work-sample tests *see* ASSESSMENT; SELECTION METHODS

— INDEX —

Note: Headwords are in bold type